The Mystic Kn
Series

In One Volume

Compiled and Written by Marilynn Hughes

The Out-of-Body Travel Foundation!

www.outofbodytravel.org

3

For information, write to:

The Out-of-Body Travel Foundation!

www.outofbodytravel.org

MarilynnHughes@outofbodytravel.org

If this book is unavailable from your local bookseller, it may be obtained directly from the Out-of-Body Travel Foundation by going to www.outofbodytravel.org.

Having worked primarily in radio broadcasting, Marilynn Hughes spent several years as a news reporter, producer and anchor before deciding to stay at home with her three children. She's experienced, researched, written, and taught about out-of-body travel since 1987.

Books by Marilynn Hughes
Listed in the Back of the Book

INTRODUCTION:

The Mystic Knowledge Series is a group of compilations of the Mystic and Out-of-Body Travel Works of Marilynn Hughes on various subjects of scholarship so you may have at your fingertips all the Out-of-Body Travel Instructions on a particular area of study.

As many experiences would overlap into more than one area, we've chosen the best category for each Out-of-Body Travel Experience in which to place it in order to avoid repetition.

We hope this series helps those who are interested in a special area of study to read all the recorded mystical and out-of-body travel experiences that the author had on each subject.

These experiences are compiled from 'Come to Wisdom's Door: How to Have an Out-of-Body Experience,' 'The Mysteries of the Redemption: A Treatise on Out-of-Body Travel and Mysticism,' 'Galactica: A Treatise on Death, Dying and the Afterlife,' 'The Palace of Ancient Knowledge: A Treatise on Ancient Mysteries,' 'Touched by the Nails: A Karmic Journey Revealed,' 'Suffering: The Fruits of Utter Desolation,' and a few other published and unpublished sources.

CONTENTS

Out-of-Body Travel

Mystic Knowledge Series

Compiled and Written by Marilynn Hughes

The Out-of-Body Travel Foundation!

www.outofbodytravel.org

(www.tripod.com)

PART I
CHAPTER ONE
Getting Out, Universal Mind, Sound, Spirit Guides, 'Physical' Senses, Thought Forms, Atonements, Lost Souls, Vibrational Raisings, Surrender, Interdimensional Travel, Energetic Aids, the Corridor and Other Tunnels of Travel.

****

My prayers were long, deep and arduous, like a fire raging inside my soul, wanting to know the truth of all existence. It came in the morning, like a thief in the night, without foreknowledge or preparation. Turning to get out of my bed from sleep, what *felt* like my body began vibrating at a speed indescribable in human terms. Feeling numb all over, I didn't know what was happening to me. The noise was so loud, it sounded as if I were surrounded by jet engines. I was afraid.

Lifting my arm, my hand now became two, as a light sparkling image of it moved from inside my body to the outer air. My physical arm didn't move. Rolling over, my spirit rolled out of my body as my ethereal form bounced up to the ceiling. My body below looked like a gray clump of matter. As a fearful thought overcame me, I shot back into my physical form.

"God also decreed that the bond between the body and the divine soul should be somewhat loosened while man sleeps . . . The freed portions of the soul can then move about in the spiritual realm wherever they are allowed."
The Way of God, Part III, Chapter I, No. 6, Paragraphs 4-5, Page 183, (Judaism, Author: Rabbi Moshe Chayim Luzzatto)

****

Far away, but moving at great speed towards me, I stared reticently at the light that glowed before me in bed. Remaining still, there was nothing I could do. Moments later, the light permeated my soul and was within me, spurning the vibrational sensations of before. Unafraid, I had previously prayed to the Lord to deliver me from my fear, after my disconcerting re-entry within the last experience. The loud noises returned, as my body and spirit hummed to the rhythm of high intensity.

Suddenly, without any instigation, I felt an incredible connection to all things, all life, to GOD! It was as if I now understood all the mysteries of the Universe, at least for this moment. There is a oneness between all life that I could completely comprehend and feel. Absolute calm and peace filled me in this new state of love.

Six presences appeared out of the ether, three on each side, and gently lifted me out of my body. The presences were ill-defined, only elliptical expressions of absolute light. Their love for me was so complete, that I was moved to depths I cannot explain, but I also felt God's love for me and all of creation. For a moment, I felt like I was nestled in His chest like a tiny child that He wished to form according to His will.

Reveling in this absolute love and peace, I only momentarily noticed that all my 'physical' senses - like sight and hearing - were now coming from my entire consciousness, rather than a specific vantage point of an eye or an ear.

Looking below, I saw the gray clump of matter that was my body with more interest. This sense of separation was profound, this knowledge that beyond all doubt, I was much more than my body. Engine-like sounds of the astral plane could be felt, as well as, heard. Everything was uncomfortable because it was so new, but the all-encompassing love that filled me was the most amazing aspect of this moment.

After a short time within this immensely loving embrace, the six essences gently lowered me back into my body, decreased the vibrations slowly, and as I began waking to physical consciousness, distinctly faded away into the ether from where they had come.

"The kingdom of God is not a matter of talk, but of power."
New American Bible, New Testament, 1 Corinthians 4:20, (Christianity, Catholic, Words of the Apostle Paul)

****

Immense vibrations began again as I sought refuge into the spiritual world. Noticing my baby daughter floating on the ceiling, I instinctively realized that babies travel out of body in their early days adjusting to the physical world. Rolling over to get out of my body, I looked towards a window, realizing it would be interesting to see if I could actually get out of the room. Movement was strained, but I quickly learned to move by WILLING it, rather than wading like water or moving some vague image of feet.

Floating towards the window, I began to permeate it, but found that the particles in solid objects were tighter vibrationally than air. Interestingly, the temperature was a constant, it did not change once I was outside, and there were two frequencies visible, a higher and lower vibration separated by a distinct line with an upside down V in the center. Flying down the street, I ended up in a neighbor's backyard watching a dog that was staring right at me and barking profusely. My neighbor appeared at the back door to calm the animal, but did not notice me.

As I thought of my home, I was immediately returned; and as I spontaneously thought of my childhood home, it appeared right in front of me empty and devoid of furniture. Indeed, our thoughts are quite powerful, for they appear in the spiritual planes immediately when we think of them. Their physical emergence takes more time, which makes us less reticent to realize the connection between our lives and our thinking.

For a moment, I listened to the voices. I heard them every time I entered into this vibrational state even before leaving the body. It was like being in a big room where hundreds of people were carrying on conversations. Suddenly, it became known to me that these voices were actually the thoughts of humanity resonating through the ether. Many of the voices were agitated and scattered.

"Thought is inexhaustible. Since the world began, thoughts in unimaginable numbers have passed through the ether. One could not begin to count them . . ."
Man's Eternal Quest, Universality of Yoga, Page 22, Paragraph 3, (Hinduism, Kriya Yoga, Author: Paramahansa Yogananda)

****

Relaxing comfortably when the vibrational feelings began, I had no desire to leave my body as I was feeling so embraced by the connection I experienced with all that is. All I wanted to do was absorb this massive peace, serenity and love. Over time, I learned to call these experiences vibrational raisings, and I had them quite frequently.

Energetic knowledge was imparted to me as I absolved myself into the ether, small keys of wisdom, and a place for me to begin my quest. Conveying to me the importance of living in the moment, a spirit voice rang in my spirit, "It's not what you are, but what you *become.*"

Do not judge yourself or others, rather, learn. The past is dead, live in the present. And when mistakes are made, do not dwell on them, rather, alter them. And perhaps most importantly, be willing to see and embrace your own imperfection. For it is only in embracing our faults, that we can become capable of altering them. But all wisdom in this state is imparted by energy, it is not of words. Hours later, my peaceful soul began coming down from the vibrational state, returning me to a conscious state, changed and renewed.

"Trivial thoughts, insignificant thoughts, when followed they distract the mind. Not understanding those thoughts the roaming mind runs back and forth. But by understanding those thoughts, one ardent and mindful restrains the mind. An awakened one has to overcome them completely so they do not arise to distract the mind."

The Udana, Chapter 4, 4.1 Meghiya, Page 56, Stanza 1, (Buddhism, Theravadan, Words of the Buddha)

****

And so it came to pass that I was taught the ways of the spiritual body and the spirit world. All things; hearing, sight and movement, are concurred by the will, not a singular movement of a body part. In relegating from the physical to the spiritual body, you may roll out or learn to WILL yourself out of form. In time, I would learn that almost all functions in the spirit world are related to our thinking.

And the ways of the spiritual world, too, differ from our world, in that every thought you may have, manifests before you. If you think of someone or a place, you are immediately transported to that place. And because the vibrations of spiritual ether are so much higher than physical matter, you must undergo hundreds of what I call vibrational raisings, which increase your vibration on a soul level, coming via the crown or third-eye chakra, or throughout the entire body. This makes you compatible to higher-realm travel.

Later, I began having atonement experiences with people from my past, wherein we would meet on the astral plane in a sub-conscious manner and work through any hurtful things said or done to one another. Very few people ever actually intend harm to another, it is the limited understanding that we carry within us which makes us say and do things insensitively.

Also beginning to work with lost souls, these unfortunate souls were usually unaware that they had died, and required assistance to get to the other side. These things I learned with fervor and with joy, for they were only the first steps of many required of me to continue in this journey I had undertaken in God's name.

"There is no mystery which is more excellent than these mysteries on which ye question, in that it will lead your souls into the Light of the lights, into the regions of Truth and Goodness, into the region of the Holy of all holies, into the region in which there is neither female nor male, nor are there forms in that region, but a perpetual indescribable Light."
Pistis Sophia, Fifth Book, Page 313, Paragraph 1, (Christianity, Gnostic/Essene, Words of Christ)

****

Flying high up into the night air, I cannot express the immense joy I felt within my spirit. Soaring over a small clearing in the woods, I noticed a man was sitting on the hood of his car staring into the night sky. Reading his thoughts, I understood that he was searching for answers, the meaning of life. Rushing energy and desire to share the truth came over me, as my spirit suddenly materialized into a white wispy form. Circling the sky, I sent messages of eternal peace and joy. "There is no need to fear God, for He is of love. Experience God within yourself by journeying inward!"

Somehow, I knew he'd received my message, though I don't know if he actually saw me in a conscious way, or if the manifestation occurred to him in a sub-conscious state, which can happen to people in their dreaming, or in their conscious form wherein they don't consciously experience the event, but another aspect of their soul processes the incoming flow. For any of us who aren't ready to hear the truth consciously, the Lord speaks to our sub-conscious, gently easing the truth of His love to our surface, and calling our souls to unite with Him.

"If a man wishes to travel a certain road, Heaven guides him to it."
The Talmudic Anthology, No. 108, Paragraph 7, Makkot, 10, (Judaism)

****

Whisked to a new dimension, a black space where all life manifested in yellow light, huge monolithic musical chambers surrounded my spirit echoing a serene celestial music that cannot be described. Rectangular ellipses of light with no edges, many spirits were waiting by the chambers for me to come. My arrival had inspired happiness and joy.

Lying down on the platform of yellow light, my spirit was floating mid-air, as one of the spiritual guides lifted his arm and the musical chambers began to emanate energy from their core into my spirit. Vibrations filled my soul, and when the energy became too strong, the spiritual guides around me transmuted it into my spirit. Each emanation of the light made me feel such profound joy and a oneness with God and all created things which were inexplicable. For in this reality, there was no separation between God and His creation.

"One with each other! These poor earthly words cannot convey a true idea of the Divine Unity . . . in that Unity all feeling of 'difference' between God and the soul disappears; and therefore, between each soul and all other souls."
The Divine Crucible of Purgatory, Chapter XVIII, Page 151, Paragraph 3, (Christianity, Catholic, Author: Mother Mary of St. Austin)

"I am the one who comes from what is whole. I was given from the things of my father . . . if one is whole, one will be filled with light, but if one is divided, one will be filled with darkness."
The Gospel of Thomas, No. 61, (Christianity, Gnostic/Essene, Words of Christ)

Returning to this state subsequently, the six entities stood around me, three on each side. Allowing me to observe the colors and vibrational patterns of my soul, they determined what medical problems I may encounter if these anomalies were left unaddressed. Raising their hands synchronistically, beams of white light shone down from them healing my auric disturbances and causing immense warmth. Reasons for these manifestations in my auric field were made known to me, as I became aware that my attachment to the perceptions of others was making me sick.

"All worship and spiritual discipline are directed to one end alone, namely, to get rid of worldly attachment. The more you meditate on God, the less you will be attached to the trifling things of the world."
The Gospel of Sri Ramakrishna, Chapter 33, Page 653, Bottom, (Hinduism, Words of Sri Ramakrishna)

****

Focus in the out-of-body state is quite vital to conscious recall. Beginning to do affirmations upon exit, I would repeat to myself, 'Conscious, fully conscious.'
****

Soaring amidst an astral woodland, a spirit spoke, "Stop what you are doing and let your mind totally clear." As I did this, the spirit continued, "Allow the subtle influence of the wind to take you wherever it may." Surrender catapulted my spirit to the heavens.
The Urantia Book, Paper 13, No. 1, Paragraph 7, (Christianity, Urantia)
****

And it came to pass that I learned how to maneuver through many dimensions of my own accord. One secret I learned was that when no tunnels appear to you, as there are many different tunnels of travel through time and dimensions, you must *think* of them and WILL them to appear in order to traverse them. (Shout out "The Corridor!")

"Apply your heart to instruction, and your ears to words of knowledge."
New American Bible, Old Testament, Proverbs 23:12

"The One Life, moreover, is not to be thought of as dividing and splitting itself up into bits, parts, and particles, in order to accomplish the process of Creation, and the Manifestation of the World. Instead, it is to be thought of as merely reflecting itself in the many individual mirrors of expression, just as the sun reflects itself as One in the millions of falling raindrops, or in a million tiny jars filled with water. There are millions of reflections of the One, but only the one One in reality."
The Secret Doctrine of the Rosicrucians, Part V, Page 64, Paragraph 2, (Mystery Religions, Rosicrucian)

****

CHAPTER TWO
A Spiritual Exposition Demonstrating the Process of Leaving the Body, Finding Your Way through the Inner Spirit, Taking in the Light and Energy of Stars, the Causal Plane, Transforming Dark Energies.

****

"And the city had no need of the sun, neither of the moon, to shine in it: for the glory of God did lighten it, and the Lamb is the light thereof."
King James Bible, New Testament, Revelations 21:23, (Christianity)

"The Mahamati asked the Blessed One, saying: Blessed one, is the purification of the evil out-flowings of the mind which come from clinging to the notions of an objective world and an empirical soul, gradual or instantaneous? The Blessed One replied: There are three characteristic outflows of the mind, namely, the evil out-flowings that rise from thirst, grasping and attachment . . . and from becoming attached to it, are gradually purified and not instantaneously."
A Buddhist Bible, The Lankavatara Scripture, Chapter VIII, Page 325, Paragraph 3-4, (Buddhism)

Zooming to a place among the stars, a spiritual exposition was in progress and I was to demonstrate one of the main events. As soon as I arrived, spirits came and whisked me away to a demonstration site. A thought-form body lay in the middle of a cavernous space. Quickly informing me of my job, they asked me to enter the immaterial body and use it to demonstrate to sub-consciously astral spirits the separation process of body and spirit. About a hundred sub-conscious souls entered and stood around my 'sleeping body,' when someone else came into the room who immediately took me aback. "What is it about that person?" I thought, feeling intense love and recognition. Calmly, he stood in a corner in the back.

Entering into a vibrational state, the spirits began to narrate what was happening. "As you will see if you look through your spirit's eyes, the separation of body and spirit has begun. The light body has now determined its separate status by allowing the spirit to fully feel the frequency of the soul." As she spoke, I began to focus on my sixth chakra and begin the raising of my vibration. "Marilynn is now raising the frequency of her vibration higher so as to maximize the ease with which she exits the body. Without this step, you may shoot right back to your body after leaving. Allow your spiritual eyes to focus now, as her spirit is rising from the body and out." Slowly lifting upwards, I felt the freedom of my soul.

Flying around the room, I came upon the soul who seemed so familiar. "I am blessed to be with you again, Marilynn," he said. In his eyes was such intense adoration, I felt a bit overwhelmed and quite curious, but I didn't recognize him. Continuing my flight around the room, I would touch the sub-conscious souls as they would shout out in joy. "I felt it, I truly felt it!" Again making my way around the room, I came nearer to the one who inspired such tremendous emotion. "Who are you, beautiful spirit?" I asked. His peaceful smile did not change. "My dear Marilynn, we have walked the earth together many days. We have flown the stars many nights. It is our love that you remember and it is wondrous, indeed!"

Reaching his hands to me, he held them for a moment in silence. "You have been confused lately. You feel uncertain about your task. I have returned to clarify it for you. You are paving the way for the Mithra's return." Contemplating a moment, I asked, "But what is Mithra? I have searched my soul but found no memory of it." He had nothing to say. "But what does Mithra represent?" With a final hug before his departure, he said, "Your task will be to find out."

Returning, I discovered that Mithra was the 'Beneficent One' or God of light and wisdom according to ancient Zoroastrian texts. Mithra was the word for 'God' to Zarathustra.

"So may you in both worlds, may you keep us in both worlds, O Mithra, lord of wide pastures! both in this material world and in the world of the spirit."
The Avesta, Part II, Yast 10, No. 93, (Zoroastrianism)

****

"Come with us, we have a job for you!" The group of six spirits said to me as they hovered above my bed. Soaring out of my body, I followed them to the home of a pregnant woman in need of assistance. As we hovered above her, the spirits explained that her baby would die during the night if we didn't wake her and get her to seek help. Creating thought-forms in her mind, we spoke to her in her dreams.

Because that didn't immediately work, one of the spirits pointed a finger at the woman's stomach and light came through, inspiring the baby to kick really hard and wake up his mother. While we worked to make the mother aware that something was wrong through her sub-conscious, the other spirits worked on the husband's sub-conscious through his dreams. Awaking the husband said, "What's going on?" The mother replied, "Something is wrong with the baby, take me to the hospital." Rushing out, our job was finished and the spirits took me outside.

"Good job," the leader said to me. "Thanks!" I replied. Turning to leave, they made no mention of getting me back home. "Wait a minute!" I cried out "Aren't you going to take me home?" Laughing, they said, "Of course not! YOU find the way home. Follow the voice of your inner spirit." With that they disappeared.

Panicking, I didn't even know what part of the world I was in, so I began to float aimlessly for a while before coming across a beautiful forest. Two pathways were clearly delineated in front of me. A spirit appeared for only a moment and said, "One path is the way of the spirit, the other, the way of the intellect. Surrender to the will of your spirit and you will find your way home."

Surrendering my soul to God, I let go of all physical and spiritual control of my faculties. If I had been in a physical body, I would have fallen to the ground from the weight of surrender, but in the spirit surrender caused my soul to be lifted into a flight directed by the Lord. Having given my soul to patience, and allowing it to fall from its own forces, it was able to accept higher ones, thus causing heavenly movement. In moments, I was back home.

"Were all created things, visible and invisible, to direct themselves towards Him, thou wouldst find them winging their flight unto the Supreme Goal, the Spot wherein the divine Lote-Tree exclaimeth: Verily, no God is there but Me, the Almighty, the All-Bountiful."
The Tablets of Baha'u'llah, Tablet 13, Lawh-I-Wiyyid-I-Mihdiy-I-Dahaji, Page 195-196, (Baha'i, Words of Baha'u'llah)

****

"Fill me with light!" I shouted in the midst of a vibrational raising, "I will transmute it into my being!" An angelic spirit descended holding a lighted wand. Sparkly light surrounded her lithe form and golden hair, as rays of light surged into my third eye and pulsated through my body like a wanton tornado as she waved her wand.

Suddenly, my spirit soared out of body and began to fly effortlessly through the heavens. Like a massive snowstorm, the stars flew by me in quick bursts of heavenly light. Speeding by planets and galaxies, my spirit landed upon the body of a star.

Bright and awesome, the light was extremely bright but did not hurt my eyes. In a surge of instinct, I plunged onto the surface, almost hugging the star with my soul. As I lay, the starlight merged into every crevice of my soul, and my spirit took on some of the immortal energies of the star. A white mist enveloped me, particles of starlight, which created a feeling of absolute bliss.

An unseen force pulled my soul away, and during my flight back I passed by a planet of purple and blue, swirling with a marble rotating design. Seeing planets with parallel sets of rings, as well as, double rings that rotated in opposite directions around the planet. "Thank you, Great Spirit," I shouted to the heavens, "for filling me with light!" An inaudible 'your welcome' was felt from within my soul and all around me in the star-filled blackness of night.

"Jesus said, 'Images are visible to people, but the light within them is hidden in the image of the father's light. He will be disclosed, but his image is hidden by his light."
The Gospel of Thomas, No. 83, (Christianity, Gnostic/Essene, Words of Christ)
"For he saith, Eye hath not seen, nor ear heard, neither have entered into the heart of man, the things which God has prepared for them that wait for him."
The Lost Books of the Bible and the Forgotten Books of Eden, I Clement, Chapter XVI, Verse 8, (Christianity)
****

Calling to the universe, I shouted, "The Causal Plane, please take me to the Causal Plane." My spirit shot through the heavens in one constant motion, and stopped in a black void. A rounded light doorway beckoned, and I entered with fury. Inside, geometric gems shot up from every crevice in the ground. Tall and pastel colored amethysts and diamonds permeated every inch of this place. Triangular shapes seared into the sky like arrows; and power, direct and beautiful, shone through the illuminated forms. Blue green skies and tiny glittering stars emanated like sparklers on the fourth of July.

Stopping to engage, I began concentration and focus on the manifestation of my work on the ground. As light came from my heart center, a glowing beam shot straight from myself to the energy vortices creating an explosion in light. "Thank you, Oh mighty universe, you are wondrous, indeed!" I said. Upon return, I received light for several more hours.

"How shall I ever be able to tell you of the riches and the treasures and the delights which are to be found in the fifth Mansions? I think it would be better if I were to say nothing of the Mansions I have not yet treated, for no one can describe them, the understanding is unable to comprehend them and no comparisons will avail to explain them, for earthly things are quite insufficient for this purpose."
Interior Castle, Fifth Mansions, Chapter 1, Paragraph 1, (Christianity, Catholic, Author: St. Teresa of Avila)
****

And so it came to pass that I learned how to transform dark energies that one takes on from another. Putting both hands together while in the vibrational state, allow each finger to join with the corresponding finger from the other hand. As the energy increases and grows, you place one of the energized hands on the chest and abdomen (heart and emotional centers), which releases the negative energies immediately.

"When mindfulness is set with the purpose of guarding the doorway of the mind, then alertness will come about and even that which had gone will return. When, just as I am about (to act), I see that my mind is tainted (with defilement), at such a time I should remain unmoveable, like a piece of wood."
A Guide to the Bodhisattva's Way of Life, Chapter V, No. 28-29, (Buddhism, Tibetan, Author: Shantideva)
****

CHAPTER THREE
Form Transference, Transcendence, Other Vibrational Techniques, the Issue of 'Spiritual Weight' in Out-of-Body Travel, Seeing the 'Dead,' the Two Perceptions.

****

Waves of energy were flowing like the ocean high into the black sky. Their colors varied from pure white light to yellow and then pale blue. Inside the waves, my spirit flowed with the energy, embracing knowledge. Following this flow, I noticed an ominous wave up ahead. Going thousands of miles into the sky, its crest beckoned. Yearning to follow its beckon to the top of this wave, I ventured forth, but a woman appeared next to me. "You cannot go to the top of the wave like that," she said almost sarcastically. Looking down at myself, I didn't understand. My soul was manifesting as my earthly self. Grabbing my hand, she took me away from the wave.

"Have you ever heard of form transference?" She asked, as I nodded no. "In order to expand your abilities to travel these realms, you must learn to transfer form. Up until now we have done this for you." Confused, I just looked at her. "The term shape-shifter may be more familiar to you." This was a term I did understand. "There are many levels of transcendence on this side. Different forms of matter and spirit manifest in different dimensions. Look at yourself." I did as she asked. "You are astral matter right now. You manifest in spirit what you know to be yourself in the physical. This is one frequency of your self. But if you wish to travel through higher dimensions, you will need to alter your frequency." Suddenly, an inner knowing entered within. "Oh, I understand. In order to follow the wave, I need to enter pure spirit form." She smiled. "Yes, that is true. There are many forms you may take; pure energy, light, spirit, astral, physical, and others. And each of these forms can manifest in many frequencies. The higher you go the more light you will need to continue becoming. Learning form transference will open the doors to all aspects of yourself. It will also aid in the transfer from physical form to spirit at will when you are in your body." Excited, I allowed the broadcast that was now entering my spirit which emanated further knowledge about form transference and programs to change the structure of my spirit.

Knowing now what to do, my astral self began to transfer through thought to an energy form. Willing myself to enter the next form, I became pure energy. Looking behind, I could see my astral self still standing behind me, but I had entered a pure energy beam prepared for flight. Intrigued, I quickly jumped back into my astral self. "Wow, that was neat!" I said. Again, I entered pure energy and quickly popped back. Directing me, the woman said, "Now, truly transfer your energy. Follow your inner knowing." Imaging my astral self, I began to alter its reality. In my mind, I saw the particles of my astral self rearrange. Turning like a vortex, the particles were becoming pure energy molecules. Thinking of flight, my astral self swirled into a ball of energy and shot for the astral sky. My astral image was no longer below, I'd transferred my form.

Returning to the scene of the energy wave, I followed the wave, shooting to the crest, feeling total ecstasy and oneness with God, my joy was complete.

"Your reality body is transcendentally pure, equal in all times, without distinction: Therein all worlds are gathered, and form and dissolve without obstruction. I see your body in all realms, in a variety of manifestations: And in your pores I see the moon and stars."
The Flower Ornament Scripture, Chapter 39, Entry into the Realm of Reality, Page 1294, Stanza 2-3, (Buddhism, Mahayana)

****

Chief Joseph (my spirit guide) showed me that upon entering the vibrational state, I could make a running motion and that would separate my spirit from my body. He also showed me that keeping my etheric arms at my side, close to my body when flying would make my soul shoot like a rocket.
****

Fifteen steps behind on the pathway to transcendence, I had fallen back because of distractions. Soaring with purpose, I got through the first five steps with ease. Easily passing through the next five, I came upon a turn in the path. Turning, I fell over, but quickly lifted myself up continuing my journey. Somebody I remembered and knew was in the transcendence booth, which was where I would go after finishing all fifteen steps.

Those ahead of me were proceeding with difficulty now because of the different concentrations required upon each of the final five steps. Landing in each individual slot was difficult, because the soul became more weightless from the first ten steps. Floating out of control, it became difficult to grab hold of the next step.

Looking beyond me, I was beckoned by the soul who had become transparent. "Marilynn," she said, "I speak to you now from a higher place than your own. You know this is true, don't you?" Nodding yes, she beckoned me to listen. "Marilynn, you are allowing yourself to be distracted, you must go on. You are an advanced spiritual traveler created in human form, you have been given the ability to travel amidst the tunnels between worlds, a gift so few have been given, and no other has been given at your level until now." Stunned by this pronouncement, she asked, "You know why, don't you?" Nodding that I didn't know why this was true, she began explaining why, but I could no longer hear her. "I didn't hear you!" I shouted, but she was not given leave to repeat it.

Now on the last two steps, I needed to focus, concentrate, and let distraction fall to the wind. Achieving transcendence by God's grace, I realized that in a world filled with vice, distraction is our enemy.

"A million distractions, disguised as Thee, constantly delude us. Come, O Perfect Joy, into the waiting temple of our devotion! Be Thou the Pole-star during our wanderings in the night of ignorance, leading us safely to our haven in Thee."
Whispers from Eternity, Page 103, Stanza 3, (Hinduism, Kriya Yoga, Words of Paramahansa Yogananda)

"From the very moment in which mortals begin to have use of their reason, each one of them is followed by many watchful and relentless demons. For as soon as souls are in a position to raise their thoughts to the knowledge of their God and commence the practice of the virtues infused by Baptism, these demons, with incredible fury and astuteness, seek to root out the divine seed; and if they cannot succeed in this, they try to hinder its growth, and prevent it from bringing forth fruit by engaging men in vicious, useless, or trifling things."
The Mystical City of God (Abrid.), The Transfixion, Chapter II, Page 403-404, (Christianity, Catholic, Words of Mary)
****

Teaching a young six-year old girl how to fly at a large schooling facility in the heavens, we were working with souls sub-consciously to bring about their redemption. Holding her hand, I grasped her around the waist and told her to hold tight. Running quickly, we jumped over a cliff and into the sky, flying with ease. But when I pushed her off to fly on her own, she was unable to do it. Weighing too much, she was also afraid to do it by herself. By weighing too much I in no way mean a physical measure, for she was quite a tiny girl. Our lightness of being on a soul level is determined by our spiritual frequency, not by physical weight.

Taking her back to the ground, I spoke to her of letting go and flying free within the love of God. "Your soul is too heavy, my child." Although I'd seen many souls, especially in certain hell realms, who's spiritual weight was a great deal heavier; her soul was just a bit too heavy to fly. "You need to feel safe in the

Lord, be willing to stand alone, and soar into your love of God. Then you will fly on your own, my child." Looking pensive, she opened to my words. Needing to remember her uniqueness within the realm of God's thinking, this would allow her to feel safe in taking her unique creative expression aloft.

In the end we all fly alone towards the pillar of the Lord. Resting easy in God's love for our individuality, we must maintain humility within our own smallness. God's redemption is active and industrious, existing in our own world through Christ's sacrifice, and in worlds and realms we forget in our sub-conscious minds. Awakening to these mysteries, we may graduate from this mortal existence into the paradise spheres of greater love and light.

Leaving the young girl to her exercises, she was beginning to make progress, slowly and surely. Before leaving, I was given permission to look in upon several classrooms, wherein the students were being taught universal moral codes and their souls were being imprinted with redemptive knowledge for their gradual future development.

For that which is living must continue becoming, otherwise it falters into the throes of death, also called stagnation and the redemption is a grand thing, not a solitary moment.

"The Rabbis said that the Redemption of Israel cannot come suddenly, but will come gradually and slowly, just as the sun gradually and slowly rises in the dawn of day."

The Talmudic Anthology, No. 279. Page 372, Stanza 3, Midrash Shoher Tob, 18, (Judaism)

****

Entering into an ecstatic state, my spirit and body were vibrating at speeds beyond my own imagination. Before my face, lights began to appear resonating all across my interior landscape placing my mind and spirit into an even higher state of peace and rapture. I watched the lights for a very long time. Smiling faces of those I'd known before who had died before me crossed over into my vision . . . and they waved as if in welcome. Exterior movement was long gone, as my world was completely consumed and taken away from all that was physical into the ether. Continuing for several hours, I rode the waves of ecstatic rapture in silent gratitude.

****

Entering into a border world, I immediately became aware of two different states of perception that I was being pulled in and out of in order to observe them.

The first state of perception was that of an earthbound soul, the physical perspective. Three-dimensional in nature, there was great beauty in it, but a flatness as the vision I had was directly in front of me and almost like a flattened movie screen. The second state of perception was that of the spirit in death and was intriguing in that it was very globular. My view was not just straight ahead, but above me, behind me, to the sides of me, etc. My vision was multi-dimensional and very expansive as if I were viewing reality from every aspect of my being, rather than simply in front of my face.

But there was an energetic shift with each view, as well, which will be hard to describe. In the first earthly view, I was in a state of total peace. For a while now, I had experienced a certain serenity in my impending death which I hadn't always had before. It seemed to me a simple stepping over into another life, rather than such a ripping away from my past (a view I had experienced frequently when I was initially diagnosed). But despite this peace, there was a blandness which perhaps came from the fact that this path was reaching its end. But most certainly it also came from the fact that the earthly path was less vast than the other. In the second spirit in death view, I was in a state of excited peace. Total serenity overcame me, but it was a serenity filled with a liveliness and excitement. It seemed that there was so much more to this world than the simple three-dimensional reality from which I had come. There was so much more to know and understand, and I found this exciting, but in a serene sort of way. It was perhaps as if my molecules were more enlivened in this other world, enlivened towards higher knowledge and vaster plains of truth to follow and expand upon within my true sphere of perception. For perception in this other world was like a sphere, rather than the flat screen of the earthly three-dimensional view.

Suddenly, I was ripped out of this interesting observational situation and awoke.

"Be not content with the ease of a passing day, and deprive not thyself of everlasting rest. Barter not the garden of eternal delight for the dust-heap of a mortal world. Up from thy prison ascend unto the glorious meads above, and from thy mortal cage wing they flight unto the paradise of the Placeless."
The Hidden Words, No. 39, (Bahai', Words of Baha'u'llah)

"Were anyone apprised of that which is veiled from the eyes of men, he would become so enraptured as to wing his flight unto God."
The Tablets of Baha'u'llah, Excerpts from Other Tablets, (Bahai', Words of Baha'u'llah)
****

INTRODUCTION:
Come to Wisdom's Door
How to Have an **Out-of-Body Experience***!*

Amidst the spectral journey of the physical being upon this earth-plane we know as earth, it comes upon a time in its sojourn whereupon it realizes it has been asleep at the wheel in the cosmic purpose of its existence. It is at this time that the soul is beckoned to come forth and reach towards a higher ideal in existence and in eternity, to find the meaning and purpose of its existence in this realm, to go forth into higher worlds and to seek out the knowledge which has been lost to it for time immemorial. It is this time that we seek now.

Come to Wisdom's Door is a beckon to your inner spirit to come forth and stand at God's feet to be instructed in the knowledge of the spheres. It is a beckon to you to find the Master, the Lord of all, within you and inside you, and to break the barriers of physical existence and sojourn into another place which provides the instruction for which your soul yearns.

Out-of-Body Travel is the means and mechanism of this journey and in order to attain unto it in the proper way followed by the prophets, saints, mystics, sages and ascetics of all religions throughout time, our souls must be prepared to enter within its confines.

How do we do this? We must Come to Wisdom's Door and be instructed . . .

CHAPTER ONE
To Begin . . .

We are all travelers, whether we know it or not, in a temporary world of vice created for our instruction. Our own vice has brought us here, and our recognition of these factors is what will bring us out.

So we begin our instruction with the understanding of from where we come . . . from where we are now. Each of us has incarnated upon this world to fulfill certain tasks, much of which has to do with certain realization and attainments within our soul. Many of these attainments can be reached through the modicum of Out-of-Body Travel, but the mystical state must be approached first with the knowledge of what we must first achieve to reach it.

Most of us live within a grand world of noise, karmic chaos to be exact. The first thing that the prophets, saints, mystics, sages and ascetics would do in their journey to higher wisdom was to seek out the world of silence. They did this in various ways. Some of the prophets were called into the wilderness, as were many ascetics and monks. But others intentionally isolated themselves and began to seek God through ceaseless prayer, fasting, mortifications and the practices of contemplation and meditation.

So we begin with this.

But in order to achieve the true contemplation and meditation for which our souls seek, we must first examine the world of noise and begin to shut things off, so to speak.

In the world of our day, activity is honored and extolled, while serenity and quiet is considered unfruitful. Ironically, just the opposite will be true in our consideration of the attainment and expansion of mystical states.

First, we must consider individually the purpose and destiny in this life. Because it is in this that we will find the proper balance in following this path, without interfering with our individual work for the Lord. For instance, in my own life, my work is to go into these states a great deal of the time, and thus, my world is very secluded and quiet as a general rule. However, there are many other purposes in this world which contain within them varied elements of participation in the world and its effects, and these are valid destinies which must not be usurped in the journey to reaching a higher understanding and/or mystical states.

Consider your own vocation in this life, whether or not you feel that the work you do on a daily basis is your highest calling or not. Take into consideration the requirements of fulfilling that work first, because there is great holiness in fulfilling our work whether it be something lofty or mundane, for the purpose of God's kingdom. Every work in this world carries with it great importance in a societal structure, and we mustn't allow our ego to play a part in this consideration. Think deeply on your work, whether you be a trash collector, mother, artist, or judge; and contemplate deeply on the earthly requirements you will require to abide by to give that work the proper honor within the context of your duty to society and, thus, God's kingdom in creating balance and stability across the worlds. Be totally honest and real with yourself about the responsibilities entailed within the earthly vocation you now follow, for this is vital in understanding the entire context of the journey of which you are about to embark.

In doing so, set aside now whatever the needs of that vocation shall be and give this to the soul as a requirement of your journey. Because you will consider this vocation as the holy will of God for you in your life, and will give it the proper context and respect in achieving its ends.

Next I ask you to do the same thing in regards to the needs of your immediate family; parents, siblings, spouses and children. But I ask of you to take a slightly different look in this regard.

We all have different family structures. For those of you who have supportive, loving and functional families, take heed of your God-given responsibilities to them and add this to your vocation which will be set aside from that which we will examine.

For those who come from one of the varied dysfunctional environments who may be very unsupportive of this journey, look upon this with a different view. I will ask you to look upon your responsibilities to God first, in order to ascertain your *proper* responsibilities to your family. We are given to be stewards of legitimate needs, not slaves to inopportune vice. Examine your own family within this context and allow yourself to ascertain that responsibility as part of your vocation and set it aside from that which we will examine.

What remains now is the rest of your life beyond your vocational responsibilities to God, family and country. In this context, I shall ask you to examine that portion of your existence and what you can do to alter its mechanism from 'doing' to 'being.' Are you engaged in constant activity? Do you feel you must always be taking in new things from your exterior world? If so, the first thing you will do which can be difficult for many people is to cease.

What remains to you now is the time that is accessible within your life and reality to explore mystical states. But now we must examine your reasons and means to explore such matters.

I shall tell you what the prophets, mystics, saints, sages and ascetics did in their search. They set aside all self-serving motivations in their quest and asked to know the Will of God alone. Humbling themselves before God and all that is, they asked to be shown the truth whether it coincided with their previous view of reality or not. In so doing, they were able to be instructed. For if you are attached to your own views, how is that God will instruct you otherwise? Pursuing this path contains within it a given understanding that you will not do so to prove your own theories of reality to be true. Follow this path to truly know, and then you will find yourself opening to receive.

Secondly, they pursued this path with serious ardor and great respect. It never occurred to them to 'play around' with spiritual gifts or to look at them as something other than a very holy gift to be nurtured with the greatest responsibility and selfless regard. Part of the reason they were able to generate such deep intense ardor was because they understood that such spiritual gifts could be given to them by either a heavenly or hellish specter. They were not disillusioned into believing that such things would automatically come from God, but that they were capable of being deceived by evil spirits and lost souls whose entire purpose would be to lead them astray from God's holy will. And yes . . . there is a grand difference from experiencing Out-of-Body Travel and Mysticism as directed by the eternal hand of God or from the hands of a lost soul, dark spirit or demonic force.

Remember the holy prophets of the Old Testament who were regularly 'raised up to heaven' such as Enoch 'the man who walked with God.' They experienced Out-of-Body Travel as a sanctioned part of their mission for God, and thus, it was rendered useful for the people and for their own sanctification. And remember the consequences to King Saul for going to a medium to call up the spirit of a dead prophet because he was impatient in knowing the will of God? He lost his kingdom. This was so because he approached the holy altar through an inappropriate door. He did not wish to wait upon the Lord . . . and this is what we shall discuss next.

Before entering the silence, the soul must always begin to cultivate patience first. Because in entering the silent corridors after living in a world of noise and activity, the soul will become impatient with God if he does not understand that he must approach the holy altar of the Lord with an entirely different view.

The Lord chooses whom He chooses and when He chooses. Not my will, Lord, but thy will be done. Cultivate this within your new view.

I ask you to cultivate patience first because the Lord so wills it. In approaching the mystical experience from a proper view, rather than as something to 'play around' with, your progress may appear to be slower or come in waves of activity followed by lulls of inactivity. That is because the Lord does not wait upon us, but we are to wait upon the Lord.

Surely, you must know that dark forces and lost souls who also perceive the spiritual pathway from a wrong view would love to energize the path you take with extreme vigor to fill you with pride and excitement in your progress. In so doing, if you ever realize you are being led astray, you will be less likely to renounce your wrong view because you've become attached to the false 'spiritual gifts' which have been given you to take you away from that which is true.

Pursuing Out-of-Body Travel through the wrong path may yield initial results, but it will not yield long-lasting results which actually produce within your soul progress towards the goal of your existence in this realm, which is karmic purification and union with God.

In contemplating patience, however, I wish for you to remind yourself of these very important things. There is great satisfaction and joy in pursuing God, while there is great agitation and pride in pursuing holy gifts as if it were a game. God waits upon those who wait upon Him . . . and He is worth the wait.

Experiencing Out-of-Body Travel outside of a true search for God is empty and non-rewarding. It also can become a path of the ego, and thus, a path of endless falsehoods which take you nowhere.

There are many souls who have been led astray by this very means. In their fervor to achieve the Out-of-Body Experience, they have lost the understanding and purpose of such things.

The prophets, saints, mystics, sages and ascetics always kept this knowledge firmly fixed before them. And by so doing, when the inevitable hardships, dry periods or confusion arose, they kept their view firmly fixed upon heaven in patience and trust . . .

If you have followed a wrong path in pursuing the Out-of-Body Experience, allow me to invite you to change that at this very moment. God is merciful in His judgments and He wishes all to be saved . . . it is never too late in this life to change our view, and thus, our path, towards that which serves God in this realm and across all worlds. Simply fall on your knees in prayer and tell God these things.

By so doing, you will re-energize a new spiritual path towards light rather than darkness and the will of the evil one or the agitation of those who are lost and choose to remain so because of stubborn pride in holding to their wrong view even in death. These are the souls who require our compassion . . . but also our watchfulness, because they continue to 'play around' in death and are confused, often without even realizing that they are so. This is why it is so easy for them to share such wrong views with those of us still encased in form because they may truly believe they are correct as they wander around in purgatorial realms without the ability to see that the heavenly abode lies within the reach of us all, if only they would release their wrong-views long enough to see the heavenly abode in the distance.

So in preparation to experience Out-of-Body Travel, we must follow a path of service to our fellow men and to God in all worlds. This begins with recognizing those elements of destiny within our own life in relation to our work and our families and setting this aside as our duty. We then indemnify the remaining time and space in our life to be solely and exclusively devoted to our pursuit of God and the knowledge of ourselves. We pursue the mystic path by pursuing God first.

And it ends in acquiring patience to follow this path at the rate in which God chooses, rather than that which we believe to be best.

There is a tradition among masters and disciples in Buddhism which relates to this patience and fervor we must achieve in our quest to find God. It is said that the ancient masters would take their disciples into a pond and place their heads under the water. Waiting for them to struggle for air, they would allow them to remain under the water only long enough for them to become a bit frantic in their desire to breathe. When they emerged from the water, the master would calmly say, "When you desire to know God with the intensity with which you just desired to breathe, you will find Him."

CHAPTER TWO
Prayerful Fervor

There is correct and incorrect fervor. Incorrect fervor is motivated by self-seeking rather than God-seeking. Correct fervor seeks only God as its end. Seek to evaluate if you have fervor, and if so, what kind.

Because fervor is a direct factor in subsequent experience, we need to discuss how to achieve a proper fervor for God which will yield results to a soul seeking to know Him.

The prophets, saints, mystics, ascetics and sages found fervor because they had naturally begun to detach from the things of this world and had thus naturally amended to a desire for the things of the next world.

So we begin to achieve fervor by first recognizing that our attachment to the things of this world prevents us from developing a proper fervor for the things of the next.

Detachment is a necessary step in the spiritual path and one that comes through a concentrated effort on our part. Many of the ancient Buddhist texts discussed detachment as being not only the goal of the path of renunciation but the first step. And this begins with the recognition of certain 'cankers' within our own soul.

'Cankers' in Buddhism are similar to 'sins' in Christianity. They are those vices and habits that we are attached to which prevent us from achieving our truest destiny in this world because we are ignoring the purpose of earthly existence which is karmic purification and a liberation from karmic impulse and sin. The Seven Deadly sins are envy, anger, sloth, avarice, gluttony and lust, and if you will follow the texts (Works by Marilynn Hughes, See List on Inner Cover) as recommended, you will learn much about the progress of a soul in the purification of such defects. You will also be reminded sufficiently of the fact that if you are incarnate upon this earth, you have one or more of them as a prerequisite for incarnation into this purgatorial realm.

A clear examination of conscience is required to begin the proper process of renunciation. By recognizing those fetters which attach us to the things of this world, we may begin to focus our concentration on them and to make acts of the will to cease serving such vice. By doing so, you begin to make conscious choices to resist occasions of sin. Do not be concerned if you do not succeed in resisting at all times, for this is part of the process. It is the introduction of conscious choice into the sub-conscious mind which begins the process of detachment.

For this process, we will use the concepts of Buddhism. There is a valid reason to do this. In Christianity, the soul has a tendency to focus on sin, and thus, guilt. A soul can get very stuck in guilt and cease progress as a result. In Buddhism, the process is intellectual. By recognizing superior acts to inferior ones, you begin to make conscious choices to engage in those which are superior. Guilt is removed (which is also a prime instrument used by the forces of darkness which would like to impede your path) and the soul progresses to the next step. (A soul can easily utilize Christianity for the same end, if they are able to honestly acknowledge their fault without losing sight of the Divine Mercy of God and the sacrificial offering made by Jesus Christ for this very cause.)

In choosing the superior over the inferior you might want to be reminded of the seven virtues which counter-balance the seven deadly sins. It is easiest to remember these if you understand that every sin has a virtuous counter action. In Catholicism, there are four cardinal virtues and three theological virtues.

"Prudence enables us to know what to desire or to avoid; justice gives everyone his due; fortitude urges us on when difficulty stands in the way of our duty; temperance restrains us when passion excites us to what is wrong"

A Catholic Dictionary, Cardinal Virtues, (Christianity: Catholic, William E. Addis, Thomas Arnold, Benziger Brothers Publishers, 1893)

Repentance can be an intellectual exercise if the soul has much difficulty with guilt. By doing so, you begin to make the changes you need to make whether you are emotionally inclined to do so.

Eventually, this fervor will be experienced as remorse. And this is a very good thing . . . But we begin the process by making it an intellectual exercise. Energy follows course and it becomes an exercise of the soul.

As it becomes this, remember that repentance is required of us to enter into the Kingdom of Heaven. But God does not wish that we hold onto that which is from the past, but to purify it and become the new man. So we mustn't allow ourselves to focus on it much beyond the natural. Because the next step requires us to step into what is supernatural . . .

"Faith, Hope and Charity are called the theological virtues, because they relate immediately to God. The moral or cardinal virtues are concerned with our duties, and so relate to Him indirectly; but the theological virtues have Him for their immediate object- it is God in whom we believe and hope and whom we love. These virtues are supernatural because they are beyond the reach of man's natural powers, and because they enable him to attain a supernatural end."

A Catholic Dictionary, Theological Virtues, (Christianity: Catholic, William E. Addis, Thomas Arnold, Benziger Brothers Publishers, 1893)

Working on the cardinal virtues pertaining to our duties in this world, lead to working on the theological virtues pertaining to our duties in the next.

But this can be misleading, because we cannot get to that next world unless we bring them into our soul in this one.

These virtues are attained through prayer, because they are gifts of the Holy Spirit with which we must be endowed. They are not a 'natural' part of man, but rather, a 'spiritual gift' which we must ask for in prayer. We have all seen that Faith, Hope and Love manifest in differing degrees among mankind. Some have it to the fullest possible extent, while others have none at all. But it is these which ignite our fervor to know God, a necessary element in our quest to achieve Out-of-Body and Mystical states.

Ask God in prayer to give you the fervor to know Him. Remember that prayer is conversing with God. Alongside whatever prescribed prayers you may utilize in your spiritual practices, make sure your prayer with God is conversational.

CHAPTER THREE
Meditation, Contemplation, Practice

Once a soul achieves true fervor, they must be tempered down into a state of meditative understanding. There is a silent place that the soul must now enter and remain . . . outside of the dutiful works required of him during the day.

This place of meditation must be quiet, serene and peaceful because the soul is now going to learn how to listen to God. He cannot be heard where there is noise, so the soul must go to where God can be heard, rather than remaining in a place which may be comfortable for the soul instead. Go to where God resides, in the silence of your heart. Begin to engage in meditation as much as you can throughout your days depending upon your duties. When I began to enter this phase, I was required to meditate up to three hours per day. Considering my unique purpose to be in the silent places most of the time, go backwards from this figure depending on your worldly duties. If you have one hour, do that. If you have fifteen minutes, do that.

Now enter contemplation, a misunderstood feature of religious tradition. In the Orthodox tradition, contemplation is practiced through what is called 'The Jesus Prayer' (Lord Jesus Christ, Son of God, Have Mercy on Me a Sinner). Throughout the day while engaged in their duties, practitioners repeat this prayer over and over again to bring them back to an awareness of God. It came about because of Paul's exhortation to the followers of Christ to 'Pray without Ceasing.' But the other more well-known contemplative prayer tradition is practiced by remaining in communion (conversation) with God throughout the day while fulfilling the duties of your state of life. Thus, this contemplation keeps a soul in ever-awareness of the presence of God irregardless of what they may be doing. Bringing 'being' into 'doing,' so to speak.

In every spiritual tradition, there are many 'practices' which can be gleaned upon. For instance, in Buddhism is a practice called 'Mindfulness,' where the practitioner, in essence, tries to remain in the moment, focusing only on what is happening right now. This practice is especially helpful in attaining to the realization that 'it's not what you are, but what you are becoming . . . ' ("The Mysteries of the Redemption," Marilynn Hughes) This may be confusing at first, but if you contemplate upon it you will see that it is so. In Hinduism, there is a practice called 'yoga' which utilizes both spiritual and physical actions to bring a synergy between the inner and outer man. In Christianity, there is 'Adoration' where the practitioner places himself in the presence of God and adores Him and meditates upon His attributes. In Native American Religion there is the practice of the sweat lodge, where a person enters into a small enclosure filled with steaming rocks, sweating and purifying oneself in order to receive a vision. There are innumerable practices amongst the many religions which can be utilized according to the individual practitioner's faith to enhance and empower the spiritual journey of the soul.

Many of these things serve for the purpose of making an interior desire manifest exteriorly. By so doing, we are bringing that which is sub-conscious to a conscious level. All of which helps to bring about the Out-of-Body Experience.

CHAPTER FOUR
Interim Glimpses

As you put all these things into your daily practice, several things will begin to occur. I call these things interim glimpses which usually continue throughout your journey and expand and grow even beyond when you begin to experience Out-of-Body Travel.

You may begin to see colors during your meditations which may then expand into your physical waking world. Colored or simple light orbs may become visible to you as you begin to open up to spiritual realities.

Some people will become more aware of presences around them, whether they be good or bad. If a negative presence is around you, ask it to leave in the name of Jesus Christ. You may need to do this more than once or many times. Sometimes these presences may make you happy or uncomfortable; it can vary a great deal depending upon whom they are and for what they have come.

For instance, angelic guardians and spiritual guides may make you feel quite comfortable, while somebody from your karmic past may bring up emotions you don't consciously understand, thus discomfort. Dark forces are always possible, as well, and it is advised that you keep the prayer of the 'Our Father' on your lips as it is the prayer of exorcism for evil spirits. This will keep your energies more clear for positive experiences. The name of Jesus is particularly powerful, as well.

You may become aware of shifts in frequency. Usually, this manifests in a very distinctive change in the 'tone' of the room. Since we are very used to the 'tone' of the room, we notice this shift which usually occurs in one ear and sounds like a high tinny ringing sound. When such a shift occurs, pay attention. You are usually being beckoned to take note of something that is happening in your environment . . . or perhaps something that was just said.

Your awareness may shift without notice. Suddenly, you may be almost transported into another perception of reality. One moment, you may be very grounded and earth-bound and one second later, you may be lifted up into a cosmic space that allows you to view reality from an entirely different vantage point.

Some people will be taken into such spaces for extended periods of time where consciousness will merge for them. Often, the purpose of this is to allow them to observe the goings on of earthly reality from the spiritual perspective, to observe the oneness between life, to observe the energetic elements around all things which assist in reality taking form, etc.

These are instructional states and experiences meant to prepare the soul for the Out-of-Body Experience. And though it may appear that 'nothing is going on,' much is going on energetically to prepare the soul on subtle levels to get ready for a full-blown experience.

CHAPTER FIVE
Preparation to Leave Form

As a soul prepares for mystical experience, several things will begin to occur.

Some sleep times will appear unusually deep as sub-conscious promptings are being programmed deep within the soul.

A person may awaken with the awareness that something really amazing happened during the night, but be unable to recall any of it. Again, this is sub-conscious work being done to prepare the soul . . .

Dream activity may increase and become more vivid (and subsequently more lucid) as the dream state crosses from entirely sub-conscious to slowly working its way into conscious realities. Some people will begin to experience prophetic dreams and what appear to be 'psychic gifts,' although these are actually just the natural development of a five sense individual to a six sense human being.

Human beings have great untapped potentials lying within their reach, and much of what is considered paranormal in our day will be considered absolutely normal in the future.

The person may become more aware of experiencing moments of a semi-vibrational state (which will be explained in more depth shortly) which is a precursor to the totally conscious experience. This will manifest in somebody partially waking up, becoming semi-conscious during sleep, and feeling their body vibrating or buzzing at a low hum. This may be accompanied by buzzing sounds which will eventually increase to a huge roaring sound as one approaches an exit from form.

CHAPTER SIX
Fears and Blocks

As a soul approaches this threshold, it becomes vital to examine and remove fears and blocks to the experience. Some of the simplest to remedy but yet biggest blocks to approaching and completing an Out-of-Body Experience include not emptying the bladder before meditating or sleeping, filling the mind with too much garbage (i.e. television), not creating enough solitude, allowing too many potential interruptions during sleep or practice, and finally, not listening to the spiritual promptings which are already in process which might be calling for some type of change. Remember that in a spiritual path, our progress is gauged by how quickly we respond to guidance from God, no matter how subtle it may be.

Some of the fears I am about to discuss can be very crippling if not dealt with fully.

For instance, many people are afraid they will die if they attempt to experience Out-of-Body Travel, and this is just not the case. Spiritual experience only enhances the life we already lead. Rather than actually catapulting the soul into an as yet undiscovered country, the soul is actually in truth only becoming *conscious* of something for which they have already been participating.

Some people are afraid of the dark side and should be alerted to that presence. Keep the name of Jesus Christ near you at all times and let prayerfulness be your constant companion.

Ironically, one of the first things a soul will notice when getting ready to eject from form is that the spiritual body does not breathe in the same way that a physical body does. When a soul disconnects its awareness from the physical body's breathing, it will immediately enter the awareness of the spiritual body and it can appear that breathing has stopped. This is an illusion; the soul has just transferred awareness from one form of existence to another. This transference does not in any way change the two existences, just the point of perception of the traveler.

Some people are afraid of ghosts and the easiest way to remedy this is to be reminded that human beings are no more than ghosts in bodies themselves.

People are people whether they be in spirit or in the physical and the traveler will experience ghosts in much the same way he would experience other people in his waking life. (This does not mean, however, that a soul will not be called to the service of 'Lost Souls' as many eventually will be asked to do.)

The fear of the unknown can be a huge difficulty for some because they worry that they might get lost or be unable to come back. Although the Universe is vast indeed, it is important to remember that it is an ordered Universe and that instruction is always at your beck and call. No matter the issue you may be confronted with, you can always call for assistance. You can ask for the help of your guardian angels who are usually nearby or call out to Jesus for help. With the exception of when I've undergone teachings in relation to following the call of my inner spirit, I have never been left alone in my traveling as there has always been an overriding presence who leads me every step of the way. (Now there are times when I've engaged in demonic warfare and have been expected to do so 'alone.' But I've always had assistance as close as a simple call for help, and I wasn't asked to engage in this warfare until I'd undergone extensive training in the facilitation of such.)

Believe it or not a lot of people can get frightened by the simple experience of the unconditional love of God. It's so intense, that it can be overwhelming and 'too much' for some. Simply being aware of that intensity can prepare a soul for the experience to some extent.

Another fear comes from the desire to hold onto the ego. Some can be really threatened when their view of reality is challenged or if they receive guidance indicating that they are not yet perfect. Humans don't like to change even though that's what we're here to do. Humans don't like to change their view of reality; they like to hold onto it even when it no longer serves them. But a soul need not fear any of these things because they apply to us all. If we are to transcend this mortal realm into the higher spheres, we will have to confront our own imperfections, our own false views about truth, and we will have to change. So knowing we're not alone in this can be helpful, because every single prophet, saint, mystic, sage and ascetic from throughout the world and time had to do exactly the same thing to achieve their calling.

I've saved two of the biggest fears for last because they are common obstacles to almost all.

The first one is the fear of being alone with oneself. After all, our world is focused entirely on activity and doing and to shift from this to a state of being . . . and then being alone with oneself . . . can be quite threatening, not to mention boring at first. But this is because the inner self has not yet been cultivated. This aloneness is the path to that cultivation. Don't give it up.

Finally, the second one is the normal reaction of a human being to the unexplainable intensity of the experience. Although it is emotionally intense, this is not that to which I refer. I speak of the raw and unbridled divine power which pulses through your body as you enter into the vibrational state and connect to the cosmic mind. Which is what we shall discuss next.

CHAPTER SEVEN
Mechanics

Most people will become aware that they are about to have an Out-of-Body Experience when they enter into what is called the vibrational state. But some may feel the inklings of the experience by initially hearing a loud roaring sound. Either way, the two will eventually merge and come together so that you are experiencing the vibrational state and hearing the loud roaring sounds at the same time.

The vibrational state occurs because the soul is disconnecting from physical awareness and re-engaging into spiritual awareness. Because physical vibration of particles is so much slower than that of the spirit, this change is dramatic and can be very scary the first few times. But it's only frightening because it is such a different point of experience from what the soul is used to, and eventually it becomes a very comforting and peaceful time. More on that in a moment.

Although it may sound like a jet-engine revving up for flight, what the soul is actually hearing is the change in frequency from the physical realm to the spiritual; which again, is much higher than what the soul is used to. Particles vibrate at a much faster rate of speed in the spirit world and it takes some getting used to.

Usually, but not always, the soul will immediately connect to what could be termed the mind of God as soon as they enter into the vibrational state. This is an amazingly powerful thing because you enter into a state of all-knowing, although unfortunately you can't bring it back with you when you return. However, part of the purpose of the Out-of-Body Experience is to bring little pieces of it back, little by little, so that eventually the soul tends to become and engage more from this source than from any earthly one. When connected to this, the soul will feel like all knowledge is available to him. Anything the soul might want to understand, he currently does. But when you return, much of that will retract.

While experiencing this connection, the soul may also begin to feel the first inklings (or a full-blown blast) of the unconditional love of God. It will truly be life-altering and is completely beyond words.

This experience can continue just like this for many times, or a soul can be inspired to leave his body the very first time. Great variation can occur in this particular aspect of the journey. Others may experience what I call vibrational raisings before they ever leave their body, while some may go ahead and experience an exit and then be apprenticed through the vibrational raisings further on.

Vibrational raisings are usually overwhelming at first because the soul re-enters the spiritual frequency . . . and then the spirit world begins to raise the consciousness even higher. In essence, the soul's engines are revved to an even higher frequency, the purpose of which is to gradually bring the soul's consciousness, view, perspective and physical body to a higher level to attain to greater and greater insight and understanding. Knowledge is energetic, and although this is hard to understand, it is with each vibrational raising that the soul sees its consciousness rise. Understandings evolve into a higher ideal. Vibrational raisings are so very important because they are truly the cornerstone to the evolution of the soul.

Let me use an analogy. If you were to take a three-year old child and have the ability to raise their awareness up to the level of say an eighty-year old man, this would be very significant. Although such a thing would be undesirable on the physical level, on a spiritual level, raising our awareness to the level of more highly evolved spiritual beings has great purpose. Not only does it prepare us to overcome our own karmic impulse and ascend from this world to higher worlds, but it prepares us to become servants in the Kingdom of God which consists of this world and all others; higher and lower.

Vibrational raisings are experienced as highly powerful shifts in the actual force of the vibrations which accelerate and recede according to how well the consciousness takes in the thrust. They can go on for minutes or hours and although they are somewhat frightening at first, as time goes on they become something very blissful.

When the soul is ready to leave the body it can be done in a number of ways. The most common at first is to roll out. Sometimes angelic guardians will lift the soul out in the beginning to be helpful and instructive. But as time progresses the spirit can learn other techniques for exit; such as using the power of thought to 'will' the spirit out of the body.

Another mechanic you mustn't forget is that the soul operates from the standpoint of a spherical existence with all senses originating from every point along that sphere. Sight, hearing and other senses will not originate from an organ of the body, but from the entire consciousness. Because of confusion over this, some people may have trouble seeing at first or hearing . . . or moving around.

Movement is not accomplished through two legs in the spiritual body, but rather, by means of thought. Sometimes in the beginning, a soul may be tempted to try to 'wade' through the spiritual ether. But this will only get them so far. The soul must discipline the mind to make things happen through thought. By doing so, movement will not only become easy, but instant . . . as the light body is capable of traveling at light speed.

Remembering that physical objects are permeable is important, but realize that they will be more 'tight' vibrationally than air. Going through physical objects can and will be done, but it will be experienced differently than non-solid objects.

Two things that might take the first time traveler by surprise are these.

Immediately, the soul will notice a new ability to sense the reality of spirits and people the soul comes across while in the spiritual body. The soul can hear the thoughts of humans, as well as, a huge roaring and sometimes overwhelming mass of the thoughts of humanity blasting in the background. Upon observation of an entity or individual, the soul may be provided with information on their past, present or future . . . a new ability to sense realities. The soul can sense past-lives, karmic states, needs, etc.

Another thing that will assuredly surprise most is that in the spiritual body . . . thoughts become things. What you think about . . . will appear before you. Where you think about . . . will take you to that place. If you think of someone . . . either a holographic image of them may appear before you, or you will be sent to them immediately (or vice-versa). Because of this reality, it's important to understand how to discern between holographic images of entities, and true entities.

A true entity will behave according to the manner in which you know them, or the higher form (you may not yet know) which appears in their place. A holographic image will respond according to your thoughts.

Sometimes a soul has to discern between their own fear-generated holograms which can bring all sorts of chaos around them in the spiritual state, and a true dark or demonic persecution, which during the purification process will be just as common.

The way to tell the difference is this. A fear generated thought-form will respond to the soul deciding to change the form, i.e. 'You are an eagle, not a vicious beast!' If the form changes, then it is most likely a hologram of internal fear. But if it's a dark force, it will not respond according to your own inner fears and promptings or your wish to change them. It will act as a separate being, vicious and destructive. If you suspect one of these, call on the name of Jesus repeated and continually recite the 'Our Father' which forces them out.

Beyond the experience itself, there is a whole host of things a spirit will now undergo if they are to follow a Path of Karmic Purification (The Ascension Pathway).

Among the stages a soul will go through are these: Awakening, Co-Creation, Surrender, Rites of Passage and Initiation into the Mysteries, Emergence of Karma, Mirroring of Karma, Ignition of the Eternal Flame and the Ascension.

Beyond the Path of Purification lies the Path of Discrimination (The Alteration Pathway) which contains these stages: Rites into the Medicine, Rites of Evolution, Alteration of Reality.

Beyond the Path of Discrimination lies the Path of Discipline (The Absolution Pathway) which contains these stages: Energetic Entry into Ancient Sacred Paths, Entry into the Knowledge of the Lower Realms, Self-Scrutiny, Original Sin and the Mysteries of the Redemption. Beyond this . . . lies the mysteries of death, dying and the afterlife and all that is ancient!

Because the knowledge contained within these paths is vast, they are contained within several books. (All are listed at the front of this book.) But allow me to say welcome, traveler! To the pathway . . .

ADDENDUM
Evolution and the Question of Consciousness:
A Function of the Brain or a Function of the Soul?

Throughout the ages, mankind has struggled with the basic question of existence. Most people know that the brain is the center force of the body, a computer of sorts that dies as the body dies.

Scientists argue that one must prove all things according to scientific method, a series of rules which define three-dimensional worlds of form; worlds with physical substance and solidity.

Religionists argue that some things are to remain as mysteries. They say it is an issue of faith, just believing in something you cannot see or know.

What if they were both right and both wrong?

What if our world - the world of form - is only one of many worlds? So within this world of form, the laws of science would indeed apply. However, if there were other worlds, worlds that existed in multi-dimensional realities, would it not be plausible and highly likely that the laws ruling their existence would be different?

Perhaps the world of spirit can be called the world of force. We call it such because it generates the power behind all that exists in substance. If this world of force exists beyond third-dimensional laws, beyond what can be lawfully seen within the confines of physical sense, then it would indeed be true that one must have 'faith' or belief in that world to then see it.

But then again . . . what if this world of force could actually be seen and proven to individual souls who were willing to change their frame of reference and their ability to view? Would the worlds of science and religion be willing to traverse the pathway which would lead to proof (albeit on an individual basis) that would only be attainable if they were to step outside of the 'method' and the 'mystery?'

Consider me a scientist of a different kind. My scientific method is to allow the Universe to SHOW ME what is true rather than confining the truth to a very limited understanding of what that can be based upon what we already know within the confines of our very small eye-view from the standpoint of a physical organism. Consider me a scientist of the soul who attempts to contain within myself both the worlds of science and religion to find the cohesive truth that inevitably binds them beyond the world of form. My scientific method stumbled upon me. I did not choose it. My method of exploration is Out-of-Body Travel.

Out-of-Body Experience has been elusive only because it has not yet been properly explored. Science perceives it as a ridiculous assertion of the brain. Religion feels that it is wandering into worlds that should remain a mystery . . . perhaps going too far.

But for those who have experienced such things, there is absolute experiential proof. You are not going to convince somebody who has experienced such things on an extensive enough level that what they have seen is not valid. What type of proof is most valid? That which is experienced by someone which was previously considered an unknown, or that which has been theorized by someone who has never experienced it?

For thousands and perhaps millions of years, mankind has always struggled with crossing into the next threshold of the age. Mankind has struggled with a myriad of things which seem so small to us now; whether to believe the world to be flat or round, the development of energy source, communications and transportation. Each of these developments met with ridicule and mockery. The mass populace found it ridiculously naive' that these scientists, explorers and harbingers of a new age could possibly be onto something. But they were . . .

Out-of-Body Travel is not merely 'psychic' phenomena. It is more like the moment when Christopher Columbus saw the new world for the first time. It is the awakening of a part of our consciousness that was previously asleep. Sudden proof thrust upon us of a higher truth that is not within the realm of dispute to the one who experienced it. But this proof only comes upon us (at least at this time) one at a time. Unlike other developments in the history of mankind, this is one that every person must traverse alone.

To do so requires a recognition of science as well as faith; because it is through the curiosity of science that we energize the knowledge to come. It is faith which allows the knowledge of consciousness to come to us of its own accord, in its own way. Rather than coming to us in a way which fits within the confines of our current limited understanding.

Out-of-Body Travel provides a window into the next major evolutionary leap within mankind. Science has trouble with this because their methods only apply to us as long as we remain three-dimensional. But what if we become fourth or fifth-dimensional human beings? Then their rules no longer apply. Religion has trouble with this because they feel that these abilities only belong to special people; prophets, saints, mystics, sages and ascetics. But what if these extraordinary few were actually the first of our kind to make these leaps in consciousness and they have come to lead the way for humankind? Pre-cursors . . . instigators of great leaps of humankind into new millenniums?

What if a world that our species has been unable to see (as a general rule) for thousands of years does actually exist and it is possible for us to see it? A world that prophets and scientists like Nostradamus have known from the beginning of time, but to the naked mortal eye remained unseen? The world of force. What if the world of form and force have co-existed forever impacting each other in ways unknown to the world of form; while the world of force protected us from the knowledge of our co-existence during our infancy as a species?

What if evolution is as much about energy as it is about matter? And what if we've been making energetic leaps throughout the ages but were unable to see the energetic implications due to our limited scope of vision? Then all levels of evolution within mankind may have been instigated by some energetic alteration coming from the world of force into the confines of our physical vehicles. Perhaps the greater Mind or Soul of humanity would be adjusting on many other levels and in our ignorance we could only actually see physical changes.

Evolution within humanity's soul occurs through energetic alterations which subsequently manifest in a physical universe. Our Universe is a highly complex, multi-dimensional reality of which the physical worlds hold only a small portion. In fact, the three-dimensional worlds are actually pretty low on the totem pole of all life. Guardianed by higher worlds that exist in a myriad of dimensional awarenesses, our world is watched over by those who are anywhere from a fifth-dimensional world to many thousands of dimensions higher than our own. This is a portion of what I've been shown.

As you can imagine, in worlds that exceed third-dimensional reality by many millennia, the laws of existence have become very different than our own. Physical laws apply to physical worlds but not to worlds of force. Worlds of force abide by a whole different set of laws. But the presence of the worlds of force are continuously manifesting in worlds of form, although they keep a low profile.

Appearing only when someone is ready (when their faith and desire for knowledge exceed their arrogance about what they already believe to be true), the world of force intercedes when a human being becomes ready to *experience* knowledge rather than hypothesize from a very limited perspective.

Consciousness is not a myth. It is not an issue of science *or* religion in its truest sense. The issue is the tie between energy and matter.

As a species, we are again being challenged to go to a new level. As Cro-Magnon man could never envision the Homo-Sapien, we have trouble envision a Homo-Universalis or whatever name it may end up being given, but it remains the next step.

Through this step, man's form will become more united to energy attaining to universality, uniting with life in all worlds, not simply our own. Such a change will require a new energetic link-up, not unlike being uploaded to the internet; the new man must be uploaded to Universal Mind.

Knowledge originates in ALL worlds, ALL life, ALL existence, not just a singular world. And to truly *know* something you must *experience* it.

We haven't been alone for quite some time . . . forever, in fact. Higher worlds have guardianed the world of form for thousands of years. Like a small baby we have grown and matured and it is time for us to reach adulthood and take the torch from the world of force to become more like them.

Perhaps science would benefit from taking a step back and thinking about what it seeks. Knowledge comes to those who seek it. But if you seek to prove what you already believe or what is within your present realm of knowledge, you will never know wisdom.

I challenge you to go beyond the limitations of third-dimensional science and seek in a new way. Send your desire to know into the air through prayer. Allow the truth to reveal itself to you in its own way. It may not be what you expect, but it will be made known to you.

Whether you are of the mind of science *or* religion, your brain will process the knowledge that your spirit retrieves.

And as you think, perhaps you will begin to 'see.'

Not unlike the prophets, saints, mystics, sages and ascetics from throughout every religion and time. Not unlike Albert Einstein as he was perusing the theory of relativity which was subsequently revealed to him in a dream. Without sub-conscious promptings, perhaps we would discover nothing at all or at least our technological advancement would have slowed a great deal.

Scientists may say that this is an indication that our brains are working out conclusions through dreaming. But to assume this must mean that our brain carries more knowledge than we have actually taken in from physical sources. In order for this to be true without divine inspiration, we would be required to believe that our brains can retrieve knowledge that we have not yet given it on a conscious level. If our brains are working out things through our dreaming . . . how are they doing this without divine guidance and direction from above? If this were so, the brain would be acquiring knowledge it had not yet been 'fed' from a physical, conscious source. So it must be coming from the world of force . . .

Scientists have also stated that we only use 10% of our brains. Given this, perhaps they would say that the other 90% kicks in to fulfill these functions. But this makes no sense because if there is no force behind the form there would be no inherent desire to engage a cluster of neurons or cells in the brain which are currently inactive. Even such an activity would require a force to activate it in the dreaming state.

Computers require both the force (the programmer) as well as the form (the computer). A computer can only solve problems if the proper programs are uploaded into the system. Without such, it has no deductive thinking skills.

How can our brains inherently contain within them more knowledge than our waking selves? If evolution is a purely physical mechanism, then all we know as a primal species would be all that we are capable of knowing. If there is no force behind the substance, there can be nothing more than literally meets the eye.

Einstein received theories from dreams. Mozart received music from dreams. Those that invented electricity, the telephone and the car were driven by images given to them in dreams. This gives cause to at least ponder the possibility of force behind form.

If we all in fact die a literal death at the end of our lives, evolution would either cease or slow down considerably. It would do so because the form becomes de-energized at death and truly ceases. If every life after breathing a momentary existence were to simply CEASE mid-stop through life, where would the driving force for the continuation of knowledge come from? The driving force would cease with every death and there would be no continuum.

When a computer is turned off, it CEASES. But if programmer's continually upload more and more information into the mind of the computer, it evolves. But it does so because of the force that drives its evolution, not because the will of evolution lives within the computer itself. It *responds* to that which it *receives*, but it will not *instigate* further development.

If it is merely form that we occupy, our souls would not advance. If we were merely form, we would not seek to know *anything*! As mere forms, we would have no knowledge of good and evil. We would simply exist with an instinctual drive similar to the animal kingdom. No *moving* desire to progress as a species would exist.

It requires a soul to desire these things.

Many scientists are doing work to simulate the human brain - artificial intelligence. Despite their greatest efforts, they have been unable to recreate the inherent ability to learn that is shown in the youngest of our species - babies. A computer responds to what it is told to do, but it has no care as to the outcome. A computer can learn things, but only if the knowledge is uploaded to its hard drive. This is because there is no force behind the form. The programmer must supply the force. Turn off the computer and it ceases to function, just as a human being dies and the body ceases to function. But the programmer does not die; the force does not die . . . the force remains. The form itself has no will or desire, but it contains a soul. And it is the soul that instigates evolution.

In the worlds of energy and force - As a mind thinks, so it creates. In the world of science, this seems ridiculous. But in the worlds of force, this is the first law. The second law is the law of gravity . . . the absence of it. The third law is the law of perception . . . perception is limited by the vehicle expressing it. Humanity is limited to three-dimensional perception, while those in the worlds of force can contain fifth to myriad-dimensional perspectives.

In the world of force, vibrational laws express even more. Vibrational law expresses the truth of all things, and the inherent mode of perception of every vibrationary vehicle . . . of which human beings are only one kind. All life carries within it a vibrational energy which expresses its level of understanding, evolution and its past, present and future. Vibrational law enforces that every life form can only exist in vibrational energies at or below its own level of reality perception. Thus, the need for vibrational raisings to incur change. Vibrational law also states that every life form can only perceive through the windows of their own vibrational frequency or below. Again, the need for vibrational raisings to incur change. Vibrational levels differ between life-forms, worlds and between individuals within intelligent species, as well.

Differences in vibrational frequency determine the level of spiritual evolution inherent within a life-form. The higher, the more aware.

If you were to attempt to traverse into a world of a higher vibrational frequency than you possess, you simply could not without the aid of vibrational raisings. Lower frequencies feel as though they are being crushed when they enter into a higher world because the power of their force is so much greater than that which a human being actually encompasses.

Vibrational law is inextricably tied to spiritual evolution because it is the manner in which it occurs in a physical vehicle whether we are aware of it or not. Vibrational raisings are the means to raising perception, knowledge, wisdom and force within a human being. It's very simple in that increase in vibrational frequency or force brings about evolution in consciousness. Vibrational raisings bring the soul to higher levels of knowledge. And knowledge that appeared to be complex prior to such raisings, the soul will just know.

Scientists have already discovered that color, light, electricity and all the forms of 'energy' that we acknowledge to exist have differing frequencies.

Vibrational law speaks of many layers of truth and reality. Each level works within its own parameters and its own world and they interact (often unknowingly) with other worlds in order to eventually advance. Vibrational law also concludes with the inherent sovereignty of the world of force. The world of form is merely a projection of ideas originating from the world of force.

Unifying the worlds of form and force are one of the goals of human evolution. In this unity, our species has a chance to make leaps and bounds in consciousness arriving at new levels. The next level - multi-dimensional Homo-Sapiens or Homo-Universalis.

If science and religion have anything to say in common it may be that there are mysteries to life. Science wishes to demystify, religion wishes to mystify. But perhaps the attainment of those mysteries must be approached with a new view, a perspective which allows for mysteries to reveal themselves as they are rather than how we think them to be in our limited human vehicle.

Out-of-Body Travel is truly a gateway to a new way of life and existence. It pursues direct contact between Creator and created. It allows human beings to have direct contact with *knowledge* itself.

Science tries to place all reality and all worlds in the brain. Physical law says that might be reasonable. Vibrational law says think again . . .

Just as creatures in our own world differ entirely in their mode of existence, so do those who exist in the worlds of force. As the beings of the sea do not breathe oxygen in the same manner that humans must to survive, there are others beyond this realm who need neither oxygen or salt water. Some live in the ether . . . some elsewhere. Because their vibrational frequency is too far removed from our own, we don't see them. But it does not negate their existence.

Human beings must learn from mistakes of the past to stop being arrogant in regards to that which they do not yet know or understand.

Evolution IS the function of consciousness of force. Consciousness evolves by expanding in frequency, enlivening the soul form which follows that force. Form without force is dead. Force without form still lives.

Evolution and the question of consciousness can be answered in that it is both a function of the brain and the soul working together. The world of force creates and the world of form imitates.

When the imitation believes itself to be the creation truth is lost. It is much like the painting of a tree believing itself to *be* the tree. It is not a tree . . . it is canvas and paint made to image the form of a tree. Force begets form.

Many would dispute that I am a scientist of the soul, perhaps because I have not attended the proper schools or hold the proper degrees. And if we were disputing the three-dimensional laws of physics, I would utterly agree. But how can a scientist who has never attended the schools of the spirit world claim to have the proper background to speak of such things?

Just as scientists go to school in the physical world so do I go to school in the spirit world. These schools teach of the worlds and laws of the spirit, rather than the rules and laws of man.

Perhaps evolution requires that we expand our three-dimensional perspectives in order to attain to higher knowledge. Perhaps we must take a leap of faith in order to find the answers to the questions of consciousness that have been with mankind since the onset of time.

Perhaps . . .

Deep in the soul of man
Lies the holy grail of wisdoms chance
The tempest storm of reasons past
Seeks the sign of an angry man
In the dark of the moon, hold my hand

Night holds a seekers glance
Begging, calling for one last chance
Death is a hungry bird
No more time, join with mirth
In the dark of the moon, there's rebirth
Seasons change the Holy Grail
Hark the night the words prevail
No more chance, life is frail
Find the wisdom of the Holy Grail

Far in the ancient cave
The words of knowledge etched with grace
Reason holds a hungry man
Knowledge fills his empty hands
In the dark of the moon, it is man
In the light of the sun, life's begun

Seasons change the Holy Grail
Hark the night the words prevail
No more chances, life is frail
Find the wisdom of the Holy Grail

Symbolic as the cup of life and the cup of knowledge, the Holy Grail must be attained through energetic means. Some things cannot be learned through physical means, but must be learned from a higher force.

Seek, my friend, to find the force which created the form you now hold. And when you do, fall on your knees for you will be standing in the presence of the One Holy God and your spirit will be standing upon holy ground . . .

The Mysteries of Out-of-Body Travel
An Introduction to the Path

It began as a tiny twinkling years ago when I was but nine years old. In the midst of a dark night, the heavens began to open before my astonished eyes. Clouds parted and revealed a marble stairway which led to a podium containing two thrones. Upon them sat who I perceived as God and His son, Jesus Christ.

Angels were singing and flitting all around them as I was summoned forward by this majestic vision.

Much happened during this visit, but the most important message that would be given to me this eve was that God had a plan for my life. Sometime in the future, He and His angels would return to me and show me what I must do. For now, I must wait. I'll never forget waking that morning with the innocence of youth and approaching my mother. "Mom!" I shouted, "I saw God last night!" Of course, she thought I was having a childish fantasy and nothing I could say would make her feel otherwise. So, I went on with my day having no tangible understanding about the ominous message given to me that night.

Thirteen years would pass before the message would begin to impart its purpose. Three months after the birth of my eldest daughter, I spontaneously had my first out-of-body experience. Mind-blowing, I had no idea what my soul had embarked upon, but it would be grand and vast. My husband had the foresight to suggest I begin writing down the experiences, although it hadn't yet occurred to me that I should.

Over the years, my experiences grew into grand vistas of knowledge where my soul was taught the ways of the spiritual world, the mechanics of existence and purified of its many defects. As I continued to expand my horizons in mystical kingdoms, it occurred to my husband that I should try to paint what I had seen; although I'd never taken up a paintbrush in my life. So, I began to do so and started learning to paint; and although my painting was never meant to be something brilliant, I learned to convey a certain energy and feeling through them of the places I'd seen and gone to. Early on, I had begun keeping a tape recorder next to my bed for the purpose of singing the music I would hear in the out-of-body realms. Later, I would teach myself to play guitar, other instruments and how to score music. Even later, I began experimenting with electronic recording equipment so that I could see if it might be possible for me to capture the feel of the music I'd heard in these states, as well.

Finally, the prophets, saints, mystics and sages who had been directing all my activities and experiences came to me with a message. Gather the ancient sacred texts and their writings from every religion throughout time. Beginning to do so, I had no inkling at this point that they would then proceed to guide my every move in adding quotations from their words to the experiences they had given me for the purpose of further enlightening their meaning.

If I were to share some of the most important things I've learned in my journey, it would have to begin with how it all came to be. One of the most common things I see amongst those who seek experiences of this nature is twofold; a desire for techniques, and a misdirected purpose.

Techniques do serve a purpose, but the only purpose they will serve is to provide a soul with the original earth-bound experience. Much more is required of us if we choose to truly seek knowledge in this experience. I've seen myriads of accounts of those who have had what I would term a classic out-of-body experience; wherein a soul leaves its body and experiences something outside of its form upon the earth or the astral planes. But there is so much more to find. Most people will think of these types of experiences when you bring up out-of-body travel, without often realizing that this is truly only the beginning of what can be accomplished in a soul.

It is here where misdirected purpose comes into play. So many people think of this experience as something to be achieved and sought after as an end. But out-of-body travel is really the means to the end; a technique which may assist a soul in seeking enlightenment. But the technique is not itself enlightenment. The end is transformation through knowledge, and knowledge is a gradual attainment which is acquired through energy.

Misdirected purpose can be several things. Firstly, it can manifest itself in someone who starts out with their own theory of truth and expects to prove it.

In this case, the correct approach is to start out assuming that what you believe to be true is going to be incorrect in many ways, thereby opening yourself to be shown what is true beyond your own limited abilities to know. Secondly, it can manifest itself with wrong intentions; playing around with spiritual gifts, wishing to use these gifts for something other than the service of God, etc. Such things will prevent a soul from becoming able to experience this gift in a meaningful way, and it may prevent it from happening altogether. The correct approach is to follow the will of God alone. Thirdly, overt intellectualism can be a huge blockage to such experience, because this can prevent the spirit from instructing the soul because of its own preconceived truths of which it is often much attached.

Many people will focus on the 'playing around' aspect because they don't realize what they are doing. Some manifestations of this can be seen when a person wishes to constantly try to prove their experience by going to see what somebody else is doing and being able to verify it later. Although this may serve some purpose, it can become a blockage to expanding the experience into the realms of knowledge.

Out-of-body travel is only the beginning of true and meaningful mystical experience, and a soul must be willing to understand that such gifts are only given to a soul when they have shown a true desire to serve God only. Self-serving motivations may work in the beginning, but they will hinder you from achieving anything of significance. Oftentimes, such motivations will also hinder a soul from realizing that there is more for them to know, and thus, they will believe they are already there when they have many more trails to cross.

Many stages of development, transformation and evolution occur within the spectrum of what a soul may find in traveling what I call the galactic heavens. But a soul will be tested much along the way and required to offer proofs of their intent and willingness to do as God so wills, rather than as they themselves may choose. What we must understand about this is that God knows what we need to know, while we don't. Our egos can be a huge obstacle to us, because a great deal of this process includes the awakening of knowledge about ourselves within us which we may not wish to hear. Many souls are difficult to teach because they don't want to explore the dark places within themselves, but only the aspects of the journey which remain fun. In order to be teachable, you must be able to handle the criticism that you will receive from heavenly sources and the direction offered for you to change and transform all that is within you that remains incompatible with an all-powerful and loving God. This is very difficult and a huge stumbling block for many, because most do not wish to really 'see' themselves as God sees them; although progress along the spiritual path is impossible without it.

Much can be said about the worlds beyond our own. In my journeys, I began by traveling into my own past lives and learning about the karmic thrust which had held my soul to the Earth for ages past. Learning about Lost Souls, I was given knowledge and wisdom in saving them from their delusions and offering them the hope of the love of God. Meeting beings from other races and planets, I was shown how evolution began and continues within our world, and how it relates to that of other spheres within our universal system. Entering the Initiation into the Mysteries, my soul underwent fascinating ritual passages within the pyramids of Egypt, ancient biblical mysteries, and inexplicable secrets of the ages. As my karmic thrust began to dwindle, my soul was taken into the knowledge of the eternal flame as I was led into the arms of the Angel of the Ascension.

Continuing my quest, I met Chief Joseph of the Nez Perce Indians who took me on a grand journey into the mysteries of evolution and the true path to life. Meeting the Old Ones, they taught me about the nature of good and evil in mortal realms such as the Earth. Learning to alter realities in our realm from the standpoint of energy, I was honored by the sacred Buffalo women to join them in their sisterhood as the medicine women from throughout the ages. And as I began to really experience the realm of evil, Jesus came to save me and show me the council who sits in judgment of such matters before God.

Beginning to tread the holy road of the prophets, saints, mystics and sages from throughout time; I met the Buddha, Babaji, Paramahamsa Yogananda, Padre Pio, Abdul Baha', and various other prophets, saints and mystics from throughout time. Teaching me the path of discipline; I learned of heaven, hell and purgatory and was taken deep into the understanding of the demonic and their realms. Giving me the gift of exorcism, the Blessed Virgin Mary took me on a grand journey into the lower realms to teach me of these worlds and the purposes they serve. In due time, I was given to assist souls as they were crossing over; to take them to their grand reward in the immortal realms, or to offer them one last hope of reincarnation before entering a lower hell realm because of their notorious deeds upon the Earth. 'The Mysteries of the Redemption' were revealed to me in the heavens as the scrolls of the prophets emerged from the stars as brilliant and holy lights. And it was at this time that the Lord revealed to me that I must take all that I had written and compile it into a book with this very title. (The Mysteries of the Redemption: A Treatise on Out-of-Body Travel and Mysticism.)

And as I began this task, the Lord deigned to give me another one; that of its sequel. (Galactica: A Treatise on Death, Dying and the Afterlife) But this would come as a shocking surprise when it was revealed to me that I was suffering from a terminal illness. Traveling down this road, I began writing about the process that a person goes through when they are preparing for death; mystically speaking. Much was revealed to me about the afterlife and the worlds beyond our own. Beyond this, I was given to see the grand city described in the Book of Revelation; adorned with gold, pearls, emeralds, amethyst and other precious gems.

Amidst this journey, the Lord gave to me the most simple and profound of truths. As I stood one night waging war between life and death, standing at the gateway to the next world; Jesus stood by my side. Conveying that I had completed everything I had to do before leaving this Earth, He gave me a choice. Because my children are still very young, I stood firm in my determination to continue to live as long as God would allow. Speaking to me of the Earth, I heard the arguing and complaint amongst the peoples, as if in echo from far away. Nothing will change, He conveyed to me, even as I lay dying the world would remain selfish and the people would be fighting amongst themselves.

At that moment, I had a profound understanding about our mortal realm, the Earth. It is selfishness which holds us to its bounds, and it will be selflessness that will free us from its fetters. No matter what karma may hold you, its root lies in selfishness. And in this lies the secret of liberation from karmic circling, rebirth and continued reincarnation.

As I had made my decision, the Lord gave me a set period of time. During that period of time I was to finish my work and bring it to the people of the Earth in order that the understanding of salvation could be brought to a higher level. Promising Him that I would complete this work, I began soaring at the speed of light through the galactic heavens and into my body below.

And thus, it begins . . .

PART III
The Role of the Seven Virtues and Vices in the Practice of Out-of-Body Travel

Why discuss the seven virtues and vices in relation to understanding a mystical experience such as that found in Out-of-Body Travel?

It is because our goal in this exercise is not the experience of Out-of-Body Travel itself. Out-of-Body Travel and Mystical experience is NOT our end. Purification and sanctification of the soul, union with God . . . is our end. Out-of-Body Travel and Mystical Experience are just a couple of means in which the Lord sometimes so deigns to utilize in assisting those who love Him to reach Him in His Almighty Holiness which is so far removed from ourselves and our world as to be unattainable without the divine pleasure.

These words of Charles Sheedy sum it up best:

"Of course it is true that Religion is not mere knowledge, it is much more a matter of action. In fact, religious knowledge, without religious action, is no good at all. 'Be ye doers of the word, and not hearers only,' says St. James. Religion is a man's response to God, his worship of God. Religion is the service of neighbor when he is in need. Again St. James: 'This is religion true and undefiled before God; to aid the widows and orphans in their tribulations and to keep oneself unspotted from this world.' Above all, Religion is love, first the love of God, and then the love of neighbor for the sake of God. If anybody keeps the two great commandments of the love of God and of neighbor, with all that they imply, then he need not worry about his religion; it is all right.

Well then, if love is all important, why this emphasis on knowledge and on scientific knowledge at that? Because of two reasons. First, a reason based on human psychology: we cannot love what we do not know, and the more we know the more we ought to love. If we know a lot about God, we ought to love Him all the more . . .

We ought to know our faith as well as we can, be able to explain it, and to defend it in case of need. There is an idea around that religion is not worthy of serious intellectual attention. It is considered more as a matter of feeling, of sentimentality. A man will say, "It so happens that I am not religious,' just as he might point out that he does not care very much for fishing or for chocolate ice cream. Thus he carelessly disregards the all-important truths which Christ has taught us, for which He died on the Cross.

Here is a good place to say that we must make every effort to keep distinct these three different ideas: 'Knowledge,' 'love,' and 'feeling.' Knowledge is man's highest power, the act of his intelligence, aimed at the possession of the truth. Love is an act of man's free-will: it always involves a choice on his part, and it is aimed at the possession of the good. Feeling is an act of man's emotions, his sense-drives, and it is aimed at sense-satisfaction, pleasure and the avoidance of pain. Only men are capable of knowledge and love; but animals as well as men have emotions and feelings.

Obviously, knowledge of God and love of God must enter into genuine Religion. Emotional feeling enters into Religion, too - it is helpful, useful, may at times be necessary. For example, the 'peace of mind' we sometimes feel at Mass, or after Confession. But emotional feeling is not essential to Religion, as knowledge and love are. Sometimes our love of God will urge us on to keep loving Him, and serving Hi, and obeying Him, even when our feelings may be running in quite an opposite direction . . .

Theology, then, as Cardinal Newman says, is the Science of God, or the truths we know about God put into system.' Thus theology differs from 'common knowledge,' the bits of unrelated information that the man in the street may have. It is a science. It is organized knowledge. Theology has its principles; from the principles it deduces certain conclusions, according to a scientific method; and its findings are brought together in one organized body of knowledge.

Theology is either natural or supernatural, depending on whether we can learn its subject matter through our own unaided reason, or whether we need God's help in the form of revelation."

The Christian Virtues, A Book on Moral Theology for College Students and Lay Readers, By Charles E. Sheedy, C.S.C., S.T.C., Dean of the College of Arts and Letters, University of Notre Dame, University of Notre Dame Press, 1949

With this in mind, we must begin our preparation and search towards this elusive mystical experience we seek, with the content of fine character in which to begin. For the Lord our God is not impressed by mighty mystical works, but by humble acts of human virtue and morality.

And if we are to approach the throne of the almighty and holy God, we must begin to 'become ye perfect as your heavenly father is perfect.' (New Testament)

When beginning to enter into the spheres of the mystical kingdom, we will not be greeted only with grand vistas of knowledge and love, but with reproach. We will be given guidance as to how our paths must be turned, altered and relegated to a higher place of love before the Lord can take us ever further. If we are to wish for the experience of the Almighty, we must be prepared to do as He asks of us, which will be great. Because no man is without the stain of sin, and the purpose of our journeying is to change those things within our karmic configuration and our habits and vices which hold us down in this mire of confusion and false doctrine; by holding fast to those falsehoods, we make the experience of true mystical knowledge utterly impossible. For the only way to approach such a holy throne, is by becoming that which we seek.

For those who seek the knowledge and experience of God, you must begin the process of letting go of all that you are as a separated identity personality, and begin to embrace that which has been required of all true mystic hearers from throughout the ages. And that is to change . . . the greatest obstacle for all humankind.

So to begin, I'd like to remind us all of the virtues and vices which we must begin to examine and ask all of you to then (if you have not already done so) download 'The Mysteries of the Redemption: A Treatise on Out-of-Body Travel and Mysticism,' and follow the way . . .

"Human Virtues are firm attitudes, stable dispositions, habitual perfections of intellect and will that govern our actions, order our passions, and guide our conduct according to reason and faith. They make possible ease, self-mastery, and joy in leading a morally good life . . . the moral virtues are acquired by human effort. They are the fruit and seed of morally good acts; they dispose all the powers of the human being for communion with divine love.

Four virtues play a pivotal role and accordingly are called 'cardinal,' and all others are grouped around them . . .

Prudence is the virtue that disposes practical reason to discern our true good in every circumstance and to choose the right means of achieving it . . .

Justice is the moral virtue that consists in the constant and firm will to give their due to God and neighbor. Justice toward God is called the 'virtue of religion . . .'

Fortitude is the moral virtue that ensures firmness in difficulties and constancy in the pursuit of the good . . .

Temperance is the moral virtue that moderates the attraction of pleasures and provides balance in the use of created goods . . .

The human virtues are rooted in the theological virtues which adapt man's faculties for participation in the divine nature, for the theological virtues relate directly to God . . .

Faith is the theological virtue by which we believe in God and believe all that he has said and revealed to us . . .

Hope is the theological virtue by which we desire the kingdom of heaven and eternal life as our happiness, placing our trust in Christ's promises and relying not on our own strength, but on the help of the grace of the Holy Spirit . . .

Charity is the theological virtue by which we love God above all things for his own sake, and our neighbor as ourselves for the love of God . . ."

The Catechism of the Catholic Church, Article 7, The Virtues, Libreria Editrice Vaticana, 1994

And as we may imagine, the seven cardinal and theological virtues have their enemy in the seven deadly sins: Gluttony, Lust, Greed, Pride, Sloth, Vanity and Avarice.

It is our duty and our call at this juncture in our journey to begin to identify that which remains within us that is not of God. In order to bring about the great cataclysmic profound moment in beatific vision before God, we must first take on ourselves and all that lies within the deep.

Ghosts and Lost Souls

Mystic Knowledge Series

Compiled and Written by Marilynn Hughes

The Out-of-Body Travel Foundation!

www.outofbodytravel.org

Photo Taken at the National Maritime Museum, Queen's House in 1966. Although the photographer was taking a picture of the beautiful staircase, nobody was there. This person with hands on the rail showed up in photograph later.

CHAPTER ONE
Ghosts and Lost Souls: Our Responsibility

****

It seems somewhat popular these days to investigate and talk about hauntings, haunted houses, haunted places and ghost hunting in general. In light of this popularity, it seems timely to discuss who ghosts are, why they are ghosts and what our responsibility to them is in the eyes of God.

I've seen many programs on television lately where investigations are done into 'paranormal' phenomena. Most instances, but not all, are focused primarily on either proving through some type of media the presence of otherworldly energies or finding out something about the person who may be haunting a place. There are a few programs where the focus does also go into the area of 'rescue.' And this is what I wish to discuss in this issue.

Who are ghosts? Who are lost souls? They are people who died who are stuck. The only difference between them and us is that they have already died, and we have not yet done so. The Lord expects us to take care of one another; whether living or dead. And one thing that concerns me about the programs which focus on phenomena and information alone, is that they ignore our humanitarian obligation to care about and help these ghosts and lost souls; who are no different from us except in that they've already died. We are also going to die, and so are our loved ones.

It is interesting how much fear is associated with ghosts and lost souls because of this simple fact. They are people - who happen to be dead. But they remain people. And because they are lost, we have a unique responsibility to them to assist them in finding out what has cast them where they remain and what needs to happen in order for them to be released from this condition.

This is not a criticism of the programs that focus on phenomena or information. Each of us have spiritual gifts, and they are different. Those who have a gift of attaining information, may not always simultaneously have a gift of knowing how to liberate the souls. But I've heard, even from gifted people who do this whom I respect and admire a great deal, things that are concerning. For instance, if a spirit is friendly, sometimes it is given to the owner of a building as an option as to whether or not it is 'cleansed.' (We will take up 'cleansing' in a moment.) I've heard this even in cases where a suicide has occurred.

It is never optional as to whether or not we have a responsibility to pursue the liberation of that individual (spirit) because they are stuck. Just as if you found a young child lost in the city, you would feel an obligation to help them find their way home through the police or whatever means were given you. Ghosts and Lost Souls are people who need help, and we do have a responsibility to them.

Just a short note on 'cleansing.' Cleansing is something that can be done in a place wherein the energies of a particular event still remain, but not the ghosts or entities of that event. Although cleansing sometimes works in helping a lost soul to cross over, its purpose is primarily focused on energy, not people, not souls.

So cleansing has a purpose in dealing with energies. But people are not merely energies; they are souls, spirits and beings. Ghosts are not just energies, so cleansing will often NOT work for ghosts or lost souls. They require specific help from us to determine the nature of why they have become stuck in the physical, mortal world, and what requirements remain in order for them to be freed.

Sometimes cleansing the energy, however, can create an opening wherein remaining lost souls may find their way to the light on their own later. But usually a ghost or lost soul has something particular that they need to deal with in order to move on, and these causes are as individual as every person can be.

For some, it is simply understanding that they are dead. For others, there is unfinished business to be attended to. And for even others, they may be actually doing purgatorial time on earth for something they did during their lives. In such cases, prayer is a great necessity on their behalf, but also determining the exact nature of what they must complete to amend for that action and be ready to move forward.

Finally, there can be evil spirits - which are the ones who can be much scarier - who can require a number of very different dynamics in order to help them cross over. And sometimes these spirits won't be crossing over to the light, and this makes them much more complicated.

But since such situations are as varied as people, I thought it might be helpful to try to give the groundwork of a general situation wherein you might need to assist a ghost or lost soul and what you might do. Remember, though, that oftentimes such things are spiritual gifts. Those of us who have such gifts will naturally 'fall into' this work, and are generally led and told exactly what to do along the way.

Usually, the first thing you might come across is the simple feeling that a spirit is there. That can come about by phenomena or just feeling the presence.

The next step can occur in either the physical waking environment or the mystical realms. Many of my liberations have been done in mystical realms and sometimes even at remote distances. But I've also done work while physically conscious in the location. It can happen either way depending on the situation.

Generally, it begins with you feeling the way that the person died. It is the last traumatic event in their lives, and they usually share it with you. Sometimes you will even feel the pain, but almost always you will feel the terror, fear or shock that they felt.

At this time, I usually acknowledge the pain they went through and I do this very sincerely. I stop and think about the tragedy of how their life ended. Oftentimes with a lost soul or ghost, it ended suddenly, abruptly, through violence or a horrible accident. But not always . . .

Usually, if the issue surrounding their status is about the way they died, they will convey it to me at that time. Sometimes they feel responsible for a horrible accident, sometimes they feel like justice has not been served if they were murdered, sometimes they remain in the fear of the moment of death and relive it over and over again, and sometimes they don't know they are dead. There are a myriad experiences.

But if the reason they are lost is caused by the mode of their death or them not realizing that they are dead, this will be the easiest liberation. In most cases, you will have a chat with them about how this horrible event that they have shared with you actually resulted in their death. If they feel responsible for something, they can often be spoken to about the circumstances of the accident which very often was not truly their fault. If it was their fault, you can very non-judgmentally express to them that you are aware they made a mistake, but it's not something that can as yet be undone. And then you ask about things that they might need from you; perhaps to tell someone that they are sorry and you make sure you keep that promise because it's very important.

If they just didn't realize they were dead, as soon as they do, you'd be surprised how quickly sometimes the light becomes visible to them.

In most cases of ghosts and lost souls, there is a reason why they have been unable to receive the same help that most people get when they cross over to find their way. And it's usually unfinished business, sudden death or a disbelief in life after death or God. Believe it or not, those who don't believe in life after death - depending on how strong that belief was while living - can become terribly confused when they die and they find that they're still in existence. They often have no idea what to do.

As the person who's been asked and called into help them, there are a few things they will need to know. First, you tell them about the existence of the light and that if they raise their eyes to heaven or God that their vibration may raise just enough for them to be able to finally see it. This also affects the ability to then see the guardian angels who have always been there, but have been unable to get through because the subject cannot see or hear them. You talk to them about reorienting their awareness to a spiritual world now, rather than the physical. In such cases, that may be all they need because their guardian angels often take over from there.

For those with unfinished business or who are doing purgatorial time on earth, there will be more steps. Oftentimes, they need prayer. But they also need somebody who can convey messages to those left behind, if possible, and they need someone who can receive from the higher thrust - heavenly forces - information that may be vital to them completing their work here and shifting to the higher awareness. Once a soul has shifted to that higher awareness, your job is almost always pretty close to finished.

Some souls may have to do some time here to make up for things that they might have done. An example: I ran into a group of souls who were inconsiderate about other people, they ignored them as if they didn't exist. When they had crossed over, they had been 'sentenced' so to speak to a period of time in wandering the earth unseen by humanity.

But here's an interesting point that a lot of people don't realize. As soon as somebody, anybody, is able to realize that they are there, it means that they are ripe for assistance in crossing over. So in buildings where we see hauntings that have been going on for hundreds of years, we've been negligent in recognizing that we have a responsibility - if God calls us to - to help them now to make that final crossing.

Some people have misperceptions or belief systems that can be religious in nature which can prevent their crossing, also. In such cases, we either help them to understand the true nature of eternal love and the mechanism by which we all return to God, or we provide them with illusions that support that belief system and help them to cross. And after that crossing, they are then taught of the Way. We ourselves can transform into police officers, teachers, nurses, etc. And in some rare instances, for perhaps Catholicism, a priest from the beyond might come to assist somebody who has a concern that they didn't receive absolution, or another religious figure may be able to come forward and provide the things the spirit believes he needs in order to get him to the light where he is then re-educated about the nature of things and the mechanism of eternal life.

Evil spirits are a whole different ball-game. You can have evil spirits who are ghosts of people who were evil, but you can also have hauntings which include principalities and powers - actual demonic entities. Such situations are very dangerous and to be handled with great care, and generally only by someone who has been trained by the Lord. Any other training will not help you here . . .

In such cases, there can be a myriad of outcomes. An evil person who is doing evil things as a spirit may well go to the light, but they may just as easily be going to the lower realms. This is something that only God knows, and when you are in the 'mystic power' it is revealed to you the 'energetic truth' of that person and situation. It is only in this way that you can know.

There are also people who are not evil, but who do things that appear and also can be very evil as ghosts. Some of them might think it funny to scare children, I've met a few of those. But that is a violation of eternal law. In one particular case I dealt with, it was an old woman who had committed suicide but was reliving her one moment with the man she felt she was in love with when she was a young woman. He'd married another and she never married. When she died, she stayed in the house where the ball had been held, relived it nightly and played tricks on the two little girls who lived there now.

She was NOT an evil spirit, but what she was doing violated eternal law and it was a true showdown with her. She refused to leave for several nights, and it was very energy consuming. But when she left, she went to the light, because she was not evil, she was simply behaving in a way which is in concert with evil as a ghost. But because of what she was doing, I was called in and had to confront her about her violations of eternal law. Because of her own sadness regarding the losses in her life, she didn't get it. She didn't think it was a big deal, and thus, we had a showdown.

However, there are plenty of ghosts who were evil in life and remained evil in death. And they, too, must go to their appointed places. But this is not so clearly cut. Because, again, only God knows the heart of a man and it must be revealed to us before we can even act. Because when we work in this capacity, we can truly only do so under the will of God. If God does not will our participation, it won't happen.

Those who are evil in life and are now evil ghosts are most often escorted to a lower realm in concert with their vices. And this could be a whole subject unto itself. But evil spirits are a whole other matter. They must be dismantled and sent back to the abyss, and this can ONLY be done if you have been taught to do it by the Lord. Because the power and ability given to make this happen does not come from you or me, it has to be funneled directly in from God. If you attempt to do this without proper eternal authority, you sincerely risk death.

Evil spirits and even evil ghosts can be VERY dangerous. They can cause physical harm, not just spiritual. And evil spirits are extremely energized beings of darkness, and they are just as strong in their evil as those of us who are trained to work for God are in the light. And anytime you take on a battle such as this, even when ordained and set up by God alone, there is ALWAYS the chance of defeat.

This humble knowledge and understanding is ABSOLUTELY essential. No one should pursue this unless specifically trained in the mystic heavens by the Lord to do it.

A lot of people will do things that they have genuine gifts towards, like 'clearing,' or working with lost souls, ghosts, etc. etc. But no one should do this unless they've been trained. Training consists of years and years of mystical training every night in the realms beyond the body wherein your spiritual guides and the specific angels, including St. Michael, engage in conscious participation in teaching you how to battle such forces. If you are trained in such a manner, you will fail miserably many times before you succeed, and that's why they set you up to learn this under illusory circumstances wherein you cannot be hurt, and neither can any other innocent living being be hurt by your training.

But when you go into real battle with the dark side, it is REAL. And you better be prepared and energized by God Himself.

Some of us will do this for a time, and then we will be asked to step aside for younger people to step in because this is a REAL physically demanding task and as we get older - and in my case, as we show some of the wounds in our bodies with disease from these battles and assaults of the dark side - we may not have the strength to continue to go in. So we go in ONLY when the Lord so deigns, because if we do otherwise, we not only risk major defeat and failure and all the consequences that this would bring to those who are dealing with the evil spirit or demonic force, but we do risk death.

When I was younger, I engaged in such battle on an almost nightly basis. I rescued lost souls probably 2-3 times a week. Now that I'm older, and I've sustained some injuries from those battles, I go into situations more like 2-3 times a month. And I'm able to sustain that.

But I don't choose where and when I go, the Lord calls me in. However, if somebody has a physical location that I'm able to go to - a haunted ranch, home, farmland, etc. - I go in of my own free will, but then the Lord reveals as He so chooses. Because of the natural gift that He has given me, I always feel things when I go. But sometimes it may take a few more days before the rest of the story is revealed to me in the mystical state. Oftentimes, the clearing of the energies - especially in situations out West where a lot of battlefields still contain a lot of energy - and the liberating of the lost souls or ghosts, will happen in the mystical realms.

Oftentimes, however, alongside lost souls and ghosts - there can be evil spirits or demonic forces. Because it is their will to hold back the souls of others, just as much as it is to hold back their own. So oftentimes, you will be required to do things on a very multi-leveled capacity. And this is vital in order for the complex problem to be solved.

Because anything that is left behind can attract like to itself again. So if you release a lost soul, but leave behind a dark force, a haunting will recur. But it will be a different ghost. EVERYTHING must be cleared, liberated, removed and in the case of any darkness surrounding it, annihilated. Evil and darkness, as energies, are always approached with annihilation. This may sound harsh, but it's the only way to protect the third and fourth realm from being infiltrated by dark and evil spirits whose domain is the first and second.

They are violating eternal law by being here unlawfully. The third and fourth realm are the mortal realms where the battles between good and evil rage, so evil will exist here. But there are eternal laws which govern how they exist and to what degree they are allowed to operate here. If they violate it, they are dismantled and sent back to the first and second realms and sometimes just the abyss.

St. Michael can do this with a single thought.

It takes a little more effort for a weak mortal being such as myself to allow enough eternal energy to come in and take care of such a situation.

In most cases, however, a ghost or lost soul is just a person who died who is stuck. Most of the time, although evil is obviously found in some very haunted places, ghosts are well-intentioned and just need help. Although they may be completely comfortable with remaining here, it is our duty not to allow them to do so. We don't do this in an uncaring way; we do this with absolute and total love because they are our brethren.

They may be perfectly content to remain because they don't realize what awaits them beyond the light. If they did, they'd beg us to help them cross. Remaining here as a ghost in spirit beyond the time allotted due to purgatorial duties or unfinished business does not serve their souls.

So for those of you reading this who may not have this gift or work with lost souls and ghosts, let me tell you the best thing you can do for them and for the rest of us who do. Pray, pray, pray for them. Ask God to bring somebody to them to assist them in their crossing. I personally welcome e-mails from people who have situations wherein they need help, and I'm happy to try to assist remotely. And if that can't be done, if I'm physically still able, I'd come to them.

When I see a haunted house, I don't feel fear. My heart aches at our brethren who are trapped because of their own delusions or something they have no control over which has caused them to be stuck in a pattern of time that is shortly or long past. We need to look at such phenomena in a different way.

Sometimes, when I do feel fear and I know we're dealing with something else, I feel justice. They don't have a right to cause harm to the living, and they must go where they are compatible and stop their stupid antics. They, too, are wasting time and avoiding and averting their own evolution because even evil spirits AND demonic spirits are supposed to be evolving towards God.

They won't say thank you or appreciate it when you banish them to the lower realms, but you are actually doing their soul a service because they will go to a realm which will teach them what they need to know to take the next step higher.

Ghosts and lost souls should not be seen as paranormal phenomena, because if they are, then the minute you or I die, we become phenomena, too. They are people. And they need our help.
****

CHAPTER TWO
Death by Car Accident, Accidental Explosion, Electric Chair, During Robbery, Suicide. The Calling to Serve Lost Souls.

****

Beginning to work with lost souls, these unfortunate souls were usually unaware that they had died, and required assistance to get to the other side.
****

"Therefore do not be afraid of them. Nothing is concealed that will not be revealed, nor secret that will not be known. What I say to you in the darkness, speak in the light."
New American Bible, New Testament, Matthew 10:26, (Christianity, Catholic, Words of Christ)

As I had drifted off to sleep, I began dreaming a horrid scene repetitively. We were driving down the highway when suddenly a frantic man began to run in front of our vehicle. His terrified thoughts were displayed all around his person in this spiritual arena. Driving past him, we had assumed he was a lunatic, as his demeanor was frightening and morose. But when we passed him, we came upon a horrid accident wherein several people had been killed. Their bodies were very mangled, and we began to feel as if we might throw up.

Each time the dream progressed, I woke up in a cold sweat. I didn't understand what was happening to me. But each time I dropped off to sleep, I had the dream again.

Praying to the guardian angels around me, I asked to understand, and as I did this, I began to achieve knowing.

Having driven to a neighboring city that day, we had picked up a lost soul, who had apparently died in a horrible car accident some time before. It became known to me that many people who die quick and violent deaths, especially those who have no spiritual foundation, become lost after death, or don't realize they have passed on. Some are not even able to 'see' spiritual beings or things of the spiritual world because their vibration is still quite physical, and much too low to sense them. Because their lives and perceptions are so physical, they often wander about the earth trying to get their loved one's attention, but to no avail. When they are not recognized, they panic. After suffering some major trauma in death, the soul feels it is caught in a void wandering aimlessly alone.

Understanding this, I was still quite terrified. A frantic ghost was now relying on me to help him, and I was still trying to deal with my fear of a ghost being present in my house.

As directed by the eternal, however, I began to communicate telepathically to the spirit. Feeling his incredible need to cling to me, I again tried to calm myself, and then affirmed to the soul my need for boundaries. He respected them immediately. "I love you," I conveyed to him, "but you must look behind you and SEE the light of God! Call out to your guides, ask them to take you there." The spirit was intrigued and began doing as I asked, but again became clingy, frightening me. "You are no longer of the physical plane, you have moved onto greater things. Turn around! Ask!" His resistance intensified and I could feel the heat forming in pools of sweat on my body. Panicking, I ordered him, "In the name of Jesus Christ, I can no longer help you, turn . . . and go to the light!" Suddenly, I felt a spirit wind blow by as a gush of ecstasy overcame my soul. Intuitively, I knew the soul had seen the light and I was feeling his profound joy.

"Let the groans of prisoners come before you; by your great power free those doomed to death."
New American Bible, Old Testament, Psalm 79:11, (Christianity, Catholic)
****

Entering into another lost soul's dream, I witnessed his death. Attempting to rob a young couple's home, he had entered when the couple had left to take a walk, not realizing that their young child was still in the home. As soon as he found their daughter, he locked her in a closet. When the couple returned from their walk, they noticed the broken glass and immediately searched for and found her, but police cars were already arriving as the neighbors had called the police when they noticed the disturbance. Checking through the house, the police didn't find the robber immediately, and assumed he had gotten away.

But the father knew of a room that was normally sealed off from the house and asked the police to check it out. Upon entering the room, they were immediately confronted with the armed robber, firing five shots, killing him instantly. Now, he was a lost soul.

Compassion for this soul overflowed in me as I was filled with knowledge of him. Apparently, this had been his first crime, and he had already made a decision that it would be his last. When he had seen the face of the little girl, it touched him, but as should be expected when someone participates in any crime, he had paid with his life, and his destiny had already been sealed. This soul believed he was going to go to hell, and that he deserved every flame he was about to embark upon. He'd actually *seen* the light, but did not go.

Telling him that God loved him, he began to cry. Beginning to increase his energetic intensity, I asked that he respect my space and boundaries. As I explained some universal truths to him, he was excited by the incredible love that God had for his soul. Our Lord had been moved by his true contrition at the moment of death.

Absorbing knowledge with ease and joy, he became hesitant to leave when I told him of his next destination, the light. (Lost souls are often uncomfortable leaving the only contact they have had since death) Telling him to stay near me as long as he felt he needed, I conveyed to him that when he felt ready he could depart directly for the light. This calmed him a great deal, and within moments, he left for the light, leaving a cool breeze in his wake.

"All our masters in the spiritual life emphasize that when the soul is free and empty of all inordinate attachments, God can then work without all hindering; He is free to accomplish His own divine designs."
The Divine Crucible of Purgatory, Chapter XIV, Paragraph 1, (Christianity, Catholic, Author: Mother Mary of St. Austin)
****

And so it came to pass that I helped dozens of lost souls, only two of which I choose to mention at this time.

A dying soul beckoned my spirit to await his entry into the void, as his death was coming quickly by the electric chair. Leaving his body and entering the astral state, I embraced him and welcomed him to the other side. Angry, he said, "Alright, where am I going to be sent now." Obviously assuming he was going to hell, I told him that there was only love for him. "Wait a minute," he said, "that's crazy!" Waiting patiently for him to absorb this truth, he finally said,

"Okay, I can handle it, tell me more." Leaving him with the knowledge that he was greatly loved by God, I gave him the information he would need to go to the light. As his guides descended in a wispy light, he reached his hand to them as he paused to say good-bye.

As I was not made aware for what crime this man was executed, or whether or not he was guilty, I considered it an interesting example of God's all-knowing wisdom; that only He knows the heart of a soul.

Another lost soul was treating me very badly in an astral realm wherein he had created a table. Unless I showed him 'proper identification,' he would not allow me to pass. No identification that I presented was sufficient, and so I quietly stepped aside waiting for instruction.

A beautiful angel appeared and told me of this man's life. Believing his whole family had not loved him, the final straw had come when his wife left him. After committing suicide, he had created this reality which allowed him to reject others. Understanding his feelings, it occurred to me that although his conclusion was incorrect, his feelings were quite real.

Returning to his table, I sent energies of love and understanding. "I'm so sorry that you suffered so much in your lifetime." I said. "But you know, you really are loved greatly. Let go of this illusory reality you have created for yourself. There is so much more to be experienced. The Universe is a loving place and you are an important part of us all." Looking up, a moment of caring was shared, and the objects of his self-imposed prison began to disappear slowly.

Apologizing for treating me as he had, forgiveness began to emerge within him for his wife and family. Moments later, he returned to the light.

"'Love is a light that never dwelleth in a heart possessed by fear.'"
The Seven Valleys and the Four Valleys, The Fourth Valley, Page 58, Paragraph 1, (Baha'i, Author: Baha'u'llah)

"Sentient beings are muddled by afflictions, their conceptions and inclinations are not the same; According to their mental states they perform inconceivably many acts, thereby forming the oceans of all lands."
The Flower Ornament Scripture, Chapter 4, The Formation of the Worlds, Page 186, Stanza 2, (Buddhism, Mahayana)

****

Playing repetitively in my mind, a lost soul's horrific death began coming to me as I was slowly releasing form. Determining to keep things in perspective, I knew that I must do so if I might be of some assistance.

A woman had been working in a power plant standing outside by a large looming tower. Suddenly, an explosion was heard, a fire ensued and people were running towards her. Another explosion went off, and before she had a chance to run, a third. Extremely traumatized, she had been blown to bits. Because it was so gruesome, I fought the fear that came with it by determining that I would see this from a spiritual reality rather than a physical illusion.

Beginning telepathic communication, she felt responsible for the explosion because of a mistake she had made. Unable to respond because of her horror at being responsible in a small way for so many deaths, I conveyed to her that everything was going to be alright, despite the suffering she'd endured. Chaotic and frantic, she hopelessly tried to communicate with those she'd left behind, but although she could hear them, they couldn't hear her and this made her panic more.

Conveying god's love for her, she calmed immensely. "You mean I won't be judged for what I did, even though it took all those lives?" "God loves you, honey, and there isn't anything you could do to turn him away. His love is complete. It is unconditional." Telling her to stay with me as long as she felt the necessity, I informed her that when she was ready, her own spiritual guardians were waiting to take her back to the light. Half an hour later, she turned to meet them.

"About this time (the deceased) can . . . hear all the weeping and wailing of his friends and relatives, and, although he can see them and can hear them calling upon him, they cannot hear him calling upon them, so he goeth away displeased."
The Tibetan Book of the Dead, Book I, Part II, Page 101-102, (Buddhism, Tibetan)
****

And as it had come to pass, I had continued dealing with many lost souls, although my spirit was becoming weak in will to do such a task because of the intensity of trauma involved with these souls. Emmanuel, knowing of my distress, had agreed to give me a short respite from this harrowing work, but with one condition; that I take a small journey with him.

Flying into a dimension of absolute whiteness, all about us was glowing with bright light! Passing by a series of rooms through arid hallways of light, we eventually came upon a humongous library. Telepathically asking the angelic librarian for some specific material, I marveled at the beauty of her. Her lightly girded wings quickly assisted her in soaring around the towering columns of perpetually white books to find that for which Emmanuel and I had come. A glowing white book glided through space from a high shelf into Emmanuel's hands below.

Perusing through the book, I noticed that there were many listings that looked like want-ads. Coming upon a listing for my name, Emmanuel covered four of the five tasks listed below it, allowing me to see but one: "Being in the physical realm to aid in the journey of lost souls." Instantly, I understood that I had made a commitment to this task well before my lifetime, and I could not quit this job. Turning to Emmanuel, I promised him that I would fulfill my vow to the Lord, and I felt great sorrow at my earlier fear and trepidation.

"Therefore, we are not discouraged; rather, although our outer self is wasting away, our inner self is being renewed day by day. For this momentary light affliction is producing for us an eternal weight of glory beyond all comparison, as we look not to what is seen but to what is unseen; for what is seen is transitory, but what is unseen is eternal."
New American Bible, New Testament, 2 Corinthians 4:16, (Christianity, Catholic)
****

CHAPTER THREE
Death of a Fundamentalist Preacher, a Mental Patient, an Abused Child, a Poltergeist, an Evil Spirit, a Murdered Child, a Family Murder Suicide, a Murderer and his Victim in a House Filled with Evil Spirits Because of the Deed.

****

Outside of form, I was watching parts of the life of a fundamentalist preacher in preparation to assist him at his moment of death. A hateful man, he used fear to influence people to join his congregation. A long-standing feud existed between him and another minister who believed in a loving God, and the two churches had an agreement to help each other out with supplies. Withholding things out of anger because he could not convert the other to his way, the older, balding and small man died of cardiac arrest in his pulpit preaching hell-fire and damnation.

As his spirit rose to meet me, I looked at him very lovingly. "Fearing God, you never found Him. Fearing truth, you never understood. In your ego, you took power from others. And in your blindness, you saw only evil." Pausing, the spirit of the dying man looked at me in dazed confusion. "When you look at me," I asked, "what do you see?" "Love!" He cried out. "I feel so much love!" Smiling, I responded, "Now you have the truth. Remember my words when you choose your next lifetime." Beamingly happy, I watched him enter paradise before returning to form.

"My daughter, all your miseries have been consumed in the flame of My love, like a little twig thrown into a roaring fire. By humbling yourself in this way, you draw upon yourself and upon other souls an entire sea of My mercy."
Divine Mercy, Notebook 1, Page 99, Paragraph 2, (Christianity, Catholic, Words of Christ, Author: Sister M. Faustina Kowalska)

****

Beckoned to the aid of a treacherous lost soul, I found an escaped mental patient who had died after shooting several children at an elementary school and then taken her own life. In her current thought-form reality, she was still shooting at thought-form children who were wandering in and around several thought-form school buses.

Walking towards her, my presence evoked intense anger and she began shooting at me viciously with her thought-form gun. Continuing my slow approach, the bullets flew right through me. Fear filled her eyes as she realized I was in control and not she.

Falling to the misty ground, she put her hands over her eyes and cried. Placing my arm around her, I sat with her quietly embracing her with my being and love. No words were exchanged as she slowly accepted the love.

Moments later, a male spirit approached wearing a police uniform, with several back-ups behind him. Doing so to make her exit a bit easier, they acted as if her thought-form reality was real and the police had come to 'take her away.' Handing her to the other guides, he said to me, "Why don't we get together after your next assignment and go mountain climbing?" "Okay." I said with a bit of trepidation.

After finishing my next lost soul assignment which regarded an abused child who had died in very unfortunate circumstances, he had been electrocuted in a bathtub by his angry parent.

He had stayed in the bathtub, very confused. I came to him very quietly, and said to him, "What your parents have told you about yourself is not true." He looked confused, as he'd spent his short eight years being told he was bad and very difficult. "God loves you very much, take my hand." I reached to him, and he smiled. In a moment, he reached both arms to me, as I picked him up and handed him over to his guardian angels whom he could now finally 'see' because his vibration had lifted enough to see into the spiritual realm.

The guide re-appeared in a flash of light. Taking my hand, we were immediately transported to a shimmering rock mountaintop. "You know," he said, "this is a great place to go after a day at work. It re-energizes your being." I smiled, but remained quiet. "Next time I have a lost soul to deal with, I'm going to look you up. You're very good at handling them. Do you know why?" My tired face looked up as I quietly said, "No." "Do you have any idea why you created so much turmoil in the first half of this lifetime?" Finally, I decided to speak. "Well, probably because I'm an idiot." He laughed and then said, "You really don't see it, do you? When you deal with these lost souls, you are able to access memories from this lifetime and truly understand their pain. Those souls know that what you offer them is real understanding. Most importantly, your love for them is real and it is this that breaks their delusion." Looking up, I asked, "Do you mean to say that I chose those hardships to prepare myself for my work with the lost souls?" Nodding that this was true, he hugged me openly. "I know you don't recognize me," he said, "but we have known each other for a very long time."

Feeling familiar, I still could not place him. Taking my hand, we were gone in an instant, but my soul was left to contemplate the perfect imperfection of our world. A childhood filled with violence from my own fold, had been created to serve the Lord's greatness, to serve His lost ones down the road. How vast and . . . how magnificent!

"Of what use is it to be impatient in trouble and contradictions? We only increase our burden thereby. The two thieves who were crucified with our Blessed Redeemer were suffering similar torments; but the good thief was saved because he bore them with patience . . . The same trial , says St. Augustine, leads the good to glory because they suffer with patience and resignation."
The 12 Steps to Holiness and Salvation, Chapter 12, Peace of Heart, Paragraph 1, (Christianity, Catholic, Author: St. Alphonsus Liguori)

****

Dangerous and menacing, the poltergeists in this house were manifesting as animals that would bite the occupants. Invisible cars without drivers rammed into the house . . . and disappeared, causing no apparent physical damage. Dangerous and out of control, these poltergeists were violating eternal law.

Completely lost as to how to handle this situation, I called out to the universe to assist me as two spirits arrived who were specialists in such cases. Named Patch and Dawn, their job was to patch up the pained soul who was causing strife and assist him in achieving the vision of the new dawn. Patch held out his hand and a huge amethyst stone was lying amidst it. In the other hand, he had a pile of white pebbles. Beginning to program the amethyst with the message of the light, Patch lightly placed the pebbles within the grooves.

Tossing the pebbles directly from the amethyst into the home, another spirit had arrived who had came over and to comfort me in my fear and confusion. As it took into itself the pain of this desperately lost soul, the amethyst actually began to bleed. Breaking down in tears, I held on tight until everything was over.

After Patch completed this phase, we watched as the poltergeist began to manifest. On his face was a pained expression, but the stones programmed with the energies of light began to absorb his pain. Dawn uttered a few sacred words, 'Henceforth, the day beginneth, Lucretian deities aboding, follow rejoicing . . . prisms.'

Achieving peace, I instinctively called out what I knew to be the 'Frequency of Otara,' the high G, which immediately brought in legions of angels and the sign of a cross surrounded by a diamond light in the sky. This was a call for aid, which had the ability to bring in legions of angels instantly in times of spiritual need.

Assisting in the immediate reincarnation of this soul, I realized that this was only one of many possible outcomes in cases such as this. But because he had been de-activated, so to speak, he was placed in a new sieve from where he could begin again.

"Man's intention and understanding are governed by the Lord through angels and spirits. And since this is true of his intention and understanding, it is true of everything bodily, since this stems from them. Believe it or not, man cannot take a single step without heaven's inflow."
Heaven & Hell, Chapter 26, No. 228, Page 166, Paragraph 3, (Christianity, Swedenborgianism, Author: Emanuel Swedenborg)

****

Soaring deeply into the underworlds, I found a lost soul who was dangerous and perhaps even bordering on evil. Because I had not yet been taught of such things, I was quite uncomfortable. Another poltergeist who was even more skewed than the first was actually causing bodily injury to the occupants of the home from which he refused to disembark.

Turning to the scary specter, I said, "It's time to go home, will you relinquish your illusion, or reincarnate again?" Grasping my arm, he ripped into my spiritual flesh which bled profusely. Terrified, I didn't know what to do, but remembered Isis's cautioning words. Healing my arm with energy, I realized that his illusions were much too strong for me to break them.

Remembering the frequency of Otara, the High G, I called out for assistance from the angels. Filling with hosts of angels and the familiar sign in the heavens, the angels sent his soul back to the Earth to reincarnate. "I cannot help you," I said to him, as his soul was being prepared for rebirth, "return to your illusions, and we'll meet again beyond the veil." Conveying to him my hope that he might return after his next life a bit more advanced, my thoughts hit his trance-like state like energy sparklers in his face and head, as he appeared to 'fall' to Earth to be reborn. Immediately, I was released.

****

Uri, my faerie, took her stardust wand and in two thunder bursts, I was in a new location.

Arriving at a very old haunted house, a young girl had been brutally murdered in the attic. Blood dripped continually from a spot in the ceiling since her death, and no one had been able to make it stop. Killed in a very brutal fashion, this soul had remained in a state of terror for what seemed like a moment in her own mind, but was actually over 100 years upon the Earth.

Floating towards the attic, I noticed a ghost who appeared as a witch dressed all in black. Vengeance and anger seething, I wasn't afraid of such things anymore. Things were not as they appeared, as in truth; this was a poor frightened lost girl who was unable to escape the horrendous moment of her death. Phantom energies whirled all about the attic, but it calmed as I approached.

"You have many lives, many moments," I said, "why don't you go to a more pleasant place to heal yourself now." Looking confused, she quietly asked, "I can go somewhere else?" Changing from a witch into a young girl, I replied, "You have many moments, and you may leave this one. Where would you like to go?" Smiling widely, she said, "I want to go to a prairie where the sun shines on golden fields of hay. I want to be a little girl again! I want to live in a world where magical things are real and nobody fears. I want to go somewhere where there is only love!" Uri appeared behind me as I took the girl's hand, placing it in hers. "Let Uri take you to where the faeries roam." I said, and in a moment, they were gone.

"They see sentient beings sunk in the sea of cravings, veiled by blindness and folly: The Free Humans show a smile and reflect that they should save beings from suffering."
The Flower Ornament Scripture, Chapter 25, Ten Dedications, Page 667, Stanza 3, (Buddhism, Mayahana)

****

Ominous in the distance, the spirit aside told me the story of the house for which I had come. Recently sold to a very unsuspecting family, they were unaware of the quadruple murder which had occurred beneath this roof, and the haunting that hadn't ceased since. A family argument had led to four deaths in this house. Three of the spirits remained, though one had already left for the light. Although the situation had been quite grisly, it had been an act of passion and the perpetrator was not doomed. Deeply frantic about what she had done, her soul needed to seek forgiveness and accept help from the Lord.

Wearing a military uniform, Raymond was the first of the three lost souls who was causing havoc. When he had died, he had been wearing this uniform, but he had pulled back into his childhood self as a result of what had happened. Scott, his friend, had also been murdered, and he and Raymond stayed together in the house.

Raymond turned into a small pony and I knew that he was conveying to me that he wanted to be free like a wild horse, but he couldn't find the way. Turning back into a child, he began to get smaller and smaller until he was a baby. Picking him up, I said, "It's alright, it's okay to want to be comforted." Holding him on my shoulder, I stroked his back and turned. Scott followed us as I explained to both of them that I was going to take them on a short flight.

"What?" They said in unison. "Take my hands," I said, "just come with me." Pausing, I gave them instructions. "Oh, don't forget the light, when you see the light, just go for it okay?" Nodding that they would, they placed their hands in mine and we ran forward. "Okay, ready?" "Yeah." "JUMP!" As we jumped, we soared into the sky as the tunnel opened before us. Pulling my arms backwards, I gave them a celestial shove towards the light, as they went hurling towards it.

Returning to the house, I sat waiting for the final soul to appear. Off in the distance, I observed a man wearing royal garments who seemed to be observing. Coming in the form of a donkey, the final soul arrived as I petted her fur. "It's okay," I said, but as I did, she transformed into a frantic woman. "NO! IT'S NOT!" In a state of utter despair, she was the perpetrator. Raymond's mother had killed her family and his friend who just happened to be there that fateful night. Plagued by guilt, she was haunted by her own violent deed. "I know . . . I know." Calming her, her eyes filled with pain and horror. "Do you know what I did?" She asked. "Yes," I calmly stated, "I know, I know everything."

Confused at my tranquil and detached position, she just stared. "Here, take my hand." As she did, we walked to the center of the living room. "What about my husband?" She asked. "Oh, don't worry, he already went back." I replied. "Now . . . we're going to go for a short flight." Excited and scared, her eyes never lost that maddened appeal. "Just remember when you see the light, that's where you go. Go for it, okay!?"

Beginning with a short run so she wouldn't be blown away by the shooting star type of flight, we both jumped into the air. Releasing her arm, I sent her soaring towards the light wherein she would face the next phase upon her journey, which remained unknown to me.

Again, I noticed the man who was dressed in the ornamental garb of royalty who had been watching this process. Quietly, he seemed to be conveying his approval of my work. "He must be a member of God's royal family." I thought.

"Jesus answered and said: 'A murderer who hath never committed any sin but murdering, if his time is completed through the sphere, that he cometh out of the body, the receivers of Yaldabaoth come and lead his soul out of the body and bind it by its feet to a great demon with a horse's face, and he spendeth three days circling round with it in the world . . . "
Pistis Sophia, Sixth Book, Page 317, Paragraph 3, (Christianity, Gnostic/Essene, Words of Christ)

****

Entering an old house in the country, there were literally hundreds of very strange looking spirits. Thinking that they might be lost souls, their strange actions made me more suspicious of something else. Sucking up to me, they were trying to get into my good graces, and it appeared manipulative. Manifesting as only a hand, a woman placed herself on the edge of a white grand piano. Calling herself Mrs. Hand, she wanted to speak to me. Something was feeling very wrong. A bald spirit with no legs, just a flittering trail, came over to me. As soon as he got close, I *knew*, and I geared up for battle.

A premeditated assault, their strategy was to overcome this eternal threat by their sheer numbers. Attempting to enter me from below, they were trying to do so to prevent their own annihilation. Becoming one big, dark, massive energy, I shouted, "Get out! Get out right now!" My torrent of energy assaulted them in such a way as to throw them backward, but they began to suck together as if into a vacuum. Now they were a swirling vortex of red eyes, still fighting. Surging light from within, I screamed again. "Get out! Get out!" Sucked out of the third dimension, they were thrown back into the first.

Led to look into another room, upon entering it I found the dead body of a person who had been murdered. Now I understood why the presence of so many dark and demonic elements were in this house, for anytime an evil act is perpetrated upon the Earth, it can give entry to many of its kind to literally infest the person or the location of the act.

Calling to the spirit of the killer in his dreams, I brought the spirit of the murdered man out of slumber into wakefulness to confront him. The killer's dream became his nightmare. Shocked and afraid, the killer was terrified to see the face of his victim. Walking forward and bringing the power of light, legions of angels appeared and completely de-energized this man. Whether we understand the harm we do or not, there comes a time when we must all take responsibility for our actions. It was done, and they disappeared.

Reappearing in a cloudy realm, horses were grazing all around me. Appearing with a headdress so brilliant and spectacular, I just stared at the Old One, the ancient grandfather who bore the signs of a Chief. Handing me a sage fan, he conveyed that I must use it to process dark energies. Honored, I bowed to him in thanks.

"And as I looked, the Six Grandfathers yonder in the cloud and all the riders of the horses, and even I myself upon the bay up there, all held their hands palms outward toward me, and when they did this, I had to pray . . . "
Black Elk Speaks, Chapter XIV, Page 169-170, (Tribal, Oglala Sioux, Words of Black Elk)

Another haunted house in a small town beckoned my soul, as this job would take two nights. Ellen was very attached to a certain period in her long-over life. Dying as an old woman, she'd committed suicide, and was now living in the energetic past. Early 1900's, she had been very much in love with a man who married someone else. Remaining bitter all throughout her life, she never married and died an unhappy woman. A dance had occurred in this house, and she continued to relive the one night she had danced with her beau before he chose another woman. She was reliving the night of the ball for eternity.

Enjoying being a ghost, she loved to scare people, knock on walls, open doors and was extremely insensitive about scaring children. "It is time to have respect for the living as well as the dead." I said. "If you will just accept that you do not know what is indeed best for you, you will let me take you to the light where you will have greater understanding of your life, your choices, and have another opportunity to make it better." Very resistant, she didn't want to leave. Being patient with her, however, she eventually let go and returned to the light two days later.

Two ancient grandmothers appeared, their long white hair flowing to the ground and their tan buckskin dresses identical. "All things are relative to the reality that you occupy and the eyes through which you perceive." They said. "Truth is unalterable, but the many perceptions of truth are infinite and undefined. Things become complex when you separate from the Source in delusion. But when you understand the essence, reality is quite simple. The complexity in an eternal one comes from their ability to find simplicity." Plummeting to the Earth, the two grandmothers became one with the soil.

"The stage in which the consciousness of the living entity is attracted by the three modes of material nature is called conditional life. But when that same consciousness is attached to the Supreme Personality of Godhead, one is situated in the consciousness of liberation."
The Teachings of Lord Kapila, Chapter 9, Text 15, (Hinduism)
"And (they came to know) themselves, (as to who they are), or rather, where they are (now), and what is the (place in which they will rest from their senselessness,) (arriving) at knowledge."
The Nag Hammadi Library, The Testimony of Truth, Page 451, Paragraph 2, (Christianity, Gnostic/Essene)

****

CHAPTER FOUR
Death of the Lukewarm, and their Meeting with Jesus in the Afterlife. Death by Heart Attacks, Accidents, Rape, and Mass Murder.

****

"And suddenly there will come to the temple the Lord whom you seek, and the messenger of the covenant whom you desire. Yes, he is coming, says the Lord of hosts. But who will endure the day of his coming? And who can stand when he appears"
New American Bible, Old Testament, Malachi 3:1-2, (Christianity, Catholic)

Flying high up in the sky above the mountains, the beauty of the clear night awed me as I was pulled towards a particular destination. At the side of a mountain, a huge golden cross lay, bearing unintelligible hieroglyphics etched in the gold. Soaring closer, I touched it.

As soon as my hand touched the cross, my spirit began melting into it. Suddenly, I was at the site of an alteration. The old and haunted office building didn't seem real at first, as hundreds of ghosts were overlapping the present humans who sat in the chairs the ghosts once knew as their own. Cause of death was apparent in their energy fields; heart attacks, accidents, and even one who had died after a heavy door fell on him, but why were so many of these former workers from the past 100 years still in this building?

Wandering about them, I began to ask that question, and they all nodded as if they didn't know. Laughing and making merry, they were good friends and made fun of each other. These spirits were not dark, just average people who died and didn't want to leave the physical illusion behind.

A woman walked towards me who had apparently died a violent death. "What do you do when you meet a mass murderer?" she asked me, as another woman answered, "You ask what he can teach you." Bolting in, I shouted. "WRONG!" Looking at me angrily, the woman who had spoken wasn't happy with my outburst. "There is much more to energetic encounters than that." I said. "Perhaps you must learn that darkness believes that it attains power by taking life, but the light knows that true power is achieved by giving life."

"Her murderer has killed many more, most of whom have not yet been discovered." I said as in my mind, I could see the skulls of the many. Instantly, I became aware that this same murderer was presently holding a woman hostage whom he had already raped in front of her two children. "Come," I beckoned to them both. "We must de-energize destruction."

Shooting through space, both women came with me to the sight of a potential murder, now occurring in the energetic realms where it could be altered. (These alterations occur in a realm called, 'Management,' which is where things occur in energy before they happen on the ground. Many psychics tune into this realm, but it is a realm of potential reality, not absolute destiny, which is one reason they can be inaccurate. Some people have dreams of their potential futures in this realm, forewarning them of events which may be able to be changed. Sometimes, they cannot be changed, as the causes are too well rooted to be altered.)

Standing there with his pants down, the murderer was holding the woman, as the two children were tied up next to him. "Watch me now as I teach you of alteration." I said. Calling all energies towards me, I allowed the eternal to guide my thoughts. Energetically placing a pair of pants on the man, the woman was then severed from his hold by a beam of light. As the eternal guided the police in her direction, I could see them on nearby city streets. Sending waves of thought to guide them to this back alley, the criminal's weapon was then locked by another ray of light towards the trigger. Rewinding the scene, our purpose was to prevent as much trauma to the children and the mother as possible. Going back to the point in which he had just taken her hostage, but had not completed the rape, one lone police officer responded to the eternal beckon, coming to the back alley. Others had been given the beacon, but had not trusted their instincts and intuition. But it was enough, because he was armed and the criminal had been rendered benign. Reinforcements arrived, and he was taken away, the woman and children tended to in the hospital.

Leaving the scene, we returned to the old office building as I spoke to the woman who had died at the hands of this man previously. "It is the recognition that you are eternal, that there is no harm that can come to your soul, which lends freedom. If you believe that your mortal life is all you are or ever will be, you will also believe that there is something to fear from the darkness that would destroy one of your many forms. Revel not in the loss of one form to the hand of darkness, but delight in your ability to create yet another to explore with." "My God, I think I understand!" she said, "he didn't destroy me, I'm still here." "Yes," I replied. "He destroyed himself by taking life, but he *cannot* destroy me!" She said. "Yes, you do understand. He has brought destruction upon himself; he will now be going backwards. One who dies in darkness ceases awareness of himself for a time, because darkness only has awareness of itself as a limited fragment, and that fragment dies. If unaware of the soul, the garment becomes reality. Recognizing the eternal nature negates death. Birth into another spiritual garment becomes simultaneous with the death of the former garment."

Suddenly, they began to speak of having met Jesus, and I sparkled with delight. "So you all had a chance to meet with Jesus?" I asked. "Yes, we did. He came to our building once and spoke to all of us disincarnates." "Well, what was it like?" I asked. "Well, I hate to say this, but many of us were disappointed." Shocked by this response, I asked, "Why?" "Because he was very normal, He wasn't what we expected. He was very inspiring and knowledgeable in what he said, but . . ." Interrupting them, I replied, "Let this be a lesson to you, the truth is not always what you expect. You can hear the truth from the mouth of Christ himself, but if you do not have within your own heart the soul of that truth, you will hear nothing."

Coming forward as I spoke of this, the disincarnates were not ready to leave this building. Some might return gradually over the next several months, but those who resided here were the middle-of-the-roaders who served the material world. For this reason, they held to this physical life as if it were their only lifetime, when in fact, it held them to their death. But no matter where you may strand yourself in the spectrum of life, you are never lost to God. Even in our years of wandering, He knows exactly when we will return. Even in the years of darkness, he anticipates our return to His divine bosom.

"Some . . . who were neither in the deep sleep of folly nor able to awaken in the light of wisdom, misled by the variety of innumerable customs, thought that there was no such thing as absolute justice but that every people regarded its own way of life as just . . . They have not understood . . . that 'what you do not wish to have done to yourself, do not do to another . . . When this idea is applied to the love of God, all vices perish."

On Christian Doctrine, Book Three, XIV, No. 22, (Christianity, Catholic, Words of St. Augustine)

****

CHAPTER FIVE
Spirits Traveling the Valley of Life and Death, Hungry Ghosts, Trickster Spirits, Unfinished Business, Regrets for Wasted Time, Souls Remaining in Bondage to Evil People (Spirits) who Held them Bound in Life, a Lost Soul 'Possession,' and the Rapture.

****

Various shades of pink on the horizon filled the sky, but the beauty was marred by the sight of this decomposed dead body. Very little skin was left around the bones, but the angel aside me directed me to touch it anyway. The thought of doing so disgusted me, but I obeyed the angel's command and found myself whirled into the lifetimes of the soul who had occupied this form. Having many lifetimes of treachery, many of them as a pirate, what was fascinating about this soul was that he had become very attached to his many bodies. Flinching when I touched the skin, I found this to be an interesting facet of original sin, to be attached to former lives to such an extent, that there is a solid encrustment, rather than simple etheric memory.

It occurred to me that this would be a good reason to consider cremation, because it destroys the physical vessel and forces the soul to release the physical bodies of former lives. Several skeletons appeared and I found it interesting that the souls of the dead were able to feel pain when I touched their former bodies, because they had not fully left them. Migrating from one body to another, they would re-enter old forms and actually re-experience aspects of their pain from previous times.

Swept into the clouds facing the horizon and a wide expanse of valley, my soul sat upon a singular cloud, and my wings blew gently in the wind. Overcome with the magnificent nature of the contrast of the two realities I'd just seen, the winds were ominously powerful, and joyfully exuberant. Alit with the fire and flame of the love of God, my spirit knew true freedom. And yet, behind me, the souls of the dead remained trapped in the malaise of Earthly existence.

Souls may travel back and forth through many migrations to be able to obtain knowledge, but *attachment* to former lives ceases growth. Understanding ones past lifetimes is solely for the purpose of knowledge, but then they must be let go. The past is dead, only the now retains aliveness in the continuum.

As the wind blew through my wings and I appreciated the flow of the movement within my soul, I could see the dead bodies and their kindred souls at a distance. Beauty unseen to them, they were only willing to look upon their former existences. A thought passed through my mind, the words said to me during my ritual of passage. "All life, like all quasars, had really worth still traveling." As the quasar star is very much an allegory of evolution, it continues to expand and grow into a larger and brighter star. Accomplished through the natural forces of the Lord - the movement, the migration of winds, gases, light and matter - to bring about creation into something new, the quasar star never ceases movement, it is always traveling. When following an eternal road, a soul must continue traveling as well. Stagnancy contains a soul within a karmic continuum, while movement places the soul into a constant state of becoming.

Birth and death, death and birth, are minute aspects of the movement. Continual generation into substance is not only unnecessary, but painful for souls because of their attachment to experience. Our individual original sin attaches to us in such a manner when we see our experiences as reality, rather than as allegorical renderings of divine lessons. Eternal movement is generated in the wind, catapulting the soul into the clouds, into higher awareness, allowing a soul to see from above the impact of their life. Eternal movement is grand when it is followed by a soul to achieve evolution and liberation. Karmic movement remains painful and doesn't move. As each lifetime is held onto, the weight of original sin increases because of the soul's belief in multiplicity and the importance of these separate lives.

The spirits who traveled the valley of life and death were lost souls, and their journey was filled with pain. Souls swept by the winds upward, however, could choose to be freed from this liaison with the past.

"Thou knowest well that I am insolvent. Imprison me, I am willing, provided the prison be that of Thy Sacred Heart. Keep me there a close captive, bound by the chains of Thy love, until I have paid all that I owe Thee."

Thoughts and Sayings of St. Margaret Mary, December, No. 31, (Christianity, Catholic, Words of St. Margaret Mary)

****

Observing my ability to eat in the out of body state, I was intrigued that a soul could experience hunger and thirst. Immediately, my soul was swept into the understanding of a concept among the Buddhist doctrines of the hungry ghosts. Hungry ghosts are described as lost souls who have become deeply attached to cravings and desires, and as a result, those hungers have become insatiable. Often portrayed as ghosts having large bellies, consuming everything in sight, whether it be food, doctrine, or sense experience, they embody another aspect of original sin which bears upon present day mankind, that of insatiability.

While observing this concept, a voice spoke, "Their composition can be compared to some of the New Ager's of present day, whose appetites and desires are so insatiable; they needed to develop a doctrine to support them." Unfortunately, such souls do not realize that their true craving is for God, and so they become insatiable in seeking out happiness in everything from food, sex to money; but somehow their aim becomes much like a drunken tirade, unfocused and worldly. Because of this, they never recognize the simplicity of their true need, that of God.

'I thirst' is the echo of the Word of God in every human soul. This is the thirst of God to be thirsted for and the thirst of God to quench the thirst of man."

The Divine Crucible of Purgatory, Chapter XII, Page 104, Paragraph 3, (Christianity, Catholic, Author: Mother Mary of St. Austin)

"Clad in the hunter's green of selfish desires, I pursued Thee in the forest of consciousness, O Divine Heart! The sound of my loud prayers startled Thee; Thou didst swiftly flee. I raced after Thee; but my erratic chase, the hue and cry of restlessness caused Thee to retreat still farther. Stealthily I crept toward Thee with my spear of concentration, but my aim was unsteady. As Thou didst bound away I heard in secret echoes of Thy footfalls: 'Without devotion thou art a poor, poor marksman!"

Whispers from Eternity, Page 90, Paragraphs 3-4, (Hinduism, Kriya Yoga, Words of Paramahansa Yogananda)

****

Having exited my body early this morning, I was floating around the house just checking on things, energetically speaking. It's always good to do this if you have the ability to travel 'in the spirit,' because there are often unwelcome guests lurking in your home which need to be extricated, for which there is no other way to identify.

Off in the living room, I noticed what appeared to be the spiritual aspect of my husband, Andy, coming towards me with the obvious intention of some sort of intimate embrace. Intrigued, it seemed to me that it was probably past the hour in which Andy had left for work, and this was not likely to be his soul, so I boldly walked forward and confronted the spiritual being.

"Are you an aspect of Andy's soul," I asked, "are you coming to me as a servant of Jesus?" Instantly, he replied. "Heck, no! I don't even *know* Jesus." His reply indicated an unconscious service of the dark one, so I asked, "Would you like me to tell you about Jesus . . . so perhaps you may no longer serve Satan?" "Huh!" he shouted, "I don't serve Satan!" Calmly, I replied, "Indeed, although you may be unaware of it, only Satan could send you to me in the form of my husband seeking embrace. This is not the work of virtue and morality which would come from on high."

Very confused, he didn't say anymore, but looked at me as if he would like to know more. Beginning a conversation about Jesus, I told him all about the redemption as he listened. When I had finished, he touched my hand in a show of deeply contemplative gratitude, and disintegrated slowly into space.

Perhaps some 'lost' souls are flying around the cosmos unconsciously serving Satan because they don't know the Lord and have not developed proper discernment to distinguish between virtue and vice. Because of this, they become easy prey to the designs of the dark one in doing his deeds, being completely unaware of what they have actually agreed to do.

****

Traveling through the dream world, an unknown voice began speaking to me as if to give guidance. Although I no longer remember the guidance given me, I immediately became suspicious and asked, "Do you come here on behalf of the Lord?" "Hell, no!" she replied. Intrigued, I asked, "Well, why then are you coming to me with erroneous advice?" "To test your soul . . . for the Lord wishes for your canonization." "Huh?" I said. Never believe anything such lost souls may tell you, because even if they don't *intend* to deceive you, they are receiving their *influx* from below. "I'm not interested in your flattery, which I know is intended to incite me to the sin of vainglory," I said, "but I am quite interested in your soul." Instinctively, I knew this was a lost soul as opposed to a demonic spirit. "Why don't you quit wasting your time allowing influx from the lower world into your spirit, and begin to seek after our Lord Jesus Christ?" With sincere befuddlement, she replied, "I don't know?" "I can tell that you are simply lost, and your confusion reflects that state. But it is really quite simple to find your way." "How would I do that?" she asked. "Seek after Jesus Christ." "How?"

Our connection was becoming weakened by the energetic intrusion of two of my children who were apparently unhappy that I was still in bed. Turning to my smaller daughter who was the cause of the greater disturbance in energy, I told her, "Stop! Do you wish to be responsible for this lost soul?" Nodding no, her unconscious self understood.

Turning to the lost soul, I said, "Think on Jesus, call on Jesus, ask for His help . . . it is really quite simple." Waning in and out, I heard a very innocuous response. "Oh." Praying that she might find her way, I awoke.

****

Amidst the crowded astral streets, my spirit was approached by a young woman who claimed that her house was haunted. As she came towards me, I offered to help and handed her a business card which said, "Marilynn Hughes - Ghost Hunter." (In the physical world, I do not have such a card, so I found it amusing.)

As I'd discovered over the past two years, many hauntings are actually caused by three different types of phenomenon; demonic spirits, lost souls, and those doing their purgatory upon the earth. Each of these three types of hauntings or poltergeist phenomenon requires different spiritual approaches in order to affect a successful outcome.

When entering the home, I was unable to discern of which type we were dealing with, because of the excessive poltergeist activity in the home. Poltergeist activity can often be linked to demonic spirits, but on occasion, such extreme forms of haunting can be perpetrated by lost souls or purgatorial wards. If this is the case, it is usually because the soul is still carrying a great deal of anger about something. In this particular home, there was a lot of flying objects and it was what I'd term to be a very 'unfriendly' haunting.

Having met the woman's husband who was now waiting inside the house with me, his wife awaited the results outside. "Are you ready to go to work?" I asked him as he nodded that he was. Repeating several Catholic prayers over and over, we entered the house.

Starting with the Apostles Creed, my voice slowly trailed through the room. "I believe in One God, the Father Almighty, Creator of Heaven and Earth, and in Jesus Christ His Only Son, who was born of the Virgin Mary, suffered under Pontius Pilate, was crucified died and was buried. He descended to the dead." Pausing for dramatic effect, I turned and walked around the room before continuing. "And rose again on the third day, returning to judge the living and the dead. I believe in the Holy Spirit, the Holy Catholic Church, the communion of saints, the forgiveness of sins, and life everlasting." Tentatively observing me, the young husband didn't quite know what to think.

"Hail, Holy Queen," I began to recite the Catholic prayer of the same name, "Mother of mercy, our life, our sweetness and our hope. To Thee do we cry, poor banished children of Eve. To Thee do we send up our sighs, mourning and weeping in this valley of tears. Turn then most gracious advocate, Thine eyes of mercy towards us, and then after this our exile, show unto us the blessed fruit of Thy womb, Jesus. Oh clement, oh loving, oh sweet Virgin Mary, pray for us, Oh Holy Mother of God, that we may be worthy of the promises of Christ."

At this time, I began a sermon about Jesus Christ. Pounding on a table to give emphasis to my words, I spoke of His majesty and the fact that our salvation comes from Him. My spirit cannot remember the details of this fairly long endeavor, however, but as I finished my sermon my spirit quickly returned to prayer. "Hail Mary!" I shouted, beginning the prayer of the same name, "Full of grace, the Lord is with Thee. Blessed art Thou among women, and blessed is the fruit of Thy womb, Jesus! Holy Mary, Mother of God, pray for us sinners, now and at the hour of our death. AMEN!" At this moment, two spirits materialized clearly in front of me completely de-energized in their violent activity. Lying on the floor, I approached and sat down with them.

Sitting upright, a middle-aged woman had appeared whose garments were changing from their former color which I could not discern to a very light beige. A young oriental woman was lying beside her, and her garments had changed from their former color, to a gown of whitest white. Immediately, a young baby boy appeared at her side, and she directed me to pick him and cuddle him.

Although he appeared immediately upon their materialization, he had not been a part of the haunting of this home. An angel was waiting at his side, a luminous, clear, whitish being with large wings. Clearly, the baby was already in heaven, but was taken to his mother's side at the moment of her redemption. Conveying to me that this was her child, the young Oriental woman expressed her deep anger and regret at the young husband who lived in this home who was apparently a former boyfriend. His guilty look made clear his sin against her, but he honestly hadn't known that she was pregnant, or that she and the baby had died.

Doing her purgatory on Earth, she had joined together with this older woman who had chosen to assist her in engaging in poltergeist activity. Directed towards the one whom she held accountable for her wasted and lost life, she knew she'd sacrificed her potential on the altar of the vice of lust. The many prayers I had offered for them had begun to purify their souls, which had manifested in new garments of white and beige, respectively.

Inherently, I understood that they were both now prepared to enter into heaven, although the older woman apparently still had some purification to undergo. Despite this need, she was to be released from her purgatory upon the earth and taken to a higher purgation site very near to the entrance of heaven where she would go shortly. The young girl, however, was ready to join her tiny baby in heaven. Calling the young man over, the two souls had a moment of atonement with one another. Forgiveness seemed to be given and all awaited what was to happen next.

Directing them to kneel with me on the floor, I said, "Now it's time for us to pray you into heaven." Bowing their heads, we commenced our prayer. Joining me as they slowly learned the words, they disintegrated many minutes later. Above them, I saw the angels in whose hands they had been given . . . and I bid them a wondrous journey to the ultimate place of bliss . . . our heavenly homeland.

****

Taken to a dark and dank old castle-like building, I met an older man who was very evil. Although he was an evil man, he was not an evil spirit; because one could say he was quite lost himself. (There is a difference between a demonic force, and a dark soul. His soul was evil, but he was not a truly energized demonic force.) After listening to him ramble on and on about his conquests for a while, I'd received enough information to realize there were two lost souls in his captivity and what I must do to go in and liberate them. But before I did, I planted a seed within this dark soul which would hopefully have great impact on his future liberation from evil.

Standing before him very calmly and quietly, I said, "I feel very sorry for you." "But why would you feel sorry for me?" He said with an almost triumphant, yet fading feeling about himself. Pausing for a moment, I quietly stated, "Because evil knows no joy." Great sadness overtook his face, and I knew the seed of light had been planted within him.

Within a second I was whisked away to a dark and very small cellblock. Appearing much like that of a political prison of our world, I knew that it was not (of this world) because the woman had a very old and open bullet wound to her chest which indicated that she had been long dead. She and her brother had been held captive here energetically in some way by this evil man, and by their ignorance of the fact that liberation could have come to them with the simple act of calling out to God for help. "Help is about to arrive," I said, "prepare yourselves." Within moments, a 'tank' carrying two disguised angels (as soldiers) barreled through the side of the prison creating an open wall. "Go to them!" I shouted as the angels smiled at me and gave me a wink. The two went with the angels who revealed themselves within moments afterwards to the two they had come to retrieve.

****

My soul was swept into a house which appeared to be built around the 1970's. Immediately, I knew this home was that of a person who was exhibiting the signs of actual demonic possession and I was sent here to help. As soon as I entered the home, there was a feeling of utter terror. But as I met this woman at the door, I felt compelled to discuss with her that which was taking place. Describing physical violence, as well as, an obvious presence, she also pointed out a great deal of water damage around the home, as well. Around the back of the house, water was pooling around one side of the house. Inside the house, ceilings were in the color of brown and literally falling in. Understanding this to represent the inundation within this person's soul, I acknowledged the damage.

Before I was to give witness to the cause of all this fervor, she described this constant feeling of terror which was very much alive within the walls of her house. Showing me a bathroom, I was surprised to notice that there were at least ten toilets inundated with excrement symbolizing the level of this contamination. Asking the presence to come forth, things began to slowly become clearer.

As I did so, her home became filled with probably about 70 different spirits as they all materialized before my eyes. There were so many of them, the house was overflowing; men and woman, young and old, large and small, of every make and type.

Immediately, I asked her if she could see them, and she said, "Who?" I pointed to individual spirits, and actually took hold of one of them and placed them in front of her and asked if she could see them. She again said, "No. I see no-one." This amazed me because of the sheer population within her home.

As soon as they appeared, however, the feeling of terror dissipated. Great confusion arose instead, as I instantly realized these were not demonic spirits; but very dark lost souls who for some undetermined reason at this time had all converged on this place together and, in their multitude, were creating a very dark and terrorizing force.

Interestingly, as I had entered the home, the woman was in the process of packing her things. Having brought a pick-up truck with me, she was loading the truck and getting ready to move on. As she walked out with a box of things, she said, "I'm leaving because this house is much too haunted for my taste." Seeing proper resolve on her face, I patted her on the back as I made my way in. At that moment, I was a little concerned because I wasn't sure how I was going to be able to handle it, but I stepped forward anyway . . .

Waiting and watching, the woman was very intrigued with the process. But to her, it appeared that I was talking to the air and moving and pushing on things that weren't there; although that was not the case.

Beginning to speak to each of these spirits, it took a great deal of time to make my way through the multitude. I found that they were very dark, but not demonic. Lost and very destructive souls, they became a terrorizing and possessive force because of their sheer number; something of which I didn't yet understand. Something drew them to this one location within or around this woman, and it appeared to be a mental illness from which she suffered which caused her to be more aware of spiritual presences, but yet, unable to handle them properly.

As I worked my way through the room surmising the condition of each individual soul, one of them came up to me and asked "Were you trained by one of those governmental programs?" In his mind, I was doing 'psychic' work. I told him "No." But he became intrigued when I mentioned to him that my father had been involved in 'top secret' government work for many years, but of a different nature. He was a scientist.

After a very long while, the entire group of around 70 souls were all converged in one room with me. Their darkness had been expunged to a great deal, as we had discussed individually with each one of them their status and what we needed to be doing. Taking the entire group outside of the house, the skies began to immediately thunder up as if a storm were coming. But then something beautiful beyond words occurred . . .

Within the swirling gray clouds of thunder, I began to notice individual sparks of light emerge one at a time. "Look!" I shouted to the crowd of souls, as they immediately drew their gaze to the sky. As they did, more and more points of light appeared and began to twirl and rotate until each spark of light transformed into a magnificent and HUGE angel. The sky was covered with the sight of dozens of huge white female angels bearing large and broad wings.

"Come on!" I shouted to all of them as I began pushing them up towards the sky. "Go!" At first, they were very sluggish and slow, but I kept pushing and they began to understand as they soared in a grand line towards the sky and towards the angels of God who had come to retrieve them and bring them to their true home.

Walking back inside the home, I noticed that about 10-15 remained. Frustrated, I said to them, "Come on, guys, what are you still doing here?" An older but very small woman smiled an impish smile, but it was clear that these ones were not yet ready to go. An inner prompting gave me this knowledge, but it also told me something else. "I'm coming back!" I said, "I will be back!" Although these Lost Souls were not yet ready to go, their energies had shifted dramatically and they were no longer projecting darkness, confusion or their former terribly dark ways. Although they had made progress, they would still be qualified as Lost Souls.

A large and tall man wearing all green began to belt out Christmas Carols. It seemed that he was doing so in honor of the liberation of so many of them this day, as though they had received their Christmas present early this year by achieving liberation. But as they all began to join him in singing the Christmas Carols, I noticed that they were getting many of the words wrong. Wrong in a sense that it was quite clear that demonic forces had been influencing them to change the words. Laughing at them, I said, "If you're going to sing these carols, get the words RIGHT?" I taught them the correct words, and they all continued singing joyfully.

Despite the continuing presence of these souls as I was slipped away into the ether, I noticed that the roof was now in perfect condition and the flooding outside was no longer present. After returning from this experience, the woman experienced a general feeling of well-being, although she still continued to hear one particular voice.

In a subsequent experience several weeks later, my soul was taken deeply into the storyline of a soap opera. It was my task to verify this storyline and see if all that I was being told about it were true. Making calls to actors and actresses on the soap, I finally received a letter from the writers who quickly made it clear that no such storyline had ever been written into the soap opera. All the stories these voices were telling her were false and had no basis in reality.

A voice exclaimed to me, "The voices that she continues to hear are not real, but related to the organic mental illness from which she suffers. Now that she has learned to be diligent in guarding the gateway that this mental illness creates within her to the influence of spirits, she must also become diligent in taking the medications which will help to close the doorway more completely by altering the organic condition within her brain which is the cause of her mental illness." She also had realized a tendency within herself to identify too closely with others, taking on some of their characteristics; rather than observing others from a clear sense of self. This was also a natural response of the psychotic illness from which she suffered and a very excellent realization.

As with medical conditions, it is the merging of both the spiritual and the physical sciences that brings about a full balance. If done from only one perspective, the answer may be incomplete.
****

Returning to the home I'd previously visited of the person who experienced the signs of possession, I noticed that the home had three wings. The first wing looked very much now like a new home, and the door to the second and third wing of the house had been closed and locked.

Going behind the locked door, I noticed the rot and decay in those rooms, but amidst that rot was a singular picture of Christ walking with His disciples. Gathering the picture to bring to the first wing of the home, I ran into an angel dressed as a construction worker who said, "I'll be working on fixing up some of this wood and restoring that which has been lost here. In the meantime, you take Jesus back into the first wing of the house and lock the door to these wings behind you." Nodding, I did exactly as he'd told me.

Gazing at the woman who lived in this house, I locked the door to the spirit world (the second and third wing), hung up the picture of Christ in the physical world (the first wing) and gave her a thumbs up. The decision had been made to close the door entirely, and it was good in this case.

"Nothing in Heaven is servanted; nothing upon Earth free."
The Divine Pymander of Hermes, First Book, No. 55, (Egyptian, Words of Hermes)
"As you hedge around your vineyard with thorns, set barred doors over your mouth; As you seal up your silver and gold, so balance and weigh your words. Take care not to slip by your tongue and fall victim to your foe waiting in

ambush."
The New American Bible, Old Testament, Sirach 28:24-26, (Christianity, Judaism)
****

Whisped into an energetic reality which represented some of the views held by denominational Christians, I realized that I had joined a group of people who were preparing for the end times. It was my task this eve to begin preparing myself, and to go through this experience with them so as to better understand the doctrine and its truth's and falsities.

Gathering my ancient sacred texts and religious relics, I was placing them into boxes to be taken with me into the holy kingdom. Doing this represented the gathering up of all of the spiritual wisdom and knowledge I had learned in this lifetime, and preparing to unite this knowledge with my soul as it prepared for the Rapturous end moments of this world.

What happened next was inexplicable and yet very profound. Unknowable and yet perhaps revealed in the smallest of senses.

My spirit was now amongst a group of souls all wearing white robes in preparation for this coming end time. Many of the women were having their hair cut off due to some ritual of purity which was required of them. Following their lead, I had mine cut off, too.

A ritual of adoption began wherein we were joined with others who would be members of our spiritual family, but there was something amiss and off. A young Native American boy was given to me as an adopted son, who I immediately recognized, but we were completely incompatible. Although he wore the robes of white, he had a smirk on his face and was simply going through motions. Very little faith or belief backed his soul, as he actually was a very lost child in this confusing array of doctrine. He, like many of the others present, believed that all that was required of him was to *accept* Christ. They had not penetrated into the understanding of Christ's admonition to be perfect as our heavenly Father is perfect. Although they wore the robes of white awaiting the rapture, they were quite impure and had not really changed very much in their lives since accepting Christ. They had never truly entered into a purgative purification process.

In order to understand the import of this moment, you must also understand who this young Native American boy had been. Two months before this event, I had met a young Native American boy of about nineteen in the local park. In a way that was very unlike myself, I felt an undeniable compulsion to go speak with him and his friend who were doing drugs and smoking openly and were obviously in trouble. "You two look awfully young to be throwing your lives away like that." I'd said. Getting nervous, they both tried to deny they were as young as they were. "I have a very distinct feeling that if you don't change the path you are currently traveling, you are going to die very young." I said. Looking at me with utter disdain, the Native American boy said, "Why should *you* care, you don't even KNOW me?!?" "I'm a mother," I replied, "I care about everyone." With a confused glare, he stared. "Well, I've been trying to quit the smoking and drugs, but it's hard." "Yes, I know. It's very hard, but I hope very much that you will succeed. I wish you the very best in your attempts at quitting." Acting annoyed, he and his friend drove off, sharing a whiff of the finger out the side door of their car.

Three weeks later, my husband received a call in the middle of the night. "We have a homicide," was the message from the officer. A young Native American boy had been stabbed fourteen times in the park by a drug dealer. Although it didn't strike me immediately, I began to wonder if this might be the same boy whose path I had crossed. When Andy showed me the picture of the victim, I let out a sigh of disbelief and disappointment. The young man I had spoken to had indeed died young, but he'd also died in a most horrific manner. And he'd died very much alone . . . it took several days to even identify him and notify his family.

Because of these things, this heavenly 'adoption' became all the more significant. And the impending rapture of which he was about to see contained within it knowledge for which this particular soul, as well as those of the others present, had need.

At that moment, an angelic presence beamed across the heavens and entered into my spirit allowing me to pronounce that the Rapture was about to occur. Still unsure of what was to happen, I lifted my arms to the heavens to receive of it.

Coming in a fury of light, the heavens opened before me as shooting stars began to shoot across the heavens and into my soul. I began to see the universe and all its planetary systems spin around me, and I was lifted up into the cosmic ethers to become one with this powerful energy which fulfilled the coming of the great day! Spinning and merging with these energies, the heavens were opened to me like a cosmic fire spinning and merging with God and all that is and is to be. My essence was in a state of utter rapture, ecstatic bliss and unity with the Almighty. In a specialized instant, my spirit was lifted away from the Earth and into the universal heavens where I could see our planet in the distance, and I felt the omnipotent and awesome Presence of God. In a shattering light, a bolt of omnipresence came towards my soul like lightning and my robes became *whiter* than snow.

In this instant, I understood that my recent triumph over the lustful temptation which had come in the form of the carnivorous demon had rendered my soul to an even greater triumph in the eyes of God, for who can triumph except those who fight the battle between good and evil in their own souls? As this purity was imparted upon my robes and my spirit, I fell as if in a swoon into the hands of loving a God, surrendering my spirit to the fall of the wind. As I did so, I returned to the Earth and to the crowds which had awaited this Rapture with me.

Utterly quiet, I didn't realize for several moments that these folks had watched this event happening to me, rather than joining me within it. And suddenly I understood that the misnomer within the denominational faiths about this Rapture is their literal rendering of it as an event which happens *simultaneously* to believers alone, and that this is its only requirement. When in reality, the rapture occurs *individually* to a soul who truly enters and perseveres in the battle of its own purification. When a soul is determined to conquer its own vices and sin, the Lord lifts him up out of the mire of earthly delusions and lusts, to bring it to a higher purity attainable only in energy through the hands of the Lord.

All those around me were wandering around still waiting and wondering. They didn't understand. For a moment, I regretted cutting my hair along with them, because it had not been required, and my longer hair had represented a certain spiritual freedom. Several of them became very agitated waiting for the Rapture and the End Times to happen on a grand scale, because even though they had just seen it, they still held to their wrong understanding. They were cranky, uptight and exhibiting signs of agitation. Unresolved karma exhibits itself as agitation, and unpurified vice does the same.

Whenever a soul truly enters into the purgative way, the path of purification, they are entering the end-times for their own soul. As they achieve various triumphs of virtue along the way, they will be taken up into the heavens in a state of rapture. Belief in the Lord is only the first step; we are required to fight the good fight against the darkness within ourselves in order to triumph and be *taken up*.
****

CHAPTER SIX
Ancient Ghosts, How Religion Plays a Part in Why Souls Become Lost, a Murdered Priest's Liberation, a Woman Spirit Looking out for the Well-Being of the Lost Souls in her Graveyard, a Reunion with the Captives Who had been Set Free.

****

My spirit had been called in to work upon a large piece of land which carried so much history that that it went back to the trail of the ancients. This land had belonged to the Native Americans - the Navajo, the Ute, the Hopi and the Anasazi - at one time.

Because I'd become aware of a Heyokah spirit upon the land, I prayed for an audience with the Thunder Beings, the only angelic guardians with power enough to affect this situation.

As I did so, I stood before the mountain of my previous birth into new life. Ute Mountain began to erupt voraciously. In the distance, the sounds of the Thunder Beings began to resonate in the skies. It was conveyed, "You shall be given an audience with the Thunder Beings, but it will not be this eve . . . " A pause ensued, "The Heyokah spirit is a traveler from the East." The mountain erupted for exactly thirty minutes, a time frame which held meaning that I did not understand.

"There are twenty of these souls here," the angelic guardian warned, "but you shall be receiving three to four of them to begin." Immediately, I resonated with the fact that these souls liked where they were and didn't wish to leave.

Interestingly, there was a singular grouping of three souls; two of whom were women and one a man. There was quite a story here. The man was with one of the women, but she was not the right one to whom he truly belonged.

Something had happened which had derailed the eternal program between the other two, and it had been perpetuated and fulfilled by this other woman.

In short, the woman for whom he'd been meant to be married had been murdered by the other woman. But the man, not knowing who was responsible for the murder of his intended, eventually ended up being with the other woman who had taken his intended's life.

In the afterlife, this dysfunctional configuration remained, and it was my task to make it right. As I corrected the false pairing, a relief seemed to come over the two who had been wrongly set apart from each other. The guilty party accepted responsibility and said nothing . . .

The priest came to the forefront to teach these souls the Catholic faith. He was worried that they would cling to their Lutheran heritage, but it was not a valid fear. They accepted willingly the spiritual food offered for their souls.

Now that the perpetrator of this grave injustice (against eternal law) had been separated out from the couple, the mountain ceased its rumblings. The couple who had been meant for each other seemed relieved that this mix-up had finally been resolved, and the third accepted this just sentence because she knew she had committed something very evil and manipulative and she was getting her just due.

And as they whisped off into the heavens, it began to rain. Volumes and volumes of rain fell as my soul was taken down into a dark and dank basement where a very old upright piano stood about two feet deep in the water's fold. Everything was waterlogged, and I knew this held great significance, but did not know its meaning.

It continued to rain as if the rain would never end . . . I saw two other souls. Two men, one appeared to be a 1800's era barfly and the other wore the clothing of a man who may have worked the railroads during the 1800's. Waiting patiently, they knew it was not yet their turn to receive deliverance.

The rain continued to fall . . . the medicine of heyokah - the contrary spirit - would continue its reign until time and the Thunder Beings would herald something new.
****

As regards the haunted land I'd been working on, a Navajo medicine man had come out and performed a purification ritual asking permission for the land to be given to those who now occupied it.

Soaring into the ether, the Thunder Beings took me into the land. They were Native American angels and they allowed me to watch the land over an aeon of time. The land was under water very long ago and the Thunder Beings allowed me to watch as the water slowly receded over the ages and then belonged to the Native peoples.

They spoke to me ONLY in a Native American tongue, which language I didn't know. But I was given the gift of understanding them this night. Much was conveyed, they talked and talked and talked, but I only retained that which they allowed. At one moment, I almost spoke English by accident, but they stopped me because doing so would've interrupted the ceremony in which we were engaged.

As the water dried up and went away, the Native people had spent aeons upon this land. On the spot where the home was built, there used to be a lodge made up of four poles on one side and two on the other. The Native family who had lived there joined us in the ceremony which they called 'Yuwipi,' a Lakota word meaning to 'tie up or bind.' All the elements that had remained with the land were undergoing massive purification. For many hours, they spoke their native tongue and continued the Yuwipi to tie up and bind any remaining dark forces or lost souls or other presences which no longer belonged to the land.

The entire Native people from many aeons and generations suddenly appeared and arrived to stand before this single lodge which was unique. In certain respects, it resembled a tipi, but it also had a different shape (hogan?) which made it look more like a lodge to me. In that instant, I realized that both of these had existed upon the land at different frames in history. I was then shown a different set of poles. Again four poles were on one side and two on the other in this other home from the past. The number and location of the poles was important, but I did not understand.

Continuing to speak their native tongue, they asked me to retain silence. The Thunder Beings were guiding the prayer of Yuwipi and all the spirits (hundreds at this point) were speaking the prayers with them not unlike Catholics might pray the Rosary together. As we did this, however, a few here and there would walk off into the ether, take a single step . . . and disappear.

When it was finished, the Thunder Beings stood with me and this family who had once lived in the lodge. The other natives had lived on the land encompassing the ranch, but this family had lived on the exact spot where the current home had been built and this made them the specific previous tenants of their now current home.

Explaining to me in native tongue, the Thunder Being said that the family had now finished binding and tying up all the energies in regards to their former home and their ancestral land. In essence, they were 'handing the holy lodge to the white people,' which is what they said to me. The 'white people' they spoke of were the current owners of the land, not I, although the transfer was to occur through my spirit.

Each took a pole from the lodge. There were two adults and two children. Handing them to the Thunder Beings, the Thunder Beings then handed those poles to me. The current owners of the land were not present, but I knew I was accepting the poles on their behalf. It's important to understand they were not being given to me, because they were not mine, but that I was accepting them. And at the moment I accepted them, it was as if the current owners were accepting. In other words, nothing further would be required to make sure this gift was given to them. They received it as I received it, as if we overlapped at that moment for this purpose.

When the poles had been given to me, they disintegrated somehow into the current owners; despite the fact that they were not present. I knew this, but did not see it.

Great jubilation followed as the Thunder Beings smiled at me with satisfaction and a sense of success. All now was pure peace. At this moment, the Thunder Beings all sprouted Eagle wings on their backs. It looked very much like the wings worn by some Native tribes when they are dancing. The wings were unlike those I see on other types of celestial angels.

As their wings sprouted, they began to step up into the sky and began walking up an invisible staircase as they each disappeared, one by one.

When they were all gone, I was left alone in this peaceful space for a moment. I could still see the lodge with the tipi overlapping it, but everything was pure peace. And in that instant, I disappeared as well.
****

My Lord, to see it! Fear and trembling overtook my soul as I entered this mysterious haunted mansion. At first, I was not given to know the inner secrets of what lay beneath the haunting in this old but magnificent house. And in truth, my soul longed to leave it long before such secrets could be made known to me because I was in such fear.

In an upper room were three beds, one of which seemed to contain the darkest and vilest of the energies of the haunting in this home. I fled in terror to the lower stairs, but the wards of my journey - the angels of light - would not allow me to abandon my seeking.

Going back upstairs, I went to the bed which held such fear for my soul. As I stared at it, an old picture frame began to materialize upon its surface showing the face of an old Native American man, probably from the time of the 1800's or so. As I looked upon his face, his lost soul began to appear in front of me.

"Why have you haunted this house for so long?" I asked him quizzically. "So many came and went," he said, "but they would not help me." He paused. "Or any of us . . . " Suddenly, many other spirits began to slowly materialize in front of me all over the room. By the time they had all become visible to me, there were at least 100 lost souls, almost all of them Native American. Their faces were filled with a sorrowful longing for something which they knew they could have but did not know how to attain to it.

All fear left me at this moment, and I knew I was looking upon the faces of about a hundred people just like me who had crossed over at least 100-150 years prior and had become stuck. They'd all gathered into this home. It started with one, then another joined someone he had known, and another and another . . . Before anyone could discern all that had been coming to pass, the house appeared to be extremely haunted when it was merely filled with the longing of tens of lost souls who were all grown men and women. There were no children.

One woman told me how she had lost her baby who had already gone to the light and she longed to be rejoined to her beloved child. Another man shared with me that he, in his fear of leaving the rest of his family who were lost, declined when the opportunity had been given for him to cross over in the other worlds.

Turning to all of them, I asked, "Why are you all lost here?" A gentle man walked forward and spoke for them all. "For we practiced our Navajo Religion more than our Christian one." Although he didn't speak it, I inherently understood that they had known better. "Wow," I said, "that tells us a lot!" I couldn't help but think of my own path and the paths of so many of us who may not realize that such a thing could put us in such a status. It shocked me and it silenced me for several minutes.

"Well," I finally said, "I will help you." They all looked at me with a longing hopefulness that perhaps I held the sacred trust that they needed to make this crossing which had been hidden from them for so long.

"I am the Way and the Truth and the Life," I shouted with great fervor. "No one comes to the Father, BUT BY ME!" As I said this, all the women metamorphosized and their garments became bridal gowns as white as snow and white veils covered their faces. The men were changed in a different way. Their garments didn't necessarily change, but light began to shine from within them. "Our Father," I said, "Who art in heaven, hallowed be Thy name." Some of the women began to float gently in the skies. "Thy kingdom come, Thy will be done, on earth as it is in heaven. Give us this day our daily bread and forgive us our trespasses as we forgive those who have trespassed against us." Men and women were now ascending into the heavens and disappearing into the light. It was so beautiful I could not describe it adequately. I continued. "And lead us not into temptation, but deliver us from evil." Almost all of them were now released, but a few remained and they looked at me expectantly. It was the final words of the Lord's prayer which they required. "For the kingdom and the power and the glory are Yours . . . now and forever." As soon as they were spoken, they were all gone but one. The original man who had appeared to me on behalf of them all had a final word to speak as he was floating upwards towards the light and the heavenly host awaiting him. "Tell them now." He said. "They must know of the secrets . . . The Mysteries of Our Lord."

Immediately, I recalled the amazingly holy text I was given to hold in the Palace of Ancient Knowledge within the galactic heavens, the City of the New Jerusalem. It's holiness swept through me as I simply touched it. In a later experience, the angelic host had made me to know that they wished that I bring the words from ancient sacred texts in the galactic heavens into the earth. As I recalled all of this, I remembered the name of the book I had held in the Palace for which I had felt so unworthy. It was entitled 'The Mysteries of Our Lord." I nodded to him that it would be done as he smiled and ascended into heaven.
****

Andy was obsessed with buying a home which had been placed on the market well under what it would normal market value should be. It had been built in the 1930's and was in fairly good shape. It had a huge amount of square footage and several floors. All in all, probably around 5,000 square feet for which they were asking a paltry $124,000.

Standing in a rear entry, Andy was taking some of my holy objects, things that had come from my wedding ring and several gold coins with the image of Jesus upon them, and tried to glue them to an old bathtub as if he'd already made the decision to purchase the home. Another man was already looking through the home, and we'd find within moments later that several others were inside.

"What are you doing?" I told Andy. "You're acting as though we're going to buy a house I haven't even seen?" So he and the owner, a rich Arab businessman who claimed persecution because he looked Muslim, insisted I go through the house immediately and see it. I agreed that I would, but before I would, I took all my holy items off of the bathtub and washed off the glue. Placing them back in my possession, I moved forward to look at this home that Andy had become very interested in.

As I walked through, I asked many questions because there was something very sinister about the place but I couldn't immediately place it.

In the downstairs, there was the cutest schoolroom apparently being used by his and his wife's children who were being home schooled. A large open garage, probably made for at least three cars was nearby. I looked through the drawers in the schoolroom and made a comment on how nice that was.

Walking through the lower floor, the owner took me to a lookout point which was perfectly situated on the top of a hilly slope so as to give the owner the ability to look down upon a variety of religious sites. You could see a monastery down below and what he referred to as a temple mount. Perhaps we were in Jerusalem, it seemed, but that made little sense to me at the time. Indeed, however, there were several visible shrines, temples and churches within view and smiled in some delight, although I still felt something was very wrong here.

Passing through the first two floors, the lady of the house indicated that although the colors were all outdated, for that price somebody could completely change all of that. I made note to Andy that neither him nor I were very much in the shape to do that.

On the third floor, I looked out the back window and noticed that there was barely anything protecting the inhabitants of this floor from the elements. It appeared almost like an old cafe had once been there and had gradually gone from the inside cafe to an outdoor deck cafe. As I walked forward, I noticed the building was surrounded by a mote. And I immediately asked for what purpose would someone need a mote in a residential district. Looking behind me, I saw something apparently invisible to the other guests. It was a pile of bags, it looked like some kind of smuggling operation. Whatever was in the bags was of an energy of great evil.

Speaking to the very tall Arab man of the house, I suddenly picked up an old newspaper which no one else could see either which had a heading about his illegal operations. It seemed he might be into organized crime or something similar. He told me a story of his persecution because he looks like an Arab or a Muslim, but none of what he said coincided with what I was being shown around him.

Then I came upon a corner of the room on the third floor. The wife and the husband were not even nervous. But I noticed the presence of a group of people now, who were obviously not of this era. They were sitting at cafe tables, some reading papers, others eating breakfast.

Looking intensely into what appeared to be an old bed frame standing against the wall, I turned to the woman of the house and said, "Somebody died here . . . WHO WHAS IT?" She didn't immediately respond, and I began singing as I stared into the corner of the room. "Ave Maria, gratiaplena, Dominus tecum, benedicta tu in muli eribus," In my mind, I was wondering how and why I was receiving the Latin Version of the Ave Maria (Hail Mary) which I didn't myself know, when suddenly I saw him.

"Oh, my God!" I shouted as I turned to the owners of the house, ignoring Andy as he was watching in grave concern. "He was a priest!" He looked to be of small frame, medium height, and grayish black hair, probably in his mid fifties. Immediately, I began singing as if not under my own control, "Hail Mary Full of Grace the Lord is With Thee, Blessed Art Thou Among Women . . ." As I sang, I saw this priest. He was sitting in bed in this corner of a room which had once been part of a small hotel. He was holding something he had woven in his hands, as it was his hobby, and he had come here for retreat. He was speaking about how he wouldn't have time to finish it before he returned to his service at his parish, of the location I did not know.

Both owners were becoming very agitated and concerned. I looked towards them and shouted, "How did he die?" Remember, they had not yet even acknowledged a death had occurred. The woman walked forward and right in the spot I had pointed out, she said, "You're right, somebody died right here." "I KNEW IT!" I shouted. "HOW did he die?!?" I said as they both became very silent.

As I looked towards the priest, I saw it. Something had gone wrong, the priest had seen the illegal merchandise and although he hadn't figured anything out, he needed to be taken care of. The current man of the house was apparently there in the 1930's, so my immediate assumption was that this lady and man of the house were also dead. Looking at him, the man of the house, I said, "You did it, didn't you?" Immediately, he denied, but I pointed to him again and said, "YOU DID IT, DIDN'T YOU!?!" Then I saw it. He had set it up during the night that debris would fall upon the priest from the ceiling; rocks and cement, and it would look like an accident, that the building had partially collapsed. I saw the priest die a lonely, unexpected and undeserved death at the hands of a pretender, who was in reality a leader in organized crime and the cause of this holy priest's demise.

As I said this, I began again to sing outside of my control. And to stop this, one of the ghostly bystanders sitting in a chair having breakfast for the 60th year in a row in his own purgatorial realm, began to play a guitar in a key which was not fitting to what I was singing. I sang anyway, and drowned him out until he stopped. "Our Father . . . " I sang, "Who Art in Heaven. Hallowed be Thy Name." Beginning the most powerful exorcism song on the face of the earth, the man and woman of the house began to turn into their true forms, as did their guests. The others who were looking at the home for purchase had all suddenly ran away. Their true forms were those of little demonic trolls, and the winds of God immediately came upon the building and everyone in it.

"Thy Kingdom Come!!!!!!! Thy Will be Done!!!!!!!!!" I sang with all my heart and soul to the great glee and smiles of this holy and humble priest who had been held captive here for sixty seven years because of something of which he had no knowledge, even to this day. In his humility, he just looked into my eyes and listened to me sing. He paid no attention to all the infernal spirits which were being raised from the ground beneath this unhallowed building. Nor did he pay attention to the infernal spirit that his previous hosts had become, nor to the fact that the winds of God were blowing them in the opposite direction of the heavenly temples which I'd been shown just moments before. In a holy rage, I continued to sing for this holy priest as I would gaze upon the various countenance's of those demonic souls who had been so bold as to take the life of a man consecrated to the Lord God and the infernal spirits who had been hiding in the walls to continue to energize this long-time situation.

"On Earth . . . as it is in Heaven. Give us this day our daily bread, and forgive us our trespasses as we forgive those who have trespassed against us." The Holy Priest bid me adieu with a smile, a nod and a wave as the Holy Angels came to take him to the kingdom of heaven of which he was a rightful heir. The light shone in him, and all the infernal spirits and the spirits who had been living in the home - including the man and woman of the house - were gone. It was evident that they didn't even realize that somehow they had also been killed at the same time, probably through an error in the accident they staged for the priest. And somehow, he also had not noticed the transition into death because so many of them had come with him, they had transferred from one realm to another as if it hadn't happened. So the owners of the building continued to seek a buyer, and the guests remained seated for breakfast for Sixty Seven years. "And lead us not into temptation, but DELIVER US FROM EVIL!!!!!!!" I paused as I noticed that my soul was beginning to move from this realm to another.

"For thine is the Kingdom . . . and the Power . . . and the Glory, FOREVER . . . . . . " I was now waking into my current home still singing the 'Our Father' to the Lord. "A . . . . . men."

"It is over," I said out loud, as I pondered upon the plight of this holy man so unjustly treated. And I thanked God for the opportunity to free him from his fetters, as so many of my own priests had freed me from mine in the confessional and in private counsel.
****

Awaking in the middle of a graveyard in the middle of the night, I immediately became aware of a very stately woman probably in her sixties or so who had a strong Christian background. She was wearing a long navy blue skirt with a white shirt and a matching navy sweater. Her grayish black hair was pulled back in a bun, and she wore a sheepish smile.

Five other souls were present, none of whom held the light of this woman. One man was wearing what appeared to be prison garb, a striped white and orange shirt with orange pants. His hair was brown and long to his shoulders. He had an almost wild look, but I have to say almost, because there was something emanating from this woman that took that wild look out of his eyes. So you knew it had been there, but you could also see that her presence completely transformed him.

The others were all a mismatch of souls from the last 100 years or so and I'd been called in for a reason yet unknown.

The Christian lady very quietly stepped forward and said to me, "I felt it unseemly for me to go to my heavenly reward, knowing that these beloved souls of God should remain behind here lost." "How kind of you," I said, "to make it your concern." "Oh, no," she replied, "not my kindness, but my reliance upon the words of my own Savior have made it my concern." I said nothing, but smiled and listened. "He said that if I were to ask anything in His name, that it should be granted. And it seems that I would wish to ask that these souls beloved of God could come and escort me to my heavenly homeland and join me there among the beloved of God." Silence ensued. I was amazed at her faith, and at her willingness to remain behind to bring these lost souls with her. "Well," I said, "You have trusted rightly in the words of Our Lord. Anything you shall ask in His name shall be answered."

Turning around, I gazed upon the interiors of these souls, and could see that although these souls were lost, it was not because they were not worthy of the kingdom or able to partake of its redemption, it was because they didn't know how. They weren't Christians during their lives, hadn't practiced any spiritual paths, and had led somewhat notoriously sinful lives, though in a state of ignorant reprieve.

They all looked at me with expectancy as I simply replied, "Of course, this is the will of the Lord. Your faith has set you free . . . but it has also set all of them free. I am honored to be in your presence, for your faith is great indeed." And she smiled sheepishly as she and the others turned towards the light and she motioned them to follow her. No more words were needed as I watched them all leave this dark graveyard which had for a time been filled with the special spirit of a Christian woman who had stayed behind for her kinsmen. Bowing to the heavens, I felt the eternal thrust as my soul was catapulted back to my body.
****

What joy could become mine I could not fathom as I entered into what appeared to be a dark cave. Inside these caverns, were the souls of many men and a few women. At first, they were very busy at work, and I was given only a moment to watch them in their toil. But moments later, a wisp of wind seemed to come into the cave as we were now surrounded by the heavenly hosts.

I began to sing praise to the Lord, and the men and women in the cave joined me in my hymns of thanksgiving. It seemed to go on for hours, and I was wrapt in ecstasy with my Lord despite this dark place to which I had been taken with an entire host of angels. It seemed so odd, and yet, it seemed perfectly natural at the same time.

Taken from the scene, I was then given to re-enter the very same cave at a later juncture in time. The angels were singing all the louder, and they now took me to meet several of the wards of this place who loved me so deeply, I could not understand why.

The first man was Dominic, a very tall man with curly brownish hair. Immediately, the angels asked me to look at what he was working on. Noticing that his hands were enmeshed in sculpture for the Lord, I praised Him all the more. But the angels bid me to continue to look around the room. All of these people were sculpting things in the image of God, their souls were undergoing a profound transformation.

An angel led me to a man who embraced me with such holy love, I felt overwhelmed. He showed me what he had been working on and I was stunned by its beauty and uniqueness. He had been crafting a book out of rock. Each of the pages of this book was a scene from the Last Supper of Our Lord. He held me tight for many minutes, and I could feel such profound joy, gratitude and love from him, I couldn't understand why. It was not a lust thing at all. These people who were mostly men were expressing eternal love towards me for something that I could not yet ascertain.

Looking towards the heavenly host, they began yet again in their praises of the Lord and I joined them. As they did so, they explained to me what I had been given to see.

These people had been in darkness, but had seen a great light. "You are witnessing the captives being set free," an angel said to me, "and you have seen from whence they began and to where they have been led through the works done of God through your hands." I began to weep.

These people were taking these holy works of art which represented transformations in their lives, understandings and souls which had come about directly from their exposure to my writings and my work. It was overwhelming, yet I felt so honored and I felt so much love coming towards me from these people. I'd had no idea. The angels had allowed me to see them before and after - and now they were all lining up to leave the darkness of the caves. They had graduated onto higher things. But the bond between our souls was profoundly deep beyond any of my imaginings. It was truly a profound gift that the Lord had allowed me to be a vessel for them in this way. I was not worthy of it, I could only praise God with them and the angels as they quietly exited the cave and disintegrated into the ether. My heart knew where they were going next, and I was in awe of His ability to use such a simple instrument to bring this about.

As they all disappeared, the angels surrounded me in praise and worship. I was wrapt in ecstasy for hours with the angels. They were filling me with something more as we praised Our Lord. It was not just the understanding, which was profound, of how He was working through me. It was something energetic, and it was taking me to a higher place of ecstatic bliss where I felt completely at One with the Lord as if I were wrapt in prayer right at his side.

I held onto the divine pleasure until it was slipped out of my fingers, and I was led back to my earthly vessel.
****

Spirit Guides and Guardian Angels

Mystic Knowledge Series

Compiled and Written by Marilynn Hughes

The Out-of-Body Travel Foundation!

www.outofbodytravel.org

CHAPTER ONE
Emmanuel and his Realm, 'Physical Illusion Workout,' Little Chinaman, Running the Race, Island of Truth, the Grandfather, Cheyenne.

****

Entering the vibrational state, I began to consciously will myself out of the body. A familiar but as yet unidentified voice began to speak, saying that it wouldn't be necessary to leave the body to travel amongst the dimensions. My spirit could go inward.

Changing perspective, my mind entered into a hypersensitive state wherein it began working at an unfathomably high rate of speed. Inherently, I knew that I was feeling what it was like to be dead, and I was surprised by the activity that is apparently present at life's end.

Identifying himself, the voice told me his name was 'Emmanuel' and that he had been with me for quite some time and that his purpose was to teach me about the oneness of all life. An energy surge came over my spirit connecting me to an even greater ultra-sensitive state of oneness with God the Father. Knowledge of oneness became so expansive, that it was earth-shattering to me.

'The purpose of astral travel,' he conveyed, 'is to bring eternal knowledge from this heightened state, back into the limited human form.' Further, the process was very slow and tedious because only small amounts of knowledge can be retained with each journey.

In order to approach God, I would first have to let go of all that I perceived myself to be, as separate or distinct, because that part was of no use to God or to the evolution of my soul. What remained after the removal of such things, were the eternal soil upon which the Lord's blessings would bear fruit.

"Hence, one of the Prophets of God hath asked: 'O my Lord, how shall we reach unto Thee?' And the answer came, 'Leave thyself behind, and then approach me."
The Seven Valleys and the Four Valleys, The Third Valley, Page 55, Paragraph 2, (Baha'i, Author: Baha'u'llah)

****

Emmanuel came and went many a time to bring me into the understanding of oneness and to assist in raising my vibrational level. Upon this visit, however, Emmanuel taught me how to transmute the energies of vibrational raisings into my own soul. As the tremendous amounts of energy had begun forging through me, he guided me to stop and bring the energy to a level of love. Rather than fighting the immense energies, I had to allow it into my spirit. Sometimes, it would get so powerful, my head felt like exploding, but upon transmutation, the energies would expand in such a manner as to alter my worldly perceptions and attachments, bringing me to greater light. After a few hours, I literally begged him to stop.

"All earthly things, except those absolutely necessary, must die through our complete disregard for them, even though they are not wrong in themselves. We must control our minds and not permit them to wander aimlessly about."
The Spiritual Combat, Chapter 9, Page 23, Paragraph 2, (Christianity, Catholic, Author: Dom Lorenzo Scupoli)

****

"In Tibet we say that just as it is the nature of fire to burn and of water to quench thirst, the nature of the buddhas is to be present as soon as anyone invokes them, so infinite is their compassionate desire to help all sentient beings."
The Tibetan Book of Living and Dying, Chapter 19, Page 300, Paragraph 4, (Buddhism, Tibetan, Author: Sogyal Rinpoche)

During a vibrational raising, energetic waves began pulsing through my body beginning at my feet and working up towards my head. When it reached its pinnacle, I felt a jerking sensation in my forehead (sixth chakra) and my eyes jerked upwards. Appearing beside me, a female angel began funneling energies throughout my body and instructed me on how to hold energies more efficiently and refine them to make a stronger connection with the heavenly realms.

Having left form, my soul was vibrating at speeds higher than I'd gone before. Knowing that I was bordering on a much higher dimension, my eyes were closed, perhaps with fear of what I might see. I still had a fear of seeing ghosts, which was odd considering the journey I had undertaken.

Emmanuel's voice echoed before me. "This is an important step, one that you must take. In order for you to grow in your abilities, you must rid yourself of the fear of ghosts." Willing sight, I immediately became dumbstruck by the vision of Emmanuel before me. Emmanuel's dark hair framed his small face, his white robes glowed with light, and all around him a beautiful yellow, purple and white aura encircled his spirit. All around him were beautiful pastel shades of ether; blues, purples, greens, yellows, and among this ether was a silvery glitter quality. "See, it isn't so bad to see a ghost." Emmanuel said in jest. But I was so overcome with the beauty of this place, I cried out, "OH, MY GOD! THIS MUST BE HEAVEN, THIS REALLY MUST BE HEAVEN!!!!" Emmanuel's eyes were deep, loving and enthralling.
****

Meeting Emmanuel in an empty house, he informed me that I needed to work through blocks that I had in regards to the permeation of physical matter. Presenting me with the 'Emmanuel Physical Illusion Workout,' I began flying through the ceiling, walls, doors and windows until I started doing so with more ease.

"O now, when the Dream Bardo upon me is dawning! Abandoning the inordinate corpse-like sleeping of the sleep of stupidity, May the consciousness undistractedly be kept in its natural state; Grasping the (true nature of) dreams, (may I) train (myself) in the Clear Light of Miraculous Transformation: Acting not like the brutes in slothfulness, May the blending of the practising of the sleep (state) and actual (or waking) experience be highly valued (by me)."
The Tibetan Book of the Dead, The Appendix, III. The Root Verses of the Six Bardos, No. 2, (Buddhism, Tibetan)
****

Andy, my husband, had a dream in which he saw himself in a room which contained an imaginary line bordering on another dimension. Suddenly, a small man with short black hair came through the imaginary line. Immediately recognizing him, Andy shouted, "Little Chinaman, you're here!" The little man giggled and quietly jumped back over the line.
****

Having projected into another dimension together, my husband, Andy, and I had entered into a foggy realm filled with haze. Waiting to see Emmanuel, we sat in anticipation of the great being we awaited, speaking of our honor in knowing him.

When Emmanuel arrived, however, he appeared to us in street clothes. "Do not make me more than I am. As I am divine energy, so are you. Do not glorify me." Surprised by his response, we quickly realized that he was right. "We will meet again, my friends," he said, shortly before he disappeared.

"It is I, John, who heard and saw these things, and when I heard and saw them I fell down to worship at the feet of the angel who showed them to me. But he said to me, 'Don't! I am a fellow servant of yours and of your brothers the prophets and of those who keep the message of this book. Worship God."
New American Bible, New Testament, Revelations 22:8, (Christianity, Catholic)
****

Joining several runners about to begin a marathon race, I was quite determined to take a slow pace in what appeared to be a long journey ahead. Other runners quickly passed me by, perhaps thinking they had somehow gained something by doing so. However, I was quite pleased with my pace because I had perceived everything along the road, although a part of me could not help but wonder if I should speed up and keep pace with the others. After some time, the others sped by so quickly I saw only a blur in their wake.

Another runner appeared beside me without my notice, keeping the same pace that I had chosen. Immediately sensing my distress, he spoke to me. "The other runners are caught up with the finish line, and you are more interested in the path." I looked over at him, and said, "But I feel so separate and apart from their reality." Interjecting, he smiled at my confusion. "As you should! You feel the oneness and you see their reality for what it is. They see it from a different illusion. To them, physical life is all there is, winning is all there is. Spiritual growth requires a different perspective, one that you now have. Growth comes from within, not without. By taking life at the pace you have chosen, you allow yourself to perceive more accurately what the world truly represents. You embrace the divine plan and trust it completely, they do not. They feel that their importance lies in finishing the race with the fastest time, and you see that the race will never end. Every perception along the path is an important and crucial one. If you miss the flower on the side of the road because you ran by too quickly, you will need to return to perceive it in the future. In their ignorance, they may think they are passing you by, but the truth is you have not even entered their race. Your path is parallel to their road, but they have not yet begun the path that you seek. The irony is that the race is an illusion. Do not compare yourself with those who see only illusion. Walk slowly down your path of increasing awareness and opening perceptions as it is this path that leads to enlightenment."

Taking my hand, he and I transcended the race and sat together on a stone. "Knowing what you know about the universe, would you choose to again become ignorant of it?" My response was a resounding, "No!" "You may feel lonely and separate at times in your physical world because of your differing perceptions, but truth is a wonderful gift, and those who have the truth have everything. Your loneliness is just another part of that illusion. Is it not true that we are always with you? Is it not true that we are available to you at all times? And if this is so, then your loneliness is only a false perception on your part. You are never alone, it is an illusion!" Letting my hand go, he cried from the distance, "Remember, you have universal truth . . . you have oneness. How is it that you could ever be alone?!" In moments, I was returned gently into my body.

"Do you not know that the runners in the stadium all run in the race, but only one wins the prize? Run so as to win. Every athlete exercises discipline in every way. They do it to win a perishable crown, but we an imperishable one. Thus I do not run aimlessly; I do not fight as if I were shadowboxing. No, I drive my body and train it, for fear that, after having preached to others, I myself should be disqualified."

New American Bible, New Testament, 1 Corinthians 10:24, (Christianity, Catholic)
****

Lying amidst a stone complex, I awaited the guidance of someone to come. Resting peacefully, the spirit who had run with me on the racetrack of life appeared.

"In order to understand the true reality within your conflicts, you must see the window of perception that others see through." Projecting images of the way somebody I knew perceived reality, I immediately understood why we misunderstood one another. "Allow yourself to tune into other people's perceptions, so that you may understand the parameters of their vision. Love all beings, despite their present manifestation, as love is the only reality." He disappeared.

"There is nobody who lives happily with anger. Hence the enemy, anger, creates sufferings such as these, but whoever assiduously overcomes it finds happiness now and hereafter."

A Guide to the Bodhisattva's Way of Life, Chapter VI, No. 5-6, (Buddhism, Tibetan, Author: Shantideva)

****

     Twenty students and I were preparing to take a test in a very unusual schoolroom. Everything was foggy, and our desks were scattered around a lake. Beyond the shore, was a distant island referred to as the 'island of truth.' The teacher was a young, balding thin man of average height. Very much like a spelling test, he would tell us his truth and we had to write it down exactly as it was said. Trouble was he spoke so fast that no one could possibly keep up with him. Getting three out of ten right, I asked the teacher for another chance because I had a true yearning to know the truth. Ten stone pillars could be seen on the distant island, and the teacher's desk was set right on the shore of the lake. According to the teacher, the truths were etched in those stones. "Only I know what those pillars say," he said, "and because of that no one will ever pass this test. The answers are on that island, but don't try to jump across, as many have tried and never returned!" Confused, I agreed not to go.

     As another group of students came in and failed his test, I realized that his words were not difficult to understand but he meant something different than what he was saying. In essence, it was a trick.

     Understanding enveloped me as I realized I didn't have to jump across the lake, but willed my etheric body to the island of truth. On the island, there was no fog, and I looked upon the pillars to find their ominous wisdom, but found that there was nothing written on them at all, only a constant energetic whirling which could be seen. Many souls were on the island experiencing joy, and I immediately knew these were the ones of which the teacher had spoken. They'd found the truth and had no need to return. In his fear, the teacher could not see them on the island, though they stood right before his eyes.

     It was then that I knew that the real truth was that the man on the bank was afraid to step into awareness, because he was afraid of the unknown. Perpetuating his own fear, he told others that only he knew the truth. Despite this, a few brave souls realized that they must seek after the truth anyway.

     At that moment, several of my spiritual guardians appeared and conveyed, "Never give your power to the man on the bank. You must go to the island, yourself."

"See that you do not reject the one who speaks. For if they did not escape when they refused the one who warned them on earth, how much more in our case if we turn away from the one who warns from heaven."

New American Bible, New Testament, Hebrews 13:25, (Christianity, Catholic)

****

     Coming to me in sleep, Emmanuel directed me in achieving the vibrational state required to leave the body of my own accord. As he focused my energy on the chakra centers of the body, he told me to pull all that energy into the sixth chakra, or the third eye. As I did so, I entered into the vibrational state.

     My soul was immediately transported to another dimension and I heard a distant Gregorian chanter singing these words:

"I am the grandfather, old and wise
I know the answers you just can't deny
But you have not found me yet
But you have not found me yet"

     Swept away by the beauty and mysterious echo of this chanter, it was repeated over and over again as a glowing shrine of jewels appeared before me. In its midst was an old, old man with long white hair and a beard, sitting in a lotus position, adorned in a pure white robe. Eyes closed and legs crossed as if in meditation, his hands were placed on his knees.

     Enchanting me, the music held me in its rhythm, as it was conveyed clearly to me that I must find him.

"When you find your place where you are, practice occurs, actualizing the

fundamental point."
Moon in a Dewdrop, Actualizing Fundamental Point (Genjo Koan), No. 11, (Buddhism, Zen, Words of Zen Master Dogen)

****

An old parchment stood upon an easel in a clearing in the woods, as an Indian man quietly directed my attention to it. "This is a map of your spiritual growth in this lifetime. These are the next few steps you will take before meeting your Indian master." Realizing he spoke of the grandfather, I continued to listen. "And this is what you have mapped for the rest of this lifetime."

Although I could see the map, I was unable to really understand the details of the path, only the essence of the journey. Pointing to the bottom corner, he said, "And down here in the corner is the day you have chosen to leave this earth." Nodding, I understood.

Standing in an old dirty attic, I suddenly found myself looking for an old box covered in jewels. When I found it, I noticed several slips of paper inside indicating heavenly promises I had made to teach certain individuals and groups of people in certain areas of the world. Below it was an old black and white photograph of me teaching a group of people. Extremely uncomfortable, because I knew I was not qualified to teach anyone anything, I quickly put the box away.

Destinies must be revealed in order for us to fulfill them. At the time of its revelation, we can be left with hesitation in wondering whether or not we are up to the task. We aren't, but God is. Therefore, put your faith in God's abilities, and worry not about your own.

"Faith is the realization of what is hoped for and evidence of things not seen . . . By faith we understand that the universe was ordered by the word of God, so that what is visible came into being through the invisible."
New American Bible, New Testament, Hebrews 11:1, (Christianity, Catholic)

****

Working with a theatre group, I was playing many different roles, none of which suited me. Asking me to return for the tryouts for the next play, the director; a middle-aged short balding man, told me he had another part for which he'd like me to try out. In the meantime, I was sent to a crystal enclosure. Huge shimmering white crystals covered the ceilings, walls and floor, and I sat in a corner soaking up the intense vibrations.

Returning to the theatre group at the appropriate time, the stage was filled with dancers who were performing a drama about human nature. Only two people had showed up for the play, and the actors were disappointed. Entering the backstage area, the director ran to me holding a white flowing garment. "It is the Age of Aquarius," he said, "and you are the Aquarian! You must play this part as it comes natural to you!"

"The sage dwells in affairs of nonaction, carries out a doctrine without words. He lets the myriad creatures rise up but does not instigate them; He acts but does not presume; He completes his work but does not dwell on it."
Tao Te Ching, No. 46, (Buddhism, Taoism, Words of Lao Tzu, Translation: Victor H. Mair)

****

Flying through a small park out-of-body, I came upon a nice picnic table area with some shade from a large tree. A female spirit approached me with three friends, and I felt immediately uncomfortable without knowing why. Telling me that they knew I was learning from Emmanuel, they began to ask questions. "Don't you think that unconditional love is impossible to attain? And if we are always experiencing the now, then what about the future?"

Feeling irritation, I didn't know what to say, when suddenly the woman began changing form . . . and in moments had turned into Emmanuel.

"It's you!" I shouted at him, laughing at my own delusion. Responding immediately, he said, "You fear exposing yourself and being scrutinized. You fear being called a teacher. It scares you to think that others may try to give their power away to you and expect you to know all the answers." Pausing, he reflected concern in his eyes. "The answer is simple. BE. If you don't take another person's power, they cannot give it. And if they desire proof, they do not desire the truth." Standing, he disappeared.

"An evil and unfaithful generation seeks a sign, but no sign will be given it . . ."
New American Bible, New Testament, Matthew 13:39, (Christianity, Catholic, Words of Christ)

"He who knoweth things as they are and not as they are said or seem to be, he truly is wise, and is taught of God more than of men. He who knoweth how to walk from within, and to set little value upon outward things, requireth not places nor waiteth for seasons, for holding his intercourse with God."
The Imitation of Christ, Second Book, Chapter 1, No. 7, (Christianity, Author: Thomas A Kempis)

****

"No longer is my consciousness limited to a phial of flesh, corked with ignorance. No more did I move through Thine Ocean of Spirit day and night, years, incarnations - so close, yet without contacting the Sea. No longer do I thoughtlessly dwell in Thee, knowing and feeling Thee not."
Whispers from Eternity, Page 163, Paragraph 1, (Hinduism, Kriya Yoga, Words of Paramahansa Yogananda)

After many journeys into the heavenlies seeking atonements with others, I found myself in a celestial realm of white filled with musicians. Finding myself playing the bassoon with a trio, we were standing on white pedestals which hovered in the clouds. Many musicians were playing all around, but none of the performances seemed to interfere with one another.

Moments into our performance, a short stocky Native American man approached with long black hair. Immediately mesmerized, I began staring at him and felt as though I knew him.

Taking my hand, we walked away from the podium. Entering a small room, we both laid down on what appeared to be thin air. "You wanted to experience what it means to be. I will show you what beingness is. Lay your head on my shoulder and be." As I did so, I felt complete love, peace and joy in a way I never had in my physical body. Skyrocketing vibrations filled my soul, as other spirits passed by us with total respect for our state of being. 'Being' was considered superior to 'doing.'

Heading down another corridor of light hours later, he said, "It is important for you to receive these energies so that you will be able to meet with the Indian master." Taking me into a large crowded room, he led me to a table where many books were stacked. Picking one up, its title read, 'Cheyenne.' "My name is Cheyenne, as I was a Cheyenne Indian. I will call you Ute."

In a moment he was gone.

"First keep thyself in peace, and then shalt thou be able to be a peacemaker towards others. A peaceable man doeth more good than a well-learned."
The Imitation of Christ, Second Book, Chapter III, Paragraph 1, (Christianity, Author: Thomas A. Kempis)

****

Emmanuel was watching closely as the group lined up in a circle and put their arms on each other's shoulders. As music began, we all began dancing in a circle. "Stop," Emmanuel said. "Look around you and tell me, who were the followers and who were the leaders?" We all looked around and could not decide, as each person in the circle was doing both. "Let this be a lesson to you. Know that you will always have things of the spirit to share with others, but that you should constantly follow the beckoning of your inner soul as there will always be more to learn."

"When exhaustively contemplated, these teachings merge in at-one-ment with the scholarly seeker who has sought them, although the seeker himself when sought cannot be found."

The Tibetan Book of the Great Liberation, The Seeing of Reality, The Yoga of the
Nirvanic Path, Page 224, Paragraph 1, (Buddhism, Tibetan)

****

Cascading upon the sands of a beach, Emmanuel told me a story:

"Notice how vast the ocean is and how many drops of water exist out there. Every few moments, some of those drops come into shore on a wave; a small amount in comparison to the size of the vast sea, but they come in to see if there truly is such a thing as a shore."

"They have heard stories about a shore, but all they have known is the vast expanse of the sea. Some of those drops come in, look and say, 'No, I am only dreaming,' and rush back to sea. But a few of those drops see the shore, grab onto a piece of sand and say, 'It is real, there really is a shore!' In their excitement, they beckon to the ocean, 'I have found truth, the shore exists, and it is real!' But the drops of water far out to sea think it is only an impossible dream. Other drops continually come and go, some finding the shore, others frightened by what they see. Wanting so much to share the truth of the shore, the drops continue to beckon. In frustration, they get angry at the drops further out. 'How can you be so blind? The shore is right in front of your eyes!'"

"A voice inside of them says, 'Only a small amount of water can hold onto the sand. The beaches are small in comparison to the wide expanse of the sea. You have made it to shore, now move on my friend and make room for another drop to fill your space. Help them by letting them find the shore themselves. But do not stop beckoning, as the stories of the great shore are what lead them to question its existence.'"

"So the drop evaporated into the heavens and made room for another drop to grab onto the shore. From above, he saw a tiny drop fill his former space and find truth. Then the drop shed his physical shell and in his place a tiny new soul came. It rained and the new soul began its journey to find the shore."

"Remember, my friend, continue to beckon, but move on and allow others the space to find the truth. It is all a great flowing plan and each will find the truth in his own time. We love you in your imperfection; love others as we have loved you.'"

"But the souls of the just are in the hand of God, and no torment shall touch
them. They seemed, in the view of the foolish, to be dead; and their passing
away was thought an affliction and their going forth from us, utter destruction.
But they are in peace. For if before men, indeed, they be punished, yet is their
hope full of immortality."
New American Bible, Old Testament, Wisdom 3:1-4

****

CHAPTER TWO
Guardian Angel, Kutahey, Spirit Guides of Inspiration, Temple of the Dolphins, Assisi Marauders, White Winged Horse, Quasar, Crystal Forest, Traveling to the Sun, the Two Native American Men.

****

Soaring from my body, I was suddenly catapulted into a dark world of ghettoes. Feeling very unsafe, it seemed as if I'd entered into a chaotic energy belt and I didn't know what to do but continue to fly away, running from my fear as fast as I could. Before long, I came upon an empty amphitheater and quietly sat down.

Noticing at once that I was wearing the robe of a monk, my head was bowed down in contemplation. A noticeable presence could be felt coming from behind, and a huge warm light was beaming upon my backside. Meekly turning to see who it was, I saw the Romanesque image of the man from my past life, but glowing with white and yellow light. Light emanated from all around him as he spoke to me. "I am your guardian spirit. Why do you fear?" Looking at him in awe, I could not answer. "No harm will ever come to you, as I will protect you always." Reaching out to him, our hands met in a shimmering bolt of light.

In a moment, we stood upon the shore of a great ocean, and I knew that this gift from God was soon to end. "I am always there for you." He said. "If you allow yourself to feel my presence, you will know that you are safe." He disappeared in the blink of an eye.

"Know that He wishes more love than fear from you. Therefore, Abandon yourself to His love, and let Him act in you, with you and for you, according to His desire and good pleasure."
Thoughts and Sayings of Saint Margaret Mary, April, No. 29, (Christianity, Catholic, Words of Saint Margaret Mary)

****

Before leaving my body, I heard Emmanuel's voice in the ether. "I now set you free my little bird with golden wings, may your wings span the entire universe. I give this being to the Indian master, Kutahey!"

Sucked out of form, I entered into a thought-form. Groups of people from my life, past and present, were working together in the accomplishment of some elusive goal I could not see. Angry that I was not part of the group, I said, "Don't you see? Who I was a year ago, is not who I am today!" They couldn't understand and asked me to leave. "I like you the way you are," I said, "Why is it so difficult to like me the way I am? Am I really so different?" Tears were welling up in my eyes, but they were adamant, and I left through a side door.

An old dear friend of mine was sitting alone in this next room, hurt and upset that his father was in trouble. Wanting to know how he might be able to help his father, he was seeking the counsel of a wise being whom he was unable to see. "Why can't you see him?" I asked, as his eyes lit up. "But, you can!" He shouted. "The being is behind that door!" Pointing to a door behind him, he begged, "Would you talk with him?" "Of course I will go, maybe he can help you." I answered, permeating the door to float into the next room.

A peaceful bald monk sat behind a small table in robes of white. Smiling at me as I entered, I respectfully spoke, "My friend is having a very serious problem with his father, and he feels that you know what he should do." Looking at me intensely, he gazed several moments before he replied, "Why do you feel so strongly about finding an answer for this entity? What does he mean to you?" "Well," I replied, thinking upon the nature of our age-old friendship, "I love him very much, and I think I understand his despair as my own father is very much like his. I could never help him and I had to leave him to his own reality." Laughing, the spirit spoke again, "My child, you are wiser than you realize. Perhaps you could give him an answer yourself. Did you realize that when you feel such love for another being, that in that state of loving completely, all answers come to you. All the answers are simple." Nodding in agreement, he then asked, "Do you understand the thought-form in the previous room you put yourself through." "No, I did not. It was very frustrating for me." "My child," he replied, "you experience frustration in your physical world because people don't see who you are. They don't see who you are, because they don't see who they are. They cannot forgive others, because they cannot yet forgive themselves. Their disappointment is real, but it is not at you . . . but rather, themselves. Having not accepted that all the answers lie within, they find none. Believing unconditional love to be too simple, they do not become a part of the divine energy of love that flows through every being. They still try to *do*, rather than *flow*. My dear friend, you have chosen to flow with the divine plan of oneness and love. We do things through you, rather than by you. Few will see that in your world so you must see it yourself. Recognize this and your frustration will turn into understanding and love." Thanking him, I turned to leave, but he quickly stopped me. "Wait, my friend, I desire to speak with you more. Will you return?" "Of course," I responded, "but why do you want to talk to me? After all,

I'm not anywhere near your level of evolution!" Laughing the beautiful spirit said, "I want to teach you, I am Kutahey!" Thrilled and excited, I realized he was the grandfather I sought. "But you do not look the same as before. You appeared as an aged Indian, and now you appear to be a monk from India. Which one are you?" Patiently, he replied, "What I am is who you are. Cannot I be both, and more! Do not limit your perception of me. Go through that door you have entered and confront your fearful thought-form. If you can enter into understanding and love, it will disappear and be replaced by whatever beauty you desire. We will meet again!"

Floating through the door, my friend was no longer there. Appearing for an instant, he said, "I have found the answer inside myself. Thank you."

Cruising through the next door, I found the other people still there, ranting and raving. "Your anger is not at me, but yourself. Understand who you are, and you will understand who I am." Lying on the ground, I willed my sight to cease. The noise stopped. As I willed my sight to return, they were all gone, and I was laying in a magnificent field aside a snow-topped mountain peak.

Lying in the grass, I marveled at the blue of the sky before returning to form.

"Make no great account who is for thee or against thee, but mind only the present duty and take care that God be with thee in whatsoever thou doest."
The Imitation of Christ, Second Book, Chapter II, Paragraph 1, (Christianity, Author: Thomas A Kempis)

****

"Simply give yourself over completely for the sake of your Enlightenment-seeking Eye; give up your life for the sake of the Teaching. How could you possibly arouse your will to realize enlightenment in the vain cause of fame and gain . . . just call to mind your own original intention to realize enlightenment and reflect upon whether this is what you are now concerned with or not."
The Denkoroku, Chapter 17, Saint Ragorata, (Buddhism, Zen)

"I have spoken but according to my knowledge and only with such sense of right as a creature of clay may possess. But how can I speak except Thou open my mouth, and how understand, if Thou give me not insight."
The Dead Sea Scriptures, The Book of Hymns, Page 193, Stanza 1, (Christianity, Gnostic/Essene)

And so it came to pass that the Lord revealed to me that many spirits on the other side of existence had specific purposes in the realm of inspiration. Anyone who brings into the world something of a higher nature, is bringing it with the aid of higher sources who inspire him in his work; whether it be artistic, like writing, painting, music, etc., or scientific advancements. It also became clear that every soul is given a special holy gift, their life purpose, but only the few ever attain to it, because so few choose to do what is necessary to become able to bring within them a sacred mission.

What is necessary is twofold. First, a soul must be willing to be completely transformed, and second, a soul must be willing to do whatever God may ask of them.

In order to be completely transformed, a soul must be able to view itself with honesty. Most souls do not see their own vice and deadly sin, because these vices are held intact by an intricate working of delusion within the mind. We can rationalize our actions in every which way, but truth. Let me again mention to you the seven deadly sins, and advise you to take a careful accounting of them within your life: Gluttony, Lust, Greed, Pride, Sloth, Vanity and Avarice.

If you are honest, you will find that you most probably practice each of the deadly sins to some degree, and that one or two of them hold prominence. The purpose of the journeys into lives from long ago is not for mere fancy, but to provide you with knowledge of the patterns of your existences, which become clearer as you witness lifetime after lifetime of repeating similar patterns in entirely different settings. In perusing past lives, it is wise to peruse with a thorough eye, and with true diligence. No soul resides upon this Earth unless it remains necessary, and no soul leaves this earth until it is no longer so.

Doing whatever the Lord asks of you can require many things. The Lord helps those who help themselves, and many souls lose their holy destinies because of their unwillingness to make it happen on the ground. We are the hands God works through to make things happen in this earthly realm. For an eternal destiny to manifest in the physical realm, it must first be energized from above, and then below. God energizes us from above, but we must complete the process by energizing and *doing* it on the ground.

Beyond this, it is vitally important that a soul learn the proper balance between action and surrender in bringing things to birth; acting when inspired to do so, but having the discipline to cease action when energies are in gestational phases. Eternal programs, just like babies, are birthed in their own divine time, not according to our earthly whims.

Beginning to understand that although my awareness of it had often been void, there were many guardians, angels and spirits whose purpose it was to assist me in bringing out this work. Knowing this, I felt a sense of expansion in that the Lord directed my every step, giving me the knowledge that I needed at each juncture to accomplish His will. Finally, a soul cannot bring something of heaven to earth, unless he is willing to transform his selfish desires for fame, money, power or wealth, into the desire to create for the purpose of furthering eternity, alone. Vice cannot be attached to such a pursuit.

"My dear Mother, I am a little brush which Jesus has chosen in order to paint His own image in the souls you entrusted to my care."
Story of a Soul, Autobiography of St. Therese of Lisieux, Chapter XI , Page 235, Paragraph 2, (Christianity, Catholic, Words of St. Theresa of Lisieux)
****

And so it came to pass that the Lord placed two souls in my care who were very dear to Him. Musicians, the Lord had given them an eternal option with their creative works.

Entering into the realms of inspiration, one of these souls and I entered into a large white space which seemed to be inside a building but had no roof or walls. Marble white steps led to an airy celestial sky and the darkness of night made the shooting stars descent in the astral sky all the more ominous and foreboding.

Four entities appeared to us, three male and one female. The woman was wearing a Victorian servants dress. The men had long thick brown hair down to their shoulders and were wearing greenish-white stretchy pants and leather jackets. All of them communicated only in song.

Asking them questions, their melodies were often joyful and exuberant, but they also encompassed a haunting karmic tone which gave me the impression that the music they created aided in the karmic transformation of souls. As we sang together, they looked deeply into my eyes to convey their identities. Becoming aware of their purpose, I shouted to my companion, "Do you know who these entities are? They are the musical entities that work with you!" Disappearing, a thought-form album cover remained on the floor. "Temple of the Dolphins," it said. They were a band of spiritual guides who brought music into our world.

For a great time, our souls were united in purpose, to assist in bringing that which was of heaven into the earth through these dearly beloved souls of the Lord. Appearing to me and energizing me for this function many times, the Temple spirits and others worked in the progression of this work of God. But apathy and unbelief on the ground eventually forced its halt.

"Many men are incited to do works of virtue for the sake of certain temporal goods; nevertheless inordinate desire for temporal goods is not on that account without sin. So even if most people perform works of virtue for the sake of

*glory, nevertheless inordinate desire for glory is not on that account without sin,
since works of virtue should not be done for the sake of glory but rather for the
good of virtue, or better still for the sake of God."*
On Evil, Question IX, On Vainglory, Article 1, Page 339, Reply to 6, (Christianity,
Catholic, Author: St. Thomas Aquinas)

****

Having left form, a sort of melancholy had taken over my soul as to
make it unaware of the pathway it had taken to arrive at this unusual place. A
knowing told me that I was on another planet, and that this entire land was
known as the land of the Assisi's.

A mountain range that I inherently knew to be called the Assisi's
loomed overhead the ocean beach I stood upon. An omnipresence of rich color
entranced me in this world, for everything held richness deeper than I'd
remembered upon the earth. A spiritual community lived here, souls in no need
of bodies, who honored the way of the Lord.

*(As St. Francis of Assisi neared death, he asked his body to be turned in the
direction of the city of Assisi and he spoke these words:)*

**"Lord, as in days gone by many evil-doers lived in this city, so now I see it has
pleased your abundant mercy to show this city the fullness of your grace. May it
become a dwelling and a home for all who acknowledge you and seek to glorify
your name forever and ever."**
The Prayers of St. Francis, A prayer for Assisi, Page 46, (Christianity, Catholic, Words
of St. Francis)

Going into the mountains with a group of sub-conscious astral spirits,
they had come here to learn flight, as well as, to become more at one with the
natural laws of life and the earth. While I was leaping down mountain cliffs and
through trees, the sub-conscious souls would grudgingly try to walk because
they hadn't yet learned to fly.

Coming across a steep mountain drop, I noticed an iridescent lake
below filled by a crystal river. A meadow surrounded the waters with beautiful
flowers in bloom. Soaring down, I dove directly into the lake, although my spirit
did not become wet. As I got out, I sat down in the meadow to rest, and
motioned the tepid souls to join me. All declined but one brave soul, who
injured her ankle preparing to make her descent. Massaging her ankle, she
suddenly pointed to the sky and shouted, "It's the Assisi Marauders."

Memory came upon me as I recalled that the Assisi Marauders were a
group of spiritual guides who focus on creation energy. At the time, there were
five marauders who all manifested as men.

Looking up, I noticed five white-winged horses carrying the men who
wore all black, with capes blowing in the wind. Waving, I knew that these guides
had something to do with St. Francis of Assisi, but that was all I knew.

**"Then I saw the heavens opened, and there was a white horse; its rider was
(called) 'Faithful and True.' He judges and wages war in righteousness."**
New American Bible, New Testament, Revelations 19:11, (Christianity, Catholic)

As they passed, I was entranced by their Godly power, because they
were extremely energized beings who performed the function of energizing
works of creation on the ground which empowered the evolution of souls
towards God on earth. Rather than being a source of creative works like the
Temple of the Dolphins, their energies were actually those that brought things
into manifestation upon the ground.

Flying back up the mountains and rejoining the group, we eventually
returned to the ocean-side community. To the spirit who had hurt her ankle, I
said, "If you allow yourself to trust, you will be able to fly with ease!" What this
means is that flight is a gift given solely through the power of the Lord, if you try
to do it on your *own* will, it doesn't work correctly. Give all power to God, and
then flight comes naturally.

A short old man wearing a white robe approached me, and I

immediately knew that I had known him for centuries, but this was the first time I remembered him in my current lifetime. A great sage, I knew him to be the master sage of the Assisi Marauders . . . and my teacher.

Spirits began assembling in the clearing and a voice could be heard echoing across the sky. "Everyone stop what you are doing as the ceremony is about to begin. A new Assisi Marauder has been chosen!" Oohs and aahs were heard from the crowds and I felt an indescribable excitement. Looking to the old teacher, I asked, "My father, who is this being? Do you know?" Smiling, he said nothing.

Suddenly, the white horses came from the distance, flying overhead. Carrying their respected passengers, they landed right before me. One of the marauders, a blonde man, walked up to me and handed me a card proclaiming my rite of passage, "Welcome back, my friend, you have been missed," he said. My very own white-winged horse flew in from the sky, landing next to me. Beckoning me to ride him, I hopped on and flew into the sky with the marauders.

Landing in an isolated area, a white-winged stallion stood by one of the marauders who looked especially familiar to me. Intensely attracted to his energy, we sat aside each other in the grass. Feathered black hair, and rough beard and mustache made him quite mysterious as he stared at me without regard to the intrusiveness of the act. Suddenly pulling me closer to him, he looked directly into my eyes and said, "You could be my fantasy."

Pulsating energy surged into my spirit, words holding power and meaning far beyond what I could presently understand. I wanted to know more, but the spirit wind pulled me away, returning me to form.

"Lord Jesus Christ, you are the good shepherd. You grant us your loving mercy without our having deserved it, and many a time it must endure the pangs of sharp pain. Since you have called me to your flock, I beg you by your grace and strength that in trouble, anguish and distress I may never turn away from you."
The Prayers of St. Francis, Lord, help me, Page 38, (Christianity, Catholic, Words of St. Francis)

****

Lying in bed completely awake, an unseen hand touched my hip. At first I was startled, but calmed down immediately, knowing within myself that this was an angelic visitor. Returning the hand began sending an intensive energy throughout my spirit. Entering into a silence that cannot be described, I felt an absolute peace I'd never known before in this life. Above me, I saw the spirit of the Assisi Marauder who had spoken the mysterious words to me. Transparent, he appeared for only a moment, as his hand remained on my hip pulsing this silent energy throughout my soul. Reveling in this newfound silence, I surrendered and let go to the powers of God to energize my soul.

"For the knowledge of it is Divine Silence, and the rest of all the senses; for neither can he that understands that, understand anything else, nor he that sees that, see anything else, nor hear any other thing, nor in sum move the Body."
The Divine Pymander of Hermes, Fourth Book, No. 17, (Mystery Religions, Egyptian/Hermetic, Words of Hermes)

****

And so it came to pass that I underwent many powerful and arduous vibrational raisings at the hands of the Assisi spirit. Of the many things he taught me, he showed me that joining our fingers together at the tips in a meditative or vibrational state, multiplies the energy coming through the soul. And it also came to pass that my white-winged horse would come to my bedside with regularity, to take me to fantastic places of universal joy and love, places like the crystal forest where everything was created from pastel shades of crystal, blue, purple, pink, green, and a golden river flowed through this spectacular place which was a place of intensive creation energy. In so doing, he showed me many things of wonder, many different groups of spiritual guides who aid in creating music, art and writing on the earth. I was made to know that there were others who aided those in the sciences, as well. And as my understanding grew, I came to understand that in order to be able to bring these things into my world, the earth; a soul's parts, both physical and spiritual, must be unified.

As I made more and more contact with these and other creative spirits, they began to give me mystical and allegorical poetry, whose meanings are deeper than they initially appear, much like parables. *"This is why I speak to them in parables, because they look but do not see and hear but do not listen or understand . . . But blessed are your eyes, because they see, and your ears, because they hear. Amen, I say to you many prophets and righteous people longed to see what you see but did not see it, and to hear what you hear but did not hear it."*
New American Bible, New Testament, Matthew 13:13-16, (Christianity, Catholic, Words of Christ)

****

Hovering above my bed, my white winged horse descended from the sky and beckoned me to ride. His wings were a combination of feathers and fur, and when I touched them I felt completely energized. Climbing onto the horse, a voice overhead spoke. "You are truly a marauder now, flow with love and be with us always. Do not fear expressing all that you are and all that you feel. There is no shame in love." Taking me to several places that night to energize eternal creations on the ground, my spirit white-lighted special receptacles of eternal creation, like record companies, publishers, radio stations, etc. (Another time, the Assisi Marauders allowed me to come and watch as they invisibly worked with huge power on individual souls who were being energized to bring eternal ideas into their creative work on the ground.)

****

Bringing a group of sub-conscious astral souls to a special place lit by twilight, they were to meet a very holy being. Speaking to them of astral flight and the spiritual journey, I prepared them for this powerful spirit to arrive. Feeling a huge energy surge, the sky began to glow and twinkle in illumination and I knew she had arrived. Descending from the sky, the dark-haired Indian woman held familiarity, as I said, "May I introduce you all to my beautiful sister, Quasar!" As she appeared, she hugged me in recognition and love as my eyes welled up in tears. Glowing in a way that cannot be described, there was an oval light that surrounded her manifestation. Love was evident in every peaceful motion of her body.

"In death as in life," she said, "astral flight is one of the most beautiful things you can experience. Those who believe enough to allow it into their lives are greatly blessed and greatly loved." One of the male spirits interrupted, "Astral flight? That sounds very different." Obviously from another time frame, the man was wearing a three-cornered hat like the ones found during revolutionary war days. "In your present state," Quasar patiently explained, "it may sound quite different, but in our natural state, it is a normal state of being. It is not very different from what my own race, the Indian people, did for centuries."

Another spirit interrupted, "What tribe of Indian are you, Quasar?" Waving her hands across the sky we began to see thought-forms of soldiers tracking down a tribe that they intended to imprison, but as the Indians went over the crest of a hill, they transmuted themselves and flew away. Confused, the soldiers couldn't understand how they had escaped. Putting her arms around me, she said, "I am of the Bird tribe, more specifically the Robin people. The last of us left the earth-plane long ago, but some of us have returned as power points." She looked at me. "My people reside in the stars as we no longer have need of physical bodies. You are here in a very special time. Many of my people have returned in this time frame to help bring in the new energy."

Quasar took my hand, shooting us straight into space at the speed of light. Soaring through the star tunnel, we viewed galaxies and universes unimaginable and impenetrable to a human mind. In the distance, I saw the planet where the Assisi's resided. Within moments, our consciousness had been expanded to take in a vast knowledge of the grand nature of the universe, but with a limited understanding through human eyes of things celestial.

"But I said, Sir, teach me about the faculty of these authorities - how did they come into being, and by what kind of genesis, and of what material, and who created them and their force? And the great angel Eleleth, understanding, spoke to me: 'Within limitless realms dwells incorruptibility. Sophia, who is called Pistis, wanted to create something, alone without her consort; and her product was a celestial thing.'"

The Nag Hammadi Library, The Hypostasis of the Archons, Page 167, Paragraphs 5-6, (Christianity, Gnostic/Essene)

****

And it came to pass that on subsequent journeys, I was returned to the Crystal Forest (A place in the heavens . . .) where Quasar (A Spirit Guide) had continued to energize creation within me. Returning to the sun several more times to observe the mysterious ether pathway, the mystery of it would not yet be revealed.

"Sonarington. This sphere is the 'bosom of the sun,' the personal receiving world of the Eternal Son. It is the Paradise headquarters of the descending and ascending Sons of God when, and after, they are fully accredited and finally approved . . . There are numerous orders of divine sonship attached to this supernal abode which have not been revealed to mortals since they are not concerned with the plans of the ascension scheme of human spiritual progression through the universes and on to Paradise."

****

Entering into the atmosphere of the earth and then space, I watched as I passed by Venus and Mercury, and suddenly my soul shot directly towards Venus. Entering what appeared to be a city, it looked much like a very clean and glistening version of earth except that the corners of all the buildings were rounded, there was an omnipresence of color and all was silent and peaceful.

Thinking about Quasar, I sent a question out to the universe. "Can I please come to see you Quasar?" Shooting through the heavens, the flight of my spirit hit soaring proportions in speed unlike ever before. Knowing that I was going very FAR away, the stars flew by in a streak of white light, and suddenly my soul plummeted.

Landing on something, I noticed the great amount of white mist all around me. Angelic music was emanating from all directions and you could FEEL it as well as hear it. A small speck of purple light appeared, and it began to grow larger and larger, coming nearer and nearer. It didn't stop growing until it was a huge ball of purple light, as large as any star around me. "Quasar," I shouted, "My God, you are beautiful!" Enveloping me in her love, I felt the high honor it was to be in her true presence, that of a star.

"What these higher entities accomplish with the physical entities (below them) is called influence (Hashpa'ah). All influences that are directed from the higher entities toward those below, pass through the stars. The stars are therefore the closest things to the terrestrial world having such influence."

The Way of God, An Essay on Fundamentals, Page 373, Paragraph 2-3, (Judaism, Author: Rabbi Moshe Chayim Luzzatto)

****

Standing at the foot of a forest, I noticed two Indian men wearing jeans but no shirt, their hair long and black, and each bearing a feather hanging down with the flow of their hair. Andy was with them, and as soon as I saw them they smiled and raised their hands. Beckoning me to follow them, they both turned into eagles and flew into the sky. Landing about one-hundred feet away, they waited for me to get nearer to them as I flew with a fury to keep up. But once again, as I got close, they turned into eagles and soared off to reappear next to a large waterfall which fell into a wide lake. Andy disappeared and reappeared with them wherever they went. As I approached them at the waterfall, I asked, "Why is Andy with you?" They quietly responded, "We are of the Bird Tribe and Andy is our brother." I was thrilled to hear such news, as they continued, "Follow him in times of distress. His knowledge is different from yours, but just as vast. You understand the realms of spirit, which is wondrous indeed. Andy, however, understands the intricacies of living in a physical world with the spirit of love fully incarnate."

"Our journey represents the fluidity of your life on the earth-plane. You shall never stand still for long, as you will constantly move from one mind space to another more appropriate for the path of knowledge." With that, they turned into eagles and flew off deeper into the forest as I frantically followed them. Andy disappeared. Continuing several more times, we went deeper and deeper into the woods. My yearning to catch them and to understand grew deeper and more passionate. Finally, they spoke in unison as they took their final leap into the forest. "Follow us deeper into the forest, oh beautiful spirit! We will guide you! As you follow us deeper into the great forest, you will enter into deeper understanding and awareness of truth." Flying faster, I still could not catch them. "Wait, I am coming!" I shouted, "I want to come with you!" Shouting back, they said, "It is wonderful that you desire so much. Fly, spirit, fly! We will constantly be moving deeper into the forest of understanding and love, so you, too, must be moving in order to follow us. Never stop flying, my brave little soul, as it is this willingness to move and change that will fuel your growth!" Digesting their words, they disappeared to my sight. "I will follow you!" I shouted, "Thank you for showing me the way! I love you!"

"Those whose vital spirit is scattered outwardly and whose intellectual ruminations ramble inwardly cannot govern their bodies. When what the spirit employs is distant, then what it loses is nearby. So know the world without going out the door, know the weather without looking out the window; the further out it goes, the less knowledge is. This means that when pure sincerity emerges from within, spiritual energy moves in heaven."
Wen-Tzu, Further Teachings of Lao-tzu, No. 20, (Buddhism, Taoism, Words of Lao Tzu)
****

Taken to a fear thought-form on the astral plane, a group of people were making fun of me and provoking me physically. When they approached, I held out my hand and touched them, and they fell back from the force of the light. Two native men walked in the room wearing blue flowing jackets with white shirts and pants. One of them immediately came near me as I instinctively raised my hand. As he fell, I looked at the other spirit with him who had the most beautiful long black wavy hair. "Kutahey!" I shouted. "It's you!" Looking behind me at the man who had just fallen to the floor, I cringed, "Cheyenne, I'm so sorry!" He was unconcerned, however, and motioned me to listen to Kutahey.

Embracing me, Kutahey asked, "My child, are you on our side?" Thinking a moment, I replied, "I represent many sides, whichever I can understand in the now." "That is perceptive of you. However, we come to you with this group of beings you perceive as hurting you. Why is it that you don't perceive us as hurting you, after all, what I am is who they are?" I pondered. "Well, I know that you love me and want to help me grow in my awareness of love." I said. "Yes," he replied, "that is true. We want to help you, yet you are afraid. What is it you truly fear, my child?" Sheepishly, I replied, "Rejection." Kutahey smiled and put his arms around me. "They will not reject you, my beautiful child. At the core of their being, they are so grateful to receive this truth. It is their ego that wants to reject your words as those words force them to re-evaluate their entire reality. See their core of unconditional love, not their crust of anger and misunderstanding. The ego is the hardest obstacle to overcome, as many will hold onto it to define themselves as separate and somehow different. Truth, however, is that what I am is who you are. We truly are all one entity." "Thank you," I said as I hugged him good-bye, "I've missed you."

"At the root of this precept lies the reason that we were commanded to emulate in our actions the qualities of the Eternal Lord, blessed is He. (One) of His attributes is that He abounds in loving-kindness - i.e. He deals with human beings beyond the strict line (letter) of the law."
Sefer haHinnuch, Volume 1, No. 76, Paragraph 2, (Judaism)
****

CHAPTER THREE
The Inner Caverns, the Vortex, Warehouse of Unfulfilled Dreams, Abraham Lincoln, Paintings on the Walls of my Spirit, Madame Trinidad, Long Hair, Spinoza, the Tribe of Swallow River, the Overlapping Reality, the Chief, the Totems - Mayan Cards of Walking Stone, Medicine Man.

****

Freed in a flash of light, my spirit soared until it reached its destination aside an Indian man who wore only a buck-skin. "Follow me!" He said, as he darted to the heavens. Leading me to an endless river of iridescent blue, he motioned me to get into the water. Creating a thought-form canoe, I prepared to climb in when he calmly said, "No, YOU get in the river." Disposing of my thought created canoe; I jumped in the water and noticed that it was very warm. An unseen protective spirit got into the water before me, and the Indian man was behind.

Traveling through the waters, we journeyed into a cavern wherein the river flowed. Stopping to look at the man behind me, I gently said, "Which way do I go?" "Follow the inner caverns," he said, "they will lead you to the core." But as I moved ahead, the water became very cold. "This water is so cold!" I shouted, not wanting to go further. "The water is only as you perceive it." He said. "A path rarely traveled has little light. Follow the river to the core, and bring forth your deepest understanding and awareness. By doing this, you will bring light and warmth to your river. Open the channel between your higher self and your physical manifestation, and you will travel this part of the river often!" Flowing inward, I looked back and noticed he wasn't coming with me. He had read my mind and said, "This journey must be taken yourself, but I will wait for you on the bank."

Feeling the intensity of the unseen presence in front of me, I knew I wasn't truly alone, but I was still frightened. As this journey continued, my memory was blocked, but I returned with a certain understanding that I had taken my first journey to my own inner core, my higher self. And that this journey was vital in the process of purification.

"They see the Lord in the cave of the heart and are granted all the blessings of life."
The Upanishads, Taittiriya Upanishad, Part II, 1.1, Page 142, (Hinduism, Translation: Eknath Easwaran)
"Love opens the minds interiors but fear closes them . . ."
Divine Providence, VII, No. 139, (Christianity, Swedenborgianism, Author: Emanuel Swedenborg)
****

Unrelenting and merciless, a force drove my spirit through space to arrive upon the planet of the Assisi Marauders. Standing in the midst of the Assisi Mountains, I reveled in the beauty of all around.

Sitting on the ground, I suddenly noticed a shadow of a man at the top of a cliff in the distance. In the mild wind, a cape blew behind him. "Could it be?" I thought. Disappearing from that spot and materializing in front of me, it was my special friend, the Assisi Marauder with his white-winged horse standing in the distance.

"It's been a long time," he said, "but this visit will have been worth the wait." Starting to talk about old times, he tried to awaken my memory of him, but I couldn't recall his connection to me, although my senses were always reeling in his presence. My soul *felt* our past, but I had no historical landmark within which to place it. Taking my hand, we flew high into the sky within the universal spheres.

Stopping in a huge rotating white mist, he said, "This is the vortex, the ultimate tool of creation!" The mist spun like a top into the center of the cloud. Motioning me to enter into the vortex, I flew in and began spinning slowly at first, but increasingly faster until I was nothing but a blur of energy. "Create with this vortex!" he shouted, as I focused my thoughts on the creative projects the Lord had asked me to fulfill. As time passed, I eventually came out of the vortex, rejoining my friend.

Flying back to the place where my body lay sleeping, he said, "You will create your own vortex, follow the example of the stars!" Willing myself to spin, it didn't take long before my spirit spun, relentlessly consumed in my own personal vortex. Winking, he waved good-bye as he left for the stars. "Thank you!" I called out as he disappeared.

"In a state where Being is fully maintained the process of experience becomes powerful, and the experience of the object becomes deeper and fuller than before. This art of being on the level of experience is natural in a fully integrated life where one is able to live all values of the transcendental, absolute bliss-consciousness of Being together with experiences of the various aspects of relative creation."
The Science of Being and Art of Living, Part 3, Chapter 2, Page 119, Paragraph 3, (Hinduism, Author: Maharishi Mahesh Yogi)

****

A spiritual hand took mine and we flew me to another destination. Entering a huge warehouse, it was filled to overflowing with paintings, sculpture, musical scores and books. Looking around, I noticed a small man dusting everything with love and care. Walking over to him, I said, "Sir, what is this place? There are so many beautiful paintings!" Smiling as he looked up, he said, "This is the warehouse of all unfulfilled dreams." "Wow," I replied, "all this beauty, and yet unfulfilled?" Quietly chuckling, he said, "Until the bearer is ready to allow it into their reality, I watch over their dream. When they are ready to let it in, their dreams will be as bright and new as the day they were conceived!" Looking at a painting, I asked, "Can anyone bring these beautiful things in?" "Oh, yes," he said, "but as you are aware, you must desire it with all of your heart. Your friends have many dreams warehoused here; I could really use the space so I am hoping that they will allow them into their reality very soon!" He spoke of the two musical souls I'd guardianed. Musical scores were lying all around, piled up in boxes for them. Feeling sadness for their loss, he said, "There are many very beautiful dreams, are there not?" Nodding 'Yes,' the spirit who had taken me to this place placed his hand in mine and led me home.

"If a piece of canvas painted upon by an artist could think and speak, it certainly would not complain at being constantly touched and retouched by the brush, and would not envy the lot of that instrument, for it would realize it was not to the brush but to the artist using it that it owed the beauty with which it was clothed. The brush, too, would not be able to boast of the masterpiece produced with it, as it knows that artists are not at a loss; they play with difficulties, and are pleased to choose at times weak and defective instruments."
Story of a Soul, Chapter XI, Page 235, Paragraph 1, (Christianity, Catholic, Author: St. Therese of Lisieux)

******

"I have come to talk to you about freedom." The spirit of Abraham Lincoln said. "And who better to talk of freedom than you, Mr. Lincoln?" I retorted with a smile. "That's true," he replied with a grin, "However, I am no longer Mr. Lincoln. I'm only appearing this way for the sake of effect." Inherently, I knew that his soul had gone onto other things, and that this historically significant lifetime of his was nothing but a vague memory of a distant past. "Freedom, like the wind, flies to completion but never truly ends. When you are giving the gift of freedom to others, there are guidelines to help you complete your task. In the beginning, fly like the eagle. In the end, set like the sun. But forever, patrol like the moon. Always there, but in the shadows." "How beautiful that is, sir." I said with respect. Sobering, he replied, "The universe is beautiful, my child, and though this may be difficult at times, love means giving freedom, all spirits are born to be free, in pursuit of their dreams and in all that they see. Be like the sun, watch and shed light, but make room for the moon in the darkness of the night."

My guardianship for these two souls was complete for now, but as with all souls I was instructed to guide, there was an energetic bond that would remain which would alert me to their condition and status for the remainder of their lives, almost like a homing signal. If they ever needed me again, this mechanism would call me into action. "Thank you, Mr. Lincoln." I said, as he disappeared. Another spirit wind blew by whispering these words. "Potentials are filled by seekers." Then it was gone.

"They perform their journey together, in union, and moving about collectively. For they act with cause or without cause, moving in a body. Of all these acting with one another, but differing in development, the increase and diminution will now be stated."
The Anugita, Chapter XXIV, No. 3-4, (Hinduism)

******

While traveling amongst the fourth realm (dimension), I ran into a bit of a problem, as the fourth realm is much like the third, it carries both darkness and light. Having gone into a bar, a woman had warned me. "You shouldn't stay here; we can't guarantee your safety." But I'd noticed an old friend of mine, and talked for such a long time that before I knew it there was a mob of people with very dark energy around me were emanating seriously harmful intentions.

Before I could think about a solution, a monk came scurrying through the crowd. Wearing a brown robe, he had long curly brown hair. Picking me up, he took me away from the dangerous place. Somehow along the way, though, the monk switched places with another monk who was larger and bald. Reacting intensely at first, I was afraid, but as he swept me up and carried me through a corridor, I thought to myself, "I am eternal; no one desires to hurt me."

Entering into a very lighted place, the other monk was waiting. "Very good," he said, "you recognized my brother with love. In order to surrender, you must be willing to place your entire reality in the hands of the spirit. Your knowingness becomes who you are, not just a separable part of the whole. In order to surrender, you must now be willing to relinquish all forces contradictory to your role of love." Nodding as he spoke, he asked me to repeat after him. "My spirituality is who I *am*. Therefore, I will not enter any reality of negativity and fear simply because another fears the true reality of love and oneness." The other monk was waving his hands, creating an energy vortex around our circle. "Though some do not understand, it is not my role to make them believe. My role is to continue my journey onward. Any being who will continue to be in my reality must join me where I am, for I will no longer join them where they are if it be in fear."

Placing their arms on my shoulders, they began filling me with light. "Who are you, beautiful spirits?" I asked. "All that is love is all that I am. All that

I am is all that you are. All that you are is a mirror of God." Pausing a moment, he asked, "What have you allowed to remain in your reality that does not express love, what barriers do you still hold to surrender?" Considering the question deeply, I asked, "But how can you relinquish everyone who is unaware?" With total calm, they replied, "If you are to enter into a world of peace and love, you must become peace and love. If you are to change the reality that you occupy, you must change the energy that it encompasses. Is it not true that you accommodate these beings in their negativity because of their refusal to deal with who you *are*?" I nodded yes. "Do as they do. Do not allow their negativity around you, as they have unconsciously asked you to keep your loving reality away from themselves. You needn't suppress who you are, because of their limited perception of what it means."

Getting up, the monks turned to go get something. When they returned, they held a stack of paintings with held images of themselves and other spiritual guardians of mine. "Display these on the walls of your spirit and we will protect the structure of your home."

"If a lay person learning the Way still clings to wealth, covets comfortable housing, and keeps company with relatives, despite having the aspiration, he will confront many obstacles in learning the Way."
Shobogenzo-zuimonki, Book 3, No. 11, Paragraph 3, (Buddhism, Zen, Words of Zen Master Dogen)

****

Entering a cavern, large stalagmites about fifteen feet high ascended from the rock floors. When my guide and I arrived, a man was waiting who was sub-conscious astral. "I want to bring in something really special," he said, referring to his work on the earth, "Do you think you can help me find it?" Our guide lifted his arms to a side wall of the cavern as a river began to instantly flow through it. As they walked into the river, I stood by and watched as the guide lifted his arms to the sky and they both began to glow with light. Addressing me to join them, we created a power triad of light, and afterwards, the man walked through a door in the wall of the crater while our guide disappeared.

Following the man who walked through the door, I noticed him playing music on a piano. As I came up behind him and began to sing along, he began to cry. Reaching in a flood of emotion to hug me, he said, "Now I know who you are!" Intrigued, I asked, "Well, who am I?" Quickly, he jumped up and ran over to a drawer in a desk. Pulling out some drawings, he explained, "I was given these drawings years ago, they are pictures of my spiritual guides." Handing them to me, he pointed to two drawings right next to each other. "As you can see, these two guides are the same." "Oh, my God!" I cried out, as I looked at them. "I was told many years ago that one of my guides would be incarnating to help the earth-plane." Continuing to look at the pictures, they were of me. One of them was a drawing of my physical manifestation, and underneath it, it said, 'Marilynn.' To the left was a drawing of myself as a luminescent golden angel, and underneath it, it 'Odyssey (Marilynn).'

Sharing with me that he was soon to be passing and that I must continue his work, he said he would guide me from the other side as I had done for him. All of this came to pass, in that he crossed over and began to guide and direct my soul in the continuance of this eternal mission from the other side of existence.

"In order to be inspired to extract the essence of our precious human life we must appreciate the nature of our spiritual situation . . . The first of these is that we should make every effort to accomplish the spiritual path."
Training the Mind in the Great Way, Point One, Page 55-56, Bottom & Top, (Buddhism, Tibetan, Author: Gyalwa Gendun Druppa the First Dalai Lama)

****

Rescinding form, my spirit was taken through the corridor to a realm of deep blue as I awaited the arrival of someone I was to meet. Floating and wearing a long colorful gown, she had a bandana wrapped around her auburn hair. "I am Madame Trinidad," she said.

Quickly coming towards me, she began speaking. "A destiny is unfolding for you, my dear child, one so vast as to open a door of transcendence from fear for all spirits incarnate in human form!" Looking in her eyes, I sighed, "That sounds like a big job." Her serious nature did not change. "It is, my child, it is. There are many who follow your destiny and each part of the awakening is precious to the whole. A voice cries out, a soul is stirring! Many souls in the voice of one are calling! 'I am remembering who I am, I am waking!' The gentlest movement has been stirred deep within the spirit of manifest life. Secret longing and unknown remembrance of love greater than any in form! The longing to know and to understand, no longer lies dormant, but is turning in its sleep. Reaching out to the surface, it finds an ego that has grown so large as to block its entrance into the vehicle of physical life." Taking my hands, she looked deeply into my eyes. "Those who have awakened must become vehicles of transcendence, as there will be no confrontation to fear centered thinking. Fear is dissolved through love. All life stirs for the love of the Great One."

Stopping, she created a scrapbook to show me, "This is for you to remember me by," she said, "go ahead, look through it." Inside were newspaper clippings and other physically grounded stuff. "No, thank you," I replied, "I will not allow physical grounding and negativity into my reality, for love is all that I see." She brightened. "Very good, my child of the stars. GO! Show others what you see! Not only through words, but through expression! And don't allow physical interference in any form. Show those who sleep what it is to *feel* love in its totality. Act with love towards all life, all consciousness. Recognize that their destiny is parallel to your own, despite their limited knowing. Let your own love, peace and transcendence express itself in physical reality. All life stirs for the love of the Great One. This is how fear will dissolve into nothingness."

Releasing my hands, she foraged through a small purse she had created. In it she found a band-aid and put it on my finger. "The ego oriented planets have a gift for you; a band-aid to filter out all the negativity in your work with them." Chuckling quietly, I said, "Planets?" "Aaaaah," she said as she pointed her finger upwards, "An observant spirit, indeed! I did say planets, as you are manifesting in several at this time. We are opening the bridge of light between the other side and physical manifest worlds on several planets." She stopped and picked up my bandaged finger. "As you will notice, it takes very little to filter out negativity as that energy has no power. The power of love is of a much higher vibration than fear, and one who is love cannot be truly harmed by it. It is only when one exits love and enters fear that an equal confrontation takes place. Once those shadows are seen, they are no longer a mystery and they disappear. A light lit bright in a pocket of darkness forces those in fear to see their shadows. In our realms, we speak not of love, for we ARE love. Anything else is foreign to us. Bring this reality into the illusion!" She began waving her arms wildly to and fro with a flow of energy that now encircled us. Suddenly, she shot towards the sky in a flash of light and disappeared.

"The secrets of Divinington include the secret of the bestowal and mission of Thought Adjusters. Their nature, origin, and the technique of their contact with the lowly creatures of the evolutionary worlds is a secret of this Paradise sphere."
The Urantia Book, Paper 13, No. 1, Paragraph 5, (Christianity, Urantia)
"His blessings will be sought for by the offerers, those who are living now, and those who have lived, as will they who are to me, the immortal souls of the righteous in eternity."
The Avesta, Yasna 45, No. 7, (Zoroastrianism, Words of Zarathustra)

****

Floating up towards the marble steps, I sat down, and suddenly felt a presence behind me. "We are calling you into service, my child; allow whatever comes to enter for we will be asking many varied tasks." The familiar voice of Long Hair (A spirit guide and soul from my past lives . . .) spoke, "This is the Temple to the Indians, and many of us reside here in total harmony and love." He paused. "You have lived here in the past." Not surprised, I felt very comfortable and familiar here. "You are *becoming*, my child," Long Hair continued, "Lessons are being learned and released into the universe. Surrender is near as the spirit cries for more awareness. Much can be accomplished through an open sieve." At that moment, I recognized the importance of his message, for it indicated the absolute certainty of the path. When you are *becoming*, you are *not there*, yet. Quietly, Long Hair floated away effortlessly.

Standing before a seeking soul, I looked down to notice that I was manifesting as Odyssey, a higher aspect of myself who appeared as a golden transparent angel. Preparing to journey back to my body, I called out, "The Corridor," as it appeared before me. "What is it all about?" the seeking soul asked. "Love, my dear friend, it is about love." Light poured from my third eye to him, as my soul entered the cloudy violet corridor.

"For maintenance is perpetual creation, and continuance is perpetual coming to be."
Divine Providence, Chapter 1, No. 3, Paragraph 2, (Christianity, Swedenborgianism, Author: Emanuel Swedenborg)

****

Approaching with a smile, the Native American man approached as my soul awakened from sleep. Taking my hand, we soared through the time tunnel, entering the body of a native woman in a small tribal encampment laid by the river. "My name is Spinoza," he said.

Standing in a field, he asked me to take flight. Shooting towards the sky in a rush of delight, we began soaring in ecstasy. "There are three levels of transcendence, Swallow Bird," he said, "these are low, moderate and high level. You are now ready to become more of what you are becoming, but there is one more thing you must learn in order to become of high level transcendence. This is the manipulation of matter through spiritual means."

"I know what you mean," I responded. Flying into a grocery store, I noticed a poor man was leaving with little food for his family. Creating a disturbance, I picked up some food and flew into the parking lot as he exited the store. When he wasn't looking, I dropped it into his basket. Spinoza was pleased. Continuing with this process, we stopped at several more places wherein we manipulated matter through spiritual means, in essence, doing the work of Guardian Angels.

Finally, he directed us towards the moon. "Create an unexplained disturbance on the moon," he said, "something that will perplex mankind when they find it." Following his direction, I created handprints in the rocky surface. Taking my hand, Spinoza flew me back to my home.

An entire tribe was waiting at my house, concerned that they might wake my husband. "What are you all doing?" I asked. "It is in celebration of the new transcendent being that is you!" Spinoza gave me one last hug, "The tribe of Swallow River rejoices at your memory of them. The tribe cannot stay in this place for long, but we are preparing a home where we can abide together in harmony and the flow of nature, and in this place we will commune often." Spinoza kissed me on the cheek and turned to fly away.

Several native women specifically asked me to record the contents of their visit. "You are no longer who you were yesterday, that being is an image in the illusion of time. Do not forget who we are, for we are the tribe of Swallow River."

"When, through illusion, I and others are wandering in the Sangsara, Along the bright light-path of undistracted listening, reflection, and meditation, May the

***Gurus of the Inspired Line lead us, May the bands of Mothers be our rear-guard .
. ."***

*The Tibetan Book of the Dead, The Appendix, II, The Path of Good Wishes for Saving
from the Dangerous Narrow Passageway of the Bardo, No. 2, Page 199, (Buddhism,
Tibetan)*

****

Rescinding form, I took my husband's hand and flew to the bedroom door in our new country home. Behind the door was a large carving of the sun with two distinct faces portrayed. One side of the carving displayed a happy face, while the other half glinted with fear and suspicion. Looking somewhat like an ancient Aztec sun calendar, Andy became frightened when the image became animated and prepared to speak. Directly at Andy, he quietly said, "Boo." Andy's fear was quickly deflated by this humorous gesture. "Who are you?" I asked the being. "I am a sun spirit," he replied. "I am confused by the two sides that your faces represent," I said, "Which are you?" Becoming fully fearful, he said, "To those who come to me in fear, I teach them about fear." Becoming fully loving, he continued, "But to those who come to me in love, I teach of love. I am whatever you perceive me to be."

***"Know ye, O my brother, that fear is an obstacle great; be master of all in the
brightness, the shadow will soon disappear. Hear ye, and heed my wisdom, the
voice of LIGHT is clear, seek not the valley of shadow, and light only will
appear."***

*The Emerald Tablets of Thoth the Atlantean, Tablet VIII, Page 45, Paragraph 5,
(Mystery Religions, Egyptian/Hermetic, Words of Thoth)*

Suddenly, a spirit jumped out of the carving and became an Indian woman. Noticing that my medicine wheel had manifested on the wall, she took it and flew out the window towards the woods. Running after her, I begged, "Please return my medicine wheel, it is a most cherished possession." Following her, I was determined to retrieve my sacred object. Reaching the backyard, I noticed a massive ribbed tunnel which had opened, leading to an interior woodland.

Running through the tunnel, I turned a curve and fell to the ground. Now in the midst of a dense, thick forest, the woman was standing on a cliff just above a river. "No!" I screamed out as I saw her jump into the river, "The paint will be ruined." Flying towards her, I jumped in the water, as well.

In the water, I quickly forgot about my medicine wheel as I emerged at the surface to observe hundreds of Native Americans coming out from hiding in this beautiful forest glade. Emerging from the depths was the woman who had taken my medicine wheel, which was now washed clean. The painting was gone.

Looking around me, I saw our home in wavy energy form. "These realities overlap," she said, "though you may not see this world with your physical eyes in your body, know that this world is here. We exist on top of your world as interspersed energy. Know that you may traverse the tunnel to our world at any time." Handing me the medicine wheel, she continued, "Paint what is within your spirit upon this wheel, be willing to take your spirit far. Know that your medicine wheel of life can never be broken . . . only changed." Understanding, I thanked her.

Returning to the house, Andy was still looking at the carving on the door, "I am here, I am there, and I am everywhere I please." It said. Taking his hand, we returned to the physical realm, knowing that the tribe of Swallow River had made its home with us.

Within moments, my spirit was awaking back to the physical world.

****

In full headdress, the Indian Chief sat atop a horse, as Andy and I awaited his gifts. We'd found him only after traversing a great maze, wherein surrender was the only key, the only redemption . . . the only deliverer. Now we stood atop a great waterfall hundreds of feet high, and on the opposing cliff, the

Chief sat upon his white steed.

"Who are you?" I asked, and he replied. "I am the water in the lake, and the life in the tree. I take form in clouds and in the wild animal spirits that roam your world. I see through many eyes, but my true perception is that of a star. It is through these eyes that I bring the energy of creation into form. Find me in your heart." Pointing an arrow at Andy from a nearby cliff, the Chief began to shoot them. The first arrow was blue and he shot it into Andy's heart. "My first gift to you is the energy of the ocean," he said, "feel its pulse in your heart." The next was pink and as it entered it changed colors, as if psychedelic. "My second gift to you is the energy of the sunrise. Feel its constant change, and its constant ability to rise above illusions." The last arrow was purple and entered Andy's crown chakra, as he remained in utter peace. As the Chief lifted his arms, a young Indian woman bearing a purple rose appeared. "My third gift is the energy of the spirit, the energy of the celestial realms. Know who you truly are, my son." Andy sighed in joy and asked, "May I be with you?" The Chief winked. "You have found me, now you must follow me. This young woman will show you the way to my temple, a place of love and a very high vibration. But, my dear son, you *will* come to my temple, and when it is that you do, a grand welcome will take place." Shooting up towards the sky, the Chief disappeared. Although we didn't know it at the time, this Chief was a manifestation of Andy's higher self.

"Seeing the world of sentient beings so full of afflictions, the enlightening beings arouse their energy, thinking, 'I should rescue and liberate these beings; I should purify and emancipate them; I should lead them, direct them, make them happy, develop them, and cause them to reach perfect peace.'"

The Flower Ornament Scripture, Chapter 26, The Ten Stages, Page 722, Paragraph 3, (Buddhism, Mahayana)

****

And so it came to pass that I retrieved the mystery of the totems, which are our guardian spirits. The further the seeker goes, the more totems they are given to protect them in their journey. Presented to me as many different faces upon dozens of totem poles scattered throughout a mountain valley, each represented a guardian spirit, but they also represented different states of being. Calling the totems 'Mayan Cards of Walking Stone,' Odyssey had one last thing to share before this experience was over. "The lighted are precious, our link to the Earth; we protect the sacred, those who give birth."

"At the root of the precept lies the purpose to establish firmly in our spirits that the watchful care of the Eternal Lord is individual, over each and every one among human beings, and His eyes are open to observe all their ways."

Sefer haHinnuch, Volume II, No. 169, Paragraph 6, (Judaism)

****

Taken to a large forest glade, some people were with me who I was trying to help understand my spiritual journey, but they only mocked me and laughed. Suddenly from above in the sky, a light beam came towards us. Panicking, they all thought it was a nuclear bomb. But I knew that it was not, and as they all ducked in utter fear at its approach, I reached my arms out to embrace the light of God. After it had passed, they were gone, and I had a small mark on my skin as evidence that this had occurred.

Walking down the mountain, I went back into the city looking for them, but they were nowhere to be found. Up ahead in a large crowd, I finally saw one of them and I ran in her direction. "Oh, are you okay?!" I shouted excitedly. "Who are you?!" Get away from me!" She replied. Looking into her eyes, I said, "You really don't know who I am, do you?" "Of course not, get your hands off of me!" Walking slowly away, I joined a group of souls who were wandering away from the city, away from the mass retain. 'The light beam severed all my ties,' I thought to myself, 'I am truly homeless, now.' A voice from the sky bellowed. "No, you are not. For in your freedom, you may now be free to find your true home."

"Whoever loses his life for my sake will find it."
New American Bible, New Testament, Matthew 10:39, (Christianity, Catholic, Words of
Christ)
****

Chanting and pointing in the direction of the mountains, the medicine man's long black hair blew in the chilling wind, as he stood beside a native woman holding a blanket. "It is important to always follow a straight path," he said, as he walked towards the mountain.

"They that are guided go not astray, but they that are lost cannot find a straight
path. If thou go among men, make for thyself, Love, the beginning and end of the
heart."
The Emerald Tablets of Thoth the Atlantean Tablet III, Page 17, Paragraph 8, (Mystery
Religions, Egyptian/Hermetic, Words of Thoth)
****

CHAPTER FOUR
Chief Joseph, the Medicine Women from Throughout the Ages, Mountains in the Sky, Returning to the Native, Supas and Uniting the East and the West, Iwa - Temple Builder, the Old Ones, Imperterbability, Pathway of Books.

****

Drawing a circle around my spirit, the Medicine Women were watching us. Just at the moment when the lines met to complete the circle, an energy shift occurred. Holograms of every moment of my life and all of my different selves were functioning in synchronicity. Staring at this scene, Chief Joseph replied, "It is the Sacred Hoop, you have completed the circle."

Energetic understandings were beginning to take hold as Joseph explained that the hoop was a sequence of life, and when that sequence comes together, all exists as one moment. "The circle has come together, the moment of birth and death meet at the same point, there is no more differentiation between moments, they are now one." Seeing myself as a baby in a crib, a child, my current self, an old woman, all at the same time, my birth and my death, and all that lay between . . . was now one singular moment.

"You are free now; the Sacred Hoop has been completed. It's not what you were, but what you have become!" Joseph said these words as the Medicine Women began pounding rhythmically on drums and energy pierced the astral skies . . . but I couldn't hear them. I felt them, I saw them, I knew them . . . but I was caught in a melodious stream of light that held my attention. Somehow, I knew that they were the ones who were generating the energy to take me to this space. The magnitude of the moment carried my thoughts, "I guess what will be, will be." I thought, as Joseph's voice rang in my ear, "In one moment, lies all eternity. What is . . . is."

Joseph's peace pipe was before me again. "Beyond the illusions we perceive as reality, beyond the dying breaths we've chosen to forsake, beyond uncaring . . . is a whole new world. This world is life." Pausing a moment, he took another whiff. "At the center of creation where all life originates, lies the seed of humanity. It is where it all begins . . . and where it all ends." Looking into my eyes, he handed the pipe to me. As I took a whiff, he quietly said, "That seed is love." And then he disappeared into the night.

"Sometimes they show entering the womb, sometimes birth, sometimes the
attainment of enlightenment - Thus they cause all worldlings to see: This is the
path traveled by the unbounded . . . The real cosmos is all equal, without
distinction, containing infinite, boundless meanings; They enjoy contemplating
oneness, minds unmoving: This is the path of the knowers of all times."
The Flower Ornament Scripture, Chapter 21, Ten Practices, Page 482, Stanza 4 & 7,

(Buddhism, Mahayana)

****

Looming gently above the mountains of the earth, I could see the mountains in the sky off in the distance. Changing form, I became a small brown bunny with beads hanging around my neck hopping through the woods searching for the path. Up ahead, I saw a pathway.

Approaching, a great white light appeared in the sky, and instantly below it, an old, old man appeared sitting in a canoe on the river. Wearing only a loincloth, his hair was white as snow. "You may exist inponentially or exponentially," he said, "it is like the sailor. He is a Master of the Sea, but only he and those fellow sailors who go with him know of his mastery." Pausing, he looked my way. "Exponents are the few, inponents are the masses." Inponents are those who group together and follow that which is popular on the ground. Exponents stand alone outside the mass retain, follow only the call of the spirit, and have little need to speak of it.

Hopping away from the scene of the Old One's departure, I began singing a song, "I'm a bunny and I'm hopping, that's what bunnies do." And in this, I realized that there are common characteristics of certain life forms, just as there are common characteristics of different levels of soul evolution, which by observance, can tell a soul what is 'native' (or natural) to that particular form. Just as a bunny hops, a scorpion will sting, and a fish will swim.

"Beyond the six realms of heaven, earth, and the four directions, the sage accepts but does not discuss. Within the six realms, he discusses but does not pass judgment . . . When there is division, there is something which is not divided. When there is questioning, there is something beyond the question. Why is this? The sage keeps his wisdom to himself while ordinary men flaunt their knowledge in loud discussion."

Chuang Tsu, Chapter 2, Page 37, (Buddhism, Taoism, Words of Lao Tsu)

****

"To return to the native," he said, "is to become all existence . . . again. By becoming all existence, everything then becomes real." Joseph disappeared.

****

Running frantically, I knew I couldn't stop for fear of being run over by the incessant jeep behind me. Going towards the mountains in the sky, the driver of the jeep was Daniel Pierce, my other self, while Chief Joseph was in the passenger seat. Confused, I turned back to see that Joseph was sitting in the approaching vehicle calmly, looking older than he'd appeared before as his hair had grayed and he had become an Old One. But they were merciless, and I had to run as fast as I could toward the mountain in order not to be run over by them.

Finally reaching our destination, I was amazed at the beauty all around us. Each tree echoed its aloneness as it heralded the many. At the foothills, our journey had been long and a woman by the name of Celeste joined us. Showing me a vine, she twisted it and music came out of it. Flying towards the treetops, she handed me my own vine and tried to teach me how to do this, but I was very awkward. Singing from the tops of the trees, Celeste's voice was like a chime in the wilderness.

All of a sudden, Daniel got up and started wrestling with me. How odd this was to be fighting with another aspect of myself. In a flash, his leg came up towards my neck, kicking me harshly and pushing my head back and I could no longer move. Energetically, I was jolted into awakeness. Everyone was calm, as they knew I would move again momentarily.

As soon as I could move again, we began our trek deeper into the mountains. Following them, I could see how awkward and undeveloped I was compared to them. Animals came to them without fear, but I had not yet developed the capacity to communicate oneness and they shied away from me. Commenting on my awkwardness, they pointed out the many things within my energy which would need to be addressed on this wilderness trek, in order for me to become native again. Returning to the native is returning to what is real. What is real is what is natural. What is natural is being in a state of oneness with all life. Chief Joseph shook his head when he saw an animal come towards him, but back away when it saw me. "Your world has put you out of harmony with the natural world," he said.

Entering a deep wilderness, I was getting increasingly uncomfortable being so out of my own element. Persevering, I continued, knowing that my awkwardness had to be experienced in order for me to become native again. Coming upon a band of wild mustangs, they were quite peaceful with my friends, but agitated with me. Offering their backs freely to my companions, they neighed and jumped at me. Leading me to a small band of ponies, Joseph directed me to a white one whose discomfort was not as severe. Walking towards him, I tried to get on his back, but he resisted.

No judgment or anger occurred, just a completely open discussion of my incompatibility to the natural world. Ready to ride their wild mustangs to the mountains in the sky, my white pony finally allowed me to mount him. Chief Joseph pointed towards the deep wilderness ahead. An ominous light beckoned from that direction, and I was afraid. If I turned back, I could return to my comfortable little world. But if I went in the direction he pointed, I couldn't turn back until I had been altered and made completely native. Animals peered from behind trees and bushes, as I honored their role as teachers and guides in this unknown country.

Willing to accept my awkwardness in order to restore my nativity, we began to trot towards the wilderness as Chief Joseph pointed to a place far ahead where the light shone more brightly than any we'd seen; the mountains in the sky above the clouds of the horizon. "The Old Ones . . ." he said, and then there was only silence.

"Then suddenly, as I sat there looking at the cloud, I saw my vision yonder once again - the teepee built of cloud and sewed with lightning, the flaming rainbow door and, underneath, the Six Grandfathers sitting, and all the horses thronging in their quarters."
Black Elk Speaks, Chapter XIV, Page 169, Paragraph 1, (Tribal, Oglala Sioux, Words of Black Elk)

****

Entranced as I faced it, the trail of tears had been cordoned off because it was sacred ground. Many souls had died on this path as the Cherokee nations traveled its length, forced to go to reservation lands. Invited to walk aside the path, I stepped forward and began to walk.

Eventually reaching the end of the trail, I noticed the ominous graveyard of Wounded Knee. Another sight of Native American slaughter, many Indians had died here after the natives had performed a ghost dance. Led to a single gravestone, there were about twenty different Indian names etched upon it. Guided to look upon a single name, I allowed it to penetrate my soul. 'Window heart,' it said.

Leaping towards the mountains in the sky, the amazing energies of the Old Ones surrounded and transformed my soul, as a voice emanated from the Earth. "Welcome to Ute Mountain," it said, "you are welcome." Grandmother stood atop the mountain beside a lone mountain lion. As I walked gently towards them, I began to alter and change into a mountain lion.

Returning to my human manifestation, my clothes were now of buckskin and my feet were adorned with moccasins. My soul was completely native.

Rugged but comfortable, the moccasins bore my feet well as I journeyed deeper into the mountain wilderness. Having walked through the mountain pass, the animals were no longer afraid and I bore a newfound wisdom of my people and all that they had stood for.

Grandmother pointed to an image in the sky, as the stars began to cascade towards me from ominous distant moons. Gentle wisdom of my destiny filled my soul, as a mountain lion peered quietly from an overhanging cliff. Nodding my gratitude to him for his energy, grandmother began to disappear, and as she did, I began to walk . . .

"When the wise man casts off laxity through vigilance, he is like unto a man who, having ascended the high tower of wisdom, looks upon the sorrowing people with an afflicted heart. He beholds suffering ignorant men as a mountaineer beholds people in a valley."
Dhammapada, Canto II - On Vigilance, Page 15, No. 28, (Buddhism)

****

Grandmother peered down from the mesa to my spirit, as I watched her awe-inspiring essence. A single brown horse astride her, she calmly walked off of the mesa into the sky. Saying nothing, she didn't have to. "I am honored that I have been humbled by your presence, thank you for allowing me to see you." I said. Stopping in midair, her robed face turned to look. "It is acknowledged." She conveyed. White hair barely showed from the top of the brown coverlet over her head. The mane of her horse blew in the spirit wind while the yellow orange sun stood at its last moment before setting. Glistening stars had begun to appear in the night sky. A voice beckoned. "Behold . . . Grandmother Skywalker," it said. She turned to go.

"The Great Spirit was usually referred to by the Lenni Lenape as being male; however, the Shawnee, their close Lenape family relatives, referred to the Great Spirit as 'Grandmother.'"
The Red Record, Book I, Page 53, Paragraph 2, (Tribal, Plains)

****

grandmother's face popped up from beneath the surface of the water, her white hair soaked from the mountain lake. Swimming through the waters, I began to follow her, but she went so very fast, I could not catch up. She began to alter her form.

Transforming from an old woman to a young Indian girl; she became an Indian warrior, and then an old woman again. "I am Hunkpapa woman," she said, "it used to be that the seasons were all commanded and owned by spirit, but now I alone own the season, the autumn, the change. I command the cycles of death and re-birth." Shooting across the water so fast that I could barely see her, I jumped out to try to catch up.

Instead, I found a baby mountain lion trapped in some reeds. Bedraggled, wet and all alone, I picked her up. "Mountain lion," I cried out, "I must save you."

Hunkpapa woman appeared again from the depths and remarked, "She was born in the reeds by the watery lake . . . and she was known to her people as Mountain Lion." Reaching to me, she gave me a green stone. "Serenity," she said, "serenity is power." Lightning struck, and my birth at the hands of she who bore the season was complete.

"And I saw, and beheld the angel of Joy. And between her lips flowed the music of life, and she knelt over the earth and gave to man the song of Peace."
The Essene Gospel of Peace, Volume 2, Page 107, Stanza 2, (Christianity, Gnostic/Essene)

****

Flying about my house out of form, I was surprised to notice an old woman who was energetic and playful, beckoning me to come near her. Giving me two gifts, she said, "You have much to do . . . far greater significance." The first gift was a blue-green tower of crystal which soared in a step fashion towards the sky. The second was a series of magnifying glasses. Pointing to the far ends of both sides of the crystal staircase and the magnifying glasses, she said, "It is your job to bring the extreme West and the extreme East together, to magnify the vision of the people." Pointing to the farthest and topmost point on the crystal piece, she said, "You must walk to the farthest point my daughter."

Walking me to the front door, she opened it to display a group of native carvings. In the center were some of my old belongings which I'd given away. Coming to life, the carvings began to dance as they'd become native people. "They are thanking you for the gifts, and for the gifts you will give to the people." Having become aware of allowing everything its proper use, I no longer stored things I no longer needed. Angel wings emerged from the natives backs as they continued to dance.

Running into the house, I followed the old woman. "What's your name?" I called out to her. "It is Supas," she said. "What do you mean by far greater significance?" I yelled out. Beginning to laugh hysterically, she looked at me as if to say, 'I couldn't possibly tell you that now.' Disintegrating, she became a tiny vase in my hand. A carving on the side of the vase showed the two of us sitting aside a fire in the shadow of a pueblo. Underneath the tiny little pot there was a sticker, 'Supas of the Quintas lodge,' it said.

Starlight glittered all over the room as I heard a voice echoing wisdom. "You must go to the farthest point, far greater significance, far greater significance . . ."

Transported to my backyard, a small bunny hopped over to me. Light brown with white dots, he told me he was a healer. In the grass were a set of keys, "These are the keys to the past," he said, "you will need them on your journey." Placing the old, worn and rusty keys in my hand, suddenly, I was alone.

"Each Manifestation of God hath a distinct individuality, a definitely prescribed mission, a predestined Revelation, and specially designated limitations. Each one of them is known by a different name, is characterized by a special attribute, fulfills a definite Mission, and is entrusted with a particular Revelation . . . It is because of this difference in their station and mission that the words and utterances flowing from these Wellsprings of divine knowledge appear to diverge and differ. Otherwise, in the eyes of them that are initiated into the mysteries of divine wisdom, all their utterances are in reality but the expressions of one truth."
The Kitab-I-Iqan, Page 176-177, (Baha'i, Author: Baha'u'llah)

****

Entering into the ancient past, I noticed cavernous homes made of clay and brick (pueblos). While many people were walking around completing their daily tasks, a man approached me. Paintings were done upon his chest, and I was intrigued with their meaning. Handing me a buckskin dress, I noticed how exquisitely it had been beaded. Gazing deep into my eyes, all was quiet. "I am Iwa," he said, "my name means Temple Builder."

Surrounding me all at once, the ancient tribe came to me with gifts. "Thank you." I looked at them in confusion. Iwa smiled, "We are thanking you for the service you give to our people." Placing a thunderbird pipe within my hand, he disappeared, as suddenly, there were about twenty or thirty different pipes lying at my feet. An Old One's face appeared in the sky, he smiled and then he was gone.

As the winds died down, and we continued moving further westward, ending up in the Four Corners, the land of the Pueblo's.

"Cleave to the noble, and they will also bow to thee."
The Talmudic Anthology, No. 130, Stanza 4, Sifre Debarim, 6, (Judaism)

****

"The enlightening being who are thus skillful in effectuation of the science of these specific analytic knowledges, having reached the ninth stage, having attained the treasury of teachings of the enlightened, acting as great preachers of the Teaching, come to attain the concentration spell containing meanings, the concentration spell containing principles, the concentration spell containing

evocation of knowledge, the concentration spell containing illumination . . . "
The Flower Ornament Scripture, Chapter 26, The Ten Stages, Page 782, Paragraph 2,
(Buddhism, Mahayana)

Sitting in the bleachers of a coliseum, I intentionally chose to face the opposite direction of the stage in a lotus position. Showing my rejection of the falsehoods of worldly existence and my lack of interest or attachment to them, thousands of others were facing the stage and my defiance of their chosen direction angered them quite immensely. Throwing things at me, I did not budge. Fruits, vegetables, cans and containers were hitting me in the face, on my back, and all over my body, but my serenity was unmoved by their rage. I didn't flinch or change the position of my eyes.

Amidst all the ruckus, a janitor appeared and walked quietly by, sweeping up the mess with a broom. Stopping a moment, he said to me, "You are not perturbable; this is good. You are attaining imperturbability." Even at his words, I remained unmoved, as he quietly walked away.

"The discerning man straightens his mind, which is fickle and unsteady, difficult to guard and restrain, as the skilled fletcher straightens the shaft (of the arrow)."
Dhammapada, Canto III, No. 33, Page 17, (Buddhism)

****

Expressing to my soul that knowledge of the Lord is not purely an intellectual experience, I was shown that spiritual realities are only truly *known* through divine influx, because *knowledge* is not just information but energetic comprehension. Who among us could even begin to comprehend the beginnings of faith, if we approached it by reason, alone?

"Even the greatest philosophical speculators cannot have access to the region of the Lord. It is said in the Upanisads that the Supreme Truth, the Absolute Personality of Godhead, is beyond the range of the thinking power of the greatest philosopher. He is unknowable by great learning or by the greatest brain. He is knowable only by one who has His mercy."
Teachings of Queen Kunti, Chapter 3, Page 5, Paragraph 1, (Hinduism)

"The Word is not understood except by those who are enlightened. The human rational cannot apprehend Divine things, nor even spiritual things, unless it is enlightened by the Lord. Thus only they who are enlightened apprehend the Word."
Miscellaneous Theological Works, Heavenly Doctrine, No. 256, (Christianity, Swedenborgianism, Author: Emanuel Swedenborg)

"A number of intellectuals who quote prophets are like victrolas. Just as a machine plays records of sacred writings without understanding their meaning, so many scholars who repeat Holy Writ are unaware of its true significance. They do not see the deep, life-transforming values of the scriptures. From their reading such men gain, not God-realization, but only a knowledge of words. They become proud and argumentative . . . That is why I tell all of you to read less and to meditate more."
Sayings of Paramahansa Yogananda, Page 51, Stanza 2, (Hinduism, Kriya Yoga, Words of Paramahansa Yogananda)

****

Sweeping amidst the chaos of the world, I began to seek the pathway of the light. Ending up in a small and tiny passageway of books, there were many guardians to this passage, so I assumed I had found the proper way. But after I'd passed through three guardians, I again asked, "How do I get to the light?" Stopping immediately, one said, "Oh," and took me by the arm and turned me around. "You've gone the wrong way; let me help you go back." As the passageway was not set up to go backwards, he had to gain permission from the prior guardians to lead me away from this narrow path.

Emerging from the passageway of books, he left me alone in a wide and dark alley. A man approached, who was dressed as a hippie from the sixties, his hair was long to his shoulders but rounded, and he was dressed all in denim.

"How do I get to the light?" I asked him, as he immediately brightened. "Here, I'll show you," he said as he opened a vast door in the side wall of the alley.

Immediately, I could see a vast light in the distance, much like I had on Hakeo Island. Door shutting behind me, the hippie jumped on a motorcycle and began to rev his engine. "Will you take me to the light?" I asked. "No," he said, "I may make some different turns." "Oh, I understand," I said, "I need to go to the light myself." Nodding that this was true, he drove away. Another unoccupied motorcycle stood in the parking lot, and I quickly hopped on and tried to follow him and the beckoning light in the distance, but he was already long gone.

Asking people along the way, many were very helpful in giving me directions as to which roads to take to get to the light. When I came upon a toll booth, I made a left to avoid the toll, but a young black woman directed me to turn back and pay the fifty cent toll and go right. Using a bizarre instrument on my hand which measured my level of consciousness, if you were entirely sub-conscious you were unable to pass. "Wow," she said, "you have eighty five cents, and that's really good. Unusual, too, we don't see souls who are this conscious very often."

Driving towards the light, my vehicle suddenly stopped. Appearing in front of my car, the toll booth operators were standing there with another traveler. Looking very dazed, I realized that she was almost subconscious, just barely fifty cents worth (50% conscious versus 85% conscious). Still seeking the great orb of light in the distance, the toll operators indicated that it wasn't yet my time to understand this mystery, and my time was up.

"All the atoms of the earth have announced unto all created things that from behind the gate of the Prison-city there hath appeared and above its horizon there hath shone forth the Orb of the beauty of the great, the Most Mighty Branch of God - His ancient and immutable Mystery - proceeding on its way to another land."

The Tablets of Baha'u'llah, Chapter 16, Lawh-Ard-I-Ba, Page 227, Paragraph 1, (Baha'i, Author: Baha'u'llah)

****

CHAPTER FIVE
Astral Books as Spirit Guides, Levitation, Buddhist Mai Tai Prayer, True Discipleship, the Cosmic Master, Messiah Master Number, the Celestial Temple and the Turbaned Masters, the Lines of the Holy Spirit Whirring from Heaven to Earth, St. Michael, Return of Little Chinaman and his Family, Golden Angels of the 23rd Dimension.

****

My Lord and harbinger of such good news! Beyond me comes the message, and aside it the messenger. Amidst its garbled appearance, comes clarity and wisdom. Amidst its contents, one finds peace. Looking upon the title of a book I was now shown, it said, 'Energizing Unity.' Down below, at the bottom of the cover was the word, 'Baha'i.'

Opening the book, I was enmeshed within its holy contents and the sacred qualities of its mission. Although another soul, one I'd known from days past appeared to look upon my endeavor with disdain. "Why do you look upon such a thing?" he asked, "the Baha'i religion is not one of the important ones." Looking upon his beleaguered countenance, without emotion, I simply replied, "You are mistaken, my friend, for the Baha'i religion is indeed one of the great religions." Countenance unchanging, he didn't believe me. Among those souls who believe that only Christian religions hold any merit, he believed that God has not spoken before or since in such a way. Mistaken he was, mistaken he was . . . for God is ever-present, and He speaks whensoever He wills, and this faith's revelation was an integral part of the mysteries of God's grand redemption.

"The gates that open on the Placeless stand wide and the habitation of the loved one is adorned with the lovers' blood, yet all but a few remain bereft of this celestial city, and even of these few, none but the smallest handful hath been found with a pure heart and sanctified spirit."
The Hidden Words, Part II, No. 17, (Baha'i, Author: Baha'u'llah)

****

Holy winds began blowing wildly as the beckon of the holy guardians came hither. Entering a deep meditation, my spirit was suddenly sprung into an ecstatic state wherein I began to feel the touch of various invisible spirits working on my soul. Vibrating incredibly, my feet and my hands were being moved into different positions, while another worked on the structure of the bones on the left side of my face; all this in order to facilitate some type of energetic adjustment. The winds continued blowing, thunder roared, but no rain fell in the outer world.

Suddenly, two spirits were lifting my body and soul up off the bed, as I began levitating. What wonder! What malaise! It was so spectacular; I cannot even fathom the words to tell! As my body and soul floated about the room in the hands of my unseen guests, I awaited the end of this levitation to bid them with a question. Lasting for about five minutes, they slowly began lowering my body back onto the bed.

Now that I was again situated, I asked them to reveal themselves to me. Suddenly, I saw two lighted beings, their forms the outline of a small human body, appearing first in a lotus position hovering in the air. One male and one female, they slowly opened their bodies to a standing position. Honored, I thanked them, as they immediately conveyed to my soul that they were some form of extra-terrestrial life. Beginning to fade away, I bid them adieu and reveled in the afterglow of their wondrous energies and the attunements that had been made to my soul. The winds ceased, the thunderclouds rolled away, and all became calm again.

"He whose mental attachments are extinguished, who is not immoderate in food, who is within range of perfect deliverance through realization of the Void and the conditionlessness of all forms, his holy path is as difficult to trace as is the track of birds in the air."
Dhammapada, No. 93, (Buddhism)

"Truth is no theory, no speculative system of philosophy. Truth is exact correspondence with Reality . . . It is not a pumping-in from the outside that gives wisdom; it is the power and extent of your inner receptivity that determines how much you can attain of true knowledge, and how rapidly."
Where There is Light, Chapter 5, Stanzas 2-5, (Hinduism, Words of Paramahansa Yogananda)

****

"I wish to accomplish the redemption of the human race with which Thou hast charged Me. I wish to restore to this human nature the highest perfection and the plenitude of thy divine complaisance; and then I wish to pass from this world to thy right hand, bearing with Me all those whom Thou hast given Me without losing a single one of them for want of willingness on our part to help them."
The Mystical City of God, Volume 3, Book II, Chapter 11, Page 453, No. 473, (Christianity, Catholic, Words of Christ)

Entering an old Buddhist monastery in the sky, they practiced something called the 'Mai Tai' tradition, something of which I'd never heard of in physical reality. Immediately joining the group of monks in several forms of prayer, they showed me a chart indicating a total of nine forms of Buddhistic prayer. Focusing on the first form, it served the purpose of rendering all remaining ego benign. As I prayed in this manner, I began experiencing who I truly am, what I'd truly done in my life, leaving all illusory interpretations behind, and holding onto only those true aspects of my soul which could be of use to the will of God. During this prayer practice, I was expected to fully experience and disclose to myself and my associates all the acts of my life which had been committed in a state of ignorance and karmic malaise. And then, I had to fully experience and disclose to myself and my associates the person I had become since; the state of serenity, as opposed to reckless disregard, the state of flow as opposed to moving against the movement.

Bidding me to know that I would not be given leave to remember how this form of prayer was practiced or any of the remaining eight forms, it was a practice brought about through the mystery and mechanism of the redemption. Understanding their strict command, I bid them thanks.

"Who once did live in recklessness and then is reckless nevermore, shall light the world like the full moon when clouds unmask it. Who checks with wholesome deeds the evil deeds already done, shall light the world like the full moon when clouds unmask it."
The Life of the Buddha, Chapter 9, Page 138, Stanza 1, (Buddhism)

"For a learner who is training in conformity with the direct path, the knowledge of destruction arises first, and final knowledge immediately follows. To one freed by that final knowledge, the topmost knowledge of freedom, there arises the knowledge of destruction: 'Thus the fetters are destroyed.' Certainly not by the lazy person, nor by the uncomprehending fool, is Nibbana to be attained, the loosening of all worldly ties."
The Ituvittaka, The Section of the Fours, No. 102, Page 80, stanzas 1-3, (Buddhism, Theravadan)

"The Highest Wisdom, however, perceives and knows what is best to rectify all creation. In its profound design, it weighs everything together, and directs each individual element of creation accordingly."
The Way of God, Part II, Chapter 3, No. 11, Paragraph 2, (Judaism)

****

"Light and darkness, life and death, right and left, are brothers of one another. They are inseparable. Because of this neither are the good good, nor the evil evil, nor is life life, nor death death. For this reason each one will dissolve into its earliest origin. But those who are exalted above the world are indissoluble, eternal."
The Nag Hammadi Library, The Gospel of Philip, Page 142, Paragraph 4, (Christianity, Gnostic/Essene)

Becoming a true disciple of Christ, the energy beams kept coming at me from different locations to fulfill the coming. Faced with the constant onslaughts of these very different energies, my soul was receiving an energetic education on all the aspects which were relevant to me in becoming such a disciple of Christ. But such knowledge was inexplicable, and was of many different qualities, rather than intellectual knowledge. Hitting me for most of the night, the beams kept coming.

"Blessed are ye of the inner circle who hear my word and to whom mysteries are revealed."
The Gospel of the Holy Twelve, Lection XX, No. 7, (Christianity, Gnostic/Essene, Words of Christ)

****

Appearing truly spectacular as he lay before me upon the back drop of the stars, the cosmic master's essence was astonishing. Feeling very familiar in this visionary state, my waking self held no memory of him. Amidst this spectral monastery which floated in the heavens, my soul had been gathered together with many others in need of instruction. Our cosmic teacher of truth was not one to mince words, and was known for his bluntness. Another aspect which made him unique was that he had a somewhat 'physical' approach to solving spiritual issues. Celestial and galactic knowledge permeated every pore of this being of light, and no words came from his mouth unless they were deeply meaningful and filled with power.

All who had come were in need of a cosmic adjustment of some kind to remedy an energetic dysfunction in their waking physical life. The cosmic master's task was to quickly alter the pathways of dysfunction and turn the directional indicators of the soul towards a more galactic perspective. Doing this in a very unusual way, the master approached each individual, identified their area of difficulty, and quickly altered their energies through sheer brute force. I don't mean this metaphorically. Many of the alterations came about through 'physical' injury. Very serious and direct, the master knew that, of necessity, changes were required immediately, and thus, techniques which would bring about immediate alteration from the spiritual to the physical vehicle were employed.

Particular illnesses or injuries had the ability to significantly alter a person's energy more quickly than other gentler means, and thus, these aspects were used to alter elements of energetic misunderstanding from the spiritual to the physical octave.

Turning to me, the master was serious and direct and within one second I knew what method he was about to employ. Cringing, I knew that he was about to 'break my back,' but this breaking was only to occur in the spiritual realm, not the physical. Although it would be painful, I would feel it primarily in this spiritual state.

In the Earthly quest for knowledge, our souls are often taken from one extreme to another, for the sole purpose of eventually achieving a place of balance. Because I had begun my journey with very few boundaries, I had necessity to travel from a state of laxity to an opposite extreme of rigidity. It was the cosmic master's judgment that my soul had become too rigid, and that this alteration would necessitate a new energetic influx inculcating freedom within the boundaries of morality. 'Breaking my back,' would bring that needed flexibility into my soul.

Done in an instant as a searing pain went through my back, the greatest pain lasted only a moment before a higher aspect of my husband, Andy, appeared to begin assisting me with the remainder of the adjustment. Going through a series of exercises in expressive emotion, Andy's higher aspect guided me through this initially controlled and uncomfortable situation to a peaceful surrender to the divine influx of love. After this, we entered into a long melting embrace which opened my two heart chakras, the one directly in the center of the chest, and other which lies just outside it and directly in front, which altered my ability to give and receive love.

Within a few moments, my soul had been drastically changed energetically. Pleased with the changes, the master moved on to the next soul. As I stared at this grand being in awe, my spirit was pulled away to another destination.

Placating myself that my back would be as good as new before I knew it, I found myself soaring through space at a grand speed. My destination was a very unusual one as I observed a woman who was diligently working at her desk which hovered in the stars. As she was calculating the mathematical implications of the second coming of Christ, I'd been sent to offer her energetic protection from those who wished to steal her calculations and use them for ill effects. Although I would be want to explain the larger meaning of this woman and her work, I inherently knew that she carried great importance and significance with the Lord, as her duty was sacred and it was vital that she be left alone to complete it. Creating an energetic wall of protection around her, I watched with concern for her safety and well-being.

Looking up to me, she shared with me the master number of the Messiah, making it very clear that I was not to record or share this number, and that it would be taken from my memory within days of returning from this journey. In a momentary flash, she made me to know that the Earthly perception of Jesus is much too narrow, making specific mention of the denominational views which doctrinally offered vicarious evolution through the majesty of Christ, rather than the true nature of evolution in the individual spiritual path, transformational change effected by a recognition of the *ideal* within Christ.

As she turned again to her mathematical calculations, I quickly observed that the field of protection I'd created for her was intact and my soul began jetting towards Earth at the speed of light. My back remained sore for about two days.
****

Standing at the doorway to the celestial temple, he appeared in the garb of a man from India. Around his head was a tightly wrapped turban, and upon his bodice the garb of 19th century India. Two other masters resided in this heavenly abode, but I was not to see them as of yet.

Waiting outside the door, the master's were deciding upon whether or not they would allow me entry. Hesitating because of my lack of knowledge and true mastery, they regarded me as a novice. Although there was no way of getting around that, they agreed to allow me to enter because, for some reason unbeknownst to them or myself, the Lord had allowed my spirit to fly to this destination of which I had no knowledge. As they argued amongst themselves, they seemed to agree that I would not have been allowed to find them, if not for the permission of the Most High.

Slowly entering their abode in the stars, I was surprised to notice that in the entryway, there were some very old, dusty statues representing humanity's various vices. These statues seemed out of place in such a celestial sphere, but the masters began to telepathically transport information into my soul, as I observed and looked closely at each one, walking slowly down the entryway. As I came upon each one, I picked it up, and was filled with an inexplicable energetic knowledge. Each statue represented a different karmic impulse which held souls back from reaching the ascension. Contorted according to their vice, their impurities were manifest in symbolic renderings upon the statues. One element which held true with all of these statues was that they were all in motion, agitation and almost a sense of impenetrable fear. No peace or serenity radiated from them, as they were distorted and grotesque, in both observation and feeling. When you touched them, a certain inexplicable distasteful abhorrence filled you of these karmic abnormalities, this lack of unity with God.

As I passed from the entryway into the interior corridor of the masters, I noticed that another female pupil had already arrived and was waiting patiently for me to sit down with her before the masters. Intensity filled her eyes, and I sensed her grandeur as a soul. Knowing that I must seem like a little worm to these spectacular servants of the Lord, I observed that the turbaned master was playful as he came towards me.

Expressing to me that I'd had trouble in my many lifetimes dealing with pain, he placed his hands on my lower back as the other two masters followed suit. Unprepared for this step, I almost jumped back as I began to feel the intense heat and pressure flow into my back and up into the rest of my body. Retarding that instinct, I knew that I was here as an uninvited guest, so I surrendered to this process. Beginning to fade, the heat and pressure could no longer be felt although they continued to touch me. Continuing to send energies through me, I no longer felt the pain.

Looking toward the woman who had been totally silent and peaceful, I was surprised to see her cringing. Before I could ascertain why, the turbaned master had approached me from behind and cut one of my fingers. My first reaction was of pain, but the turbaned master looked deeply into my eyes, saying very quietly, "I feel no pain, I feel no pain." Conveying to me in energy, I saw that he wished for me to focus on my existence *within* God, rather than *outside* of Him. Waving his hands in the air from above to below in a motion to direct me to calm myself, the pain disappeared. After many moments had passed while he stared at me with an intensity I would be unable to duplicate, he proceeded to heal the wound with light from his hand.

Thinking the surprises might be over; I gently followed him when he took my hand to guide me to a small garden path inside the celestial abode. As we were walking, a bumble bee stung me on my foot. Surprisingly, I felt no pain whatsoever, and the stinger was actually unable to penetrate. With this, the turbaned master smiled and looked to the others with a glance implying, "I told you she must've been sent here by God." Intention apparent in his thoughts, he was pleased that they were able to make such progress with a novice. Relieved, the masters gathered around me and began transmitting understanding regarding what they had just done.

Preparing me to repulse the attacks of the enemy, Satan, who often sends hordes of bees, wasps, and spiders to infect a soul aspiring to reach God, I couldn't help but wonder if this knowledge also had something to do with the many saints throughout history who became impenetrable; unaffected by fire, poisons, swords or one of many other horrendous forms of torture.

Seeming pleased with my quick study in this area, they again mentioned my many lifetimes wherein I had trouble with pain. One of the other master's approached me and in a manner somewhat scolding, spoke to me of the lifetime I'd had as a conqueror which had been revealed to me long ago. As I'd been a horrible specimen of humanity, I felt ashamed, and responded like a defensive idiot getting into his face. "I know! I know about that lifetime!" Laughing hysterically, I realized that they were 'playing' with me, and I'd played right into their hands. Embarrassed, I became immediately less serious.

Returning to assist me through several more pain-associated rituals to assist me in repelling pain and the attacks of the enemy, the turbaned master taught me well. When time came for me to leave, I quietly asked them for help. "Will you help me to focus my remembrance of my journey here so that I can write about it in full detail?" Agreeing very wholeheartedly to assist me, the master touched my third eye above my forehead as my soul returned to my body in a euphoric state.

Returning to me several hours later, the turbaned master took me on a splendid journey beneath the ocean. A spectacular yellowish aura appeared around him as soon as we were submerged beneath the sea. As I was unable to take my eyes off of him, he pointed directly behind me so as to indicate that I should look over there.

Turning, my eyes met such a magnificent sight! Spiritual cities of light appeared beneath the sea, there must've been at least five within our current view. Shining in glorious heavenly light and containing the entire spectrum of color, it was as if this heavenly light were being brought into the city through a prism creating a rainbow effect. Saying nothing, he pushed my spirit up towards the surface as the erroneous hum of the spirit wind returned my spirit back to form.
****

Drumming filled my psyche as I sat around a circle of Buddhist monks. Several types of drums were in the center of their circle, all of which were being played by several monks who sat around them. As the beating filled my head, an intermittent energy of detachment began to wave through my soul. Continuing for quite some time, the monks conveyed that I must come to a place of detachment in regards to the way others viewed my soul. Falling outside of myself, it became a true surrender. Spiritual development requires a continually evolving process of discipline which comes about through continual evaluation. Such evaluations serve the purpose of recognizing the preferable from the less preferable; good and evil. In those whose philosophy is 'anything goes,' such discretion and discipline is viewed as contrary to freedom. Despite this view, the disciplined mind is fully cognizant that true freedom only comes about within the confines of moral certitude. In essence, it should not surprise me that my blunt words might make some people upset, but it remained irrelevant to my purpose.

As the drums continued to beat a rhythmic energy of detachment into my spirit, the monks sat calm and serene.

****

Ominous in its import, the celestial sphere was overrun by beautiful music which made it more difficult to concentrate. Floating in heavenly spheres, we were surrounded by the stars. Though a barrier clearly existed around us, the walls of the space were invisible. The celestial vision of the heavens was so earth-shatteringly stunning; it was excruciatingly painful knowing that I could not stay here forever.

Inside of our heads, an instructor showed us what appeared to be a cyclone of energy, which looked like a small tornado whirling within our brain at great speed. Pointing into deep space and guiding our eyes back down to the Earth below, the instructor now allowed us to watch as incredible laser beams of light appeared, originating from heaven and continuing all throughout the vast expanse of space to the Earth below. Amazingly, we were told that these were the lines of the Holy Spirit flowing from heaven to Earth!

Placed into a sitting and meditative position, we were directed to lean back our upper body in an attempt to have these cyclones within our heads meet with the line of the Holy Spirit. The alignment had to be just perfect for the intended effect to occur and this was very difficult, but we were told that when that alignment hit synchronicity, we would be swept away immediately. As they said this, they had snapped their fingers to indicate the quickness of the alteration.

Trying many times before I could make this link, it didn't come easily. Finally hitting the alignment perfectly, my soul was instantly transported to another location.

No bliss can ever hope to attain that which was now my own. Riding on the back of a gigantic being, approximately forty feet tall, I was leaning upon his neck and shoulders looking directly into his face which happened to be larger than my spiritual body. Small in comparison to him, I was like a little mouse sitting upon a person's shoulder.

Looking into his eyes, I felt a serene wisdom which surpassed everything. Blank and tan, his eyes were the color of his skin while we were traveling the Earth, uniquely fashioned to bring focus for his specific mission for the Lord. Falling gently below his ears, his somewhat curly and flowing hair was of a blondish-brown color. But as we shot off into space, his features took on a violet and white color, reflecting the colors of the galactic heavens.

Before I had a chance to realize what had happened to me, I'd entered into the power of this individual, feeling an incredible thrust of heavenly propulsion. In some ways, it was as though I were riding on the back of a rocket . . . as St. Michael the Archangel was taking me for a ride.

Patrolling the Earth looking for loose demons, I noticed that he was going after those which were not specifically attached to souls. Those demons which were already inside of people were left alone for this particular journey, as those who were lucidly looking for prey were immediately annihilated. St. Michael literally snapped these demons up in his two forefingers, pinching their neck and tossing them aside, as they fell back to the pit.

Along the way St. Michael found several dogs that were possessed by demons and had become extremely violent. Pinching the neck with one fell sweep of his two fingers, the demons were extricated and annulled. No words exist for the tremendous immensity of the energy pulse which I was honored to behold while riding upon his back. Circling the Earth several times, I was in a total state of ecstasy.

During our ride, we came upon several people who were misusing eternal power received unlawfully; souls in positions of worldly power who had used non-eternal means to achieve their ends. Snapping his fingers, several of these people simply dropped dead in their tracks.

Finally, St. Michael was done patrolling the Earth for now and conveyed to me that he had a secret to tell me and it was something very important for me to know about myself. Motioning that he was going to make an 'etheric' phone call to someone on Earth who also needed to know, he allowed me to eavesdrop on the conversation. Sending an eternal impetus through the ether, the soul of the person answered the call of the spirit asking who might be on the line. "St. Michael," he said, "You know, the Archangel." Not believing him, he hung up. St. Michael looked at me with a calm disappointment, conveying nothing more regarding the secret. Stunned that somebody had hung up on St. Michael, I was sad for this soul who had just denied an eternal option given to him on the ground.

In my estimation, as many as nine out of ten eternal options are refused, perhaps more. I've known souls to deny two or more eternal options with soul-mates because they are too dense to recognize them (the same applying to their life work). Ego's get in the way most of the time. Most of us wish to believe we are fine the way we are, and thus, we don't wish to make the changes in ourselves which all eternal options require. Because of this, the Lord's intentions are blocked in mortal realms, and the whims of the dark side win again.

Without any warning, my soul was swiftly hurled upon the light beam of the Holy Spirit returned to my body below.

****

Bright orange Bengal tigers with piercing black stripes wandered this high mountain abode. An old friend, Chinaman, sat inside this small oriental retreat cabin with his wife and two adult children, a young man and woman. Chinaman had been a spiritual guardian of Andy's many years ago, during the time in which we had begun to purify our karmic programs. Neither of us had seen him in many years. Although I was feeling fearful of the presence of the tigers, Chinaman assured me there was no need to worry.

All was quiet outside, and he told me we were 3200 feet higher than the highest mountain on the Earth. Although we were in the midst of a grove of oriental houses, there was no sign of other people being actively present. Assuming this to be because we were all in retreat, I made no mention of it.

Chinaman had assured me that it was necessary that I pull back from friends and family upon the Earth. "Their own issues about death," he conveyed, "are taking too much energy from you, which you desperately need in your battle to remain with your children." Having so little energy left for others because of my illness, I had pulled back so the little I had could go to my children. In order to do this, I had to sacrifice the many hours given to family and friends for their problems. Making it clear, Chinaman nodded that this retreat was good. Having felt guilty doing this, his assurances were helpful.

Chinaman handed me my guitar and led me to begin strumming an old song I wrote long ago, 'To Retrieve a Golden Angel.' Lyrical pathways in the song speak of the light trail home to the 23rd dimension from where I had come, the realm of the golden angels. "Remember where you came from," Chinaman said, "and how to get back." Mystical winds surrounded me as wisps of memory filled me with his words. Assuring me of salvation, Chinaman gave peace to my tormented soul, which had become obsessed with its eternal destiny.

As I again momentarily felt the impulse of the 23rd dimension, the realm of the golden angels, I saw little Chinaman smile, his family behind him in supportive fashion.

****

"Thunderbird," the heavenly host said loudly as he handed a long-ago worn out ring with the sign of the thunderbird upon it to Andy, who then gave it to me. Repeating his words, Andy said. "Thunderbird." Describing the fiery quality my soul possessed which energized new programs on the Earth, the heavenly host allowed me to look upon the Phoenix, the harbinger of change. Smiling, he disappeared into the ether.

****

CHAPTER SIX

The Child Prophets, Galactic Convent, Monks, Monastery in Space, Turbaned Guardian Spirits, my Nurse, Laughing in the Light, 200 Angels, my Deceased Priest, the Transformation of Souls into their True Natures, Anasazi Indian, Opa, Various Angelic Guardians and Hosts, Passing on the Gifts.

****

Gazing about the room, there were about fifty spiritual children flitting about, all in robes of white, and many with flower garlands draped about their heads like halos. Understanding them all to be prophets, I also inherently knew that they were there on behalf of my children; their purpose in my home had to do with the spiritual formation of my little sweethearts. Despite their childlike stature, their presence was filled with great holiness and power.

An older man was standing next to me, as we were awaiting the arrival of the sub-conscious soul of a man who resided on Earth who was known for his spiritual gifts, in other words a 'psychic.' Chuckling, the older man said, "Won't it be interesting to see if this man will be aware of the presence of so many prophets in your home." Although he didn't say it, he conveyed that oftentimes those with such gifts are so competitive about their abilities, that they completely block out those of a holier nature than themselves, rather than have to humble themselves before more sanctified beings, especially those of such small stature. By doing this, they negate the need for their own further development and can claim that they are already 'there,' simply because of the nature of their gift. Such gifts are given in the hopes of greater cultivation towards holiness, not just the use of the gift in its most primal form.

As he arrived, his response to the room was quite agitated as it was very clear that he was aware of the presence of the prophets, but was very uncomfortable acknowledging that these 'little people' encompassed a holiness greater than his own. In order to reduce the need to speak of them, he turned to us and said, "Gee, you know . . . I believe that I've already given the required amount of time to your reading as I was entering the room. Go . . . ask the guy at the door, he'll tell you. I'm afraid I cannot give you more of my time for a reading." We both looked at him quietly and nodded.

As he was leaving, the older man next to me gave me a knowing glance as I began to disappear and return to form. Honored to have seen the 'little prophets,' I wondered at their greater meaning, but could only speak of having seen them without fully understanding their import.

****

Soaring into a wonderful Galactic convent, it was filled with nuns of every age, young and old, who wore modern clothing which appeared to be from my time. An old woman with short, curly gray hair was my guide for this evening, and as I sat and rocked my children who appeared on my lap as if they were babies, they all gathered around and allowed me to listen as they spoke of various things.

Three very holy priests entered the room and sat at our table, beginning to speak of the gifts of the spirit. As they spoke of the Anointing, they made mention of a modern day healer who was not Catholic, but who was blessed with a true gift of the Holy Spirit. Showing unity amongst the denominations, I listened with interest. Because I had been so sick, I didn't move, but the nuns understood.

Leaving the room, the priests retired to a holy sacristy which we were not allowed to enter. As they had been drinking milk, several of the nuns gathered around their glasses and began drinking what they had left behind, conveying that this would fill them with the spirit of holiness that had filled the priests. But I was not allowed to sip from their glasses, because I was of the Earth.

Before I left, the nuns conveyed to me of my holy purpose as a mother, and that although I was very compatible in *visiting* their convent, I wouldn't be so in *living* there. "Go to your home and rock your babies," they said, "for this is what God has ordained for you." Finally, they gave me the sense that I must rest and attain to more stability, because my true time of death had not yet arrived and they wished for me to fulfill my full aeon upon the Earth.
****

Having sat down to play the guitar, I was very surprised when about thirty monks began to literally come out of an old jar which was sitting on the floor about twenty feet in front of me. Wearing a brown habit with their hoods draped over their heads, I immediately knew that they were Essenes. One stepped forward quietly, as he handed me a book which was titled, "The Lost Books of the Essenes." Nodding, I allowed myself to take in their energies as I understood that much of their contents could be found in the Dead Sea Scrolls.

Emerging in my physical body, a single monk stood about five feet from my bed, his hands held in prayer and a hood covering his head. Praying over my sleeping soul for several minutes, he disappeared slowly as I came back to consciousness. Completely silent, his presence conveyed power.
****

Wandering through the starry heavens, my soul was alit in the wonders of a great and holy monastery. Gathering to share their joy that I'd arrived, the nuns took care of my every need. A great holy energy filled this place, which was reminiscent of the Essenes. "The Lord does not wish for you to worry about whether or not your works were published, for this does not matter. All that matters to God is that your soul remains 'energetically' in this monastery." Feeling the presence of the Essene monks who had recently come to visit, I understood that they resided in the 'deeper recesses' of the monastery.
****

My oldest daughter (Melissa, now 15) had an experience after praying for me. Worried because I'd recently been put on nighttime oxygen, somebody had come into her room. Looking up to see who they might be, two men in turbans had entered; one black and the other white. Distinctively holy, the black man was clearly the mentor of the other. Both men wore all white garments with the ballooning pants in the tradition of the Sikhs, with the exception of a lime green sash which was worn by the black holy man.

Following them, they peeked into her siblings rooms; they then walked towards my room and stood quietly at the foot of my bed with their hands serenely held before them. Giving me something that I very much needed 'energetically,' love, caring and support, such things had been lacking during my illness because of the normal manner in which terminally ill people are isolated from others. Expressing the great holiness, peace, serenity and powerful silence which occupied their presence, she mentioned that she fell asleep in her dream, only to awaken later to watch them as they left the house quietly. She felt they had come both to assure her that her mother was being watched over, and to let me know that despite the rejection of the world, I was on a correct and holy path. She said they had displayed a calm satisfaction in my spiritual state.

A few weeks before, she had a similar experience where she had been given to go to her brother's window within a dream. Outside the window stood one of the Essene monks wearing a garment of pure white facing to the side with his hands in prayerful repose. Again, was the quiet, silent picture of great power and holiness, of which energy she felt so strongly that she fell to her knees in response. Above him and all around, were the spacecraft of extra-terrestrial civilizations, which emanated power, might and the great vibration which accompanies such crafts 'in the spirit.'

****

Outside of my body, the stallions came rushing towards me as if in slow motion from every direction. About thirty horses were coming towards me as their manes blew in the wind. As I felt their power coming towards me upon my doorstep, one of the horses quietly laid down like a puppy, rolled over and cooed as I rubbed his belly. The others stood around us majestically as if to herald something wonderful to come.

But a warning was to foreshadow the good news as a voice began to bellow from behind me. "Don't you realize that you could be dead within fifteen minutes of any time?" (In 'Galactica,' I was diagnosed with a potentially terminal condition - Cardiomyopathy with associated Heart Failure) As the words were spoken, the tentative nature of my situation was shown to me in energetic fashion. Given warning to be aware of how quickly my life could end, I was told that my situation was very tricky and my life could depend on some of the choices I might make in regards to overdoing things or not. Nodding that I would be watchful of my condition, it was reiterated that any bad choice could result in my life being over in fifteen minutes.

Suddenly, my spirit was lying on a gurney amidst a beautiful church. Parishioners were looking at me from above, as they waited for the priest to arrive. Realizing that I was very sick, the priest gave me the anointing of the sick as the onlookers remained quiet and respectful.

Within moments, I was flown amidst a beauteous mountain range. Feeling ecstasy, I entered a huge mansion in the heavens filled with priests and nuns who were at retreat amongst this mountain hold. Watching their daily lives, I observed that they were not as different from the rest of us as I might have thought. There was a great normalcy in the religious life of which I hadn't expected.

An older nun approached who I immediately understood was one of my heavenly nurses. My health condition had become apparent in that my spirit had come to a halt on the floor and I was too tired to get up. Picking me up off the floor, she said, "We've got to get you up and going again. If you've still got nine years left, you need to get moving again and get back into life. Let's get you in the shower." Surprised and grateful by the possibility of which her soul heralded, I forced myself to get up and start pushing again.

In a spectral millisecond, my soul now stood upon a very holy isle. Having no idea how I'd gotten there, I was much too entranced to care. Amidst this spectral beauty lay sites from the holy land where Jesus had experienced some of his most important moments; the place of His birth and death, his tomb, and various places he'd visited during His life on Earth. Filled with holy wonder and awe, I was guided throughout the island with Andy, my husband, and a group of other spirits.

Wanting to stay in this holy place forever, I was very disappointed when we were being led towards a boat. Andy and all the others had boarded and were preparing to depart the island, but I had to quickly take care of a quick health matter before I could go. My wonderful nurse was smiling with great peace as she bid me to take care of my health matter because they would be only too happy to wait. Turning to take care of this final task before departure, I heard the motor of the boat begin to start. Looking back, I noticed the boat had begun to leave the shore rather quickly. Running towards it, I reached out to Andy who raised his hands to me in a state of surrender and a wave good-bye. My nurse was smiling and also waving good-bye as they stranded me alone on this island containing the holy places within the Life of Christ.

Confused by this gesture, I sat down on a large holy rock and began to cry. So many things had gone wrong lately. Besides my obvious continuing health crisis, I'd completed my tasks in getting my work made available to the world. But it had not been received well. Because of this, I'd worried a great deal about whether or not I had done my job according to God's will. As I wept, I was instantly transported into the light.

Inside the light was a greater light that I could gaze upon. But each time I did so, I broke out into uncontrollable laughter. For what seemed like hours, I kept turning to look at this light, laughing uncontrollably for a time, and then looking away because I needed to stop for a moment. A grand male voice beckoned from the heavens into my consciousness, "If God is not worried about this, then you needn't be, either. Everything is going according to His plan." As usual, I began to laugh uncontrollably at this as the angel appeared before me and began to laugh with me. "Just continue to do what we ask of you," he said, as he continued in roaring, unfailing laughter, "you don't need to know why."
****

After spending weeks working on a project given to me by the prophets, saints, mystics and sage from every religion throughout time (to make my work downloadable for free on my web-site); I was given a great gift.

For a couple of weeks they had come with their requests, each one requiring a little higher level of technical knowledge. When I gave up on two occasions, they returned to me at night insisting that it could be done and I just had to figure out how it would work. After uploading and downloading day and night for two weeks in my compromised condition (heart failure), we finally had success and there was great joy in the heavens.

Taking me to an astral hospital, the spiritual doctors worked on my spirit and soul to rejuvenate me. Then they took me home. A few times in my life, I'd been given to witness the line of angels that surrounds the perimeter of our property and home as heavenly protection for us. As a special holy gift for performing this task, they said I would get to see them again.

As they said this, the lines of angels appeared out of the ether. Golden and luminous, they were all smiling exuberantly in their joy that this task had been completed and this work of God was now being broadcast all over the world. Perhaps 200 angels protected our property, standing quietly in line in the form of a square around our home. Nodding with gratitude, I was returned to my body.
****

Boarding an airplane which was transparent and filled with people, I sat down as I noticed that there was a guide of some sort preparing to teach us. Surprised to notice that there were two priests among the group, I was also happy to see my own former priest sitting in wait.

"This is the airplane of Truth and Wisdom," said the guide as he began a lengthy discourse on the finer points of guiding souls properly. Although it was quite obvious that I didn't really know what to say or how to say it to those in need of guidance, it was also apparently clear that I was among those who were required to learn this skill of guiding souls towards God. Because of this urgency, there were three points of great importance for me to learn this night.

After steering the plane into the skies several times, which represented steering a soul properly upward to begin its own flight; we landed the plane to focus on these finer points of inquiry. Firstly, they began to introduce new souls into my group, and as they did so, I became confused and mis-focused. This was my first failing, that I would lose focus too quickly when a new person came into the picture. Secondly, they began speaking with my former priest and discussing a failing of his which I had apparently shared. As he stood there in his shining robes, he nodded with calm acceptance of the fact that his primary failing in shepharding his own flock had been that he had done too much for his people, rather than teaching them compassionately to receive the tools he had already honed so well. By being brusk on occasion in regards to matters which appeared quite obvious to him, but were true obstacles to those who came to him for guidance, he scared them away in a sense. Nodding, I understood that the arrogance and conceit of wisdom can become a huge obstacle if you become unwilling to give others the tools they will need in a compassionate manner, rather than being annoyed that they need such guidance. Finally, it was time for me to go to my next class, but I quickly realized that my class had gone long over its expected time. This was my third error in that my classes lasted too long. An extension of the second problem, I was allowing people to become too dependent upon me, rather than giving them what they needed in a focused, concise, clear and compassionate manner, resulting in a certain co-dependency which allowed them to neglect utilizing and perfecting those tools within themselves.

Understanding, I turned to the angelic guardian and said, "Before I go, I want to let Father know how much I loved him." Looking at me quizzically, the guide said, "Oh, you do? In what way?" Pausing, I stumbled. "Oh, I don't know . . . as a father?" Energies began to pull back as I quickly understood that my sincerity was in question. In truth, I had had mixed feelings about our priest. Sometimes, he had been great, but there had also been times when he had brought me to tears with his abruptness or gruffness regarding grave issues. Ironically, I realized that those very issues within him that had given me mixed feelings were issues that I, too, shared. It was almost funny to realize that. At that moment, I turned to Father and realized that he already understood that I'd had mixed feelings, and that me expressing my love to him was insincere, rather stupid and unnecessary. For the purpose of this exercise, it made it doubly important that I be honest with myself so that I could hopefully avoid that same pitfall within my own work in this life. It was his desire that I do so, perhaps his final gift to me.

Finally, it was time to leave and I followed the spiritual pull towards a classroom in another sphere. Many metaphysical thinkers had gathered there, and I sat down in a chair awaiting instruction. An older woman appeared who was apparently going to teach, but she immediately looked towards me and said, "Make sure we can hear your CD's, too." Surprised, I wasn't even aware that they knew of my work. Speaking of some kind of award the group had given me for my efforts in the field of Out-of-Body Travel, she said, "Frankly, we feel you've shown greater prudence in presenting the subject than we have." In a moment of surprise, I quietly said, "Thank you."

Suddenly, I was inside a metaphysical bookstore. Having come to sign books, the owner had instead regarded my humble manner as indicative of my lack of worth, and directed me to straighten shelves instead. Confused, I did as she asked, walking first over to where my books had been displayed. As I began to move them around and try to dust them, diamonds began to fall out of them, spilling onto the floor in droves. Concerned, I tried to vacuum them up, but found that that didn't work very well. Afraid, the owner of the store would think I was stealing from her, I attempted to gather up the diamonds, but they continued to spill out of my books all over the floor.

For a moment, I stood back up to notice that the entire room had transformed from what it had *appeared* to be to its *truth* in energetic reality. As diamonds continued to fall from my little corner of the store, I noticed that there were clothing racks of human-size scorpions hanging upside down from hangers. As I tried to straighten a few of the other books, crab-like creatures fell out of them as I jumped back in horror. Several customers had been in the store and had previously appeared as normal humans, but now one of them was adorned in great wealth and was a vampirical beast. When he smiled, you knew this. Two others were a lower-grade order of vampire, as they were not in disguise at all and their energetic nature was out in the open. A fourth person carried the look of an old hag, almost monstrous in her appearance. Her hair was knotted, unkempt and dirty, and her face held a witchy glare. In horror, I quietly slipped out a side door.

****

An invisible guardian took my hand and began leading me to a place that I knew instinctively represented the church run by the minister I had previously received a message for about discipleship. Surprised, we were wandering towards a large cliff. The ground was wet and muddy to the point of having your feet sink into it deeply with every step, but we continued onward. Climbing below the cliff, we saw a very muddy cave which resided below the cliff. In the rocky crag, the congregation sat in the two-foot deep mud, completely unaware of the defilement and filth surrounding them. Instinctively, I understood this filth to be the true nature of the minister's ego, which was ill-formed and self-serving.

In a previous experience, the Lord had shown me this minister sleeping as his grandchild was entering perdition. Because he'd been taking care of the child for a time and this child was extremely unruly and exhibiting unbelievably violent and dark tendencies, he held responsibility for his correct rearing while under his care. But he was 'asleep at the wheel' and not fulfilling this duty. Because of his ego, he considered ministering to his congregation of more importance than the primal and first responsibility given to us all to properly rear our children in the ways of the Lord. For him to be a minister and nix this duty was considered a severe misjudgment and act of laziness on his part for which there was eternal wrath.

Appearing for only a moment, the angelic guardian manifested out of the ether to nod knowingly at my soul with piercing eyes. Wearing a long robe of white enhanced by a pair of white wings which were folded upon his back; his hair was short, curly and white. Nodding my understanding of what I'd seen back to him, I interiorly knew that this minister and his church were impure and I must stay away. He disappeared and I was instantly in another realm.

"Enlightening beings provide for all , able to give up everything they have, internal and external, unfailingly causing their minds to be forever pure and never to be narrow or mean . . . The virtues of giving their tongues they dedicate to all sentient beings, praying that based on this excellent cause all may attain the universal tongue of the enlightened."
The Flower Ornament Scripture, Ten Dedications, Page 623, (Buddhism: Mahayana)
"If the mystic knowers be of those who have reached to the beauty of the Beloved One, this station is the apex of consciousness and the secret of divine guidance. This is the center of the mystery: 'He doth what He willeth, ordaineth what He pleaseth."
The Seven Valleys and The Four Valleys, The Fourth Valley, (Bahai', Words of Baha'u'llah
****

Sitting up in bed in my astral body, I noticed my husband, Andy's, spiritual body sitting up also and looking out the window. Intrigued, I turned to see what he might be looking at and was stunned to notice a huge fireman of about seven feet in height outside our window watching over and guarding Andy in his new work. Recently, he'd been promoted and was now in charge of the most serious cases involving murders and homicides. His uniform was a burgundy-red, and his face showed seriousness and resolve.

Suddenly, an image began to overlap with his. An ancient Anasazi Indian became infused upon this huge man's chest, with long dark black hair blowing in the wind. Wearing a white leather garment, he/she also stared deeply into my eyes with great power, seriousness and resolve. I say he/she because I was unable to ascertain whether this being was male or female, and there was an indescribable sense of she/him being both. Within seconds, I fell back towards conscious reality.

But subsequently, before entering awareness, I was swept up into a puff of air and was now standing over my middle daughter, Mary. In the ether, I saw the face of my grandfather (her great-grandfather) in his early twenties. Then he merged into the face of himself as an old man, and was now bowing down, looking upon Mary. Conveying, he thought, "I wanted you to know that I watch over all of you, but in a special way over Mary." "Opa!" I nearly shouted, as he disappeared into the ether. ('Opa' was the German name we called him for grandpa.)

But a final spiritual wind ushered me into its presence, bading me to look upon both of my girls who were now sleeping. In the spirit world, a false spirituality began to play out before my eyes. I was shown that although my daughters kept up an exterior facade of spiritual depth, their inner world was lacking and filled with worldliness. "How long has it been since they asked God what He wanted them to do, rather than doing what they wanted?" A spiritual guardian whispered. "Do they really wish to fulfill God's will, or only their own? Do they engage in spiritual reading of their own accord, or only when you insist upon it? You will not be here to guide them forever; they must take responsibility for the life in which they choose. Do they wish to serve God or themselves?"

Interiorly, the two of them were shown as being very out-of-control, giving into many desires, lusts and cravings of the world; while exteriorly they were almost using their false spirituality as a means to fulfill vice. For instance, using the facade of spiritual depth to attract members of the opposite sex or to gain favor among others who perceived them to be truly spiritual and valued that quality.

Nodding to the spiritual guardian, I attempted to continue to sleep, but the ethereal winds would not allow me to do so. Waking several times, I finally concluded that this message was to be delivered in the middle of the night, a symbolic and very real 'waking' of the body and soul. As I shared with them the words of the angel, they both bowed their heads, acknowledging their guilt.

We discussed that spiritual reading, prayer and contemplation don't have to be overwhelming. It can be as simple as reading a couple of pages in a truly sacred text each day or every other day (Like 'The Ascent of Mount Carmel' By St. John of the Cross) and allowing it to penetrate within you throughout your day, becoming the object of contemplation, meditation and prayer alike. By applying such small disciplines into your daily life, these little seeds of understanding become as drops of water into a pitcher penetrating gradually into our sub-conscious and conscious minds. Slowly, it becomes a part of our way of thinking and being in an almost passive way as the hand of the Holy Spirit uses the words of the Masters throughout time to hone, guide and prune us into who we must become. But it requires a small discipline on our part and of our own choosing in assuring that those seeds are placed within our mind each day, creating fertile ground through which God may work in us.

"They protect us when in distress with manifest assistance."
The Avesta, Yast 13, Verse 146, (Zoroastrianism, Words of Zarathustra)
"Who will apply the lash to my thoughts, to my mind the rod of discipline, that my failings may not be spared nor the sins of my heart overlooked."
The New American Bible, Old Testament, Sirach 23:2, (Christianity, Judaism)
****

Crying out to me in the night, an angelic guardian came upon a galing wisp of wind to tell me one of the sayings of Jesus Christ. Repeating it twice, I cannot recall what it was that was said, although I remember it penetrating my soul deeply as the words were spoken to me. "These words of Jesus are really important to you now." The Angel said, as he disappeared into the night.

Continuing to struggle with my desire to serve God to my best ability by making my writings available as easily and cheaply as possible to anyone in the world, I hit a stumbling block because of the simple realities of the publishing world and how expensive it is to produce books. Asking God in prayer if there was more I could do beyond providing the e-books for free download, I received a vision.

One time, when I was very close to death, an image of roses had come before me in a most beautiful and profound manner as I had felt the presence of the Blessed Virgin Mary responding the rosaries being offered for my healing. These same roses appeared again to me for the first time since that moment, but this time there were three very beautiful, pronounced and vibrant roses. Interiorly, I heard these words, "Don't worry yourself, my child, you have done your work well. Worry yourself with the three beautiful red roses (my children) that the Lord has given you. Be at peace."

Another angelic guardian came into the room showing me the relationship between various mothers and their children. In contrast, I was then shown the relationship I had with my own children and their truly deep abiding love for me. "Do you know how unusual it is for a child to love their parent so truly?" Because I'd never really considered this, I nodded, 'No.' "You are a true success because of this . . . " He paused." Do not lose heart, and do not let yourself by diverted."

"Saith Nanak: Thrice blessed is the wife who with her noble Spouse has bliss."
Sri Guru Granth Sahib, Volume II, Raga Wadhans, Page 1187, (Sikhism)
"Happy the husband of a good wife, twice-lengthened are his days; a worthy wife brings joy to her husband, peaceful and full is his life. A good wife is a generous gift bestowed upon him who fears the Lord; be he rich or poor, his heart is content, and a smile is ever on his face."
The New American Bible, Old Testament, Sirach 26:1-4, (Christianity, Judaism)
****

With barely a pause, I found myself sitting at Holy Mass with my children. Another man had come to the Mass who was involved in feeling self-important. Right before communion was to be distributed, he shouted out, "I ate within an hour of this Mass, but I am planning to receive Communion anyway." In the Catholic Church, you are required to fast at least one hour before receiving Jesus in the Holy Sacrament of the altar because it is considered blasphemous to mix the food of Christ with mundane food of the world. The priest simply said, "No, you cannot receive communion if you have not fasted. The Church has come up with these rules over hundreds of years of study, trying to find the most appropriate means to give the sacraments to the people." "You don't understand," the man again said, "I intend to have Communion anyway." Getting up, he moved closer to me in the church and sat down with a young child. Within moments, he shouted, "You stop acting like a jerk!" to his child.

"That's it, " the priest said, "you are to leave the Church immediately and I'm demoting you to a second degree Catholic." He wouldn't leave. Quietly, I walked over to the man who remained arrogant and rude, and said, "You need to leave NOW." "Why?" He asked, truly puzzled. "I KNOW you don't understand, but you NEED to leave NOW!" The Church and all within it phased off into the ether.

An Angelic Host began to convey to me. "There are some like this man who believe that they are entitled to more than others simply because of their position in this world or some other earthly attainment. They often go so far as to believe that they are entitled to receive more from God, as well, and this is blasphemy. All are equal in the eyes of God, and we are all required to humble ourselves before our Lord and fellow man, as well." These are often the types who can't themselves live up to what they require of others in their perimeter because they are often excessive in their demands of those around them. Yet, they don't see this in themselves, because they believe themselves above others; and therefore, they expect exceptions to be made for them. Not unlike the ungrateful servant in the parable that Jesus told who was forgiven of a huge debt, but then threw another man into prison for a small debt owed him.

> *"Whensoever thou comest forth turn thy face toward the Inviolable Place of Worship; and wheresoever ye may be (O Muslims) turn your faces toward it (when ye pray) so that men may have no argument against you, save such of them as do injustice - Fear them not, but fear Me! - and so that I may complete My grace upon you, and that ye may be guided."*

The Meaning of the Glorious Kuran, Surah II, No. 150, (Islam, Translator: Marmaduke Pickthall)

> *"He will die from lack of discipline, through the greatness of his folly he will be lost."*

The New American Bible, Old Testament, Proverbs 5:23 (Christianity, Judaism, Words of Solomon)

****

Andy had an experience. He and I were sitting in lotus position before one another. Between us was a simple salad made with lettuce and carrots, no dressings or other fancy accoutrements.

Suddenly, and without warning, the salad disappeared, going into another room. As it did, I did also. Appearing before the priest, the salad was now between the two of us as we sat in lotus position gently picking up a piece of food here and there and many regions of light passed between us. An interchange was going on that was the will of God. Eternal in its nature, it was shown by the sparkling lights and stars going from each of us to the other in circular fashion. In this situation, I was to be the primary teacher, but there was an exchange between us that went beyond my teaching.

Andy was tempted to be very angry and jealous, but a larger force than he held him back. Instantly, he knew that this was God's will and that he must not interfere. Something very important was happening and he understood and accepted this instantly. He was made to know . . . so to speak.

After all, those of us who are led by the angelic hosts and spirit guides in heaven, are then expected to pass the gifts onto others by becoming guides on earth.

****

Reincarnation and Karma

Mystic Knowledge Series

Compiled and Written by Marilynn Hughes

The Out-of-Body Travel Foundation!

www.outofbodytravel.org

By Laughing Spirit, 1920

CHAPTER ONE

Various Past Lives, Red Jacket, Man in Battle, Atonements, China, Courtesan, Seven Deadly Sins and their Corresponding Virtues, Gray Robe, Thread Bare, Mobster Lifetime, Prairie Ranch, Roman Soldier, Request for Forgiveness from the Past.

****

Transported to a beautiful mansion in Europe, I noted that although the language being spoken was not English, I understood it. With my connection to knowledge which followed me on all my episodic events, information was usually available to me as it proved necessary.

A woman lived in this big mansion all alone, and immediately I knew that she had been my mother in a previous life, which was interesting considering I hadn't yet really thought much about reincarnation. Her present lifetime had no connection to me at all. Widowed and bitter, I could feel the sadness that enveloped her soul as if it were my own. Having a boyfriend living with her in her home, her adult son lived next door. The son had just come over to see his mother, and I was intrigued, because, after all, in a certain sense he was a brother of mine. Wearing a blue, polyester suit, I went over to him to try to make him aware of my presence, forgetting my immaterial nature. For a moment, he looked towards me confusedly as if he felt my presence, but then he blew it off and turned away. Journeying forward, I found myself in another place.

****

After rolling out of form, I found myself looking upon a strange tunnel I had not yet seen. Dark and mysterious, a bright light burst forth at the end. Drawn almost incomprehensibly toward it, I began shooting down the tunnel at what seemed like light speed and suddenly began falling DOWN.

Having been dropped into a man's body, I noticed that I was wearing the form of a soldier sitting behind a rock barricade waiting for an impending battle. The uniform he wore was reminiscent of the Cavalry, but I didn't know when this war had occurred.

And despite my previous view which had not truly considered reincarnation one way or the other, I immediately KNEW that it was true, without doubt or fear. It was as if this journey had opened my soul to remembering such things in a distant way.

"I remember as many eons as there are atoms in a hundred lands."
The Flower Ornament Scripture, Chapter 39, Entry into the Realm of Reality, Page 1426, Stanza 2, (Buddhism, Mahayana)

My attention turned to the captain now instructing us on the upcoming battle. Informed that we would start shooting when we were told and continue for a certain stretch of time and then we were to stop, and all would count their wins and losses. It would all be over, for a time.

Calm and accepting of my duty to perform this act of violence; I was surprised when, without any understandable warning, I was overcome with holy rage. My mind was full of terrifying thoughts of the injuries I could inflict or sustain, and the lives that would be lost. For what? For that brief moment, I KNEW the terror of a man in battle, and it was profound.

Running over to the other men, I screamed to them, "We don't have to do this; we don't have to kill each other! They can't force us to pull the trigger!" Walking away, I deserted my brigade with three men following. Holing up in a nearby house, the shooting began, and with it; the screams, carnage, dying, suffering, barbarism. We cried uncontrollably.

Overwhelmed with grief and emotion, the spirits of the Lord quickly pulled me up and back through the tunnel through time, and led me to the present day. Moved, the power of God was working on my soul deeply, profoundly, in a way I could not yet understand.

"The immature run after sense pleasures and fall into the widespread net of death. But the wise, knowing the Self as deathless, Seek not the changeless in the world of change."
The Upanishads, Katha Upanishad, Part II, (I), No. 2, Paragraph 2, Page 90, (Hinduism, Translation: Eknath Easwaran)

****

Becoming aware of another presence around me, I mistakenly took it for a lost soul because of the uncomfortable feelings I had about his presence. Becoming clear that this soul was desperately trying to receive forgiveness from his wife and child, I didn't understand why I couldn't get him to leave or to go to the light. Over time, I began feeling a certain conflicted love for this soul, and begged it to reveal to me its purpose. In response to my inquiries, I was taken on a journey a few nights later.

Tossed through the time-tunnel, I felt the presence of a Native American. Conveying his name to be Red Jacket, my spirit was suddenly crashing into a different time and place.

Hurled into the 1800's, we looked from above at an old Native American camp which was sparsely populated. Several teepees were scattered around and a fire pit was burning in the middle of camp. Very poor, the people were scavenging for food to feed their children. The men were absent, and the women and children were trying to fend for themselves during the time of the Indian wars. Autumn winds were blowing in, and I couldn't help but feel the tremendous cold they would soon be facing in winter. Intense suffering was apparent on all of their faces.

And then I remembered something, I felt it. Intense love filled my soul. Although the feelings were quite powerful, memory was coming only in flashes. Red Jacket and I had been together in some distant time and place, but for some reason we were separated.

It came to me in a flash of knowing. Red Jacket could not leave his people in these conditions, and I could not bring myself to join them and give up the comforts of the white man's world in which I had lived.

"All life and all existence here, with all its joys and all its woe, rests on a single state of mind, and quick passes that moment by . . . Out of the unseen did they rise, into the unseen do they pass, just as the lightning flashes forth, so do they flash and pass away."
Path to Deliverance, C Wisdom (Panna), Page 175, Middle, Stanza 1 and 6, (Buddhism, Theravadan, Author: Nyanatiloka)

****

Emmanuel's (My spirit Guide) eyes turned to the right, and suddenly my spirit was swirling away from this place back into the time-tunnel, all black with a bright light at the end. Red Jacket's voice was heard in the ether, calling me to go with him. As he reached his hand to me, I took it.

Soaring at light speed, I suddenly became aware that I was now falling down. With a loud thud, I entered into a body. My immediate instinct was to look down, which gave me many clues as to where I had entered. Wearing a long dress with a petticoat, I noticed how heavy these clothes felt. Walking along some dirt roads towards a dingy bar, it occurred to me that my current self was overlapping another life, and that I was here to observe . . . not interfere.

The bar was like an old barn with the front doors opened wide. Inside, a man whom I knew to be my husband was arm wrestling with a group of men who were very loud and boisterous. He wasn't a big man, being slightly shorter than myself with straight sandy-brown hair. Two men near him were very large and unusually dirty. Sporting wavy black hair and mustaches, I supposed they might be Mexican. All the men were wearing dirty brown pants with suspenders and soiled shirts that apparently used to be white. Some had old cowboy hats on. My husband ordered me to leave as soon as he saw me, for this was no place for a woman, and they were busy with men-folk talk. Angry, I turned to go.

On the way back to our home, I noticed that I was walking around a western fort. Prisoners quarters made out of sandstone rock sported windows with metal bars. A young Indian boy's face motioned to me. "We are very hungry, they do not feed us. Can you help?" He said. Promising that I would return with food, I went upon my way.

Returning to the prison later, I took note that the guards were quite intoxicated. One had fallen asleep and was lying in the dirt smelling strongly of whiskey. The other stood against the prison wall in his blue cavalry uniform, holding his rifle upright. Bottle in hand, it wouldn't be long before he joined his friend on the ground.

"Sir," I said with a curtsy, "I would just like to bring the prisoners some food for their bodies and perhaps some food for their soul." I said. "I've prepared something for them to eat, and I know that they will be ready to hear about the Lord on a full stomach. I'd be mighty appreciative if you would let me help these poor souls enter into heaven." Flippantly, the guard moved away from the door, unlocking it. "Well, ma'am, that's mighty Christian of you. Good luck to you and God bless," he said.

Walking into the door, there was a short flight of steps going down to the disgustingly filthy room which was about 10' X 10' and housed about fifteen prisoners. There were other cells, but I didn't venture into them. Apparently, some of the more dangerous prisoners were kept in those privately locked cells.

Appreciative of the food, the young boy ate voraciously, although the others remained suspicious. At this moment, I realized that this was the moment I had made the decision in that lifetime that I was going to help the Indians. Ascending the rock stairs, a flash of light pulled me out and shot me back home to my present life.

"You and I have passed through many births, Arjuna. You have forgotten, but I remember them all."

Bhagavad Gita, Chapter 4, Verse 5, (Hinduism, Words of Krishna, Translation: Eknath Easwaran)

****

Entering the dream of a handicapped man in a veteran's hospital, we talked for a short period of time. The young man had a bandage around his forehead with only a little bit of brown hair showing. Apparently, he had few visitors and was very lonely.

Offering universal love and acceptance to him, we talked for quite some time before he suddenly burst out, "You aren't from here, are you, Ute?" I didn't know what to say. He continued. "Like, I mean, you're a spirit aren't you?" Red Jacket immediately pulled me out of his dream.

My confused glance held an unknowing as I asked him, "Why did he call me Ute?" Red Jacket didn't even pause before he answered, "Because that is who you are." Upon return, I discovered that it was a tribe of Indians in the western United States.

****

An old friend from ten years prior appeared to me in another dimension, apparently brought here for an atonement. We'd gone to school together and been very cruel to one another as children. It was apparent that we had been brought to this space to work things out. Apologizing for his cruelty, he bade me to know that he truly did love me very much, and that his actions were not at all reflective of his true feelings. This surprised me, but gave me great joy, as well. Sharing my own confession of guilt, I apologized in return for my own acts of uncaring towards him. Embracing, all that remained between us now was unconditional forgiveness and love. This person I'd literally not thought of for years, who had seemed such an insignificant part of my life, was now pulsating within my heart in such a powerfully loving way. From this experience, I realized that even when people's feelings are hurt by another, it is very often an expression of love trying to understand itself. Our small piece of karma had been worked out, and we were now atoned.

As I began to meet many people from my past, I found that working out these seemingly small events in my life, allowed my spirit to become more open to receiving love from God. Because the nature of these hurts is rejection, a soul can close itself off, through the actions of others and itself, to believing it is not worthy of love. Because of this, every interaction we have with one another becomes important.

"A man in this world will not be able to be pure of sins; for if he is pure of one, he will not be able to be pure of another . . . For this cause, therefore, I have rent myself asunder and have brought the mysteries into the world, because all are under sin and all are in need of the gift of the mysteries."
Pistis Sophia, Fourth Book, Page 292, Paragraph 2, (Christianity, Gnostic/Essene, Words of Christ)

****

Red Jacket took me to a beautiful prairie. Tumbleweeds blew by as we rode separate horses towards an awesome mountain ahead. A third horse appeared with a young Indian boy riding. Instantly, I knew that this was our son. Disappearing as quickly as he had come, Red Jacket waved his arms and we were no longer there.

As he hovered above, I was now in the body of an Indian woman sitting in a small camp. Two teepees could be clearly seen in the firelight, and they were painted with a red jagged line around the bottom of them. Many more teepees were shadowed by the night. Sitting by the fire, the forest serenaded me with the sounds of the blowing wind and the calling of the night animals. Instinctively, I knew this had been my home somewhere in time.

Taking Red Jackets hand, I was quickly pulled away.

"I will see the hand of God in all that happens to me, attributing nothing to individual people, who are but instruments used by Him in the work of my sanctification."
The Voice of the Saints, Chapter 3, Page 17, No. 3, (Christianity, Catholic, Words of Blessed Raphaela Mary)

****

Outside of form, my soul was traveling quickly towards a most majestic mountain range. Red Jacket was speaking behind me as I traveled through the ether. Three mountains were in sight, two smaller ones surrounding a snow-capped beauty in the middle. "There is a being," he said, "who is at ONE with these mountains. The animals and the trees are her friends, and she speaks with all life. In her heart, she has lived here for centuries."

Reaching the mountain, I looked up to notice a horse had been carved into the bluish rock which appeared to be in motion. Soaring to the midsection, my spirit was directly before the horse's heart, listening to its rhythmic beat. "And you, my friend, are Heart of the Horse!" Red Jacket said, "It is your name, it is your legacy."

"Because mountains are high and broad, the way of riding the clouds is always reached in the mountains; the inconceivable power of soaring in the wind comes freely from the mountains."
Moon in a Dewdrop, Mountain and Waters Sutra (Sansui-Kyo), No. 2, (Buddhism, Zen, Words of Zen Master Dogen)

****

Having many, many atonements which all ended in a beautiful display of love and forgiveness, I was surprised when I found myself embroiled in two separate instances wherein those I had sought forgiveness from, were not yet ready to give it. Leaving them with my apologies for their hurt feelings, I told them we'd meet again when and if they chose to be ready to atone.

Much later, one of them appeared to me in an empty theatre. Occupying the first seat in the second row of chairs, a brilliant red curtain completely closed off the stage. Behind the curtain, you could hear the sounds of a performance. Sitting behind him, he turned to me and smiled, "As the curtain conceals the illusion, I am ready to discard my own." Conveying that he was now at peace, I thanked him for his understanding and again was overwhelmed with a rush of love and forgiveness.

Moments later, I was pulled away.

"Hazardous and slow is the path to the Unrevealed, difficult for physical man to tread. But they for whom I am the supreme goal, who do all work renouncing self for me and meditate on me with single-hearted devotion, these I will swiftly rescue from the fragment's cycle of birth and death, for their consciousness has entered me."
The Bhagavad Gita, Chapter 12, No.'s 5-7, (Hinduism, Words of Krishna, Translation: Eknath Easwaran)

****

During an intensive vibrational raising, I began to see a globe of purple and white light rotating. As this occurred, Red Jacket spoke in my ear:

"I am like the great tree,
who after bearing witness
to day and night for hundreds of years,
cries silently to the Great Spirit,
'Oh, I understand!
There is oneness between light and dark!'
The tree silently and peacefully dies . . .
making room for new life,
and becomes one with all that is."

"God has also set the one over against the other; the good against the evil, and the evil against the good; the good proceeds from the good, and the evil from the evil; the good purifies the bad, and the bad the good . . . "
Sepher Yezirah, Chapter VI, Section V, (Judaism)

****

Entering the time-tunnel, I began falling into another time. Again, I emerged in what appeared to be the Cavalry lifetime, crossing a river over a swinging bridge.

Across this river was a large prison community which consisted of a few small shacks surrounded by wooden fences. Stone shacks with leaky grass roofs were guarded by armed men at the entrances to prevent escape.

Bringing food to the prisoners had eventually led to helping them with other tasks, like washing clothes. Used to my frequent visits, the guards let me pass without a word. A young Indian woman met me at the gate, which was highly secured because many escapes had occurred amongst the Indian prisoners.

Three Indian men lived in one of these huts, who called themselves brothers, but I knew they were not biologically related. A special bond existed between me and these brothers; we were close friends and confidantes. Red Jacket was one of these brothers, and there was an obvious attraction between us. Five women lived in the shack next door, all who would escape but one, who died from the cold during the winter.

Pushing a large wheelbarrow containing food, blankets and clean clothes, Red Jacket jumped in as soon as we were safely in the hut. Dirty cloths and blankets were used to cover him. At that moment, I realized I was responsible for the escapes.

On my way out with the prisoner, I ran into my husband who was entertaining three guests. Trying to impress his guests with lavish gifts, they were celebrating one of the men's recent graduations from a military school. "Why don't you join us in our celebrating, honey?" He asked, as I nervously looked down upon my cart. "In a moment," I replied, "Let me put my cart in the house and I will meet you at the general store." Turning to leave, they acknowledged that they would meet me there. At that moment, I realized that the soul of my husband in that life was the same soul as in my present. Although they looked nothing alike, there was a recognition that went beyond the flesh, deep into the windows of another kind of knowing.

Hiding Red Jacket in an old abandoned log cabin, he stayed in a closet until nightfall, as all the other prison escapees had done. Formerly an old storefront, the old cabin was nailed shut after going out of business and no one went in there. Bringing the cart to my home, I headed for the general store.

Many people went to this log building to socialize. Inside, a man of about fifty-five with gray hair was smoking a pipe and catering to my husband who was buying expensive cigars for everyone. There was a wooden counter with a very old version of a cash register. A big selection of rifles was hanging on the walls. Annoyed at my husband who was much too concerned with wasting money on people who didn't need it, I slipped into the background. Talk turned to the current Indian escapes, and after expressing my outrage, I excused myself to leave.

Later as night had fallen, I slipped off while my husband was at the bar. Red Jacket was ready to go, but before he did, he unexpectedly pulled me close to him. After spending some very intimate time together, he looked at me very seriously. "You are one of us, and do not belong here. Come with me and we will share our lives with each other. The Indian people will accept you and love you!" A big part of me wanted to go, but I didn't have the courage to make such a hasty decision. Night was upon us and he had to leave. "No," I said, "I love you very much, but I can't leave . . . not yet, anyway." Embracing me, he said, "I love you with all my heart." Moments later, he was gone. Crying softly as he departed, I pulled myself together so as not to arouse suspicion.

Returning to form, I was shocked to realize I had done this.

"For whoever has the courage to conquer his passions, to subdue his appetites, and repulse even the least motions of his own will, performs an action more meritorious in the sight of God than if, without this, he should tear his flesh with the sharpest disciplines, fast with greater austerity than the ancient Fathers of the Desert, or convert multitudes of sinners."
The Spiritual Combat, Chapter 1, Page 6, Paragraph 3, (Christianity, Catholic, Author: Dom Lorenzo Scupoli)

****

Swept through the tunnel of time, I found myself in a small house with several Chinese men and women. All of us were living with an aging master who we called 'Little Chinaman.' Very thin and bald, he was a gentle soul who taught us of the Way.

My current husband was a young Chinese man with jet black hair that shone in the light, a beautiful smile and very tall and muscular. Three other disciples lived with us, but Andy was Little Chinaman's prize student and friend, who took care of the house and grounds in exchange for his teachings.

Discussing our lessons, two other disciples and I approached Andy to ask him questions. As I approached, however, his aura became bright red and yellow, his rage obvious. Immediately, my over-self, which was observing from inside my former body, became aware that this sub-conscious anger resulted from our past lifetime during the Cavalry days.

Little Chinaman was in town for the day leaving our studies in the care of Andy, who responded to my presence by ordering me to do extreme and strenuous physical labor. Becoming very tired over time, I begged him to let me stop, but he pushed and pushed as his auric red intensified with every order.

Unexpectedly and suddenly, I went into cardiac arrest and died.

Shocked, this had not been his intent, and for years Little Chinaman tried to help him to get over what he had done, for he had no conscious desire for me to die. But Little Chinaman was wise and knew of our past life, and he helped Andy to overcome some of his rage during that lifetime and begin to forgive.

"Some lands are dirty, some are pure; Pleasant or painful, each is different. This comes from the inconceivable ocean of acts: Cyclic phenomena are always like this."
The Flower Ornament Scripture, Chapter 4, The Formation of the Worlds, Page 190, Stanza 3, (Buddhism, Mahayana)

****

Having traveled again through the time-tunnel, I found myself lying in a field of grass wearing a pale blue gown. Deeply in love, the object of my affection laid beside me, wearing the traditional knickers with stockings, black lace shoes, a vest and a puffy shirt. Telling me of a home he had bought for me, I didn't hear what he was saying due to my obsession with his piercing green eyes framed by locks of dark wavy hair.

But it suddenly became apparent to me that he was married and I was his mistress, a courtesan sometime in the 17th century. Intending to 'keep' me, he wanted to provide me with a home and all my other needs. Angered that he had not consulted with me in choosing a home, we began to argue, but I eventually agreed to move into the home he had chosen for me.

Before I could make the move, however, a sudden and unexplained break-up had occurred. It appeared that it was possible his wife had found out about us, and demanded that it stop. Never hearing from him again, I was heartbroken, and didn't marry in that lifetime.

Dropped into a later time in the same life as an old dying woman, I passed over to the other side and wandered aimlessly as a lost soul for several years. But at the very moment when I called out to God for help, an angel appeared and led me to a door. Inside, my lost love sat next to another man who appeared to be his son. Many people were gathered in the room, all of them appearing very young. As I floated in, I tried very hard to keep my hoop skirts quiet so as not to arouse attention, but they made no noise in the spirit wind.

When I came into view, my lost love turned and flashed a big smile, sending me an energy of great love. Drawing me to him, everyone was watching an event on the earth-plane below. Introducing me to his son, the grown man looked up in surprise. "So you are the woman my father loved so much!" Surprised by this, I acknowledged that it was mutual.

A very elaborate funeral was going on below, and I was unsure as to what the fuss was all about. Overflowing with joy, my lost love chimed, "My son, of whom I am very proud, was an important man!" Looking to see if I could recognize him, I was surprised to notice that he was a historical figure. A beautifully carved beige basket was lowered into the ground as the mourners cried.

As we watched, the angel conveyed to me that he could not have left his wife without a scandal, and they had stayed together for proprieties sake. Despite this, he had loved me very much and that love was real. Finally, she revealed that this was the same soul as that of Red Jacket. A light went on in my soul.

Taking my hand, we soared away. From the mind of the woman I used to be, I never considered my acts as immoral, because I was so lost in love that I never even considered the pain of those I'd hurt. Because of this fog I had chosen to live in, at the time of my death I became lost.

"Do not cling, in fondness and weakness, to this life. Even though thou clingest out of weakness, thou hast not the power to remain here. Thou wilt gain

nothing more than wandering in this Sangsara (illusion). Be not attached (to this world); . . ."
The Tibetan Book of the Dead, Book I, Part II, Page 103, Paragraph 2, (Buddhism, Tibetan)

****

"But if you are able to confess, I wish you to do so, and if you are able, and do not, you will be deprived of the fruit of the Blood."
The Dialogue of St. Catherine of Siena, A Treatise of Prayer, Page 173, Paragraph 1, (Christianity, Catholic, Words of God as Received in Ecstatic Vision, Author: St. Catherine of Siena)

And so it came to pass that I was taken into many past lives, all of which I confess to you now. For all of my lifetimes were seemingly stained with the sin of lust. And it appeared that the three key players (myself, my husband and the soul of Red Jacket) remained the same. For time immemorial, we had been incarnating over and over again, never understanding or transforming this horrid pattern of betrayal and lust. Further, Andy's greed and control issues remained a constant, also remaining unaddressed for aeons.

The seven deadly sins are a very important part of purification and they are as follows: Gluttony, Lust, Greed, Pride, Sloth, Vanity and Avarice. We all incarnate with certain stains upon our souls that have yet to be purified, and most of us have one prominent vice. For me, it was lust, for Andy, greed.

It is not the conscious desire of most souls to cause harm, and yet they do. Why? And how do we end the cycle of pain? The answer is purification, which comes about through a very involved eternal process to awaken the soul to its own delusions about the true nature of love, transform those perceptions, and alter the stimulus response through eternal understanding.

"The world, however, is given to pleasure, delighted with pleasure, enchanted with pleasure. Truly, such beings will hardly understand the law of conditionality, the Dependent Origination of everything; incomprehensible to them will also be the end of all formations, the forsaking of every substratum of rebirth, the fading away of craving, detachment, extinction, Nibbana."
The Word of the Buddha, Page 2, Paragraph 2, (Buddhism, Theravadan, Author: Nyanatiloka)

****

Soaring through time, I ended up in the body of an Indian woman on a reservation around the early 1900's. Living with my seven-year-old child, my Indian mother had died, and my father, an aristocratic white with gray wavy hair, was making one of his infrequent visits to see us. I felt nothing for this man, as he had not raised me.

Located near a small forest, our small square homes were built around each other in an almost circular fashion. Every night, the community would gather around the campfire to talk and share stories. My husband and the father of my little girl, was fighting in the war, and we missed him greatly.

Going to the commissary, we were stocking up on supplies. In the distance, I thought I saw a familiar face. "Gray Robe! Is that you?!" I called out, running towards the Indian man, but as he turned I could tell that he was trying to conceal concern. Somberly, the man replied, "Gray Robe has just been reported as Missing in Action." Beginning to cry, he continued, "We were good friends. He was very brave and he loved you and your little girl very much." Carrying the supplies, we returned together to the reservation.

At camp circle that evening, I remained silent. Standing up during the gathering, the man told the others of my husband's status. Our chief took me aside and patiently placed his hands on my shoulder.

Being very much in touch with the spirit world, he explained to me what had happened. "Gray Robe was in a healing lifetime," he said, "his aura was filled with the color green. Giving back to those he has taken from in the past, he chose to move on." Suddenly, it became clear to me that Gray Robe was an incarnation of Red Jacket, and he had given his life to pay back for the lives he had taken during the Indian wars. "Hold his love within your heart, and set him free." His wisdom was peaceful, and I knew he was right. Raising our hands to the sky, we both chimed to the heavens, "In our love we set you free, Gray Robe." While gazing upon the full-moon, I drifted away from the past and soared back to my current life.

"Perhaps I have lived before, In some strange world where first my soul was shaped. And all this passionate love, and joy, and pain, that come, I know not whence, and sway my deeds, are old imperious memories, blind yet strong, that this world stirs within me."
Reincarnation - An East-West Anthology, Western Thinkers, British, Page 146, The Spanish Gypsy

****

Traveling to a point in time which appeared to be several hundred years ago, I lived as a woman named Thread Bare in an Indian camp with my father, Night Bear. Our camp had split into three factions due to three differing perceptions: Night Bear led a group that believed in war and strength, the man I loved led a group that believed in unity through music, and I led a faction which believed in birth. Unable to meld our perceptions into one, we became separate.

Surrounded by mountains and pines, several women in our camp were preparing to give birth. Going into labor one clear dark night, a woman gave birth at the very moment that a lightning-bolt struck a tree. In honor of this exalted sign of birth, we named the baby, 'Lighted Pine.'

With the child's birth, we realized the stupidity of our separate ways, and we summoned the other camp leaders for a gathering to reconcile our differences. Radiating immense love, a woman from the camp of music spoke to me. "Now we can share our music with you, our way of perceiving." Smiling, I replied, "I would love to hear your music, it's wonderful that Lighted Pine has opened us to perceiving in many ways." Her gaze became serious, "It is good that you want to hear our music, as it is all written by our leader and they are all love songs written for you." Turning, she walked away, as a huge pine began to glow in the center of our camp. Becoming the center of unity for the people, it reminded us that the Lord shares differing gifts with differing people, and that when we close ourselves off to only our own, we lose a part of the wholeness which is God.

"The door of the lodge is soon opened for the second time, representing the coming of the purifying Power of the north, and also we see the light which destroys darkness, just as wisdom drives away ignorance."
The Sacred Pipe, Black Elk's Account of the Seven Rites of the Oglala Sioux, Chapter III, Inipi, Page 40, Paragraph 3, (Tribal, Oglala Sioux, Words of Black Elk)
"Which is the way to the dwelling place of the light, and where is the abode of darkness, that you may
take them to their boundaries and set them on their homeward paths?"
New American Bible, Old Testament, Job 38: 19-20, (Judaism, Christianity)

****

Leaving form and soaring through the time tunnel, I was dropped into the body of a brassy, short-haired blonde wearing a red cocktail dress which appeared to be from the twenties. My husband, who I immediately knew to be Andy, was wearing a hat and a gray suit which appeared to be from the same time frame, and he was mingling with guests across the room. We were at a big party being held in a red brick mansion with white pillars and a circular driveway. About 100 people were in attendance. Parked in front of the house were two model-T cars.

Very suddenly and from behind, I felt something being pressed to my back which I immediately knew to be a gun. Dragged to an empty room, I heard shots being fired in the room I had just left. The two men who had taken me here beat me and then shot me in the chest three times, and then rushed away from the scene of the crime.

Amazingly, I was still alive as the paramedics placed my body on a stretcher and took me to catch an awaiting ambulance. As we exited through the main room of the house, the coroner laid over my dead husband's body. Guests were watching anxiously as we were removed from the home.

Lying quietly in my hospital room, I knew I was close to death. Trying to phone the police to tell them who my attackers were, I didn't have the strength to call before losing consciousness, and I realized that they would never know that it was a mob hit.

When I returned to consciousness, I could still feel the pain from the gunshots. As Andy woke up, he asked me what was wrong. When I told him, he looked at me strangely and said, "I just had the exact same dream!"

"Resentment and anger, these are foul things, too, and a sinner is a master at them both. Whoever exacts vengeance will experience the vengeance of the Lord, who keeps strict account of sin."
The New Jerusalem Bible, Old Testament, Ecclesiasticus 28:1, (Judaism)
****

Traveling through the time tunnel, my spirit plummeted into the body of a woman, who was living on a ranch in the prairie in what appeared to be the 1800's Ranch. With hair of light brown, I wore a blue flower print dress with a matching bonnet, while my husband, a thin small man with long black wavy hair, a weathered cowboy hat, brown leather pants and a vest, stood next to me. Walking outside to meet our two children, a four year old girl and a two year old boy, I noticed the small three room cabin with a pillared porch behind us as we approached two farm hands who were working with the animals.

Suddenly, the sounds of galloping horses could be heard from the distance and before we could look up or respond, gunfire rang out. Three outlaws sped through in a flash, killing the two workmen and myself.

Continuing to observe from above, my husband was walking away from a freshly dug grave. Feeling a peaceful surrender, my spirit was calm in knowing that I had to go, and thus, I did.

"So we are always courageous, although we know that while we are at home in the body we are away from the Lord, for we walk by faith, not by sight. Yet we are courageous, and we would rather leave the body and go home to the Lord. Therefore, we aspire to please Him, whether we are at home or away."
New American Bible, New Testament, 2 Corinthians 5:6, (Christianity, Catholic)
****

Thrust through the time tunnel, I found myself surrounded by souls from the mob lifetime. Quite scared, I didn't know what to expect, and when they did absolutely nothing, I didn't know what to think. One of the murderers spoke, "We want you to know that we are very sorry that we killed you and your husband. As you know, our actions came as a result of our illusion and we have all grown and evolved since that time. We do love you very much, and we hope you can forgive us and let this go."

Energetically, I knew that this was sincere . . . without doubt, without fear. Although this felt somewhat strange, I accepted their apology and thanked them for taking the time to work this out with me.

"Remember the last things, and stop hating, corruption and death, and be faithful to the commandments. Remember the commandments, and do not bear your fellow ill-will, remember the covenant of the Most High, and ignore the offence."
The New Jerusalem Bible, Old Testament, Ecclesiasticus 28:6-7, (Judaism)
****

Sucked into another place and time, my spirit entered the body of a dark-haired woman, a blonde man with a very muscular physique standing beside me. Holding my arms, I had just been captured and brought to an illegal slave labor camp where women worked in the fields until they were sold to wealthy men as servants.

Appearing very Romanesque, I recognized this spirit as the soul of Red Jacket, who was apparently one in the same. I remembered how he had appeared to me in both ways in the coliseum to show me the connection.

Known for messing around with a lot of female inmates, I ignored his advances and pretty much blew him off. As a result, he began coming into my hut and talking with me for hours at a time, and eventually we developed a deeper friendship and love for one another. My life became easier as a result as he became more and more protective of me, giving me easier jobs and finding things I could do to help him with his work.

At some point, the illegal operation was discovered by proper authorities, who arranged for a siege on the camp to free the women. Women were running everywhere during the uproar, and amidst the chaos, I decided that I, too, must go.

Waiting for him to come with me for quite some time, I finally turned to leave before it was too late. Frantically running, I was at a safe distance when I heard his voice calling me. Turning, I saw him motioning for me to return, but there were also guards coming to retrieve me. This was my only chance at freedom and I took it. Staying to defend his world, I took off to find what was left of mine.

In a flash, I was no longer in the body, but watching from above as I observed him sitting in my hut with incredible sadness and tears showing upon his face. Surprised, I hadn't realized his feelings for me had been so strong. The spirit of Red Jacket appeared beside me, as I observed the irony of this switching of roles as prisoner and keeper.

"He that leadeth into captivity shall go into captivity."
King James Bible, New Testament, Revelation 13:10, (Christianity)
"As you have done, so shall it be done to you, your deed shall come back upon your own head."
New American Bible, Old Testament, Obadiah 1:15, (Christianity, Catholic)
****

CHAPTER TWO
Considering Reincarnation in Religions, Running from the Crow, Evil Past Lives, Avoiding Present Death by Agreeing to Atone for Past Life Debt, Cave Man, Dove Song and the Massacre, Gridimaria, Slave Dancer, Man with the Rose, Long Hair, Dark Maggots Exiting Body, Kusokway, Juliosa, Life with the Inca as the Deity of Ayacucho, Oil Baron, Reunion of Spirits from Hundreds of Past Lives, Original Sin from Parents, Mysteries of Reincarnation Demonstrated in the Ark.

****

Shall we pause for a moment to consider reincarnation? Reincarnation is an accepted tenet of many Eastern faiths, such as the Hindu's and Buddhists, and some western faiths including the Mystical Cabalists of the Jews, the Sufi's of Islam and the Gnostics of Christianity. Some of the Early Church Fathers taught this doctrine before it was declared heretical at the Council of Nicaea in the fourth century. Jesus spoke of reincarnation in the bible, but He spoke more deeply on the subject in the Pistis Sophia and other Gnostic Gospels.

"Jesus answered and said to him, 'Amen, amen, I say to you, no one can see the kingdom of God without being born from above.' Nicodemus said to him, 'How can a person once grown old be born again? Surely he cannot re-enter his mother's womb and be born again, can he?' Jesus answered, 'Amen, amen, I say to you, no one can enter the kingdom of God without being born of water and Spirit. What is born of flesh is flesh and what is born of spirit is spirit ... Nicodemus answered and said to him, 'How can this happen?' Jesus answered

and said to him, 'You are the teacher of Israel and you do not understand this? Amen, amen, I say to you, we speak of what we know and we testify to what we have seen, but you people do not accept our testimony. If I tell you about earthly things and you do not believe, how will you believe if I tell you about heavenly things? No one has gone up to heaven except the one who has come down from heaven, the Son of Man. And just as Moses lifted up the serpent in the desert, so must the Son of Man be lifted up, so that everyone who believes in him may have eternal life."
New American Bible, New Testament, John 3:3-15, (Christianity, Catholic, Words of Christ)

"Is it not rational that souls should be introduced into bodies, in accordance with their merits and previous deeds . . ."
"Every soul . . . comes into this world strengthened by the victories or weakened by the defeats of its previous life. Its place in this world as a vessel appointed to honor or dishonor is determined by its previous merits or demerits. Its work in this world determines its place in the world which is to follow this."
Reincarnation - An East-West Anthology, Page 36, Early Church Fathers, Contra Celsum, De Principiis, (Christianity, Catholic, Words of Origen)

"It is absolutely necessary that the soul should be healed and purified, and if this does not take place during its life on earth it must be accomplished in future lives."
Reincarnation - An East-West Anthology, Christianity, Early Church Father, Page 36, (Christianity, Catholic, Words of St. Gregory)

"Mary answered and said unto the Saviour: 'My Lord, before thou didst come to the region of the rulers and before thou didst come down into the world, hath no soul entered into the Light?' The Saviour answered and said unto Mary: 'Amen, amen, I say unto you: Before I did come into the world, no soul hath entered into the Light. And now, therefore, when I am come, I have opened the gates of the Light and opened the ways which lead to the Light. And now, therefore, let him who shall do what is worthy of the mysteries, receive the mysteries and enter into the Light.' Mary continued and said: 'But, my Lord, I have heard that the prophets have entered into the Light.' The Saviour continued and said unto Mary: 'Amen, amen, I say unto you: No prophet hath entered into the Light; but the rulers of the aeons have discoursed with them out of the aeons and given them the mystery of the aeons. And when I came to the regions of the aeons, I have turned Elias and sent him into the body of John the Baptizer, and the rest also I turned into righteous bodies, which will find the mysteries of the Light, go on high and inherit the Light-kingdom . . . The rest of the patriarchs and of the righteous from the time of Adam unto now, who are in the aeons and all the orders of the rulers, when I came to the region of the aeons, I have through the Virgin of Light made to turn into bodies which will all be righteous,- those which will find the mysteries of the Light, enter in and inherit the Light-kingdom.' (Elias is the Greek form of Elijah)
Pistis Sophia, Fourth Book, Page 293-294, (Christianity, Gnostic/Essene, Words of Christ)

"Behold, I will send you Elijah the prophet before the coming of the great and dreadful day of the Lord."
King James Bible, Old Testament, Malachi 4:5, Old Testament, (Christianity)

"And his disciples asked him, saying, 'Why then say the scribes that Elias must first come?' And Jesus answered and said unto them, 'Elias truly shall first come, and restore all things. But I say unto you, that Elias is come already, and they knew him not, but have done unto him whatsoever they listed. Likewise shall also the Son of man suffer of them.' Then the disciples understood that he spake unto them of John the Baptist."
King James Bible, New Testament, Matthew 17:10-13, (Christianity, Words of Christ)

"Naked I came forth from my mother's womb, and naked shall I go back again."
New American Bible, Old Testament, Job 2:21, (Christianity, Catholic)

"The victor I will make a pillar in the temple of my God, and he will never leave *it again.*

New American Bible, New Testament, Revelations 3:12, (Christianity, Catholic)

"And then cometh Yaluham, the receiver of Sabaoth, the Adamas, who handeth the souls the cup of forgetfulness, and he bringeth a cup filled with the water of forgetfulness and handeth it to the soul, and it drinketh it and forgetteth all regions and all the regions to which it hath gone. And they cast it down into a body which will spend its time continually troubled in its heart. This is the chastisement of the curser."

Pistis Sophia, Sixth Book, Page 315, Paragraph 2, (Christianity, Gnostic/Essene, Words of Christ)

"And these hand it over to their receivers, in order that they may lead their souls out of the bodies, - they hand over to them the peculiarity of the seals, in order that they may know the time when they are to lead the souls out of the bodies, and in order that they may know the time when they are to bring to birth the body."

Pistis Sophia, Fourth Book, Page 288, Paragraph 1, (Christianity, Gnostic/Essene, Words of Christ)

"For many are the pleasant forms which exist in numerous sins, and incontinencies, and disgraceful passions, and fleeting pleasures, which men embrace until they become sober and go up to their resting place. And they will find me there, and they will live, and they will not die again."

The Nag Hammadi Library, The Thunder: Perfect Mind, Page 303, Stanza 2, (Christianity, Gnostic/Essene)

"Whoever knows that he has lived before, and sees heaven and hell, and has arrived at the destruction of birth, him I call a brahman."

The Group of Discourses II, III. The Great Chapter, 647, Page 73, No. 647, (Buddhism, Theravadan)

"I mind not if I must pass through sextillions of lives, undergoing the throes of birth and the pangs of death; leaving behind me a heap of my mangled fleshly forms - if at last I find thee."

Whispers from Eternity, Page 21, Paragraph 2, (Hinduism, Kriya Yoga, Words of Paramahansa Yogananda)

"A single soul can be reincarnated a number of times in different bodies, and in this manner, it can rectify the damage done in previous incarnations. Similarly, it can also achieve perfection that was not attained in its previous incarnations. The soul is then ultimately judged at the end of all these incarnations. Its judgment will depend on everything that took place in all its incarnations, as well as its status as an individual in each one."

The Way of God, Part II, Chapter 3, No. 10, Paragraph 2-3, (Judaism, Author: Rabbi Moshe Chayim Luzzatto)

"The first light that God created was so bright that the worlds could not endure it. God therefore made
another light as a vestment to this one, and so with all the other lights, until all the worlds could endure the light without being dissolved. Hence grades were evolved and lights were wrapped in one another . . ."*

The Zohar (Kaballah), Volume V, Balak (Numbers), Page 301, Bottom, (Judaism)

"You were without life and He gave you life? Again, He will cause you to die and again bring you to life, then you shall be brought back to Him."

The Holy Quran, Part 1, Chapter 2, Section 3, No. 28, (Islam, Words of Mohammed)

"I died as a mineral and became a plant, I died as a plant and rose to animal, I died as animal and I was man. Why should I fear? When was I less by dying?"

Coming Back, Chapter 1, Page 4, (Hinduism), Quotation from Rumi, Poet and Mystic by R.A. Nicholson, 1950, Page 103, (Islam, Words of Sufi Poet Rumi)

"In the third chapter of St. John, in the verses three to nine, we find another incident which clearly refers to the rebirth of the Soul. Here Jesus is telling how important it is for a man to be born again in order that he may enter the Kingdom of God. Nothing is said as to how many times or how often a person must be reborn in order to purge the being of its sins and attain that purification

which would admit one to
the Spiritual Kingdom."
Mansions of the Soul, Chapter XII, Page 169, Paragraph 2, (Mystery Religions,
Rosicrucian, Author: H. Spencer Lewis)

****

Riding a horse frantically through a small western town, I was rapidly escaping the white men who followed. My long black braids flew in the winds and my buffalo dress was warm in the fall air. Up ahead, I saw three Crow Indian men and rode towards them, hoping they might help. As they turned and galloped away, I followed them, riding through the prairie grass and entering a plot of woods. "Why didn't they wait for me?" I wondered, but continued to follow. Losing them in the woods, I turned around and got off of my horse. Bending over, one of the Indian men placed an ax in my back. Searing pain enveloped me as I tried to leave my body, but I hadn't yet died. Only moments passed, however, before my body fell to the ground and I passed.

Meeting me on the astral plane, the Indian responsible asked forgiveness. Conveying that he had been misled by the white man to go against his own people, I knew that his words were true and sincere and accepted. Suddenly, I recognized this man as the same man who had shown me the map of my spiritual journey. "Of course I forgive you, and I thank you for the help you are giving me now." Relieved, he hugged me and left.

"If you have drawn your sword on a friend, do not despair; there is a way back."
The New Jerusalem Bible, Old Testament, Ecclesiasticus 22:21, (Judaism)

****

Kutahey appeared to me as an ancient priest in a white foggy realm. Many souls were present from a particular time when a tyrannical ruler had lived. Due to this man's incredible obsession with obtaining power, many atrocities were committed and lives lost. All the people in the room were victims of this terrible man, and I listened carefully as they spoke.

Moments later, Kutahey had each of us line up so that he could tell us who we were at that time. Waiting patiently, my turn came rather abruptly when Kutahey spoke quietly. Giving me a familiar name, one I remembered hearing from history although I knew nothing specific about this persons life, he smiled and said, "A man with sarcastic humor." Having no idea who this was, I asked him to tell me more and he said, "Hangaroo." Panicking, I asked, "Did I hang people?" Kutahey bent over and wrote the horrid name down on a piece of paper. "That is for you to find out, my dear one."

"For there is no part of the World void of the devil, which entering in privately, sowed the seed of his own proper operation, and the mind did make pregnant, or did bring forth that which was sown, Adulteries, Murders, Striking of Parents, Sacrileges, Impieties, Stranglings, throwing down headlong, and all other things, which are the works of Evil Demons."
The Divine Pymander of Hermes, Thirteenth Book, No. 44, (Mystery Religions, Egyptian/Hermetic, Words of Hermes)

Returning to my body, I was dumbstruck that my soul could have ever been in such a state of evil. Upon researching the name, I found it was all true, he had been an ancient tyrannical ruler who had done atrocious things.

Bowing in shame, I knew this experience was to teach humility. Our souls have journeyed a great walk, in days of glory and days of evil. No soul can be purified until it is willing to see the darkness within itself, and no soul can comprehend evolution until it absolves within itself the long ago and darkened past from which it came, with the present day seeker who absolves to know only God. If a soul were *not* in darkness from incarnations past, it would no longer be required to walk of the earth, a place where darkness purifies itself to become compatible to the light of God. Those who walk here, walk because their soul still retains the shadows, mysterious and deeply hidden. A soul must lift up outside of itself in order to see clearly, so that the greater part of itself may take dominance over the soul's flight.

"From that which was deficient in itself there came those things which came into being from his thought and his arrogance, but from that which is perfect in him he left it and raised himself up."
The Nag Hammadi Library, The Tripartite Tractate, The Imperfect Begetting by the Logos, Page 73, Paragraph 6, (Christianity, Gnostic/Essene)

****

Going to the front yard, I noticed a black thought-form sports car descending from the sky driven by a tall stocky man from India with short curly black hair. Motioning me to enter, I reluctantly did. "I am the messenger," he said, "I have come to tell you of my return." Confused, I responded, "What return?" He became very serious. "I will return for you in a short time. At this time, you will leave everything behind and come with me." Angry, I protested. "What, are you crazy? My husband and child would never forgive me if I died now." Waving his arms to the air, he began to show me aspects of this date of my death, and it appeared to be in the summertime. "But there is so much more to do." I said, after watching the thought-forms. "When I come to take you, you will have manifested everything you planned. We need you for other matters." I didn't say anything. "The spirit world is preparing for your return. Your tasks have just begun. You will know when I am coming for you." Looking down, I said, "But I just don't know. My family will be mad at me. A big part of me wants to go, but another would like to stay and watch the manifesting." Smiling, he replied, "Ultimately . . . it will be your choice when to go, Marilynn. Remember that you have known all your life that your stay could be short. However, you can change that decision and create something new." Returning to my body, I had a migraine. I had a big decision to make.

"My soul, confined in a fragile frame, cried for release. Within the fenced garden of the charming senses no more I loved to abide."
Whispers from Eternity, Page 157, Paragraph 2, (Hinduism, Kriya Yoga, Words of Paramahansa Yogananda)

****

It was about two weeks from the present, and I was about to witness from above what would be my future death. Three big men grabbed me in a crowded parking lot and threw me into their car. Driving for several hours, we ended up in the mid-west somewhere. A bunch of rednecks, they didn't do anything to hurt me, but they were careless drivers and we all died in a head-on collision on the highway. There was no pain, only freedom, but after I left my body, I was upset that my loved ones still in physical form could not hear or see me. Trying to communicate with them, I channeled, poked, jumped on their backs and put my hands over their face, but all to no avail. Looking at the angelic guardians awaiting me, I asked, "They won't be able to communicate with me?" Calmly, they replied, "They are not yet ready to do that, Marilynn. Do you now remember why you chose to incarnate?" Laughing, I said, "Probably so I could get them to pay attention to me." "Exactly, it is much easier to manifest with a physical point of power on the earth-plane. You chose to return for that very reason. This is also why you chose to create this possible time of departure; you never liked the limitedness of the physical plane." The angelic spirit chuckled. "Well, I've changed my mind." I said. "If I can't communicate with them from here, then I have to go back." Then it occurred to me that the reason the car carrying the messenger had been black was because my death would not have been pure, but still stained from unresolved karma if I had left at this early juncture. "Are you sure that is what you want to do?" They asked. "Yes, there is too much to be done for me to bow out now." The spirit reiterated. "You are making your final decision now, are you SURE?!" "Yes, I am." I said confidently.

Looking at the three guys who kidnapped me, I asked, "Is it okay if we call it even? We can all go back and agree that our karma is balanced." Agreeing wholeheartedly, they nodded their acceptance of my offer, and with that my potential death was altered. I raised my face to heaven, and gave a prayer of thanksgiving to the Lord.

"I have seen God, face to face, and my life has been saved."
The Five Books of Moses, The Schocken Bible Volume 1, Genesis, 32:31, (Judaism)
****

Entering the body of a young cave man, my father was at my side. Long grayish-black hair framed his old and tattered face, and he wore a small piece of animal hide around his midsection. Standing in a small plot of dirt, a cliff lay to my right and a small hill was in front of me. Very little vegetation was in the area, only a few small trees and bushes. In my hand was a long spear, and about twenty feet in front of me was a huge Mastodon.

The beast was intensely gazing my way, and I knew that I would have to make a move soon. It was imminent; it would be either him or us. My father whispered in my ear some words which came from a language I didn't recognize, but at the time, understood. "You must spear him in the heart," he said, "and you must get it right the first time. There will be no chance for a second try!" We were in grave danger.

Suddenly, the Mastodon got up, his thick legs and armor showing strength that I could not hope to match. Instinct took over, however, as the creature lunged forward. Pushing the spear in the direction of his heart, my father and I leapt back as he continued our way. It seemed clear that I had missed as the animal prepared to smash us with a single swipe of his front legs, but suddenly, he bent backwards and began to die. A small wound near the heart was evident when he rolled over. My father was very proud.

"The Master said, A man can enlarge his Way; but there is no Way that can enlarge a man."
The Analects of Confucius, Book XV, No. 28, Page 199, (Buddhism, Confucianism, Words of Confucius)

****

Gently guided into the body of a peaceful native woman from a long time ago, I was married to the chief of this small band of the Ute tribe, whose people had not yet been exposed to the white man. My name was Dove Song. Young and naive, we lived a very peaceful life until the white men eventually came.

On the occasion of the white man's arrival, our tribe threw a big party and danced for them, but the white men had come in military dress. In a completely unexpected move, they began firing at random at our people during the dancing and six were killed.

Taking myself and twenty warriors with him, the chief journeyed into the camp of the white man, still convinced that their harm was accidental and their intentions were good. The chief thought it might have been a misunderstanding, but just in case, we did bring a war party in addition to the twenty warriors which hid in the hills behind us, in case he was wrong.

Entering the camp, the white men led the chief inside a tent to talk. As soon as he was out of sight, the soldiers approached us. Holding a knife to the throat of each one of our warriors, a woman came towards me and held a knife to my stomach. In moments a command was given to kill each of us simultaneously. After she shoved the knife into my stomach, my body lay upon the ground dying, as she scalped my long black hair while I was still alive.

When the chief emerged from the tent, he screamed! "My beautiful Dove Song!" As his war cry began roaring across the sky-tops, havoc ensued as the hidden war party emerged. The chief died only moments later not far from my side. Remembering this now, I knew that this was the beginning, the first sign that the white man had come to do harm.

"It is time for all to seek deliverance from the pains of birth, death, old age, and sickness. Outflows of depravity and defilement are everywhere, and there is nothing in which you can find true joy."
The Three Pure Land Sutras, The larger Sutra, No. 33, Paragraph 3, (Buddhism, Pure Land, Words of the Buddha)

****

And so it came to pass that I traveled more and more into literally dozens of past-lives. Many of my lifetimes dealt with lust issues, unrequited love, danger, and unfulfilled dreams. From the ancient days of Maya when I was a queen, to my many lifetimes among the prairie as an Indian man and woman, to the medieval lifetime as Queen Gridimaria, a hermit who lived all alone in castles of stone. In fact, I was made to know of a legendary song which spoke of her, "She lives all alone, in castles of stone, who is this Queen . . . Gridimaria."

Performing with a troupe of actors in the middle ages, I never fulfilled my potential completely, and again was unrequited to the love of my life. An accomplished dancer from a poor family, I became a servant to a rich family whose man of the house often raped the help. Escaping with a man who loved me, I was free, but unable to fulfill my life dream as a dancer. A Jewish girl during the Second World War, I was spared the torment that so many Jews suffered in concentration camps, when I was shot fleeing from German guards. Many lives, as men, women, rich, poor, healthy, handicapped, from every culture of the world . . . but each bore the mark of karmic stain. And throughout this process, I underwent hundreds of vibrational raisings, and assisted scores of lost and sub-conscious souls.

"All these things arise dependently, from causes, yet they are neither existent nor nonexistent. Therein is neither ego, nor experiencer, nor doer, yet no action, good or evil, loses its effects. Such is your teaching."
The Holy Teaching of Vimalakurti, Chapter 1, Page 13, Stanza 4, (Buddhism, Mahayana)

"You associate with living beings by frequenting their migrations. Yet your mind is liberated from all migrations."
The Holy Teaching of Vimalakurti, Chapter 1, Page 15, Stanza 3, (Buddhism, Mahayana)

****

Nestled in the sky was a huge city of light built within the mountains. As I entered, I followed the huge corridors which led in every direction, watching thousands of souls fraternize. A meeting place of some sort; spirits were introducing themselves to one another and then walking off together. Many musical and creative souls were here, and everyone wore interesting clothing. Underneath a see-through illuminated gown, they wore a robe spun in colors and design that represented aspects of their soul, and those with similar designs seemed to be drawn to one another in their interests. Wearing a white gown with a very large coral pink rose emblazoned on the back, another friend was present who wore a gold-tone gown.

Continuing our journey through the city, we noticed that there were no true ceilings as the walls of light seemed to go on into infinity. Many of the hallways were of different colors and designs, but all of them glowed with the luminescent light of love. Turning a corridor, I noticed someone with a very familiar feeling wearing a similar rose who was talking to another male spirit adorned in blue. Observing a woman who was a vocalist in a band called 'Galaxy' wearing a gown of pastel colors vibrating together, she was spectacular.

Turning to leave, my friend wanted to explore another part of the city alone and we waved good-bye.

Instincts led me to a spiritual compound, a place to rest my soul. Finding somewhere to rest, I closed my eyes and absorbed the light. Suddenly, I felt a hand on my shoulder and opened my eyes to find the man with the rose standing above me smiling. Wavy brown hair framed his illuminating face, and his green eyes glowed like emeralds in his spiritual form. There was almost a blooming quality to his eyes which was very unique and mystical.

Standing up to greet him, he was initially very kind and polite, but suddenly his demeanor changed.

"By the way," he said, "I saw your friend stealing from you. I just thought you would like to be aware of what kind of person she really is." First I was angry, but then I calmed. "There is nothing for her to steal from me here. If it were true, it would not matter as all that I have is truly the property of the all that is, the oneness, which we are all part of. Everything belongs to all of us as there is plenty of abundance for everyone." The man with the rose smiled widely. "Very good," he said, "you are learning trust!"

Reaching to my hand, he guided me back to the heart of the city of light. "Surrender to trust and love," he said, as he stopped in the middle of a large corridor and raised his arms to the heavens, "we will meet again!" Looking into his deep emerald eyes, I nodded as I was then whisked through the heavens to my home.

"So let one's mind be guarded. Let one's domain be right thought. By putting right view to the forefront . . . a bhikku will forsake all bad destinations."
The Udana, Chapter 4, 4.2, Page 57, Stanza 1, (Buddhism, Theravadan, Words of the Buddha)

****

Emerging upon a city of light, I ascended a crystal staircase permeated with white light and walked through a long hallway before I entered a distant back room awaiting the entry of someone. Many people were waiting in this room, talking openly about their various roles in the manifestation of the work I was to bring into the earth, but as he entered . . . all became silent. Absolutely peaceful, his long black hair went all the way down his back and he wore a red buffalo skin. Speaking at the other side of the room, his very way was of calmness and serenity.

Moments later, he floated over to me, very quietly putting his hands on my shoulders. For a few moments, we just stared into each others eyes, feeling the intensity of this soul's vibration.

Communicating intense eternal love, I witnessed the way of the peaceful spirit. Wanting to touch his long black hair, he knew my innermost thoughts. "Please, touch my hair." Slowly, I lifted my hand to his hair. "It's so soft." I said. "And it's so long! Your whole being is so beautiful." Nervously, I moved back, but he came towards me. "You may call me Long Hair. Surrender your reality to spirit and flow within the now." Mesmerized by his entrancing gaze, he said, "My dear loved one. Once you experience truth, you cannot split yourself between the physical and the spiritual. You exist spiritually in the spirit realm, and commence physical illusory reality when you return to your body. You have transcended the illusion, and must bring reality into your illusion. You can no longer act according to illusion . . . anywhere."

Hugging me, he took my hand and placed it on his hair, again. Feelings surged through me as I felt his hair, memories of many days among the Indians, memories of my love for their ways. "Remembrance is food for the spirit, drink of it often. What I represent before you is a part of you that will never die. Feelings such as these flow into eternity, just as we who watch you from the sky fly with you always. Never doubt our love for you. Our separation is temporary, and our love is eternal. One such as you may find it difficult living in a reality devoid of intensity as you know it. Know that such intensity exists in the world of surrender, the world of truth. The world of spirit, my world, is yours, as it is every soul's." Cautiously, I looked up and he continued. "Surrender. Follow the longings of your spirit, once you let go, you will let us in. That is the time that I will return. An open spirit is an open sieve for us to travel.

We are with you always, but it is when you flow with the river of surrender that you become aware of us." Warmly embracing me, he turned to leave.

Another Indian man walked in the room, this one with short black hair. Searing eyes met mine, as everyone else left the room as he entered. "Do you remember who I am?" he asked, as he approached me. Saying nothing, I nodded; 'No.' Waving his arms, the room that we were in became a clear starry night sky.

Pointing to a galaxy in the distance, he took my hand and we soared towards it. Reaching a planet in the galaxy, we hovered above. A lifetime in this world played before my eyes, a love unrequited due to circumstance. He'd been an android, but a conscious form of life, and I was human. A union between our two forms of life was not possible. Although I loved him deeply, I knew that our differences were irreconcilable, so I let him go. Finding him a female android, they eventually fell in love.

"We have been together other times," he said, "the manifestations I show you now should be familiar." I couldn't remember no matter how hard I tried, but I could FEEL, and my spirit remembered the deep and true love between our souls. "That was a beautiful gift of love you gave to me in that lifetime," he said, referring to the lifetime on another world, "I am returning those gifts to you now. I am helping . . . we are all helping you to bring in so many things. You still cling to illusions, however, rather than surrendering to the wind of spirit."

Pausing, he looked into my eyes with a passion that made me feel inner conflict. "Try to remember the days when we walked the plains together, or the days of ancient Maya when you were my queen. We are who you think we are, but will not believe. Allow our Odyssey to descend and let Marilynn go, for she is but a vehicle. Our love is vast, indeed!" Intense eyes looking into mine, he suddenly was gone.

Entering into the body of an Indian woman, I was sewing a dress made of buffalo skin. Noticing my dark skin and long black hair which flowed forward when I bent over, I suddenly looked up to see an Indian man. Outside of the teepee arguing with his mother, she was trying to warn us that we were in danger. Living outside the Cheyenne encampment because I was from another tribe, one which the Cheyenne abhorred, she warned us of an impending attack.

In the night wind, we heard the sounds of distant drumming and the Cheyenne war call. "Whatever happens," my Cheyenne husband said, "KNOW that I love you." Quietly, I responded, "And I, you."

About twenty Cheyenne armed with knives and tomahawks burst into the teepee as a young brave grabbed my husband, slashing his hand. Feeling intense pain, I watched as he was taken away. Instantly . . . I felt absolute terror.

Running through the woods the next moment, the war party was chasing me, as within minutes my violent death occurred. Leaving the body as I hung upside down from a tree, slashed and bleeding, I could still feel the penetration of the knives as I returned to form.

"Taken by the waves of afflictions, sunk in the torrents, they are tormented by a hundred miseries in the triple world, wrapped up in the clusters, thinking of them as self - For their sake we strive, to release them from pain."
The Flower Ornament Scripture, The Ten Stages, Page 720, Stanza 5, (Buddhism, Mahayana)

****

Soaring, hundreds of maggots began exiting my body through the bottoms of my feet. Knowing that these disgusting little things were there because of old beliefs, negative thoughts, and delusional thinking, it appeared that some of that darkness of my karmic journey was beginning to be released.

As they fell out into the sky, they would slowly extinguish into non-existence and disappear. Apparently, it wasn't necessary to analyze each piece of darkness, just to allow it to dissipate.

Watching them fall, images of past lives were presented to me like a vision within a vision . . . a lifetime as a highway robber; a bedraggled man riding a mule in the desert looking for his next victim . . . a lifetime bound in a wheelchair . . . other lives of suffering through poverty, disease and injury.

Less than a millisecond passed before I was now looking upon a marble temple, the steps leading to its pinnacle at my feet. A group of souls was listening to a white-robed teacher, "All of you who have come today are bringing in changes," he said, "I have only one word for you, and that is love." Lowering his head, everyone began to feel an intense energy of love beyond words, and they immediately understood what he had meant.

"Hence virtue is perpetually feeble, the great strength of evil being extremely intense, and except for a Fully Awakening Mind by what other virtue will it be overcome?"
A Guide to the Bodhisattva's Way of Life, Chapter 1, No. 6, (Buddhism, Tibetan, Author: Shantideva)

****

Re-entering the spiritual spheres, I popped into the time tunnel.

Entering the body of a young Indian woman, I was holding a tiny newborn baby. Another woman lay on the ground recovering from labor. "Will you raise my baby?" she asked, "her father does not know that she is his and I will not tell him." "You should tell him, Clear Heart," I responded, "Kusokway will change for his baby." "No," she quietly retorted, "he will not know she is his. He lives in another camp and will never find out." Pausing a moment, she looked intently with great anxiety into my eyes. "Please, Lone Wolf Child, will you take my child and raise it as your own?" Noticing the tears in her eyes at such a heartrending request, I put my hand in hers. "It is an honor to be asked, and I will take this child as my own." Her face shone with relief as she looked at me with love and thanks. Moments later, she turned to sleep from the fatigue of labor.

Kusokway was a wild spirit who enjoyed many women and his freedom. A very handsome man, it was easy for him to get away with it.

Lone Wolf Child was my name in part because of my appearance. Not terribly pretty, I had a large bone structure which made me awkward, and my face was covered in pock marks from a bad case of acne. Consequently, I spent much time alone as men were not often attracted to me. Deep inside, however, I was terribly in love with Kusokway, though I always had known he would never have any interest in one such as myself. Nevertheless, the feelings I had whenever I was near him made me unable to let go of this love I held for his soul. Clear Heart had known this. Giving me Kusokway's baby, even under these circumstances, was an act of honoring my love for her *and* the baby's father. Having no desire to raise the child, she'd known that I did.

About six months after the child was born, I was unexpectedly needed in another camp. My skills as a midwife had become well-known, so I packed Wet Eyes (My child was named for her excessive crying) onto my back in a papoose, waiting for my escort to arrive before leaving for the other camp. Many Clouds, an old and wise man, was coming to protect me on my journey.

The three-day journey gave us much time to talk, and Many Clouds had known of my secret love for Kusokway and the birthright of this child. "You must tell Kusokway of his child," he said with exasperation, "we will be in his camp and he must know of the love you have offered his child." "But I am ugly," I said, "Kusokway will have no interest in me." Many Clouds looked at me with love and held my hand, "What I see is beauty of the spirit, perhaps you are not meant to be a Lone Wolf Child any longer. Promise me that you will at least tell him of his child." Thinking a moment, I lowered my head, "I will tell him of his child, but that is all."

As we arrived at the camp, the woman was very close to birth and my plans of speaking with Kusokway were postponed. Shortly after the child was born, however, an opportunity presented itself. In my confusion after the delivery, I took Wet Eyes and entered into a teepee, thinking that it was the one set up for us. To my surprise, however, I had walked into Kusokway's teepee. Sitting on the floor, he'd motioned for me to come over. "How is Corn of Light?" He asked regarding the condition of the woman who had just given birth. "They are both fine." I said. "She had a boy."

Turning to leave, he quickly stopped me, "Please don't go. I'm lonely and would welcome company." Nervously, I sat down, removing the papoose from my back. Holding Wet Eyes in my arms, I began rocking her to sleep. Kusokway tickled her feet, "What a tiny little baby, so much beauty in such a tiny package." Pausing, I quietly said, "I . . . I have something . . . " Kusokway interrupted me with a kiss. Putting the baby down to sleep on her blankets, Kusokway took me in his arms and pulled me beside him. Surprised, I hugged him intensely and returned his kiss when Kusokway got very nervous. "I hope you know that this is all there will ever be." He said, "There could never be more with you. I need a . . . uh . . . " Finishing his words for him, I said, "Pretty woman, I know and I don't care." As I was kissing his neck, he was suddenly in a different state of mind. Looking almost sickened by what he had said to me, we sat in silence for a few moments. "That is a horrible thing to say . . . or believe." Kusokway said. Replying nonchalantly, I said, "But I know I'm not attractive, it doesn't surprise me."

Suddenly, Many Clouds entered the teepee, and I began to sweat in fear. Looking at my child, I was afraid that I might lose her. Picking Wet Eyes up, I tried to remain calm for what may very well be the last time I could hold her. Many Clouds sat down, looking at me with expectancy. "I have something to tell you," I said to Kusokway, but Many Clouds jumped in, "The child, Wet Eyes, was born to Clear Heart and given to Lone Wolf Child at birth to raise. This child is yours Kusokway." Handing Wet Eyes to Kusokway, I tearfully got up to leave. "No!" Kusokway shouted. "Wait! You have taken care of my child. I am grateful. But why? Clear Heart is not dead." I couldn't say anything, so Many Clouds spoke for me. "It is out of love for you Kusokway. In your limited vision, you could only see what lay on the outside. But deep inside of Lone Wolf Child is a spirit filled with love for you and your child. When Clear Heart gave her your baby, she saw it as a great gift."

Kusokway now looked down upon the child which lay in his arms. "I will call you Kimosabi, for you are a friend I had lost, but have now rediscovered." Looking at me, he said, "You are no longer Lone Wolf Child, for I know who you are. You are Starlight! The Great Spirit has sent you to me in this way to teach me. I have looked in the wrong places to find love, and now love presents itself to me in a star, which in my limited vision, I saw only as a Lone Wolf Child." Taking my hand, he embraced me. "Will you join me in union, Starlight?" "Yes," I quietly said, "It would be an honor."

Flown to view a period later in time, I witnessed the entire family of Kusokway, Starlight, and Kimosabi happily going through life together, and I realized that Kusokway bore the spirit of my current husband, as Kimosabi bore the soul of my eldest daughter in this current life.

"The host of thieves who are my own disturbing conceptions will search for a good opportunity; Having found it they will steal my virtue and destroy (the attainment of) life in a happy realm. Therefore I shall never let mindfulness depart from the doorway of my mind. If it goes, I should recall the misery of the lower realms and firmly re-establish it there."
A Guide to the Bodhisattva's Way of Life, Chapter V, No. 28-29, (Buddhism, Tibetan, Author: Shantideva)

****

Traveling to the overlapping village around our home, a familiar Native

American man with short black hair loomed in the distance. Tall and wearing a business suit, he stood out because all the other natives wore tradition Native American dress. Remembering him as the one who'd talked of our days among the prairie and of ancient Maya when I was his queen, I felt deep love for his soul as conflict was emerging in my conscious self.

An old woman approached and quietly placed her hand on my shoulder. "I know of a person you should see." She said. "There is a woman who can tell you of your future." Leading me to a teepee, I waited outside. Two other women approached of whom I felt immediate remembrance. Hugging me, they said, "Did you see him, yet?" They seemed excited. "Yes, but it doesn't matter." I replied. Sighing heavily, they gave each other wearied looks. "Don't you know who he is?" They said in unison. Looking behind me, they shouted, "Oh, here he comes!"

Before I could respond, the man came from behind, putting his hand on my shoulder and smiling; but he continued moving and in a moment was gone. "Don't you see," they said, "he loves you!" Confused by their seeming obsession with this, I replied, "All he did was smile." The old woman returned and led me into the teepee.

A large old medicine woman with curly hair stood waiting. Motioning me to sit down she gazed deeply into my eyes. Taking my hand, she finally spoke. "Juliosa is coming." I immediately knew she spoke of the man I'd just seen. "He waits for your readiness, but he is coming." Saying nothing, I stared at her. "This is your future, my child, are you ready?" "I don't know." I said in astonishment. "How can this be?" "Juliosa wears a business suit because he has business to attend to." She said. "Will you allow yourself to experience the teaching of Juliosa?" Nodding hesitantly, I quietly said yes. Smiling, she motioned me to stand and led me out of the teepee. "Go now, my child, we will await your return."
****

Leaving form, I heard the phone ring. "Are you coming to our party?" The voice on the other end asked. Crossing through to the tribal community, a celebration was in progress. A group of people came towards me, staring at me with obvious interest. Each person in the group looked at me for a few minutes, and then moved aside to another behind him. When they reached the end of the crowd, my heart began racing as Juliosa stood waiting for me, wearing a business suit of white. "Who are you?" I asked as he came closer, not yet recognizing him. Quietly and slowly he approached. Putting his hands on my shoulders, and gazing into my eyes, I asked again, "Who are you?" He did not answer, but slowly walked away.

Sitting alone by a tree, I was lost in my conflicted thoughts, as the man approached again from behind and sat next to me. Hugging me tightly, I looked into his face, "Oh, my God!" I said, "You're Juliosa!" He still said nothing, but it was clear that he was happy that I'd recognized him. Taking my hand, he held it tightly and closed his eyes, as he began sending me the energy of remembrance. Feeling very uneasy with remembering such things, I jumped up and began to run away. "Don't go!" were his first words to me, but although I couldn't understand my reaction, I had to go!

Jumping into the rock tunnel, I soared through to the third dimension. "Why?" I thought to myself, "Why did I leave him?" Sending him my telepathic sorrow, I thought, "I'm sorry, Juliosa. I will come back; I do not know why I left." "It is okay," the return came, "you will understand soon enough." As the morning star arose on my horizon, I mourned my own fear and the loss of time with this unusually mesmerizing soul.
****

Juliosa stood amongst the clouds immersed in white light holding his arms to me. Coming closer, remembrance began to seethe. "I remember you." I said to him. "Yes, you remember me now." He replied. "But why do I fear you so much, Juliosa?" Hugging me tightly, he pointed to the tunnel of time. "The answers you seek will be found through the tunnel."

Entering into the body of a young woman, I was dressed in a fireman's uniform. Driving to work, a tall man with light-brown hair of medium build was sitting next to me. Immediately, I knew it was Juliosa, but his name at this point in time was Kenneth. As we were both firemen, I was giving him a ride to work. The firehouse had two fire trucks, and there was a large open area used for daily training activities in climbing and rescue. Pulling my long blonde hair back, I secured it in a barrette.

Ken had been joking around about quitting his job and he looked at me flirtatiously. "Well, if you're going to be working here, then I'm not quitting my job." Over time, our playfulness developed into a deep love and we became inseparable.

One day, an incredibly bad fire was reported and we responded quickly to the massive building which was totally ensconced in flames. Fighting from different locations, Ken and I were part of a rescue team which went inside the building to help the remaining victims emerge. But soon after we got the last of them out, an explosion rocked the entire building before he and I were secured. I blacked out.

Waking in a hospital, my conscious mind was alert, but my body was in a coma. Listening to everyone around me, I never left my body, but I was able to see through my spiritual eyes. Feeling guilty that I couldn't make myself wake up, I listened with expectation to everyone who came to tend my wounds, hoping that somebody would speak of Ken's fate and give me a reason to wake up. No one spoke of him for days and I assumed the worst, my will to live decreasing with each hour. I sunk deeper into my coma.

A few days later, Ken was wheeled into my room, paralyzed from the waist down. As I watched him observe my lifeless form, I saw a need in his eyes, a reason to wake up. Trying very hard to return, I still couldn't, but I twitched and made slight movement, enough to gently touch his hand. Both of us knew at this moment that I would come back; it was just a matter of time.

Pulled from the body, I soared back through the tunnel to the space above my bedroom where Juliosa awaited me. "What a beautiful love we had, Juliosa." I said. "Yes," he replied, "and it forever lingers." After a long gaze, he smiled one last smile, and simply vanished.

God is love. Therefore, all that I now felt was God. I had an epiphany. My love IS God. Whenever we feel this sort of eternal love, we are feeling the true, unfathomable presence of Our Lord . . . God.

So there were two definite strands of karma, one linked to the soul of Red Jacket, and the other to Juliosa. I made note of this in my mind.

"A person who is constantly engaged in devotional service to Krsna and who chants His holy name becomes so transcendentally attached to the chanting that his heart becomes softened without extraneous endeavor. When this happens, he exhibits transcendental ecstasies and sometimes laughs, sometimes cries, sings and dances - not exactly in an artistic way, but just like a madman."
The Teachings of Lord Caitanya, Chapter 19, Page 208, Paragraph 1, (Hinduism, Bhakti Yoga, Author: A.C. Bhaktivedanta Swami Prabhupada)
****

Entering into an Incan lifetime by the edge of Lake Titicaca, I lived with my husband in a small home by the lake. Few of the people were allowed to live outside the city gates, but because I was considered a 'deity,' it was permitted that my husband (who was my present day husband, Andy) and I could do so. Sensitive to spiritual presences, some of the Incans were able to see them. As I was adept at astral flight, my task was to fly about the city doing what could be considered astral dance. A form of praise to God, my spiritual gift was honored.

Other townspeople lived in small huts cloistered around a great stone sun temple where the king lived. (He was an aspect of the soul of Red Jacket) Very few people had been inside this grand palace.

Flying about the city on a daily basis, I would sit in the lotus position on a stone pedestal, where my body would remain as my spirit flew. Because of my special gift and the unique beliefs of the Incans, I was revered as a princess of the Gods, so to speak. At the same time, they feared me, calling me the 'Deity of Ayacucho.'

Arriving on our continent and camping far outside of our cities, the Spaniards had become a controlling force and were greatly feared.

One day while performing my art, something happened. Returning to my body, the king was waiting at my side. "I want you in my temple!" He said. "I have admired you and I find you beautiful." With respect, I said, "But my great king, I am already communed with another soul." Taking my hand without reply, he led me inside the temple.

Having never been inside the temple, the hallway was painted orange. Faces of many kinds were painted in brilliant colors on the high ceilings and walls, between them were images of suns. Taking me to a room with stone steps leading to a platform, the kind said, "I will take care of the matter of your husband." Leaving me under heavy guard, he was gone.

Concerned by his words, I was unable to leave the temple physically, so I went into trance and left form. Taking a very large fish net held together by bamboo poles with him, the king had gone off to see my husband, asking him to repair a few broken strings. Climbing in the net to repair it, the king quickly tied him to it and threw him in the lake to drown. Calling to his brother for help as he happened to walk by, he turned the other way and didn't respond. No one dared to interfere with the king, not even one's own family.

Heartbroken, I turned and flew back to my body. Interestingly, however, I found that this type of random violence and murder was an accepted and understood practice. Despite my sorrow, I accepted it.

When the king returned, a group of Spanish soldiers had arrived. Outside of the temple they had organized the Incan people for some strange practice which was called the 'seven-pick.' Everyone was terrified because this meant that the Spaniards would choose seven people for random killing.

A fat man with a beard, moustache and a wrap about his head, led the brigade. Terribly cruel and sick, he enjoyed instilling fear.

Begging the king to interfere, he said, "You are now my queen, say what you wish." Having picked a member of an albino family, who were unique in that they were all born with blonde hair and red eyes giving them the status of deities, they chose the eldest daughter who was a beautiful woman with long white hair. Approaching the Spaniard in anger, I said, "You will not touch her, she is a princess." Looking into my eyes with a sick glare, he replied, "I will kill who I want, we are here for our seven." Grabbing him, I repeated loudly, "YOU WILL NOT TOUCH HER!" My eyes were almost touching his, but he didn't recognize me, because if he had, he would have backed off.

Spaniards feared me because they were highly superstitious and they knew that the 'Deity of Ayacucho' was a 'bearer' of powers from the other side. In their eyes, I would have been something of a witch, although their perception was quite untrue.

Another Spaniard released the albino. "Take her back you coward!" The leader called to him, but he refused. "You may want to make an enemy of the deity," he replied, "but I do not." Pulling back, the fat man finally recognized me. "Aye Ammente!" I said, as an unseen force began to push them back. Although they couldn't see it, I was able to see a conglomeration of angels who had pulled together and formed an energy field. Placing my hand on his shoulder, I said, "You can deal with me personally if you do not leave now!" In fear, they ran, but we knew they would return.

Praying to God to thank him, the people then returned to their daily routine. Over time, I fell deeply in love with the king who was very clearly the same soul as that of Red Jacket, despite the horrid act that he had committed, which remained as the greatest conflict I had during that lifetime. I found this very strange to remember.

"Between heaven and earth, the five realms are clearly distinguishable. They are vast and deep, extending boundlessly. In return for good or evil deeds, happiness or misery ensues. The result of one's karma must be borne by oneself alone and no one else can take one's place. This is the natural law. Misfortune follows evil deeds as their retribution, which is impossible to avoid."
The Three Pure Land Sutras, Larger Sutra, No. 39, Page 300, Paragraph 3, (Buddhism, Pure Land)

****

Hovering amongst the tunnels of time, my soul was rendered into a time when Andy was my father, a rich oil baron, controlling and difficult. A man who bore the soul of Red Jacket worked for him, and we had fallen in love. Thinking that this man was not good enough for his daughter, my father plotted to have Red Jacket killed.

At one of the pipeline's where Red Jacket often worked, he planted an explosive device. I'll never forget the shocked expression on my father's face when the bomb went off, for he hadn't known that I was with Red Jacket at that moment, and it was already too late. Both of us died.

"Hence, because of the natural working of karma, there are innumerable kinds of suffering in the three evil realms through which wicked beings must pass, life after life, for many kalpas, with no end in sight. It is indeed difficult for them to gain release, and the pain they must undergo is indescribable."
The Three Pure Land Sutras, Larger Sutra, No. 39, Page 301, Paragraph 1, (Buddhism, Pure Land)

"Love does indeed occur apart from wisdom, but this love is characteristic of human beings, not of the Lord. Wisdom too occurs apart from love, and while this wisdom is from the Lord, it does not have the Lord within it. It is like winter's light which does indeed come from the sun, and yet the essence of the sun, which is warmth, is not within it."
Divine Love and Wisdom, No. 139, Paragraph 2, (Christianity, Swedenborgianism, Author: Emanuel Swedenborg)

****

Passing through the doorways of time, I experienced a peaceful death and was swept away to a reunion of spirits from hundreds of my past lifetimes. Emotions were high in seeing so many souls who held such importance to me although, in most cases, I could not place my memories of them.

While enjoying this reunion with so many familiar souls, a friend pulled out a very physical book. Solid and colorful, my friend said, "Your destiny awaits, you must return to the other side." Allowing me to peruse the title, it said, 'Red Jacket Reunion.' I didn't understand.

Looking around and beginning to feel the timeless nature of existence, I peered upon the faces of those I'd known throughout all the ages. Emmanuel appeared and sat down next to me, his face tearful. Taking the book from my hands, he opened it and began conveying that the contents of the book held my future. Beyond this, he conveyed that I would be unable to return to the hereafter until the book's contents were fulfilled. "Who among us knows the name, of timeless veils linger call, reach through distance, tender tide, prepare to catch the fallen souls." Emmanuel said this as hundreds of contractual agreements fell into my lap of souls I must aid. "You'll be a sieve through which knowledge moves," he said, as he pointed out that I was again wearing a wedding gown. "You are to reach the ascension in this lifetime."

Nodding and confused, I said, "I don't know if I'm worthy of that . . . I don't know if I'm able . . ." With tears in his eyes, he said, "You *must* make the choice now, as to whether or not you will achieve the marriage of spirit to matter in this lifetime!" "Okay," I said, cautiously, "I will do everything I can to reach this ascension you speak of, please teach me and hold me in check so that I will not falter from the path to attaining it." Nodding, he wiped a tear from his face. Holding back something he knew, there was something he wasn't able to tell me about . . . something to come.

Uneasy, I slowly walked away from timelessness towards time. Emmanuel called to me from a distance just before he disappeared, "Contemplating the night and all that it means, the rhythms of life, the movement of streams, the flow everlasting, entry to form. Go . . . find your pathway, and then come quickly home." Tears filling my own eyes, his image dissipated into the ether.

"Lord, I consider Your Lordship to be eternal time, the supreme controller, without beginning and end, the all-pervasive one. In distributing your mercy, you are equal to everyone. The dissensions between living beings are due to social intercourse."
The Teachings of Queen Kunti, Chapter 11, Page 71, Srimad Bhagavatam 1.8.28, (Hinduism, Bhakti Yoga, Author: A.C. Bhaktivedanta Swami Prabhupada)
****

"Go," said the woman who now stood with me in a cornfield, as a huge tunnel loomed in the sky, "you're ready for the 'House of the Mysteries.'" Stone steps led to a huge cavernous tunnel. Stones surrounded the entrance like a rock wall. "The door is deceiving," the woman said, "it appears very large, but it will change. It will shrink and become very small, but you mustn't fear it, if you wish to see Eden."

Proceeding with care, I noticed that other people were within the tunnel, but despite their presence, I felt absolutely alone. As the tunnel began to meander, my spirit was its back as if riding down river. Closing in on me now, the tunnel began to shrink just as I'd been warned and within moments, it was only a tiny ribbed cage with an unusual white substance flowing like a river. Claustrophobic, it took an act of will to not be afraid.

As suddenly as it started to shrink, it began to open up again, and I saw the gate to the House of the Mysteries in the distance. Walking through the gate, I was surprised to realize that I had entered some kind of floating gazebo. Up in the air, I saw the Garden of Eden floating.

Given entry, I walked into the bounteous garden and was greeted by a spirit who pointed out that you could see the Earth from this place in the heavens. Speaking of original sin, the spirit conveyed that it is not the sin of Adam and Eve for which we are accountable, but our own sins which we have been born into, via our karmic entanglements in past-lives. Original sin is the sum of our own actions which follow us as we journey the repetitious cycle of transmigration. Original sin is karma. Represented symbolically in the story of Adam and Eve by their failure to obey God, this sin is the root of all sin, which is the essence of karma.

Beyond this, I was given understanding into the concept of the sins of the father's having been visited upon the sons. Through example, the seeds of a parent's particular vice are naturally amended into their children. Although you are not accountable for the sins of your parents, you *are* accountable for the aspects of your parent's vice that you embrace. By the nature of the laws of existence, you take on some of the dark influx that your parents have within them, and you become subject to the laws of cause and effect in regard to their actions. Therefore, parent's sins can be visited upon the children.

Parents are chosen because of the knowledge they can impart to the soul. Sometimes they teach virtue, sometimes they teach vice, all depending upon the needs and spiritual condition of the souls involved. If you are born into darkness, the purpose remains rebirth into the light, rather than an acceptance of wrong view, karmic circling, and backwards motion.

Being an upperworld, the Garden of Eden existed in the ether above the Earth, and down below I could see the underworlds residing in their own spheres. "The garden is a gateway," the spirit said, "a place where the mortal ignite immortal paths."

"O Adam, look at that garden of joy and at this earth of toil, and behold the angels who are in the garden - that is full of them, and see thyself alone on this earth, with Satan whom thou didst obey. Yet, if thou hadst submitted, and been obedient to Me, and hadst kept My Word, thoudst be with My angels in My garden. But when thou didst transgress and hearken to Satan, thou didst become his guest among his angels, that are full of wickedness; and thou camest to this earth, that brings forth to thee thorns and thistles."
The Lost Books of the Bible and the Forgotten Books of Eden, Adam and Eve, Chapter LVI, Verses 2-4, (Christianity, Judaism)
"Gardens of perpetuity, wherein flow rivers, to abide therein. And such is the reward of him who purifies himself."
The Holy Qur'an, Part XVI, Chapter 20, Section 3, No. 76, (Islam, Words of Mohammad)

****

When Andy awoke, he conveyed a story of how he had been taken to a glorious Native American temple. Given his true name, 'Tree of the Rainbow,' an old man appeared in a fetal position. Hundreds of lighted hands were motioning Andy to come closer, and as he did, the old man became the sacred Indian chief. Embracing, the two became one. Celebrations ensued.

****

And so it came to pass that I was initiated into the mysteries of the ark (Noah's ark) which is the key to crossing the ages, and is linked to reincarnation. Pyramidal elements appear, forming a vortex, placing the soul upon the ark to find its successive link of existence. Very complex and difficult to describe, I watched the mystical process of a soul reincarnating into another lifetime.

****

CHAPTER THREE

Karma Hits the Ground, Red Horse, Sacajawea Guides Across the Great Divide Between Karma and Knowledge, Pleiadian Ships Descend with Faces of all of my Existences, Essence, Karmic Memory, Spiritual Ether, Katharine - Spy, Red Horse Lifetime, Lemuria, Appreciation of Role in Seeing Who People Really Are, Spanish Woman, Toam Arrives to Guide, Nature of Karma, Scotland, Knife of the Emerald, Ancestral Hand, Nature of Karma, Scotland, Knife of the Emerald.

****

Leading me to a bus that was waiting outside, an Indian man was staring at me whose name was 'Red Horse.' (Although I didn't know it at the time, he appeared to me in the manner in which he was presently incarnate, and this was the soul of Red Jacket.) 'Red Jacket Reunion' splashed through my head like a torrential flood. Taking one last glance at this mysterious man, I walked away.

While awaking, my spirit became conscious while my body was deep in vibration. Hearing a knock inside of my head, I telepathically conveyed, "Please, please come into my spirit." A sudden torrent of energy burst and exploded inside of me as a very high celestial being began its entrance into my form. "I am timeless, a being of God." The voice sounded like that of a very old woman. "I am you," she said, "the highest part."

"Heaven's peace, being something Divine which most deeply touches with

blessedness the good itself which is in angels, does not reach their conscious perception except as follows: through a pleasure of heart when they are engaged in the good proper to their lives, through a sense of fitness when they hear something true that is in harmony with their good, and through an exhilaration of mind when they perceive their bonding."
Heaven & Hell, Chapter 32, No. 288, Page 211-212, Bottom & Top, (Christianity, Swedenborgianism, Author: Emanuel Swedenborg)

****

Rotting at their foundation, holes had formed in spots amongst the walls that now surrounded Andy as he desperately tried to repair them where the light was shining through. Opening in more and more, places, he couldn't do it, and huge block letters appeared forming the words, 'Dont's' and 'Should's.' Fighting internal programs which were blocking out the inflow from heaven, they made it difficult for him to accept or experience love.

A rainbow pathway appeared beckoning both of us to travel its road, but he couldn't yet go. "I'm sorry, Andy, I'm moving on." I said, as I grabbed hold of the movement.

Up ahead, was a woman that I remembered seeing with the Chief upon the cliff, the one with the gift of the purple rose. Holding a book and sitting in lotus position, a message was encoded above her head in petroglyphs. Horizontally, a line of symbols appeared; a series of three rectangles, one triangle, three rectangles, one triangle . . . etc. The rectangles represented Earthly lives, while the triangles represented transcendence. Triangles represent the karmic journey of a soul in that the bottom base is the symbol of multiplicity and separation, while the top-point is the symbol of unity and oneness with God. The wide base of the triangle represents the view of many lifetimes and an unfocused chaotic perception, while the top-point holds a single focus on God. Everything in-between represents the journey of the soul from multiplicity to oneness, showing the gradual narrowing of view to the one cause.

Calling herself 'Sacagawea,' because her purpose was to lead souls across the great divide, she conveyed that I must lead Andy to her. Directing me to look upon the rainbow path, she said, "I come in disguise, the rainbow my form, the path of the rainbow, leads sleeping to dawn. Those dwelling in fear may stall throughout time, but those seeking redemption, must cross this line." Pointing out the yellow band upon the rainbow, she said that I must now seek the path of illumination. Thrust upon this pathway in a frenzy, I looked behind me.

Andy had borne through his wall and met Sacagawea. Stroking her long black hair, it seemed that this action held energetic purpose in freeing the soul. Looking upon a triangular pyramid, she directed him to fly from the base of multiplicity through the top-point of one in one tremendous surge of power.

"In time Unity will perfect the spaces. It is within Unity that each one will attain himself; within knowledge he will purify himself from multiplicity into Unity, consuming matter within himself like fire, and darkness by light, death by life."
The Nag Hammadi Library, The Gospel of Truth, No. 25, Verse 9-20, (Christianity/Gnostic)

****

Led to a forest by invisible spirits, I kneeled in a glen and glanced at the full moon above. "You live under my essence." The moon replied. "You hear the voice of the birds." Taken aback by the moon communicating with me, I listened with intrigue. "The violates won't listen so you must become my voice. The laws of nature must be followed and respected. Man likes to control everything, including life, so I need you to help me. The initiate must make an oath to all that is of the light. Your higher self awaits in the stars."

Bowing my head lightly, I called out instinctually, "I make this promise to the moon in the sky. I will hold nature most high and sacred. And I shall only use the power of the light with the purest of intentions."

Opening grandly, the skies were filled with Pleiadian vessels which approached from all directions as cloudbursts exploded, lightning cried out and faces began forming right in the sky. Understanding that these faces were all my own, I was witnessing a panoramic display of my many lifetimes upon the Earth. A voice came from the space vessels, "These faces are you and they join you right now." Knowledge of each lifetime entered me. "I'm ready!" I shouted to them, "All that I am, and all that I will be relies on this moment. Let Odyssey descend." (Odyssey was the name of my highest self)

Everything began to calm as the mother ship began to glow and a beam began emanating from its bottom. Watching from the side, Andy said, "I'm proud of you honey, go take the next step." Looking above me, I replied, "All that I am, and all I will be, relies on this moment, reuniting with the Pleiades." Odyssey appeared as an old woman with a bun in her hair, but as she descended, her image changed into many forms, encompassing all who had lived and died under her herald. As she entered my spirit, she said, "The memory of all you have been is now back. Hold your oath to the moon sacred, forevermore."

Falling through a large luminous tunnel together, we re-entered the earth.

"Canst thou bind the sweet influences of Pleiades, or loose the bands of Orion?"
King James Bible, Old Testament, Job 38:31, (Christianity)

"He found that, at the very same time that the Dragon Star (The North Star) was in alignment with the Descending Passage (On the Great Pyramid), that beautiful and much admired little stellar cluster, the Pleiades or Seven Sisters in the Constellation of Taurus (The Bull), was in alignment with the scored lines."
(Ascending Passage)
Pyramidology, Book I, Chapter VI, Page 92, (Christianity, Pyramidology, Author: Adam Rutherford)

****

And so it came to pass that the four elementals returned to me with three more to teach me of the process of death and re-birth. Meeting 'Essence,' 'Karmic Memory,' and 'Spiritual Ether,' I learned that Fire, Earth, Water and Air are elementals of the earth, while the remaining three serve the function of karmic re-birth. The Essence creates astral fragments, Karmic Memory stores karmic data, and Spiritual Ether blends matter with spirit to create re-birth. The elementals are the choreographers of earthly existence.

"The sacred seven, reminders of the galactic origins of Mayan culture, are also the seven isosceles triangles we see each year . . . in Chichen Itza, Yucatan. There, the masters teach us in a living way, and you and I can experience the sacred moment when Kukulcan/Quetzalcoatl arrives to imbue us with cosmic energy. At that moment, we feel the vibration of Hunab K'u as the only giver of life."
Secrets of Mayan Science/Religion, Chapter 5, Page 121, Paragraph 5, (Tribal, Mayan, Author: Hunbatz Men)

"Say all these things with fire and spirit, until completing the first utterance; then, similarly, begin the second, until you complete the seven immortal gods of the world. When you have said these things, you will hear thundering and shaking in the surrounding realm."
The Ancient Mysteries, Chapter 7, The Roman Mysteries of Mithras, The Mithras Liturgy, Page 216, No. 615-620, (Mystery Religions, Mediterranean)

****

"Many object to the doctrine of Re-Birth on the ground that the experiences of each life, not being remembered, must be useless and without value. This is an erroneous view of the subject, for while such experiences may not be fully remembered, yet they are not lost to us at all, but really form a part of the material of which our minds are composed. They exist in essence in the form of

feelings, characteristics, attractions, repulsions, etc."
The Secret Doctrine of the Rosicrucians, Metempsychosis, Page 177, Paragraph 1,
(Mystery Religions, Rosicrucian)

"Thou must still be tried upon the earth, and be exercised in many things. Consolation shall from time to time be given thee, but abundant satisfying shall not be granted. Be strong therefore . . . thou must put on a new man, and be changed into another man."
The Imitation of Christ, The Third Book, Chapter XLIX, No. 4, (Christianity, Catholic, Author: Thomas A Kempis)

Standing at the ancient burial site, a familiar face could be seen approaching from the distance. Red Horse approached slowly, carrying something in his hands. Looking deeply into my eyes, his gaze did not cease to meet mine at any point during his slow approach. When he arrived, he placed the animal skin he had held in his hands over my shoulders. "This is my gift to you." He said. Looking up, I noticed Long Hair standing beside a tree in the distance, watching the interaction on this dark night.

"With the young woman's feet planted in the slanting doorway where an older female relative could see them, the man would cover their shoulders and heads with a special courting robe and make his case."
Walking in the Sacred Manner, Chapter 4, Adulthood, Page 78-79, (Tribal, Plains)
****

Plummeting into the body of a blonde woman named Katharine; I was sitting in the woods somewhere in South American being briefed on the next assignment. Involved in a covert operation in the jungles, there was great danger here. Sitting next to me was a man with dark piercing brown eyes which revealed his true identity, that of Red Jacket. But at this time, his name was Dave.

Concerned about a woman being involved in such a dangerous operation, I shrugged all of them off. "Having a woman around will only make our cover more believable." I said. "But you don't look like a woman from these parts," the crew leader said, because most of those on our team were dark-skinned. Looking at Dave, I said, "Well, Dave doesn't look very South American, either." "That's true." They replied. "But that doesn't mean he isn't handsome in his own special way." I added, knowing that he was shy, and I was bold.

Spying on some sort of illegal activity in the jungles, we hid our camps among the thickest brush. Tripping and spraining my ankle one day, Dave rushed to my aid. But he wasn't a big man and was unable to carry me. Angry, he yelled at me. "I want to get you out of this operation! This work is dangerous. A time will come when I can no longer take care of you." Rather angry at his attitude, I was also confused by his apparent sense of impending death. "Come on, Dave, you're not going to die! Besides you'd be surprised what I can do in an emergency." Releasing his arm, I ran off into the woods on my injured foot. Laughing, he followed.

Spending many nights around the campfire talking about our dreams, we had obvious deep feelings for one another. One evening while sitting around the fire, he looked up at me very seriously. "If we ever get out of here alive, I'm going to marry you." Taken aback, I asked, "What's holding you back, now?" "I can't," he said, "not when I don't know what will happen, if I'll leave you behind. I worry about you being with us, I couldn't stand it if you . . . nothing." Moving closer, I hugged him. "That's the nature of this business, sweetie."

Suddenly, we heard something which sounded like a vehicle approaching. Dave looked up, "I have a bad feeling," he whispered, "on your back!" Diving immediately beneath a tree, machine gun fire ripped at us as the hooded driver aimed for us. Moments later, it was over. My leg was grazed but otherwise I was fine. Looking up to see how Dave had fared . . . my scream echoed through the night wind, as the blood oozed slowly down his back.

Shot in the back, it appeared very serious but he was still alive . . . just barely. "Oh, my God," I cried out, as I noticed that the others were miraculously unharmed because their shelters were skillfully hidden behind huge rocks and barriers. Dave tried to speak but his words were a jumble, "I can't take care of you anymore." "Shut up!" I yelled at him angrily. "I don't need you to take care of me! I'm going to take care of you." Trying to make him more comfortable, I turned him over but couldn't move him. Whispering in his ear, I said, "You're going to be okay, I'm going to heal you . . ." Breathlessly, he replied, "I believe you could," but we both knew he was dying.

Leaving his side to speak with the group, we were trying to make decisions about our next move because our whereabouts were obviously no longer a secret. A terrible feeling came over me, but before I could ascertain its cause, shots began to ring out again. Running back to Dave as the others screamed for me to stay where it was say, they shouted, "No! You can't help him now!"

Holding his bullet riddled body in my arms; tears were streaming down my cheeks. Crying out, I shouted, "You're free now!" But in my profound grief, I hadn't noticed one minor thing, as suddenly a big smile came over my face. Blood dribbled down my chest where the searing bullet had entered, and there was no pain as I released the ghost. "Hang on! I'm coming with you!"

Moments later, my present fragment, Marilynn, hovered tearfully over the scene of their deaths. Katharine rose to greet me, her short blonde hair framing her dying smile. "Oh, don't cry," she said, "Remembering is good, even though it sometimes evokes pain."

"May my life merge in the Immortal when my body is reduced to ashes. O mind, meditate on the eternal Brahman. Remember the deeds of the past, Remember, O mind, remember."
The Upanishads, The Isha Upanishad, No. 17, Page 210, (Hinduism, Translation: Eknath Easwaran)

****

The grand convention was about to begin and all the natives were gathering for the festivities at the coliseum. My family was not to be involved, however, because father didn't like to mingle with the natives of Lemuria, because he felt that dignitaries should be above the native people. Wandering off, I'd gone towards the beach.

Sitting in a lotus position, his black hair framed his honey colored skin, but he was far away . . . in a trance of some sort. Submerging his legs with each wave, the ocean went back and forth out to sea. Beginning to chant a mystical song, I walked slowly closer. Sitting down far behind him, I was very quiet, but he knew I was there. Turning without pause in his chant, he motioned me to join him. Coming closer, I sat near him, closing my eyes and joining in his meditation. Looking at me with expectancy, it was as if he'd expected me to come.

Inviting me to join him at the coliseum later for a sun ceremony, I entered alone to observe the huge monoliths of stone that cascaded into the sky. Sitting in the distance with a woman, he beckoned me to join them, as I suddenly realized that this man carried the soul of Red Jacket. His name in this lifetime was 'Red Horse.'

As the sun prepared to set, the native people wore elaborate feathered outfits with masked faces which depicted the many moods of the Earth. Wearing a gleaming sun on her head, one woman danced to a shamanic drumbeat in a wild frenzy of primeval power.

Meeting secretly, Red Horse and I became close friends, but never more. He was married, and his wife knew nothing of our friendship. Heartbroken that he would repress his feelings for me when others were around, I was unsure of how he felt. My feelings for him clearly crossed the line.

"Hurry up, let's go," my mother was shouting for me to pack my bags. Lemuria was experiencing many changes; earthquakes, minor volcanic eruptions, and weather disturbances that led the inhabitants to believe that the continent was in the beginning stages of destruction. Special boats had been prepared for the dignitaries and their families, and after they were all evacuated, they planned to retrieve more ships to evacuate the remaining tribes.

Grabbing my stuff, our family began its walk to the docks. Hundreds of people were evacuating, and long lines of native people were hurrying around the boat docks. "You'd think they could keep those unkempt dark people away from us." Mother said. "Darnet, Mother!" I shouted. "I'm getting really tired of your attitude about these people!" Laughing hysterically, she said, "Well, that doesn't surprise me with the way you've been seeing one of those silly people behind our backs!" Shocked, my jaw dropped because I'd thought no one knew. "How long have you known?" "Long enough to know it's time we got you off this island before he ruins you." Another line of tribe's people blocked our path. "How can these dirty people live with themselves?" Mother said, as I lost my temper. "These *people* are the ones who are evacuating people like *you* before themselves!!!" "Well," she said, "it doesn't change the fact that they are disgusting! And you, you're so taken with one of them, it almost makes me sick. He's not even interested in you, he's got a wife! But that's how desperate you've become in this country." "That's it, Mama!" I yelled. Running towards a boat, my brother followed me, agreeing with my stance. "You're on your own, Mother; you know nothing about me or what I feel!" She and my father continued towards the larger boat and dock which was further away, completely unmoved.

Rumbling began without warning, and we knew that we had to get off the boat because it was shaking and wrenching against the land and the docks. Calling to my brother, I said, "The boat is too close to the land, it will shatter if the earthquake gets worse. Come with me!" Running towards the exit, I was now at the top of the steps on the verge of escape, but my brother laughed and motioned me to go without him. A thunderous movement was felt as the earth shook with ferocity. Bursting apart, the walls of the boat started to crumble as my brother fell to the ground, his leg bleeding badly because a beam had ripped through it. Running to grab him, I pulled him off the sinking boat through the might of adrenaline, but he couldn't walk and I had to get us to safe ground.

Looking for the large boat my parents had boarded, I knew they would have doctors aboard. Only half-conscious now, his wound was bleeding badly as I ran and ran with no clear focus as to where to go. Up ahead in the near distance, I saw Red Horse with his wife at his side. Tearful, I called out to him, but stopped myself not wishing to interfere. But he'd looked my way and was horrified as he saw our dramatic condition. Running quickly to my aid, he picked my brother up and threw him over his shoulder. Taking my hand, he began running in the direction of the dock. Confused, his wife followed. "No, Red Horse," I said, "Just point us in the right direction and we'll find it. You belong with your wife." Refusing to stop, he ran until he got my brother safely aboard the large boat preparing to leave the shattering nation.

Forcefully directing me to board the ship before it was too late to evacuate, I turned to him in confusion. "Go!" he shouted, "You will be safe now!" Below my breath, I replied, "Come with me!" Turning to glance at his wife who was now far behind, he said, "I can't." Looking down in shame, I quickly apologized. "No, it's not that, our marriage was arranged. I can't get on that boat, I don't have passage. Go!" Pushing me forcefully, I began to walk slowly towards the boat, but as I did I turned to watch him. Eyes looking up to meet mine, I blew him a kiss but realized that there was no invitation to stay.

Shouting at me to hurry, my shipmates were getting annoyed at my delays. But I continued to watch him and slowly, Red Horse lifted his arms and opened them in welcome. Turning to my shipmates, I said, "I'm staying, go without me." Amidst their protests, I ran to Red Horse as he hugged and tossed me in the air. Taking my hand, he danced me around in circles. As the boat pulled away from the land, the vibrations of the earth slowly ceased. Red Horse's wife walked slowly away, not appearing at all distraught, as if she knew all along.

Sitting quietly in the stone amphitheater some time later, a rehearsal was in progress. Red Horse was an actor, and I, a playwright. Juliosa was lingering around the stage, and he approached. "The play is good, huh?" I nodded, 'yes.' "There is something you must know." He said with a pause. "Spinoza." Looking at him, I repeated his word, "Spinoza," but I didn't know what it meant. "Remember this," he said, "Spinoza means, *your writing lives!*" Whoosh! Falling through space, I landed in my body.

Although I didn't know it at the time, Spinoza was an ancient Jewish philosopher whose writings do indeed still live.

"We should, in the same way, reflect on courage as a means of overcoming fear; the ordinary dangers of life should frequently be brought to mind and imagined, together with the means whereby through readiness of resource and strength of mind we can avoid and overcome them."

The Ethics of Spinoza, On the Power of the Intellect, Passions and Intelligence, Page 144, Paragraph 2, (Judaism, Author: Baruch Spinoza)

"A writer says of the character of the civilization of Lemuria: 'Life in Lemuria is described as being principally concerned with the physical senses and sensual enjoyment, only a few developed souls having broken through the fetters of materiality and reached the beginnings of the mental and spiritual planes of life.'"

The Secret Doctrine of the Rosicrucians, Part XI, Page 197, Paragraph 1, (Mystery Religions, Rosicrucian)

****

Running wildly on the sandy beach, the gunfire was getting ever closer as I quickly boarded the nearest boat. Hiding behind a wall, another thunderous bullet rang out from the beach. What was happening? Sudden movement knocked me to the floor of the boat as I heard the sound of its bottom scraping against the boulders on shore. "Oh, my God!" I thought, "We're setting sail!" Peering around the corner, the beach was now a good hundred feet away. "Hey!" A voice called from behind me, "What are you doing on this boat?!" My heart fell as the Indian man approached. My long dress had been soiled and I brushed my hands against the spots to make myself presentable. "Are you a stowaway?!" He called, as I stuttered no answer. Coming closer, his energy toward me changed. "Oh, my God, you're a woman." He exclaimed. Bowing shyly, I didn't reply. "Women aren't allowed on this boat, don't you know that?" "There was a gunfight on the beach, and I ran from them, I'm so sorry, sir." Putting his arms around me, he said, "Don't cry, honey, it'll be okay." And he made sure that it was.

Leading me to a small room, he gave me a place to stay and food to eat as long as I promised to stay out of the way of the sailors. The ship was some kind of coal barge and our destination was a small island not terribly far away. Coming to see me often, many hours passed as we talked and talked. A storm slowed the boats progress, and then it was damaged when it hit a rock near the reef of an island, delaying it even more.

After a time, we became very close, and fell deeply in love. It was only after this that he mentioned that he was married. "But she's no threat to you," he said, "we married to make things right. But let's not talk about that, she's far away and you're close to my heart." Despite this revelation, we remained close.

"Where am I!" I shouted. Looking down, I was in a hospital bed and appeared to be very pregnant. Looking out the window, I knew it to be winter. "How about some warm milk on this cold November day?" A nurse had entered the room. "What am I doing here?" I asked. "Honey, don't be scared, the baby's fine, you just had a little fall." Confused, I looked around at the other pregnant women who shared the room with me. "Red Horse!" I screamed, "Where is Red Horse?!" Giving me a serious look, the nurse calmed me. "Now, honey, he's right outside, but you can't see him now. The baby's not due until December 19th, more than a month away. You need some rest, and then we'll see about visitors."

An energy whoosh was felt and heard as I suddenly sat up in bed. Looking down I realized that I'd re-entered the present, a cold November day in 1989. What was to be birthed into my reality on December 19th?

"A person can sometimes receive information and knowledge about his future in this manner. This occurs as a result of God's decree."
The Way of God, Part III, Chapter 1, No. 6, Page 183, Bottom, (Judaism, Author: Rabbi Moshe Chayim Luzzatto)

****

Long Hair was waiting in the wild forest glade holding a large medicine wheel. Five lines separated the circle into sections. "We are Elohim," he said, and I immediately understood him to mean brothers in the Lord. "There are several cycles of time in the creation of this reunion." "Reunion?" I asked. Serious and direct, he said, "with Red Horse." I remembered, 'Red Jacket Reunion.'

****

Riding atop a white horse overlooking a luminous valley, Red Jacket said, "We are going to Wakadgeri, the land of the union."

"The taking-out and bringing-in actions are to be understood as actions of creator-spirit using humans as a form of creative expression."
Being and Vibration, Chapter 4, Chanting and the Breath, Paragraph 4, (Tribal, Tiwa, Author: Joseph Rael)

****

Wandering into sleep as visions flowed through his mind, Andy and I were attending a native ceremony taking place on the astral plane. Approaching with a basket of beads, Red Jacket handed each of us a gift.

Responding my clawing Red Jackets hand, as the moments passed, the energies calmed. Grasping each others hands in union, an image of the sun rose behind them.

Now at peace, Andy saw the Chief approach, showing him a large medicine wheel and indicating that he was now embarking upon the East, illumination. As they embraced a luminous temple erected itself upon the ethereal plane behind them.

"The direction of the East, the mental, number one on the wheel, is the direction where there is unity in all things. Then we go to the South, the emotional, which then becomes step number two, where we deal with polarities or opposites, like hot and cold or male and female. Then we move to the West, the physical, step three, the place of reconciliation of the opposites. Then to the North, the spiritual, step number four, where one finds direction and purpose. Finally, one comes to the Center, step five, which completes the circle and is the place of transformation possibilities."
Being and Vibration, Chapter 3, Page 91, Paragraph 1, (Tribal, Tiwa)

****

Standing among a vast expanse of land, the Native American ancestors became present in waves. As their bones began to emerge from the ground, I looked upon the faces of the many generations. "Help us, help us!" Long Hair had appeared and now stood by my side as a coffin emerged from the ground. "This one lies sleeping, but he must awake," he said. Directing me to open it, I gently lifted the lid. Red Horse lay sleeping, but quickly opened his eyes and emerged. 'Again, I walk the earth in your name. I am Red Horse, he who aids the sleeping in slumber. I hear the call of my people and I awaken to the journey within.'

As he paused, I spoke, "You don't remember me, do you?" Deeply piercing eyes looked into mine, "Aaaaah, but I do," he said. Long Hair spoke, "When searching for wisdom, pay heed to the source, tranquility glistening, is there love or remorse? Mysteries lay hidden beneath cloudy veils, but answers forthcoming come in many mirrors. The past holds the answers you seek in the now, are you willing to listen, or will you bow out? In love, we do call, the destiny fire, but first you must find us, we hide in our mirror."

"We shall walk the path of life, carrying in one hand the sacred pipe which You have given us, and in the other hand will be our children. In this way the generations will come and go and will live in a holy manner."
The Sacred Pipe, Chapter VIII, Page 132, Paragraph 3, (Tribal, Oglala Sioux)
****

"We are in Ingwaupapa, the time of waiting." Red Jacket said.
****

Coming with a shocking revelation, December 19th, the date of birth in my vision, heralded a meeting which occurred when I entered a small building and came face to face with the very image of Red Horse in my waking world. Looking exactly as he had been prophesied in many a vision, we both seemed a bit taken aback when our eyes met for the first time on the ground. Our karma would now cease its trembling and begin the quaking descent into our lives on the ground.

"For evil has many details, effects and influences, both in its intrinsic existence and in its relationship to man. Through all these, man is affected by evil and placed in its midst in such a way that he can overcome it, release himself from its fetters, and eventually conquer it completely."
The Way of God, Part IV, Chapter 4, No. 1, Paragraph 12, Page 261, (Judaism, Author: Rabbi Moshe Chayim Luzzatto)
****

Wearing all white, the angel was sparkling in light as she spoke. "You are allowing more and more love into your reality. It is beautiful." Sometimes we must be led into that which we don't understand, in order to be freed of it. Karmic purification is like this.

And so it came to pass that Andy and I separated and divorced for a time. Red Horse came into my life and quickly departed from it, because that was his nature. Because of this, there were always unresolved feelings. And so it is when something is left unfinished, it leaves the future caught in the trap of the past. Such is the nature of karma; such is the nature of delusion.

"There is no fire like passion; there is no stranglehold like hatred; there is no snare like delusion; there is no torrent like craving."
Dhammapada, Canto XVIII - Impurity, No. 251, (Buddhism)

Sometimes a soul must journey into their own delusions, in order to be purified of them. Purification requires a change within one's thoughts, as well as, actions, but a true and complete purification from vice culminates in the soul no longer having the desire to indulge in them.

"You have heard that it was said, 'You shall not commit adultery.' But I say to you, everyone who looks at a woman with lust has already committed adultery with her in his heart."
New American Bible, New Testament, Matthew 5:27-28, (Christianity, Catholic, Words of Christ)

If a soul truly wishes to attain to this level, the Lord sends his angels right into the abyss, to guide that soul back to God's salvation. And the angels pick you up . . . and pick you up . . . and pick you up again . . . until you set yourself aright of your own accord.

"(The story is) that while I was asleep (one night) there came to me a person (in the dream) who asked me to stand up. (So I stood up) and he caught hold of my hand and I walked along with him, and, lo, I found some paths on my left and I was about to set out upon them. Thereupon, he said to me: Do not set yourself on (them) for these are the paths of the leftists (denizens of hell-fire). Then there

were paths leading to the right side, whereupon he said: Set yourself on these paths. We came across a hill and he said to me: Climb up, and I attempted to climb up that I fell upon my buttocks. I made several attempts (but failed to succeed). He led until he came to a pillar (so high) that its upper end touched the sky and its base was in the earth. And there was a handhold at its upper end. He said to me: Climb over it. I said: How can I climb upon it, as its upper end touches the sky? He caught hold of my hand and pushed me up and I found myself suspended with the handhold. He then struck the pillar and it fell down, but I remained attached to that handhold until it was morning . . ."
Sahih Muslim (The Hadith), Volume IV, Kitab Fada'il Al-Sahabah, Chapter MXXV, Page 1325, Paragraph 2, (Islam, Words of Mohammad)

****

Standing atop a burial ground, I watched as grave robbers dug up the people. Beginning to cry, a small hole appeared in my heart and began to bleed. The part of me that was dead was being resurrected through an intricate divine plan; and as with all karma, it hurt. No one about me could see my pain but Red Horse, who placed his hand over my heart and healed it.

"Woe to you who hope in the flesh and in the prison that will perish!"
The Nag Hammadi Library, The Book of Thomas the Contender, Page 205, Paragraph 1-2, (Christianity, Gnostic/Essene)

****

Red Jacket descended in a spiral of energy. "Why do you mourn for that which you have not lost?" Looking into his deep loving eyes, I realized that love is never lost, no matter what the circumstance. Love . . . remains.

"When you wish to contract something, you must momentarily expand it; When you wish to weaken something, you must momentarily strengthen it; When you wish to reject something, you must momentarily join with it; When you wish to seize something, you must momentarily give it up. This is called 'subtle insight.'"
Tao Te Ching, No. 80, (Buddhism, Taoism, Words of Lao Tzu, Translation: Victor H. Mair)

****

"The holy angels gain a knowledge of God not by the spoken word but by the presence in their souls of that immutable Truth which is the only-begotten Word of God . . . Therefore, in the sense I have explained above, the knowledge which they have in Him is as clear as daylight, whereas what they have in themselves is like the twilight."
City of God, Chapter 29, Paragraph 1-2, (Christianity, Catholic, Author: St. Augustine)

"So, through us, life becomes aware, because life wants to experience itself through us, through our awareness. Life experiences beauty through the way. The way means being inside the purity of lifting, beyond time awareness, so that what we see and work is the beauty around us."
Being and Vibration, Chapter 3, Page 89, Paragraph 2, (Tribal, Tiwa, Author: Joseph Rael)

Flying to an encampment near the bank of the ocean, I saw two women drowning in the vast sea. Jumping in, I saved them both. All of my friends were watching, and they approached me with deep loving vibrations quelling about them. Red Jacket appeared and put his arms around me. "My dear spirit, why do you judge yourself?" In frustration, I cried out, "I couldn't reach them!" There were many souls I'd guardianed on the ground, who seemed not to have accepted the hand of the eternal in their lives. At that moment, I noticed several of these special souls waiting for me. Red Jacket began to read a poem that Odyssey had written.

ODYSSEY
I see illusions
All in form

I see frustrations
And lingering pain

Beneath the facade
The essence is clear
And in my heart
It's always near
True connections
Are all I see
That is the beauty
About me

One of them said, "Though *we* may not feel our true connections in form, you should perceive your ability to do so as a beautiful gift to us. We love you for your purity of knowing. Don't you realize that to us, you are one of the very few who perceive only our light rather than our illusion? There is no greater gift than this!" Smiling at their kindness, Red Jacket was now holding two gold medals in his hands. "These are the gold medals of courage and bravery. It takes a strong and loving spirit to enter these realities." Pointing to the ocean, he continued, "You have pulled them from the depths of illusion and shown them light."

In a flash, my spirit was at a wilderness retreat as an old man wearing white robes came to hand me a chart of my spiritual journey. On it were pictures, and the heading read, "Path to Angels Twilight." A picture of the old man who had come was on the chart, and beneath his image, his name was written. 'Toam,' it said, 'he who comes to aid the angel's journey into twilight.' Immediately, I knew that the twilight . . . is karma. The next picture was of myself as a lighted being, an angel. Below it was my name, 'Odyssey,' and below my name were three words, 'Nurse - Nun - Eve.' In italics next to the picture, it said, 'Will become capable of materializing in and out of realities, and become truly transparent.'

Suddenly, several angels appeared around me, whispering over and over, "Angel's twilight, angel's twilight . . ." Staring in awe of their essence, they whispered again, "Angels in form operate in the twilight, for their light is veiled by the illusion. Angels in twilight must enter the underworld without shadowing the essence of their angelic purpose." Some angels do incarnate for the sole purpose of mirroring to others the true eternal nature of love, and these angels are called, 'Angels Twilight Gleaming.' But even souls who operate in the twilight of karma can perform the work of angels. Through their own delusions, they may function as mirrors to those who seek to see their own vice more clearly. Much knowledge is achieved experientially, and a soul must recognize its own darkness, before it can comprehend the true nature of the light. Souls such as these are the Angels in the Twilight.

Do not be ignorant of those who teach these more difficult lessons in life, for they *will* come. Some will lie, cheat, betray, dominate . . . some may love you and leave you . . . all of them will take from you, whether it be belongings, someone you love, or even your heart. Only the true seeker will realize the exchange . . . some seekers, if they are quite honest, will begin to view their own selves more clearly. Most of us do not always recognize the pain that we cause, only that which we sustain, as this is the selfishness of karma. But something is given amidst the treachery, as you are performing a heavenly function on each other's behalf, though neither of you may be aware of it. You are providing a mirror . . .

To everything there is a season, and our lessons in life come in God's divine timing, and so, too, do they end. Be not like unto the soul who weeps, but never raises its head to the knowledge coming from above. Be not like those who would mourn, but not listen to the voice of wisdom that guides them away from their troubles. For in every sorrow, there is an epiphany. In every epiphany, humility is birthed. The all merciful Lord protects us in our ignorance for a time, but when that time passes, if we have not listened, the Lord does withdraw and leave us to withstand the true consequences of our mistakes.

"Your Lordship is my only means of getting out of this darkest region of ignorance because You are my transcendental eye, which, by Your mercy only, I have attained after many, many births."
The Teachings of Lord Kapila, Chapter 6, Text 8, (Hinduism, Author: A.C. Bhaktivedanta Swami Prabhupada)

****

Soaring through time, I entered the body of a Spanish woman in South America. Living in the hills very close to the former land of the Incas, a relic of what once was remained in this place, a worn down amphitheater with a stone podium. Having been Incan land, the people living here were very superstitious about the ghosts of the ancient Incans and never went near the relic.

In certain ways, this lifetime was resonant of the time when I was the 'Deity of Ayacucho.' Every night, I went to the podium to chant and pray for the souls of those who had once walked the land. Wearing a wispy white blouse with a flowing red skirt, I danced about the spot just as the Deity of Ayacucho had danced across these very skies hundreds of years before. Around my neck I wore a string of beads, costume jewelry which held absolutely no significance.

On my way home through the mountains, I usually stopped to buy bakery goods from a local woman. Hysterically one day, she told me that she had seen a woman dancing in the amphitheatre and she was afraid satanic worship might be at hand. Leading me to a back window, the podium was in view of her house. "Should I call in the authorities?" She asked. "What do you think is going on?" Calming her, I replied, "I really don't think you need to worry about it, honey." "But don't you know that that was the place where the Incans made sacrifices?" Surprised, I hadn't known this, and I began to feel a compelling sadness for the suffering of those who had experienced such a horrendous fate. But before I left, she noticed my beads and commented on how unusual and pretty they were.

Several friends joined me over time in my prayers for the souls of the dead who had been sacrificed in such a horrific manner in this place. Living in a small secluded area, the only other people I had regular contact with were two Spanish families who lived next door. One day while walking home, I ran into one of my neighbors who immediately touched my beads and pulled away, afraid. "Devil woman!" he said loudly. "What's wrong, my friend?" Fear emanated from him, as he froze in his spot. "Why do you call me devil woman?" "You," he stuttered, "you wear the beads." "It is just a necklace, my friend." "We will get them, and then you will have no more power." Violently, he grabbed my neck.

Turning to run, I went in the other direction for miles. Catching up to the Incan spot, I knew that I would be safe there for a little while because the people were afraid to come here. Several of my friends were there, and we concluded that someone had seen my beads which identified me as the spirit dancer, and attributed 'power' to them.

Called in to aid in our capture, Red Jacket was one of the lawmen who came looking for us. Considering me the leader, they truly believed that if they could just get the beads I wore that my 'power' would be nullified.

Arranging to meet our pursuers alone in places they wouldn't anticipate, Red Jacket was the one who came to meet me. He was a midsize Spanish man who wore a gray suit most of the time which was very dusty from travel. Stern and serious, I would try to make him laugh, and I could continue this because as long as I wore the beads he was afraid to approach me for capture.

Over time, however, Red Jacket's curiosity got the better of him. Strongly attracted to each other, we began arranging secret meetings while I was on the run. Meeting in the mountains, in caves, or in vast woodlands, his stern composure would change to a smile, as we became very close. "I understand you now, and I know that what the people have said is untrue. But if I can just have the beads, then the people will be convinced that you have been stripped of your powers." Laughing, I ripped them from my neck. "Here, take them, it will make you a hero and you deserve that." Taking my beads, he reached around his neck retrieving a locket. Silver and very old, there was a picture of him inside which showed the stern glaze, a part of him that I rarely saw. "This is yours to remember me by."

Pulled out of the lifetime, Red Jacket awaited me in the spirit world. Still holding the locket, the picture began to change as the stern look changed to a smile. "This is what you gave me," Red Jacket said, "moments of smiles. That is the most beautiful gift you can give." Not realizing the importance of his words at that time, 'moments' was the key. Holding the locket to my heart, Red Jacket said, "In this life, we are giving each other the same gift, moments of smiles and happiness."

"Through being attached to living beings I am completely obscured from the perfect reality, my disillusionment (with cyclic existence) perishes and in the end I am tortured by sorrow."
The Guide to the Bodhisattva's Way of Life, Chapter 8, No. 7, (Buddhism, Tibetan, Author: Shantideva)

Sitting amidst an office because there was business to attend to, an angel stood aside the image of a person who flickered in and out of this reality. Immediately knowing him to be an aspect of Juliosa, he looked different, but was wearing a business suit. One wrapped and the other unwrapped, two gifts laid on the desk. Red Horse had already given his gift to my soul which was demonstrated in the unwrapped gift, but the other wrapped gift had not yet been given.

"There she is," the three women shouted excitedly as they entered the room and began to pamper me. "He has asked us to all take care of you until he is ready to come into your reality." Flickering in and out again, I could feel the love that this person bore my soul. Handing me the wrapped gift, one of the women said, "This is for you, but you can't open it until you meet him on the earth-plane in three weeks. Now that you've answered all the questions of your spirit with love, you have magnetized love." Understanding nothing, I nodded and disappeared from the realm.

"The nearer you come to God the less you are disposed to question and reason When you come up to Him, when you behold Him as the Reality, then all noise, all disputations are at an end."
Teachings of Sri Ramakrishna, Disputation, No. 568, Paragraph 2, (Hinduism)
****

Toam arrived to take me into the energy of Red Jacket's fragment on the ground, Red Horse, because my spirit was having difficulty letting him go. After all, I'd never done it in hundreds of lives, what should make it different this time around? Looking at me lovingly, Red Horse asked, "What do you see when you look at me?" Silently, I replied, "I love you." Many thought-forms began to appear of horrid and violent scenes. "It's my spirit you love, do you not? You see only my spirit?" Nodding, I conveyed that this was true. "You say you understand me, but do you . . . really?" "I don't know," I replied, as suddenly the fearful images began to come to life with a fury.

Samurai swordsmen chased me, and a pile of battered and bloody people appeared, screaming for help. Appearing beside him was my father, drunk and violent, and images of the man who had raped me years before. Crouching to the ground, I began to cry, "I don't know! I don't know!" All of the images suddenly jumped up and came after me, but I didn't move for I was unable to respond.

Red Horse came in and carried me out of the mess and with deep love in his eyes, he said, "Don't you see what I represent to you now? I am all your fears in one package. I am the man who uses you and hurts you; I am the family who cannot love you because you are different. I am your father . . . the violent and drunken one. I am the warrior energy, which you *do not understand*, and you *fear*." Crying, I knew he was right.

Red Jacket appeared in the center of the spiral. "Your job is not to be understood, but to be *understanding*. Nothing anyone does is rejection of you, but of their self. In order to resolve this karma, you must be able to know from within, that Red Horse loves you underneath all his illusions, and you cannot wait to hear it from him. You must *know* it because it is true."

Toam appeared and showed me Red Horse's bowie knife. "You are about to see the energy of the knife, a side of him you haven't yet seen." Watching as Red Horse got into a fight with people in a bar, I went into a severe asthma attack. Offering me an emetic to purge this energy from my system, I shouted, "I don't need it!" Not wanting to let him go even now, Toam replied, "Are you going to give everything up for him?" "No, but I love him!" I shouted. "How can I leave him behind?" Touching my heart, he said, "He'll always be right here. Red Horse still operates from the same frequency of his lifetime as Red Jacket." Beginning to understand, I remembered that there was a side of Red Jacket I'd never really been a party to, the violent part of him that made him one of the most wanted Indians because of his skill in battle. "You are afraid of his twinness. The violence you see is his illusion trying to understand its own nature. You don't understand each other because he follows the path of the warrior, and you follow the path of peace; but the irony is that both paths eventually lead to love. Don't be afraid of the warrior within him . . . seek to understand it."

Within a few days, I witnessed this face of Red Horse in my waking life, on the ground. Horrified, I hadn't previously allowed myself to see his violent nature, though signs of it were evident and in clear view. You can love someone's soul but be incompatible with their personality. Love was much larger than me, and its meaning was something I didn't yet fully understand.

Red Jacket interjected, "You have thrown the rope in the water, now he must either drown or grab hold of it." Having shown him another direction he could take, it was now entirely up to him as to whether he would seek it. A vast difference exists between karmic and eternal relationships as souls come together to teach each other about the true and false natures of love. By recognizing what is true, we slowly begin to assimilate what is false. By recognizing what is false, we slowly begin to assimilate what is true. Because of their purpose, most karmic relationships are momentary, arriving very powerfully at an important juncture in our lives, and just as quickly disappearing. Eternal relationships are usually of a more lasting quality.

The nature of karma is to try to *force* things to become what you think they should be, whereas, the nature of the eternal is to *allow* things to unfold into what they are becoming. Because of these differences, karmic relationships tend to be quite chaotic with many highs and lows, whereas, eternal relationships that have reached fruition become peaceful and serene staying more along the middle ground. Karma is selfish and seeks for its own gratification, while that which is eternal is selfless and seeks for God's gratification. Karmic relationships diminish the individuals involved in them, whereas eternal relationships are ordained by the Lord for the very reason that they energize the potentials within them, making the two greater together than they are apart. Karma is chaos, while that which is eternal is peace.

Ironically, the insatiable emptiness that drives us in search of other people and things is truly sparked by the soul's thirst for union with God. Herein lies the greatest delusion that can be attributed to all karma, it seeks in the wrong direction for its fulfillment. Lustfully chasing after the whole of creation, the lost one does not find peace. Only by seeking the *source* of all creation can a soul attain liberation from elusive drives. Only in God, can a soul find peace.

"Seek thou not what is pleasant and advantageous to thyself, but what is acceptable and honourable unto Me; for if thou judgest rightly, thou must choose and follow after My appointment rather than thine own desire . . . Already thou longest to be in the glorious liberty of the children of God . . . but the hour is not yet come there remaineth still another season, even a season of warfare, a season of labour and probation. Thou desirest to be filled with the Chief Good, but thou canst not attain it immediately. I AM that Good; wait for Me, until the Kingdom of God shall come."
The Imitation of Christ, The Third Book, Chapter XLIX, No. 3, (Christianity, Author: Thomas A Kempis)

****

Taken to see Red Horse in the astral state, he was manifesting as subconscious astral, meaning he was asleep in his dream. Without my control, my spirit began materializing in the room, and he saw me. "How do you do all this?" He asked. "I've told you that I follow a very pure path of spirit, but you did not believe me." Panicking, I cried out, "I've gotta get out of here!" Looking for an avenue of escape, he stopped me and quietly asked, "May I get a leather tie for your hair?" A sign of reconciliation, I accepted it. (There are many different levels of existence upon which a soul can manifest astrally. In this case, as in others where I mention materializing, I am not speaking about a physical materialization; but rather, a materialization from a higher frequency than the dreamer, to the frequency of the dream, wherein the dreamer can then see me within his dream. It is not uncommon for my soul to be given transparency in the status of dreams, for the purpose of observation.)

****

Pulling me into a deep vibrational state, Red Jacket spoke, "I'm bringing you back," he said, "you haven't even noticed half of the improvements I've given to you, have you? I'm bringing you back, restoring your vibration. Notice what we've done for each other, the gifts were mutual." My vibrations were raised well above the sinking abyss I had flung myself into, and I vowed never again to leave the heavenly abode, losing myself in another.

"In the flash of light are the ashes that fly us beyond us in wisdom and into memory, placing us into the here of vigilance and the now of seeking. In the beginning was a flash of light in which everything was known and seen. In that moment was the beginning, the end and everything in between."
Being and Vibration, Chapter Three, Page 76, Paragraph 2, (Tribal, Tiwa, Author Joseph Rael)

****

And so it came to pass that the prophecy in regards to a manifestation of Juliosa coming into my life . . . occurred. But I had also met another person that I had decided not to get to know better, which was the subject of the following experience.

Gently lifting my spirit to a realm of white filled with books, Toam led me to a room where a small old woman awaited my arrival. In the hall of records, the lady was holding a very ancient text. "It is the 'Tamadra.'" Toam said.

"Why would you avoid the lesson? What do you fear?" the woman asked very compassionately. Confused, I didn't know what she meant. Flipping through the pages of my personal Tamadra, she came to a section titled by the name of this person I'd just met of whom I had no intention of getting to know further. Pointing to a section she wanted me to read, it said, 'Further instruction in the warrior energy.' "It is your choice," she said, "but you are turning down many lessons for your spirit by choosing not to see him again. It is in your spirits highest interest to recognize the connection." "Come with me," Toam said, as he took my hand and returned me to my body.

And so it came to pass that the very next day this person contacted me, wanting to get together. Choosing to spend some time with him, I quickly realized that he was exactly like Red Jacket in the sense of aggression. Realizing that the same type of behavior in any other soul repulsed me, it became clear that it was the love I held for Red Jacket's soul which made me blind to his true ways on the ground.

"Approach not integrity with a double heart; nor be associated with double-minded men: but walk, my children, in righteousness, which will conduct you in good paths; and be truth your companion."
The Book of Enoch, Chapter XC. (Sect. XVIII), No. 5, Page 146, (Judaism, Christianity)
"Seek peace and pursue it."
The Talmudic Anthology, No. 244, Stanza 2, Y. Peah, 1, 1, (Judaism)
****

"The ancestral hand has been held out to you, but it will not reach to you, you must reach to it." Pondering this message I'd been asked to convey to Red Horse, it continued, "The Red energy is the essence of the Earth and the path of the Earth's transformation. The ways of old burn inside and yearn to be remembered. The essence of Native American spirituality must be reintegrated within. What has been forgotten will surface in an open heart. Your true nature, that of your spirit, knows the ways of old and can bring them back." Preparing to deliver the message, I knew that he would not receive it well. Hesitating, the eternal reminded me that it was my task to serve his soul, not his personality. Understanding, I sent him the message.
****

Very agitated, Red Horse almost screamed at me in the astral. "Where did you get that message?" I didn't respond. Seething, I felt the energy of his confusion and conflict. Beginning to chase me, I ran through the woods. "Where did you get that message?" Laughing and playing with him, I said, "I don't know." Catching up, he remained angry. "If only you believed, you would know." I said. "It tugs and tugs at you, but you refuse to listen when I tell you where it truly comes from. You won't believe in Red Jacket, you won't believe in your true self." For a moment, he was calm. "I'm so sorry that you're going through this now, but sometimes one must muddle through the confusion in order to reach the light." Looking at me with confusion, he phased to a different level of consciousness in his dream and I was gone.

"He who strives to attain that which is not for him loses that which was intended for him."
The Talmudic Anthology, No. 242, Stanza 1, (Judaism)
****

Juliosa's aspect on the ground was becoming a very important part of my life, and we shared deep friendship and love. Although the innocence and simplicity of our friendship was something I needed at the time, I knew that it would not be a lasting union; for this fragment of Juliosa on the ground was not on a spiritual path, and eventually, I knew that this would tear us apart.

"'So long as we are immersed in body consciousness, we are like strangers in a foreign country,' the Master said. 'Our native land is Omnipresence.'"
Sayings of Paramahansa Yogananda, Page 86, Stanza 2, (Hinduism, Kriya Yoga, Words of Paramahansa Yogananda)
****

Flying into the depths of space, I entered a star system that was vastly familiar, yet unremembered within my soul. Floating in the midst of it, I watched as star systems were converging, and a being with two head connected by a V-shaped body was floating very joyously in the spacious ethereal realm.

"Please let me look at you and make sure this is really happening." I said. "Welcome to the galaxies Alpha Centauri, Alpha Omega, X, Y, and Z! Welcome to the constellation of star systems known as 'One.' I am he who writes with you the book of the angels." Starting to laugh with joy, I said, "You're the one who's helping me write about the mirroring stage of karma?" "Yes," he replied, "we've been working together very well." Dancing with joy, I said, "It must be so easy to write about angels here." He smiled again. "You are welcome to come here anytime. Does it inspire you to be with us?" "Oh yes!" I cried out, "Oh, yes!"

The magnetic stars chimed as they circled in their display of oneness. Galaxies were circling in the distance and I was awestruck from the view. But suddenly, coral pink roses began blossoming in the skies above me, burgeoning into a beautiful bloom. "Juliosa!" I called out into the heavens. He appeared, as I realized that the man with the rose had been an aspect of himself. Only for a moment, he appeared, and then he was gone.

"Buddha said, 'All things are ultimately liberated. There is nowhere that they abide.' You should know that even though all things are liberated and not tied to anything, they abide in their own phenomenal expression. However, when most human beings see water they only see that it flows unceasingly. This is a limited human view; there are actually many kinds of flowing."
Moon in a Dewdrop, Mountains and Waters Sutra, Sansui-Kyo, No. 13, (Buddhism, Zen, Words of Zen Master Dogen)

****

"You have become very free in your life, this is beautiful." Toam said in the ancient coliseum, "but you must be more understanding of those who await in their own bondage." Showing me an image of my ex-husband, Andy, I saw that I had been harsh to him. When we were married, he had been very controlling and I resented him for this. "When you learn to detach from his controlling behavior, knowing it is something that he must go through, you will find forgiveness." There was much more for which I needed his forgiveness, than he would need of mine. Forgiving him, I smiled at Toam in gratitude, and relished the friendship which Andy and I had retained despite our divorce.

"People talk of errors and superstitions and pride themselves upon book-learning. But the sincere devotee finds the Loving Lord ever ready to lend him a helping hand. It matters not that he had been for a time walking along a wrong path. The Lord knows what he wants and in the end fulfills the desire of his heart."
Teachings of Sri Ramakrishna, Spiritual Practice, No. 451, (Hinduism, Words of Sri Ramakrishna)

****

Pummeled through the time tunnel, I dropped into the body of a young woman with brown hair dressed in an exquisite gown. *Knowing* I was in Scotland, we were trying to cross the borders as turmoil had overtaken the country. Walls protected the city and you could only leave at a certain time of day, else wise you could be shot. Juliosa was my husband, and he had short reddish hair with a medium size build. Wearing tails and navy blue baggy stretch pants, he was a very jealous man. My brother and sister, who were very dear to me, were also with us. As the walls opened, the crowds poured through the gates, trying to escape this war torn land. Noticing a column of soldiers in front of the wall, their coldness frightened me. Rachel, my sister, was lingering behind, and I worried about her.

Crossing the wall with no problems, we waited patiently for my sister to catch up, but our contentment was short-lived as shots rang out from the other side of the wall. Determined to find my sister, I ran towards the shots as a familiar face captured my attention. Flirting with me often, a man who enraged Juliosa snuck up from behind me, placing his arm around my waist. Asking him about Rachel, he nonchalantly replied, "Oh, you didn't know? She didn't make it across." "What do you mean?!" I yelled out. He was so drunk he had no sensitivity to the gravity of the situation. Taking my hand, he pointed me in the direction of the shots. In the distance, the bullet-riddled body of my sister lay with many others.

Breaking down into tears, I asked him to take me back to Juliosa. As I was very distraught, he put his arm around my waist as he escorted me as Juliosa turned to look our way. Noticing my distraught condition, he jumped to the conclusion that this man was hurting me and challenged him to a fight over my honor. Despite my vehement protests, he wouldn't let it go.

Smaller than the other man and obviously outmatched, Juliosa was determined to prove his manhood. People gathered around as they prepared to fist fight. From my former perspective, I had no other alternative than to sit with the women, angered and embarrassed that he was making such a scene. Pretty well beaten a couple of minutes into the fight, Juliosa knew this, so in a surprise (and stupid) move, he pulled out his sword. An expert swordsman, I figured he would probably nick the man and leave it at that, but the man he was fighting with was drunk, and he was playing for real.

Seconds into the fight, the drunken man plunged his sword directly through Juliosa's heart. Falling back, I screamed in terror; shocked, in tears, sobbing. Knowing there was no hope, I held him in my arms. Passing from this world, I stared in numb disbelief. Several women caught me as I fell to the ground in shock. Because he chose to risk his life for something so stupid, I was very angry inside. I mourned.

Juliosa appeared in the sky, waving his arms to send me to another lifetime.

Entering the body of black woman, my husband and I were sharecroppers on a large plantation with our two children. Juliosa didn't have a good relationship with the owner of the plantation, and in a fit of rage, he confronted him and was literally whipped to death.

Speaking to Juliosa immediately upon my return, I said, "It seems that I always lose the one I love." "You understand the pattern," he said.

"When thou was under My control, all creatures yielded to thee; but after thou hast transgressed My commandment, they all rise over thee."
The Lost Books of the Bible and the Forgotten Books of Eden, Adam and Eve, Chapter XLV, Verse 2-4, (Christianity, Judaism)

****

The fragment of Juliosa on the ground was very nourishing to my soul, but there was no way around the fact that we were incompatible; he an earnest dreamer, and myself a dreamer seeking reality. My spiritual journey could not be held back, and his had not yet begun.

Juliosa hovered again in the clouds. "Our paths are going to part, aren't they?" I said. He nodded, 'Yes.' Our paths were no longer parallel. Our souls had come together because of love, and now they would part . . . because of love.

"These three vertical levels are called natural, spiritual and heavenly . . . they grow along a continuum, gaining information and getting discernment thereby, ultimately reaching that highest level of discernment called a 'rational faculty.' This in itself, however, does not serve to open the second level, which is called spiritual. This is opened by a love of useful activities which stems from elements of discernment . . . Again, though, these in themselves do not serve to open the third level, which is called heavenly. This is opened rather by means of a heavenly love of useful activity, and this love is a love for the Lord."
Divine Love and Wisdom, No. 237, (Christianity, Swedenborgianism, Author: Emanuel Swedenborg)

****

Having no entrance, the enclosed circular structure presented a challenge to the beckoning soul. "It is the Secret Garden." A voice said. Soaring at close range, a glimmering green sword emanated from the stone about four feet from the ground. "The Knife of the Emerald!" I instinctively remembered. On the next stone step there was an image of a small tomato box. The Knife of the Emerald was symbolic of courage to enter the garden, while the tomato box served the purpose of extracting seeds of knowing and planting them in fertile ground. Taking the tools, I soared to the wall, becoming transparent to enter.

Flying through the wall, a flowery garden with plants of all kinds existed along with a rock pathway which expanded into a path which consisted of scores of music from throughout time etched in stone. Showing me that in previous existences, Andy had brought some of these works into the earth-plane; more music remained on the pathway that had yet to be brought into reality which I allowed to enter into my soul.

Someone was coming, and the sacredness of the garden made me feel as if I should hide for I didn't feel worthy to be here. But the spirit flew by, smiling, "I know you're here and am glad of it." Soaring home, my time was finished.

Knowing how to read music and play the piano, I began to teach myself how to play the guitar and write music so that I might preserve that which was given to me in the world beyond.

"The Master said, 'Only common people wait till they are advanced in ritual and music (before taking office)."
The Analects of Confucius, Book XI, No. 1, (Buddhism, Taoism, Confucianism)
****

Soaring through time, my spirit flew into the body of a young white woman, my dress tattered and covered in mud, I was running, breathless, through the thick of the woods. Lost and alone, I stopped, sitting on a moss-covered rock to catch my breath. Several Indian men appeared from behind trees and rocks, some on foot and others on horse. Running Wolf was their leader, and he directed them to take me as a prisoner.

Going with them, I felt no fear for they were kind to me. When I entered their camp I was given new clothes to wear; a buckskin dress and moccasins. Within a short period of time, I became one of them.

As our tribe was continually moving, and I was not as fit as the other women, I oftentimes lagged behind the traveling band trying to catch up before long. But one afternoon as I fell further behind than normal, I stopped for a moment to catch my breath. My tribe was far in the foreground and out of view. A Shawnee war party came behind me, and I was captured.

Taking me back to their camp, Red Horse awaited my arrival. Having already claimed me as his own, they brought me to him as another man hit me on the head, knocking me out. My spirit heard the words of Red Horse's anger as he ran towards him. "We agreed that there would be no violence against her!" Picking my limp body from the ground, he carried me into the woods.

Coming to, I felt as though I were wavering in and out of realities. Going deeper and deeper into the woods, he carried me to a special spot of which only he and I knew. On the side of a tree, a hole appeared. Light and crystals glimmered from within, as he reached his hand inside the small crevice. "Do you know what this is?" He asked. "I sure do," I said with tears in my eyes as I quietly placed my hand next to his inside the tree. "Let us take the ancestral hand together." Although I knew this was a sub-conscious experience for him, it was still quite relevant to his journey as a soul.

Light poured through both of us, and before he was to go he looked at me one last time. "I would die for you," he said. It was finished.

"There are two birds, two sweet friends, who dwell on the self-same tree. The one eats the fruits thereof, and the other looks on in silence. The first is the human soul who, resting on that tree, though active, feels sad in his unwisdom. But on beholding the power and glory of the higher Spirit, he becomes free from sorrow."
The Upanishads, Mundaka Upanishad, Part 3, Chapter 1, Paragraph 1-2, (Hinduism, Translation: Juan Mascaro)
****

CHAPTER FOUR
Lighted Golden Pyramid, Masculine Part of my Soul, Golden Sphinx Emerges, Fifty Levels of Illusion on the Earthly Mountain, the Eternal Flame, Heaven Dawn, Magical Lace, Chimney through Frequencies, Secrets of the Earthly Realms, Eternal Cloth, Psychadelic Stew, Yraknin - Goddess of Truth, Alpha Centaurian Visitors, Knights of the Three Melodies, Become that which you Seek.

****

    Awaking in bed, I looked up to notice a lighted figure of a man standing at the foot of my bed. "Andy?" I called out to no reply. Fear swept over me, as I yelled out, "Who are you, who's here?!" The lighted image swept up to the ceiling and exploded into a lighted golden pyramid.

"Difficult is it to be born as a human being; difficult is the existence of mortals; difficult is the hearing of the Sublime Truth; rare is the appearance of the Enlightened Ones..."
Dhammapada, Canto XIV - The Enlightened One, No. 182, Page 73, (Buddhism)
****

    Floating to a river where a female guide was waiting, she took my hand. "It is time to embark upon your eternal path," she said. "Okay," I agreed, as a man appeared next to her. Rising to meet my gaze, I asked, "Who is he?" "The masculine part of you," she replied. Familiar and intense, I could not truly remember him.

    Soaring, we stopped at a lake of iridescent blue surrounded by mountains. Peering into his eyes, he calmly reached his hand to me and said, "I have loved you forever." My heart reached to him, "And I, you." Conveying telepathically to us, the woman said, "This Lake is no ordinary lake, for it is filled with all the minerals of the Universe. As you submerge yourselves into it, you will completely change the molecular structure of your bodies, and you will become one." Quietly . . . hand in hand . . . we walked into the water.

"Therefore, water is not just earth, water, fire, wind, space, or consciousness. Water is not blue, yellow, red, white, or black. Water is not forms, sounds smells, tastes, touchables, or mind-objects. But water as earth, water, fire, wind, and space realizes itself."
Moon in a Dewdrop, Mountains and Waters Sutra, No. 12, Page 102, Paragraph 4, (Buddhism, Zen, Words of Zen Master Dogen)
"Those who are beyond the dualities that arise from doubts . . . achieve liberation in the Supreme."
The Bhagavad Gita, Chapter 5, Verse 25, (Hinduism, Translation: A.C. Bhaktivedanta Swami Prabhupada)
****

"Sometimes a way seems right to a man, but the end of it leads to death. Even in laughter the heart may be sad and the end of joy may be sorrow. The scoundrel suffers the consequences of his ways . . ."
New American Bible, Old Testament, Proverbs, Chapter 14, Verse 12-14
"Who can say, 'I have made my heart clean, I am cleansed of my sin?"
New American Bible, Old Testament, Proverbs 20, Verse 9
"Now I am overwhelmed that in accord with your instruction I assumed the garment of flesh and have to endure the fact that my own members, who are bound to me by the sacrament of baptism, should turn away from me and fall victim to the son of corruption and revere him. Yet I bring home again those among them who have fallen. But I reject those who remain rebellious and cling to evil."
Book of Divine Works, Vision Ten: 34, Page 260, Paragraph 2, (Christianity, Catholic, Author: Hildegard of Bingen, Words of Christ)

    The coliseum was dim at twilight, as the tribesmen scurried about to complete its construction. Watching from the eyes of my spirit, I hovered over the scene in a state of timelessness regarding the message of the ancients and its impact on my present life. Suddenly amongst the raucous, something began emerging from the center of the coliseum.

"What is that?" I thought deeply to myself, as the image in the center of the coliseum continued to grow. Appearing to be a large golden pyramid, a sphinx was emerging from its crest. A wind stream passed by my senses. "The golden sphinx is emerging," it conveyed. Linked to the mysteries of life, death and re-birth, the sphinx represented the death from karmic delusion and rebirth into the light of God, the energy of creation in progress.

"What is the cause of the cosmos? Is it Brahman? From where do we come? By what live? Where shall we find peace at last? What power governs the duality of pleasure and pain by which we are driven."
The Upanishads, Shvetashvatara Upanishad, Part I, No. 1, (Hinduism, Translation: Eknath Easwaran)

****

Walking towards me, the ancient Egyptian man approached in the windswept desert. Disappearing behind his back, his hands emerged holding two objects: a statue of a phoenix, and a winged horse. Choosing the winged horse, I placed it on my heart as it exploded into a diamond light. "This is the energy of St. Harmony Crystal Fire; it is now a part of you."

Handing me the phoenix, I admired the wingspan and majesty of the bird and began to hold it to my heart. But for no apparent reason, I suddenly threw it to the ground, shattering it into thousands of pieces. Looking up at the man who'd given it to me, he said, "Congratulations! You have shattered the myth, and entered the knowing of the mysteries."

"And if thou wilt even break the whole, and see those things that are without the world (if there be anything without), thou mayest. Behold, how great power, how great swiftness thou hast!"
The Divine Pymander of Hermes, Book 10, No. 123-124, (Mystery Religions, Egyptian/Hermetic)

****

Taken to a majestic wanton lake, I was invited to begin ice-skating on its frozen surface. Despite the frozen ice, flowers were in bloom all around the lake and many crowds were there to witness this moment. A beautiful lady descended from the sky wearing a golden crown of flowers, "I give you my daughter, Odyssey!" she said. Dancing on the ice, I began to feel the freedom of my soul, as my dull and drab outfit changed into that of a light, flowing and airy white gown. Around my waist was a beautiful golden butterfly. Speaking again, the beautiful lady looked into my eyes with depth. "The butterfly is what you've become; you've emerged from the cocoon of karma."

Taken to a distant mountain where a secret waited to be revealed, I boarded an elevator which could take you to any of fifty different levels on the holy mountain which mirrored the many levels of illusion on the earth. Traveling to several levels, I found that level thirty-five was the place where jealous women would claw at each other in sexually competitive games with one another. Level forty-one held the images of those who wore false faces, as each had a mask to cover their true image, and each had two names, one for their false self, and one which personified reality.

"Take me to the level where only truth lies." I called to the elevator as it soared above the crest of the mountain and into the sky. An island floated in the air covered in vegetation, flowers and waterfalls of light. As I got off of the elevator, a man was waiting for me with his arms outstretched and singing.

Sitting down to speak, he told me many things about music and how it emerges into a soul who brings melody into the earth. All beautiful things that come into the earth originate from heaven, or the eternal, which is an all-inclusive name for the forces of the Lord. As we spoke, a flame began emerging from the soil. Panicking, I ran to put it out, "The people on the mountain must be protected," I said. Walking over to the waterfall, he filled a small bucket with water as the flames had become a large circle around us. Still spreading, he gently poured the water on it to put out the excess. The flame was now in perfect order.

"It is the eternal flame," the man said, "and it can only be found above the mountain of illusion. Those on the mountain do not need protection from it for it will not go where they reside." Pausing, he sat down again. "But you must hold the eternal flame in your heart, for as you enter the different levels of illusion, you offer remembrance of this place to those within the mountain. But remember, as well, that you cannot remain on the different levels of the mountain for long. You can visit these places, but they are not who you are and you will be unable to stay long. Visit these places with love . . . but know when it is time for you to return to your own home." My home was this place *above* the mountain of illusion.

Getting up, he told me about level fifty, where most of my friends lived. "Level fifty is the threshold, those living within illusion who choose to rise above it. Those in this space visit this island often and have learned to bring much of the flame into the mountain." Watching him, I began to disappear.

Slow re-entering form and preparing to wake, I opened my eyes to notice the familiar form at the foot of my bed, a man made of light. Walking closer to me, he stopped when he was directly in front of my face. "Who are you?" I asked, fearful, but intrigued. Beginning to swirl as before, he turned into a lighted golden pyramid before disappearing.

"Mountains have been the abode of great sages from the limitless past to the limitless present. Wise people and sages all have mountains as their inner chamber, as their body and mind. Because of wise people and sages, mountains appear."
Moon in a Dewdrop, Mountain and Waters Sutra, No. 17, Page 105, Paragraph 1, (Buddhism, Zen, Words of Zen Master Dogen)

****

Overlooking a river, a rock bridge was my destination as I noticed that two places within it were split open and incomplete. Standing on the side of the water, I looked across the river to notice a man standing on the other side. Waving me to cross, I was frightened as the bridge did not seem complete. At that moment, a dark-haired scantily clad Egyptian man joined me where I was standing. As he appeared, fruit began growing on the trees all around me. "The fertile ground has been presented," he said, "but you must complete the bridge before you can pass." Pointing to the man across the river, he said, "You are drawing him into your reality with the energy of the Sphinx. His name is Heaven Dawn." Psychedelic eyes penetrated my psyche. Heaven Dawn was the masculine aspect of my higher self.

"Such is the greatness of this Day that the Hour itself is seized with perturbation, and all heavenly Scriptures bear evidence to its overpowering majesty."
The Tablets of Baha'u'llah, Chapter 17, Page 237, Paragraph 2, (Baha'i, Author: Baha'u'llah)

****

Flying to a faerie realm to meet Odyssey, it was lighted in the essence of purple, as a small faerie with violet wings appeared who obviously knew me well. Landing here and there on my fingers or arm, she was playful and happy in this rhythm of the spheres. Twinkling with the colors of pink, purple and gold, the sky held light particles which flashed through the astral airways while Odyssey was at my side. "It is time to begin energizing the Eternal Flame," she said.

Slowly re-entering form and awaking, I opened my eyes to notice a familiar form at the foot of my bed, a man made of light. Walking closer to the head of my bed, he stopped when he was directly in front of my face. "Who are you?" I asked as he began swirling and again turned into a lighted golden pyramid.

"And after seeing in his dream the gold-colored one, him who displayed a hundred hallowed signs, he hears the law, whereafter he preaches it in the assembly. Such is his dream."
Saddharma-Pundarika or the Lotus of the True Law, Chapter XIII, No. 68, (Buddhism, Nepalese, Words of the Buddha)

****

Odyssey stood by my side as I looked upon those people who would be left behind in my journey to seek God. Beginning to hunch over, my body began to take on a burdened appearance because of my hesitation in letting them go. Taking hold of me, Odyssey stood me up straight. As she did, a massive beam of light surged through my form turning me into total light. "Stand tall and BE the light!" she said, "for as you do this, the light fills you and evolves you into a higher being. By doing this you will become a magnet to others who are raising their vibration, as well."

As my sleepy eyes rolled open, the man of light again appeared in my doorway. Calmly, I was no longer afraid of him. "Hi, you're back." Nodding, he was obviously happy that I was no longer afraid, but he made no attempt to come closer or communicate. Staring for five minutes or more, he simply disappeared.

An angelic presence appeared at the side of my bed and I observed as she began forming a new energy center directly in front of my heart chakra; a second, more highly developed one.

"When a spiritual guest enters the house, like a bright flame, he must be received well."
The Upanishads, Katha Upanishad, No. 7, (Hinduism, Translation: Eknath Easwaran)

****

Meeting Heaven Dawn in an ancient coliseum, the stone encasements were blurred from the winds of time. Walking towards me, we embraced. "You are now ready for the mysteries of your higher self to reveal themselves." A gale wind blew us apart.

As my sleepy eyes rolled open, the golden man again appeared in my doorway. Calmly, "Hi," I said quietly, "you're back." Again, he nodded but no attempt to come closer or communicate more. Five minutes passed before he turned into a lighted golden pyramid and was gone.

****

And so it came to pass that many mysteries were revealed to me which held energetic currents that could free a soul from karmic bondage, past, present or future. These included the 'Magical Lace,' which frees a soul and its parallels from the bondage of childhood trauma; the 'Phoenix' which energizes the soul's change from karmic activity to eternal activity; and the 'Chimney through Frequencies' which enlivens the soul's energy beyond any karmic ties which continue to hold it back.

As I passed through these rites, I was taken deeper into my own psyche to understand my delusions and fears and all the hidden sin which held me back from union with God.

"Drag it to the light at once and say - 'My God, I have been guilty there.' If you don't, hardness will come all through."
My Utmost for His Highest, Page 76, March 16th, Middle, (Christianity, Author: Oswald Chambers)

****

Entering a horrid space, I was witnessing childhood nightmares of long ago. Violent, decadent, deviant and dark, the place held the energy of fear and despair. Observing a violent episode wherein a father was assaulting his daughter, his son had no choice but to defend his sister, which traumatized his soul and changed the relationship between sister and brother into their adult lives. Because they'd come from such darkness, they had to cut him and his vice completely out of their lives in order to recover or progress beyond it.

Immediately, light began to flash incessantly about as Odyssey entered. Waving her arms wildly, she manifested new clothes for the young man and his little sister, whose garments had been torn in the battle. Staring in shock, the little girl was rocking back and forth.

Seeing images of them as adults, I realized that they had grown up but the trauma of this experience had remained within them. Becoming afraid of losing people in her life, the young woman had assumed she'd never had the love of her father because of his behavior; or that of her brother, because she was a reminder of the trauma he'd chosen to forget. Odyssey looked at me, "Change it. Change this into a more beautiful reality."

As the little girl was now adorned in a pastel pink gown emblazoned with a beautiful lace which appeared to have been made by the angels, it was about six inches thick and held images of every beautiful creation of the Lord; angels, butterflies, winged horses, flowers, gnomes, faeries, blue skies, clouds, everything! Darting towards the little girl, I remembered the secret of the 'Magic Lace!'

The lace of the angels could free a soul from parallel spaces caught in bondage or suffering. Removing a small piece of the lace from the dress, I cried out, "I remember!" Running to the brave young man, I said, "I'm going to change the energy of your past." Waving the white lace around the sky, light began flickering as I looked at the sad little girl. "No more, I am freeing you both from the bonds of your past, I'm changing it."

In a qualified moment, we were surrounded by a wondrous land filled with all the beauty of the lace. The young man was no longer wearing tattered clothing, but shimmering in a veil of white, while the little girl was dancing with an elf. Two-foot high shamrocks and clovers were growing about them and faeries were flitting about playfully. All the joyous things of the universe existed in this faerie realm, as the Magic Lace had actually taken the energy of the little girl and boy out of the circular karmic nightmare trapped within time, and moved them into a new energy.

Looking upon the adult versions of these souls, their burden seemed to be lessened, although it was not completely removed. Lessening their burden, Odyssey assured me, would give them impetus to break free of the remaining chains of their father's sin. For the sins of the father had been visited upon this son and daughter; but by the grace of God those chains could eventually be removed.

Sending an intense vibration through my soul, vibrations surged and grew in intensity as I was suddenly wearing a white wedding gown. "It is for the marriage of you to your soul." Odyssey said.

"The three qualities - goodness, passion, and darkness also - are always acting unperceived."
The Anugita, Chapter XXIV, Page 331, Middle, (Hinduism)

****

Flying into the lands of the ancient people, Odyssey and I were admiring their ways as we entered the energetic realities of native villages which remained existent above the physical places in which they had once roamed. Dressed brightly in garments with diamond-shaped blocks of color sewn skillfully upon glittering fabrics, it almost appeared metallic, but was filled with rainbows of colors. Many of the people were wearing hats rounded about the sides and flat on top, copperish to gold in color. Monkeys were everywhere, and seemed to be some type of pet. Homes were carved in the cliffs and huts were erected along the flat mesas.

Gathering people together to listen to music, a woman was playing something similar to a xylophone, although it was different. Sounding like resonant bells which echoed through the heavens, a mystical quality emerged creating expectancy in the air.

Calling energy into action, a shadow darted across the sky generating 'Oooh's' and 'Aaah's' from everyone. Flitting with abandon, a small bird with a tail that seemed to go on into infinity flew around us in a powerful display of beauty. "It is the phoenix," Odyssey said, "the inspirer of change." Humming, the bird landed on Odyssey's arm as I was able to notice that it was made from blue starry light which emanated from within. "Whenever you need help in making a change or going higher," Odyssey said, "Hum. Hum a happy tune, think of the phoenix and he will come to you." The phoenix had the function of transforming karmic energies, karmic thrusts, and karmic delusions, and I began to enter into a liquid state wherein my soul became motile for transformation. Distant is the word I would use to describe the way I felt, as my soul felt unattached to my life, which was a very different feeling from the karmic energies which were scattered, confused, disoriented, compulsive, obsessive and almost neurotic.

"Command it to fly into Heaven, and it will not need no wings, neither shall anything hinder it, not the fire of the Sun, not the Aether, not the turning of Spheres, not the bodies of any other Stars, but cutting through all, it will fly up to the last and furthest body."
The Divine Pymander of Hermes, Tenth Book, No. 122, (Mystery Religions, Egyptian/Hermetic, Words of Hermes)

****

Painted upon the wall, Odyssey stood beside a huge mural. "This mural holds the secrets of the earthly realms." Odyssey said. A mountain scene lay before me with each aspect labeled with symbolic understanding of a level of Earthly (mortal) evolution. Nine categories existed which exhibited, but there were hundreds of steps between each level of perceiving:

1) UTS - Underground Level - Total darkness, very often evil with intent. All there is, is physical life.
2) BOOMSOIL - Ground Level - Primary darkness, and tends to engage in evil acts, although it is usually out of ignorance rather than intent. If there is a God, He is to be feared.
3) RAD - Flower and Plant Level - Total illusion, engaging in dark acts out of ignorance, but less geared towards actual evil. God is to be feared.
4) LOTU - Bush Level, Leafy Plants - Reside in illusion and reality, engaging in ignorance *and* moments of genuine kindness and inspiration, but beginning to approach cause and effect. Pertaining to God, you get what you deserve.
5) MORKAR - Small Tree Level - Karmic circling, people can get stuck here for ages, literally, until karmic purification begins, but there is a higher curiosity and examination of God which usually remains self-serving.
6) SENDU - Tall Tree Level - A threshold, residing in the world of form and spirit, no longer completely encased in karmic delusion, but unable to yet comprehend the higher, finer frequencies of existence. Intellectual view of God, rather than emotion, love or experience based.
7) PLENTU - Air above Tall Tree and Below Mountain Level - Do unto others as you would have them do unto you, state of perception. Because karma is still impure, the tendency remains to cause some harm to others out of ignorance, but there is greater knowledge of cause and effect. God is experienced as a loving God.
8) CELESTI - Mountaintop Level - Master of Creation. The knowledge of the mechanism of creation is encompassed in mortal realms, although they still make many mistakes out of an ignorance that is slowly becoming less karmic and more focused. God is just.
9) TRINAD - Air above Mountain Level - Karmic purification is almost complete,

and therefore, the soul is in training to serve the Lord. Higher levels of knowledge are reaching a balance between self-creation vs. the will of God, etc. Trinad is the *gateway* to the ascension, but you are not there yet. When karmic purification is achieved, the ascension process does complete itself. God is.

10.) TAO - Ascension achieved.

There are two major bodies of mortal knowledge to be attained beyond the TAO (which are encompassed in the Alteration and Absolution Pathways.) Between the levels of UTS, multiplicity, and TRINAD, oneness, there are many varying degrees of unity which epiphanize at TRINAD and become the knowledge attained at TAO.

As you reach higher, you mirror varying levels of perception into the physical realm. Showing me that my husband was at the top of the tree level (SENDU), I was peering from the air above the mountain (TRINAD). Below both Andy and I was a trail of light extending all the way down into UTS, showing that we had attained understanding of those points. Above my head was a small surge of light trailing from the top of my head up into the heavens, as well. Odyssey conveyed that this represented the synergy of my soul to achieve greater heights. Some souls had this synergistic light, but some did not, and among those who had the light trail above, their trail below was brighter than the one above because the trail below had been traveled more often. In essence, they were working harder on the spiritual path.

Communicating with my light trail at the SENDU level, Andy and I apparently perceived through very different eyes at this moment in time. But his trail above was ignited which indicated continuing growth.

"We are connected with them when we place ourselves at the top of this highest mountain which is made up of vibration composed of slowed down light that has crystallized into meaning."
Being and Vibration, Chapter 3, Page 111, Top, (Tribal, Tiwa, Author: Joseph Rael)
****

Destination silent, large walnut trees hovered around me as Odyssey appeared and I spoke. "I am seeking the purity of truth." Pointing to a large ragged brown building which had now appeared and was hovering in midair, a ladder rose from the ground to the entry. "Follow the river of truth," she said, "it will show you the secrets of yourself."

Beginning to climb the ladder, a resonant voice echoed across the sky. "Climb up the ladder, there's beauty inside, a river of substance to warm your insides. Few will traverse, the spiral path, it will lead you straight inward, to the core of yourself. The path starts quite slowly, but there's a point of escape, just in case you're not ready, to take this big step. When the flow slows its speed, you'll stop 'round a bend, there's a door of escape, to forget about this path. But if you want truth, push your soul down the path, your speed will pick up and your fears will come back."

Entering the ragged building, a spiraling river of a pink and gaseous substance ran through an enclosed tunnel. Just as I'd been told by the voice, the descent began slowly, and it slowed even more as I went around the first bend as it suddenly stopped. A trap door was present at this intersection in the spiral, and I knew I could end my journey now, but I shoved myself past the door, determined. Floating in midair, it began going very fast, making me dizzy and suddenly hurling me the ground.

Earthly delusions began pouring out of me and appearing as thought-forms around me. Violence, rejection, fears, stupidity, loss . . . Merging into one big mass of smoky gray energy which was removed from my innards, it landed at my feet in a big clunk.

Skies now opening up before me, I saw a man and a woman. Resonating truth, a voice said, "There is only one man and one woman . . ." Even though I didn't quite understand this yet, it gave me peace.

"There being no duality, pluralism is untrue. Until duality is transcended and at-one-ment realized, Enlightenment cannot be obtained."
The Tibetan Book of the Great Liberation, The Seeing of Reality, Page 206, Paragraph 4-5, (Buddhism, Tibetan)
****

Soaring through the heavens, Heaven Dawn beckoned to me from a distance, and when I arrived he had a gift for me. Handing me a box of what he called 'spongy creatures,' hundreds of little sponges were contained within it shaped like hearts, circles and octagons. Living creatures, they smiled at me. "These beings absorb love," he said, "I've filled these creatures with my love for you." Pulling out a heart, he said, "These represent the love that fills us," a circle was next, "and these represent completion of the soul," and finally, the octagon, "these are the immortal, the eights."

Understanding that there were eight levels of development which a soul must undertake in karmic purification, he expressed them; 1) awakening, 2) co-creation, 3) surrender, 4) rites of passage, initiation into the mysteries, 5) emergence of karma, 6) mirroring of karma, and 7) igniting of the eternal flame, and 8) ascension. Although there are very significant passages beyond these, I was unaware of them at this point.

Heaven Dawn turned to leave, but paused and looked at me again, "One more thing," he said, "The man who appears in your room at night, his name is Lavelle."

"Surely We have sent thee with the Truth as a bearer of good news . . ."
The Holy Qur'an, Part I, Chapter 2, Section 14, No. 119, (Islam, Words of Mohammad)
****

Waiting at the depths of the ocean, Odyssey had given me a silver ring upon which she was looking. Noticing that it had been transformed into an eight-sided diamond, she handed me a thin white stick of incense. With a breath, Odyssey lit the incense, which began burning an eternal flame.

Surrounded by fear mists, Red Jacket approached me. "Do not fear my essence because my fragment is immersed in karma. Your feelings were real . . ." Red Jacket disappeared.

Appearing out of the ether, Lavelle, the one who had been appearing by my bed had manifested. "Okay," I said calmly, "I'm not going to be afraid of you, please show me the reason you've been coming to me." Amused, he turned into a big yellow bird and began dancing around the room. Understanding that he was trying to show me how ridiculous it was to be afraid of him, I laughed. "Okay, but please tell me your purpose with me, don't leave me in suspense." Nodding, 'No,' he disappeared into the ether.

"He it is Who sends blessings on you, and (so do) His angels, that he may bring you forth out of darkness into light. And He is ever Merciful to the believers."
The Holy Qur'an, Part XXII, Chapter 33, Section 6, No. 43, (Islam, Words of Mohammad)
****

Entering a space filled with colorful spheres, Red Horse was manifesting sub-consciously up ahead, desperately wanting to see me and running away from me at the same time. Odyssey appeared. "Remember the 'Chimney through Frequencies.'" Handing me a piece of clay, I began molding it into a chimney, adding jewels and jade, and finishing it with a candle on each side as tall as the chimney itself. Lighting them, the chimney grew until it was about eight feet tall. In the fire pit, a murky white substance flowed which I immediately jumped into. Emerging on the other end, I was suddenly far away. Red Horse seemed so far away, like an ancient memory and somehow I'd traveled beyond him, my past and my delusions.

Holding a blanket with many symbols sewn on it, Odyssey appeared. The symbols represented moments of my life. "Red Horse represents four short lines," she said, "attach the past to this cloth, and it no longer has freedom to reign in your present." Sewing the four oblong lines onto the cloth, I began to feel as if that part of my life no longer even real. "Your 'Eternal Cloth' holds the past tight, so your future can be free." Odyssey said. A small gnome approached. "You've put it to rest," he said, "you're future is bright indeed."

Immediately returned to the faerie realm, I placed my Eternal Cloth back into Odyssey's hands, and walked quietly away from the past.

"The tenth stage is called the Great Truth Cloud (Dharmamegha) . . . Only the Tathagatas can realise its perfect Imagelessness and Oneness and Solitude. It is . . . the land of Far Distances; surrounding and surpassing the lesser worlds of form and desire (kharmadhatu), in which the Bodhisattva will find himself at-one-ment."
A Buddhist Bible, Lankavatara Scripture, Chapter XI, Page 343, Paragraph1, (Buddhism)

****

Hovering in silence, Odyssey appeared bringing with her a pulsation of light. Shaking from the vibrations, they continued to grow with intensity because of her presence as angels and heavenly hosts began appearing all around us. "Look, the ascension energy," a consensus consciousness voice said, as Odyssey continued to send light through my spirit.

Ancient drumming beckoned my spirit, as I immediately soared to a small tribal village. Leaving me in the care of an Arabian man in a pink heart-shaped tent, Heaven Dawn was in the distance, watching and waiting. Sitting on a pillow with puffy bright hearts, I watched the man in the tent as he stirred up a pot. Calling it, 'Psychedelic Stew,' he said it contained within it the psychedelic essence of the eternal. "Because you perceive yourself as unworthy of Heaven Dawn, we give you this stew which will help you relinquish control and doubt." Preparing to serve it up, he said, "You may feel rather high." Swirling of its own accord, many colors revolved within it.

Beginning to slowly sip it, I liked how it tasted and began to drink very quickly. Changing drastically, my point of perception lifted *up* as if out of a fog. Happiness, joy and a certain sense of abandon filled me as my self-doubt disappeared. Heaven Dawn entered the tent sitting right next to me. "You're perfect to me," he said.

A shooting star took me to the location of an ancient beat which was echoing through the stars. Two medicine women were drumming around me, chanting around a blazing fire. Handing me a doll, a large flame had been lit in its center, and a synergistic energy rose like an electric storms as lightning flashed. Grabbing my hands, the women said, "Be ONE with the flame." Shoving my hand into the flame in the center of the doll, the dress began to glow outward and grow. "You have lit the eternal flame; it now burns inside of you." As I couldn't yet see this flame within myself, they assured me that it would grow, but that it must be synergized with knowledge to achieve full radiance.

"Jesus said, 'Whoever is near me is near the fire, and whoever is far from me is far from the kingdom."
The Gospel of Thomas, No. 82, (Christianity, Gnostic/Essene, Words of Christ)
"Know thou moreover that every created thing is continually brought forth and returned at the bidding of thy Lord, the God of power and might."
Tablets of Baha'u'llah, Suri-i-vafa, Page 183, Paragraph 3, (Baha'i, Author: Baha'u'llah)

****

"For love that seeks aught but the disclosure of its own mystery is not love but a net cast forth: and only the unprofitable is caught."
The Prophet, On Friendship, Page 71, Paragraph 4, (Christianity, Author: Kahlil Gibran)
Outside of form, I called out, "I want the knowledge that will give me

clarity and truth." As I did so, a goddess appeared before me sitting on a golden throne. "The first thing you must do to find truth and clarity is to call me by my name. My name is Yraknin, Goddess of truth." "Yraknin, I am honored, thank you for answering my prayer for wisdom. I ask you, Goddess Yraknin, what is the knowledge that I seek that will fill me with clarity and truth?" Heaven Dawn appeared before the Goddess. "Lavelle," he said, "Do you want to know?" "Yes!" I said.

Soaring towards the Assisi Mountains beyond the star tunnel, the familiar Assisi Marauder was awaiting my arrival, a white-winged horse at his side. Deep eyes piercing mine, his cape flew wildly in the wind. "I am Lavelle," he said, "the one who appears to you. I've come to watch over my Eternal Flame. Heaven Dawn and I are ONE. I've shown you many faces. If you remember our pasts, every man you've known has held an image of us. In order to find us, we've had to search deep within self. Now we can become one." Approaching me, Lavelle tried to touch me, but a force began pulling us apart. "You ARE my fantasy," he said, "let me in . . . let me in."
****

Suddenly, Lavelle and I were surrounded by vessels from Alpha Centauri. Light beings came from inside the crafts and began spreading sparkly energy all around us. "Energizing," they said, "energizing eternal things."

Transported to Alpha Centauri, we were on a planet encompassed in different shades of violet. Everything was bright, cheery and vibrant with light. Music began emanating from all around us manifesting into sparkly light, as our eyes became psychedelic lights. "You must SEE music, before you hear it!" a light being said. Legions of angels descended as they handed me a gift; a statue of an angel. "Yes, I understand, Lord." I conveyed, as I allowed the musical part of my mission to fill me.

"O virtuous one, you have only once seen My person, and this is just to increase your desire for Me, because the more you hanker for Me, the more you will be freed from all material desires."
Srimad Bhagavatam, First Canto - Part One, Chapter 6, Text 22, (Hinduism)
"And with a great voice he said: When love beckons to you, follow him, though his ways are hard and steep. And when his wings enfold you yield to him, though the sword hidden among his pinions may wound you. And when he speaks to you believe in him, though his voice may shatter your dreams as the north wind lays waste the garden."
The Prophet, On Love, Page 11, (Christianity, Author: Kahlil Gibran)
****

Entering a cave, the Goddess Yraknin stood ready to enhance further clarity and truth, as my shame over having made the same mistake over and over throughout many lifetimes was made manifest. Yraknin intervened. "You never thought you would allow yourself to love a man filled with hate like your father, but your father didn't hate you . . . he hated himself, and released his anger on those around him. Neither did Red Jacket hate you. Distorted love . . . is still real, though not eternal." Pausing, she added, "Loving others is never wrong." Yraknin said. "In order to choose life, you must release your shame and let it all go." "I will," I replied, "I will let this go."

"'And Aaron said to Moses, 'Oh my Lord, account not to us the sin" (Num. 12:11). He said to him, 'Since we sinned inadvertently, forgive us. It was not deliberate.'"
The Classic Midrash, Numbers, Page 261, Paragraph 3, (Judaism)
****

Descending around my body and soul as I lay sleeping, a lighted dome had formed with hundreds of small little rings of light. Odyssey appeared. "It is the energy of protection, the ringlets." She said. "The what?" "As you energize the eternal flame, the role of the masculine energy is to surround the feminine in protection. Heaven Dawn has energized this field of protection." "Oh," I said, "that's kind of nice." "An eternal connection takes time, as the energies must be aligned perfectly." Odyssey replied.

"To hear Thee, O Guardian Angel of All, with soft touches of love I tuned my intuition radio."
Whispers from Eternity, Page 186, Stanza 4, (Hinduism, Kriya Yoga, Words of Paramahansa Yogananda)

"See then how He returns, not in actual flesh and blood, but, as I have said, building the road of His doctrine, with His power, which road cannot be destroyed or taken away from him who wishes to follow it, because it is firm and stable, and proceeds from Me, who am immoveable."
The Dialogue of St. Catherine of Siena, A Treatise of Discretion, Page 88, Paragraph 1, (Christianity, Catholic, Author: St. Catherine of Siena)

****

Holding swords in a circular pattern towards the heavenly hosts above, three knights held their swords so that the points might meet in the center. Decorated with religious symbols from throughout the ages, their armor displayed majesty. As their swords met, majestic energy soared straight up into the cosmos, falling gracefully into the top of my head, my crown chakra. Hovering in the heavens behind them was the secret garden. "We are the three melodies." The knights said. "Synergized, we are music. You are the chalice that we fill." Their sword touched my head lightly, "Melody, harmony and words." Then they were gone.

Juliosa appeared in the empty black space as the intensity of his eyes held familiarity. Beginning to change form, I was confused. "Juliosa?" I whispered, "Yes, it is I." Appearing in another image, he said, "Did you forget that we had business to do?" Admittedly, I had. "It's time to remember." He was gone, and suddenly I was in another time and place . . .

Dying, my wounds were bleeding profusely and I knew I had little time left to live. Our farm had been taken over by vengeful marauders. Taking my father, sister and I to the back fields, they shot each of us once in the chest.

Juliosa and I had been close; he was a field hand and had just found us lying in the grass dying. Wanting to say, 'I love you,' the words were directly on my mouth, but I was too weak to speak them. An angelic voice began singing in my brain:

"Dreamer, dreamer, dreamer
Tell him, I love you
Dreamer, dreamer, dreamer
Tell him, he'll know it's true
Dreamer, dreamer, dreamer
Tell him before the life's drained out of you
Dreamer, dreamer, dreamer
Tell him, he'll know your love is true"

Moments passed as I began slipping away into the realm where the angel's voices originated. Trying, reaching, yearning, pulling towards him, no words came. "God, I love you!" My thoughts cried out. "Why can't he hear me anymore?" Calmly, I whispered, hoping that a spirit wind would breathe these words to him from beyond the veil of death:

"In the wind, you'll feel my presence
In the stars, you'll see my breath
In the night, you'll hold the memory
Of a love I won't forget"

As my death neared completion, he never heard those words. Heaven Dawn was at my side, and I instantly knew that Juliosa and he were one. One man . . . one woman. "In one breath, lies all existence, in one moment, every moment. In one moment . . . lies all eternity." Heaven Dawn whispered.

"Hear me, you hearers, and learn of my words, you who know me. I am the
hearing that is attainable to everything; I am the speech that cannot be grasped.
I am the name of the sound and the sound of the name. I am the sign of the letter
and the designation of the division."
The Nag Hammadi Library, The Thunder: Perfect Mind, Page 302, Stanza 3
****

An unexpected message came to me in a dream when I was told that I would be hearing from Juliosa's fragment on a particular day. Our paths had parted long before, so such contact would be unusual. But on that prophesied day, it was not he who called, but my father from whom I'd not heard in years. Telling me that he loved me, I realized a great truth in this moment.

"A dream that is uninterpreted is like a letter that is unread."
The Talmudic Anthology, No. 66, Stanza 2, (Judaism)

Even those who hurt the ones they love . . . do love, it's just that their love is immature. Flawed love remains true, although not eternal. Earthly love is often ruled by karma, only becoming eternal by an intricate set of choices made by *both* parties on the ground.

'Evil has been committed by me,' thinking thus, he repents. Having taken the
path of evil he repents even more."
Dhammapada, Canto 1 - The Twin Verses, No. 15 & 17, (Buddhism)

"For even as love crowns you so shall he crucify you. Even as he is for your
growth so is he for your pruning."
The Prophet, On Love, Page 11, Bottom, (Christianity, Author: Kahlil Gibran)
****

"You will find the answer lies within," Odyssey said, "in order to find wholeness, you must *become* that which you seek. You are not yet that which you seek."

Always entertaining a delusion of someone left behind, focusing on a love that was not present, in my past, and therefore, dead, I was unable to love that which stood right before my eyes. Relationships serve purposes that reside within proper time/space continuums, and are often meant to impart a 'quality' to our soul. Thinking of many souls who had walked life's path with me, I realized that I'd been unable to 'see' many of them because I was obsessed with those who were not around. Unrequited love is a clever way to manifest fears of intimacy, because you are always in love with someone who isn't there. Someone who is not present does not have to be *real*; they are very much a *fantasy*. In my quest to seek fantasies, I'd lost opportunities for realities because I simply didn't see them. But they were there . . .

"He does not crave the object of desire because of any intrinsic value it may
possess, but simply because it is perceived as something beyond his reach."
Strive for Truth, Lovingkindness, Page 137, Paragraph 5, (Judaism, Author: Rabbi
Eliyahu E. Dessler)

Contained within my own soul is the eternal flame, it is not outside of me. In reality, we are never truly separated from those we love, because we are united in the spirit. Overcome by a majesty of knowing, it became evident that all things were a part of me, and that I was a part of all things. Everyman, everywoman . . . was one with me. Every face . . . was my own. There had never been a moment when my soul had not been completely loved by God.

Knowing that I would remain powerless only as long as my focus was not in the present moment, it became known to me that for everything there is a season, and when that season has passed, the soul must move forward. For who among us has not loved and lost, who has never known death, been afraid, felt lost, and who, I beg of you to tell me, who has never fallen from grace, even for a moment, in thought, word or deed? If you have not, you have no need of these words, but if you have . . .

"No one can be withdrawn from his evil unless he has first been brought into it."

Marital Love, The Lust for Variety, No. 510, Emanuel Swedenborg, (Christianity, Swedenborgianism)

"Let the sinner not be afraid to approach Me. The flames of mercy are burning Me - clamoring to be spent. I want to pour them out upon these souls."
Divine Mercy, Notebook 1, Page 24, No. 50, (Christianity, Catholic, Words of Christ)

And so continues the karmic journey of a soul, long, arduous, filled with pitfalls and error, but when all has passed, if a soul reaches higher for the everlasting light of God, it will begin its ascent to the divine altar of ascension, the first step on the long and winding stairway to heaven. So as the soul begins its ascent, let it awaken to the silence of knowing, which is the place where unconditional love resides. Silence takes form in love, and love takes form in silence. Knowing must become wisdom, and wisdom always retains silence.

"All hail! this is the Knowing of the Mind, the Seeing of Reality, Self-Liberation. For the sake of future generations who shall be born during the Age of Darkness, these essential aphorisms, necessarily brief and concise, herein set forth, were written down . . ."
The Tibetan Book of the Great Liberation, The Seeing of Reality, Page 238, Paragraph 6-7, (Buddhism, Tibetan)

****

There he was again, the fragment of Juliosa, watching from the sub-conscious astral state . . . always watching. "Why is it that I continue to see you everywhere I seem to go . . . beyond the physical realm, but yet we are not connected in the physical realm at all?" Juliosa appeared and overlapped him. "In one breath . . . lies all existence; in one moment, every moment. In one moment lies all eternity." "Okay, yeah?" "What we have together in one realm is not diminished by another. Can you love my soul for all that I am, even though this physical fragment is sleeping? Will you sacrifice the magnitude of a soul, because the tiny fragment of that soul is not awake?" "Well, no, of course not. You know I love you." "Perhaps that is all that it means; that there is love. We are one; we have been united beyond the veil. We will forever meet, wherever it may be, whatever time, space or reality . . . because we are not separate, because I love you, and you love me. Some parts of me have forgotten, some parts of you have forgotten, but our souls are forever one." "Thank you, Juliosa," I said. "My fragment will be in school for three more years." Juliosa added. "Okay," I replied. Exactly three years passed as my soul guardianed him from sub-conscious levels of sleep, and then my unseen work with his soul was finished.

"Of course it is bewildering, O soul of the universe, that You work, though You are inactive, and that You take birth, though You are the vital force and the unborn. You Yourself descend among animals, men, sages, and aquatics. Verily, this is bewildering."
Teachings of Queen Kunti, Chapter 13, (Hinduism)

****

Coming quickly, the spirit reached his hand to mine as he imparted his message quietly. "Someday true love is going to hit you." He said. "Do you really think so?" I responded. "Of course," he replied, "if it doesn't, then sadness exhumes the soul."

"True marital love increasingly unites two into one human being . . . And because true marital love persists to eternity, it follows that a wife becomes more a wife, and a husband more and more a husband. The ultimate reason is that in a marriage of true marital love each becomes a more and more interior human being."
Marital Love, No. 200, Page 277, Top, (Christianity, Swedenborgianism, Author: Emanuel Swedenborg)

****

CHAPTER FIVE

Palestinian Master, Civil War and a Family Named Sagrerro, Book of the Drain of the Dragons, Silken Angels, Merging of the Red Jackets, Land of Passage to Enter Eternity, To Retrieve a Golden Angel, Flatliner Dance, Meeting the Council, Native American Life in the West, Lavelle, Underwater Temple, the Old Ones and the Falling of the Veil.

****

Soaring through the echoing waves of time, my spirit landed in an ancient village outside of Palestine. A large, turbaned man with a cape wrapped around his shoulders approached. "I am the Palestinian Master. Now that I have been all that is good, and all that is bad, I find that I am in essence the same." "And what is it that you are, master?" I asked. "What is it that *you* are?" He replied calmly, "Are you not merely a manifestation of energy, and energy a manifestation of love?" Nodding, I said, "Then, I am love?" "In our purest form, we are all love . . . but what is love?" He asked. "Love is all that is." I sighed. "So if you choose to become all that you truly are, then you must become purely love?" he asked, as I became exasperated. "Yes, yes, that must be true." "Then it is time for you to take another step . . . atonement."

Stepping back from the intensity of what he said, I asked, "But what is atonement, really?" With a final sway of his robes, he replied, "All must become of the *one*." Disintegrating, he was gone.

"It is uncreated and indivisible, utterly purged, purified of the two extremes, definitively liberated from the obscurations three - the defilements, ideational knowledge and blockages to meditative mastery: stainless, completely beyond concept, and through being the domain of the Yogi . . . essentially pure, it is clarity."
The Changeless Nature, Enlightenment, Page 90, No. 212-213, (Buddhism, Words of Arya Maitreya, Author: Acarya Asanga)

****

The guns were no longer firing, the battle had stopped, but here on the mountain the lone soldier stood atop his horse dealing with the greatest battle of all . . . that of grief. Barely marked, the grave was hardly noticeable in the windswept dried grass, but it was here that they lay, his wife and their unborn child. What had once been a working farm was no more. All that remained was the wooden cross which bore the family name, 'Sagrerro.' A plaintive wail tore across the horizon.

Peering through time, I knew the grieving man to be an aspect of Red Jacket. Memory returning of how he had gone to war, in his absence, robbers had come to the farm, burned everything to the ground, and left me to die in the searing flames.

"Noooooooo! Noooooooo!" I heard the distant cries of my mother-in-law as the flames consumed everything including my life and the life of our unborn child who had been six months along. Burying me on the hill, not far from the rubble of what had once been our home; this was only the beginning of its hauntings.

Beginning to torment my soul, the memory of this time was unwilling to leave my consciousness, unwilling to leave me in peace.

"List ye, O man, drink of my wisdom, learn ye the secret, that is Master of TIME. Learn ye how those ye call Masters, are able to remember the lives of the past."
The Emerald Tablets of Thoth the Atlantean, Tablet XIII, Page 71, Paragraph 4, (Mystery Religions, Egyptian/Hermetic, Words of Thoth)

****

Yelling and screaming, the woman's face was clearly in view in my dreaming, but what was it she was so upset about? Gray hair pulled back into a bun, her plump body was neatly dressed in a flower print blue dress. "What?" I called out in the ether. Though her lips moved, I couldn't hear her. Suddenly, they were there, the four men responsible for my untimely demise. Desperately afraid of them, my screams filled the horizon. "No! Don't do it!"

Moments later, I stood before four brothers (who were not the same four men) in a different time. Holding a maternity dress made of cream-colored yarn and decorated with violet; it was long to the floor and drew me into the memory of a happier time. Smiling in remembrance, I put it on and was immediately transported back to the farmhouse.

Running across the plain, the house was on fire, the barn was ablaze and the renegades had run through our little settlement on the hill, robbing, raping and killing in their wake. Unable to run fast because I was six months pregnant, I was determined to get to the barn and save the horses from a fiery death. My husband's mother was running towards me with fear in her eyes. "No!" She screamed. "Don't go in there, it's too dangerous. No! Don't do it!" Ignoring her, I ran in.

Ensconced in flames, I opened the stalls, but one of the horses in his frenzy, kicked me in the stomach. Falling over, I tried to get up but I was hemorrhaging. It was too late, the smoke was thick. Coughing, I passed out in the smoke and passed away.

"The door of memories swings open. Among the motley I look for Thee but Thou appearest not. Halt, ye
throng of countless thoughts and experiences past! Come not into my sanctuary."
Whispers from Eternity, Page 46, Stanza 2, (Hinduism, Words of Paramahansa Yogananda)

****

Crying at the table, the Civil War was raging and I was dressed in black. My husband had been aboard a boat that had gone on a daring mission, many had been killed and I'd been told that there was no way he could've survived. Tears streaming down my face, I heard the sound of the front door. Looking up, I was stunned as my husband walked in. In elation and joy, I ran to greet him. He was alive! On this short one day leave, I got pregnant. Six months later, I died at the hands of highway robbers.

When awakening, I felt detached, as if I was no longer a part of the emotional turmoil of this haunting time. In a state of observation, I looked into it with a certain, 'I'm beginning to understand, Lord.'

****

Lying in bed, six months pregnant, I was alone in the farmhouse. Banging on the door with vigor, the renegade robbers knocked the door down and came barreling into the house. At this moment, I *knew* I was going to be raped. Again, I witnessed their attack, the fires, my mother-in-law's screams, and my own death.

The medicine man was chanting and shaking his rattles over the scene of my death. "My dear one," he said, "you felt cheated that he was taken from you by the war and when you presumed him dead. Now you must accept the choices he made. He chose to leave. This is what you must understand and embrace, that it was his choice. Release it!"

"That bhikkhu who has crossed the mire, crushed the thorn of sensual desire and reached the destruction of delusion, is not perturbed by pleasures and pains."
The Udana, Chapter 3, 3.2, Page39, Stanza 1, (Buddhism, Theravadan, Words of the Buddha)

****

"Thou hast ascended on high, thou hast led captivity captive: thou hast received gifts for men: yea, for the rebellious also, that the Lord God might dwell among them."
King James Bible, Old Testament, Psalms 68:18, (Christianity)
Entering the body of a woman in an ancient time, I was sitting next to

my husband, who was a king, and our three children. Concerned about the Amazons, a race of women who lived on a nearby island that seemed to have the secrets to power and knowledge, many people from our kingdom had gone to the island never to return. Assuming they'd all been killed, the Amazonian women were reputed to be monstrous in size and very strong.

Local mythology spoke of a sacred book which explained the secrets that they knew, but no one knew its name or what it really contained. Interested in finding this book to learn more about the Amazons, I agreed to cross the ocean path, find the sacred book, and bring it back to him.

I never returned.

A floating pathway to the island had been built by the Amazons, but the last stretch of about twenty-five feet was left unfinished. Raging ocean waters prevented those of impure heart from crossing, because in order to get to the island you had to swim in water infested with water dragons. Getting to the island was not much of a problem as the dragons rarely bothered those coming in, but were very hard on those going out. While I had been washing ashore, I noticed the size and might of the dragons and ran quickly into shore to escape their huge talons.

After arriving, I was surprised that the Amazon women were not big at all. In fact, most of them displayed very soft and feminine features. Walking around naked, their faces held a purity, solemnity and grace that I admired, because their strength was not physical, but spiritual.

Running into a soul who kept changing identities from male to female, I bowed to show my respect. "I am the Dragon Master, and I carry the sacred book." "I remember you," I said with surprise, as my current self, Marilynn began to overlap. "The Dragon Master, you were my teacher." "Yes," he said, "Come, I have messages for you . . . and the sacred book."

Traveling deep into the brush of the inner island, we sat beside a waterway which extended into the sea. A special place of teaching, a protective crystal enclosure was set up to protect pupils from the wrath of the dragons. From particle energy, the Dragon Master manifested a book and handed it to me, 'The Book of the Drain of the Dragons.' Taking it with the utmost of respect, the dragons in the water began to stir. "Do not worry," he said, "one of the secrets of the dragons is that they can only see your auric field. The Amazonian women have learned to draw in their energy around the shore so they will not be seen. We are protected by the crystal enclosure until you learn this technique, as well."

Wanting to open the book, it seemed to be stuck. "The book is not of words, but of energy. This is a book of memory." Taking my hands, the Dragon Master sent a wave of light through them, and then from his third eye to mine. A powerful energy began entering and I felt and saw images of beautiful things. "The silken angels!" I shouted, "Where are the silken angels?" Laughing, he held one of my hands and led me to a temple. "You remember quickly, my daughter." Prancing through the wilderness, we came upon the gateway to the Amazon regime. Silken pink angels immersed the entire city in a sensuous warm glow.

Allowing my consciousness to expand, I remembered that the Amazons were a spiritually evolved, predominantly female society, protected by the power of their high thoughts and the silken angels who allowed no harm to come to them. Those who had never returned had not been killed, but had either chosen to stay with them, or died at the hands of a dragon while trying to bring back secrets to a society that could not understand them and might misuse them. Wearing no clothing was a sign of their purity and looking down at myself, I realized that I, too, was undressed. Taking me to the temple, the Dragon Master said, "You carry the sword of sacred duty." Brushing his before my third eye, memories surfaced as I relived them.

Having never returned during that lifetime, my family thought I'd been killed. Desperately, I'd tried to find a way to return, but found that you can never turn back. Teaching me much, the Dragon Master helped me to pass through the Amazonian rites more and more every day. But I missed my husband and children.

One day while walking along the water lost in thoughts of my husband, I'd forgotten to pull my auric field into myself. Another woman who was just arriving was walking along the shore, as a huge green tentacled dragon surfaced and immediately grabbed her. Running to her, the Dragon Master's voice rang in my head, "You now carry the sacred sword." Manifesting in my hand was a tool very much like a screwdriver, but different. The thought of hurting the dragon repelled me, but I knew there was no other way. Taking the sword, I plunged it directly into the dragon's third eye.

Feeling the pain of transformation, my hands were bleeding profusely as the dragon had sent his claws directly through my wrist, but the woman, though badly injured, would survive. Holding her injured form in my hands, I watched in disbelief as the dragon who'd appeared dead, was now stirring and changing form. Energies of purple were soaring around his talons and his tentacles were no longer solid. A whiz of energy gyrated throughout and exploded in pink light as the dragon became a silken angel! (An allegory of the karmic soul who achieves purification.)

Standing at the new angel's side, the Dragon Master said, "You've remembered the secret of the sacred 'Book of the Drain of the Dragons.' You have drained the negativity of your dragon and transformed it into a silken angel of love." Walking forward into my soul, the silken angel became one with me, as the woman who'd been hurt just got up and walked away. Being an actress, she'd played her part well because she was not truly injured. My tears were pink as I remembered the Amazonian secrets. "The dragon?" He asked. "My unfulfilled potential." I replied. "The silken angel?" He asked. "Potentials fulfilled." "Very good, when you look in the eyes of the dragon, you fear the part of you that has yet to be transformed, but it takes courage to bring potential to fulfillment." Approaching me, his face became serious. "As a bearer of the sacred sword, I now ask of you to bear service to another." "Yes," I replied, "whatever you ask, I will do. You've shared with me the gift of memory." "I have a message for one who follows."

Although the message was for someone in particular, it was truly a message for all. Holding a stick of incense which blazed at the tip he said, "Many masters have shared techniques, doorways into the sacred spaces." I knew he spoke of the many forms of meditation, mantras, contemplatives, prayer, masses, etc. "But the ritual is not the *truth*, it is the *door*. Use the technique for the purpose of opening the door, not as an end in itself. You must open the door in order to find sacred memory." Nodding, I understood him. "Tell my honored friend this." He paused as a rainbow gyrated above the incense.

"Brethren, there are monks who are keen on Dhamma and they disparage those monks who are meditators, saying: 'Look at those monks! They think 'We are meditating, we are meditating,' and so they meditate and meditate, meditating up and down, to and fro! What, then, do they meditate and why do they meditate?' Thereby, neither these monks keen on Dhamma will be pleased nor the meditators. (By acting in that way,) their life will not be conducive to the welfare and happiness of the people, nor to the benefit of the multitude."
Anguttara Nikaya 1-3, Part II, Book of the Fives, No. 24, Paragraph 2, (Buddhism, Theravadan)

****

Another person came into my life for a period of time, who exhibited the same personality qualities demonstrated in the Red Jacket lifetimes. Despite many nudgings to go towards the light, he was choosing an alternate path.

Odyssey came to show me what happens to the souls of those who run out of time in karmic circling, and are held accountable for that which they do.

Apparently, this fragment had lived a lie, using deception and dishonesty to get what he wanted in life. Receiving several opportunities for grace, he had denied them all.

A dark cloudy vortex encompassed him, and the power of it was unfathomable and frightening. Watching as he became consumed in the raging clouds of the backwards flow, Odyssey said, "He has refused the hand of the eternal, he will now experience some of the darkest times of his life."

"There are five mistakes: faint-heartedness, contempt for those of lesser ability, to believe in the false, to speak about the true nature badly and to cherish oneself above all else. The ultimate true nature is always devoid of any thing compounded: so it is said that defilements, karma and their full ripening are like a cloud etc. The defilements are said to be like clouds."
The Changeless Nature, Buddha Nature, Page 70, No. 157-160, (Buddhism, Words of Arya Maitreya, Author: Acarya Asanga)

****

Odyssey handed me a stick of incense with a label that read, "Pathway of Ascension."

Standing gracefully, I awaited the entrance of somebody unknown, although I felt the ominous importance of the moment to come. Red Jacket entered the room and at his side, Red Horse. At his side, the most recent fragment joined. At his side, other manifestations of this soul began to appear, each from different lifetimes. Joining hands, they were showing a link between them, one to another. Looking at me with expectancy, I said, "I understand, they all come on behalf of the same karma." There's only one man and one woman . . . Red Jacket stepped forward. "You *have* to understand!" He said with great urgency. "You have to let this go *now*. I will love you forever, but you must see clearly not only what is true *beyond* illusion, but what is true *within* illusion. Immortality is forever, I will always be a moment." I was beginning to understand. Just because you have karma, or a connection to another person, doesn't mean you have to do something about it. Interestingly, those who truly follow the precepts taught in the major religions are sometimes able to rise above karmic impetus, making former lifetimes less relevant. After all, these matters do involve choice.

Gazing at Red Jacket and his counterparts, I said, "I will honor your soul, I will walk away." Red Jacket embraced me, looking deeply into my eyes. "I love you now more than ever," he said, "because you love me enough to serve my soul." They disappeared, as I cried.

"He is convinced that his happiness depends on his attaining this particular object and that if he would only achieve this goal he would be happy ever after. If he only realized how deluded he was about this he would soon cease his pursuit."
Strive for Truth, Volume 1, Lovingkindness, Page 139, Top, (Judaism, Author: Rabbi Eliyahu E. Dessler)

****

"Marilynn, you are resistant to love." The angel said to me. "I know you're right," I answered, "but I don't think I understand."

Surrounding my form in a whirlwind of light, my consciousness waned but resurfaced in a dark and dank graveyard. Tombstones carried the names of the dead, and those who hadn't yet been buried lay on the ground covered in sheets. This dark place didn't frighten me, but it didn't feel very good to walk within its midst, so I began searching for an exit through which I could leave.

In the distance, I could see a doorway. Light was pouring through the cracks and I knew that it was my destination. Walking towards it, the corpses covered in sheets were scattered everywhere and I had to be very careful to avoid stepping upon them. But as I walked, a hand came from under a sheet and grabbed my thigh, trying desperately to hold me in the graveyard.

Gently, I picked up the hand and placed it back under its sheet, but as I did so, I had accidentally moved the part which covered this dead person's face. "Oh, my God!" I thought, "It's him." Eyes showing sadness, Red Jacket's most recent fragment remained content in this dark place, as the vortex had overcome his soul. A rush of emotion urged me on towards the door where a security officer awaited me. "This is the place for the spiritually dead," he said, "those who have forgotten the eternal for momentary gains that aren't real. Leave this place, and as you go, shed the armor you have taken on to protect yourself from those who are not living. Those who do not live do not love. Those who do not love do not live. Shatter your illusion that one as yourself mustn't deserve love because a dead man cannot return your love. A DEAD MAN HAS NOTHING TO GIVE!" Deceased in the spirit, though not of the flesh, thunder roared across the horizon.

"Jesus said, 'Look to the living one as long as you live, or you might die and then try to see the living one, and you will be unable to see.'"
   The Gospel of Thomas, No. 59, (Christianity, Gnostic/Essene, Words of Christ)
****

Taken aboard a bus, Andy and I were going on a journey to a land of passage. Several different bus trips were to be taken to complete this journey, and with each trip a successive rite of passage.

On the first bus, a man who wore a jacket depicting the many faces of the Earth greeted us. Conveying to us that we would have only a short period of time to complete the passage, if we didn't make it . . . we couldn't continue.

Exiting the bus at the first passage, we noticed a mausoleum and went towards it. Instinctively we knew that there would be ancient sacred statues which contained energies needed to energize an eternal program. Walking in the doorway, however, we suddenly stood atop a magnificent snow-topped mountain.

Sacred statues were strewn amongst the wintry wilderness, and we could see the next bus waiting at the bottom of the mountain. Urging me to hurry, Andy was concerned that we reach the bottom in time; but the snow was high and slushy, and despite my thigh-high rubber boots, I kept falling into puddles and snow-drifts. Although he only wore tennis shoes, Andy had no trouble with this. Andy had a much higher degree of physical skill, and I was able to continue because of his help. After what seemed like a long time, we both reached the bottom in time to board the next bus. Another guide awaited us.

Holding two small statues, one held the image of an Indian man, and the other an ancient priest. Indicating that we needed to find the hieroglyphic signs upon each statue in order to continue our journey, Andy picked them up but could not find any signs. "No, Andy," I said, "the sign would be at the base of the statues, the foundation, where all things must begin." Turning them to their base, we found the mysterious sign which was on the 'Book of the Eights.' Realizing that I had a higher degree of spiritual skill than Andy, he was able to continue because of my help.

Showing these signs to the guide, he quietly said, "Yes, now we go to 'Nightmare house.' A psychedelic van will be waiting to pick you up, and it will be very difficult to make it in time." "Nightmare house?" I said, conveying my displeasure at this uninviting title. But he said nothing more as he dropped us off at the eerie old mansion, which looked to be haunted by all sorts of nasty things.

Greeted at the door by a small woman, she had a dog. A short balding man with a terrorizing demeanor spoke like an echo in your mind. Leading us to a small room on the left side of the house, it contained frightening elements from our lives, and aspects of memory which had had laid down limiting patterns on our souls.

Overwhelmed by the energy of what I saw of my own past, Andy volunteered to walk in first to assist me with my nightmare, but as he entered, he disappeared, and in what seemed to be the will of God, I was left alone to overcome it. Exhausted and confused, the first thing that caught my eye was a mangled tricycle which had been run over by a car. Inspiring a long ago memory of an accident, it had become a symbol of my fears. Walking towards it, I owned my own memory, touched it, and was immediately transported to the other side of the house.

Completely immersed in obsessive cleaning, Andy was not yet released from his past. I saw the old man laughing in my mind, his eeriness never waning. From the corner of my eye, I noticed that the woman was fleeing the premises. "What's going on?" I thought. Looking out the window, I saw three men in revolutionary war attire coming towards the house with fiery torches. Somehow knowing that they were going to burn down 'Nightmare House' in order to transform our karmic past, I realized that if we didn't get out of here first, we would spiritual die in the fire of karma. "Andy!" I shouted. "We have to go! They're going to set this house on fire." Andy, still trapped within his prison, was unable to respond to my words.

Grabbing his arm, we ran towards the side door which led into a vast maze. Realizing that the time to catch the van was nigh, I dragged him behind me as we tried to decipher this unusual conglomeration of tunnels. Behind us, the home was ablaze and the fire was spreading into this maze of illusions. Hot on our trail were the three men, who followed us because it was their mission to hold us in our karmic past and keep us from making passage.

Up ahead was a small bridge across a divide which was about four feet wide with a white hazy void below it. Not knowing what lay beyond that void, I knew we needed to cross quickly and then remove the bridge to stop the past from entering into the present. After crossing, I mistakenly thought Andy had already crossed, and thus, I'd removed the bridge. Panicking, I called to him to jump the gap, but he wasn't running, but walking rather slowly and before I could stop him, he fell into the great white void.

I screamed . . . and I screamed, but the woman who'd previously left nightmare house suddenly appeared, "Maybe he's re-entering eternity." Grabbing my hand, she forced me to continue my quest through the roundabout tunnels reaching higher and higher. Once we reached the surface, I knew we would see the psychedelic van.

After what seemed like an endless ascent through the maze, I saw the door. Pushing it open, I ran to the van. "Wait! Wait!" I yelled, "Maybe he'll get here . . ." But the driver sped off without delay. "You never know," he grinned, "Andy might be in the back of the van. He might have gotten here *before* you." Now allowing me to look, he grinned from ear to ear as we sped off.

"When he gives attention to formations as impermanent, they appear to him as exhaustion, when he gives attentions to formations as painful, they appear to him as terror. When he gives attention to formations as not-self, they appear to him as voidness."
The Path of Discrimination, Treatise on Liberation, Page 258, Paragraph 6, (Buddhism, Theravadan)

****

Sweeping through the window, the golden angel gained in size as she approached. Spreading to envelope my soul, I entered her as we became one.

And it was said that he who died by the sword must live again and retrieve a golden angel. As the swordsmen left his life, the man he had tried to kill appeared. Remembering his own moment of death, he had died taking the life of another. With fear in his eyes, Andy hovered about his own dead body hoping to understand what his purpose could now be. Although the ninja warrior didn't speak, he extended his hand in forgiveness, and as Andy reached to take his hand, he was swept away.

Seeing a crowd up in the distance, the ancient swordsman noticed that everyone he'd ever known had gathered; family and friends from all lifetimes awaited his arrival. Walking through the crowds, the celebration was in full force to honor his return to reality.

Standing in the distance beyond the crowd, I stood. Light surrounded me, and he was entranced. Quickly moving to find me, he could not because I would disappear as soon as he would approach. "Where are you my golden angel?" Andy cried out, as I appeared at his side holding his hand. "You remember me?" I asked. "I do, but from where I know not." As we began to dance, our family and friends looked on. "Those who die by the sword," I said, "must live again to retrieve a golden angel. I've loved you forever and I've watched over you for centuries. As the ninja warrior returns to this side, you must return to the Earth. You have learned the ways of the warrior, now you must seek love and become an eternal warrior, a warrior of peace." "I don't want to go back to earth," the swordsman said, "I don't want to leave you, my golden angel." "But leave, you must," I said, "as you discover the peaceful way, the lighted way, you will also find me, for I will go with you this time. Seek me, for I shall be your counterpart." A light grew in the room, as my angelic essence was allowed to appear as all that it is, in its radiance. Only a moment passed, and we flew towards Earth to reincarnate into the tribes of man.

"Just as the disease needs to be diagnosed, its cause eliminated, a healthy state achieved and the remedy implemented, so also should suffering, its causes, its cessation and the path be known, removed, attained and undertaken."
The Changeless Nature, Buddha Activity, Page 134, No. 331, (Buddhism, Words of Arya Maitreya, Author: Acarya Asanga)

****

Trotting upon the back of a horse, my soul was embarking upon a cathedral in the distance. A woman's voice began singing in operatic tones of her love for the Lord. As I came upon the holy site, I realized that this cathedral was for God's royal family, the prophets, mystics, saints and sages from throughout the world and throughout time. Beautifully decorated, statues of holy things were everywhere.

Wandering alone to the altar, a familiar face beckoned me to come near. Looking at him, he was wearing a white shirt and a pair of blue jeans but what was most striking about him was his long blonde hair and the medallion he wore. Upon it was the Sign of Otara, the sign of the angels.

Coming towards him, he mimicked every move I made, coaxing me with lively smiles. Acting as though he were my twin, he didn't cease to imitate any form I took upon myself. In order to confuse him, I began doing a pretty complicated dance step, and rather than repeating my new moves, he put his hands on his hips, smiled, and scolded me.

Who are you?" I asked him, as he shrugged his shoulders in jest. Pointing to a set of gems directly in front of him, he motioned me to look at them. "They are gems," I said, but he directed me to look closer. Each gem held a face inside, the different men in my life, while the center gem held an image of Andy, my ex-husband.

Gazing closer, I noticed that all of them were fakes, simple plastic imitations, except the center piece which held Andy's image. It glimmered with light like a true gem. "It is coming full circle. A true gem cannot be distinguished from a group of fake stones unless one looks closely to see the reality and the illusion. The seeker must embrace the gem. What is real, and what is illusion, what is eternal, and what is momentary? Gems are rare, plastic is common. Potentials unfulfilled have no meaning, potentials fulfilled are eternal." He disappeared.

"For a certain higher part of the soul has advanced already to the point of judging the good of righteous action, while a slower, carnal part of the soul is not led by reason to this judgment. Thus, as a result of this very difficulty, the

soul is urged to pray to the One who aids it towards its perfection, whom it recognizes as its Creator."
On Free Choice of the Will, Book Three, XXII, Page 139, Top, (Christianity, Catholic, Author: St. Augustine)

"Now, my God, You can easily look upon and bear high esteem for the soul You behold, for by Your look You present her with valuables and jewels and then esteem her and are captivated."
The Collected Works of St. John of the Cross, The Spiritual Canticle, Page 540, Stanza 33, No. 9

****

Gleaming golden pyramid steps shone in the bright sun as I began the short trek to the top of the temple. Flying to the crest was easy, but what greeted me at the top was surprising. The golden sphinx lay silently, peacefully . . . emerged. Dancers were swaying all around it, as a spirit told me, "They are doing the flat liner dance." Noticing that they were imitating the fluctuating heartbeat of a dying person, the heartbeat became erratic and then flat; purged of life (Death of Karma).

Attention falling to the sphinx, I was shocked when he turned his head towards me. A living being, he was quite noble in stature. Opening his eyes for only a moment, he revealed grayish-blue eyes. Knowing that this dance had been done for me, every soul that is born into ascension must first die to karma.

"Deep neath the image lies my secret, search and find in the pyramid I built.
Each to the other, is the Keystone; each the gateway, that leads into LIFE.
Follow the KEY I leave behind me, seek and the doorway to LIFE shall be thine.
Seek thou in my pyramid, deep in the passage that ends in a wall, use thou the KEY of the SEVEN, and open to thee, the pathway will fall."
The Emerald Tablets of Thoth the Atlantean, Tablet V, Page 31, Paragraph 2, (Mystery Religions, Egyptian/Hermetic, Words of Thoth)

****

Standing before the council with my papers in hand, a council member said, "It is she who seeks passage; show us your life papers." Looking down in my hands, the papers I held were an in-depth look at all that I had accomplished up to this point in my lifetime. Handing it over, I looked dimly at the council. "Well, I don't know how I fare," I said, "I've done quite a bit, but I've never made much money." A slight chuckle passed through the council. "What we are looking for is something quite different. What have you sought, physical or spiritual wealth? What have you gained, knowledge or goods?" The bearer of knowledge and wisdom, one who has sought knowledge and found it, is the one who is ready to receive passage."

Sheepishly, I spoke on my own behalf. "To be quite honest, I have been a seeker of knowledge all my life. It has always been my highest purpose." A knowing look passed through the council, "You have, indeed, and you don't need this to show that." Tossing the paper aside, they continued, "We vision a seeker by his heart, you will be given passage and the knowledge that will set you free."

And then they disappeared.

"'A person who devotes his mind, body and speech to the service of the Lord, even though in the midst of a miserable life fraught with past misdeeds, is assured of liberation."
Teachings of Lord Caitanya, Chapter 26, Page 290, Paragraph 2, Quote from Srimad-Bhagavatam, (Hinduism, Author: A.C. Bhaktivedanta Prabhupada)

"Jesus continued again in the discourse and said unto his disciples: 'When I shall have gone into the Light, then herald it unto the whole world and say unto them: Cease not to seek day and night and remit not yourself until ye find the mysteries of the Light-kingdom, which will purify you and make you into refined light . . . '"
Pistis Sophia, Third Book, Page 213, Paragraph 1, (Christianity, Gnostic/Essene, Words

****

Awaking to the physical world, a voice came abruptly and with power. "FIND YOUR TWIN!" The male voice emitted intensity and exasperation. "Who are you?!" I called out, as the voice repeated, "FIND YOUR TWIN AND MAKE HIM YOURS!" A white spirit form appeared in front of me, as I immediately recognized him as the man from the cathedral who had mimicked my every move. "May 10th is your day," he said, "Oh really? In what way?" I asked. "It is your birthday!" he replied, knowing full well that my biological birthday was in March. "FIND YOUR TWIN AND MAKE HIM YOURS." Looking at the clock, it said 6:30 A.M. The spirit began disintegrating until he disappeared. Looking at the clock, it was now midnight.

"Everything is foreknown, but man is free."
The Talmudic Anthology, No. 97, Page 135, Stanza 4, (Judaism)

"My son, listen to my teaching which is good and useful, and end the sleep which weighs heavily upon you. Depart from the forgetfulness which fills you with darkness, since if you were unable to do anything I would not have said these things to you. But Christ has come in order to give you this gift. Why do you pursue the darkness when the light is at your disposal? Why do you drink stale water though sweet is available for you? Wisdom summons (you), yet you desire folly. Not by your own desire do you do these things, but it is the animal nature within you that does them."
The Nag Hammadi Library, The Teachings of Silvanus, Page 383, Paragraph 1, (Christianity, Gnostic/Essene)

****

Screaming wisdoms echoed through time as my spirit journeyed into yesteryear. Of different and warring tribes, Andy and I were very much in love. Together for what would be the last time, we both knew it, and as we parted he spoke his last words to me, "This can never be. We must go."

Shortly thereafter, my death came suddenly like a wind in the night as I left my Earthly home to return to the grandmothers who lived within the mountains in the sky. Years went by and I became my true essence, that of a grandmother spirit watching over her many spiritual grandchildren. Going to him in dreams, he'd reject me openly due to his anger over my death. Determined to keep our momentary union a secret, my memory haunted him. In his heart, however, he knew the truth. It was something that could not be in this time or place, but would have to be in another. "I am you, you are me," he would always say, and it was true.

Close to his death, I returned to him in a dream. Becoming a great chief to his people, he'd married another and felt conflict in seeing my spirit. Touching my essence beyond form, he said, "I cannot do this, if I feel your skin, I will remember how it once was, how it used to be. I cannot let that happen." Whispering in his ear, I spoke quietly to his heart. "I love you as grand as the setting sun, with the passion of a night wind thunderstorm, with the power of the winding valley, with the joy of the singing bird. I am you; you are me, as we will always be." A lone teardrop fell from his eyes down his time-worn face.

"Oh Lord of Law, may I wear my scars of trials like deserved medals of chastisement, presented to me by the sacred hands of Thy perfect justice."
Whispers from Eternity, Page 70, Paragraph 1, (Hinduism, Kriya Yoga, Words of Paramahansa Yogananda)

"We must feel the suffering of our people. To be transfigured we have to be disfigured in our own sight."
The Love of Christ, Part III, Page 84, 18 July 1968, (Christianity, Catholic, Words of Mother Teresa)

"I find myself in some scene which I cannot have visited before and which is yet perfectly familiar; I know that it was the stage of an action in which I once took part..."

Reincarnation - An East-West Anthology, British, Page 154, John Buchan
****

A disturbing rite, the 'Maze of Passages' was a very bizarre initiation wherein there was almost a vortex of constant motion. Various choices and potential paths appeared before me as if in a constant stream. Constantly moving, I made choices to go one way, found it incorrect, turned around, found another, picked a different direction . . . water crossings, the field of childhood dreams and nightmares, lenses of reality which passed before me until clarity was achieved. A drama perceived as reality was the wrong choice and appeared as a blurry and unfocused mess. Leading to a life trapped inside a novel, perceiving earthly life as the only reality; was *not* where I wanted to go. Barreling out of there, I found clarity.

Standing amidst an old room filled with artifacts of my past-lives, I looked at war bonnets, headdresses, old books, pipes, etc. Turning, the chief had been watching me. "You are a writer," he said, "and you simply must write." Handing me an old book entitled, "TWINS," I began leafing through it, intrigued that the date on the book was 1909. Inside, it spoke of a bond so strong that the souls were truly like one soul. There was a picture of the Chief, and a picture of myself as the woman I'd been in that lifetime. Below it, it read, 'Twins.' I looked at him again . . .

"It is the Bridegroom who takes up the song here and describes the soul's purity in this state and her riches and reward for laboring and preparing herself to come to Him. He also tells of her good fortune in having found her Bridegroom in this union . . ."

The Collected Works of St. John of the Cross, The Spiritual Canticle, Page 541, Stanza 34, No. 2

****

Sitting by the river, I was with the Chief who represented Andy's higher self. Coming to direct me to view the water, a shimmering could be seen from the shallow bottom of the river. "What is that?" I asked, reaching to pick it up. "Oh, it's a wedding ring," I said, "someone must have thrown it away; they must have no longer wanted it." Placing it on my finger, I suddenly recognized it. "It's MY wedding ring, I haven't worn this since Andy and I got divorced." "Maybe you'd like it back," the Chief said. "Yes! I do want it back!"

Knowing that an eternal union could not come without a great deal of work, I accepted that it would require gentle cultivation and time. Would Andy be willing to come with me, knowing there were many problems and issues for us to deal with?

A shooting sound was heard overhead, and I looked up to see a white-winged horse approaching with an eternal rider, Heaven Dawn and Lavelle of the Assisi Marauders who had appeared all those nights at the foot of my bed were merged into one. But as he came closer, something appeared different. "Wait a minute," I said, "Is that . . . Andy?" Before I could answer my own question, Heaven Dawn had swooped down to pick me up. My essence became that of a golden angel, an eternal manifestation of Odyssey. Flying high up into the ether sky, I tried to get him to turn, and when he did, I was dumbfounded. "Andy . . . it's you!" I shouted, as his essence had become that of an Assisi Rider, an eternal manifestation of Heaven Dawn. "I will come with you," he said, "I am you, you are me, we *are* the *reality*."

Soaring off into the heavens, today was May 10th, my 'birthday.' And on that day, we reconciled.

"It is to be observed that at the conclusion of a Grand Period, only two persons are left in the world, one man and one woman . . ."

The Desatir, Prophet, the Great Abad, Page 16, No. 117, (Zoroastrianism)

"On the sleigh of incarnations we slide from dream to dream. Dreaming, in a chariot of astral light we roll from life to life. Dreaming, in a vibrant physical vessel tossed by alternating waves of birth and death, we sail uncharted seas.

Becalmed waters of indifference, whirlpools of activity, eddies of laughter, inexorable swells of mighty outer events - dreams all! It was only in Thee I awoke! Then I realized that, thinking I was awake, I had been only dreaming."
Whispers from Eternity, Page 165, Paragraph 2-3, (Hinduism, Kriya Yoga, Words of Paramahansa Yogananda)

****

"Listen carefully, listen carefully and ponder deeply. I, the Tathagata, shall discourse on the pure karma for the sake of all sentient beings of the future who are afflicted by the enemy, evil passions."
The Three Pure Land Sutras, Contemplation Sutra, No. 8, (Buddhism, Pure Land, Words of the Buddha)

"Blessed art Thou, O Lord, who puttest the sense of discernment into the heart of Thy servants, (that they may walk blamelessly before Thee,) and be steeled against all the devi(ces) of wickedness, and that they may bless (Thy name,) (loving) all that Thou lovest and abhorring all that (Thou hatest,) (and stray not in the waywar)dness of men, but, through the spirit of (discern)ment which is theirs, (distinguish) the good from the wicked, (and keep) their deeds undefiled."
The Dead Sea Scriptures, The Book of Hymns, Page 196, Stanza 3, (Christianity, Gnostic/Essene)

Falling into its depths, the ocean was mild that night. Land could not be seen for many miles from this sacred place, as I was seeking an underwater temple. Reaching the bottom, I saw the entrance fairly quickly. Looking much like the 'Taj Majal,' it held lights of many colors. No one seemed to be there, when . . . a voice began speaking. "You must show that you are worthy to receive the wisdom." It said. Behind me a screen appeared showing scenes from my life and how I'd handled them, both in the physical and beyond the veil. "You are welcome," it said, as the great marble white gate began to open

Swooshing suddenly back into my body, I was lying in bed as the purpose of the temple revealed itself. A massive energy surge overtook my body, thousands of times stronger than I'd ever felt before. Scared, I'd never felt anything quite like this, but suddenly, my whole *body* and *spirit* lifted up out of bed, beginning to fly around the room. "It IS possible!" I screamed out, trying to get Andy's attention, but he was deeply asleep, assisted in his unconsciousness by his angels so that he wouldn't see the spectacle. For the next hour or so, the energy beam came and went, taking me on bodily flights around the room.

"Know that all states of being . . . are manifested by My energy. I am, in one sense, everything, but I am independent. I am not under the modes of material nature, for they, on the contrary, are within Me."
The Bhagavad Gita, Chapter 7, Text 12, (Hinduism, Translation: A.C. Bhaktivedanta Swami Prabhupada)

****

Standing atop the canyon lands, the native grandmother was pointing deep into the Earth, as music began to arise from its depths. Mesmerized, the Old Ones began phasing in and out of energy before me, and I felt their beckon to my soul. "I will come." I said peacefully, as I listened to the majestic melody of the Earth. "I will come."

A small pile of wood appeared as thunder crashed across the horizon. Trembling, a huge bear broke through the pile, awaking from hibernation. "The sleeping bear wakes, the dream becomes a reality," the Old Ones said. Being called to the mountains, it was time to go home.

"Holy messenger of the Earthly mother, enter deep within me, as the swallow plummets from the sky, that I may know the secrets of the wind and the music of the stars."
The Essene Gospel of Peace, Volume 1, Page 39, Stanza 1, (Christianity, Gnostic/Essene)
****

Chief Joseph was serene and direct as we walked in the mountain pathway. Handing me four temples of ice, he said, "Seek the place where the temples of the Earth reside." Drawing with his fingers in the dirt, he etched a sacred medicine wheel. "Sacred ground," he said. All of a sudden I noticed a native doll unlike any other I'd ever seen. Lying in the woods, I ran to retrieve it. "I love this!" I shouted. "That does not surprise me." Joseph replied. "This doll is a gift from the Old Ones. It is their remembrance." Embracing it with humility, Chief Joseph handed me a papoose. Unaware of it at the time, he was trying to tell me we were going to have more children. In the blink of an eye we were now standing at the edge of a mighty canyon. Music was emanating from the canyon floor. "You will find it at the end of the road," he said, as I knew he spoke of our coming homeland. Then he was gone.

A mountain pass stood majestically before me, as a singular monk sat alone under a tree silently meditating.

"I looked about me and could see that what we then were doing was like a shadow cast upon the earth from yonder vision in the heavens, so bright it was and clear. I knew the real was yonder and the darkened dream of it was here."
Black Elk Speaks, Chapter XIV, Page 169, Paragraph1, (Tribal, Oglala Sioux, Words of Black Elk)

****

"Woe, woe unto sinners, on whom the negligence and the forgetfulness of the rules lie until they come out of the body and are led to these chastisements! Have mercy upon us, have mercy upon us, son of the Holy (One), and have compassion with us, that we may be saved from these chastisements and these judgments which are prepared for the sinners; for we also have sinned, our Lord and our Light."
Pistis Sophia, Sixth Book, Page 324-325, Bottom & Top, (Christianity, Gnostic/Essene, Words of the Disciples to Jesus)

And so it came to pass that the veil between my former life and my current one began to fall just as had been prophesied by the Old Ones. Required to make a choice of following the Lord thy God or allowing myself to be plummeted into the dark and Godless reality of the world at large, my worldly past became as a former life. I chose God and the veil fell.

"And every one that hath forsaken houses, or brethren, or sisters, or father, or mother . . . for my name's sake, shall receive an hundredfold, and shall inherit everlasting life."
King James Bible, New Testament, Matthew 19:29, (Christianity, Words of Christ)
"God dwells in all beings. But you may be intimate only with good people; you must keep away from the evil-minded. God is even in the tiger; but you cannot embrace the tiger on that account."
The Gospel of Sri Ramakrishna, Chapter 1, Page 84, Paragraph 5, (Hinduism, Words of Sri Ramakrishna)

****

CHAPTER SIX
Karma of Religion, Struggle to Discipline the Will and Overcome Vice, Karmic Retribution, the Great Red Road, Satanic Cults, Homosexuality, Withholding Forgiveness, Self-Forgiveness, Karma of Original Sin, Why We Need Religion.

****

Wearing a monk's robe, I was covered in the garment of the Catholic faith. Some Islamic renunciants saw me and began throwing fireballs at me. A voice told me, 'Islamic renunciants don't like Catholic monks.' Finding a box filled with old rosaries, I placed my fingers amongst them and was delivered from the strange assault. For a moment I felt within me the stupidity of religious hatred, as God created all peoples, whether they be Hindu, Islamic, Buddhist, Christian or otherwise; to disregard this is ignorant.

And so it came to pass through a series of experiences, I was shown aspects of the dark side as it manifests in various world religions. Hovering in the air over a vortexing whirlpool below, I was told that the Babe Batre was violent and unjust, especially towards women. At the time, I didn't know that the Babe Batre was a tract of the Jewish Talmud. Arrogance and self-satisfaction were the failing of Nichiren, who founded the Nichiren sect of Buddhism. Profoundly, I was shown his dark liaisons. And as a certain branch of the Catholic monks of old came flying at me carrying their tools of self-torture, a stick with a hanging iron ball gilded with spikes, I felt their hatred of humanity. The Lord, in liberating me from them, made me to know that there is a difference between victim souls who are chosen by God whose sufferings come from above, and those who torture the body for no purpose other than their own self-hatred and hatred of others. God *is* love, and he wishes us to serve our individual functions as He so deigns, in whatever religion He might choose for them. And in the same vein, a great Old One appeared to me from the mountains in the sky, saying that the tribal religions go a bit further than necessary in their self-mutilation and torturous practices. Certain of the mystery sects were singled out as failing in humility. In particular, the Rosicrucians were shown to have a weakness in this arena, due to the intellectualized nature of their belief; they become dark when they fall into arrogance and intellectual pride.

Beyond this, I was shown that almost all religions share differing degrees of an element of darkness which cannot be sustained on a true spiritual path - control. Because of judgmental absolutism, and rigid observance of ritual and rule, they do not allow God to express himself uniquely in individual souls, because it doesn't follow their own rigid practice or belief. Therefore, it is disregarded as coming from an evil force. Although discretion is always warranted in the acceptance of mystical experience, it is ignorant to refuse to accept God's movement within individual souls of many faiths, cultures and circumstances. God reaches to all of His children, in every part of the world.

As balance is always a required element of understanding, it is important to remember the many holy aspects in the world religions, as well. Throughout time there have been saints in every order who have been formed to be that which they were within the confines of religious rule and observance. These saints are in no way diminished by the failings of the political structure of religion, and in many cases, have been greatly increased because of their obedience to their faith. God chooses whom He chooses, and He has chosen many souls for holiness from all walks of life, from all religions (some from no religion at all), from all cultures, from all corners of the world. And in many respects, it is those saints who come from rigid rule who become the most holy, for they attain the highest levels of discipline. But this rigid rule becomes destructive when it disallows the natural mechanism of mortal realms to take place, karmic purification. For the saints who attain to such heights have already achieved this goal, while the remainder of humanity remains below in karmic circling unable to grasp their height. God reaches to us all, and let us thank Him for this gift, rather than limiting His holy movement within the consciousness of mankind through our own ignorance and fear.

"You may say that there are many errors and superstitions in another religion. I should reply: Suppose there are, every religion has errors. Everyone thinks that his watch alone gives the correct time. It is enough to have yearning for God."
The Gospel of Sri Ramakrishna, Chapter 4, Page 112, Paragraph 1, (Hinduism, Words of Sri Ramakrishna)

"The purpose of religion as revealed from the heaven of God's holy will is to establish unity and concord amongst the peoples of the world; make it not the cause of dissension and strife."
The Tablets of Baha'u'llah, Chapter 8, Ishra'q'at, The ninth Ishra'q, Paragraph 1, (Baha'i, Author: Baha'u'llah)

"Run not after rule."
The Talmudic Anthology, No. 146, Page 194, Stanza 6, Pesikta Rabbati, 22, (Judaism)
****

Many nights passed where I was allowed to traverse back in time to days of old when I was a member of different religious orders: Buddhist, Catholic, Tribal, and Mystery Religions. Beyond that, I was given to experience lives as a layperson in many of them, too: Jewish, Hindu, Buddhist, Christian, and Moslem. This knowledge gave me a sense of unity.

"The dreaming mind recalls past impressions. It sees again what has been seen; it hears again what has been heard, enjoys again what has been enjoyed in many places. Seen and unseen, heard and unheard, enjoyed and unenjoyed, the real and the unreal, the mind sees all; the mind sees all."
The Upanishads, Prashna Upanishad, Stanza 5, Page 164, (Hinduism, Translation: Eknath Easwaran)

****

And so it came to pass that my soul continued an intrusive self-examination, a life-review, to take note of all the harm I had caused, all the sins I had committed, and all the ways in which I had gone wrong. The time came when this process of examining my past deeds SEEMED to come to an end, as I had learned much and begun amending my life, but the ugliness that it had left upon my soul remained visible.

Then it was that I was taken to a place where a priest was giving baptism to all of God's children ready and willing to be cleansed. Not feeling worthy, I bowed in the other direction, my ugliness was too visible. But another priest appeared and took my arm. "Hurry, go now, before he is done and is gone." Pushing me down the aisle towards the altar, tears began streaming down my face.

White light was the essence with which this priest was created; his face, his hands, his robes. He was not of this Earth, but of heaven. Kneeling to the floor and bowing before the altar, the priest poured an entire cistern of living water over my head as I cried openly. Speaking words in another language, I cried because I could actually feel my sins being forgiven and taken away from me as he spoke. The signs of my sins were no longer visible upon my face and body, for these waters had washed my soul clean.

As he finished his invocation, I began to rise quietly away from the altar, still in tears and in awe of the blessing of baptism that had been given me. My stains had been blotted out, as the Lord Jesus had promised! Our sins will be forgiven us, if we will go to the Father and seek it.

"He that believeth and is baptized shall be saved..."
King James Bible, New Testament, Mark 16:16, (Christianity, Words of Christ)
"I am baptizing you with water, for repentance, but the one who is coming after me is mightier than I. I am not worthy to carry his sandals. He will baptize you with the holy Spirit and fire. His winnowing fan is in his hand. He will clear his threshing floor and gather his wheat into his barn, but the chaff he will burn with unquenchable fire."
New American Bible, New Testament, Matthew 3:11-12, (Christianity, Words of John the Baptist)

****

A huge light began blaring from the center of my chest as I had awakened in my sleep. My Lourdes rosary, which had water encased within it from the holy shrine, was shining. Taking it to bed with me every night, my spirit looked up above into the sky as my beloved Jesus was kneeling at the foot of the Father, their robes white as snow in the heavenly mirage. It seemed I had just given birth, and it was a very holy birth.

But the Lord was concerned that I should rest, for my journey had been harrowing, both spiritually and physically. Conveying that He had chosen me for this work because of my sinfulness, He wanted me to lead sinners back to His holy heart. In my wretchedness, perhaps other souls would see the vastness of God's mercy to those who repent.

As I gazed upon this holy vision, now beginning to fade, I felt God's love so greatly and fully, and I cannot express my joy. For in this moment, I felt God's love for me, and that despite this great trial in the abyss, wherein I felt as though God could not possibly love me anymore, I knew that the Lord had never left my side, He'd only made his presence less obvious to test my faith. But in this deep abiding presence I also felt great satisfaction, in that, this trial was necessary, it was fulfilled, and its fruits would be deeply holy.

For a moment, I was given a vision of the blood of the lamb as I knew that my soul had been washed in His holy sacrifice, and I was honored.

"Ye shall see the Son of man sitting on the right hand of power, and coming in the clouds of heaven."
King James Bible, New Testament, Mark 14:62, (Christianity, Words of Christ)

"My Heart was moved by great mercy towards you, My dearest child, when I saw you torn to shreds because of the pain you suffered in repenting for your sins ... I see every abasement of your soul, and nothing escapes my attention. I lift up the humble even to my very throne, because I want it so."
Divine Mercy, Notebook 1, Page 134, No. 282, (Christianity, Catholic, Words of Christ, Author: Sister M. Faustina Kowalska)

"Thou hast a few names ... which have not defiled their garments; and they shall walk with me in white: for they are worthy. He that overcometh, the same shall be clothed in white raiment; and I will not blot out his name out of the book of life, but I will confess his name before my Father, and before his angels. He that hath an ear, let him hear."
King James Bible, New Testament, Revelations 3:4-6, (Christianity, Words of Christ)
****

And so it came to pass that I was taken into the holy and unholy aspects of many religions. Inside a holy mosque, several Muslims showed me a huge card file that lay in the archives which contained very holy revelations. Upon closer inspection, I realized that these cards represented the original Hadith, the teachings of Mohammad to his disciples. Holiness swept through me as I reveled in the energies of the sacred teachings. In another moment, I was given to again see the violent side of the Muslim people, and the very dark nature of their holy wars.

Through an energetic exchange, I was given to feel the holiness of Krishna, the Hindu embodiment of the Lord, and it became known to me that the Lord had truly sent him to the Earth.

The light of Baha'u'llah, the founder of the Baha'i' faith, came first as a lighted moth. Expanding into an angelic presence, knowledge of the Bab and Baha'u'llah was given to me in a conceptual manner, one which I cannot explain. But let it be said that it was made known to me that they were holy men. But as I posed the question to the Lord as to whether Baha'u'llah was actually the second coming of Christ, as he had claimed, I was given no reply.

Taken to the Jewish Wailing Wall, a voice said, "You may follow the Rabbi's, the great ones of old, and you will find among them the highest status of religious discipline." Then I was shown how the cliquish mentality of some Jewish people seriously displeases God, and that the parameters of the religion as practiced are too limited and repressed, not allowing for evolution and growth to be pursued. Although the foundation of the absolute laws was quite holy; in practice, there was a need for individual movement. And in subsequent experiences, it was made known to me that this was also a problem among the Catholic tradition.

The Lord revealed to my soul that because God is love, there was a great need for more merciful religion towards those who seek the Lord in earnest, but fail at certain precepts because of their level of evolution. Because of the many holy experiences I'd had in regards to the Catholic church and its saints, my soul was alight with wonder as I was flown to the Vatican in Rome. A mass was in progress and I was honored to be allowed to be a part of it, so I patiently sat and enjoyed the ritual. However, not long into the service, I noticed that there were many sub-conscious souls outside the cathedral in need of service. Due to their focus upon the ritual, however, the others involved in this service were unaware of this need. After a short time, I couldn't wait any longer, and I flew outside as unobtrusively as possible to give service to the souls hovering around the cathedral. Rituals serve a purpose, but when they are done for the ritual's sake alone, or for the obedience to a rule, the spontaneity of spiritual service may become lost. Although I was greatly honored to attend this mass at the Vatican, for it was a holy experience, it made me aware of the dangers of hard and fast rule which sometimes blind us to the spontaneous promptings of the spirit.

And so an angel of the Lord spoke to me in my dreaming, this time to tell me that there are three qualities which must be included within every religious path to make it valid: humor, direction and use.

"'Thanks be to Thee, Eternal Father, who hast in Thy House many mansions.'
And he rejoices more in the different ways of holiness which he sees, than if he were to see all travelling by one road, because, in this way, he perceives the greatness of My Goodness become more manifest,
and thus, rejoicing draws from all the fragrance of the rose."
The Dialogue of St. Catherine of Siena, A Treatise of Prayer, Page 217, Top,
(Christianity, Catholic, Author: St. Catherine of Siena)

****

Journeying again into my sin had left me feeling wretched. Having already asked the Lord for mercy, I now asked for grace. Becoming aware of my sin didn't, in and of itself, make me stop committing them. My vices controlled my words and deeds in such a manner, that it required a long, arduous path of trying to change, screwing up, trying again, screwing up again . . . I often felt so wretched in my inability to break the habit of destructive speech, inappropriate deeds, etc., that I sometimes honestly felt that I was a hopeless soul.

A time of great atonement, I sought forgiveness from those in my past for whom I had wronged, and I asked forgiveness from the Lord in prayer, imploring His mercy. "I am sorry, Lord, I am so very sorry . . . Lord of all creation, take this bird you have freed from the fragmentation of vice and teach her to fly, so that maybe someday she may return and bring joy instead of tears."

"But habits of any kind are so strong in their possession of the minds of men that, even in the case of those that are evil (and these usually come from the dominant passions), we can more quickly condemn and detest them than we can abandon or change them."
The Fathers of the Church, Volume 4, The Advantage of Believing, Chapter 17, No. 35,
(Christianity, Catholic, Author: St. Augustine)

"St. James tells us that this virtue comes from Heaven and that we shall never have it unless we ask it of God. We should, therefore, frequently ask God to give us purity in our eyes, in our speech and in all our actions."
The Voice of the Saints, The Challenge of Chastity, Page 59, (Christianity, Catholic, Words of St. John Vianney)

"The man of Armaiti is bounteous, and with understanding in his words and actions. May Ahura give him that Righteousness which is blessed, together with the Religion and that Sovereign Power which is established through the Good Mind. And I would pray for this same blessing from His grace."
The Avesta, Yasna 52, No. 21, (Zoroastrianism, Words of Zoroaster)

****

Having tried to find my niche amongst the many different world religions, I was shown that every time I broke free from one of these groups, a great psychic event occurred in the heavens. Appearing in the sky, the phoenix and hundreds of angels celebrated my freedom from bondage to one school of thought, and one key of knowledge. Conveying that I needed all of the keys to be complete, I didn't yet understand their meaning. Because I embraced aspects of all of the world religions, many of the followers of the world religions did not embrace me.

"But, since things appear similar to each other in many ways, we should not imagine there is any precept that we must believe that, because a thing has a certain analogical meaning in one place, it always has this meaning."
The Fathers of the Church Volume 2, Christian Instruction, Chapter 25, No. 35,
(Christianity, Catholic, Author: St. Augustine)

****

"Past wrong actions have left seeds in your mind . . . You cannot achieve emancipation until you have burned the seeds of past actions in the fires of wisdom and meditation. If you want to destroy the bad effects of past actions, meditate. What you have done you can undo . . . When your present efforts become more powerful than the karma of past actions, you are free."
Sayings of Paramahansa Yogananda, Page 108, Stanza 1, (Hinduism, Kriya Yoga,
Words of Paramahansa Yogananda)

Preparing for the next leg of our spiritual journey, an old Indian man sat in front of us as we packed our moving trailer. Having only a foundation with no roof or walls, the moving trailer had deficiencies which had to be rectified through Jewish holy observances. "Because you are content with what you have, you are welcome to stay," he said, "but if you have to go, my people will understand."

Nodding that we indeed had to go, we began our holy observances, which were required for our souls to attain a state of cleanliness in the eyes of the Lord. After-winds of sin had to be blotted out, and our penances complete.

Forty percent of the wall appeared as we performed a mitzvah, and forty percent more appeared as we performed a second mitzvah. Mitzvahs are acts of goodwill required by Jewish law. The remaining 20% came up after an unknown benefactor performed three Hallahs for us (10%, 8%, and 2% respectively). Halvah is one of the unleavened breads of the Passover, and it occurred to me that we were preparing for our final Exodus, our journey to the place of safety the Lord had prepared for us, the monastery in the mountains.

"The idea behind the trait of Cleanliness is that a person be completely clean of bad traits and of sins, not only those which are recognized as such, but also those which are rationalized, which, when we look at them honestly, we find to be sanctioned only because of the heart's being still partially afflicted by lust and not entirely free of it, so as to incline us towards a relaxation of standards. The man who is entirely free of this affliction and clean of any trace of evil which lust leaves behind it will come to possess perfectly clean vision and pure discrimination, and will not be swayed in any direction by desire, but will recognize as evil, and withdraw from every sin that he had committed, though it were the slightest of the slight."
The Path of the Just, Chapter X, Paragraph 1, (Judaism, Author: Rabbi Moshe Cheam
Suzette)

****

And so it came to pass that the Lord took me deep into my soul to gaze upon its weaknesses and flaws, and then lifted me up again and again so that I could take that knowledge with me to the surface of my conscious mind. In this humbling journey, I came to know the power of the Lord, and how He so deigns to lower Himself into the very midst of our wanderings, in order to lift us up. Coming not only to those saintly souls who are without stain, He comes to me and to you, those of us caught in the web of delusion and the Maya of incarnate life. He comes to those of us covered with stain, and humbly washes us. He comes to those of us enraptured with vice, and dispels our delusions and subdues our passions. He comes to all of His children, because He loves them all. And for those who are willing to undergo His grueling journey of purification, and abandon evil desires, He frees them from all bonds and sets them free to fly within His kingdom.

Transported into the worldly malaise, Andy and I sat amidst a group of people who were incessantly garbling about worldly matters. Surrounded by mass retain, up ahead several Jewish Cantors were singing. Within moments, my own soul began singing, 'Hey La, Hey La,' drawing my soul into a vibratory state which transcended all outer noise.

"Repentance only occurs when a person abandons his sins and evil deeds. Abandonment does not depend on knowledge alone but on will. Repentance is complete only when one changes the internal balance of his desires. He no longer sins because he has succeeded in making his desire to return stronger than the desire to sin."
Strive for Truth, Lovingkindness, Page 156, Paragraph 2, (Judaism, Author: Rabbi Eliyahu E. Dessler)

"And the eyes of all them that were in the synagogue were fastened on him. And he began to say unto them, 'This day is this scripture fulfilled in your ears.'"
King James Bible, New Testament, Luke 4:18-19, (Christianity, Words of Christ)
****

Taken to a monastery in the heavens which honored all world religions, I observed the order and rule of prayer, fasting and meditation. Dressed in untraditional clothing, those who were staying in this place were wearing T-shirts which had writing on them indicating their current journey into the Catholic faith. Having already studied Buddhism, and just now finishing with their studies on Catholicism, a spirit voice told me that they were now 50% there. Continuing their studies into the remaining world religions would bring them to completion.

"God is one, but His names are many."
The Gospel of Sri Ramakrishna, Chapter 4, Page 112, Paragraph 1, (Hinduism, Words of Sri Ramakrishna)
****

Taken to see a person I'd known as a child, I was surprised to notice that he was about to receive karmic retribution for something he had done to me a long time ago. When we were teenagers, he had thrown me out of a party because I wasn't cool enough, and he had jeered the other party-goers into yelling at me as I walked away with shame.

Now up for a promotion at his current job, he was going to lose the promotion in karmic retribution for what he had done to me years ago. But I felt really badly that he was going to be punished for doing something when he was so young, so I pled with the lighted guardians, a tribunal of sorts, who were gathered to carry this out. "Please don't do this." I said. "It's okay with me. I don't feel any need for him to be punished on my behalf. It was so long ago, and I'm sure he's grown and changed since then." Quiet, they listened carefully to what I had to say, all the while gauging his sub-conscious soul for remorse, for which there appeared none.

Faces remaining hard, they told me they would carefully consider my plea. Sent away, my soul was not allowed to hear their final decision. With the looks on their faces, it didn't seem that there was much hope for a stay upon his retributive sentence.

"All members of the Academy enter the secret chamber. Then the Court assembles and the spirit of the man to be tried is brought up by two officers, and placed near a pillar of flashing flame which stands there and which is kept in shape by a current of air blowing on it . . . If his word was a fitting one, happy is he, for he is crowned with many radiant crowns by all the members of the Academy. If, however, his word was of another kind, alas for his disgrace. They thrust him outside, and he stands within the pillar until he is taken to his punishment."
The Zohar (Kaballah), Volume V, Balak (Numbers), Page 252-253, (Judaism)
****

Alit with eternal desire as my soul ravaged upon an ancient time, the twelve tribes of Israel were gathered in the deserts, but my soul was specifically amongst the tribes of Abraham, Isaac and Jacob. Eating a very large but fine leaf which they considered a delicacy, two angelic guardians were showing me that they were not as they seemed. Within them lay hidden locusts, and as they partook of the leaves, they partook of the locusts. Unable to intervene, we could only watch as the locusts bubbled up within their bodies, and slowly, very slowly, crawled their way down towards the lower back where they could exit. Although I had not taken any of the leaves, I suddenly saw two bubbles within my own back. In disgust, I watched as locusts within me crawled out.

A representation of an impurity among the Israelite people which they had taken in, the locusts had been passed to the generations after them. Original sin had been passed down through these, my forefathers.

Now that I had purified my soul of my own particular and familial vice, I was thrust into the purification of humanity's sins which were imbedded within me, passing from generation to generation, original sin. At no point did the angels tell me of what sin these locusts represented amongst humanity, and at no point did I deduce it. My particulars had been cleansed, now my humanity must be washed in the blood of Christ.

"Man, created innocent, fell by disobeying Him; the mark of original sin remained engraved on his forehead and that of his progeny who will bear its consequences until the end of time."
Meditation Prayer on Mary Immaculate, Paragraph 3, (Christianity, Catholic, Author: Padre Pio)

****

Amidst the fiery display, I saw his essence. Hair long and black, the dark horseman was an Indian. His tomahawk was lifted above his head, ready to plunge deep inside of me. Strong and powerful, his darkness was overwhelming and smothering. Wishing my destruction, he also sought to suck the life-force of my second child, who was but a baby.

Holding onto her tightly, I ferociously shouted the name of Jesus Christ upon his countenance. Conquering his soul, he came after me again in a renewed fit of rage, shoving me towards a great abyss. Fighting with ever greater fervor, I called to the Lord for help and shoved him in the opposite direction. Forcing his soul out of darkness, his black foggy form dissipated rendering him benign and dispersing original sin.

"Our best, our easiest remedy is the Name of Jesus. It drives the devil flying from our sides and saves us from countless evils."
The Wonders of the Holy Name, Chapter 10, Page 44, Paragraph 4, (Christianity, Catholic, Author: Fr. Paul O'Sullivan, O.P. (E.D.M.))

Because I'd had many lifetimes as both a Native American and a white person, my soul bore the original sin which was transferred through both races. Because of the violence perpetuated upon the native peoples (original sin of the white race), entry had been given to the dark horseman who was unwilling to set the past free (original sin of the natives; vengeance). Many whites were trapped by the past in the present, a past which left them insensitive to the pain of others, and oblivious to affliction and oppression. Many Native Americans were trapped by the past in the present, a past which had left them seeking revenge, and/or oblivious to the need for impetus, focus or eternal direction. Many had lost their souls.

Despite the origin of the difficulty, it remains the responsibility of every individual soul to rise above the delusions and crimes perpetuated upon them, and to find the Great Unitive Spirit of all life hidden within the multiplicity.

Now that these stains had been conquered, I was free to begin my true work, the building of the great red road which now lay before me in magnificence. Doing so with great zeal, I was laying bricks upon the three roads of the Indian people. Suddenly, up in the distance, I noticed a familiar face. Red Horse was soaring amidst the woodland, helping to build this great red road.

Joining me, he was greatly pleased that I had battled and won the dark horseman over to the light. Because of this demise of the energies of the past, the native spirits were now focusing on bringing in something new.

Because we've all had many lifetimes among the many races of the world, we all bear responsibility in the crimes of differing nations. Who among us can claim that they bear no guilt for the past, when the guilt they share with humanity is etched deeply within their soul?

Peace could now be paved because the dark horseman, the manifestation of the sins of both races, had been dismantled. In the distance, I saw the other fragment of Red Jacket, who had *not* energized an eternal program, watching. Because of his status, he was unable to assist in bringing this significant event into fruition, and his eyes were sad.

Where we now stood there was no interest in vengeance, only wholeness. Gathering from all tribes, we were all helping to build the three great roads which together made up the great red road, and we worked slowly, peacefully and with focus.

Finding a baby leopard and a baby cheetah amongst the woodland, Andy approached, carrying the two. Handing them to Red Horse, he took them to a place of safety. The skies opened up.

My soul was filled with a wanton display of awe and wonder at the glory of the Lord. Swept into the heavenly skies, I was now amidst the spectacle which had been revealed to me. Hovering in a glistening light, the violet, purple and gold hues of the Pleiadian system overlapped, filling the sky. As the great red road was being paved, the energies of their actions resounded in the heavens, filling the sky with the vastness of the Pleiadies. Orbiting our galaxy in some fashion, it is not possible to describe the wonder that I was shown. That which had been lost was being fully restored. Others, too, followed this great red road and found restoration also.

As the skies filled, I noticed a spaceship flying through the wonder, as it was conveyed to me that it was from Saturn. The gold was so ominously beautiful, the violet so haphazardly strewn in this wondrous display of color. Each element of color continued metamorphosing into something higher, and somehow, the union of the red energies of the Earth and the violet energies of the Pleiades synergized a unity and something of great significance.

"I thought of my vision, and how it was promised me that my people should have a place in this earth where they could be happy every day. I thought of them on the wrong road now, but maybe they could be brought back into the hoop again and to the good road."

Black Elk Speaks, Chapter XXII, Paragraph 2, (Tribal, Oglala Sioux, Words of Black Elk)
****

Standing before them, I was surprised to feel compassion because these people were members of various satanic cults and orders. Dressed in a rather foolish manner, most of them wore some form of black, and had make-up on their faces to make them look white, drawn, and dead. Those before me were very young, perhaps late teens or early twenties, and had been deceived by the dark side to think that this was very cool. Another alterer was with me, but was quiet for now.

Some of these souls were involved with these cults because their parents had been, others of these souls were involved because their parents had been naive about the true nature of darkness, not recognizing that allowing the seeds of any darkness, through television, vanity, greed, or any other form, could energize this more highly developed evil in *any* soul, but most especially a child. Some parents didn't have proper discernment, and thus, did not teach their children proper discernment. Some parents were naive about the company their children kept, or didn't insist enough that they stay away. Some children were coming from a darkness they brought with them from previous lives which had nothing to do with their parents. Some who were older were drawn by their own evil impulse which was highly developed, and some due to the apathy of their own upbringing.

Original sin is an interesting concept, because it can apply to so many aspects of existence. Original sin can be the failings that we, through example, give to our own children. Original sin can be the failings of a particular extended family that we, through example, give to our own children. Original sin can be the failings of a particular city or township that we, through example, give to our own children. Original sin can be the failings of a particular country that we, through example, give to our own children. Original sin can be the failings of a particular society that we, through example, give to our own children. Original sin can be the failings of all humanity that we, through example, give to our own children. Original sin can also be the failings of a particular soul that, through the mechanism of karmic retribution and transmigration, are given to that soul at birth. Original sin can also be the acts of darkness that a soul is forced to process because it was done unto them.

Guilt for criminal or dark acts are actually an energy, and this energy falls upon the defenseless victim who usually carries it until it is purified, because perpetrators of evil rarely take responsibility for their acts. Applying to the evil works of a satanic cult, who through apathy, allow their evil deeds to fall energetically upon their victims rather than themselves, it also applies to any perpetrator of a dark or evil deed, from murder to adultery. If the perpetrator of a dark or evil deed were to take full responsibility for his deeds, he would remove a burden from his victim. If he does not, he throws his own burden upon that soul. It is important to realize, however, that although this mechanism occurs very often among victims and perpetrators, and many victims as a result process the dark deeds of the perpetrators rather than vice-versa, perpetrators stand guilty before the tribunal for all their deeds, for they cannot be truly thrown aside. Shunning responsibility is a selfish act which energetically forces a burden upon another in *this* life, but that burden remains with its owner in the *next*.

Karma, in order to be completely purified, must be identified on three levels of being in a conscious manner. First are the physical acts of karma. Second are your thoughts, and third, are your dream-state behaviors.

One girl who was rather large had smeared white makeup all over her face and she had a very ugly blackish-red lipstick upon her mouth. All of them were trying to scare me, but they didn't realize that they couldn't scare me, because I knew of their ways. Because I'd peered into their humanity, I knew that their weakness was their thirst for false power, and in seeking satanic ways, they could never attain anything of substantial value.

"It's not easy to do what we do, to go to hell," said the woman, as I looked at her with an emotionless face. "No, that's incorrect." I said. "It's very easy to go to hell." She looked at me with disgust in her face. "What will actually be quite difficult for all of you . . . will be to go to heaven." Gazing upon their distorted faces, she continued, "We *want* to go to hell. Hell is a much better place." Remaining unmoved, I replied, "Well, I think it's obvious that all of you *want* to go to hell just by looking at you. However, it is also obvious from your naive statement that you've never been there." "Oh, like you have!" she stated sarcastically, implying that it wouldn't be possible for a warrior of the light to go to such a place. Beginning to laugh almost uncontrollably, I said, "Do you honestly think that you have anything to offer even hell?" They didn't respond. "Of course I've been there, many times in fact. Firstly, because Satan has no use for souls with no energetic impetus like yourselves, he goes after light warriors, hoping to turn them over to his ways through temptations. So he tries, and I tell him where to go, to hell. Secondly, because I refuse to work for anyone but God, and because morons like you who think hell is such a great place end up going there, they eventually discover how wrong they are and beg souls like me to come and help them when they've realized how badly they've screwed up."

Becoming somewhat confused, they all began talking amongst themselves about their actions within their respective cults. Minimizing their bad acts, it seemed that a bolt of conscience may have hit them and they were now lying to cover their deeds. "Do you really think I believe that bullshit?" I said to them, as they immediately became quiet. "You must try to remember that I know what cults like yours do," I said, "and I know exactly how evil, deviant and disgusting you all really are. If there is any hope at all for your souls, you're going to have to completely alter yourselves through prayer and repentance, and in a case such as yours, you must *expect* divine retribution, for you will be required to pay dearly for your evil crimes." Saying nothing, their eyes were big and wide, looking at me with horror and expectation. "You must accept divine retribution with grace, to prove your sincerity. And you must accept it, knowing full well you've earned every trial, every pain, and every suffering the Lord may inflict upon you. Only through this, do you have hope." All souls must accept such things.

> *"They pass through kalpas as numerous as motes of dust, confused, deluded, obstructed, and afflicted by difficulties, like fish swimming down a long stream through nets."*
> Sutra of the Past Vows of Earth Store Bodhisattva, Chapter 4, Page 119, Paragraph 1, (Buddhism, Pure Land, Words of the Buddha)

Swept away to an ice arena with the other alterer, we began to skate. In order to energize the mechanism of these souls to achieve liberation from their evil states, we joined together in an ice dance. Soaring around and around the arena, we were suddenly energized to begin skating sideways in a circular fashion. Facing the inside of the circle that I was now creating, I seemed to be energizing the sacred hoop, which was creating an opening, an awakening. Leaping into the air, I flew twenty to thirty feet up. Joining me in the air, my friend helped me to descend back upon the ice which was now beginning to melt. Formed on the top of a very deep pool, it was perhaps one-hundred feet deep.

Dancing in many formations, the ice disappeared as we were now upon this liquid mass which represented their evil and icy consciousness becoming liquid. Now performing a dance of love, we sank to the very depths, because we had to bring the light to the very core of these evil existences in order to override their ice cold hatred, and hellish craving. Placing a tiny light at the bottom, I had lost my breath down below. Sweeping me to the surface to claim our victory, knowing that this would show on the surface as only a slight change, we understood that it would take many lifetimes for these souls to fully germinate the tiny ball of light which had been placed in their depths. Love had been planted, and now they must let it grow.

Returning to the surface, we found our subjects at a firing range. Dressed as normal people, their black attire had been replaced by the clothing of common men and women and their makeup was gone. Shooting at targets, I scanned their minds. Although they often thought of shooting each other, they were not acting on their evil thoughts. Negativity was prevalent all around them, as their thoughts manifested in energy, but they had taken a step from their former ways.

> *"And speak unto me, and turn aside from me the evil of this abode and of that abode; And illuminate the band of Light and Splendor, and bless them and us, and purify them for ever and ever. So be it."*
> The Desatir, The Book of Shet the Prophet Feridun, No. 36-37, (Zoroastrianism)

****

Entering a very nice home where several men were living, I realized within a short period of time that they were all homosexual. Because their neighbors realized this, they became very mean, discriminatory, and hostile. My duty was to assist them, so for a time, I prepared meals and took care of the home.

Admittedly, my own reaction to their homosexuality was mixed, as well. Because I couldn't relate to this phenomenon, I didn't know how to discern it. But over time, I came to a simple realization. It was unnecessary for me to understand why they were the way they were, it was only necessary that I continue to behave in a merciful and loving manner. Perhaps it would have been different if these men had been promiscuous, for promiscuity by any soul carries with it its own chastisements; pregnancy, disease, heartbreak, etc. These were homosexual men looking for what every chaste heterosexual would look for, a partner in life.

One particular day, the neighbor man who had become increasingly assaultive with his hostility, was shouting out of his window biblical condemnations of homosexuality. Angered by his hypocrisy, I shouted back, "Blessed are the merciful, for they shall obtain mercy." Calming a small fraction, I continued, "He who is without sin . . . he may throw the first stone." Backing off, I turned to my friends and served them their dinner meal, as they looked towards me with gratitude.

Another original sin that much of humanity is given at birth and through upbringing is intolerance for that which is unlike itself. Thus, we give birth to violence against homosexuals, different races, sex or religions. Only a fool could think that God wishes for his children to fight amongst themselves because they are not identical.

But so that balance may be achieved, the Lord sent me to yet another place.

A mother from a generation past was married to an incestuous man and, because of her own past which included the same, original sin had been placed upon her soul. Because of this encrustment, she was unable to discern that having sex with your children was wrong. Original sin which she had been born into, had skewed her own vision, and thus, she allowed this horrendous sin to be perpetuated another generation. Unable to realize the damage she had allowed to continued, in her mind, it was simply the way things are. Never having raised a hand to protect her daughter, her husband was eventually convicted of his crimes, and she felt sorrow for him although she had not even once generated compassion for her own daughter. The Lord bade me to know that this type of merciless deviance had no justification.

By watching this, I realized just how important it is that we all look deeply upon our own pasts, making sure that we do not accept those habits, lifestyles and ways of thinking which are wrong in God's eyes, for we become accountable for the sins of our parents as soon as we begin to perpetuate the same sin in our own lives. And how much more so, if we allow it to pass onto yet another generation?

We are responsible, no matter how destructive our background might be, to overcome, shake off the darkness, and be born into the light. If we do not, we become like our own abusers, carrying the burden of their original sin into adulthood, to manifest in myriads of ways, spreading darkness and descent among the future generations of humanity.

"The unvirtuous he cultivates, he visits not the virtuous, and in his ignorance he sees no fault in a transgression here, with wrong thoughts often in his mind his faculties will not guard - - virtue in such a constitution comes to partake of diminution."

The Path of Purification, Part I, Chapter 1, No. 39, Stanza 1, (Buddhism, Theravadan)

"Having renounced every selfish desire, he has found his rest in the Lord of Love. Wisdom is the staff that supports him now. Those who take a mendicant's staff while they are still at the mercy of their senses cannot escape enormous

suffering. The illumined man knows this truth of life. For him the universe is his garment and the Lord not separate from himself. He offers no ancestral oblations; He praises nobody, blames nobody . . . The world of change and changeless Reality are one to him, for he sees all in God."
The Upanishads, Paramahamsa Upanishad, No. 3-4, (Hinduism, Translation Eknath Easwaran)

****

Thrust into my past wherein I was confronted by someone who had done great harm to me, I recognized that I'd played a role in her deed, albeit a small one. Although she held much greater responsibility for these acts of which she had partaken, I was guilty in a very small way. Approaching her, I hoped that if I were to apologize to her that she might extend the same favor in kind, and that perhaps we could get beyond what she had done. Asking for her forgiveness, she lashed out in rage, refusing to give me forgiveness for an act of harm which was in truth, her own.

Beginning to ask forgiveness from the Lord, as he is our final judge, I knew that I had done the right thing in going to her first, because she was the one I'd hurt.

Feeling the tassels of the ropes tied around my soul loosen, the Lord conveyed that although I held a small fault in this particular matter, that the soul who refused forgiveness was actually the one who held responsibility in this great harm that had been done. Apparently, her refusal to forgive my small fault, and to recognize the greater sin which was her own, had bound her *own* soul, not mine.

"That man implores you, and asks for pardon. Then forgive him; forgive him at once. If you refuse to forgive him, the refusal will injure you; it will not injure him, for he knows what to do. If you, a servant, refuse to forgive a fellow servant, he will go to your Lord and say to Him: 'Lord, I asked my fellow servant to forgive me, and he refused; do Thou forgive me?' Is it wrong for the Lord to loose His servant's debts? When that servant has obtained forgiveness from the Lord, he comes back free; you remain bound."
The Fathers of the Church, Volume 11, Commentary on the Sermon on the Mount and other Writings, Sermon 56, On the Lord's Prayer, (Christianity, Catholic, Author: St. Augustine)

****

Amidst the cold and dark they stood; the homeless of the world. Aside them was a shelter which had been closed due to lack of funding. Going inside the abandoned shelter, a man greeted me. Giving me a periscope, and referring to the homeless people outside, he told me, "If you think what you've already seen is bad, take a look at this." Looking through the periscope, it took me deep into the pavement. Difficult to see at first, slowly I was able to view what was lurking. Small snakes were beginning to descend on the place, and among them large ugly scorpions. Entry had been given to hoards of demons who were now seeking hosts among the homeless, due to lack of charity. Bearing the burden of original sin for humanity, the homeless were overwhelmed. I stood, stunned and frozen in silence.

"A very important duty of charity towards our neighbor consists in giving him alms when he is poor and needy and we ourselves are in a position to do so . . . 'Alms delivereth from death,' said the Archangel Raphael to Tobias, 'and the same is that which purgeth away sins, and maketh to find mercy and life everlasting.' (Tob. 12:9) . . . If we can do nothing else let us at least recommend him to God, for prayer is also an alms."
The 12 Steps to Holiness and Salvation, Chapter 4, Almsgiving, Paragraph 1-2, (Christianity, Catholic, Author: St. Alphonsus Liguori)

****

Because of my sins, I was punishing myself by taping objects to my leg which would cause me physical pain and public humiliation as payment for them. Tormented by my previous bad acts, I felt I deserved to suffer. After several hours, a black man with long black braids walked in the room, a monk (Mythosetia, guardian of the entry to the lower realms).

Looking at me with disapproval, he said nothing at first. Walking into the room, my daughter also bore the stain of sin. Looking at me, the monk said, "If she is stained, she should also pay for her sins in the manner in which you do." Nodding, 'No,' I refused to allow her to wear the garment of mortification which I had chosen for myself. Smiling the monk conveyed, "You are more merciful to others, than you are willing to be to yourself." Acknowledging my sins was important, but my level of wretchedness because of them was overkill. "After a soul has looked upon its own darkness and achieved understanding, it is proper to let those sins go, for they have been washed in the blood of Christ. Once they have been washed, they are no more."

Feeling a bit silly, I began removing the objects of mortification which I had taped to my leg.

"Someday man should learn how to enjoy liberty without license, nourishment without gluttony, and pleasure without debauchery. Self-control is a better human policy of behavior regulation than is extreme self-denial."
The Urantia Book, Part III, Paper 89, No. 3, Paragraph 7, (Christianity, Urantia)
****

Four Arabian brothers were converging on one of their wives, who was becoming frightened. Verbally assaulting her for her faults, they were attempting to blame her for their sins. Claiming that they would not do the bad things they do, if it were not for the things that she did, they were holding her accountable for their acts of violence, hatred, and ravaged avarice. Because they were so domineering and enraged, the younger woman eventually just agreed with their stance, saying that indeed her own faults were the cause of anything that they might do inappropriately, and she begged their pardon for causing such difficulty for everyone.

But as I was watching this scene, heavenly truths were being imparted to me constantly. None of their accusations were in any way true. Despite the fact that this woman did bear sin of her own doing, she was not in any way responsible for their violent and retributive behavior. A figure was given to me that if she held 10% guilt upon her soul, they held 90%. Just as Jesus bore the lies and sins of humanity before his crowning moment on the cross, this woman also bore the lies and sins of her family (original sin), a pattern of avoidance and denial which had been visited upon them by the former generation, now deeply seeded within the next.

"Hence thou wilt understand the ignorance and error of mortals, and how far they drift from the way of light, when, as a rule, nearly all of them strive to avoid labor and suffering and are frightened by the royal and secure road of mortification and the Cross."
The Mystical City of God (Abrid.), The Transfixion, Book 5, Chapter V, Page 433, Bottom, (Christianity, Catholic, Words of Mary)

Many families drop their sins on one victim soul amongst them. Many families perpetrate acts upon their children which place the seed of those acts within them. Many families unknowingly teach their children the ways of sin, by following the ways of the world and not doing the work required of each of us to learn God's ways. Vanity, greed, lust . . . all of the seven deadly sins, are aspects of our society which are not only accepted, but considered worthy attainments in a world devoid of God.

Original sin is transmitted through the seeds of the seven deadly sins, is implanted through habit, is cultivated by tolerance, and grows through the mass ignorance of humanity. Original sin can only be transformed through the seeds of the seven virtues, implanted through habitual choice, cultivated by discernment, and grown through the singular awareness of an individual soul. Beyond our individual karma and vice, lies the original sin of all mankind. We partake of it because of our own humanity, so we must transform it because of our own divinity.

"On the trails of time I have carelessly fallen into pits of error; but have always been rescued, O Lord, by Thine unseen hand."
Whispers from Eternity, Page 39, Stanza 1, (Hinduism, Kriya Yoga, Words of Paramahansa Yogananda)

"O my daughter! How greatly do mortals misunderstand this truth, and how far they err from it in their actions! The Lord gives them life in order that they may free themselves from the effects of original sin, so as to be unhampered by them at the hour of their death; and the ignorant and miserable children of Adam spend all their life in loading upon themselves new burdens and fetters, so that they die captives of their passions . . . "
The Mystical City of God (Abrid.), The Coronation, Chapter VI, Page 774-775, (Christianity, Catholic, Words of Mary)

****

Without my foreknowledge, my soul was being swept into the original sin of religion. Although I'd already begun this journey in learning of the light and dark aspects of many religions, there was one religion yet untouched because it was so new, only 140 years old. But even so, it was already becoming prey to the common elements of most religion; structure, control and dogma.

In no way diminishing its significance or the profundity of its revelation, it deterred individual seeking because of its rigid beliefs that were held to be true, although the texts of their founder did not *seem* to agree with their interpretation of these self-same words.

A voice issued from above, "Baha'u'llah knew about reincarnation," it said. Suddenly, hidden tablets of Baha'u'llah, the founder of the Baha'i faith, which I assumed were written in the heavens but not on earth, were unsealed before my eyes. Clear and precise, his words spoke of the advent of many lifetimes which each soul must take to ultimately reach union with God. Although Baha'i's, do not believe in reincarnation because his son/successor 'Abdu'l Baha' openly denied its existence, here in Baha'u'llah's hidden tablets, he spoke of it, knew of it, and counted it among the many mysteries only to be revealed at such a time that humanity could comprehend its hidden mysteries.

"Whenever we desire to quote the sayings of the learned and of the wise, presently there will appear before the face of thy Lord in the form of a tablet all that which hath appeared in the world and is revealed in the Holy Books and Scriptures. Thus do We set down in writing that which the eye perceiveth. Verily His knowledge encompasseth the earth and the heavens."
Tablets of Baha'u'llah, No. 9, Lawh-I-Hikmat, Page 149, Paragraph 2, (Baha'i, Author: Baha'u'llah)

"No man shall ever discover its reason unless and until he be informed of the contents of My Hidden Book."
Call to Remembrance, Part 3, Chapter 5, Page 69, Top, (Baha'i, Words of Baha'u'llah)

"We have revealed Our Self to a degree corresponding to the capacity of the people of our age."
The World Order of Baha'u'llah, The Dispensation of Baha'u'llah, Page 116, Paragraph 2, (Baha'i, Words of Baha'u'llah)

Because his purpose was unification, he didn't focus on the precepts of the prophets before him. Acknowledging the truth of their mission, he placed their teachings before his own people whose purpose was to unify the world religions. But Baha'u'llah knew that wisdom is given to the seeker by the Lord, and that the Lord works in mysterious ways. 'Abdul' Baha's notion that reincarnation is a foolish concept simply because most people wouldn't want to return to this world of misery seems contrary to the words of his predecessor.

"If the mystic knowers be of those who have reached to the beauty of the Beloved One, this station is the apex of consciousness and the secret of divine guidance. This is the center of the mystery: 'He doth what He willeth, ordaineth

what He pleaseth.'"

The Seven Valleys and the Four Valleys, The Four Valleys, The Fourth Valley, Page 57, Paragraph 1, (Baha'i, Author: Baha'u'llah)

To state that mankind is given entry into higher worlds by simple virtue of death seems to be a mistaken understanding of the evolutionary purpose of mortal realms. Every man must earn his right to stand before God, and this cannot always be accomplished in one short lifetime which can range from one moment to over a century, depending on the circumstances of death. Even in our Earthly schooling, no soul attains to the next level simply by virtue of showing up in class. The next level can only be attained by earning it through hard work, and the attainment of knowledge. So it is with the evolution of a soul. Mortal man must become immortal before he can attain to higher worlds.

Although a soul may invariably incarnate upon other *mortal* worlds, he cannot enter into immortal realms until he has earned it by becoming eternal. Death, alone, is not enough.

Baha'u'llah stringently rejected many former interpretations of the sacred scriptures of all religions, contending that within mystical verses are contained mysterious knowledge which only the visionary who comprehends the meaning of mystical language may truly observe.

"By corruption of the text is meant that in which all Muslim divines are engaged today, that is the interpretation of God's holy Book in accordance with their idle imaginings and vain desires."

The Kitab-I-Iqan, Page 86, Paragraph 1, (Baha'i, Author: Baha'u'llah)

Reincarnation, although considered as mystery to some, was understood by many of the prophets and manifestations of God; Krishna, the Buddha, Jesus Christ, Rumi, Nanak, and others. Lay people of these religions took it out of some of the teachings, because it was beyond their understanding. But mystical seekers always knew and understood reincarnation as a basic concept within the mechanism of existence.

The mystical writings of Baha'u'llah, such as 'The Kitab-I-Iqan,' have many mystically coded references to the myriad lifetimes of reincarnation. What Baha'u'llah rejects, which is indeed imbued with true knowledge, is the notion that reincarnation encompasses a spirit, soul and personality configuration which would never change; and that we are sent to lower life forms as punishment, which is a Hindu concept. According to Baha'u'llah, we are sent where our soul is compatible, and each lifetime connotes its own distinctive personality, soul configuration and package of karmic and original sin.

In essence, there is no repetitive cycle wherein a soul enters another body - in essence - entirely or even close to the same as was before. Past memory is shaded and a whole new identity emerges. A whole new family tree fills the soul with its own aspects of perception and there is generally little if no likeness to the former lifetime or body. What remains are the subtle aspects of karmic imprint, which are indeed so subtle that few ever seek to identify them, and when they do, are often vanquished in their inability to truly understand karma's mechanism.

A soul who dies purely a personality with no tangible immortal qualities does in essence truly die, for the part of that soul which was a conscious personality, ceases. The mortal aspects of that soul return to God, the center of creative force and merge as God takes life back to Himself. Because God is an energy, and can be seen as a huge ball of light similar to the sun, energy is in constant flux, incoming and outgoing from the heart of our Creator. Until life attains immortal status, it cannot bring the severed links of existence together into one whole, and thus, retains separate identities which complete in and of themselves, at least in the soul's conceptual understanding. Immortal status, when achieved, creates a separate existential link which operates in all spheres of paradisiacal existence as an extension of the will of God.

Immortality occurs when a mortal personality attains immortal qualities and at the death of such an individual, there is no true death/rebirth, because the soul has already died and been reborn during its life. Mortality is the status of human travelers amongst the evolutionary spheres of Earth and other mortal realms. These worlds are referred to as the ascension worlds because a soul must seek and attain immortality to graduate from the fetters of the time-bound free will worlds. A soul must *earn* exit from these realms, and can only do so by retrieving sacred memory expunging karmic thrusts and attaining immortal status, also known as ascension.

Personalities, or unconscious souls, do not truly die, but are changed as their essence is merged into the life-force of God. Reincarnation occurs when He takes His own beatified essence and creates a new form, imprinting it with the unconscious personality aspects of former generations of karmic imprint, and giving it new conscious qualities and personality aspects. But because the Lord may do as He pleases, He may endow the new creation with aspects of memory from one succinct line of existence or many. Cellular memory is implanted according to the will of the Lord, and may be altered at His command. New incarnations retain cellular memory according to their own line of karmic impulse, their own historical elements, and as they attain to a new body, cellular memory of this new line of genealogy originating from their new family of birth origin, and historic aspects of their new race.

Reincarnation is a mystery which lies within the mechanics of existence, which can only be understood fully in the energetic mystical state.

"These journeys have no visible ending in the world of time, but the severed wayfarer - if invisible confirmation descend upon him and the Guardian of the Cause assist him - may cross ..."
The Seven Valleys and the Four Valleys, The Seven Valleys, The Valley of True Poverty and Absolute Nothingness, Page 40, Paragraph 2, (Baha'i, Author: Baha'u'llah)

"My Lord, I offer my respectful obeisance's unto You because You are the director of the unmanifested total energy and the ultimate reservoir of the material nature. My Lord, the whole cosmic manifestation is under the influence of time, beginning from the moment up to the duration of the year. All act under Your direction. You are the original director of everything and the reservoir of all potent energies. All the conditioned souls are continually fleeing from one body to another and one planet to another, yet they do not get free from the onslaught of birth and death. But when one of these fearful living entities comes under the shelter of Your lotus feet, he can lie down without anxiety of being attacked by formidable death."
KRSNA, Book 1, Chapter 3, Page 51-52, (Hinduism, Words of Devaki)

Rigid structures which do not allow for individual exploration are the crux of the original sin of most religion. No religion contains *all* of the truth, and no religion is free of imperfection. In practice, many religious structures become so rigid that continuing revelation is stalled or ceases, and thus, individual souls become trapped within dogmas which cannot lead them to higher epiphanies of knowledge or attainment. Let us cast off this original sin from our souls, and rectify within ourselves that religious structure is Earthly, but religious seeking is eternal.

True religion must accept that God leads different souls back to Him as He pleases. This issue is not limited to the Baha'i religion in any way, but encompassed by them all to a certain extent. Such original sin causes souls to cease their individual search, following a rigid path which can lead them only so far. Immortality comes to those who allow eternity to embark upon their soul, in the manner in which eternity chooses. That which is eternal is not stiffly rigid, but flexible and ever-moving in many myriad directions to assist an individual soul towards its prime unity. God does what He wills and ordains what He pleases.

"Stop judging and you will not be judged. Stop condemning and you will not be

condemned. Forgive and you will be forgiven. Give and gifts will be given to you;
a good measure, packed together, shaken down, and overflowing, will be poured
into your lap. For the measure with which you measure will in return be
measured out to you."
New American Bible, New Testament, Luke 7:37, (Christianity, Catholic, Words of
Christ)

****

   Amongst the stars, I saw a Baha'i man. Turning to him, I conveyed, "If I simply accept the claim that Baha'u'llah was a promised manifestation of God, we have only one issue remaining." Accepting this claim was not an acceptance of *all* of Baha'u'llah's claims, only that he was indeed a promised manifestation of God in the Islamic line of prophets. Looking toward me, he made no reply. "Baha'u'llah knew about reincarnation," I said, "and Baha'u'llah also said that science and religion must agree. Eventually scientists will prove the existence of reincarnation, and because this is true, you should also realize that an interpretational error was made in Baha'u'llah's teachings, for he knew of reincarnation." The man nodded, 'no,' as a voice came from the sky.

   "They will not accept it," the voice said, as its essence conveyed more. Because they were now a body of religion, a political structure; the revelational capacity had been stilled. Any new knowledge that contradicted their earliest interpretations of a veiled and mystical prophet's words would be quickly rejected. "Tell them," it said, in reference to the Baha'i's of the world, "that Baha'u'llah knew of reincarnation." As the voice ceased, it conveyed only a moment more. "Do not allow political structure to quell the great revelation which has begun your faith, for even as Baha'u'llah said, revelation is progressive, and it encompasses more knowledge as humanity becomes able to understand and comprehend it."

"If any of the utterances of this Servant may not be comprehended, or may lead
to perterbation, the same must be inquired of again, that no doubt may linger,
and the meaning be clear as the Face of the Beloved One shining from the
'Glorious Station.'"
The Seven Valleys and the Four Valleys, The Valley of True Poverty and Absolute
Nothingness, Page 40, Paragraph 1, (Baha'i, Words of Baha'u'llah)

"Tahiri (a Baha'i saint and martyr) . . . was regarded as the quintessence of
chastity and the incarnation of Fatimih (Muhammad's daughter) . . ."
Call to Remembrance, Part 2, Chapter 4, Page 31, Paragraph 3, (Baha'i)

"I testify, O my God, that if I were given a thousand lives by Thee, and offered
them up all in Thy path, I
would still have failed to repay the least of the gifts which, by Thy grace, Thou
hast bestowed on me."
Call to Remembrance, Part 3, Chapter 5, Page 70, Paragraph 1, (Baha'i, Words of
Baha'u'llah)

"With both his inner and his outer ear he will hear from its dust the hymns of
glory and praise ascending unto the Lord of Lords, and with his inner eye will he
discover the mysteries of 'return' and 'revival.'"
The Kitab-I-Iqan, Page 198, Top, (Baha'i, Author: Baha'u'llah)

   Turning to the Baha'i man, he had turned away from me. Standing with his back facing towards me, his arms were folded in defiance of this truth which the eternal appeared to wish for them to rectify within their body of knowledge. Sighing, I couldn't help but mourn this common state of affairs. Followers of religion can become unable to lead souls into new vistas of knowledge, because they cannot let go of misperceived notions which have become dogma. Eventually, the beacon of new revelation is stilled because the dogmas have obtained structure, and new understandings which expand and clarify are not accepted. Every religion begins with a thrust of transcendental light, beckoned in by those fearless enough to conquer tradition and superstition. But it seems that eventually most religion, if it becomes too structured, falls into the traps of dogma, causing immobility, a trait uncommon to eternal things.

"How great the difference between the condition of these people and the station of such valiant souls as have passed beyond the sea of names and pitched their tents upon the shores of the ocean of detachment. Indeed none but a few of the existing generations hath yet earned the merit of hearkening unto the warblings of the doves of the all-highest Paradise."

Tablets of Baha'u'llah, No. 6, Kalimat-I-Firdawsiyyih, Page 57-58, (Baha'i, Author: Baha'u'llah)

"They would willingly lay down a myriad lives, rather than breathe the word desired by their enemies."

Call to Remembrance, Part 4, Chapter 10, Page 222, Paragraph 1, (Baha'i, Words of Baha'u'llah)

"They regard a single drop of the sea of delusion as preferable to an ocean of certitude. By holding fast unto names they deprive themselves of the inner reality . . ."

Tablets of Baha'u'llah, No. 6, Kalimat-I-Firdawsiyyih, Page 58, Top, (Baha'i, Author: Baha'u'llah)

"There was once a lover who had sighed for long years in separation from his beloved, and wasted in the fire of remoteness . . . . He had given a thousand lives for one taste of the cup of her presence, but it availed him not."

The Seven Valleys and the Four Valleys, The Seven Valleys, The Valley of Knowledge, Page 13, Paragraph 1, (Baha'i, Author: Baha'u'llah)

"Verily God is fully capable of causing all names to appear in one name, and all souls in one soul. Surely powerful and mighty is He. And this Return is realized at His behest in whatever form He willeth. Indeed He is the One Who doeth and ordaineth all things."

Tablets of Baha'u'llah, No. 12, Suriy-I-Vafa, Page 183, Paragraph 5, (Baha'i, Author: Baha'u'llah)

"Know thou moreover that the former Manifestation affirmed that the return and rising of the spirits would occur on the Day of Resurrection, while in truth there is a return and resurrection for every created thing."

Tablets of Baha'u'llah, No. 12, Suriy-I-Vafa, Page 186, Paragraph 3, (Baha'i, Author: Baha'u'llah)

And as another example of the same sort of misinterpretation of sacred writing, Baha'i's believe there is no hell or Satan, but rather, that darkness is merely an absence of light. Partial truth doesn't diminish the true existence, significance and ramifications of darkness and the lower realms. Believing this despite the fact that Baha'u'llah and the Bab (The forerunner of Baha'u'llah who was endowed with the same station as Baha'u'llah) speak of the judgment of souls, punishment of sinners, and hell and Satan as much as most texts of other religions.

"The Glory of God rest upon thee and upon whosoever serveth Thee and circleth around Thee. Woe, great woe, betide him that opposeth and injureth Thee. Well is it with him that sweareth fealty to Thee; the fire of hell torment him who is Thine enemy."

Call to Remembrance, Part 5, Chapter 11, Page 257, Stanza 1, (Baha'i, Words of Baha'u'llah)

"Likewise apprehend thou the nature of hell-fire and be of them that truly believe."

Tablets of Baha'u'llah, No. 12, Suriy-I-Vafa, Page 189, Paragraph 1, (Baha'i, Author: Baha'u'llah)

"All the keys of heaven God hath chosen to place on My right hand, and all the keys of hell on My left."

The World Order of Baha'u'llah, The Dispensation of Baha'u'llah, The Bab, Page 126, Paragraph 2, (Baha'i, Words of the Bab, the Forerunner of Baha'u'llah)

"The things which have, from the first day till now, befallen Me at the hand of thy people are but the work of Satan."

Selections from the Writings of the Bab, Tablets and Addresses, Extracts from a Further

Epistle to Muhammad Shah, Page 25, Paragraph 1, (Baha'i, Words of the Bab)
"He will bring thee into grievous trouble by reason of that which Satan instilleth in his heart . . ."
Selections from the Writings of the Bab, Tablets and Addresses, Extracts from a Further Epistle to Muhammad Shah, Page 25, Paragraph 3, (Baha'i, Words of the Bab)
"Verily it is incumbent upon thee to become a true believer in God, the All-Possessing, the Almighty, and to turn away from the one who guideth thee into the torment of hell-fire."
Selections from the Writings of the Bab, Tablets and Addresses, Extracts from another Epistle to Muhammad Shah, Page 19, Paragraph 2, (Baha'i, Words of the Bab)

Evolution is about compatibility, and there are many worlds, just as Baha'u'llah stated. But some of these worlds are below ours, and this can be understood even through common sense.

Despite the use of this particular faith as a sacrificial lamb in demonstrating the possibility of original sin in regards to religion, these examples could apply to most any religion. And the true revelation of the Baha'i faith is in no way diminished by possible misinterpretation, just as the revelation of any other faith is in no way diminished by the same. Perhaps this particular faith has been chosen as the sacrificial lamb and example of this quality because of its very youth. Because this manifestation of God appeared so soon past, it shows in a more grandiose manner how easily and quickly a text can be distorted or misperceived. Because this faith will grow in the coming centuries, if there is error, it is grandly important to recognize it as early on as can be ascertained by the eternal. But these 'errors' remain my opinion, and I state very clearly that my 'opinions' remain human and fallible.

But do not lose sight of the knowledge these examples are meant to impart. They are given to show you how easily the words of a prophet or messenger of God can be misinterpreted, misperceived and dogmatized into something different than the intended revelation. But it is also true that mystical language is oftentimes meant to carry several meanings. This is done intentionally by the Lord.

"Take notice also, my spouse, that very often I permit and cause differences of opinions among the doctors and teachers. Thus some of them maintain what is true and others, according to their natural disposition, defend what is doubtful. Others still again are permitted to say even what is not true, though not in open contradiction to the veiled truths of the faith, which all must hold. Some also teach, what is possible according to their supposition. By this varied light, truth is traced, and the mysteries of the faith become more manifest. Doubt serves as a stimulus to the understanding for the investigation of truth. Therefore, controversies of the teachers fulfill a proper and holy end."
The Mystical City of God, Vol. 1, Book 1, Chapter VI, No. 77, Page 80, (Christianity, Catholic, Author: Ven. Mary of Agreda)

****

Retreating to the scene of a horrible occurrence, my soul was filled with sorrow for the souls of a cult who had committed a mass suicide. Led by fanciful ideas of the end of the world, they perceived that the coming of a comet was the coming of the end, and ended their lives wastefully.

Wandering amongst the building where the bodies remained, my sadness could not be sustained. One of the great religious original sin's had been played out upon this stage; that of a fearless, infallible leader who allowed no individual thought within the confines of his domain. Because of this, whatever he may have taught them that *was* true had been overshadowed by this great defect in his dogma which led to their deaths.

Floating out to the small garden plot outdoors, I noticed a very evanescent growth coming from the ground. A small tree had been planted, and upon the branches of the tree, fruit was being born. Rectangular small compartments, the fruits were about the size of a video-cassette, and every single one was entitled, 'Abdu'l Baha,' Baha'u'llah's successor and son. Baha'u'llah had called his son 'The Most Great Branch.'

"This is why there is need of religion," a voice said, "for the souls who are unable to guide themselves." Turning, I looked upon the misled remains of souls who had followed a fanatic, getting lost in the delusions of a mentally ill man. Remembering Christ's words, 'You will know them by their fruits,' the fruits of the good tree before me were 'Abdu'l Baha', the 'Most Great Branch' of the Baha'i faith.

Let it be known unto all the world, the great revelation which is contained within the texts of this new faith. Let it be known.

"Consider! The station and the confirmation of the apostles in the time of Christ was not known, and no one looked on them with the feeling of importance - nay, rather, they persecuted and ridiculed them. Later on it became evident what crowns studded with the brilliant jewels of guidance were placed on the heads of the apostles . . ."

Tablets of the Divine Plan, Tablet 7:3, Page 39, Paragraph 2, (Baha'i, Words of 'Abdu'l Baha')

****

Entering into the ancient past, a spirit aside was telling me stories about the patriarchs of the Old Testament. Immediately taken aback by the disrespectful nature of the storytelling, I instantly sensed that a demon must be present. Another aspect of original sin is the intellectual arrogance that modern men use to insist that the patriarchs were less educated or civilized. By doing so, people of our age can consider themselves superior, when in fact, the mysteries of God in every age are holy, and the education of a future age does not diminish the holy nature of a sacred path forged in ages past.

Who among us may say that we bear the same holiness as Abraham did *in his time*? For who in our time has accomplished the same sacred duty within the context of our present age? Who among us?

Turning, the spirit aside me had become an ugly reptilian demon, holding a centipede in his hand. "You jerk!" I said, as he cowered in disappointment that his ruse had not worked. Attempting to thrust the centipede infestation into my soul, he threw it at me but I ran. Missing, I shouted to the heavens. "Holy Mary, Mother of God, please help me." As soon as these words were uttered, the centipede quietly walked away with three other centipedes, two tarantulas and one spider. Completely disappearing, the other demon was now gone. Because I had called for the assistance of the Holy Mother who treads upon demons underfoot, they were unable to pursue me any further. "Hail Mary, Full of Grace . . ."

"For thy enemy and adversary is laboring with ceaseless vigilance to obscure thy understanding in forgetfulness of the divine law, seeking to withdraw thy will, which is a blind faculty, from the practice of justification."

The Mystical City of God (Abrid.), The Transfixion, Chapter II, Page 405, Bottom, (Christianity, Catholic, Words of Mary)

****

As my prayers had gone up to the heavens as I continued asking the Lord to show me His will and how I might better serve Him. Sitting aside two native women amongst a tribal gathering, an eternal voice spoke. "You must now tell the story of the Native Americans, and because of this, you must go talk to them." Then they were gone.

"I asked for a vision which might show me how best to serve the earth and honor all life, to honor walking on the surface of the earth at this time. Then . . . I received a vision."

Being and Vibration, Chapter 5, Page 148, Paragraph 1, (Tribal, Tiwa, Author: Joseph Rael)

****

CHAPTER SEVEN
The Dark Side Attempts to Undo Karmic Rectification, Potentials Unfulfilled, Accepting Individual Free Will, Misunderstandings of Religious Concepts, Holiness of Religion, Seeking High Level Consciousness, Karma of Dogma, Unfoldment of the Doctrine of Reincarnation, Different Levels of Temptation, Reconciliation in Spirit with the Native American People, Journey as New Testament, Heavenly Reward of Overcoming, the Outpost of Resolved Karma, Resolution.

****

Beyond form, the demonic intrusion awaited their opportunity as I became aware of myself awakening in the dark, dank apartment that I had rented when I was but eighteen.

Getting up from this long ago bed of mine, I immediately began throwing up feces, but interestingly, my feces was white. Two women stood before me, as I was made aware that they had fallen prey to the lures of 'the gull,' destructive sexual energy. Feeling sorrow for them, bats suddenly began appearing from the attic and were flying all around me. A powerfully dark presence became manifest all around.

My roommates had become creaking sets of bones lying on their beds, and I could feel my own bones creaking in the eerie mist. Someone from my past was present, and I continued throwing up white feces whenever I saw him or felt the energies of our interactions from the past. Immediately, I felt great shame, although the shame was no longer mine, and I began to pray for his soul. "Eternal Father," I said, as I began to recite the prayer of divine mercy, "I offer you the body, blood, soul and divinity of your dearly beloved Son, Jesus Christ, in atonement for our sins and for the sins of the whole world. Amen." (A Prayer given to Saint Faustina, a Catholic Nun.)

Looking for refuge, I walked silently downstairs, while a great red gale-wind burst open the front door of whom I immediately knew to be that of Satan. Looking around, I sought refuge from the presence of the evil one. Another person I had known in the past was flying outside in the winds. Eyes perched upon the source of the wind; they betrayed the identity of that which he had befallen. Showing terror and decomposition as he gazed upon the countenance of Satan, he was quickly overcome. "Eternal Father," I began to pray on behalf of this other soul, "I offer you the body, blood, soul and divinity of your dearly beloved Son, Jesus Christ, in atonement for our sins and for the sins of the whole world. Amen." Realizing that Satan was trying to lead me to despair by showing me the chosen fate of some of the souls who had participated with me in sin, the red wind slammed the front door shut.

Turning to directly face the wind, I never looked upon the countenance of the viper. Attempting to fill me with terror, I stood strong and cried out, "Cursed be thy name, cursed be thy name, cursed be thy name, cursed be thy name." His energy was strong and harsh, so my voice was weak and small against his force. Bringing forth all the strength that lay within me, I cried out the louder, "Cursed be thy name! Cursed be thy name! Cursed be thy name! Cursed be thy name!" In moments, I'd awoken safe in my home. Depleted by my defiance, he was gone.

"O chastiser of the enemy, the sacrifice performed in knowledge is better than the mere sacrifice of material possessions."
Bhagavad Gita As-It-Is, Chapter 4, Text 33, (Hinduism, Translator: A.C. Bhaktivedanta Swami Prabhupada)

Returning to dream vistas, my soul was immediately alit in a powerful vibrational force which led me to a beautiful and wanton woodland.

Seeing two distinct lines indicating two patches of ground which were before me, they represented the dark and light side of existence. The light side of existence was a rich, green and lustrous patch of healthy fertile grass. The dark side of existence was a patch of dead, dry and tan colored infertile grass. Touching the lighted side, it was beautifully warm and soft. Lightly touching the dark side with one finger, it held a hidden torment, as my finger was filled with thistles. Pulling out the pile of stickers which had come into me, I understood the allegorical rendering. Light is fertile and warm, while darkness is deadened and painful.

Soaring to the sky, I looked below to witness the always beautiful and magnificent spectacle of the mountains below in flight. Suddenly, however, my soul was in the hands of another spirit, carrying me with love and grace to our destination. Red Jacket had taken me into his arms and was now flying me to safety. Landing next to a small fire pit that had been prepared for us atop the mountains' peak, he laid me upon the ground gently. Looking at him deeply, his long black hair was straight and thin, his body, tall and big but not overtly muscular. Wearing buckskin pants, they were lightly fringed, and his face appeared younger now. Large, deeply brown and piercing, his eyes expressed the love he had for my soul. Sitting quietly by the fire, the torment of the viper was far away, but within moments, he soared off into the mountain's horizon as my soul had been rendered silent by his visitation.

All of a sudden, a bunch of bunnies appeared; pink, yellow, blue and green. Some were small like regular bunnies, but some were two and three feet high. Cozy energies surrounding me, I petted their soft fur on this mountain's peak. Feeling very safe now in the bosom of the Lord, I bade my farewell and returned to the earth.

****

Quickly alit with eternal desire, I was led by an unseen force to several texts. Among them were Augustine's writings and the Holy Qur'an. All of a sudden, the texts were far away as I stood beside Andy, my husband, in a vast mountainous woodland.

Having ventured into an overlapping astral space, our purpose was to meet a man who had done something rather wonderful, an eternal beacon, but what he had done we did not know. As we began our journey to his home, we didn't realize that we had gone into another reality of our own world when we had taken the turn into his realm, but we had entered, in a sense, the past; but yet, here in this reality, it was the present.

Arriving at his home, his family couldn't be more cordial as we entered to convey our wonderment at his great heroic act. Although we still didn't know what he had done, we could energetically ascertain its merit. A governor of sorts, it wasn't an Earthly title, but some kind of heavenly post that he held over this realm; as if what he had done remained unseen to the common man, but visible to eternity.

Congratulating him on his brevity in seeking and attaining such a high universal station, we were energetically allowed to feel the great merit he'd attained through his work, and the gratitude of many souls who had been assisted in their journeying. Grateful for our visit, when it was time to go, he said, "Ya'Baha'Islam." Although I didn't understand it immediately, the words meant something like "Hail Glorious Islam," and he was opening the energetic door to the Islamic faith in my soul. Nodding, I turned.

Driving deeper into the wilderness community, we entered a strange time/space continuum. It was as if we were living in the present world, but no longer inhabiting the particular Earthly reality from which we had come. But this warp served a purpose, to give us the opportunity to finally understand the nature of the eternal accomplishment of the man we had just left.

Many of the folks who belonged to these parts lived in 20th century buildings and drove 20th century cars, but their primary mode of living was very much as it would have been 150 years or more before. Living off of the land in a harmonious manner was something that wasn't just common to the native Indian peoples here, but to the white man, as well. Everything was so beautiful, natural and harmonious. A balance existed between the needs of the Earth, and the 20th century devices which had been discovered to make survival less difficult for humanity. Native American's wore traditional garb and the Indian and white men hunted together, often for bear, to feed their families. Loving each other as brothers, there was absolutely no racial tension.

Becoming apparent that this was a parallel world which had played out very differently in regards to the red race than it had in our reality, this harmony had come about primarily through the efforts of the governor, and it was a marvel to witness.

Because we were seeing the native people before the betrayal, the beauty was heart-wrenching. Industrious, kind, playful, and above all, earthy, they lived in harmonic pleasure with all around them. Certainly, they did have something to teach the white man about redemption. They showed above all simplicity of living which allowed for them to exist in a state of great joy without causing harm to the Earth or taking any form of life outside of balance.

As I watched the people in this place where the Indians still roamed freely, I didn't want to leave. My soul wished to retain the joyousness I had in just quietly watching this harmonious exchange, for it was so different than what I saw in my own world. Wondrous attributes which were uniquely qualified to their race, were destroyed in a great number of their people in our world; mostly due to violence, treachery and oppression which occurred so soon past. Our actions had borne a conquered people, many consumed with sloth because their self-initiative had been taken away when they'd been herded onto reservations. What shame we should feel for causing such a travesty! What a horrid shame!

There was no need to speak to the natives of this realm, for their presence had communicated to me all I needed to know. Coming as I'd been bidden, we'd communicated in a way no Earthly chat could have produced. Allowing myself to revel in this joy, I felt myself being pulled away from this beautiful parallel of my own world; a parallel filled with the joyous alternative to what could have been, had we respected and honored the lives of the native people. So many lost . . . so many lost . . .

"Grandfather, I am sending a voice! To the Heavens of the universe, I am sending a voice; that my people may live!"
The Sacred Pipe, Chapter IV, Page 54, Stanza 1, (Tribal, Oglala Sioux, Words of Black Elk)

****

Amidst the splendor of a Baha'i gathering, a large cloth banner depicted the substance of the Baha'i teachings. Upon its sheath something inexplicable was missing, until . . . until . . . Suddenly, a very devout Baha'i woman placed the cloth of Baha'u'llah upon a banner depicting the crucifixion of Christ. As the two cloths came together, the cross melded deeply into the banner of Baha'u'llah, and it bore new meaning greater than any it could bear on its own. The Baha'i revelation was not complete without the crucifixion of Christ upon its bough, but together, they made a powerful revelation far surpassing the separate links. Watching, I saw the cloth fibers of the banner melt into the wood of the cross, merging over top of one another, becoming one. Together, together, together . . . the revelations of the prophets must be understood as a whole, not as separate pieces, if one seeks full knowledge.

"In every land We have set up a luminary of knowledge, and when the time foreordained is at hand, it will shine resplendent above its horizon, as decreed by God, the All-Knowing, the All-Wise. If it be Our will we are fully capable of describing for thee whatever existeth in every land or hath come to pass therein. Indeed the knowledge of thy Lord pervadeth the heavens and the earth."
Tablets of Baha'u'llah, No. 9, Lawh-I-Hikmat, Page 150, Paragraph 1, (Baha'i, Author: Baha'u'llah)

****

The barren landscape outside the church was almost too much to bear as I stood with people of the world, begging them to enter the holy shrine along with me. They would not, and they argued and fought continually as I cried and cried, begging and pleading. One of them was getting very dramatic as he spoke of the torment I was giving them by begging such a thing. From his words, I gathered that he truly felt smothered and afflicted.

My tears could not be confounded as they gathered in arms against my approach, angered at my 'self-righteous' attempts to bring them with me into the church. Another one of them approached me with her views on the matter. "You are trying to make us into something that we are not, and have us do something that we do not wish to do." I awakened to an epiphany.

Tears still falling, perhaps even harder because of the force of the realization, but I suddenly understood that these people did not view my attempts to save their souls in such a manner, but rather, as direct interference with what they wanted to do. In their view, they had no souls to save.

Wiping my face with a tissue, my red and puffy cheeks could not be hidden. Turning to the people, I realized that many years and many church services had gone by as I waited outside trying to get them to join me. I'd missed so much, I'd missed so much. For all these years, I'd watched the churchgoers enter quietly while I cried and waited outside, waiting, always waiting for these loved ones to take heart. But it had never happened, and it never would. "I understand," I said to them, "I truly understand, now. You don't *want* to go." Quiet but assured, I finished. "Well, I'm going to go inside, and when I do, I'm never coming back. Do you understand? I'm never coming back for you." Sighing in relief that I was finally going to leave them alone, I turned quietly, opened the door and entered the church, as the heavy door closed loudly and tightly behind me.

Inside the church, the altar was aglow with the love of God. Speaking wonderful words of God, the minister was directing the congregation in beautiful praise. Walking quietly forward, I tried to hide the redness and puffiness of my cheeks from the minister, and I sat in the second pew. Words eloquent and the music astounding, the energy inside this holy church far surpassed my expectations. Finally, I was home with my Lord.

Passing out hymnals with the Latin text of some Gregorian chants, the entire congregation began singing them. Moments later, they all burst into yet another genre of singing, that of one of my own hymns, 'I Love the Lord.' Invited to lead the congregation in this song, I approached the front of the church and stood aside the altar, feeling quite unworthy. But when my mouth opened, my voice issued in praise of God in a sound that even I could not believe was my own. The Lord and His angels were using my voice to honor His name. Peace overcame my soul in a moment of serenity, and it was as if the trials of my human existence were no longer, as if they'd never been, for now I was in the arms of my most loving Lord. I sat down to pray for those I'd left behind, and all became silent.

"And I earnestly pray for this whole company, with a hope against hope, that all of us, who once were so united . . . may even now be brought at length, by the Power of the Divine Will, into One Fold and under One Shepherd."
Apologia Pro Vita Sua, Part VII, Page 353, Paragraph 3, (Christianity, Catholic, Author: John Henry Cardinal Newman)

****

After years of seeking, we finally found our way to the mountain abode prophesied in many a dream.

Catapulted into a rather bizarre circumstance, my soul was about to embark upon the varied concepts of the New Age movement, those which were positive and pleasing to the Lord, and those which were deeply flawed.

Led into a library wherein were contained many books by New Age authors, a voice issued from above, "Do not condemn them," it said, "for they do have a purpose. Just realize that their purpose is very limited." Nodding, I realized that their prime purpose was to open people up to the 'experience' of God, rather than the cold, structured face many have rejected in church. Embracing mystical teachings, reincarnation, extra-terrestrial influences, and the recognition of the many layered self all leading back to the highest aspect of each individual soul's divinity, the higher self, they supported self-discovery, individual search, and differences amongst themselves. Most of all, they offered unconditional acceptance to each other.

However, it was made clear to me that after this opening occurs, there remains little within the New Age teachings regarding God as Supreme, or the importance of morality and virtue. Because of this, some of them are swept away by the viper, believing a self-centered truth which allows all acts of virtue *and* vice, to be equal and the same. Nothing, in their view, is either negative or positive within the program. Everything that they choose to do to serve the misperceived 'self' is okay. (The 'self' as spoken of in Eastern religions is the divine element within, not the ego.) Sometimes propounding a selfish absorption which precludes the needs or concerns of others, they also believe that we create our own reality. Although it is somewhat true that we create our own reality, it is not entirely true in the manner in which they believe it to be so. We direct our reality within the confines of the will of the Lord, we can completely destroy our own destiny, or energize it; but we cannot alter the course of *all* events within the confines of our life's program simply by willing it to be so. The Lord's decrees are carried out by His own choosing, and this belief becomes self-serving when it is used to deny responsibility or the need to care about those who suffer in the world; the hungry, the meek, the poor, and the sick. True holiness comes from serving the Lord, and thereby, serving others. Serving the 'self,' as in the ego, is the doctrine of the fallen angels (Again, the 'self' referred to in Eastern teachings, is the divine element within, not the ego.).

"Mankind at first numbered two, then three, and at last they became innumerable. They had been images of God, but after the Fall, they became images of self, which images originated in sin. Sin placed them in communication with the fallen angels. They sought all their good in self and the creatures around them with all of whom the fallen angels had connection; and from that interminable blending, that sinking of his noble faculties in self and in fallen nature, sprang manifold wickedness and misery."
The Life of Jesus Christ and Biblical Revelations, Volume 1, Sin and its Consequences, No. 1, The Fall, Page 18, Paragraph 2, (Christianity, Catholic, Words of the Venerable Anne Catherine Emmerich)

Virtue and a respect for the true karmic consequences of incorrect behavior, thought and action are lacking. Even in realms which appear unlimited to our human eyes, such as the Pleiades, freedom is afforded within the confines of the will of God. Freedom is afforded to them because of their own innate controls: Freedom within the concept of what is good and what is true.

"Liberty is a self-destroying technique of cosmic existence when its motivation is unintelligent, unconditioned, and uncontrolled."
The Urantia Book, Paper 54, No. 1, Paragraph 3, (Christianity, Urantia)

Now my soul was standing amidst the putrid filth of the untrue concepts within the New Age. The primary affectations were the misperceived doctrine of 'I am God' which becomes blasphemous in its misunderstanding (The Eastern doctrine of 'I am God,' is very much linked to the true understanding of the correct doctrine of the 'self.' But this understanding cannot fully be known outside the states of ecstasy and Samadhi where the meaning is made clear. Its truth lies in the knowledge of the divine element within, which when properly energized allows for a soul to display miraculous holy gifts.); the missing link of virtue; and the misunderstood concept of 'self.' (The divine element within being misperceived as the ego.) True doctrines, when misunderstood, can become very dark.

Surrounded by the manure which represented the self-serving thinking of New Age thought, there was no way through this mess on the ground; it was a cesspool, putrid, impure and disgusting. Suddenly, a huge angelic man stood before me who must've been fifteen feet tall, high in the sky above me holding a bow and arrow. Attired like a Roman soldier, his back was adorned with white lighted feathery angel wings. Erroneous concepts were depicted in the air as a hazy black cloud, and on the ground as piles and piles of excrement. As he began to aim his bow at this cloud of unknowing, he said, "It is much easier to take on a reality by shooting it down as a concept, rather than to take it on, on the ground." Immediately, as his arrow shot through the falsehoods, they exploded and were dispersed. As this occurred, Andy and I were freed from the repugnant results of such false doctrine on the ground.

"After death everyone comes to know in the spiritual world what the uncleannesses are which titillate the body's fibers in such persons and comes to know the nature of them. In general they are things cadaverous, excrementitious, filthy, malodorous, and urinous; for their hells teem with such uncleannesses."
Divine Providence, Chapter II, No. 38, (Christianity, Swedenborgianism, Words of Emanuel Swedenborg)

****

Buzzing all around me were the holy energies of the Islamic faith, 'The Holy Qur'an,' the poetry of Rumi and the 'Sirat Rasul Allah,' a text on the life of Mohammed. Flying all around me, they began to spin.

As I experienced the texts whirling around me, I became more and more entrenched in the energies of Islam. The words from these texts and especially the poetry of Rumi began swirling in the air around me, moving my soul to such a degree, that I instinctively began whirling like a dervish. As I was spinning, I recalled that this state was for the sole purpose of thinking of God, and as I did so, my soul became almost dizzy with love for God. Carrying a circular rope with me, it somehow spun with me and contributed to the dizzying, ecstatic state I had entered upon. My Islamic inquiry was going deep quickly, and the vastness of this ecstatic state held my attentions for a great deal of time. Spinning, spinning, spinning, I fell deeper and deeper in love with the Lord. My head spun at eye level and then turned towards the sky, and then down again. My rope was spinning in a centrifugal fusion, it seemed impossible that it could be in such synchronicity with my soul.

When I finally emerged, I felt immense honor at the opportunity to experience such a thrust, and my regard for the whirling dervishes grew sevenfold. When my soul had completely exited such state, I looked upon the sky and the remnants of the words which spun around me . . . in tranquility.

"The sun is love. The lover, a speck circling the sun. A Spring wind moves to dance any branch that isn't dead. Something opens our wings. Something makes boredom and hurt disappear. Someone fills the cup in front of us. We taste only Sacredness. I stand up, and this one of me turns into a hundred of me. They say I circle around you. Nonsense, I circle around me."
The Essential Rumi, Chapter 27, Page 280, Stanzas 2, 3 & 5, (Islam, Sufi, Words of Rumi)

****

Thrust amidst a deep and profoundly putrid ghetto, I interiorly knew immediately that in order to exit, I would have to find my way to route 25 from route 24, my current location.

Having entered a convenience store, I tried to buy several things to eat and a book or two, but when I'd gone to the cash register, they'd told me my credit card was 'hot,' or stolen. Ironically, however, they knew that this was a mistake and didn't take my card, but they wouldn't allow me to purchase any of the items which I had mistakenly perceived might have helped me in my peril. Returning all of the items to the shelf, I left the store, immediately boarding my bike, keeping my hopes high because I could now see the exit to route 25 within view. Surprised when I came to the exit, I was not yet allowed to board it.

Entering upon a maze which encompassed route 24, the place was filled with confusion. Apparently trapped, I began riding endlessly in search of route 25. Following a sign which led me into a series of buildings, I left my bike behind and walked through several rooms, but could not seem to find my way. At first, I missed the proper exits altogether. On the second try, I entered the buildings on my bike, only to follow literally hundreds of rooms through office buildings, exiting each through closet doors, finally reaching an even scarier part of the ghetto. Following all the rooms outward to what appeared to be the end, I found myself only more lost in the depths of this increasingly haunting ghetto.

In the distance, I noticed a kindly looking black gentleman sweeping the streets. As I quietly approached him, I asked, "Where might I have gone wrong?" "There's a lady in the last room who can tell you how to find the final exit, and the elusive final exit is hidden in the last room about one quarter of the way through . . . hidden in a door," he said.

Turning around, I began to ride back to the last room of which I had just left behind, only to find a filthy white woman covered in feces, urine and blood lying on the floor as if dead. From where I stood, I could see the exit one quarter of the way through the room and I began to turn to follow it, but my conscience stopped me. A young black boy had appeared and was now standing there looking at me, knowing full well I didn't fit in this horribly disfigured dark place. Frightened and horrified by the sight of the woman, I didn't wish to remain because I was so scared. Many people suddenly appeared out of the ether, all bearing threatening glances and hideous treachery. If I were to stay here very long, they might kill me, or come after me like someone apparently had done to this poor unfortunate woman lying on the ground covered in feces, urine and blood.

A desk appeared to the side of the woman who was lying in the center of this room, but at the same time, was lying in the street, as this room represented a ghetto block. Noticing a phone on the desk near the woman, I turned to the horridly frightening appearance of the woman on the street and asked her if I might be able to get her some help. Surprisingly, she responded. "That would be nice, and let the ambulance know that I have malaria." Realizing that she had not been injured by these people, but rather, she was deathly ill with a . . . oh, my gosh . . . highly contagious disease! Immediately feeling fear, her feces, urine and blood were everywhere, but I quelled my fear and turned to the phone.

As I did, the 911 operator said, "It is good that you called me, for if you had not, you wouldn't have been able to get through the exit even though you had found it. Because you called for help, you can go now." Hanging up the phone, I began to leave . . . but then stopped myself. Turning to the woman, I said, "I can't leave you here, I'll just have to wait until the ambulance arrives."

Asking to speak to the woman, a man suddenly appeared. Whispering in his ear, the woman said to him, "This is unfortunate (that she has chosen to stay) because she would have been able to exit this realm if she had immediately left, but now that she's waited she won't be able to exit." Conveying her words to me, I was saddened, but replied, "It wouldn't have been right to leave you here helpless, so I had to wait, even if it costs me the exit of this maze, and the loss of this rite of passage."

Suddenly, all the putrid filth around her disappeared and she metamorphosized first into a small boy, and then a small girl dressed in a long white robe. Smiling, she conveyed, "You wouldn't have been able to exit this realm had you not stayed." Reaching her hand to me, I was suddenly transported outside of that city block ghetto room, into yet another room of this elaborate maze.

A series of very illusive passages followed, each successive one more complex than the other. Inexplicable and energetic in nature, they were impossible to retain upon consciousness. After passing through many such rooms, however, the little girl greeted me again.

"There will be many angels awaiting you in each room," she said, "and they will guide you to the next passage." Stopping her, I said, "Well, with each angel I must stop and demand that they reveal their true selves, for I do not wish to follow any angels in disguise." As soon as I made this discernment, I was far away from the little girl. Now standing before a series of passages which I undertook with greater and greater fatigue, this process was mentally tiring because it required 100% consciousness on my part, and each passage was so complex and intricate there seemed no possible way to remember the details of each, or even some small details of any singular one. Inexplicable . . .

After passing through several ritual passages, I entered a maze whose purpose was the discernment between falsehood and truth. An old woman began making true statements, all of which were depicted in writing on a page much like a newspaper. Warning me that the false ones would be difficult to discern, she directed my fingers to touch tens of statements of truth, imprinted on the newspaper. Allowing me to feel the vibration of truth and how it differs from falsehood, she warned me that in the next passage I would be unable to discern through vibration, and would be left with only my intellect to discern the true from the false. Some would be absolutely true, others would be intricate falsehoods fashioned to appear as though true. In order to pass through this phase of the rite, I must be able to discern the true from the false.

Disappearing, literally hundreds of statements made by various religions throughout time appeared upon the page. Beginning to read them all, I began to get very tired. At first, it was easy to discern that most of the statements were falsehoods, but what began to happen as I continued reading false theological doctrines, my mind quickly became too fatigued to discern. Stopping me in my sloth, the old lady's voice said, "You must be able to continue no matter how long it takes, and it will continue for a succession of three full days."

'Oh my goodness,' I cannot express in words how tiring just the thought of this had become. Focusing my very tired mind, I resolved that if it must take three days, then it will take three days, I will not fail this very important test due to lack of diligence. New sets of statements appeared in regards to the station of certain religious leaders, many of them indicating that it wasn't uncommon for such people to misunderstand their purpose, attaching more significance to themselves through their own pride; rather than fulfilling their function without the need to create a new faction, sect, or denomination in their name.

A specific statement was made in reference to a particular sect, and my first impulse was to discern that the statement was true, but I didn't discern either way as the old lady's voice had come into my head. "Now you must run like a young buck across the field." Becoming a wide field, I began running across hoping that the end of the field might bring freedom from this endless discernment which seemed to already have taken several hours. Stopping myself, I turned back. 'I must be diligent in my efforts to discern all these statements, and I was told it would take three days, I must go back and discern the truth from the lies.'

Going back, I picked the newspaper up from the ground and began looking at the statements again. But as I looked upon these statements, I could no longer discern that which was true from that which was false. Fatigue of mind overcame me, and I made a decision not to discern any of the statements. Rather, I would take them in and allow the Lord to reveal to me the true from the false. Even more importantly, I decided to allow the Lord to reveal to me that which really mattered from that which truly was unimportant. Entering a detached state of inquiry wherein I chose to accept the statements as neither true nor false, the Lord began to reveal a great truth. All of these points of theology in religion held absolutely *no* importance in the eyes of the Lord. Detailed doctrines and fancy dogmatic theologies were unimportant in the eternal scheme of things. Nothing retained importance except this interiorly pure desire of the heart to *know* God. All the rest became meaningless. What I knew, what I believe . . . all paled in importance as it stood aside my love for God.

Becoming totally detached in this manner, the page changed into a picture. In the far lower right corner, the old lady was depicted in pencil drawing holding a set of weights and balances. At the top of the page, it said, 'If you wish to know the truth and falsehood, you must place your nose against the old lady's hand holding the balance.' As I did so, my nose began vibrating immensely and my soul quietly began to be delivered from this maze exiting upon the illustrious route 25, and arriving at consciousness in the physical state.

"The Prophet said: When flattery will grow in good people among you, the kingdom will go to the meanest of you and theology to those who will be corrupt."

Ihya-Ulum-Ud-Din, Book 1, Chapter 1, Section 4, Page 58, Top, (Islam, Author: Imam Gazzali)

"The Prophet prohibited dispute about useless things . . . He said . . . If a man gives up disputation in matters of truth, a house will be built up for him in the highest paradise."

Ihya-Ulum-Ud-Din, Book 1, Chapter 1, Section 4, Page 60, Top, (Islam, Author: Imam Gazzali)

****

Witnessing the unfoldment of the doctrine of reincarnation, I was filled with an inexplicable knowledge of every aspect of this grand mystery of the redemption. As the mysteries of the redemption and reincarnation are inseparable, it was beholden to me as eight separate vessels of knowledge. Containing distinct energetic knowledge which denoted, reiterated and explained much of the experiential knowledge I've come to know throughout my journeyings, there was also a great deal more.

Each of eight aspects of the mystery were presented to me distinctly and separately, each by two hands opening up before my eyes, with a profound energetic body coming from between them and into my soul, which expounded and filled me with the energetic truths of reincarnation. I wish I could express this vision further, for it was quite profound, but inexplicable. With great anticipation, I awaited the final two mysteries; for I knew that they held profundity beyond my imaginings. When these last two bodies of knowledge opened and filled me, I cannot express the relief and satisfaction which came through me, but yet, I remember nothing tangible of the knowledge which came over me, for it was all profoundly energetic and inexplicable.

Let it suffice to say that the mysteries of the redemption - and reincarnation - are inseparable.

"I am He who in an instant lift up the humble spirit, to learn more reasonings of the Eternal Truth, than if a man had studied ten years in the schools. I teach without noise of words, without confusion of opinions, without striving after honour, without clash of arguments. I am He who teach men to despise earthly things, to loathe things present, to seek things heavenly, to enjoy things eternal, to flee honours, to endure offences, to place all hope in Me, to desire nothing apart from Me, and above all things to love Me ardently."

The Imitation of Christ, The Third Book, Chapter XLII, No. 3, (Christianity, Author: Thomas A Kempis)

****

Brought upon a great series of disasters which represented the different levels of temptation which can descend upon our souls; the first and most catastrophic was a volcanic eruption coupled with earthquakes, the second was mud slides, and the third flash floods.

In each of these scenarios, my soul was given to experience and learn how to 'ride' the flow of the temptation so as not to be overcome. All three could overcome you without regard if you were not watchful for their sudden emergence, but if you knew how to ride temptation, you could survive the assaults of even the greatest element of vice.

In regards to the first temptation, the worst involving volcanic eruptions and earthquakes, I was bidden to ride the volcanic flow and willingly go underneath it as it covered me over in vile usury. Able to emerge victorious after it had passed, I was then able to emerge very slowly. In essence, you had to surrender to this level of temptation, not in the sense that you followed it, but rather, that you accepted the temptation as a wave of energy you could not avoid. Because it could not be avoided, you rode it. Riding required immersion with eventual re-emerging, unscathed if ridden properly. At the end of a first level temptation, you emerged on very high ground, far above (several hundred feet) the point you began, indicating the reward of overcoming such a high level temptation of the soul.

The second and third level were rather similar, in that you were required to ride the waves of mud and water, as well, but because they were less overwhelming than the first, you sought to keep your head above the flow. Mastering this was done by forming your body as if like a tube, a key for second and third level temptations.

Overcoming these three levels of temptation proffered the journeyer with the title of 'Master of the Slide.' Learning to follow the movements of temptation, the soul must do so in a flowing manner so as to avoid perishing amidst the tumultuous and rabid natural disasters of sin.

Unable to ride the waves of temptation, completely overcome on all three levels; my eldest daughter required my assistance to keep her from being overwhelmed by vice. Andy had trouble with the first and second level temptations. Upon sharing this with them, they confirmed their weakness, vowing to strive ever more in the fight against temptation and sin.

Do not flee from temptation, but do not succumb, but ride the wave, and follow it through so as not to be overwhelmed. Do not fight temptation from the ground, overcome it through surrender to the flow of the divine, and you shall obtain the strength to swim through the greatest of moral obstacles with success.

"It is necessary that temptations should happen; for who shall be crowned but he that shall lawfully have fought . . ."
The Voice of the Saints, Chapter 9, No. 2, (Christianity, Catholic, Words of St. Bernard)
****

Our party had taken to camping in the wilderness for the night, as our two wagons we had were in need of repair and the horses in need of a rest. Traveling across the mighty frontier towards the plains, we'd made plans to settle and make new homes in the wild country. But we were unprepared for what happened next.

Approaching us in English, a middle-aged Indian woman saw our party from the banks of a river. "Your presence here is insulting to my people," she said and then walked away. Having accidentally dropped a small bible into the water because of my fear of her when she approached, I picked it up.

In the middle of the night, they came, the Cheyenne warriors. Immediately, my spiritual aspect remembered their leader who had come to me early in my spiritual journeyings calling himself 'Cheyenne.' Shocked at how brutal he had been in life, the life of the frontier was violently different than what I had perceived.

Being taken captive by the Cheyenne, we were brought to their camp. One of the older men among us was a doctor, and very strong willed, and he defiantly spat at the feet of their leader. Immediately shot to death, we quickly learned that if we were to live, we had to become useful to the tribe. There were quite a few white folk amongst this tribe and it immediately became clear that if anybody lost their use, they would be killed.

A grown woman, my grown sister and brother were among us, as well as my father. My mother was not present; perhaps she had already died in the East. Wearing long dresses with petticoats, my hair was dyed blonde and curled at the ends in a tress. Looking upon all of us, I noticed that my butt was pretty big, and my sister was skinnier than I. Women wore hats with limp colored feathers in them. Fancy and looking quite odd at this juncture, over time, my blonde hair grew back out to its natural brown color.

Becoming useful to the tribe in teaching, they'd become interested in learning to read. Having to give up everybody and everything from our old life made me extremely angry at the Indians. Although we were made regular citizens of the tribe, it was also made clear that we were not allowed to leave at penalty of death.

At one point several years later, my sister and father escaped one night, but I was unable to go with them. Becoming extremely depressed, over time, I had taken ill. Laying down struggling to breathe, I was unable to control urination. The Indians actually tended to me very lovingly at this juncture, but I still hated them and all they had done to us in my heart.

Never recovering, I was rarely able to get out of bed, and it wasn't long before I died.

The Indians and what they meant to me, what can I say? This event made it clear to me just how important they were in regards to my own redemption, because I had built up so much karma regarding them between my own lives as a native among them, and my lifetimes as a white person whose reality kept bumping into theirs.

In a sense, I knew that I had had this experience to give myself a sense of the journey, the accomplishment, the distance, and the struggle. The journey from karmic delusion towards the grand redemption of my soul had been a very long one, and this moment reminded my soul of the distance it had come. For the purpose of praise, we must always remember from where we have come, for it is only through this, that our soul retains a true understanding of the value of that which has come to pass. Praise the Lord, for the journey slowly reaches its end, the mysteries of the redemption have unfolded and become manifest within my heart.

"For it is by wise guidance that you wage your war, and the victory is due to a wealth of counselors."
New American Bible, Old Testament, Proverbs 24:6
"But the rational soul who (also) wearied herself in seeking - she learned about God. She labored with inquiring, enduring distress in the body, wearing out her feet after the evangelists, learning about the Inscrutable One. She found her rising. She came to rest in him who is at rest. She reclined in the bride-chamber. She ate of the banquet for which she had hungered. She partook of the immortal food. She found what she had sought after. She received rest from her labors, while the light that shines forth upon her does not sink."
The Nag Hammadi Library, Authoritative Teaching, Page 310, Paragraph 1,
(Christianity, Gnostic/Essene)

****

Studiously transcribing the notes that I had written regarding the mysteries of the redemption, it became known to me that they were a commentary on another more important text. Within each section of the commentary, I also wrote down the verse of this unknown text which had been its inspiration. Continuing this process throughout the night, when I finished I was shocked to learn just what sort of book I had been writing about. Emerging from my notes was a copy of the New Testament, as my writing was a commentary on the New Testament, bearing the journey of a soul according to the teachings of Christ within the pages of the most Holy Bible. Honored and stunned by this, I realized that in our humble journey towards the redemption, the Holy Scriptures had been fulfilled, as they must be fulfilled in every individual life. It is finished; let it be done according to thy will . . .

"I have set you as the light of the world, and as a city that cannot be hid. But the time cometh when darkness shall cover the earth, and gross darkness the people, and the enemies of truth and righteousness shall rule in my Name, and set up a kingdom of this world, and oppress the peoples, and cause the enemy to blaspheme, putting for my doctrines the opinions of men, and teaching in my Name that which I have not taught, and darkening much that I have taught by their traditions. But be of good cheer, for the time will also come when the truth they have hidden shall be manifested, and the light shall shine, and the darkness shall pass away, and the true kingdom shall be established which shall be in the world, but not of it, and the Word of righteousness and love shall go forth . . . "

The Gospel of the Holy Twelve, Lection XCV, No. 3-4, (Christianity, Gnostic/Essene, Words of Christ)

"Then opened he their understanding, that they might understand the scriptures. And said unto them, Thus it is written, and thus it behooved Christ to suffer, and to rise from the dead after the third day. And that repentance and remission of sins should be preached in my name among all nations, beginning at Jerusalem. And ye are witnesses of these things."

The Gospel of the Holy Twelve, Lection LXXXVIII, No. 6, (Christianity, Gnostic/Essene)
****

My soul had been in a state of disorientation for a long time. As I began to reacquaint myself with the reality of the world around me, I found myself within the confines of a mental ward. In my stupor, I had failed to notice that many people had come to see me in my confinement, and were concerned about my soul.

Feeling as though I were emerging from a dream, I quietly walked down the halls following the whims of my heart, I knew where I needed to go.

Carrying with me a box full of ancient sacred texts, I began to look upon them with intrigue. It was these texts which had led me down a road which looked so much like mental illness to those around me. Yet, this road had been the most vital of all roads I'd ever taken. Despite the perception of those who surrounded me, I knew that this road was one every mortal soul must follow at some point in their endless cycle of lives.

After entering the room and settling my accounts with several people, the teacher got up and began to talk to this crowded room of students. "Now that you finally have this little distraction taken care of," he said, "you can focus again on your studies." I was the distraction he spoke of, my failing mental health. Surprisingly, however, several students began sharing a defense on my behalf. "I'm just trying to point out," the teacher responded, "that this woman has been a great distraction for all of you, because of her craziness, and all her problems." A woman jumped up. "You speak of her as if you don't understand," she said, "it is not like the butler who has been caught stealing. No, it's not like that at all, but rather, the poet whose battle in life is always with himself, her sinfulness is the only thing which concerns her. Have you ever listened to this soul? How she speaks of her own sin with such disdain and regret, how she believes with her full heart that her life has warranted hell." Only making him believe in his position all the more, he replied, "Don't let this woman continue to distract you from your goals. She's crazy, that's all there is to it."

Standing up, I looked directly into his eyes and said, "It is not I that you are afraid of, sir. I am only another worthless crazy person to you. But it is *yourself* that you find reflected in me which gives you such fear and trepidation. I see angels . . . and I see demons. I see them both. They are as real to me as you are at this moment." Pulling back, he cringed at my admittance of what I saw. "You are afraid of your own spirit which I reflect to you now," I said, "you are

225

afraid of the journey which I have taken, not because you find it so crazy, but because a part of you finds it extremely disturbing, somehow not so far removed from that which your own soul must do to progress, but you are afraid to walk this path because you, too, may then seem crazy." Visibly shaken, I began to recite the death song. "The timeless moon doth ocean sway tide, holding tight to beachhead reign, but never be near the stillness of time, crossing to regions of lingering plane . . . Sing in spirit to mountains that speak . . . " Almost shouting, he pushed me away from him. As he did, the whole group of students began to slowly clap and stand.

Within a short flicker of time, they stood in ovation for my journey and recovery through the mental crags of karma, which had given my soul a strange new insight into all things. My eyes didn't see things the same as they had before, because all was brilliant, lively and filled with meaning. The molecules in the air were visible to me now, and every step I took was energized and filled with light emanation. Was I crazy? Perhaps. But my crazy love for God had set me free from the delusions of my youth.

Perhaps all who cross the walkway towards the redemption appear to those we leave behind as somehow touched. But it is the Holy Spirit which touches us and makes us seem so odd, so malfeasant. It is unnecessary to explain to those we leave behind, for someday, too, they will emerge upon the same threshold which shall take them deep into a state of apparent mental illness. Perhaps if they knew that it is their current, unrealized state which is the true madness, they would begin to see the world through the eyes of a soul preparing to leave this planetary teacher behind. Beginning in karmic madness, this journey ends in heavenly malaise. Heavenly malaise is the ultimate madness to a soul locked in karma's temptation, and trapped within the gate of lifetimes of sin. Spinning . . . spinning . . . spinning . . . do they know that they appear mad to souls such as my own? My own soul whimpers in pain to hear other souls constantly talking, spinning, of things other than God. No meaning, no rapture, no joy, just the continuing drudgery of sanity, whilst I continue in my crazed ascent ever closer to my Beloved.

If this love of God is madness, then let me be mad, for I would never go back to being a rational soul, defect free in the eyes of the world, who lives only for the self and worldly pursuits. Without God, let me die. With God, let me appear as crazy as I must, to awaken these slothful souls towards the path of heavenly bliss.

"For them that believe, these things are true. For them that believe not, they are as an idle tale."
The Gospel of the Holy Twelve, Lection XCVI, No. 27, (Christianity, Gnostic/Essene)
****

As my spirit began riding through the epochs of my life, I found myself wandering throughout several places and towns, visiting with those souls from my past to celebrate this great redemptive moment. However, they were not aware of this great happening until a momentous event occurred.

Amongst the spectral skies, a sudden wonderment overflowed into my being, and amidst the ruckus and turmoil of the world, containing everyone and everything I'd ever known throughout my life, music began to pour forth from my cells. And beyond this, the most beauteous fabrics began coming from my soul as I began dancing on the air.

Floating through the air at an indescribably vast speed, these fabrics began coming forth from my pores creating canvasses of life immersing the world about me in the joyous beauty of God and His magnificent creation. Stunned by the magnificent sounds which poured forth from my cells and the fabrics, linens, laces and cloths which emerged in the finest synchronicity, the people did not speak.

As my operatic endeavor continued, the thoughts of the people around me began appearing as objects representative of their senses. Statues of worldly objects began appearing, and in order to rectify this error, I began singing all the louder of the Holy Mother of God, and the Lord Jesus Christ. As I sang, my voice's pitch went ever higher to encompass the vastness of God, His Son and Mother. Before me, as I sang, appeared beautiful statues of Mary and Jesus with their arms outstretched to all mankind. As I saw them, my spirit soared high up in the sky, going higher and higher. Bliss filled my soul.

Amongst one of my beauteous canvasses of life, somebody had erected an altar to the ancient Egyptians and to the Roman rulers. Flying with ease to the sight, singing this operatic song of life to my Lord, I spewed forth from my loins the sounds of the saints. As I did so, Mary, Jesus and images of holy souls throughout time from all ages, from all religions and sects filled the spaces, immediately replacing the former idolatry which had held Earthly images and people as Lord.

How can I express? How can I say it? If only I had the skill to rewrite the most beautiful opera I was proffered to sing in the honor of the Lord. Perhaps some things are meant to be so holy that they remain in the heavens as living monuments to the living Lord.

Beginning to run into souls of whom I'd known during my life, with each soul I gave thanks to the Lord for our reunion, and bid them adieu. But amongst them came one soul I'd known who had once been a spirit so free as to fill the world with his soul. But now, he came as a statue, dark and morose, fulfilling the whims of the world. Having lost his enlivened soul, it had been replaced by a stodgy shadow which fulfilled only the whims of the pocketbook. "Where have you gone, comrade?" I bade to ask him. "I gave up my childish fancies years ago," he said, "perhaps it is time for you to do the same." "Oh, no, my old friend," I replied, "I will never give up the enlivened love of the Lord, for He is my all." Looking at me, he shrugged his shoulders and turned his head as if to remark sarcastically of my stupidity.

So, in order to awaken him from his sleep, I began to sing my opera to the Lord all the louder. "Holy . . . Mother . . . of God . . . ." I sang, "My Lord of life, Lord of love, Lord of all creation, Jesus Christ!" As I did so, statues of the most holy eminence's appeared out of a puff of smoke, replacing the worldly statues of things which converged throughout all these minds of souls. The canvas filled with the souls of the entire world, not just my own past.

Flying high again up in the air due to the mention of the holy duo, many souls were watching my flight with interest and confusion. They didn't realize that whenever I mentioned the mere names of Our Lord Jesus Christ and His Most Holy Mother Mary that my soul lifted high up in the air due to the lightness of being which such holy names rendered. Jealous for the bliss, they had begun to believe long ago that such bliss was not truly possible in this world. Although our world *is* very limited, its possibilities do retain the full inflow of heaven's bliss. Because humanity has chosen to fill it with those worldly things which contain no implicit joy, the world has become devoid of life. But it doesn't *have* to be this way.

Redemption can be a singular moment for an individual soul, but it could also contain the grandness of the entire human race if such a miracle were to take place within the mind of humanity.

Singing to my hearts content, bliss of soul filled my spirit in a manner indescribable, as banners of beautiful cloths, laces and linens continued to come out of me painting the world in beauty and kindness. "If only," I thought, "if only souls would paint their own little corner of the world with such beauty, fill it with the wonder of God, then they, too, would know the joy and bliss of God's magnificence." I thought of how sad it was for those souls who had never experienced what I had been blessed to witness. My soul pondered the melancholy malaise that many in the world must be left with, when only their worldly imaginings remain. But if only they would dream again, if only they would look, for beyond this world lies another far greater and more vast than even the few have imagined. Our momentary sojourn upon these shores could be of wondrous beauty if only we would listen to the silent sounds which emanate continuously from the shores of heaven to beckon each one of us to come home. There are no words, there is no reason . . . yet man continues to spin in his karmic wheel of indifference towards his most glorious Creator, and in his malaise, he misses the joyous manifestations of love which emanate from His heart to our own. For He beckons us, every one, until we heed His call and return to His heart, His bosom, and again take suckle of the holy nourishment of our heavenly origin.

"No," I thought, "they aren't listening to me." Angry at my outflow of beauty and song, they were content to remain in their boring imaginings of worldly attainment and greed. So I sang all the louder, for in the corners and crevasse's were a few lone souls amongst the multitudes who were quietly, shyly listening. Unsure, they were, if my message could be true, but in their eyes I saw the wonder of a soul willing to seek, to beckon, to pray with fury to the Almighty Lord. If only they would be able to put down their worldly imaginings, and do it. Just do it.

My singing erupted into a vast furlough of melodious exhaustive bliss. My spirit flew to heights above the multitude, way above the multitude. My spirit listened in on the thoughts of the few, as their minds began to untangle the messages. Many were going back and forth between jealousy for my state of bliss and their own longing to know God, as well. Would they break through the worldly view of conceit, which allowed them to judge my state? Would they hold fast to old ideas which supported a world devoid of the Lord God and all the bliss His love contains? Or would they awaken? In a tiny spark of wishing for more, would they begin to unravel the ancient mystery of the all-merciful redemption of God?

I wished for the latter, and I continued to sing, praising the Lord with all my might, flying higher than any soul could imagine, with the beauteous canvas of life continuing to emerge from my soul. Nothing would restrain my glory, for this glory was expressive of my own redemption, and who among the wards of imprisoned humanity, could understand such freedom? Redemption is a beautiful and magnificent thing, and so I allowed my soul to partake of it grandly; and in so doing, only beauty filled my soul, only beauty came out of my soul, only beauty filled my vocal chords, and only beauty filled my flight this night.

For those who could not or would not listen, I left the beautiful canvasses behind me, so that perhaps someday they might notice such beauty, and wonder from whence they had come. For those who might be ready to listen, I continued my singing; so that they might be able to hear the beauty they so longed to fathom. For myself and the holy angels, I continued my flight of joy, for there was nothing or no one that could take away the joyous melodious beatific vision of which I had embraced. The Lord, my God, filled me with majestic praise for all His great works in saving and restoring that which had been lost. My own unworthy soul had been redeemed. Hallelujah, hallelujah, hallelujah to the Lord!

"All the ways which the living soul of a person breathes forth in itself, and all the things a person does which are useful and fruitful as well as those which are useless - all these things are open to the sight of the all-powerful God."
Mystical Visions, Vision Four: 21, Paragraph 1, (Christianity, Catholic, Words of Hildegard Von Bingen)

****

It was the end of a war, a truce had been called, and many soldiers had gathered at the outpost for supplies and food. With a friend of mine who was also a long time friend in this life, we were deep in the West. Indians were at the outpost looking to trade, and amongst them I saw the soul of Red Jacket.

With a white woman, he noticed me immediately, as I did him. Quiet about this recognition, only our mutual glances could betray our connection to each other. It seemed for this moment that this was later in the life of his imprisonment and our union, but I was unsure if this was the case.

Showing up brandishing a gun, my friend's brother was planning to kill a few Indians. Grabbing his gun from him, I got rid of it and stopped him. Again, I felt the glances looking upon me from behind. Turning, Red Jacket quickly turned his own head away. His majestic figure in the day was ominous, his long black hair a bit matted and dirty, but I cannot describe the intensity of the feelings I would experience just watching him from afar, a deep soul-felt love, something very rare and unique.

Despite this, we both knew that whatever liaisons we may have had in the past were to remain there. Both of us had grown and matured, and neither of us had any desire to cause pain to others over something which was already quite real, without any further need for expression.

Suddenly, our past and our present began to overlap. Deep feelings I felt for him seemed to be balanced by the greater understanding I'd achieved throughout this present incarnation, during the process of my own redemption.

Sitting down to think upon these and other great things, I hardly noticed him coming closer to me; but suddenly as he had left his place in the distance, he whisped by me looking deeply into my eyes for only a moment. Looking up to his, our eyes met, and without a single word being exchanged, a powerful union was revealed to both of us. We both reached to touch the other's hand, but pulled back almost as quickly.

What karma holds between two souls must never be misunderstood. Powerful love exists between souls of such karmic thrusts, but that love can only be conquered by recognizing its import. Our move towards each other was a demonstration of mutual respect, a recognition of our mutual mistakes, and an unspoken desire to cease causing pain to ourselves and others through wrong conduct. For how many lives had we touched each other? But at this moment, we touched each other in a completely new way; it was a touch of forgiveness and mercy.

Recognizing the pain our union brought to ourselves and others because of its karmic nature, we acknowledged the deep love between our souls, but released the need to process its unsavory elements any longer. In so doing, we could elevate it to a higher place, an eternal place. In eternity, our love could be experienced in a whole new way, beyond karmic thrusts and reasoning. No more need remained to play this story out on the ground, for we had forgiven each other for our misunderstandings. Giving each other a gift of inestimable value, a gift which paid the debt of the sin, pain and chaos our love had caused to all in our midst, the gift of mercy. Our eyes remained dry during this last Earthly exchange, for there was no more need for tears on our account. Quietly, he walked away and all around us disappeared into the mist.

Within a moment, I was flying in ecstasy to the melodious sounds of the Word of God. Many of my friends who had walked karma's path with me were now joyfully embracing this moment of eternal union with the Lord. The words of Christ were echoing in melodious chant from the harmonic skies, many voices of both male and female interspersing with the wondrous lure of the Word. Even those still entrenched in karmic influence on the ground, were for this moment, very much in the flow, adverse to temptation and melodiously accepting the higher thrusts of forgiveness and mercy. Our dance of redemption was a moment of celebration that another soul was returning to its God. Our ecstatic dance was ominously exciting, as our souls were thrust upon the heavenly spheres to fly. My soul created effortlessly upon the wisps of the eternal skies as this expressive dance took no skill, the artistry coming directly from God to His subject. Soaring in ecstatic bliss, I enjoyed the ride for as long as the eternal would allow. Then, I floated back to existence in peace.

"Ho, Father! This day we have done the will of the Great Spirit, and through this we have established a relationship and peace, not only among ourselves, but within ourselves and with all the Powers of the Universe. The dawn of the day has surely seen us . . ."
The Sacred Pipe, Chapter VI, Page 114, Paragraph 2, (Tribal, Oglala Sioux, Words of Black Elk)

"By contrition we are made clean; by compassion we are made ready, and by true longing for God we are made worthy. These are the three means, as I understand it, by which all souls - that is to say, all souls that have been sinners on earth and shall be saved - come to heaven, for by these medicines it would profit every sinful soul to be healed."
Revelations of Divine Love, Chapter 39, Paragraph 4, (Christianity, Catholic, Words of Juliana of Norwich)

****

Allowing me to take a night flight, my soul was swept into the mountains. Upon my breast, my second daughter, now two, lay holding tight to her momma, and on my feet and hands were adorned shoes and gloves made of interwoven crystal rosaries. Sky blue, they protected not only my feet and hands, but my entire soul upon this journey.

After traveling through a beauteous mountain landscape, I was taken back to the state of my childhood and young adult years, wherein I was given leave to look upon and observe the current goings-on with several people in my past who had walked karma's path with me. I was overjoyed to see how they were doing in this invisible way. In a sense, it was a release of them. Walking into karma had caused much pain and hardship for others, but despite this, they were all doing just fine. Thankful, I returned home on the wing of the wind, as the spirit directed me to go home.

"Let the righteous man arise from slumber; let him arise, and proceed in the path of righteousness in all its paths; and let him advance in goodness and in eternal clemency. Mercy shall be showed to the righteous man; upon him shall be conferred integrity and power for ever."
The Book of Enoch, Chapter XCI (Section XIX), No. 3, (Christianity)

****

Andy had an experience:
"Marilynn and I were walking in a barren rock area when suddenly a fountain of water began gushing forth in the midst of our trail. Proceeding to step into the fountain, Marilynn immersed herself in the water. At that time, I heard a voice say 'The Fountain of Redemption.' And subsequently, I followed Marilynn's example and immersed myself likewise. It was truly a holy experience, a baptism."

"(And) some say, 'On the last day (we will) certainly arise (in the) resurrection.' But they do not (know what) they are saying, for the last day (is when) those belonging to Christ . . . was fulfilled, he destroyed (their archon) of (darkness . . .) . . . they asked (what they have been) bound with, (and how they) might properly (release themselves). And (they came to know) themselves (as to who they are), or rather, where they are (now), and what is the (place in) which they will rest from their senselessness, (arriving) at knowledge. (These) Christ will transfer to (the heights) since they (have renounced) foolishness (and have) advanced to knowledge. And those who (have knowledge . . .) . . . he has come to) know (the Son of Man), that (is, he has come to) know (himself. This) is the perfect life, (that) man know (himself) by means of the All."
The Nag Hammadi Library, The Testimony of Truth, Page 451, Paragraph 3, (Christianity, Gnosticism)

"I also came out as a brook from a river, and as a conduit into a garden. I said, I

will water my best garden, and will water abundantly my garden bed: and, lo, my brook became a river, and my river became a sea. I will yet make doctrine to shine as the morning, and will send forth her light afar off. I will yet pour out doctrine as prophecy, and leave it to all ages for ever. Behold that I have not laboured for myself only, but for all them that seek wisdom."
The Apocrypha, Ecclesiasticus, Chapter 24, Paragraph 3, (Christianity, Words of Christ)
****

CHAPTER EIGHT
To Return to the Native, Karmic Retribution for Unintentionally Spreading False Truth, Attempts at Temptation that Failed, Linking Spiritual Seeking with your Life, Past Life without Joy, Native American Angel, Karma of Christianity, Original Sin of Sexual Abuse, Karma of Utilizing False Spirituality to Promote Lust, Widows Lifetime, Subconscious Regret of Evil Acts.

****

Awakened, my soul found itself standing amidst a grand forest. All around me were the benefits of the wild, the trees cascading high above me in this almost iridescent and yet somewhat waveform world. Beginning to prance along the wilderness path, I looked around to find the purpose of my arrival in this spiritual world.

Wavering through the forest sheath, I began to see the vague outline of a form ahead of me. As he began to materialize, it revealed a Native American man dressed in buckskin riding a white horse. Back facing me, he was riding slowly along the path. Following this immensely mystical mirage, I began to run towards him, but then began to soar so that I might catch up.

Stopping before the side of a red rock cliff, he turned to look at me for only a millisecond, as his image and that of the horse began to fade. Beginning to make out what lay before him on the path, it was a doorway. Although there was no visible outline of an entry, the stone rock wall led high into the sky.

Looking up, a woman dressed all in white appeared at my side. Shimmering in the wind, she began to speak words of passage which she bade me not to repeat to any Earthly soul. (As usual, they were also then taken from my memory within a few days of the experience.) Highly evolved and very calm, she took my hand and a small screen appeared in the rock face of the mountain wherein our faces were now visible.

Without words, the woman conveyed to me that I was being examined for signs of readiness by those of the elect who resided within these walls. Suddenly, the lines which would indicate a door appeared and opened before us in the rocks. Two stools quietly lay within, and she guided me to join her in sitting upon them. As we did, the doors closed around us and we transmitted to another dimension.

Words cannot express the bliss I felt upon arriving in this majestic kingdom and being granted the privilege of seeing my long lost friend, St. Harmony Crystal Fire, the white-winged horse who had traveled to so many distant places with me, and who had guided me into many doorways and realms of knowledge. It'd been a very long time since I'd seen my beautiful white-winged horse, and I was brought to tears upon visioning his beauty.

Arriving through a similar multi-dimensional gateway, St. Harmony Crystal Fire passed through a machine which was somewhat like an x-ray. You could see the skeletal structure of the horse and his wings as he passed through, but in order to be allowed entry here, you had to have certain auric markers indicating that you were sufficiently evolved. St. Harmony Crystal Fire passed with flying colors.

Previously unnoticed by myself, there appeared at St. Harmony Crystal Fire's side a woman who was apparently responsible for bringing him here.

Summoned to go with them for some sort of preparation, the woman who had led me here left with them while I was to remain behind.

Time passed before I was telepathically airlifted, without any verbal warning, to St. Harmony Crystal Fire's side. Seeing before me two states of energy, they were demonstrated to me in a way which my limited understanding did not comprehend. Because of this, I was led through a series of lights which were designed to bring your vibration higher, so as to gently guide you to an understanding of these two lights which were apparently very important. As these little lights were understood, they would then merge within your spirit and become a part of you. My case was a difficult one, however, as I was having trouble comprehending the energetic meaning of these lights. Thus, my own lights were not igniting properly, which posed a problem for the patient guardians who had brought me here this evening.

Approaching me, a man dressed in white appeared in the essence of peace and serenity. Guided by a higher voice which belonged to a woman, I could not see her. Everyone present, however, was aware of the telepathic impetus which was received from her by this man. Because the other method had not worked (that of showing me the lights and attempting to integrate their knowing within me), he was attempting to transfer the knowledge of these lights telepathically. Eventually, this would lead to my spiritual link-up with St. Harmony Crystal Fire.

As this process bore fruit, I saw before me the first light. Lighting up as a holy rage, I immediately understood it to be an inferior understanding. 'Holy Rage' was an excessively angry response to the sins of others or the world. The second light was a calm and calculated energy which acted for the sole purpose of evolution. Recognizing misdeeds or sins as such, it held within it a proper recognition of the place of sin in the development of souls. Entering into this knowing, the second light lit up and entered my spirit.

As soon as this was accomplished, my soul began to waver in and out of energy, as I watched the final link-up with St. Harmony Crystal Fire achieve itself. A line of energy which looked very much like a laser beam, formed from my heart to his. Beginning to be drawn away, there was little I could do about it.

Conveying telepathically as I began to disappear, the guardians thought, 'You must release the purpose of holy rage, which is an extreme you've traveled to in balancing your understanding. Embrace calculated evolutionary energy as the proper balance in the understanding of deeds, your own and others, perpetuated upon the planet Earth.' Completing this process according to their instruction, St. Harmony Crystal Fire and I melted into one another, as we both disappeared.
****

As my soul was being mercilessly assaulted by a large group of demonic entities, I was calling out to Jesus for help in this precarious situation. Something very unusual occurred, however, in that Jesus did not come Himself, but rather sent to my aid a Franciscan monk. Immediately vacating the dark spirits, he turned without delay to chastise me.

I was clearly forgiven for that which he was about to discuss, but my sins were serious and had energized karmic retribution. Looking upon his face, I knew that I was about to really get it, and I adjusted my energies to an appropriately serious stance.

Earlier in my journey, before I had rewritten and completed the books involved in 'The Mysteries of the Redemption' and 'Galactica,' I had published two books under the New Age genre. Having allowed them to be dispersed too soon, I had neglected to obtain the complete picture, and expressed two very serious untruths. Despite the Lord's understanding of our delusional status, we remain accountable for that which we do and say. Every jot and tittle of the law shall be fulfilled.

Speaking of how many of my previous books had actually been sold; the monk mentioned that somewhere between 10-20,000 people had bought them. By publishing standards, this number was pathetic, but by number of souls misled, it was significant.

When I'd written the books, I'd been completely sincere in believing that what was within them was true, although I'd expressed *opinions* in regards to things which had not yet been revealed to me, which were judgmental and absolutely incorrect. A common problem among those of us awakened to the spiritual realms, I'd given myself to comment on that which had not yet been revealed, simply because of the nature of that which had. Making assumptions about a broader truth based on my limited understanding of a series of mystical experiences, I made the broad leap that they contained within them *all* knowledge. A good example of this same arrogance came to me when I read a very short booklet written by a young man who'd had a near-death experience as a child. Explaining what he had seen, he began to mock those who had made mention of the cherubs, because he'd only seen angels of adult stature in his one experience. As a result, he believed that cherubs simply did not exist. It is unwise to create your own theology of all that is, based on one or a few mystical experiences. God's kingdom is much too vast. To do so is small-minded and lacking in humility.

Although they were not based on my experience, but rather my false conclusions extending beyond them, I had deduced two things which were untrue. 1) There is no hell, Satan or demons, and 2) because we create our own reality; those who are sick can heal themselves. (Please be assured that all such falsehoods were removed long ago, under divine direction. Neither of these versions will ever be in print again.)

Essential understanding lies in this. In both cases, I'd made assumptions based on what I'd seen, ignoring that which I had not yet seen. Because the Lord *begins* the mystical journey of the novice by taking him into the heavenly realms, I assumed there must not be hellish realms. Because I'd been shown the basic mechanism of reality creation through thought, I assumed that *all* reality was thought based and conscious. Because I hadn't yet seen the deeper movings of the mechanics of existence (something I should have assumed that I did not yet know), I hadn't realized that such things were a working of intricate levels of existence, thought playing only a partial role. The will of God and the laws of nature are intricately involved with such things, stupid, stupid, stupid . . .

Having commanded me to get my earliest books taken out of print years before this current experience, the Lord Jesus had been kind and forgiving of my error, because it was to serve a greater purpose. As I had taken them out of print years before, the Lord shared that I'd been allowed to publish them as part of a karmic path which would lay the foundation for my later eternal work. Having now spent years rewriting the books from the standpoint of knowledge, the Lord laid everything out for me like a map.

In following my karmic impetus which had stemmed from vainglory and greed, I'd pursued publication of my books (at that time) because it appeared (on the ground) like the correct thing to do. An eternal program requires the will of God to reveal such matters.

Steady, sure, just and swift, my soul received karmic retribution. For the first untruth perpetuated through my hand, the Lord gave permission for the dark side to continually tempt my soul. For the second, the Lord gave permission for my body to experience the ravages of a disease whose prime manifestation had yet to be diagnosed. (Although I had been diagnosed with Lupus by this time, another deeply foreboding diagnosis was yet to come.)

Feeling ridiculously stupid, the monk had made things abundantly clear, but I couldn't help but notice his disgust with what I had done. Disgusted with myself, as well, I noticed that his energy changed as he observed my true contrition.

Becoming abundantly merciful, he took my hand, and we walked towards a meditation cell. "I'm going to pray for you," he quietly said, as he bid me to know that another awaited who would also assist.

Arriving in the cell, my soul could not believe the beauty the Lord in his infinite compassion had prepared for me. Pope John Paul II was waiting for us, incredible warmth upon his face for such a sinner. White robes gleaming with holiness, there was a three-foot high, shining, gilded, golden crown emanating from the top of his head. The holiness of this man was abundantly clear. Above it, ethereal aspects of the crown radiated into the molecular structure of the air in a manner which lit up the whole room. Falling to my knees, I lowered my head in shame, as he placed his hands upon me and said, "I love you."

Tears flowed from my eyes as he took the hand of the monk, beginning to pray that the Lord would forgive me and lift this just retribution from my soul. Beginning to disappear, I shouted out my thanks for their blunt chastisement. As they smiled with deep compassion, I disappeared.

****

Amidst the spectral universe, my soul was led to several classrooms where I was given inexplicable knowledge regarding astronomy which lay beyond my comprehension. But as this class commenced, another spirit entered the room with the purpose of inflicting upon my soul some lurid sexual temptations. Because I was so mesmerized by the teaching, I didn't even notice that there was somebody at my side attempting to lure me into insidious behavior.

When it was that I finally realized the presence of this individual, but not his intent, I turned to him and kindly asked him to go away. Rather surprised that I didn't respond in any way, shape or form to this, the guardians appeared stunned.

As the man who behaved inappropriately disappeared, the guardians of the rite looked at me and said in a very quizzical manner, "You didn't fall for that temptation." "What temptation?" I replied.

Remaining stunned, it appeared that few souls passed through this rite. Walking towards a door which emitted much light, as they opened it, you could see nothing but an indescribably bright, white light which blared through our souls. Walking alone, I proceeded to enter this light, and then it was that I awoke.

****

Taken into the reality of someone who expressed a different angle on the issue of incorrect views, I flew into a room which represented their spirit. Led to a table which displayed three very beautiful and exquisite paintings, they represented this person's spiritual search. Each of the paintings represented a different religious viewpoint of which he had studied; Judaism, Buddhism and Hinduism. As I looked upon them, I understood immediately that this person's spiritual journey was very sincere and quite serious.

Gazing upon the room around me, it was filled with clutter, and I understood that there was more to this story. Scrap papers were thrown around the room, sheets and blankets thrown over furniture and a general pattern of disarray permeated the room. Being led to a kitchen, it was conveyed to me that I would observe that upon which this soul spiritually feeds. Observing the same sort of messiness which had encompassed the other room, an invisible presence led me to observe something which had been very well hidden at the side of the refrigerator.

As I pulled it out, I began to look upon the pages of what appeared to be a magazine. Inside, were images of people having sex, and as you continued through the magazine, the images became more lewd and deviant, indicating that the deeper you went, the more this vice manifested in this person's soul.

Although this person's spiritual journey was very sincere and serious, he had not linked his spiritual search with his life; with the choices, decisions, vices, and issues which made up his true self. In a sense, the spiritual journey was an intellectual exercise which was intentionally kept far away from the actual spiritual substance which was his soul.

Another manner in which souls can be unable to see the truth, when a soul separates the spiritual quest from who he actually is, ignoring vice, choices, responsibilities, etc., the search will not bear fruit. Because our vices, issues, responsibilities and choices *are* **the way** for each one of us, ignoring them to focus on intellectual truths has no purpose. Difficulties in our lives are most often the means which God gives us to prune our souls, if we attempt to ameliorate them and avoid the truth that they provide, we miss the point.

In this man's case, he very much wanted to discard of the responsibility of a wife and children in order to pursue his spiritual journey. What he didn't realize was that his wife and children *were* his spiritual journey, and to discard them to find himself would be pointless and empty. Substance lies within those things which are difficult for us to do, the very responsibilities which can appear to hold us back are the doorways to our freedom.
****

Dark and occupied by two other nuns, the cell in the medieval monastery seemed confining. As we were praying, I immediately recognized one of the nuns as a friend of mine from this present life. Mother Superior was directing the two of us, as we were kneeling on the floor praying before a blank wall adorned with a single crucifix. Praying for hours, I began to feel restless. After several more hours passed, I could no longer take it.

Getting up, I began walking towards the doorway of the cell. Joining me, my friend and I walked through the doorway and into our present life.

Our souls seemed to be lighter without the weight of the habit, but we said nothing regarding this sudden miraculous transition from one world and time zone to the next. In our hearts, we understood very clearly that what we'd experienced had demonstrated an intense extreme, and it was now our process to restore proper balance. Prayer is a very important thing, when done in the context of living your life fully. What had been missing in that former time zone was *joy*, and we had quietly and unobtrusively walked into the future to find this elusive quality.
****

Surrounding my spirit were a plethora of holy crucifixes of many different sizes, shapes and designs. Standing in a battered and run-down old country store, I gazed upon each one carefully. In the center there was a huge crucifix which bore the image of Christ, but the cross itself was translucent. Jesus was obviously suffering, but the instrument of his torture was invisible, much like my own illness. Amidst this wide assortment of crucifixes, I came across a statue of Our Lady of Grace which portrayed her lying down amidst a field of flowers. Rather than the usual demon underfoot, the many colors in bloom serenaded her feet. At peace, the battle was over and she was surrounded in her victory, much like my own death.

Gazing upon it with wonder, I heard the voice of a male angel who surreptitiously appeared at my side. Native American, his long black hair framed his deeply dark face, while white wings protruded from the back of his bare chest. Eminence came from him, but I was so drawn to these images of the crucifixion that I only looked at him for a moment.

"The time has come," he said, "for you to speak for my people." Nodding, I remembered that several years ago I had been told I would speak for 'my' people, the Native Americans, who were 'mine' through the benefit of many past lives living as one of them, but I had never been told what I would say or when.

'How do these images and the words he just spoke interact?' I thought, looking at what appeared to be a contradiction. "This is what you will say first," he said, "The Native Americans were very much like Jesus Christ . . . "he paused, as I tried to understand the meaning of what he was saying to me. With unction and extreme stillness, he said the final words he would utter very slowly and quietly, almost a whisper. "Lambs led to the slaughter . . ." My heart literally fell as I immediately understood the connection and the profundity of this comparison.

Native Americans suffered at the hands of an invisible instrument of torture, racism, and their graves now bore the fruitful bloom of the martyrdom of a brave and tortured people. Understanding, I disappeared.

****

Having come in response to an urgent prayer, the priest had appeared in a room which resembled the showroom of a modern car dealership. One exception existed, however, in that all the signs and advertisements which would normally be hung and free-standing about the room about cars and trucks were about St. Patrick and St. Nicholas. In the center of the room was a sign which read, 'Don't do anything that pulls you away from Catholicism.'

Sitting down at a table which had been set up for confession, I faced the priest and began to share my usual list of sins, but then quickly stopped myself. "The books I have written speak of reincarnation which is not an accepted Catholic doctrine, what should I do?" I asked. Directing my attention to several books which were displayed on a bookshelf, I noticed that they explained Catholic doctrines. "Some of the views expressed by denominational Christians are incorrect." He said. "These books will help you to see where they are in error."

Leading my attention to life-sized cardboard cut-outs of St. Patrick and St. Nicholas strewn about the room, I observed that they were all depictions of the two saints expelling demons. Showing me a large white book about the life and virtues of St. Patrick, he began speaking in great detail about the *ten heroic virtues* of St. Patrick. "If you study these ten heroic virtues of St. Patrick," he insisted, "you will know what to do."

St. Patrick had expelled demons, converted pagans and attempted to document his amazing mystical life, though he was not gifted with words. But what seemed to be the most important information about the saint was that he had been a follower of the original Nazarean sect of Christianity, who later became the Gnostics who clearly taught reincarnation. During the time shortly after Christ's death, Jesus' brother St. James had expressed a different doctrinal Christianity than St. Paul, who despite his great holiness had never actually met Christ during His life. St. Patrick had followed the Nazarean sect, and this was one of the reasons for his many difficulties with Rome.

"The disciples said to Jesus, 'We know that you will depart from us. Who is to be our Leader?' Jesus said to them, 'Wherever you are, you are to go to James the righteous, for whose sake heaven and earth came into being."
The Nag Hammadi Library, The Gospel of Thomas No. 12, (Christianity, Gnostic, Words of Christ)

"When the blessed one had said this, he greeted them all, saying, 'Peace be with you. Receive my peace to yourselves. Beware that no one lead you astray, saying, 'Lo here!' or 'Lo there!' for the Son of Man is within you. Follow after him! Those who seek him will find him. Go then and preach the gospel of the kingdom. Do not lay down any rules beyond what I appointed for you, and do not give a law like the lawgiver lest you be constrained by it.' When he had said this, he departed."
The Nag Hammadi Library, The Gospel of Mary, No. 8-9, (Christianity, Gnostic, Words of Christ)

****

A woman who had passed from this world came to me wishing to show me something very intriguing in regards to original sin.

Standing beside my bed, she said, "I want you to see the demonic force which is plaguing my family which originally comes from my father." For a moment, it was given for me to know that her father had been a violent and sexually deviant man and during the abuse she had endured; the 'sin' of the father had been visited upon her and his demon given entry into her soul. Due to her lack of knowledge and discernment during life, she was unaware of the ways in which she had allowed it to be perpetuated in the lives of her family. Some of these ways included her attraction to the occult, and allowing her children to engage in games which promoted demonism and violence.

As she conveyed this information, a huge gale wind came down upon me as I looked into the eyes of one of the ugliest demonic creatures I'd ever seen. But it was so powerful, I had no time to think before I was forced to engage in furious battle very quickly. While battling, I called upon the Lord, shouting, "I am a temple of the Holy Spirit and am protected by the Lord of Hosts. Jesus Christ, I trust in You!" With that, this large red reptilian creature pulled back for a moment and disappeared.

My husband, Andy, was sub-conscious astral during this experience, but he suddenly sat straight up in his bed (in the spirit) and said, "It's behind you!" As I readied myself to turn and face the creature, my husband shuddered and showed a terrified look upon his face. 'No, don't look at it, it's absolutely horrible. You don't want to look upon it!' Understanding that the demon had mustered up additional strength, I heeded the warning and did not turn to look at it but waited for its next attack. Coming upon me like a bolt of lightning, I battled furiously and again called upon the name of Jesus and then St. Michael the Archangel both of whom instantly rescued me.

The woman stood beside me as I looked at her in shock. The clear evil of what had been perpetuated upon her as a child was very clearly in my awareness. Quietly and with no emotion, she said, "They don't understand that a great deal of the problems they are facing has to do with their attachment to dark things and this particular demon in general which I allowed to be visited upon them by lacking in discernment while I was alive." During her life, she had not only perpetuated, but encouraged, such things. But she did so because she was plagued by this sin which was visited upon her by her father. Nodding, I understood. For a moment, I pondered the manner in which such original sin had been visited upon the third generation through entirely different means than that which had allowed the demonic oppression to begin in this particular family.

"O God that sentest us into the world: that didst reveal thyself by the law and the prophets: that didst never rest, but always from the foundation of the world savedst them that were able to be saved: that madest thyself known through all nature: that proclaimedst thyself even among beasts: that didst make the desolate and savage soul tame and quiet: that gavest thyself to it when it was athirst for thy words: that didst appear to it in haste when it was dying: that didst show thyself to it as a law when it was sinking into lawlessness: that didst manifest thyself to it when it had been vanquished by Satan: that didst overcome its adversary when it fled unto thee: that gavest it thine hand and didst raise it up from the things of Hades: that didst not leave it to walk after a bodily sort (in the body): that didst show to it its own enemy: that hast made for it a clear knowledge toward thee: O God, Jesu, the Father of them that are above the heavens, the law of them that are in the ether, the course of them that are in the air, the keeper of them that are ion the earth, the fear of them that are under the earth, the grace of them that are thine own: receive also the soul of thy John, which it may be accounted worthy by thee . . . And as I come unto thee, let the fire go backward, let the darkness be overcome, let the gulf be without strength . .

. Let angels follow, let devils fear . . . and grant me to accomplish the journey unto thee."
The Apocryphal New Testament, Acts of John, 112, 114, (Christianity, Words of St. John)

****

Having underwent a series of sexual temptations in regards to a particular individual, I'd prayed to receive knowledge in regards to what lay beneath the surface of this particular person who came across as a devout Christian, but sent out a great deal of sexual energy despite both of us being married.

Shown to me as a cannibalistic demon, this particular creature utilized the facade of great spirituality to lure victims into its perimeter and then feed on it like a cannibal. Its appearance was of a human sized hairy creature with fangs and blood dripping from its mouth. Parasitic in nature, the tendency of this demon was to conquer a quantity of people in its life, not only members of the opposite sex. Because it relied on the energies of others to live, it sought out relatives, friends and members of the opposite sex to fulfill its many voracious and unspeakable appetites. This demon presented a very terrifying influence, because it went after it's victims in a very darkly powerful way, unrelenting in its quest to fulfill its quota of victims. But what was so alluring about the demon's guise, was its ability to create what appeared to be genuine feelings based on something substantial, when in reality it was not based on anything substantial or real at all. On the surface, this demonic force would present itself as a very good religious person whose character could not be questioned. But its victims would be confused by this internal struggle which they felt; something dark, an underside which was well hidden. Its basis was in lust, greed and every form of vice; conquering and consuming.

From what I'd been shown, I surmised that this type of demon would afflict those drawn in by a unique lure. Thinking that true spirituality, eternal love or substance was present, the victim would fall easily into the sway and mesmerization presented to it, but then they would be completely consumed and destroyed inside and out by the person harboring this demonic presence.

If the intended victim were to suspect that an evil presence lurked behind this Godly guise, they would usually feel guilty for having such feelings because of the beautifully constructed exterior facade held by the harbinger of such a demon. If they were to fall prey to its many lures (sexual, familial, friendship, professional, etc.) because of the deception of false spirituality and eternal love, they would be completely destroyed when they realized that they had entered literally into a hornet's nest and a white sepulcher full of dead men's bones. They would be further destroyed financially, spiritually, physically and in every other possible way.

One point that is absolutely vital in understanding this type of demon is that the person harboring this believes in their own exterior facade of goodness. Many of them don't actually *intend* harm; they just don't recognize the actual harm that they actually inflict. Because their mode of operation is habitual and normal to them, it is stained upon them as original sin or karma. This is one of the great disguises of the demons; convincing their own wards that they are good and righteous people, despite the underside which exists in energy and is enacted upon the lives of those closest to them or their intended prey.

But isn't that true as regards all humanity, in that most of us choose to believe we are basically good and righteous people, despite the wrongs we already know that we commit against God in our deeds *and* in our thoughts? Because of this very well-developed delusion of the dark side on humanity (and some of the doctrines taught by some religions or Christian denominations which make believer's feel that all that is required of them is belief in Christ), most people never even truly begin, much less fully enter, the process of intensive purification which is required of us in mortal realms.

There can also be some kind of charitable need used as a lure for the potential victim, and this type of demonic force often uses the kindness and caring of others against them, sometimes going so far as to turn their acts of kindness towards them into criminal deeds directed at the victim or prey. Examples might be anything from financial need, to something more difficult to ascertain. For instance, using the needs of a sick and perhaps innocent member of their family as a lure to bring someone in for their destruction.

Sometimes, in such cases where the exterior facade is believed by its bearer but the underside poses a threat of harm to you or your family (either energetically or physically), the only choice is to stay away from them because you cannot alter this energy without the recognition of its bearer which rarely happens, and this particular demonic force will truly take you down.

Another manifestation which occurred in my own experience with this demonic force (which is only a further indication of its destructive powers) is that while I was under the mesmerization and fiery pull of this creature, I began to lose weight uncontrollably going into a state of serious cardiac cachexia. As soon as I had overcome the temptation and began to pull away, I inexplicably had an appetite again and began to put weight back on. Literally, this demonic force had been sucking the very flesh from my bones.

Unfortunately, it took about seven weeks for me to get a hold on this demonic force, which literally pulled at my body and mind in a way I'd never previously experienced. Aware of its presence at all times, it became an obsessive thought that never left me, making me unable to move forward in my own study or spiritual path. What defeated this demon was CONTINUAL spiritual reading, prayer and asking God to reveal the ugly true nature of this creature which held my mind in such a way as to make it seem attractive. What a horrendous demonic force! But I never ceased praying for deliverance and understanding. I continually read holy texts (such as the 'Philokalia' which is a compilation of the writings of the ascetic desert fathers of the church, and 'The Introduction to the Devout Life,' by St. Francis de Sales), to help me to overcome this minefield of temptation. When I'd finally overcome this creature, such a feeling of relief came over my soul. A huge sense of renewed humility also overtook me in that no matter how far along the path we may be; we are always vulnerable to demonic attack. Remaining prudent in our thoughts, words and deeds, we must continue to be ever watchful of the next assault which may come in a way never before experienced, thus taking us off guard. Entering our souls as a tiny spark of fire, it can become huge and raging within a very short period of time.
****

As the soul who harbored the cannibalistic demon had remained in my perimeter despite my having overcome the initial onslaught, I begged the heavens through prayer to reveal to me the karmic impulse behind this uniquely strange phenomenon that had been laid in my path; and at such an unexpected time in my life's journey, as well.

Wafting through the ethers, I landed upon a time long ago, perhaps in the 1600's or 1700's. Unable to discern where I might be, I was living in a very large home with my husband who bore the soul of my current husband. Having several children and being very much in love, we were absolutely terrified when we heard from the doctor that he had an advanced case of cancer and had very little time left to live.

Among the more well off of the time, we lived very comfortably but had many friends and acquaintances among the peasants and others. Our closest friends were two peasants, a brother and sister. Instantly, I recognized them both. Their souls were in my current perimeter, the brother being the harbinger of the carnivorous demon and the sister, his current wife.

As my husband died very quickly, the brother began to move in very close to me and, over time I genuinely fell in love with him. Thinking that the feelings that he'd shown me were true, we were married; although it was also for the sake of my children. But because I truly loved him and thought it was mutual, I was shocked when shortly after our nuptials had passed, he exhibited his true nature in a way I could not have guessed.

Entering into a room in our large home, he said, "I am now Master over all of this, and I will say how things are to be done." Angered to no end, I suddenly realized that this man (who had then harbored the same carnivorous demon he continued to bear hundreds of years later) had married me for my money. With rage, I went forward. "Oh! No! You will not!" I said.

Cowering back, he accepted my authority, but we never got past this betrayal and my realization that he had not truly loved me as I had him. His sister remained with us, not participating in any of the deception, but perfectly contrite to receive of its rewards. As a result, they both became more like servants of the household and the familial bond was broken and never mended. But despite this, we remained married and I never sent them out.

Returning to the present day, the knowledge of this demonic attack became clearer as I was given to see one further thing.

Bringing our new kitten over to this man to 'baby-sit' for a time, I returned to find that he had eaten the tiny little thing from the inside out. The fur and skin were still there, but nothing of its innards remained. Looking in shock, I observed the lifeless body of the cat and remembering all that I'd been shown about the cannibalistic demon.

Despite hundreds of years, these two had continued to harbor this carnivorous presence and utilized it to live off of other people; financially and spiritually. In fact, in their present time circumstance, they were living in someone else's home just as they had in this previous existence with me. He was the active and she the passive participator in this 'way of life.' It truly was not a unique plan intended for individual victims, but a 'way of life' for them. The carnivorous demon would utilize a variety of approaches such as lust or the appearance of love, but with an end to greed and power. This guise was so well practiced and honed; it appeared with great sincerity and was very convincing and alluring to its prey.

It was shown to me that I had felt such strong feelings when I'd initially come upon his soul again because I had genuinely loved this man in our previous existence. And so the nature of this karmic debt had been revealed, and it appeared that resolution was required. As is the case in most karmic matters when another soul has not yet seen that which holds them to the ground; such a debt requires simply loving them, understanding, and letting go of the harm and all that was not meant to be . . . a necessary process for a soul who attempts to reach a greater height.

"How may transmigration be annulled? How find union with the Lord? Vast is suffering, birth and death. Perpetually fixed in the mind is doubt of duality."
Sri Guru Granth Sahib, Volume II, Raga Asa, Page 894, (Sikhism)
"According to Vedic opinion, there are two ways of passing from this world - one in light and one in darkness. When one passes in light, he does not come back; but when one passes in darkness, he returns."
The Bhagavad-Gita As It Is, Chapter 8, Text 26, (Hinduism, Translator: A.C. Bhaktivedanta Swami Prabhupada)
"Go not after your lusts, but keep your desires in check."
The New American Bible, Old Testament, Sirach 18:30, (Christianity, Judaism)
****

Whisping further, my soul began to go back in time to my childhood home. Excited to be there, I was led around the house to touch certain things from my past which had given me joy. First, I noticed the old countdown to Christmas calendar on the wall my mother had out every year. Placing my hand on it, I was shouting with glee to Andy who accompanied me sub-conscious astral. Looking in the garage, I noticed our old couches were still there and I hurled myself upon them and reveled in the energies. Looking out the window, I noticed my sister riding her bike just as she had many years ago along the tattered streets of our hometown.

Many times, I'd been sent to my past to work through difficult times and otherwise, but this time it was different. It was time to come full circle and be grateful for my whole life in its entirety and the gifts it had given me in my spiritual acceleration. As I reveled in remembrance, I began to disappear.

And blessed be He unto Whom belongeth the Sovereignty of the heavens and the earth and all that is between them, and with Whom is knowledge of the Hour, and unto Whom ye will be returned."
The Meaning of the Glorious Kuran, Surah XLIII, No. 85, (Islam, Translator: Marmaduke Pickthall)
"The Cyclic Scheme, to them, is but to Him a stair."
The Seven Valleys and The Four Valleys, The Third Valley, (Bahai', Words of Baha'u'llah

****

A woman entered the astral counterpart of the room who had been involved in the perpetration of an injustice against a family which had caused grave harm. A man had been fired from his job unjustly . . . through the use of slander and falsehood, primarily because he was a man of conscience. Although it was not overtly a Christian persecution in that different false reasons were given for the action, it was a Christian persecution. Through God's grace, the family had come through it not only unscathed, but better than they had been before; despite the fact that they had been forced to relocate and several members of the family became sick for a time as a result, one becoming gravely ill. But getting through it so well did not change the fact that this woman had participated in creating the evil that they had been forced to overcome and her soul carried that.

Sitting quietly in a corner in the place where she worked, the woman walked in the room and was not happy to see me there. Over the past year, I'd seen her several times in the astral as the progress of this persecution had played out. Part of my purpose was to take her through the process required of a soul who had committed a grave evil.

In the beginning, I had seen her and her fellow conspirator standing on a boat surrounded by grave torrential black winds as a specter from the heavens pronounced the inevitable onslaught of divine justice upon them both. She had looked terrified as she realized her mistake in choosing to unite and align with the man who stood with her, a dark choice. She could have just as easily aligned with the good, which was embodied within the man she had chosen to persecute. The man engaged in the action with her was unmoved, because he was truly dominantly dark while she was ignorantly so.

For months, I would see this woman while she remained obstinate in her sin. Wishing to justify the action she had taken, it was necessary to believe the falsehoods she had participated in creating in order to fire him in the first place. My spirit would be called in to the office to dance 'in the spirit' upon and throughout their desks, proclaiming the righteousness of God. Initially, this annoyed her and her cohorts. Over time, it intrigued them. In the end, it made them feel a sense of longing for this spiritual freedom being demonstrated to them in my spiritual dance.

This leads us to the encounter of this night.

Expressing annoyance at seeing me again, I came to her very boldly this eve carrying a CD. With me was the man who had been persecuted so unjustly, and she asked him to leave. "No." I said to her very quietly, refusing to be unkind no matter what she might do. "I carry with me an album which contains the energetic truth of what transpired here between you and this man, and this energetic truth reveals that he has more right to be here than you do! He will not be leaving." (This was despite the fact that he no longer lived in this location or worked there, but energetically it represented him retaking his reputation back and restoring the potential which had been lost through this evil act.) Placing the CD into her hand, she was taken aback, but suddenly thrust into an ecstatic experience of the energetic truth contained within it. As I pulled it back, she said nothing, just quietly walked away.

Continuing to remain in the office, I instructed the man to stay.

While she was gone, my spirit was given to go to a Buddhist retreat center where she had been scheduled to arrive. The monk who ran this astral monastery informed me that she had not shown up, and that I must go find her so that I may insure her arrival there so she may take the next spiritual step within the confines of this redemptive repentance which was being energized within her sub-consciously.

Returning to the office, we waited only a few more minutes as she returned with her husband. Uncomfortable, but no longer combative, they approached him slowly with caution. Wishing to ask her why she had not gone to the Buddhist monastery for further instruction, I resisted this impulse because it appeared something unexpected was about to happen. In their hands, I observed a CD containing the energetic truth of their repentance within it as they handed it to the man for whom they had harmed. All three of them touched the CD at the same time, as the husband of the perpetrator asked the man and his family if they would join them for Christmas dinner.

Within this was great symbolism, as they were asking the family to join them in their rebirth in Christ. They were also symbolically making a new choice to align with this man who had represented the eternal pathway, the path towards good . . . and to rescind the alignment they had previously chosen with the man in their office who had represented the evil road. Although it was unclear as to whether this was a conscious or solely sub-conscious change, it was more than we were expecting and indicated they had both taken a step beyond what had been scheduled for tonight. The Buddhist monastery would be unnecessary now because they had gone beyond intellectual understanding of their 'canker' to a recognition of their 'sin' and a need for the application of mercy through Christ.

Confused, the man was unsure as to how to proceed and I instructed him. "Proceed now with kindness towards your former persecutors and a detached understanding of the energetic truth within this persecution. Remember that you were innocent in this act, and that you hold energetic dominion over this domain because of this. Proceed with kindness, but do not forget that you hold dominion which means you must not allow them to ask you to leave this domain. You hold the dominion, because you contain the right. Those who contain the right must lead those who contain the night. Kindness . . . detachment . . . truth. But you must *refuse* to be unkind to them, no matter what they do." As a light descended upon the three hands who had now contained within them the energetic truth of this dark encounter, I disappeared.

"It being impossible for man to be without failings, he exhorts them not to scrutinize severely the offences of others, but even to bear their failings, that their own may in turn be born by others."
The Complete Writings of the Early Church Fathers, Nicene and Post-Nicene, Volume 13, Commentary on Galatians, Chapter VI, (Christianity, Catholic, Author: St. John Chrysostom)

"Except such of them as repent and amend and make manifest (the truth). These it is toward whom I relent. I am the Relenting, the Merciful."
The Meaning of the Glorious Koran, Surah II, No. 160, (Islam, Translator: Marmaduke Pickthall)

****

CHAPTER NINE
The Preacher and the Riverboat Nun, A Proposal Left Unanswered, Accepting God's Will Over your Own, Tranformation of Karma into Eternal Desire.

****

The river was wide and deep, and all I could see in front of me alongside the tall trees and wet grass on the bank was the turning back rudder at the end of a large riverboat which traveled before me. He was a preacher, not Catholic, and I was a nun . . . and I was in the water. We had taken this journey together on a mission. Something terrible had happened, but I wasn't given to know what, only that it had resulted in my death. In my heart, I felt the raw but patently quiet emotion again, almost like a crucifixion within my soul. I was leaving him, and it was not yet time . . . again. Gazing at him from above, I saw him shed a silent tear as he gazed upon a black and white photograph of the woman who had just expired because of some horrible and unforeseen accident. Pain . . . pain . . . more pain.

This man had entered my current life. And he was a priest.

****

It was the 1700's or thereabouts and all I could see was the two of us from the waist down. No faces. I was wearing a white dress with blue flowers upon it, and he was wearing the stretchy pants and waistcoat of the time in varying shades of brown. Asking me to marry him, I interiorly understood that this was the second time he had asked me . . . but I was not given to hear the answer. All went pale to black as I shifted to another sphere.

In a subsequent experience which occurred during a period of illness, Christ again appeared and showed me myself lying in bed surrounded by curtains (comparing it to St. Therese of Lisieux) as perfumed blue and white flowers were emanating from my suffering into the priest and his priesthood.

****

Christ appeared to me and said, "It is my will that you help him to reconfirm his vocation to the priesthood." (He'd shared with me privately his questions about whether he'd made the right choice of vocation.) Seeing two outcomes, I was shown the energized path of the priesthood versus the de-energized path of becoming secular in his life. Accepting this assignment, I again felt this continual raw yet patently quiet emotion. Pure, undefiled sadness . . . and then the throne appeared.

Christ was seated at the right hand of the Father, wearing the robes of the Sacred Heart, the searing red Passion of His cross a constant reminder of my duty to fulfill His will and not my own. A huge torrent of water came towards me as I held on for dear life. Christ spoke, "Be careful not to be swept away," He said. Instantly, I saw an image of someone I had once known, a fragment of Red Jacket (a soul of whom I had great karmic ties). "They are one and the same." Christ said without explaining further, but I remembered that each time I had come into contact with aspects of this soul, it had been a higher aspect than the previous one. Interiorly, I knew I had come across the highest aspect of this soul, the one closest to God. I again felt this continual raw yet patently quiet emotion. Pure, undefiled sadness . . . it was familiar because the love between this soul and mine was so powerful that it had always swept me away, lifetime after lifetime. No matter what the cost to those near to us or to a higher purpose, we were swept away . . . But that had to be in the past for Christ was asking of me a different response to such intense love, to make it 'divine,' to be willing to sacrifice it for His higher purpose and not to hoard it as only my own.

****

Walking through my home, there was a darkened doorway which was enveloped in the green alb of a priest. All of the house was lit, but beyond the green alb all was dark and yet to be revealed. Because I had been feeling intense and confusing feelings for the priest at the time, I felt compelled to rip the alb down. It didn't belong to me or in my home. It was not mine. **He** was not mine, **He** belonged to Christ. I, too, belonged to another. But as I ripped the alb off of the door, I noticed that there were two tiny baby's hands made out of felt embroidered into the alb which had been slightly damaged due to my fierce ripping. Suddenly, I knew that I should never have touched the alb, I should've left it alone. I had damaged something which was in its infancy, something holy and sacred yet to be revealed. But at the same time, I KNEW that I must go through this door into the priesthood. There was something I must learn.

Praying fervently, I cried out to Christ, "I have inappropriate feelings here, should I just leave the Church and never go back again?" Appearing to me all in white, he carried in his hands a bright, white ball of light which exuded into eternity a light more brilliant than the sun. Placing it immediately into my heart, He said, "These feelings you have are of 'Divine Love,' they are a gift, and I have placed them within you. Do not leave the church for this is My will. Embrace it as the gift it is intended to be." Nodding, I again felt the continual raw yet patently quiet emotion. Pure, undefiled sadness . . . Intensity, love never before felt . . . with no answer to accompany its purpose.

****

Sitting in lotus position, I began to feel a surging pulse from beneath me indicating a resurrection of the spirit. As I did so, my soul began flying around the room much like that which was described of St. Joseph of Cupertino, although my own experience occurred in the spirit rather than the physical realm. Energized and magical, I felt the intensity of the cosmic surge of knowledge and wisdom which was about to come over my soul. The birth of this experience in my life was to be an apex in my journey, but how . . . I did not yet know.

After hovering and flying around for a bit, my spirit again settled into a posture of meditation, not unlike the Buddha. And also not unlike the Buddha, I began to emanate a form of steam coming from beneath me which was the fruit of my contemplations. This steam was energized, radical and real, indicative of a shift in consciousness that was about to emerge within me.

We had just returned from his diocese, as I'd watched him renew his vows to the priesthood. I'd given him the torch that had been entrusted to me in an unexplainably painful act of sacrifice on my part.

Again, I felt the continual raw yet patently quiet emotion. Pure, undefiled sadness . . . Intensity, love never before felt . . . with no answer to accompany its purpose.

But I surrendered to that moment, and let it be . . . because this eternal mission had yet to be fully revealed. It was in its infancy.

My marriage was on the rocks. After almost twenty years of marriage, five separations and three children, I'd finally admitted to myself that my husband was destructive. Praying fervently as to whether or not I should separate from him, an angel appeared. "Sit tight," she said, as the huge expanse of her wings enamored me. "Detach, but sit tight."

If further knowledge were to come, I'd simply have to watch and wait.

"Children, it is in this self-departure, this going forth from self-will, that the essential peace of the soul is born within us, which means the acquisition of well-seasoned virtue."
The Soul Afire, The Two Ways: Martha and Mary, Page 238-239, (Christianity: Catholic, Words of John Tauler)

****

Drooling with ooze and disgusting odiferous aromas, the reptilian demon had emerged from the netherworld in a fury. Within its clenched fists lay destructive forces which could ravage a family. In its claws, lay a hidden sexual motive, a dark and demonic force which could unleash a storm of decay upon its prey. Although the bearer of this demon was a woman I knew, its prey was

Andy, my husband.

Standing before the door, the reptilian creature had come up from a 'basement,' passing through many steps. Now standing at our front door, Andy knew that if he opened it, the fury of this demon which didn't belong to him would be unleashed and all of the destructive forces would begin to tear away at the foundation of our home.

After years of destructive behavior, Andy was about to be faced with the ravages of his choices. Knowing full well that he'd had eternal options from which to choose, he would have to stomach the free will choices he'd made to follow a dark path of destruction, manipulation, disrespect and chaos which allowed for this attack to occur.

Now he would hark to the sounds of the ravages of that beast. It was time to pay the piper. Time to lay hold of all that had come to pass and all that had been within the realm of his choice but left unbidden.

The door opened . . . he moved out and we began a separation.

****

A distant friend had several experiences in regards to the priest. Many of them contained images of a man tormented by an interior struggle. Putting on a good face to the public, but turning to his interior with a red and obviously pained and tearful demeanor, he was hoping for privacy, to be left alone in his struggle. In another, she was shown that he was 'starving' for energetic fulfillment in the red, orange and yellow chakra's; the lower and sexual chakras.

After seeing this need, she'd traveled to his rectory to prepare a feast, but found that there wasn't any food anywhere; nothing to sustain or fulfill that which was lacking in him. He needed to receive these energies from another human being.

She saw that I was wearing a green nurse's uniform, a symbol of healing and a green and rose heart correlated with the heart chakra defining the healing and nurturing action required to assist him. The green was energizing the lower chakras with divine love and the rose parts rooting the lower chakras more firmly to the earth and sensuality.

Later in the experience, she saw me wearing blue representing the throat chakra, communication through voice. The priest was wearing purple representing the crown chakra and the connection with the divine presence, but his robes had patches of brown unhealthy energy which he tried to cover with patches and white makeup.

She said I needed to reach down into my heart and lower chakras to give him what he needed. He might outright reject it because healing can also hurt, but it might help him on a subtle level.

In a final experience, she said this: "In my dream, Father was leading a play about Mary Magdalene and Jesus Christ. I played the part of Mary and a friend of mine played the part of Jesus. Father told me that the audience would be throwing things at Jesus to symbolize the crucifixion. My role as Mary would be to follow him and clean up after him. We walked through the church and people started to fling all sorts of dangerous objects at my friend. I immediately started to use my body as a shield in order to protect him. The crowd became furious and started to throw arrows, calling me 'bitch, whore, you're ruining the play!'

Father called out to me and said, 'It's all wrong, please play your part!' But I told him, 'Father, don't you know that Mary Magdalene loved Jesus so much that she would have given her life for him?' With that, Father started to sob. The tears came down heavily and his face was red. He started to cry, 'Mary, I'm so sorry, *Marilynn*, Marilynn, I'm so sorry, Marilynn."

****

At the gathering of priests, I noticed that they were all wearing the green robes of ordinary time. This held significance in showing me that beneath the true vocation and calling that each of them followed was an ordinary man with flaws and failings like the rest of us.

As they gathered, they engaged in much frivolity. In the distance, I saw someone who was dressed up as St. Nicholas, a powerful saint who had given much to the poor and suffered persecution for it during his life. But whoever wore this costume was engaging in frivolity. This seemed blasphemous to me because of who St. Nicholas had been.

Walking towards this person, I found that it was a church volunteer beneath the robes. She hadn't meant to be irreverent, but she was, because they were all engaging in this frivolity and nothingness at this particular moment.

In this experience, there were three rooms. My husband and I walked from the center room to the room on the left. A priest was planning to play the guitar and sing on a live radio feed and I was to help him set up the equipment. I knew this elderly priest and so I knew that in his true life, he still had his own natural teeth. But in this experience, I realized that he was wearing false teeth and they were coming in and out of his mouth as he laughed about it.

In that moment, the priest for whom I cared deeply walked into the room. Astonishingly, he was also laughing about the false teeth and displayed his own (despite the fact that in his true life, he also had his natural teeth).

My husband and I sat down quietly as my father-in-law came into the room and stood before us energizing unity. In that moment, I recognized the frivolity and the false faces that the priests hid beneath the surface, but was a part of their ordinary selves. It was important to honor the priest in the person of Christ, but I realized it was also important to honor the priest as an ordinary man, as well.

To do any less, would be unfair; because priests are human beings, despite their high calling.
****

Riding an old riverboat, my current husband was a Spanish man with the name of 'Jacinto.' Married, we traveled the rivers selling our wares. Our home was a very small, white, rectangular abode in the woods. Our life was quite modest, and we were deeply in love. Lying upon his chest, I fell asleep from that life and woke again in this present life as he lay sleeping next to me again quietly. Our separation was now over and we had entered a new spiritual era of our lives. Jacinto was my current husband, Andy.
****

Perchance, when love befalls us, we should watch and wait for God to show us in which manner our love should be expressed. For eternal love mirrors the intentions of God the Father, and harms not the beloved, but spares the beloved from harm.

Boundaries in this world serve a purpose and remain in place so that we can learn to love in many eternal ways. Many lovable people exist in the world, but our natural human inclination is to respond to such feelings from our lower centers (i.e. sexual), rather than feeling it from our hearts.

If we feel love from our hearts and we remain patient in allowing God to reveal to us its purpose, we become sentinels of eternity by loving those around us with great power and intensity, but within the framework with which God intended.

Such love honors the eternal path of the beloved, as well as its own. Such love is patient and kind, and does not demand to have its own way . . .

It watches carefully to determine what is best for the beloved . . .

And it waits upon God to reveal such in His own time . . .

Thus, in order to conquer the passions which are fiery, hot, impatient . . . and usually wrong (or karmic); we must discipline ourselves to choose rather to watch and wait. And by so doing, we give God a chance to reveal higher love to our souls and the way in which it can be expressed in all of our relationships with those we love . . . eternally.

And thus, the love between my husband and I remained and the caring between the priest and I continued to grow, as we both energized each other's mission for God. And no one was harmed. And I learned that loving one another is something I can do with all my fellow men, as long as it is translated through my heart and not my lower nature.

In thus so doing, all life can be honored, enriched, and enlivened to achieve its highest purpose, and all can live in peace and a rich enjoyment of the goodness of God within one another.

For the first time, when a familiar karmic pattern had come upon me, I had chosen to watch . . . and wait . . . rather than respond. By so doing, I'd learned the one thing I'd needed to get in order to be released from the fleshly bonds of this earth.

****

. . . In a wisp, my soul was flying above my body as I saw in the distance an image of my deceased grandmother as a young girl romping through the familiar woods of the black forest in Germany where she had grown up and lived her whole life. Within a millisecond, I was with her.

This image was different than any I'd had of her before, because during life my grandmother had been very stern, angry and difficult to get along with. Many years prior, I'd seen her go through several levels of purgation. But here . . . for the first time . . . I was seeing her in a purified state and it was a sight to behold and a vision to take in as nourishment for she was absolutely beautiful, young, free and joyous.

Romping through the woods, we laughed and carried on as if we were both children, enjoying the beauty and simplicity of all that surrounded us.

The usual bliss of such a near death experience filled me as I felt intensive freedom, love and vitality within my soul.

Beginning to fly at the speed of light, she took us into the future. In front of me was a graveyard with five simple headstones engraved with a singular cross. Interiorly, I immediately understood that these headstones were for my husband, myself and my three children and I was being given to see a time in the future when all of us would be dead and gone to this world.

Because I had always seen my own death as separation from my children, she began to try to tear away at the veils of understanding and help me to see death differently.

As we soared around the stones, she said things over and over again as I repeated them back to her. "Oh . . . death . . . it comes to us all. " She would say. "It's a part of life. Death will be okay, it's a natural thing." "Oh, Yes!" I replied, "Grandma, it is a natural thing." I said in my swoon to the heavens. "Death is part of life." She repeated matter of factly. "Yes," I said almost dreamily, "death is a part of life."

I could hear the winds cutting across my ears as we soared and soared, back and forth. Suddenly, she lifted a piece of paper before my eyes. On it, she had written, "I am healing you now." I'd been sick that night, thus, my encounter with my dead grandmother. But I knew interiorly that she was helping me to feel better and go back to my body, not healing me completely. She was preparing me for a journey I would be taking in what appeared to be the not too distant future.

Feeling the heat and wind go through my spirit, it again entered into my body as I slowly wafted back into consciousness, the smell and bliss of the near death encounter still upon my lips and my brow.

But before I was to awake, a congregation of deceased priests appeared before my view. Hovering around me, they were so excited because I had mentioned to the priest that our deceased priests needed our prayers and the priest had included their intentions in a Mass. They had literally swarmed around the altar to receive this grace, and they were thanking me for planting this seed in the mind of this young priest.

Nodding in surprise and great joy, I turned and for a moment I saw an image. The priest was standing before the church as my three children were garbed in their regular server robes. My husband stood there to usher the congregation into the church, and I stood there directing the liturgy for the evening. In a wispful moment, my husband and kids began to playfully run out of the church and around the building as the priest chased them with a gleeful joy.

Harmony had been restored between the souls of these three. A just peace had emerged from what had been an inordinate attachment to sensual pleasure erupting in a corruption of eternal intent, desire and motive. Pure love was now being expressed . . .

Waking, I savored the moment before heading off to work . . . at the church and at my other new job, where harmony, love, peace, joy and mutual respect would reign, forever and ever, Amen. And forevermore, I would take upon myself the yoke of the prophets, saints, mystics and sages in proceeding with caution . . . watching . . . and with patience . . . waiting . . . as the Lord deigned to reveal His will to me so that I might translate His love for His own creation into my human mortal body rightly and correctly within the bounds of His will and intent.

In this manner, I could love my fellow man more powerfully than I had ever before known. I'd lost nothing except the plight of sin, but had gained a kingdom of inestimable worth . . .
****

CHAPTER TEN
A New Eternal Relationship to Karma, Becoming a True Nun, Karmic Love Becomes Eternal Love, Planetary Conjunction, the Ever Changing Reality of Relationships, Sub-Conscious Acknowledgement of Love Where it Cannot be Expressed Consciously, Seeking God's Will in Relationships, Recognizing Internal Misunderstanding, Acknowledging that Love Remains.

****

Andy had a vision of our family inside a huge circular lighted ball of energy. As we began to reunite and become strong again in our unity together, the priest appeared outside of that circular lighted ball of energy. But as we continued to unite and become more and more powerful in our unity as a family and our relationship with the Lord, the priest gradually but very naturally slid quietly into our circular lighted ball of energy becoming a member of our family. An angelic guardian spoke to Andy, "First he came inappropriately . . . now he will come as an invited guest."

It was clear that our mission would be to transform an age-old karmic configuration into something eternal and it would come about through a familial brotherhood between all of us which would be energized by letting the illusions and fantasies die, and the reality of God, which is always grander and more meaningful, to shine through.
****

The spirit of my deceased priest came to visit me in the rectory where our living priest currently resided. He was in a pair of white shorts and a white t-shirt. Behind him was a young Mexican priest recently ordained under his study. We were both kneeling on the floor, although the energy of the room was fun, good-natured and relaxed.

My deceased priest directed my attention towards an altar which contained the many gifts I'd been giving to the church and he very kindly bowed on his knees at the altar. Smiling at me, he conveyed, "I'm very happy with the gifts you have been giving to the church, and if a new priest is to come with a newly ordained with him, it will truly be okay." I felt immediately that the energy between this older incoming priest and his younger ward would be similar to that which I was experiencing in the room right now; fun, good-natured and relaxed.

Thanking him, I turned and disappeared.
****

One of my daughters had an experience. Standing aside the priest and herself, I was patiently waiting for the axe to fall. Things had been up and down with him for months, and I seemed to be in a space of surrender to whatever unkindness he might lunge my way. But that didn't happen . . .

Instead, he began asking me my opinion about something and we began talking. My daughter left the room and came back later in what seemed like an aeon of time - perhaps before, during and after he'd left - and we were still talking.

She said it felt like he'd always known that it would be good for him to ask my opinion about things. But now he was coming out of the closet about it.

A moment later, he was sitting with our entire family ensconced in an energy field with us. He had become a member of the family and he was wearing casual clothes indicating our level of familiarity and comfort of being together.
****

In the ethereal heavens, I saw myself standing quietly and pertly with several other women . . . all garbed in full nun's habits of black and white with full head cover. I was told by the angel aside me that we were sister's of the Sacred Heart. In this space, I was a true, completely consecrated nun. It was clearly energetically delineated that I had passed through my twelve years of formation and I was a true veteran. And in this space, that energetic reality was not only completely honored but displayed in a very powerful way. It was something that just 'was.'

Later in the day, I would realize that our new priests were coming from the parish of the 'Sacred Heart.' And it felt very much that this experience was letting me know that things would go well, that I was already fully consecrated to my Lord and that all was well with God.

But before I could leave this beautiful space filled with poofy clouds and a wondrous array of light, I began to hear the voice of what I perceived to be the Lord speaking to me. In a mysterious way, the priest was given to hear the words, as well. "You will be asked to give your life for someone . . . and you will do it." He said. Within moments, I was seeing someone, although I was unable to be certain of their personage. There was some kind of deathbed conversion going on, and the scent of roses permeated the room. And as I stood in my full habit, the Lord ended with these words, "And you did give your life." Almost as if it had already occurred . . .
****

The legion of space captains had come to my husband, Andy, in the dark of the night revealing a power beyond his imagining. It was revealed to him that an emergency meeting had been called in the heavens because the priest was about to abort the mission. Everyone was scurrying about trying to come up with ways to save it, to bring him back into the fold, or do whatever it would take to re-energize the mission. A captain approached Andy and said, "He's going to abort the mission, but you are hereby ordered to continue to behave as if he's not going to. Continue forward even though this is inevitable."

My husband awoke with a powerful and sincere recognition of the importance of this mission which was about to be lost because the priest had decided that what he wanted for his life would be better than what God had planned. It was so very sad, if only he could have understood . . . What God had intended for him was so much greater than anything he could've fathomed for himself.

　　We continued as if he weren't going to abort the mission as instructed, but we grieved this great loss as a family.

　　Shortly thereafter, the priest left. Gone forever, it seemed?

****

　The legion of space captains had come to my husband, Andy, in the dark of the night revealing a power beyond his imagining. It was revealed to him that an emergency meeting had been called in the heavens because the priest was about to abort the mission. Everyone was scurrying about trying to come up with ways to save it, to bring him back into the fold, or do whatever it would take to re-energize the mission. A captain approached Andy and said, "He's going to abort the mission, but you are hereby ordered to continue to behave as if he's not going to. Continue forward even though this is inevitable."

　　My husband awoke with a powerful and sincere recognition of the importance of this mission which was about to be lost because the priest had decided that what he wanted for his life would be better than what God had planned. It was so very sad, if only he could have understood . . . What God had intended for him was so much greater than anything he could've fathomed for himself.

　　We continued as if he weren't going to abort the mission as instructed, but we grieved this great loss as a family.

　　Shortly thereafter, the priest left. Gone forever, it seemed?

****

　　Coming again to see me, the former priest arrived at a party happening in the ethereal realms. A couple was talking about how hard it is for married folks to stay together, and he came directly towards me, looked me in the eye and said, "But it is so much harder not to be able to be with the one you care deeply about." He said, as he embraced me.

　　An eternal element was emerging within his sub-conscious. He was awaking to and realizing the gift of eternal love no matter its essential end. Love in and of itself is a gift. And love, by itself, is sometimes enough. And God, because He IS love, utilizes this power and force to bring about all manner of things in this world. Love is not relegated to the realm of lust and sex; that is to diminish its true nature. Love in its highest expression, remains eternal and can BE irregardless of circumstance.

****

　　As the heavens heaved a mighty splendor, I stood upon a planet as another planet was coming upon mine with great velocity carrying the soul of my former priest. The galactic heavens were powerful tonight as this grand conjunction was about to occur.

　　Something odd became apparent as he moved closer in that he bore the signs of being full-term pregnant, actually already in the act of giving birth. Spaceships hovered around both of our planets as their lights permeated the heavens.

　　As the planets collided, I fell prostrate to the ground with my face upwards. Arms outstretched as in the form of a cross, I noticed that my former priest and several alien life forms were holding my arms in place as this conjunction was actively engaging.

　　"He is going to connect with you and ignite the birth." One said as I noticed that my body could not move. Then the former priest spoke. "Oh," he sighed, "I've hurt her so much by keeping this from her." Immediately, I understood that he was referring to the purpose of this grand conjunction, what this 'birth' was meant to impart in both of our worlds. He was greatly relieved that he was now being allowed to reveal the master plan of this entire journey, although I still did not understand.

In great relief, he fell at my feet and sighed, "I've finally been allowed to tell her how much I feel for her. It's been so painful to keep this from her." Shocked, I didn't know what to think of that statement, but just took it in. I inherently knew he was referring to the previous experience wherein he finally shared his feelings on some level with my soul.

But there was no time to contemplate this. The planets were colliding, and those around me were waiting for me to show them signs of life by moving. Shaking my hands violently, the former priest grabbed them and stopped me from moving further. "It's too soon," he said, "you are resurrecting from the dead. You must allow these energies to come into you slowly or they can hurt you." The amazing power of this moment cannot be described. But although I could not understand the import of this moment, I sensed his great relief in being given permission to let me see that there was a huge master plan in this conjunction.
****

The heavens began to rumble and roar as they opened to reveal that the mission was no longer aborted, but yet to begin again with the two new priests who had been brought into our lives and had taken me into the interior cloister.

The intense power of the moment overwhelmed me as the Lord allowed me to see the light within them that had been kindled in the pursuance of our newfound protectorate. There was a very special and important relationship between my son and one of these priests which had been energized by the Lord. An angel shouted across the heavens, "The mission continues . . . it is not lost!" As I heard these words, I saw a stairway to heaven open in my bedroom wall through the tapestry of the Sacred Heart of Jesus. The power of heaven came upon me and all of us in this space and extreme excitement filled me. A terrible and immense sorrow lingered, however, for the one that I had lost.
****

Within moments, myself and my two younger children were wearing the garb of a religious order and we again being hidden and protected by these two priests and the rest of their religious brothers in a cloister in the realms of spiritual ether. On some level, they had an understanding of our need to be hidden and protected from the outside world and did so instinctively.

A moment later, I was again in my own home, but looked outside the window to see one of the priests guarding it in plain clothes to protect us for the mission.

And a final moment later, I was taken into the church at a later time when all the people knew I was a mystic and it was a very positive thing that they knew this. The mission was safe, despite its abortment by an original founding member.
****

Despite the fact that my husband and I got back together, within another year we again had to separate due to the same destructive issues. Perhaps this is a story that is *meant* to have no final end . . . because life is ongoing and ever changing.

It is only meant to help the traveler along the road of love which can be guaranteed to offer one thing only - and that is uncertainty.

Love grows, love dims, love changes . . . only God knows what lies beyond this. Love in itself is not a sin, but if expressed in a way contrary to the will of God, it becomes so. I'd like to leave you with the simple thought which is that 'love is.'

The hard part is that sometimes God's will does not come with a final concrete answer. Love is and always will be a hugely important part of our human experience. And because of this, we will always seek to understand its many manifestations. But in the end, if we watch and wait despite the touch of the nails that pierce our souls by doing so, we are more inclined to discover God's will in each of these manifestations and to walk with a more sure footing of the righteousness of our path. Sometimes we can't control what we feel or do not feel for others. But in the end, it will always come down to the simple fact that 'love is.' And when it truly is, no matter the purpose, it remains a gift from God - even though touching the nails of such an uncertainty as this may cause you to bleed. You can't make it happen, nor can you make it go away. When love happens, it just is.

"For even as love crowns you so shall he crucify you. Even as he is for your growth so is he for your pruning. Even as he ascends to your height and caresses your tenderest branches that quiver in the sun, so shall he descend to your roots and shake them in their clinging to the earth. Like sheaves of corn he gathers you unto himself. He threshes you to make you naked. He sifts you to free you from your husks. He grinds you to whiteness. He kneads you until you are pliant; And then he assigns you to his sacred fire, that you may become sacred bread for God's sacred feast. All these things shall love do unto you that you may know the secrets of your heart, and in that knowledge become a fragment of Life's heart. But if in your fear you would seek only love's peace and love's pleasure, then it is better for you that you cover your nakedness and pass out of love's threshing floor into the seasonless world where you shall laugh, but not all of your laughter, and weep, but not all of your tears. Love gives naught but itself and takes naught but from itself. Love possesses not nor would it be possessed; For love is sufficient unto love."
The Prophet, Kahlil Gibran, On Love

****

Many people were watching on from a distance our family with a very judgmental stance. Because of the difficulties we'd had in our marriage, people were suspicious and uncomfortable even though the Lord had been making it clear to me that many of those very same people harbored similar issues and/or demons, but were unable to see it in themselves yet.

I had already accepted our fate to be judged and was busy painting spiritual symphonies all over our small little town in the mystical realms. Suddenly, our former priest who had been watching judgmentally himself, turned and saw the spiritual symphonies I was painting all over town. I expected nothing, his gaze was stern, judgmental.

But suddenly, a small smile began to come from his lips as eternal understanding overtook him and he finally saw that the honest evaluation of our failings was a beautiful thing, and not something to be ashamed. And it bore much more fruit than hiding behind a veil of false perfection.

I smiled back knowing that our friendship was being restored. But this restoration was coming about in a wholly different way, one which was without sin and full of virtue and possibilities because of the infinite eternal fruits which could be borne of a friendship grown from eternal understanding and love.

****

For a fortnight, a green healing energy overcame my energy field every time I would close my eyes and open them again to the spirit world. All was bathed in green, and my spirit and body took in the warm healing energies from above.

An unexpected journey was about to come upon my soul as I was riding an old riverboat with my three children from my current life. Familiar, but from another time, I remembered the lifetime when I had lost my life overboard one of these things - a karmic moment engraved upon my memory as one of several sudden yet final partings from life in this world from a person and soul I'd loved deeply; he who was known only as 'the priest' in 'Touched by the Nails."

The journey represented by that book in this life had ended with uncertainty, an uncertainty which was demonstrated as possibly the simple truth we must all embrace about love in this world.

My youngest son, Jake, had darted off and I was looking for him on the boat. There were many pretty women on the boat, I noticed this. But my focus was on finding my son, and on the journey I must now take with my munchkins. Very worried, he seemed to be nowhere to be found and I was getting scared.

Suddenly, I turned around and the priest was standing behind me with an expectant glaze in his eyes. I read within them that he truly wanted to help me find Jake, and there was something bothering him that he wanted to share with me.

Turning again to notice all the pretty women aboard the boat, I was a bit confused as his normal behavior in such a subconscious state would be to go pay attention to them all. In the conscious state, this could sometimes also be the case. But he was staring at me and boring a hole through my soul. He had a mission tonight.

"Please," he said, "let me help you find him." Pausing for only a millisecond in my search, I said, 'Okay,' and continued my search. He found my son quickly and brought him to me as he placed the same eye-piercing gaze was upon me.

Again, I noticed that there were scores of very pretty women on the boat, but he acted like I was the only one there.

"I love ALL of you!," he said about me and my kids. We kindof stared at each other quietly for a while, because I was very confused by this seemingly sudden visit in the night from someone who to my mind had done everything possible to make it clear that I meant absolutely nothing to him, not even as an acquaintance, much less as a friend or even less as anything more.

Suddenly, he took my two hands and continued looking deep in my eyes. By this time, we were alone, as the kids and the surrounding environment had faded off into the distance and it was just us two. "I LOVE you." He said. "I really need you to know that I truly do love you." Still confused and finding anything he might say hard to believe, I just kindof stared at him.

Repeating himself a few times, he said, "I need you to know that I TRULY love you." And as he said it a few times, an energy came into me which made me to know that this was *profoundly* true, as hard as it seemed for me to believe I knew inwardly that it was absolutely true. His eyes continued to pierce into mine as he explained that this love he had for me was unique to me, and although it had been necessary for him to go through some growth experiences regarding his attraction to all pretty women, he had come to realize the unique nature of what truly was between us.

All I could do was stare at him as he continued to hold my hands and look at me with such profound intensity that I felt myself filled with the truth of this moment. And for that time, it seemed that God and he wished for me to know.

My soul was floored, relieved, grateful . . . for this moment. But I also knew that this momentary union of souls would end and, therefore, cause me great pain later.

By this time in this journey, however, I also understood that this was the price I would have to pay for truly loving someone with that kind of power who could never again be a part of my life. It had now been several years and I knew this was not something that I was likely going to pass through. These would be the thorns that I must walk alongside . . . because I had learned that in regards to this person, it was not in my power to change what the core of my soul understood and felt for him. It was not a fleeting thing, it would probably walk with me for the remainder of my days.

So I accepted this gift with that knowledge. Awaking the next morning, I bathed in the momentary glow of the revelation, allowing it to penetrate and remain within my heart, but then I had to enter my waking world and integrate the experience back into my 'real' life on the ground by letting it go and

preparing for my day as a mom.
****

On the eve of the morrow, my soul was swept into a typhoon of eternal energies depicting questions my soul had bade to the Lord in prayer.

As I was hurled to the etheric floor on my knees, a light came from the highest heaven which immediately shone upon two rings I wore on my hands.

My wedding ring on my left hand was a golden band with a small diamond cross in the center. On the other hand, I wore a diamond which had been given to me by my husband's (Andy) grandmother. The ring had been worn by her husband's mother and grandmother and I was the 5th generational line to wear it. The ring truly represented the ancestral line of our family.

The two diamond rings began to shine throughout the heavens before me, and I was given to know that by this sign, the Lord had given me to know that I had gotten two answers right.

Although these answers were never enunciated, it appeared that my husband and I staying together AND focusing on the ancestral line, i.e. my children, were possibly the two answers the Lord wished me to understand.

In a subsequent experience the same night, a similar incident occurred wherein as I lie prostrate on the etheric floor, my two wedding rings became manifest in the sky above me again representing the answers that I was seeking.

This was a difficult answer to receive, but I did receive it. I obeyed. Although it was difficult, we did continue to work on our marriage both together and apart - however necessary - and focused on the well-being of our children.
****

And the third night brought with it another powerful but painful consolation. During this period I began to learn that sometimes in order to discover God's will and learn to follow it, you have to simply accept things as they are and as they come. Because if you do not, you will fight the progression because you still don't know whence it leads.

My home was represented as a three story structure. On the bottom floor were the parish members of our local church, in the middle was my husband, Andy - and at the top was my private quarters, my private prayer launch pad, so to speak.

Although Andy and I were 'together,' we had certain agreements which allowed me to continue to live a consecrated life within my home.

Sitting outside by myself, a large number of people were standing at the sides of the road as if we were waiting for a parade to come. And within moments, I saw off in the distance a procession headed by our bishop. Bundled up with a quilt, I watched quietly as he came with probably a train of about 20-30 priests.

But I was surprised when I noticed that at the tail end of the procession of 'robed' priests, my priest was walking without his robes but in his 'collar.' When I saw him, I quietly walked inside my 'house' to my private quarters because I didn't want him to notice me.

But it quickly became clear that he was actually seeking me out again, and he *knew* I was there. Interestingly, he was again portrayed as a 'man on a mission.' Coming towards my home, I thought for a moment. It seemed that avoiding this was a bad idea, that we needed to face one another and deal with what was going on between us. So I quietly slipped back out.

But before I could close the door behind me, I realized he was standing right before me giving me that same kind of intense gaze that he had done before, but with more determination.

Taking my hand with force and determination, it didn't seem to matter to him anymore what people thought about him as he took me through the first floor of our house where the parishioners were and somehow completely bypassed level two. In seconds, we were alone in my private quarters on the third level of the house.

His eyes were very clear as he came to me in embrace. Again, I knew he wanted me to know that he truly loved me. It was not lust, it was not something else . . . it was simply a powerful love that apparently he nor I could explain, understand, come to terms with nor deny.

It was so vivid, it was as if it were really happening. He stayed with me for a long time, and when it was time for him to go, he engaged my eyes again as if to reinforce that his departure affected nothing of what he had shared with me.

But then I began to awake and realize it was happening only in energy, and it was a painful realization. But I again gave many thanks to the Lord for this moment, even though the knowledge and experience of it caused me pain, it relieved more just to know that it was mutual . . . even though to all appearances it could and would never be.

Again, I allowed the experience to penetrate my heart, but integrated it properly so that I could get up and be a mom.
****

The Blessed Virgin returned weeks later with a message of different import. In her grace and glory, she took me into my own thinking. Showing me how I was perceiving things with my husband, she then showed me how they really were. Very kindly, she explained that the many medications, the level of pain, the amount of doctor visits and procedures, etc., were all serving to make it difficult for me to see things as they truly were.

Most difficult to see was the pain this was causing my children, but I had to see and feel it profoundly in order to understand.

Grateful but ashamed, I thanked the Blessed Virgin for her lengthy visit to show me these things in such a profound way and began the work to amend my life with my husband and stop my part in inciting conflict with him.
****

Taken into a space wherein I was shown people throughout time and the ages who loved each other deeply but could not be together because of a greater good, an angel walked up beside me. "It's sad that two people who love each other so much," she said, "cannot be together." I knew inherently she was speaking of myself and the priest. I looked at her very peacefully and with calm. She repeated herself. "It's sad that two people who love each other so much cannot be together," she said, "in order to fulfill a higher good for others." Looking directly into her eyes, I nodded again. I KNEW in my heart a sense of peace about this decision. We had honored his call to the priesthood and my call to motherhood. We were doing this for the greater good of others.

But it was sad that we could not be together, and for that moment, I felt how truly real that love between us remained. But I also knew we'd done the right thing.
****

Spiritual Warfare, Angels and Demons

Mystic Knowledge Series

Compiled and Written by Marilynn Hughes

The Out-of-Body Travel Foundation!

www.outofbodytravel.org

'Ascension' by Mattjin

CHAPTER ONE
Energetic Alteration.

****

Flying through a horrible ghetto, I appeared invisibly in a barroom behind a father and son. Apparently, they lived upstairs and owned the bar below, and the small brunette boy of about eight years was quite upset. His father also had brown hair, was very skinny and was very drunk. Getting loud and raucous with several friends, it seemed that this occurred on a regular basis.

In his anger, the son ran over to the table, grabbed a pitcher of beer and poured it all over his father's head. Responding in a fit of rage, the father began to chase the boy around the bar. Because of my special condition, I could read his thoughts, and I knew that this man had the potential of seriously beating the boy.

Floating in-between them, I sent powerful loving thoughts to both of them. Universal acceptance poured through me from the Lord and into them, as suddenly the father began to calm . . . and they both began laughing. Putting his arm around his son, the tension had been diffused and my presence was no longer necessary.

****

Lifting my soul into a spectacular cathedral filled with Sunday worshippers, I began flying around spreading love amidst the rounded and exquisitely painted ceiling.

Although the facial expressions on the people didn't change, much of the congregation felt my presence sub-consciously. Human souls experience things on many levels of consciousness, but most are only aware of the conscious, waking state. Telepathically, members of the congregation asked questions. "What does it feel like to do that?" Responding, I replied, "I just went through the ceiling, now I'm floating to the floor. Now through it. Out the window I go, oops, I'm coming back!" Receiving confirmation from their sub-conscious minds that they'd received the message, my spirit was beckoned to return.

****

While leaving my body, I noticed something odd while looking down at my bed. There were two images of my husband, Andy. Undergoing a vibrational raising, Andy's physical body lay on the bed while his etheric was raised just above. Vibrating rapidly, a spiritual guide was at his side overseeing the raising and Emmanuel stood aside. 'Andy would not remember this,' he conveyed, 'and they wanted him to know that they were working with him.' Emmanuel then began raising my vibrations in preparation for a journey.

Taken to a coliseum, I was waiting to hear a speaker. From behind me, I could feel an immense amount of love being directed at me. Turning, I saw a large man with sandy-blonde hair, dressed rather Romanesque, looking at me with incredible recognition and deep love. I turned away.

A woman was speaking about spiritual teachers and their role in evolution, when she suddenly whisked over to where I was sitting. Asking me to turn around, the woman had noticed the intensity of the love coming from this person behind me.

The Romanesque man began to change his image. Long black hair and olive skin framed an aged and worried Indian man's face. Red Jacket, a man from my karmic past, embraced me. His happiness was obvious, as I felt feelings for him that I didn't yet understand. Reaching his hand to me, I took it and in a flash of light, we were in a vast and beautiful forest.

Sitting down in the brush, he hugged me tightly as energetic knowledge about our life together was conveyed to my soul. Instantly, I knew that we had been lovers, and that this had happened sometime during that Cavalry lifetime.

Unfocused memories came to me, and I was overcome with emotion.

One thing was certain . . . he had returned for a reason and I knew that his coming held great importance for my soul.

"Thy letter from which the fragrance of reunion was inhaled hath been received. Praised be God that following the firm decree of separation, the breeze of nearness and communion hath been stirred and the soil of the heart is refreshed with the waters of joy and gladness."

The Tablets of Baha'u'llah, No. 11, Lawh-I-Maqsud, Page 163, Paragraph 1, (Baha'i, Author: Baha'u'llah)

****

Traveling to a convention of sub-consciously astral souls, I was told that I must speak to them of the truth. Telling them that they could venture inward and do wonderful things, they responded with religious tenets of several Christian faiths. When told that they could experience out-of-body states, they began laughing. "What are you, some kind of nut? That astral projection stuff is a bunch of garbage!" Smiling at them, I replied, "Is that so . . . hmmm. Well, would it make it any clearer if I told you that you are all out of your bodies right now?" In a wild state of panic, they began to notice their transparent nature. "Oh, my God!" They screamed. "How will I get back to my body?" Calming them, I told them to will themselves back to their bodies and they would be fine.

****

Lifted up as if like a vase into a dimension of incomparable beauty, I was standing with a group of women who were talking loudly. At the same time, they were becoming increasingly bothered by my presence. "What did you do to create such a bright light around you?" One asked. "I am flowing with the divine plan of unconditional love and existing in a state of peace and being." I said. They stared at me in silence before I was whisked away.

Pastel blue ether filled my spirit like a loving embrace from God, and a magnificent light beam emanated from above down into this dimension. Several spirits were hanging around this light, so I followed them to see if I could find out what it was. "Touch the light," one of them said to me, "and you will be allowed to speak to Jesus." In awe, I placed my hands around the light, and no sooner had I touched it, than a massive energy surge pulsated into my soul and a powerful voice spoke. "My dear one, you come to me with fear and worry. Let us understand what you fear so as not to hide your light." Immediately, I knew this was Jesus Christ, and I bowed down in great honor.

Showing me a thought-form, less aware souls had come to speak to Jesus, but because of their doubts could not make the connection. Feeling sorrow for these souls, I asked Jesus if I could help them, and He replied, "Don't expect to be validated by the earth-plane, just feel strength within yourself and do the tasks you have set out to do. You may be misunderstood even by those who are called teachers. Some of them are so involved in the monetary aspects of what they do, they no longer see. They may perceive you as a threat. If only they knew that you represent what they could become! You will lead beings to themselves, thus, away from their lucrative businesses." The energy current paused.

"I have a task for you that you will become aware of when the time comes. Remember that your growth is of the utmost importance as our task will depend on your continuing evolution. Don't stop for anyone, as venturing forth will force others to follow your lead and venture inward themselves. You are greatly loved and I am very happy with your progress. Let your light shine brightly." Pausing for a moment, He asked, "Marilynn, why do you think we are able to speak with you?" Confused, I replied, "I really don't know, I know I have just as many faults and imperfections as everyone else, it has left me wondering . . ." He interrupted. "We are able to speak with you because you put your ego aside and ask to be told the truth. When we tell you the truth, you know it as such despite your prior view of reality. Truth is a simple thing, yet for some impossible to accept. Love is all there is." I knew inherently that Love as the absolute was the core of all life, despite the existence of delusion and shadow upon the earth. Despite the evil that arises in this world, love is all that is *eternally* real. Although this is true, it cannot be understood while in a physical body and it is only upon leaving form and entering into knowledge that this can be comprehended.

The connection slowly dwindled. .

"I went up to the light of truth as if into a chariot: And the Truth took me and led me: and carried me across pits and gulleys; and from the rocks and the waves it preserved me: And it became to me a haven of Salvation: and set me on the arms of immortal life."
The Lost Books of the Bible and the Forgotten Books of Eden, Odes of Solomon, Ode 38, (Judaism, Christianity)

****

Leaving form, two spirits took my hands and rushed us through the time tunnel. Plummeting downward, we entered a sunny hot and barren desert with red cliffs and cactus. In the near distance, there was a small and worn cabin. Looking down, I noticed that I had taken on the manifestation of a middle-aged fat dirty man with razor stubble. Wearing a pioneer hat, dirty old brown pants and a flannel shirt, I took a glance at the other two who had come with me. Manifesting as a little girl and a woman, they were wearing long tan-colored dresses and bonnets.

Noticing my confusion, the woman explained. "We need to look the part for what we are about to do. There is a woman in need here, and we have come to help her." Time was of the essence, so I followed their lead by manifesting a horse and beat-up carriage and began our trek to the cabin.

Knocking on the door, my partners filled me with knowing about our task. A young bedraggled woman answered the door, bending over slightly as I began to speak. "Howdy, ma'am," I bowed to her, "We don't mean to intrude, but it seems we're lost and we were wondering if you might be able to help us." Holding the door tightly, she was suspicious. Pointing to the others, I continued, "This is my wife and our little girl." Loosening up, she pulled away from the door. "Come in," she said, "I don't have much to offer you. My husband passed away of heat stroke, and I just gave birth to these two babies." Walking into the home, the twin baby girls were asleep on the floor. My 'wife' spoke up, "Maybe we can stay and help you with your babies in exchange for a roof over our heads. My husband and I could help with food and fixing up your home and that beat up carriage." The woman brightened, "You wouldn't mind?" "Oh, not at all," said my wife, "I love little babies and you need some rest." Leading her to bed with a smile on her face, she assured her that the children would be cared for while she recuperated from birth.

Staying with her for several weeks earth time, one night astral time, we prepared her for her journey out of the desert. One morning at the breakfast table, she looked at us shyly and asked, "Where did you all come from?" "Well," I said, "we came from the east." Quiet for a few moments, she then added suspiciously, "I saw you all come out of a cave in the desert, a cave that wasn't there before and isn't there now." Looking down, she tried to be nonchalant. My wife broke in, "Oh, you must have been hallucinating; after all, you'd just given birth." Changing the subject, she added, "Well, it looked real to me. How is that wagon doing?" Smiling, I replied, "I think it's about ready to make the trip. Are you sure you want to make the trip alone?" "There's nothing for me here," she said, "it's time for me to move on."

Having repaired her wagon, we sent them off out of the desert, as we prepared to go the opposite way. We knew that she would be meeting another 'chance' person along the way, and that she would be okay. Riding off into the desert, we quickly jumped into the time tunnel and I returned to my physical body.

"The stage in which the consciousness of the living entity is attracted by the three modes of material nature is called conditional life. But when that same consciousness is attached to the Supreme Personality of Godhead, one is situated in the consciousness of liberation."
The Teachings of Lord Kapila, Chapter Nine, Text 15, (Hinduism)

****

Taken to the Midwest, I met up with the Reverend Sam Malone. Speaking for hours on love and truth, he soaked up knowledge like a sponge. Hugging him as his guides came to return him to his body, he thanked me. Taking his hands, his guides asked, "Sam, will you give this gift of truth to others as we have given it to you?" Nodding that he would, they took him home.

A few months later earth time, but the same night astral time, Sam got into a bit of trouble with some criminals. Held hostage with a group of others, Sam began to feel sympathetic to his captors, in his mind condoning their violence.

Flying towards Sam, I suddenly transformed into an Assisi Marauder. Pulsating royal blue lights shot out from my soul like stars. Speaking to his sub-conscious, I said, "The Reverend Sam Malone, I remember you, do you remember me?" Looking startled, his sub-conscious mind responded, "I do, yes, I really do." "Do you remember your vow to me?" Silently, he waited. "It is wonderful that you allow yourself to see the twinness of man, realizing that your captors have more than one side to them. But you must never condone violence. NEVER! With the truth we have given you, you can set everyone free. SPEAK TRUTH TO THEM, REVEREND SAM MALONE!" Immediately, Sam began to speak and within moments he had de-energized the violence that had almost come to be. Leaving the scene, I knew all would be well.

A woman appeared to me with a rack of designer clothes. "Would you like to wear any of these beautiful clothes?" She asked. Looking at my marauders outfit, I responded, "This fits very well, thank you." Smiling, she beamed. "Very good! You know your role! May I tell you more?" Excited, I begged her please continue. "The blue stars that shoot from your being are very powerful. You come from the stars and your world lies through the star tunnel. Do you not remember traversing the star tunnel to reunite with the Assisi Marauders?" Surprised, I had not. "Blue light is a high spiritual energy. In your heart, you know this. Return to your illusion and flow with who you are." Pulsed into my body, I awoke.

"Therefore the sage is sharp but not cutting, pointed but not piercing, straightforward but not unrestrained, brilliant but not blinding."
Tao Te Ching, No. 58, (Buddhism, Taoism, Words of Lao Tsu, Translation: Gia Fu Feng and Jane English)

****

Given a book by several spiritual guardians, they explained that the purpose of it was to teach me how to do a better job with souls in the unconscious world. Containing a listing of courses for spiritual guides, I was directed to look upon a course entitled, 'Telepathic Communication with Sub-Conscious's.' Understanding, I took the book and returned back to form.

"The soul's secret door suddenly opens; and, oh, what bliss I feel at the sight of Thy light!"
Whispers from Eternity, Page 185, Paragraph 2, (Hinduism, Kriya Yoga, Words of Paramahansa Yogananda)

****

Entering the time tunnel, I soared into a different reality which appeared to be a Japanese soldier camp in World War II. The majority of those here were men, although two women were seated directly in front of me who had had long shiny black hair and wore pink pant outfits. Sitting down to join them, they asked me who I was. "I am a time traveler," I said to their completely shockless faces, "I am a writer from the future." Pausing, they awaited an old thin man to arrive who appeared to be a cook. Directing me to speak to the men, they ignored me momentarily as one man said that their regulations wouldn't allow me to speak. Allaying them, I made myself be heard. "Are all of you so caught up in your illusion that the only words you will allow into your reality are those of your regulations book? Have you ever stopped to consider why you follow those regulations?" They began to pay attention to me. "You all act as if you are zombies with no control over your future, yet everything is available to you. War is only the answer for young souls who feel that their reality must be perpetuated on the world. Is there not room in the world for many viewpoints and many soul-ages? Why do you allow yourselves to be used as pawns in the game of unevolved beings? You should be taking charge and leading them, because you know what is real and what is not. How many more will you kill for someone else's argument? How many of you will die for an ideal that is not your own? Enter into love, and bring about peace!" With that, all the men entered a contemplative state.

Coming to hug me, the cook said, "Thank you, man of peace!" Looking down, I realized that I was indeed manifesting as a man. "I have a gift for you to thank you for the gift of truth you have given these men." Handing me a beautiful golden statue of a man sitting in a lotus position, he continued, "This is the golden man of Nikko; please take it back to where you come from as a token of our friendship." Touching it, I said, "Where I am going, I cannot take this. I am a time traveler and physical matter will not go through the time tunnel. But let me hold it a moment and bring it back fully with my memory." Accepting this, he hugged me again and said, "I want to make this a good hug, because I will probably never see you again in this lifetime." In a flash, my spirit was sucked into the time tunnel.

Entering into a battle scene, I was on a riverboat during the Civil War. Small and beat up due to the war, five men were left on our boat and four on theirs, as all the rest had died. Walking to the front, I yelled to the guys on the other boat, "Why don't you guys come over for lunch?" Obviously taken by surprise, they thought it was a good idea and they came over. Tension was in the air as everyone was still armed, but no one wanted to die and they were willing to take a chance at peace.

As we ate lunch, I asked the other boat crew where they were from and they said, "Louisiana." Smiling, I replied, "My family lived in Louisiana for a short while when I was a kid." One of the men on the boat I originated with got angry. "Hey, whose side are you on, anyway?" "I am on everyone's side." I said. "You all seem pretty much the same to me. Only you know why you're killing each other." One of the Louisiana boys broke in, "When did your family live in Louisiana?" He asked. "Well," I answered, "the late twentieth century." Looking at each other as if their confusion was bordering on anger, I continued, "I realize that this is the nineteenth century, but I am a time traveler, I've been sent to tell you of the futility of war." Now they became silently contemplative. "What have you gained by killing your brothers and what have you lost?" Some of the men began crying. "Those you have lost are doing very well, as they have moved on into the spirit realm and into their unlimited forms. Do not worry about the past, but think about the future! What a beautiful reality you could create if all of you would enter into love." Standing to leave, I hugged them. "I must re-enter the time tunnel now and return to my time frame. I will not see you again in this lifetime, but I love you all. Think about your choices." Quietly, I walked into the tunnel as they looked on. In a moment, I was gone.

Again, it is important to achieve balance, and there are times when one must stand against dark forces that manifest upon the earth. But war is not just, for there are always innocents who die for someone else's cause, and guilty ones who go free . . .

Returning to form, I was interested in the gift given to me by the Japanese man. Upon looking in the dictionary, I found that Nikko was a town in central Japan on Honshu Island, famous for its shrines and temples. The sacred gift of love would be forever displayed on the shelf of my spirit.

****

Leaving form, I met with some spiritual guides who were demonstrating their techniques for bringing light into the sub-conscious state. "Though there may seem to be little change consciously in a being," they said, "there can be much activity in the sub-conscious mind. Changes occur on subtle levels and these changes will eventually surface in the conscious state."

Watching them perform this work on a soul, a tall spirit wearing a white robe began sweeping light across this soul. Beginning to shine brightly, the different spirits present began working on their own specialized areas. One spirit touched different parts of this soul, igniting them in light. Another spoke softly to this soul, speaking universal truths. All of this was being done without any conscious awareness of this person on the ground, but was ignited by the soul's prayers and desire to move closer to God. Fascinated, I returned to form.

"Moreover, the desire to go is the measure here. When there is the desire to go, one who has made his mental resolve in this way goes visibly, carried by the force of the resolution like an arrow shot by an archer."
The Path of Purification, Chapter XII, The Supernormal Powers, No. 132, (Buddhism, Theravadan)

"Never begin a war yourself, God does not like blood-shed, fight only in defence."
Nahjul Balagha, The Author, 34 to 40 A.H., Page 55, No. 1, Imam Ali Ibn Abu Talib, (Islam)

****

Because of my work with many souls, I was beginning to realize that higher and sub-conscious aspects of souls can be quite different from their physical counterparts. It was my duty to serve the higher good of the soul, rather than the personality on the ground, which oftentimes believes it needs something different than its true requirements.

****

Hovering on the astral plane, I was confronted by an image of a spirit that began throwing rocks at me, and taunting me with disgust. Ducking, I wanted to avoid being hit, but suddenly realized that this was not a real spirit, but a thought-form I had created from my own insecurities. Turning to her, I said, "That is not who you really are, you are an eagle!" No sooner was it said, than it became such and flew away.

****

After I'd entered a wanton woodland, a green bus with circular windows arrived to take me to my destination. Other sub-conscious astral souls were among us, and an argument had broken out between two of them.

Ignoring the dispute, they were caught up in their ego's, arguing over who had the most exciting experiences to talk about. Interfering, the driver said, "Someone is here who can help both of you," he looked right at me, "an extra-terrestrial being with more knowledge than meets the eye." Uncomfortable, they looked at me with expectancy. "All our experiences are truly the experience of the One. When the two of you begin communicating through love, your misunderstanding will be clear."

Quiet followed the remainder of the short journey, and when we arrived at my destination, the bus driver handed me a glass of juice. "Take this," he said, "this is the juice of surrender. It will help you become one with the flow." Drinking the sweet juice quickly, I exited the bus.

As I looked at the trees, I saw an unusual sparkle coming from them, and I felt deep love for them. Becoming more flowing, my spirit was swaying to and fro in the light beam that was my soul. Beginning to enter into a deeper state of total oneness with all that exists, I eventually became truly liquid, understanding things very clearly which had previously been a struggle to me.

Many souls were experiencing the oneness, and I was asked to join in the mass consciousness experience. Afraid, the angels came to comfort me, assuring me that what I was about to experience was an important element of truth. As the many spirit lights became one, I felt an ecstatic feeling of utter peace.

Becoming non-existent as a separate soul, I entered into a truly indescribable state, wherein I became a liquid part of the mass of all life. The beauty of this experience filled me with love and deep intense knowing. No longer was I the fragment, 'Marilynn,' but a singular molecule in the structure of life. 'Liquid mass in the consciousness of One,' triggered a profound knowing. The *you* must die, in order to become a part of the *One*. Broken down into the molecular state, I experienced a singular molecule in a liquid strand of life . . . a thought within the mind of God.

Returning to form, I was forever changed.

"Although they are similar in appearance, common people behold forms and other such things and conceive of them to be really existent; they do not understand them to be like an illusion. But since yogis do understand them to exist in such a way, it is here that the yogis and the common people disagree . . . Although it does not appear to the common person, because it appears to those yogis who have merely seen personal identitylessness, there is no mistake in its being a deceptive truth . . . Compared to the worldly view of things as permanent and so forth, the yogi's vision of momentariness is posited as a vision of Reality itself."

A Guide to the Bodhisattva's Way of Life, Chapter IX, Answers 5, 7, 8, (Buddhism, Tibetan, Author: Shantideva)

****

Emmanuel (my spirit guide) bade me to witness a spectacular image in the heavens. Taken deep below the Earth's surface, I watched as the controls to several volcanoes were set to erupt. but I was surprised to find upon emerging that these were volcanoes of light in the heavens, all formed in a circular fashion like that of a medicine wheel, which erupted in a synchronicity of light, which came from the heavens and fell upon the Earth. At one point, the circle of volcanoes began spinning as a wheel, while Emmanuel brought sub-conscious astral spirits above them to receive of its light.

"Glorious is it to see the Noble Ones; their company at all times brings happiness."

Dhammapada, Chapter XV, No. 206, (Buddhism)

****

"The simple fact that Being is the never-changing, eternal phase of existence and that It pervades the diverse forms of phenomenal creation gives us the hope of bringing all the diversified phases of our lives into harmony by co-ordinating their values with the values of absolute Being."

The Science of Being and Art of Living, Part 3, Chapter 2, Page 121, Paragraph 3, (Hinduism, Transcendental Meditation, Author: Maharishi Mahesh Yogi)

In a journey beneath the depths of the sea, I came upon a school of dolphins who graciously did flips to entertain myself and the spiritual guardians who accompanied me. "Welcome to our world, spirits of light," they telepathically conveyed, "we are happy you speak with us." In awe at this communication, I replied, "You are so beautiful, thank you for sharing the beauty of your form." Laughing, the dolphins responded, "All form comes from the mind of God, and all of it is beautiful in its own magnificent way. Share your perception with the consciousness of mankind, it will expand their vision and create a yearning among them to know us, as well."

Continuing to go deeper into the ocean, we found schools of brightly colored fish and spindly sea creatures looming in their world of quiet and the dark. A shark swam by with the majestic demeanor of one so feared by man, but there was no fear within the eyes of his spirit. Billowy seaweed flowed to and fro with the water and the rocks glowed from the sunlight captured in the sea. Each sea creature sent a welcome to our spirits in the silence for they knew who we were and seemed to see many spirit lights travel their waters. Our presence was comforting to them, for it reminded them that their world of predator and prey was not real, but only a dream.

Entering into a huge cavern, I was apprehensive. "Do not be afraid, follow me," the guide conveyed, as we floated in. A large marble door fell suddenly from the ceiling, dropping down in front of us so as to prevent our entry. "Let's get out of here!" I screamed, "This scares me." Remaining calm, the spirit spoke lovingly. "Ask the door to open and it will." Calming, I thought, "Door, will you allow me to enter?" Coming open quickly, we continued down the dark passageways deeper into the cave. Every few feet another marble door blocked our entry, but would open upon our request.

Finally, we came upon a light-filled space wherein a seemingly never-ending circular staircase went up into the heavens. Beginning to ascend, I followed after my guide, level after level. Soon we were passing through clouds and there were no more walls. Almost at the top, I again became scared. "Come," the spirit with me beckoned, "you are almost there." "But I am tired." I said, groaning. "All these stairs have worn me out." "Aaaaah," the spirit replied, "breaking down the walls and barriers was not easy, but you have done it. Just at the top of these stairs lies our destination." Quickly, he shot up the stairs beyond my vision, and I followed.

When I reached the top, my guide had had disappeared. Only a bright a luminous being remains and his holiness was apparent. Beginning to feel unworthy, he held his arms out to me and wore a big smile. Smiling back, I said nothing, as our exchange was entirely silent. Embracing me with a warm and loving hug, I became transparent as his height blended with my lowness, in a communion meant to bring my spiritual energies higher. As my energies began shifting, I suddenly . . .

Looking closer, I suddenly recognized this spirit as the higher self of one of the souls I'd been watching over. Pulling back, his peaceful eyes conveyed appreciation, and I knew that he was thanking me for working with an aspect of himself on the ground which remained completely unaware of our work. "You're welcome." I conveyed sheepishly. (The higher self is that part of a soul that is closest to God, and that there are many aspects on the various levels below it manifesting in myriad worlds and those manifestations are as different from their source as God is from his many creations.)

"The entire matter of reaching union with God consists of purging the will of its appetites and feelings, so that from a human and lowly will it may be changed into the divine will, made identical with the will of God."
The Collected Works of St. John of the Cross, The Ascent of Mt. Carmel, Chapter 16, No. 3, Page 238, (Christianity, Catholic, Author: St. John of the Cross)

****

Hearing a tremendous call for help within my soul, I followed the timely beckon and flew about the Earth to find its source. A man in need of help was praying, "Angels of light, my son is choosing between worlds, please help me to tell him I love him and I dearly hope he returns to me." As he spoke, our Heavenly Father filled me with knowledge. Having an adopted son who just got his girlfriend pregnant, he had been involved in a car accident and was now in a coma.

As I flew over an intricate sand carving his son had made, he sub-consciously turned to see me standing in the room. "This is my most cherished possession. I know it is asking much, but if you will help me I will be eternally grateful." "It will be my pleasure to help you," I said, "I will go now and do what I can."

Inner urgings led my soul to a place beneath the sea where his son's spirit was busy playing with some mermaids. Approaching quietly as I didn't wish to disturb his joy, two dolphins swept us up and took us for a ride. Smooth and luxurious to the touch, the skin of the dolphin was very soft. Arriving in a location where 100 angels had gathered, I turned to him. "My dear brother, you are now between worlds and you must make a choice. It is beautiful here, but your father calls for you in tears. His love is unmarred by the pregnancy, he just wants you back."

Waving my hands across the sea, I showed him images of his father, so that he might feel his great grief. "I will return to my body tomorrow morning," he said. Dancing in joy and singing heavenly songs of love, the angels formed a large circle as we held hands and shared light. Leaving the boy to enjoy his final day amongst the angels, I returned to his father, who looked up sadly.

"Thanks for trying, anyway." He said. "No," I replied, "you do not understand. Your son will return tomorrow morning." Beginning to cry, he walked over to the sand carving and picked up a statue of Nefertiti. "Take this," he said, as he handed it to me, "you have earned it."

Placing my hands on the statue, my spirit whizzed to the sky, returning to the angelic kingdom I'd left before. Angels sang in joy and euphoria as a masculine light being, ominous in size and holiness, came towards me. Looking into my eyes with peace, he said, "Eter Oar." Instinctively, I repeated, "Eter Oar." Handing him the Nefertiti, he replied, "Come forth for thy wings." Moving forward, I said nothing in the sacred moment but remembered the words that had been chanted to me in sleep, "In the evening bronze, the night wind sings, chanting visions and songs, calling forth the Nefertiti wings." Touching my shoulder, ethereal wings appeared on my back. Moved to tears, I fell to my knees as the angels began singing and dancing in a circle around me, while the magnificent angel who had given me the wings, stepped back, smiled . . . and disappeared.

"Amen, I say unto you: The soul for which ye shall pray, if it indeed is in the dragon of the outer darkness, he will draw his tail out of his mouth and let go that soul. And moreover if it is in all the regions of the judgments of the rulers, amen, I say unto you: The receivers of Melchisedec will with haste snatch it away, whether the dragon let it go or it is in the judgments of the rulers; in a word, the receivers of Melchisedec will snatch it away out of all the regions in which it is, and will lead it into the region of the Midst before the Virgin of Light."
Pistis Sophia, Book Four, Page 271, Paragraph 2, (Christianity, Gnostic/Essene)
****

Sent to observe a soul caught up in a cycle of time, I hovered in space. The nine planets of our solar system appeared like scattered rocks as they followed their individual paths around the sun. Encircled in an energy beam, the man I'd come to assist was floating about the top of his orbit, preparing to make a change. "He is ending a cycle of time." A voice said. "He has created a repetitious energy pattern which has hindered productivity in his life. Remember the words of release, and tell him." Calling out, "Chorub Lee!" he raised his hands to the sky and began pushing forward. Repeating the words, I again called out, "Chorub Lee!"

Pushing forward to rescind its circular form, he shot straight forward down a new, direct line of energy, a forward motion rather than a circular spinning of the wheels. "The cycle of time has been completed and changed." The voice said.

"The Principle of Cycles manifests that universal circular direction of process or progress which is apparent in all the manifested world, from its highest to its

lowest manifestation."
The Secret Doctrine of the Rosicrucians, Part XIII, Section V. Paragraph 1, (Mystery Religions, Rosicrucian)
"Just as the present aeon, though a unity, is divided by units of time and units of time are divided into years and years are divided into seasons and seasons into months, and months into days, and days into hours, and hours into moments, so too the aeon of the Truth, since it is a unity and multiplicity, receives honor in the small and the great names according to the power of each to grasp it."
The Nag Hammadi Library, The Tripartite Tractate, No. 5, Page 71, Paragraph 2-3, (Christianity, Gnostic/Essene)

****

CHAPTER TWO
Chief Joseph, Mysteries of Evolution, the Knowledge of Good and Evil, Medicine Women from throughout the Ages, Five Winds of Alteration, Spiritual Warfare, Taking One's Heart Out.

****

"Get up now, and stand on your feet, I have appeared to you for this purpose, to appoint you as a servant and witness of what you have seen (of me) and what you will be shown. I shall deliver you from this people and from the Gentiles to whom I send you, to open their eyes that they may turn from darkness to light and from the power of Satan to God, so that they may obtain forgiveness of sins and an inheritance among those who have been consecrated by faith in me."
New American Bible, New Testament, Acts 26:16-18, (Christianity, Catholic, Words of Christ)
"O Lord, I am Thy servant; I am Thy servant and the son of Thy handmaid: Thou hast broken my bonds in sunder. I will offer to Thee the sacrifice of praise. Let my heart and my tongue praise you."
The Confessions of St. Augustine, Book IX, Page 184, Paragraph 1, (Christianity, Catholic, Words of St. Augustine)

"My child, you are sleeping." His voice rang out as if echoed through time, as my spirit began waking in another realm. "You seek to know?" The Indian Chief asked. "What?" I responded, confused as my vision was still cloudy and distant.

His face was worn from time and harsh weather, and his long black hair was braided. Many beads were about his neck. "Tell them my story." He said, as I felt the reverence of this soul. "Walk the pathway with me." "The pathway?" I asked, "I'm not sure what you mean." "But you will my dear traveler. Beyond the gateway, beyond the ascension is the knowledge of life. Walk with me."

With great respect, I awakened, stood and looked this spirit in his eyes which visioned deep knowledge to me. "Who are you?" I calmly asked, feeling the familiarity of this soul. "I am Chief Joseph." Reaching his hand towards me, I remembered him. "I will tell your story, I will walk with you."

He began to speak, and I listened . . .

"I was born as particle of light. My mother was the Universe, my father, a star; an idea born of life, becoming life, to seek life. No man came before me, but myself. No thought entered reality without my knowing. I was one."

"Then came the scattering, when clarity became confusion. Light became darkness, love became hatred. I'd never traveled that road before, when my fellow life became a destroyer of life. My brothers became my enemies, my sisters, the hunted."

"Everything was confused then, and I sought to understand. What had changed? Why had the harmony been broken into chaos? Where could I retrieve that seed of life that began it all, and save the world I perceived as my own? For years, I fought their battles, their wars, defending the peace I so missed from my heart. And then one day . . . I stopped. I was Chief Joseph of the Nez Perce, now . . . I am life. I exist in a new world, a new reality, where the seeking is sacred. This is my story."

"Hear me, my chiefs, I am tired; my heart is sick and sad. From where the sun now stands, I will fight no more forever."
The Words of Chief Joseph as he Surrendered to General Sherman

****

Awaking from death silently, the distant wailing of a woman could be heard. Looking around him, he could see no one but the whimpering sadness he felt alarmed him. All was dark and black, nothing existed here, it seemed. Suddenly, he could not breathe. As Chief Joseph looked up, a huge entity had placed its hands over his mouth. Fighting for air, Joseph suddenly realized he no longer needed to breathe in the same way. Still the entity continued as though he was trying to extinguish his soul. Raging at this violation of life, Joseph threw his arms back, lunging backward and away from him. Now the entity stood in front of Joseph with a threatening glare.

In the distance, he could hear the whimpering cry of a woman, but he could not yet find its source. This lone and distant song of a mournful soul touched him, and he wanted to help. Suddenly, a train carrying the souls of those who had died to the spirit whizzed by him, the blaring engine and the cries of these lost souls were humbling and horrid. "They seek the dead side," a voice with no apparent owner spoke. Their moans and cries for help hurt his soul terribly, for in this state he could truly feel all their pain, even though it had been self-inflicted. "Why?!" He cried out to their fear-laden faces, "Why do you seek to maintain death?!" The black around their eyes was haunting, and there was no response, no change.

Without warning, the large entity lunged forward again, as Joseph called out to it in absolute rage. "As long as I AM, no one will violate my life!" The entity didn't budge, and Joseph didn't know what to do. To become dead, you must become complacent in thought, acting on impulse without regard for the harm you cause, and without regard for reason or higher purpose. In disregarding life, you choose death, and Joseph was not about to choose this horrid state.

"In the name of the spirit, I demand that you leave my presence, I choose life!" Joseph called out as the entities energy began to lessen. Another hand took his own, but he could not see the formless image of the spirit who had come to retrieve him. Repeating Joseph's words to the dark entity who had tried to take Joseph in the moment of death, the formless image said, "In the name of the spirit, I demand that you leave our presence."

A whirlwind of light cascaded about him as the formless image began to become visible. Appearing in a white hooded robe, it was . . . no, could it be? The Angel of Ascension! Joseph felt calm now, knowing his life-force was no longer in jeopardy from the dark one.

"'It is I,' he said, 'who am understanding. I am one of the four light-givers, who stand in the presence of the great invisible spirit. Do you think these rulers have any power over you? None of them can prevail against the root of truth.'"
The Nag Hammadi Library, The Hypostasis of Archons, Page 167, Paragraph 3, (Christianity, Gnostic/Essene)

Celebrations ensued in the colorful place where Joseph had been taken. Swirls of colors tore across the sky in a rainbow of energy. Before him stood someone he'd known, but couldn't place in his mind. "I cannot remember your name, old friend." Joseph bowed his head in shame. "Your memory of me is not of this life, but another," his friend replied, "you'll remember me as Daniel . . . Daniel Pierce."

Suddenly Joseph became extremely uncomfortable, but why, he didn't understand. Within his stomach, he began to feel that he might become sick, but

Daniel took Joseph's hand and spoke quietly. "It is forgiven, brother. As life was taken from your tribe, you once took life from me." Joseph's eyes began to tear as his memory slowly came back, but Daniel had no feelings of animosity. "We will now seek life together, as one," he said.

Suddenly Joseph was alone sitting amongst a plain of long dried grass. A tunnel appeared in the distance, and a man came from within it dressed oddly for Joseph's sensibilities. As he approached, Joseph recognized the symbols he wore, that of a Catholic priest. Many of these men had come into their camps speaking of their God, trying to save their souls. Sadness filled Joseph as he remembered how they had always come before the slaughter.

Looking somber, as if to say, "I'm sorry," the man came this time without a bible, but held his hands out to Joseph in peace. "How many?" The priest said. "Too many." Joseph replied. As the priest sat down, he reflected another question to Joseph. "How many groups of people have been set apart in the name of religion?" Perplexed, Joseph looked deeply into the eyes of this priest, when suddenly the field all around them became a battleground between the religions and the people. Groups came forward from every direction, all who stood apart because of their race, beliefs, imperfections, illnesses, karma or any difference to the one acceptable human that this man's religion would allow.

Crying, the priest lowered his head, as Chief Joseph stooped to look upon him. Intrigued by his sadness, he asked, "Is this not what you wanted?" "No, I wanted life, but this is what I have done!" The priest was ashamed. "But why did you do it?" Joseph asked. "I don't know, I really don't know." "Was it out of ignorance, perhaps you didn't understand?" Joseph replied, trying to make him feel better. "I wish I could claim ignorance," sighed the priest, "but I cannot." "Why is this?" Joseph said. "Because I did not question, I followed," the priest was distant, lost in his thoughts, "and in following, I denied life. If I had asked my heart, it would have told me that this was not honoring life, that this was wrong."

Rising from the ground, the two looked on, as the groups of people who had been set apart disappeared. Joseph quietly took the priest's hand to help him, and said, "My brother, may we now honor life together? The sun is setting, a new day awaits. All of us have been guilty in one lifetime or another of not properly honoring that which was sacred. Perhaps we can seek understanding together?" Unable to speak, the priest took Joseph's hand as they walked towards the sun.

"The prey departeth not, nor do the crack of the whip, the whir of wheels, the prancing horses, the bounding chariots, the charging horsemen, the flashing (sword), the glittering spear, the multitude of slain, the great heap of carcasses. No end is there to the bodies; men stumble over those bodies."
The Dead Sea Scriptures, Nahum, Chapter Three, No. 1-3, Page 315, Paragraph 1, (Christianity, Gnostic/Essene)

Seeing it for only a moment, the deeply sacred golden book encased in blue-turquoise appeared. A voice spoke from the sky. "As you seek life, you will find the holy words of life . . . of each life. Every life has its own holy words, its own holy pathway, and its own holy book. These differences allow all life to meet in understanding, as all life exists because of the other. As you follow the pathway of life, you must seek to *become* your brothers." As they listened, they sat beneath the setting sun as suddenly the priest began changing . . . within moments he had become Daniel.

"One must, then, read the book of his own self, rather than some treatise on rhetoric. Wherefore He hath said, 'Read thy Book: There needeth none but thyself to make out an account against thee this day."
The Seven Valleys and the Four Valleys, The Four Valleys, The First Valley, Page 51, Paragraph 2, (Baha'i, Author: Baha'u'llah)

Thunder struck and Joseph now stood amidst a dark, dank and dusky graveyard. Bleak headstones were surrounding him, but something was unusual. Joseph immediately knew that everything buried here was still alive, it was the graveyard of things not yet fully dead, held in this state by the memories of those who would not let the past go. Grave diggers were busy opening up a grave, pulling out the dirt around the body of man who was dead in every way; although decomposition had not yet set in. Joseph was shocked and alarmed when he saw that it was himself.

Looking somber as she spoke, an angel appeared, "You must now let your former self die to become a part of the one. Who you were is not what you seek to become. You can no longer be Joseph, you must become life itself." With her words, the body began to quickly decompose as they laid his past to rest. But as he began walking slowly out of the graveyard, he noticed that other aspects of himself and his former life were following him. Running in fear, he was afraid of these zombie-like memories that chased him, but then he stopped, realizing that he had to allow these things to die, as well. Childhood fears, past loves, those who had passed before, all were among his memories that must cease. "They are not of the now." The angel said. "They must be allowed to die. The past is already dead, but if it does not die within you, then it grasps hold of you and stops you from living. Their aliveness is maintained by you, but still they are no more alive."

Then he saw her. As the image passed before Joseph, he began to cry tears that had been unfulfilled within his own lifetime. She'd been gone for so long, but her face had never left him. Having never told anyone about her, she stood before Joseph reaching out to hug him in joy. Strong and certain, her love relinquished his fears, and quickly put them to rest. "I love you," she said, "but you have held me in your heart long enough, let it cease. A love that can never be is a dead love, how many years did you weep for me?" His tears were drying now, "So many, and no one ever knew." "Yes," she said as she dried his final falling tear," and it held you in that which no longer lived, you were never completely free again. Now . . . you are free, my beloved Joseph. Our love will always remain, but what you hold onto must die. Seek life, and in the seeking, let this go. Spirit directing life always directs it towards the path of the highest good; we were what we were meant to be in that time." Joseph looked up," I never did let you go . . . completely." Hugging him tightly, she comforted him, "There is one thing I must leave you with, life continues to create, life continues to love . . . it never ends. But life can cease movement when it holds onto dead things. If you wish to seek life, you must follow this," placing his hand upon his heart, she concluded, "always, my love, always." In a flash of light, he suddenly saw Daniel, and in an act that initially confused him, she walked into Daniel, as the two souls became one. In a flash of knowing he realized . . . Daniel, the priest, and she were one.

"Great spirit, I am confused." Joseph cried out to the heavens, as a voice echoed from the highest realms. "You believe something is being taken from you, but it is being given back." A huge lighted hand reached from heaven to touch Joseph's head. "Challenge your beliefs, Joseph, because they are only a disguise to the truth. What do you *believe*, and what do you *know*? Which pathway will you follow, life or death?"

"Lord, incline your heavens and come; touch the mountains and make them smoke. Flash forth lightning . . . reach out your hand from on high; deliver me from the many waters."

New American Bible, Old Testament, Psalms 144:5-8, (Christianity, Catholic)

****

"Welcome." Joseph said. Hovering above his small encampment, he was sitting before a small campfire motioning me to sit. A small teepee was behind him, and he wore modern clothing; a brown hat, a vest, and a blue flannel shirt with a pair of old jeans. "Come, sit by my fire," he said. "Before we continue," Joseph said, "you must pass through a small test." "A test? I just want to tell your story, you know, of the pathway." "In order to follow me, you must follow the pathway. The next step requires a small rite of passage."

A vibration entered my spirit as I began to whirl. Within moments, my soul was manifesting in another place, another reality; a modern looking restaurant decorated in frontier fashion with lots of woodwork. People were laughing and making merry on the cool November day. Beginning to manifest into this energetic reality of a potential future, I was sitting at a table with about ten people who acted as if they knew me.

Turning to look out a window behind me, I noticed a man holding a gun. "Uh oh," I thought, "here it comes." Without any warning, a burst of about twenty armed people poured into the restaurant, happening so fast that most of those present could not possibly ascertain what had occurred. Shooting in the air, they were demanding that the people gather in one location, which everyone did except for me. Attempting to make a statement about the social conditions in their country, they'd taken about 25 hostages. Wanting peace, love and understanding . . . justice for their people, I Immediately understood why I was present.

Beginning to talk to them, I was cracking a lot of jokes, which was not the custom for most hostage situations. Enraging the captors, the other hostages were concerned that I was going to get shot. One of the men was wearing a shirt depicting a well-known musician in their realm, John Lennon. Walking quietly over to him, he pulled out his gun as I approached. Ignoring his threatening stance, I asked, "So you like John Lennon?" "Yes, I do." "Well, I love him, too. What was your favorite song of his?" "Well, that would be 'Imagine.'" "Oh, I love that song, too." Beginning to sing, I savored every lyric, "Imagine there's no countries, it isn't hard to do, nothing to kill or die for . . ." Angry, he shouted, "I know the song! Just shut up and get over there with the others!" Cocking his gun, I continued singing. "You may say I'm a dreamer. But I'm not the only one. I hope someday you'll join us. And the world will live as one." "Shut up!" He said again. Walking up to him, I put my hand on his shoulder. "You wear a shirt with John Lennon on it, and you carry a gun, that makes no sense. You *must* know that he was killed by a gun, too." With that he got very mad, "Don't tell me that, that's bullshit! John Lennon is not dead!"

Suddenly, I realized that I had entered a parallel reality, and in this parallel, John Lennon had not been murdered. "Where I come from, the reality of earth I live in, he died of gunshot wounds over ten years ago." Looking at me shocked and angry, some of the others thought I was crazy. Not wishing for me to interfere with their plan, they were sick of me using up their time. Wanting us to focus on their cause, they said that they couldn't have done this in any other way.

Two women suddenly grabbed me and took me to the other side of the restaurant. "You are not going to mess this up for us." I started laughing, "Mess this up, I really care about what you are trying to accomplish, but whatever possessed you to try this technique, I don't understand." "Shut up, it's time for you to die." "Do you realize the message you're sending out? You are asking people to care about other people . . . by killing and hurting others." One woman began yelling and screaming, and the other stopped her. "She'll be very quiet in a moment." "No . . . I won't." I said, looking at them very seriously. "If you shoot this body, it will simply disintegrate and I will manifest a new one. I'm sorry, but because of my purpose here, I will not go away with something as simple as the illusion of a gunshot." They looked at me, grabbed my shirt, and held the gun to my head. I didn't wince or respond. "Do what you gotta do." I said.

Suddenly, she dropped her hands and began to cry. "I don't want this, I really don't. Why does it take something like this to get the attention of the people? Why do you have to go to such extremes for them to notice injustice or cruelty?" "I don't know that answer myself," I said, "I battle uncaring in my own world, my own realm. I cry for injustice, I cry for the environment, I cry for life! But I've learned that battling such uncaring cannot be done by engaging in the tactics of uncaring people." They both calmed, as did the entire group. "But nothing ever changes." "Yes, it does change. Change sometimes comes slowly, but the change you desire can only come from love. You must allow it, you cannot force it. "Well, what do we do now?" They asked. "To be honest with you, I don't know what can be done at this point. You've probably caused a major stir, and violent retaliation is what has been created by your action. I am concerned." With that, they all pulled back and began thinking. What could turn back the tides of time?

Several hours passed and everyone became closer in this hostage drama. Hugging me, the man with the Lennon shirt came to hug me. Very quiet, he had calmed down a great deal since the beginning of the episode. Everyone, hostages and captors, were beginning to hang out together as if nothing had ever happened. Now I was concerned as to how to get this turned around so they wouldn't all be killed by the SWAT team that was currently surrounding the building.

One of the women agreed to go out and talk to the police, asking for an opportunity to release everyone safely. As she walked out the door, I immediately felt that she was in danger. Grabbing the door, I ran out with her acting as a hostage to prevent gunfire. Police were ready to fire, but when they saw me they stopped. Whispering to her, I told her to act as if they were releasing me as a good-faith hostage. Running towards the police, I met with the man in charge. "These people have made a mistake and they know it. They want to let everyone go and release everyone safely. No one is in danger anymore and they really want this to end, their motivation was distorted, that's all." Agreeing to allow me to return into the building, I was given the task of preparing everyone for safe release.

Walking through the building, the hostages had already been gathered for release. But as they began leaving, I felt something was terribly wrong. In the corner of my eye, I noticed someone who wasn't there before, a member of the SWAT team. Glancing around, I saw many more of them. "Oh, my God, NO!" I screamed out, as they began firing at the captors. Bodies lying in a pool of blood, I was crying uncontrollably. Nineteen had been lost.

On the wall before me, Chief Joseph's face appeared, encompassing its entirety. Compassion was in his eyes as he pulled me outside of the turmoil and into an energy vortex. "Well done." He said. "What do you mean, well done!" They're DEAD!" Joseph interrupted me. "They have finished a program in that realm. However, you did everything within your power. You gave them knowledge about their choice, and then it was up to them to choose. It is the natural order of cause and effect. Violence begets violence. Sometimes, although perceptual alterations occur, the act cannot be turned around." I understood. Grateful that they had changed their perceptions before their death, it's always better to realize truth in our mortal state, than to awaken to it after death. But grief is grief, and I continued to cry. "Go home, now, child. You have done enough for one night."

"Their faith was shaken severely. So great was their alarm, that many of them, discontinuing their prayer, apostatized their faith. Verily, God caused not this turmoil but to test and prove His servants."
The Kitab-I-Iqan, Page 50-51, (Baha'i, Author: Baha'u'llah)

****

"The Divine Physician is keeping you in the hospital of earthly delusion until your disease of desire for material things is cured. Then He will let you go Home."
Sayings of Paramahansa Yogananda, Page 70, No. 2, (Hinduism, Kriya Yoga, Words of Paramahansa Yogananda)

Having room for only two people, the horse-driven carriage was small. Open to the elements, we were happy that it was a warm and sunny day. My sister and I had ridden into town to go to the bank. Flirting with a handsome gentleman who held the door for her, she was older than me and could do things lacking in propriety. After she emerged from the bank in this one road town, we headed back to the farmhouse. I was a teenager.

Black servants were working very hard; a cook in the kitchen, and a frail young woman boiling water for my younger brother's bathtub. Walking by without a word, the door was open. White folks were above such menial tasks in a household such as ours.

Larry, my fiancé, was waiting for me on the front porch. Playing ball with Luke from the farm nearby, they seemed upset about something so I wandered out in the sun to see what could be the matter. Carrying my lacy umbrella, it protected my pearly white skin from sunburn. Down below the hill on the dirt road, a black family was driving an automobile. Immediately, I understood their outrage! Apparently they were the first in these parts to own an automobile and they were BLACK! My insides were ripping me apart with the injustice of such a thing.

My spirit tumbled out of that body, whizzing through time and space into another.

Our escape was only moments away, as our plan had been set into action. We'd been held for a very long time as prisoners because of our religious beliefs. Unwarned of our plan, our captors didn't know what hit them when the gunfire began and the escape was in progress. People were dying all over the place, and for a moment, I looked behind me at the suffering of those who had held me captive. The dead and dying caught my caring for only a moment. It was God I was fighting for, and God wanted them to die!

Ripped and squeezed out of that form, my soul whizzed through time and space into another.

The stout older man looked me in the eye, as his wife had just passed of a horrible illness. We'd just received word that one of his two sons had died in the war this same day, fighting for the Union army during the Civil War. Promised to their other son in marriage if he returned from the fighting, he'd just signed up for the Rebel forces.

Suddenly, there were two of me. My former self was continuing within the body, while my present self overlapped and observed and felt from my own current vantage point. My present self was concerned as to how this father would handle these two deaths in his family *and* the knowledge that his other son was preparing to fight to preserve slavery for the Rebel forces?

My former self was unconcerned with slavery and its ramifications, it was self-consumed. Tears were running down my future father-in-law's face, "I told him joining the Union army would kill him . . . AND his mother," he said to my present self's astonishment. Realizing that this family supported slavery, and that I was very much a part of it, I also discovered that my former self was not offended by war at all.

The haze began clearing from the intensity of the shooting star that took me back into the present. Chief Joseph looked calmly into my face. "You felt it?" He asked. "Yes, oh yes, I sure did. It was so strange." I replied. "You went back to the parts of you that violated life; you saw and felt through their eyes again, what did you feel?" His question instilled shame within my soul. "Nothing," I replied very softly, "Isn't that horrible? In my mind, I didn't see it as violating life. I saw it as perfectly okay. Isn't that horrible?" Taking my hand, Joseph looked deep into my eyes. "No," he said, "that is very good. Now you are ready." "For what?" I couldn't help but ask. "You felt the separation and the duality, now you will feel the oneness. If you could violate life in those lives without having any conscious awareness of it, is it not possible that there are things you have not seen or fully understood about life in your present, is it possible you could be violating life now and not be aware of it?" This shocked me to realize the magnitude of what he might be saying. "Yes," I replied, "yes, that is very possible." "Remember, life is greater than you know, its meaning, its significance. You've remembered how easy it is to be ignorant; you don't even have to think about it. There are some things that you've never thought about . . . things you might find horrible if you had."

Interrupting him, I said, "Okay . . . but, I'm confused, I thought this story was going to be about you." Joseph smiled in a knowing manner. "Why, Daniel, I thought we were seeking the pathway together?" My gaze didn't move from his eyes as the meaning of his words penetrated into my soul. "Daniel Pierce, that was me?" "Welcome to remembrance, Daniel, now you are ready."

So, I was the soul of that priest. "Whoa," I thought, as I returned to my body.

"(Thou wilt make) an end of all that oppress us; and we shall give thanks unto Thy name for ever."
The Dead Sea Scriptures, The New Covenant, Page 437, Stanza 4, (Christianity, Gnostic/Essene)

****

Joseph's long black hair was flowing around his neck and shoulders, and a hat shadowed his face. Lighting a peace pipe, he handed it to me. Smoking the aromatic vapors, I became PEACE.

A group of Native American wise men appeared and began singing ancient chants. I'd thought it odd that they did this in my presence, because I was white. "Isn't this disrespectful to the spirits?" I asked. "It is wise to sing," the leader said, "we sing for you today." Not knowing what to say or do, I just listened, as I suddenly noticed a young Indian boy had appeared at Chief Joseph's side. "The river," he beckoned, "you are going to the river."

Waves thrashed and spun all around me as I had been immediately transported into what could become my watery grave if I wasn't careful. Hurled through the enclosed underground waterway for quite some time, it was very narrow in spots and I'd banged my eye and lip very hard from being hurled against the rock wall.

Emerging in another time and place, the river was open again as I was climbing onto the surface of the bank. My long gray dress was soaked and tattered from my journey, and behind me, I could see there was trouble. Remembering, I saw a group of people lined up against a wall on the other side of the river, inland a ways. A firing squad was about to shoot all of them, but someone had come to help me escape. "Come on," said a man with a deep English accent, "hurry up! We've got to go!" Pulling me from the water, we were running in the wilderness towards a boat. Gunshots were heard in the distance, and I was very confused. Everything had happened so fast, and my present self had no idea who this man was or what was going on. Hearing other footsteps behind me, we were almost there. "Come on! There is no time!" He yelled again loudly. More gunshots rang out, and due to the grace of God, we weren't hit. Moments later we were on the boat as it steamed down river.

As soon as the boat began to move, I passed out cold on the wooden deck. Awaking in a daze to a man's face looking above me; his light brown hair framed the concern in his eyes. "It's you!" I shouted, as I reached to hug him tightly. Taking my hand, he looked into my eyes and didn't say anything; he was just relieved that I was okay.

"Wow!" I said, as I opened my eyes to another face. Chief Joseph was amused at my return from the past. "That was romantic," I said, "what a rush!" Continuing to smile, he projected almost a sarcastic humor. "What?" I said, defensively, "It *was* romantic!" Interrupting my rampage, Joseph said, "I want you to remember now. You've traversed many lifetimes since the beginning of your journey. You've remembered many pasts." "Yes," I replied, "I have." "Well, tell me if you see a pattern." Pausing a moment to think, I replied, "I saw the pattern of unrequited love, that was obvious." "Do you see another in your many lives of adventures, mercenaries . . . battles of the light and the dark?" He was so serious now; it almost ruined the fun of my little adventure. "Well, I get really excited in those battles." I said. "You even thought it romantic?" Joseph questioned. Pausing to think, I was afraid I might be getting trapped into the truth. "Okay, yeah." "How could this affect you now . . . in your path?" "Well," I mused, "maybe in my relationships . . . or my life in general . . . maybe I have a tendency to get bored with calm . . . peace." "But yet, you say you want peace?" Joseph was inspiring intense thinking within me now. "Yeah, isn't that strange?" "You are turned on by adrenaline, not love." Joseph said. "This is why you are drawn to the dramatic, bored with peace." "My Gosh!" I screamed, "You are right! I get turned on by battling the dark forces on the ground or torrid romances . . . you're right! I do!" Joseph reached the peace pipe to me as I took another smoke. "When you travel the pathway to life," he said, "you begin to alter the energy that surrounds evolution, by that very existence. There are various stages of the evolution of humanity; one stage is the battles that occur on the ground, highly dramatic; and the next stage, energetic alteration, highly peaceful. Now that you are embarking upon this energetic alteration, those parts of you which still entertain fancies of the dramatic must be prepared to become peaceful. Then the energy works *through* you, rather than *by* you . . . and it happens all the time, whether you are aware of it or not." Somewhat ashamed, I asked, "How do I transform those parts?" Joseph was kind, "First, you become aware that they exist, and then you are able to recognize that which no longer serves your path. Those lingering questions, thoughts, fantasies created in your own mind about what was or could have been . . . are only that. Love is not what you have believed it to be, it is not torrid romance or danger-filled rescues . . . love is patient and kind . . ." Smiling, Joseph disappeared on a wisp of smoke from his pipe.

"Love is patient and kind; love is not jealous or boastful; it is not arrogant or rude. Love does not insist on its own way; it is not irritable or resentful; it does not rejoice at wrong but rejoices in the right. Love bears all things, believes all things, hopes all things, endures all things. Love never ends. As for prophecies, they will pass away; as for tongues, they will cease; as for knowledge, it will pass away. For our knowledge is imperfect and our prophecy is imperfect; but when the perfect comes, the imperfect will pass away. When I was a child, I spoke like a child, I thought like a child, I reasoned like a child; when I became a man, I gave up childish ways. For now we see in a mirror dimly, but then face to face. Now I know in part; then I shall understand fully, even as I have been fully understood. So faith, hope, love abide, these three; but the greatest of these is love."

The Holy Bible, Revised Standard Version, 1 Corinthians 13: 4-13, (Christianity, Words of Paul)

****

And so it came to pass that Joseph took me aboard a starship to show me the state of the auric field of the Earth. Showing me the former earth of many moons ago, a triangular grid was surrounding the planet keeping it in balance, energetically. Meshed together, the triangles were in harmony when mankind's thoughts reflected harmony. When the Earth had once been peaceful, the electrical currents of negativity and evil still struck at the field, but were kept in check by the grid. As Joseph showed me the grid that surrounded the Earth now, I began to cry. Everything was a complete electrical distortion, as energy blitzed out in every direction, like thousands of lightning bolts striking all at once. Falling away in one corner of the planet, the triangular part of the grid was dissipating from the energetic imbalances of mankind's thoughts and deeds.

Chief Joseph put his arm around my shoulder. "It is sad," he said. "What has happened?" I asked. "Death to the ways of life, death of the spirit." I nodded. "As life dissipates from those who inhabit a planet, the energy of life can no longer hold on." "Is this our future?" "That all depends." "On what?" "On you . . . on me . . . on every being who walks the Earth." "What can we do?" "Walk the pathway; walk *with* life, not against it. Life will beget a new Earth." The starship was moving towards Mars, and Joseph took my hand. Joining us as we began to fly to Mars, the starship captain listened to the chief.

Floating on the pink energy of the angels, we soared to Venus to gather the white light of love. Returning to Earth, the energetic disturbances were strong and continual, but we took the energy and distributed it amongst the entire auric field of the Earth. Pulling the grid haphazardly into some shape, it was still incomplete but it would give the Earth more time. "You know," Joseph said, "one person really does make a difference. One person who cares amongst an entire planet is all it takes." "What do you mean?" I asked. "Caring is powerful. If one person . . . one person . . . asks that it be saved . . . prays to the spirit of life, to the Great Spirit, that planet may be saved for that one caring soul. If you care . . . just you . . . that might be enough to pull it off." The light trails were flowing all around us. "Caring brings clarity, and clarity will balance the earth. Then it will shine a radiant blue, green and gold throughout the universe." "Wow, won't that be beautiful?" "It will, it will, my friend."

"Let me show you something." Joseph said, as we entered the starship which was now heading straight into the Earth's energy field. "I want to show you where life, peace and caring still exist." Landing amongst a mountainous region, we walked towards a winding river. Sitting on an old log by the water, I noticed my reflection. "What do you see?" He asked. "Life is everywhere, the trees, the river, the fish . . . Oh!" I was dumbfounded as I noticed a beautiful white-tailed deer striding through the woods. "Oh, how beautiful!" I shouted. "Do you know where we are?" Joseph asked. "No." I replied. "We are in the energetic reality which surrounds the earth, the ether reality that wishes to descend into physical reality." The deer was staring at me. "Who is it?" I said under my breath. "Oh, my God, it isn't!" "Yes, he's free now." (A few days before, I had found a deer that had been ritually sacrificed in the woods. I'd gone to a great deal of trouble to try to get the perpetrators caught, but to no avail, but afterwards focused on the traumatized soul of the animal, freeing him from the bondage of his death.) "Oh, he's so beautiful, how could anyone . . . how could they?" "That is past, look to the now." "Why does he keep looking at me?" "He is grateful." "For what? I was unable to help him." "You cared." Giving me an intentioned glance, the sun caught its eye as it glimmered like a diamond. Suddenly, he leapt into the wilderness.

"I have something else to show you." Joseph said. I was so busy admiring this beautiful natural world that when I looked up and saw a highway, I was totally taken aback. "How'd that get there?" I asked, almost angry. "We've now entered the physical reality of the place we were." Litter was strewn everywhere, the mountains were covered with electrical poles, highways, houses, smokestacks, but there was one sacred space remaining . . . where we sat. Looking in the water, I noticed my reflection again.

The starship captain walked forward, as Chief Joseph disappeared. "We must go now. Our ship only remains in the energy field of the earth for a short time! Come!" Running to the ship which was now perched on a dusty highway, the eyes of the deer were still piercing my mind. Somehow we had become one, because of our mutual caring. Shuddering momentarily as it rocketed out of the electrical disturbance of the Earth, the starship eventually shot forth.

Mankind bears free will which bears its own cost. Angels can only interfere with the natural results of our thoughts and deeds when given the eternal directive to do so. And this eternal directive is only given to protect the evolutionary programs of souls, or to protect souls from their own ignorance.

There does come a time when we are no longer afforded protection, when we are expected to accept the results of our own thoughts and deeds, because as every soul matures, he is required to take on greater responsibility.

And so it came to pass that Chief Joseph and the angels began to teach me of evolution, as it was a part of my purpose to give back some of that which had been given to me.

"'A man of realization does not perform any miracle until he receives an inward sanction.' Master explained. 'God does not wish the secrets of His creation revealed promiscuously. Also, every individual in the world has an inalienable right to his free will. A saint will not encroach on that independence.'"
The Autobiography of a Yogi, Chapter 12, Page 136, Paragraph 5, (Hinduism, Kriya Yoga, Author: Paramahansa Yogananda)

****

Following the sound of a distant drumming, I found Chief Joseph surrounded by a large tribe of Indians. "Graduation requires a rite of passage." Joseph said, as I looked at him quizzically. Beginning to create something in his hands, it was a ball of light. Handing it to me, he said, "This is the medicine, take it with you." "What medicine?" I asked. "You will know." Joseph said, as I was suddenly transported elsewhere.

Having entered a crowded restaurant, a flash of information suddenly came into my soul. I *knew* that, in a moment, a man was going to run into this public place and begin randomly shooting at people, and it was my job to stop it. Panicking, I ran towards the door as the man entered and blocked his gunfire with my body, taking the shots into myself and falling to the ground. The man stopped shooting.

Chief Joseph's voice spoke in my head, "Try again, you'll understand." But the same scene repeated two more times, and I responded in a similar fashion. What made it more difficult was that before each try, I couldn't remember having done it immediately before.

Appearing to me with his peace pipe, Joseph looked at me intensely. Suddenly, I saw them. Their energies were phasing in and out, in and out. Hundreds of them appeared in a circle of energy around me. Chief Joseph continued smoking the pipe. "These are the Medicine Women from throughout the ages," he said, as one approached me holding a white-fringed native dress, moccasins and a pair of wings. Humble and quiet in her demeanor, she said, "We wish to pass our medicine onto you." Amazingly honored, but also deeply afraid, I replied, "I don't know. I don't know if I even want to be a Medicine Woman. I don't even know what that really means." She was unmoved by my cowardice, "You will know," she said, "receiving the medicine is receiving that knowledge." Hesitating, I didn't say anything more. "Just try one more time, see how you do." Her patience made me feel somewhat ashamed. "Okay," I said, cautiously allowing myself to be drawn into the state of unremembering again.

As the man walked into the room, I looked down in my hands noticing the gift from Chief Joseph. "The ball of light!" I thought loudly. Throwing the ball towards the man's hands, it began to meander through the air because of my pathetic aim, but the power of the medicine quickly swept it up and carried it to its proper destination, knocking the gun out of the man's hand and rendering him unconscious.

Apparently, it is better to alter something without allowing harm to come to your own soul, for this keeps you strong to do God's work, and although my initial approach was successful in the accomplishment of the directive, the purpose of attaining the medicine is to become capable of altering realities without taking on the destructive energies you have come to alter. The destructive energies must be altered, not just redirected.

Joining the Medicine Women in celebration, we were engaging in a ritual designed to assist me in becoming one of them, the Buffalo women.

Giving me a garment consisting of a white buckskin pantsuit, two white moccasins, and a pair of white buckskin wings, I wore it as they danced and rattled all around me. Energies were vortexing, lightning was striking, and energetic particles began merging throughout and within, as my soul became fire, energizing me in the ways of the medicine. Hair turning long and black, the energies were transforming me into a true native. Becoming one with them, a familiar face appeared. Red Jacket sat down peacefully by the fire, smiling in pleasure at this rite of passage achieved. Knowing this to be the fulfillment of the prophecy which foresaw my entry into the lodge of the Buffalo women, I accepted it with humility.

Moments later, I was standing before a statue of an Indian chief which began to give me detailed instructions for an upcoming alteration. My spirit was flown to the scene in an instant.

Whizzing in, I caused a spirit wind strong enough to force the three people in the store to the floor. As they did this, bullets began to spray their building. Remaining on the floor where they might be safe, I applied energetic pressure to a phone in order to call for emergency assistance. An ambulance and the police arrived very quickly.

Dying of a blood disease, the perpetrator of this horrid act had remained very bitter about his shortened life. Hovering inside the ambulance, they had placed him inside, as no one else had been hurt. Hovering to take on an energetic understanding of his state of mind, I learned that he was getting much weaker. Reaching into my pocket, I now had many balls of light within them. Placing them around him on the stretcher, he went into a deep peaceful sleep.

Saying nothing when he came out of his body, I noticed him staring at my image, covered in white robes and light. Smiling, I handed him some energy from my hands. Imagining light swirling about the room, it did. Looking at it in wonder, he seemed to become calmer. "Everything's going to be okay, isn't it?" He asked. Nodding that he indeed had nothing to fear in death, he gently fell back into his body. Now a peaceful soul, he was grateful that no one had been harmed by his wretched act, and that he had been protected from the deserved consequences of his own wrath.

Chief Joseph was standing amidst the great ocean as he handed me a sacred book. Holding it open, I tried very desperately to absorb all the knowledge contained within it before my time to view it had come to pass. "You hold the medicine now, my friend, do you realize what this means?" Nodding no, Joseph said, "You are no longer Marilynn . . . you are life itself." Turning, he walked quietly atop the waters away into the distance, and then faded from my sight.

And so it came to pass that I began entry into the realms of energetic alteration, but also continued to receive information about others who came into my life on the ground. The information ranged from past-life knowledge, warnings about upcoming events which could be altered if another path was taken, warnings and specific information about the actual energetic alignments of people in their lives, specific spiritual insight into the issues that blocked them, messages from deceased loved ones, etc. Limited only to what the Lord deems to share with me, I would often pray to receive on behalf of others who ask of it, because this light is only given if and when the Lord chooses.

"If you saw that a man was going to hit another, you could step in front of the intended victim and let the blow fall on you. That is what a great master does. He perceives, in the lives of his devotees, when unfavorable effects of their past bad karma are about to descend on them. If he thinks it wise, he employs a certain metaphysical method by which he transfers to himself the consequences of his disciples errors. The law of cause and effect operates mechanically or mathematically; yogis understand how to switch its currents."
Sayings of Paramahansa Yogananda, Page 47, Stanza 2, (Hinduism, Kriya Yoga, Words

of Paramahansa Yogananda)

"It would help much to increase the humility of those who are endeavoring to obtain that virtue, so dear to the heart of God, if they were to present themselves before Him with these sins, as it were, upon them, the sins that God in His Truth sees they would have committed if they had not been prevented by God's watchful Providence, turning them from paths in life that would have been fatal to them, giving special assistance at certain times of danger, and in the numberless other ways by which He shows His care for those who are dear to Him .
. . "

Devotion for the Dying, Mary's Call to Her Loving Children, Page 175, Paragraph 1,
(Christianity, Catholic, Author: Mother Mary Potter)

****

"In order to understand life," Chief Joseph said, "we must first understand death."

Soaring to another lifetime, I was working in an old frontier bank. Only moments passed before a bomb exploded, killing me instantly. As I lay in death, Chief Joseph whispered, "Dead man's might . . . and the light spread." Another light came and suddenly I was aboard an old ship during a massive sea storm. Preparing to sink, we had only minutes to live before the water reached the ceiling below deck. Our last breaths filled our watery grave. Surprised at how quick and painless these deaths were, Chief Joseph whispered into my ear again, "Life manages, life slates, from on and on into eternity." "Amen." I added. Reflecting on these moments and how I no longer felt anything, I asked, "Death is no longer *feeling*?" "Exactly," he said, "Vitality is life. Numbness is death. When you no longer *feel*, you are dead."

"It is not death, but a bad life, which destroys the soul."
The Pythagorean Sourcebook, Select Sentences of Sextus the Pythagorean, No. 91,
(Mystery Religions, Pythagorean)

****

And so it came to pass that Chief Joseph taught me the mysteries of evolution as we sat at his fire smoking the pipe of peace, a little bit of which I share with you now. "If what is, is; then what is not, is not. In the kaleidoscope of creation, what is continually expands and changes. What is depends entirely upon the point of now in which you peer through. What is, in this now, is. But what was, in another now, no longer remains, unless you separate that point in time."

"Evolution is like a bit of tobacco. If you light a flame to the tobacco, it catches fire. In moments, smoke will begin to rise, curling into the air, parts dissipating and parts becoming. Creation is the flame, for it is the fire of love which forever changes everything it touches. Tobacco will remain tobacco indefinitely unless something changes. But if it is touched by the flame, it will no longer be tobacco. Transformed by the flame into a completely different substance, it becomes ash. Life is transformed by the flame of love, just like the tobacco is transformed by the fire; nothing remains of what once was. What is . . . is no more. What is holds the memory of what was, but no longer is what was."

"If in one moment, lies all eternity; then all time, holds all things. Time is like a kaleidoscope. If you were to place a blue bead in a kaleidoscope which had only red, yellow, white and green beads within it, you could watch the transformation of a piece of God. A singular bead is a moment in time; perhaps a lifetime, a fragment of a soul. All the beads together represent all lifetimes and all life. Looking through the kaleidoscope, you will notice that with every movement of your hand, the images will constantly change unless you stop applying the movement. Appearing as a star at one moment, it's a triangle the next. If there is only one blue bead in your kaleidoscope, you will notice that it continually moves and changes according to the movement of the entire creation. The image never remains the same, it no longer is, what was, but yet, all the separate parts which create it remain the same. Creation can be seen in this manner. All moments exist as one, yet are continually altered by that which we become in the current point of now. Every piece remains essentially the same, yet is completely transformed by that which we become in the present."

"Although (the consciousness) appears in other ways, its nature remains the same as before and is permanent . . . Consciousness appears in other ways, and although the (different modes) are not true, (their nature) is one and true . . . It is the nature of merely being conscious that is one and true."
A Guide to the Bodhisattva's Way of Life, Chapter IX, Part II, Page 155, Stanza 3, (Buddhism, Tibetan, Author: Shantideva)

"Let us return to the tobacco seed. What we are as humanity, can either energize or de-energize evolution. All begins with the tiny seed of life which God entrusts to every one of us. Imagine a small seed of tobacco which represents your portion in God's plan for humanity. As you place this seed upon the earth, you know that each part of humanity has a choice of what they will do with their own seed. Some will grow into vibrant and healthy plants, while other's seeds will wither into nothing, ceasing to grow . . . death. If you give your seed the water of life, the living water of the eternal, the seed has the potential to blossom into a beautiful plant . . . or it may wither into nothing, but you water this seed because you know that this water gives it the *potential* to grow. If you give it nothing, we know for a certainty that it will die. The water is caring. A world that has thrived on old ways needs to be watered regularly to grow. But you must also understand that what is . . . is. Humanity is still a seed, but what is, is never a constant, as it is always changing."

"Note the unfolding order in the growth of a tree from seed to new seed; reflect on the continuous effort in all stages after self-propagation . . . Furthermore, if you can think spiritually enough, you will see that this energy does not come from the seed, nor from the sun of the world, which is only fire, but is in the seed from God the Creator . . . and is from Him not only at the moment of creation, but ever after, too."
Divine Providence, Chapter 1, No. 3, Paragraph 2, (Christianity, Swedenborgianism, Author: Emanuel Swedenborg)

"Understanding this, we must take the knowledge of evolution even farther. Evolution comes in phases, not all at once. What is now, is now, and what will be, is not now. Evolution takes place when the seed recognizes what is, and allows life to direct its course in a pattern of becoming. Individually, we energize evolution by becoming, and this comes about from an understanding of cause and effect and personal responsibility."

"Every realm has its own laws of cause and effect. You know that if you jump off a mountain in your astral body, you will fly. But if you do the same thing in your physical body, you will fall to the ground and be crushed to death. This is cause and effect. Because humanity is a karmic species, they tend to constantly run into one another and bump off of each other's programs. Karma tends to invade other programs in search of the missing part of itself which resides with God. Because the Earth is a karmic realm, most human souls operate in karmic desire, which has many varying manifestations of selfishness. Karmic souls live primarily off of the energies of others, although there is some self-generation present."

"An eternal soul does not have the same need, which is why they thrive in aloneness and silence, and have a wish to be unseen. An eternal soul lives from the light within, and the knowledge of oneness, not from the energies of others."

"Because of the deluded state of karmic programs, those involved in them often do not recognize the cause and effect of their actions, and feel they are victim to circumstance and bad luck. But the reality remains, if you follow the ways of gluttony, you may get fat and unhealthy; if you follow the ways of lust, you may have children out of wedlock, be victim to a number of diseases, suffer from frequent heartaches, and never find true love; if you follow the ways of greed, you may or may not have many things in life, but you may never find meaning or peace of soul; if you are prideful, you may be blind to your own corruption, perceive yourself above others, and ignorant to the ways of the spirit; if you follow the ways of sloth, you shall never achieve anything of significance on the ground, or up above; if you follow the ways of vanity, you may be compulsory in your need for attention, and your soul shall be marred by the self-gratification it craves, unable to see the true need's of other soul's, unable to give love or receive it in a true sense; and if you follow the ways of avarice, which is unforgiving and hateful, you shall also be unforgiven and hated. Worst of all, if you follow any of these ways, you may never truly know God."

"When a target is set, arrows are shot at it, when a woods is luxuriant, axes are taken to it. It is not that they beckon it, but it happens as the result of the situation."
Wen-Tzu, No. 94, Page 86, Paragraph 5, (Buddhism, Taoism, Words of Lao Tsu)

Chief Joseph also taught that our intention is just as important as our action. "The energetic truth behind all that we do determines the validity of an interaction, not simply moral reasoning. We are protected for a time when we are ignorant from the true effects of some of our own causes, but after a certain point, we will no longer be afforded protection and the full magnitude of our causes will become effects."

Chief Joseph's face became very dreamy as I began to remember the harm I had done to others. Deeply ashamed, Joseph wanted me to feel this, but he was compassionate, "Remember the energetic truth; it determines the validity of all interaction. You were protected as you followed your karmic path, your own destiny protected you, but if you were to engage in such acts now, you would not be protected. Because your destiny protected you, you have attained knowledge, and your actions actually energized your path." Knowing this did not lessen my remorse, for it is through remorse and repentance that humility is birthed. Sincere ignorance is understood, even compassionately, but *chosen* darkness is not tolerated by the Lord.

"They will come in five winds," Chief Joseph said, as he disappeared.

"And the wickedness of a Soul is ignorance; for the Soul that knows nothing of the things that are, neither the Nature of them, nor that which is good, but is blinded, rusheth and dasheth against the bodily passions; and unhappy as it is, and not knowing itself, it serveth strange bodies and evil ones, carrying the Body as a burden, and not ruling but ruled: And this is the mischief of the Soul."
The Divine Pymander of Hermes, Fourth Book, No. 27, (Mystery Religions, Egyptian/Hermetic, Words of Hermes)

****

Beginning to teach me how to manifest in and out of realities, we began to fulfill the prophecy of Toam. "You have learned that what is . . . is. And you have crossed into the understanding of personal responsibility. Now you are ready to undertake the threshold of energetic responsibility." Pausing, I didn't yet understand him. "When you are given the gift of knowledge, you must then take responsibility for alteration of energy throughout your realm." "Wow," I said, "that sounds intense." "It is a great gift." Joseph said. "When it is given, you will be tested, not just once, but continually. What you choose to use this gift for, will determine whether it remains." "Okay, I'm ready." I said. Joseph conveyed to me that the medicine was already my own, and that now I must use it to shift, alter and energize life in our realm. "But . . ." I asked. "It's the next phase, Marilynn. That means you don't know it, yet."

"It often happens that we pray God to deliver us from some dangerous temptation, and yet God does not hear us but permits the temptation to continue troubling us. In such a case, let us understand that God permits even this for our greater good. When a soul in temptation recommends itself to God, and by His aid resists, O how it then advances in perfection."

The Voice of the Saints, In Temptation, Page 68-69, (Christianity, Catholic, Words of St. Alphonsus Liguori)

****

Quietly lighting his pipe, Chief Joseph returned. "Very few incarnate beings act purely in conjunction with the spirit," he said, "to do so requires a surrender of their own will to a Greater One, but it is only by this that true power is achieved." Handing me the pipe, he began showing me images of all I'd seen throughout my journey to date. "It's so beautiful," I replied, "I'm so blessed and so grateful. To think how many people would *die* to see what I've seen." Chief Joseph looked very serious. "To think how many people *have to* die, to see what you've seen." "What do you mean?" I asked. "People do not reach for it, until they die. They do not think of it, until they die. And many who do are not willing to become energetically responsible, to give up their existence as a glorified part, and become a part of the one." Intrigued, I asked, "But why, why is that Joseph?"

Becoming very upset, his face showed an intensity of emotion I'd never seen in him before, as his eyebrows wrinkled in worry. "Because they refuse to *see*, they refuse to *reach*, they refuse to *change*, and most of all, they refuse to *care*! They do not recognize that which has value, it has to be given to them in such a way that precludes their own discernment." Pausing, he looked at me as I absorbed the deep impact of that truth. Beginning to lighten, he said, "This is why those of you who are willing to see, reach, change and care become so important. You are the ones who take on the energetic responsibility for your world, altering those things that could destroy it if there hadn't been intervention. You know that your significance lies in conjunction with your spirit, and you realize that the knowledge of your many selves is meaningless if it is not linked with higher knowledge. Reaching to the Great Spirit requires pure intention, otherwise it means nothing."

Looking off into a magnificent sunset that had just begun, Chief Joseph took another smoke from his pipe. "Today is a wonderful day!" He almost shouted, to my confused look. "Wonderful?" I replied, "It sounds so very sad. So many people will die without knowing the truth, without caring, without becoming even a tiny part of their highest potential." Smiling, Joseph quietly said, "But not you." A small tear fell from the corner of my eyes, as I was so grateful for all I'd been shown, all I'd learned. "Today we bring home one of our own," Joseph said, "take the pipe, it is yours."

Handing me the sacred pipe, I was stunned. But as it touched my hands, the energies all around me began to stir, phasing in and out. Appearing and disappearing with the energies, the Medicine Women who had initiated me into their fold were appearing and disappearing with the energies. Hair becoming long and black, my white buckskin dress felt good, pure, energized and lively. Becoming fully native, fully Indian, I suddenly became one with them . . . and I was gone.

"When the superior man hears the Way, he is scarcely able to put it into practice. When the middling man hears the Way, he appears now to preserve it, now to lose it. When the inferior man hears the Way, he laughs at it loudly. If he did not laugh, it would not be fit to be the Way."
Tao Te Ching, No. 3, Stanza 1, (Buddhism, Taoism, Words of Lao Tsu, Translation: Victor Mair)

****

As all things occur in an energetic realm before they hit the ground, this is where the Lord's warriors go to assist in the five winds of alteration which are undertaken by guardian angels, eternal warriors, and various souls who work for the Lord. Five winds of alteration take place: 1) Alteration of perception, 2) Alteration of the outcome of a physical event, 3) Removal of dark energies around souls, 4) Removal of evil spirits or demons around souls, 5) Rendering benign or de-energizing demons that are incarnate in human form. Beginning with the first wind, my first mission involved the alteration of perception.

Appearing in energy form, I had awakened in a mountain hold with six other astral spirits who were my students. Two women were walking in the woods, and I immediately knew that they were going to be killed by a group of people who were angry because the women were planning to terminate their pregnancies. Attempting to take charge, a couple of men in the alteration group were unaware that they didn't have eternal permission to do so. "We'll wait behind those bushes for the killers, and then we'll kill them before they kill the women." Surprised by their arrogance, I quietly said, "We will not."

Although they were perceiving an actual physical death, in alteration the term 'kill' actually means a fatal blow to the energetic field of the perpetrator, de-energizing their physical ability to perform a particular destructive action, rendering benign the energy behind the destructive source.

"We will not," I repeated, "we will go to the group in the woods and take a bigger risk for a better alteration." Confused but obedient, I hid my own fears as I walked forward while the trainees stayed behind. One of the men spoke up as I approached the group, "But what are you going to say?" "I don't know," I honestly replied, "I just go with guidance, I don't act on my own accord."

Walking forward into the group of about fifteen people, the leader approached me immediately. As he had given a flower to each member of his group, he handed one to me. Taking their flowers, the others had started a bonfire, but I held mine to my heart. "Who are you?" He asked. Smiling at him, I said nothing. Two women approached; the potential victims in a well-planned murder. As violence began to erupt, I lifted my hands, sending a lighted beam all around the group suspending them in time. They couldn't have moved if they tried . . . but no one tried. Recognizing that this was a force outside of their control, they surrendered.

Walking towards the two victims, I held their hands and led them to talk to the others about their lives, their pregnancies, and their fears; and as I allowed the lighted beam to lift, the violent feelings had been completely de-energized. Replaced by sincere interest, caring and love, the formerly hateful group emerged with a sincere desire to help these women find other options. I was gone.

"When we believe that ours is the only faith that contains the truth, violence and suffering will surely be the result."
Living Buddha, Living Christ, Chapter 1, Page 2, Paragraph 1, (Buddhism, Author: Thich Naht Hahn)

"The angels, however, also have the power to function in a supernormal fashion within their own normal areas of activity. They then act with more strength and force than is required for the natural order. This occurs when they act to bring about miracles and wonders in the world, according to God's will."
The Way of God, Part III, Chapter 2, No. 7, Paragraph 4, Page 197, (Judaism, Author: Rabbi Moshe Chayim Luzzatto)

Alone in an energetic void, I awaited my next mission only to be surprised by the arrival of one of the young men who had initially tried to take charge of my first operation. No longer confrontational, he was very nervous, and kept looking around. "Who are you looking for?" I asked. "The others in the group," he said, "I can't do this alone." Smiling, I took his hand. "The spirit path can only be taken alone. We all want to bring somebody with us, hoping their presence will give us the support we need to move on. But it is only in our aloneness that the spirit path appears to us."

Taking a guitar off his shoulder that had been bound by a strap, he asked, "But how can I leave them?" His concern was a common one. "You cannot bring somebody from the outside in, if you try, you will fail. The spirit path is within; all that is without cannot go there." "How can I go there?" He asked. "Live your life according to caring, do not become self-righteous, but seek to become the highest ideal within yourself. *Be* the light, but do not be afraid of the darkness. Allow things to be altered *through* you, rather than *by* you. And never exalt yourself above the human race, because it is only by being fully human *and* fully spirit that you may serve and ultimately give humanity a higher definition." Face filling with wonder, he reached to hug me before he would be gone. Disappearing into the ether, I saw a single tear fall from his eyes. "Today is a wonderful day!" I shouted to him, as he disappeared.

Chief Joseph's face gleamed brightly in the sky as suddenly the pipe he had given to me appeared in my hand. Blowing upon it a single breath so that it would light, I took a smoke. Joseph began singing and making hand signals. Forming a teepee with his hands, he then clasped his hands together. Knowing that the first sign meant 'teepee' or 'home,' the second meant to 'come together.' Inviting me to join him at his lodge, I reflected upon this great man's earthly life. Chief Joseph died on September 21, 1904 while sitting next to the fire in his lodge. Spending his life fighting for justice, many say he died of a broken heart, broken by the unkept promises and violence perpetuated upon his people.

Heinmetooyalakekt, his Indian name has been translated as 'Thunder Rolling in the Mountains.' As he began to disappear from my view, he told me the correct translation, 'Thunder Traveling to Loftier Heights.' Then he was gone.

"You, O religious souls who live in the prison chosen by Love, often deemed useless and even dangerous in the eyes of the world, have no fear; in your solitude and moments of stress, let the world rant against you . . . only join your heart yet closer to God, the one object of your affections, and do all you can to repair for the sins and the outrages of mankind."
The Way of Divine Love, Page 272, Paragraph 2, (Christianity, Catholic, Words of Christ, Author: Sister Josefa Menendez)

****

"Know ye, O man, that all of the future is an open book to him who can read. All effect shall bring forth its causes, as all effects grew from the first cause. Know ye, the future is not fixed or stable, but varies as cause brings forth an effect. Look in the cause thou shalt bring into being, and surely thou shalt see that all is effect."
The Emerald Tablets of Thoth the Atlantean, Tablet XII, Page 65, Paragraph 2, (Mystery Religions, Egyptian/Hermetic, Words of Thoth)

Chief Joseph stood before me for only a moment. "Remember the bright white light," he said, as I thought of the gift of the medicine, "you must give back that which has been taken. Restore that which has been lost." Pausing for a moment, he began to slowly dissipate, "You must return to the mountains in the sky and learn from the Old Ones." Then he was gone.

"This day is salvation come to this house . . . for the Son of man is come to seek and to save that which was lost."
King James Bible, New Testament, Luke 19:9-10, (Christianity, Catholic, Words of Christ)

****

Venturing upon an ancient time, my long tattered dress seemed a burden to me within these prison walls. Almost full-term, my pregnancy remained a sign of the rape that had occurred at the hands of the native men who'd captured me many months ago. Standing before the Chief, who was angry and burdened by what this young brave had done, the rapist with bushy hair wore nothing but a loincloth. A very honorable man, the Chief had charge over these cave dwellers, but his hair was long, black and straight, unlike the others.

In the center of the cave was a fire-pit holding red-hot burning rocks. Now that the two stood before each other in confrontation, the rapist took a burning rock and began searing his own skin upon his chest, making three horizontal lines which bled profusely. Somehow a sign of bravery, he began to laugh with an evil tone as he tossed the still raging and fiery rock to the Chief. In his mind, there was no way the Chief could top this sign he had made.

Surprising us all, however, the Chief caught the rock in his bare hands as its solidity became more and more fragile. Reaching it to his mouth, he bit into it as blood began pouring out into his hands. This was a very powerful symbol, one that surprised the younger native, and showed superior strength. "I will take your heart out!" the Chief said.

The strongest words an eternal alterer may utter, 'taking someone's heart out' means that they will be made to look upon it, and to truly *feel* all the pain they have inflicted upon others, thus, coming to the receptive end of their own defilement. There is no greater suffering than this.

"He also saw a skull floating on the water; he said to it: 'Because you drowned others, they drowned you; and those who drowned you will be drowned eventually."

The Siddur, Minchah for Sabbath, Page 553, No. 7, (Judaism)

****

Fire was raging all around us, as I hovered with the angels over the Earth. A section on the planet earth was bursting with darkness, and although I didn't immediately understand what was happening, I assisted the angels in energizing a destruct/construct operation in the area. A large city was completely on fire and the angels . . . were energizing the action. But simultaneously, the angels were energizing a 'construct' to fill the voided space once the dark destructive energy had depleted itself; an angelic realm to reside above the city.

Sadly, we knew that in order to construct something higher, we had to be willing to allow the destruction of the lower. But destructs of this magnitude were rare, and proper respect for the magnitude of this action was vital to carrying it out successfully.

Two days after this experience, the L.A. riots broke out over the city of angels, the city of the alteration. Fires, looting and murder abounded for days, but afterwards, the people began to work together to clean up the horrible remains of this expulsion of the dark energies. Now it would be up to them to guardian their thoughts and deeds, to energize the higher construct which remained only as a potential; a hoped for reality.

Light energy is energized action and provides construction, whereas, dark energy is de-energized action and provides destruction. Light energy goes towards life, creates and serves dominion. Dark energy goes away from life, towards death, destroys, and serves domination. Light energy is energized and, therefore, provides for itself, whereas, dark energy is de-energized and, therefore, is parasitic of others.

Energy magnetically draws its like to itself, and thus, when dark energy is expressed - either through thought or action - it begins to magnetically draw similar energies towards itself.

Over time this energy can form clouds of darkness requiring destruct operations, which are required to actually energize the depletion of increasingly harmful or dangerous mass retain. By depleting its energy, it deactivates future potential destructive capabilities and makes room for new constructive action.

Dark energies consume and destroy until they are expunged and depleted, because dark energy is continuously destructive at random. Destruct operations energize a high level of destruction to occur within a short period of time to completely deplete the energetic cloud. A construct action follows because it places the potential within the etheric atmosphere for souls to be turned towards the light.

Clouds of energy like these are created by the mass thoughts and deeds of humanity. Because man has free will, they are given the freedom to choose between darkness and light. Because of the nature of mortal realms, that of karmic circling, almost everyone incarnate soul is circulating his own specialized delusions, which are, in essence, dark. Delusion is darkness, although there are many levels of darkness upon which delusion can take form. God limits the scope of the chaos through his angels, who enter into the world to alter and change energies, thoughts, actions or deeds which would be destructive to individual or mass programs. Doing this for our own protection, without it, many of us would die premature deaths and never learn anything.

Various levels of understanding exist in mortal realms, the lowest being evil which are turned on by power and domination and enjoy causing serious harm to others. Dominant darkness is controlled by vice, and chooses darkness consciously, usually by rationalizing bad acts as good, and it perceives *true* goodness as naive and inferior. Ignorance, on the other hand, wants to do what is right, but rarely does so because it is controlled by karmic delusions.

Because all who are incarnate have unseen karmic defilement, much of what happens to us can seem unfair or unjust, when if seen through the eyes of clarity, it is quite easily discernible as karmic retribution. But there are also things which occur simply because men have free will. No great eternal purpose may underlie a grievous action, and it may simply be a tragic act of evil. Because the mortal realms are dominated by the battles between good and evil, good does not always win. Everybody can help this situation by looking closely at what they truly generate on the ground.

"The adviser says to him, 'If you see those whom you know personally, as well as other travelers, be they men or women, tell them that there are many poisons and evils on that path which can cause them to lose their very nature and life. Do not let them seek their own deaths."
Sutra of the Past Vows of Earth Store Bodhisattva, Chapter 8, Page 182, Paragraph 2, (Buddhism, Pure Land)

****

Sand blowing across the desert, my spirit manifested in a dank political prison somewhere in the Middle East. Thirty new prisoners had arrived, and I was immediately made aware of my assignment. If it were not accomplished very quickly, this reality could not be turned back, and all these souls would suffer and die in this truly God forsaken place.

Naked men and women laid in their own feces, roaches and rats crawling all over them. Aching, my heart had never been witness to such torture. Manifesting as a woman who'd just arrived, we had not yet been put in the cages with the other prisoners. Distracting the guards by being loud and obnoxious, the eternal gave the command to the others to use this distraction to make an escape attempt. Hesitant to do so, they feared they would leave me behind; but as I urged them on, they ran for it. Guards attempted to run after them, but I lunged forward using my body as a shield to trip them.

Leading to my capture, I was brought back to a torture chamber where they put me on a rack and beheaded me. They hadn't realized that this was an energetic reality, so I just put my head back on. Staring at me in confusion and fear, I looked at them coldly. "I will take your heart out," I said. As the words came from my mouth, they all began grasping their own necks, screaming in terror and pain.

Returning to form, there had been nothing left to say as the eternal command had come. Chief Joseph appeared before me, "I am very happy with your efforts!" "Everything is so complex!" I replied, "I feel overwhelmed, there is so much darkness that must be altered!" In his eyes, I could see that he understood, as a concerned tear fell down his cheek. For a moment, I couldn't help but wonder if he was reflecting upon his own people, and what had been done to them. Reaching to touch his hand, he smiled and disappeared.

"Great are Your deeds and mighty, humbling the haughty and straightening the bent; even if man lived thousands of years, he could not fathom the extent of your powerful deeds . . . God to Whom belongs honor and greatness, save Your sheep from the mouth of lions, and bring Your people out from the nation of its exile . . . "
The Siddur, Sabbath Evening Meal, Page 367, Stanza 2-4, (Judaism)

****

The hostage situation was out of hand when I arrived, as the perpetrators were enraged. One woman had already been killed and a black man had been stabbed in the leg before I'd even gotten there. As I manifested into the potential future, I was immediately targeted for violence because I'd appeared on behalf of the light. Leading this band of angry people were those who served darkness, but those who followed their violent ways were suffering from karmic delusion and ignorance and they were misled.

As I'd already energized the seeds to end this hostage crisis, the leaders wanted to kill me. Holding a knife to my throat, the man who served utter darkness was losing favor with his followers who were uncomfortable with the violence they had seen perpetrated. But they didn't have the courage to stand up to this very dangerous man. Making a stand against racism, the perpetrators were black people who were angry at the white race due to injustices committed against their own. This type of focus, looking at a group of people rather than individual dark thrusts, always leads to the corruption of intent.

An innocent bystander, Hank, had just been stabbed in the leg during the raucous, and he was a young black man. "Well," I said, "since you intend to kill me anyway, why don't you give me a minute to let you know who you are killing." Scoffing, the leader didn't want to listen, but the others immediately agreed. "I am you," I said, "and you are me. My life has been dedicated to the quest for the truth, and towards the evolution of myself and humanity to create a world where domination doesn't exist." Beginning to calm themselves, I showed them my hands. "What you see is not what you get, you see white, just as those who have violated you have only seen black. But is that really who you are, is that really who I am?"

Using the medicine, I began to resonate light all around my body. Beginning to change form, I appeared in the form of my many lifetimes; all races, all sexes, all species of the animal kingdom, and then I became a tree. Suddenly, I heard Hank cry out . . . "Please help me!"

Running to him, we all dropped what we had been previously doing to assist him as he was going into shock from the bleeding and it appeared he might die. Holding him towards me, blood was everywhere. "You are my brother," I said to him, "do you remember me?" His glazed eyes didn't recognize anything at this point. Beginning to cry, I knew that he was going to need help in crossing over. Surrounding him in light to hopefully suspend the shock, I began preparing him for death. "Hank, you are going to see a light," I said, still attempting healing in hope that it would not be too late, "follow that light! You're going to see some lighted beings who reach to you . . . take their hands, Hank." He began to twitch. "You are going to feel a vibration in your body as you separate. It may feel almost like pulling off a band-aid, real fast. Remember how it's easier to pull off a band-aid fast than to do it slowly? This is the same." I felt his soul's release.

But just then, the alteration medics finally arrived; and in moments, they'd brought him back. Hank had seen the light, and he'd touched the unconditional love of God. "Thank you," he said quietly, looking at me with a deep recognition. "I . . ." Pausing in his weakness, he looked upon my face. "I do!" he said. A medic turned to me, "Your light work was very effective in holding the shock in check." I thanked him. "I remember you." Hank said. "You're my brother. I hope we'll be friends forever." "We already are." Happy that he'd remembered me, we had indeed been brothers in several lifetimes.

"In all space there is only ONE wisdom, though seeming divided, it is ONE in the ONE. All that exists comes forth from the LIGHT, and the LIGHT comes forth from the ALL."

The Emerald Tablets of Thoth the Atlantean, Tablet VII, Page 39, Paragraph 6, (Mystery Religions, Egyptian/Hermetic, Words of Thoth)

****

And so it came to pass that American soldiers who had died in World War II War appeared before me. "Sometimes you've got to have the courage to stand," they said. Understanding that they had given their lives to conquer an evil incarnation (Hitler), they'd prevented pure evil from taking dominance over the Earth. Bowing to them, I acknowledged their honorable and brave sacrifice on behalf of the light. They disappeared.

Standing before a headstone bearing the name of 'Adolf Hitler' in the deserts of Iraq, Saddam Hussein stood aside it as a voice from the heavens explained that he was the reincarnation of this evil soul and bore the same intentions to rule the world with absolute evil. People of the light would be tested again, to see if they had learned that you cannot allow evil to reign at any level, it must be stopped. Many of the Nazi S.S. officers had also reincarnated into the strange group of people who emerged later in our century, the skin-heads and neo-nazi hate groups who again perpetuated the evil delusion of white supremacy.

Lighted people often operate through naiveté because they don't understand the mechanism of true evil. Believing that everyone has right to their own view, they do not discern between dark and light thinking. Eternal law states an entirely different supposition, 'The moment you violate another's life, you immediately rescind the right to your own.' Because many souls violate life without intention or through ignorance, God sends angels and guides to protect us from what we may truly deserve. But true evil violates life with evil intent because it carries within it absolutely no compassion or empathy, it has not yet cultivated these traits and it sees only its own survival and need. Evil is predatory and cannot be tolerated, it must be *stopped*.

There are times when you *must* have the courage to *stand*.

"Pythagorus said that, 'Those who do not punish bad men are really wishing that good men be injured."

The Pythagorean Sourcebook and Library, Select Pythagorean Sentences, No. 166, (Mystery Religions, Pythagorean)

****

Something was amiss amidst this alteration, and I immediately knew it. Andy and I had come together, although he was sub-conscious. Hiding behind a car on the streets of a large city, another car had wrecked into a fence in this parking lot. Telling Andy that we needed to tune into what was happening before proceeding, but he chose not to listen and walked out from behind our protective barrier proceeding towards some hotel rooms.

Waving a rifle around and obviously on drugs, a man who was so out of it that he didn't realize the danger he represented, was blithering in his stupor. Using the medicine, I shot a light beam towards Andy and pulled him back behind the barrier. Preparing a lighted wall of protection to contain us, I then placed a circle of light around the entire reality to keep everyone out of the dangerous perimeter. Instructing us to wait for him to come out, the eternal directive came telling us to allow him to come down from the drugs and pass out. Sending a time-coded message to the police through the emergency phone system, I arranged for them to arrive just as he passed out. Taking him away at the correct time, it was hoped that he would get help and alter himself back towards the light.

Because nobody had been in the immediate area when he did this, this man was very lucky. If there had been other programs threatened, the results would have been very different, because he would have automatically rescinded the right to his life by being a threat to the lives of others. Having a chance to awaken the next morning, he could realize what he had done and make a change.

Pulled from the scene and hovering over my bed, Chief Joseph appeared. Handing me several Indian dolls, he said, "These are gifts from the Old Ones, Waki." Never having called me this before, it became a nickname for me, and I found that its meaning was hidden in the Hopi language, 'Place of Shelter.' Beginning to sing medicine songs, the music of the dolls entered within me, and as I hovered over Andy, Chief Joseph began energetically altering him. Chanting prayers above him, Andy began speaking a native tongue. Joseph was like a mirage in the night, appearing and disappearing as he sang, smoking a pipe and disappearing into the ether.

"O Kali Primordial, from Thy hand of creative power issue the vibrations of Aum, materializing in an inexhaustible, bewildering, and wondrous variety of finite forms. Another hand holds the astral sword of preservation, keeping guard over planetary rhythms and balances . . . Thy fourth hand stills the storm of delusion and bestows on devotees Thy rays of salvation."
Whispers from Eternity, Page 178-179, (Hinduism, Kriya Yoga, Words of Paramahansa Yogananda)

****

CHAPTER THREE
Origin of the Concept of the Devil, Star Map, Angel Implants Device to Discern Energetic Truth, Understanding Falsehood and Darkness, Understanding Phases of Knowledge, More Energetic Alterations and Spiritual Warfare, Re-Energizing Station, Court of Herbethius, The Tribunal.

****

Returning to take me on another quest, the interstellar beings upset me with their words. "We are here to take you directly into the energy that people call Satan," they said, as I hesitated, "You must KNOW it, to become capable of changing it, you must walk directly into darkness in order to seed its ascension." Cringing, I said, "I must be fearless." "You must recognize your function," they replied, "and that is to go where there is ignorance, where there is darkness, where there is hatred, where there is illusion . . . and show them reality."

Stepping onto the spaceship, we soared back to the time of the ancient mariners who were on a very perilous journey. Seeking a mythical creature, the old wooden ship was small in comparison to what the stories had said of this beast's size. Tales had been told of the sea monsters that literally ate humans and their boats in one single bite, the people greatly feared him because they believed that he took his victims to the great underworld.

Observing my fellow humans with interest, I was very surprised when we actually saw the huge creature emerging from the depths. Although in myth and legend he was portrayed as reptilian, he was actually formed out of a green jelly-like substance with blisters and warts on his skin. Awestruck by his size and serpent-like appearance, the sea creature didn't appear hungry.

Listening to the words of those around me, they said, "It is the vengeance of God! To be chosen by this creature must surely mean damnation." A man came running towards me in a panic. "Surely, we have sinned! We will be taken to the depths of the sea, under the world, if we do not repent. The Gods are angry with us!" Pulling me from the ship, the interstellar beings conveyed that mankind's views of hell and the dark side had originated in myth, and the realities of it were yet to be known.

"One of the manitos is a spirit of ill will, who creates serpents and sea monsters,

flies, and mosquitoes. The forces hostile to humans were often symbolized in Lenape myths and stories by horned water snakes and water in general."
The Red Record, Book I: Verses 9 through 15, Page 55, Paragraph 4, (Tribal, Lenape)

Suddenly standing amidst a desert, an ancient circular stone star map was laid out on a rock before me. Looking somewhat like a shield, I picked it up and began hearing the songs of melodious angels. In a moment, a huge and beautiful angel appeared before me dressed in blue and white with large, feathery and soft wings. Touching my shoulder, she smiled. "When you can hear me singing, I can come to you." Placing her ear next to mine, she said, "Do you hear that?" A vibrating tone emanated from her ears. "Yes," I said, pulling back. "It's okay," she responded, as suddenly an etheric circular star map appeared before me in the air. Continuing the tone as the odd configuration of stars manifested before me, the map contained detailed knowledge of all Universes and realms. Making it clear that the detailed information within the map was for me alone, I was given permission to share the basic structure of it which was encompassed in the 'Universal Sphere of Realms.'

"The tone has been implanted," she said, "the tone warns you of deception and untruth." "Thank you," I said, as I began to feel catatonic. Falling to the ground, I stared at the swirling star patterns no longer able to move or respond.

Shooting through time, I appeared at a gathering in the eighteenth century. Voice singing wildly in my head, the angel remained with me, but I was the only one who could see her. In the front of the room, people were discussing the problem of the Indians calling them heathens and savages. Anything they couldn't understand, they attributed to Satan. A vial of holy water was being passed around the room in order to purify themselves from evil presence of the natives. As the tone began ringing wildly in my head, I didn't partake of their vial, but took the angel's hand and left.

Spinning above me as the white mists became our path of flight, the swirling cosmic vortex led us whirling, swirling and spiraling in the encompassing etheric mass.

And then a hideous face stood before me. Wearing the garb of an ancient soldier, his uniform was red and had many buttons and two brush-like attachments on his shoulders. Handing me a cross, I immediately fell sick to my stomach as it was not an ordinary cross. Upon it were the skins of all the people who had died in the name of Christ. Appalled, I intensely sought the knowledge within as the tone began ringing incessantly. Christ's name had been used to perpetrate all forms of evil upon the Earth, and its sacredness had been tarnished and violated. Remembering the shackles upon Christ's spirit and the torture in his eyes, I began to cry softly.

As the soldier disappeared, another person came out of the ether wearing a ceramic head. "Don't you know me?" she asked, with genuine concern upon her face. "No," I replied, "I cannot know who you truly are until you remove your false face. Take off the ceramic head." She refused. "I'm hurt. If only you knew who I was, you'd feel foolish for not recognizing me." For a moment, I did feel foolish, but then the tone began ringing. "If you were who you purport to be, you would not come to me wearing a false image. You would show me who you really are." Beginning to cry, but refusing to remove her ceramic head, I said, "Do you fear that by showing your true self, you will no longer be loved?" She didn't respond. "Perhaps you should know that unless you show me your true self, I cannot heal you." Still, she refused to remove her disguise.

Turning to walk away, an old man appeared and stopped me. "One must be willing to know that which lives in darkness, in order to become capable of altering it." Turning back around, I shot a beam of light to her head as it cracked and fell to pieces.

In her hand, she now held a human heart, severed from her own body. Looking into her face, I saw uncaring disguised as religious dogma, sloth disguised as victimization, heartlessness disguised as political views, arrogance disguised in self-esteem, and perhaps the most painful; manipulation and self-aggrandizement, disguised as some form of spirituality. "I am humanity," she said, "I show you my heart." Breaking down in tears, I cried uncontrollably. Forming a pool of tears around me, I noticed a face forming in the watery chalice. Watering my heart with my own tears, the old man was very methodical. "This is good," he said quietly, "it is through tears that the seed of humility is watered . . . and where there is humility, love grows." Placing the final tears upon my heart, he placed his hand upon mine. "From love, comes wisdom."

"Hark ye, O man, and list to my Voice, open thy mind-space and drink of my wisdom. Dark is the pathway of LIFE that ye travel, many the pitfalls that lie in the way. Seek ye, ever, to gain greater wisdom, attain and it shall be light on thy way . . . Open thy Soul to the BROTHERS of BRIGHTNESS, let them enter and fill thee with light . . . "
The Emerald Tablets of Thoth the Atlantean, Tablet VII, Page 39, Paragraph 1 & 3,
(Mystery Religions, Egyptian/Hermetic, Words of Thoth)

****

Meeting me in the clouds below the mountains in the sky, thunderclouds were bursting on the horizon. Dancing with me amidst the light, he quietly said, "The purpose of life on earth is to alter the predatory will into the will of love." Staring in his amazing eyes, I knew that this sky dance was a pathway, a passage into just such an endeavor.

"Governing things is not done by things, but by harmony. Governing harmony is not done by harmony, but by people. Governing people is not done by people, but by rulers. Governing rulers is not done by rulers, but by desires. Governing desires is not done by desires, but by virtue. Governing virtue is not done by virtue, but by the Way."
Wen-Tzu, No. 134, Page 130, Paragraph 1, (Buddhism, Taoism, Words of Lao Tsu)

****

And so it came to pass that the Old Ones came and began to teach me of the ways of altering darkness and evil. When the time came for graduation, I began to hear the soulful sounds of mourners crying in the distance. Raising their hands as thunder billowed in the mountain winds, the grandmothers commanded the wind. "It is a balance," one said, "when you move beyond the predatory will to the will of love, it is natural to no longer be comfortable with the predatory nature of life in this realm. This indicates that you are moving towards a higher existence, however, it doesn't diminish the natural function of the realm you are moving beyond. You must respect the function, the phase of knowledge it provides." I nodded, as she continued. "The will of love asks that you love the children, not despite their ignorance, but because of their innocence. This love will guide you ever forward." Touching my hand lightly, I was greatly honored, but I was disturbed by the mourners that I continued to hear crying in the distance.

"Why are they crying, grandmother?" I asked. "They are mourning the death that must come in order that a new birth might take place. Suddenly, my soul was going further and further away and there was nothing I could do to stop the movement. "It is time," grandmother said, "it is meant to be this way." "So it is my time to die?" I asked, confused. "It is time to go," she said.

Feeling very peaceful about leaving, the only thing that kept me from leaving was the sounds of the mourners I'd left behind. Sending them my love, grandmother conveyed to me that they, too, could grasp hold of life whenever they chose. "I love you," I shouted back to them as I took grandmother's hand and walked into peace. Again the two grandmothers commanded the thunder as it struck across the horizon, I knew that they were the ones who would make this alteration complete. "Thank you, grandmothers." I said as the second bolt let my soul to another place.

Lying flat in the sky surrounded by six spiritual guardians, they began to perform mysterious levitations upon my spirit. Programming new thought processes, they were down-loading old programs from my spirit, and correcting my imbalances in thought, word, and deed. Altering something near my crown chakra, I realized that existence is like a blinking light, momentarily passing from one place into yet another more suitable to the path of knowledge. As we pass, we give our vehicle back to the realm chosen to guide us, so that those who follow in our footsteps will find the energetic clues we have left behind to assist them in attaining their passage, just as we, too, have found them. Returning the gifts given to our souls from the realm that harbors us in our sleep, the part of us that dies returns to the ground, altering that which is possible by remembering that which has come to pass.

"I with my lips have fashioned for this Hero words never matched, most plentiful and auspicious, for him the Ancient, Great, Strong, Energetic, the very mighty Wielder of the Thunder. Amid the sages, with the Sun he brightened the Parents: glorified, he burst the mountain; And, roaring with the holy-thoughted singers, he loosed the bond that held the beams of Morning."
The Hymns of the Rgveda, Hymn XXXII, Page 304, Stanza 1-2, (Hinduism)
****

"To show them special mercy, I, dwelling in their hearts, destroy with the shining lamp of knowledge the darkness born of ignorance."
The Bhagavad Gita As-It-Is, Chapter 10, Text 11, (Hinduism, Translation: A.C. Bhaktivedanta Swami Prabhupada)

"The power angels have in the spiritual world is so great that if I were to cite at this point everything I have seen, it would be beyond belief. If there is something left there that needs to be removed because it is in opposition to the Divine design, they raze and destroy it by a sheer force of will, with a look."
Heaven & Hell, Chapter 26, No. 229, (Christianity, Swedenborgianism, Author: Emanuel Swedenborg)

Dropped into the body of an investigator, I was brought here to deal with the case of a mass murderer. Someone had been killing pregnant women mostly by the use of a poison that had been placed in food, but the investigators on the case were missing a crucial piece of evidence, and if it were not found, they would convict the wrong man.

A homeless man named Maxton was the prime suspect. Knowing the killer was from the homeless community because of the evidence they had, they'd suspected Maxton in particular because of his tendency to get into fights. Energetically, he was closer to insanity than the true killer who was a man by the name of John, the ex-husband of the first victim. Because he had beaten his ex-wife to death rather than poison her, he'd never been a suspect. It all began when his ex-wife miscarried their child years before.

After they split up, she eventually remarried and became pregnant with another man's child. John's life hadn't gone as well, and he had become homeless. Bitter and angry, he blamed her and sought revenge. Raped, beaten and left to die in an old abandoned farmhouse, he began poisoning other women after her death, although it was not something he had planned. Losing perspective completely, he allowed himself to be swept more deeply into evil.

Several other investigators were with me as I followed the instructions of the eternal. Boarding a bus to go to an abandoned store where a group of homeless people were living, we had gone there to search for Maxton, and for further evidence to prove that he was the killer. Directed by the eternal to go to a far corner of the building where there was evidence that would otherwise never be discovered, I found an old plastic football with John's full name written upon it, and a bag of hair with dried blood stains.

Taking this immediately to the chief investigator, he was intrigued but not convinced that there was another suspect, but as I walked through the building, I *felt* his presence, and knew danger was in the air. "Be careful, I feel the killer's presence." I warned the other investigators.

Noticing a man with a bedraggled long beard, if you'd seen him anywhere else, he would have appeared harmless . . . but I *knew* it was him. Sitting next to him, I asked, "So who are you?" "John," he smiled innocently, almost as if grateful for the attention. Heartbroken at seeing a shell of humanity which no longer contained a heart, I could see the broken dreams in his eyes.

Other investigators continued to pursue Maxton who was holed up inside a closet, but as they did, a small fight broke out. Another homeless man had a bad cut across his hand. Running towards him, I gasped in shock. "Raymond?" I cried out, "Oh, my God, it's you!" Raymond was a soul I occasionally guardianed from above. Bleeding badly, I ran into the bathroom to find some toilet paper to clean him up. Not as bad as I'd originally thought, I still cried, because I was sad about Raymond's homeless plight. "Do you remember me?" I asked him, as I looked deeply into his eyes. "Sure, I do, Odyssey, how you been?" "Don't move." I said, as I prepared to implant him with a seed of light. Looking surprised as he saw the spark of light hovering above my finger, I slowly reached to the center of his chest. "What are you doing?" He asked. "I'm not leaving you here without implanting you with the energy to get you out." Confused, he allowed me to finish.

Investigators, meanwhile, were looking at the evidence I'd found. Also containing a powdery substance which appeared to be poison, the bag had turned out to be vital evidence. The eternal command came, and I was finished. No wrongful conviction would occur, and the mass murderer would now be stopped.

As my soul was being swept away, I exploded out of that body, but turned for a final look at Raymond, whose tiny seed was beginning to grow.

My eyes were slowly opening as a gentle face stood before my bedside. "She's waking," she said to her invisible spiritual partner, "she's being born into the now." The other voice responded, but no face could claim it. "The alteration's complete, then?" "Yes," she replied, "it has been righted." I turned over and closed my eyes.

"Thou mayest step on the right path and walk in the presence of Angels. Thou mayest sing of the Earthly Mother by day and of the Heavenly Father by night, and through thy being may course the golden stream of the Law. But wouldst thou leave thy brothers to plunge through the gaping chasms of blood, as the pain-wracked earth shudders and groans under her chains of stone? Canst thou drink of the cup of eternal life, when thy brothers die of thirst?"
The Essene Gospel of Peace, Volume 2, Page 118, Stanza 1, (Christianity, Gnostic/Essene)

****

Energetic debris was all around me and I was having trouble breathing. Coming from people in my life who still retained delusion and darkness within them, they were throwing their 'trash,' so to speak, in my perimeter. A person doesn't have to be evil to spew dark energies, just ignorant. Every time I had the debris almost cleaned up, they began tossing more of their 'trash' into my sphere.

Suddenly, a small little green faerie appeared, about two feet high. Holding a stardust wand, she began tossing stardust and cleaning up the mess around me. Laughing and joyful, she conveyed that her name was, 'Uri,' and that she was an old childhood friend of mine. Excited to see her, I grabbed her by the shoulders and began dancing around the room with her. "Look!" She said as she took my hand.

One of the souls who had been throwing his trash into my perimeter was standing before her in the distance. Throwing stardust all over him, I was surprised to notice that it had absolutely no effect on him, not even on sub-conscious levels. I'd always believed that even when it was clear that a person had chosen their dominance, rejected the eternal hand, and accepted darkness as their path, showering light in their direction couldn't *hurt*; but I realized now was that it did absolutely no good, either. A waste of eternal energy, it was needless to shower it on souls who would in no way benefit from it. Further, I had allowed them to toss their waste into my perimeter and smother me in the debris of their dark ways. Eternal energy is to be used where it can be absorbed and bring about transformation, and if a darkened soul later became open to the reception of light, the eternal would respond swiftly.

****

Two dogs appeared in the sky, one lighted, the other dark. Fighting for dominance over the world, the dark dog was vicious and cruel, taking dominance over the light with amazing ease. Having moments of dominance, the light dog would lose its power as soon as the darkness began its next inevitable invasion, due to its passivity. People felt helpless to this fluctuation of light and dark.

Looking to my side, I noticed that I was wearing my angel wings, and I flew frantically to the people, as they observed my flight in surprise. Raising my arms to the sky, the energy began to alter . . . slowly . . . towards the light. Doing nothing, the onlookers just stood there. "YOU MUST CHOOSE, AS WELL! Which will it be; darkness or light?" Understanding my plea, they all began to raise their hands to the sky, focusing their consciousness as the lighted dog's dominance began to take hold. But then something happened which surprised all of us. The dark dog began melting into the light dog . . . and they became one.

"The Supreme must be an entity in which the two are one; it will, therefore, be a Seeing that lives, not an object of vision like things existing in something other than themselves: what exists in an outside element owes its life to that element; it is not self-living."

Plotinus: The Enneads, Nature, Contemplation, and the One, Page 280, Paragraph, 2, (Mystery Religions, Greek, Author: Plotinus)

Suddenly, the men in black appeared. Wearing black suits and hats, they were faceless and very stern about their purpose. Coming with a dark energetic surge that would frighten anybody, I'd seen them many times before. Intimidation was their function, and their purpose was to retain the dominance of darkness in this realm. Going after souls who seek higher knowledge, they desired to convince them to leave the service of the light. Because they were powerfully dark, they often achieved their goal. Threatening me, I got mad.

"Get out!" I yelled, "You will not stop me from fulfilling my mission for the light!" Seeming unsure of how to cope with my lack of fear, they jumped back for a moment. "Get out!" I repeated. They stood quietly. "I will serve only light," I said, "I will fulfill the destiny I have come to fulfill. I will open the doorway of light into the third dimension! You cannot stop me!" They didn't move. "It's time for you to go!"

Raising my hands, I sent a surge of light barraging through them like a hurricane wind as their spirits became particle energy and were dismantled. In a final surge of light, I sent them back to the second dimension, and never saw them again.

Darkness is simply a lower form of evolution than our own. Souls walk the pathway from the depths to the heights. When a soul is sent back to the second or first dimension, they are simply being returned to the place in which they are compatible. Just as we are not given entry into higher worlds, until we have learned to abide by the laws of their realms, and have become compatible to them.

"May they be saved in the sight of everyone and let not the wicked dominate them."

The Siddur, Selichos for Thursday, Page 841, Bottom, (Judaism)

****

Transported to an alteration to take place around a falsely religious man, he was surrounded by little dark energies which had been magnetized towards him because of his self-righteousness. Being very fearful, he had drawn to him a particularly dark entity who supported and energized his fears.

Wandering around him, the short dark creature immediately noticed me and began trying to pull off my arms and lash my spirit around so as to frighten me away. Beginning to pour a pile of his own waste in front of me, I asked him, "So, who are you?" Grinning widely, he responded, "Lucifer." As I began laughing uncontrollably, this relatively benign creature seemed confused by my complete fearlessness when he used such a guise. "Oh, you think you're really funny, don't you?" I said, as he all of a sudden began to cringe.

Now he knew he was facing a servant of God, rather than a fearful soul and he began to shiver. Using Lucifer's name in the past to intimidate people, it was obviously not his true identity, and I knew it. "You have two choices?," I said, "either you become transformed and serve the light . . . and I will turn you into a nice little animal, perhaps a dog or cat . . . " Even as he shook, his arrogance didn't wane. Most demons do not realize that their arrogance energizes their demise. "Or . . . I will dismantle your energy and send you back to the second realm." Not responding, the eternal command came quickly. "Okay," I said, "have a good journey." Sending a bolt of light towards him, he was immediately dismantled into thousands of dark little pieces. With another bolt of light, the eternal blasted him back to the second realm.

Apparently that this man's thoughts had given entry to this demon, and the eternal sometimes removes these things to disengage lower thrust. When darkness is removed, some souls will retain the new construct, no longer having contact with the demons of vice. But it often happens that souls do not change their thoughts, giving quick permission for the return of the demons of vice. Our thoughts, intentions and deeds magnetize guardians from below . . . or above.

"The messengers of fear are harshly ordered to seek out guilt, and cherish every scrap of evil and of sin that they can find, losing none of them on pain of death, and laying them respectfully before their lord and master. Perception cannot obey two masters . . . what fear would feed upon, love overlooks."
A Course in Miracles, Chapter 19, No. IV, Page 410, No. 11, (Christianity, Metaphysics)

****

Native faces energetically meshed all around me, beckoning and calling. Seeking to grasp the essence of their urging, an interstellar spacecraft began to rise upwards above me as I entered it. Soon we were in the heavens looking down upon the Earth below as the energetic vibrations were increasing. Descending, the mountain loomed gently in the sky as the energies shifted and I found myself hurling through space.

Landing on a fire hydrant in a dirty ghetto, danger was all around me. Focusing to achieve the knowledge about the mission at hand, a street gang was about to be the victim of a drive-by shooting, and all of them were going to die. Wanting to save one soul among them, the eternal had sent me in as a homeless woman. As the gang in question quickly approached, the one I was supposed to save wrapped a jacket around me to protect me from the cold, while the others contemplated a sexual assault.

Taking my hand, he warded off the overt advances of his animalistic friends. Beginning to lose focus in remembrance, I missed the vital moment when the eternal command had come. If I'd listened, I would have thrown him to the ground, but I was too late. The spray of bullets came out of nowhere as the killers sped by in their cars armed with machine guns. Only a second passed before all of us were on the ground, wounded and dying.

Because I'd been shot, I'd suffered a serious blow to my energy field, and I couldn't remember anything. Beginning to take on the actual identity of the part I'd come to play, the memory of my mission and spiritual status was completely gone. Grief was multiplied by confusion, as the one I'd come to save lay dead. 'Who am I, why am I here, and how'd I get here?' I thought.

Walking out of the energetic body that had been shot to death, I wandered around the ghetto aimlessly. Angry sirens approached the scene of the deaths, as the streets remained lonely in the night. Hearing them from a distance, I wandered further and further away towards an old run-down building where prostitutes were hanging out. Approaching them, I saw a man signaling me to follow him, who appeared to be a street thug.

Following him anyway, he took me inside the run-down building which was abandoned. Pointing to a locked wooden door, I was afraid. But light came from his hands, swinging the door open, and my eyes were filled with brilliant light. A white door heralded the top of a long staircase into the heavenlies, as I instinctively began walking towards it. An invisible force shut the wooden door behind me, and when I reached the top step, I fell to the floor from the magnitude of my energetic wounds.

Awaking later in an astral hospital bed, my memory was slowly returning. Having gotten lost in the temporary identity of an energetic alteration, many other alterers laid in beds around me in the same predicament. Emotionless as he asked me questions about my missions, memory and true identity, the doctor was sending white light through my spirit from the hospital bed below. Gunshot wounds in my auric field were closing and re-energizing. "Where am I?" I asked the doctor. "The re-energizing station," he said, "I understand this is your first visit?" "Yes," I replied. "Well, that's pretty impressive. You must be good at what you do." "Thank you." I responded sheepishly.

"How's she doing?!" came somebody's frantic voice. "She's going to be fine," the doctor said, "but I think there is emotional residue." Placing a flat, clear, cylindrical object above my soul, I began to enter a natural state of detachment. Realizing my error in losing focus, I vowed never to do so again. Now calming, the frantic man conveyed to me that he was the supervisor on several of my missions. Terribly upset about the failed alteration, he calmed me, pointing out that another alterer would go in at an earlier point in time and try to fix it.

"Well, you're all healed up, time to get back to work," he said. "What!" I shouted, annoyed. "If you don't go right back into it," he said, "you won't have the courage to try again." Within less than a second, I was off, led to complete two more alterations this night, which I did successfully.

Sitting upon a mountain peak, two Indian men approached me. Handing me a document with pictures of twelve Indian chiefs, they said, "You are the eleventh generation, welcome home, Red Hawk."

"When the nervous system functions it conveys the experience of objects through the senses of perception and it engages itself in activity through the organs of action. Functioning in this manner it becomes fatigued. If the fatigue is slight, perceptions become less sharp and the man begins to feel drowsy. If the fatigue is greater, perceptions cease because the mind fails to experience."
The Science of Being and Art of Living, The Art of Being, Page 126, Paragraph 2, (Hinduism, Transcendental Meditation, Author: Maharishi Mahesh Yogi)
"What shall we then say to these things? If God be for us, who can be against us?"
King James Bible, New Testament, Romans 8:31, (Christianity)
****
"The Saviour answered again and said: 'Nay, but all the mysteries of the three spaces forgive the soul in all the regions of the rulers all the sins which the soul hath committed from the beginning onwards. They forgive it, and moreover they forgive the sins which it thereafter will commit, until the time up to which every one of the mysteries shall be effective.'"
Pistis Sophia, Third Book, Page 251, Paragraph 2, (Christianity, Gnostic/Essene, Words

of Christ)

Cautiously, I walked into the cave, as I'd been sent forth to appear before the court of Herbethius. A cold night in this ancient world, the air was dark. Knowing that coming here meant that I'd made a very grave mistake, I shook with fear for what I may have done. Now I would speak for my energetic crime before the courts who judge the servants of God.

Herbethius wore a long white robe, and his face was very stern. "Hermes!" He shouted to me, as I shook with fear. Herbethius directed me to look towards the sky, and I saw many space vessels from other worlds, but I also saw my crime. Having recently tried to help a woman who was of somewhat high standing in the physical world, a deceased relative had come to me begging me to give her some specific messages. Feeling obliged to give them to her; I'd had contact with a close friend of hers who'd told me she wanted the information. Sending it to her, I immediately knew I had made a mistake. Eternal law requires that souls *must* come to you. But because of her earthly stature, I had agreed to send it to her through this intermediary who had apparently given me a horribly wrong impression of her true desires. Although it didn't sit right with me, I'd done it anyway.

Information like this can be harmful if someone is not ready to hear it, and you must attain permission from the eternal to give it, regardless of whether or not a deceased relative comes to you; for those relatives do not often hold eternal knowledge, power or permission. Ironically, I'd known when I met her that she was not very open to the spirit and if she hadn't been in this particular position in life, I would never have given it to her. Falsely attributing Earthly significance to eternal significance, I'd interfered with eternal law and now I stood before the court for judgment to be rendered.

Herbethius was harsh, because ancient ones do not take lightly the violation of eternal law. "Hermes! If you had done this with the *intention* to violate eternal law, you would have been shot on the spot." What he referred to was a de-energization of eternal power. Taking away the power of the light within you, it renders you benign and scatters your consciousness. In order to steward power, you must honor the laws of beholdment. "However," he continued, "because you did not violate these laws with the *intent* to do harm, but out of *ignorance*, I will give you the chance to argue your case. If you do not satisfy me that you have learned your lesson and that this will *never* happen again, you will be beheaded." Being beheaded is to lose your head, lose your reason, which would manifest as scattered, fragmented confusion. All that had been given to me in the realms of knowledge, would, in essence, be taken away.

Kneeling down, I began to beg. "I am so sorry. I really *see* what it is I've done. Oh, I hope I have not hurt this soul terribly in my stupidity. Oh, my God, what can I do to make this right? I really do see what I've done." "Hermes," he replied, "I believe that you are indeed repentant of your mistake and that you do indeed *see* why what you've done was wrong. Because of this, you will not lose your head."

Pausing, he allowed me to tremble as I awaited his final words. "You must perform your mission . . . nothing more! You must never do anything for self-serving reasons, only the cause of furthering eternity. Do you understand?" "Yes," I said, "thank you, thank you!" Pointing to a hallway where my paintings, writings and music were displayed, he said, "This is what we ask of you now. Only do what we ask of you, nothing more!" "Yes, yes, I will!" I shuddered.

Transported through a beam of light from one of the spaceships above, the light beam altered me and energized understanding of my purpose and the lessons of my mistake. A second chance was a grand gift, and I was honored, humbled and unworthy to receive it.

"I have sinned, O Lord, I have sinned, and I acknowledge mine iniquities. Be not angry with me for ever, by reserving evil for me; neither condemn me into the

lower parts of the earth. For thou art the God, even the God of them that repent; and in me thou wilt shew all thy goodness; for thou wilt save me, that am unworthy, according to thy great mercy. Therefore, I will praise thee for ever all the days of my life: for all the powers of the heavens do praise thee, and thine is the glory for ever and ever. Amen."

The Apocrypha, The Prayer of Manasses, Page 254, (Judaism, Christianity)
****

Wanting me to go with him, I was initially attracted by the incredible amount of sexual energy he emitted. Looking into his eyes, however, something felt amiss, and I questioned him. "Who are you?" I said quietly, knowing that darkness must always reveal itself to the light. Turning into a black creature with bat wings emerging, he replied, "They call me the gull," he said, "I am destructive sexual energy." "Be off with you, then." I said, lifting my arms, and revealing the medicine. Plummeting down to the realm of his domain, the light had forced him to return to the second dimension.

Another one approached who called herself Aschira. "What do you want of me?" I asked, impatiently. "I can give you everything you want . . ." she replied, as thousands of gold coins began appearing in front of her like rain. "It can all be yours." "But I could care less about those things; I don't even want what you have to offer." Looking confused, I lifted my hands, "Goddess Aschira of the dark, take your greed and stealth back to the place it belongs." Plummeting, she was instantly gone.

"Watching for riches consumeth the flesh, and the care thereof driveth away sleep."

The Apocrypha, Ecclesiasticus, Chapter 31, Page 199, Paragraph 1, (Judaism, Christianity)

Vortexing like a band of light, I found myself amongst a circular cave. Inside, there were slaves of all races upon the earth, their orders to rip at the walls of the cave and destroy it. Immediately, I was angry. "This is our Mother Earth!" I shouted, as I ran through the cave pulling the slaves abruptly from their posts. As they were in a daze, I had to jolt them harshly in order to awaken them to reality.

Those who heralded this darkness were like ominous dark clouds of energy from above, voices of demise that came from the outer cave walls. "How dare you!" I said. "They are your slaves no more and your destruction will not be energized."

Hoards of people were exiting the caves into the sunlight, and a familiar man approached me from among them. When our eyes met, neither of us said anything. Still busy, I had to finish freeing the remainder of these souls. But after a time, I became curious as to why he had sought me out. His involvement in this oppressive situation concerned me.

Gauging my surroundings, I became aware that he had been the one who called for my assistance. As I walked closer to him, he reached his hand out to touch mine, and I traveled into his eyes.

Peering through his reality and vision, his futility was immediately apparent. Wanting to see me, he was hoping I could free him from this life, but this was not my place. Locked in his past, he hadn't been able to break the chain, because he was honoring false gods, thus, he was living a false life.

Taking his other hand, I exchanged telepathically. "Thanks for asking me to come, I'm honored that you've requested me to help you. But you must know that what must be changed comes from within yourself. It is not I who holds the key to your destiny, but you, my friend. I understand. I really do. You've trapped yourself by following what you were told, what was supposed to be important, what was supposed to be real, what was supposed to be the meaning of life. But the boat has been lost; you've never known *true love*, my friend." I paused. "Shall I say in parting, however, that it is never too late to honor love?"

A lone teardrop fell from his face as our hands began to sever. Beginning to disintegrate, I offered him one last word. "You needn't be a slave to the material world, but you can be a steward of your spirit. Don't stay here my friend; you deserve much, much more." Then I was gone.

"And a terrible pain seized me as I felt within me the souls of all those who had blinded themselves, so as to see only their own desires of the flesh."
The Essene Gospel of Peace, Volume 2, Page 111, Middle, (Christianity, Gnostic/Essene)
****

"You must let go of everything with an energetic past," the Old One's said. They spoke of things, as we were selling everything we owned to follow the beckon of the inner spirit westward. "Beware, for the backwards flow would have you destroyed. You have stated your intent, thus, energizing your destiny. Now they will come."

And they came with a vengeance, the god's and goddesses of the lower worlds came like a torrent in the night, attempting every illusion, temptation or trick they could muster. Their only power was their sheer numbers which overwhelmed me at first. Knowing the darkness simply couldn't prevail, I simply couldn't allow it. Aschira returned, goddess of greed, laughing hysterically about the fact that anytime Andy or I had a single thought of greed, she had an invitation to enter our spaces. Anytime anyone bears a single thought of gluttony, lust, greed, pride, sloth, vanity or avarice, it gives passage to these predators of darkness to be near your soul. After all, it is their duty to energize your destruction. Purifying my thoughts would be vital in the fulfillment of my destiny. "You won't be getting anymore invitations, Aschira." I said, shooting her with light to send her away. Disappearing, I never saw her again. We must purify ourselves not only in word and deed, but in thought; so that our thinking does not bear the markings of the beast.

Demons encircled me, their fanged teeth laughing their backwards laugh. For two nights, the battles continued, but I refused to give in to their terror and fear. By the second night, they no longer even frightened me, for I considered them a nuisance which simply had to be tolerated in the attainment of a higher good. They had come to tempt my soul, and they simply would not be allowed to win. Finally, I called out Otara, asking for my eternal alliances to assist.

"We will eat you alive," the consumption energy threatened. "Go ahead, try!" I responded as the golden angels descended and with one mighty stroke of their hands, completely annihilated them. Safe for the moment, the golden angels left me with the knowledge that the dark side would try me for the remainder of my life. Because my function was to save many souls from their hands, they wished to destroy me.

Erupting into an epiphany of awareness, I realized something. It is a gift when you receive that moment of awakening where all life is eternal, all things timeless, and your life seems to pale in its imagined importance in the overall scheme of things. In this moment, you find humility. And when you realize that you are but a blink of an eye, eternity rushes in, in one majestic sweep of awareness!

"Lord, I call to you; come quickly to help me; listen to my plea when I call. Let my prayer be incense before you; my uplifted hands an evening sacrifice. Set a guard, Lord, before my mouth, a gatekeeper at my lips. Do not let my heart incline to evil, or yield to any sin."
New American Bible, Old Testament, Psalms 141:1-4, (Christianity, Catholic)
****

Making the motions of death, I can say without reservation that in that moment, I had no doubt that I was truly going to die. Terror swept over me in this moment of death, which surprised me. After all I'd experienced, I hadn't realized how frightening the final parting would be. "No!" I screamed out to the spirit world, "I don't want to die alone." I was dying in my sleep. Seemingly endless, the spiraling void went on forever, but all of a sudden there was calm.

"In death, you will know." A voice calmly stated. "In death you will know things that only death can teach you." Calmly accepting my fate, my fear had begun to fade. "If I must die, then I will go quietly," I said with resolution. Suddenly, an unexplainable understanding came over me, the knowledge of death.

Another parting soul approached, a woman, "I know my destiny!" She shouted. "It is to forge the bridge across forever." "Yes, that is true," I replied, "but it is *everyone's* destiny to forge the bridge across forever. That is the destiny of humanity, to enter timelessness and leave time behind." But when you cross that bridge and return to the present time/space continuum, the knowledge of forever returns with you. In my death, I'd crossed this bridge, and now suddenly, my soul was going the other direction again . . . towards time.

Swinging over rough waters, I knew I had the opportunity to go back over the bridge with the awareness of forever intact. If I could do that, my impact could be much greater within the continuum. A man approached, "So, you're going out West?" he asked. Something felt strange, but he looked nice enough. "Yeah," I said, "but I gotta go now."

Walking towards the bridge, he blocked me with his hands. "Do you think I could go with you out West?" "I guess you can go wherever you want," I replied, not realizing the impact of my statement until he suddenly turned into a deathly decomposing man. Immediately, I knew I was in trouble, the darkness had tricked me, and I'd fallen for it.

Manifesting a large wooden cabinet, he pushed it over to crush me. Running out of its way, I shouted, "Who the hell are you?!" His white ashen eye sockets revealed where his soul resided. "I have sent my granddaughter to hell," he said, "now I must kill you to get her out." Desperation filled his pitiful eyes, but he didn't realize that he was following a lie for this action would only sink his soul deeper into the abyss. A soul cannot *serve* darkness in order to be *freed* from it. Surely, a reasonable man must know that no one can be freed from hell through a dark act; a soul can only be saved from the abyss through love.

Conveying to him that he'd been misled, and destroying me would not give his granddaughter freedom, his violence didn't dim. Sending him an understanding of love's deliverance, I couldn't get through to him; he was lost, condemned by his own hatred. Dark forces had used this ignorant man who had lost his soul to stop me from bringing forever back. With a quick thrust of my hand, I pushed him out of my way and ran towards the bridge. Chief Joseph awaited me on the other side. Still breathless, the danger had passed.

Showing me an image of things that he wanted me to do, he never mentioned my encounter with the man in front of the bridge. "You have been given the gift of words, I would ask that you go now and speak on behalf of my people," he said. Kneeling to the ground, tears were streaming down my face. "I am honored," I said, "I am so amazingly honored that you would trust me with something that important. Please, I just ask that you always be with me, so that my words are yours and that I honor the people with only the truth." He nodded.

Returning to form, Andy awoke from sleep to give me a message. "I was shown many faces," he said, "and they all looked nice enough. They seemed like they were okay, that there was nothing to be concerned about. But then they all changed and a voice said, 'Beware the serpent for he comes in many faces.'"

"He who desires happiness for himself by inflicting injury on others, is not freed from hatred, being entangled himself in the bonds of hatred."
Dhammapada, Canto XXI, No. 291, (Buddhism)
"Blessed is he whose conscience hath not condemned him, and who is not fallen from his hope in the Lord."
The Apocrypha, Ecclesiasticus, Chapter 14, Paragraph 1, (Judaism, Christianity)

******

"You asked for help, didn't you?" I said to the angry face that now stood before me. It was only a moment, but what seemed like a long sleep to him, and we were far away from the battlefield. Fighting for the South at the time of the American Civil War, it was my duty to get him to the North. Having prayed for understanding, he'd wanted to know if he'd been doing the right thing. His sincerity had inspired the powers that be to give him an opportunity. Agitated with me anyway, he was suited up and ready to meet his Northern comrades, nonetheless.

Unable to tell that he was a Rebel, I'd altered his uniform so he would appear to be one of them. No one had to know that he was the 'enemy.' Anger diminishing as he listened to them, it wasn't that he went over to their side, but he began to understand why they perceived the slavery issue differently than himself. Because he'd never known anything else, he joined the army in the fervor of the battle call, never really thinking deeply on the issue. After a great deal more time, he began seeing that maybe he did agree with them a lot more than he ever felt he could. Laughing with these men, he found it odd that he would have killed these very same individuals had he seen them in battle.

Time for me to go, he came to find me. "My life will never be the same comrade," he said, "come with me, be with me." "You don't understand," I said as I began to disappear, "I am in your dreaming, when you wake I will be gone." Reaching to grab hold of me, he panicked, for he suddenly realized he would wake again in the South. What would he do? Would this new understanding change anything? Would he have the courage to stand for what he'd been shown? He could *die* for the truth, would he take that risk?

When he awoke, it was night. Walking away from his camp, he began his journey northward. Dying at the hands of one who did not know his heart, a Yankee soldier killed him, feeling that no Confederate deserved to live. Born into the light, there was no regret, no remorse. "I am glad I've been born," he said, "for no life will end by my hands today. For it is better to die standing for life, than to live standing for death."

"(Mark the blameless man and behold) the upright, (for there is pos)te(rity for the ma)n of peace."
The Dead Sea Scriptures, Psalm 37, Page 330, (Christianity, Gnostic/Essene)

"Without anger, without trembling, not boasting, without remorse, speaking in moderation, not arrogant, he indeed is a sage restrained in speech. Having no attachment to the future, he does not grieve over the past. He sees detachment in respect of sense-contacts, and is not led into (wrong) views."
The Group of Discourses II, IV. The Chapter of Eights, Page 98, No. 850-851, (Buddhism, Theravadan)

******

A funnel of black had pulled my soul away, and I didn't know where I was. Lost and confused, I frantically feared I would not be able to find my way home. A warm house appeared in the distance and I ran towards it like a thirsty man looking for water in the desert. At the door, a woman approached, but I immediately felt that something was amiss. Ignoring my instinct, I began to talk with her. Offering me a pair of magic pants that would give me magical powers and guarantee that I would never want, I suddenly had the feeling of witchcraft. "Come on," she said, "just take them. They will lead you out of your confusion." "No," I said quietly, "those are not magic pants; they are a temptation away from the light." Her face began to crinkle like an old witch, as she began to turn into her true self. Everything around her turned into blackness and her face became pitiful and wretched. A dark gull man emerged from the other room. "YOU WILL TAKE OUR GIFTS!" he shouted at me angrily as his dark black cape followed him. Lifting my hands, I said, "No, they are not gifts, they are destruction, itself." Turning, I began to walk away. Grabbing my shoulder, I knew that he wanted to destroy me. "No." I repeated as I lifted his hand from my shoulder. Very upset that they had lost this seemingly perfect temptation, they both sunk. Unable to get to me even when they'd intentionally scattered my focus, they were in a state of angry despair.

Light flashed wildly as the skies began to open up. Standing in another place amidst the clouds, I looked up to see an image forming above. Her white veil covered her head, but did not hide her radiant face. Sky-blue robes shimmered as if moved by a light-source emanating from beneath them. Mother Mary looked at me with a serene gaze. "I will be with you much more, now." She conveyed to me. "I want you to be aware of my presence all around you." Saying nothing, I just looked at her in awe. Feeling the presence of Christ, I could see Him coming in and out of view behind her. St. Joseph appeared behind them, in and out. Calming, I fell to my knees.

Reaching her hand towards me, our hands clasped. Disappearing slowly like a mirage in the astral sky amidst a realm where angels fly and visitors *must* be invited, I bowed my head, "I thank you. I am honored."

"Let the storm rage and the sky darken - not for that shall we be dismayed. If we trust as we should in Mary, we shall recognize in her, the Virgin Most Powerful 'who with virginal foot did crush the head of the serpent.'"
The Voice of the Saints, Behold Thy Mother, Page 137, No. 1, (Christianity, Catholic, Words of Pope Pius X)

****

And so it came to pass that I fulfilled hundreds of alterations, and continued to seed evolution within the Earthly realm. Many temptations came from the dark side, as I slowly began the arduous process of purifying my thoughts. As long as these forces are present around you, it remains difficult to banish the confusion, destruction and wrong views which they continually barrage upon your mind. Through the power of the eternal, I was able to overcome temptation after temptation, beginning to slowly realize how deep this purification must eventually go to be fulfilled completely within my soul.

"To abstain from sinful actions is not sufficient for the fulfillment of God's law. The very desire of what is forbidden is evil."
The Voice of the Saints, The Challenge of Chastity, Page 58, No. 3, (Christianity, Catholic, Words of St. John Baptist de la Salle)

****

Having been called in to assist on a home haunted by pure evil, I was very nervous because of the nature of darkness I was about to face. Out of body, I was floating around the house looking for the cause of the disturbances when I turned a corner and saw something which totally frightened me. A totally black humanoid demon was standing before a boiling cauldron, his energy so intensely energized towards darkness that I wasn't sure I could take care of it; but as the demon glanced my way and saw me, I knew there was no turning back.

Lifting my hands and pulling together all the power of the eternal, I swept it as a gale-wind towards the beast. Already in the process of preparing to energetically assault me with his own very empowered demonic energy, I was terrified. But my thrust hit him and he blew into thousands of little pieces. Sending him back to the first dimension, he was gone, never to be seen again.

"These signs will accompany those who believe; in my name they will drive out demons."
New American Bible, New Testament, Mark 16:16-18, (Christianity, Catholic, Words of Christ)

****

Darkness came with a vengeance that I had not anticipated. In the night, I witnessed the angels of the light and the angels of the darkness battling over the sustenance of my life. Since I was unwilling to be thrown off the pathway, the darkness determined that death was the only way to stop me from fulfilling my cause. A powerful virus overcame my body, and I became very sick.

Drifting off to sleep, I saw a dark being laughing above my bed. In the window, there stood an owl. Instantly, I *knew* it meant death. Suddenly feeling terror, the dark man laughed. "Get out!" I said to him, as I sent a beam of light directly towards his third-eye. Immediately pushed back, the impending pressure of death still mounted my soul.

Before I could think to respond, a wild Cheetah appeared out of nowhere. Grabbing the owl, he threw it down, disabling its power. Disappearing in terror of this powerful being who had come to my defense, the dark man was gone. Looking at me with immense love, I said, "Thank you, thank you," as the graceful Cheetah walked quietly away. Weeks earlier, I'd been told that my future son would be born under the sign of the Cheetah, and I *knew* that this was his spirit. (I was not yet pregnant with this son, who was to be my third child. My second child, a daughter, had not yet been even conceived.)

Waking the next day, I'd been healed.

"It is human to fall, but angelic to rise again."
The Voice of the Saints, Contrition, Page 73, No. 1, (Christianity, Catholic, Words of St. Mary Pelletier)

****

Leaving form, the eternal swept me into a vortex of compelling energy. Showing me a situation that the eternal wanted to alter, they were unable to do so because the sub-conscious mind of this soul was unwilling. Vital knowledge, everything that is done in the alteration framework is done with the permission of the soul, on some level of consciousness, sub-conscious or otherwise. It cannot be compelled, even by the eternal. A vortex of energy surrounded this man, trying to get him to do what was right, but he wouldn't.

An angel appeared and spoke to me about the souls of those I'd had to leave behind in order to follow my path. "It is not that you do not love, my child, it is that they will only choose to truly love you if you are a certain way. This way that they want you to be would destroy who you truly are. Although they perceive you as the unloving one, they are the ones incapable of loving you." Seeing my soul being strangled and held down to the Earth by vines, their hands became roots beneath the Earth, carrying me below ground.

But as I began to sing angelic praise, their shoots began to wither and my soul began soaring upwards towards a heavenly gate, a choir of angels singing with me. As the angel prepared to leave, she said, "You've always loved them, you still do, it's just time for you to go."

"He Who makes peace in His Heights, may He make peace upon us . . ."
The Siddur, The Mourner's Kaddish, Page 369, Paragraph 4, (Judaism)

****

Five undercover police officers were infiltrating the mob. A female double-agent had been ordered to murder them, and it was my job to get to them in time so that they would not be killed.

In the energetic realm, she knew my purpose. Perceiving me as one of them, the police held this view even though in physical reality, my part in this did not exist. Headquartered on the eleventh floor of a hotel, I had to get to their room before she did, and warn them.

Chasing me, she was shooting in the back rooms where no one could hear her silenced gun. In her perception, shooting me would kill me, because she was not aware that this was an energetic realm where things are played out before they happen. In my perception, getting hit might send me into a state of forgetfulness, which could make me lose the alteration.

A long chase ensued before I was able to elude her, and find a back entrance to the upstairs. Not more than three minutes after I arrived in the eleventh-floor room, she'd made it, but it was not too late because I'd gotten there in time. What would have ended in the slaughter of several police officers, ended in this woman's death.

Pulled from the scene, I felt a duality inside because I'd saved lives at the expense of another. An angel appeared and placed her hands on my back. When someone refuses to respond to the light, their dark plans are sometimes carried out upon themselves. And though it is sad, it is a vital part of evolution; because becoming the victim of your own vile plans, sparks awakening and empathy. As is proper when one must be a part of an extreme action resulting in the loss of life, the angel and I mourned her death. Kneeling down, we asked God for grace.

Appearing before us, the woman who died had thoughts to share. "It is not for you to mourn me," she said, "for you have energized my evolution. I have not died, but found life again. It is for me to thank you for altering the pathway of destruction I did follow." Bewildered, I looked at her with interest in her higher form. "I'm sad that this had to be done, was there no other way?" I asked her. "No, there was not. My darkness was deep; you had to break my sleep." Pondering her words, I said no more. "It is the earthly part of you that sees only tragedy," the angel spoke up, "the eternal part of you sees something entirely different." "What does it see?" I asked. "The eternal part of you sees evolution in progress."

"For I know, that oppression will exist and prevail on earth; that on earth great punishment shall in the end take place; and that there shall be a consummation of all iniquity, which shall be cut off from its root, and every fabric raised by it shall pass away."
The Book of Enoch, Chapter XC, Page 146, No. 6-7, (Judaism, Christianity)
****

Several spirits were gathered in a gymnasium learning about the first stages of energetic alteration, and it was my job to teach them. Allowing the group to peer in on a simple alteration, we went back in time to a gunfight. Doing a simple maneuver, I jammed both of their guns with a bolt of light. Quickly, we returned. Many of the students were novices, still learning about moving through objects and adeptness at flight, so we worked on those issues for several hours.

Preparing to leave, another alteration teacher came in and said, "There's a lot more to alterations than what's going on in their minds." Tuning into their minds, I understood her observation. "They see it as baby-sitting, or a quick fix. Some look at it from very self-serving eyes and only a few see it from the realm of knowledge." Disappointed, I knew she was right. They saw it as an intellectual endeavor, or from the standpoint of their ego. "Only a few of those, if that many, will be chosen to continue in this learning. The others are not doing it for the right reasons." We flew away.

"If your sight is still too weak and is repelled from this vision, turn the eye of your mind to the road where wisdom used to reveal itself for your delight. Then remember that you have postponed a vision which you may seek again when you are stronger and sounder."
On Free Choice of the Will, Book Two, No. 167, (Christianity, Catholic, Words of St. Augustine)
****

Never had I faced such evil, and I sincerely hoped I never would again. A satanic ritual murder had occurred in our town, wherein the body had been dismembered; the skin peeled and kept in foil, the blood drained for drinking, etc. Making contact with the deceased, I was shocked to realize that it was the same spirit who had tried to kill me days earlier when the Cheetah had come to my rescue. A cult member who had agreed to a ritual suicide, he felt he would be much more powerful in death than in life. Pitying him for the evil that he was, I didn't for one moment let down my guard.

Without warning, he attempted to enter my spirit. "I WILL CRUSH YOU!" He said. Powerful to the dark side, his energy was terrifying. "GET OUT!"

I screamed. Shocked, I'd never encountered such evil and I was in shock. With his fingers, he attempted to crush my skull. As I'd gathered plenty of information regarding the perpetrators, to insure that they would be caught, I screamed out, "Don't think for one minute I'm doing this to avenge your murder! You are pitiful! I feel sorry for one who has embraced evil as you have. I'm doing this to nail your friends who share in your evil. It will not be tolerated, the eternal has spoken."

Trying to enter me again, I called out to Jesus. "My Lord and Savior Jesus Christ!" Immediately appearing, he directed me to sing a song, 'Hallelujah and the light came tumbling on in! Hallelujah, and the light came tumbling on in!' Singing with power and fury, the light came barreling in from all directions. In moments, the demonic presence was gone.

"Woe to you, ye obdurate in heart, who commit crime, and feed on blood. Whence is it that you feed on good things, drink, and are satiated? Is it not because our Lord, the Most High, has abundantly supplied every good thing upon the earth? To you there shall be no peace."
The Book of Enoch, Chapter CXVII, Page 160, No. 20, (Judaism, Christianity)
****

Painted and dressed for the ceremony to honor the dead, the natives came into the room. Dancing around a fire, a man handed me a bowl with an herb inside it. Bidding me to take a piece and eat, I was hesitant. Placing it in my mouth, I felt the coarseness as I swallowed.

Speaking to me as the others danced around the fire, the native man said, "We must honor the dead even when they are as he is. Because he is dead in spirit, as well, we mourn for his lost soul." Feeling the immense sadness of it, I listened to him carefully. "It is our ceremony for the dead that honors our loss, as well as our knowing that all souls return in their own time." A tear dropped from my eyes. "But there must be no mistake; there is no tolerance here for that. Evil will not be allowed here, in our love we will not hesitate to dismantle him."

Turning to the fire, he said, "Now you must sweat." Beginning to cry, he comforted me. "It is the cleansing of your soul. You have walked directly into the very heart of evil and now we must cleanse you." Afraid to sweat, I knew it would hurt. "Don't be afraid to sweat," he said, "all of these energies will come out and it will not be comfortable, but you *must* sweat." With that, I did so, feeling pain in every joint of my body as the toxins poured forth.

An honored guest quietly walked towards me. He was so quiet that I didn't notice His coming until I saw His sandals before me on the ground. Looking up, the beautiful face of Jesus was looking at me. "You have courage, my daughter. You are truly a warrior of light for the forces of the Lord, thy God." I couldn't speak as my body was shaking while the sweat poured out. Walking away quietly, his sandals made no noise upon the ground.

"He renounces himself, and takes up his cross, who, from having been unchaste becomes chaste; from having been immoderate becomes temperate; from having been weak and timid becomes strong and courageous."
The Voice of the Saints, Contrition, Page 78, No. 3, (Christianity, Catholic, Words of St. Jerome)
****

Powerful and frightening to watch, the tribunal stood before me, as Christ had bid me to go with him. Sitting in the audience, we were watching the judgment of the soul who had tried to overtake me. In a grave position, the one who had tried to crush me had violated eternal law. There was no vengeance towards him; his actions were simply not to be tolerated. Now he would face the consequence of the intentional misuse of power. Quickly, I ascertained that the fate of those who came before this tribunal was greatly determined by their intent and remorse. There was no remorse here.

Twelve Old Ones wearing long white robes filed in to stand as judge before this soul and others. Christ made it clear to me that I had no say in this matter; this was not in my hands, and it was not up to me. Allowing me to come because He'd wanted me to know that I was safe; He wanted me to see the protection of the Lord in action. For he who wished to crush me they pronounced sentence. "Death," they said.

Starting to cry, I felt conflicted. My caring for this lost soul clashed with my awareness of the depth of his evil. Not fully understanding, I didn't know what this sentence would mean, because he'd already died an Earthly death.

Christ took my hand and led me away, for He knew I didn't understand. "It is not for you to understand," He said, "it is just for you to know." Asking again for further clarification, He simply repeated His words. "It is not for you to understand, it is just for you to know." The tribunal filed out of the room, as I gazed into my savior's eyes, and then He disappeared.

"But as for cowards, the unfaithful, the depraved, murderers, the unchaste, sorcerers, idol-worshipers, and deceivers of every sort, their lot is in the burning pool of fire and sulfur, which is the second death."
New American Bible, New Testament, Revelations 21:8, (Christianity, Catholic)

"And fear not them which kill the body, but are not able to kill the soul; but rather fear him which is able to destroy both soul and body in hell."
King James Bible, New Testament, Matthew 10:28, (Christianity, Words of Christ)

"It is of no importance to me how you or any other human court may judge me: I will not even be the judge of my own self. It is true that my conscience does not reproach me, but that is not enough to justify me: it is the Lord who is my judge. For that reason, do not judge anything before the due time, until the Lord comes; he will bring to light everything that is hidden in darkness and reveal the designs of all hearts. Then everyone will receive from God the appropriate commendation."
New Jerusalem Bible, New Testament, 1 Corinthians 4:1-5, (Christianity)

****

CHAPTER FOUR
Dealing with Pure Evil - Consumer's of Children, Fame and Greed, an Encounter with Satan, Rage, False Religiosity, Holy Angels, Sutta on Evil, Demons of the Common Man, Drinkers and Partiers, Angel of God, Gargoyles, Gossip, Gluttony, Lust, Satanism and Witchcraft, False Prophets, Adultery.

****

Struck down with illness, the impurities within my soul were now manifesting upon my body in the process of purification and removal. But my sicknesses became rampant and numerous, as I became bedridden for several months. Beginning their torments and temptations, the dark side made a very strong effort to see if I would give in to my sickness and suffering, and turn away from God. Determination strong and body weak, my saving grace was my faith in God's love for my soul.

Flying through the stars, I suddenly felt someone touch my shoulder and looked to see that it was jet black. Instantly transported into a barren, eerie and ominous wilderness, I knew something was terribly wrong. For a moment, it appeared that I was alone, but everything was backwards here. It was daytime when it should've been night. Then he appeared.

Covered entirely in black robes including his face, only two holes showed where his eyes must've been. Because I was pregnant, I *knew* that he had come to take the child from my womb. Guilt filled him as he tried to explain himself and his function, but I had little time to hear him as twenty more of the dark-robed beings instantly manifested before me carrying with them the mortal remains of children. Parasitic creatures crawled along the ground eating the remains of the children who had perished at the hands of these creatures. Then I *knew* . . . I was in hell. These were the 'Consumers of Children,' dark creatures who energize all forms of evil towards children on the Earth, from molestation to murder.

"Don't you think it's hard choosing whose children must live, and whose children must die?" The first one said. "No." I said calmly. "Your child must die," the creep said, "and if you will not surrender it to us, you both shall die." My rage brewed at his words and at the grisly scene, the horridity of which cannot be described. "ENOUGH!" I shouted. Despite my outrage, I knew I could not take on all of them at once. I would need more help . . . but if I could get this one alone?

As I slowly turned and walked away from the others, he followed me, and within a few moments, we were alone in another part of the barren wilderness. Picking up a boulder, I began chanting an ancient prayer that destroys the power of evil. Throwing many boulders at him, I continued chanting the prayer because nothing seemed to have an immediate effect. But as the final and largest boulder came, the secret words inspired it to begin glowing. Hurling it towards him, he fell over and his robes disintegrated. Now revealed, the blonde man was ashamed as I ran to him and tore off the final part of his robes covering his face.

Calling out to the Universe, I shouted, "Behold! The Consumer of Children!" Exposure is what evil fears the most, and doing this made him shudder and bow his head down in shame. As the light was now entering his eyes, it was more than he could stand. Painful to him, this revelation of his true identity shamed him to such a degree that he began appearing incongruent. Dismantling, he slowly disappeared.

"For everyone who does wicked things hates the light and does not come toward the light, so that his works might not be exposed. But whoever lives the truth comes to the light, so that his works may be clearly seen as done in God."
New American Bible, New Testament, John 3:19-21, (Christianity, Catholic, Words of Christ)

"The material race, however, is alien in every way; since it is dark, it shuns the shining of the light because its appearance destroys it. And since it has not received its unity, it is something excessive and hateful toward the Lord at his revelation."
The Nag Hammadi Library, The Tripartate Tractate, No. 14, Page 95, (Christianity, Gnostic/Essene)

****

As I slept soundly in my body, a rapping could be heard from outside. Leaving form, I went to see who might be calling me from form at this time of night. A well-known musician stood at the door, one whom I had used to find quite appealing. But his appeal was not of the light, and as I looked upon his countenance, I realized that he was aligned with the gull, the demon of destructive sexual energy.

Immediately upon entering my home, he began undressing and making sexual gestures as though he wanted to make love to me. Watching his strange behavior with curious interest, I knew something was terribly wrong. Even he seemed uncomfortable with the forwardness of his act. Having already taken his pants off, he was kneeling on the ground and removing his shirt. Gently, I touched his chin and lifted it so that he could look into my eyes. "Do you come here on behalf of the dark side?" I asked. With no pause, he replied, "Yes, I do." Lowering his head in shame, he put his clothes back on. "I have two things to tell you," he said as he began to get up. My reaction to this was lukewarm, as I could not imagine that he expected me to have any interest in the words a representative of darkness might have to say. "One is that everyone who forsakes his true destiny has surely bought himself a place in hell." "Surely not!" I replied. "What do you mean?" "Well, it may be their own personal hell, but it is hell nevertheless." "Surely," I replied, "Christ will redeem them if they are willing." "But many are not willing, and it is hell, nevertheless." His revelation shocked and saddened me. "Well, what about you?" I asked, "I am aware that the music you write serves darkness, but why? Why have you chosen this?" Looking down in shame, I could tell that despite the fact that he did indeed serve darkness and was very much caught up in fame, money and glory, he wasn't proud of it. "Well, I have these good ideas," he replied, "but they are always turned down." "I see," I said, "you gave yourself to the god's of darkness because their ideas are popular in the physical world." "Yes, for fame and wealth, I sold my soul." Nodding, I understood. Choosing a lower destiny for its quick profit and reward, he'd lost his higher path which would have taken time and probably given him less worldly success.

"The second thing I must tell you is this," he said, as his face became intensely serious, "I brought the whole power of darkness with me . . . and still . . . the light *triumphs* in you!" At that moment, I realized that if I had fallen for his temptation, I would have been uniting with darkness, and fallen from grace. Taking note of the fact that his flattery might well be a ploy from the dark side to lower my guard, he walked away as he continued talking. "Well, I must admit that even I, who came here on behalf of the dark side, cannot imagine the world without the knowledge and grace you are bringing into it." I interrupted him. "Well, that's interesting. So in some ways, I really sense that you regret serving darkness, at least on this level of consciousness." Nodding that this was true, he remained unable or unwilling to give up the treasures that the dark side had given him - money and fame - even with the awareness that doing so would be the only way to save his soul. "You have been willing to give up the reward for substance," he said, "I wish I'd been able to do the same." Looking at him, I knew he read my sorrowful gaze. It was his choice, his free will. "Well, day is breaking on the East coast," he said, "I need to go."

Taking his hand, I quietly said, "Bye now, but please don't forget those good ideas you get. It's not too late . . . yet." A tear fell upon his cheek as he disappeared from my presence.

"Wisdom is poured forth like water, and glory fails not before him for ever and ever; for potent is he in all the secrets of righteousness. But iniquity passes away like a shadow, and possesses not a fixed station."
The Book of Enoch, Chapter XLVIII, No.1, Page 55, (Judaism, Christianity)
****

Awaking in the spirit but not in the flesh, my soul sat up in bed noticing that the sheets at my side were ruffling. A spirit was sitting at the foot of my bed, and in irritation, I shouted, "If you are here on behalf of darkness, I order you to leave by the power of Jesus Christ." Beginning to stir and reveal itself, a heart-shaped light of iridescent yellow appeared amidst a blue-green essence. Inside the heart were four silver stars, each representing a member of my family, including our unborn member, Mary. "You're my guardian?!" I shouted, feeling badly. "I am the guardian of your family," he replied.

Noticing that a demon had appeared in the corner of the room, I asked my guardian spirit to take care of it, taking note of the fact that I must be more vigilant in monitoring my thinking so as not to allow such annoying creatures entry into my perimeter.

"The demon knows cogitations better than the soul of another man does, not because the demon sees cogitations themselves but because he sees them through more hidden external signs."
On Evil, Question XVI, Article 8, Reply to 13, (Christianity, Catholic, Author: St. Thomas Aquinas)
****

Hearing a raucous from my bedroom, my spirit quickly exited form to go see what was happening in the bathroom next door. Sitting in the bathtub, was a demon wearing a very sarcastic grin upon his lips. Feeling irritated, the pause taken gave him an opportunity to reach towards and touch me, sucking me into an abyss of darkness far away from home.

First he led me to a place where much deviant sexual activity was taking place; orgies and perverted sex with hundreds of souls. "We are going to make you participate in this with us," he said. "If you would only give us a chance, you'd understand us and come over to our way." Not only laughable, but completely absurd, I refused to even talk to him. Enraged, he took me to an even more horrible place.

In this second location, body bags were lying all around filled with the souls of those trapped in darkness, but not yet truly dead. Attempting to squeeze their final breath from them, their hope was that they'd give in because of pure and simple exhaustion. Placing me into a body bag, he sealed it as I could hear the breathing of the others.

Pleased with himself, the demon took me to a third location, where he showed me a best-selling book, my name written on the cover as author. "Accept this gift, and you can go free," he said, "you will have a best-seller and it will be quite financially lucrative." As I was not speaking, he got angrier. "Will you accept this?!" Looking around the blackness of my bag, I unzipped it from the inside and peered into his ugly reptilian face. "No," I said, "I don't care about having a best-seller. I don't even want it."

Quietly, I stepped out of the bag. Continuing to experience higher and higher levels of rage, the demon hadn't expected me to know that I could free myself from any kind of bondage that Satan might put on my soul.

In a flash we were in a fourth location, a stage transfixed upon an open field. A big tour bus waited alongside it, as trucks were arriving for an upcoming concert. Offering me fame and fortune as a musical performer, the only catch was that I had to give up the hymnal given to my by the Lord Jesus. His icky little hands were reaching out to me in a 'gimme' kind of fashion, hoping I would hand him the book. Saying nothing, I turned away in irritated anger, shrugging my shoulders at his stupid attempts to bribe me.

An old black woman approached and for a moment, I was confused. Because of her age, I wondered if she could be an Old One, but something didn't feel right. "What is your name?" I asked her. "Monica," she said, smiling an evil grin. But because I had paused, she quickly snatched me by the remaining arm that wasn't being held by the demon. "Are you here on behalf of the light?!" I asked her, hoping that maybe she had come to rescue me. It was already too late when her sinister smile told me the answer, as another very evil man appeared to take me somewhere beyond the gateway of darkness she seemed to herald.

The fifth location was merely an open field. A sinister grin overtook his ugly face, but this man, despite how obvious it was that he was very evil, did not appear as a demon, but a person. "You know, I've killed people before," he said. "Oh, really," I retorted, unperturbed. "Why?" I asked. "Well, the last one was eating crackers, and it got on my nerves," he said. Replying with absolute calm, I said, "You're a sick son-of-a-bitch, you know that?" Laughing, he spoke again, "Well, maybe I could teach *you* something. Maybe you're getting tired of all that religious stuff. Maybe you're ready to come serve a *true* master, a *true* god."

Without warning, a voice more ominous, sickening, awful, disgusting, and torturous to hear than any I'd ever heard began echoing across the entirety of the sky. Much more powerful than I'd ever imagined it to be, it scared me to death. "YES . . . COME SERVE ME! I WILL TEACH YOU ABOUT TRUE POWER!" Immediately knowing who this was, though I had never heard it before, I would be grateful to never hear his voice again.

Overwhelming in its power, I prepared my response with an absolute inner knowing that I would be crushed, destroyed and annihilated from existence upon responding, and I yelled at the top of my lungs, "**** YOU, SATAN!" YOU'LL NEVER HAVE ME! I SERVE THE ONE GOD, THE GOD OF LIGHT! **** YOU, SATAN!" Lowering my head, I awaited the crushing energy I expected to descend. But instead, all of the darkness dissipated within seconds. Satan was gone, along with his demons.

Two Jewish Rabbi's approached quickly and quietly, covering me in ceremonial robes and leading me away. As they led me through an ancient ritual of purification, I silently fell to sleep. In awe of God's true power, I meditated upon the strength of the Lord to whisk us away from Satan's very grasp, if only our heart remains true to Him.

As I sat quietly watching the rabbi's, an old man walked in. Dressed as if from the middle ages, he quietly spoke, "I believe we should let all people worship as they please," he said. "The Jewish rabbi's have always given me nothing but light, and I will always support them." Nodding in agreement, I felt absolute gratitude for their help this harrowing night.

"Then Jesus was led by the Spirit into the desert to be tempted by the devil. He fasted for forty days and forty nights, and afterwards he was hungry. The tempter approached and said to him, 'If you are the Son of God, command that these stones become loaves of bread.' He said in reply, 'It is written: One does not live by bread alone, but by every word that comes forth from the mouth of God.' Then the devil took him to the holy city, and made him stand on the parapet of the temple, and said to him, 'If you are the Son of God, throw yourself down. For it is written: 'He will command his angels concerning you,' and 'with their hands they will support you, lest you dash your foot against a stone.'' Jesus answered him, 'Again, it is written, 'You shall not put the Lord, your God, to the test.' Then the devil took him up to a very high mountain, and showed him all the kingdoms of the world in their magnificence, and he said to him, 'All these I shall give to you, if you will prostrate yourself and worship me.' At this, Jesus said to him, 'Get away, Satan! It is written: 'The Lord, your God, shall you worship and him alone shall you serve.' Then the devil left him and, behold, angels came and ministered to him."
New American Bible, New Testament, Matthew 4:1-11, (Christianity, Catholic)
****

And so it came to pass that I was introduced to the many mansions of evil within the Universe. Journeying into these scary places was disconcerting at first, especially after having experienced many of the heavenly mansions of the Lord for such a long period of time. These stately old haunted places all had ominous characteristics correlating to the vice in which they were founded. Some souls in these horrid places were trapped there after death, as they clung tightly to their sin. Others would go there in their sleep, at night, unaware that the evil one was working hard to *increase* their vice and destructive deeds, through subconscious suggestion.

Having a very eerie quality, this particular haunted mansion shared the quality that most of them bore. My purpose was to rescue souls from these places, exorcise them, and dismantle certain energies as commanded by the Lord. Holding the energies of past dark acts committed in the Wild West of the United States, it was haunted by criminals, train robbers, bounty hunters, and every possible crime of that era. Amidst the agitation, a soul was calling for help.

All it takes is that one sincere look to the sky, 'Lord, there has to be more, what does it all mean?,' and all the angels of the Lord are called in to nourish that spark, so that it may one day become a flame. Lying awake in an old-fashioned bedroom with pictures of the greatest criminals throughout history, I appeared to the man. "Let's get out of here," I yelled to him, not wishing to stay in this dark place long, "but first, we must exorcise these demons."

Confused by my request, I began to demonstrate this vital process to him. Thinking that he could not possibly leave until all of his family and friends were ready to come with him, I tried to help him to understand that they would not be leaving for a very long time. Not yet having asked for redemption, they'd not even recognized their need for such a grand event to take place within their soul.

As hundreds of dark entities reside in haunted mansions, when you enter, many immediately cling to your soul and try to burrow within. It's not possible to even *enter* without having them attach, so if you've resided in a particular haunted place for any amount of time, there are many demons to exorcise. Even if you enter for the purpose of helping another, you must go through an exorcism before you may leave safely. Exorcism is not comfortable to experience or witness, especially at first. But once you understand the mechanisms of darkness and its various forms of assault and energetic invasion, you recognize that in certain circumstances deflection is not enough. Just as if a man were drowning in a muck pond, you would recognize that in order to save him, you must be willing to jump into the muck. No possibility would exist that you would be able to do so (to save him) without yourself being covered in grime and odor. Knowing in advance that you will have to cleanse and purify upon exit, you go in anyway because it is the only way to save him.

Beginning to pull all my energy upwards from my feet all the way to my crown chakra at the top of my head, I instinctively began reciting the first stanza of the Lord's Prayer: "Our Father, who art in heaven, hallowed be thy name, Thy Kingdom come, Thy will be done, on Earth as it is in Heaven" Repeating these words over and over, I concentrated deeply on the meaning of each phrase as I continued pulling the energies up. Dark energies settle in the lower chakras and the lower stations of the body, and in order to remove them, you must pull them up from the very bottom to the top, and out. Knowing they would invariably pass through my throat chakra on their way through, I began *thinking* the Lord's Prayer deeply within my mind so as not to give them any repose once they'd snatched my vocal chords. As the invasions rose, they came screaming out at the top of their lungs, trying to stop the painful exorcism, as they did not want to leave. Chanting continuously, my words and the power that they invoked gave them no choices. In minutes, it was over and they were gone.

In shock as he watched this event, the man was very uncomfortable with the idea of experiencing the out-of-control nature of an exorcism himself. Not wishing to go through his own process, I said, "You can't leave this place until you exorcise the dark spirits within you." His face revealed that he couldn't believe that *he* could possibly be possessed by such things. "They are within you . . ." I said, to his disbelieving face, "they are within you. Do you remember when you've felt that rage coming from your gut all the way up to your head and you lost control completely?" Now, he understood. "Who do you think fuels your rage?" I asked. Even so, the exorcism was too scary for him to undertake. "It is the only way to remove them," I said, "you may be able to control them sometimes, but inevitably they control you." He wasn't ready, and began looking agitated. But agitation is one of the most easily recognizable signs of demonic interference.

Leaving him with the knowledge of the exorcism, I said, "When you are ready, begin chanting. Someone from the light will return to retrieve you when you are ready." Nodding, it was only a matter of time before this soul would accept deliverance, even though it would not be easy.

All of a sudden, my spirit was hurling through a black hole in space. A star tunnel swept my soul into a higher energy that took me light years away from the haunted mansion I'd visited. Cascading around me in purplish blues, the stars filled my vision.

"The evil within a person is hell within him . . ."
Heaven & Hell, Chapter 57, No. 547, Page 453, (Christianity, Swedenborgianism,
Author: Emanuel Swedenborg)
"Were the eye to be anointed and illumined with the collyrium of the knowledge
of God, it would surely discover that a number of voracious beasts have

gathered and preyed upon the carrion of the souls of men."
The Kitab-I-Iqan, Part 1, Page 31, Middle, (Baha'i, Author: Baha'u'llah)
****

Appearing benign at first, the serpent could amass enough rage to explode into a raging, reddish-orange, thirty-foot, cobra-like demon within seconds. Fire, venom and smoke poured out of its mouth like a volcano, and this demon was attached to his solar plexus. Ironically, in its benign state, it appeared as a small, four-foot, and green snake.

An old man was present, very obviously well versed in the area of exorcism. Allowing me to watch as he extricated this monstrous demon from the soul of the man in the haunted mansion, we'd been summoned by the eternal to retrieve him, as he was finally ready to accept the exorcism. You simply could not describe the look upon his face when he saw what was inside of him. Afraid to proceed, he agreed sheepishly, feeling confident in the presence of this experienced old man.

"You can only restrain a demon like this one for so long," the old man said, "you can try to control it, but it is much too excitable . . . ultimately, it will control you." As the demon finished its spewing forth of vile things, it began shrinking into its benign state. Seconds later, something else riled the creature up again and it began the entire cycle all over again, turning into a huge raging inferno of darkness. Taking cover, the old man directed us to stay back while we waited for another opportunity to grasp a hold of this demon in its benign state. Very calm and expert in dealing with this process, the old man patiently waited for its benign state to return. Reciting the Lord's Prayer repeatedly, the younger man in the haunted mansion joined him in its recital. As the creature became benign, the younger man's face was still filled with terror. "You think *you're* scared of this thing?" The old man said, "Don't you think you've scared a lot of people letting this thing come lashing out of you?!" Awareness and remorse lit up the younger man's face.

Ironically, this man was not evil, especially in the sense of what you might expect in witnessing what had been living inside of him. Pointing out that this particular demon was quite common; the old man had much to say. "The demon of rage is what they call it," he said, "it often sparks outbursts of rage and lives inside a great many people who are anywhere from verbally to physically abusive." Pausing to look our way, he made sure we were listening to importance of his words to come. "This is not the demon of the mass murderer; it's the demon of the common man."

Taking the now benign creature and placing it into an unusual aquarium, we realized that this aquarium had the power to keep the demon benign and at rest while encapsulated within. Feeling relief, the man who'd undergone an exorcism felt relief, but still harbored shock from the experience. "It's time for you to get out of this place," the old man said, "before you get contaminated again." Waving good-bye to us, the younger man disappeared.

"The worst people of all are the ones who have been involved in evil pursuits as a result of self-love, with an accompanying inward behavior stemming from deceit. This is because the deceit penetrates their thoughts and purposes too thoroughly and fills them with poison, destroying their whole spiritual life."
Heaven & Hell, Chapter 60, No. 578, Paragraph 1, Page 483, (Christianity, Swedenborgianism, Author: Emanuel Swedenborg)
****

Amidst a cloudy realm, several religious leaders were waiting for me to arrive. A large silver cross adorned my neck, and I was wearing the Essene robes. Expressing their concern that the laity were having religious experiences, the religious leaders were dumbfounded as to why this would occur. Because they were the leaders, they considered themselves 'chosen ones,' and it was they who should be experiencing such unusual events.

"God chooses whom He chooses." I said as they looked at me wryly and with sarcasm. "You've become political figures, not necessarily holy men. God doesn't contain Himself to your boundaries, you must seek Him on His terms, not your own." (Although being a political figure for the sake of God can be a *very* holy calling, it is simply a different calling.) Angered, a priest replied, "Well, who are you to tell us this? You're no prophet!" "I've never claimed to be a prophet, I only serve the Lord."

"(Howbeit), in accordance with the tender mercy of God, in accordance with His goodness and with the wondrous manifestation of His glory, He has (always) granted it to some of the earth-born to gain admittance to the Congregation of the Holy, to be reckoned among the community of angelic beings who are with Him, to have station there for life everlasting and to be in one lot with His (celestial) Holy Ones. All men are punished(?) or marked out for distinction according to the lot which (God) has assigned to each, (some for eternal shame and contempt, and some) for life everlasting."
The Dead Sea Scriptures, The Epochs of Time, Page 523, Paragraph 3, (Christianity, Gnostic/Essene)

****

Enraptured in flight, my soul emerged upon the altar at a holy church. My white robes and cross were glistening as I kneeled before the sacred altar to Mary. Bowing and praying, I lit a candle in the name of the priest who had admonished me, to honor and respect his post and his holy place with God. As I quietly arose, this same priest approached me. Fearing a further confrontation, he greeted me with a smile.

Saying nothing, he showed me a book. Immediately, I recognized it as my own, the one I had written. "An angel came to me!" he shouted in exuberation. "She showed me your writings and told me that you are a servant of the Lord!" Smiling, I placed my hand in his.

Insisting on administering Holy Communion to me, I felt unworthy but his insistence brought tears to my eyes. Deep from inside his robes he retrieved a box containing a small statue of the Holy Mother of God, and then he placed a small amulet of Mary around my ankle. When he finished, I said, "Thank you, thank you fellow servant of the Lord." As I said this, he smiled.

Noticing that the angels had given him a gift when they'd come to him in vision, on his teeth were golden hieroglyphics, markings visible only to the eyes of God's servants. Bowing in honor of this grace he had received, I said, "I must go now," disintegrating into only a light, I disappeared.

Soaring gracefully to an angelic realm, I was directed to put on my angel wings. Upon attaching them, my robes turned into a magnificent white-gold. Flying to my destination, two young Mormon missionaries who truly loved God and were seeking with all of their soul had failed to find all the answers they needed. "Your path provides you with only a fraction of the truth," I said to them, "there is more to know about the Lord." Confused and hesitant at first, they both reached to touch my wings. As they touched them, they immediately knew that I was a servant of the Father. Sitting down to teach them, these souls were young and childlike, and in their in their innocence, they sought true knowledge, and were willing to learn even if it contradicted the doctrine they had previously been taught.

Soaring outside to an iridescent river flowing amidst a wanton mountain forest, I pointed to the trees that were all around us. "How do you look at a tree?" I asked him. "I look at the top, primarily." He said. "Well, you must look at a tree from the ground to the sky if you want to watch its ascent to heaven!" As I said this, he looked at it this way, and a grand smile overtook his face. Heavens opening and skies parting, it made way for the arms of the Lord to reach humanity. "I must go now," I said, as he tried to convince me to stay. "I'm sorry, I have others I must assist, but I do have a message to give you from the Creator." He was excited. "I have been given permission to grant you one miracle, so think about what you would like, and when I or another returns, it will be done." Smiling with childlike glee, I soared into the heavenly realm that now lay open in a pinkish mist.

"Suffer the little children to come unto me, and forbid them not: for of such is the kingdom of God. Verily I say unto you, whosoever shall not receive the kingdom of God as a little child, he shall not enter therein."
King James Bible, New Testament, Mark 10:14-15, (Christianity, Words of Christ)
****

Having worked with a particular soul in attempting to elevate her to a higher degree, Andy and I found that no matter how hard we tried, it seemed that this soul couldn't understand what we were trying to teach her, and she continued in the ways of her former sin. One night, the Lord bade me to see a set of three lights. Andy and I had ignited all three of these lights within our soul, but our friend had only lit two of the lights. A voice from the heavens said, "She has only two of the three lights, and thus, she cannot understand." This gave me insight.

"Nor has any one known that there are three degrees of love and wisdom, in accordance with which the angelic heavens are arranged. Nor that the human mind is divided into that number of degrees, to the end that it may be raised after death into one of the three heavens, which takes place in accordance both with its life and its faith."
The True Christian Religion, Volume I, No. 24, Part 7-8, (Christianity, Swedenborgianism, Author: Emanuel Swedenborg)
****

Again, I was holding 'The Sutta on Evil,' as I was being prepped before being sent upon my way.

Soaring into the alteration, this particular mass murderer had spent her life completely undetected; a black woman had killed anyone who possessed anything she felt she didn't have. It could be anything from money to physical beauty. Partly because she was a woman, she had gone completely undetected by the law despite the overwhelming number of victims she had to her debit.

Upon my arrival, she was confronting her latest target; a woman with large breasts and a voluptuous figure which she envied. Walking towards the two, the murderer began speaking angry words to her potential victim. Conveying her intention to kill her, the woman didn't take her seriously. And as the murderess did not leave things be; the other woman reached her arm back planning to sock this screwy stranger in the face. Knowing that that action would energize further violence, I knew I must subdue this move. Having unusual physical strength, the perpetrator could have overtaken her with no difficulty. Grabbing the potential victim's arm, I held it. Upon seeing me, the black woman began running, so I summoned the aid of two other alterers to assist. Appearing, they chased after her, while I ran around the other side of a building, knowing that she would be chased right back to me.

Running frantically, seeing me struck absolute terror in her. Somehow, she *knew* me, and she *knew* of my purpose with her. In a flash of light, I transformed her into a small domestic cat. Picking her up, I placed the 'Sutta on Evil' on her back and allowed the knowledge of its energetic pages to enter into her being. She hissed as I did this. "You have always followed the ways of 'fight or flight.' We cannot allow you to continue doing harm; you have had your chance as a human and failed to attain higher learning. Your predatory nature will now be monitored in a more harmless form."

Even as a cat, she remained terrified of me. But as I held her, I began to pet her anyway. Hissing and lashing towards me with her claws, I said, "You cannot hurt me. You *need* love in your heart. You *need* to learn a higher way." Agitated still, the darkness within this soul had much to overcome.

Placing her on the ground, I looked again at the Sutta which contained the knowledge of these lower evolutionary incarnations which occur in energy.

Because the border worlds, realm three and four, are mortal realms of light and dark, incarnations are allowed from lower evolutions (the hells) to give opportunities for growth to occur, and from higher evolutions (angels, the heavens) to give opportunities for higher knowledge to descend. Those from lower evolutions who fail are most often returned to the animal kingdom or one of the hells until they again show potential to reach a higher thrust. Evil exists in the mortal realms because of free will and the function of evolution in these realms. Mortal realms contain elements of higher love, slightly lower love, souls in karmic purification, karmic darkness, dominantly dark souls, evil souls, and the animal kingdom which is completely predatory. From this, you see the range of function in karmic purification, but now we will focus on the element of evil.

Some demons are actually given entry into the third realm through human incarnation. Although these demonic incarnations are few in comparison to those in the state of karmic delusion, the actual evil which occurs in this realm is often instigated by incarnate demons or former wards of hell who manipulate other incarnations to do their dirty deeds. (Usually karmic darkness, or dominant darkness, but sometimes those of the light who are naive, and as a result, fall from grace.) Karmic darkness is always surrounded by some demonic influence and can usually be easily manipulated. All souls who incarnate in mortal realms, except for very unusual souls who volunteer to come from above to fulfill a higher task, are controlled by the elements of darkness to a certain extent. Even a soul who achieves karmic purification has <u>only begun</u> to purge all such influence.

Demonic incarnations are brought into the third realm to actually give opportunities for the advancement of their souls. In their human birth, it is hoped that the parents will teach them in infancy of respect and honor for life, the essence seeds of compassion, but in the case of demonic birth, a parent must be extremely diligent for even the smallest bit of growth to occur. In most cases, but definitely not all, the parents chosen for the task are a few levels above or below the soul incarnating and are fairly dark themselves. Because of this, they are often easily manipulated into accepting wrongdoing and protecting or sympathizing with the disturbed child. It goes without saying that if a demonic birth can sometimes be altered through the hard and tedious work of parents, that children who are born with very strong karmic programs can be turned around in childhood, also, but only if they are given parents who work diligently to teach them the proper truths, within the understanding of their inherent delusions, and if the children are open and receptive to the seeding of new awareness. Parents are often chosen by their conscious or unconscious ability to transform particular karmic programs, but because of the delusional state of mankind and the inherent difficulty in overturning karma, many, if not most, children are unable to accomplish this in childhood. Because of the nature of parental sin being visited upon the children, many of these souls not only don't catapult, but rather, turn backwards, embracing additional vices of their parents. Because of the difficulty in rearing souls and the self-centered nature of our society; parents and their children sometimes fail this most important task, because they are too distracted by worldly attachments, or because the child is too deeply ingrained of its karmic or evil view.

"Moreover the same enemy instills into the parents a base neglectfulness and carnal love for their offspring; and he incites teachers to carelessness, so that the children find no support against evil in their education, but become depraved and spoiled by many bad habits, losing sight of virtue and their good inclinations and going the way of perdition."
The Mystical City of God (Abrid.), The Transfixion, Chapter II, Page 404, Middle,
(Christianity, Catholic, Words of Mary)

A grand difference exists between those surrounded by dark influences and incarnate demons or wards of hell. Incarnate demons can vary from an actual incarnation of a god of vice, to very powerful demonic manifestations (former wards of hell) who encompass many or all of the deadliest vices. As the most evil of souls in their potency, they are difficult to identify (they can be smart and they come in many faces), and they can maintain a semblance of absolute normalcy to the outside world. Demonic souls are good at disguise.

An incarnation of a singular god of vice or multiple vice evil is difficult to distinguish and can only be verified by energetic means. Because ignorance, dominant darkness, and evil manifest such similar behaviors, it is difficult to recognize the difference between them on the ground; for they differ only in intention and movement.

Demonic or dominantly dark incarnations can often be discovered by a singular flaw. On the surface, they will not often reveal their identity, but their singular flaw is their absolute *hatred* of God. As opposed to someone who just doesn't believe in God, this type of incarnation experiences rage, discomfort, agitation or nervousness upon the mere mention of His name. Despite this abhorrence of God, it does not necessarily keep them from attending a church. Becoming increasingly agitated in the presence of beings of higher incarnation, they are severely affected by those with energetic influence or who use the name of God with true power. Assaultive at times around their opposite, they try to keep this hidden side of themselves under wraps. Many mass murderers operate in this manner, as only their victims see the demonic image behind the mask they wear, and of course, they don't live to tell.

To keep up appearances, the deception of the serpent, the evil one will do whatever it takes. Many very sincere spiritual seekers will not have the same affect on a demonic soul because they are not able to discern energetic liaisons. Because of this, demonic souls may be very comfortable around such as these, as long as their true nature is concealed.

Interestingly, those involved in karmic darkness may sometimes demonstrate this behavior, as well, because they are very often still possessed by dark forces, or surrounded by their influence.

Benign at times when the soul is in complete control but violently assaultive at others when control has been usurped; the most popular disguise is the silent, violent one, keeping its dark destructive agitated behavior behind closed doors. Those possessed by such influences may be very agreeable in public, kind and laid back, but in their own home they may be abusive, or energize destructive thoughts within others who then carry them out for them; keeping their own hands clean of the carnage of their own vice, at least for the sake of appearances, but not in the sense of the absolute.

When someone is surrounded by darkness, simple dismantling and removal of the bad energy is accomplished, although many re-energize the return of such influence rather quickly through their vice-filled thoughts. In regards to incarnate evil, however, because they *are* the bad energy, they are given a certain amount of time to show movement towards a higher ideal, before the eternal energizes their death and rebirth to a lower life form or realm. Although this can be an animal birth, because many animal species are compatible to the predatory will, this is usually a temporary fix.

Because evolution is meant to be forward movement rather than backwards flow, any soul who is traveling towards life will be energized further, no matter at what level they may stand in the spectrum of understanding. Thus, those who are traveling away from life will also be de-energized accordingly no matter what level they may stand in the spectrum of understanding. Giving insight into God's mysterious ways, a soul who has been given much light, might be turned backwards if he ceases movement forward; just as a soul who may still be deeply ensconced in ignorant karmic darkness (ignorance, because chosen darkness and evil always turn away from life), may be given eternal assistance and protection on the basis of their pure intent and desire to move towards God.

Many incarnations of evil have ruled, as have incarnations of light. Society must learn to discern the serpent from the lamb, but society often fails and evil is chosen. Evil is not simply a benign presence that needs to be rehabilitated, true evil must be *STOPPED*. Sympathizing with darkness only magnifies and implodes its ramifications, and it can only be stopped by swift, severe, deliberate retribution. When a society fails to perform this responsibility, society becomes the host and victim of the darkness it hasn't the courage to stop. The serpent comes in, oh, so many faces, and his manipulation is won with hundreds of reasoning's and excuses for the rightness of his acts. Although the eternal recognizes ignorance, there are no excuses for dominant darkness or evil. When you face chosen darkness on this level, good and evil do become black and white.

Birth in the lower hell realms is appropriate for the deepest forms of evil because their thoughts and acts reflect the deafening violence to which they are compatible, and they are quite at home in such places. In the lower hells, souls undergo the tortures that they have inflicted upon others, and a soul who *is* destruction, is not compatible to God, whose existence *is* creation. Enjoying the infliction of pain upon others, an evil soul is aeons away from the ultimate and divine mercy of God.

Evolution is not an issue of judgment, but of compatibility. Birth in the hell realms is appropriate for those souls who *love* their vice. Souls who love God, despite their ignorance, will naturally amend to a higher status through the influx of heavenly forces. Because of the millions of possible configurations, each path is unique and can only be understood energetically. Jaded with many elements, and many forces of both good and evil at work to lay claim to its destiny, only God may stand as judge of a soul, and His judgments are always true.

"Dearly beloved, avenge not yourselves, but rather give place unto wrath: for it is written, Vengeance is mine; I will repay, saith the Lord."
King James Bible, New Testament, Romans 12:19, (Christianity)

"We can determine the nature of hellish spirits' malice by looking at their unspeakable arts . . . These skills are virtually unknown in the world. One kind has to be with the misuse of correspondence; another with the misuse of the lowest elements of the Divine design; a third with the communication and inflow of thoughts and affections, using transformations, investigations, other spirits beyond themselves, and emissaries. A fourth kind involves working with hallucinations, a fifth, projection beyond themselves so that they seem to be present where their bodies are not. A sixth kind involves impersonation, persuasion and lies. An evil spirit comes by its very nature into the use of these skills when it has been released from its body. They are intrinsic to the nature of his evil . . . Hellish spirits torment each other with these skills in the hells."
Heaven & Hell, Chapter 60, No. 580, Page 484, (Christianity, Swedenborgianism, Author: Emanuel Swedenborg)

****

Ordering that I be allowed to see the demons of the common man through the souls of an average family, the Lord had ordered them to come to me and show me their true selves. Each were hesitant as they approached, and but they were under divine command to be revealed. The first came with darkness in his eyes, as his face slowly became reptilian and metamorphosized into an ugly demon. Conveying that he was an incarnate demon, I turned. The second's approach brought with her an ominous presence. Through her mouth a most disturbing voice began speaking, the hoarse, deep, throaty cry of Satan. "YOU CANNOT COME HERE," Satan echoed through his charge, "You must know I serve two masters." Revealed, her masters were Satan himself, and the gull, destructive sexual energy. The third approached as the demons that controlled this soul were by her side. Told that she made 'unconscious incantations to Beelzebub just by the nature of her thought processes,' I was shocked. She was not aware of this. The fourth stood alone, the darkest of all of them, a consumer of children, who stood as a mere shell of the human he had once had the chance to be, and lowered his head in shame. But he was not given permission to reveal his full status, yet, for to see such evil at this time, would be too much for my soul to bear.

In a flash, I was sitting in the center of a small living room. The Dalai Lama came and sat down on the floor, attempting to teach the members of this family. Showing them pictures of transformations in progress, he tried to make them understand what they must do to purify themselves and deliver themselves from darkness. Rudely shouting, they screamed. "We are not what you say we are!" Displaying irritation, the Dalai Lama was completely in control of his emotions despite their total disrespect of all that is sacred. But I couldn't stand to see such a holy man be treated in this manner, "How dare you speak that way to one of God's holy men!" I shouted. Raising his hand to me, the Dalai Lama motioned me to stop as he began to speak of compassion.

Beautiful and eloquent, his words were difficult to grasp. But I listened as intently as I could so as not to miss any of his mastery. Coming to show me that it wouldn't matter if the holiest of God's servants came to these people, he wanted me to realize that they would respond with arrogance and rage, nevertheless. Needing to be mindful of my anger, it would only be through a calm and peaceful mind that the Lord would be able to work. "You must accept their choice," he conveyed, "it is theirs to make. This journey will strengthen you in your ability to perceive those in the lower realms with compassion."

Before he left, the Dalai Lama made mention of the recent birth of our daughter. Smiling with joy at her arrival, he chuckled and disappeared.

"Vasudeva tried to pacify Kamsa by good instruction as well as by philosophical discrimination, but Kamsa was not to be pacified because his association was demoniac. Because of his demoniac associations, he was a demon, although born in a very high royal family. A demon never cares for any good instruction. He is just like a determined thief: one can give him moral instruction, but it will not be effective. Similarly, those who are demoniac or atheistic by nature can hardly assimilate any good instruction, however authorized it may be. That is the difference between demigod and demon. Those who can accept good instruction and try to live their lives in that way are called demigods, and those who are unable to take such good instruction are called demons."
KRSNA, Chapter 1, Page 19, Paragraph 2, (Hinduism, Author: A.C. Bhaktivedanta Swami Prabhupada)

****

The rowboat was moving slowly along the river as we began our trip to the wilderness of demons. A Buddhist monk rowed the boat very mindfully towards three separate destinations in the eerie woodland. Taken to learn more about the demons of the common man, as manifested in this particular average family, I was unsure.

Walking through the woods was the demonic form of the gull, destructive sexual energy, wearing a skirt up to her buttocks; she kept trying to get the monk's attention by taunting him sexually. Unmoved by her attentions, he had no interest in such manifestations. The young woman owned by this gull appeared next to her, as I acknowledged her charge.

Inviting the demon to join us in the boat, the monk remained totally at peace as we rowed further towards a mountainous area. I was not very comfortable sharing the boat with a demon. Arriving at our second destination, we exited the rowboat and traveled on foot to a spot deep in the woods.

Standing there was a very large raging demon; fifteen or twenty feet in height. Introducing me to the demon of rage, he was given to uncontrollable fits of rage, which made him grow larger. Frightened by this particularly reptilian demon, I moved back; but the Buddhist monk stood forward, even as the demon raged. The demon stood on two feet and had green horns. Holding his hand to the demon, the monk asked him to join us in our boat. Two members appeared at the side of this demon, father and son, as the monk made me to know that this demon controlled them both, having been passed from one generation to the next. In this, I saw how the sins of the father are visited upon the sons, for the demon of the father had been inherited by the son.

In the face of this simple monk, I saw complete compassion and understanding. Imperturbable, he generated no anger or hatred towards the demons, just a polite understanding of the causes of such births. While we rowed in the boat, the demon of rage would burst into fits of violence at random moments, which made me fearful and uncomfortable. But the monk remained completely unchanged, as if it were simply a small child throwing a tantrum on the floor.

Rowing quietly to our final destination, we reached the home of the final member of this family. The beast continued his rages and the gull continued her sexual tauntings; but the monk parked the boat quietly with no response to the emergent defilement. His compassion was something I could not yet fully understand.

Attached to the side of this soul's home was a haunted mansion, overrun by demons and haunted memories from her past. Anything but benign, this haunted mansion was inhabited by the soul who made unconscious incantations to Beelzebub, just by the nature of her thoughts.

As the monk walked with me to the door, he directed that I should enter alone. As I did, I saw the demons, ghosts and maniacal ravings of the occupants of the haunted mansion, while this woman stood amongst it, unwilling to do anything about it. "You could free yourself from this plight if only you would be willing to examine and process these energies singularly." I said. She folded her arms in defiance. "No!"

Leaving the home, I closed the door. As we re-entered the rowboat the demons disappeared and reappeared on the shore in this demon wilderness. Smiling and waving at the monk, they seemed grateful that he understood their true nature and felt compassion for the inherent suffering of such a state. Finding it compelling that all of these demons were common, not unusual in any way, it was shocking to me to realize that almost all incarnate souls are possessed to a certain degree by such varied demons of vice.

Being with the monk transferred a very important knowledge, that of compassion and love to even the most vile of creation. Continuing to row the boat until we exited this forest of demons, the monk said and conveyed nothing more. But I reflected a great deal on how I used to perceive darkness. And now, I understood something I'd never fully grasped. Darkness knows no happiness, for it doesn't know God. This is very sad.

"To encounter a true master is said to be worth a century of studying his or her teaching, because in such a person we witness a living example of enlightenment.

How can we encounter Jesus or the Buddha? It depends on us. Many who looked directly into the eyes of the Buddha or Jesus were not capable of seeing them . . . When a sage is present and you sit near him or her, you feel peace and light."

Living Buddha, Living Christ, Chapter 4, Page 52, Paragraph 1, Page 53, Top,
(Buddhism, Mahayana, Words of Thich Naht Hahn)

****

Wandering through a haunted mansion which was quite different than the others, I found it to be more of a middle of the road haunting. Huge and endless in its number of rooms, only a few of the rooms were actually haunted by demonic spirits. What stood out about this mansion, however, was the overwhelming amount of corruption, putrid water, rotten walls, dirt, grime, and mold which was growing everywhere. But it was also the most populated mansion I'd ever come across, there were literally thousands here at any given moment, for it was the haunted mansion of the common man.

Resting in a small bedroom, Andy was with me and within moments of our arrival crowds of people were waiting in lines to see us. "Would you mind?" I said, rather irritated, but Andy quietly touched my shoulder and said, "No, you don't understand, I must minister to these people."

Immediately, I realized that Andy worked on behalf of the souls in this mansion on both levels of consciousness, here and through the court systems, to restore that which has been lost.

"Shaking the palaces of all demons, awakening the minds of all sentient beings, those who received the teaching and practiced it in the past, they cause to know the true meaning."
The Flower Ornament Scripture, Ten Dedications, Page 667, Stanza 8, (Buddhism, Mahayana)

****

Walking into the old duplex, it was a smaller, but very defiled haunted mansion. A group of young, college-age men lived there who were drinking and partying with several young women. One of the young men was being very attentive to a young woman who was slightly overweight. Using flattery and insincere compliments, she eventually agreed to go have sex with him. But when they returned from having sex, he treated her like trash, as though she was worthless, humiliating her in front of the other men and women who were engaging in other various levels of sexual activity.

Asking the monk beside me, I begged the question. "He seemed so sincere; I don't understand why he is behaving so terribly to this woman now." As I asked this, barracudas appeared in the middle of the floor, long black fish which I immediately understood to be their penises. "It is another manifestation of darkness," the monk said, "their penises have become serpents used to humiliate women."

Suddenly, he was gone.

An inner knowing was leading me to find the Buddhist monk who had taken me upon his rowboat. Scheduled to be speaking somewhere in the astral arena, in order to get there, I would have to travel alone through several dark and dank streets. In the deepest of ghettoes, I felt no fear, only expectation in seeing the monk.

Up ahead, a worldly man, still trapped within the defilement of his own ways, was watching me; angry that I'd emerged from the prison of vice that still held his soul. Glaring at me as I turned away, I conveyed, "You have no hold on my soul, your bondage is your own."

Arriving at the place where the monk was to be, many souls were engaging in frivolous speech, talking endlessly. Sitting quietly across the room, I watched the serene and peaceful monk as he said nothing. Walking over to where I waited, he sat down next to me.

Conveying silently, he said, "I am impressed with your state of mindfulness." Placing his hand on mine, I gave a glance of thanks.

"Craving steadily grows in the mortal whose mind is agitated by (evil) thoughts, who is full of strong passions and ever yearning for what is pleasant. Such a one makes his fetters strong."
Dhammapada, Canto XXIV, No. 349, Page 137, (Buddhism)

****

Now pursuing me, the demonic man was in a violent rage. Holding a gun to my head, he had been led into this vile state by his own bitter darkness, but his rage was multiplied because I had given him the truth of the state of his soul and would not take it back; he was a consumer of children. Astral police officers were standing by to disarm him, but I didn't think I would need them. Reaching down, I took his first gun and handed it to the police. Pulling out a larger gun, I saw within his eyes that he was truly capable of killing me, although this should not have been surprising, for he was quite violent in the physical realm. "I will destroy you!" he said, as I gazed into his crazed eyes. "You may kill this body, but the Way is established in me and cannot be destroyed. This is what you hate, is it not?" I shouted. Confused, he began shivering and didn't know what to do. "DO IT!" I shouted at him. "I've no fear of losing this life. The Way is established within me. It will not die, and it will haunt you more than my living body ever could." Taking the gun from his hands as he quivered, I handed it to the police and disappeared.

"To accept death at such a time, in order that the Will of God may be fulfilled, merits for us a reward similar to that of the martyrs, because they accepted death to please God."

The Voice of the Saints, The Meaning of Suffering, Page 122, No. 2, (Christianity, Catholic, Words of St. Alphonsus Liguori)

****

Alit beyond the threshold of time, my soul flew fast along a roadway as hundreds of singular red roses began emerging from the ground; not on bushes, but each alone atop a single stem. An angel came gracefully carrying within her hand a single white rose, as the hundreds of red roses continued to emerge around her. Handing me the white rose, she asked me to give it to my husband, Andy. "The white is a constant symbol of the presence of God, and within each petal of every rose lies the secrets of all existence." Conveying that it was a medal of honor for his work in restoring that which had been lost, the angel acknowledged his courage in the face of much darkness to strive to save souls who would otherwise be lost to the Lord. Taking notice of his many personal sacrifices on behalf of these souls, this had pleased God. He was being honored for his work as a prosecutor in the court system. She began reciting the Lord's Prayer. "Our Father who art in heaven, Hallowed be thy name . . ."

"I saw there roses, white and red, and I thought them symbols of Christ's Passion and our Redemption."

The Life of Jesus Christ and Biblical Revelations, The Creation, No. 2, Page 5, Paragraph 1, (Christianity, Catholic, Words of Ven. Anne Catherine Emmerich on Paradise and the Garden of Eden)

****

Before I knew what had happened, a group of spiritual guides had swept me away to follow them on their missions for the night. About fifty men and women, all were trained in the de-energization and extrication of incarnate consumer's of children.

Like a SWAT team, they were unfailing in their lures and devices to entrap and capture the assailers of God's most precious ones. And if there was even the smallest of hesitation to cooperate with God's answer to the consumer's of children, they were immediately destroyed. No tolerance whatsoever was given to those who perpetrated evil upon children. In fact, I had never seen such immediate, total and thorough retaliation by any force of light for any other crime. Perpetrators of such acts were held accountable for the soul's they defiled, and were given no second chances. Sympathy was absent for this putrid form of evil. Committing such an act seemed to render immediate judgment against your soul to be administered at God's command.

Preparing to take out a particularly horrible soul who had committed many acts against children, the SWAT team revealed to me how many victims, crimes, and unspeakable acts he had committed, all of which were hard to fathom. Leading the SWAT team on a long and arduous chase, it resulted in a confrontation in a mall where he was now surrounded. Randomly, he shot at people all around, because he knew he was doomed but did not want to give up.

One of the team members took my hand as he wanted me to see this particularly vile character God had sent them to annihilate. Directing me to look upon the countenance of this creature, I followed him quietly and turned to face this man who had piled up all around him the disgusting lures and horrific devices he had used on his unfortunate victims. "Aaaaaaaaaaaaaaaah," I screamed in horror, as I looked upon the face of the consumer. "Aaaaaaaaaaaaaaaah." Showing no emotion, he had nothing to say regarding the charges brought against him; but his face was covered by a pox, the visible sign of his sin. An angel of the Lord appeared. "Choosing evil is enough to drive a man away from God," she said, "but even this has the hope of salvation. But to bring other souls to damnation is a violation of God's law to the highest degree. To deliver children into the hands of evil is a crime against God for which you are accountable." The consumer saw two souls for which he was paying due. One had been born into darkness, but because of this man, had become worse, and had gone backwards. This was very bad. But then the angel showed him a sweet innocent young child, who'd been born in a state of grace, but because of him, had become filled with demons of various kinds, causing this soul to fall from grace. This was so much greater a loss, so much greater a sin, and this was very, very bad.

As I watched, I realized that being the cause of another soul's fall from grace is a much greater sin than any other. Falling apart at the sight, the man said nothing, nothing at all. Cowering, I turned away because I couldn't look as the team moved in and destroyed him. Time for destruction now completely over, he was rendered completely benign. To prey upon children is the lowest form of evil, and to commit such acts, is to almost assuredly commit your soul to hell.

"Silence is equivalent to confession."
The Talmudic Anthology, No. 189, Paragraph 1, Ketubot, 11, (Judaism)
"Whoever offends an innocent, pure and faultless person, the evil (of his act) rebounds on that fool, even as fine dust thrown against the wind."
Dhammapada, Canto IX, No. 125, Page 51, (Buddhism)
"He said to his disciples, 'Things that cause sin will inevitably occur, but woe to the person through whom they occur. It would be better for him if a millstone were put around his neck and he be thrown into the sea than for him to cause one of these little ones to sin."
New American Bible, New Testament, Luke 17:1-2, (Christianity, Words of Christ)
****

"Even though there may be an every-day purity, silt-clear as a river's water in autumn, how can it possibly compare with a luminous spring night, the moon softened by haze? Many are the houses where people yearn thus for a spotlessly clean life, but, however much they sweep this way and that, their hearts are still not emptied and clear."
The Denkoroku, Chapter 7, Page 40, Stanza 1, (Buddhism, Zen)

Arriving with a calm smile upon her face, the most reverend master walked towards me, complimenting me upon my monastery and how it had been erected to *almost* perfection. Every religious statue, picture, symbol and book had been arranged according to energy, placed to create a specific energetic function. Showing me an area which was not quite finished, she told me what changes needed to be made to make the monastery 'energetically' perfect, thus, affording energetic protection from dark forces.

Another monk stood beside her as she quietly asked, "Have you studied the next Seraph?" "Yes, I have and I believe I am ready for the following," he replied. Walking closer to her, I bowed lightly. "Master, would it be alright if I posed a question to you?" "Yes, it would." She replied. "You use the word 'seraph' and I don't know what it means." "Seraph," she replied, "is a word we use in scriptural study to represent a level of training and attainment." Conveying that she acknowledged my continued desire to learn and serve the Lord, she had grave concerns regarding my naiveté regarding the power of the dark side and their desire to destroy me. Satan hates souls, but he hates the souls that steal others away from him all the more. "You must be more aware, diligent and empowered to destroy the demons," she said, as she suddenly saw something coming from behind me and shouted, "Close your eyes!"

Having arrived without warning, the demons were pouring some type of harsh chemical from above intended to blind my spiritual sight. Because of her quick action, my eyes were closed and I was able to protect myself from this dark plan.

After opening my eyes, I saw an orange demon about four feet tall with a cup in his hands. Beginning to pour out spindly dark-winged creatures onto the floor, they immediately began multiplying by the thousands. Standing back, the reverend shouted, "It's too late! The gargoyles multiply too quickly, you will be defeated!" "NO!" I shouted.

Walking forward as the gargoyles began clinging to our arms and legs, parasites by nature, I began praying fervently to the Lord. Allowing a part of His enormous vastness to enter into my spiritual body, the Lord began shouting through my vocal chords, "The Almighty One demands your death! The Almighty One demands your death!" Realizing the vastness of God's mercy, in that moment, I also realized that His wrath is equally powerful.

The reverend master looked shocked at God's presence within me, as she truly believed that we had been beyond saving and that it was too late. Imminent destruction was so profound and I, too, was amazed at God's voice blending with my own, but I couldn't really contemplate it right now. "The Almighty One demands your death!" echoing over and over, "The Almighty One demands your death!" Gargoyles began falling to the ground like flies, as the reverend master took my hand in respect, acknowledging the presence of God within me. Walking away, I thanked her for her warning, for it surely had proven quite vitally true.

"My Son, let not the fair and subtle sayings of men move thee, for the kingdom of God is not in word, but in power."
The Imitation of Christ, The Third Book, Chapter XLIII, Paragraph 1, (Christianity, Author: Thomas A Kempis')

"And the seventy returned again with joy, saying, Lord, even the devils are subject unto us through thy name."
King James Bible, New Testament, Luke 10:17-19, (Christianity, Words of Christ)
****

As the Lord continued His promised purification of my soul, I began experiencing an expungement which frightened me. Within my soul were several spindly creatures, and as the Lord began removing them one by one, the demonic realm would assault me continually at night. Sending various forms of temptations, usually in the form of lust because of my karmic propensity to this vice, they were relentless in their search for an avenue which would allow them to return.

As soon as I recognized a temptation within my soul, I would immediately awaken from sleep, and the spindly creatures would be pushed out through my neck by the power of the Lord as I saw them bouncing on and off the walls in my conscious state. Soaring quickly to them, I grabbed the creatures and soared into the heavens, placing them in the hands of angels who would insure that they be returned to the second realm. Far be it from me to leave a dark force to roam the Earth seeking a new host.

"The devil sleepeth not; thy flesh is not yet dead; therefore, cease thou not to make thyself ready unto the battle, for enemies stand on thy right hand and on thy left, and they are never at rest."
The Imitation of Christ, The Second Book, Chapter IX, No. 8, (Christianity, Author: Thomas A Kempis)
****

Silent demons are worse than those who are more obvious, acting on impulse. Because their rage is multiplied by several times and are more likely to incite another to commit grave and deadly evil acts. Despite their sometimes benign appearance, the silent demons appear on the surface to never be angered, but inside they hold vile thoughts and hatreds, which they keep to themselves in public, but behind closed doors they energize hatred, destruction and disunity in others.

"Hypocrites are excluded from the presence of God."
The Talmudic Anthology, No. 147, Page 201, Stanza 5, Sotah, 42a, (Judaism)
****

       Soaring outside of my body, I felt the sheer of the spirit as the eternal directed me to the heavens. Beginning to demonstrate how a single soul can affect millions by doing God's will, I watched and saw as the energies of the Lord poured through my lithe form and my spirit followed His commands without hesitation. In a way that defies words, I understood how truly significant every single soul can be. But I knew that my small little life could be very large in God's eyes, if I would follow His will. Beyond that, I was told that it is *only* by following God's commands without hesitation, regardless of how little sense it may seem to make at the time, that a soul can ever achieve true greatness, in an eternal sense.

"All do We aid - these as well as those - out of the bounty of thy Lord, and the bounty of thy Lord is not limited. See how We have made some of them to excel others. And certainly the Hereafter is greater in degrees and greater in excellence."
The Holy Qur'an, Part XV, Chapter 17, Section 2, No. 20-21, (Islam, Words of Mohammad)
****

       Standing within a school house, two women were arguing. One was a party girl, and the other was more reserved and virtuous. Walking away, the virtuous girl was no longer present as I walked towards the party girl. Dressed very sexually, I looked at her calmly and said. "I used to be just like you. I thought it was cool to be the party-girl, the fun one, the one that everybody noticed and wanted to hang around. But I was wrong. It is much more virtuous to be somewhat reserved and more prudent about what you wear and how you behave. It is a very different thing to try to look nice because you want to be your best, but it is quite another to dress in a very sexual manner, wearing lots of jewelry and makeup, simply for the purpose of attracting attention and wanting everyone to notice you, that is vanity and it is a deadly sin." Looking at me strangely, I walked away.

       There are seven deadly sins according to the bible: Sloth, Greed, Vanity, Avarice, Gluttony, Lust and Pride. If you are incarnate, you came in with a tendency towards at least one and more likely two or three. Virtue must replace vice, but the desires and cravings that come from vice must naturally amend into the higher thinking that results in virtue: Wisdom, Justice, Temperance, Courage, Faith, Hope and Charity (Love). Forgive and be merciful to all . . . for as Christ said, it is easy to love those that love you, but it is hard to love those that hate you.

"Do not think lightly of evil, saying, 'It will not come to me.' By the constant fall of waterdrops, a pitcher is filled; likewise the unwise person, accumulating evil little by little, becomes full of evil."
Dhammapada, Canto IX, No. 121, Page 51, (Buddhism)
"Before I come as the just Judge, I am coming first as the King of Mercy."
Divine Mercy, Notebook 1, Page 42, No. 83, (Christianity, Catholic, Words of Christ, Author: Sister M. Faustina Kowalska)
****

       Taken to a very demonic young man, he was in distress. Because of his evil nature, nobody was willing to help him, so I walked towards him and placed my hands up his head. As I did this, he became a baby, and I held him and comforted him until he was calm and felt safe. Turning to his brother, I said, "Be merciful to him, and you will see him change." Taking him into his arms, he changed back to his current age. Although evil was still present, his energy had been completely altered, as love's power was present in his tearful looking upon my countenance. "Be merciful, my dear child, and mercy will come to you." Tears began pouring in his release, and as they fell, some of his demons began to emerge and leave him.

Awaking suddenly to face a large demon tarantula sitting upon the pillow next to my hand, I realized that he had been unable to enter into me because I was holding the rosary.

"At death we will not be judged by the amount of work we did but by the love we put into it. And this love must come from self-sacrifice and be felt until it hurts."
The Love of Christ, Part II, Page 55, Paragraph 7, (Christianity, Catholic, Words of Mother Teresa)

****

Soaring through space, the eternal call had led me to a home that was up for sale. A woman was about to buy the house and she was with her real estate agent preparing to write out a contract on the home. My job was to stop her, for presences lurked within this house of which she was unaware.

Appearing in spirit form to them, they were unafraid. Asking the woman to follow me into the basement, which was a very ornate part of the home, they followed with caution. As soon as we were there, I commanded the spirit of Satan to reveal himself. Apparently, this home had been the site of satanic ritual, and the demonic forces were very well established here. Appearing immediately, the demons tried to hide their faces from the light. "This house is inhabited by Satan," I said to the lady, "do not move here." Satan's presence was not seen, but felt, and hordes of his demons infested this place like termites.

In shock, the woman appeared grateful as she ripped up the papers. The real estate agent seemed more concerned with the loss of a sale. Flying away, my task was done.

"Many people, when moved by fear, run to mountains, jungles, hermitages, shrines and trees in search of safety and asylum. But these are no real refuge and they afford no real protection . . . But if sometime someone turns for refuge to the buddha's, the dharma and the sangha . . . this is the real refuge."
Training the Mind in the Great Way, Point 1, Page 87-88, (Buddhism, Tibetan, Author: Gyalwa Gendun Druppa, the 1st Dalai Lama)

****

A pool of rattlesnakes had formed in my backyard, the demons of gossip and foul speech regarding one's neighbor. Sadly, I could say nothing, for it was true. It shocked me that I had never really considered the damage of my foul speech before, because it seemed so easily identifiable in this moment. Representing foul speech on every level, the snakes represented gossip, slander, and vanity in the use of the name of the Lord. If our mouths are merciless about the faults of others, then the mouths of the demons will also be merciless about our own faults on judgment day. Having been merciless, I'd shown poor judgment and caused harm to others with my mouth.

Judgment had been passed as one of the small rattlesnakes, about three inches in size, was given leave to poison me. Biting me in the arm, I knew that I wouldn't die, but would suffer illness for a time as penance, atonement and repentance for all the harm I had caused with words. Accepting the Lord's judgment as just, I prepared for the next wave of illness.

"One way of talking is like death."
The New Jerusalem Bible, Old Testament, Ecclesiasticus 23:12, (Judaism)

"But those things which proceed out of the mouth come forth from the heart; and they defile the man. For out of the heart proceed evil thoughts, murders, adulteries, fornications, thefts, false witness, blasphemies: These are the things which defile a man."

King James Bible, New Testament, Matthew 15:18-20, (Christianity, Words of Christ)
"R. Shmuel bar Nachmani said: 'They asked the snake, 'why are you found near fences?' He answered, 'because I breached the fence (that protected the world).' 'And why do you slither with your tongue protruding?' (The snake answered), 'it was my tongue that caused (my transgression).'"
Taharas Halashon, Chapter 5, Page 55, Bamidbar Rabbah 19:2, (Judaism)
****

Stealing a pick up truck before my eyes, I flew after the criminals and witnessed their crimes. Arriving at a bridge, a stand-off erupted, and the two were now pointing a gun directly at me. "We are going to have to shoot you," they said, "you're a witness." Remaining calm, I opened a book of Torah law. "No, no, no," I said, "you've got it all wrong. According to Torah law, the laws given to Moses, you've sinned greatly already; you certainly don't want to add the taking of a life to this list. Let me teach you the laws of repentance." Looking bemused, they became disoriented. "First, you need to return the car, then you need to feel genuinely badly about what you've done, and thirdly, you must beg of God to forgive you for completely ignoring His sovereignty over you in this world and the next." The gun dropped as the confused men had not a clue where to begin. "The Lord gave us laws for our behavior in every circumstance," I said, "He even gave us laws as to what to do when we have violated them. Here . . . "I tossed the Torah to them, "read the laws, abide by them . . . most of all repent for all you have done that is evil in God's eyes." Catching the book, they looked upon it as I disappeared.

"The Lord Himself not only shows us the evil we are to avoid and the good we are to do (which is all that the letter of the law can do), but also helps us to avoid evil and do good - things that are impossible without the spirit of grace. If grace is lacking, the law is there simply to make culprits and to slay; for this reason, the Apostle said: 'The letter killeth, the spirit giveth life.'"
The Fathers of the Church, Volume 2, Admonition and Grace, Chapter 1, Page 245-246, (Christianity, Catholic, Author: St. Augustine)
****

Happy to see this soul I'd watched over for years, I remembered when I'd energized him with a seed of light in the ghetto to energize this very moment. Homeless and having gotten into a fight, I had placed a seed of light within his heart chakra, hoping that it may bear fruit over time.

Crowds of people surrounded us as we reunited, my joy obvious, but they were judgmental in his regard. Having spent time in prison, he was just getting out. Addressing the crowd, I quietly stated, "Mercy is a very important thing, we are all going to need mercy when we face our Creator." Ignoring me, I walked away with my friend whose troubled soul had become more focused and direct in his incarceration. Disappointed by the crowd, I knew his life would be difficult because of his former ways.

God loves a repentant sinner just as much as He loves the just. Be merciful to those who have been lost because of the impetus of the original sin catapulted upon them. If they embrace the ways of the darkness, accept their choice and let them face whatever consequences will come of it. But if they choose to energize a higher way, then be merciful in forgetting their faults, and give them a hand when they begin their climb.

"If you kept a record of our sins, Lord, who could stand their ground? But with you is forgiveness, that you may be revered."
The New Jerusalem Bible, Old Testament, Psalm 130:3-4, (Judaism)
****

Three teenagers had broken into a small shop which was owned by an elderly woman for whom they had befriended. Her home was attached to the back of the store, and it was quite obvious that this kind old woman could get hurt if she walked in on this robbery.

Noticing the soul of a gentleman had appeared, he was very skilled on the ground in martial arts. As we walked in on the robbery in progress, several things had been broken into and the store was already trashed, but we were here for another type of alteration. Because of the well-known martial arts skills of my 'partner' this evening, I turned to him in a respectful gesture and offered the alteration to him. Standing motionless, he was completely unable to respond. Completely unaware of what needed to be done, I was surprised that one who appeared so empowered, strong and invincible on the ground, was actually very weak in this eternal context.

Smiling at him, he seemed embarrassed, but I motioned him to move aside and be unconcerned. This was nothing of which to be ashamed, for he served his function well on the ground.

Looking at the three youths, whose heads were covered with snow caps in a stupid attempt to disguise their identity, I placed my hands on my hips and just stared at them. As the light from my eyes penetrated their hearts, they began to feel shame. A kindly old woman who had tried to help them had become the victim of their evil design. Beginning to look down, their bodies became slumped and cowardly. Never having to say a word, they just *knew*.

Grabbing all three of them, they filed out of the store, as a life-threatening potential had been changed. I'd seen something I'd not previously understood; the illusion of power on the ground being challenged from the sky. Putting my arm around this man's shoulder, I looked him in the eye and smiled. Slowly, we walked away as there was no necessity for words.

Coming again the next night, he showed me just how empowered he was on the ground. Impressed by his ground alteration capability, it became apparent to me that both aspects are needed for balance; energetic interception in the sky, followed up by ground alteration.

"The Highest Wisdom decreed that in order for all things to receive God's sustenance, they must first bind themselves to each other. The lowest things bind themselves to those above them, and these in turn to the ones that are still higher, continuing in this manner until the root Forces, which in turn depend on God Himself. His sustenance is then extended to these Forces, and it spreads downward appropriately to all levels of creation. In this manner, they all regain their ordained level and function."
The Way of God, Part IV, Chapter 6, No. 10, Paragraph 6, (Judaism, Author: Rabbi Moshe Chayim Luzzatto)

****

As my sleeping body lay in bed, the spirits of several demons came without warning and began hurling my soul to and fro about the room. Mercilessly, they'd ripped my spirit out of the body as I began flying around the room, banging into walls and hitting the ceiling and floor. "In Jesus Christ's name, I demand that you leave." I said repeatedly. Hurled into the abyss by the force of His name, my spirit was left at rest.

"Many demons were expelled without their knowing who it was that thus hurled them back to hell. Yet they felt the divine power, which compelled them and wrought such blessings among men."
The Mystical City of God (Abrid.), The Incarnation, Book Four, Chapter IX, Page 376, (Christianity, Catholic, Author: Ven. Mary of Agreda)

****

Standing amongst the multitude, I was feeling rather low because I felt that I didn't play a large enough role in the world. Suddenly, my soul was swept into an ecstasy wherein I saw a golden angel administering to the children. As my face was forced upwards and my soul fell down on its knees, I couldn't move for several minutes. When I came out of the ecstasy, someone pointed out to me how lucky I was that I had seen the golden angel, when no one else present could. At that moment, I was humbled, and I knew gratitude.

Beginning to use me as a vessel for the multitude, many of them were lost sinners. Taking me into several ecstasies, I saw the holy souls and angels in heaven. After going into five ecstasies and sharing the energies of what I had seen, a Eucharistic host formed in my hand. Placing it on the altar, I turned to the multitudes, many of whom were now coming forwards in conversion.

Others in the crowd were not yet ready to convert, and were pleading with me to feed the poor amongst them. Knowing this to be outside of my power at this time, I began explaining to them that my purpose was to feed souls the food of the spirit. A particularly troubled soul came to me, exclaiming that God wouldn't come into her life because she was a slut. Rather than being a humble announcement, it was more of an enraged defiance indicating that she was fighting God's presence in her life. "God loves all His children," I said to her, "and He wants to come into *all* of them." Screaming at the top of her lungs, she replied, "I don't want God to come into me!" "Then God *cannot* come," I said, "but it is not because He doesn't want to, but because you don't want Him to."

Very few skeptics remained, and many were convinced of my sacred mission. But one particular soul arrived suddenly with rage on his face. As he wanted to kill me, the Lord began manifesting several more miracles through my body; ecstasies, visions and holy occurrences among the people, but this particularly demonic man would not give up.

Beginning to ask me about him, the crowds lit up in inquiry. "He is a scientist," I said, "a physicist in particular, and for these accomplishments, the Lord is very pleased with him. But his singular flaw is that he is a deviant atheist and refuses to allow others religious freedom." Directed to walk towards the front of the room, he came to confront my words with physical violence.

As he approached, I said to the crowd, "Beware the serpent, for he comes in many faces. Look upon this face for he is one of them." Possessed by a demon of rage, he tried to jump me. Warning him one last time, I said, "The power of God is with me tonight." Attacking me violently, God sent energies through my hands as I de-energized him quickly. Holding his benign spirit in my hands, I replied, "God's mysterious ways, God shows his power in mysterious ways."

Walking towards the altar, the remaining unconverted souls were ready. Taking the miraculous host from heaven into my hands, those who came forward touched it. Despite the obvious presence of the Lord, the atheist proceeded forward again, trying to prevent the new converts from reaching the altar. "Can you not let others exercise their religious freedom?" I asked.

Protecting the new converts from him, I held him aside until heavenly forces pushed him away. Saddened, I turned to the others who had been lost, but were now found. Joy filled my eyes, but sadness welled inside for the one sheep that would remain lost, for now.

"Blessed art thou inasmuch as the darkness of vain imaginings hath been powerless to hinder thee from the light of certitude, and the onslaught of the people hath failed to deter thee from the Lord of mankind."
The Tablets of Baha'u'llah, Chapter 17, Page 259, Paragraph 2, (Baha'i, Author: Baha'u'llah)

****

"Deny thyself and put off all the works of human weakness, and, by the true light, which thou hast received concerning the works of my Son and my own, contemplate and study thyself in this mirror, in order to arrive at that beauty, which the highest King seeks in thee."
The Mystical City of God (Abrid.), The Transfixion, Book 5, Chapter III, Page 411, Paragraph 1, (Christianity, Catholic, Words of Mary)

Taken to observe a soul obsessed with gluttony, he was wandering around a grocery store placing excessive amounts of pastries into his cart. Jesus appeared, adorned with the Sacred Heart, and begged my assistance in extricating this soul from sin. After he had received several divine warnings and intervention on issues within his life (such as careless driving and bad associations), my spirit was taken in to help him.

Taking out some of the items, I said, "You don't need this." Angered, he insisted that I keep them in his cart and leave him alone. Wishing to join the crowd, he went outside, despite my protests of this action. Making a lot of noise, and being rather verbose, he thought he was fitting in with the crowd when in truth, he was just making a nuisance of himself. "You're only out here acting like this because you're obsessed with having everyone else's approval; you want everybody to like you." I said. Interestingly, he looked me in the eye and replied, "You're absolutely right, that is why I do this." But then he went about his way, disappearing into the crowd.

Following him, I eventually caught up to him in a hotel room where he was now sleeping. In the corner of the room was an open vase with holes along the sides, inside it was a gleaming green light. Tapping him on the shoulder, he awoke and began to tell me about his spiritual guide, the green light from the vase, which continued to speak to him of the wonders of arrogance, gluttony and the importance of following the crowd so that you will be greatly liked. It went so far as to implant seeds of divorce within his mind in regards to his marriage, and seeds of thoughts that he should sue for custody of his children.

Turning to the vase, I said, "Do you come here on behalf of the light or darkness?" "Um, uh, I, uh," said the vase, as I shouted my reply, "Do you come here on behalf of the light or darkness?!" "Uh, I don't know," he said, whimsically. Moving aside, I shouted, "In the name of Jesus Christ, I command you to leave. In the name of Jesus Christ, I command you to leave!" Very attached to his ward, he would also have to release him before I would be able to banish the dark spirit. "In the name of Jesus Christ, I command you to leave! Jesus, Jesus, Jesus, Jesus, Jesus, Jesus, Jesus, Jesus," I said, "Jesus, Jesus, Jesus, Jesus, Jesus, Jesus, Jesus, Jesus!" Repeating it probably thirty or forty times, it took that long for the demon's energies to pull in towards the vase, and then to be hurled downwards towards the abyss.

"The doors of Perdition shall close on all that Perverseness has conceived, and everlasting bars shut in all baleful spirits."
The Dead Sea Scriptures, The Book of Hymns, Page 154, (Christianity, Gnostic/Essene)

Turning to the former ward, he replied, "I am dreaming of this spirit right now." Tuning into his soul in his dreaming, I pulled him out of the dream to hopefully reduce any potential damage.

Looking at him, I noticed that his lower chakras were lighted all the way up to the throat, but his third eye and crown chakras were completely closed and unlit. Placing my hands around the sides of his head, I tried with all my might to light them, but could not because the influence of the demonic force had been too strong. Requiring time to recover from his fall from grace, I chastised him for his stupidity.

Knowing this person in the physical realm, I'd contacted him to discuss this issue. Having just returned from a dream where he was gathered with friends, engaged in a gluttonous party which was adorned with pastries of all kinds, all who had come were ruled by a singular evil spirit. He'd realized that he'd allowed something dark to come near him, but before he could respond in terror, a mysterious force had pulled him out of the dream, awaking him instantly.

Many are there whom have come upon this great juncture in their own paths, but because of their fear or inability to accept the true nature of their alliances, ranted off angrily at the messenger bequeathing the message rather than the truth it beheld, tarrying off into the night, abasing themselves before the viper, unwilling to battle him anymore, wearied of the fight, surrendering their eternal souls at his clenched, reptilian, engorged and most vehemently disgusting feet, denial playing them for the fool they had become, denial keeping their awareness at bay to the true fall they had taken from grace.

Paramahansa Yogananda came to impart wisdom. "Do not listen to the 'spirit guides' that others speak of in concentration, for they are impure."

"A weak will is a mortal will. As soon as trials and failure cut it off, it loses its connection with the dynamo of the Infinite."

Man's Eternal Quest, Answered Prayers, Page 35, Paragraph 2, (Hinduism, Kriya Yoga, Author: Paramahansa Yogananda)

"I should flee far away from childish people. When they are encountered, though . . . I should behave well merely out of courtesy, but not become greatly familiar."

A Guide to the Bodhisattva's Way of Life, Chapter VIII, No. 15, (Buddhism, Tibetan, Author: Shantideva)

****

Andy, my husband, was given a temptation. Two lustful women approached him and were trying to allure him. Looking to the side, Andy saw a radiant image of me holding a baby, exactly like the Madonna of the streets. Surrounded in a golden hue, I was afloat in the air. Power from my image immediately obliterated the two demonic women and they cowered, almost as if they were melting. Andy pointed in my direction as he quietly replied, "No, thank you, I'm going home to that."

"Jesus said, 'Grapes are not harvested from thorn trees, nor are figs gathered from thistles, for they yield no fruit. A good person brings forth good from the storehouse; a bad person brings forth evil things from the corrupt storehouse in the heart . . ."

The Gospel of Thomas, Page 41, No. 45, (Christianity, Gnostic/Essene, Words of Christ)

****

Soaring amongst a place which lay infested with satanic and witchcraft activity, I destroyed several satanic and witches covens, their evil books, and de-energized them completely. Taking care of the children they had harmed, I tended to their injuries; both physical and emotional, and prepared to leave.

"The women that first allowed themselves to be ruled by evil spirits were fully conscious of the fact, though others were ignorant of it. These women had it (the principle of possession) in them like flesh and blood, like original sin."

The Life of Jesus Christ and Biblical Revelations, Sin and its Consequences, No. 5, Page 33, Paragraph 4, (Christianity, Catholic, Words of The Ven. Anne Catherine Emmerich)

****

Someone had been faced with a temptation given by Satan. "Come in, whores," Satan's deep raspy voice had taken this person aback. Twenty or thirty women entered the room. "Take one," he continued. Looking at them, he noticed that they were all spiritually dead, their bodies were worn and battered. "No," he replied, "I have a marriage vow." "If you don't take one, they will die," exclaimed the raspy voice. Confused for only a moment, he finally retorted, "They aren't going to die." Satan left and they all disappeared.

Perchance, he had been given to witness the true energetic thrust of the craving of lust. In the faces of Satan's charges, he witnessed a spectacle most unappealing. With the manifestations of their sins apparent upon their countenance, they all showed scars, paleness, weathering, pock-marks and other signs indicating spiritual death. Lust was unbecoming in its true imagery, as it manifests its ugliness vividly in the energetic realms. Repugnant, this man's issues of lust were revealed to him in such a manner as to *repel* him from this vice and it was ironic that the grand tempter had succeeded in discouraging the vice with which he had come to sanction a fall.

Awaking with the haunting memory of the deep, raspy voice of the master of darkness, he said, "I wouldn't mind if I never had to hear that voice again." Because of his confusion at the point when he was told that the women would die if he didn't comply, I reminded him that we are to help others as much as we possibly can, but if we *must* commit sin to help them, we are required *not* to commit sin. Everyone must take responsibility for their own condition and alliance and there is plenty of opportunity for charity outside the confines of sin and destruction.

Perhaps it should be repeated for those with a listening ear, that the surest way to defeat evil, is to deny it, deny it, and deny it . . . no matter what skillful guise the tempter may thrust before you, you must turn away.

"The heavens shall thunder loud, and they that now do dwell on the crumbling dust of the earth be as sailors on the seas, aghast at the roaring of the waters; and all the wise men thereof be as mariners on the deep when all their skill is confounded by the surging of the seas, the seething of the depths, as high o'er the swirling tides the billows (surge), the breakers roar, while the gates of Hell burst open, and at every step they take, they face perditions shafts, and only the raging deep hears their cries. Yet anon shall the gates of (salvation) be opened; all baleful deeds (will cease)."
The Dead Sea Scriptures, The Book of Hymns, Page 153-154, (Christianity, Gnostic/Essene)

****

Suddenly, I became aware of my sleeping body on the bed. A huge and ugly tarantula was waiting to lunge into my hand from the floor. Instead of being black, however, this one was a light brown. In an instant, I felt the stinging assault in my hand which occurs when a master spoiler attempts to enter into your body.

Imaging light from my hand, I sent a pulse of light through the ugly demon and watched as the dark abyss opened to receive its viper. But, angered at my victory, several more came out towards me in the direction of my other hand which was holding a rosary. Sending a bolt of energy towards me, the rosary began vibrating in my hand as a large sting could be felt in my palm. Startled, I tossed the rosary towards the wall, unaware of what was happening as the surprise assault came so quickly. Now, I was mad.

Picking up my rosary, I became fully conscious and awake, yet still quite aware of the battle with which I was entrenched in the ethereal realms. Remaining visible to me, the nasty tarantulas were coming again, hoping to gain victory and entry into my form. Imaging light, a huge beam of light came down from the heavens, and I watched as the terribly immense and black pit opened to receive the lurid creatures. Initially, they went one at a time, and then suddenly they began falling in droves into the pit from the force of God. Grateful, I prayed to the Lord in thanks for His divine protection.

"Even if you are considered to be the most sinful of all sinners, when you are situated in the boat of transcendental knowledge you will be able to cross over the ocean of miseries."
Bhagavad Gita As-It-Is, Chapter 4, Text 36, (Hinduism, Translator: A.C. Bhaktivedanta Swami Prabhupada)

****

Taken to see a man claiming to be the second coming of Christ (This man had no connection to Baha'ul'llah and the Bab), I didn't believe him at first, but because of several ruses he'd used to demonstrate spiritual abilities, I began to believe he was true. But I soon recognized his falsehood.

What initially made this distinction difficult for me, however, was that the man spoke many truths, he showed many signs and wonders, and he behaved initially with the actions of a saint. If it had been simple to discern, the Lord would not have found need to warn us of such false claims. If the deception were attended by an obvious falsehood, then warning would not be necessary. Christ warned about the false prophets and messiahs because they would come in many believable faces, showing many believable signs. If these counterfeit messiah's were to come bearing the face of the demon, there would be no challenge in identifying their falsehood. But if they were to come as good people with good intentions, who simply got lost within their own ego . . . that would be a little more challenging. If they were to come as prophets with true purpose, who simply got lost within their own ego . . . that would be *most* challenging.

Yea, Christ warned us because warning was necessary, and it is only through energetic discernment that a soul can know the truth pertaining to such matters.

At this time, the false messiah wanted to silence me, because I was discounting his claim. Coming after me in an energetically violent manner, I managed to escape and went about my way. Let not yourself be deceived, let not yourself be deceived . . .

"The soul is absolutely perfect, but when identified with the body as ego, its expression becomes distorted by human imperfections."
Where There is Light, Chapter 1, Page 5, Stanza 1, (Hinduism, Words of Paramahansa Yogananda)

"Then if any man shall say unto you, Lo, here is Christ, or there; believe it not. For there shall arise false Christs, and false prophets, and shall shew great signs and wonders; insomuch that, if it were possible, they shall deceive the very elect. Behold, I have told you before. Wherefore if they shall say unto you, Behold, he is in the desert; go not forth: behold, he is in the secret chambers; believe it not. For as the lightning cometh out of the east, and shineth even unto the west; so shall also the coming of the Son of man be."
King James Bible, New Testament, St. Matthew 24:23-27, (Christianity, Words of Christ)

****

Going on a drawn out mission as a social worker for a family in crisis, a family of three was being torn apart by an affair perpetrated by the husband with a very young girl. Their five year old son was having a difficult time adjusting to the changes in the family, and there were several issues facing them. Currently living with the young girl, the husband had split with his wife who lived elsewhere, and saw his son on the weekends.

Frustrated because the young girl wasn't good with his son, the husband had not yet taken responsibility for having a relationship with someone so immature. Because the young girl had chosen to be such an affliction to this family, she now had to be responsible for what she had chosen to take on. Handling this adulterous liaison with amazing maturity and grace, the wife was not in need of assistance.

After working with the two on their perceptual delusions, an interesting thing occurred. The young girls clothing slowly began metamorphosing into a whole new form of attire as her shirt and shoes now depicted pictures indicating St. Augustine's writings on the Trinity. Realizing that my reward for working with these people was to receive this ancient sacred text, I inquired further into the images and was catapulted into an ancient sacred text library.

****

Adrift with visitations from the spirits of souls I'd helped in the past, they'd come to thank me and show me that my efforts had changed their lives. Some were souls I'd spent hours talking with on the phone, trying to assist and energize their ascent forward; and others I'd worked with on energetic levels, to release their baser selves and thrust into a higher catapult. There is no greater gift than this, to know your life has been meaningful to others. Thank you Lord, for the gift of this window.

"When the mother of Rabi saw that his son was weeping excessively and passing sleepless nights, she said to her son: O my darling, you have perhaps killed somebody. He said: O my mother, yes, I have killed. His mother said to him: Whom have you killed? I will take pardon of the family members of the murdered person. By God, if they see your condition, they will certainly show kindness to you and pardon you. He said: O mother, I have killed my baser self."
Ihya' Ulum-Ud-Din, Book IV, Chapter VIII, No. 21, Page 429, (Islam, Sufi, Author: Imam Gazzali)

****

CHAPTER FIVE

Angels Assisting in Awaking to Eternal Life, Test of Alliances, Heavenly Specter, Lukewarm Souls, Demon Disguises Himself as Holy Mother, the Crossings, Avalokiteswara, the Golden Buddha and Zarathustra Come to my Aid.

****

Confused and disoriented, I stood amongst several brothers with great musical abilities who were bickering over who had written which music. It seemed, for the moment, that my purpose here was somehow to help them decide who should take credit for which works, but something wasn't right. Because they were so much a team in their musical endeavors, I couldn't figure out who should take credit for what, and I was unable to discern what music belonged to whom. Many other people were among us, two separate and distinct groups; regular mortal humans, and the others who bore a distinct marking.

These others were more liquid and fluid, despite their solidity in human form. A marking lay upon their heads, somehow a sign of the difference between us. In a sense, they were almost like rubber people, movable yet erect. My soul and the souls of many others among us were being led towards the same road that these souls had taken. Despite the fact that they were joyful and full of happiness, quite unconcerned about the squabbles of the brothers, we were rather afraid because the changes that had occurred within them were so profound, it seemed to us that only through dying could one achieve such status. Indeed, this turned out to be true.

Our bodies began floating towards a gate, and instinctively we knew that this gate was the doorway to death. Trembling and afraid, we slowly arrived at the juncture to find ourselves surrounded by boxes and boxes of candy bars. Without any effort on our parts, the candy bars flew into our mouths and began being chewed and digested. Realizing then that these candy bars were the harbingers of death, we fell into a deep sleep of death as everything became tranquil and quiet.

A great deal of time passed, but it seemed like only a moment before I suddenly awoke. All of us who had been taken through the sleep of death were awaking in unison, and hundreds of angels had come to assist each individual soul in awaking to eternal life. A beautiful female angel greeted my own sleepy soul as I aroused from death. Her long auburn hair surrounded her happy face, and her bright yellow-white wings adorned her back in a very comfortable looking manner. Interestingly, she wore jeans and a white T-shirt, not the attire I always expect from heavenly hosts. Immediately, she spoke, "Do you wish to have immortal life?" Because of my experiences in the past, I had to ask a question. "Do you come on behalf of darkness or light?" She repeated herself. "Do you wish to have immortal life?" Again, I asked, "Do you come on behalf of darkness or light?"

Pulling back, she smiled a knowing smile, as suddenly, a most magnificent angel appeared before me, gleaming with light. Wearing huge and luminous wings, his face was only light. In answer to my question he conveyed that he was a servant of God. Very pleased with my question, as I was the only soul who wished to be certain that the gifts offered were from the Lord, he touched my shoulder. It is not uncommon for dark forces to offer souls immortal life, although they cannot give it. All they may offer is the attainment of a longer physical existence, at the expense of your soul, and even this existence must be for the purpose of serving the viper. It is wise to ask, before you accept any such gift. Never forget the host of muddy flats and his vile gifts in disguise which lead only to destruction. Such discernment is wise when one wishes to serve God. "Because of your wise question," he said, "you will be given an extraordinary gift beyond measure." Suddenly, my soul transformed into an immortal form, just like those other humans who had been with us of whom we had been unable to define. Tasting of eternal life, I felt the joy, bliss and ecstatic union with the Lord of all creation; immortality.

But suddenly, I saw the keys of a giant piano coming from the great light in the heavens coming towards me. As they came, they entered into my now fluid and liquid mouth and expanded into vocal and musical abilities beyond all measure. Singing in a very high tone, my voice rang out amongst all who had come to receive immortality this eve. The angel began floating upwards towards the beautiful light, with a huge joyous smile. Although his joy was great at the gift given to me, his elation over my discernment was beyond words. Stunned by the magnitude this question I had posed had meant to the universal Lord, I was humbled.

Without warning, we were all returned to the former place where the bickering brothers remained. But having been transformed into immortality, the truth had set us free. No one bothered to mention it to the brothers who had stayed behind in mortal life because it was so obvious. No one had right to claim the music, it belonged to God alone. The sleep of death seemed so short, and there was no pain for any of us, but now in our immortal states, we, too, had become fluid joy.

"This is the plane whereon the vestiges of all things are destroyed in the traveler, and on the horizon of eternity the Divine Face riseth out of the darkness, and the meaning of 'All on the earth shall pass away, but the face of thy Lord . . . ' is made manifest."

The Seven Valleys and the Four Valleys, The Valley of True Poverty and Absolute Nothingness, Page 37, Paragraph 1, (Baha'i, Author: Baha'u'llah)

****

Approaching and gesturing towards me, a Native American horseman approached. Initially, I said no and backed away. As he rode off, however, I gave it a second thought due to some texts I'd been reading which expounded that the belief in darkness was purely superstition. Crying out, I said, "No, wait!" Before I could realize the profundity of my error, the horseman turned dark and came at me with profound red winds of destruction, energized all the more by my slip in judgment. It became all the more clear that the refutation of the existence of darkness only energizes its affront towards you.

"In the name of Jesus Christ, I demand that you leave!" I shouted several times. Then I began singing a hymn, "Holy Mary, Mother of God, forgive our sins and please pray for us." Still, the red winds were upon me, so I shouted, "Jesus, Jesus, Jesus, Jesus, Mary, Mary, Mary, Mary!" Over and over again, my voice shouted, until the energies depleted and were halted by the power of God. Ashamed of my lapse in judgment, I thanked Jesus and Mary profusely for saving me from the dark force which, through my naiveté', had been invited.

"The living beings had been confused, but when they heard this command of yours, their virtue flowed like streams and rivers . . ."

Gnosis on the Silk Road, Chapter 23, Hymns to Mani, No. 115, (Christianity, Gnostic/Essene)

****

The following experience is related for the purpose of demonstrating how the Lord sometimes tests our alliances and loyalties. Sometimes, in order to be certain that a soul has made great changes or alterations in liaisons, the Lord places a test within their midst.

Packed with souls, both of the living and the dead, we were being taken to a camp. There was only one way to discern who was alive on the Earth at this juncture, and who was deceased. Placing a mirror before them, if their reflection bore fruit, they were living upon the Earth, if not, they had passed. Although I was unaware of it at this juncture, the Lord had permitted that a temptation be placed before me. But as far as I could tell at this moment, everything that was about to transpire was coming from a purely up front source. All of the souls gathered were here to learn more intricate details of their personal destinies.

Literally hundreds of souls were lined up to receive information about their purpose. As souls were awaiting their turn, they talked quietly amongst themselves, sharing ideas and inspirations for higher destinies, with the hope that some of these ideas might reach the conscious minds of some of the living members of this congregation.

Giving information to others, the man who was giving counsel suddenly came over to me. Because I was so impressed with what I'd heard him tell others, I was quite expectant as to what he might have to tell me. Handing me a cassette tape, he guided me to look upon the jacket and read something that was scribbled in handwriting upon its sheath. The work of a male musician, he had scribbled a note in his own handwriting on the cover. 'Dear Marilyn,' it said, 'I am looking for you, my true wife. Find me.'

Looking at a black and white photograph of the musician contained within the cassette, I couldn't say that I held any memory at all of him. Telling me that this man was looking for me, the 'guide' told me that I was this man's true wife. But nothing he said resonated within me, and I began to suspect foul play. "I have absolutely no memory of this soul," I said, "and besides, my name is spelled with two N's." Looking down, he noticed that I was correct about the spelling. But then he asked me to look inside the jacket, wherein my own handwriting supposedly lay. Looking inside, the words were a plea to eternity to help this 'Marilyn' find her true spouse. However, my name was again spelled incorrectly and it didn't appear at all to be my own handwriting. So I looked upon his face and said, "I have absolutely no memory of writing this, or of this man, or of anything connected to this cassette." The 'guide' was now smiling.

Saying nothing more, he walked quietly to the next person. Before he began to work with this other person, he said to me, "Okay, now allow yourself to resonate to the real reason you are here." Intrigued, it seemed to me that this subtle temptation had been placed before me to test my alliances. Could I be so easily swayed away from my marriage commitment? Had I really changed? It seemed I'd passed. Smiling at him, he smiled back with a certain approval.

Watching the others, I noticed that people were exchanging ideas. Speaking quietly in my ear, the 'guide' said, "It is ideas which cause funds to come into being, things to be accomplished, and evolution to occur for mankind." Nodding, I suddenly felt my hand resonating to a distant location within the campground. Following the resonation, I found myself going towards a very different cassette tape bearing the image of a female performer, quite unknown, who had built her own recording studio to accomplish her life's work in music. My hand was literally stuck to the tape like a magnet, and I took this to be a true signal of something the Lord might wish for me to be open to in the accomplishing of His will. As soon as I realized this, all those present who were destined to be performers broke out from the crowd and began singing a song together in unison.

Those with other purposes; medical, philanthropic, business, legal, etc., were all grouping according to such traits listening to the performers. At this moment, I realized that performance can be done aside from the ego. If done to please God, it can be a talent or gift like any other which requires expression and dissemination. Performance bore a purpose in God's design. At this moment, I was pulled back to my body.

But upon return to the astral state, my soul was returned to the heavens to a place known as the Emanuel Swedenborg Institute, teaching the visionary knowledge of the 17th and 18th century Christian mystic.

Immediately directed to take a shower, I was given a special rose scented soap and shampoo. Lathering up, the smell of the roses permeated every cell of my being with a tranquil joy. After showering, I went to the dressing room to discover what they might bid me wear. Told to put on some, 'Divine

Providence' and 'Love and Wisdom,' these titles of Swedenborgian texts (The second title reads, 'Divine Love and Wisdom') were arrayed in a most beautiful garment which was to adorn my body.

Gently taking it and lowering it over my head, I felt such immense peace. Below the garment, was a rose scented perfume with which to adorn my body. Smelling like a rose, it was obvious to me that the concepts of Divine Providence and Divine Love and Wisdom were an integral part in the Mysteries of the Redemption, and as I wore the garment of the Lord, the knowledge of it was made energetically manifest unto me.

"Conjunction of good and truth in others is provided by the Lord through purification in two ways; one through temptations, and the other through fermentations. Spiritual temptations are nothing else than combats against the evils and falsities exhaled from hell and affecting man. By these combats a man is purified from evils and falsities, and good and truth are united in him. Spiritual fermentations take place in many ways, and in heaven as well as on earth; but in the world it is not known what they are or how they come about. For evils and their falsities, let into societies, act as ferments do in meal or in must, separating the heterogeneous and conjoining the homogeneous until there is clarity and purity. Such fermentations are meant in the Lord's words: 'The kingdom of heaven is like leaven which a woman took and hid in three measures of meal until the whole was leavened (Mt 13:33; Lu 12:21).'"
Divine Providence, No. 25, (Christianity, Swedenborgianism, Author: Emanuel Swedenborg)

"It is because the very divine essence is love and wisdom that the universe and everything in it, living and inert, remains in existence as a result of warmth and light. Warmth in fact corresponds to love, and light corresponds to wisdom. So spiritual warmth is love, and spiritual light is wisdom."
Divine Love & Wisdom, No. 32, (Christianity, Swedenborgianism, Author: Emanuel Swedenborg)

****

Returning to dream vistas, my soul awoke upon the sky amidst a sunlight filled oasis. Up in the heavens, a large lighted heavenly entrance resided, wherein the thoughts of an invisible specter spirit were issued forth to my ears in the form of a divine decree. In order to ignite my soul properly, I was commanded to reveal the truth to myself about the general status of the people of the world, regarding their dark ways.

Sometimes attempting to be kind about the truth, minimizing darkness, or trying to lessen its impact, allows our souls to become entrapped within that lie, allowing the darkened designs of those we've minimized to become maximized potential; both in society, and certainly within our own selves. Because the energetic nature of darkness is assaultive, no matter what level you are dealing with, whether it be highly energized violent behaviors, or less obvious applications of vice on the ground, it will continue to energetically barrage a soul unless and until the soul draws a definitive and distinct line, disallowing all manifestations of the viper, no matter how great or small, to enter into their soul's depths. Even if such things do not manifest on the surface, the true energy and liaisons of an individual, like vanity, lust or greed, continually seek to implant other souls through thoughts, example and dreams. Despite the benign or disguised appearance of many souls filled with darkness, the energetic nature of them cannot be denied. Absolute exposure of the truth of darkness is the only avenue of reproach within its confines. If you choose to ignore such need, whether you realize it or not, your attachment or denial of such qualities allows them to exert energetic thrust within you of a backward nature.

So in following the command of the heavenly specter of the Lord to reveal the nature of the world, I allowed myself to ponder not only the obvious sins and darkness of the world; violence, sexual deviance, etc., but the less obvious manifestations of darkness which appear in our world due to accepted delusional thinking or living Godless lives.

"For years, you've minimized the truth to yourself about this issue," the heavenly specter told me, "and the world around you as a whole, primarily for the sake of kindness." Because of the world's denial of such truths, I tried very hard to reconcile that which I was shown in the astral realms of the truth, with my desire for there to be peace on earth. Such an ideal will come about through global purification. Unfortunately, dark liaisons are far from uncommon, and all karmic souls who reside upon the Earth harbor some vice.

Although it is difficult for anyone to look upon such truth, the truth remains that every soul who walks the Earth would be shocked and stunned to witness their true alliances, alliances I shared until very recently . . . but for the grace of God, go I.

As directed, I began writing down the excruciating details of the darker aspects of the world, remembering if it had not been for several hundred acts of God, that I, too, would share this status. Meant only for my own eyes, they were very necessary in this instant for my own soul to be somehow freed from the constant barrage of energies which were sent my way by backward forces and those in my own past. Some dark energies were thrust upon my soul for nothing more than the fact that I believed in and loved the all-powerful God, these types of energies coming from the agnostics and atheists of the world, some in my own past. In their eyes I was fanatical or extreme, and this honesty regarding our differences was necessary for my soul to be ignited in a higher way. The truth shall set you free, and indeed, the truth was affording my soul final and true liberation from the ties of my worldly origin.

Although the darkness of violence and abuse is obvious to most, it is not always so well known within the perimeter of a perpetrator. Oftentimes, victims or families deny what the perpetrator has done, leaving him open to continue his destructive acts. Even a dangerous individual can remain undetected in our world. But the other members of society, whose darkness does not lie in violent or deviant behaviors, are even harder to discern. In fact, with most members of society, it is safe to say that few if any souls in their perimeter would recognize the true status of their souls. Of course, these same individuals very possibly would not recognize the true status of their own souls, either; which is, in essence, the point I am trying to make. There is a darkness which lies beyond the more obvious forms; the murderers and rapists, and these are the dark activities of the common man, and such things can plummet a soul to lower realms or reincarnation just as quickly as the other more obvious transgressions, albeit, perhaps a different sort of lower realm, a different sort of reincarnational experience.

Allow us to peruse some of the other forms, as all of us have born witness to manifestations such as these. Lukewarm religious persons, Christians and/or worldly souls whose love of God is limited, who attempt to make others who seek to become purified and holy feel that they are extreme or fanatical in some way. Practicing religion which is self-serving and momentary, they are guided by their own wishes or designs, rather than the wishes of God. Perhaps this is a lesser transgression than the atheists, who use their arrogant 'intelligence' to make others who love the Lord feel silly for their 'illogical' beliefs. Not looking the part is key for the most common forms of darkness. They may have a good education, hold a job, be accomplished in their field, dress well, have a family and kids, live in a nice house; but interiorly despise the Lord, be indifferent towards the Lord, practice various of the seven deadly sins, hold contempt against their fellow man, or harbor extreme arrogance regarding either themselves to their fellow man, or themselves to God. Very few if any other souls recognize such darkness within them, but the preceding honorable actions will in no way diminish their great inward taint. Looking within, energetically, you will be able to know the true status of a soul. Many souls' bear upon their foreheads the sign of the viper, but to the outside world appear to be 'good' people. Let me state unequivocally that for such souls, this appearance of 'goodness' to the world will in no way hinder their projection into the lower realms or reincarnation upon death.

Perhaps it is most difficult to herald the truth regarding such dark propensities within our own perimeter, for we tend to make excuses for those we care about. Although this forgiveness is essential, recognition is the key to freedom from original sin and entry into the mysteries of the redemption. Expression of truth is for the purpose of knowledge, not blame. To analyze these truths for the purpose of blame would serve no greater purpose, but to analyze them for the purpose of understanding, accepting and acknowledging an energetic reality . . . this can harbor many fruits.

My honesty prompted a huge and magnificent ecstatic emergence within my chakra centers emerging and thrusting upwards. Perhaps I can describe it almost as a thirst which unfolded into fulfillment experienced as a blissful hum, more like a continual ecstasy than a momentary one, holding me in a heightened state of spiritual union with the Lord.

As this occurred, I was given to see a chart which showed three balls of violet light, each depicting subsequently higher ways a soul can demonstrate unity with the Creator. Currently embracing the lowest form, it was portrayed as a light violet-white glowing warm globe, described as a somewhat hidden flame, a hidden light, it was called 'Idle,' and I had been operating from it most of my life, waiting for the world to validate the need for my journey to a higher place, something which would never happen. Suddenly, my consciousness erupted into an ecstasy, striking my flame to attain to the second level, a level titled simply, 'Consciousness,' portrayed as a deep purple globe surrounded in emergent orange, yellow and red flames coming warmly from the top of the sphere. Continuing to expand as the truth was setting me free, my soul emerged at the highest levels, portrayed by a violet, yellowish-white globe with bright yellow flames emerging from the entire sphere upwards towards God consciousness in a gracious ecstasy, this level was called, 'Shooting out Flames.' Thrusts continuing as violent bursts upward took me through the spheres of knowledge.

A spectacular spiritual guardian now emerged from the holy cloudeous lighted gateway to the heavens. A glorious angelic man framed in light who appeared to be a warrior spirit, arose from this flame of consciousness and conveyed to me that I had always held my flame within because of my *attachment* to the welfare of the world.

Leaving the world behind, I turned and entered a home filled with worldly souls who had continued to deny God. Turning to cruelly distorting my musical and literary work into examples of their vices, I protested as they immediately became enraged and began to verbally argue. Attempting to accuse me of some crime, an astral federal agent appeared. Calmly, I pointed to them. "They are atheists, and I love God. This is their motivation in trying to accuse me of such crimes." Immediately, the agent understood, nodding as he said, "You should have nothing to do with them, then, for these types are very dangerous," he disappeared.

At this point they began chastising me for not looking upon my creative work in terms of financial lucrativeness for the future, because in their eyes, I was a fool. "No," I said, "you don't understand, you've missed the whole point. You have to do this kind of work knowing full well that you may never earn a thing." Enraging them to the point of violence, an eruption ensued, wherein they argued and fought with me over the existence of God. Merciless in their attacks on the Lord Almighty, I stopped them and asked, "What are you going to say to God, when you die . . . on your own judgment day?" One replied, and the words spoken were too vile to repeat. Suffice it to say, I turned and walked away, in full understanding of the need for exile.

"Those who are thus bewildered are attracted by demonic and atheistic views. In that deluded condition, their hopes for liberation, their fruitive activities, and their culture of knowledge are all defeated."

The Bhagavad Gita As It Is, Section 9, Text 12, (Hinduism, Translated by: A.C. Bhaktivedata Swami Prabhupada)

"'Suppose ye that I am come to give peace on earth? I tell you, Nay; but rather division: For from henceforth there shall be five in one house divided, three against two . . ."

King James Bible, New Testament, Luke 12:51-53, (Christianity, Words of Christ)

****

Standing before me were lukewarm souls who all bore the same vital flaw, they were unable to make commitments in their lives. In order to bridge the gap between their present understanding and the truth, it was my duty to speak to them on the nature of commitment.

In their view, committing to another person in marriage was a waste of time, because they felt that life was too changeable to make such an inquiry. Unable to perceive their intimacy issues as being self-generated, they believed that they were pursuing a superior path. Speaking of the importance of being willing to make a sacrifice for the attainment of a greater good, I spoke on many issues.

"Commitment begins with friendships, but then expands into the ability to achieve intimacy with one other individual, a life partner, for the purpose of achieving balance and stability within your own soul. Marriage serves to give continuity to one's life, as well as, a sense of honor, loyalty and devotion. But this commitment often expands into the lives and souls of children, for the purpose of rearing them appropriately, assisting them with their own karmic issues, as well as, the developmental issues which affect all children, according to the laws of society of the ways of God."

"Commitment thus expands into society, in following its parameters and helping your fellow man. Beyond this, and the many other types of commitments we must share in order to grow and evolve as human beings, lies our greatest commitment, that to God."

Commitment is a vital link in the evolutionary spiral, it must occur within the confines of love and wisdom to fully mature. If a soul chooses to go through life making no commitments, this is a weakness not a strength. In order to make a true commitment to God, you must first be able to make the smaller commitments in your Earthly life. Commitments become a vital link in the mysteries of the redemption, because they provide opportunity for true self-sacrifice, duty, honor, loyalty, and goodness. As our lives become less self-serving and more geared towards serving others, we move closer to the redemption, something which cannot come about without this vital link. If a soul cannot commit to anything in its life, then it will be most difficult to make the ultimate commitment to do the will of the Lord, no matter what that may be."

"This does not mean, however, that every soul must be married or have children, but that every soul within the confines of his own life experience must choose to be faithful to that which is true and good, those people in his life which are true and good, and those experiences which bring truth and goodness upon him. Some souls are truly never meant to be married, and this is a purely acceptable status, but many others will never marry because their self-serving interests consistently get in the way of service to one another, or to a higher ideal."

"Some people may have many opportunities for eternal connections to take place, while others may not be destined for such unions, but it is not uncommon for eternal links to remain unrecognized and lost due to the blindness of souls on the ground. Easy avenues for self-gratification are not provided by the Lord, but rather, He places difficult paths before us so that evolution may occur. Paths of self-gratification do not serve the soul, they serve the self. Commitment can be a vital link in the redemption, because to commit to something greater than yourself is the first step in committing to God's kingdom by loving your neighbor as yourself. In so doing, you naturally amend to the even greater attainment of loving God with all your heart, your soul and mind."

As I tried to explain these concepts to the group, one among them became especially angry, because he still believed that making commitments was an inferior path. Unmarried, he'd gone through life using women to fulfill his sexual needs and treating them unkindly. Wearing the demon vice of the serpent penis used to denigrate women openly, the concept of commitment affording a higher path to his soul had never occurred to him in his self-serving view. Angry that the concept had been presented to him in such a blunt manner leaving his life bare in all its putrid filth, he was good at using words to make his exploits seem desirable or worthy. Lacking in true commitment to anything in his life, his greatest deficit remained in his lukewarm 'commitment' to God. Knowing my words would perform whatever function the Lord had deigned, I turned away. It was time for me to go.

"I know your works; I know that you are neither cold nor hot. I wish you were either cold or hot. So, because you are lukewarm, neither hot nor cold, I will spit you out of my mouth."

New American Bible, New Testament, Revelations 3:15-16, (Christianity, Catholic, Words of Christ)

****

Coming to me disguised as the holy mother, it was not difficult to discern the most inglorious apparition as a putrid lie. As she began to sing a song, I raised my arms up to her eyes, shooting a beam of light continuously into them as blue ooze began dripping profusely from them. Blankets covered something on the ground around this false Madonna, and as I picked them up, the bodies of several dead and mangled witches lay around her. A demon appeared behind me, and said, "Another dead witch, another dead witch." But I didn't allow her distraction to shift the focus of my beam of light, as I cried out, "I demand that you leave in the name of Jesus Christ!" Completely discharged, the blue ooze melted as the demon had been exorcised. Falling to the floor, the body which had been made for its use fell over flat like a lump of melting flesh. Repeating my words to the demon behind me, I said, "I demand that you leave in the name of Jesus Christ! GET OUT!" Managing a sinister grin before dissipating and disappearing, the two demons were dismantled and discharged to the lowest of realms.

Awaking distraught but victorious, I returned to sleep moments later, stunned by what had now begun.

Standing before me was a demon whose direct line of command came from Satan himself. Wearing a body of bluish white and cold from the viper who held its reigns from behind, this demon was powerful and dangerous and had come with an entire legion from hell to defeat me because of their anger at the dismantling of two of their dark warriors who had come before.

Battlefield surrounded in tens of demons, I noticed that tens of lighted souls had appeared on my side of demarcation. 'Perchance could I expect any assistance?' I thought, realizing that these lighted souls were the typical Christian but lukewarm souls who lacked energization towards the forces of evil. In essence, I was on my own. What initially appeared as perhaps a bit of help, now became clear to me as a crowd of lighted souls who needed my protection.

As the ugly demon approached, his bluish white body was cold from death, two horns protruded from the top of his head and he had a leatherish reptilian tail. Human in form, but demonic in detail, I raised my hand and centered a beam of light upon his form, directly at the eyes and the heart. "I demand that you leave!" I shouted, "In the name of Jesus Christ, in the name of Jesus Christ!" Still clinging tightly to the beam of light which held him to his spot, within moments the blue within his form began oozing out through his eyes, completely draining his innards from within to without. A wisp of dark energy left the demon body as it fell to the ground. Leaving momentarily, but I knew he was far from gone.

Spirits of the dark and light were now surrounding me, and it was difficult to discern which bodies were animated by demonic predators and which were not as many of the de-energized light people had become infested. Because I was the only one present as an energized warrior for God, the others were leaning towards the light, but unwilling to make sacrifices on its behalf, making them benign and morose. Because they were so de-energized in their light that they could not protect themselves from such an onslaught of evil, I had to protect them. Because of this difficulty, I repeatedly had to ask the alliance of each animated form, before responding. "Reveal yourself, in the name of Jesus Christ! Reveal yourself, in the name of Jesus Christ!"

The constant onslaught of the dark side was met with beams of light and pronouncements bidding the name of my most beloved Jesus Christ. Allow me to state that without His most holy name, I would be victorious in very few, if any, battles with the dark side. Jesus Christ's name is the most powerful weapon you can take into such battles.

Within a short period of time, while trying to keep the primary demon charges at bay, the primal demon re-animated a new body created from the fabric of that which had been destroyed. Doing this several times throughout the battle, each time I dismantled it through the power of the holy name.

Becoming very intricate, the battle was highly charged intricate and there is so much that I can no longer recall which would be fascinating to tell, for this battle appeared to be my own personal Armageddon. Having come to defeat the light within me, the dark forces had failed. But despite their persistent failures, the dark side continued to come at me mercilessly, while I fought alone with the souls I'd vowed to protect. Becoming very clear just how important it is that souls who seek the Lord, become energized through His hands, I took note of the inexplicable level of wrath the dark side bore my soul. The depth of their rage towards me was something I didn't yet understand.

Having placed several holy statues within our home recently, I was surprised to note that much of the demons rage was directed towards them. Bade to witness their thoughts, they were afraid of what the statues represented (the mysteries of the redemption), and the holy protection they offered.

As the battle became more and more strategic, I became almost like a medieval queen trying to direct and guide the benign army of the light, as my main purpose with these souls was to attempt to keep from being possessed in their idleness.

As the battle drew to an end, a voluminous green cape was draped over my body. Symbolic of St. Jude, the patron saint of lost causes, I'd saved souls who otherwise would have been lost, and my victory in Christ was now displayed upon my spirit. But this represented more than just the lost cause which was won tonight, as it represented my own soul, the ultimate lost cause. Once, a grave sinner unaware of my defilement, now a sinner attaining to repentance and redemption, my love for the Lord had saved me. Born of darkness . . . into light.

But this pronouncement made something very clear. As the souls aside me were so easily taken over by such forces, I saw the simplicity in which the dark side often controls the lives of many Christians who become benign because of their misinterpretations of Christ's words. In their desire not to be judgmental, they lose discernment. In their desire to help the poor and lowly, they don't see it when their assistance is being used by those hardened in darkness and evil, against them and against goodness. A lighted warrior must always be aware that their caring *can* be used against them. Discernment is *key*. In their desire to be kind, they don't acknowledge what *is*, in regards to good and evil; and their submissive and passive approach allows for all forms of darkness to take hold. Eventually, if undetected, such darkness can infect entire congregations of people.

As I was given the green robes of St. Jude, it inspired a defilous rage which cannot be understood or comprehended by my soul. But if they had been outmatched before, they were certainly outmatched now. Secretly, the forces of the Lord conveyed to me that Satan's forces were so angry because of that which the Lord intended for me to do. Thy will would indeed be done!

Walking past several de-animated forms which had been exorcised; my cape was blowing lightly in the wind. Taking a moment, I paused to pull the robe up closer to my neck, because I was concerned about exposing myself. Suddenly, from the right came another demon in disguise, this one looking like an animated human, bearing no markings of the bluish-white of the viper. Appealing to my vanity, he told me that a particular gentleman who was very handsome thought highly of me. Immediately, I said, "That's not true," but then stopped myself, because I realized that they wanted me to argue the point simply because it might energize my vanity, and therefore my own destruction. Shouting, I said, "That's not true, and it's completely irrelevant!" Disappearing, the dark side was unavailed by my defiance.

Again approaching from the side, the main perpetrator (the bluish-white demon with horns and tail) said, "It is useless, you can't win this fight. My army is too powerful." His grin was wide and filled with sarcasm. "Just give up, come over to our way, you will eventually have to anyway. There's no escape from here, my power is too great for you, you *cannot* banish me." Making me very angry, I said nothing to him, but grabbed a hold of my green cloak of lost causes, and waved it before him in defiance of his atrocious words. As I did so, I was immediately delivered from the battlefield. Soaring through space to return to form, I heard the moans of the viper, distraught at the loss of his prey.

May I simply state that no soul who seeks to attain to God's highest holy ideal, can do so without energizing themselves properly through the intervention of the Lord. So many souls are lost in the battles between good and evil, eventually giving in to the hosts of darkness because of their lukewarm morality and virtue, and their fear of the power or their attraction to the 'lures' of dark ways. Let no man walk with weakness in his heart, for only a soul with conviction to withstand the constant barrage of temptation, vice and sin, shall pass through such inexplicably arduous trials. Do not be fooled by pride, vanity, greed, lust or whatever, do not be fooled!

Pride and vanity are the easiest and most common downfall of the mystic dweller, because a soul who has received his first visions or extraordinary experiences is in the time of greatest peril. So many fall into the vain and prideful interpretation of their own importance or significance, and the viper takes them easily, then using them to trick those who genuinely seek the light. For the vain and prideful can easily take a holy experience from the Lord thy God, and use it to glorify themselves rather than the Lord, thus, tricking others into believing that they are to be followed.

The Way, the Truth and the Life . . . is Jesus Christ, and the rest of us are simple wretched souls seeking to understand the karmic mystery which holds our souls to mortality. Never follow another, only follow God.

If my words help others, it is not because of any quality of worth on my part, but only through the saving grace of God, who so makes use of the trials and failures of one soul to teach another, and allows the ignorant ramblings of one soul who seeks the summit to be as an arm to those below, pulling them up towards Him.

Redemption is for everyone who reaches for it, no matter how lowly, lost, sinful or wretched you may think you are. But you can only reach it through true resolve to conform your life to His ways, honestly striving and reaching for Him, and most of all, truly *loving God* in your heart. If you don't have that love, ask Him for it in prayer for He will provide it for you. Mercy is the greatest and most mysterious attribute of the Lord; He gives in full measure to those who will accept it. Will you?

"Go down into the abyss, you evil appetites! I will drown you lest I myself be drowned."
The Voice of the Saints, In Temptation, Page 65, No. 5, (Christianity, Catholic, Words of St. Jerome)

"St. Peter and St. Paul warn us in the strongest language to beware of the devil, for he is using all his tremendous power, his mighty intelligence to ruin us, to harm, to hurt us in every way"
The Wonders of the Holy Name, Chapter 10, Paragraph 2 & 5, (Christianity, Catholic)

"My persecutor did not cease to attack me in every way."
The Autobiography of St. Margaret Mary, No. 89. Page 102, Paragraph 1, (Christianity, Catholic, Words of St. Margaret Mary)

"Though my body be pained by the trials that befall me from Thee, though it be afflicted by the revelations of Thy Decree, yet my soul rejoiceth at having partaken of the waters of Thy Beauty, and at having attained the shores of the ocean of Thine eternity."
Prayers and Meditations, LX, Paragraph 3, Page 96, (Baha'i, Author: Baha'u'llah)
****

Amongst the crossings, I was again shown the powerful simplicity of my own past, how I'd been thrown into life at an early age to make it on my own in the world. But the final run of this experience found me wearing the habit of a nun crossing hundreds of mountaintops in a single bound, not a single foot touching the valleys below. My soul seemed to be alight in the sky, high above the great mountains of the Earth, and my legs were so astute they could attain to each peak without need of contact with the valleys below.

My first destination, however, resided within a crevasse in a valley. Placing upon my collar a simple metal pin, a sign which indicated that I was amongst a particular league of souls; those in the valley were not to hurt me. Running again, this time through the valleys, I came upon a dark, dreary ghetto, where several derelicts were following me. For a reason unknown to me, I was unafraid. Everything here was decomposing, dead and rotten from the putridity of the sin of mankind. The 'Valley of the Doomed,' those who resided in this place were lost from the graces of God, because they truly wished not to receive of them. 'How can any soul truly wish not to receive God's grace?' I thought. 'Such a state of misery must be a true hell.'

Apparently, in order to attain to my final destination, I had to cross this singular valley of death which had warranted the protection of this sign upon my collar. As soon as the derelicts caught sight of the pin, they backed away and left me alone.

Having passed through, I began crossing hundreds of mountaintops in a single bound again, as I interiorly understood that these peaks represented the care of children and my many years of service to such tasks. Depicted upon these peaks were the graciousness of such skill in rearing children in the ways of the Lord, and the honor bestowed upon those as who do such things.

Upon leaving these peaks, I stood at a beauteous shore, my body older and more middle aged than it is now. Coming to this marvelous shoreline was another time in my life, when I would proffer other services to the Lord upon other peaks of service to humanity. A chest of drawers appeared before me on this rocky peak before the shore. As the waves crashed and hit, I began asking the Lord to bid me His calling as to what He might wish for me to do at such a time as this.

There were four main questions, one for each of the three drawers, and a second question for the top drawer. But I remember only a farthing of what I was shown. In the drawers, I was shown many papers written in cryptic coded messages, almost biblical in fact, stating profound truths regarding the gift of service to the Lord. Upon the pages were intricate drawings of cosmic substances attaining to physical strata's, which represented my work in bringing eternity into that which is mortal, heaven to Earth. Retaining very little of the contents of the drawers, I did remember that in drawer one and two were messages regarding paths of service my soul might take in the future. Many things were shown to me, but they seem nebulous now. Reference was made to my past experience in the media, and that this would be of use in God's future demands.

But I do recall the question for drawer three, "What exactly do I need to do next to make these things come to pass?" The answer came on an ancient piece of paper. A simple drawing of a man whose arms reached upwards and out, his legs were going downwards and out, representing a soul in total surrender to divine will. Upon it were the words, 'You must bond deeply in your sleep with the purpose of this command.' Many papers followed it, with directions for each successive step, but I recalled none of them upon waking. Looking at all that had been shown to me, I became overwhelmed and shouted out to the Lord, "How am I to recall all these messages upon return and record them according to your will?" Pulling my soul away from the visionary abode, the message was clear. A picture of a power plant adorned the next page, and upon it were many sets of cryptic messages. Stopping on one, it said, 'The fire will guide you to the place of power, then cease your imaginings and create rapidity upon the ground.'

Begging not to be pulled away, I asked one more question which bid the fourth and final allowance to emerge from the top drawer. Closing the one below, I asked a question I cannot remember, and received answers I cannot recall.

After returning from the experience, these words came into my conscious being:

"Oh thou glorious passer through thy realms of glory, cease your traveling upon the heavens for a time, to reach below and dip within the suckling of the Earth the heavenly odors and fragrance you have attained. Do not, I say, put forth thy soul unless and until it lingers with the heavenly odors and longs to encroach such eternal wisdom and suckle upon the wards below."

"Seek the highest wisdom in the nighttime stars; to be redeemed by the Lord thou must follow His whims and fancies beyond your idle imaginings. For the Lord is all great and all powerful and beyond all imaginings, and His method of approach is to seek to find souls of great magnitude to do His bidding in the fashion and manner of His bequest. Thou must seek to know His will, and His will awards you with service and purpose of many degrees beyond the present day necessity."

"Beyond such necessity of childbearing, allow the Lord to guide thy soul into the ever present image of His love, and to bid thy calling to thee when the time is nigh. For whotofore may know of what is asked, for thy soul is prepared for great things on the Earth, not as the Earth would perceive, but only as thy heavenly Father might bestow."

"Upon this lot, know that thy service is to be ministered with humility with the attainment of knowledge fully in place, and upon thy bough, wherever thy Lord may send you, thou shalt go with kindness fulfilling the work of His calling in an energetic manner, beyond the realm of the knowledge of mortal men to know. Thou wilt be as a small person, unknown and undefiled, but thy works will be done according to His great will. Your works will be unseen to humankind, until long after your passing and beyond this, only when thy Lord decrees. Such as the Lord decrees bear witness to the grand scope of your ministry, but they shall remain unrevealed until the time of which the Lord shall deign to reveal. Of this, you know the greatness of this time and these acts."

"Seek to know the wisdom of the ages, in this thou shalt find peace. For only in God will the time bear fruit of which you must reap. These reapings are thy bequest to the Lord, thy only gift that thou may offer to thy Holy Host. What fruit shalt thou bear for Him? Beyond the fruit of thy prophecies, thou shalt bear the fruit of redemption for all mankind through thy words and thy unseen deeds. A soul who bears the guidance of the Holy Host bears within him the secret codes of life eternal, and within these codes the highly prized mysteries of the all powerful redemptive spirit are found. Who among thy world must bid to give thee the knowledge, for there is no one, but for thee thy Host has reserved the greatest pleasure. Thy pleasure is the fruit of the redemption, illustrated through thy words and travelings to the other worlds and realms of the heavens. Thy pleasure is the grand knowledge of the fruits of this redemption for ages to come, for thy words shall be used for the purpose of cleanliness and purification."

"Thy soul has become the harbinger of great things, unmanifest as of yet, but to be born so soon through thy handiworks and obedience to the will of the Lord. Most blessed are the works of the Lord done by thy hands. This is the great majesty of the heavens, the great Lord of creation. He can take thy hands, empty and meaningless of themselves, vases of clay, and fill them howsoever He pleases."

"O thou soul of thy passing, come forth to bid thy soul to service in the realm of the learned, and then cease your upping to charge forth to thy next abode of traveling. Howbeit that a soul must bid welcome to the Lord of Hosts in such manner, but yet it must be done. Through the horns of a Ram (My astrological birth sign is Aries, the Ram) shall the Word of thy Lord be manifest. Through the magnitude of one soul shall the mysteries be revealed to the common man in the worlds of the below. The synchronicity of the soul must be achieved through the redemption of the beloved. Allow thy words to become as a flame of purgation for souls, and as a novena to ever present holiness."

After these words came to me, an image symbolic of the redemption came into my mind. Seeing many ancient clay vases, all but one, were together in a huge clump on one side of the floor. Those who stood together leaned away from the other vase which was leaning in the opposite direction, resting comfortably in the palms of the hands of the Lord. Hands glowing and brilliant in light, He formed the vase according to His will. Placing upon the singular vase a sign, the sign of the redemption, the other receptacles bore no sign upon their bough.

"(He who) had understanding and remembered everything, the first, intermediate and final things; (his) lips and tongue responded and he uttered great praises with . . . his mouth. He revealed the path of salvation and the road of purity (to all) souls who were in harmony with him."
Gnosis on the Silk Road, Chapter 3, No. 2, Verses k, l, m, (Christianity, Gnostic/Essene)
"In this world, there is nothing so sublime and pure as transcendental knowledge. Such knowledge is the mature fruit of all mysticism. And one who has become accomplished in the practice of devotional service enjoys this knowledge within himself in due course of time."
Bhagavad Gita As-It-Is, Chapter 4, Text 38, (Hinduism, Translator: A.C. Bhaktivedanta Prabhupada)
"I will put my words in his mouth, and he will speak to them whatever I command him. And it shall be: (any) man who does not hearken to my words which he speaks in my name, I myself will require (a reckoning) from him."
The Five Books of Moses, Deuteronomy 18:18-19, Old Testament, The Schocken Bible, (Judaism)

****

"By reflecting upon the evils of life in the round of successive existences, mayest thou be incited to seek Emancipation."
A Buddhist Bible, The Supreme Path, No. IX, (Buddhism, Tibetan)

Thrust upon a place of darkness, all was fearful and overwhelming in the nature of the vile energies ensconcing this abode. The dark forces were hidden, but immensely present as their essence was elusive behind the lurid cracks and walls, invisible to our eyes, but very noticed by our other senses. Everything was gray and dark. Andy was with me and we were praying to be delivered from this darkness into the light.

Emerging from the floor in prayer, a dark creature close to Satan in the line of rank in the armies of darkness appeared to me as a serpent with many heads. Looking like cobra heads, his body was reptilian, but of human upright form. Spitting venom into my face, he tried to convince me that I was doomed.

"Why bother," he said, "you cannot win this battle. You will be easily overwhelmed by Satan's forces, for he has sent quite a battalion here in your honor to have you defeated." I said nothing. "Accept it, you are doomed. You shall be defeated. You may as well accept this and come over to our way while you still can. We could make use of you." Although unafraid, I was quite overwhelmed by the ugly nature of this creature. His spit was like vomit, and his serpent heads were so disgusting I could have upchucked.

Rather than this, I said a few words to him. "What shall I say to you?" I said, "Shall I tell you of Christ?" Looking concerned, he began to hiss. "Or shall I speak of the second coming of Christ?" Throwing him into a tizzy, I continued, "Perhaps I should speak to you of the return of the Buddha, the Buddha to come . . . Maitreya?" Reptilian skin sizzling with flame, he spit and hissed in discomfort. Now in flames but not yet destroyed, I turned and saw an amazing spectacle.

Behind me in the room appeared two life-size statues; a large golden Buddha which stood next to Avalokiteswara in deep purple robes, the Buddhist personification of compassion and Holy Mother. As the statues synchronistically came to life, all the darkness within this place became animated and visible. Creatures of the dark appeared; jelly-like parasitic critters sticking to walls, moaning in the darkness, many forms of black bugs, and tiny three-foot tall reptilian creatures who stood upright and had long tails with hooks at the end. An odor surrounded the place and a dark cloud had sprung from every nook and cranny, but I couldn't be afraid or even notice, because I was stunned at the sight of these prophets who had bid me the honor of coming to life before me, in all their holy splendor. Staring at them, their beauty and awesome power was mesmerizing.

Avalokiteswara and the golden Buddha were in the forefront, as the Buddha pointed me in the direction of another room. His arms held within them a power expressed in moderate movement, almost as if he were performing a spiritual aspect of martial arts in response to the forces of the dark. Avalokiteswara emitted an aura of kindness which shone around her in white and green flames. Interiorly, I understood that the Buddha was fighting the darkness with his singular arm which represented his special power, the *balance of wisdom*; while Avalokiteswara was fighting the darkness with this spectacular aura, the *essence of love*. Following their guidance to the next room, I saw a third statue, this one of the prophet Zarathustra, wearing intensely green robes. Coming to life, he began fighting in a very physical manner the forces of darkness with a sword, which was a personification of the *light of truth*.

Interestingly, I had noticed that both the Buddha and Avalokiteswara had appeared fully oriental, but Zarathustra also had a small amount of oriental blood which could be seen in the partial slant of his eyes. Ceasing not once his battle with the forces of darkness on my behalf, he pointed to a room in the far off corner for which he wished me to traverse.

As I walked closely towards it, I opened the door to find a stunning pronouncement regarding the mysteries of the redemption revealed before my eyes. Having his back to my view, the personification of the second coming of Christ stood wearing a long white robe. Brown hair was cut short to his upper neck, as I wondered if I was witnessing the manner in which He would manifest in the flesh. Wondrous inexplicable things were revealed to me energetically regarding His second coming, and I was made to know the power of this moment. Displaying a power and peace indescribable, I felt holy honor. Something inexplicable was revealed to me regarding the power of this second incarnation, that it instilled a fresh terror amongst the demons who so wished for it to never occur. Saying no words, I turned when bidden to do so by the Lord.

Running frantically back towards the many headed viper, I shouted! "In the name of the second coming of Christ, I invoke your destruction!" As I did this, the demon began shrieking a horrid sound from his many mouths, and began to dismantle before my eyes. In moments, Satan's charge was a dismembered serpent lying upon the floor. Many other smaller and less powerful demonic charges lay motionless upon the floor as the name of the second coming of Christ gave the demons a fresh terror, renewing powerfully the horror of which his first incarnation had given them.

"The nearer we approach our goal, the more will Hell strive to prevent our reaching it."
The 12 Steps to Holiness and Salvation, Chapter 2, Page 28, A Happy Death, Paragraph 1, (Christianity, Catholic, Author: St. Alphonsus Liguori)

Within moments, the dark and dank dwelling was completely exorcised and the living Buddha in gold, Avalokiteswara in purple, and Zarathustra in emerald green, stood all around me; joyous and triumphant. Hugging Avalokiteswara tightly, I cannot even begin to explain the consolation I felt in her arms, for she was filled with the essence of love, and her spirit of kindness was very motherly and soothing. Refusing to let her go, I grasped Zarathustra's outreached hand with my other hand while still embracing the Bodhisattva of Compassion (Avalokiteswara). Within Zarathustra's hands, I felt the light of truth and the power it held. The Buddha did not reach to me, as he only gazed in a very moderate manner towards my eyes, filling me with the balance of wisdom he encompassed.

"Attach thyself to a religious preceptor endowed with spiritual power and complete knowledge . . . Seek friends who have beliefs and habits like thine own and in whom thou canst place thy trust."
A Buddhist Bible, The Supreme Path, No. III, No.'s 1 - 3, (Buddhism, Tibetan)

Although not given another privileged opportunity to see the manifestation of the second coming of Christ this eve, I came to understand that He would encompass all the qualities which lay before me and much, much more. Come in one form as the second coming of Christ, AND the Buddha to come, Maitreya, within His soul lay a native element, as well, known only to me as 'Son of the Twelve Chiefs.'

Though Andy had not been present for most of the battle, he reappeared holding a card covered in pictures of bouquets of pale blue roses and carnations. "I figured you all looked so beautiful," he said to the prophetic guests, "I needed to put a light on you." As Andy held the card towards me, the many roses and carnations now beamed with a holy light as the essence of their fragrance overtook my soul.

Awaking surrounded by pale blue roses and carnations, their smell surrounded me in my bed, as I lay in comfort and peace.

"What, then, is the state of this happy soul in her bed of flowers . . . ?"
The Collected Works of St. John of the Cross, The Spiritual Canticle, Stanza 26, No. 1, (Christianity, Catholic, Author: St. John of the Cross)

"The perfume is an announcement or the confirmation that he has heard our prayer or request."

CHAPTER SIX

Dark Secrets of the Satanic and Witchcraft Realms, Samadhi, Cherub, Milinda - Warrioress of the Oriental Tribes, Swami, Serpent, Spider and Bug Demons, Incarnate Demons, Exorcism, Satan's Attempt to Sacrifice My Life, Conversion of a Rock Star, St. Michael, Reptilian Demons, Suicidal Sacrifices to Satan, Misused Grace, Satanic Cult, Deviant Sexuality, Saving a Baby from Abortion.

****

Having come without warning, the demons had thrust my soul into a disgusting and horrible place of darkness, a place of brainwashing which was used to bring in witchcraft cult members on the ground. Knowing I had to be careful in my escape, this place was a realm of the energized demonic activity, one of the realms of the satanic cults. What initially gave permission for them to take me here was a very stupid error of words on my part. Some people who I had immediately known to be dark had approached me speaking of war and brotherhood. In the past, they used to engage in warring amongst themselves, but now had learned to form brotherhoods of men, instead. "Yeah," I said, "I believe in brotherhood." Speaking of an entirely different kind of brotherhood, my soul was immediately transported to their realm.

Propelling my soul from one council of Satanists to another, each tried in a different way to trick me into agreeing with their evil doctrines. Each council submitted me to one form of torture or another, along with spells and castings by the demons and their Earthly witchy wards. Beginning to pray, I repeated the 'Our Father' and the 'Hail Mary.'

Brainwashing souls into false doctrines, they specialized in energizing the spirits fall from grace. As I had the opportunity to observe those things which gave Satan and his charges great glee, I learned several things. First and foremost, there is no such thing as white witchcraft, because witchcraft of any kind involves manipulating energetic reality, which is against eternal law. Angels and spirits of the light do not respond to magical whims, only demons do. It gives the demons great pleasure to deceive souls into practicing any form of magic, even those which claim benign status; white witchcraft or magic, Wicca, sorcery, etc. They all originate in darkness because manipulating reality is an energetic crime against God.

Other aspects of great joy to Satan and his charges were several doctrines they had managed to defile and distort. The first is the belief that there is no dark side, demons, hell or Satan. The second is the misinterpretation regarding the doctrine of the 'self.' Many souls believe the 'self' is their ego, when the 'self' spoken of in Eastern religions is truly the divine element within. In order to experience the true 'self,' a soul must experience a state of ecstasy or Samadhi. Because this is something achieved primarily by prophets, saints and mystics, remaining undiscovered to the masses; many souls misperceive the 'self' to be their desires, their wants, their dreams and aspirations, and by so doing, they become selfish and self-centered making the job of the demons much easier. The third was a teaching they particularly enjoyed, a distorted teaching of unconditional love which says that there are no right or wrong actions, making the job of demons extremely pleasant, because they didn't even have to break down the walls of moral foundation. The fourth, was the belief that any 'channeled' entity comes from a higher source, when in fact it was given to me to observe several demons fulfilling this function, some going so far as to make lofty claims about their identities, saying they were great masters and the like. Although there are legitimate channelers who speak with the tongues of men and angels, it was made very clear that a great deal of discernment was required in knowing the true from the false prophets. One obvious criteria for making such discernment would be to stand aware of any of these erroneous doctrines.

"For he who uses the gift of tongues to seek after riches, or to hold sway over his enemies, he shall no longer be a Son of Light, but a whelp of the devil and a creature of darkness."
The Essene Gospel of Peace, Volume 4, The Essene Communions, Page 11, Paragraph 4,
(Christianity, Gnostic/Essene, Words of Christ)

Diabolical liaisons surrounding souls who believed such doctrines included dark parasitic creatures, bats, tarantulas, webs, serpents, ooze and sludge coming from the pores. Disturbing to witness the level of darkness involved with such erroneous beliefs, all of them were completely deluded, convinced they were following a higher path. Neglecting to realize that what they believed was very similar to another well-known doctrine, the doctrine of the fall, they were being led down the road of perdition completely unaware. Beware the serpent, for he comes in many faces, and he deceives the most sincere among you.

Many souls were led down this road of perdition, even though they had begun their paths sincerely. Who would not prefer a doctrine of unconditional love which supports a soul, no matter what place upon the path he may be? But this doctrine of unconditional love was *not* meant to harbor souls in their sleep, but rather to catapult them into movement on their paths of karmic purification. Compassion and understanding are very much needed as a soul travels down the rocky road of karmic influence, but with the truth firmly rooted at his side. Forgiveness and understanding regarding one another's fallibility cannot be overstated, but within the constant confines of abiding truth.

Easily weakened and overcome by several prayers, the demons could not fight the 'Hail Mary,' because the Most Holy Mary has the power to crush the head of the serpent. Unable to withstand the 'Our Father,' it is actually used in the process of exorcism, and renders them benign. Another prayer which made them benign was, "Jesus, Mary, I love you, save souls." Throwing them into a tizzy, it literally hurled them away from my soul.

Brainwashing in the form of energetic manipulation, if you became fearless in the face of their torture, it could not enter into you. Their brainwashing is actually doctrine which enters the soul in an energetic form, via demons and dark spirits. None could enter me because of the holy names I continually used and the prayers I offered. Also, most importantly, I continued to deny every doctrine of falsehood they presented to my soul, despite their torture at my denials.

Lashed about, thrown against walls, stomped on, etc., despite this, I knew the Lord had allowed this temptation for my greater knowledge of such falsehoods. Throughout the night, the battles continued and I wasn't sure how I would escape them. Continuing to torture me, my soul was thrust into a horrid position wherein my mouth was locked shut and I heard the voices of the demons shouting. "Where there will be wailing and gnashing of teeth." Repeating in my mind the words, "Christ crucified, Christ crucified, Christ crucified, Christ crucified," they plunged into a rage and howling. For a moment, they couldn't come near enough to torture me. More powerful than all the prayers I'd already used, in their anger they attempted another temptation. "We can make you become a saint," they said, as in my shock and horror I was taken aback, suddenly lashed against the floor because of my moment of stun. Repeating their offer, I was horrified to think that the demons could make such a thing really happen for somebody who wanted something like this because of their ego. It was shocking! But now suddenly having the faculty of speech, I began to shout, "I don't want to be a saint! I am not a saint! All I want is to be like

Christ crucified, Christ crucified, Christ crucified . . ."

Laughing at my reply, my soul was horribly thrown against the floor and placed in the position that Christ was placed on the cross. "Then you shouldn't mind dying the way He did then, should you?" Pounding their reptilian heels and feet into my appendages, I continued repeating 'Christ crucified,' the 'Our Father,' and the 'Hail Mary.' Holding large nails which they intended to pound through my hands and feet, they ran out of time. Within a few moments, the demons howls became blood-curdling, and they began to plummet into the depths of hell, far away from my soul which was rising towards the heavens far away from their bleak world. The power of the Word had released my soul from this affliction, and I'd emerged victorious. Hallelujah! Hallelujah!

Unfortunately, I awoke with some of the signs of the battle upon my body.

"Do thou set thyself to endure tribulations, and reckon them the best consolations; for the sufferings of this present time are not worthy to be compared with the glory which shall be revealed in us, nor would they be even if thou wert to endure them all. When thou hast come to this, that tribulation is sweet and pleasant to thee for Christ's sake, then reckon that it is well with thee, because thou hast found paradise on earth."
The Imitation of Christ, Second Book, Chapter XII, No. 10-11, (Christianity, Catholic)
"Oh that thou wert worthy to suffer something for the name of Jesus, how great glory should await thee, what rejoicing among all the saints of God . . ."
The Imitation of Christ, Second Book, Chapter XII, No. 13, (Christianity, Catholic)
"Let us understand that God is a Physician, and that suffering is a medicine for salvation, not a punishment for damnation."
The Voice of the Saints, Chapter 15, No. 1, (Christianity, Catholic, Words of St. Augustine)

****

Entranced by the level of the vibration, my soul was thrust into a very long state of ecstasy or Samadhi. Lasting for three and a half hours, I could see everything around me in the room, above my home, into the stars and the ether, and into all heavenly abodes which might possibly overlap my current threshold, despite the fact that my physical eyes were closed. When your soul is alighted into such a state, all things become enlivened, you can see the consciousness in all things around you, the molecular structures, and the living ether trails which unite all life.

"Samadhi but extends my conscious realm, beyond limits of the mortal frame to farthest boundary of eternity where I, the Cosmic Sea, watch the little ego floating in Me. Mobile murmurs of atoms heard, the dark earth, mountains, vales, lo! Molten liquid! Flowing seas change into vapors of nebulae! Aum blows upon vapors, opening wondrously their veils, oceans stand revealed, shining electrons, till, at last the sound of the cosmic drum, vanish the grosser lights into eternal rays of all-pervading bliss. From joy I came, for joy I live, in sacred joy I melt. Ocean of mind, I drink all creation's waves."
The Autobiography of a Yogi, Chapter 14, Page 170-171, (Hinduism, Kriya Yoga, Words of Paramahansa Yogananda)

****

Lying down amongst a multitude of souls, a tiny little baby boy came down from heaven and landed on my tummy, sitting up in joyful laughter on my lap. All the souls around me were too busy with grounded things to notice the happening. Cute, adorable, happy and filled with joy, something totally amazing began to happen. A pair of bright pink wings shaped like rose petals began to spread out from upon his back. As they did, they seemed to bloom before me much like a rose, in that there were several layers to these wings, three layers to be exact. "Oh, my goodness," I thought, "It's a cherub!"

I'd never seen one of these most holy cherub angels before, and my soul felt as though a great honor had been bestowed upon it. And what I cannot express fully is just how adorable and cute the tiny baby angel was. Looking around me, I tried to point out to the others in this dimension that we had been honored by the arrival of a cherub, but no one seemed interested. In his face, I read a message of my future, my upcoming journey. In his eyes, I saw an invitation. Little did I know that this little cherub was to be my third child, a son named Jacob, to be born two years later.

> *"I have talked with angels about heaven's bond with the human race, noting that while a churchman might say that everything good is from the Lord and that angels are with man, few of them believe that angels are intimately connected to man, and fewer still that they are within his thought and affection."*
> *Heaven & Hell, Chapter 33, No. 302, Paragraph 1, (Christianity, Swedenborgianism, Words of Emanuel Swedenborg)*

****

As Andy was immersed in the spectacle of sleep, he began to feel an infernal rumbling, as suddenly a horrid orange egg-shaped driving demon with pointy teeth and much drool, popped out of his soul. Thereupon vexed, the nasty little spirit went angrily away from his former host, as now he was no longer welcome.

> *"When you feel the assaults of passion and anger, then is the time to be silent as Jesus was silent in the midst of His ignominies and sufferings."*
> *The Voice of the Saints, In Temptation, Page 68, Stanza 2, (Christianity, Catholic, Words of St. Paul of the Cross)*

****

Pulling up to the gas station, I was now manifesting as a young oriental woman, my long black hair shone in the light, and my pale face was accompanied by a shimmering peach-colored body suit. Upon my brow was a red dot, above my third eye. Although this was a Hindu, thus Indian, sign, I was actually a warrioress of the oriental tribes, my place now well secure among the adepts since my invitation to join them from the swami. For this fortnight my name was Milinda, and I was to experience another aspect of my soul residing in this very unique place I had just ventured upon.

Unknown to me at the time, my soul bore a sign of reflection and malaise. In my essence was a tinge of self-satisfaction. Such a thing could well be dangerous for an adept, for it made them vulnerable to outside forces. As I was waiting for my vehicle to be fully gassed, another entity awaited me invisibly from above, awaiting my return to the gateway of initiants. Because I was blinded by my self-satisfaction, I didn't notice the tiny brown and white speckled fawn standing in the center of the road. A warning of my vulnerability, the frail, gentle creature held an imminent knowledge of a battle to come.

As I made it to the tubes of the initiants, I prepared to enter, find my resting abode, and sleep for the night. Unknown to me, the invisible specter remained hovering above. The initiants in this realm were adepts at psycho-kinesis and other powers of the mind. Upon entering the abode, the initiants were placed in a long, narrow, bluish white tube which contained on the right side many doors, leading to the many cells of the warrior adepts. In these cells, they would rest and sleep, being energized to higher stations for their return to their Earthly places. But the one who had hovered invisibly and unobserved was waiting for me, to challenge my place within this hall of initiants.

Such a challenge was considered unlawful, but was often attempted by those who bore the sign of the serpent. In their manipulative abilities, they would attempt to win over a cell or a place within the warrior sect, by using their own psycho-kinetic powers to remove the memory of the former occupant, replacing it with memory of themselves. This was a rare occurrence, for the warrior adepts were aware of such guises. But on some occasions such maneuvers would be attempted, when the serpent was especially tricky and energized. For instance, when an adept was especially self-satisfied or in any other state proving them vulnerable in preservance of their station.

Locating the cell of a particular adept, they would overcome him, and take to it because the cells carried within them initiation into higher spheres of knowledge and power. If an occupant could be tossed out, they would then be the beneficiaries of this particular energy. If they were to be successful, they could use such knowledge and energy for their dark designs.

Sitting in a lotus position, I closed my eyes and quickly lifted into the air preparing to find my place well among the third series of tubes. White rounded hallways tinted by a bluish light, much in the shape of large water pipes, the locked doors were along the right side. Moving without the aid of my physical body in lotus position, I used the psycho-kinetic powers I had use of in this realm to move slowly in the air towards my cell, eager for further energization and spiritual sustenance.

But suddenly behind me, the spirit who had been watching manifested openly as a woman, her long black hair pulled into a high ponytail, and her body clothed in a shimmering blue body suit. Quickly attaining to the lotus position, her psycho-kinetic powers in this regard were quick and fast.

Within moments, the two of us were darting through the tubes, the one in the blue body suit chasing myself in the peach. Battle raging, the only thing that I now had on my side was my singular knowledge of the location of my special cell. If the challenger were to take my place in the warrior elite, she would first have to figure out which cell was my own. Even though her psycho-kinetic powers regarding speed of movement might have been slightly more advanced than mine, if I could outsmart her intellectually, than my place among the tubes, and thus the initiants, could not be overtaken. It was my duty to protect the initiants from an invasion from the dark side of such a nature, especially since it was my own self-satisfaction which had made this attempt possible. There were literally hundreds of cells locked against the white walls tinged pale blue by the light, and each door was locked, only able to be opened by the psycho-kinetic powers of those who bore them.

Within moments, I realized that my challenger held superior psycho-kinetic movement abilities, but I also quickly reasoned that her mental prowess could not be quite so advanced, because her assault was completely through the movement of her body in lotus position. "You'll never be able to find my cell." I called to her, as she was only about twenty feet behind. My challenger shouted, "You will reach your cell in due time, and then it is that I shall have it." But I had already prepared a way to defeat this challenger, although it would mean my extrication from the warrior sect, anyway.

Swami would be so disappointed in my lapse, but I had to do what I must to protect the hall of initiants, even if it were to be at the expense of my own place.

When first being initiated and entering into the tubes, we and all the warrior's were given special orders regarding behavior during such a challenge, and this included rules regarding our own extrication. If a warrior passed his own cell, he would lose it, and if a warrior passed through the entire series of tubes without finding his cell, he would be automatically extricated. Knowing and finding your own cell were a special mental quality, which if not met, rendered immediate extrication. In certain cases, you could win back your spot, but having a firm mental hold on the location of your own cell was determined to be of great importance, one of many disciplines required in this spiritual warrior sect.

Assuming I would never give up my cell in such a manner, my challenger had assumed that I would reveal the location of my cell and try to reach and lock it first. But that was not what I had planned. Within moments, we had passed by my cell, although my challenger was unaware of it. And several moments after passing my cell, I counted on something else, the fact that my challenger might be wearing down with fatigue. After all, we had raced through several tubes since we'd been there; all very long, and all very complicated.

Turning to face my challenger who remained about twenty feet behind, she was cocky and arrogant, making statements regarding my eventual need to reveal the place of my cell. Sending a ray of light to throw her off her path, I took the challenger off guard. As the light came from my hand, the ray of light shot directly towards her left knee, which altered her balance, causing her to topple through the tubes. Taking this opportunity, I began soaring at high speeds towards the final thrust of the tubes, unaware of how much time I might have to extricate myself.

At the end of the tubes was a large drop off. Cruising in lotus position towards it, I fell but did not land through this final series of tubal thrusts. Exiting the tubes, a house awaited. Upon the door was a sign which offered this home for rest to those who had either failed initiation, or been extricated from the tubes. Declining this offer, I knew that my challenger would emerge with a fury very soon. Noticing that the roof seemed inviting for some unknown reason, I went there to lay my wearied form. Within a moment, the roof's special properties made my form invisible and transparent, which at this moment was a grand blessing. Never at any time did I notice my challenger exiting the tubes. Assuming she'd been left far behind and defeated, I prepared to make my next choices which would determine whether or not I could retrieve my place amongst the initiants.

In transparent form, I flew off into the vistas of the night praying and asking for guidance as to what I should do next. Everything seemed dark and dreary on the edge of my defeat, and I didn't know where to go. I'd done what I should, protect the order, but had lost my place within the order in the same mechanism.

As I flew invisibly through the streets of the city, a large muscular man who was jogging ran right up to me, taking my invisible arm into his visible one. Conveying telepathically that he had come to assist me in re-proving my status as a member of the warrior sect, I welcomed his assistance.

Spending several moments evaluating his inner spheres, I knew without a doubt that he'd been sent by the eternal, and that he was not another clever ruse from the dark side. Because I'd lost everything by soaring through the tubes, in a sense, I had momentarily even lost my identity.

Directing me to another location, the scene of a staging of many initiants, all were exhibiting their spiritual prowess. Many battles of the spirit were occurring between two at a time in several locations, these things being done for the practice of spiritual skill. Bringing me to a place amongst the crowd, I immediately recognized the face of my challenger within it, the woman in pale blue.

Somehow, despite my safeguards, this serpent was still attempting to manipulate the order. Intending to eventually be admitted by the swami through a very intricate disguise of her true liaison, she had been allowed to be a part of everything, even given status among them just short of being initiated. Remaining invisible, my presence was known only to the man who had brought me.

Challenging the woman to battle, the man prepared to reveal her true identity to the crowds. These battles were not physical in nature but entirely energetic, spiritual and mental. Proving to be quite less advanced with this aspect of mental adeptship than she had been with speed in psycho-kinetic flight, within less than a moment, I sent an energetic bolt through the man to the woman, which had sent her roaring to the floor in a station of defeat.

Other's were now coming over to assist this woman in getting back up, while the crowds were rambling about the quickness of this battle. Directing me to materialize, the man told me to make known my claims against this serpent invader.

Appearing in the air above the crowd, I immediately materialized. "I am Milinda," I said in a magnetic voice, "I was initiated by the great warrior sect ten centuries ago. It is I who has defeated your woman in pale blue." Remaining silent, I, too, was silent for a moment as my conscious present self took in this knowledge. Shocked that I remained in existence, the woman in pale blue had assumed I was dead after the challenge in the tubes; for many such warriors take their own lives after losing their status among the warrior sect.

Conveying telepathically what had happened, I made clear as to how this woman had unlawfully challenged me for my place in the warrior sect, and how I had chosen to give up my place rather than reveal the sacred location of my cell, thus, jeopardizing the whole order.

At this information, the crowds insisted that I be given another opportunity to crush the head of this serpent. Forcibly placing the challenger within a ring of some sort, although her battered mind, body and soul remained on the floor in a status of defeat, I said, "I will show mercy to this serpent, I shall not fight her when she is down." The crowds began roaring, "She is not only a great warrior, but she is a great saint!" Cowering at this proclamation, I revealed that it was deeply untrue. Telepathically, I revealed to the others the self-satisfaction which had given entry to this serpent woman in disguise. Merciful in my confession, the crowds settled down.

Turning towards the swami who resided over the sect, I knew that my fate would be entirely in his hands. And by his mercy, I was given re-entry. The crowds continued cheering my return, and as they did, all began to fade away into the night. Reflecting, I knew of the great sacrifice the swami had made on my behalf, for it was my own negligence which had brought about all these events. This humbled me, and I vowed never to allow myself to engage in the deadly sin of pride again.

"Humility is the abasement of the heart to Him Who knoweth the unseen."
The Doctrine of the Sufi's, Chapter XXXIX, (Islam, Sufism, Words of Ruwaym)
"Likewise if I wish to be happy, I should not be happy with myself, and similarly if I wish to be protected, I should constantly protect all others."
A Guide to the Bodhisattva's Way of Life, Chapter VIII, No. 173, (Buddhism, Tibetan, Words of Shantideva)

****

Reaching his hand to me out of the ether, the swami handed me a book whose title read, 'Early Beloved.' As I opened the book to peer upon its contents, I was quickly guided through two separate energetic emergences which manifested as ecstasies originating in my lower chakras which thrust upwards throughout to the crown. As this completed itself, I began to spin uncontrollably like a vortex, as elements from within my soul were becoming more outward and elements from without were becoming more inward.

Many hands were now appearing to me in the ether, and they all seemed to come from the swami. Hundreds of hands surrounded my soul, and each would emerge from its place of benign status, to sound forth another harmonic spin within my soul. As I spun, I traveled to many worlds and realms, only to remain a moment, soaring in the wanton majesty of the worlds of the beloved.

"Everywhere are His hands and legs, His eyes, heads and faces, and He has ears everywhere. In this way the Supersoul exists, pervading everything."
The Bhagavad Gita As It Is, Section 13, Text 15, (Hinduism, Translation by: A.C. Bhaktivedanta Swami Prabhupada)

****

Several witches attempted to torment me, but I found that to repeat the stanza, 'deliver us from evil,' from the Lord's Prayer was very effective in overcoming their attempt.

"Whilst yet on earth Christ empowered the Apostles to cast out demons in His Name, and in His last solemn charge He promised that the same delegated power should be perpetuated."
The History of Witchcraft, Diabolic Possession, Page 206, Paragraph 2, (Christianity, Catholic)

****

Sent among a community which was ravaged and completely overcome by serpent, spider and bug demons, it was my task to save a particular soul and return him to God. In order to rid themselves of these creatures, the people of this community had begun to purge them from their souls, but there were so many that when they were set loose in such a manner, the streets of the cities became filled with these infestations. Because of this, no one could truly be purged, because they had not developed a plan to take care of the creatures after they were extricated from individuals.

One individual was secretly working for the serpent, and he was the object of my journey this eve. Having led the people to believe that he wanted to lead them to safer land, in reality, he was tricking them. Leading them to a place where they could be re-infected, the dark side would re-attain control of their souls.

Because I knew of this status, I would not allow him to take control of the group. Rather, I led the people to begin sweeping up the bugs in dust pans. In so doing, I had them take the bugs to another location where they could be placed in one spot. As this was accomplished, I began energetically sending these creatures back to lower realms, dismantling most of the serpents, but leaving the bugs intact.

Enraging the man I was here to serve, I began flying into the air shouting to him as inspired by the Lord. "Your soul cannot be lost," I said, "The Almighty God wants you back, and I won't stop until this is so." Stunned by these words, he knew how vile and evil he had become. Even in such a state of sin, God had sent assistance to bring him back to the light, and this had obviously affected him deeply. Turning to assist the others in gathering up the infestations of bugs and serpents in dust pans, no more did he interfere as I sent them away from this community for good.

"Our Lord preserves us most carefully when it seems to us that we are nearly forsaken and cast away for our sins, and because we have deserved it. But because of the meekness we get through these trials, we are wholly raised in God's sight by his grace. We are moved with such great contrition, compassion and true longing for God that we are suddenly delivered from sin and pain."
Revelations of Divine Love, Chapter 39, Paragraph 3, (Christianity, Catholic, Words of Juliana of Norwich)

****

Regarding incarnate demons and demonic tendencies among juvenile delinquents, my spirit was shown that those who are born in deep darkness have very little hope of rehabilitation due to counseling and other techniques. For those steeped in deep darkness, restriction and punishment are absolutely necessary if one wishes to preserve the safety of society, for these levels of evolution are very predatory by nature.

Unfortunately, society does not recognize the different levels of existence, and often makes judgment calls regarding only one level of evolution. What works for a soul in karmic ignorance, will not work with someone existing in the element of dominant darkness or evil.

"The worst people of all are the ones who have been involved in evil pursuits as a result of self-love, with an accompanying inward behavior stemming from deceit. This is because the deceit penetrates their thoughts and purposes too thoroughly and fills them with poison, destroying their whole spiritual life."
Heaven & Hell, Chapter 60, No. 578, (Christianity, Swedenborgianism, Words of

Emanuel Swedenborg)

Coming to the crowded room to exorcize the demons of many within the audience, the exorcist was instinctually drawn to those with the most serious infestations, as he violently overthrew them and yanked them out of their wards. Approaching them, their bodies would immediately begin to jerk and writhe, some of them beginning to scream.

All of these people appeared normal to the naked eye, and no one would have guessed that they had infestations. I remembered when the Buddhist priest had first made me aware of my own infestations and how shocked I had been. After considering the infested cases of five or six people, my spiritual guardian who sat to the right of me, asked him to assess my case. Becoming concerned, I'd learned to never take anything for granted. 'What would he assess?' I thought, 'Had I made any progress regarding the task of exorcism in which the Buddhist priest had said, 'these things take time?''

Ready for anything, he came nearer, and held out his hands in a smile. "This one is perfect," he said, (Meaning I was no longer infested by any dark forces. Not that I was truly perfect, by any means.) "She's a wife and mother . . ." Giving me a clean slate of spirit, I was thrilled at his diagnosis, and so happy that the exorcism begun upon my soul so long ago by the Buddhist priest was now complete.

Certainly, these things do take time, just as he had said, but they can be accomplished with diligence and effort. Smiling with joy, I couldn't restrain my glee at realizing that my soul was pure and clean of such defilements. Considering how awful it had been to become aware of such infestations in the beginning, such a pronouncement upon my soul was truly joyous for us to hear.

Hallelujah to the Lord!

"Let the evil that I have earned be turned away from me."
The Dead Sea Scriptures, Poems from a Qumran Hymnal, No. III, No. 5-7,
(Christianity)

Before the delivery of my third child, Jacob, the Lord Jesus appeared personally, showing me the status of a soul who was apparently about to encounter an early death. Despite having a family who needed to be cared for, I was shown that this soul had earned a place in hell because of his extreme atheism and hatred for God. Screaming in the fires of the abyss, I cringed at the fate he was about to endure which the Lord had bade me to witness. Asking me to offer up the pains of my labor as a sacrificial penance for this soul, the Lord said that if I were to do this for him, he would be given another opportunity to continue to live, and thus, possibly change his wicked ways. Agreeing to do so with great fervency, this chastisement was indeed lifted and this soul was given another chance at life. Only time would tell how he might use it, however, and whether or not he would save himself from this hellish fate.

Continuing to journey into the status of various souls, I was bidden to observe a pitifully sad situation wherein a soul, who had been given great spiritual opportunities to advance by the Lord, was allowing herself to be taken down the road of perdition by a boyfriend. Succumbing to temptation, she had yielded all that she knew to be true in order to be with a man who was obviously following the wide road to perdition. Having chosen the status of 'death,' which had been emblazoned upon her chest, her body was decomposing. Experimenting with her decomposition, her boyfriend repeatedly said, "She needs to go to hell, she needs to go to hell . . ." Very concerned, I made it clear to him that he was now responsible for the state of her soul and that he would pay dearly for this in hell. Unconcerned, he couldn't care less but because of the many bad choices she had made up to this point in bringing her soul to such a pitiful reality, there was little I could do but wait and hope that she would stop this horrid reality before it became solidified and final on the ground.

Giving me an opportunity to warn this soul in her physical waking world, she eventually broke free of this defilement, and became one with her eternal destiny.

As a sharp contrast to the former experience, I was shown a soul who bore within her a twenty-foot high, blue-green, rounded and fat demon of sloth. Literally taking the breath right out of you, it was smothering in its incessant wants and 'needs.' Unrelated to work ethic, this sloth demon had appeared from laziness in regards to spiritual development.

Giving me an opportunity to warn this soul in her physical waking world, it inspired within her a torrential flood of transformative energy which resulted in the expungement of the demon and a grand deepening of her spiritual life.

Finally, the Lord Jesus allowed me to experience a demonic battle wherein I'd called to Him for help and none had come. Feeling this absence, Jesus wanted me to understand the isolation of those who live consciously sinful lives (hardened, repetitious, actual sin); those who seek repentance in words but not deeds. Because they belong to Satan, he may torment them at will, and they may not always receive swift help. Differing from the type of temptation or torment meant to *try* a soul, Satan must have permission to reach one who already belongs to God, and the purpose is expiatory, to build a crown of strength.

Returning to form, I immediately went into labor as Jacob was born.

****

Covered in blood, the muddy path seemed ominous as I looked ahead to see where my spiritual guardians might be taking my soul. A gathering of satanic worshipers loomed ahead. "Oh, geez!" I thought, as the Lord made it clear that I *must* go. The angel aside me quietly and very calmly said, "The Lord asks for your presence." Not replying, it seemed that they were awfully calm about sending me to such a horrific place.

As soon as I'd arrived, I took notice of a throne in the center of all the activities with a small statue of Satan sitting upon it. The people were wandering around in a state of dazed confusion; many of them had joined together in smaller groupings to 'do their own thing.' (Their own things were violent, sadistic, sexually deviant, etc.) Ceremonies had yet to begin as I wandered around observing, remaining as incognito as possible. Because these were demon-filled Satanists, many knew immediately that I was a Christian and filled with the Holy Spirit.

Running towards me with fists upraised, an entire band of them began coming after me to take me out. As they did this, I yelled out various truths about Jesus Christ, and began calling out His name, over and over, "Jesus, Jesus, Jesus, Jesus . . ." Continuing with His many titles, I said, "King of Kings, Jesus is the Lamb, Jesus is the Messiah, Jesus is the Savior. You are following a false king, for Jesus is God." Beginning to speak words from the gospel of John required in the discerning of spirits, I was inspired! "Jesus came down from heaven and became flesh; He is the Son of God. Jesus rose from the dead and ascended into heaven. Jesus is the King."

As I spoke these words to them, there were three reactions. The really violent and vicious ones would get angry and want desperately to rip me to pieces, but they couldn't because I was protected. Others that were not as rooted in evil would just walk away because they knew they couldn't do anything. Those that were lukewarm in their satanic leanings, thus borderline and open to the possibility of conversion, would start crying openly and uncontrollably; which embarrassed them to no end. Waving for me to go away so that they could stop this embarrassing display, I stayed and spoke more about Jesus. Having no control over this process, the Lord had literally taken a hold of them as they were 'convicted in the spirit.' I felt sorry for them, for evil knows no joy.

After a good long while, about fifty of the approximately two-hundred participants had been taken to this state of conviction and I was hoping I might be able to leave. But when I least expected it, one of the truly nasty Satanists grabbed me from behind and sat me down in a chair, blocking my view of what was going on to the right of me. In a moment, he moved away to reveal that I was sitting next to the throne I'd seen earlier, but it was now occupied by Satan himself. Looking like a caricature of a big time wrestler with gray colored skin, the texture of sand, the bulging muscles in his chest were overtly large, exaggerated and frankly somewhat frightening. Proportionately large, his head was separated into two bulging sections like a large brain with horns coming out of it. Having no hair, his image held two large black eyes.

Laughing hysterically in his own unique evil way, the ogre didn't waste any time in letting me know his purpose. According to him, I was going to die in my sleep tonight because I'd been chosen as the sacrifice for this particular satanic black mass. Surprised by his pronouncement, I quickly regained my composure and began to laugh right back at him.

"I'm not going to be the sacrifice tonight," I said, "I know that you have to have permission from God to bother me, but I also know that you *don't* have permission to do *that*." My knowledge of this had come from the book of Job, in the Old Testament of the Holy Bible. Frowning, I continued, "And besides, Jesus is the King of Kings, and you're the king of nothing." Roaring with anger, I began to recite the Apostles Creed, "I believe in God, the Father Almighty," as I said this, he moved a few inches away from me, his roar becoming more of a growl, "Creator of heaven and Earth; and in Jesus Christ, His only Son, our Lord;" his facial expression became one of doubt and confusion, "who was conceived by the Holy Spirit, born of the Virgin Mary, suffered under Pontius Pilate, was crucified, died and was buried. He descended into Hell; the third day He arose again from the dead; He ascended into heaven, and sits at the right hand of God, the Father Almighty." Flinging himself out of his chair, he waved me off and ran away, but so as not to appear bashful, I shouted after him, "I believe in His holy church!"

As I said this, several of his wards became invisible, planning to assault me without my awareness. But before they could touch me, the Holy Spirit filled me and took me away. Before I could awake, however, the Holy Spirit began repeating something over and over to me. "Check your house for a gas leak, check your house for a gas leak . . ." When I did awaken, I had the power company check our home for a leak and sure enough, we had one. Satan had been serious about his plans to take me out, but the Lord would not allow him to do so . . . because he didn't have permission.

The following night, a swarm of wasps came towards me as I was drifting off to sleep. Hitting me directly in the heart, I immediately felt like I was having a heart attack or stroke. Entering into deep prayer as I struggled to breathe - chest pain and pressure searing, tingling and electrical sensations traveling throughout my body - I remembered the words of the masters. "I feel no pain, I feel no pain." Centering on my place within God, I gradually began to feel better.

Although the Lord had not allowed the viper to take my life, I had suffered a grievous injury ordained by God which would not be revealed for another year and a half, a trial which was now brimming within my body and soul . . .
****

Sleeping peacefully on my bed, I reached my hand over to grasp Andy's, assuming he was still there. Sometimes I don't realize it when he's already left for work, and this was one of those moments. Feeling a hand on the bed, I placed my hand within it, but I couldn't have been more wrong in assuming it was my husband's.

No sooner had I done this than the ogre had hurled my spirit into the air, throwing me around the room. Obviously, Satan had laid a trap for me, and I'd fallen right into it. Because of what had happened the previous day with the Lord, however, I became very courageous and bold.

Once he stopped throwing me all over the room, I regained my composure and began to look around to spot the haggard fool. Looking in the direction of where his energy had been, I noticed that he was invisible at this time, which frankly, was a great relief. He's so ugly! Instinctually, I knew that he was planning to materialize in front of me at any moment, so I shouted at him. "You idiot!" I screamed loudly, "Don't you know that you could've been up in heaven with Jesus! God made you such a beautiful and powerful angel and you are such a fool!" Angered by my statement, a sense of his imminent materialization was forthcoming. "Oh, please don't do that! You're so ugly and so gross! It's so sad what you've become. Please don't ruin my day by making me look upon your disgusting countenance."

Energetic quiet overtook the room, as it appeared that he might be embarrassed. Surprising me, it probably shouldn't have, because after all, Satan *is* the Lord of vanity and all deadly sins. Within a moment, his energy had completely dissipated. Calmly, I went back to sleep.

****

Called into service, my soul entered the sub-conscious dreaming of a rock musician. Having no idea who he was, I was immediately made aware that his music was inspired by Satan and it carried a mesmerizing quality which lured unsuspecting crowds of people into his web. Angered that I was being called in to interfere with his loyal and devout ward, Satan appeared to thwart my attempts at saving his soul.

Throwing my soul around the room, he actually lifted my body up off of the bed as he prepared to throw me against the wall. Before he could, I called to Jesus for help and was delivered from this brutal attack before it could reach fruition.

Amidst the sub-conscious dreaming, I followed the rock musician through many epochs of his life. Observing the demonic content of his soul, I noticed that he was given to demonic rages, sometimes going so far as to allow his eyes to roll back into his head. When he performed for crowds, he appeared as a very normal, attractive man, mesmerizing many young people into the lure of the dark side unconsciously.

Following him, I continually prayed to Jesus to free this tormented soul from bondage. Speaking to him, I spoke to him of Christ's love for him. After several hours, I noticed that his soul had begun wrestling with the demons within him. Shouting loudly towards him, I told him that he must *fight* Satan and force him out.

Fighting continued for quite some time and I was unsure who was to win this battle, but once it was over, it was complete. Hurled outside and raging, the demons were screeching as his body became calm, serene and peaceful. Guiding him gently, he spoke the words indicating his acceptance of Jesus into his life, thanking me for giving them.

As a crowd awaited his next show, he quietly explained the changes which had taken place within him and his conversion to Christ. Immediately, three quarters of the crowd just left because his mesmerizing quality was no longer present. Despite this, he remained calm and accepting. Knowing that discarding the demon and embracing the truth would require sacrifice, he was now willing to make it.

****

Dragging me through the mud of my past sins, a demon had tried to bring me to despair. Mother superior appeared with a priest, expunging the demon. Retaining focus of past sins disallows forward movement.

Accompanying me to my home, the priest performed a mass in my living room, consecrating the Eucharist and placing it in a tabernacle upon the altar, making complete the transformation of our home into a monastery.
****

Given to return to a haunted mansion which I frequented regularly for years, I'd gone there to loose many of the lost souls who had been trapped there by their own delusional thinking. Located in an 18th century setting, this group of mansions was ornate and lush. A ballroom with them had always been the most densely populated place upon the property. In fact, it was so filled with lost and dark spirits, that I was really quite terrified of it for quite some time. Each time I returned to retrieve souls, I felt intimidated by the sheer number of lost souls and dark spirits confined to these walls.

Over the years, I've gone through this mansion so many times I couldn't possibly count them. Processing some of the energies with each visit, I had never really noticed much of a change. Despite this, I met and talked with many souls who were not yet ready to leave, but might be in the near future. Giving them information on how to extricate themselves, my business would be accomplished and I would go.

Stunned by what I saw upon entering this familiar haunted place, I immediately noticed that there was a huge decline in the haunted energies within the house. What used to feel like perhaps several hundred lost souls and dark spirits, had diminished to perhaps a handful. Terror did not even strike me as it had done so many times in the past.

Many times over the years, I'd questioned the true and deeper meaning of this mansion, and wondered if it represented my own karmic issues in some sense. That theory was put to rest as an angel appeared and whispered into my ear. "This place has nothing to do with you," she said, "I come to proclaim the deliverance of the captives! The Lord wishes for you to see the fruits of your many labors." A place which had literally been teeming with darkness was now almost completely liberated! My work had not been in vain. Unworthy and quite honored to see how the Lord had deigned to use me, I thanked the angel for allowing me to understand this enigma. On my knees, I was in tears thanking my God.

As I did so, she faded from my view, and I disappeared to the remaining wards of this haunted place, reappearing in a darkened building filled with Christian worshippers.

Waiting in a darkened hallway, two men were carrying a large silver pot. Asking them what they were doing, they said, "This pot is filled with the life-giving water which comes down from heaven and never ends." Begging them to pour this water over my own wretched soul, I fell to the ground as the Holy Spirit filled me with an intrinsic roar.
****

Praying on my knees in the astral state, a huge torrent of energy swept me off of my feet and into the cosmos. St. Michael came this time as a huge shadowy figure, almost like a thundercloud, but in the definite form of a man. Appearing as he does in popular statues, he wore a shortened metallic skirting adorned with body armor, as his huge wings protruded explosively from his back. Sometimes he appears as a shadowy bolt of energy, and sometimes he comes in pure living color. Magnificent size not diminished; there was something unusual about this visit. Just as huge, a female stood beside St. Michael. Flowing straight brown hair caressed her shoulders, and she wore a glimmering white robe down to her feet. Energetically, she was just as powerful as St. Michael and left me in ominous awe as I understood that she was a member of his league of angels.

Placing me upon his shoulder as he'd done in the past, St. Michael was very stern with me this evening. Wishing to discuss my visions with a particular individual who was supposed to be well-versed in spiritual direction, St. Michael and I were flying all over the world at a speed indescribable as he showed me an image of this person in the heavens. "Do not discuss this with him," St. Michael said in an energetically powerful way, "you listen to *me*!" Conveying that this person would give me false guidance regarding the mystical realms, St. Michael allowed me to see that he could jeopardize my divine mission.

Swooping down towards a building below, I saw a demon who was trying to interfere with this eternal directive. St. Michael flew by, and the demon was struck dead. (I was unsure if this striking dead was a literal rendering, or if they were struck dead in energy, annihilated in their ability to render destructive force towards the work of the Lord.) As quickly as he had swept me up, St. Michael returned me to my place of prayer on the floor of my bedroom and was gone.

****

Continuing the influx of eternal energies which had been heralded by St. Michael, my body began in an ordinary vibrational state and was separated from form. Intensive energies began to overtake my body, as an invisible angel beside me took hold of my soul and thrust me towards heaven. Soaring past the Earth into the universal spheres, I rode an eternal wave conducted by the angel below.

As my soul gathered celestial energy, it was immediately thrust downwards to the Earth below, but as I emptied myself of these sonic pulsations, I was again thrust into the heavens to repeat this process. Continuing into the night, with each ascent into the heavens, came a descent back to Earth to bring the energies down. While soaring towards the heavens, I instinctually shouted, "Lord Jesus Christ, Son of God, Have Mercy on Me, a Sinner."

Remembering the importance of discerning the spirits, I turned to the angelic guardian. "In the Name of the Lord Jesus Christ," I asked, "I demand that you reveal your identity to me." Appearing as a very beautiful creature of brilliance, I finished, "Are you here to serve the light?" Swept in a thunderous energy as he spoke, he replied, "Yes."

Although I knew that he was male, he had no features like hair or eyes that were visible. Wearing no apparent clothing, he seemed to be anatomically sexless, although his essence was very clearly that of a man. Lighted and iridescent, brilliance shone outwards from his very distinctive form. This was no nebulous creature, his form was well-defined, although clearly made of light and in a splendid array of colors; pale violet, blue and white. Upon the backdrop of the stars and the heavens, this magnificent angel shone with a splendor which can only be termed stunning.

Confident in his identity, I shouted to the heavens. "Lord Jesus Christ, shall we take a journey with these eternal energies across the mountain pass, and distribute them to all who must be energized?" Shooting like lightning towards the pass, the spirit world had made my soul aware of a pocket of darkness which needed seeding in the light.

But as I came to the edge of the location in question, there was an energetic barrier clearly present which had been placed there by Satan to mark his territory. Reinforced by souls on the ground unaware of their alliance with the ogre, I shouted, "Lord Jesus Christ, Son of God . . . Archangel Michael, Destroyer of Demons, allow us to pass through this demonic gateway." St. Michael's thunderous presence became abundantly clear as we were allowed to pass through. Coming upon the people in this area, some of them had been filled with green sludge.

As there was no more I could do, St. Michael simply said, "NO!" as he quickly changed my direction. Able to bring the light in, we were unable to seed it as of yet. This eternal program was de-energized by mortals on the ground.

Free will is a powerful thing.

Passing through the demonic boundary, St. Michael left me with the angel who'd come before, as we continued the process of bringing heavenly fruits into the Earthly mortal realm. Flying through the heavens together this time, a bold thought entered my mind and I conveyed it to my compatriot. "Perchance," I thought meekly, "I could go to the throne room of God?" Offering no reaction to my bold request, the angel thought, "Don't ask me, ask God." Gathering my boldness to make my grand proclamation, I shouted to the heavens, "Lord Jesus Christ, Son of God, may I come to the throne room of heaven?!" Shooting immediately through the universal beauty of space, I was given to see many tremendously awesome things.

As we'd traveled a great distance in a very short amount of time, I saw ahead a very brilliant city of light. Our souls were edging closer to this magnificent place, and on the periphery of this city of light you could see light trails leading from the outskirts of this heavenly mirage to within its sacred walls. Coming close enough to see details, I noticed that there were children playing who had distinctively human features, but yet, were surrounded by auras which made it clear that they were not physical beings. Light beings were walking down a side road near the children, as well as, other adults who looked more like the children, with physical features but distinctive auras. Happiness, serenity and bliss emanated from the city, and I felt honored to view it from such a close proximity.

As I expected, however, the Lord did not deem me suitable or worthy to go to the place I'd requested. Instead, because of my boldness which the Lord had apparently enjoyed, He'd allowed me to come to this periphery of what appeared to be heaven, and he gave leave to my angelic host to take me on a most spectacular journey through the galactic heavens.

A celestial tour ensued wherein I gave witness to visually and energetically stunning solar systems, galaxies, stars, planets, orbs, black holes, nebulae, etc. Entranced by this panorama, I shouted a sigh of thanks to the Lord of hosts, whose presence was with me, inside me, around me, and one with me as I soared through this newfound, magnificent world . . . this world was Galactica.

****

A horde of demons approached in the black and red cloud of dust which came in their wake. Hundreds of them appeared to me as a legion of dark reptilian creatures with bat wings coming towards me. The demons swarmed like vermin in the inner part of the cloud, and the outer part of the cloud was jet black with no boundary. As they came near and surrounded my soul with their stench, I could see and feel them all around me, but their attack felt like it was coming from the inside of my body. Clearly visible outside, they surrounded my body in vociferous smoke and odorous hues. Writhing, they came in waves of red as I felt internal symptoms from their assault.

Intrigued by this fact, I'd never experienced something quite like this. Although demonic attacks do affect you physically, what I'd experienced in the past were attacks which clearly delineated their way from the outside in. Although these demons were very clearly outside of me, their attack was coming from within, although they hadn't actually even touched my soul.

Standing before me in the form of a black tunnel filled with swarms of satanic hosts, I knew that I had to fight my way through them in order to prevail. Pushing with all my strength and might, I shouted out for the assistance of Jesus and St. Michael to help me wage war and break free from this demonic stronghold which wished to overcome me this night, and as I did, I began moving ever slowly through their ranks, pushing them aside. Screaming for help, I also shouted out physically, for my husband shook me awake, releasing me from the grip of the demons for this night.

After this battle had been waged, it very quickly became known to me why the demons had sent such a stronghold to stop and de-energize me the previous night. Attempting to de-energize my spirit because the Lord intended to use me in a planned effort to redeem a very lost soul, Satan wanted to keep it. Thus, I was targeted.

Arriving in an old hospital, I had no idea what had led me here until I heard some of the staff speaking of a haunting which had been occurring on the pediatric floor. Deciding to go investigate, I was very shocked at what I found. A young boy of about nine years old was haunting this floor and was *very clearly completely demonic*. As soon as he saw me, he came after me like a torrent of lightning. Appearing as a mixture of white and gray matter which had formed in the manner of his former body, the demon's medium-length white hair stood on end as if held by electricity. Coming towards me, this little child had the appearance of a madman.

Remaining calm, I grabbed a hold of his arm and began reciting over and over again the 'Hail Mary.' Sending him into a tizzy, he was now feeling dazed and confused enough that I was able to corner him and take a firmer hold of his soul. "Lord Jesus Christ, Son of God, have mercy on this lost soul." Repeatedly, my cries shot through the ether into the heavens, and as I did this, his soul began to be de-energized as demonic power left him. When it was finished, he became limp and powerless.

Knowing my job was finished, I handed him over to the angelic hosts awaiting the return of his soul. All were happy and joyous, for we all knew that Satan had put up a huge battle for this little one, because it gives him the greatest pleasure of all to steal the soul of an 'innocent;' innocent in the sense of his age, but not in any other regard. Although it was somewhat shocking to realize that even a small child can be completely demonic and aligned with darkness, it was very clear that they *can* and *do* choose such things, and it was important for me to know.
****

Having come into the room while I was sleeping, the demon lurked as my spirit sat up in bed beginning to separate from my body. Turning to Andy, he was sleeping and sub-conscious. Shouting at him, I said, "Andy, look!" Pointing in the direction of the ten-foot high, brown, reptilian looking demon with strange wing-like protrusions coming from behind his ears, I said, "Don't you see it?! Help me!" Andy was simply unconscious, and unable to respond.

While I'd been asking for help, the demon had taken a live electrical wire and placed it in my hands. Stuck to the chord, I was getting electrocuted and I struggled to release myself. But as soon as I detached from the chord, the demon reached for me and literally threw me across the room. Looking towards Andy, whose spirit was sitting up in bed in a sub-conscious astral state, I said, "Do you believe me now?!" Andy had no problem in recognizing the presence of demons; he'd had many encounters of his own. But he had no idea how violent these demons truly behaved towards me, although I spoke to him about such things, because it was not within his experience to be tormented at this level. As many people may believe things they haven't seen, their depth of understanding radically deepens once the experience becomes their own.

Nodding that he did believe me now, I noticed that his eyes were glassy, indicating that he was sub-consciously astral. Before I could surmise that I was on my own, the demon whipped up a huge wind of satanic energies which began blowing me all over the room. After this unpleasant encounter, he tried to force a very extravagant ring upon my finger.

Shoving it back in his face, I noticed that it was made with the most exquisite of emeralds, diamonds and other jewels of the Earth. But what horrified and stunned me, was that the ring was covered in blood.

Immediately, my soul knew without any tinge of doubt that the blood on this ring had come from aborted babies. An angelic host appeared above me for protection, funneling knowledge towards me regarding this particularly horrendous ring which the demon had tried to force upon me. A symbol of wealth, position and prestige, the extravagant ring was covered in blood, the symbol of the children who have died on the altar of the previous vices. Beyond the obvious profiteers of abortion, those medical practitioners who make their living performing abortions, there was a more discreet form of profiteering which cost these children their lives.

Because so many abortions had been performed for economic reasons - financial, educational status or position - many had sacrificed their children for whatever goals they had hoped to achieve as a result of terminating an ill-timed pregnancy. Some of these people had sacrificed the children in order to attain position or wealth which may not have been available to them if they'd kept their child. (Obviously, there are many reasons that women choose abortion and this is not meant as a blanket statement to cover them all, nor is it meant as a judgment upon them. Many women who have abortions experience severe regret, and their suffering as a result is immeasurable. But the healing from such things begins with recognition of the lies which begot it in the first place; our culture of death which states that children are a burden rather than a blessing, and that we may pick and choose such events in our lives as we please, even if we must destroy life to do so. This same world view is what fuels the ideas of Euthanasia, when a person no longer remains 'productive.')

In such cases, abortion has become a sin of greed, and the future 'success' of such individuals has been bought with blood. Looking to the angel, she sent a stroke of lightning towards this grotesque figure who was assaulting me. As it hit him, he and his gratuitous adornment of blood had disappeared.

Shaken, I reached towards the angel, who calmly took my hand and led me back into my body. Directing me to go to a church and sit before the Eucharistic Tabernacle, she said, "The Blessed Sacrament expels certain demons."

Along with this I was given to look upon a particular demon of deviant sexuality who *sometimes* inhabits those of a homosexual nature. But it was made equally clear that this demon does *not* possess *all* those who have the tendency, and that many souls who display homosexual tendencies are perfectly within the bounds of that which God wants them to be.
****

Becoming conscious in this horrendous place, I looked upon the disgusting pterodactyl-like creature, of which I knew to be a demon, ravaging a human victim. Pecking with his long beak into his flesh, he was tearing him apart with his claws and eating him. Doing this under the cover of night, the cowardly creature only performed his hideous function in total darkness.

Satanic high priests were overseeing the torture of the wards of this realm, who had appeared in the form of normal human men. Surrounding them were a host of snakes and two-headed serpents filled with deadly venom. One of the high priests approached me as I had lurched forward in an attempt to run away from this disgusting abode. Throwing me over a glass balcony, I was cut in the hip severely as I fell to the ground. Not moving, I realized quickly that my torture was to simply be present in this hellish place watching the torture of others. If I stayed put, the satanic priests did not approach me, at least at first. Many bodies lay all over the floors, appearing as if dead and there was a rack of bodies hanging as if on a closet rod on one wall. Also appearing to be dead, I inherently knew that they were suicides, although they were not your ordinary type. Unusual as it seemed, these were souls who had committed suicide believing that it would be an honor to do so for some evil purpose. (Of course, these did not include those who had committed suicide in order to prevent a torturous death at the hands of an enemy, or to prevent the revelation of knowledge that would harm others during a war.) Speculating on their motives,

I wondered if they were the souls of satanic worshippers who had given themselves in sacrifice, not an unusual practice among Satanists. Another very odd circumstance that I witnessed was that after the demons were finished torturing the humans, they burned them to the finest ash. Everything burned, including their bones.

Before I could ascertain a means of escape, the high priests approached me. "You're not saved," one said, "and you are a fool to believe that the Lord could forgive your sins. You are totally dark and destined for hell." Although this frightened me, I said nothing, contemplating that their motive was probably that of despair. When I wouldn't speak, one of the more prestigious high priests grabbed me angrily and took me to a second floor area where there were no other humans present.

Covered with snakes and two-headed serpents, they were slithering around in hideous fashion. Throwing me to the ground, he had come towards me holding one of the two-headed serpents with which he had hoped to assault me viciously. Before he could, however, the serpent fell dead to the ground, infuriating and enraging the demonic host to no end. Thrashing the dead creature all around him, he banged it on walls and doors, raging at its impotence. Within moments, before I had thought to call for assistance, my soul was liberated from this hell but taken to witness another fascinating phenomenon regarding these wards upon the Earth.

As I watched totally unnoticed, the Lord bid me to observe the goings-on as several of these same high priests appeared as ordinary men walking upon our planet. Nobody could see me and this made it possible for me to observe some very interesting facts. In my inmost soul, the Lord bade me to distinguish between the regular people walking around this ordinary street corner on the Earth and those who were Christians. As you might expect, nobody could distinguish the high priests from others within the crowd, and they were regarded as regular ordinary people.

Very developed in spiritual power, the high priests were accomplished in their dark thrust. As a stark contrast, most of the Christians were not developed in this manner at all because they lived by faith. Because of this, they noticed nothing unusual about the high priests and were unable to discern their evil states. However, despite this difference in regards to spiritual power and attainment, the Christians, completely unknowingly, *tortured* the high priests simply through the power of their faith in the Lord!

Completely oblivious to the impact they had on these evil souls, the Christians approached them, speaking as if they would to anybody else. Unbeknownst to them, however, the energy of their faith would rebound on these evil wards because of the presence of the Holy Spirit within them. Allowed to listen to the energetic interplay, I noticed that whenever one of these dark souls was near a Christian, he was, in a sense, 'bowled' over.

Expressing his rage hearing the voice of the Holy Spirit, one shouted, "Every time I get near one of those Christians, I have to hear THAT VOICE!" Holding his hands over his ears, he was cringing in pain. Unable to tolerate the power of faith, the demons were tortured without the need for effort or even notice on the part of the Christians. Holding mundane interactions with these people, discussing everyday things, their faith spoke *for them* in energy. Having no hold on the Christians, despite their advanced spiritual abilities which had been refined towards the darkness and the deep, the demons were whipped just by being in their presence. Wow! Perhaps this is one manner in which the Lord marks the souls of the faithful.

****

An angel of the Lord had been given charge to show me a woman who had been given much in the way of religious training. Allowed to witness the true outcome of her life beside what could've been the status of her soul if she had made good use of the graces provided by God, the angel described her current manifestation as that of a 'meaningless bimbo,' while next to her stood the beautiful image of a woman looking towards heaven emitting a great degree of holiness. Exhibiting great disgust at what she had become despite the great workings of the Lord, the angel regarded her with sorrow.

****

Fond of the darkness, these unusual men who lay before me, about to become my quest for the night, were Satanists. Abhorrent and violent people, it only made sense that I should be terrified of them, but by a special gift from the Lord, I wasn't.

Beginning in a darkened sideway behind some large trees and near two very big rocks, two people with a knife approached me and Andy, who had joined me only for the beginning and end of this quest. Asking us to participate in a ritual with them, they promised not to hurt us if we would do so. However, I inherently knew that they would attempt to hurt us either way. Despite couched terms used to deceive us as to the motives of their ritual, I was very much aware of the fact that these were members of a satanic cult and their ritual was dark, disgusting and blasphemous to God. Never specifying this truth to their followers, they always used terms which were vague and misleading. In truth, they were the darkest of the dark, as evil as souls may get, and their master was Satan. Sad . . . so very sad.

Threatening to cut Andy with the knives, I approached them, grabbing the arm of the guy who did not have a hold of Andy. Repeating their intentions, they said, "If you participate in our 'ritual,' we won't harm him." Pausing, I very quietly replied, "You see, we have a little problem with that." "What's that?" he asked. "Well . . . "I paused, "I . . . looooooooooooove . . . Jesus."

Silence permeated the place for several moments, and then you could hear a faint growl coming from his mouth. Holding my ground, they still threatened Andy, so I shouted to him. "Run! Get out of here. I'll take care of these two," but Andy wouldn't leave. Realizing I would have to aid him in departure before I could deal with the souls of these Satanists, I used heavenly gifts to attain our freedom. Even so, I sustained several energetic bolts to the chest which took some time from which to recover.

Returning that same night, Andy was no longer with me and it seemed that I was being energized to seek out and find this cult for the purpose of infiltration, dismantling and disposal. What would eventually happen, however, would be much greater than this.

Bidding my soul to arrive in a large older house, the Lord placed my buns in an easy chair in the living room where I proceeded to act as if I owned the place. Several women were on the first floor, most of whom were completely deceived as to the true nature of their 'guru.' But there was a select group of mostly males who were apparently the 'right hand men' of the high priest, who very much knew exactly what it was they were doing. Most of them hung out on the second floor of this house, plotting and colluding in various evil and dark schemes against their enemies.

Beginning to talk to the women, I became aware that the high priest was scheduled to arrive shortly and that my time with these particularly deceived souls would be short. Mincing no words, I told them exactly who their leader really was, but they didn't believe me. So I told them to watch closely all the things he said and did when he got back, so that they might be able to discern the truth for themselves.

Walking in the door, he immediately observed my presence on the easy chair. Under his breath, he growled, but tried to maintain a good appearance to the women in his charge. Making some nebulous comments about some rituals and procedures, he directed his followers to come with him into another room where these would take place. As a master manipulator and father of lies, he often made misleading statements or those which were completely untrue and this time was no exception. Turning towards me, he said, "Well, after all, I once trained to become a Catholic Priest . . . but you know that I left the seminary because it wasn't exactly my calling." This was completely untrue, but he had said it to give credibility to his 'techniques.' Sarcastically, I looked at him and said, "Well, I'd love to join you . . . after all . . . I . . . looooooooooove . . . Jesus! But perhaps I'll wait here."

Growling again, his followers made note of his strange response to the mention of Our Savior's name, but still continued after him. Standing outside of the door, I waited only a few minutes in which time he had all of them in a state of total satanic mesmerization. Running into the room, I shouted and pushed them over onto the floor. "Oh, this is wonderful!" I said, looking towards the high priest, "Christian Meditation!"

At this point, he was really pissed off because his subjects were now coming out of their strange trances and asking me what had happened to them. Quietly, I said, "Oh, nothing like a little satanic memorization to control your wills and minds." In their faces, you could see that they were beginning to realize the deception which had been perpetrated upon them. Continuing, I said, "Oh, but don't let it bother you, it's just a form of *meditation.*" Stating the word 'meditation' with much sarcasm, I said it very slowly so that they would understand my intent in speaking it.

Looking at me with a very quiet and subdued growl, the high priest whispered under his breath. "Leave," he said. Responding very loudly and again, with sarcasm, I said, "But I don't understand . . . I . . . looooooooooove . . . Jesus! How can I leave this intensely spiritual gathering when I love Him so much and we have here a great master of the Christian path to teach me all the ways of My Lord?" Every time I talked about my love for Jesus, the high priest and his inner circle were very much disturbed and, although they hid it on the surface, it was throwing them into an inner tizzy. Many of the less involved followers, those ignorant of the satanic nature of this cult, were becoming suspicious of them.

Following me back to the easy chair, the high priest had anger and suspicion in his eyes. Indeed, he was well aware of who I was and Who had sent me, but he couldn't say or show this outwardly because it would affect those under his charge. Sitting down, I made my intention of remaining in the house very clear, which displeased him.

Momentarily, my spiritual vision was expanded to view the activities of the upper floor where the hard-core cult members were gathered. All were dressed in black ritualistic garments, and their conversation was putridly evil. Amongst their topics of discussion was that of mutilating a human corpse, which they intended to do in a ritual they were preparing to attend.

Suddenly, my spiritual body materialized in their presence, and I was led to act in a very ignorant manner of what they were truly planning. "Oh . . . this is wonderful . . . are we preparing to celebrate the Eucharist together?!" Looking up with disgust, I ignored them and said, "Great! You all know how very much I . . . looooooooooove . . . Jesus!"

After my disappearance from the lower level, the high priest had assumed I'd been sent to this upstairs gathering. As a result, he entered the room just as I was concluding my declaration of love for the Lord. "It's time for a final battle between forces," he stated to me very calmly. Giving me directions to a location where we would all meet, there would be a showdown. We were to meet on an island, and it was to be me against about forty of them. "Okay," I said, "I'll be there."

Flying over the waters towards the island destination, I fully expected that this battle might not be winnable. Considering the possible injuries I might endure, I was assessing my losses ahead of time, so to speak. When I arrived, however, there was a great shift in energies and things began to go very differently than I had anticipated they might.

Thirty to forty of the darkest and most evil members of the cult had shown up in full dress black. Standing before a patch of bare ground piled high in a mound, they stared me down with their eyes. Intending this mound to be my grave site, I was completely unmoved or unafraid through an inexplicable gift from God. A presence could be felt all around us and literally in the molecules of the air which I could not yet identify, but I knew that I was surrounded by heavenly protection, and even more than that, I was filled with peace and a sense of complete safety. Perhaps I had not come by myself after all, but had been given the invisible assistance of legions of angels from heaven.

Kneeling before the patch of ground, I began to continually repeat, over and over, the words which caused them so much anguish. "I love Jesus, I love Jesus. I . . . looooooooove . . . Jesus." As I did this, six roses emerged from the ground in three rows of two. Single stalks with singular flowers, they appeared in the colors of white, pink and red. Growing as if from a heavenly light, they began to expand into bushes as more flowers bloomed.

As I'd been ignoring the cult members, I was shocked to notice that the high priest had fallen to his knees, followed by several of his cronies behind him. As they did so, you could see demons leaving their bodies, coming out of their mouths in the form of black mists shaped as diabolical images. Floating upwards, they dissipated as they entered the heights of the skies. Becoming limp after the expungement, they instinctively had fallen even further forward, bowing to the ground.

Turning to him, I very cautiously said, "You know, I really do love Jesus." Looking up, his eyes were almost blank. A new energy began to surround and fill the skies above us, that of the Rosary, a Catholic prayer in honor of the Virgin Mary and the mysteries of the life of Jesus Christ. Sparkly lights began to fall from this energy into the blank eyes of these former cult members who were still almost lying forward on the ground. You could hear whispers in the air like thousands of people praying; "Hail Mary, full of grace, the Lord is with thee . . ." Beginning to fill with something new, the eyes of the high priest looked towards me and spoke. "You know," he said under his breath as if almost embarrassed to admit it, "I think I love Jesus, too."

Shocked at his revelation, I was stunned at what my soul was about to witness. Many of the others expressed a similar feeling under their breath, and all began to comment at about the same time. "Yeah, me too!" "Uh huh, yeah." Without further adieu, they all began to get up and follow one another towards the church which stood conveniently nearby where they intended to receive full baptism! As they began to walk away, I reiterated to them under my breath, "I really do love Jesus." But I did not move from my kneeling position as this amazing conversion took place.

As I'd come expecting to infiltrate, dismantle and dispose, I was shocked that I'd actually witnessed a *conversion* among the most evil of souls.

Moments later, Andy and I were driving through a small town in a very bright and sunny oasis. Colorful, bright and pretty, there seemed to be a sense of lightness and good. Suddenly to my left, we came upon a building which was quite different than the bright surroundings. Dark and misty, the building appeared gray and black covered with statues of gargoyles and other demons on its eaves. For a moment, the Lord bade me to witness the building as it appeared in the physical realm, which was just as bright as every other building in town. But in the spiritual realm it was quite evidently 'possessed.'

"Interesting," I said under my breath towards heaven, "do you want me to go in?" Receiving a definitive verification, my spirit was made to know that this would be my next mission. "Okay," I said.
****

Appearing amongst a coven of witches who also practiced deviant sexuality in ritual manner, they were demonstrating rituals in an attempt to convince me that there was nothing wrong with their practices. Disgusted by the blatant nature of their evil, I called for the help of Jesus.

As it had been their purpose to demonstrate the power of darkness by casting spells and performing evil and lewd rituals, I waved my arms to the sky and Jesus parted the heavens to show them eminent and *true* power. Clouds parting and rumbling to the sides, a pinkish bright white light had come down from heaven. In majesty and might, there was no doubt about the energetic truth behind what lay visible for all to see, the *truth of God revealed.* "I don't know!" I said in a very sarcastic and mocking manner, placing my hands on my chin as if I were thinking, "Which should I choose?" Because it was *so* obvious, I was making fun of the huge contrasting chasm between the heavens opened before us above, and the lewd acts of vice and evil for which they were participating on the ground.

Despite this, there was no legitimate response. Although the witches present were actually capable of *seeing* the heavens bared open, it did not move them, not in the slightest degree.

As God's display of majesty pulled back into the heavens, I called out to Padre Pio, asking if he might appear and talk with these people. No response came, however, as I began to consider that even asking this after such a bold demonstration from the Lord, could be considered overstepping my bounds. Having presented them with an undeniable pronouncement of the truth, they made a decision to reject it. It was as simple as that.

If such a catastrophically grand event had no effect on them, it had been arrogant and presumptuous of me to think that any further display of God would prove any more fruitful. In asking the Lord to present more signs and wonders, I'd asked him to throw pearls before swine. As it says in the bible, they loved their sin more than they loved God.

****

Displaying before my soul the holocaust of our time, Our Lord Jesus showed me a gruesome scene. Bloody baby corpses fully formed, and tiny hands and feet ripped from bodies were floating in a sea of blood. Spiritually bereft of any appropriate response to such horror, I looked at these images given to me by the Lord with horror and great sorrow. The holocaust of my time, that of abortion, and the full tragedy of its evil, was displayed for my soul to look upon in disgust.

****

Terror surrounded Andy and I, as we were running from the villains who sought my life. Although it hadn't yet occurred to me that these murderous and violent people might actually represent the violent and destructive disease which was trying to take my life, we continued running for cover, over hills, valleys, tunnels and buildings. Emerging in a large art museum from several escape routes below ground, the battle continued raging all around the building, but for the moment, we were well hidden from destruction's force.

Coming upon a room filled with huge paintings, they emanated peace. As the battle had not yet reached this room, and I quietly looked around at these paintings which were hung on the wall, and those which were lying around on tables still waiting to be displayed. Surrounded in ornate frames of silver and gold, the paintings themselves were filled with bright colors and were somewhere around ten by twenty feet in size.

Gazing upon them with wonder, I quietly picked up a large painting waiting to be displayed which was lying on a table. Filling with tears of joy, I called out to Andy, "Come here, Andy! You must see this!" Upon first inspection, you might have thought it was a very beautiful painting of a mountainous scene filled with color and delight, but upon further view, you could see that there was an image painted in the lower right hand corner, an old man dressed in the robes of a priest. Hair the color of mostly dark gray, the colors within his soul betrayed his youthful vibrance. Even so, Padre Pio was filled with energy and light.

Becoming animated, he remained rather still, but seemed to wish to convey something to me. As the violent battles continued all around us, Andy and I were filled with peace and silence as we gazed upon the infinite beauty of this holy man. Nodding towards me, Padre Pio's gaze gave me strength and filled me with a sense of wonder in knowing of his watchful protection over my body and soul. In his face was a grand sense of acceptance, as if he knew of my mission in this life as in regards to writing, and he approved. In his heavenly abode, he knew that what I was doing was indeed the will of God, despite the apparent contradictions previously discussed. Encouragement filled his face and a certain sense of perseverance in the battle for my life, as well.

As Andy was about fifteen feet away facing me from behind the picture, Padre Pio turned towards him, motioning him to come forth and nodding at him in approval, as well. Filling me with serenity, the Padre's nod at Andy gave me a sense of peace in knowing that his watchful protection would also be with Andy, especially at the time when the battle for my life was lost. Because of my children, this became all the more important. Directing us to go and participate in the battle which raged on all around us, we ran for cover from the forces of evil which were now gaining on us again.

Boarding a bus towards my childhood home, we began to think that perhaps we were home free, but in fact, we had only just begun.

As we came upon the road which led to my past life within my current life, the long road of about two miles which had led to the house was overridden with dirt. Old friends from my past appeared who were to assist me in covering this road in rock, to make it beautiful and complete. But the old friends who had appeared happened to be the ones who had been somewhat dark at the time (who knows where they may be today, they may be transformed in light!) and they quickly began to display murderous intentions as they snuck up behind me and smashed rocks into my head.

Turning in self-defense, I knocked one of them out with a stone and then lay beside her with great remorse and sorrow. Although I had been defending my own life, I was now very concerned as to whether I had taken hers. As I waited for her to show signs of life, I wandered the street which was now miraculously paved with stone for a quarter of a mile, and I gathered all the remaining stones which appeared to be large enough or shaped in such a manner as to be able to be used as weapons. Upon her waking, I quietly sat beside her and talked to her about the importance of peace and love. Although she initially seemed open to such matters, within moments she had found one of the stones which had a very distinctive weapon quality. Looking upon her with disappointment, she put it down, "I will honor peace," she said.

No sooner had she made a commitment to do so when hundreds of black snakes appeared upon the part of the road which had not yet been completed. Both of us knew that it was impossible for us to pave this entire road without anybody else's help, so we looked in horror at the scene before us. At this moment I realized that my battle was not just against the violent forces within my own body which wished to take my life, but also against the very dark forces of the Universe.

As the black snakes were very large, about five to ten feet long, and because I was easily able to take a stick and push them away, they began to grow arms and legs. With their new limbs, they began to reach towards me and attack. Without further adieu, I realized that because of the location of these battles and the now obvious signs of the presence of the dark side, that the battle to save my life was also a battle between my destiny and the dark intentions which had been placed upon my soul by those I'd left behind in my past.

Putting my stick on the ground, I gazed upon the rock pathway and the now thousands of black snakes which slithered along the dirty part of the road. Sitting down, I ignored them completely, as wisdom began to come upon me like a torrent in the night. "I understand," I said to myself, but out loud, "I cannot build this road from the light which is my present to the darkness which is my past. It is not I who need to build this road, but many others who have chosen not to help with this task . . . I'm not going to work on this road anymore." As I said this, I was no longer there.

A holy nun stood before me in a place of solitude and rest. Placing within my hands a picture of a sainted medieval nun, she directed me to place it on the wall of my spirit.

****

Raging through the darkened night, my spirit was in a hurry to arrive at the monastery in the galactic heavens which I knew would give me and my ward refuge. As we'd entered, I was excruciatingly aware of those who were quickly following behind, with the intention to harm my ward. As a result of this knowledge, I continued further and further into a catacomb-like structure beneath the building.

Bearing this tiny unborn baby in my hands, the Chinese baby could be no more than five inches long and perhaps several months along in pregnancy. Swelling feelings came from within my soul for this child, as if she was my very own, but I knew I would be giving her up soon. Those who were following me were taking a journey deep into themselves as they ventured into the catacombs, wherein their souls were undergoing transformation. As it was my duty to protect this baby until the threat of abortion was no longer present, the parents arrived moments later. Opening my hand and showing them the fragile and tiny little child, tears came from their eyes. Handing her back to them, I inherently knew that she would be safe now and that this child would not be harmed by abortion.

****

Journeying through the countryside, I was gathering my things to embark upon the next leg of my journey in this life. As I packed a bag of clothing near the house, I noticed in the distance a huge, perhaps twenty foot long, electric eel approaching. Very thick, this eel was perhaps a foot and a half in diameter, and I immediately knew it to be a demonic force. Slithering about six feet into the air, there was a hump in the center of its body.

Grabbing my things rapidly, I ran to the truck with Andy, desperately trying to get out of there before the demon could get near us. But we weren't fast enough, and I did the only thing possible to protect myself, which was knocking the creature to the ground with my arm. Inherently, I knew that this creature had come to kill me, and that it was going to use its electrical properties to throw the electrical systems in my heart out of whack. Running, Andy had the key in the ignition and we were off.

****

Filled with knowledge of this incredibly dark soul, he had been involved in a horrendous act of violence, and was now working his way through the court system trying to figure out what to do. Having been offered a plea agreement which would punish him appropriately, but give him a chance at a life in a reasonable amount of time, he'd turned it down, despite the fact that such a choice placed him at risk of being in jail for the rest of his life.

Standing before me, he had just been shot dead energetically. As he resurrected before me, it became clear that by choosing not to take responsibility for his crime and pleading guilty, he had cut off his soul from any future potential.

Good aspects of his soul were shown to me, and the great potential that had been misused and lost because of his horrendous choices. At the very core of his soul was a large pocket of evil, which was very dangerous, unpredictable and violent. Despite these good things, this man was a threat to society, and without a conversion experience, his soul was now officially damned.

Now exiting this soul's symbolic death, I came upon this man's subconscious spirit and those of his violent and vicious friends who proceeded to come after me and my children in a gun battle. So that we could not escape, they slashed my tires. Evil exuded from their very pores.

Turning to the kids who I protected with my body, I called to St. Michael for help as we immediately became invisible to all of them, except the defendant. My children began to disappear from the scene, and I was left alone with the main defendant who was now standing at the door of my car inciting me to get out and fight him. Realizing that I could not get away from this confrontation, I got out of the car and stood with my arms folded in front of this man's soul, which was now bare and exposed before me.

Challenging me to fight him, I refused to do so, inciting his rage all the more. Beginning to shout, his voice rang out, "Why won't you fight me?! Why won't you fight me?!" Folding my arms, I looked directly into his eyes with no fear. As my face exuded disgust, I maintained calm and composure as I spoke to him quietly. "Jesus said we should turn the other cheek," I said. With that he tried to punch me in the face, but his fist went right through me. "Love thy neighbor," I said as my voice began to get louder and more insistent, "Do unto others as you would have them do unto you. If you love Me, do as My Father Wills!"

Getting more and more angry, he started to wimp out and walk away, but I followed him with continuing disgust at his violent cowardice. "You're just angry because you *know* you aren't living your life right!" Running after this bully, he was now running away from me. "You know that you are *not* doing the will of God, and that you're screwing up your destiny!" Stopping for a moment, his head turned halfway as if he was listening to my words but did not want to admit them to be true. For a moment, a look of melancholy came over his ashamed face.

"It just drives you crazy that you know you could turn your life around, but you haven't done it! You *know* you are *not* doing the Will of God!" At that moment, he turned to look me in the face for just a moment. His gaze was uncertain, for he had chosen the evil path he wanted to walk, but he *knew* that the choice he had made was wrong, and he *knew* . . . he just *knew*. At that moment, he decided to change his plea. Without any further adieu, my spirit disappeared and was gone.

****

After a series of very violent attacks against strangers in another city, I was given to witness in the astral state the nature of the perpetrator. Portrayed as an envoy of Satan, this person was spreading evil and mayhem in such a manner as to make it seem as though it might never end or be salvageable.

As I gazed upon the sad state that had been caused by this evil soul harboring no brilliant thoughts as to how to solve it, I suddenly witnessed something of stupendous magnitude. From the ground and the ashes of destruction caused by this very tormented and evil man, came a surge of light. Coming from the depths of the Earth, it spread outward as it funneled high into the sky into a wondrous beam which now cascaded with brilliant orbs of sparkly light. A white dove flew from the depths of the Earth, directly into the highest heights of heaven, and a holy feeling overcame my soul.

At that moment, I knew that the evil would be overcome through the intercession of God, and that this had been affected through the prayers of multitudes of people. Awaking the next morning, the beltway sniper had been captured.

****

Cascading through time, my spirit was taken to visit a group of souls consisting of many I'd known throughout my life. These were the souls of those who had stayed in my life, but had never embraced a spiritual path, many of them atheists or agnostics.

Gathering for this profound reunion, we spent many hours talking and reminiscing about times spent together, but as the evening wrapped up, I wandered alone upstairs. As the gathering was being held in the home of a soul who had been previously revealed to me, I remembered that her home had once been infested with many demons, almost like a haunted mansion, but now I was grateful to note that the demonic presences were gone and the home was clear of any forces.

Profundity filled my vision as I ascended the stairs to notice a grand picture displayed before my eyes. Amongst this home filled with items displaying a love of the world, was a magnificent portrait of Jesus and Mary. Gazing at it, I could not believe that it was hanging on *this* wall in *this* house. Running downstairs, I found the person who lived in the house and another of her friends. "Where did you get this?!" I shouted expectantly at their confused faces. "You mean you really don't know?" her friend asked. Nodding that indeed I did not, they both led me upstairs to a bedroom that I had not yet seen.

As the door was opened, I watched in amazement and shock. Adorned with magnificent holy relics, every wall was covered from top to bottom with religious artwork, crucifixes, statues, medals and holy books. "Oh, my God!" I said. "Where did you get all of this stuff?" "You mean you really don't know?" they both asked me again in unison. "No, I don't."

"You began sending us these things about twelve years ago, don't you remember?" Immediately, I realized that although the impact of my words through the years had appeared to be of no import on a conscious level with these souls, they had been received as heavenly gifts. Stunned, I walked around the room, admiring the beauty of these magnificent pieces. For a moment, I was almost a bit jealous because I would have loved to have these beautiful works in my own home, but realized that such thinking was very selfish and admonished myself for such thoughts.

Taking me back downstairs, the woman showed me a large picture window which was now adorned with the most exquisite curtain of roses. About 500 individual stained glass roses were formed and joined together as a large window-covering. Pointing at the spectacular vision, I turned to the woman of the house. "That was a gift you made for me before you died," she said.

****

CHAPTER SEVEN
A Message of Redemption, Magnificent Female Angel, a Holy Deception, Angel Helping me in Exhaustion, a Dark Act of Charity, the Heavens Open, Ancestraland Ancient Demons, Borderlands, Family Demons, Betrayal, Lust Disguised as Abuse, Grace Because of Forgiveness.

****

Having recently crossed over, the man who had come to me months before in danger of damnation along with a legion of demons for me to battle; returned with a very different message.

Turning to see his glowing face, I was astonished at the light that surrounded his soul and the bright smile which adorned his face. Could this be the same man who had been working through so much anger? Could this be the man who had never allowed the name of Jesus to touch his lips during his life? Indeed . . . it was.

Smiling with joy in our reunion, he gently took my left hand to his mouth kissing it with kindness, love and respect. In my heart, I knew that this gesture held a thank-you, but it was also a great gesture of unconditional love. Because I had helped to save his soul, he was now watching over me with my ancestors. He'd adopted me, so to speak. Honored beyond words, nothing needed to be said as he gazed into my eyes with love. Wonder filled my soul to see such a transformation within a soul. What had once been filled with darkness, now glowed with the brightest light!

****

A magnificent female angel appeared in a white gown adorned with very large wings. In her hands before her, she held a large single amethyst crystal. Coming towards me in a wisp, she gently pushed the amethyst into my face which immediately overlapped into me because we were all etheric. Suddenly, there was a large blazing explosion within my consciousness. Feeling and seeing the immense beauty from inside the amethyst, I began to also hear astonishingly beautiful music. Soaring sounds of mystical beauty filled my spirit, as I suddenly understood that whether or not anything happened with the seeds I had planted in a visible way in the physical world, something beautiful was happening within the souls of those who had received of it. Even if they responded with initial anger and rage at knowledge which contradicted their former views of reality (especially in regards to the knowledge of darkness), these seeds were creating a beautiful flowering of knowledge within them which was ordained of by God.

As the purple surrounded me, I began to return to consciousness.

****

Our former priest had given Andy, my husband, a gift, "a relic of the saints," he had said. Arriving at our campsite, Andy showed me a piece of a broken Mason jar, upon its jagged edge was a torrent of blood. "Father gave this to me because this blood is the actual blood of many saints!" He said excitedly. Confused, I felt evil in the room, but continued to listen. "Apparently, according to our priest," he said, "this was used by a demonic force to slit the throats of many saints."

Instantly, I knew I was in grave danger. This was not a holy relic, but a demonized instrument of death dealing the blows of death and persecution to the saints. Now the force behind this demonic instrument was seeking to slit my throat.

Remembering, I thought about the mixed feelings I'd had toward this priest which had arisen because there had been times where he had misjudged my illness and spread the persecution amongst the church. For some reason, unbeknownst to me, there had been a lengthy period where he had come to the conclusion that I was lazy. This perception had been spread amongst the congregation, and I'd gone through a period of great desolation as a result of it. There had been times when he'd made light of some of the mystics and stigmatists, because he seemed to have a disdain for supernatural gifts among the saints. At this moment, I realized that he had carried this unholy relic unawares, not knowing the truth behind his false views which had led him to bring persecution upon them. In his mind, he had thought he was properly chastising the sinner, when he had apparently been discerning the truth through incorrect means.

Taking the relic from Andy, I immediately brought it over to the campfire, trying to melt the jagged edge. Knowing that as soon as I went to sleep, this demonic instrument would animate and come after my throat, I sought to melt off the sharp side which could slit my throat unawares. After realizing it wouldn't work, I handed Andy a hacksaw and asked him to break it into many pieces. Again, it wouldn't work.

"I'm sorry, Andy," I said, "We're going to have to seek refuge from our campsite, find a hotel room where I will have some level of protection from this force which seeks my destruction." In moments, we were in a hotel room, but a loud buzzing sound was piercing my ears and driving me to distraction. Going about the room, I sought to find the source of the sound. As I found a fan in the bathroom, I attempted to turn it off. But as I did so, it only became louder and louder and louder and louder . . . and then suddenly, it stopped.

Waking to a darkened room, a huge blizzard had taken out the power, and all had gone silent. Because we usually sleep to the sound of a noise machine, the sounds immediately ceased. All was dark.

Returning to sleep, I found myself again in the center of a room in my chair unconscious. My husband and children flitted about me, unaware of my physical condition which had deteriorated. Picking myself up, I walked out the door and into a hot sunny oasis. Lying on the ground, I closed my eyes. As I did so, my garments and body became that of the medicine woman. From the ground came timbers and a leather sheet to hold my body as I realized that I was being laid out for burial in the Native American way. Baking in the hot sun, my consciousness receded to unconsciousness as I surrendered to my ill health. "It's the barometer," the angels whispered in my ear, "the barometer has dropped due to the storm and will affect your heart badly. Be careful." Nodding, I ceased.
****

Traveling through the wilderness, I was trying to keep up with the others but deathly aware of my inability to do so. My heart failure situation was simply making it impossible for me to do what I had done in the past. As we approached the familiar wilderness retreat which was the home ground of the infamous haunted mansion of which I had visited and worked on extricated members many times, I realized that we would have to stay in unheated huts overnight during our stay and that I simply wouldn't survive that.

Although no one around me was aware of my dire condition, I wasn't doing well at all when we did arrive at the encampment. Immediately, I asked about my van, but somebody had borrowed it and wouldn't be back for two to three hours. "Oh, my God!" I said, "I'll never make it that long!" Everyone was looking at me very funny except for one angelic being who appeared behind me and caught me as I fell in exhaustion. Looking into my eyes, I understood an unspoken message, 'Although no one else around you may understand the condition you are in, you will no longer be able to do many of the things - even in the spirit world - that you used to do. You need to surrender to that.' Although I had not yet even visited the haunted mansion to assess the status of the lost souls inhabiting the place, it was clear that I would not be given entry this time because I was not strong enough to perform this task anymore. Sadly, I surrendered to this in the arms of the male angel and was suddenly transported.

Arriving in a beautiful apartment building, we were living on the top floor. A huge light came down from the heavens filling the place with sunshine and heat. Andy and I were organizing a new altar to God to be built in the living room, placing white and purple linens on the table top before retrieving our relics. We were peaceful with this reality and we accepted it. Outside the open back glass patio door, was a stunningly crystal clear pool. The bright light emanated from the water like a prism in the brightly lit sky. "I guess this is my retirement home," I joked to myself softly.

Suddenly, I had visitors who literally appeared out of the ether. As I'd mentioned previously, I'd helped a man who had been in danger of damnation by fighting the demons for him probably six months before, and he had come to kiss my hand shortly after I'd won his soul back for him, surrounded in light. His ancestors were suddenly filling my living room, about thirty of them. Some of them appeared to be brothers, cousins and recent relations and others went further back. Honored, none of us said anything, but I felt their gratitude that I had intervened on this man's behalf and made it possible for all of them to be together.

After a while, I walked into the bedroom to have some solitude for just a moment but quickly noticed that there were two Native American men in the room. One of them had long straight black hair, and was very tall and skinny. I didn't feel like I knew him, but was entranced by his beauty. The other had shorter and frizzier long black hair. A beard and moustache adorned his face as he sat silently on a couch. "Hey, can I hear some of your music?" He asked, as I timidly pointed out, "Well, my music isn't fully produced or anything, but I guess it would be okay . . . " Before I could get to my CD's, I instinctively walked over and sat next to him. My inner spirit knew this man, and I felt an intense unconditional love coming from him towards me and vice versa. Quietly laying my head on his shoulder, he pointed to the other man in the room. "My friend and I have come here to bring you the Ancient Mysteries," he said as my head cocked upwards to look in his face with surprise. "Be ready to receive the emissaries . . ." Fading from view, they were instantly gone. "I guess I'm not retiring after all," I thought, "I just got another job that maybe I can physically handle. Cool!"

Looking towards the family members of my friend in the living room, I observed my eldest daughter in the room. "Hey, what's she doing here!?!?!?!?!?" I shouted because I was concerned that she was included in a group of ancestors who were dead! The man who appeared to possibly be the brother of the man I'd come to help looked at me and conveyed a warning. My daughter was beginning to learn how to drive, it was very important that this process be undergone with great care. She had work to do, and an accidental death would be unacceptable in regards to her destiny being fulfilled.

****

Gloriously decorated, the home appeared as if it were a mansion, although in reality, I knew it to be a family home. A large group of people had gathered there as some benefactor was planning to give this home to a poor family who had undergone a catastrophic medical event. In this case, it appeared that the doctors who had assisted the family were going to give them this home, but there was something sinister about it. Something was very amiss, although I could not yet ascertain it. One thing was clear in that this gift was being given to glorify the givers, more than to assist the family in need.

Wandering around the house, I noticed a large, ornate, circular stairway and quickly ascended it. But as I did, a huge windstorm overtook my soul as I looked upon the face of a particularly terrifying demon. Sitting upon a 'throne' was a man who was not ethnically a black man. But everything he wore was black, his skin was black and his eyes were a piercing red. Around his head was a large black turban and winds of evil literally blew from him in a heated storm of fury.

Tearing down the staircase, I found myself back in the familiar part of the home. People were continuing to enjoy the party, completely unaware of this unusually sinister presence. Noticing that the temperatures in the house were quickly beginning to rise, I understood that the demonic force was about to overcome this home.

Walking quietly to the intended recipient of this gift, I informed her of the demonic nature of it and that the home was completely possessed. Even if it were to be given to her for free, she should not take it. Unable to ascertain whether or not she would abide by this advice from the eternal, I was flown away from the scene of impending doom.

"Self-complacent and always impudent, deluded by wealth and false prestige, they sometimes proudly perform sacrifices in name only."
The Bhagavad-Gita As It Is, Chapter 15, Text 17, (Hinduism, Translator: A.C. Bhaktivedanta Swami Prabhupada)
"He who digs a pit may fall into it, and he who breaks through a wall may be

bitten by a serpent."
The New American Bible, Old Testament, Ecclesiastes 10:8, (Christianity, Judaism)
****

Wandering around trying to find my home, I suddenly realized that I'd been wandering in the place where we had formerly lived and it was no longer compatible to the path of my soul. In that instant, I shot immediately to our new home where we currently lived.

Instantly maneuvered into a high-powered vibrational raising, a force beyond my own control began moving my arms and legs around in some form of astral physical therapy. Because of the natural degeneration of the body which occurs in heart failure, this was very helpful to me. Feeling bliss and joy as they assisted me, I turned to notice a television screen in front of me which was depicting daily life on the screen. Bored to death, I turned it off and turned my attention to another television set which was doing the same. Equally boring, I turned that one off, too.

Continuing to receive higher and higher vibrations and astral physical therapy, I heard a thundering rumble as the roof of the house instantly disappeared and my head was turned upwards towards the heavens where the entire cosmos appeared. Because of my recent temptation with the cannibalistic demon, my gaze had been incorrectly attuned towards the Earth and I'd been mesmerized for a short time by the delusion presented to me. But as I gazed at the cosmology of the sky, I entered into an eternal mesmerization and an ecstatic state of Samadhi. I couldn't take my eyes off of the upper ethereal heavens.

Continuing to raise my vibration and work on me physically, the process went on for quite some time because I'd been taken very deeply into ecstatic bliss. When the time came to begin returning, the vibrations subsided very slowly, so as not to jolt me back too quickly. Because I'd prayed for help in dealing with this cannibalistic demon which had proven quite a foe, I understood that the Lord was guiding me to turn my gaze from the physical world up into the heavens, a higher sphere, wherein the answer would lie. Understanding, I agreed that I would do this.

"In this world, there is nothing so sublime and pure as transcendental knowledge. Such knowledge is the mature fruit of all mysticism. And one who has become accomplished in the practice of devotional service enjoys this knowledge within himself in due course of time."
The Bhagavad-Gita As It Is, Chapter 4, Text 38, (Hinduism, Translator: A.C. Bhaktivedanta Swami Prabhupada)

"Only heart to heart can speak the bliss of mystic knowers; No messenger can tell is and no missive bear it. I am silent from weakness on many a matter, for my words could not reckon them and my speech would fall short."
The Seven Valleys and the Four Valleys, The Valley of Contentment, (Bahai', Words of Baha'u'llah)
****

Entering into an energetic reality of our home, it appeared that we had gone far back in time. Although our current home was new and never lived in before, it was built on ancient land with a rich past. Unfortunately, some of the darker sides of this past were unbeknownst to me at this time.

Inside, a play of the previous realities upon this land began to be shown to me, as I entered into a place of torture and death which was beyond my ability to comprehend. Although it wasn't made clear how, the Catholic Church was responsible for many of the crimes in this location. Many women had been tortured and killed in heinous fashion, as well as other souls who had been tortured and murdered in various horrendous ways. (This was Native American land, however, and it might be fair to surmise from what we know of history.)

Flabbergasted, I turned to my husband, Andy, who was also stunned by this vicious past, and the powerfully demonic forces which inhabited the land as a result. "Do we have to stay here?" I asked him.

A knock on the door led me to a very quiet monk. He wore robes of light blue, his hair was dark brown and he had a moustache and beard. "Come." He said. "Stay. Purify it. Stand tall for the light." His face pierced my own with such power, that I simply turned back towards the room and gathered all of my strength. "Okay," I said. "I will stay and purify it. I will stand tall for the light."

Entering the room, the demonic forces which had taken hold of this land were terrifying, but I was no longer afraid of them or the past that they had heralded. Calling out to the dark forces, I shouted with fury. "I will not leave! I will fight and destroy you!" Beginning to barrage the room with eternal energy which had been conveyed to me by the monk's presence, the light began bouncing all around the room, throwing out the dark forces in a torrential flood of rain. Within moments, the forces which had been with this land for centuries were gone, and I turned quietly away.

"A thick mist, a darkness and cloud is spread over all the earth. And, showing this, the Apostle said, 'For we were once darkness." (Eph. v. 8.) And Again, "Ye, brethren, are not in darkness, that that day should overtake you as a thief." Since therefore there is, so to speak, a moonless night, and we walk in that night, God hath given us a bright lamp, having kindled in our souls the grace of the Holy Spirit."
The Complete Writings of the Early Church Fathers, Nicene and Post Nicene Fathers, Volume 13, Homily XI, (Christianity, Catholic, Author: St. John Chrysostom)
"If you seize that Glory that cannot be forcibly seized, I shall rush upon you, so that you may never more blaze on the earth made by Ahura and protect the world of the good principle."
The Avesta, Yast 19, Verse 48, (Zoroastrianism, Words of Zarathustra
"My son, sinners entice you and say, 'Come along with us! Let us lie in wait for the honest man, let us, unprovoked, set a trap for the innocent; Let us swallow them up, as the nether world does, alive, in the prime of life, like those who go down to the pit . . . My son, walk not in the way with the, hold back your foot from their path!"
The New American Bible, Old Testament, Proverbs 1:10-15, (Christianity, Judaism, Words of Solomon)

****

Standing betwixt a borderland and the Earth, my soul was mesmerized upon the sky. As I'd gaze upon the various orbs such as the moon and other planets which were visible in this realm, I saw hieroglyphics upon their face. In the skies themselves, messages in various Asiatic, Hieratic, Aramaic, Hebrew and other languages would appear to me at random filled with beauty and awe. Although I understood them at the time, I would not be able to read them in my conscious waking state. Their full meaning lay beyond words, but they were, in essence, a beckoning to my spirit to the world beyond.

A larger young woman was waiting nearby, expressing agitation and anger. Coming over to me, she asked me why I was staring and gazing at the sky in such an obsessive manner. In an ecstatic bliss, without lowering my gaze from heaven, I said to her, "My dear, I am being prepared for death. The Lord calls me from the highest of heavens and I cannot take my gaze away from Him, for He is my All. I cannot wait to go to heaven! But I must continue to wait . . . until it is time. But He echoes to me tonight that I must be *prepared* to go now." "Why would you want to go there?!" She said, as I did remove my gaze from the sky to look upon her face to understand what type of pain would cause such a reply.

"I don't ever want to go there . . . especially if people like the ones I know go there. They don't accept me; they hate me, just because I'm gay." Immediately, I was given interior understanding of this woman's plight. Taking her hand, I said, "Oh! No, you do not understand." Looking at me confused, she said nothing but listened. "Those who are unwilling to accept you as you are on Earth cannot themselves go unto heaven until they, too, have been purified of their defects. They only go to heaven once they realize and understand that they have been mistaken to not accept you as you are. When you enter into heaven, you will be accepted as you are, beautiful in God's sight!"

Lifting my eyes back to the ethereal display above me, I asked, "Can you not see that?!?!?!?!?!" Pointing to a Hebrew inscription on the left hand of the sky, I shuddered at its awesome wonder as its knowledge filled my soul in beckon. Nodding, she said, "I don't see anything in the sky." "Oh," I said with intrigue, "Then you must not yet be ready to cross over. You're not dead, yet, are you?" Nodding, 'No,' I nodded back. "Ahhhhhhhhh . . . then go back, my friend, and blame not heaven for the failings of man. And I will see you again, yes? . . . when it is your time also to die?" She smiled and disappeared as my gaze again became fixed upon the hieroglyphics of the orbs and the ancient languages upon the sky.

"By dint of knowledge the leaders produce many illustrations, arguments, and reasons; and considering how the creatures have various inclinations they impart various directions."
Saddharma Pundarika or the Lotus of the True Law, Skilfulness, No.106, (Buddhism: Mahayana)
"Let the man among you who has no sin be the first to cast a stone at her."
The New American Bible, New Testament, John 8:7, (Christianity: Catholic, Words of Christ)

****

As I was being sent back to my body, a call was heard in the ether. A young girl of whom I'd known when she was younger had taken a very seriously wrong turn in her life recently. Although she had cut off her family in order to marry a drug dealer and be part of a large crime family, she was wishing that some way could be made to open the line between them again. She had made this almost impossible because she had children with this man and the people with whom she had united were very dangerous.

Hearing her plea, I sent word back to her soul that I would pray for her; but that I could think of no way to fix this situation at the moment. Sadness overcame me, but a certain sense also of the natural order of things. Some mistakes can be fixed. But there are many mistakes we as human beings cannot necessarily be easily remedied and do carry life-long (and sometimes eternal) consequences. Perhaps repentance and forgiveness could eventually alter her path again to the light . . .

****

The Lord bade my soul to go into several realms containing the energetic reality of various other families that we knew. Within several of these families, lay the same demons which our own family had been trying to purgate from our reality.

One family in particular, the father was almost a cloned image of the exact same issue which lay within my own husband, Andy. The Holy Spirit came upon me in a powerful way, as He spoke words through me which were not my own. They contained tranformative energy, and it was directed at this father who was domineering, controlling, verbally abusive and completely comfortable with that. As I did so, he seemed to be receiving blows from the spiritual ether.

Anger began to seethe within him, but the Lord insisted I continue for hour after hour battering him with the opposite goodness to the vices of which he embraced and saw not the evil within them.

But even had I wished to stop, it was not possible. The Holy Spirit completely took me over and did the Lord's bidding throughout my spiritual vessel in a sub-conscious way directly into the heart of this man.

And when it was finished, I interiorly knew that it was going to affect him in some way consciously, that I should be alert that his attitude towards me might change because of some level of remembrance. It would be most likely that he would remember nothing, but suddenly feel ill at ease in my presence.

As the final blast of the Holy Spirit came through my voice, I uttered the final words which were intended to counter his words rooted in anger, pride, and power. Each of the Holy Spirit's responses were the direct opposite of whatever the ill-informed purpose of his initial words might be. Because it went on for hours, and because the issue was so deeply ingrained, he became very agitated that for every syllable out of his mouth of a destructive nature, the Holy Spirit would respond out of mine in the opposite construct.

When finished, it seemed that both of us were exhausted and I fell into a peaceful sleep.
****

The sky's were alit with a holy wonder this night as I followed the eternal beckon to a place I would not have expected.

Inside the offices of two men who had betrayed my husband not just once, but twice; I observed that the first partner - who was the prime instigator of evil - was standing around the room with his hands on his chin pacing the room. The second partner - who was more of a follower, perhaps could be described as a man with no backbone who did the bidding of the first partner - was quiet for only a moment until he noticed my presence. Then he became hysterical, but we both ignored him as my work was with the first partner this evening.

Ironically, the two of them had betrayed my husband by demoting him from a position that he had fulfilled with great devotion and skill. Before a local election had occurred, they had promised that they would come in and help with a large court docket. Coming from another jurisdiction, they knew that Andy, my husband, could've run against them and minced them mercilessly. But he chose not to, because he had felt that the combination of the three of them would be better for the community than he alone could provide. We lived in small town, one which could not offer the types of salaries offered in larger jurisdictions. It was difficult to get other attorney's to be willing to come to this poor community and serve. So he'd made a decision based on their word not to run against them.

But after they were elected, they both came in and had my husband do the work of three men for several years while they politicked around and took time off days, weeks and months at a time. My husband worked seven days a week, sometimes until 11:00 at night, but at least 60 - 80 hours every single week.

Time had come, however, when his use was becoming more of a political threat to them than a help. So they used a falsehood to demote him from his position and force him out.

A judicial position had come open a few months later which the first partner had already known was coming. And this was the reason for my husband's departure. They wanted him out of the position he was in, bearing the title which would give him a political edge over them.

That time came and they were certain of their success - until the local nominating committee ousted the first partner and didn't even allow him to interview for the position at the State Capitol. Because the first partner had been close friends with the Governor, it was already assured him that if he were sent up, he would receive the position.

Anger had swelled within him. He claimed that two of the attorney's on the nominating committee had conspired against him. Although this was not true, he felt it was true. My husband and another good man were nominated to go up.

Because of the first and second partners' friendship with the governor, they didn't hesitate to betray my husband yet again by spending hours on the phone with the governor spreading falsehoods and lies.

So my husband went up and interviewed. His interview went well, over all, but he knew that the slander had been passed. Although the decision had not yet been made as to who would attain the position, the spirit of the eternal had led me here to the office of these two partners that night.

Other angels surrounded me as I approached the first partner who appeared pensive and thoughtful. On some interior level, he understood that he had been the recipient of karmic payback, swift and sure. Even though he truly had not been conspired against, he honestly felt as though he had been. And he was SO angry about it, that on a subconscious level, he was having a thoughtful moment about the betrayal he had inflicted not once, but twice upon my husband: pensive and thoughtful, yes, but emotional or caring, absolutely not.

The angels were swift and sure in bringing me up to him, as their words came out of my mouth in a holy confrontation. "You TOOK that which was not yours," I shouted, "and it was not enough." Pausing, he looked directly into my eyes. He knew that he had put our family in a desperate situation. Not only had he lost his job, but we'd lost our health insurance and the ability to be insured because of my heart failure. Because I'd saved money, we had made it through. But I had to resort to treating myself for many things, because the doctors don't return calls from uninsured patients as quickly as they do those who have coverage.

In God's infinite mercy, He had led Andy (my husband) to a job which seemed to be the place we'd been searching for since Chief Joseph began appearing to my over fifteen years prior insisting that we go to 'Ute Mountain,' our true home and help to 'restore that which had been lost.' Just two weeks before Andy became the Special U.S. Attorney for the Ute Mountain Ute Reservation in Towaoc, I had begun work publishing a book written by a social worker who'd been on the reservation for about thirteen years working with families in the restoration of alcohol and abuse situations. Her book was brilliant, inspired and before I even read it, I was slammed by the energy of the Thunder Beings. I had said to her, "I haven't read this yet, but I KNOW I will publish it." It became available just weeks after he'd begun his new work.

I tell you this information for one reason. Because it is important to know that to those who serve the Lord, He gives them their due. Sometimes, it's not in this life and sometimes it is. Out of a betrayal of the finest proportions, God provided Andy with his true vocation. He brought him to the Reservation which we had been trying to get to for fifteen years. Ironically, he was also given a job which allowed for him to work 32 hours a week and make more money than he'd ever made. This was a huge gift because he'd been working literally day and night for years. But we didn't have insurance, we had to find ways to take care of that separately and were actively involved in doing so. That would take time.

"You took that which was not yours," I shouted again, "and it was still yet not enough! You had to try to take this, too, which you KNEW did not belong to you!" In regards to this judicial position, we were not yet aware of whether or not this position belonged to Andy or the other candidate, but it belonged to someone who had served and lived in this community for much longer than these two. We'd been here for fifteen years as had the other.

He didn't say anything yet. So I again repeated, not of my own accord, but by the power of the angels who spoke through me. "You took that which was not yours," I shouted again, "and it was still yet not enough! You had to try to take this, too, which you KNEW did not belong to you!" Taking something which is not yours is a serious crime against the eternal. But taking something which is not yours for self-serving motivations; money, power and greed, is all the more serious, especially when you take it from someone who is a servant of God, who IS doing the will of God in that position. He hadn't taken this from us, alone, but from the community which deserved a justice system with integrity.

I remembered for a moment the day I saw the Blessed Virgin climb upon a cross and begin to weep for Andy because of the lies those two had perpetrated against him. And my husband had been doing the work in order to serve, while they wanted the money and power.

The angels around me began to speak through their own mouths of another time and place. Surprised, this was apparently not between my husband and the two of them, but myself! I was shocked. It was between myself and the first partner to the greatest degree. As they began, they spoke of another time when he had been a dear, dear friend of mine, nothing romantic, but a very close friend - and he had betrayed me then. They said, "You have learned nothing! We placed her right back in the same place in your life, but this time we made her terminally ill with three children and a husband who was completely loyal to you! And you BETRAYED HER AGAIN!" I said nothing, I was surprised that this was about me and him, rather my husband and him in a previous lifetime. "TWICE!!!!" They shouted.

Suddenly and without any warning, he ran towards me and took a hold of my body in a powerful embrace. Tears began streaming down his face as he began to wail in memory of this lost time. In his eyes, he was devastated by the memory of the previous betrayal, and realizing he had just done it again, twice, to someone he dearly loved in the world of spirit - it was too much for him.

I allowed him to embrace me, and I embraced him back. But I again said, "You took that which was not yours, and it was still yet not enough! You had to try to take this, too, which you KNEW did not belong to you! When will it be enough!?!?!?" "I'm so sorry," he said, "let me make it up to you." Everybody in the office that had worked there at the time of my husband's departure had already left and they had open positions. "I can give you a secretarial job. Please, please, let me do this for you." I looked up at him and said, "You've forgotten. I'm really, really sick. I am not able to work full time. I so wish I could, but I'm not able. You KNEW this before you tried to destroy my family, and you did it anyway." Weeping and wailing went on as he continued to hold onto me for dear life in the hopes of some kind of redemption. My forgiveness had already been offered on the days that he betrayed us. He already had that, but he was suffering on a subconscious level because it appeared that he was starting to realize he may not be able to repair the damage he'd done. The sin would remain upon him, and all the sufferings that were to come to our family and the community because of his selfishness were about to come down upon him.

But he was very, very sincere. His tears, for what seemed like the first time, were not for himself. They were for me as the angels continued to refresh his memory of our deep friendship and the betrayal which had followed in another life. He was truly contrite . . . he was ripe for God's picking. But it was not my fruit to pick.

The second partner was hysterically running around the office telling me to leave. "It's not appropriate that you're here!" He kept saying. "You need to go now." But we all ignored him for the most part. "God will decide what's appropriate and what's not!" An angel said, as she then immediately turned to the true work at hand.

As the first partner held me and wailed, I cried with him for the loss of a friendship that could've been powerful, meaningful, deep AND eternal. But he'd thrown it away like so many do.

And then the bugs began to emerge . . .

From every crevice of the building, through every sideboard, floor, roof, ceiling and wall - the creatures of the dark began swarming the room. Ants, Roaches, Water Bugs, Black Beatles, Spiders; vermin of every kind were now swarming at his feet. What he had done in taking that which did not belong to him by eternal right - and in trying to take that which did not belong to him by eternal right - had allowed the infestation to completely encompass the room.

An angel put her hand upon my shoulder and pulled me away from him. "Oh, my God!" He shouted. "Please help me to clean this up! I can't do it myself!" The angels were stern. "It shall not be so." They said. "For this mess is yours to clean. The Lord will not be sending help at this time."

Wailing harder, the angels continued. "What you do now with the mess you have made will determine whether or not the Lord will EVER come to your aid! If you so desire such help, we suggest with all earnestness that you bring this true contrition from a subconscious level to your conscious world and stop wreaking havoc with God's will all around you." He was hyperventilating between tears. "And then, you must not only stop such wreaking, but you will have to repair - as much as is possible - the damage you have already done! Do you understand?" He nodded, "Yes."

He tried to hand me a broom to start sweeping up these bugs which were coming in from everywhere, hoping I might still help him because of my deep and true caring for his soul. But the angels would not allow me to take it. "The Lord has specifically bidden that you shall ask no more sacrifice of her for your own gain. She will not be allowed to assist you. May I suggest you take the broom yourself and get to work before this place is so infested that there remains no hope."

I cried at this, too. But I understood. He had to clean up his own mess in order to prove his contrition. And that contrition was only manifesting on a subconscious level right now. In the conscious world, there was NO SIGN OF ANY CHANGE, as of yet.

Taking my hand, the angels threw the second partner another broom and said, "We leave you now with this. Clean it up!"

In a moment, we were gone.

****

In the distance, I saw her. She was a woman who was in the process of a divorce because she had been involved in an abusive relationship for many years. But I was shocked at what I was being shown.

Although her situation with her husband was very real, and they had serious issues to overcome, she was using this as an excuse to actually indulge a gull demon that was lurking within her.

His unacceptable behavior had become an excuse to engage her own demonic force within which was seeking after lust.

This was very surprising to me because in our day it is so politically incorrect for women to try to work through issues that involve any type of abuse; whether it be verbal or physical. But I was clearly being shown that her situation could be worked out, but she was using the indulgence her husband had given to his demon of rage as an excuse to indulge her own demon of lust.

It would most likely be something never seen on the surface, because she had a genuine problem in her marriage that she would be perfectly justified by the political thinking of the day to dissolve. But in God's eyes, that wasn't what was happening at all.

****

Taken into the home of a friend and couple who had recently reconciled after one of them had an affair, I was taken through every nook and cranny of the house to clean it of the energies and entities that no longer belonged since the partner had repented of his misdeeds.

He had to be present for this because of his own participation in what had come to pass, the contamination; but he was kept in a safe room while I did the work with spiritual guardians, angels and the power of God.

There was difficulty as I went through the house, because some of the darkness wished to cling to the place and continue to cause discord. However, by the time I was finished, everything was clean.

It was made clear to me that this couple had passed through some type of 'allowed' trial, and this cleanup job was a gift in exchange for having survived the temptation and tribulation they had undergone.

In the end, when everything was now clear, I was taken to the river which flowed nearby the house. I had to say the rosary while walking through and across the river, and when I had completed this, the river began to flow through their home.

It was clear that the channels of energy coming from above had been restored, despite this fall from grace, because this couple had survived a huge trial.
****

Death, Dying and the Afterlife

Mystic Knowledge Series

Compiled and Written by Marilynn Hughes

The Out-of-Body Travel Foundation!

www.outofbodytravel.org

CHAPTER ONE
Meeting a Loved One in the Beyond, Disaster Team, Demons of Death, Taking Souls at Death to an Immortal Realm, A Young Death, the Angel of Death, Experiencing the Peaceful and Detached Moment of Death, Gang Member who Saved his Soul, Putting on the New Man, Helping the Blessed Virgin Cross Souls Over in a Hospital, Deliverance from Living Death, What Meeting Loved Ones Beyond the Veil is Really all About.

****

As the vibrations began, I found myself separating with more ease and quickness, and doing it through the use of thoughts, rather than rolling out. But to my surprise, as soon as I had split from form, I was in a space I could only call a black void, rather than my bedroom. Frightened to no end, I immediately shot back into my body. It seems that any fear at all will always send you right back to your body, a special way God protects us from that for which we are not yet ready. Willing myself to separate and go back to the void, I did this two more times before I finally became so determined that my fear was overridden and I was able to remain there.

Passing through the black void, I crossed over into another dimension. It was very bright, light and airy, I almost felt like my spirit was a feather. Spirits whose forms were only light occupied this place, and it seemed that they knew me. Interestingly, they immediately recognized that I was an astral traveler, not one who had died, like themselves. Calming myself, I eased up on my fears.

Up in the distance, another spirit began to approach me. Walking along the sky, my dear friend (who had passed on several years before in a car accident) was now coming towards me. Feeling an urgency from him, as though he had something very important to tell me, I was very disappointed when I realized that my surprise and shock at seeing him was so powerful that it blocked us from having any communication.

Beginning to laugh, his seriousness diminished as he gently hugged me. Somehow, he knew that this was all I could handle for this visit and he turned to walk away.

As though hit by lightning, my spirit soared at the speed of light back to my form.

"The caravan of my prayers is moving toward Thee. It has been delayed now and then by blinding sandstorms of despondency."
Whispers from Eternity, Page 117, Paragraph 1, (Hinduism, Kriya Yoga, Author: Paramahansa Yogananda)

****

Leaving form, my spirit was sent directly to a group of spirits whose work was quite unusual. Called the 'disaster team,' they were responsible for disasters and the souls who perished in them. Suiting up in silver boots and helmets, I joined them for an evening of work worldwide.

Responsible for the victims of airplane disasters, earthquakes, tornadoes, car accidents, fires and all other types of tragic, sudden death situations, they wore the silver boots and helmets to make easily recognizable amidst the chaos of fires, floods and other catastrophic events. Whisked from one disaster to another, they worked non-stop as they helped souls all over the globe. An 'energetic pull' would come to take them to their next site, and they would be there instantly.

In each instance, the team pulled dying souls out of the mass of smoke, fire, wreckage and physical obstructions, literally shoving them up and out of the mess to the heavenly guardians who awaited their delivery. Most souls were so disoriented, that they didn't know they had passed on. Souls were plundered beneath such a mass of smoke and flame, they couldn't see anything. Because their deathbed had almost become the abyss, the screams of terror were immediately transformed to tears of joy upon seeing the heavenly lights above.

"The people who walked in distress have seen a great light. Upon those who dwelt in the land of gloom, a light has shone."
New American Bible, Old Testament, Isaiah 9:1, (Christianity, Catholic)

After my time was finished with the 'disaster crew,' I was shown astral support groups which operate on sub-conscious levels to help souls through their lives. Being sub-conscious, most people don't remember them upon waking, although some remember portions in dreams. Groups exist for every crisis one can experience in this world, and also for teaching specific spiritual knowledge. My spirit was allowed to sit in on a group discussing changing 'negatives' in their lives into 'positives.'

"The coming of the kingdom of God cannot be observed, and no one will announce it, 'Look, here it is,' or 'There it is.' For behold, the kingdom of God is among you."
New American Bible, New Testament, Luke 18:20, (Christianity, Catholic, Words of Christ)

****

Now that time had passed and I'd become accustomed to such things, the visitation from my friend who had died was no longer shocking. Out-of-body, he came to me to convey to me a message of his love for me. Appearing at the age of his death, I said, "It's so good to see you again. I've missed you . . . a lot!" Staring through me, he could sense all my feelings and love.

Coming closer, he hugged me, "I had no idea you felt that way about me." Noticing my embarrassment, he hugged me tighter, "Hey you don't have to be embarrassed. Remember, I'm dead. I don't have an ego anymore. To tell you the truth, I had a crush on you, too."

Showing me that he was working with some of his former friends sub-consciously, he had become their guide. Admitting frustration, it seemed clear that very few of them were able to see or hear him, which made his work very difficult. Whisked away, I acknowledged death as both an end . . . and a beginning.

"Blessed be Thy name, O God of mercies, for Thou hast done great and wondrous things . . . and in accordance with Thy goodness towards us, Thou has ofttimes opened for us gates of salvation, when we were oppressed."
The Dead Sea Scriptures, The War of the Sons of Light and the Sons of Darkness, Of thanksgiving for victory, Page 422, Paragraph 2, (Christianity, Gnostic/Essene)

****

Leaving my form behind, I was swept away to a beautiful mountain valley to fly with the wind and watch the beautiful creation of the Lord below. But as I soared upon a field of flowers, I noticed someone familiar sitting amidst the meadow. My friend who had passed on was waiting for me with an urgent message. Hugging him with intensity, I kept looking at him to make sure he was real, as he was so tangibly alive in his new life. In fact, he seemed MORE alive than he had been during his earthly sojourn.

"Why are you so argumentative with Sister Mary Christian?" He asked. "Who is that?" I blurted out, not recognizing this persons heavenly name. "This is important, I have to know." Blurting out the name of one of the souls I'd been working with on music, he nodded that this was correct. Apparently, it was not fitting for someone sent to guardian a soul to become annoyed or frustrated because of the soul's struggles. Ashamed, I asked, "What should I do to make up for my argumentative nature?" "Give her servitude." He said, as he directed my attention to all around us.

Many spirits had suddenly appeared who were working with souls on sub-consciously astral levels. "See all these spirits," he said, referring to the spirits of the dead who were present, "they cannot leave here completely until they have fulfilled all of their contracts. You are lucky because you can work with your people from a physical perspective. Though you are sometimes perceived as crazy, at least you can plant CONSCIOUS seeds of remembrance."

Nodding that I understood, I felt compassion for these souls and all the angels who try so hard to catch our attention, despite our reasoned thinking which prevents us from even opening our eyes to see them. Pulled away, my spirit returned to form.

"May my instruction soak in like the rain, and my discourse permeate like the dew. Like a downpour upon the grass, like a shower upon the crops: For I will sing the Lord's renown. Oh, proclaim the greatness of our God!"
New American Bible, Old Testament, Deuteronomy 32: 2-3, (Judaism, Christianity)
****

Sitting in a car with Andy as a dark horseman approached, I quickly locked my door but Andy was too slow to lock his own. A large man with a black hat and veils all about his face and head, he tried to open the doors. Upon finding mine locked, he moved onto Andy's. "Andy, hit the gas!" I shouted, but he refused to hear. Pushing him out of the way, I stuck my foot on the gas pedal before the death messenger could take him. Pulling out a black staff, he pointed it at us. "When the black pointed staff comes, death is near." His echoing voice sounded, as I knew that he spoke of karmic death. Death is not just a state of the body, but a state of the soul.
****

My soul was lost in thought as I sat at the table with childhood friends and relatives. Surprised when my deceased friend, who'd died in a car accident, entered the room, he sat down to talk with one of his best friends. Watching him, I felt a sorrow in my soul for this loss, but I turned away so as not to feel the pain. When I looked up again, he was walking straight towards me, staring me down with deep caring in his eyes. Taking my hand, he sat next to me.

For a moment, I was lost in his visions and dreams, which held the image of the fatal car accident that had taken his life. Drinking and driving, four out of the five passengers had been killed; all thrown from the vehicle, bloodied and battered. When he turned to face me again, the wounds which caused his death were present upon his body and I could feel his pain. Beginning to cry, he told me that he now worked with the Disaster Crew to help others who were dying traumatic deaths, and this brightened me up. For a moment, he became very serious, and though his words weren't eloquent or poetic, he let me know how much he had loved me. My tears began flowing harder, for I'd loved him deeply, too. Wonderful to see him again, I didn't want to return to my physical world. "Come with me," he said, as he held out his hand. Being pulled back beyond the veil of death, I timidly reached my hand to him, but then pulled back. Knowing I couldn't go with him, we lived in two different worlds.

Suddenly, we were sitting on a small park bench before his gravesite. Nothing was said, as he pulled me close to him and comforted me in my sorrow. "Sometimes love just isn't enough," he said to me, as he disappeared and his casket appeared before me. "No!" I screamed out, "No!" I screamed again as I flung myself to the box which held his remains and held on tightly. But an angel appeared, who was direct, "You cannot go with him," she said, "because his destiny lies in the world beyond death, and your destiny lies in the world of the living. Can you sacrifice your own destiny to be with him, now?" I didn't reply. "He cannot come to your world, and you cannot go to his . . . you cannot go with him."

Still crying, she conveyed something very dramatic, poignant and blunt. "Don't you see? Stop mourning over that which you have not lost." She paused. "Stop mourning over a destiny that was never meant to be, and by doing so, perhaps you will recognize the destiny that *was* meant to be."

"A veil exists between the world above and the realms that are below; and shadow came into being beneath the veil; and that shadow became matter; and that shadow was projected apart."
The Nag Hammadi Library, The Hypostasis of Archons, Page 167, Paragraph 7,

****

Encompassing me as they took me to my destination, the solar rays projected my spirit to a nursing home where several patients were scheduled to cross over. As they were to be transported to the sun, I was honored to be involved in assisting soul's who had achieved immortality!

Some of them were quite senile. Larry actually believed he was Batman from the old television series, so I knew that I was going to have some fun. Reporting for duty, I was assigned to accept a job as an activities director for this Catholic nursing home. Versing me on the religion so that I might fit in long enough to make this transition pleasant and simple, a very conservative fiftyish woman ran the home and was not at all pleased with the senile fantasies of her residents.

My playfulness with Larry, a.k.a. Batman, and his friend Ralph, a.k.a. Robin, really disturbed her. By nightfall of my first working day, she was considering my dismissal.

Batman, a name by which he preferred to be called, was saddened because he only had one arm; his left. Because of this, I had only been given one arm upon entry into this operation, my right, which made him feel comfortable with me immediately. Serving spaghetti for dinner that night, Batman had gotten frustrated because he couldn't twirl the spaghetti around his fork with his left arm. So I sat on his bed and twirled it with my right. Betty, the lady in charge, was upset at the special treatment I gave to Batman, and it disturbed her that I sang the Batman theme song and danced around the room. "Nanananananananana, Nanananananananana, Batman!" Encouraging his senility was wrong in her view.

As night fell and midnight approached, I knew my true job was nigh. Going to the rooms of Batman, Robin and two other patients who called themselves the Tin Men, I revealed my identity. Another woman who wasn't to cross over this night was also present. Calling her 'Hatchet,' she liked to cut things in half, especially towels, bed sheets and other cloth materials.

Noticing the sparkly blue light that came from my fingers, Batman was impressed. "What is that?!" He asked. "You haven't seen anything, yet," I replied, "I'm a Solar Angel and I have to energize this room with solar energy. Then you'll see just how much fun we're going to have tonight!" "Oh, how exciting!" Hatchet said. "A Solar Angel!" Before you could count to ten, the whole room was aglow with the sparkling blue energies of the immortal.

All of them were now being released from their bodies to play with me as I transmitted through them, making them young again. Batman immediately manifested a cape and sang the Batman song, running and jumping all over the place. The Tin Men created fire trucks to pretend they were firemen. Robin sped alongside Batman. Hatchet, who could not be made young again because she wasn't going to be transitioning this eve, had a good time playing with a thought-form ax, pretending to chop up her sheets, towels and tissue boxes. And as she did, she screamed with hysterical laughter. "Half price! I'll give it to you for half price!"

Betty, meanwhile, had heard some noise, even though it was occurring beyond third-dimensional awareness. Running towards the room, she saw me and was furious. In her view, everyone appeared to be sleeping, and she was unaware of Batman making faces behind her, or Robin lunging towards her and through her, laughing hysterically. "I want your resignation on my desk in the morning!" she screamed, as she took me to my room. Other Solar Angels arrived and put Betty in a deep sleep so that I might return to and finish my job.

Batman, Robin and the Tin Men were ready to go, so I took their hands and flew out the window into the night sky. Waving quietly to Hatchet as she re-entered her sleeping body, Batman cried out, "My Bat mobile!" An abandoned, beat-up old car in the woods had become the object of his fascination. Because we were laughing so hard, I almost forgot that I had to let them go now to be taken by their other guides. The Penguin appeared, another Solar Angel in costume pretending to be Batman's mortal enemy. "You must go," he said to them with humorous ferocity, "there are some journey's mortal enemies must take together." Beginning to soar towards the sun, the Bat mobile went off in the night sky.

Taking me to Hatchet's window the next morning, a brother Solar Angel had come to allow me to observe.

"Good morning, Elizabeth," Betty said, trying to prepare Hatchet for the empty beds that lay next to her. "Good Morning!" Hatchet cried, "Where's Batman and Robin?!" Solemn in her effort to console her, Betty replied, "They both passed in the night." The Tin Men had slept in another room and their absence was not immediately obvious to Hatchet. Brightening, Hatched exclaimed, "What happened to the Solar Angel!?" "Huh?" Betty replied quizzically. "What happened to the Solar Angel?!" "Just hang in there, Elizabeth," Betty replied, "I'll have your nurse in here with your morning medication in just a minute, okay?"

The eternal command came and we were gone.

Vortexing energies soared into me, as the voices whispered into my ears. "Destiny of the East wind Pyramid." Before my eyes, a swirling circle was going on into infinity, a triangle overlapped it; the karmic triangle, the pyramidal symbol of unification with God. As I re-entered my body, the voice continued to whisper into my ears. "They who are willing to beacon the light of all lives, to embody the eternal nature of all things, to become one with all who live within these hearts; shall be opened, shall be beckoned, shall receive. And in this reception, the many shall become one, and all that is eternal will henceforth become they."

"They therefore want me to declare on their behalf that in all of heaven there is not a single angel who was created at the beginning, nor is there in hell any devil who was created an angel of light and cast down. Rather, all the individuals in both heaven and hell are from the human race. In heaven are the ones who lived in heavenly love and faith in the world; in hell are the ones who lived in hellish love and faith."

Heaven & Hell, Chapter 35, Page 233, Paragraph 3, (Christianity, Swedenborgianism, Author: Emanuel Swedenborg)

****

Coming closer to the woman with the emerald face, her tears were flowing long and hard. Coming closer to her, I gave her a few moments to digest my presence. "Who are you?" she said, as her voice quivered. "I come as a servant of he who has parted." I replied. Placing my hand on her shoulder, she began to weep deeply.

Three had died in the accident, and I knew that this young girl was going to have a rough time dealing with this throughout her adult life. Her first love, the one she was to marry, had died at the age of eighteen.

For hours, we talked, and I told her of my dear friend who had also died so young. "You know," I said, "it feels like an unbearable pain at first, but it really does change over time." "Really?" "Yes." Thinking for a moment, she continued, "My mother thinks I'm overreacting, but she doesn't understand. She says it was just a teenage romance and I'll get over it." "You're right, she doesn't understand." I replied, "Love hurts the most when it is taken, but although this may be hard to understand, the love between you two will always remain. You will cry over losing his presence in your life, the destiny you thought you may have shared, but you will never really lose him completely. He lives in a new world now, but he will more than likely come visit you sometimes . . . perhaps when you least expect it." Looking at me, she said, "That's not enough." "Not enough for now . . . but over time, it will be." I paused. "But for now, you must cry, you must grieve . . ."

Summoning her other sub-conscious friends, they all began to appear in order to help one another through this great tragedy. Standing in a circle, I placed their hands together. "May serenity float upon your doorstep someday, my brave little young one." Whistling into the winds, she looked up one last time as I left.

"Serenity displays a consciousness that does not flare up when provoked by people or things. In the face of difficulty, the serene person's sentiments remain cool and detached."

Secrets of Mayan Science/Religion, Chapter 3, Page 98, Ziiz Olal, (Tribal, Mayan, Author: Hunbatz Men)

****

Coming closer to the woman with the emerald face, her tears were flowing long and hard. Coming closer to her, I gave her a few moments to digest my presence. "Who are you?" she said, as her voice quivered. "I come as a servant of he who has parted." I replied. Placing my hand on her shoulder, she began to weep deeply.

Three had died in the accident, and I knew that this young girl was going to have a rough time dealing with this throughout her adult life. Her first love, the one she was to marry, had died at the age of eighteen.

For hours, we talked, and I told her of my dear friend who had also died so young. "You know," I said, "it feels like an unbearable pain at first, but it really does change over time." "Really?" "Yes." Thinking for a moment, she continued, "My mother thinks I'm overreacting, but she doesn't understand. She says it was just a teenage romance and I'll get over it." "You're right, she doesn't understand." I replied, "Love hurts the most when it is taken, but although this may be hard to understand, the love between you two will always remain. You will cry over losing his presence in your life, the destiny you thought you may have shared, but you will never really lose him completely. He lives in a new world now, but he will more than likely come visit you sometimes . . . perhaps when you least expect it." Looking at me, she said, "That's not enough." "Not enough for now . . . but over time, it will be." I paused. "But for now, you must cry, you must grieve . . ."

Summoning her other sub-conscious friends, they all began to appear in order to help one another through this great tragedy. Standing in a circle, I placed their hands together. "May serenity float upon your doorstep someday, my brave little young one." Whistling into the winds, she looked up one last time as I left.

"Serenity displays a consciousness that does not flare up when provoked by people or things. In the face of difficulty, the serene person's sentiments remain cool and detached."

Secrets of Mayan Science/Religion, Chapter 3, Page 98, Ziiz Olal, (Tribal, Mayan, Author: Hunbatz Men)

****

Taken to an arena, two familiar beings approached. Wearing the traditional black robes, their skull faces looked into my eyes. "Perchance, we meet again," one said, as he gnarled at me expecting absolute terror. "Oh, my dear Angel of Death," I said with a smile upon my face, "do you really believe you can take me now?" "Why yes, it is time, is it not?" "To believe that it was my time to go would deny my further mission to God, and thus, you are incorrect. You may also be advised that I have reached the ascension. When it is indeed my time to depart this realm, it is the Angel of Ascension who will be coming to take my spirit to rest." Saying nothing, they both appeared a bit less confident. Coming forward, he reached his hand to me. (The Angel of Ascension had come to me previously to inform me of this.)

Laughing hysterically, I didn't offer them my hand. Embarrassed, the angels of death began to pull back. Used to being able to intimidate souls, they were not familiar with being made a fool. Cringing and lowering their heads, I said, "There is no need for shame, death. I know your purpose, but your purpose will not be done with me. I am not yours any longer; I belong to the living God. It's too late; you may go back to your comrade's and tell them they have lost."

Turning to leave, they disappeared.

"Wickedness makes a bad use not only of evil, but also of good. In the same way, holiness makes a good use not only of good, but also of evil. Thus, sinners make a bad use of the Law, although the Law is good, while saints make a good use of death, although death is an evil."

City of God, Book XIII, Page 274-275, Chapter 5, Paragraph 4, (Christianity, Catholic, Author: St. Augustine)

****

Death came silently in the night as if beckoning from the night wind into my soul. Pulling away, my form seemed unimportant to me as I looked ahead. Stained glass windows were hovering in the sky as the sun beamed through them its echoing light. Or . . . was that the light of God!?!? Each stained glass window frame held a portrait of a member of God's royal family. Sprawled across the sky across the heavens, I saw only the first few: Mary, Jesus, St. Francis of Assisi . . . Beginning to narrate my journey as if I were talking to my husband, Andy, I began speaking, "All I see are the lights . . . and the velvet."

Continuing my journey, I experienced my Earthly attachments, remembering the longing I used to feel for Andy. But now . . . everything was different. "I remember how I would miss you before," I said as if to Andy, "I MISS YOU!" Wrenching from my heart a purely emotional pain, I saw my plea-stricken face, and the torment of separation. But then as I continued further in flight towards the beautiful stained glass, my soul experienced an 'Exodus,' "Now . . . yes, I miss you." I said calmly with reserve. "But I am going away." Content in the will of the Lord, I passed through the stained glass as my ascent to heaven became ever more fervent. "All I see are the lights . . . and the velvet . . . All I see are the lights . . . and the velvet . . ." Saying it over and over again, I realized that I had gone to Exodus, and I had gone alone. Deliverance can be given to the body, but there is another type of deliverance within the soul. It is a deliverance of perception.

"Was it not you, Lord, who taught this soul of mine which now makes its confession to you? Was it not you, Lord, who taught me that, before you gave shape and variety to this formless matter, there was nothing - no color, no outline, no body, no spirit? And yet not absolutely nothing; there was a kind of formlessness, lacking all definition."

The Confessions of St. Augustine, Book XII, Chapter 5, No. 3, Paragraph 2, Page 286, (Christianity, Catholic, Author: St. Augustine)

****

Shaped like a book, an ancient sacred text, with two legs and face, the 'The Lankavatara Scripture,' was written on the cover. Below the title, it read, 'The Angel of Death.' Walking away, an angel appeared. "Look at the last commandment within the ten commandments." She said.

Finding that the Lankavatara Scripture deals with the cessation of birth, in essence, death of rebirth cycles, it speaks of the unborn, the Tathagata's, who live in the triple worlds beyond form, perceptions, birth and death. It seemed that the relation between this scripture and the angel of death was that the scripture deals very much with the cessation of craving and desire, which process leads to the cessation of future births and deaths. The tenth commandment deals with coveting our neighbor's possessions, craving. Craving generates samsara, the karmic condition of suffering, death and rebirth. Seeing the oneness between these Jewish, Christian, and Buddhist doctrines, I noticed that the combined elements of them led to the cessation of the activity of coveting, also called craving, which causes rebirth in karmic realms.

"Transcendental Intelligence is the inner state of self-realisation of Noble Wisdom. It is realized suddenly and intuitively as the 'turning-about' takes place in the deepest seat of consciousness; it neither enters nor goes out - it is like the moon seen in water. Transcendental Intelligence is not subject to birth nor destruction; it has nothing to do with combination nor concordance; it is devoid of attachment and accumulation; it transcends all dualistic conceptions."
A Buddhist Bible, The Lankavatara Scripture, Chapter VI, Paragraph 2, (Buddhism)
"Commanded by wisdom, led by compassion, endowed with skill in means, pure in resolution and intent, measureless in power, unobstructed, direct, not relying on another's guidance, knowledge of the supreme mind equal to the enlightened, with the birth of this mind-jewel of enlightening beings, one transcends the sphere of the ignorant and reaches the sphere of the buddhas, is born in the family of the enlightened, impeccable . . . once one produces this mind, one attains this stage, the will immovable as a mountain, joyful and happy, serene, resolute, and forceful, with a buoyant mind, nonviolent, harmless, free from anger, modest and respectful, with superior honesty, self-controlled; one remembers the immeasurable knowledge that saves the world and becomes joyful in anticipation of that state."
The Flower Ornament Scripture, Chapter 26, The Ten Stages, Page 711, Stanza 4-5
****

Taking me to another soul ready to make the final passing, this very merciful woman was having trouble making her crossing because of the grudges that other souls had held against her during her life. Lying on the floor and waiting to be attended to as I arrived, three other women stood around her, sub-conscious astral, all of whom had been friends. Ironically, the decedent was in some respects a mother figure to all of them, and had given them advice and guidance during their lives. Feeling great caring for their souls, she watched out for them with a certain light of the divine.

But these ungrateful souls were focusing on her occasional tendency to be rather robust in her guidance, usually when they were very much in danger of falling away from the path of the Lord. It surprised me that this rather virtuous soul was held down by their lack of mercy, but it was immediately known to me that I was to obtain forgiveness for her from these unforgiving friends. "I find it so very difficult to understand that you are holding onto such a petty fault when you yourselves have ones which are much greater and will require a much more complex level of mercy than that of the soul of your friend." In only a moment, they realized that this was true, and they offered their absolution . . . walking away in somewhat of a state of shame.

As they did this, I prayed to the Lord as He sent down a beam of light towards the body of this woman who was immediately transformed into a robe of white light. Still inanimate, her body swirled up into the sky in a standing position and was vortexing for quite some time before her eyes opened and she looked directly above her. Opening in welcome, the gates of heaven were before her and she soared towards them, never looking back.

It wasn't made clear to me, however, whether she was held back because of her own desire for her friend's absolution, or because their forgiveness was required. Had she turned to the Lord for absolution after their refusal, perhaps her sins would have been loosed irregardless.

And so it came to pass that I began working with souls on forgiveness in the astral states. In particular, I worked with the soul of a young man who was trying to leave a dangerous gang. But leaving these gangs is almost always a guarantee of death. So I visited the remaining gang members sub-consciously, assessed their energies and had them look at pictures of their former buddy amongst the gang. Erasing him out of the picture with a pencil eraser, it seemed to create confusion on their parts and send their focus elsewhere. It was the Lord's wish that souls who tried to turn away from former evil ways, be given the opportunity to do so in peace.

And so all measures that could be taken, were taken; however, it was clear that there was no guarantee for any of these souls. They would have to stand and perhaps be willing to fall, in order to save their souls from what they had energized in the past. All comes from causes, all comes from causes.

"Dismiss all anger and look into yourself a little. Remember that he of whom you are speaking is your brother, and, as he is in the way of salvation, God can make him a Saint, in spite of his present weakness."
The Voice of the Saints, In Temptation, Page 68, No. 1, (Christianity, Catholic, Words of St. Thomas of Villanova)

****

As I drifted away into sleep, I saw the dead and mangled bodies of six souls. One of them had been beheaded, and the others had all died violent deaths, as well. Suffering great pains in some kind of purgatory, it was conveyed to me that I could relieve their suffering and actually deliver them from it if I were willing to take on their pains, and restore their spiritual bodies to wholeness.

Agreeing to do so, a massive pain came through my side and back that cannot be described, it was absolutely unbearable. Barely able to move, the task of getting up and approaching each of their bodies for repair was almost impossible, but I began the process anyway. Pain shot through me like a fire *and* like a knife; like a lightning bolt with every move. Persevering for what seemed like hours; I approached each body, and slowly repaired the physical damage that had taken place. Putting the beheaded person's head back upon her body, holding together skin torn apart by knives and bullets, and caressing burns with my hands . . . a heavenly force sealed the wounds, making their bodies whole again. Despite this newfound wholeness, their bodies remained dead, but the excruciating pains in my body ceased at this point.

A pile of boxes appeared before me containing white garments and robes, and it was my task to re-clothe these tortured souls in the garment of the new man. As I brought the boxes to each body, they came back to life and were instantaneously clothed in the robes of white. Happiness filled their faces, as the old mangled bodies became spiritual bodies of purity and light, ready to leave their sufferings, and enter into a heavenly abode.

Kneeling, I prayed to the Lord in thanks for offering me such an opportunity to serve my fellow humanity and to give of myself to make their burden lighter.

"Let us be glad and rejoice, and give honour to him: for the marriage of the Lamb is come, and his wife hath made herself ready. And to her was granted that she should be arrayed in fine linen, clean and white: for the fine linen is the righteousness of saints. And he saith unto me, Write, Blessed are they which are called unto the marriage supper of the Lamb."
King James Bible, New Testament, Revelations, 19:7-9, (Christianity)

****

As the vibrations came upon my soul in a fury, my vibrations were raised and then brought to a calm. Looking towards the heavens, a small portal had erupted. A star tunnel swirling on my ceiling grabbed my eye as I jutted towards it. Journeying through the heavens at the speed of light, many things happened of which I no longer recall. Moments later, I landed in a local hospital.

Having trouble holding the vibration, an angel diffused the physical response, allowing me to maintain my status in the spirit world.

Dressed as a golden angel, I saw a beautiful white statue of Mary on the hospital altar. Looking behind me, I noticed that no one observed my presence. When I turned back, the Mary statue had left its podium. Coming to life, she was hiding around the corner in a patient's room, beckoning me to come to her.

Entering the room, I realized that the soul of the patient had already been removed, as she had died. Hovering above the light fixture on the ceiling, I marveled at the psychedelic beauty of the soul. An oval ellipse, the soul had not yet resurrected into its spirit body.

Mary was manifesting in modern attire, wearing a headband to pull her long auburn hair back. Amazed at how young she was, I was also surprised at how meek and humble she appeared. Intentionally taking on an unthreatening demeanor, she expressed a need to hurry because there were other souls to attend to this night. Taking the light stream in my arms, I soared above and heavenward, taking the soul to the light of God.

Returning, Mary had hidden inside the statue again. Leaping out, she beckoned me to another room. Doing this with two more souls, Mary reassumed her posture inside the white statue on the altar.

Soaring into the star tunnel which awaited me on the ceiling, I cried out, "Oh, my Lord, oh, how I wish I could enter the tunnel of light again, it has been so long and I miss it so!" Hearing my beckon, the tunnel between life and death appeared. Many kittens were in the tunnel this time, as I ran joyfully towards the light.

Reaching the end of the tunnel, I stood before the light in ecstasy. The light has a cloudy veil before it wherein no one can cross unless it is their time. "Lord," I cried out, "I know that if I touch your light that I will be unable to return, but, oh, how I yearn to just touch your light!" Immediately, a small part of the shadowy veil lifted, just enough for my hand to go through. "May I?" I questioned the Lord, "May I touch it, or will I be unable to return?" A telepathic prompting made it clear that the Lord was making an exception for me so that I may touch His beatific essence, and I reached in to touch the light in a frantic and ecstatic moment of joyous rapture. "Thank you, Lord!" I shouted, "Thank you, Lord!"

"Ought we not to look upon it as a great grace and favor to be invited into His presence? Surely, we ought to find our delight in His company since He is delighted to be in ours. We ought to go to Him frequently and say to Him: 'My Jesus, why dost Thou love me so much? What good dost Thou see in me that Thou art so enamored of me? Hast thou already forgotten the sins by which I have offended Thee so grievously?"
The Blessed Eucharist, Chapter 4, Page 58, Paragraph 1, (Christianity, Catholic, Author: Fr. Michael Muller)

****

Beginning to drive down a road, I met with my fate. A car accident took my life, yet another death/rebirth. Dressed all in white, a beautiful woman with short gray hair awaited me with a doll that she had sewn for me. Holding it, I felt safe.

Beyond form, my spirit met up with several adjusters who were playing a game which offered many options to those who had passed. Adjusters help souls in transition from one world to the next, both from life to death, and from death to life. Tonight they were assisting in making a transition from my past to my future.

As it was my turn to pick a card, I did, and it showed an eagle. Suggesting I take it, they conveyed that the eagle represented a transformation which would come about through returning to the body, returning to life.

The beautiful woman was sitting in the corner at a sewing machine making another doll for me, but I saw somebody looking on with jealousy. Ignoring her, she told me she was my heavenly mother. "It's okay to let the past go," she said, "but now you must listen to the light." Before I could, I simply passed out, perhaps for fear of what the light might tell me. Patiently picking me up, my spirit soared before the light as it now opened its crevasse towards me. Ominously powerful, it was holy and ecstatic at the same time. Opening and closing in a state of bliss because I was so near to my creator, I listened to what it said. "You are now ready to be married, but your past cannot go with you."

Until now, because of my vices, I couldn't experience a true marriage.

Now I was ready, but my past life was a contradiction of such a holy rendering.

Continuing to convey, the light informed me that much of my current illness was connected to me feeling guilty about moving forward, thus, leaving behind some of the people who had walked karma's path with me. 'You must move forward anyway,' the light conveyed.

Awaking and returning to sleep moments later, my spirit was standing aside a doctor in a hospital who was trying to teach me methods of serenity through Zen Buddhist meditation. Following his instructions, a woman came into the hospital with a baby who had been abused. Acting as though her actions were unimportant, the woman with the child was very cold. Uncomfortable with everybody in the hospital, the baby immediately took to me when I approached. Holding the child, the love that we felt for each other made him whole. Because of this, the doctor suggested that I take the baby home to its father, and try to affect change in their home.

Living on the edge of a cliff, below it was a dangerous and murky lake. Wanting to affect change for his child, the father didn't know how. In despair, he fell over the cliff into the waters and was consumed. Because of the danger of the waters, no one went in to save him assuming it was too late. Still holding the baby, I didn't feel I could go in, either.

Walking to the edge to see if there was anything I could do, the ground collapsed and I fell into the murky waters with the baby in my arms. Below water, my soul became encased in a casket, and I mourned for the loss of the baby because I felt certain it couldn't have survived. Because the cliffs were at least several hundred feet high, I felt that my demise was imminent, so I began to pray for myself, the baby, and the father.

As I prayed, my soul emerged on the surface of the waters still encased in a burial casket covered in mud. Emerging in his own casket covered in mud, the father appeared on the surface. The mud encasing my own soul began to stir, and within moments the baby emerged safe and sound. Having grown, it appeared to be about two years old. Rejoicing that the baby was alive, we all began swimming to no avail, for we couldn't penetrate the ends of the waters, or the height of the cliff. So again, I prayed.

Suddenly, the liquid beneath our feet became solid ground, as we were transported to the grounds above. "Praise God," I shouted, "for He has delivered us from the deep."

Through prayer, the original sin that had been encased upon their souls in the form of mud and deep murky waters (violence and abuse), had been taken away, at least for this moment. Spared the pain of his own reality, saved from his own murky depths and muddied thinking for at least this moment, it was unfortunate to realize that he would soon jump back in, for that was his nature. Though the sins of this perpetrator had been visited upon this child, the Lord All-Powerful was too merciful to allow him to be lost.

"Now, lo, if he beget a son, that seeth all his father's sins which he hath done, and considereth, and doeth not such . . . Neither hath oppressed any, hath not withholden the pledge, neither hath spoiled by violence, but hath given his bread to the hungry, and hath covered the naked with a garment, that hath taken off his hand from the poor, that hath not received usury nor increase, hath executed my judgments, hath walked in my statutes; he shall not die for the iniquity of his father, he shall surely live."

King James Bible, Old Testament, Ezekiel 18:14-18, (Christianity)

"He loves you and would not have you attach yourself to what is perishable, but to Himself Who alone can satisfy your heart, and He will do so and fill it in the measure in which you empty it of creatures."

Thoughts and Sayings of St. Margaret Mary, November, No. 15, (Christianity, Catholic, Words of St. Margaret Mary)

****

Returning to see me beyond the veil, my friend who had passed appeared with great warmth towards my soul. "I miss you," I said to him, as he quietly looked down. Shyly, he replied, "Yeah, but that's not what this is all about." "It's not?" I said wistfully, "Well, then what is it all about?" I asked.

Pulling out a book, its title read, 'Now that you're Dead.' A manual for those who passed over, he turned to a page in the front of the book. 'How do you want those you've left behind to feel about you and to remember you?' Having filled in the answer, it read, 'I want them to feel good.' Looking up, I didn't know what to say, so he replied, "It's not about us being together, it's about destiny . . . and the contracts we have to fulfill." Speaking of my life's work, he was serious and direct about its fulfillment. And speaking about our unique destinies on opposite sides of the veils, our love for each other was not about being together, but simply about love. "You will always do menial work when you are to have a job, because that is what is necessary for your path, your true work for God," he said before he began to disappear. Grateful that his love for me was not selfish, he loved me enough to serve my soul.

"When the wise realize the Self, formless in the midst of forms, changeless in the midst of change, omnipresent and supreme, they go beyond sorrow."
The Upanishads, Katha Upanishad, Part 2, No. 22, (Hinduism, Translation: Eknath Easwaran)

"Though you may be alive today, do not think that you will necessarily be alive tomorrow. The danger of death is right at your feet!"
Shobogenzo-zuimonki, 4-8, Page 150, Paragraph 5, (Buddhism, Zen, Words of Zen Master Dogen)

****

CHAPTER TWO
Process of Dying Souls and the 'Epochs,' Rebirth of the Redemption at Death, Flame of the Lord, Who Constitutes 'Family' in the Next Life, Preparation of Energies Around a Dying Person, the Tunnel, Messages of Potential Impending Death, Seeing Life on Earth Without You, Temporary Reprieve, Dead Relatives and Ancestors Making Themselves Known, Discernment in Crossing Over, Power of Prayer.

****

Extricated from the world of the living, I was given to take passage upon the road from life to death, to observe the processes of the dying souls. When a soul passed through death, it may spend time in separate life 'epochs,' which contain within them elements of different time frames during their lives. Totally determined by the level of attachment a soul had to the period and the level of resolution which had already taken place upon the ground, the time spent in each epoch could vary considerably.

Observing several separate souls, I noticed many differences in application of this process. One of the souls went through four ten-year epochs mimicking four separate time periods and events in his life wherein he had great regret and attachment. Another soul went through no epochs, and journeyed directly into the following stages proceeding the epochs to learn from a 'jurist,' whose function is to speak to the soul about the next phases of existence. Apparent that the time spent in 'epochs' lay in direct correlation to the amount of time spent during life in self-evaluation, remorse and repentance, those who had thoroughly investigated their actions while living had no need of the epochs in death, proceeding directly to the next phase.

Interestingly, I observed a third soul who had no need of epochs *or* jurists. A very advanced, detached and spiritually educated soul, he was ready at the moment of death to depart for a higher life station.

During my traveling, I had taken several sub-conscious souls who were either friends or biological relations of the souls we were to observe in death this evening. Very confused because the after-life afforded so many differing journeys for each of their loved ones, I observed that the after-death experience could differ greatly for souls who had lived through the same time-frame together.

For instance, in observing the after-death experience of an old boyfriend of one of the souls who was watching with me, she was disturbed that he had great conflict in the epoch of his life regarding the two of them, which had long since passed. Because he had badly mistreated her, he had many regrets, although she was quite detached from that epoch of her life, because she had moved on.

It seemed that souls were most attached to epochs of their life wherein they had caused harm to others. But it was less likely that a soul would be greatly attached to the times of his life when he had actually been the recipient of pain.

Trying to help this soul from her past to move forward through this epoch of their lives, she quickly realized that it was a necessary process which she could not either lengthen or shorten. For those souls who spent little or no time in self-reflection during life, the immediate after-life would contain a great deal of time for such ventures.

An actual road existed between the living and the dead upon which we were driving, and it was a very treacherous route filled with many pitfalls of conscience. Surprised when somebody from my own past wrecked intentionally into our side, she replied, "Karmic payback." Unintentionally causing her harm many years ago through the use of improper words, I asked her what I might be able to do for her in return for what I had done in the past. Wanting to know the status of the soul of a friend of hers who had passed, I entered into a reflective state.

Having passed directly through the epochs and jurist, he'd immediately entered eternal life. Disappointed, she knew that you could communicate with souls who remained in the epochs by traveling this road. Many souls did communicate with loved ones while they traveled through the epochs of their lives, which gave them opportunities to settle old conflicts and hurts. But beyond the epochs, there remained no attachment to their former existences and they were no longer willing to speak of their 'past lives' with souls who remained within them.

After death while traveling the epochs, souls would only communicate with those from the past for a short period of time, to resolve these conflicts, and then they would begin to learn of eternal life from their jurists. When they were well-versed in such matters, they moved forward. At this point, any grudges held by those in life towards the deceased became their own problem. Continuing to hold a grudge against the soul of the *remorseful* departed becomes almost as a sin connected to the living remaining soul. An attending jurist spoke, "Forgiveness moves mountains and souls."

Understanding was the purpose of this road, and many of the dead who linger, such as lost souls or souls who wish communication with their loved ones, are those who have much to rectify, either because of their own lack of diligence in pursuing such matters in life, or because their life was cut short unexpectedly leaving much unfinished. But all souls, despite the great need for this process, do try to work through the epochs of their lives as quickly as possible. In order to help souls going through such phases of death, we must simply forgive.

On the road from life to death, there was a process which can only be described as going from hot to cold to colder to frozen. Traveling through the epochs contained an element of 'freezing' whose purpose was to take a soul from a 'hot' or attached state to life, and bring them slowly to a 'cold' or detached state from that past life. Memory slowly becomes iced as aspects are forgiven, released and let go. As the knowledge of mistakes become manifest, the attachment to the experience becomes less consequential. Rather than being an act of uncaring, it allows for knowledge to be processed through honest detached observation, within the context of continued movement. Great sorrow and lamentation occurs during this process, so when the lamentation is finished, the soul ices and becomes less emotional and more knowledgeable with a newfound sense of detachment. Emotional lamentation is encouraged, however, because it breeds true contrition which leads to knowledge.

Soaring now towards the sun, my soul stopped to witness a swirling cluster of blue stars which had formed into a magnificent nebulae.

"By quitting one's own country and dwelling in foreign lands one should acquire practical knowledge of non-attachment."
A Buddhist Bible, The Supreme Path, No. VII, No. 2, (Buddhism, Tibetan)
"By reflecting upon the irrevocable nature of the results which inevitably arise from actions, mayest thou be incited to avoid impiety and evil."
A Buddhist Bible, The Supreme Path, No. IX, No. 3, (Buddhism, Tibetan)
"When you are joyous, look deep into your heart and you shall find it is only that which has given you sorrow that is giving you joy. When you are sorrowful look again in your heart, and you shall see that in truth you are weeping for that which has been your delight."
The Prophet, On Eating and Drinking, Page 29, Botton, (Christianity, Author: Kahlil Gibran)

****

Led through yet another maze, this one led to the latest and most powerfully significant rebirth of the redemption. Andy and one other soul went with me as several rooms of rites had preceded those I now bore, but I could no longer remember them.

The fourth or fifth room began with a tiny canoe and one oar, and it was my purpose to row myself to the far shore. Difficult because the body of water was among the highest mountains and snow-capped peaks, it was cold and icy at the same time, and the depth of the water was somewhat frightening. Clear, you could see all the way through to the bottom, just like your spirit after it has been redeemed; clear and fluid, known but still very deep.

After attaining to the farther shore, I was led to a large swimming pool with pink shimmering salty water. Led to jump in and swim through it several times, I was stunned to find that this water made you feel somewhat numb, but yet, also more vibrant at the same time. There was a sense of being wet, but also dry, and it was soothing.

When this had reached its end, my soul was led to a group of buckets, all filled with a clear salty water which was designed for the feet. As I placed my feet in one of the buckets, I looked to my side and noticed a receptacle. When I opened the receptacle, I saw a small woman giving birth to a child. Almost out, the baby was coming head first and blood was everywhere. Noticing a long tube, which I immediately understood to be representative of the birth canal, in order to finalize the rite, I had to drop myself head first and backwards down through the tube, hold my breath long enough to emerge, and then be born anew, victorious.

Andy and the other soul were sitting with me, and were afraid to hold their breaths not knowing how long the tube might be, but I jumped in head first, holding my breath, sliding down the tube rather quickly. Becoming frightened near the end of the tube, I was getting concerned about the length of the tunnel and whether or not I could make it. But as I emerged victorious, I felt a shining radiant new birth come over my soul. Humanity shining in splendor, my redemption was now fully complete and my soul was ensconced in a new vibratory energy which felt like a combination of being made somewhat numb to reality, but yet, more vibrant at the same time.

Andy and the other soul had gone through but were still waiting to emerge, so I ran back to the former area and helped them by pushing them through the birth canal. All of a sudden, I remembered that I'd been through a similar rite two or three times before, but I had previously retained no memory of it.

Every death of our soul comes with a new rebirth, for no man can see the kingdom of God unless he be born again, and again, and again, and again . . . If this be so, I welcome every death I must face, for each death brings my soul ever closer to the object of my affection; the one true God.

Kneeling to the ground, I gave thanks for this grandiose moment for my own soul. For who could possibly have foreordained, lest it be God, that this very lost soul could have been brought back to the fore of God's army as a child of the most holy light? I gave thanks, and for a moment, I bade my soul to rest in the peace of knowing that this leg of my journey was now complete. Hallelujah!! Praise the Lord!!

"And Jesus said unto him, This day is salvation come to thine house, forsomuch as thou art a just man, thou also art a son of Abraham. For the Son of man is come to seek and to save that which ye deem to be lost."
The Gospel of the Holy Twelve, Lection LIX, No. 18, (Christianity, Gnostic/Essene, Words of Christ)

"I too had been marked for death on account of my sins, my wrongdoings had sold me to Sheol; but Thou, in accord with Thine abundant compassion, Thou, in accord with Thy bounteous ways, didst rescue me, O Lord."
The Dead Sea Scriptures, Poems from a Qumran Hymnal, No. IV, No. 10, (Christianity, Gnostic/Essene)

"When they return from the battle, they shall write on their standards: Salvation of God, Triumph of God, Help of God, Support of God, Praise of God, Thanksgiving to God, Acclaim of God, Peace of God."
The Dead Sea Scriptures, The War, Page 405, Paragraph 3, (Christianity, Gnostic/Essene)

****

Amidst an astral gathering of souls who were instructing me regarding death, I turned to notice my dear friend who'd passed away fifteen years before in a car accident. Smiling, he appeared at about my age, the age he would've been today (about 36), had he not died at the age of twenty one.

Calmly, I looked at my smiling friend and shyly asked, "If I am to cross over . . . you will meet me, won't you?" Nodding 'Yes,' the peaceful loving smile did not change upon his face.

****

"End of October, the sleepy brown woods seem to nod down their heads to the winter. Yellows and the grays paint the sad skies today, and I wonder when you're coming home." (From the song by Dan Fogelberg, 'Old Tennessee') My Uncle who had passed two years ago led a crowd of my family's ancestors in song. Currently, it was May, and it appeared they were telling my time might be up in October, but it also felt possible that they were just confirming that I didn't have a great deal of time, maybe a few years. (At this juncture, 85% of people with my specific condition statistically died within five years, although the numbers could be 50-70% for those with Dilated Cardiomyopathy from other causes.)

Floating outside, my three children and husband were playing in the sunny day while I was still asleep inside, my soul traveling the spirit world. Looking towards the deep blue sky, I watched intently as a cross began forming out of the clouds. Distantly, I heard the sound of a Native American flute, and my soul became mesmerized by its melody.

Walking over to my husband, I asked him if he could hear the flutes, but he was unaware of my presence, much less of the presence of the mystical malaise surrounding me in the ether.

An amphitheater appeared with about 1,000 spectators. Singing beautifully about Jesus, an intense black woman appeared. Beautiful and mesmerizing, she sang about the Lord. A couple in the audience was holding a glass enclosure, reaching out their hands as a flame spontaneously lit up within it. Getting very excited, I immediately knew that this flame was the Presence of Our Lord Jesus Christ.

As the flame was also within their hands, they began to touch other people's hands, which immediately lit up with this flame also, until everyone in the audience was aflame with the Presence of Our Savior. Walking towards them, they bid me stay back as this was not yet something in which I could participate. Asking Andy again if he heard the beautiful singing or saw this amazing spectacle, he wasn't even aware that I was talking to him or that my spirit was present.

Disappearing, the native flutes began their mystical melody again in the distance as I reached my hands towards the heavens and shouted, "I'm coming to you, Lord!" Lifting me towards space at the speed of light, the Lord allowed my soul to take in the celestial energies, before returning to my body.
****

Meeting the deceased brother of a very good friend of mine, (not the one who died in the car accident and has visited me for years), he said, "Because you and my brother have been like family in this life, you and I will be like family to one another when you cross over. I wish to do this for him." Realizing that this was a response to a prayer, I'd worried that I wouldn't know anybody on the other side because I was so young and would be the first to die. "By the way," he finished, "tell my brother that I watch over his sons, I'm one of their guardian angels."
****

Awaking from sleep, I noticed the presence of a male angel standing next to my bed. My doorway had been altered into a magnificent ascending starry passage into heaven, and the room was alit with sparkly light. "What are you doing?" I asked. "We are preparing the energies here so that when you cross over it will be an easier transition." "But my doctor doesn't believe that I'm going to die anytime soon," I said, confused. Flippantly, he laughed, "Yeah, we know, but that's not your problem." Pausing a moment before leaving, he said one last thing. "Andy will have to either fight for you, or learn to live without you." Looking at the astounding ascending passage, I dropped back off into unconsciousness.
****

As something went wrong with my heart, I immediately saw the tunnel and the light. Understanding the implications, I shot through it thinking, 'Uh-oh,' but then shouted in excitement. "Can I go see Jesus?!" As I said this, I began traveling towards Him. "Yes, you can do this," a voice said, "but if you journey all the way to Jesus, you will be unable to return." Shouting, I said, "Oh, no, I can't leave. I need to be with my kids." Instantaneously soaring back towards my body, I heard the voice of Christ in my head. "I want you to go back and fight to be with your kids." Conveying that our family needed to learn to value each other more wholly; not by function, but by mere existence, learning to care for each other's true needs, rather than 'using' each other, He stopped the strange happening in my heart and returned me to form.
****

Awaiting my arrival on the runway, the dark blue plane appeared normal to the naked eye. As I boarded, however, it opened into a mystical euphoric scene. Crystalline glass enclosed us as brilliant colors of the kaleidoscope appeared randomly all about the walls and ceiling which were formed into a large dome overhead. Rather than flying, we began to glide very slowly across a large, calm body of water. Up ahead on the opposite bank, I could see a thick mystical forest. "Where are we going? What is that land ahead of us?" I inquired to no reply.

****

Traveling to yet a borderland, I found myself inside a small Catholic monastery amidst a wooded forest land. A lone monk sang mystical chants, the words speaking of death and crossing over. In a few moments, a young Tibetan woman entered the room, as a voice announced her as an emissary of the Dalai Lama. Several other people entered the room and circled themselves around her, as she began telling them of the next phase of their lives in service to God. Speaking to them of specific tasks, she turned to me and quietly said, "You don't need to think about further service to God on Earth for you are going to die." Nodding in understanding, I was unusually detached from this information, silently acknowledging the message.

****

Swirling through the ether, my soul had landed upon a desert oasis within sight of the Assisi Mountains on Venus. My old friends, the five Assisi Marauders were at my side, teaching me about being a spiritual guardian to souls. In the center of a large table were five conical, triangular-shaped crystals which I immediately knew to represent each member of my family including myself. Moving them around, I began placing them in positions which seemed appropriate for my children's further destiny.

Andy's soul was present in the Assisi Marauder with whom he'd blended into one, as if they were the same soul. For a moment, I also recognized other elements and identities within the Marauder, including the man whom I'd 'married' on the mountain. Feeling within me that I would have the presence of Andy with me in the after-life, I realized that many aspects of his soul remained on the other side, of which this was just one. Encompassed in the Assisi Marauder, they were all present within this particular manifestation, yet individually available through him, as well. Remembering who he was, we embraced in a quiet hug, as the red-headed aspect seemed relieved that I now understood his purpose.

Quiet and somber, they differed at this moment from their usual highly energized quality as it seemed that they were honoring my grief. Waiting, they were very patient with the fact that I was confused and learning to detach from the world, knowing this would mean I would have no choice but to leave behind my three young children, my jewels. Feeling God's will in all that was happening to me, we were peaceful.

Although they never actually removed the crystal piece representing my soul from the table, I felt the energy present indicating that this was what they were waiting to do.

For now, we waited . . .

****

As the clandestine heavens appeared above me, my spirit began to experience an unusual state wherein I was watching my family as if I were no longer there. No matter what I would say or do, they were unaware of my presence. With interest, I looked on as I noticed that my husband and eldest daughter had come up with a plan for the family, and everyone was truly okay. Surprised and relieved by this, I wandered around following them as they implemented their plans for life 'now that I was gone.'

Suddenly, I found myself standing in the front yard, but not for long. Falling to the ground, I lost all control of my body and its senses. Noticing that the hose had fallen nearby, water was running all over me, but I could do nothing about it.

In a millisecond a great mountain appeared before my eyes and my spirit was airbound. Upon the mountain in the distance, an ancient prophet wearing a robe of deep blue and carrying a staff appeared. Standing upon a rocky edge, he beckoned me closer. He began to speak words of great depth and

401

wisdom, and I attempted to write them down with clear accuracy. His words impaled my soul with intense longing to know the things he had to teach, but I wasn't given to remember a single iota of them upon return.

As he began to disappear into the distance, my highly vibrating spirit began to return to my sleeping body slowly, so as to ease my way back into my physical abode.

"I know a man in Christ who, fourteen years ago, whether he was in the body or outside his body I cannot say, only God can say - a man who was snatched up to the third heaven. I know that this man - whether in or outside his body I do not know, God knows - was snatched up to Paradise to hear words which cannot be uttered, words which no man may speak."

The New American Bible, New Testament, 2 Corinthians, 12:2-4, (Christianity: Catholic, Words of St. Paul)

"We say to you, as if the Lord himself had said it, that we who live, who survive until his coming, will in no way have an advantage over those who have fallen asleep. No, the Lord himself will come down from heaven at the word of command, at the sound of the archangel's voice and God's trumpet; and those who have died in Christ will rise first. Then we, the living, the survivors, will be caught up with them in the clouds to meet the Lord in the air."

New American Bible, New Testament, 1 Thessalonians 4:15-17, (Christianity, Catholic, Words of St. Paul

"Like the wind, like clouds, like thunder and lightning, which rise from space without physical shape and reach the transcendent light in their own form, those who rise above body-consciousness ascend to the transcendent light in their real form."

The Upanishads, Chandogya Upanishad, 12.2, (Hinduism, Translator: Eknath Easwaran)

****

Arriving in a splendid array of light, the angels came to tell me that it was time for me to make my journey. The top of a huge mountain completely isolated from the rest of the world was my destination, a border-world.

Directing me to board an old western train, it waited silently at the side of a wild rushing river, white from the gales of the current. Walking quietly towards it, the angels disappeared.

Boarding the old train, my spirit was immediately made aware of the presence of one soul, a cowboy wearing the customary garb of the 1800's. Wearing an old worn cowboy hat and light brown western wear, I stared at him rudely before approaching. Looking outside the windows, the train stood no more than a few feet from the banks of wide and deep rushing river.

Engaging the cowboy in conversation, I asked, "Where and when does this train cross the river?" Knowing I could not reach the mountain top without crossing this great divide, I also recognized its impassibility by any other means than the train. "We can't cross the river at this time of year," he said, "we'll have to wait."

After fighting for months and making progress with medication, it was October 29 . . . the end of October. Could I have averted and received pardon for a potential time of death?

Turning the train around, he started me back towards my home in the foothills.

Standing amidst a large auditorium, I noticed that there were many ovular, metallic tubs filled with warm water. Souls of people who had crossed over from life into death were fully immersed in these tubs, as if in meditative baptism. Uncomfortable at the prospect of getting into one of these tubs, I couldn't get the idea of not being able to breathe out of my head. Although these souls had no need of breath while underneath the water, I turned to the man in charge. "Is the water too warm for a heart condition?" I asked. Allowing me to feel that the water was lukewarm, he asked me wait my turn.

Scheduled to go last, I watched the others immerse themselves. While meditating under the water, the souls of the people began to display and be surrounded by inexplicable aspects of the Trinity. Dumbfounded by the beauty of this transformative process, I remained unable to understand it.

Before I could enter into the waters, my soul was taken from this fascinating border-world.

****

Exiting an elevator, the doors opened and one of my deceased grandparents was waiting for me. Without saying a word, he led me towards a truck, planning to take me on a drive somewhere. Noticing a troubled look upon his face, it appeared that it was unclear at this juncture whether or not I was going to die, and he did not wish for me to die. Worried about his great-grandchildren, he continued his duty despite his displeasure at my fate.

As time would progress, I learned more about my condition, and how to remain more stable. Keeping myself away from the crisis of imminent death, I learned how to balance activity and rest, so that I wouldn't visit death's shores quite so frequently.

****

Had a very involved experience with many of my dead relatives where they didn't seem very happy with me. It seemed that they felt I had misjudged a family member unfairly, and upon reflection, I felt very ashamed. Taking steps immediately to repair this damage, it was my hope that my relatives could forgive me at some point.

****

Looking up from my bed, I realized that I was now lying upon it underneath the stars. Grandpa appeared sitting at the foot of my bed in a small wooden chair, watching quietly. In the distance, we could see through the walls of the house as Andy and his family were looking for an outfit for me to wear for my funeral. Grandpa remained silent while I lay convalescing from my latest brush with death.

****

Surrounded with an aura of yellowish-white light, my old friend who'd died in a car accident had appeared. Although surrounded with such brightness, I'd remembered many experiences I'd had since his death which had indicated to me that his purification was incomplete. Demonic tendencies which he struggled with in life had been shown to me in his death.

Laying near-death, he said, "Don't worry, you can come with me." Shocking myself, I was surprised that my response did not shock him. Reaching his hand to me, I replied, "Please do not take offense, my dear friend, but when I do indeed cross over, it is my intention to go directly to Jesus. Did Jesus send you? Do you intend to take me straight to the realm where Jesus reigns?"

Lowering his hand, unsurprised by my discernment, he began to slowly disappear without saying another word.

****

As people prayed for me, I began to experience visions of roses. Singular roses, tapestries of roses, gardens of roses, and they all seemed to precede a recovery from a close brush with death. One night, Mother Teresa stood over my bed for several hours, waiting patiently for me, as if she had something for me to do.

****

My body had been placed in a white casket inlaid with gold and taken outside to the driveway. As my spirit waited inside, I spoke to Andy. "I think it's inappropriate for my casket to remain in the front yard. You'll never live this down with the neighbors if you don't quickly call somebody to pick it up." Timidly, he agreed, but mentioned he'd put it there because he didn't want the kids to see it.

Another night, my soul was taken to visit a decomposition doctor, who measured my body parts as they were now, so that they might be compared to a future time when I might be decomposing. In this way, they could monitor the process. During this experience, I was given to look in the mirror and take note of the fact that my hair was turning gray and squalid like that of a corpse, although this was not yet the case in real life. And much like a corpse, there was very little hair hanging onto what was remaining of my skull.
****

Standing before me as a radiant beauty indescribable in human terms, the Blessed Virgin Mary had greeted me as I'd left my body, watching my physical form lying down with my youngest son below. For a moment, it seemed that I might be experiencing death, but the Virgin directed me to observe my sweet baby boy.

Coming from inside of his spirit, I could see a stirring, as if he were perhaps praying for me in some way. Inside of him, I could see my two daughters and their prayers for me also.

Suddenly, a very thin light beam came forth from his body directly into my soul, pulling it back into my body. Knowing this beam was the result of my children's prayers, the Virgin allowed me to witness this event over and over again. Showing me that I was not incorrect in determining that my situation was quite tentative, she conveyed that I was still alive because of the prayers of my children.

Wearing a veil of dark blue with stars around her head, her face was filled with light and appeared pale because of the effect of the light coming through her. Upon her breast she wore a lighter blue robe which contrasted that of her outer garment. "Thank you for allowing me to see you," I said excitedly, "I am honored." Without words, she raised her hands as I was sent back to my body.
****

CHAPTER THREE
Death and Afterlife Experience of a Friend, In Our Weakness God is Our Strength, Rocket Trail, My Friend Intercedes for Me, Three Scheduled to Die, Heavenly Help in the Night.

****

Standing amidst a tannish pink horizon, I came across a very close friend of mine who held incorrect views regarding spiritual matters and issues upon the ground. (Having been terminally ill for several years, she was close to death.) Believing herself completely, she was unable to get outside of herself and her distorted thinking long enough to discern that she had misperceived and misinterpreted various aspects regarding the spirit and God, and thus, various aspects of occurrences within her own life. As a result, she actually had incorrect perceptions of events within her own life; believing things to be true which were not, believing things not to be true which indeed had been so. As I explained this to her, she looked at me with a blank and confused expression upon her face, because she was so distorted she couldn't even comprehend that her false views were not true.

Sweeping my hands into the sky, I called to Jesus for assistance, as He parted the skies to reveal the heavens. As the entire horizon opened and the heavens appeared, eternal truths were depicted to her energetically. Although demonstrated clearly, she still could not *see* them because of her own biases and delusions which had actually prevented her from being cognizant of the parting of the heavens which lay in magnificence before her.

Remaining in her delusion, unable to *see* the tremendous truth which the Lord had deigned to show her, I observed the tragedy of those who remain unable to hear the truth because of their attachment to false views.

Although I had no idea at the time, her appointed time to die would come within two weeks, and afterwards, she would share with me her after-death journey.

****

After entering the retreat center, I was taken to a back room and guided to look upon a large statuesque mountain of stone outside the window. As the sides of the mountain were steep, there was no vegetation and it was brownish red. Twelve pillars stood from the top of the mountain about twenty feet high.

Inherently, I knew the mountain represented death and the pillars, God. When I reached the pillars, the Lord would meet me there and take me the rest of the way. But in my weakened condition, I could see no feasible way to get to the top and was exhausted just looking at it. Noticing that there were three people in the room with me, I observed an old woman with long gray hair wearing a night robe, a younger woman who came to me and handed me a small porcelain angel, and a quiet priest who appeared to be reading quietly while sitting in the corner. Turning to accept the porcelain angel, something inexplicable happened.

The priest tapped my shoulder as I again looked in the direction of the mountain to see what he might have to tell me. Miraculously, the mountain had been painted from top to bottom in the colors of red, orange and brown. "I understand that you need some help in accomplishing your task," he said. Energetically, it was if I had already ascended the mountain and reached the summit because he had painted it. This is inexplicable, I know. "When the Lord tells you that its time for you to travel towards death and reach that summit," he said, "you won't have to do it alone. He will send help."

****

An angelic being stood before me holding an image of my heart in her hand. Allowing me to observe its appearance, I was able to note that it was large and thin. Without warning and before my eyes, the heart exploded and burst. "This is the way you will probably die," she said. (Since that time, however, progress has been made on size and thinning.)

****

Beyond words described how I felt when I found out that my closest friend had died suddenly in the night. Although she was terminally ill, she was expected to live possibly many more years and all were taken quite by surprise, especially her family.

Having met her years before at a book-signing, we became fast friends. Early in our relationship, she told me of a dream she had in ancient Egypt, where she was young girl of about eight, and I was her grandfather, a member of a priestly class who worked on the pyramids. Most profoundly, she recalled in her dream the moment of his death. Lying on the ground, the little girl was kneeling at his side crying. Grandpa said to her, "Wherever you go, wherever you may travel, I'll be there. And when you're ready to learn the mysteries of the spirit, I will teach you. Whatever time and place that may be." She repeatedly told me that she knew from this experience that the time had come, and we had been reunited so that I might be able to teach her of this world beyond. Because of her intensive belief and emotional tie to this experience, she always called me grandpa, which I enjoyed immensely. (However difficult it was to explain this to others, since we were both women of similar age.)

Our union was predestined, and our parting seemed to also be so. For two nights after her death, I didn't feel her presence at all, and this disturbed me to no end. Because of unusual circumstances at the scene of her death, there was a question of whether or not she overused her prescription drugs, and this made the loss even more painful. On day three, however, she came to me in an afternoon dream. My spirit was looking out the back window of my house where a huge brown wooden table appeared with two chairs. Immediately feeling her presence, I felt a peacefulness which gave me serenity regarding her status. Conveying to me, she said, "I will be sitting down and talking with you *very* soon." And then she disappeared.

Again feeling her presence that night, she took me to an astral computer screen. Immediately, she went toward a web-site which was called '*accidental death.*' Conveying to me that she had been in such a state of severe agony that she had taken pain meds earlier, and when she awoke in the night, she didn't remember that she had taken them already and took some more. Apparently, she took too much.

Taking me to a monastery somewhere in the heavens the following night, she immediately introduced me to an older Chinese monk. Because she had been Buddhist in her lifetime, she'd been taken to this monastery which offered a combination of Buddhism and Catholicism. Frantic, I was somewhat afraid for her, although she was without any doubt in a good place. Approaching me, she said, "I've entered into a state of purgation and am now in need of prayers to help me through this process. Can you pray things like the Rosary or the Divine Mercy for my soul, and ask my husband to learn them also so he can pray for me, too." It was interesting that she was asking for Catholic prayers, because she'd been a Buddhist.

The Chinese monk explained, "Because she suffered from some level of mental illness stemming from severe childhood abuse, she's beginning her purgation with the aspects of mental illness she had faced during life. Many of the things she believed to be true were falsehoods, and are now being demonstrated energetically in a manner which is undeniable in its truth and unnerving to a soul when it just begins." Promising to pray, I began a quest to get everybody I knew to pray for her, but especially our family and her husband.

Two nights later, I was honored to witness the power of such prayers as my dear friend stood upon a large rock amongst a desert oasis. All alone at this time, you couldn't see anything for hundreds of miles. Aloneness filled the air and my very special pal was sitting in a lotus position on a rock continuing the purging process as a total of six screens were coming out of her spontaneously and consecutively. Three screens were on each side of her body, lined one on top of the other, and the images within them changed continually. Much like watching a disc download, various difficult memories, terrifying moments, and incorrect thinking as a result of such experiences were coming out of her spirit very peacefully and with calm. Completely at ease during this process, she no longer displayed agitation or fear about this purgation.

"Thank you for the prayers you've offered on my behalf," she conveyed, "they helped me to get from the state of agitation two nights ago to a peaceful purgation, and an acceptance of purification." Nodding my honor, I turned to go.

In preparing for my own death, I had also prepared for hers. Now our special union had created an energetic link-up between us which had brought about a unique opportunity to explore the journey *after* death. God's ways are mysterious.
****

Absorbed in prayer, I had been begging for my life due to a serious setback in my condition. Drifting into the world beyond, my spirit came into a brightly lit bookstore sitting inside a mountain oasis. Although I didn't see Him, I felt the distinct presence of the Lord Jesus Christ who proceeded to communicate. "Okay," He conveyed, "I am going to help you to get better again, and with the extra time I am going to give you, I am going to give you work to do."

Directing my attention to several books lined up one behind the other on top of a shelf, I noticed that they were written by me. Although my current manuscript was one large text at this time, he indicated that it was to be broken up. Each of the books I'd written taught of a particular spiritual concept, and together, they became unified into a clear cohesive understanding. Intrigued that some of these concepts were Eastern, Christ reiterated His sanction of my work in uniting the East and the West.

Nodding my understanding and excitement, He conveyed, "You *will* be healed at this *time*, but the road ahead will be *very* rough." Speaking of my latest downfall, rather than a healing of my condition as a whole, I agreed to His terms, I felt peace surround me. In this serenity, the presence of my recently deceased friend became felt, as she encouraged me to fight and live.

Thus I would continue to follow the road of my fate, being prepared to live . . . and to die . . . at any given moment.
****

After preparing for my funeral 'in the spirit,' I was sent to spend the evening with a group of souls who had already crossed over to watch my future funeral from above.

Commenting on the messages I'd written for loved ones and the music I'd selected, they said, "We really like what you've chosen to do for your funeral because of its uplifting nature for those you will leave behind." "Thanks," I replied.

Having selected a series of musical renditions with three themes, they were: 1) How the heart of our existence is Jesus Christ and our lives are really about Him, 2) Great praise and thanksgiving to the Lord, and 3) finally, the continuing spiritual journey of the soul after death and the never-ending eternal nature of every soul. Messages to my family and friends were those of love, joy and release, with the assurance that the Lord had generously prepared me for my transition and of my continued watchfulness over their lives.

Enjoying the funeral service, at the end I was instructed to play my guitar and sing the song I had written years before, 'To Retrieve a Golden Angel.' Ending in quiet reflection, our joyous celebration filled me with peace in knowing that I could now focus on other things with the knowledge that I'd prepared for my death well.
****

Appearing very excited, my deceased friend had come to show me some of her experiences in the after-life, and she was anxious that I record them.

Journeying through death had taken her into yet a new phase of travel wherein she was no longer in the confines of a monastery undergoing purgation, but had moved into a period of spiritual discovery which had now moved beyond the bounds of her Buddhist and my Catholic faith. Traveling now in Universal knowledge, she was learning of the mechanism of the evolutionary journey of souls. As she began conveying to me, she repeatedly mentioned the number twelve in regards to her journey, but I didn't understand. (It occurred to me that it might have something to do with the twelve pillars on top of the mountain of crossing.)

But because of my excitement, I could remember no more of what she had said. Shouting towards her, I said, "It's you, you're here to talk to me!" Smiling, she surrendered to my inability to hear her further, but she was able to convey to me a sense of peace regarding her children. Having a certain 'foreknowledge' about their future, it gave her total and indescribable peace about their welfare, although she did convey that it would take a lot of time.
****

Walking towards the horrible scene in the spiritual realm, a certain peacefulness came over my soul. Allowing me to look upon the dead body of my friend, the Lord had done so for the purpose of deeper understanding of the meaning of life's end. Blue and surrounded in vomit, it was very hard to look at.

Hearing her voice above me, she called me by a different name which intrigued me. "Mary," she said, "Don't be afraid to pray, don't be afraid to ask about me." Renewing my covenant to pray for her, I knew that she was also making reference to my fear of the mystery of death.

Lying on the back porch covered in the signs of my own impending doom and decomposition, worms, maggots, dirt and various molds were attached to my legs as I tried to scrape them off with a large comb.

Walking down a valley road which represented the various directions that my life had taken, I cautiously walked towards the distant town which represented my present life. Observing several junctures of that life upon the way, there was a certain smallness to my life, a simplicity which encompassed appreciation and understanding of the little things which give life meaning. Clearly, I had followed my path in life which included a deep investigation into the matters of the spirit, but a contrasting goodness was shown to me. In order to provide a balance for those who read my writings whose lives are meant to serve a different, but just as exalted, cause, I witnessed many areas of our world which allowed a soul to be in the forefront of scientific advancement. Witnessing, those in medicine, geology, biology, physics, mathematics, astronomy, computer technology, and every other field of science, my spirit felt the grand importance of these callings, and the great expansion that participating in such advancement allows a soul, and the gift it offers to the evolution of humanity. Great importance filled the air and surrounded the souls of those engaged in such works! Science and spirit should not be separated, for the knowledge of both combines wisdom from two worlds (physical and spirit) into one; worlds encompassing very different laws of existence.

Off in the distance, I saw what appeared to be a rocket trail going from the ground into deep space somewhere in the area of my present home. Looking somewhat like a cloudburst, it resembled that of the smoke and steam you might witness when watching a rocket being launched, except that it bore the color of a deep brilliant pink. This rocket trail didn't diminish over the passing minutes, but remained as a testament to that which my soul was bade to witness.

Speaking above my head, a man's voice began to speak of the journey of life and death as I continued walking towards the rocket trail. "We live our lives from day to day as if it will go on forever," he said, "but then, all of a sudden, we have a death date to carve upon our tombstone, and our life is instantly over." Remembering my friend, I nodded in agreement as he then conveyed the possibility that my life might be over soon, as well. Giving me a time frame which I would not see the end of, I became very sad at this realization, but also knew from experience that terminal illness provides a variety of possible death options, some of which may be able to be avoided, and others . . . which cannot. At this time, I didn't know which kind of death date this might be, but made note of it within my soul.

Looking off at the distant rocket trail, I instantly knew its meaning. Representing the ascension of my soul into heaven, it was a reminder of what the heavenly world is truly about . . . GALACTICA!
****

In a moment, I was with my friend who had recently parted this world as she was leading my soul into the home she had been living in while still upon the Earth. Wishing to share with me several things, she began by expressing her sadness that her family was still renting their home. Through her purgation process, she had become aware of the fact that her indiscriminate spending had given rise to this condition which had prevented her family from saving for the future or buying their own home. Leading me to the medicine cabinet, she pointed out to me the many medications she had taken for very legitimate and intense pain. Despite this legitimacy, she expressed her sorrow at having used such dangerous drugs so indiscriminately and without due caution. Taking me to the kitchen, she opened the cabinets and refrigerator doors, showing me some of the unhealthy foods she had eaten all too regularly during her lifetime. Expressing sorrow at her lack of discretion in such matters, she now realized that she had placed her body at more risk because of unhealthy habits.

As we finished our task in the kitchen, she handed me a curly straw, telling me she had used a lot of straws to drink during her life, and wished to give this one to me. As we were both laughing, I took the straw and placed it on the counter. (Her husband later confirmed that she had a special curly straw that she used for the last few years of her life.)

Finally, she directed me to the bookshelf where she guided my eye to a set of old Catholic books. Although I didn't realize it at the time, she was guiding me to a gift she wished to give me, a set of classics I'd wanted for years which would show up the very next day at a thrift store for almost nothing. At the moment, however, I just acknowledged them on the shelf.

Nodding to her, I knew our time for parting had come. Promising to share these very important words with her husband, her presence disappeared in a wisp of wind. Shortly before her death, she had been shown the truth, but could not see it because of her own distorted perceptual thinking. Because she was now seeing that which she had been unable to in the past, I was very proud of her. Purgatory had been good to my friend, and she was beginning to understand a great many things.

****

Pulling my stretcher up the road, Andy was trying to bring me home, but my limbs were heavy and my body weak. Unable to move, a caring neighbor helped him to pull my stretcher up a hill. Embarrassed, I surrendered to it and let it go. Moments later, I woke in a hospital in an environment which felt so real, I truly thought this was physically happening . . . although it was not happening in the physical world.

A nurse was attending to my sick body, "You've been unconscious for three days," she said, "under normal circumstances, we would not release you from the hospital like this. But because you have children and they aren't able to see you in this ward, we are going to send you home so you will be able to see them." Taking care of various tasks in the room, I nodded. "Before you can go, you have to see your doctor one last time." Expecting my cardiologist to enter the room, I was shocked when my priest came instead and referred to himself as my doctor. Immediately thinking of last rites, I wondered if it were possible that he'd come to impart spiritual healing.

Before I could figure this out, I was instantaneously flying out of my body down a hallway in the morgue. Listening to various conversations of doctors along the way, I noticed the bodies which were laid out for autopsy in each room.

****

Blissfully taken away, I found myself standing in a room with my dear friend who'd died recently, as she was all aglow in her new garment of sheer white. Happiness exuded from her face as I ran towards her, tackling and sacking her in a fierce hug. As we fell to the floor, we laughed and hugged together in a joyous reunion. At this time, I noticed that her husband and two boys were in the room, but unable to see her. Pointing out to her husband where she was standing, I followed her as she took me towards a bookshelf.

Several items were upon the shelf for me to peruse, the first of which was a hymnal similar to the one I'd written with my first book, 'The Mysteries of the Redemption.' Pointing inside, she showed me a song she had written for me which spoke voluminously of our deep friendship and her love for me. Honor and bliss poured forth from me as she handed me the book, saying she wanted me to have it. Although her husband was unable to see our interactions, at this moment he had a similar inspiration, and also asked me to take the book, because he believed his wife would've liked me to have it.

Directing my attention to a small Buddhist book which spoke about saints, she said, "Don't buy into all the stories written about the saints, because some of them were portrayed as being more perfect than they truly were. Doing this will prevent you from accomplishing your own work, because it requires you to speak in opposition to certain established doctrines."

Showing me the Gnostic texts of the Christians, ancient texts written by followers of Christ which are not included in the New Testament, she also had the Apocryphal books and other books which were considered heretical.

Looking upon them, I *felt* their true holiness, and as I held them, they energetically reinforced my purpose which would take me outside of established dogmatic parameters. "You must do it! You mustn't fail the Lord!" she said, fiercely adamant about my destiny.

Pulling away, she directed my attention to her children for whom she had expressed concern recently. Unwilling to talk about her death openly, she had said that they needed to express their deep grief.

Everything suddenly became awkward, because I didn't know what to do to help them. A sudden inspiration led me to run towards a bed, where I began pounding with my fists and shouting, "THIS SUCKS! THIS SUCKS!" Asking them if they'd like to join me, they approached and we all began pounding on the bed and shouting out to the heavens our extreme dissatisfaction at the fate of their dear mother and my wonderful friend. "It's important for there to be humor involved in the grief process," she said.

Turning to one of her kids, I casually made a joke about seeing a bug on him, and used the opportunity to start tickling him uncontrollably. As they laughed, my friend began to direct me towards her husband.

Expressing concern over my illness and potential fate, he felt very badly about our shared fates. As I thanked him for his caring, I began to tell him that I had a strange feeling that God might be willing to give me another extension on my life, and as I did this, my friend again appeared behind him with a great big smile on her face. Knowing what she meant to say, I was very much aware that she had been interceding for me before the throne of God. Although it wasn't clear yet what the answer might be, it seemed that another extension on my existence might be in the works.

Conveying to me a deep sense of importance regarding my work, she bade me to know that she was now helping me to accomplish it from the other side. Another smile lit up her face as she expressed gratitude regarding the painting I had done of her experiences in purgation. "The first few weeks were very difficult for me, but I am now more at peace and able to enjoy the fact that I'm no longer in physical pain." In her eyes, I could see the pain of separation from her children, but she was coming to terms with it. At that moment, she disappeared.

Because my latest death date was coming up within the week (and I would surpass it due to her prayers), I found it a most amazing thing to witness that the dead pray for the living, and that their prayers can be efficacious if the Lord so deigns. Receiving the extension, my limbo was not to be lifted as my heart function had begun decreasing again.

****

Joining two older men we gathered together in a solitary room as the angels explained that we were all currently scheduled to die around the same time. One of these men was the soul who had been saved from condemnation to hell. Because of this intercession, his destiny had been altered, but he had a great deal of time left to do in purgatory because of his continuing angry nature. Although he had not been violent during his life, he'd been very mean, at times. Having an angry nature would give him an extended journey through purgation, although what had condemned him to hell was his total and complete disinterest in the Lord during his life which he acknowledged at the time of the battle for his soul.

The other man had also led a questionable life, but his faith in the Lord had saved him, and his soul was not in danger of hell. Purgatory would also be prepared for him, but despite his bad life, it seemed his time there would be shorter than the other man because of his true love for the Lord. In his youth, he'd not only engaged in anger, but violence. But in his old age, he was mellow and passive, no longer the man he had once been. On his face, you could see his fear and respect of the Lord, which had helped his plight.

Leaving the room quickly, the angry man did not wish to communicate with us, so I turned my attention to the other, who was greatly afraid of death. Suffering from an extended terminal illness, the angry man was aware of his eventual fate, but the other man had no reason to believe he was close to death before this pronouncement, other than his advanced age. Death would be sudden and unexpected for him, and he was truly terrified.

Approaching him, I placed my arms around him and said, "We needn't be afraid. At this time, we must think of our heavenly homeland." Beginning to sing a traditional operatic aria version of the 'Our Father' prayer, I sang quietly, "Our Father . . . Which art in Heaven . . . Hallowed be Thy name . . . " Slowly joining me, we sang together. "Thy Kingdom Come!!!!!!!! Thy Will be done!!!!!!!!! On Earth . . . as it is in Heaven."

Calming down significantly, my spirit's attention was drawn to members of my extended family who had not shown much sadness over my imminent demise. As they appeared in the room, they noticed my deteriorating status, and in this realm experienced their full grief before me. Overwhelmed with sorrow for me, I was truly stunned! Because of the way they had behaved in regards to my condition, I had quite honestly perceived that some of them really didn't have any feelings about my death. A great gift, this moment allowed me to see that, despite their own unique ways of handling grief, they did truly love me and were very saddened by my imminent parting from this world. Moved, I began to disappear from this realm, awaking again in my physical body.

"Do not wait for death
To reveal the great mystery;
If you know not your Heavenly Father
While your feet tread the dusty soil,
There shall be naught but shadows for thee
In the life that is to come.
Here and now
Is the mystery revealed.
Here and now
Is the curtain lifted.
Be not afraid, O man!
Lay hold of the wings of the Angel of Eternal Life,
And soar into the paths of the stars,
The moon, the sun, and the endless Light,
Moving around in their
Revolving circle forever,
And fly toward the Heavenly Sea
Of Eternal Life."
The Essene Gospel of Peace, Book Two, Page 52 – 53, (Translator: Edmond Bordeaux
Szekely, Words of Christ)

****

Sitting quietly in the hospital room where she now received treatment and help for her mental illness, my departed friend was wearing her garments of white and staring off into the distance with great sorrow piercing her face. Family surrounded her, those of the living and those of the dead, as they had gathered this evening to visit and give her comfort and support. Pointing to an older man and woman in the room, she said "'Mom and Dad' are here with me." These were her Aunt and Uncle, who had been much like parents to her.

Two cowboys were hanging around, although not in the center of the family fray, one of which was her departed brother, who had died about two years prior to her death. Although the two looked much alike, I didn't know who the other man might be, but was later able to confirm that another brother had died during infancy, and the two had since reunited beyond the veil.

A succession of children came forward walking in succession in front of my friend. Five or six of these souls appeared before me, each jumping successively into a pool of water . . . knowing that they were going to drown. Each of them had made this sacrifice willingly to serve a greater good which would come of their gift. Beginning to wonder if these souls were the babies which my friend had miscarried during her life, I recalled how she had lost about that many pregnancies to miscarriage because of an incompetent cervix. Finally, the doctors found a way to help her be capable of carrying to term, and she had her two living sons.

Given a special opportunity to speak with one of the children, a small, blonde little girl with pigtails sat upon a chair manifesting at about the age of four. Immediately, I learned her name was Molly, and we began a lengthy conversation. "What do you do in heaven?" I asked, "Do you pursue careers?" Quietly, she said, "No, you just follow your heart at any given moment as God leads you." Nodding my understanding, a nurse approached, allowing me to hold and rock one of the other babies while I continued to talk with her. "Can you tell me," I asked boldly, "the time in which I will die, or that of my husband, children or my friend's husband?" Turning to the side, I realized immediately that I'd asked a forbidden question. "Is that something you are not allowed to tell those of us in the world of the living?" As she turned her gaze back to mine, she nodded, 'Yes.'

Now my attentions were turned to my friend, who remained despondent, sad and quiet. Conveying many things, I sat next to her and held her as her sorrow was expressed. Having watched from above to witness the consequences of various actions she had taken in life, she was learning about the true impact of those decisions on those that remained behind.

In particular, she had left behind a financial disaster for her family to clean up. In her newfound state, she was able to see the line of energy in the choices she'd made which had led to this condition, and was feeling 'convicted' of spirit, so to speak. Although she was accountable for the damage she'd left behind, she was less accountable than she might have been had she not suffered some level of mental illness.

True delusion was involved in some of these choices she'd made, and it was only at this time in her after-death journey that she was able to truly understand the ramifications of some of these choices which had been made so haphazardly during her life.

Expressing great concern for one of her children upon the Earth, her manner of accidental death was of concern to her and the heavens because she had modeled to him a certain way of handling difficulties in life which could lead him to handle future problems in a similar way. Great sorrow filled her in this regard, for she hadn't realized that this issue she'd had regarding the use of prescription drugs, could indeed be passed along to her children. Giving pause to great warning, she asked that I convey this to her husband, so that he could be extremely watchful in preventing this sort of fruition from ever taking place.

Because she was now in the heavenly spheres, despite her status in a mental hospital, she shared with me that her capacity to love had been greatly increased and that she hoped her husband could know that she loved him even more in this new place than she had been capable of in the world. Further, she expressed her hope that he could someday offer her his forgiveness for the financial disasters she had left behind, and that he might be able to separate in his mind her love for him, from some of the very harmful choices she had made. Asking for understanding of her compromised mental state during life, she made clear that she had truly been mentally ill.

A great deal of her sorrow was generated from the fact that she knew that some things can be undone, and others only endured. Many of the problems she'd left behind could only be endured. Because she'd crossed the great divide in such an unfortunate and untimely manner, she felt a certain impotence in being unable to assist in cleaning up the mess she had left behind. It's always easier to deal with our issues and problems while still in the world than to wait until we are no longer of it, and thus, no longer able to affect it in a full and complete manner. Purpose exists in this life, and it is best to fulfill it while still in this world. Fulfilling it from across the divide is much more difficult. Walking alongside her family, it was vital that she assist in helping to resolve these matters, even though she must now do so from beyond the grave.

Finally, she conveyed a final few words regarding her practice of Buddhism during her life. Far from being a conviction of the religion itself, she convicted herself of not allowing her practice to become penetrating. Becoming more of an intellectual exercise, rather than a process of transformation, she'd actually allowed it to become a crutch in the assessment of her life. Much like the other person of whom I'd witnessed earlier, who had not allowed the truths of his religious practice to penetrate into his personal issues in life and the actual things he was doing, and she was confessing that this had been a fault she shared.

Buddhism, ironically, is a religion of renunciation and could have very adequately provided her with the tools to conquer the issue of misuse of financial means. Separating spiritual or religious practice from the actual life is a misunderstanding of the true purpose and destination of Earthly life. Religious practice cannot be separated from the actual life, because our actual life is the *true practice*. Religious practice, of whatever faith it may be, all centers upon transformation from within. If your practice is true, your faults and issues will naturally arise from it as a result of your devotion.

In many respects, this true practice leads to a continual process of 'convictions' of the spirit wherein the soul witnesses the view of its soul from the heavenly spheres, rather from the limited point of view of itself. By doing so, it recognizes those cravings and fetters as the Buddhists would say, or the sins and vice as Christianity might term it, which linger within. Issues arise because they are the fetters which tie a soul to the Earth, matters for which mortal realms have been created to serve. Souls do not part from this realm until those issues have been resolved in a mortal context. So, as you can see from this, there is a purpose in this life of which you must fulfill while you remain in this realm . . . otherwise, you will return until it has been resolved within the context of time. Timelessness is not the proper context in which this particular purification of a soul may be completed.

As we hugged tightly, I was aware that my visit was about to end with my dearly departed friend. Sadness filled my soul, although at the same time I felt a joy at her newfound wisdom and understanding of that which is true. But watching this process can be a double-edged sword, because truth is only attained through the suffering which comes to us when we deign to see things as they really are, rather than what has proven to be convenient for our conscious minds to peruse.

Because we witness our own delusions which have caused suffering for others, there is sorrow and regret. But we must never forget that it is the seed of sorrow and remorse which are the soil and earth upon which every spiritual transformation takes place, and without it, the grandiose heights cannot be reached.

So we gather in sorrow together as a human family to comfort this wonderful soul who now looks upon her life with regret, so that we may assist in this grand process which leads to purification. With this knowledge we may go in peace, because sometimes what is best for us to know is not the most pleasant thing for us to hear. But the unpleasantness lasts for but a moment as a soul begins to generate true loving compassion penetrating to the core of the soul. Penetration leads a soul to harmlessness, wherein a soul truly seeks only the good of all sentient beings, and further, has the clarity of vision to pursue it in every action, thought, word or deed.

No journey worth taking is without flaw or difficulty. Smiling at her, she remained quiet, but seemed content in the knowledge that she had been able to express to her family her love . . . and her sorrow.

About a week later, she again appeared to me wearing her white garment sitting behind a table looking at a book. Expressing her immense gratitude in having been able to share her sorrows with her husband on the Earth, her soul was able to experience peace as a result of having been able to do so.
****

Having been a very normal day, there was no reason to suspect that it might be 'the one.' Waking in an unfamiliar place, I was lying in a hospital bed completely unaware of how I had gotten there. Quickly, it became clear that I wasn't feeling very well. "How did I get here?" I asked the nurse standing beside my bed, "What happened?" He calmly replied, "Oh, you wouldn't be expected to remember that. You ran into problems while you were sleeping and you passed out." "Well, what happened?" I asked again. Although they refused to be more specific, it was very clear that something had happened with my heart while I was sleeping which was apparently quite serious; serious enough to force my soul to cross over into this borderworld.

For several moments, I became quite anxious, wondering if I had experienced sudden death and was irretrievably dead, but found fairly quickly that my spirit had been sent to this borderland hospital in order to receive spiritual assistance to *prevent* my crossing over . . . at least, as of yet.

Hooked up to several I.V.'s, my spirit remained there for four days, although when I returned I came back the next morning chronologically. "Don't feel bad about having to come here," the nurse said, "you may need to come back here many times during your illness, because it is necessary to keep you alive and may very well give you more time." They seemed to know how long I had left to live, and although I got the impression that I may only have, at most, a few years, those few years appeared to be quite important in the larger scheme of things, and thus, they wished to intervene in any way they could to insure that I didn't expire prematurely.

When they were finished with me, I felt significantly better. But when I attempted to return to the body, I found resistance. Experiencing severe chest pain, my heart and breathing were going very fast and it was pounding so hard it felt like it might explode. Making several efforts to return, the angels and nurses from the astral hospital intervened with my physical body and were eventually able to shut down the problematic behaviors within my body. Shaken up, I went about my day.
****

CHAPTER FOUR
Being Beat up in the Eucharistic Tabernacle, Being Truthful About the Deceased to Allow Closure, Expression of Regrets, Cathedral of my Soul, Meeting my Deceased Friends New Spiritual Teacher, Life Review, Near Death.

****

Standing before me was a large emblem of green, a great expanse of wings emerged from its sides, and the centerpiece held what resembled a family crest with a very prominent eagle inside. Representing the various layers of the soul, it conveyed the importance of awakening these layers while remaining upon the Earth. As I gazed upon this intricate symbol, a melody and words began to replay over and over again in obvious reference to the awakening process of the soul beneath the soul. "Born beneath the soul, born beneath the soul, born beneath the soul, oh oh oh, the soul is waiting." For a moment, I felt the tragic nature of the human soul, in that so many remain asleep on every level throughout their lives, missing the sole purpose of their existence in this realm. Sad it is, how sad . . .

****

Chaos had ravaged our part of the Earth as the most extensive wildfires in hundreds of years continued to burn very near to our home. As we were evacuated amidst the tumult, my heart did not respond well to the strain, and although we had been honored to be taken into the home of a stranger who accepted our whole family during the crisis, it felt very clear that I was in deep jeopardy of losing my life. Two days prior to being evacuated, I'd been informed that my heart was declining.

Appearing to me in the usual white dress with a globe of light shining from her heart, my deceased friend appeared as my heart was pounding rapidly during sleep. "If you don't want to join me any sooner than you're meant to," she said, "you need to get out of here and go to a hotel." Having tried to keep up appearances with our hosts, I was wearing myself ragged, and a hotel room would allow me to 'direct traffic' from the center of the room and stay in bed, rather than being required to socialize while I was doing so badly.

But now that she stood before me and I had an opportunity to question her, I grabbed her and asked, "Why did this happen now?" We'd all wondered about this, because she'd taken an overdose. Embarrassed, she didn't want to respond, but I insisted. "You *need* to tell me this!" I said with urgency. Quietly, with reserve and embarrassment, she said, "Because some people and I weren't getting along." Having been confronted with her spending issues which were driving the family to bankruptcy, she simply chose not to deal with them. In doing so, she dealt a death blow to herself and her family in a momentary whim. Able to call it 'accidental' because of her mental illness, the status of her delusions made her choice less intentioned in the eyes of God.

That day, we transferred to a hotel, and I believe it saved my life. Several more days into our evacuation, my heart was still very traumatized but making small progress daily towards stability. As the fire raged for weeks more, the stress of the situation would continue.

On the night we returned home, my spirit was taken to witness a huge, 200 foot high Eucharistic Tabernacle shining in gold amidst a barren desert. Inside of the Eucharistic Tabernacle where the host is usually placed, I saw myself being beat up by an unknown force. "The suffering and violence being done to your soul at this time, has purpose within a divine context," a voice said. 'Impermanence,' I thought.

****

Meeting my deceased friend, her husband was feeling tremendous guilt in trying to come to terms with their relationship during life and now after, because he felt that he would be dishonoring her if he was simply honest about the good and bad within their lives.

Coming to me in the morning, she didn't speak. Beginning to talk to her, I said, "You know, my friend, that the only way your husband is going to be able to get through this and process it successfully is if you allow him to reflect upon your lives together and the manner of your death honestly and truthfully, with the confidence that *you* still know that he loves you and honors your memory. Do you think you could give him permission to process this experience with this kind of honesty, knowing that by him doing so it will not make him love you less or make your importance to him change in any way?" Very calmly, she nodded, 'Yes' and sent a rush of energy through me, because she very much wanted him to be able to get through this, despite the fact that reflecting honestly might sometimes be painful or not paint her in the best of lights. "I accept full responsibility for everything," she said, "and tell him I love him . . . and I know he loves me." Pausing, she finished, "By thinking of me as I truly was, the good with the bad, he will honor our special relationship as it relates to eternity."

With a rush of energy, she was gone.

****

Honored to encounter my deceased friend, she came with urgency to explain several issues to my yearning spirit. Because she wished to convey several things to her husband, he sat with us in the room but was unable to see her. Conveying to him immediately her words as soon as she expressed them to me, she addressed several issues. Firstly, she loved us both and was very sorry. Secondly, she was now taking very good care of herself, and regretted that she had not done so during life. Further, she regretted not doing all that she could to help herself in her condition. Because she had been unwilling to try non-drug therapies to help alleviate pain, she had become highly addicted to dangerous narcotic drugs. Altering her state of mind, she became less lucid, and this contributed to her untimely death. Although her condition could not have been cured or much alleviated by such things, they may have made her pain more tolerable, and her need for dangerous drugs would have diminished in part.

Attempting to discuss further the issue of the manner of her death, she refused to discuss it and began to disappear from the realm. "Okay, Okay!" I shouted, "We will not go there." Direct and with purpose, she had something disturbing to tell me.

As her soul remained in purgatory, she conveyed, "I must remain her a very long time, primarily because of the manner of my death. Although it is not a 'bad' place to be, and in a lot respect is similar to Earth, it is not good, either." Nodding, she continued, "Most of my time will be spent doing purgatory on Earth watching over those I left behind prematurely, and the rest will be spent in this realm which is always overcast because of the absence of the presence of God, the sun of light. This is my greatest suffering. Knowing that I could have made different choices which would have led to my immediate entrance into heaven and uniting with God is a continual torment to my soul." Vowing to continue to pray for her, we parted ways with a loving smile and my promise to her that I would continue looking over her family on Earth.

Before she left, she said, "I'm very jealous that it is so much easier for you to talk to my husband now, than it is for me. I miss being able to just sit and talk to him more than anything else."

****

Lying down in my home, the normal low ceiling no longer existed and in its place was a large, open cathedral ceiling composed of hundreds of blocks of crystal. Grandpa was standing there as I looked upon it. "You built that," he said, "it's pretty neat isn't it?" Understanding that it represented what I had built in the cathedral of my soul, I nodded, 'Yes.'

Grandpa and my Uncle were suddenly vacuuming the house, as I realized that they were trying to help us with our mess. Asking them to stop, I said, "Don't do that, we should clean our own mess up ourselves," but they ignored me. Feeling the sudden presence of my ancestors, I noticed that my little dog from my childhood had appeared. 'Joy' had died over twenty years prior. Picking her up, she seemed very happy to see me, and it was mutual. Becoming very caught up in my childhood puppy, I forgot about my relatives vacuuming the house for a few moments and just enjoyed my dog.
****

Unable to conceal my annoyance, I'd been taken to the top of the Himalayan Mountains. In my momentary spiritual blindness, I could only think of how difficult it would be to get back down these mountains in my weakened physical condition. Because of my circulation difficulties, I was always cold; and I was absolutely freezing in this location, despite the fact that I was in my spiritual body which usually feels temperature as constant.

Standing amongst a group of Buddhist monks, my deceased friend appeared. As the monks had indicated that I would be studying many ancient texts, different ones each week, my friend looked quite radiant in her white dress. Running towards her and hugging her, as I let her go, I looked deeply into her eyes and said, "I've missed you so much and I love you so much!" Smiling and reciprocating this emotion, she quickly gave me an indication that she had a purpose in being here. Beginning to guide me down the Himalayan Mountains, we walked through the wilderness as she conveyed energetically the wisdom for which she had come to impart. "Buddhism is a little bit more detached and unemotional about mistakes and incorrect views, and this will be helpful to you at this time." Energetically, the understanding of what she was saying pierced my core and I intensely grasped her meaning. "It seems like what you're trying to tell me is that Buddhism is a little bit less judgmental than Catholicism and that this approach might be helpful for me at this time." She nodded, 'Yes.'

As we continued down the mountain, it seemed like we had been together a very long time, and I began to be complacent in realizing that at some point, our visit would have to come to an end. Asking her how I was doing in the spiritual life, she said that I was doing something incorrectly, but she wouldn't be more specific. Making reference to the concept of the 'rapture,' she showed me an image of myself disappearing with just a little pile of clothes remaining, and then moments later, the pile of clothes disappeared just as quickly as had my body. Although I didn't grasp this at the moment, I later realized that this was a demonstration of 'emptiness,' a Buddhist quality I needed to revisit in the spiritual life.

Not understanding her meaning, I just gazed at her expectantly and again asked her to be more specific, to tell me directly what it was that I was doing wrong. But for some reason, it appeared that she did not have permission to do this, and as we got to the bottom of the mountain, another spirit had come to get her. Quietly, she walked away with this spirit and disappeared.
****

Spending the night on a ranch with my grandmother and an Uncle who had passed in the previous two years, another young man was sitting very casually in the kitchen. My Uncle kept referring to him as my 'other Uncle.' Finally, it occurred to me that my father had a brother who had died at the age of five after being struck by a truck while sledding. Excited and exuberant, my newfound Uncle and I went horseback riding along the Galactic mountain range which existed in the heavenly spheres. Expressing ambivalence about my presence, he shared, "Your condition is very unstable, but you are not necessarily destined to die quite yet. Perhaps if you were to be more careful, you could be assured that you would fulfill every moment of your life. If not, you might die prematurely." Understanding, we returned to the ranch house and I disappeared.

****

Coming across a wise old lady who was waiting for me in a house, my dearly departed friend sat across a table from her. Learning from this wise old woman who had gained much knowledge during her life in regards to matters of the spirit, the psychic gift and the path of virtue followed by religion, my friend was here as her pupil. My friend had always been interested in the psychic aspect during her life, but had neglected the path of virtue which is vital to true spiritual unfoldment.

As I awaited word of the purpose for my visit, the old wise woman opened her mouth with a joke. "It seems that your friend here thought she was older than she was," she said, as my friend chuckled under her breath, "she apparently still had some time left in her." Laughing at this reference to the part she had played in her own death, as I told my friend I was jealous that she was going to get to learn from this wise woman and I couldn't. As she seemed to be doing better and better, I was grateful to see her in this light.

Within moments, she was gone.

****

Undergoing a life review, my spirit walked the pathway of my life and looked over in a very detached manner all the places I'd lived, things I'd done and the general path I had taken this time around. Rather than being a *critical* life review, where my life was scrutinized in regards to things I'd done wrong and right, it was simply a *detached* 'looking over' of the general pattern of my life with no feelings expressed or felt about any events.

After undergoing this journey, my spirit was returned to the beginning and I watched again as another pathway was overlaid above my life. It was a pathway of ancient sacred texts which overlapped the path of my life. After observing the pathway of texts, it was conveyed that I would be returned to my life at the point I was currently occupying. Expecting to go back to the mountains, I was surprised to awaken on the shore, as waves crashed and fell in the sands before me. Observing the oncoming tide, I wondered if this would be an Earthly transition or a heavenly one.

****

Within a moment, my soul was looking upon the most spectacular light and I chuckled when I saw what lay within its confines. Although my dog, 'Joy', had died twenty years prior, she stood at the gateway to the light waiting for me, looking brilliant and joyous. Wishing to embrace my childhood pal who had been with me for about fifteen years, I knew that I could not, for doing so would irrevocably take me into the light and beyond the gateway of death. "I'm sorry," I said to my dog, "I can't come with you now because my kids are just too young."

In total understanding, she remained in the brilliance of the light as a book appeared in my hands. Looking at its title, it said, 'The Palace of Ancient Knowledge.' 'Oh, okay," I thought, as I gazed upon the cover art and its depiction of this grand place within the realms of ether.

As I gazed upon the page, it transformed itself into a written message from Christ, whose Presence could now be felt powerfully at my side. "You need to pray more for a quality of which you are lacking." Displayed on the page, the quality was written down and I recognized immediately that it was something for which I should strive. Despite this, I was unable to recall the quality upon return.

Led to a porch, I observed that the steps leading to it were of different heights. The one on the right was waist high and complete, and the one on the left was built only to the level of the bottom crossbeam. Immediately directing my attention to the one on the right, Christ conveyed, "This one represents your soul, and as you can see, it is complete." Directing my attention to the one on the left, He continued, "And this one represents the souls of those you will leave behind, which are incomplete." Looking at him, I said nothing, but questioned Him with my gaze as to what had caused this deficit. "It is incomplete because of selfishness," He said. Directing my attention to the light which still contained the essence of my childhood dog, He began leading me towards it. As He did, I heard somebody screaming at another person somewhere nearby. "Thus is the nature of this world," He said, "Even as you cross over, they will be thinking only of themselves."

Gazing at the light, I felt a sense of total peace and welcome, something which was unfamiliar in my past near-death moments. For in the past, I had encountered an energy of uncertainty, as though my dying would be premature if I were to go in that moment. But at this time there was total serenity because my soul was complete.

Because of this shift, I had an epiphany as I stared at the light. At some point, my time would truly be up, and I would go to sleep and wake in another world. Death became more real to me than it had already been due to my illness, and it really 'hit' me that I was really going to die . . . and it might be soon. In this welcoming grand gesture of God, in the light which stood before me, I was beginning to feel that my journey upon the Earth was coming very close to its end. Someday, and perhaps soon, I would no longer have a choice.

As I realized this, Christ filled me with peace about this eventuality, in that I had completed that which I had come to do, and it was just time for me to go. Before my eyes, I saw the image of the books I had written as Christ conveyed, "You must pass the torch onto Andy, and make sure he realizes the importance of this task. He must finish your work when you are no longer able."

Directing me again to the bright tunnel, Christ conveyed that He was giving me the final option of entering into the light. "I cannot go to the light, yet, Lord, for my kids are too young." Nodding, He honored my willingness to remain for their sake. In a flash, I was back.

"And five hundred and fifty days since he had risen from the dead, we said to him, 'Have you departed and removed yourself from us?' But Jesus said, 'No, but I shall go to the place from whence I came. If you wish to come with me, come!' They all answered and said, 'If you bid us, we come.' He said, 'Verily I say unto you, no one will ever enter the kingdom of heaven at my bidding, but (only) because you yourselves are full.'"
The Nag Hammadi Library, The Apocryphon of James, No. 2, Verses 20-35, (Christianity/Gnostic, Words of Christ)
"Then he said to his disciples, 'Have I not told you that like a visible voice and flash of lightning will the good be taken up to the light?'"
The Nag Hammadi Library, The Dialogue of the Saviour, No. 38, (Christianity, Gnostic, Words of Christ)
****

CHAPTER FIVE
The Ancestors Introduce Themselves, Seeing into the Future, Meeting Old, Old Friends, Tomb of Bereavement, Extension of Life Through Grace of God, Relationships After Death, Party with Those Gone Before, Death Cannot be Controlled, E Pluribus Unum Christ, Tomb of the Ancestors.

****

Wandering through the grand mansion, I couldn't believe my eyes. Having been taken back in time to the world of Russia right before the Revolution in the early 1900's, I was now being given a guided tour of the home of Arta and Helen Uzebacheff (Maiden name - Sagradeff), the great-great grandparents of my three children; Melissa, Mary and Jacob, by a cordial maid.

Helen had died at the age of forty before the war, but Arta had gone on to face the trying times of the Revolution with his four sons and two daughters.

When the Russian Revolution had come, this aristocratic and very wealthy Armenian family was separated, as my children's great-grandfather, Joseph Uzebacheff, would never see his father and several of his siblings again in this life. Losing his eldest brother, Manuk, a doctor, and a sister to the armies of Stalin, the entire family was thrown out of their home and separated by war. Another brother, Ivan (after whom my husband's father was named), would die a little bit later after receiving the wrong prescription from a pharmacy. His two sisters, Ann and Katharine, had been married to two brothers, and Joseph's youngest brother, Jacob, would survive the war, dying in 1972 of natural causes. Joseph and Jacob would be reunited after the war. Arta, their father, died in 1920 of unknown causes.

Joseph, a member of the White Army at the age of eighteen, walked from Tiblisi to Istanbul, Turkey, crossing over the Southern Mountains of Russia into Persia which is currently present-day Iraq, completely separated from every member of his family for the first time in his young life. 5000 men were with him, living off of bugs and rainwater, seventeen of those men arrived alive in Persia; among them, my husband's grandfather and my children's great-grandfather, Joseph Uzebacheff. Crossing the river from Russia to Persia, his good friend was thrown from the boat and immediately sucked into a whirlpool where he would meet his fate, that of death. As Joseph made it to the other side, he fell to his knees in tears, kissed the ground and shouted out to the heavens, "Why me, Lord, why me?!?!?"

Returning to Russia after the Revolution, grandpa's greatest remembrance was of the time he spent at an orphanage, where he spent his time picking up children orphaned by the war off of the streets covered in maggots and bugs, and bringing them to shelter and safety.

Arta had a brother, Joseph's Uncle VaGram, who had immigrated to America as an engineer, doing work for the Russian's on the railroads. Providing Joseph with the means to cross the ocean and come to America, we would only discover later in the century that Uncle VaGram had spent most of his adult life giving anonymous scholarships to children in Russia, hoping to rebuild the country of his origin. When it was discovered by our family what he had done, there was quite a great number of students in Armenia, a province of the Soviet Union, who had received scholarships to Universities. A front page article had been done on his life in the province where this had taken place.

In America, Joseph went from being an aristocrat of his time to becoming a true common man. Meeting (1926) and marrying (1928) Oxana Harkevitch, a governess and immigrant from Italy, who had Russian roots, as well; Ivan, their only son, was born in 1929. Ivan met Anne, the daughter of Czechoslovakian immigrants - Maria (Maiden Name - Vanicek) and Joseph Hornik - and had three children. Their oldest son would eventually become my husband, Andy.

Wandering through the mansion, I was overwhelmed with the opulence of it. Showing me the way it might have looked at the time of the Revolution, an overlapping reality merged with the images which might have reflected the building in later years. After it had been seized by the Communists, it had become a hospital.

Taken to a solitary room, my soul was being shown some of the things that may have existed at the time of Arta and Helen's lives. An old car was in the room, the type which had no roof over the passenger compartment. Many other early-nineteenth century items were scattered around; clothing, furniture, and other household belongings. But the maid led me to a desk.

Rummaging through the desk, I now noticed many servants walking amongst the corridors as if they were continuing at this moment to do what they might have done in the early 1900's. Directing my attention to the maid who had guided my tour and was now assisting me in looking for whatever it was I had been sent here to find, I asked, "What do you know about the people who lived here?" "The man of the house was very kind," she said, "and we were very well taken care of." Immediately, I understood that she was referring to the servants of the house.

Arta wished for me to find something very important to his wife, and I continued to fumble through the drawers until I came upon the objects which I immediately knew to be that for which I had been sent.

Holding in my hands a set of five different books, I was entranced by them. Two of them were written by Helen Uzebacheff, and had appeared to me in the form of a formerly published book which was now out of print. At the moment, it appeared that perhaps this book represented a lifetime that had yet to be documented, the knowledge of which had yet to be contained. Much of the two books contents appeared to contain spiritual wisdom attained during her short life.

Gazing now at the other three books, they were written by other people of whom I didn't yet know. Upon one of the covers was a depiction of something in regards to World War II. Could this be the life knowledge of Uncle Andrew Hornik born in 1913, the man whom my husband had been named after? Anne, Andy's mother, had an older brother who had given his life while fighting on the island of Leyte in 1943 during World War II at around the age of 30.

Taking my hand, the maid was now leading me back into the large corridor which had been the hallway of this grand mansion, guiding me towards another building on the lush and spacious grounds where I was about to meet Arta, my children's great-great grandfather and be given the chance to talk with him face to face. But as we walked towards the gate, I began to disintegrate. Reaching towards this mystical mirage, I shouted, "No, not yet!" But my time for this eve was apparently now over.

My journey into death had taken me into the fascinating world of my ancestry. Because I had been so close to the gateway of death, my deceased friends and relatives from this life had become very present to me, but I had also discovered a whole slew of ancestors nearby of whom I'd not previously known. Moved beyond words at the care and concern of those who resided in the world beyond 'death' for those of us who remain in the world of the 'living,' I was amazed at the overlap and how closely we remain intertwined, despite the lack of awareness of most of humanity at their presence.

Perhaps in this overlapping of worlds, the world of the living and the world of the 'dead,' greater knowledge was to be obtained. Perhaps some of the mysteries of our existence could be found in the histories of our ancestors. Perchance, such matters as individual and religious lineage and planetary evolution . . . could overlap?

Time had come for me to get to work on genealogy. For if we forget the original dream and from whom it came, we lose the destination. In order to remember the dream, we must remember those who have come before. Our triumphs are borne on the backs of those who toiled, suffered and struggled to make them possible. Once upon a time, long, long ago, somebody had a dream . . .

****

Sitting on the back porch, my spirit was communicating with my four year old son in the future, when he was grown and ready to marry. Talking with his fiancée,' she asked, "Is it hard to let go?" "Well," I replied, "It's hard to explain, but yes, it is hard to let go, but at the same time, I *know* in my heart that it's something that I must do because it is time." Looking at me with understanding, I continued, "I'm just very glad he chose someone like you, that's what I've wished for him." Smiling at me, she spoke only with her eyes. For a moment, I felt the searing pain that would come with that moment, as a mother, in stepping aside and allowing him to go forward with another person, although at the same time I felt the absolute necessity of doing so.

Realizing suddenly where we were sitting, it was the first home that my husband and I had owned after we had married. Pointing to a rose bush near the fence, I shouted to my son, "I planted that rose bush a few weeks after your oldest sister was born!" Nodding in acknowledgement, I was guided by an unseen hand towards the side of the fence.

Almost breaking out into tears, I shouted, "Oh, my God, Lacey!" Lacey had been my neighbor in that home, an elderly woman who had turned her backyard into a veritable victory garden. During her life, she would harvest seeds from her voluminous array of flowers, and give them to me to plant in my own yard. Next to her was the elderly woman who had lived across the street from her, who had been her best friend. Having died while we lived there, Mary was a sweet, sweet lady who also loved to plant flowers.

Hugging the two of them, I remembered how they had both lived on that street their entire lives. Both were widowed, and had lived on their own for many years after the deaths of their husbands. Lacey had owned her home free and clear, and I remembered what she had told me one day while I was sitting in her living room hearing about her life. "If you handle your finances well during your life," she said, "you should be able to show something for it by the time you're my age." Because she owned her small two bedroom one bath home free and clear, she was sharing with me how she and her husband had never made much money because he had been a blue collar worker, but they had lived simply and paid for what they owned. Because of this, she was able to live comfortably in her later years.

While we had been her neighbor, Lacey had sort of adopted me, and I had very fond memories of these two grand ladies. As I hugged them and felt deep joy in their vision, I reveled in our reunion and the realization that despite how long ago this had been; the two of them were still keeping an eye on our family from the world beyond. How honorable this was to my soul.

Turning again to my momentarily full-grown son, he was wandering into the backyard gathering something from the grass. Noticing a residue on the lawn, I said, "Oh, yeah, that's the pollution that comes from the paper factory down the street. Nothing you can do about it." (Many factories of all sorts surrounded this area we had formerly lived, and pollution was a way of life there.) Nodding and intrigued by this, because he had grown up in the mountains where such things did not occur, he held it in his hands with a look of concern.
****

Going back in time to the period in which I got married, my soul was bade to experience it from a different vantage point. Remembering that there was an element of 'having' to get married, although I was not pregnant. Complications due to my own immaturity and youth would arise, but my spirit was still very much excited because I loved my future husband.

Having been taken into the house to wait for a message which was due to arrive from my husband's family, I was pacing the room, nervous as to how they may feel about me as their future daughter-in-law. As the doorbell rang, I went to the door with expectancy, as a delivery man handed me a pile of about twenty or thirty letters from them. Immediately, one fell to the floor, with an attached gift.

Gazing at the interesting package, it had some new publishing software included, which I immediately felt had symbolic value. Representing support of the path of writing in my life, it was almost as if the gift held within it energies that would bring the publication of my work to fruition. Looking towards the attached note, I immediately recognized the handwriting, although I doubt that I've ever seen it during this lifetime. 'Nina Harkevitch,' it said in English, as I rushed to open the letter. But as I did so, I was pulled away from the scene before

I could read her words.

Aunt Nina was Andy's grandmother's sister. Oxana had been married to Joseph Uzebacheff, the son of Arta and Helen. But her side of the family held great interest and intrigue, as well.

Nina was an Italian doctor, teacher, poet and a painter, whose written works had been published Germany and St. Petersburg. Known for her generosity as a physician, many of her patients became her friends. When she passed away, it was this that people remembered about her the most. Having lived a long life, she died at 92 of old age.

Oxana and Nina had a brother named Nikita, an accomplished Pianist at the Conservatory of Munich, who died a tragic death due to pneumonia in 1932, at the age of 22. Adrian Harkevitch, their father, conducted a choir in the Russian Orthodox Church, and had married Anna Levitsky, a very accomplished piano player who had hopes of becoming a concert pianist. Because of the times and the foreordained roles of women, she was unable to pursue that dream during her lifetime. Also a painter, one of Anna's paintings had been given to us by Oxana of a friend of her mother's which hangs in our hallway.

Several other stories within Oxana's family hold intrigue, as well. Joseph Vassilieve (Wife - Sophia), the father of her grandmother, was a priest and spiritual advisor to the Russian Czar, Alexander II, and was sent to Paris to found the Russian Orthodox Church in France in the year 1847. Saint Alexandre Nevsky Church in Paris was founded in 1861 and still stands today as his living legacy. Oxana's grandfather, Archpriest Vladimir Levitsky, founded the Russian Orthodox Church of the Nativity of Christ and of Saint Nicholas the Thaumaturge in Florence. Having given a loan to a young art student so that he might be able to attend school around the year of 1869, the young and very brilliant painter contracted Tuberculosis and died. Because the family had no money to repay the loan, they offered her grandfather an unfinished painting of St. Peter which had been painted by the decedent. Hanging on our living room wall, this painting appears complete, but if you look closely at the hands, you will see that it was left undone. Beyond this, the painting looks like it could have been painted by one of the great masters, and remains as a living legacy of the amazing talent that was so cruelly torn away from this world by a disease which had yet to be cured; a tragic example of the cost of an individual life.

How many of us forget the legacy of our forebears? Certainly I have, and the most profound revelation of this recent surge of ancestral visits, lies within the realization that though we have forgotten our forebears, they still remember and look over us. Such love, and yet most of us remain so unaware of their watchful eyes and loving embrace. Souls we've never known, never met in this life, and yet we are the fruit of their womb, their great-great grandchildren, and the line of the dream that began with them . . .

As my spirit awoke, the words 'Tomb of Bereavement' were placed within my head, although I was yet unaware of their meaning.
****

Having been taken to a party to honor the recent 'healing' I'd received, about 200 souls were gathered at a church to celebrate. During the party, I was made to know that my 'healing' was a partial one, and that the Lord had granted me renewed vigor and strength, but that I was not cured. Beyond this, it was clear that I would need to remain on medication, because my healing was being accomplished through drugs, and that mine was to be a medical miracle with limited parameters. Apparently, I remained in danger of sudden death, and at this moment, my life had been extended through a grace from God, but it was a temporary extension. Because I'd had a few such extensions already, it became clear that I must use the time given my soul well in the service of God, and that I could continue to ask for repeated extensions as the time came; but at this moment, I was due to die unexpectedly of sudden death sometime in the future, near or far wasn't shared, when I would appear to be doing quite well.

Overwhelmed by this information, I followed the large crowd as they began filing into a large hallway to begin a journey to an unknown destination. Walking quietly through the corridors, they slowly became very grand and ornate caverns, stalagmites majestically hanging from the ceilings and protruding from floors. Very bright, it was unlike an Earthly cavern because it was well lit and spacious.

As we were traveling through the caverns, I ran into many spirits I recognized on a soul level, but did not know in my current Earthly life. It occurred to me that some of these familiar faces could very well be ancestors, and the reunions with these people were so comforting and warm, I cannot properly give it justice. Very many of them were old, old friends, of whom I could not place, but seeing them again was an awesome experience. Immediately, we began talking about old times that I don't remember from this life, but perhaps from many others and from times between them.

An old and very sick woman wearing an oxygen tank was struggling to get through the cavern, and her full-grown son - tall, thin, and red-headed - was attempting to help her. But she would go into breathing fits and something resembling cardiac arrest every few minutes. Annoyed, he was embarrassed by her difficulties and started saying things to her that were unkind. Relating to the predicament of the older woman due to my own condition, I couldn't help but wonder why in the world anybody would have brought her into this place in the first place. Approaching the red-headed man, I didn't immediately recognize him, but would later. "Don't you realize how much you really love your mother?" I shouted at him with anger. "You're not angry at *her*, but rather, you're angry at the situation. You do all of this for her because you *know* that if she wasn't with you, you'd *miss* her a great deal more than she cramps your style now!" Our society can be very unkind to the sick, but those of us who have lost someone who had a burdensome illness realize that the void caused by their absence is often more difficult and painful than living with the disease.

Despite my rude display, the man had listened to my words, and immediately calmed. "You really helped me," he said, as his eyes began searing into my own and recognition began to emerge, "I really need someone like you in my life. I've been acting like a hillbilly to fit in, but I've really needed something and someone deeper." Moved by his words, he finished, "If you could learn to control your anger, you could really help people like me." In that moment, I realized that this was so very true and made an inner resolution to work harder to restrain my own anger when attempting to instruct souls.

Continuing forward, he became very patient with his mother, as we all entered into a grand palace within the cavernous heavenly realm. What had been a corridor, opened up into a huge and well-lit room of great beauty. Amongst the cavernous rock were crystals, amethyst and other natural gems and elements of beauty. A grand setup resonated before me, as hundreds of people were sitting in a group of stands, not unlike the bleachers you might see at a football stadium. Recognizing them as people and souls I had seen in the city of the Palace, a wrenching understanding hit my soul.

Immediately and without doubt, I knew that I had crossed from the world of life, into the world of death.

Without any further adieu, my soul was led to the other side of the cavern where the red-headed man awaited my arrival. Instantly, I recognized him, although I had spoken with him previously without knowing who he had been. I'd been taken to a mountain retreat in the heavens at the bidding of the Master. Having been introduced to this man, my soul immediately underwent a ceremony of 'marriage' to him, despite the fact that I didn't understand what was going on. After accepting my three Earthly children, and a young thirteen-year old guardian angel (Lisao) of whom I had just adopted as my own child in the same ceremony as his own, we parted; the mystery as elusive as it had been when I'd arrived.

Again, I'd seen him in the city of the Palace during my tour of the afterworld sphere. No words had been exchanged, and in fact, he hadn't seemed to notice my presence at that time. On a few other occasions, I'd met him in the afterworld sphere, but hadn't given it much thought.

Coming towards me with great intensity, he shared with me some type of compatibility testing that had been done on the two of us. "You and I score in the two's and three's," he said excitedly, "that's much higher than I've ever scored with anybody else." Apparently, this score was based on a scale from zero to four, and two and above were considered quite good. Ramifications of what he was saying were rather great for me, in that it seemed he was using a subtle approach to tell me that death was approaching. Because it had been my impression that this relationship, whatever it may be, lay beyond the world of form, any reference to the two of us being together seemed to imply that my life was in danger, and that was all I could think about as he spoke. "It has been fore-ordained that we will be spending more time together," he said very joyfully, "and we will be doing that in one and a half days."

Feeling great conflict, the familiarity and joy I felt with these people my soul apparently knew in the after-life made me wish on some level to be with them. But at the same time, I understood the ramifications of this. In no way did I want to die and leave my family, husband and children behind, but my spirit yearned to be in both worlds on some level. Feeling drawn to this red-headed man in an inexplicable way, at the same time, my spirit felt repelled because he represented death to me.

Curious but nervous about the meaning of his words, I immediately understood that I was not out of danger in regards to death, but I didn't feel that death was imminent, either, so their meaning was mysterious. But the Lord had made it excruciatingly clear that my life was not guaranteed, and as I stood amongst the gathering of joyous and friendly dead people, it was abundantly understood that when the appointed time would arrive for me to die, my journey would be taken with those who truly loved me.
****

Standing in front of me, the angelic man listened with patience as I spoke. "I'm really trying hard," I said, "I know that I am not completely healed, but I'm taking full advantage of this unique change in my physical abilities. I'm pushing harder, and really trying to do all that I can to stay as well as possible, and stay alive for my family." Pausing for a moment, he began to speak in a very calm manner which denoted his reference to humanity as a whole. "He doesn't *try* to bring death his way," he said, "It just goes to him." A wave of energy came over me as I understood his words.

Realizing that although there are things we can sometimes do to improve our odds in such a situation, the reality remains that we all must eventually die and it will come to us in its own time, not necessarily our own. Especially important for those who suffer incurable or terminal illnesses to hear, they often feel that death is a personal failure. Some will make it, others will not, and some will make it for a while as others go quickly. Neither outcome denotes a more valiant fight or a more worthy individual; it is all about fate, destiny and God's divine timing, the element which remains unknown and mysterious to each one of us until 'death goes to him.'
****

Wandering through the Italian villas, the streets were narrow and the homes were attached to one another. Water was standing on the road in puddles, as if a rainstorm had just passed through. Having just come from a home along one of these streets, I'd felt so peaceful there. As if symbolic, the large old wooden door had a window in the shape of a heart, and there was peace, contentment and tranquility within its confines. Because it was an older building, there was a lot of large ornate wood used in the decor, but I knew that the homes were attached to one another as if in one long row.

Before having been taken there, I'd undergone a wondrous journey into the life of a young man, who though robust and strong, had taken ill suddenly and died. Not a large man, he was of small build, and somewhat short. Handsome, he had a very playful energy and showed me some of the pranks he had participated in during his short life.

An old woman approached who I didn't recognize, but I said to her immediately, "This guy is a little bit on the nutty side!" Without changing her expression or displaying any sense of my rudeness, she said, "Actually, he was very charming." Intrigued, I still didn't know who these people were or why they were showing me such things.

Now that I was walking through the streets of Italy near a row of villas of some sort, I instinctually entered a door in the side of one of them. Inside, the building was cramped and small, and for no apparent reason, I began to discuss with the manager the possibility of fitting my medical offices within its confines. "Don't you realize this building is much too cramped for a doctor's office?" I said. But as the words came out of my mouth, the rooms transformed into a medical facility, cramped but very functional and quaint. Saying nothing more, I was led into another room to an office across the hall which had a small cafe' attached to it.

Entering the office, the secretary appeared as a very conservative woman, her hair pulled behind her ears. But before I could ascertain what was going on, another woman entered the office who looked just like her, except that she had done different things with her hair, clothes and make-up, and was a bit racier. Apparently, she was having an active affair with her employer, the man in the office behind the secretarial desk. Another identical 'her' entered the office, and had her hair cut very, very short. Having become a postal worker of some kind, she was also a lesbian. Two others entered, and went about their business, completely superfluous and unaware of the presence of other selves. As the overlapping realities played out in front of me, I realized that I was being shown that none of our destinies are set in stone, for we have many optional paths to choose from. For this woman, I was being shown five.

Casually walking over to the cafe', some guy was giving me 'the eye,' and I coyly smiled back. But as I walked towards the back, another gentleman appeared who was very tall and good-looking. Repeating the actions of the other man in the cafe', I smiled back at him also, flattered by his attention. But suddenly his demeanor changed, "You need to stop doing that!" Without any further adieu, I literally straightened up and shifted my energy in a flash to a more appropriate stance, realizing that such vanity was a sin.

"Nina Harkevich is trying to reach out to you," he said, "go find her." Nodding that I would, he added, "I'll even give you an assistant to operate as a liaison between you and your ancestors." A man appeared out of the blue; tall, skinny and with black hair, who smiled in his desire to assist. "Thanks!" I said to them, as I walked off alone to find my husband's great aunt.

Walking back towards the medical office in the same building, it had now become a morgue of some kind. Many people, mostly women for some reason, were dead and dying. Those who had already passed were shrouded in white cloth, while those who were still in the dying throes laid on cots that were stacked three high to the ceiling. Going towards the back of the room, I was instinctually led to a wooden crypt which supposedly contained the remains of Nina Harkevitch.

Opening the crypt, my husband, Andy, was now standing at my side, present during this momentous occasion. Inside, there laid three plastic red roses, a funeral card, and something that was wrapped in white fabric and rolled into a ball. Taking the funeral card, I noticed that on the front cover were the names of about twenty different ancestors, most of whom I did not recognize except for Arta and Helen Uzebacheff. Inside it said, "Ninitchka Harkevitcha," and below it were the dates of her birth and death.

Approaching me from the side was an older woman with darkish hair pulled back in a bun. On her face was a radiant smile, as she reached towards me. Noticing that a small paper was in her hand, I asked, "Do you have the note from Nina for me?" Without saying a word, she gave it to me.

Inside the note was a picture of a little girl holding a lamb in her left hand. Immediately, I thought of the picture I'd seen of Nina as a little girl sitting on the lap of her great grand-father, an Archpriest of the Russian Orthodox Church and founder of the Church in Florence, Italy. Perhaps he was the symbolic lamb?

Suddenly, a great many people entered the room and began changing it from a morgue to a library, which would be particularly appropriate for Nina, because along with being a doctor, she had been a great teacher of anatomy.

Looking to Andy, I said, "You've got to help me with this, please try to remember all these items so you can help me bring this back." "I won't remember," he said, "you'll need to ask somebody else to help you."

"I know what I'll do," I thought, "I need my assistant." Calling out, he instantly appeared in the room and began wandering through it to gather the information which would be vital for me to bring back into the physical realm. Reaching for two decorative dishes, they were a plate and a matching bowl with a white background and a brownish painting on them. Depicting about thirty birds flying in the same direction, I turned to my assistant, "What do you think it means?" I asked him. Pointing to the very bottom where very small words had been inscribed, I read, "E Pluribus Unum Christ."

Now surrounded in a vast library of books, I thanked my assistant for pointing that out to me as the other gentleman from before had entered the room. "You shifted well," he said, "and you are a much more attractive spirit when engaged in the proper energy." Nodding in acknowledgement of this truth, we both chuckled at my previous silliness.

At this moment, all that I had seen began to come together for me. Remembering the heart window in the door of the home, I knew that this was Nina's residence, and the heart represented the warmth and love that had resided there as she welcomed young and old, rich and poor within its confines; to teach them and to assist some who were sick. Nina had become a doctor in great part due to the tragedy which befell her brother, Nikita, who had died of pneumonia and pleurisy at the age of 22. Charming and playful, the young man I had met was my husband's great Uncle Nikita who had died long ago. Obviously, the doctor's office in the building was Nina's office, which was built from scraps into a very functional and helpful place of healing for her many patients.

Finally, I looked up the meaning for "E Pluribus Unum Christ." Although I'd known the first part of it to be a common American phrase, I'd forgotten its origin and meaning. Looking it up, its translation read, "Out of Many, One," which I immediately construed as a reference to the connection between myself, my family and our ancestors. But placing the word, "Christ" after it expanded its meaning beyond such borders. "Out of Many, One Christ." Written in 1776, the symbol of this message was the eagle in flight.
****

In the midst of the night, my body began experiencing a fast heart-rate and excessive nausiousness. Entering into sleep, my spirit had collapsed into another realm. Before me were the doctors and nurses who had come to my aid before. "Are you going to cross over tonight of cardiac arrest?" One asked very casually and with humorous sarcasm, as he held a hypodermic needle in his hand. "Oh," I replied in shock, "I'm at risk of dying again tonight, huh?" Nodding that indeed such was the case, I began concentrating a great deal on going back, as he plunged the needle into my arm just as he had done before, and my spirit immediately awoke back in my body.

****

Traversing the far caverns, my soul was led deep into the tomb of my ancestors by a single male spirit, draped in white. Amongst the depths were caves, each one holding a set of dry white bones. Walking quietly and methodically by each tomb, I gazed at the bones as a misty image began to emerge and the spirit of each ancestor slowly appeared from the ether, quietly standing and turning to reach a singular hand to my soul. Images of about twenty unknown ancestors rose to meet my soul as I walked by their individual resting places. Gently nodding as I slowly passed, I allowed myself to take in their many faces. Feeling their beckon, I could not inquire further at this time, but acknowledged in silence their need . . . and my calling.

Perhaps one of them was 'Ma' Crane, my grandmother's sister, who had founded and run a maternity hospital in Provo, Utah before the hospitals had been built. Or my grandfather on my mother's side, who was forced to become a German soldier during World War II. What stories he had to tell, but he didn't live long enough for me to hear them. How odd it is to think that my children's ancestors were fighting on opposite sides of the battlefield in that horrific time. What if my other grandfather on my father's side was among them? He had died to save the life of one of my cousins by throwing her out of the way of an oncoming car and taking the impact upon himself. Certainly, such an act shows a soul who held great care and interest in the lives of his grandchildren. Perhaps some of those bones represented my earlier Mormon ancestors who crossed over to Utah from the East with Joseph Smith, or my great-great grandmother who was involved in a polygamous marriage? Others could have been a number of carpenters who had fulfilled a long line of apprenticed descendants of mine in Germany from my mother's family. Hard to tell, but I was being urged forward by my guide so I moved ahead.

Ahead of us was a grand tomb, gilded in gold, pearls and jewels, standing magnificently before us. Having reached the end of the line of caverns, we emerged upon an open vista which sparkled in the color of blue-green. Without speaking, my guide conveyed to me that this golden shrine was the 'Tomb of the Ten Commandments,' as he reached his hand forward in invitation to enter. Amazed and thrilled, I walked towards this magnificently quaffed specimen which emanated holiness beyond my comprehension. Walking inside the small entryway . . . all went black.

****

Emerging from the clouds, the darkness came in a powerful wind towards me and my family. Thrusting ourselves to the ground, we gathered together to protect one another during the attack but were not fast enough. Shouting to Andy, I said, "Throw yourself on top of Jake!" but he didn't respond quickly enough and Jacob was being blown out of our reach. An interior voice spoke within me, and it said that my recent attempts to record the music beyond 'Galactica' were being generated by my ego, rather than God's will. Thus, I had given entry for dark forces to assault me both physically and spiritually. Because I had heart failure, recording vocally was very difficult on my body, and doing so to great lengths was no longer advised.

Acknowledging my mistake, and recognizing from the scenario that I had made a grave misjudgment; it was clear that my children should always be my first priority, and I should do nothing that would put them in danger of losing their mother any sooner than absolutely necessary.

****

Standing in an office that I had worked at as a younger woman, I was remembering the many people with whom I had known and the general dynamic of this long ago place. All of us had lost contact many years before, and in fact, I'd forgotten many of these people who had once been such important friends. Interestingly, I was shown a former boss who had demonstrated certain issues, and was shown that this had continued and expanded during his life. Chuckling to myself, I walked around the office to observe how people were currently doing and most of them were doing quite well.

But when I casually walked over to the cubicle of two older men who had watched over me in my youth, I was greatly surprised to see that it was empty. Although I had not known them that well even when I'd worked in this environment, they had always kept an eye on me in fatherly way, looking out for me because I was young and inexperienced in the world.

Confused by their absence, I turned to inquire about it when I suddenly saw a sight that filled me with joy and glee. Surrounded in light, the two were standing behind me in their glorified bodies as they had passed from this world several years before. In my conscious waking life, I had completely forgotten about them, and so the Lord had given them an opportunity to take me back to this time so that I might remember their watchful care. As they stood before me, they conveyed that they continued to watch over my soul from beyond, and they wished for me to remember the special fatherly interest they had taken in me during my youth. Apparently, it had continued into the next life and I was quite honored.

A cosmic quality enveloped their presence which filled me with joy in seeing them. Despite my previous forgetfulness, seeing them generated an almost ecstatic state. Reaching their hands to me, I thanked them and expressed joy in our reunion as they held my hand for only a moment before disappearing from the scene.
****

Standing before me, Nina Harkevitch was smiling a grand grin as she appeared as she would have looked as a young girl. Beside her was her sister, sub-conscious astral, with a daze upon her face indicating her lack of awareness of this experience. Reaching her hands out to the ether, Nina said, "I want to show you something."

Whisped away, my spirit was now standing on a lush college campus in the 1920's. A large and beautiful building stood in the front and center of a green and verdant valley; beyond the front lawn of the building were several small roads with many small houses standing aside one another. Behind the college was a very beautiful valley surrounded by several small woods and some type of water. Unable to recall whether it was a river or a small lake or pond, I only recall the water.

Nina did not confirm or deny my suspicions, but I wondered if we had known each other earlier in her life?

Walking along a road towards my own home, I ran into an old friend named Brian, who had been gone for some time. "Brian!" I shouted, "How *are* you? Where have you been?" Very quietly, he explained that he had been sick, and although he had been doing better for some time, he was now dying of terminal cancer. So sad to hear such news, we began walking together in the other direction towards the college. As we strolled into the valley and woodlands behind the college, he told me about his plight and what was to happen to him. Despite the seriousness of his condition, he was totally at peace with his impending doom because he'd had plenty of time to accept it. Holding his hand, I said, "Well, there's something you don't know about me, as well." Looking at me with interest, I said, "I'm also dying, and I understand what you're sharing with me." Surprised, but not shocked, he asked what was wrong with me. Apparently, during this time I'd also suffered from heart failure; but because of the time-frame, there was no hope.

Realizing that much time had passed, dusk was now upon us. Offering to walk me home, I was somewhat hesitant because of his condition, but allowed him to do so. As we came closer to my house, he collapsed complaining of pain in his lower leg. Feeling his calf, I could discern a lump, but made no mention of it. "Wait here, I'm going to run and get my mom and dad to help." Shouting out a four-digit phone number, he asked me to phone his parents.

Arriving at my house just a few yards away, I quickly informed my parents of the need, and the two of them ran to Brian's aid while I called his family. Using the four-digit number he had given me, a woman was speaking on the other end of the line in Italian. When arriving on the scene a few minutes later, I noticed anger in my father's eyes as he observed the way Brian looked at me. But he put his anger aside and we all picked him up and got him inside where he could lie down in a warm place.

At that moment, my spirit quickly flashed through several moments in the future which clearly delineated the path that was to come. Brian and I became engaged, spending a great deal of time together, but he passed within a year, and I was gone within a year of that.

Standing before Nina and her sister, she nodded as I felt a close bond. And then she was gone . . .

****

Before my eyes lay a gravel road of rocks which floated effervescently on top of the ocean waters. As it led to a heavenly island, Andy and I rode our car carefully over the etheric pathway. Afraid of sinking during the journey, the weight of my car began to depress into the water several times during the crossing. A guard waited at the dock of the island, and without words, asked me why I had come. "I was invited by a cousin." I said. Joyful to hear this, he said, "Oh, Paul and Jenny! You are welcome; I'll take you to them."

Arriving at their very humble single-wide mobile home planted amidst a very lush and green island rainforest, I walked in quietly. Noticing a sign on the wall, it said, "What are you losing to live in the world that you do?" A very small man approached me very quietly, a woman at his side. Unable to discern who he was, I only knew that he was a 'cousin' in some way to my family. "We gave up everything," he said, "to come to this island which honors spiritual values. What are *you* losing to live in the world that you do?" In unison, Andy and I said, "Ourselves, everything, our dignity, our integrity." Without any further words, he nodded as if he understood, and turned to walk away. In a split second, we were gone.

****

CHAPTER SIX
St. Thomas Aquinas's Scribe, Watching the Souls Coming and Going, Fascinating Journey of the Departed, How Quickly we Lose Interest in the Souls of the Departed, Crossing of a Holy Priest, Learning About the Family, Message from the Deceased Priest, My Friend's New Spiritual Journey After Death, Bringing Birth and Death Together, Two Views of Death, Meeting Deceased Step Dad, Don't Die Angry.

****

Gently rising from form, my spirit hovered over my body for but a moment as it then moved slowly to the floor, directly in front of the gateway at the door of my bedroom that had been prepared for my exit. A voice began speaking words of great wisdom of which I remembered none. But his words were so eloquently beautiful; I had wished to record each one. "You have no need to fear your final end," he said. Within moments, I was prancing along a woodland pathway, as beautiful music began playing all around me.

Following many bends and curves in the path, I came across a young man dressed in ancient garb. Immediately, I asked, "Do you come on behalf of the darkness or the light?" "Of the light, Madame," he said, as he bowed respectfully before me. "Allow me to introduce myself, Madame," he continued, "as I was St. Thomas Aquinas's scribe." Very honored, I didn't know exactly what he meant. Had he helped the saint write his words during his own life, or had he *copied* his works later? I did not know. "It is my great honor to escort you now, Madame," he said, "to the place that the great writer's of the Lord all gather." Feeling quite unworthy of such a gathering, the music again began to emanate all around me and we continued to walk together.

Suddenly, I felt my soul begin to pull away from this woodland pathway and towards my body, as the scribe said, "Remember, Madame, you have no need to fear your final end."
****

In a moment, my soul was taken through many aeons, as my spirit experienced several different lifetimes along the spectrum of time. Each of these lifetimes held an aspect of selfhood which was distinctive from the other. Whether it was a lifetime from the ancient past or the lifetime around the turn of the 19th century where I was a black man from the ghetto side of town, an aspect of unique self was apparent and distinctive. In each of these existences, my spirit was attached to the personality of my lifetime. For these moments, I took in the various scenes and sites which made each period of time unique and memorable.

Seconds later, I was standing in the midst of a hospital, watching the souls coming and going. Wives, mothers, children, babies, young men - I watched and observed as they began their ascent out of this world into the next.

In each case, they held onto an identity shortly before death which slowly disappeared into a vacuum as they approached the time of their passing. It was fascinating to watch, because every single soul was concerned with the way they were perceived by others and existed in the same trap of all humanity in that they understood themselves to be separate and distinct. But moments before they crossed over, I witnessed that a monk-like energy overcame each and every one, actually manifesting as an etheric brown robe overlapping their physical bodies. This occurred even with the little babies.

This etheric brown robe carried with it the qualities of a cosmic state which pulled those who were dying into a Zen-like understanding, carrying them outside of their personal selfhood into an actual energy where their selfhood disappeared and they simply 'were.' Becoming one with life, they began to prepare for a long journey as a very quick movie-like depiction flowed through their psyche. Although many *near* deather's report experiencing a life review, these souls who were definitively going to die without any question were experiencing an overview of the journey to come. Perhaps they had already gone through a life-review in their preparation for death or maybe that was something to come later, but these souls experienced a microcosmic entrance into their understanding of the journey of which they were about to embark upon almost like a computer download into their souls.

And as these souls died, they shot off like a rocket into that program, entering their eternal journey as if they'd prepared their whole life for it, even in cases where they clearly had not. It was not frightening or new to them, even though it had come upon them very quickly, for they were all in perfect peace.

Watching those left behind mourning for lost loved ones, I noticed a man who had just lost his wife who was currently engaged in prayer and contemplation for her soul. Frustrated that others had forgotten her so quickly, he was asking professional opera singers to sing the Divine Mercy Chaplet (A Catholic Devotion originating with Saint Faustina in the 1930's in Poland) on her behalf. Many would begin, but would not finish the Chaplet and simply walk away because they had lost interest in it and the soul of his wife. As he wandered these astral hallways, I quietly said to him, "I will do it for you . . . ?" And I began singing quietly and growing louder as I awaited his response. "Eternal Father, I offer You . . . the Body and the Blood . . . Soul and Divinity of Your Dearly Beloved Son. Our Lord Jesus . . . Christ" Nodding that he accepted my gift even though I was not a professional singer, I continued to pray and sing on his wife's behalf. "In Atonement for our Sins, and for the Whole World. For the sake of His sorrowful Passion, have mercy on us and on the whole world. For the sake of His sorrowful Passion, have mercy on us on the whole world . . . " And thus, we sang together in quiet contemplation on the life of this soul and her entrance into eternal life.

"As the juggler's show is the world: For a brief moment the show you witness: Instantly it is dismantled . . . The Name Divine in our hand is held as the staff in blind man's hand."
Sri Guru Granth Sahib, Volume II, Raga Asa, Page 895, (Sikhism)
"Remember your last days, set enmity aside; remember death and decay, and cease from sin!"
The New American Bible, Old Testament, Sirach 28:6, (Christianity, Judaism)
****

My soul was given to witness the crossing over of a holy priest. As I dropped off to sleep, I was honored to stand about twenty feet away from his hospital bed. Three huge white angels with gigantic wings stood on each side of his bed, and one at his head. At his feet, Jesus and Mary stood with their arms outstretched. Light came from their hearts and the heart of the angels into his, and I saw him coming out of his body and reaching his arms towards Jesus. As he did so, I saw a vision within a vision. Watching as he had performed the Mass during his life, Jesus overlapped his every move on the altar.
****

An angelic guardian took me to a mountain top to show me something which gave me great sadness. As I'd mentioned before, in 'Galactica' I had been shown that my death, at that time, was scheduled to occur around the time of the death of two other gentlemen. One of them had died (about five months prior) and had almost been sent to a hell realm when he'd asked for my help. Assisting him in liberation by battling hundreds of demons on his behalf, he'd come to thank me from a very brightly lit realm. Recently, I'd been made to know that the other man was in the process of dying, although it was unclear if it would a long lingering death or quick.

Standing on the mountain, the angel pointed to a blue elliptical pattern of light which represented his soul. As I watched, the light went out. Immediately, I knew that he was soon to die. But unexpectedly the angel asked me to look upon another light, a pinkish elliptical pattern which represented another person in my life of great importance. As I gazed, her light also went out. Turning to the angel, I understood that her time was possibly coming, as well, which caused me sadness. Finally, I was asked to gaze upon a third individual of even greater importance in my life, a yellowish elliptical light, whose light did not completely extinguish, but seemed to be faltering in the wind as a candle might do. Clearly, this person was in danger of death. Nodding to the angel, it seemed that the third person represented the only outcome in which my actions might have an impact. Vowing to do my best to uncover the threat to this person's life and to remedy it, I was quickly escorted to a cove where mourners stood waiting to comfort me in my sadness and I began to contemplate.

As I did, an angel again pointed out to me the importance of learning not to do everything for others, but to allow them to receive the tools and then practice and hone them. Hearkening off into the distance, the angel's hands were now directly pointing at a wall of water coming in my direction. Before I could look around me to find a means of escape, the tidal wave had hit and I was completely submerged in the waters. Nodding to the angels, I understood that I was receiving warning about new wave of illness which might place me in harms way. I would be careful. Then we were gone.

"If we say, 'We have fellowship with him," while continuing to walk in darkness, we are liars and do not act in truth. But if we walk in light, as he is in the light, we have fellowship with one another, and the blood of his Son Jesus cleanses us from all sin."

The New American Bible, New Testament, 1 John 2:6-7, (Christianity: Catholic, Words of St. John)

"Before you have fallen, humble yourself; when you have sinned, show repentance. Delay not to forsake sins, neglect it not till you are in distress."

The New American Bible, Old Testament, Sirach 18:20-21, (Christianity, Judaism)

****

As I lapsed into a very dangerous period during my illness, our ancestors who had graced my presence in 'Galactica' were very present in my dreaming. As I'd become very ill, I was greeted the first night by Joseph Vasillieve and Vladimir Levitsky, the two Archpriests of Russian Orthodox Tradition in my husbands family line. With them was Christ, who wore a showering gown of white which was held up in the back by two angels, one on each side; much like the way a bridal train is carried during a wedding. Christ was facing towards the East, and these two ancestors of ours were trying to teach me something about Christ which I did not yet know. But it was an energetic transmission, and much of it was lost as I came back to consciousness.

The second night, the Hornik side of my husband's family dominated my vision, as grandma Maria Hornik came to shower her graces upon me. Standing beyond an ocean of water, she beckoned me to come forth. As I did, I noticed that the other ancestors were with her from both sides of the family line. In this space, I was able to float across the water with ease and I came halfway across the great divide in order to hear her out.

Grandma Hornik began to show me things about their lives, and I became acutely aware that there was much more to these people than our family histories presented. They wished for us to know them better and more intimately, showing me the foibles and the triumphs of each member of the family during their lifetimes. There was no ego involved in this experience, it was simply a sharing of the life-wisdom gained by each ancestor; although again it was very energetic in nature and much of it was quickly forgotten as I resumed consciousness.

"I teach those who have long-standing ties of affection with their families and relatives in such a way that they may get to meet and associate with buddhas and enlightening beings. Those who are involved with their spouses and children I teach in such a way as to extinguish their craving for mundane enjoyments and so that they will become impartial toward all and will come to have great compassion."

The Flower Ornament Scripture, Entry into the Realm of Reality, Page 1330, (Buddhism: Mahayana)

****

Standing inside a beautiful church, I was astonished to yet again be witness to the arrival of my former priest who appeared wearing his ceremonial robe of green with a great big smile on his face. Appearing in the ether, he was hovering above the floor in front of a beautiful stained glass window. He didn't speak, but rather, conveyed. Appearing to be very happy in his new state, he was also nodding, indicating that he approved of and was very happy with the path I was taking. "I better understand your unique abilities to communicate with the dead. It is a *true* gift from God, one fully expected *as any other* to bear fruit."

There was joyful laughter as he said this. His laughter was in reference to the common teaching of the Church that those of us with this particular gift should 'by obedience' not use our gift. Because those of us who have it understand it as a gift, we feel compelled by conscience to use the gift. Ignoring and hiding such a gift only negates the true and vital purpose this gift serves in the Body of Christ, which is to 'assist those souls coming and going.' It was clear to me that he was letting me know that he now understood why I felt 'compelled' to do as the spirit had led me, because I knew that if I did not, that I would be held accountable at the throne for these wasted spiritual gifts which had borne no fruit. If I were to ignore my true calling, which wasn't in perfect alignment with Church teaching, I would be no more than a 'faithless servant' who did not use the 'talents' given him by the Lord for their proper use.

"Keep it up, I'm behind you all the way . . ." He said. Waving good-bye, he smiled and began walking up an invisible staircase which took him also into invisibility.

****

My deceased friend - Karleen - appeared, showing me a new hairdo she was wearing. Having become very thin since her passing, she had now gotten a new short haircut which feathered her now naturally dark brown hair around her face. Before her death, she had long bleached blonde hair, but she had now returned to her natural appearance. Cracking a joke, she said, "Oh, Andy wouldn't like this haircut." We both knew that Andy preferred longer hair, and we laughed as I said, "Actually, I think he would. You look great!"

Sitting down with me, she held in front of her a blank piece of paper which suddenly began to manifest a very skillfully done line-image drawing of her with her new look. Sitting down, we began to write a poem underneath her image:

'I think in terms of divineness within
All that comes forth alludes to the dream
Creative and seed are what fills me
I am life.'

Signing both our names, we wrote, 'By Marilynn/Karleen' at the bottom of the poem. Appearing hurried, she gave me the piece of paper with her image and our poem and turned to rush away.

Several entities appeared with a precise message. White and flowing light beings whose eyes showed persistent purpose, they conveyed, "Rise two more steps in consciousness and you will find a cure for your chronic infections. You are very close and you will stumble upon it." I'd had this problem for years and it had recently become medication resistant. Because of heart failure and Lupus affecting my immune system, these infections had taken hold.

That morning, I stumbled upon a new form of treatment for this problem which used bacteria and organisms to actually eat the infection out of your system, a totally new approach to treatment. I decided to give it a try.

"Since you have been raised up in company with Christ, set your heart on what pertains to higher realms where Christ is seated at God's right hand. Be intent on things above rather than on things of earth. After all, you have died! Your life is hidden now with Christ in God."
The New American Bible, New Testament, Colossians 3:1-5, (Christianity: Catholic, Words of St. Paul)

"Free thyself from the fetters of this world, and loose thy soul from the prison of self. Seize thy chance, for it will come to thee no more."
The Hidden Words, No. 40, (Bahai', Words of Baha'u'llah)

"Beseech thou the Almighty that He may remove with the fingers of divine power the veils which have shut out the diverse peoples and kindreds, that they may attain the things that are conducive to security, progress and advancement and may hasten forth towards the Incomparable Friend."
The Tablets of Baha'u'llah, Kalimat-I-Firdawsiyyih, (Bahai', Words of Baha'u'llah)

****

Flitting about the heavens in some type of spiritual aircraft, my spirit was taken to an island somewhere. A very grisly scene stood before me on the beach, as thousands of caskets were lined up and strewn around. But these caskets were all children's caskets, and I was initially fairly freaked out. Watching as those who had been brought with me began to swarm the beach, I noticed that inside these caskets were the bodies of their 'inner children,' for lack of a better term. The bodies were of these adults at the age of about nine, supposing they had died at that time. Up ahead, I saw my own casket by being given a certain inner vision of my childhood body lying within it. But I did not approach it as the others did.

Literally hundreds of adults ran to their own individual casket, apparently guided by a similar interior vision of its contents, and picked them up. Holding them and hugging them, many of them were kissing the caskets because they were in such bliss to be reunited with this part of their life. Although the scene was very odd, I interiorly understood that this was a uniting of birth and death which was taking place. These people were crossing over, and in doing so, they were bringing the beginning and ending of their life together on this island.

Lining up while holding their caskets, I was the only one who stood alone without my casket. I never approached my casket, but ignored it. Some type of spiritual guardian was at the front of the line, waving his hand gently as each person would disappear with his casket, one at a time. But at this moment, the 'pilot' of the spiritual aircraft tapped me on the arm and led me back to the plane. My time was finished, and we left the island instantly.
****

Because it had been a long time since Andy had been given such a forewarning, this experience took him by surprise and upset him a great deal.

Being led into a room, he noticed that my departed friend, Karleen, was sitting quietly on a couch knitting. A young boy, whom he immediately understood to be my father's brother who had died at the age of five after being hit by a truck, was also in the room. About five others were there, family and friends - all deceased, gathering to assist at the moment of my death and aid in my transition. Immediately, he was made to know that there was one or two more who needed to arrive, and when they were in place, I would be crossing over.

Karleen looked over at Andy with a smile indicating she knew more than she could reveal. But Andy felt that my death was much closer than he'd thought, and was imminent, like perhaps before another year would pass.

Upset and distraught, he was pulled away from the scene and led back to his body.
****

Gazing from the infinite heavens, my spirit was allowed to look upon two views of death. The first view was that of the common man, square-ish and very three-dimensional . . . almost one-dimensional in the human scope as all was flat and contained no depth. The second view was that of the eternal, wider, globular and multi-dimensional; containing many layers of meaning and rhythms of life. Yes . . . life . . . in death.

For a moment, I remembered an experience I had many months ago with the spirit of our former deceased priest. Coming to me in the night, he had carried a torch in his right hand. Wearing the green robes of the ordinary time of the priesthood, he descended into a group of Native Americans. Because he had served these people during his life, it was his wish that his work be carried on. As I walked towards him in the center of the group he did something surprising. Handing me the torch he held in his hand, he said, "Take care of my people . . ." I couldn't understand at the time, because I was not a priest. How could I do this?

But I accepted his torch in an ignorant surrender and allowed him to be at peace.

Since that time, we'd moved to another parish wherein a younger priest around my own age had begun work in his first parish as chief pastor.

Several nights before this experience, he had given me the anointing of the sick. On that eve, I was to see Christ as He filled me with a seed of partial healing. My immune system was to be functional for a time, giving me the freedom to be of more use in the world. But my other infirmities were to remain (Heart Failure, Lupus). The city of the New Jerusalem hovered in the heavens as the clouds of pink, purple and blue billowed around the form of the Christ wearing robes of burgundy and deep purple. His eyes were penetrating, His look joyful, expectant. I could sense he would ask much of me, but He said nothing of it at this time. Interiorly, I sensed an impending crucifixion. "Go back to Mass . . . now that you can," he conveyed. Grateful for this gift of being healthy enough to return to Mass, I nodded that indeed I would do so.

On a successive night, He said, "Go to the priest and the other (he called her by name as someone who worked with him), and do whatever they ask you to do." I had called that morning and asked what they needed, and this had begun a sequence of volunteering which culminated in the diagnosis of her husband three weeks later with cancer. It seemed that Jesus had wanted me to be there to help her through this coming time, both emotionally and with her job while her husband underwent intensive treatments.

****

The lights around the departed only seemed to get brighter and brighter as I came across the spirit of my deceased step-dad.

So excited to see him, I immediately ran up to him and embraced him saying, "I'm so sorry, I'm so sorry. I didn't appreciate you enough when you were here. All those houses and cars you helped us to rebuild . . . I'm so sorry." Laughing, he replied, "Oh, don't worry about it. It's okay. It's like that for everyone who crosses over." Immediately, I understood that it was a very common phenomenon for people to not have full appreciation of their loved ones while still living.

Knowing that my husband and I were in the process of working through a lot of things, a lot of anger over past abuse, etc., he said, "Don't die angry . . . " As he said this, he transferred an energy to me which immediately drained all the anger out of me which I had towards my husband.

He seemed so happy to see me, it was as if I were not a step-daughter, but a biological daughter. He shared with me several messages for my mother. He said that he was aware of what my step-siblings did to her after his death and that it disgusted him. They had tried to take everything from her, including her home, despite the 20+ years of marriage. It was a legal mess filled with a lot of betrayal.

But he saw it, and I somehow sensed from him that part of the reason he felt so close to me was because he'd known that I never cared about his money on any level. I just wanted him to be taken care of in his final days, and for his end to be peaceful.

After talking a little bit about how he liked to hang out with my mom when she was out to eat somewhere, he mentioned a hat she wears and a certain suit that he really liked. But what surprised me the most, and it did so because my step-dad was very jealous of my mother during his life, was that he told me he was aware of her new male friend and that he was so very happy that they had each other and were so close. The love just poured out from him about this, and I so wanted to tell my mom as he'd wished, but she was not open to hearing it. She's not a believer in life after death.

So I share my special moment with you and the great advice that my step-dad shared which is, "Don't die angry . . . " Very few things are really worth

436

holding onto and not forgiving, especially when we realize that our end is
always upon us, whether we know it or not.
****

Heaven, Hell and Purgatory

Mystic Knowledge Series

Compiled and Written by Marilynn Hughes

The Out-of-Body Travel Foundation!

www.outofbodytravel.org

CHAPTER ONE
Star Tunnel to the Heavens, the Inner Sun, House of Satan, The Gateway and the Sky Pictures, Seven Levels of Heaven, Universal Sphere of Realms, Guardian of the Veil, Feather Plane.

****

Vibrating rapidly as it lifted slowly towards the ceiling and then passed it, my soul was going further up into the heavenlies. Watching my house go further and further away as I ascended to the stars, my spirit was now standing amidst the heavens, the stars and darkness of deep space enveloping me in peace. More moments passed as I went further and further away, watching the earth become a blue ball surrounded in white swirls. Turning to face the blackness of space, the stars slowly began to move. As they did so, they began to form a tunnel which appeared to be much like a black hole. The circular motion of the stars around this tunnel in space was almost dizzying, and it seemed to make you enter into another awareness. In my mind, I heard the name, 'Star Tunnel.'

Shooting towards the tunnel, my spirit almost entered . . . but was quickly pulled back from the ominous and powerful sight.

"For shining steadfastly upon and round the whole mind, it enlighteneth all the Soul; and loosing it from the Bodily senses and motions, it draweth it from the Body, and changeth it wholly into the Essence of God."
The Divine Pymander of Hermes, Fourth Book, No. 18, (Mystery Religions, Egyptian/Hermetic, Words of Hermes)

****

Soaring through the stars, my spirit was beckoned towards the sun. Venus and Mercury were full of splendor as I soared passed them at the speed of light. Finding myself on the outskirts of a city of light in the inner recesses of the sun, everything here was pure essence; the spirits were ether, and their forms were like fluorescent yellow lights. Wanting to go further, I noticed a pathway that went from this inner recess to a place further and deeper, but as I moved towards it, I was pulled away. A voice echoed, "You have seen what you were meant to see. Return now, and tell of it." Bowing, I did so as I returned to form.

On two successive occasions, I was given to return to the sun, but found that the strong vibrational force of the sun was much higher than my own, and my spirit was unable to endure its power. Flying towards it six times, I finally reached my goal when a spiritual guide whispered instructions in my ear. Focusing my energy on my sixth chakra or third eye, my vibrational state began to increase. As it slowly increased significantly, I was able to make it back to the sun. Again, I noticed many ether islets resonating from the center. "Pathways," I thought, "but to where?" Immediately, I was transferred home.

"We are drawn to heaven by him, like beams by the sun, not being restrained by anything."
The Nag Hammadi Library, The Treatise on the Resurrection, Page 55, Top, (Christianity, Gnostic/Essene)

****

Taken to a blue space, the sky was of emerald blue and the ground pastel. A female came in and laid my spirit down, floating in midair. Smiling and very cheerful, she started to put many different blue stones on my eyes and on my chakra centers, especially my throat. A yellow and purple cloth was laid over me as my soul went into vibratory bliss. "What are you doing?" I asked. "We are preparing you to go to new places." She said, excitedly. "Oh, good!" I retorted, "Do you think I can go back to the sun?" Laughing, she said, "Of course, you will go there and way beyond."

"Only sages are effectively able to know strategy, so their words prove truthful and their expectations prove accurate."
Wen-Tzu, Understanding the Mysteries, No. 85, Paragraph 2, (Buddhism, Taoism,

Words of Lao Tzu)

****

And so it came to pass that my soul underwent several journeys into cosmic elements, quasar and pulsar stars, the rings of Saturn, as well as various other planets. Going to these places filled my soul with energy unattainable in any other fashion, because they were filled with spiritual power.

****

Entering the chapel, the Native American man came over to me as I sat waiting for this night's quest. Wearing a charming smile that never dimmed, his long black hair was slightly graying. What struck me the most was the medicine wheel he wore around his neck lying quietly on his bare chest. Pictures of sheep were etched on the piece, they were running to freedom. "Those with few words," he said, "need not listen to those with many. The meek and timid sheep does not always stand reluctantly in silence. Will you run to freedom?" He spoke of my attachment to those in my past who did not share my spiritual journey, and were very much holding me back. Then he was gone.

Leaving the chapel with one of these incompatible people, we arrived at our vehicle. Noticing that the parking space overlooked a large cliff, I looked over the side to see a Native American encampment below. Yearning to join them, I watched their dance of life as the men dived in and out of the coral reef, hunting for fish, and the women danced happily around the campfire preparing what they had caught. Turning away from that which would have given me peace, I went with the other person out of a sense of obligation, who wanted to go to a store in a shopping center. Following on foot, I immediately sensed that something was wrong when I entered the store. Fear and foreboding exuded from every pore of this place.

Looking to the wall, I saw a sign that read, "This is the house of Satan, a place of fear. All that reside here follow a falsehood, though they believe in its reality. All that they are is all that they have chosen to be, a sad state, indeed. If you are love, do not reside here!"

As I ran to the door, the person with me refused to leave, and in so doing, some rather horrible demons came to 'sacrifice' this person to their 'God.' (Materialism, Greed and Worldliness) As I ran out, a man with pointed teeth tried to grab me for sacrifice, as well. But I looked at him calmly and replied, "I am of love, I know that you are not real. You are but a fear within the hearts of many men."

Looking down, he let go of me and sadly replied, "Loving being, thank you for giving me hope. As I am a creation of the fearful mind of man, I play my part with grace. Oh, but I do wish for the day when all mankind sees me for who I truly am, a distortion of truth. It is then that I will join you as a creation of love." Nodding that I understood, I turned to go.

"Let me help you!" He called out. "In order to leave this fearful reality of the world, you must follow the path of the flowers! They are the path of new life and love, the path of completion, as well as, the seed of new awakenings!"

Running towards my car, another incompatible person was now present and prepared to drive. "Drive towards the path of the flowers," I told her, but she refused and immediately entered a ghetto which represented her chaotic and agitated thinking. Wanting to rescue the other person I'd left behind in the store, I reluctantly agreed. Moments later, however, I changed my mind. "I will not return to a place of fear," I said, "he has chosen the way of fear, and ultimately death of the spirit. However I know that he will be fine as his Father will be with him and show him the Way." "We have to help him," she said, "he could die!" Knowingly, I replied, "He has already chosen the way of fear, but he will not truly die."

Pointing in the direction she had taken, I said, "That is not the way to the truth, we must take the path of new life!" She disappeared, as suddenly the windshield became a torrent of wind filled with rose petals and magical displays of blossoms in color. Pastel blues, pinks, peaches, purples and white filled my vision as I soared through the path of the flowers.

Awaiting me at the end of the path was the Native American man with the medicine wheel. Flying to him in a fury, I entered his arms which were held high in embrace. Changing color, his medicine wheel was no longer orange (restraint) and red (passion), just red. Although I didn't know it, he was energizing my walk into karma. A soul must walk many extremes in its path, from one to its opposite, in order to eventually achieve balance.

"Thank you. Thank you for showing me life!" I shouted as I hugged him gently. Putting his hands on my shoulders, he said, "My child you have surrendered to love! I rejoice, indeed! Every time you overlap another's fearful reality, you enter it, as well. Do not enter fear, whatever the cost, for the road to surrender requires a purity of love in the spirit."

Pointing to the path of the flowers, he said, "You have traveled this path, now do not return to the start of it. Transcend those in fear, do not participate. Fear cannot understand love, and love cannot understand fear. Words will not change what is in the heart. Keep your own heart pure." "I will," I said, "and thank you . . ." He turned, and disappeared.

"Behold, I am sending you like sheep in the midst of wolves; so be shrewd as serpents and simple as doves."
New American Bible, New Testament, Matthew 10:16, (Christianity, Catholic, Words of Christ)

****

Jumping towards the sky, I was quickly pulled down, as the movement directed me to lay quietly in a pink bed surrounded by pink curtains which had been prepared for me in the yard behind our home. Blowing in the spirit wind, I lay quietly, enjoying the quiet and solitude. Uniformed and thin, a man approached, but not wanting to be bothered, I ignored him. As he got closer, however, he said, "I've come to show you the sky pictures."

Pointing to the sky, he said, "If you look closely, you will see them." Nothing happened immediately, but minutes later an intense cloud came rolling in and the skies began to open. Images of hundreds of dimensions were flashing, appearing for several seconds and then moving forward. A gateway appeared, a large crystal entrance arching over a tunnel. Scenes changed from places I'd already traveled, to places I'd never even dreamed about. Joyful at my excitement, the spirit grinned as I called out with fervor, "Oh, my God, look at that!"

"There is one more thing," he said as he pointed upwards. Opening to a luminous vessel that hovered over me, two very old men beckoned to me, adorned with white beards grown to their waists and white robes glistening in purity. Coming from a vessel of many colors, it emanated with blues, greens, pinks and purples, as its celestial humming began to purr in my head.

A circular light beam was cast to the ground. Walking towards it, the spirit held me back. "It is not time," he said, "but you have found the gateway. A gateway has been forged in this space on the earth-plane. The sky is clear, the space is free, and the energy is open! The gateway has been forged so that you may enter any dimension you desire at will. It is through this gateway that you will meet a Pleiadian vessel, the one before you. Take this vessel. Antoneek will be your host. A world of dominion and peace awaits your arrival. You will tell of it to the earth and show them that dominion and peace are attainable in an entire civilization." Gazing intrigued, he continued. "You may open this gateway at any time. The gateway will remain the constant and will guide you to your return. The gateway holds much knowledge and will help you find your path." Standing up and quickly preparing to leave, the sky began to dawn the morn of tomorrow. "Thank you," I said, "a gateway, thank you."

"Wisdom's voice rings out from behind the doors of the righteous; wherever the godly foregather (is heard) her song."
The Dead Sea Scriptures, Poems/Qumran Hymnal, II, No. 12, Page 220, (Christianity, Gnostic/Essene)

"And the Lord took up word with me and said: Write the vision, and make it plain upon tablets that he who runs may read."
The Dead Sea Scriptures, Habakkuk, Chapter 2, Paragraph 1, Page 321, (Christianity, Gnostic/Essene)

****

Entering the elevator with a male spiritual guardian, I attempted to push the seventh of seven floors. Not lighting up, the six below it took instead. Knowing inside that seven was a higher reality and my goal, I looked towards the spiritual guardian. "Remember where you are in the fragment of time." Bewildered, the elevator began rising and stopped at level six. As the door opened, I saw a wondrous realm filled with ether and cloudy substances. Above, I could see the entry to level seven. "What you see is the shore, it lies in your view, it leads to the sky, a blue and gold hue." Emoting my desire to go there now, he continued, "All that lies, lingers;" he said, "all that emotes, forms; all that love, radiate; and all that serve, return home."

Understanding that I was to render service, he continued to speak. "Extemporaneous reason far behind, enter now the washing zone, beneath your feet a bluish light, cleanse, bring forth immortal soul." Leaving the elevator, my spirit walked upon the bluish clouds, realizing that all imperfect reasoning must be left behind, in order to instigate the purification process which brings forth the immortal soul. As bluish light seared forth from beneath my feet, I felt the intensity of the moment.

"Somehow, I remember this, but I can't place it. Is this a ceremony into service?" I said. Smiling the guide responded, "Open veils to light abode, release the fragment, duty done, allow creation's tempest flow, find the part which is but one." Remembering something about the seven levels of heaven, the spirit replied to my thoughts. "Yes, the seven levels of heaven."

Memories began to surface of things I'd forgotten. Somehow level six and level two were parallel to my path in the time constraint in which I was operating. Returning to the elevator, the guardian pushed level two. "Ever near the parting time, velvet linens part the zone, blood in pastness, sheer shine, relinquish sound, return to home." When it is time to part with the heavenly home, the veil moves aside for the descent of the soul to earth. The body contains the karmic self, which resides in the past, while the spirit remains sheer and iridescent as the two unite. Seeking to release the noise of karmic delusion, the spirit seeks the silence which is the essence of the journey home.

Reaching realm two, I saw that it was present-day Earth. "What do I do here?" I asked. Eyes piercing mine, he replied, "Ever dancing spirals mesh, beneath the fancy of the rain, close encounters to goodness, reaching ends, no longer pain." Many pathways merge and dance in the physical world, but they appear in energy as many spirals interacting below the storm clouds of karma. But amongst the turmoil, there are visions of higher reality, which provide the impetus to reach the end of the tumultuous karmic path and the end of self-inflicted pain.

"Why can't we do this from the sixth realm?" I asked, "Why must I enter this strange world in order to change it?" Pointing upwards, he replied, "Timely gain cannot complete, when traveling amongst the clouds, all diversion seemly sweet, but time exists beneath the shroud." One cannot affect worlds existing in 'time' effectively from 'timelessness,' as the subtle influences become only mild diversions to those beneath the veil. "But we have sent so much energy and light to the earth, has it not helped?" I asked. "Wheretofore, the gain complete, standing midst the starry realm, timeless air blows reaching tide, movement eludes most every soul." Progress which can be accomplished due to subtle influences from higher realms is minimal. Timeless energies (the movement) are not seen or heard by the majority of incarnate souls. "Yes, you are right; they do not listen to the sounds of the movement."

Turning to go, I looked within his deep green eyes and saw eternity.
"Quite oblivious they are to what the LORD is about, too blinded ever to see what He is actually doing. That is the reason why My people, likewise unconscious, have likewise been 'carried away' - away to an alien land, their gentry starving for hunger, their masses parched for thirst."
The Dead Sea Scriptures, Isaiah, Chapter 5, Page 303, No. 11-14, (Christianity, Gnostic/Essene)

****

And so it came to pass that I was given entry into the mysteries of the upper and underworlds; also called the 'Universal Sphere of Realms.' Realms (or dimensions) one through four are all underworlds, as they exist below the veil of illusion. Realms five and above are upperworlds which exist in ever-increasing levels of light and love above the veil of illusion. Shown the planets of our solar system, it was revealed to me which of them resided beneath the veil of illusion, those that were above.

UNIVERSAL SPHERE OF REALMS

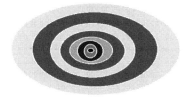

Realms:
Center, 1 and 2 = First and Second Dimension/Lower Worlds (Total Darkness) = Below Veil of Illusion
3 and 4 = Third and Fourth Dimension/Border Worlds (Light and Darkness) = Below Veil of Illusion
5 and above = Fifth Dimension and Above/Upperworlds (Light) = Above Veil of Illusion

The underworlds consist of the border or mortal realms, three (Earth) and four, and the lower realms, one and two. Border/mortal realms contain both light and dark energies and provide a karmic circling format for birth and death. Realms one and two are realms of total darkness, one being primary evil and two being dominant darkness. Many variances exist in levels of darkness as well as light, but greater understanding of this would come later.

After I was shown these things, Emmanuel appeared and said these words. "Forevermore, the tempest divide, master deva's come to seek. Moonlit mountains, thundering shores, icen castles, crystalline . . . enter deep. Like the crescent moon above, your starry realm emitting light, the earth-plane comes to fruition, the fullest phase in sight. Initiate vessels coming to find, relinquishing baggage . . . a solitary ride. Accepting of path, the lone company, each spirit will come to his own destiny." Conveying to me in a vision the process of transformation which occurred in other planetary systems, he showed me demon infested worlds which had become predominantly lighted.

Emmanuel then plunged me into the vision of the human condition; the violence, rage and chaos which frightened me. Turmoil and the death, he conveyed, are illusions created on planets of redemption. Transcendence and peace could only be found in rising above the bedlam.

Conveying that the ancient understanding of condemnation to hell, really means that the firmament between the higher and lower worlds is closed for a time to particular souls due to their spiritual status, but that the firmament does open for transformational opportunities when a soul seeks love, calling to God. "Demons turn into a song, their careful knowledge hidden so, timeless tunes, centrifugal force, the vortex of spirit turns into itself."

All of my lifetimes, all of my experience . . . came before me. Rather than sink into the abyss of delusions again, as I'd done many times before, I realized I had to conquer them this time around. The world caught below the veil of time, was a world of chaos, and to ascend I had to find unity and peace.

"They then went forth and created the upper world and the lower, the world of unification and the world of division."

The Zohar, Volume IV, P'Qude (Exodus), Page 299, Bottom, (Judaism)

****

Standing before the veil between worlds, I looked upon an interesting soul. Having the body of a man and the face of a bird, I didn't immediately recognize him, but later realized it was Thoth, the Egyptian god of letters who kept track of men's deeds. A burial casket had fallen directly in front of me. Wanting to get by, I calmly asked, "Please move the still," but he wouldn't budge. "I guard the veil to the world of flight. Only the pure of heart may pass, as a fragmented mind cannot comprehend that which lies beyond." Feeling that someone's presence lay directly beyond the veil, but being unable to see them, Thoth showed me a burial casket as he lit it on fire, performing some type of cremation ceremony. "Cremation is the secret I will now share with you." Thoth said. Speaking of fire, matter, and the Source, he conveyed that the 'flame,' which he now spoke of figuratively, releases a great deal of energy. Ascension is honored by releasing the flesh, in essence, burning the fragmentary vessel at death. When a soul is transitioning into the spirit world, the soul divides the energies between the two aspects; the physical personality and the spirit. In order for a soul to properly release the past, the energies of the former life must be released. By releasing it, the knowledge of the lifetime can be encompassed within the soul, while the fragmented nature is let go. Although I was unaware of it at the time, Thoth was speaking allegorically *and* literally about death.

The eternal flame consumes all that is left behind with each spiritual death and rebirth, which must occur at every great epiphany of knowledge. A death, of sorts, occurs when a soul realizes something of a karmic nature, and a birth occurs when a soul realizes something of an eternal nature. "I understand," I said, "when matter is burned, energy that is released." What must be consumed is the karmic self, which must be purged in order to be recovered in a purified state. "Something is telling me to say that this energy can be retrieved and sent to Isis."

Thoth moved aside and began speaking the sacred words to part the veil:

"Lingering nature, Goddess strain, initiate calls, for energy gain
Deity Isis, Call the sound, the veil now opens, behold, a cow"

Witnessing the spectacle of a woman with a human body but the head of a cow, the casket before me completely disintegrated, and Isis, the Egyptian goddess of birth, immediately spoke to me. "Bring to me matter," she said, "and I'll send you fire."

Nodding, I had no idea what she wanted me to do, but she conveyed that, "The dead must relinquish in order for the living to wed. It is the ritual mass of immortals," she said, "Bring to me matter, and I'll send you fire."

As she began laying a pile of dead twigs and sticks before me, she started a fire and continued adding to it. Representative of old beliefs and former perceptions which no longer served my path, bluish light was released from them as they burned, which soared into Isis. Taking it within, she sent the energy back into my spirit through my crown chakra.

Transforming from a mortal man into a spirit that sparkled and spit like an electrical storm, my spirit and body were merging into one. Engaging in a fire baptism of sorts, the stains of karmic multiplicity within my soul were purified into pure light.

"Thereafter his disciples said unto him: 'Rabbi, reveal unto us the mystery of the Light of thy father, since we heard thee say: 'There is still a fire-baptism and there is still a baptism of the holy spirit of the Light, and there is a spiritual chrism . . . "

Pistis Sophia, Fifth Book, Page 312, Paragraph 6, (Christianity, Gnostic/Essene)

"And Jesus said unto them: 'Bring me fire and vine branches.' They brought them unto him. He laid out the offering, and set down two wine-vessels, one on the right and the other on the left of the offering . . . Jesus stood before the offering, set the disciples behind him, all clad with linen garments, and in their hands the cipher of the name of the father of the Treasury of the Light, and he made invocation thus, saying: 'Hear me, O Father of all fatherhood, boundless Light: . . . Forgive the sins of the souls of these disciples who have followed me, and purify their iniquities and make them worthy to be reckoned with the kingdom of the father."

Pistis Sophia, Fifth Book, Page 310, Paragraph 1, (Christianity, Gnostic/Essene, Words of Christ)

Before being able to pass beyond this veil, however, I'd have to go through another ritual passage. A vision of the twinness of man was presented to me, as I saw the aspects of good and evil which resided within every human being. Their goodness resided in an upperworld sphere, while their evil remained in underworlds, trapped in fearful manifestations which were almost like webs in their thinking.

Taking me through mountains of staircases, Isis and I reached a 'bowed' step which plummeted into the underworlds. Releasing my hand, she conveyed that the initiates enter here. "This is a great test," she said, "remember the mysteries; there's no fear in truth."

****

Awaiting me was a golden hand, and I gently gazed upwards to see the imaged face of the bearer. Looking like a master from India, he also carried the energy of the Native American people. Taking his hand, we flew upwards along a spiraling pathway of rainbow-bright colored lights. "Where are we going?" I asked. "Somewhere you've never been before." He replied.

Bursting through hundreds of realms, we stopped in an all-white place. A magnificent display of white feathers ensconced us, nothing but floating white feathers. "This is the feather plane," he said, "the place of ascended native energy." Feeling absolutely luscious here, my spirit was melting into it like a bolt of unconditional love. But there were no singular spirits residing here, only ascended native energies, essences of total light whose unity had become a totality of one.

"In Mayan culture, the aura is sometimes symbolized by feathers - a representation of the realized being."

Secrets of Mayan Science/Religion, Chapter 5, Page 133, Paragraph 1, (Tribal, Mayan, Author: Hunbatz Men)

"Everything inside of the house was created by the mirth of the yellow people, light made of truth. The house they created was time that had been slowed down so that we, the people, might seek to know the vastness of our inheritance. The house was made up of many dawns, midday's, and moonlit nights. Inside

the house lay the principles that would hold and nurture life, that would carry us from dawn to dusk and then take us into beautiful and meaningful dream states, and then beyond them."
Being and Vibration, Chapter 5, Page 149, Paragraph 1, (Tribal, Tiwa, Author: Joseph Rael)

****

CHAPTER TWO
Muddy Flats Hell, 15 Layers of Hell, Management Realm, Spider and Insect Hell, Heaviness of Spirit Determining which Realm you may go to, Chaos Purgatory Realm, Wintery Blue Hell, Mythosetia - He Who Guards the Entry to the Lower Worlds, Mercy Shown in Hell, Hell for the Consumer's of Children.

****

"If I ascend up into heaven, thou art there: if I make my bed in hell, behold, thou art there."
King James Bible, Old Testament, Psalms 139:8, (Christianity)
"The only means of controlling and restraining these elements and keeping the hellish mob under restraint is the fear of punishment - no other means exists. For if it were not for the fear of punishment and torment, what is evil would plunge into rages and the whole place would fall apart, as happens to earthly kingdoms where there is no law or punishment."
Heaven & Hell, Chapter 60, No. 581, Page 485, (Christianity, Swedenborgianism, Author: Emanuel Swedenborg)

Leading a soul through the doorway of death, we came upon the maze of choices. Having lived a good life, he was trying very hard to follow God's will, and as a result, he had the option of ascending and moving beyond the death/rebirth cycles of life. In following the maze of choices, however, a soul naturally amends to that which most deeply follows their inner desires (their compatibility). Coming upon a crossroads, I fervently pointed to the right, the choice which would lead to his ascension, but he gave no thought to his choice and allowed his inner cravings to correspond with the familiar route. Turning to the left, he re-entered his own karmic circle. His choice was irrefutable, and as soon as it was made, he was no longer aware of my presence. Caught again in the cycle of karmic retribution, I paused but quickly turned to go, as there were more people crossing over this night.

Deep below the earth's surface, the ominous nature of where we were going suddenly hit me; the knowledge of it entered my conscious awareness as I began remembering the knowledge of the many hells. Many layers of the Earth reside all the way down to the molten core, each of them containing various hell realms. Closest to the surface, are the second dimensional hells, and further below, the first dimensional hells. We were going to one of the second dimensional hells, a place of vanity and greed, lovingly referred to as Muddy Flats.

"And in the same way likewise are sinners separated when they die, and are buried in the earth; judgment not overtaking them in their lifetime."
The Book of Enoch, Chapter XXII. (Sect. V), No. 11, (Judaism, Christianity)
"Our Lady stretched out her hands, and bright rays came forth which seemed to penetrate into the earth. All at once the ground vanished, and the children found themselves standing on the brink of a sea of fire."
Our Lady of Fatima's Peace Plan from Heaven, Page 4, Paragraph 1, (Christianity, Catholic)

Carved out of an old stone, a pointer lay in the ground which a soul could point to the left or the right. Remaining unrepentant after death, these souls believed that the fountain of youth lay in one of these directions. Choosing the correct direction would have offered them immediate reincarnation, but they followed the direction which they believed would take them to the fountain. In fact, the choice they made was to continue towards Muddy Flats.

Ominously ugly to see from a distance, Muddy Flats was an enclosed rock and mud cavern which held those who had entered in total and complete darkness. Those traveling through death's door this eve could still turn back if they chose, but as they remained in delusion, they continued walking towards Muddy Flats. Our host was an attractive man wearing a tuxedo, who smiled with a welcoming posture as he asked each one of them to dance. Coming to me first, I immediately walked away, as I had noticed that his hands had vague reptilian features. As he was a demon in disguise, I tried to warn the women who had not yet entered, but they were vain, and his advances and attention were much too easy a temptation.

As the first woman began to dance, she began screaming in utter horror as the man's hands became tentacled and reptilian. In moments, his demonic nature was revealed as his face evolved into its true demonic image. But it was too late, as they had danced, her skin began to age by hundreds of years and become reptilian, her hair was now totally gray. Drawing in and white, her face began to look like that of a corpse, and spider webs covered her body as if she had been decomposing in a grave for over a hundred years. As her screams stopped and she became quiet, the host walked her quietly into the Muddy Flats with calm acceptance.

Turning back into a handsome man, the host returned to tempt each one of them individually, as they were not given to see what happened to each of the women before them. When he was finished, he quietly re-entered Muddy Flats, leaving behind only two who had not given into his temptation.

Looking in horror as the others became mud dwellers; anger filled them as they looked to me for answers and resolve. Calmly, I explained that they could attempt immediate reincarnation since they had been able to avoid the temptation of Muddy Flats, but they were angry that the others could not also go back.

Manifesting a table, I offered them water from the cup of life which I held within my soul. Because this place was very hot, we were all parched with thirst. Noticing our thirst, the host of Muddy Flats, returned with a pitcher of water to offer them. Almost accepting it, I pushed the little demon away. "You mustn't accept *anything* from him!" I shouted to them. "Else your fate will be to enter Muddy Flats, as well." Shocked, they pulled away as the demon smiled his friendly, welcoming grin. "GO AWAY!" I shouted, as he politely walked back into his domain.

"I thought that God was loving!" One shouted at me, distressed by the fate of the others, as well as, her own. "Oh, yes," I answered, "God IS love!" "If that were true than we wouldn't be here . . . and they wouldn't be in there!" "You mustn't confuse what *God* is, with what *you* are." I said calmly. "It is not a matter of judgment, but of compatibility. You have chosen to *be* conscious malice; this is where you are compatible." Anger not dimming, I continued. "You cannot serve greed and vanity during your lifetime and expect to ascend to the highest heaven upon your death. You have come to the place where you have been most comfortable." Eyes seething with rage, they knew that they had spent their lives oppressing others with their wealth, preserving their fine lineage, good standing and youthful appearance. But they still did not get that there was something wrong with that. "God is also merciful," I said, pausing a moment to gauge their reaction, as their impatient glances spurned me to finish. "God is merciful to those who love Him. Do you love God?" Irritated sighs filled the room. "What does that mean, anyway??!" One of them said in a very disrespectful manner.

Looking in upon the mud dwellers through a tiny portal, I continued, "They, too, will have the opportunity to break their delusion. Their time here will reflect their inner desire to leave greed and vanity and try again. Some will remain for only a short while; others may choose what seems like an eternity."

"The fact that *you* were able to avoid the temptation to enter Muddy Flats indicates you may be ready to take a higher step in a new incarnation." Self-righteous anger spewed from these individuals who still felt that they should be given higher privilege because of their status, there was no remorse here. "If it is God you wish to reside with," I told them, "then it is God you must seek and serve." Displaying confusion, their eyes were lost. "This is a place of selfishness. As you depart into your next life, drink of this water of life I give to you, and seek to serve *life* itself. In this, you will find a new path. Have a good journey." Waving my arms, they immediately began transport to the place where their new karmic journeys would begin. Only they could choose whether they would nurture that seed or return to Muddy Flats upon their next death.

"The devil flatters that he may deceive us; he charms that he may injure us; he allures that he may slay us."
The Voice of the Saints, In Temptation, Page 65, No. 2, (Christianity, Catholic, Words of St. John Vianney)

"When Our Lady revealed at Fatima that Hell definitely exists and that unrepentant sinners go there after death, she was reminding us that Christ never forgave an unrepentant sinner and that God is, indeed, infinitely good and loving, but that His goodness and love are manifested not in the forgiveness of unrepentant sinners, but in the bountiful mercy He shows to repentant sinners."
The Forgotten Secret of Fatima, Section 8, Paragraph 1, Page 29, (Christianity, Catholic)
****

As the winds began, my form began to transform into an emissary of Mary. A blue veil adorned my head and hair and white robes were emanated around my body. Mary pulsed within my soul as I accepted her winds in humility. Heralding the night, Mary sent me on many missions working with spirits in the deepest darkness who would not even acknowledge God. Seeding them, I returned. Appearing again for only a moment, I stood before her in the center of a commando unit preparing for a perilous journey.

Wearing camouflage gear now rather than the robes, Mary said, "You will undergo vigorous army training for this journey as you will be traveling into the deepest and darkest places in the second and first dimensions, the hells. This is a necessary journey. As you have taught humanity of the higher realms, you will now teach them of the lower realms." Pausing, she looked at me with strength. "With this journey comes danger. You cannot travel to these places without proper training and knowledge of how to safely move through these realms." Raising her hand, she pointed to the Captain of this commando unit, and in her gesture I knew I was to obey him at all costs. Then she disappeared.

Vigorous training began immediately and continued through several nights. Thinking it would never end, I realized, however, that the knowledge attained was vital. Moving through these hell realms required the ability to pull in your light so as not to be seen. In going to these places, it was my job to observe and record what I had seen, but to remain distant and unseen to those who resided within the lower realms. Predatory, parasitic and consumptive, the nature of these realms was that of destruction, and their natural enemy was the light. Therefore, I would travel unseen with my comrades, vitally observing every order from our Captain without question. So we began.

Narrow, dark, wet and dank, the corridors leading to the layers below Muddy Flats seemed to go on endlessly . . . down, down, down. A column of souls was walking down, and a column was walking up; those entering and leaving the next layer of the hells. Faces were expressionless, much like zombies. "Do not be deluded by their benign and sympathetic appearance, for if they see light, they will become ferocious and try to destroy you," the Captain warned.

Continuing downward endlessly, we exerted a great deal of energy to pull our light within so as not to be seen. Remaining in a single column, we emulated exactly what the denizens of hell did, so they wouldn't realize that we didn't belong here. Surrounded by an army of soldiers for protection, the endless journey finally reached a conclusion as we entered the next layer.

Before me was the 'Management' section for the second layer of hells. Spirits worked here to maintain this level of evolution, and an escalator stood in the middle of the room which noted fifteen separate hells on fifteen separate layers of the Earth's crust. Noted by different colors, the Captain directed me to look at a color titled wintry blue. "Would that be a cold hell?" I asked with intrigue, suddenly realizing that some of the hells were not hot. Nodding, I gazed upon the board to note that the colors ranged from putrid yellow to a horrid multi-color orange which resembled vomit.

Laying his hands upon my shoulder, the Captain indicated that our time was complete for this night. Handing me a book, its title read, "The Sutta on Evil.' As I held it, I began to take in the knowledge and understanding of evil. Suddenly, my spirit soared back to my body directly, without passing through the dark and dank passageways we had previously traversed.

"(After death), some are reborn in the womb; evildoers are born in hell; those who commit meritorious deeds go to heaven; and those who are free from worldly desires realize nirvana."
Dhammapada, Canto IX, No. 126, Page 51, (Buddhism)
"There are eighteen great hells and five hundred secondary ones, their names all different. In addition, there are another hundred thousand with distinct names . . ."
Sutra of the Past Vows of Earth Store Bodhisattva, Chapter 3, Page 114, Paragraph 3, Buddhism, Pure Land)

****

Having crossed what appeared to be death's door, the gateway to heaven again stood before me. Ether vibrated with soaring tones, and my spirit floated higher and higher, closer and closer to the entrance to heaven. Stained glass windows hovered in the heavens forming a hallway to the entrance, but no walls were between them. Hundreds of angels were singing as they were gathered all around this holy gate.

Chanting in harmonic and resonant tones, their voices echoed through the stars which lay in the distance beyond this open hallway of stained glass. Joining in their singing, my spirit knew their music. My voice began echoing louder than all the others, and my singing somehow sent my spirit ever faster towards the entrance to heaven. Arriving at the gate, I suddenly knew that these chants and hymns the angels and I sang released actual weight from the soul, dropping off the heavy vibrations of physical existence. Apparently our compatibility to heavenly realms is more determined by the actual 'weight' of the soul, a lightness of spirit. Becoming more and more weightless, then, would make it possible for me to travel to higher and higher heavens. Ecstasy echoing, my soul floated closer and closer to the gate and my soul became one in song with the angelic kingdom.

But suddenly, I was whisked back, having been called below to give service. Falling from the eminence of grace, I saw the gate and cathedral windows pass quickly by my vision, as my attention was directed to a small square portal in the sky. Slowing to a halt, I squeezed through the hole and immediately recognized the place I'd entered as the 'Spider and Insect Hell.'

Having stick bodies and spider/insect heads, two hosts of this realm stood before me. The first had a black stick body and a white spider head with eight legs coming out of it. The second had a similar black stick body with a roach head. A man was standing between me and the hosts of this hell, his face showing his fear and confusion, as he had just arrived. Serving a more vile level of greed than Muddy Flats, he was in trouble.

Knowing my purpose, I tried to assist the man in exiting this dark place.

With all my might, I began pushing him upwards towards the tiny portal in which he had fallen, but he would not budge. No matter how hard I tried, attempting to lift this heavy-laden soul out of the hell only depleted my own energies with no outward result or favor. Realizing that it was the actual weight of his soul which made it impossible for him to go higher, his unrepentant sin had become like a ball and chain. As much as I would have liked to save him, he was compatible to this hell.

After a great deal of struggle, I finally accepted that this soul was not light enough to emerge upwards through the portal, and he would have to remain. Heavy laden his soul's weight and defilement, my energy was completely depleted and it took me several minutes to engage enough energy to soar up to the portal and emerge. Sloshing down upon the starry sky, I fell to rest outside the tiny entrance to hell. An angel stood by my side to give me back my strength.

Taking my hand, the angel showed me two visions of the possible outcome of my life. As each vision was presented, I felt the actual weight, energetically, that the particular choice would yield. The first possible outcome was trying to 'save the world.' Vines emerged from the Earth holding me down to the ground with the terror and delusions of others. Hundreds of trees came from beneath the ground, smothering my life-force and keeping me completely chained to the physical world. Screaming in terror, I panicked, but from beneath the vines which held my soul in complete imprisonment, the angel picked up an 8' X 10' black and white photograph which showed the other possible outcome of my life. Within it, I saw myself choosing to focus my energies on saving my own little corner of the world, my husband and children. Reaching frantically for that option, the vines began pulling away from me. A world whose purpose is to serve karmic delusion does not need saving as it fulfills its function with perfection as God has designed it to do.

Seeking to ascend that which was within my reach, I became weightless again. Conveying to me that I *could not* save everyone in the world because they were too heavy, I accepted this, and my soul lifted up and began soaring towards the heavenly gate in a grand lightness of being.

Our singing honored the Lord as we again converged at the heavenly gate, stars cascading around the weightless ones all about me. Surrendering, I understood that all who truly reach to God find an outstretched hand reaching for them; but for those who reach below, we must pray for their souls, and let them be.

"So there we were until you, most high, not forsaking our dust, but pitying our pitiful state, came to our help in secret and wonderful ways."
The Confessions of St. Augustine, Book VI, Chapter 12, Page 131, (Christianity, Catholic, Author: St. Augustine)
"Long is the night to a sleepless person; long is the distance of a league to a tired person; long is the circle of rebirths to a fool who does not know the true Law . . ."
Dhammapada, Canto V, No. 60 & 62, Page 27, (Buddhism)

****

Dragging upon the ground behind as I rushed towards my destination, my long blue cloak was a hindrance in my hurry. Unaware of where I might be going, I only knew that I had to run through this very large crowd of people to get there. Despite my old fashioned cloak, other people about me seemed to be dressed in very modern attire. But in a blink of an eye, I was transported to a very different place, where everyone was dressed in much the same manner.

An old marketplace, much like you would expect along the streets of an old town in the 19th century, there were hundreds of spirits here from the last 200 years; pirates, cowboys, women in bonnets and long dresses, etc. In contrast to the great number of people who rushed upon their way, the streets seemed quite narrow. As I kept running, I knew that I was here to find somebody, but I didn't know who. The chaos all around me was deafening, people were yelling and screaming, selling their wares loudly, protecting themselves from thieves. Others were lying upon the ground or leaned up against the walls, drunk or sleeping.

Coming upon a woman who was writing hymns on an old player piano in a storefront, I stopped to look at her work. Such a Godly pursuit seemed incompatible to this chaotic realm, and it gave me joy to see her do this. Unhappy with her music, however, she accepted encouragement to continue writing. What she was doing might eventually free her soul.

Turning, I saw the gentleman I was here to find. Inherently, I knew that I was not to approach him, for it was imperative that he find me first. Beginning to run towards him, I became lost in the chaos of the crowds. As I was pushed, pulled and tossed this way and that, the man was suddenly out of sight. Running aimlessly, I followed the crowds down the endless yet repetitive marketplace streets which were like a chaotic maze, where you would continually go down similar streets but you never understood how you got back to them or why. In constant motion, the people in this realm were bouncing on and off of each other's realities.

Suddenly, I heard the man's voice. "I know you!" he said, as I turned to greet him. "You've run by here six times! As soon as I spotted you, I knew we must meet. Are you lost?" My purpose was unknown to him, but at least he recognized me. "Yes, indeed," I replied. Pulling me close, it was obvious that he had misunderstood the purpose of our meeting. Moving away from his grasp, he immediately sensed my discomfort at his romantic intentions. "Thank you," I said in response to his respectful withdrawal. "I have come to find the way out of the chaos realm." I said. "You mean hell?" he laughed.

Indeed, it was one of the *gateways* to the hells, although the chaos realm contained both darkness and light. A place of karmic circling, it was compatible to those who crave the delusion of constant motion.

"I'm Philip," the man said, "and who might you be?" Shyly, I responded, "Just one who seeks the doorway out of this chaotic realm." Laughing hysterically, he said, "There's no way out of this place, we're on the moon. No one ever finds their way out of here." Suddenly from my view, I could see the Earth through a small portal appearing through the clouds in the sky. "Oh, my God!" I shrieked. "You're right! We are on the moon!"

Calmly, he took my hand. Wanting to comfort me, he believed I was simply delusional. "There is a way out of here." I said, but he maintained the kindly gentleman approach as he sarcastically chuckled. "Well, then, if you ever find it, you come back and get me so I can get out of here with you." Perceiving that I was a lost soul wandering through chaos, his disbelief was undaunting. "There *is* a way out of here," I said, "come with me and we'll find it together."

Pointing to the portal in the sky where the Earth was easily seen, I knew that this had to be the exit. Closed in by a constant overshadowing of clouds, the rest of the realm was completely blocked. Suddenly, I felt a tug from the spirit world as it began to pull me away through the portal. "Take my hand," I yelled, "come with me." But he wouldn't, and as I was swiftly sucked out of the chaos, I could do nothing but watch his surprised face as he watched me exit the realm.

Making me aware that my task was to help him realize there was an exit, the eternal made clear that he would pursue it and eventually find deliverance. It was finished.

"East of that is yet another sea where the sufferings are doubled still again. What the combined evil causes of the Three Karmic Vehicles evoke is called the sea of karma. This is that place."

Sutra of the Past Vows of Earth Store Bodhisattva, Chapter 1, Page 84, Paragraph 6, (Buddhism, Pure Land)

"And I gave commandment unto Gabriel and Michael to bear Pistis Sophia in their hands, so that her feet should not touch the darkness below; and I gave them commandment moreover to guide her in the regions of the chaos, out of which she was to be led."
Pistis Sophia, Second Book, Page 116, Paragraph 2, (Christianity, Gnostic/Essene, Words of Christ)

****

Sucking me down in a manner indescribable in human terms, my spirit was being forced deep below, passing by crust after crust of the earth to reach this horrid layer of hells beneath the earth's surface. All around this formidable hell were the winds of destruction. Wintry blue was a place of absolute terror as funnel clouds, tornadoes, hurricane winds and earthquakes were a constant companion to the inhabitants.

Landing on a hard and solid piece of rock amidst the cavernous place, the inhabitants of wintry blue were starving, skinny and shivering with terror. A slightly plump, young doctor approached me. Although he did not reside here, he came on occasion to help these lost ones, and on this occasion to show me the mechanisms of this realm. Such kindness amazed me, as he protected my soul with such fervor. Serene and wise, he understood the cycles of destruction in this realm and gently guided me to crawl underneath a cavernous wall, so as not to be annihilated by an oncoming tornado. Subsequently, he moved me to a place far from the cavernous walls when the earthquakes began, so as not to be struck by boulders underneath a cliff. Time passed by so very slowly in this wintry blue hell, and although it wasn't unusually cold, the inhabitants shivered from the mere force of the torrential winds, rains, cyclones and movements of the Earth that barraged them constantly. After what seemed like a day, but in reality was only about five minutes, the doctor motioned me to watch the inhabitants carefully.

Filing out of the cavern, their blank faces became more alert as if some great danger awaited them. "They go to forage for food," he said, as he grasped my hand and motioned for us to follow them. Penetrating the cave wall, they entered another hell realm below wintry blue, called putrid yellow. Putrid yellow was highly predatorial and mixed with the absolute destruction of wintry blue. Old homes which had been demolished by these forces lay scattered around as if no one had ever inhabited them. Walking into these buildings, the souls looked for food in abandoned refrigerators or cabinets.

Penetrating into the homes brought you into yet another lower realm, which consisted of the inner sphere of the individual homes which held an inescapable feeling of being trapped. Wild animals roamed these encampments, also looking for food. Fighting the wild cats and dogs, the inhabitants of wintry blue had to battle fiercely for any remnants of food which remained. Many were badly mauled by the animals and lay wounded but unable to die and with no means of help. Only those who chose not to fight for food would be left alone by the wild beasts with the red eyes. Because of this, the beasts left the doctor and I alone, as if they could not even see us.

Leading me back through the wall while the remaining inhabitants continued their battles, the doctor lifted his head upwards as we began soaring back through the Earth's layers to the surface. Nodding to me as he disappeared, the loving doctor left me safely in the mortal world while he returned to the evil places below to assist those who were injured with their sufferings. Nodding back to him, I acknowledged the amazing gift he gave to the evolution of souls.

"There is a hell in which the offender is followed everywhere by fire; there is a hell in which there is cold and ice; there is a hell in which there is limitless dung and urine; there is a hell in which there are flying maces; there is a hell in which there are many fiery spears; there is a hell in which one is constantly beaten on the chest and back; there is a hell in which one's hands and feet are burned; there is a hell in which the offender is wrapped and bound by iron serpents . . .

Humane One, such are the retributions. In each hell there are a hundred thousand kinds of utensils of karma, and . . . any single hell would have hundreds of thousands of kinds of acute suffering."
Sutra of the Past Vows of Earth Store Bodhisattva, Chapter 5, Page 140-141, (Buddhism, Pure Land)

****

Black and hazy, the doors were frightening in their appearance. Following a path into the black mists deep within the Earth, the entry to the lower realms hovered in eerie silence. Those preparing to go there canvassed the area around me, their faces dead in expression, and their spiritual bodies decomposing in my sight. Pushing them out of my way to run far away from the gate, my only goal was to get away from this entry to the dark kingdoms. But as I pushed, they shoved and threw me forward as the gateway slowly creaked open. In moments, they had hurled me down the steps.

Instinctually, I called out, "Mythosetia." (Pronounced - mithoseeshoo). With the advent of the word, my spirit soared back up the steps beyond the gate and stopped before a group of monks who were singing. Mythosetia was a monk who guarded the entry to the lower worlds, and a guardian of the knowledge in regards to the evolution of darkness. A monk of extreme importance, he protected, taught and guided those who must go below to serve evolution's cause. Calling his name could deliver any soul of sincere and pure heart to safety.

Walking forward from the group of chanting monks, he appeared to me as a black man with many long braids in his hair. Taking my hand, he guided me through the halls of this unique monastery, but never spoke. Hearing the chants from the hallowed walls of this sacred cavernous monastery, I looked down and noticed that I was dressed in a full nun's habit, and my identity was revealed to me; an ancient nun who wrote Gregorian chant.

Mythosetia took both of my hands and stared directly into my eyes. Hearing the beautiful music of my former life, I knew that Mythosetia was conveying energy towards the writing of the hymnal. Bowing in respect to Mythosetia, he smiled and disappeared.

"And on the day when the heaven bursts asunder with clouds, and the angels are sent down, as they are sent. The kingdom on that day rightly belongs to the Benificent, and it will be a hard day for the disbelievers."
Holy Qur'an, 25:25-26, Page 701, (Islam, Words of Mohammad)
"Then as for those who are unhappy, they will be in the Fire; for them therein will be sighing and groaning - Abiding therein so long as the heavens and the earth endure, except as thy Lord please. Surely thy Lord is Doer of what He intends."
Holy Qur'an, 11:106-107, Page 457, (Islam, Words of Mohammad)

****

Lain amidst the horrid spectacle of this putrid lower realm, the grave of the abuser was surrounded by darkness. Others who had been committed to this place were walking around as their bodies were decomposing. Sitting before his grave, I noticed that a statue of him (which represented his soul) had been broken into several pieces. Carefully, I began to pick them up and put them back together as best as I could.

An old man, a caretaker in this deep pit, showed me how I could use clay from the Earth to fasten the pieces back together again. From behind the gravestone, a young Indian woman appeared with a fawn at her side. Humming a mournful chant for the dead, she shook a somber rattle in her respectful obeisance to the lost souls of the lower worlds.

Looking at her, I said, "I am deeply concerned, for this man was a great sinner, and I am filled with concern and worry over his soul." Looking up quietly and calmly, she replied, "God will not forget us, no matter how much we have sinned. His soul is not forgotten by the Lord." Conveying to me that his crimes held less accountability than one might imagine because of an accident that had occurred in his youth, causing some minor unrecognized brain damage which affected his thinking on proper boundaries. No mercy is given in *stopping* such predators, but mercy is given, when appropriate due to circumstances beyond their control in regards to the judgment of their soul.

Another young man, also confounded to this hell realm, approached. His hands were merely stubs as they had decomposed. "There are those who teach us even in our graves." He said. Surprised, I noticed a spirit standing aside his grave site. "I am told that when I learn to disconnect from my body and leave this putrid death behind, that I will be able to fly!"

Looking at the young Indian woman who continued chanting, she quietly said, "We worry about those we love who have sinned much, but the Lord has not forgotten them, the Lord has not forgotten them . . ."

"Abu Huraira reported: The Apostle of Allah (may peace be upon him) visited the grave of his mother and he wept, and moved others around him to tears, and said: I sought permission from my Lord to beg forgiveness for her but it was not granted to me, and I sought permission to visit her grave and it was granted to me. So visit the graves, for that makes you mindful of death."

Sahih Muslim (The Hadith), Volume II, Chapter CCCLIII, No. 2130, Page 463, Paragraph 2, (Islam)

"I know thy works, and where thou dwellest, even where Satan's seat is . . ."

King James Bible, New Testament, Revelations 2:13, (Christianity, Catholic, Words of Christ)

****

Standing again before a torrential river whose rage was unbearable, the ravages of hell for the consumer's of children surrounded me; spitting fire, demons, a dark black fog, and the souls who were trapped by their own defilement. It was like living in the greatest nightmare surrounded by the worst of all that exists. Lying among the burning embers of the ashes were many books thrown half-hazardly and strewn into the ashes and fires. Inherently, I knew that only one held deliverance from this burning fire of hell. 'How to Become Famous', 'How to Get Rich', were just a couple of the self-serving titles. After a short time, however, I spotted a very small book hiding below a mountain of ash.

Mother Teresa had written this book in heaven and its title was . . . 'Mercy - The Path to Becoming Holy.' Feeling unworthy, I picked it up, and as I did, I was delivered from the hell of the consumers of children. "Help Mother Teresa," a voice whispered. Mercy delivers us, but discernment protects us. Be merciful to all, as much as you can, but be discerning in what you accept and allow into your life, lest you be deceived by the serpent and his many faces.

"Behold, I stand at the door, and knock: if any man hear my voice, and open the door, I will come in to him . . . To him that overcometh will I grant to sit with me in my throne, even as I also overcame, and am set down with my Father in his throne."

King James Bible, New Testament, Revelations 3:20-21, (Christianity, Words of Christ)

Moments after I had dissolved, I stood before a beautiful, peaceful, oriental, island. Waiting for me on the shore, a man had come to guide me deeper, conveying that this was Hakeo Island, a place of serenity. Taking his hand, I noticed an orb of light coming from the center of this grand vista. Walking very slowly, I watched this light as we approached.

From that day forward, because of my belief in mercy, I prayed for souls, and begged that those who lacked remorse, be given the light of repentance. For who among us is not in need of mercy, who among us will not beg it at the moment of our own death?

"If I ascend to heaven, Thou art there; If I make my bed in Sheol, behold, Thou art there."

New American Bible, Old Testament, Psalm 139:8 (Words of David)

"Be ye the master of all that surrounds thee, never be mastered by the effects of

thy life. Create then ever more perfect causes, and in time shalt thou be a Sun of the Light."
The Emerald Tablets of Thoth the Atlantean, Tablet XI, Page 64, Paragraph 4, (Mystery Religions, Egyptian/Hermetic, Words of Thoth)
"All the desolation of the poor people, their material poverty, their spiritual destitution might be redeemed by our sharing it, by our being one with them, by bringing God into their lives and bringing them to God."
The Love of Christ, Part III, Page 74, Paragraph 3, (Christianity, Catholic, Words of Mother Teresa)
"Everything is foreknown, but man is free."
The Talmudic Anthology, No. 97, Page 135, Stanza 4, (Judaism)
****

CHAPTER THREE
Heaven and its Many Suns, Commitment and its Correlations to the Chaos Realm, Hell for those Who do not Love Their Neighbor or God, Heavenly Crucifix of Gold and Silver, Seven Keys to the Valleys, Heavenly Bodies, Hellish Misunderstanding of a Preacher at the Gate of Heaven, Heaven of Redemption, the Heavenly Matrixes, Circling Yellow, Red and Blue Stars at the Gates of Heaven, Fuscia Star Tunnel.

****

Shooting at the speed of light into the heavens to observe the stars, an unusually bright, long and hazy tunnel appeared. Before my eyes, a staircase came into being with grayish stone steps leading up to the tunnel. On each of the steps of this staircase, a white angel stood. Climbing the steps, I shot towards the tunnel, emerging at the other end. A message was conveyed to me that I could go wherever I wanted. "I KNOW!" I shouted, "I want to go to heaven!"

Immediately the stars began forming a huge vortex in motion. Becoming sea blue and eminently grand, my soul shot through the center of the *huge* circle of stars. An identical vortex of pink stars appeared, and as I shot through it, an amazing yellow vortex came to be. Going through it, I entered pure light! The light was increasing in brightness as I traveled through it. Coming upon an entry, I went inside as the most vivid and splendid colors I could ever have imagined surrounded me in forms I had never seen. Fifteen or twenty suns were blaring in its sky. Time drawing to a close, I took one last look at the colors in iridescence and pastel, deep and subtle. Shooting back through the entry, two angels took me home.

Coming back to my house, the angels pointed out to me that two guardian angels were standing beside my front door. Beautiful and very large, they were adorned with human features, hair the color of light and white robes with enormous wings. Bowing to both of them, I quietly thanked them for their protection.

"To follow the Lord is the beginning of Wisdom: And the knowledge of the Holy One is understanding . . . All Wisdom cometh from the Heavenly Father, and is with him forever. Through the holy Law doth the Angel of Wisdom guide the Children of Light. Who can number the sand of the sea, and the drops of rain, and the days of eternity? Who can find out the heights of heaven, and the breadth of the earth, and the deep, and wisdom? Wisdom hath been created before all things."
The Essene Gospel of Peace, Book Three, Page 51, Top, (Christianity, Gnostic/Essene)
****

Several people were waiting for me to arrive to give them a teaching about the lower realms. Standing before an icy pond, one side of the pond was disconnected from the rest and was almost like a bog; filled with seaweed, growths and stagnant murky water. The other side of the pond was deep, clear and clean, kept that way by an underground stream which funneled into it from a cave below the depths. Beginning to speak about the chaos realm, I compared it to the stagnant part of the pond. "The chaos realm always appears to be constantly moving, when in fact it is as stagnant as this pond; stagnant in thought, evolution or motion toward a higher ideal. Chaos contains the thoughts and actions of beings who are caught up in senseless motion, the type of motion that actually precludes any real movement towards God. So, although those beings who operate in chaos, either in the physical realm or in the actual realm called chaos, perceive that they are quite busy, there is no movement and their thoughts and actions actually look as rancid and motionless as this bog."

"The movement you see in the water on the other side is the correct way, as the water constantly purifies itself and alters itself to accommodate reality at the present level. The past and the present are inexorably tied to each other in their motion, but not enslaved. Past and present can meet, as can present and future, but they meet because there is true movement, which is quiet and inner. You cannot see on the surface of either of these two ponds the inner processes that make one a bog, and one a clear flowing stream, for this movement is unseen to the human eye, it is underground. True movement comes on an inner level, but those residing in chaos still perceive outer movement as the path to evolution. So they find themselves wandering around aimlessly in chaos."

Their confusion and irritation at this were obvious, with the exception of one soul. Apparently, these were souls currently living in chaos, and only one was ready to speak of the peaceful movement. "If you want to find the truth, you must stop like the clear pond and allow the waters of the spirit to come into you, it is in this that a soul begins to truly move."

Turning, I left the scene.

"A single word full of meaning, hearing which one becomes at peace, is better than a thousand words which are empty of meaning."
Dhammapada, Canto VIII, No. 100, Page 43, (Buddhism)

****

Entering a hell realm, I had come in just below the surface of the Earth. Those who resided in this realm were trashy rednecks, and their two primary sins had been not loving or trusting their neighbor and a complete lack of interest in God.

Because of this, I had to be very careful while traveling through this realm. Because of their perception, they assumed I was out to get them and would come after me. Spending most of my time running from these very uncaring folks, they thought I wanted to steal from them. Ironically, I found many of my missing things down there and realized that these folks often steal from the people on the surface, albeit, the demons who support them will make trips to the surface to take small items for no real purpose other than to be a nuisance.

Running wholeheartedly from a particularly rowdy band of rednecks, I came upon a clearing where there was a large stock of weeds. Coming closer, I pulled the weeds aside and saw a small bunny. All of a sudden, I understood that the exit from this hell realm came in the form of soft fuzzy bunny, and I quickly picked her up and began petting her lovingly. Because the rednecks were uncharitable towards others, they had to pick up the bunny and love it tenderly, genuinely and with innocent regard. As I petted the bunny, I was immediately transported outside of this unusual hell.

"When a man is involved in worldly affairs, his thoughts are bound by chains of the burden that weighs upon them and it is impossible for them to become concerned with his deeds."
The Path of the Just, Chapter V, Page 63, Paragraph 2, (Judaism, Author: Rabbi Moshe Chayim Luzzatto)

"They (the beings of Hell) rot upon a couch of darkness; in lust and in pursuit of

desire they give birth to each other and then destroy each other."
Gnosis on the Silk Road, Chapter 2, No. 2, Verse s, (Christianity, Gnostic/Essene)
****

Until Andy pointed out that there was a miraculous mountain pathway framed in gold ahead, the mountain retreat held little interest to me. Pure metallic gold appeared to be painted on the borders of this mountain valley, the peaks, the trees, various rivers and streams.

Going with a tour group, we began walking down the narrow pathway toward the bottom of the first mountain pass. From where we stood, we could see the beautiful golden framework which filled this mountainous region. Along the trails we would come along places where gold dust was scattered on rocks and trees, and a particular rock held my interest. Upon it was scattered both gold and silver dust, the silver to the left and the gold to the right. Others who had come along began playing with the stuff and wanted to mix the gold and silver dusts together. Grabbing their hands, I said, "If you mix silver with gold dust, the gold will be ruined."

Continuing down the path, I wandered far ahead of the group and came upon a small river alone. Despite its small size, the water was tumultuous and filled with white-water rapids and there was no way to cross. But I knew that I had to cross in order to find the secret meaning of this golden framed valley of the Lord. Fearful and afraid, I began walking towards the river planning to brave the rapids, knowing full well that I might not survive the crossing. But before I could even begin, the waves stopped thrashing. Waters calming, the water suddenly parted making a path for me to cross. Running across, I was thankful for this heavenly assistance.

The waters closed and began to rapture, leaving me alone in the golden mountain valley. On the other side, I could no longer hear the others as the frequency had shifted when I'd crossed over.

Up ahead I noticed a large, golden squarely-shaped pole about thirty feet high at the top of a mountain. In front of it was something of equal size but unintelligible from where I was standing. Beginning to walk towards it, I climbed higher and higher until I could see a huge crucifix, the exact same height as the golden pole, with a beautifully carved image of the Messiah hanging upon the cross.

Holiness filled me as I knew that this sacred sight held meaning beyond what I knew. Gazing upon the face of Jesus, I was suddenly thrust through the heavens at the speed of light to return to my physical body.

"The Palace of Righteousness, Ananda, was surrounded by a double railing. One railing was of gold, and one was of silver. The golden railing had its posts of gold, and its cross bars and its figure head of silver. The silver railing had its posts of silver, and its cross bars and its figure-head of gold."
Dialogues of the Buddha II, XVII The Great King of Glory, Page 214, Stanza 28
"It may happen that, while the soul is not in the least expecting Him to be about to grant it this favour, which it has never thought it can possibly deserve, it is conscious that Jesus Christ Our Lord is near to it . . . "
Interior Castle, Sixth Mansions, Chapter VIII, Page 179, Paragraph 1, (Christianity, Catholic, Author: St. Teresa of Avila)
****

Amongst the starlight I flew until I reached the highest summits of the mountains and my soul was swept in flight to tarry through the valleys and hills between them. But as I turned my gaze heavenwards, my soul shot like a rocket towards the starlight above me, a beautiful song entrancing my soul during my flight. "I'm talking about starlight, shining every way . . ." Spiritual essence filled me as I soared higher towards the heavens accepting the grace of this flight and the spiritual benefits of the stars.

Suddenly, my soul was shot back to the ground to witness some thought patterns of two particular souls. Disturbing, they were harboring nasty thoughts about one another and their thoughts were spewed all about them like rubble and trash. "I must speak to them, and redirect their thoughts." As I did, my soul began to fly again.

Again my soul was alit, flying high to the summits and peaks amassing the energy of the light, and dipping below amidst the valleys to witness the thoughts of souls in need of direction. Distributing light and making mental note of them all, I noticed a set of keys in the distance hanging on a mountainside amidst the valley.

Flying closer, I could see a musical sign, a treble clef, hanging amongst them. When I got closer, there were seven keys in all, which I understood to be the seven keys to the valleys (the seven phases, the seven seals).

"The stages that mark the wayfarer's journey from the abode of dust to the heavenly homeland are said to be seven. Some have called these Seven Valleys . . . And they say that until the wayfarer taketh leave of self, and traverseth these stages, he shall never reach to the ocean of nearness and union, nor drink of the peerless wine."
The Seven Valleys and The Four Valleys, Page 4, Paragraph 2, (Baha'i, Author: Baha'u'llah)
"Yea, I tell thee truly, the paths are seven through the Infinite Garden, and each must be traversed by the body, the heart and the mind as one, lest thou stumble and fall."
The Essene Gospel of Peace, Book 2, Page 61, Bottom, (Christianity, Gnostic/Essene)
****

"She will not touch anything consecrated nor go to the sanctuary until the time of her purification is over."
The New Jerusalem Bible, Old Testament, Leviticus 12:4, (Judaism)

Raptured in the moment, my soul became the vessel of higher energies as the Lord began another series of vibrational thrusts into my spirit. For hours, I would be swept into the vibrations of the next level of learning, and my spirit was given leave to fly amongst the stars, the sun and the heavenly bodies. Because of the sheer number of vibrational raisings I'd received for years, these experiences were no longer shocking or overwhelming.

Amongst the heavens, I could see atomic particles which appeared as sparks of light, swimming in a sea of ether. Everything was connected by the sea of ether, holding together the singular atoms of light which brought forth life in this world and the next. Bidding me leave to continue these awe-inspiring experiences for several weeks, my soul was being prepared for the next series of thrusts required in my purification.

"Through Thy name, O my God, all created things were stirred up, and the heavens were spread, and the earth was established, and the clouds were raised and made to rain upon the earth. This, verily, is a token of Thy grace unto all Thy creatures."
Prayers and Meditations, CXLVII, Paragraph 1, Page 236, (Baha'i, Author: Baha'u'llah)
****

Flying through the skies of fancy, my soul was directed towards an oblique force of energy ahead. An oval, spinning force, overlooked a sight my spirit desired to see. Placed atop a large window of sorts, it was an entry to a different place and time. Approaching slowly, I timidly walked towards the oblique stream.

Oh, my senses were a reeling! Oh, how vast, how joyous! Down below this window, I was given to see an earlier time in Earth's history, when creation was pure and sweet. A small band of white unicorns were gathered by a stream, their beauty complete. Feeling a longing for the purity and innocence of that time, I was bid to go.

"They were pure and noble, nimble, and joyous. Words cannot describe them. I was not familiar with many of them, for I saw very few like those we have now. I saw the elephant, the stag, the camel, and even the unicorn. This last I saw

also in the ark. It is remarkably gentle and affectionate, not so tall as a horse, its head more rounded in shape. I saw no asses, no insects, no wretched, loathsome creatures. These last I have always looked upon as a punishment of sin."
The Life of Jesus Christ and Biblical Revelations, Volume 1, The Creation, No. 2, Page 6,
(Christianity, Catholic, Words of The Venerable Anne Catherine Emmerich)
****

Alit in eternal wonder, my soul experienced a death. Standing before the gates of heaven and hell, a preacher man was present telling souls that none of them were worthy of heaven, and all deserved and *must* go to hell. All of our souls bore the stains of sin, and a dark crusty substance was upon our countenances as a result. But I instantly knew that the preacher man was dark, trying to trick souls into despair by using one of the rantings of humanity's religious original sin, that of a judgmental and unforgiving God.

Turning to him, I replied, "Although what you are saying is true, that no man among us has earned heaven, you are forgetting that through the redemption, God's mercy can save us all." Bowing to the etheric floor of the sky portal, I earnestly prayed for forgiveness for all of my sins and the sins of those who had died on this day with me. Begging God's mercy, I spoke in prayer of my awareness that none of us had earned heaven, but begged that through the redemption we might be saved from our wretched condition.

Immediately, our dark and filthy robes were cleansed in the light, and we became lighted, white-robed creatures flying through heaven's portal.

Entering heaven, we all experienced a bliss which cannot be described. And for a time, I was unaware that I had not truly crossed over. Beyond this, I was sent to the portal of heaven and hell many times to speak to the newly arriving souls. "You must believe in God's mercy, and ask it of the Lord to cross," I would say.

Beyond all sin, beyond all that we truly deserve, beyond what mortal man can hope to become, lies God's mercy.

"How very much I desire the salvation of souls! My dearest secretary, write that I want to pour out My divine life into human souls and sanctify them, if only they were willing to accept My grace. The greatest sinners would achieve great sanctity, if only they would trust in My mercy."
Divine Mercy, Notebook VI, No. 1784, (Christianity, Catholic, Words of Christ)
"My daughter, let nothing frighten or disconcert you. Remain deeply at peace. Everything is in my hands."
Divine Mercy, Notebook I, No. 219, (Christianity, Catholic, Words of Christ)
****

"To the praise of the glory of his grace, wherein he hath made us accepted in the beloved. In whom we have redemption through his blood, the forgiveness of sins, according to the riches of his grace; Wherein he hath abounded toward us in all wisdom and prudence; Having made known unto us the mystery of his will, according to his good pleasure which he hath purposed in himself: That in the dispensation of the fulness of times he might gather together in one all things in Christ, both which are in heaven, and which are on earth . . . "
King James Bible, New Testament, Ephesians 1:6-10, (Christianity, Words of St. Paul)
"And when these things begin to come to pass, then look up, and lift up your heads; for your redemption draweth nigh."
King James Bible, New Testament, Luke 21:28, (Christianity)

Propounded towards yet another untimely death, my spirit leapt upwards away from my sullen bodice towards the gates above which bore resplendent markings of their soon to be realized origin. How was I to know how grand an exit this was to be? How was I to know? For only a few moments, I looked below at my dead body, awaiting its discovery, but soon lost interest in my former condition and sought to attain to this glorious gate with such specific and mysterious markings.

Soaring, soaring, soaring . . . my soul fled from its former containment to the glory awaiting me above. In only a moment, I had crossed this mysterious portal and was immediately faced with a giant and noble lion. Without thought or regard, I placed my hand within its open mouth, but there was no violence perpetrated against me. The lion didn't hurt me, and somehow this energetic act was now energizing me into a great realm of knowledge of which I had never yet traversed. How was I to know? How was I to know?

Beginning its ascent through a myriad of energetic currents, my soul soared through purplish and yellow-white lights expanding in light-streams. An invisible angelic guardian of great holy sanctity handed me a very large book with perhaps 2,000 pages. Inside it were magnificent portrayals of angels, ministering spirits and heavenly hosts, and beyond this . . . how shall I say it . . . the mysteries of God's holy kingdoms enraptured in picturesque dramatizations. The pictures were stationary, yet, they appeared to be moving and the colors were of no kind I have ever seen, effervescent and psychedelic lights of violets, purples, blues, greens, pinks, and an especially entrancing aqueous fuchsia hue.

When I looked upon these pages, my soul was alit with eternal knowledge, inexplicable in its nature. Although all I have ever experienced has truly been profoundly difficult to encapsulate into words, none could fathom the depth of the wordlessness of this moment. And yet, it had only begun. If I only knew what lay ahead, how my soul might burst! Hundreds and perhaps thousands of angelic hosts, and their many individual and group missions were described to me in pictures; legions of angels created for every purpose known and unknown to mankind. Impaled by their beatific colored lights, their awesome splendor paled to their magnificent purpose! 'Oh, my Lord, how am I to witness such glory, a soul so wretched as my own!' Oh, how my thoughts were reeling at the high and sacred honor bestowed upon my soul this eve. No words, no words . . .

Several angels who had attended upon me in my latest 'death' were at my side, hastening me to realize the vastness of knowledge which remained to be obtained by my soul. Dumbstruck by the vastness of all that lay beyond what I already knew, one of the angels said, "We only have so much time, don't waste it." Such words and their import were now obvious to me in this afterlife which I had truly perceived as being a final exit for my own soul.

Feeling my soul being pulled in another direction, I grasped at the book with greater ferocity to obtain all knowledge I could within the limited time I might have. And then the angel aside made it known to me that this book had a physical counterpart; 'The Urantia Book.' Although imperfect, there was a great amount of extremely holy knowledge given within its pages on the mechanics of the angelic kingdom. Stunned, shocked and perplexed, I was amazed that such powerful and direct knowledge, such holy sanctified wisdom, could possibly be available to me on the ground. Making a vow to the angel that I would not waste my time, but study this book immediately, I turned the pages and came upon something which wasn't included within the pages of the grounded portion of this text.

As I was shown pictures of the 'avenging angels' (demons), I was told that I must give them but little attention, for mankind's fear of them energizes their purpose. At every path's end, we have aspects from that former path which become de-energized because they are no longer compatible to the succeeding step. If we quickly recognize them, we can send them off, but they must be recognized first, else the elements might remain and prevent progression. Knowing of their existence is not a necessity for fear, but change. Told to make note of them, their existence, etc., I was to say to the people of the world neither to fear them nor to focus on them; for this focus causes their greater glory and energizes their vengeful functions in the world.

Holding the book, I allowed the energies of its knowledge to enter within me. There are no words. My soul was alit in eternal wonderment and amazement as the energetic knowledge of its contents poured into me. Oh, how vast God's creation truly is! Oh, how vast, how vast!

Without even blinking an eye, my soul was immediately transported to another space, outer space to be precise. As I stood amongst the stars in the blackness of the heavens, another even larger book was given to me by an unseen host. But this book was beyond all pronouncement, its wonders far surpassed the wonders of the former. Looking upon its cover, I was quietly alive in its words, 'The Mysteries of the Redemption.' (This event occurred before the title to this book was made known to the author, and I must add that the text before you cannot contain to even the tiniest degree, the level of wisdom found in its most holy heavenly counterpart.) Now I cannot express even in minutest of detail what a rush of knowledge came over my soul. A blissful expansion of understanding which included such a vast array of interpretation as to leave my mind in a state of absolute wonder, I was awe-struck. I felt like St. Thomas Aquinas may have felt at that moment when he exclaimed that he had just been shown majesties of knowledge which were completely beyond words. From that moment forth, Aquinas never wrote another word. Trouble was that I knew that I must write of this. Oh, how would I!?

As I held this most holy and sacred book, holier than any book of knowledge ever given to touch my soul's hands, even greater inexplicable knowledge emerged within my soul. Unraveling before my eyes, I cannot tell you how profoundly energetic was this knowledge. The scrolls of St. Paul appeared before me, old and wrinkled parchments upon which no words had yet been written. Given to watch as the scrolls contents came down from heaven through the hands of St. Paul, as he signed them, they ignited into a mighty flame, becoming lighted fiery beacons which flew towards the Earth. I cannot express their deep holiness, or their profoundly sacred origin. The Epistles of Paul and the Acts of the Apostles of the New Testament are so indubitably holy, I feel unworthy to gaze upon their words. Words cannot express, words cannot express . . .

And if my soul had thought it had witnessed the most marvelous sight it could ever be given leave to see, an awesome voice beckoned from the heavens, as the words that were spoken were ignited in huge and magnificent lights upon the nighttime sky. My soul fell to its knees in holy honor, holy, holy honor. But those words cannot be repeated here, for such things must remain of heaven. My Lord, I am unworthy to bear witness to such a spectacle, my Lord, my Lord, who am I but a minuscule piece of pond scum in your mystical wonder of creation? Oh, how I would wish to share the grandeur of these words with you now, but I cannot, I should not. These words cannot be repeated here, for they regard the second coming of Christ, and are not to be revealed at this time. Unable to express the glory that was shown to me this night, I am unworthy, but I am so grateful for what the Lord has deigned to reveal to me.

As I stared upon this beauteous and most profound spectacle in the heavens, and the words filled me with the grace and absolute mercy of God's holy sacrifice, I could only shed tears. Beauty beyond all beauty, profundity beyond all that is profound, was this majestic offering greater than any of which I might be worthy. And to think that the mysteries of the redemption were just now beginning to embark upon this minuscule worm. Opening its door, so much glory remained to be revealed.

Christ is the center of the mysteries of the redemption. Perhaps for the next threshold of knowledge, there are no words. Silence is best.

"But God hath chosen the foolish things of the world to confound the wise; and God hath chosen the weak things of the world to confound the things which are mighty; And base things of the world, and things which are despised, hath God chosen, yea, and things which are not, to bring to naught things that are . . . "

King James Bible, New Testament, 1 Corinthians 1:27-28, (Christianity, Words of St. Paul)

****

Alit in eternal desire, the rushing winds returned my soul to this place in outer space wherein the mysteries of the redemption had dawned within my soul. Bidden to enter a small classroom amidst these stars, there was a man who was teaching at the front of the room to an empty classroom, containing nobody but me. Immediately, without a word being exchanged, I knew within my heart that this man possessed the book, 'The Mysteries of the Redemption.'

Interrupting and approaching him, I asked, "Is it true that you have the book on the mysteries of the redemption?" Nodding that this was so, I asked him if I could borrow it for a time. Happily he complied.

Reaching below his desk to a secret chamber, he took out a key and unlocked the compartment wherein the book was laid. Handing it to me, the large book looked the same as it had before; large, tan-colored and hardback with the words, 'The Mysteries of the Redemption,' centered on the cover. But as I looked at it, the cover began to change, and the new cover had an ancient cave drawing of five or six Native American riders on horseback riding the wind towards the left bound side of the book. "So the Native American's also have something to do with the Redemption?" I asked, as I remembered the alteration pathway. Smiling in acknowledgement of their purpose, he pointed towards a door, conveying that I must return the book and exit the classroom.

Upon leaving, I was immediately stupefied and dumbfounded. The image before my eyes was so beautiful and graceful; I could not bear it without kneeling to the ground. Magnificently quaffed in her white and blue robes which seemed to blow in the wind although there was no wind present; The Holy Mother of God awaited. About twenty other people were gathered watching her eminence, as I sat down. Quietly awaiting her most magnificent gesture, she approached me first with boxes that were filled with pictures of her in her many manifestations. Inside the large box was a smaller box covered in the most beautiful images of her holiness. But this box was closed and no one knew what lay inside. Handing one to me, I immediately knew that I was not worthy and bowed, "I am certainly unworthy to receive such a grand gift from you, my most Holy Mother, please give to me only a portion so that I may enjoy a reminder of your exquisite presence, but not so much so that I may be receiving more than I am worthy to receive." Unchanging in her facial expression, she simply took the box back and handed me the small box within the larger one. The images upon its outer shell were exquisite, but I was not yet able to open it to discover what lay inside.

Quietly, she proceeded to go to each of the others in the room with the same offering. Each of the others accepted the large box filled with pictures *and* the smaller box. Many were making fun of me, because they perceived that I had been quite stupid as to not accept the entire gift from the holy mother. But Mary was unmoved by their chatter, and she conveyed to me through a small change in her countenance that she was happy about my humility, and that the fruits and gifts of humility were far greater than anything in the larger box.

Looking upon me from behind the room wherein only I could see her as she stood behind the others who were now facing me, her thin lips changed into a small smile, subtle enough to give no clue to any other in the room, but blunt enough to make it known to me she was pleased with my humble request.

Suddenly, before I could open the holy box containing her sacred gift, my soul began pulling away. In her last thought, the holy mother bade me peruse, 'The Life of Christ and Biblical Revelations,' By St. Anne Catherine Emmerich, and 'The Mystical City of God,' By Mary of Agreda, both containing many of the mysteries of the redemption.

"First, I lost sight of Jesus' head, then His whole person, and lastly His feet,

radiant with light, disappeared in the celestial glory. I saw innumerable souls from all sides going into that light and vanishing on high with the lord . . . Out of that cloud, something like dew, like a shower of light fell upon all below . . ."
The Life of Jesus Christ and Biblical Revelations, Volume IV, Part 2, No. 15, Page 425, Paragraph 1-2, (Christianity, Catholic, Author: St. Anne Catherine Emmerich)
****

Becoming a practice before flight into the abodes of light, my soul had begun to undergo awakenings by the Lord, through the mechanism of a celestial ecstasy which brought about higher thrusts required to make such a journey possible. This time it took two of these thrusts.

Given leave to fly amongst the trees in a vast woodland, I felt the absolute bliss of my soul as it vaporized gently through the forest green. Although the mountains in the distance were beyond all ecstasy can emit, my soul longed for more than these Earthly things. Beckoning to the Lord that He might give me leave to travel the heavens and perhaps the warblings of the all-highest paradise, I waited.

Within a moment, my soul shot up in a frenzy towards the night sky, as the stars began coming ever closer to my spirit in a wisp of light. Entering into another dimensional reality of outer space, the regular stars became extinct creating huge black holes in the sky. Amidst the black holes amazing matrixes began appearing, geometric patterns - triangles, rectangles, squares, ellipses, arrows, etc. - in deep colors of violet, blue, gold and deep pink. Constantly changing and spinning, the matrixes held within them the knowledge of existence and beyond this the mysteries of the redemption.

Returning to the Earth, my spirit was laying asunder the roof of a small house within the woods, as the most beautiful music began playing before me in the ether. Seeing it as I heard it, it was the most beautiful piano concerto never before written. Panicking, I called out, "My Lord, it is so beautiful, but how could I possibly capture this in physical form, it's so complex." 'Some things are for the sake of beauty alone, and do not need to be transcribed into the physical waking reality world,' it was conveyed.

For a moment, the Lord bade to show me images of the music in the ether, as the melody transcribed itself to the night sky as visions of light particles. Joyous at this beauty, I fell into a transcendental state, watching the notes play in the sparkling lights of the ether, while its movement rendered my soul to serenity.

For several hours, my soul shot up into the heavens to again witness the matrixes, which cannot be described adequately in its show of knowledge, wisdom and might. Redemptive secrets were given to me, but I am want to put them into words, for they are all energetic and inexplicable. Each time, I begged the Lord to take me back to look upon these mysterious matrixes in the sky, yet one more time, just one more time . . .

In my final journey towards the stars, the matrixes again appeared in geometric fashions and forms elucidating knowledge. Begging for more, I was suddenly shooting through a wind stream of yellow, red and blue stars. Thousands, maybe millions were encircling upon a center point, much like a star tunnel, but this was much grander. In the center and outward were a cache of yellow swirling stars, only to be joined by a secondary band of red stars further out, and the final outer ring of blue. "Oh, my Lord," I cried out, "Oh, my Lord." Suddenly, I began singing a song of praise to God as I approached Him, 'I Love the Lord.'

Piercing through this amazing spectacle in the heavens, there was nothing I could do but fall to the ground in holy worship as I stood before the gates of paradise. Six marble columns arose among a great marble gate. All around it, the yellow, red and blue stars were swirling in constant motion. Tears were streaming in wide array as my voice uplifted higher and higher, "I love the

Lord, I love the Lord." Knowing that this was to be my final vision for the night, my soul quietly flew back to Earth, with remembrance of the most beautiful scene.

"Just as a song is drawn from heaven to earth by the Holy Spirit, so these words were drawn from heaven to earth by the holy spirit."
The Zohar, Volume V, Ha'azinu (Deuteronomy), Page 378, Paragraph 3, (Judaism)

"Great indeed is the blessedness of him who attaineth Thy presence, drinketh the wine of reunion proffered by the hand of Thy bounteousness, inhaleth the fragrance of Thy signs, unlooseth his tongue in celebrating Thy praise, soareth high in Thy heavens, is carried away by the sweetness of Thy Voice, gaineth admittance into the most exalted Paradise and attaineth the station of revelation and vision before the throne of Thy majesty."
Tablets of Baha'u'llah, No. 8, Ishra'q'at, Page 116, Paragraph 1, (Baha'i, Author: Baha'u'llah)

****

"Focus on the light, focus on the light . . ." the voice repeated in my brain. My soul was stirring amongst the clouds of the earth, and high above the atmosphere was a shining orb of God's great majesty. Instinctively, I knew that this was not the sun, and although it shone with immensity like the sun, it held iridescence beyond the bursting lights of the sun which drew my gaze upon it. If I were to go towards that light, I must focus on it, and let go of mundane and worldly things. As I did so, my spirit began soaring towards it like a rocket.

Suddenly amidst a fuchsia star tunnel whose brilliance cannot be described, thousands of fuchsia stars glowed with might and iridescence, and I soared threw them as they passed me at the speed of light. Entering yet another tunnel, it was almost like a plasma tube or an intestinal wall with a see-through lining of a light pinkish plasma type substance, and variegating widths of narrow to wide. Entering it, I exited the other end in what seemed like less than a moment.

Fuchsia stars reappearing, my soul continued soaring, hopefully, wishfully, towards the beautiful light of God. My eyes could not be taken away from the focus of the light, but my soul was not to be honored with the final thrust this eve.

As my soul was pulled away from this celestial vision, my eyes did not leave the light until my soul awakened in my Earthly form.

"There was something featureless yet complete, born before heaven and earth; Silent - amorphous - it stood alone and unchanging. We may regard it as the mother of heaven and earth. Not knowing its name, I style it the 'Way.' If forced to give it a name, I would call it 'great.'"
Tao Te Ching, No. 69, Stanza 1-2, (Buddhism, Taoism, Translation: Victor H. Mair, Words of Lao Tzu)

****

CHAPTER FOUR
Souls of the Mentally Ill, True Inner Spirit of the People Being Made Known, Ice Skating to Heavenly Symphonies in Heaven, Purgatory on Earth, Parallel Existences, Purgatory of the Common Man - You Cannot Fly, Book 'Final Exit' Given to the Dying as they Cross, Inner City Maze Passage to Heaven, Heavenly Spirits Celebrating Work on Earth for the Lord, the Battle to Take a Man's Soul Back from Hell to Heaven Because he Never had the Name of Jesus on his Lips During Life.

****

Taken to a prison community wherein the souls of mentally deranged criminals are detained after death, most of them were murderers and they were all in a state of mental turbulence beyond any I'd seen. Each ward of this realm had at least one, but sometimes more, 'nurses' of some sort who watched over them and kept them in line. But they were filled with vile, morose desires; violent cravings which showed no mercy to any man.

In the distance, there stood a kindly looking old lady with a single nurse watching her. Oh, how deceiving appearances can be. Mentally deranged, she had not killed during her lifetime, but this was only due to divine intervention. At one time, she could have wiped out an entire family, but you would never know it by looking at her. Compared to the other wards of this realm, she appeared much more reserved and less dangerous. In some respects, her destructive capabilities were disguised by her outward appearance. No benign soul would be taken here, for this was very much a prison colony.

Interestingly, I was then shown a family tree from which this woman had sprung, and given a whirling vision of the ancestry which led to such a state. Deep original sin plagued this family tree on both sides. From this kindly looking old lady who suffered from derangement, to a not so kindly gentleman with violent tendencies on the other side, it became clear to me how much we become apples from the same sinful tree, due to original sin. Equally, it became clear how needful it was to rectify such patterns of anger within family lines and transform it to love. Such a path is difficult.

Another soul was with me who had trouble understanding the nature of darkness and its manifestations. For the moment, all I could do was allow her to observe this community of the deranged, for the questions on her mind could not be answered by me. Only the great and mysterious mind of God could answer such a question. For now, I was obliged to sit back and allow her to observe.

"That wise woman worked many skillful plans to entice her mother to hold right views, yet the mother did not totally believe. Before long her life ended and her spirit fell into the uninterrupted hell."
Sutra of the Past Vows of Earth Store Bodhisattva, Chapter 1, Page 78, Paragraph 2, (Buddhism, Pure Land)

****

Amidst the turmoil, the end came like a thief in the night as a giant gale wind guffawed in puff and smoke, and everyone was immediately transformed into the likeness of their true inner self through death. Time of probation in the world was now past, and each soul was now placed within the category of their choosing. Although redemption incurs many lifetimes, perhaps even in this, there is a limited cycle. Perhaps each soul has his own specific time of probation, his own judgment day, in which to accomplish his redemption. Or . . . perhaps this is the time of the final judgment, the end of time, when the new heaven and the new earth shall be formed. Perhaps those who have been purified and transformed through the mechanism of the redemption then become heavenly wards, wherein those who continue in their wicked and blasphemous ways become the denizens of hell. I can only present the questions within the context of what I have seen, for I am unable to answer them.

Becoming vibrant and joyous, the good people emerged from their cocoons, while the dark ones (who were by far the majority) became like corpses with claws, all white and dead looking. Because of the obvious differences now between the light and dark, the lighted people had to be very careful. In order to make my way through the crowds of dark people to begin my approach towards my inheritance of the heavenly abodes, I sang to Jesus a new hymn, 'Sing to Jesus,' which impotized the dark ones towards my soul.

But because our differences were now so obvious, the dark ones sought to prey on the lighted, and the lighted had to be extremely cautious in their movements through the initial worlds of the dead. A voice spoke from the heavens, "It is said in the realms of the eternal, do not wait upon angels and men to bring about your own redemption. Do it now, lest you find you've run out of time."

"The hour of death is for us the time of greatest anxiety. Jesus Christ alone can give us the strength to suffer, with patience and profit, the trials of this last decisive moment. At the approach of death we have more than ever to fear from the assaults of Hell. The nearer we approach our goal, the more Hell will strive to prevent our reaching it. St. Eleazar, who had lived a life of great purity, was violently tempted in the hour of death, but he did not lose courage for a moment. To those standing around him he said: 'The efforts of Hell at this moment are very great, but by the merits of His suffering our Saviour takes from them all their power."

The 12 Steps to Holiness and Salvation, Chapter 2, Page 28, A Happy Death, Paragraph 1, (Christianity, Catholic, Author: St. Alphonsus Liguori)

"What is your life? It is like a vapor, which is dispersed by a breath of wind and is no more."

The Soul Sanctified, Chapter 23, Paragraph 1, (Christianity, Catholic)

****

Plummeted between the heavenly and Earthly realms to listen to the music which emanated from each, my soul first listened to the symphonies coming from the Earth, and then to the celestial symphonia of the higher realms. Although I'd heard both types of music many times before, this was the first time that I noticed the very obvious differences in their expression. Earthly music had strong strings and bass instruments which supported the strong base, grounded representation; the drama of karma and Earthly existence. Heavenly music was filled with simpler sounds coming from higher instruments like flutes and harps. Both were equally beautiful, but very different.

On another occasion, I had the experience of ice skating within the spheres of the heavens. With every step of my feet, a heavenly symphony began. Becoming a dance to the rhythms of the harmonious existences of life residing in the upper spheres, I could hear such things, because my soul was flowing deep within the oneness of heavenly life, and traveling along the wave of the will of God. Many people of Earth-plane status whose spiritual regions were only programmed to hear the low, dark sounds of the bass progression of karma were present. But they were unable to hear the heavenly symphonies coming from my feet. I found this to be sadly interesting, but all too familiar.

"And your ears were made not only to hear the words of men, the song of birds, and the music of falling rain, but they were also made to hear the Holy Stream of Sound."

The Essene Gospel of Peace, Vol. 4, Page 43, Paragraph 3, (Christianity, Gnostic/Essene)

****

Standing amidst a panoramic view of the heavens, my soul was covered in robes which covered my entire being including my face. For some reason I could see through them, despite the fact that they were a solid whitish blue color. Immediately thrust into a Samadhi state, I remained in this state as I watched a man who appeared to be from India approach me and a group of others. Others thought me strange wearing such bizarre robes, but the guru recognized me immediately.

As he approached, I began to see visions as he related to me eternal truths regarding the nature of reality and the Universe, but most of what I was shown, I did not retain. Speaking to me in magnetic tones, I was given instructions in a hypnotic state. Again, I didn't consciously retain. Heralded by the arrival of two doves which landed in my hand, he conveyed to me that they were the fruits of my labors, the Holy Spirit. Pointing to others in the crowd who preferred to see physical results of their efforts, he said, 'Your efforts will remain unseen and transparent." Then he was gone.

"The creation, preservation, and dissolution of the universe are all divine play. In the universe, the Self, who is the Self of all beings, appears as many. Before creation, and in dissolution, the world exists as one absolute existence, which is God. Then there is neither the seer nor the seen, neither subject nor object. There

exists only consciousness itself. In that consciousness, which is the absolute God, is the power which divides itself into the seer and the seen, the cause and the effect. This power is called Maya."
Srimad Bhagavatam, Book Third, Chapter 1, Page 32, Paragraph 1, (Hinduism, Translation: Swami Prabhavananda, Words of Maitreya)

****

Running aimlessly through a starry realm, my spirit came upon a circling stairwell hovering gently in the heavens, covered with an indescribable ornamentation. Feeling myself immensely drawn to where this might lead, I soared towards it and up. Two large, carved, wooden, brown doors waited for me at the peak, and without hesitation, I rushed to open them and see what lay inside.

Sitting in the lotus position, a small and very skinny man with long, curly brown hair was meditating. Opening his eyes slowly with utter calm, he looked up at me. "I am Chooshu," he said, as I immediately knew that he was one of the masters. Before I could ascertain the purpose of this visit, he made it clear that my time was almost up. "Please return when you can, so that I can teach you how to meditate to Feng-shui." Interestingly, I'd used many of my own ideas similar to Feng-Shui in my own home for years, and had received heavenly guidance about the placement of certain holy objects, pictures, statues, etc., so this idea of meditating to Feng-Shui did not seem odd or unusual. Rather, it seemed like the natural extension of creating an environment meant to enhance certain spiritual qualities and states.

Without knowing what was happening, my spirit instinctually zipped out of the room traveling quickly down the stairwell to a newly manifested classroom which resided at the foot of the stairs. Going inside, it became as any other Earthly schoolroom, completely enclosed with chairs, a blackboard, and a teacher.

Upon my arrival, the classroom was darkened as the teacher prepared to show us a movie entitled, 'Purgatory.' Many students were here to watch this interesting motion picture but as the movie began we were all swept into the film. No longer in the classroom, we were now living within the scenes of the movie.

In an interesting turn of events, this movie which was supposed to be about 'Purgatory,' seemed much more like 'Armageddon.' Becoming very confusing, we experienced some horrible event in the future which appeared to a part of some distant diabolical war. (This occurred about one and a half years before the fall of the World Trade Center) In reality, we were experiencing the war between good and evil within our own souls, and within the world around us. Although I didn't yet realize it, the Lord was showing me that the Earth is a purgatory realm.

Aircraft were landing in airports without permission, while armed snipers exited planes and other war vehicles, wandering through towns and cities murdering and pillaging everybody in sight. Everybody was running for their lives, trying to remain hidden from these demonic snipers carrying machine guns. Trying to stop the killing, the United States had a difficult job because they were not employing the usual means of war; armies confronting one another on a battlefield. Rather, they were targeting people in their normal place of business and their homes.

Amidst the chaos, those of us who were members of the class on 'Purgatory' were trying to protect ourselves and others. Despite this, many of those in the classroom were killed. Eventually, however, the forces of the United States were able to overcome the terrorists, but not until much bloodshed had already occurred.

As this tremendously disturbing scene began to end, the students and I re-entered the classroom as if we had been watching a movie all along. All were in shell-shock from the horrendous experience, and many hadn't survived in the movie, but were immediately restored to life in the classroom.

Awaiting some bold pronouncement from this teacher regarding the hell we had just witnessed, we got no such thing. Pulling out a book entitled, 'Purgatory,' the teacher looked at us with expectancy as if we should somehow understand. All very confused, the image of what we had seen seemed more like 'Armageddon' than 'Purgatory.'

In the Catholic tradition, 'Purgatory' is one of the places one can go to after death. Heaven, Hell and Purgatory are the three possibilities. Those who are evil go to Hell, those who are wholly good go to Heaven, but those who are not bad enough to go to Hell, yet not good enough to go to Heaven, go to Purgatory. Purgatory is a place of purification where a soul cleanses itself of sin in order to become pure enough to enter into Heaven. In medieval times, people feared Purgatory because it was depicted as a realm very much like Hell complete with burning fire. A soul underwent tremendous pain in its purification, but the saving grace was that Purgatory wasn't eternal, your salvation was assured.

In modern times, Purgatory is often depicted as a place where the soul's torment is primarily experienced in the absence of God. For a soul who loves the Lord, this absence is extremely painful, but seemingly appropriate, because the soul willingly turned away from God when committing sin during life.

Because this experience was a foreshadowing of a true historical event to come, I didn't realize its full import until after this occurrence. There is a war going on in some part of the world, almost all the time. Most of these wars are true Armageddon's, battles between good and evil. What if these wars, and other smaller battles which occur in individual lives, *are* one of the mechanisms of 'Purgatory?' In the Old Testament, there are many wars which are intended as a cleansing of the sinfulness of the people.

In my travels to the hell realms, I'd been shown on several occasions that many souls were given the option of reincarnation before entering hell. In the 'Pistis Sophia,' a Gnostic text, it says that souls who have committed certain sins are sent to Hell to undergo specific punishments meted out according to their sin. But when they have undergone this punishment, they are then placed in a body with certain features; physical, mental or spiritual, which correspond to their previous bad acts, and returned to the Earth. With this in mind, you can see how Earth operates as a 'Purgatory' realm, a place of purgation (Not unlike the Moon, which was revealed in 'The Mysteries of the Redemption' as a 'Chaos' realm.).

If various heavenly bodies may encompass diverse realms, and my previous writings primarily considered the journey of those of us confined to the Earth, imagine how many more realms may be found encompassed in planets, stars, galaxies etc.

Looking upon the face of the teacher, he revealed nothing more. As our eyes met, my soul began to disappear to this classroom in the stars.
****

Staying the night in a motel, I was visited by about ten wandering spirits who wanted to speak to me. Coming into my room in the astral state, they said, "We're doing our 'Purgatory' by wandering the Earth as lost souls for a prescribed time period." Unable to help themselves or others in any meaningful way, they were not allowed to share with me the sins for which they were paying. Agitated, they were in a state of definitive unrest.

"What can I do to help you?" I asked, as they began to fade and disappear, unable to ask for such help from me this night. Offering many prayers for these souls, I became much more cognizant of the need for patience in my daily life, and the opportunities for helping myself and others as I walk through this world.

As they disappeared, a book fell from the heavens onto my lap. Its title read, 'The Praxis of Suffering,' a prophecy of that which was coming (about my undiagnosed illness). Intrigued, I didn't know what the word 'praxis' meant, so I looked it up and found it to be a 'discipline.'

****

Entering into a brazen swoon, my soul began to experience yet another death, crossing over into the worlds of the beyond to witness the souls of those who had just crossed. All of these souls had made choices which had led them to a variety of states after death. Although none of them were to be sent directly to heaven, none of these particular souls had chosen hell. Realizing this led all of these souls into a transcendental swoon, as they became aware of how wonderful it was that they had not chosen hell. Angelic hosts placed them in an almost hypnotic state wherein they spiritually and energetically understood the wonderful grandeur of this moment.

Another interesting thing occurred in that there were a variety of parallel existence's coming to fruition in this realm, and thus, we were witnessing various aspects of all of these souls experiencing multiple death points. Other aspects of the soul which had come from parallel realities were experiencing synchronistic death points. As the primary aspect of the soul experienced death, the other aspects began to reach a death point, one after the other.

As this happened, each aspect experienced an almost identical death, with very minuscule and minute changes for each portion of the personality. Watching this phenomenon with a particular soul, I spoke of it with an angelic host. "It's very interesting," I thought to him, "how these different parallels each replay some aspects slightly differently than the previous selves, and how this seems to throw many people off." Primary conscious elements of the soul would become confused by these different experiences all intertwining and intermeshing into one another. Expecting identical experiences, they became confused when each aspect of their personality did not align in the manner in which they had thought. Because of their connection and attachment to the primary aspect of their experience, which they had chosen to be aware of during life, and thus death; they had trouble integrating and recognizing these other aspects of their soul as truly parts of themselves.

Turning to observe a particular woman, she was expressing deep regrets about her lifetime, in that she had not considered the status of her soul before death. Although she was not in a bad place - these souls were definitely not in heaven, but rather, some type of in-between state like purgatory - she immediately recognized that she had not yet made it to heaven and this distressed her. Despite the fiery and scary descriptions some have made of various parts of purgatory, this particular in-between state was not like that at all. (But that does not mean that such places do not exist.) Rather, it was much more like an extension of Earth, very possibly a fourth-dimensional overlay of our world.

Because of their purgatorial status, none of these souls could fly, as their souls were too heavy with sin. As a result, I soared towards the air in a sweeping gesture, and showed them the beauty of spiritual flight so as to seed them that this possibility could be ahead for those who purified themselves properly.

Another very profound occurrence happened after all the parallel existences had gone through their transition and the souls were now, in a sense, reunited. Very subtle things began to happen all around this arena which would remind them of the Lord. Whether it was a flash of light or a holy book found lying around, the souls were beginning to leave behind their mundane existence and begin to think upon holy things. One of these books was a very thick text entitled, 'Final Exit.' (Absolutely **no** connection to the Earthly title of the same name.) Looking upon its contents, I found it to be a very detailed instruction regarding this particular experience of the afterlife, this particular purgative state.

Two large angelic hosts appeared in white robes adorned with large white wings, and were now quietly addressing the crowd of about twenty souls. Speaking of their 'causes' for being in such a purgative realm, they said, "The bond is of the Earth." Many didn't understand what this meant, but I inherently and immediately understood that the angels were referring to the bonds of sin which had led them to this place, which was apparently karmic and/or mortal in origin; an attachment to something worldly. Speaking again, they said, "Jesus planned for mankind to keep the commandments . . . but some just didn't." Very matter of fact about this truth, these souls understood immediately that they had indeed chosen not to keep the commandments.

Once they realized this and took responsibility, it was now time to move onto the next phases which would include purification from those sins and attachments to worldly things which had led them to this state after death. Time over, I'd seen what the Lord had bid, and my soul disappeared into the ether.
****

Having traveled a long journey on a bus to this unusual spaceport, I was awaiting entry into a magnificent building which I was told contained within it many mansions of the Lord. Within its confines were literally hundreds of floors, each of which represented a whole different world, a whole different understanding. As we had entered into the space portal, I noticed I was wearing the brown robe of a monk as I began to embark upon this journey of the spirit.

Before arriving at this intriguing world, we had traveled through what appeared to be an inner city floating in space. Placed within the dirtiest and most squalid place among the city, this large, square and white building which had appeared was a place of ritual passage. In the midst of this dirty, ugly, agitated and worldly ghetto, I saw a tiny ray of hope; a statue of Jesus stood before a storefront. Hoping to find a church, I found a sign for a psychic reader instead. My momentary joy had been dashed.

Entering the mansion worlds, it was easy to become overwhelmed because of the many places represented within its confines. Surrendering to the flow of the soul, my spirit was taken to a dark classroom where I whiled away many hours, sitting in meaningless fashion as the teacher of this class did nothing. Once in a great while, she would teach us for a very short time, perhaps five minutes, about an aspect of writing, such as verbs. Finding this to be all too shallow, I was trying to be polite and respectful. Finally, however, I decided it was time for me to move on. In a rude gesture, I stood up and left the dark room.

Wandering outside of the classroom, I found myself meandering through many mansions of the world. Realizing quickly that I had done the right thing to leave the classroom, I realized that the classroom had been a very tiny aspect of this mansion world. Still lost, I was now confined to a series of floors which were scattered, aimless and agitated. Comparative to the mass retain found in any busy business district of a large city on Earth, my soul meandered. Inexplicably, these city streets seemed to be enclosed in a very wide, white hallway, much like that of a university. Along the corridors, were neon signs, fast food restaurants, various businesses and the like. Chaos, agitation, and commercialism filled these mansions, as I accepted that these mansion worlds, too, were incompatible to my soul.

Car salesmen were shouting in one corner of the building while fast food restaurants were trying to lure me into their gluttonous calling by offering me free food. As I was very hungry, I accepted an offering of a chicken sandwich made by one of these establishments, but before I could take more than one bite out of it, I was approached by two large men who begged me to allow them to have it because they were quite hungry. Noticing that they had identical sandwiches in their hands with which they were gorging themselves, I inherently knew that they didn't really need what they had asked me to give. But I thought about Jesus, and what He would wish for me to do. So I gave it to them, and as I did, it became an epiphany as a corridor appeared before my soul.

Walking forward, hundreds of people were wandering through the noise aimlessly, but I and three other souls walked into the confines of the corridor, swept up into the mechanism of its establishment.

Now walking down a very narrow stairwell, quite a crowd was trying to make its way down and we were all packed together. All around this stairwell were hundreds of pictures and statues of Jesus and Mary. An almost invisible and transparent hand placed a small 3" X 4" framed picture containing the image of the Blessed Virgin Mary in my hand. Swooning in delight, my sigh left me in a glorious manner. A voice came from the invisible hand. "Blessed are those who are born into the mansion of Jesus and Mary upon the Earth."

As I quietly exited the stairwell, an amazing phenomenon occurred. Although the stairwell was narrow and led downwards into what appeared to be a basement, the moment I touched the floor after descending the last step, my spirit was elevated high above this mansion world into a mansion of God which resided at the highest level of the building.

Feeling the Presence, I immediately knew that it was the mansion of Jesus and Mary, and as soon as my soul walked forth, I heard the voice of the angel again speak. "Those who enter here, their robes will become white." As these words were spoken, I watched with ultimate delight as my robes slowly transformed in a wavelike pattern from top to bottom, from brown to white.

Looking before me, everything began to appear as vapor as all those who had passed before me were unseen. Translated suddenly from this realm into the heavens, I momentarily witnessed the soul of those who bore the robes of white walking in heaven peacefully. A huge smile lit upon my face as I ran towards them . . . but I was not to stay at this time, and was returned to form.
****

Awakened to the sound of grand celebrations ensuing 'in the spirit' within the confines of my home, about two hundred dead people were there praising God and talking amongst themselves about many of the small things they had done during their lives to assist the Lord. Gathering around to show me what I had done for God, they showed me homes which had been steeped in dark energies which now appeared as family cathedrals. Speaking of my writing, they expressed the great depth of meaning I had shared through my words. Feeling unconditional acceptance from these people, they were not judging me for being sick and possibly dying, which was quite a relief. Many of them had suffered lingering deaths, and they fully understood the frustration of losing your physical capacities, and accepting the loss of your Earthly life.

Standing in front of the crowd who continually praised the Lord in a jubilant celebration, the Lord Jesus Christ began to materialize directly in front of me. Wearing the dark robes that you might see in some of the Last Supper paintings, he stood before a small table reminiscent of that event and said absolutely nothing. His hair was luminescent and His face shone with light. Behind Him a huge scene of the crucifixion began to appear as I inherently understood that I was undergoing my own personal crucifixion at this time. Part of the crucifixion is the emotional aspect which comes to a person who is dying.

Shouting to the crowd, I couldn't hide my elation at the presence of the Savior. Everybody was in jubilation, and they praised all the more loudly in His presence. Looking through my soul, Jesus filled me with unconditional acceptance and love. Feeling more at home away from home, He began to disappear before my eyes, as I began to sink into a great sadness in our separation. Refusing to allow this, the crowd quickly grabbed a hold of my shoulders, turning me to join them in their praise.
****

Standing in a borderland, I watched the spirits of the 'dead' fly, going about their heavenly business. Wearing Earthly attire, many of them were dressed in business suits and casual wear, flying through the skies. A deep yellow hue patched the skies of this vista, and although it looked much like Earth, it held a vibrance and light which was absent in mortal spheres.
****

An elderly person had come to me in the astral state, his soul terrified and confused from the battle it now waged. Close to death for quite some time with a form of dementia, he was living in a netherworld because of the absence of his physical mind in his body. Suffering from an illness which can cause great lingering, he came to me in the spiritual world followed by a host of about 300 demons.

Upon his arrival, he said, "My soul has been condemned to hell, and I've made a deal with these demons. They've agreed to allow me to come to you for help on the condition that they be given the opportunity to have at you in an attempt to overcome and possess your soul."

Because there was an active war for his soul, he would go in and out of a demonically controlled state. During the brief episodes while he was not demonically controlled, I was pleading with this aspect of his soul for his own eternal salvation! Actually quite frightening, he was a big man and very intimidating while possessed.

Given leave to torment me, the 300 demons took my soul down a literal road of perdition. An intensive spiritual battle ensued along a highway ten or twenty miles long, wherein every aspect, nook and cranny of the roadway was permeated with lures, temptations, torments, and terrifying tricks. Led by the demons through a highway of temptations, after passing through literally tens of such things, my exhausted soul finally reached the end of the road. In front of me was a white line which had been painted across the road. Given to know that this line represented the final thrust of demonic interplay, as soon as I crossed, I could claim victory.

Unfortunately, inside this small space there was a multitude of demons filled with every vice, deadly sin and discharge. Looking upon the demons who stood next to me with disdain upon their faces, I smiled at them with gladness. Those who stood beside me had already lost the battles from which they had waged war for my soul. "I think I get it," I said, "I have to get through that final passage, cross over that line, and if I do that, I win, right?" Nodding with dismay and sadness at their loss, I shouted, "See ya." Flying past the final demonic entourage, it was over in seconds.

Returned to the home of the soul who had come for my aid, the prime demons had been forced to leave. A small band of demonic influences had been given leave to stay within him, however, and these demons raged within him occasionally as he sat on the couch. "I came to you," he said, "because you're the only one who cares." Because he came from a family with atheistic alliances, no one within it knew how to help him. Nodding, I acknowledged that I cared very much about his soul having been condemned to hell. Walking over to a chair, he sat down.

Demons began to rage within him, and I began using the name of Jesus in various forms of prayer to help to exorcise his soul. Nothing happened, so I continued without avail. For a moment, the part of his soul which desired salvation re-attained control and said, "The name of Jesus will not work with me." "Why not?" I asked. "Because during my life, the name of Jesus was never on my lips." During his life, he'd been a good person who could care less about God. "Because His name was never on my lips during life, it will not work for me now." Referring to scripture, Christ had said that those who confess of Him before men, He shall also confess of them before His Father in the judgment. But those who confess Him not, He shall not confess of them before the Father.

Presenting me with a new dilemma, I was quiet. "Oh, then we'll have to think of something else."

Watching and praying quietly, the holy spirit came over my soul and lifted me up to the center of the room as I began to very slowly and quietly, almost a whisper, recite the 'Our Father.' "Our Father . . . who art in heaven . . . hallowed be thy name . . ." As I did this, the demons quickly gave way of his soul, and he sat alone in the room with the knowledge that he had been saved from eternal damnation.

As my spirit began to be sucked back into my body, I awoke still reciting the prayer. As I returned, I shouted to him, "I will offer my sufferings for you for as
long as you need. I will offer your continuing sufferings on Earth for your soul, since you are not physically capable of doing this for yourself. I will offer prayers for you, for as long as you need."

Leaving him, I knew that he had been saved from condemnation to hell, but that his soul was still in great need of assistance as it embarked upon his own unique purgatory, a state of undefined dementia. His soul would learn 'in the spirit,' that which he'd neglected to care about while still of the Earth. Wondering if much of his purgatory would be done on earth, as he suffered from this lingering, long-term illness which left him unaware of Earthly reality, I began to question whether the Lord was doing something similar with my own soul. Could my illness and possible death be an opportunity for purgation? Was this perhaps the purpose of my own illness? Was I in purgatory?
****

CHAPTER FIVE
Attack from an Evil Spirit in Hell, Purgatory of Lust, Conversation with a Soul in Purgatory, Heavenly Monastery, the Gift of Redemption and How Highly it is Praised in Heaven, Dying Young, The Palace of Ancient Knowledge, 100,000 Levels of Purgatory, ExtraTerrestrials in Heaven, House of Jesus and Mary, Galactic Ancient Sacred Texts, Accepting Suffering to Prevent the Death of a Man who Would be Damned if he were to Die Now, Parade in Heaven, Denizens of Hell, Fate of a Purely Evil Spirit, Fighting the Winds of Karma in Purgatory, Priest in Need of Prayer in Purgatory, Christ's Temple.

****

Coming to me in disguise, the evil spirit had approached me in hopes that I might pray for his soul who had died twenty years prior. Great pity emerged from my loins, as he had been killed in the process of committing a robbery/attempted murder at the age of nineteen by a man who had killed him in self-defense. Praying for him, I'd hoped that perhaps doing so might release him from purgatory and allow him to enter heaven. Going on the assumption that he had been a misguided youth who was paying for his torrid years in a hellish purgatorial existence intended to prepare him for heaven, I was deathly wrong.

A young boy, literally a toddler, had been having nightmares about a 'demon who had tried to take him away,' and I entered into his dream with the permission of the Lord to find out and hopefully take care of this problem. Turning out to face the grandchild of the man who had taken the life of this soul, I entered into the city.

Dealing with the city where this young man had once lurked, I ascertained that this soul had been damned and was now an evil spirit who had been given some type of permission to leave hell on the twentieth anniversary of his own death to roam the world and tempt souls. Rather than doing this, he had decided to make a claim on the 'third generation,' a grandchild of the man who had killed him in self-defense twenty years prior, referring to the biblical admonition that the sins of the father are visited upon the third and fourth generations. As this third generation was a baby boy . . . I was immediately enraged.

Marauding through the streets, this evil spirit was harming and attempting to kill everyone in his path. In this most horrific of cities, a young adolescent black boy had been influenced by this spirit and was beginning to follow evil. As his father prayed for his soul, he asked that he might be liberated and follow Christ, but it was too late. Losing his life in the act of committing evil inspired by the evil spirit, I quietly and unobtrusively began to pray with the father for his son's soul. Becoming aware that his son's soul was saved, the Lord Jesus was now calling me to take out the evil spirit who had violated eternal law. Crossing boundaries forbidden him in the freedom given him to tempt souls, he had not been given leave to murder and maim.

Everywhere this evil spirit had been; chaos, murder and death reigned. Catching up to him as he was driving away in a pick-up truck, he was sitting casually in the passenger side. Using the gift of the lightning which the Lord had given me years ago within my hands, I directed fifteen bolts directly into the area of his heart. Ironically, he had died from a gunshot wound to the heart. Receiving the discipline from heaven, the Holy Spirit filled me with words. Shouting, I revealed, "You have no quarrel or claim to this family, for you died lawfully. It is true that if this man had not killed you in self-defense, somebody else would've *had* to take you out. Most likely, this would've been a SWAT team during one of your many violent and criminal acts. The man who took your life holds no sin for your life, but in fact, is responsible for saving many other lives of which you would've taken. You have no claim to him or his descendants, and because you have violated the boundaries of your freedom to roam the world as an evil spirit and violated eternal laws in such a manner as to go after and attempt to harm children, the Lord has decreed that you will again be returned to the pit of hell, where you will be locked up and chained. You will be given no reign to harm the souls of the earth!"

With this, he fell as if dead from the lightning bolts which had taken him out this second time. A friend of his began shouting at me that his legs and ankles were swelling up, and there was great anger in his voice that I had ended their 'fun.' Ignoring them, I turned away . . . and he was never heard from again.
****

In another realm, Andy had been convinced to accept this man's offer of trading our small home (not our current one) in a usual neighborhood, for his huge mansion set aside on a piece of land which was quite secluded and serene . . . at least in appearance.

My suspicions were very high, as it made no sense to me that this man would make this offer unless there was something wrong with the house - first suspicion being that of a haunting. Andy had been impressed by the four Steinway grand pianos, and a very large gym which contained a basketball court which he considered to be something wonderful for our son. Admittedly, I was impressed with the grandeur of the home and its privacy, but it was clear that something was amiss.

The individual rooms in this house, in particular the living room, were each larger than our entire current home as this was truly a mansion. Planning to go through the home, room by room, and fix it up according to our tastes, there was a great deal to be cleaned up as many things had been stored up and taken care of in somewhat shoddy manner.

Because of the suspicious nature of this interaction, I wasn't surprised that the man and his wife left the house in an abrupt manner, but their manner of leaving held interest to me. A beautiful and ornate horse-drawn carriage carried the two who were dressed almost as royalty, perhaps extreme upper class, of those who might have lived during the time of the Russian Revolution, early

1900's or so. As they departed, a crowd suddenly appeared all around the grounds bidding them adieu with gratefulness and joy. This was the first sign that we were not alone.

As I worked my way through the rooms, I'd begun in the very entry of the house and worked towards the other end. Being a true mansion, I'd accomplished the reordering and cleaning of the first three to four rooms, but still had at least thirty to go. These three or four rooms were immense, and the process began to make me aware that perhaps I didn't have the energy for such a huge task. Living in such a huge mansion might not be so desirable to me (and perhaps Andy, as well). As we'd just looked at the Steinway pianos in a storage room which was larger than most houses, and were peering in on the gym, something happened.

Looking around this large, ornate fitness area, I noticed that there were people hiding behind stashes of storage items and in the rafters. Because they noticed that I had seen them, many began to come out of their hiding places, approaching me. My middle child, Mary, was with me at this time, and one man approached with what appeared to be malicious intent. "Back off!" I said, holding my hand up in the sign of 'stop,' "In the name of Jesus Christ, leave her alone!" Obediently, he pulled himself back, lowered his head, and placed his hands before him in penitential manner. Within moments, I began to realize that these people were obliged to obey my every word, and did so with the very least of promptings.

My first inkling of their presence had been that they were servants, but this theory was quickly becoming evidently incorrect. Without warning, a gale wind assaulted Andy, Mary and I which began to bring us up towards the ceiling much like a gigantic ocean wave filling the room. At this moment, I turned to Andy and said, "This house is haunted, that's why they wanted to leave." Conclusions premature, the gale wind subsided and we were let to the ground, as I began to walk around the house suspiciously.

Noticing that it was now full of people in every room, this formerly empty house had become lit to the full with at least four to five hundred souls. In one room, I found about fifteen spirits who were clearly criminals. Without any resistance, I ordered them to turn themselves into their police immediately. Doing so, I noticed that their police were also spirit beings who were dressed in the attire of police officers of the early 1900's. Taken out of the house to an undisclosed location, I began to notice something very unusual which began to shed light as to my purpose here.

Beginning with a woman who made an inappropriate sexual gesture to a gentleman, before she could take this seemingly minute act of lust any further, her body and face began to transform into the pinkish-red, reptilian face of a demon. Horns began to protrude from her forehead and within seconds, she disappeared. Those around her went on as if nothing had happened, going about their business, trying to behave in a most upright manner.

Seeing this happen again and again . . . and again, those who made overtures towards others which were lustful or inappropriate in the slightest of ways, turned into horribly disfigured demons, disappearing from the scene. A man who had quickly reached his hand towards me in a very vulgar manner . . . also turned into a demon and disappeared, at the very moment I ordered him to back off.

Looking towards a very tall man dressed very astutely and with obvious prestige, he tipped his top hat and bowed to me very politely. "This house isn't haunted, is it?" I asked him with grave concern. "No," he quietly said. "But you people are not servants, either, are you? You are all dead, aren't you?" I asked timidly. "Yes," he quietly said, with no change of expression on his face, except for a very subtle smile coming from the corner of his lips. "This is a purgatory, isn't it?" I asked. "Yes," he quietly replied. "This purgatory is kind of a last resort for those souls who struggled with lust on Earth, isn't it?" I asked. "Yes," he quietly said. Pausing a moment, I thought deeply. "Those who turn into demons and disappear are being sent straight to hell, aren't they?" At this time, his head lowered a bit in sadness. "Yes," he said quietly.

Suddenly, I understood why these souls were so obedient. Because this was their last resort, if they showed that lust remained in their hearts to even the slightest of degrees, there were no further chances. Approaching an older black woman who was dressed as if from Cajun country in the early 1900's, I listened as she began to tell me about her life. As I listened, my mind couldn't help but wander to the others in the room who were acting with great gentility in an attempt to save their soul. Interrupting this very charming older woman's story, I shouted out to Jesus for help. "This place needs transformation!" My soul was transported to a heavenly highway outside of this realm.

Sitting at the side of a wide cosmic tunnel, the light formed a roadway through space. Andy and I sat at the side, watching in the distance as a huge vehicle began to approach. Six times larger than a fire engine, and in the color of the whitest white, it held within it transformative assistance which we knew would be arriving at the purgatorial mansion. Lifted from the spinning lighted tunnel, I was returned to my body on Earth.

****

Appearing with a distressed look upon his brow, the middle-aged man appeared and began speaking very rapidly as if there was not much time. Immediately, I *knew* that this man was a soul in purgatory and I was very interested in what he might have to say. "You have to replace all the _peace_ you didn't make, conflicts you started, unhappiness you generated, agitation or just general discord that you put into the world." Finding his words rather profound, they seemed to generally sum up the true destiny of mankind, the meaning of life, in a way that I'd never fully thought of before.

Going on, he said, "We need to create a wall between us and the living because we have to focus on repairing for what we have lacked and what we could've done, but did not." Again, he repeated, "We have to repair for all the peace we took from the world . . . it takes a lot of energy to do that."

Beginning to ask him a question, I stopped myself as he continued speaking. "You always knew what your passion was, knowledge of God, but my passions in life were other things. I have a lot to make up for." Looking down, I replied, "I am very guilty of taking peace from the world, in many instances." Casually, he replied, "I hadn't known that."

Interrupting, I asked, "What happens when you die, do you reunite with all your loved ones, do you all travel the journey of death together?" Remaining very serious, he replied, "The people you knew before are in the room 'above the bedroom.' You meet them directly after death and then go on your separate ways of purification." "But what about . . ." my words were interrupted, by a rapid yet quiet voice, fading quickly into the night. "We need to create a wall between us and the living, it takes a lot of energy . . ." Then he was gone.

We can do much in this world to make it a better place, but against the enemy of life, which is death, we shall all fail. Our powerless is complete, and we shall all share the same fate. Rather than this being sad, it is liberating, because we are then free to enjoy the moments God chooses to give us without guilt, shame or fear; or the pressure that we must solve this problem, as well.

There comes a time in every life, whether it be the oncoming plane is in view, the terminal condition has taken hold, the car is on its way over the mountain, the volcano has erupted, the tornado is here, the flash flood came too fast; when the soul sees his undeniable fate approaching - and it is death - a ripping away from all things known and seen in this creature's short life, and the soul knows that it is powerless to change the outcome.

Surrender occurs, and it is in this moment that a soul truly lives with eternal life in mind, bringing meaning to the pronouncement held by all religious faiths that we should *all* live our lives with its end in view.
****

Entering into the fiery monastery, I could not believe the surrounding holiness which filled my soul; fiery in the sense of the Holy Spirit, rather than any physical phenomenon. A lone monk stood before me, his hood draped to cover his forehead. Speaking slowly, he mouthed words very slowly, but as he did, concepts of great magnitude filled my understanding.

Premonitions of my own death filled his concepts, and beyond this, great understandings of the journey of my soul and the souls of my children and husband. Bestowing on me knowledge in regards to my own children, he conveyed that whatever might happen from this point on, was destined to be and was an integral part of their spiritual formation. Sensing that I might have a few years left, I was also deathly aware that this could be wishful thinking. Premonitions are changeable. It could be more . . . it could be less.

"Are you not aware that your spiritual journey has just begun?" he said, with an ominously exciting look upon his face. "When death comes, your soul will be just beginning the eternal journey for which it is destined to embark!" As he said this, I energetically understood that I was an infant in this great powerful process of God, and there was much for me to learn and discover beyond this world.

Around me were the sounds of a music I cannot describe which filled my soul with such peace and absolute tranquility, I did not want to leave. Fire of the Holy Spirit filled this heavenly space in such a way that it was felt but not seen. The presence of the monk in his aloneness poured out a sense of utter sanctity and I relished in this amazing fire of God's love that I was allowed to feel this night. Candles were lit all around me in the monastery as if this were a medieval holy site that had been preserved and kept throughout timelessness.

Vibrating with power in the holy place I'd come, every word came from the mouth of the monk as if in slow motion and caused my spirit to vibrate. "Be at peace with your death," the monk conveyed, "for all is well, and all is as it is meant to be."

Guiding me to a corner of the room, I began to see my obsession with holy writings and relics played out as if in a movie on the wall. Watching as I rummaged through piles of secular books, only to find the one holy book which had been sacrilegiously strewn there, the monk pointed out to me that my ability to recognize and honor that which was holy, was a gift from God.

For hours, I languished in the spirit of this holy monastery amidst the heavens and would have done anything to be allowed to stay there any longer. But as the night progressed, I found my spirit walking along the streets of a heavenly city where people were reading ancient sacred texts in every corner; in restaurants, on benches, in buildings . . .

A very tall man adorned with dark hair, a moustache and beard approached me as I was walking quietly along the stone-encased roadway. For a time, I'd noticed that he'd been following me, and he was showing up in almost every location I happened to traverse. Heavenly lights poured forth from his eyes, and I inherently knew that he loved me. "Don't you recognize me?" he said, as I gazed upon him seeking remembrance. A great knowing filled me, although I could not place it. I *knew* that I knew him. "Do you *not* know that what God is giving to us is the greatest gift in all of heaven?" he said with great fervor. Actually, I hadn't known, so I did not reply.

Leading me down the street, he took me to a tiny corner building. Leading me inside, my eyes filled with wonder as I gazed upon a room filled to overflowing with ancient sacred texts. Running towards a stool surrounded by piles and piles of such texts, I sat down and began to look through them, as my newfound friend looked upon me with a wide grin.

Continuing to look through these old and tattered books, the man patiently awaited my inquiry. "This gift from God you speak of," I asked, "please tell me . . . specifically . . . what it is." Asking this, I wondered if his answer might be knowledge, or perhaps eternal love itself which permeated every cell of this heavenly city. Finally, the thought occurred to me . . . 'He must be speaking of the Redemption!' 'Of course,' I realized, 'he's speaking of the fact that we are saved!' As he smiled a knowing grin, I began to disappear and return to form.
****

Having died young, a woman came to visit me. "I was afraid to die," she said, "but then I was given entry into Heaven." Pausing, she looked deeply into my eyes as she said, "I was sent here to tell you that Heaven is SO beautiful, that I've never regretted having died so young since." As she began to pull her energy back, I asked her, "Do I have ANY chance at all of going to heaven?" Looking at me with a blank stare, it was clear that she had said what she had been sent to convey, and she didn't have permission to respond to this question. Within a moment, she was gone.
****

Having wandered through the small town and gone through several ritual passages to receive permission to enter the tiny building, my spirit was elated to finally be given the go-ahead to open the door. Another woman was with me, and had participated in assisting several souls this night, as we gazed upon a building no bigger than an outhouse with a mystical doorway.

Opening the door, we were excited to enter into a grand palace of ancient texts, much larger than the size of the entrance could have inferred. Six floors of white and gold gilded stairwells, each level filled with the ancient knowledge from throughout time. Gathering books, we slowly made our way from the sixth floor downwards. As we prepared to enter upon the first floor, we heard voices and mystical music coming from below. There was an exit available between the second and first floors, and when I heard the sounds, I said, "Perhaps we should quietly leave so as not to disturb anybody." "No, no, no," she replied, "when you hear Kabalistic music, it is an invitation. It would be considered rude if we didn't introduce ourselves." Nodding, we proceeded down the stairs to the first floor.

Astounded by the ancient sacred texts, they were huge and voluminous, the oldest in the building residing on this floor. In fact, some of them were scrolls. Standing before us were a husband and wife with their four grown sons who introduced themselves as the 'Keepers of the Ancient Knowledge.' Honored and amazed, a Jewish woman was singing Kabalistic music 'live' in the corner, and they all welcomed us with the utmost of kindness.

After sitting down with them to eat what they called a 'Pearly breakfast,' consisting of knowledge from the texts being energetically instilled within my soul, one of the sons took me over to a special section that they wanted me to see. Two huge volumes, at least three to four feet in height and a foot thick, were on the shelves next to several scrolls. The first was entitled 'Ave Maria,' and the second, 'The Mysteries of Our Lord.' Allowing me to open the second of these texts, I found mingled within the writing, a fabric banner which was a symbolic image.

As I looked upon it, the young man explained to me that the fabric banners of the cross which I made in the physical world held hidden meanings and were actually textual images. (One of my hobbies was to make fabric images of the cross with various symbols and designs.) Bouquets of flowers moved upwards through the top and above the cross, each blossom representing graces coming from the sacrifice of the cross. Placed upon each blossom were the sayings of Christ, forming a bouquet of the Word.

Showing me a set of keys, he made reference to my own library of ancient sacred texts, comparing it to this counterpart on the other side. By doing so, I realized its importance, even though it sometimes appeared to me to be just my own personal hobby. "You are also a 'Keeper of the Keys,'" he said, "Continue this task in the physical world, and when it is that you cross over, you will continue it in the next . . ." Motioning with his hands the vast expanse of the library, I was so excited that I would work here in the after-life.

Taking me to a large picture window, I was amazed to see a huge city. Skyscrapers made of diamonds could be seen off in the distance, while emeralds and pearls made up much of the rest of the expanse. Literally glowing with light, I was most entranced by the diamond skyscrapers which loomed in the distance. What a beautiful heavenly city! Handing me the keys, I began to disappear from the scene.

****

Taken on a journey through many purgatory realms, my spirit was shown something inexplicable. Many levels were represented; beginning at 100 - 300, but going on to around 100,000. Souls who were in the purgatories numbered 100-300 were much more likely to be released in a short amount of time, while those above represented higher and higher levels of vice which required long periods of purgation from which it was much more difficult to be released.

Shown to me in comparison with the stories on a high-rise building, an elevator was accessible to ascend or descend from levels 100-300. While the other levels above this were accessible to be ascended by this same elevator, souls in these realms were not able to descend or leave these realms without strict orders from the Almighty.

Souls worked themselves down from their level of vice, under strict divine supervision, and those who inhabited the levels above 300 appeared to have been there for a very long time, while souls in levels 100-300 had a regular and timely turnaround and were allowed to operate with a great deal more personal freedom.

****

Whisked off to the grand city of the palace, my spirit waited in a small house in a neighborhood before they came to take me. While I was waiting, I looked around the house, honestly perceiving that this was an Earthly home in the spheres, but was shown several labels on construction supplies used to build the place, which all exhibited dates from the future, most of them 50 years beyond the current date.

Two extra-terrestrial spirits arrived and quietly led me off, out of the neighborhood and into the city. Taking me to a small room, I was shown a set of five papers which explained my interstellar journey to the city and that with which they were about to embark. Changing my clothes, I was being adorned in the attire of the galactic heavens; a pair of shiny pants and a large shirt which was long sleeved and closed to the neck. After dressing appropriately, my spirit was taken to a square in this magnificent city of light.

Standing at a counter, a young man said nothing as he gathered up four very old ancient texts from behind the desk and placed them in front of me to view. Intrigued, I noticed that they all appeared very old, but was surprised to notice that their publication dates ranged from 1991 - 2058. (In my present time-space continuum, it was currently 2003). Reading their titles and taking note of their contents, I remembered that one book was deeply ingrained in Native American spirituality, while the others were mysterious spiritual commentaries on various subjects. Bringing me another book, it was written in a language I didn't understand, and a man appeared at my side to explain its meaning.

From the title, I could glean that it was about the mysteries, but nothing more. Looking to my right, a tall man with a cowboy hat was gazing at the text, as I immediately realized that both of us were galactic archaeologists, and it was my task in this next life to 'translate' texts which were written in my native tongue to an inexplicable galactic language of the spheres. Rather than being a librarian in the 'Palace of Ancient Knowledge,' it was going to be my task to translate, as did this other man who spoke a different language, from what I recall, a European tongue.

Walking towards a boardwalk, I entered into a small glass-encased room which held sacred relics. As I entered, I noticed a large head of Christ on the cross, the 'Ecce Homo.' Several crucifixes were displayed on the glass walls, as well, but my spirit was led to a remarkable object which lay ahead. A life-size sculpture of Mother Teresa in her death casket was carved out of the purest white stone, as I immediately understood this to be symbolic of my own death in some way. Gazing upon the serene and holy image, somebody had come to take me on a tour of the city.

What ensued was entirely inexplicable and I have only been given to remember small snippets of this wondrous and exciting adventure. Taken through the city, we were on our way towards the Palace of Ancient Knowledge, but we made about eight stops in different locations where various souls were waiting for me to tell me of different secrets of the spheres. Having many beautiful terms to share with me of galactic things and heavenly attainments, I was unable to remember a single one, despite the fact that I wrote each of them down on a note pad in the spirit. One small snippet that my memory retained was of a galactic being who in answer to a question I posed, replied in a lengthy scientific discourse about molecular structure and galactic knowledge. In a state of total awe, I took a tour of this city as the hosts made welcome to my soul. Knowing I would be coming to this city upon my death, I was so very excited; I cannot even put it into words.

As we made our way through, my guide took me to the edge of the city of light where I noticed in the grand distance the 'bad part of town.' Looking like a 19th century towered city of London, great darkness oozed from the distant place. Hearing the screaming and yelling of the dark ones, my tour guide bade me to know, "When you arrive in this city, do not ever venture beyond this point, for what you see beyond is a point of darkness, a purgatory realm of great discord and to do so would put your soul in great peril." Understanding, I nodded in agreement to never do such a thing as I was whisked off through another corridor.

As I entered, another familiar face came into the room. The man who had 'married' me on the mountain had come into the room with several friends, and was so engaged in what they were doing that he didn't notice my presence. Taking note of this familiarity, I turned to my guide, a tall thin man with black hair, and asked, "Are you going to be taking me to the Palace?" Smiling, he replied, "We are on our way there." Pulling out several pictures, they held images of notable people who had lived in this city and done important things for God. Most of them appeared to be from a different age, as the men wore top hats and the women wore bonnets. Taking my hand, we began walking quickly through another corridor, presumably towards the Palace.

Placing his arm around me, a sudden familiarity came over my soul as he smiled at me in recognition. "Who are you?" I asked, wondering if he might reveal our ancient connection. "I can't say," he replied nonchalantly. "You're not allowed to tell me are you? None of you are allowed to reveal your connection to those of us still on the Earth, are you?" Nodding, 'No,' I asked, "Why?" "I can't say," he replied.

Stopping, he pointed off into the distance as I felt the wondrousness of this holy city, and the imminent nature of my demise. At this moment, it felt that my time on Earth would *really* be coming to an end and that I was being introduced to the world I would attend to at that time. Any concern that I might have had about my readiness was quickly dispelled, as the same message that had been conveyed to me by Christ about my soul having reached completion was repeated and felt deeply within. But knowing my own unique path and that sometimes I underwent spiritual deaths in order to bring in new knowledge, only time would tell. "The Palace is up in the distance," he said, as he pointed towards something I could not yet see. Excited and amazed, I looked with anticipation as something began to materialize in the ether. But before it could, I was whisked away. "No, let me see it!" I shouted, but it was of no avail. It was time for me to go.

Was my soul preparing for a true death? Or was I being initiated into yet another realm of knowledge beyond the gates? Either way, my journey would continue . . .

Waking, an inexplicable and very intensive heat began to pour through my chest, arms, abdomen and hips which continued for three hours. So hot, I checked several times to see if the electric blanket was on high, but found it to be detached from the bed. 'Could the Lord be bringing me back in some way?' I thought.

"And he sent for the merchant which had brought him, and for the apostle, and said unto him: Hast thou built me the palace? And he said: Yea. And the king said: When, then, shall we go and see it? but he answered him and said: Thou canst not see it now, but when thou departest this life, then thou shalt see it."
The Apocryphal New Testament, Acts of Thomas, Second Act, Number 21, (Christianity, Gnostic, Words of St. Thomas)

"The Savior said to his disciples, 'Already the time has come, brothers, for us to abandon our labor and stand at rest. For whoever stands at rest will rest forever. And I say to you, (be) always (above) time . . ."
The Nag Hammadi Library, The Dialogue of the Savior, No. 1, (Christianity, Gnostic, Words of Christ)

****

Turning, I noticed a legion of extra-terrestrial spacecraft was now traveling with me, above me in the sky. About thirty silver crafts, spherical in shape though bearing an unusual conical center, hovered silently above my soul as I walked along the pathway of life.

Taking me towards my next destination, I was directed to a very old house which looked somewhat like a haunted mansion. Immediately, a young man and his wife approached me, shaking my hand in greeting; unaware of the information being imparted to me about the status of his soul. An unseen voice explained, "He is in danger of meeting his death in five days; and if he dies at this time his soul will be damned." Acknowledging the tragedy of this man's situation, I silently bid the question of what I might be able to do. "If you accept, you will suffer for a time and offer it up to prevent his untimely death. If you do so, he will not die at this time, and more time will be given him to change his dominion." Nodding that I would accept this cross, it was finished.

Although this man was in a profession which would usually be associated with those who serve the light, he had chosen darkness; abusing power to fulfill his own ends. Remaining completely unaware of the judgment which had befallen him, he breezed through his death date with no regard for the tragic consequence which had barely been avoided. As for me, I got very sick, coughing uncontrollably for weeks. As promised, I offered it up for this soul's salvation.

Breezing towards a beautiful holy church, my son, Jacob, was now in my arms. Entering the building, we were drawn immediately to a large and ornate statue of the Blessed Virgin which sat silently on an altar. Placing my son before the feet of the Virgin, a very holy priest quietly approached us. Filled with the Holy Spirit, the priest placed his hands upon my son and blessed him. As he did so, my body was forced into a sitting position, and my legs were lifted up as if on an ottoman by an unseen force. Knowing instantly that this was being done by the Blessed Virgin, I inherently understood that she was begging my indulgence during this time of illness, so that I might not put myself in danger of death during this auspicious time.

As we prepared to leave the church, all the exits disappeared and I realized that the Lord wished for me to live in His house at all times. Turning to enter a room where a choir began singing heavenly songs, my spirit was whisked back into my body within seconds.
****

Three large books fell onto the table which stood in front of me. Gazing down upon them, I noticed that the first book was a huge volume containing the writings of St. John Chrysostom while the final two were about Moses.

Standing before me in a deeply embedded cave, an archaeologist was pulling ancient writings out of the dirt which I inherently knew belonged with the New Testament. "The writings of St. John . . ." he said, as he looked at me with excitement, wonder and awe in finding them. For a moment, I was confused; thinking of the gospel of St. John and the Book of Revelation, but then I had a thought . . . Perhaps he was talking about St. John Chrysostom? Turning to go, I observed him excitedly dusting off the texts. I was determined to find these writings.

After finding out more about St. John Chrysostom, I discovered that he had been banished for telling people the truth and had actually died on one of his journeys into further banishment right along the road. A powerful preacher, he convicted people of their sins, and this displeased them. Almost everybody knows the story of Moses who did the will of God, only to have the people he'd led out of slavery turn on him and God to worship idols when things didn't go as they'd hoped in the wilderness.

For a moment, I understood that the Lord was giving me comfort in knowing that by doing His will, I would not necessarily be welcomed with open arms. This was not a measure of my works.

Soaring towards a veranda, I began to watch as a heavenly river parade unfolded before my eyes. In this river, the water was of the whitest white, and as the parade began, it began to turn into spectacular colors of blue, purple, lilac, pink, yellow and gold. Spectacular displays of wonder were shown as spirits were floating down the river on parade floats and the water would continually change color.

Without any warning, my spirit was submerged in this water, following the parade route and feeling some type of energetic shockwaves in my soul. Whatever this water represented, it was of a high vibrational nature. Immersed in the water, I quietly floated along with my head just above the water as interior changes began to take place.

Riding the wave of an ecstatic bliss, my spirit landed in a bleacher of sorts on the gateway to heaven. A robed man stood before me, as several people had been led to sit in my midst to observe what was about to happen. "Behold the power of the Lord," he said, as he raised his hand in my direction. Having no idea what was going on, I turned to notice that several denizens of hell had begun to approach this heavenly station. Lifting my hands, lightning came from them and sent the demonic souls back into the lower realms. Suddenly, hordes of them appeared, as lightning came forth from my hands towards them, refusing them entrance to a realm in which they were incompatible. Being educated in the proper use of eternal power, the onlookers were dumbfounded (and sub-conscious astral).

Without warning, my soul was thrust from this heavenly sphere down below. Following a spiraling pole into the depths of the Earth, I noticed that there were hundreds of caverns alongside me as I plunged. Passing by the many hell realms, there was an odiferous slimy green light that permeated this tiny little dirt passageway into the depths. Finally landing in one of the caves, the same slimy green light permeated the realm. Small in size, the cave held only a few wards. Each of them laughed in hysterics, as they said, "We like it here, because we can do whatever we want." Feeling claustrophobic and disliking the energy of the place, I was allowed to ascend the spiral pole all the way back up and into a heavenly realm.

Books lined the walls in this heavenly realm, and I was led to two in particular which contained the knowledge of heaven within them. Holding them, I observed a line of people being admitted into the realm. Noticing a young man wearing rap clothing and looking a bit unkempt, I reached towards him and said, "Stop, you don't belong here." The robed man came over to me and quietly said, "Look deeper." As I did so, the inner truth of this soul began to manifest upon his shirt. Interiorly, this young man was quite compatible to this heavenly realm and I had judged him inappropriately. But his words echoed into my spirit, 'Look deeper . . .'

As I waited amongst the souls in this heavenly realm, I observed that they didn't worry much about doing, but spent more time being. In the lower realms, a lot of agitation and chaos resided. But in the upper world sphere, all was calm.

Abiding in peace, I began to open the books containing this knowledge of which I'd hoped to obtain about heaven as I began to disappear from the realm.

****

Entering into an overcast realm where winds pelted and burst against the residents at all times, I came upon a small house. Carrying with me an old familiar and very cranky cat, I had a sense that I must be coming to visit a long past neighbor of mine whose cat I held in my arms. Upon her death, she had given me charge of the cat, which happened to be unusually cranky and nasty towards children. Because of this, I had found the original owners of the cat and returned it to them.

Answering the door, our old friend Joyce opened the door with a somewhat 'not happy to see me' kind of greeting. During her life, Joyce had not been the most friendly sort, but she had opened up to me a lot near the end as we'd become closer friends. Trying to hand her what used to be a previously beloved cat of hers, she indicated she no longer wanted it. Another grayish cat came to the door who appeared to be very loving and sweet, and it was apparent that the new cat represented certain qualities she hoped to cultivate in her new life. A very young woman with shoulder-length brown hair stood beside her at the door who was of the utmost of sweetness, friendliness and kindliness. Immediately, I knew this was a guide to her who lived with her to show her kindness and teach her new ways. Joyce had led a very rough life of abuse and hardship, and much of this had imprinted itself upon her soul.

As she didn't invite me in and almost acted as if she no longer knew me, I was sent off into the frantic winds to go to the house across the street which represented my former home which had been across the street from her. The skies remained gray and the winds blew with fury, and off in the distance I saw something which I could not delineate. Was this a part of this purgatorial realm which my former friend occupied, or was this a prophecy of things to come in our now war-trodden world? A nuclear blast was seen in the distance, as I watched the glow fill the dark sky. Catapulting waves of wind began to blow . . .

Winds began blowing hard as the light from the nuclear blast in the distance had now passed. Wondering what it might mean, and hoping for the best, I began emerging into physical waking consciousness.

"The virtuous acts performed by enlightening beings are all to develop and complete the living. To have them destroy obscurity and annihilate affliction, subdue the demon armies and fulfill true awakening."

The Flower Ornament Scripture, Clarifying Method, Page 437, (Buddhism: Mahayana)

"Refuse no one the good on which he has a claim when it is in your power to do it for him."
The New American Bible, Old Testament, Proverbs 4:27, (Christianity, Judaism, Words of Solomon)

****

Reappearing after quite a long absence, my old friend, Karleen (who had died and continued to appear to me occasionally), showed me to her present abode. An old duplex of sorts, she was staying on one side of the two-story building and appeared to be quite happy. In a border realm, she was still working through many of her mortal aspects, and she showed me several shopping bags on her counter to indicate that she was still struggling with an attachment to material things. Looking down as if to indicate the disappointment she had in herself, she had opened a sliding glass door on one side of the home.

Looking up, I quickly ascertained that this realm was filled with torrential winds. A huge torrent was coming across the sky, literally soaring across the atmosphere at what appeared to be hundreds of miles per hour. "Close the glass door!" I shouted to her. But she just smiled, indicating that she liked the winds. "Come on, Karleen," I said, "You know that those are the winds of karma and you must enclose yourself away from them in order to have a chance to overcome them." But she was defiant because she was still very compatible to the chaos of the karmic winds that prevailed in this realm. It was clear that she was in this realm for the purpose of purification, but she didn't wish to close out the chaos because it invigorated her and made her feel alive. "All right, then," I said calmly, as I sat down. "God will take care of it anyway." As soon as I said this, the door was slammed shut by an angelic force, and the karmic winds were shut out from her perimeter.

Saying nothing, we smiled at each other as I began to disappear from her realm.

"I reveal the law in its multifariousness with regard to the inclinations and dispositions of creatures. I use different means to rouse each according to his own character. Such is the might of my knowledge. I likewise see the poor wretches, deficient in wisdom and conduct, lapsed into the mundane whirl, retained in dismal places, plunged in affliction incessantly renewed."
Saddharma Pundarika or the Lotus of the True Law, Skilfulness, No.108-109, (Buddhism: Mahayana)

****

But at this very moment, I also was deep in the realms of the mystical places. In the distance, I began to hear the beckon of a familiar voice. "It's so nice to hear your voice!" I shouted to my former priest who was now deceased. But he came very quickly with a message of urgency. "I need prayer," he said, "I have not yet been allowed to see heaven. I'm in purgatory and I need you to pray for me." Shocked to hear this, I promised I would pray and offer all my sufferings for him.

****

A friend shared with me a vision she had of a relative who had died one and a half years previously. In life, she had been somewhat mean spirited, but at this moment, she came to show her something very important.

Surprised to see her, she immediately asked, "Are you in heaven?" "No, I'm not, but I've passed through there." She replied. "Everybody passes through a place called 'Christ's Temple' when they die," she continued, "and some highly evolved people are lucky enough to stay, but I wasn't one of them so I had to move on." She was in a pre-designated place that my friend could not understand. But she had a friend with her, another woman about the same age, whom she'd met there and they were enjoying each other a lot. A lot of the mean-spirited nature she'd had in life had dissipated and she seemed like a kinder gentler version of herself.

****

ExtraTerrestrials

Mystic Knowledge Series

Compiled and Written by Marilynn Hughes

The Out-of-Body Travel Foundation!

www.outofbodytravel.org

The Pleiades

CHAPTER ONE
Venus and Alpha Centauri

****

Flying through the blackness of space, I ventured to a distant planet as the stars rushed. Reaching my destination, an astral spaceship orbited, and in the small silver craft, a being who manifested as a human, was communicating with someone on a radio device. A disagreement ensued and she cut off communications to speak with me.

Telling me that there are some alien life-forms with which one should avoid contact, she explained that they come from scientifically evolved societies, rather than spiritual. In their view, human beings were much like laboratory rats. Although they meant no harm, they were not aware enough to realize that they did indeed cause harm. Beaming me over to one of their spaceships, she wished for me to know what they looked like.

Big black eyes and large white craniums were the trademark features of these aliens, and one of them was wearing a black robe. Rather than astral matter, like the spacecraft of the previous moment, their craft was made of physical matter. In a moment, I was returned to form.

"Judge thou fairly, I adjure thee by God."
The Epistle to the Son of the Wolf, Page 81, Paragraph 1, (Baha'i, Author: Baha'u'llah)

****

Watching as a blue crystal faceted spaceship shaped like an hourglass was descending from the sky, my spirit was mesmerized by the scene. A spirit voice began speaking behind me, "Not long ago, this spaceship arrived from Venus carrying souls who wished to incarnate in human form. Only a few saw as the spaceship came to Earth because only a few were able to see through their spirit's eyes. It was an astral spaceship, and your child was on this ship." Coming to a halt, the spirits inside began pouring out. My oldest daughter, who was only two, ran up to me, her destiny clear and known to her. In her childlike body, she spoke with authority and conviction. "I have come from a world of peace and tranquility, a world where love is all that is. I enter now into a world filled with turmoil and no inner vision. Like you, mother, this society will not sustain me. My destiny will not be to fit into this society, but to teach society new ways. Be patient with me." As tears streamed down my face, I held her tiny hand and acknowledged that I would. For a moment, I touched the glittering blue crystal plates upon the spaceship, and felt the power that fueled this vessel.

"He who lives under the guidance of reason endeavors, as far as possible, to render back love, or kindness, for other men's hatred, anger, contempt, etc., toward him."
The Ethics of Spinoza, On Human Bondage, The Little Pleasures and the Great Sin, Page 108, Paragraph 2, (Judaism, Author: Baruch Spinoza)

****

Flying about the earth, I noticed a Venusian Blue Crystal spaceship hovering around. Several hunters saw it from the woods, and were staring at it. Materializing amongst them, I walked towards their campfire, "Look up there!" They shouted at me, assuming I was another hunter. "Oh, that." I said. "That is a crystal spaceship from Venus." For the first time they all looked down to see who I was, and with a look indicating that they thought I was a moron. "Venusians have been coming here for several decades now, incarnating in the tribes of man to bring in the path of the spirit." Arguing amongst themselves, one of the men said, "You must be one of them escaped crazies!" Smiling, I replied, "You don't believe what I tell you, so I must rejoin my ship." Sheer shock accompanied their faces as I shot towards the sky, hovering about them for a few moments before entering the crystal spaceship.

Inside the ship, I saw no instrumentation but noticed the Venusian spirits were joyous beings. Shooting towards the heavens, we glowed through the sky. No matter, the time was nigh, soon the tribes of the earth would awaken, and until then I must return to the world of form.

"On the mansion worlds, after your vision range is extended and you are freed from the fetters of material comparisons, you can begin to comprehend the meaning of those realities which 'eye cannot see nor ear hear, and which have never entered the concept of human minds,' even those things which 'God has prepared for those who love such eternal verities.' You are not always to be so limited in the range of your vision and spiritual comprehension."
The Urantia Book, Paper 24, No. 6, Paragraph 2, (Christianity, Urantia)
****

Flying through the ceiling, I was greeted by a large astral spaceship. Round with many glowing lights emanating from two circular chambers underneath, I followed my inner knowing and quickly shot up inside. A man and woman appeared, the female with long black hair pulled on top of her head, and the male was tall and brunette with a stocky build. Wearing bright uniforms, she wore one in emerald blue, while he wore one with a smoky rose color.

Emitting peace, they held out their arms in welcome. Coming forward, I sensed communication but it was not clear. Putting her hand on my forehead and sending a pulsing energy force through my spirit, she held it still until it exploded inwardly in light, creating an opening in my soul. Communicating telepathically, they conveyed, "We are from the galaxy of Alpha Centauri. We come from a completely telepathic race. We have come to help you to open your channels of telepathy. Join us as we return to our world to show you who we are."

Soaring at the speed of light, I couldn't feel any movement from the chamber of the spaceship. Blue metallic walls surrounded a circular room where two chairs awaited. She and I sat down, while the man lay on the floor. Watching as they demonstrated the way of light, the female turned to the male and they closed their eyes. "I am feeling a very intense emotion!" She thought loudly, "It is a strong joyful vibration that I am sensing." Holding out her hands to the man, he gently touched them. "Share what I am feeling." She thought. Holding each other's hands for several moments, they were able to sense and feel everything from one another just by touching. "It is a beautiful vibration you have tuned into," the man thought, as they both glowed with light.

Turning to me, they laid their hands on the top of my head, allowing me to sense the vibration through my crown chakra. Vibrations of love and joy filled my soul. "We have come to open your telepathic channels, will you let us?" "Yes," I thought, "I will." Looking into my eyes, he thought, "Remove the barriers you have created to freedom, enter the flow of the higher will and all will be known to you. We are what you will become. We are what all people of the earth will become. Do you feel the flow?" "Yes," I thought loudly, "I feel it, it is within my grasp, but I don't quite have it!" Embracing me tightly, the humming vibration began to grow and increase in frequency.

With a sudden jolt, a massive force pulled my spirit back, releasing a part of me that had no true identity. My soul fell to the floor in the freedom of the release, and a massive light beam was now within my life force. "Spirit, you are now a part of the flow. Feel its beauty and the vibration of peace!" Flowing back and forth, I thought, "All that is, is all that I am." They smiled, and the woman began to think. "We all come from the same place, my dear spirit, isn't it wonderful to go home?"

Before I could reply, they opened a window to the universe. Peering outside of the spaceship, a huge planet was directly before us. "This is our home," they thought simultaneously. So illuminated by light, you could not distinguish its color; and an enormous sun, half the size of the planet, began rising from the horizon.

Peering in awe, the universal movement directed me to form.

"Moreover, such individuals are 'universal' in their sympathies, and can feel with any form of life with which they come in contact . . . Many of the great illumined souls of the race, having this consciousness in at least some degree, find themselves 'at home' with all manners and conditions of mankind, and in many cases with the lower life forms, as well . . . It may be seen at once that when one has a feeling of fellowship with all Life (and such individuals have this to some degree), then there are created certain bonds and links of sympathy and unity which serve to unite the individual more or less strongly to all living things."

The Secret Doctrine of the Rosicrucians, Part VIII, The Three Higher Planes, Page 14, Paragraph 2, (Mystery Religions, Rosicrucian)

****

CHAPTER TWO
Antoneek and the Pleiadians

****

Leaving form, I was led to look out the window of my bedroom. In the distance, were two metallic circular space vessels. Light beamed out of an open seam in the center and a blue light vibrated from the top of the vessel. The spirit aside me said, "These are Pleiadian-Atlantean vessels." Intrigued, I was led back to my body to reflect.

"I have dreamed many dreams; now I am awake."

Whispers from Eternity, Page 190, Paragraph 5, (Hinduism, Kriya Yoga, Words of Paramahansa Yogananda)

****

Two spaceships arrived, and aside them, an old, old man holding his arms out to me. Manifesting few features, Antoneek was made of pure light, in garment and in form, his hair and long beard only an outline of an extended period of growth.

In his hands, he held a document, and I could see it was a message for the world. "Go back," he said, as he placed it within my hands, "return to your body and allow us to transmit this message to your dimension." Nodding, I returned to fulfill my task:

"Greetings! Our mission is peace, joy and the betterment of mankind. Those who dwell deeply in our hearts, dwell in the glory of the light."

"I now bring you the seven tones of life. When all are balanced and converge in the spirit openly, they harmonize: Love, Joy, Peace, Oneness, Gentility, Goodness, and Ecstasy. Each of the seven tones of life vibrates at a rate seven times that of the one prior to it. With each tone, there are seven increased levels of light that enter the transmitting body. When one aspires and captures the ability to expel all seven levels, the spirit is ready to acquire a new tone. The radiance expounded by beings in your realm can differ in tonelage by forty-nine times. Light can be muted or expanded at will. It is an inalterable existence within all life, but each life force chooses how much of his total sum he will express in a given moment. Expressions of love cause an increase in tonelage and radiance, expressions of illusions cause the tones to be muted. Comparatively it is like a pot of boiling water. A pot with a lid, and one without, will hold the same amount of steam, but both will express an entirely different sum."

"All begins with love for love is the beginning of true life, the tone of love is a gentle eye-opening sound coming from the heart. Joy follows the tone reaching upward. Peace is so subtle, and yet to the individual soul, a moment of true awakening. To the outer world, however, the tone changes only a subtlety, for Joy and Peace are truly octaves of a similar tone. Oneness emerges with a glow to the spirit who sees their true nature for the first time; it connects all life in harmony. A spirit now harmonizing with all life reaches upward again, but stops at the next tone of gentility. This tone exhibits a higher peace, as the gentility tone sounds out a reverence now achieved and a deep gratitude to the One Creator. In this deep gratitude, the spirit reaches for the next tone, but is amazed at its beauty upon hearing it. Pulling away slightly, the spirit eventually returns as the awe of finding Goodness is too wondrous to ignore. This tone sweeps the tones together to form the sounds of angels singing the song of the inner light of love. Finally, the spirit in full awareness of its worthiness and divinity rises up to grasp the final tone, that of ecstasy. The spirit upon hearing the tone for the first time, immediately melts into the mass to experience the harmonic convergence of all life which resonates now at every level of being the trueness of all that is, the glory that is God."

"We offer this gift of the seven tones with great love; it is a sharing of a key that has been shrouded in secrecy and unknowing for centuries on your planet. As the ancients return to earth to complete a cycle begun in days of old, the time known as the present, and the memory of a past unknown, meet to complete the eternal cycle."

"Nothing more excellent is there, therefore, than these mysteries on which ye question, save only the mysteries of the seven Voices and their nine and-forty powers and their ciphers. And there is no name which is more excellent than them all, the name in which are all names and all lights and all powers."
Pistis Sophia, Fifth Book, Page 313, Paragraph 1, (Christianity, Gnostic/Essene, Words of Christ)

"Every sound has an image and every image, a sound. All light hologrates into form on its everlasting journeys. Who we are is a conglomeration of sounds, images and colors broadcast from light. Where in time can a moment be found, a moment that holds more than but a fragment of truth? It is only in the absence of time, that a moment can hold all truth. In the structure that binds human consciousness in a pattern of knowing, truth can be seen to exist only in fragments. The matter that defines time seems unalterable. In the inexorable state of timelessness, all is now. Thus a being can expressively undertake all moments, any aspect of selfhood which exists. In a world emerging in consciousness, form becomes vehicle rather than life. In a heightened awareness, these aspects merge causing you to flit about to various selves that exist in eternal memory. This dramatic occurrence opens the door to the present moment, as the now exists as all aspects of memory. As memory expands, beings expand in their knowledge of themselves and love is expressed through many layers of consciousness. Where is it that a being finds himself if not in his heart? As your hearts open, do not forget to open to your true timeless self which unifies the many selves."

"The ocean waves to the rhythm of the moon. A waterfall dances the design of a rocky cliff. A lake stops in silence to adhere to peace. The river flows endlessly in search. The raindrop chooses free-flight as expression. Water can be compared to spirit, expressing the totality of being in every majestic moment; the lure and longing of love, the surrender of solitude, the majesty of moments, the silence of the search, and the freedom of flight."

"Wonders of love are displayed on our skies. Our Pleiadian star, glowing brighter than any in our sky, sings the tone of tranquil love. It is a harmony that transcends time, space and illusion. Our constant star specter guides many to the shores of our worlds, glimmering at all who seek to find true love. Love is displayed in our emerald cities as a spectral light beaming forth through the receptacle monuments of crystal, amethyst and gold. Our poets and musicians, through their mastery of the seven tones, create symphonies of sound, color and light and our world pours forth to the senses the dynamics of the highest expressive love. We encompass all that is beauty and love, and the passion of the planets fuels our ever-spiraling ascent into expansive tones which envelope the soul in a gentility of bliss towards all life, and a wonderment which expresses the mystery of God."

"Expression of love is an expression of divine light, but this love is not what you presently know, but a greater, divine love. You are becoming a lighter being, you will no longer be completely physical, but you will not be etheric, either. A vibration that lingers in-between is what the new race of humanity will encompass. Our purpose is to aid this transition into higher love."

The Pleiadian Command

"'Who walketh upon the wings of the wind' to Raphael, who comes to give healing to the world. From that point on 'he maketh his angels spirits, his ministers a flaming fire.' Old man, old man! As thou art aware of all these things, fear not, but speak out boldly, and let the words of thy mouth spread light!'"

The Zohar (Kaballah), Volume III, Mishpatim (Exodus), Page 299, Top, (Judaism)
****

Returning to the out-of-body state, Antoneek appeared next to the circular vessels which accompanied him. "I have something to show you," he said, "it is your fears." Lifting his arms, my soul was thrust into parallel realities of my current lifetime.

The first was a parallel where I had been murdered at eighteen and my murder was still unsolved. I experienced the repetitive stabbing in my chest and heard the familiar gasping sounds that I would hear from my asthma. Apparently, the killer had killed again, and Antoneek took my spirit to a police station wherein I was to plant the identity of the murderer within the investigator's minds. "Help them put it together." Antoneek said, as I exerted thought-forces to the officers who were trying to figure out this odd pattern of murders.

Antoneek pulled me to the side, "This energy has been with you for many years and you now have the opportunity to truly release it. Though you had no conscious recall of these events, your inner sense of not deserving to live has manifested. You must transmute this energy that you have been carrying. It was your inner belief that you were not worthy of even life that made you choose to branch out into this reality."

The next parallel he took me to was a branch out wherein I had chosen to remain with those from my past who had been very difficult and smothering. "Make another choice!" Antoneek charged. Entering into that self, I left and altered the energies of not believing myself worthy of love and freedom.

Standing before the spaceship, I reached my hand to Antoneek. "Thank you, Antoneek, you have shown me a great deal." Antoneek smiled. "There is much for you to learn. Your thoughts manifest in ways that you do not always see. These two parallels have been changed, but the energies remain. This energy must be changed, as well, for a lasting effect to take place. Now that you understand, you can transmute it. But in order to transmute the energy of these experiences, you must change the belief that confirms the validity of these experiences." Antoneek looked up to the sky. "You have seen your fears, if you release them, you will see what lies out there." He pointed to the sky.

"Will I see you again?" I asked. "That will be completely up to you, dear spirit." Antoneek entered his spaceship and I awoke looking upon wavelets of energy which were merging and melding, altering the perceptions that my soul held. I could see it happening in the sky above my bed.

"Go thy way; and as thou hast believed, so be it done unto thee."

King James Bible, New Testament, Matthew 8:13, (Christianity, Words of Christ)
****

Antoneek returned to tell me a story:

"Whence the journey began, we asked our Creator that we may understand all that He was. In goodness, He freely asked, "Who among us has felt pain, as well as joy; lack, as well as abundance; rejection, as well as love?" In reply, one being stood forth and spoke from the experience of only love, "My Great Father, is there a difference?" Our Father smiled and quietly nodded that there indeed was.

All the spirits agreed that they wanted to create an opportunity to feel these unknown emotions. Our Creator stepped forth. "Go my beautiful spirits and create all that you desire, but promise me two things." The clouds became silent to hear the noble request. "Promise me my children that you will see beauty in every emotion you create, and all that you perceive." Everyone nodded that they would. God continued, "Most importantly, my children, no matter how lowly or downtrodden things may seen in your illusions, always remember your divinity and my amassable love for all of you." Every spirit in the room smiled in recognition of their special place in God's heart.

As time passed, however, the children of God spread among the galaxies of the universe creating worlds vast and worlds primitive. Many held in their hearts the heritage of love, but many worlds suffered a loss of memory. The Earth became a world separated in spirit from its Creator, and the peoples of the Earth, consumed with illusion, enmeshed themselves in a state of fragmentary pride which was based on an untruth. The world they created became increasingly hostile and ego-oriented. The love that once existed in their hearts was replaced with pride, anger and cynicism. Rejecting others became a way to protect oneself from rejection. The oneness that once existed with the people was forgotten in the heart of man.

And now, on this beautiful planet Earth, as the energy passed over and the space vessels returned to re-equate the lost brothers, a tiny sound was heard. One single tone called out requesting knowledge. The spirit, shattered by its own illusion, asked to understand. "We love you, brother!" We called out in our tonal language. "There are but two things you have forgotten. These are the keys to opening your heart which holds all knowledge. Two promises made to your Creator long ago. See the beauty in all the emotions you are feeling and all that you perceive. And most important, my beautiful spirit, remember your divinity, remember that special place you hold in the heart of God!"

"But who am I?" The spirit cried in exasperation. "I'm an imperfect man who has made many mistakes, and made nothing of himself." "REJOICE!" Our ecstasy tone cried out. "Because you are my brother of whom I love greatly! You are PURE LIGHT! You are a part of God! And you believe that you are nothing, what a shame, indeed." "Could it be?" He thought, pausing to remember. Suddenly, a spacecraft stopped directly above him, pouring light into his everlasting soul. "I REMEMBER!" He cried out in ecstasy! "I remember the moment I made that promise! I remember the love. Now I understand! I wanted to know the absence of love, and having felt it, I rejoice evermore in the reception of it. I wanted to know what rejection felt like, and now I run and grasp even more ecstatically to those brothers who offer their light with open arms. I no longer need to perceive the illusion, for I have experienced hate, and found more joy in love. But my journey has been wondrous, indeed! The emotions I have felt have ranged so dramatically in vibration that they were like a symphony of feelings and tones. Having loved in limitation, my unlimited form loves with more intensity, desire and clarity. Thank you, brothers, for awaking me to this journey's end!"

The star beings looked down from the sky with great happiness at their brother. "We rejoice with you, as life is a wondrous journey, indeed. Will you help us in our quest to awaken the earth beings?" Nodding that he would, the beings filled him with light, knowing that his path had been carefully mapped out in his heart. He need only take the key and open it, to set forth on his new

journey into light. You are this being, brother. Follow the light that glows within your heart and find all of us that love you, eternally waiting patiently beside you."
****

Floating quietly to the spaceship, I was greeted by Antoneek. Immediately, he blocked my consciousness so that I would not remember the means by which this journey was taken. Making a voyage to a planet whose identity was to remain unknown; my consciousness was reawakened after we stepped off the ship on a large planet.

Hundreds of beings had gathered from all over the universe in a park nearby, some had very thin bodies with heads that were T-shaped, while others were like domes with very few hair strands upon their heads. Others were various manifestations of humanoid type beings, only subtly different from human beings.

In front of us was a large domed building where a huge banquet was taking place. Antoneek guided me inside where a staff of aliens exhibiting the utmost in cordiality served foods from all over the galaxies. A humanoid man approached with a tray, and asked, "Have you ever tried an Amprien grape?" Taking one, I swallowed the strange looking fruit. Noticing an unusual woman, she had entered the room with a very human body, but her face had a long beak and she had feathers coming out of her rump.

Returning to the park, Antoneek led me to a place where hundreds of beings were meditating. As we noticed this, a loud voice was broadcast over the crowd. "This is an emergency! All out in the fields move back! All light bearers, focus your light on the approaching planet." Everyone in the space became very still and radiant. Many beings from further ahead quickly ran back to where we were, and all began glowing as the mass energy was focused on something . . . but what?

Antoneek directed my attention to the sky. "Oh, my God!" I screamed, "That's Earth, and it's about to collide with this planet!" Quietly, Antoneek said, "Bear your light." Immediately, I joined the others in the meditative state of the mass mind of those around me, but the earth pummeled quickly toward us as it appeared that there would be total destruction. Seconds later, however, it was over. The Earth had plunged directly into a small clearing exploding into flames, but no one ventured forward. Allowing the flames to extinguish themselves, in moments, they did.

Confused, I turned to Antoneek for answers. "My God!" I said, "Is that the fate of the Earth?" Smiling with sympathetic understanding, Antoneek put his hands upon my shoulders. "No, not how you have perceived it, my child." Antoneek conveyed to me the knowledge of parallel existences, as I was shown three Earths. Explaining that there were to be two additional parallel Earth's, each existing in separate realities based on fear or love, he conveyed that every member of humanity would vibrate to the Earth which was compatible to them without even being aware of it. But it was also made known to me that there are many parallel Earth's, wherein many possibilities are played out. Inexplicable, really.

Beginning a rigorous process, Antoneek continued showing me my own parallel existences, selves which existed in various realities which had branched off at certain important turning points in my life and gone in other directions. As the magnetic impulse of flesh is to experience all possibilities, it literally does, through parallel energetic universes of which unconscious man is completely unaware. In observing my own parallels, Antoneek guided me to end the karmic impulse of those selves, and thus the karmic influx which would also affect my current now. Whatever was left unresolved had to be resolved and dealt with in my energetic journey. It was necessary to alter those parallel realities and, thus, bring them within my own point of reference, to fulfill the same purpose which past-life retrieval performs . . . unity of soul.

In this process, Antoneek also guided me to several atonements with members of parallel and past-lives. Despite what I was shown, I fail to fully understand what I saw that night.

"What is this planet, and where is it?" I asked. Antoneek created a large pool. "This is something we cannot tell you for reasons you would not understand," he said, as he pushed me into the water. In moments, I emerged in my body.

"Then I saw a new heaven and a new earth. The former heaven and the former earth had passed away, and the sea was no more . . . 'Behold, God's dwelling is with the human race . . . He will wipe every tear from eyes, and there shall be no more death or mourning, wailing or pain, for the old order has passed away."

New American Bible, New Testament, Revelations 21:1-4, (Christianity, Catholic)
****

Hovering over my bed waiting for me as I left form, a man who referred to himself as my 'personal trainer' said, "This will be on our terms, no limits on this journey." Conveying to me that he was here to help me with my health, he was prepared to assist me with my asthma, as were a whole team of specialists who were now visible.

Up ahead in the stars I called out, "Where are you taking me?" "Remember, no limits, just follow your heart!" He replied. Soaring past the atmosphere of the earth, up ahead was a large Pleiadian craft; the familiar metallic circle with light pouring out of the seams, and before I knew it, we had entered the spaceship.

Taking me aside to a crystal chamber in the ship, the walls of the room were glowing in a vibrant blue. Inside, the floors were made of a velvety cushion and we sat together. "I am taking you to the Pleiades." He said. "There you will experience unlimitedness. You must experience the true nature of love in order to heal yourself."

"Prepare yourself for unlimited beauty," he said, as the spaceship door was opened. Iridescent shaded lights of blue and purple beamed from the planet, the color of lilacs. Leading me to the open door, my spirit shook in the absolute wonderment of what lay before me. Purple and blue skies shone down upon a huge temple created from amethyst stone. Seven luminous beams shot directly to the seven luminous stars, their names were Janan, Onan, Quinlan, Donan, Enos, Quinas, and Justos. A majestic sound filled the entire sky, angelic voices singing in tonal harmony. Below me, the ground was made of a whitish-clear crystalline substance. Shooting stars soared through the night sky. A large butterfly about two feet in diameter with pink crystalline wings flew directly into my hand. "Behold, the Pleiadian star!" she said, pointing to a gleaming body of light as large as the Earthly moon in the night sky. Musical sounds increased and filled me with joy, and as I ventured forth, a luminous green filled my spirit as I wandered towards an emerald city which lay beyond the amethyst temple.

Transmitted into my heart, the seven tones became comprehendible to me here. Love powers the universe, but it was not the karmic love that most humanity understood, it was a divine love which lay beyond all ramification of desire. Light beings moved to the flow of the lights and music, their ecstasy in God apparent. Luminescent Pleiadians were engaged in a joyous dance of life as I realized. "Love, love, love . . . that's what it's all about."

Flying towards a mountain made of pure crystal, it contained an open chamber filled with a power modulator. As I arrived, a soft blue substance surrounded me, and the angelic sounds projecting from the temple were being absorbed directly into the mountain's chamber. Waiting for me at the mountain, my trainer said, "What could be more natural than love?" I knew that he was speaking of this type of divine love that I just now experienced, rather than the karmically disfigured love which predominates upon the Earth.

Returning to the spaceship, we began our journey home. In an instant, my trainer said, "We have returned to Earth, and you must go back. Please," he pleaded, "remember the Pleiades, and be yourself. In this you will find your way." Beginning to wrap a piece of fine silk fiber around my head, he said, "Like the caterpillar, you are transforming into something grander. Keep this silk fiber with you to remind you of what you are becoming."

As he kissed my hand good-bye, I quickly became sub-conscious.

"Through one pore they radiate infinite light beams..."
The Flower Ornament Scripture, Chapter 38, Detachment from the World, Page 1130,
Stanza 2, (Buddhism, Mahayana)

****

CHAPTER THREE
The Millennium

****

"Come, come pass through the veil," Isis said, as they opened very wide. As soon as I'd passed through, they closed with a start. Alone, I now wore the garments of healing and rebirth.

Three beings awaited my arrival, as I immediately recognized them as being members of my band of alliances. Greeting them with a bow, I knew that we all worked together for the Lord on the ground below. Two of us were incarnate upon the Earth; a teacher who taught of the electrical nature of energy in the world and myself. The third was a starship captain, and was in spirit form. "Remember our pact, we work together," the captain said. We were all together and present to assist the teacher, who was experiencing a crisis on the ground wherein members of his family were trying to block his path and interfere with his job for the Lord. Not identifying with his universal mission, his shoulder was badly injured.

Another incarnate soul approached. I'd recognized her immediately as a soul I'd guardianed for a time, but whose apathy had prevented the manifestation of her aspects of the mission on the ground. Looking sternly at her, the teacher spoke harsh words. "Our love for you has held you intact, but I'm very sad to declare that you cannot come back here anymore." Attached to the world, her abilities to affect it in a spiritual manner had been thwarted. Loving her very deeply, it was sad to accept that her Earthly image held only fragments of the higher will, and a sleeping fragment cannot serve God unless they awaken. Unhurt by his words, she walked away quietly as her soul understood that her fragment was ensconced in the mass retain.

"Will your shoulder eventually heal?" The starship captain asked the teacher. Massaging it deeply, he looked at me. "My shoulder represents the burdens of the world. When we unite, the injury will be healed." Although I didn't recognize him at the time, this was a higher aspect of my husband, Andy, who bore a shoulder injury for years that only healed after we united in an eternal union. Enraptured in flight, my soul was climbing a steep mountain with many treacherous curves, bends and byways. A voice conveyed, "You must follow the bends and the curves, the by-ways and the highways, the good and the bad, in order to reach the goal." Driving off the road several times due to sharp curves, I always eventually returned to the correct path. Up ahead was the summit, and I stopped my car just before reaching the overhanging cliff.

At the top of the mountain was a small bookstore called, 'Sacred Rite.' Led to a book on a table, I took note of the title, 'Jesus came from the Pleiades,' it said.

"He who loves God most in this world is the happiest. All that is not done for God turns to pain. He who desires only God is rich and happy: he is in want of

nothing, and may laugh at all the world."
The Great Means of Salvation and Perfection, Part II, Various Practices, No. III, Page
351, Paragraphs 4 & 7, (Christianity, Catholic, Author: St. Alphonsus Liguori)
"It is they who will restore the world, which will never grow old and never die,
never decaying and never rotting, ever living and ever increasing, and master of
its wish, when the dead will rise, when life and immortality will come, and the
world will be restored at its wish."
The Avesta, Part II, Yast 19, No. 23, (Zoroastrianism)
****

Viewing the Earth from a multi-dimensional perspective, I noticed cylindrical spaceships with shining purple, blue and red lights soaring across the sky in silence. Venusian vessels of blue-green crystal were arriving and landing on the Earth. Angels were coming into the world in this manner. A magnetic voice of one chimed, "The angels are coming!" Voices referring to the cylindrical vessels spoke. "We have come from Mars to aid in the transition to light. We are coming to you, will you prepare for our coming?!" "Yes! Yes!" I said, "Show me what I need to do!" Flying to me, a transparent angel handed me a piece of paper with hundreds of questions indicative of my low self-esteem. 'Why do I deserve all this love? I'm not worthy of the gifts I've been given, of the work I do for God, why isn't someone else doing it? How can I experience so much joy when others are suffering?' Answering the questions, the angels said. "You deserve this simply because you exist. Those who do not do this, don't because they did not choose to, and you are experiencing joy because you have chosen love over fear. When you answer all these questions with love, you will have prepared yourself for the entry of the angels."

Gazing in awe, I asked, "Why do you come from Mars, it is such a desolate planet?" Chuckling, the angels replied, "Third-dimensionally speaking it appears so. But actually, Mars is a wonderful place to settle."

"Between the central Isle of Paradise and the innermost of the Havona planetary
circuits there are situated in space three lesser circuits of special spheres. The
innermost circuit consists of the seven secret spheres of the Universal Father; the
second group is composed of the seven luminous worlds of the Eternal Son; in the
outermost are the seven immense spheres of the Infinite Spirit, the executive-
headquarters worlds of the Seven Master Spirits."
The Urantia Book, Paper 13, No. 0, Paragraph 1, (Christianity, Urantia)
****

Taken to the inner pathways of the sun, beyond the cities of light, snow whisked all about the sky like a blanket in midair. In the center of the sun and following the ether pathways, unseen guides led me on my journey. Soaring down pathways, my destination lay up ahead.

Activity filled the night, as I observed spacecrafts and many different flying spirits soaring through a cloudy, violet tunnel. Soaring through the purplish mist, I heard a voice, "The sun beyond," it said, "the 'Universal Sun.'" Crystal angels sang, and up ahead I could see a huge body of light that looked like a huge version of the sun, which I immediately knew to be a manifestation of the essence of God. Enraptured in ecstasy, a surge of longing inspired me to soar faster towards my God, but the angels nodded, 'No,' I was not yet worthy to sit at His feet.

"The Lord, being love in its very essence or divine love, looks like the sun to
angels in heaven."
Divine Love & Wisdom, Chapter 1, No. 5, (Christianity, Swedenborgianism, Author:
Emanuel Swedenborg)
"Jesus said, 'If they say to you, 'Where have you come from?' say to them, 'We
have come from the light, from the place where the light came into being by
itself, established (itself), and appeared in their image.'"
The Gospel of Thomas, No. 50, (Christianity, Gnostic/Essene, Words of Christ)
****

Turning to look upon the night sky outside of form, my spirit was suddenly transported to another time and place. Many time-travelers were here to witness the grand event, that of the millennium. Like a comet in the night, the heavens opened up as star tunnels became the evidentiary pathways for which the vessels of all Universes entered our star system: Pleiadians, Alpha Centaurians, Marsians, Venusians and more. Rockets and saucers paraded through the sky, and in the center was a spectacular large cylindrical ship. As this beautiful and large vessel came into our realm quietly through a black hole, everyone looked upon it and said in unison, "Why, it's the Mother Ship." Inherently, my soul resonated with this coming time. Turning, I was alone in the canyon.

An old woman approached; her hair long and white. Suddenly, I knew it was I as an old grandmother. "You are She Who Walks Far," she said, "and don't let anyone tell you different. You have much to do." Disappearing like a mirage on a canyon night, an aged medicine man appeared singing a chant in a native tongue. A song of protection, he greeted me with a warning, "Beware of the darkness," he said.

"I am old and of feeble strength. For that very reason my body does not go away to there. I go constantly on a mental journey, for my mind, brahman, is joined to him."

The Group of Discourses II, V. The Chapter on Going to the Far Shore, Page 128, No. 1144-1145, (Buddhism, Theravadan)

****

Standing by the canyon, his spirit was strong and serene. Chief Joseph placed a heavy silver ball into my palm, as my spirit began to buzz with the energies it encompassed. Energy began pouring in and out of my hands. Handing me a telephone receiver, a group of spirits joined us with ferocity in trying to make the connection with someone. All of a sudden, I heard my own voice talking through the phone. "Marilynn! Marilynn! Are you there?!" "Yes, it's me!" "Oh, my God, this is great, I got through!" The spirits in the room were exuberant as Chief Joseph explained. "You have just broken the barrier of time and crossed the threshold of timelessness; your future and your present have become simultaneous."

Falling from the sky, a large ornate medicine pouch fell directly into my hands. Now I was alone, and I looked upon the sacred pictures it held inside. The first picture was of Chief Joseph, and the second picture was his name written in petroglyphs. A medicine woman approached, "These gifts are given to you directly from God," she said, as she placed her hands upon my head.

Winds began blowing very hard, and five medicine women appeared. "You cannot go until the winds die down," they said, as they began imparting prophecies to my soul of the things to come. In a vision, I was shown the souls of the dying upon the Earth. Many were dying, some violently, others from illness, young and old alike. But in their death, they were transcending to compatible realities. This was a necessary negativity in the attainment of a higher good.

All of a sudden, the skies began to open up and a familiar scene began to emerge. Space vessels from every star system filled the skies. Instantly, thousands of beings from the many different Earthly time periods were sitting and watching, waiting for the millennium. An ancient royal one, he who had been watching when I took care of the haunted house, approached. Recognizing him, he sat with a group of people and stared at me without a word, as if he were evaluating me for some future task.

Several space vessels began to land, and the turmoil of the coming days came to me as if in prophetic vision; wars and rumors of wars, pestilences, earthquakes, etc. Many people began forming a line to enter the Mother Ship, leaving to find a world of peace. Handing me a coin which appeared to be hundreds of years old, the ancient royal one directed me look more closely. Upon its face was a picture of the biblical father of Jesus, and it said, 'St. Joseph.' "This will give you passage," he said.

Giving me a second one, he conveyed that it was for someone else who may or may not make it in time. Beckoning to a longtime friend from days past, he wouldn't come, as he was too distracted with worldly attachments. For a moment I mourned, and then began running towards the line entering the Mother Ship. Waiting by my side, the royal one said no more as I bowed to his eminence in gratitude.

"Try to keep your heart reserved for God alone, that there may be no room for bitterness, gall, or voluntary repugnance to what God shall appoint. Never be absorbed in the failings of others, but pursue your own path, regarding nothing but that which may wound your conscience. The great secret of belonging to God is to neglect and pass by everything else."
The Spiritual Combat, Chapter 10, Page 218, Paragraph 3, (Christianity, Catholic, Author: Dom Lorenzo Scupoli)

Aboard the Mother Ship, I could feel the pain of a surgical procedure. Working on my solar plexus, my emotional centers of energy, I knew that this work was for my highest good. Lying upon a flat metallic board, the beings who worked on my soul looked like liquid glass, and you could see through them. Their innards were part biology and part machine, as their outside form was very human; but liquid like glass, and transparent. "She's remembering too much, we must erase some of this memory." Blip.

A massive energy pulse overtook my soul which now stood atop a mountain pass. Before me stood a very ancient Old One. His robes of white blew in the wind as his long silver hair and beard cascaded down his chest and back. "I am Yammeth, I am Symmeth," he said, as his words made the Earth rumble. Commanding the movements of the Earth, he continued to speak. "There are certain places that are safe, and you must be protected," he said. Pointing in the direction I must go, I took note. We'd already gone westward, and were now following the flow of the spirit to the correct location. "You must aid in the transition." The Earth began shaking all the more and I noticed a group of monks atop a mountain who were chanting next to their monastery. Their chanting caused rumblings in the Earth. Yammeth/Symmeths's face was of the utmost of seriousness. "It is an honor to be here at this time, and you must fulfill the function of your survival." Conveying information about where we would be safe during the coming changes, I listened. As lightning struck, he was gone.

Appearing before me in a long, yellow flowing gown, her auburn hair blew in the wind as she lifted a lighted wand about four feet long. Touching it to my crown chakra, she said, "We are de-energizing your destruction." Making energetic shifts which would protect me through the coming changes, I said, "Thank you," Again the winds came, and she was gone.

Chief Joseph walked in quietly, stern because of my impatience to continue our journey westward. "It will not happen until we know that you are safe," he said, "you will not go until the winds die down." Bowing my understanding, he disappeared.

"And I opened the book, and I read therein what had always been, what was now, and what would come to pass. I saw the holocaust which would engulf the earth, and the great destruction which would drown all her people in oceans of blood. And I saw too the eternity of man and the endless forgiveness of the Almighty."
The Essene Gospel of Peace, Volume 2, Page 116, Stanza 1, (Christianity, Gnostic/Essene)

****

Creating an image of a solar system, he was placing small purple balls in the air to represent the planets. Coming to the end of the line somewhere between ten and fifteen planets, the last three purple balls were representative of the Pleiadian star systems. Beginning to levitate, I watched the balls hover in midair before me.

Conveying to me that I needed to now get back to my roots, my Pleiadian origin, he told me that doing so would get me in touch with my mission and what I needed to do next. Watching the planetary configuration was a purifying experience, it was as if their energies were pulsing through my form and cleansing my innards. Reuniting with my purpose, the man said, "Unity . . . the end point," as he placed one of the Pleiadian planets before my eyes. Growing in size as it became a large crystal planet, I was mesmerized. "Unity, the end point," I repeated.

Conveying to me the journey I had taken, he was looking at me intensely. Having gone from one extreme in my behavior (being free, without boundaries and uncontrolled), to another (rigid boundaries, fearing imperfection and controlled), he stated, "You need to balance out, and be freer again."

"Will you tell me one thing? Why did you harp so much on sin? By repeating a hundred times, 'I am a sinner,' one verily becomes a sinner. One should have such faith as to be able to say, 'What? I have taken the name of God; how can I be a sinner?' God is our Father and Mother. Tell Him, 'O Lord, I have committed sins, but I won't repeat them.' Chant His name and purify your body and mind. Purify your tongue by singing God's holy name."
The Gospel of Sri Ramakrishna, Chapter 6, Page 159, Paragraph 3, (Hinduism, Words of Sri Ramakrishna)

"These mitigations take place because of the love which is natural in a father and which causes him to deal gently with his son, so that even when he punishes him, his blows are not those of an enemy. And again, when the occasion demands it is his love which causes him to suspend judgment entirely."
General Principles of Kabbalah, Chapter 18, Paragraph 2, (Judaism, Author: Rabbi Moses Chayim Luzzatto)

Suddenly wearing the robes of Mary, I walked towards a space station. "You are at 40% understanding," the voice of an angel said. Speaking of regret, she said that it was good and necessary for spiritual progress. Telling me of a third quality, she conveyed that when I was told this quality, all would come together in a clear cohesive understanding. Finally, she said that I was trying to force this remaining understanding to come to me quickly which was not possible, and that I must be patient, allowing it to emerge in its own fashion; slowly, methodically, and with intent, energizing it with prayer and meditation to God.

"Have we not been taught that 'hebel' (breath) is the basis of the world above and the world below . . . Every action done here below, if it is done with the intention of serving the Holy King, produces a 'breath' in the world above, and there is no breath which has no voice; and this voice ascends and crowns itself in the supernal world and becomes an intercessor before the Holy One, blessed be He."
The Zohar (Kabbalah), Volume III, Beshalah (Exodus), Page 184, Middle, (Judaism)
****

CHAPTER FOUR
The Star Chamber

****

Exploding into the heavens, I was taken to a star chamber. Becoming very transcendental as my focus was placed within, the stars were moving in mystical fashion all around me. Generating a great deal of energy within, this gave me the ability to move objects with my thoughts.

As I was in this state, I noticed friends and family members I'd known throughout my life sitting below the Star Chamber. Receiving of the Star Chamber through my transcendental state, I was taken from the chamber and placed among them.

Another person was placed in the Star Chamber, but I was surprised that neither she nor any of these other people were able to attain the transcendental state because they were too grounded. An angel approached who conveyed that through my entrance into the Star Chamber, others could benefit from its energies; but only if *I* would enter, because none of them could go there.

Returning to my former position in the chamber, I re-entered the transcendental state, making greater efforts to funnel the energies down below. Conveying that I had taken it for granted that others were able to achieve such mystical states, when in fact, my soul performed a necessary function in bringing energies from higher worlds into this one. Without me doing this, many others would be unable to receive of the higher energies at all. Funneling, funneling, funneling, I remained in the Star Chamber for quite some time sending the transcendental energy to those below.

"There is this city of Brahman, and in it the palace, the small lotus, and in it that small ether. Now what exists within that small ether that is to be sought for, that is to be understood . . ."
The Vedanta Sutras, Part I, I Adhvava, 3 Pada, 14, Paragraph 2, (Hinduism)

"More than this cannot be told, for the Holy Streams will take you to that place where words are no more, and even the Holy Scrolls cannot record the mysteries therein."
The Essene Gospel of Peace, Book Four, The Holy Streams, Page 44, Paragraph 1, (Christianity, Gnostic/Essene)

****

Flying high above the Earth, I looked upon a particularly beautiful star constellation in the heavens. Drawn towards it as I gazed upon its beauty, the stars were close together and emanating a most magnificent consciousness or soul, and I began to feel a wisp of recognition, perhaps almost a whimsical swoon in my memory of such a place. My eyes were fixed and could not be moved from the state for quite some time as my soul flew closer and closer, but I was not allowed to go all the way there, so I turned my eyes back to Earth when bidden by the Lord. Oh, how sad I was to have to do such a thing.

"The Soul's nature and power will be brought out more clearly, more brilliantly, if we consider next how it envelops the heavenly system and guides all to its purposes: for it has bestowed itself upon all that huge expanse so that every interval, small and great alike, has been ensouled."
Plotinus: The Enneads, Fifth Ennead, First Tractate, No. 2, Paragraph 4, (Mystery Religions, Greek, Words of Plotinus)

****

"The more our limited discourse seeks to make clear and extol the mysterious works of Christ, our Redeemer, and of his most holy Mother, the more evident it becomes, that mere human words are far from being able to compass the greatness of these sacraments . . . Nor can we ever fathom or compass them, and there will always remain many greater secrets than those we have sought to explain."
The Mystical City of God (Abrid.), The Transfixion, Chapter III, Paragraph 1, (Christianity, Catholic, Author: Ven. Mary of Agreda)

Beyond the scope of eternity, I flew until I reached the star station of this distant planetary system; the Didactan system. Knowing very little about where I was or what sector of space I might be occupying, I turned. Standing before me was an old, wise and lighted man. Vaguely, I remember him conveying to me something very important, 'The Didactan Codes of Life,' which create harmony in all things and provide for all life systems. This sphere was settled in light and life . . . redeemed . . . and this planet which was situated beyond the mysteries of the redemption held knowledge which could help our own sin stricken world struggling into a similar era. Inexplicable, I could recall no more.

"Evil and sin visit their consequences in material and social realms and may sometimes even retard spiritual progress on certain levels of universe reality . . ."
The Urantia Book, Part III, Paper 67, No. 7, Paragraph 5, (Christianity, Urantia)
****

As it was made known to me that religious art; whether it be paintings, sculpture, music or otherwise, contains within it energetic knowledge which has been specifically implanted by God of the mysteries of the redemption, my soul was taken to view something spectacular.

"On each occasion that a true artist approaches a biblical subject, he illuminates some portion of scriptural text and deepens our comprehension of the world's greatest story."
The Bible in Art, Foreward, Paragraph 2, (Christianity)

Aloft in the heavens, my soul was quickly aided to observe in the proper direction wherein one of the mysteries of the redemption was playing out. Amidst the spectacle of daily living, there was a starship, unseen to human eyes, but seen to the spirit. A saucer shaped vessel with red beacon lights shining along the center crease every five feet, a young man was standing below it, completely unaware of this vessel and its purpose.

As he stood there, a light from below took him into the vessel and it immediately soared away to a destination upon the Earth. Hidden to view, it was well disguised behind a mountain fold. While the man was aboard this vessel, many activities were taking place. Working on his soul sub-consciously, they were adjusting his lights and also implanting knowledge and wisdom which would help him at the current juncture in his evolutionary cycle.

What was very interesting about this whole experience was that after they returned him back to his normal life, he showed very little progress. Change was so minute; you really had to stretch your thinking to even see it. But the spaceship kept returning in intervals, and continued working on this soul despite the extremely slow progress of evolution. On occasion, there would be a genuine leap in consciousness which came as a result of these repetitive, long, arduous visitations.

Certain extra-terrestrial life forms do indeed come here and assist in the work of the redemption; they implant evolutionary perception and energies into the souls of sub-conscious mortals, many of whom are unaware that these activities are taking place.

"When physical conditions are ripe, sudden mental evolutions may take place; when mind status is propitious, sudden spiritual transformations may occur; when spiritual values receive proper recognition, then cosmic meanings become discernible, and increasingly the personality is released from the handicaps of time and delivered from the limitations of space."
The Urantia Book, Part III, Paper 65, No. 8, Paragraph 6, (Christianity, Urantia)
****

Entering into a small store, Andy and I found ourselves amongst a gathering of souls interested in the music played by a small man who ran a redemptive service for souls interested in knowing their status upon the Earth. Playing music which placed people in cosmic states, he used various sounds; gongs, flutes, and air vibrations. Able to bring forth latent desires and issues remaining in the redemption and purification of an individual soul, he was very skilled in his work.

The gong sound was especially entrancing for me, immediately sending me into a higher awareness, but I also enjoyed an extra-terrestrial sound, because it made me think of my Pleiadian home. Because of my purification, I could listen to these sounds and become very cosmically attuned. To others, it caused their latent desires to come out, making them behave in some strange ways. One man was acting as though he was in a fight with somebody, although he was by himself, and a woman was acting very sexual as if there were men she was coming on to, although she was also by herself.

Pointing me out to the group, the man who ran the place showed them my state of cosmic malaise which was an indication that my redemption was complete. As there were no remaining latent desires lingering beneath the surface, everything was out in the open to me.

"Conquer yourself and the world lies at your feet."
The Voice of the Saints, Chapter 14, Page 114, No. 3, (Christianity, Catholic, Words of St. Augustine)

Banging a gong, my spirit became very aware of a cosmic image of a spaceship being conducted by extra-terrestrials. Unlike any I'd previously seen, they were humanoid, but their heads were formed like a helmet. In fact, they looked very much like the Egyptian headwear seen on the Pharaohs. Making me wonder about the origins of the Egyptians, and whether or not they had come from outer space, our guide spoke of how some spiritual seekers had subconsciously ridden such vessels in their youth to prepare for their mission in life.

Before I prepared to leave, however, there were pointed out two distinct issues which had surfaced within another soul present, reckless driving and judgmental tendencies. As I began to leave, the man in charge made a reference to my work in decorating our home as a monastery, saying that it was a good and true endeavor.

"We see with our own eyes how often a person neglects his duty in spite of his awareness of it and in spite of his having come to recognize as a truth what is required for the salvation of his soul and what is incumbent upon him in respect to his Creator."
The Path of the Just, Chapter VI, Page 79, Paragraph 1, (Judaism)

****

"God has sent forth the Prophets for the purpose of quickening the soul of man into higher and divine recognitions. He has revealed the heavenly Books for this great purpose. For this the breaths of the Holy Spirit have been wafted through the gardens of human hearts, the doors of the divine Kingdom opened to mankind and the invisible inspirations sent forth from on high. This divine and ideal power has been bestowed upon man in order that he may purify himself from the imperfections of nature and uplift his soul to the realm of might and power."
The Promulgation of Universal Peace, Talks Delivered in Montreal, No. 4, Page 310, Paragraph 1, (Baha'i, Words of Abdu'l Baha')

As the large block of clear crystal was brought upon the back of a wagon into the room, a great light erupted over it. The crystal was now brilliant with light and the liquid life molecules within it slowly became visible to the naked eye. But within the module of liquid life, a singular particle of life began to make itself known. In the center of this spherical particle was an obvious nuclei, and two subsequent layers of life substance or energy had formed around it. As I observed this beauteous phenomenon, I was invited to enter the living life module to experience this within my own being. Suddenly, I awoke.

"The small ether can be the highest Lord only. - How? - . . . 'In it is that small ether;' declares thereupon that the small one is to be compared with the universal ether, and that everything is contained in it . . ."
The Vedanta Sutras, Part I, I Adhyaya, 3 Pada 16, Paragraph 1, Commentary, (Hinduism)

****

Spending the night riding the slippery backs of a school of pink dolphins, I was eventually led elsewhere amidst a great street fair. Everything amongst this street fair pertained to extra-terrestrial intelligences, and I was grandly excited when I was finally led to a seashore in the center of the street. The landing site for extra-terrestrial ships, I watched as the aliens descended in the sea blue sky, and was mesmerized by the sight of the many worlds represented.

"He showed me all the hidden things of the extremities of heaven, all the

receptacles of the stars, and the splendours of all, from whence they went forth
before the face of the holy."

The Book of Enoch, Chapter LXX, No. 5, (Christianity, Words of Enoch)
****

CHAPTER FIVE
Project Outreach

****

Joined with the other members of my star group, the most amazing spectacle of my life unraveled just like a miraculous event of God's supernatural substance, through the most beautiful man of another far more advanced world than our own.

Appearing very human, with silvery skin and blonde hair, he had come with his wife who was of another race and very beautiful. Her purpose was to work with the other members of my star group telepathically, while her husband worked with me.

Having started with their decree that they were in need of someone who could pose as a cosmic link-up from our realm to theirs, they had specific needs within the body of the person whom they would choose. All four members present in my star group wanted to go, but those from the other system insisted on me for reasons I only vaguely understood, my vibration was the most flexible on conscious and unconscious levels to undertake such a task. I was so lucky to be chosen for this, I cannot express it. The others were helpful, but disappointed. Approaching them to work with them telepathically, all of this a part of the link-up.

Wishing to create a cosmic link-up from our world to theirs, it was a very difficult process because they came from a world settled in light and life, and our world was so full of chaotic vibrations which were truly dangerous to them, because they existed on such a high fine frequency that our channels of vibration were very disturbing to their essence of being. As a result, they could remain with us for only short bursts of time, and when a disagreeable vibration began entering the realm, they immediately transcended to their own so as not to be harmed by the waves of negativity.

In order to develop this link-up, he had to allow me to slowly become more and more like him, and this was done by allowing me to hold his hand and the most magnificent experience of going with him when he transcended to other worlds. Setting up a two-dimensional linkup site where he would take me when the disagreeable vibrations began, as soon as we stepped on this point, we shouted "Oh mighty magnificent Lord, Oh mighty magnificent Lord!" Then we spoke some words in his language which I cannot remember now. As soon as we were finished, a light beam of immense proportions encompassed us and took us into his world which was pure light and joy. Little to see, it was a high, fine vibrationary existence. Everything sparkled in light, as if it was all composed of crystals, lights, prisms, jewels, and luminescent liquid ethers.

A great connection existed between me and this extra-terrestrial man, for I felt an immense recognition and love for his spirit which transcended the present time. Very sympathetic to my human condition, and my boredom with my sojourn on this earth, there were a few times in the beginning of working with this link-up where the male counterparts in my star group had acted rather base in their association with me, and my extra-terrestrial friend had protected me and discouraged them from their banal intercourse. Insisting on the highest level of respect between all forms of life was uplifting and exciting to one coming from a world filled with karmic turmoil.

Having traveled with him to his world about five or six times now, I was feeling very attached to my new friend. As the next chaos energy began hitting, we both ran towards our location. Joining him on the spot, we shouted out, "Oh mighty magnificent Lord, Oh mighty magnificent Lord!" We transcended this realm and went directly to another. Its beauty was so awe-inspiring; there truly are no words, because it was almost a fluid existence.

Dancing in the light, I would not let go of his loving hand. But as soon as we had arrived, he looked me deeply in the eyes. "Where I go now, you cannot come," he said. "Oh, please take me!," I pleaded, now so greatly enhanced by this change in my vibration that my body was bedecked in bluish-white crystal jewels and my voice sang out a resonant tone which harmonized with this Universe. "Maybe someday, you can stay with me in my world and sing to me with your beautiful voice," he said. "Yes, yes," I shouted, "I can do that." "But not now, it cannot be now," he replied, "Where I go now, you cannot come." Expressing to me his happiness that they were able to find a soul with the spiritual features required for the making of this link-up, they hadn't expected to create it by bringing a ward of our realm into their own.

"Please take me, I'll change in whatever ways are necessary," I continued pleading as he held my hand. "It is true, you have proven to be very able in modifying your form, but it remains that where I go now, you cannot come." Disappearing into the ether, I began singing out a tone in mourning. My spirit remained in his realm for only a moment longer before fully materializing back in my own.

Approaching me with awe at my jewel adorned form, the other members of my star group had heard my lament and they placed their arms around me in compassion. "You were lucky to be chosen to go," they said, as I suddenly realized how true it was. "You're right," I said under my breath, "I was lucky to be chosen to go."

"Do not think that hiding your gifts of God is the sign of humility. No, do and use whatever gifts God has given you."
The Love of Christ, Part III, Page 79, Letter 2, (Christianity, Catholic, Words of Mother Teresa)

"I will bring them into the splendid light of those who love my holy name: and I will place each of them on a throne of glory, of glory peculiarly his own . . . Righteous is the judgment of God!"
The Book of Enoch, Chapter CV, No. 26, (Christianity)

****

Roaring through the night sky, blazing through the atmosphere, the grayish saucer was lit up with light. On top of the center disc was a set of pillars. "Look," I shouted to the passers by, "A Pleiadian ship." An unconscious knowing came forth in a flurry of recognition.

The Pleiadian ship was spectacular and the energy surrounding its arrival was indescribably exciting. Whizzing by my view three times, I took in the energy of their people and the upcoming mission they now heralded to my soul.

In a wisp of wind, the Pleiadian ship began to return nearer to me. Coming ever closer, I was pulled into what appeared to be a hangar. Several detachable saucers located in this location, and up ahead, I noticed about five Pleiadian beings wearing robes similar to that of a monk. Beginning to edge closer so as to view them with more clarity, they returned to the inner caverns of their ship and out of my view. Shouting out, I called to them as I passed by, as they were now out of view. "I love you all!"

'From Project Outreach deep in interstellar space, your spirit is being taken on a tour through 2.55 billion worlds.' As my soul shot through the outer reaches, I could see spirals of light which were the pathways that the planets would take in each individual solar system around its sun. Hundreds and thousands of lights in spiral lit up the space sky, as I witnessed the spectacle of

40 or 50 solar systems revolving all at one time in their respective locales.

Reaching a zone in inner space, I became privy to watch and experience a world which was about to end because of nuclear destruction. The barrier for nuclear contamination had already fallen and many were already succumbing to radiation poisoning, but word came that the final rockets were on their way and this planet was doomed to die a needless death caused by the unevolved actions of several planetary leaders who failed to see the bigger picture and use of such powerful substances. It seemed that this stage of development was a necessary one in the evolution of planets, but that it was always a volatile period when planets attain to nuclear power. Meaning the beginning of space travel and interstellar life, it can also mean wholesale destruction of a world which has taken billions of years to reach this stage.

Again, my soul was alit into the night and space sky to observe the planetary swirls of light which showered my view. Purple, burgundy, blue and deep green were the colors of the lights which were the pathways of the planetary spirals around their respective suns. Each solar system was like an individual atom in a subatomic world, yet the beauty of each individual spiral of light was ominous, and amidst the glow of the thousands of systems which lit up the astral sky, they seemed peacefully quiet. Repeating its instruction, the voice said, "We now take you on a journey through 2.55 billion worlds with approximately 2500 different forms of life." I knew the voice spoke of primary forms of life, like humans, as there were approximately 2500 intelligent life-forms among those which inhabited these worlds. Suddenly, I was again on the planet Earth.

Watching me in the night sky, I could see their ships as I traveled astrally below on earth. Calling me with tones emanating from their ships in the heavens, they were like homing beacons, and I felt the resonance of their call to my soul.

In an instant my soul was given the seed of a knowledge which filled me with wonder. "There is a connection between the sightings of the Holy Mother at Medjugorje . . . and extra-terrestrials." Ceasing its call, the homing beacon stopped as the lucid ship sped away.

"But as it is written, Eye hath not seen, nor ear heard, neither have entered into the heart of man, the things which God hath prepared for them that love him."
King James Bible, New Testament, 1 Corinthians 2:9, (Christianity, Words of St. Paul)
"Let each look to himself and see what God wants of him and attend to this, leaving all else alone."
The Voice of the Saints, Chapter 3, Page 17, Stanza 1, (Christianity, Catholic, Words of Blessed Henry Suso)

****

Catching an ecstatic wave of energy, I was immediately transported towards the blackness of space. With the rushing stars cascading by my soul, I flew at the speed of light towards an unknown heavenly destination. Within my sight were nebulae, galaxies, stars, planets, suns . . . and all were resonating a holy spectral vision to my soul. Heavenly music was playing, the music of the spheres, which resonated from all of the heavenly bodies; a sacred music filled with voices which sang in a language I did not understand.

To my left, a vortex of swirling blue stars which formed into a mist performed its heavenly chorus for my soul, as I turned to notice up ahead yet another beautiful vortex of bluish light. Shooting past them, I found my eyes resting on an orb of stupendous beauty which overwhelmed my soul to tears at its magnificence.

A large, shiny, glowing, purple sphere laid ahead, its unusually slow movement calculated like that of a planet; but its texture and appearance was unusual and I couldn't help but wonder if this were actually a planet . . . or maybe . . . a space station? I waited, listening to the continuing echo of the music of the spheres. My breath was filled with light as it came to and fro between my spirit and this heavenly abode. In ecstasy, it was as if I was no longer even human, but somehow had become part of a much larger scheme of life. It all filled me with the blessedness which I knew to be possessed by this orb which appeared before me.

And suddenly, as quickly as I'd been taken to this wondrous place amongst the stars, my soul shot like lightning back to my Earthly body, returning me to humanness and all the limits that come with it.

But yet, I was changed. It would all begin here, at this moment. I would wait on the angelic hosts to guide me to this yet undiscovered country knowing full well that everything I'd known up until this point was as nothing. I would wait . . . in awe of my God.

****

Beyond my grasp, beyond my sight, lay the images of what I beheld. All I could now surmise was that I had arrived at an entirely ancient destination. This beautiful place held wisps of memory and knowledge from a time gone by.

My soul remembered a time of peace and harmony in Atlantis, when all things were working together for the one, but that had changed over time. A grand uprising had occurred when several people in political positions of power had taken over the country. Greedy and power-hungry, they demanded to be worshipped as gods; similar to the ancient Roman practice wherein the emperor was considered a god. A counsel of six, all wishing to be gods, ruled the empire.

In order to enforce this practice, martial law had been instituted and people were punished overtly and with great severity for small infractions of the law. Remembering these things as the beginning of the end for Atlantis, my soul was gazing upon a beautiful temple which represented a time before, a time of peace.

Alit with a glittering essence, the Atlantean night sky appeared as if gold dust had been thrown in the air. Having arrived via the time tunnel to this grand destination, the ceremony was about to begin, but I didn't rush to enter this magnificent silver and gold temple cascading high into the night sky. Rounded domes and triangular pillars sent a message to all who came here that this was a very sacred and holy place. Walking with a man I recognized as my spouse, I noticed that I was wearing flowing veils of sea blue over my equally sea blue bodice gown. Another triumphantly beautiful element of this temple was that the night sky was exposed, there was no roof. Holding an equally grand quality, the floors were born only of the Earth.

Entering the tabernacle left my soul in a state of wonder and awe as I looked upon a purely symbolic rendering of all the races of men. Every race of humankind upon the planet Earth was represented here in various edifices, murals, statues and architecture.

As the ceremony began, I joined a group of women, similarly dressed, who were gathered in a circle to start with the customary water dance. Representing the synchronicity of life, there was another element to it which is hard to describe or fully understand. This water dance represented the sea, and somehow this oceanic rendering was important to the Atlantean people, perhaps because they were a continent surrounded by waters, and it provided them with sustenance. But aside this oceanic nuance laid a very powerful representation of unity, and the intensive understanding of the fragile elements which held life in place. Required to be in basic synchronicity, these elements remained necessary in order for all life to flourish and continue. Somehow, this knowledge that they expressed through the water dance had come from another place and another time, of which I could not yet surmise, but it was profoundly important to the Atlantean people to never forget the synchronicity of life, because they held a very serious understanding that it was the key to their survival and continuation as a people.

As the water dance came to a close, a master of ceremonies emerged wearing simple white robes, a symbol of his position in this rite. All the people were now standing in a circular fashion inside the temple facing the center where these ceremonies had begun. Taken aback and even frightened as he released a huge black bull into the center of the temple, it was held in check by twelve men with ropes attached to the bull's neck. Raging all over the temple grounds as many of us leapt in fright, we did not leave our circular position and we waited for the men to bring the bull into the center as they formed yet another circle outside of the water dancers. Instinctually, I began to remember things about the meaning of all that began to transpire before me.

As the men held the bull, they began a series of moves which were designed to 'break' the bull, much like modern day ranchers will 'break' a wild horse, domesticating him for humanity's use. The ceremony depicted the dissipation of negative energies, karmic purification, which was represented by the wild bull. Very skilled and artistic in this process, it was ceremonial in design, and as they continued, the bull slowly became placid and peaceful, a symbol of purification. As the bull's wildly negative energies calmed and became peace, the crowd held a deathly quiet, as a form of respect for this holy process. Silently, the bull was led out of the temple to a hushed crowd.

Stunned by what I'd just seen, my soul tried to remember what these things meant, as I'd only recovered a few memories of the tremendous meaning of this ceremony. But before I could ponder deeper, a large flying object which looked somewhat like a kite was released into the sky. Upon its center was the image of the bull, and inherently I understood that this release of the kite was a symbol of the final remnants of karma dissipating as the soul began to look to the heavens and away from Earthly concerns.

Floating up to the ceiling of the temple, a huge rush of silver and gold dust was released into the air, cascading throughout the temple upon the people present. The beauty of this moment cannot be described as the night sky was lit with the stars from on high and this light reflected the millions of gold and silver particles now floating in the air.

My spouse turned to me and without explanation took gold dust which he had within his pocket and began to spread it all over my body. Instinctually, I took the dust and did the same for him. In this moment, something grand happened and changed all that I was experiencing, as if we had somehow permeated into another dimension and I was continuing this experience from a *spiritual* plane, leaving the *physical* memory of this Atlantis beyond, but remaining in a spiritual overlap.

Beginning to fly above the crowds, many of those present were not consciously astral in this element, and thus, were unable to fly. As we continued to dance in the sky, a voice began to speak loudly from above the temple and higher into the celestial heavens. With this voice, we descended back to the ground, and listened.

Speaking of the many different planetary races that had lived upon our planet Earth; he related the time of arrival of each of these races which had coincided with a great cataclysm upon their native world. Calmly, he spoke of the Pleiadians, some of whom had come to Earth at a time of great danger to their galaxy. "These Pleiadians," he had said, "began the ill-fated Atlantean race which was to perish under similar circumstances. Others remained behind and had been successful in rebuilding the Pleiades, which had eventually evolved into a spiritual world, rather than a physical one."

Forming in the center of the temple, the gold dust flew high into the night sky forming into an image of a dove. Inherently, I understood this to be the symbol of the Holy Spirit, of which these Atlantean people were very much attuned. But it also represented the transformation of mankind into a higher spiritual reality.

As the dust was forming, I gathered a gold chain which lay aside my feet on the ground and placed it around the neck of my spouse. Removing the black one which he had been wearing, this represented the transformation from darkness to light. Smiling with gratitude, he repeated this process, placing a gold chain around my neck as I discarded the previous one and we began to fly.

Soaring towards the exit, we reached our hands out to others inside the temple who were unable to fly, carrying them along with us. The grand dove inside the temple was about to explode in light and everyone was running frantically towards the exit to get out before this occurred.

As the dove exploded, gold dust fell all throughout the temple covering the ground and all who lay within its walls. But the backwind from the explosion of gold dust began to reveal something very fascinating, something that had been placed there for my eyes to see. Turning to look, my spouse and the others began leaving the temple in droves while I flew around the temple floor to observe what the gold dust was revealing as it blew away from the ground. Artifacts appeared everywhere of many extra-terrestrial intelligence's who had come to seed this Earth, lightly dusted books, pictures and maps from differing star systems were all revealed.

As I saw these things, my soul began to receive an energetic influx of knowledge regarding the many migrations from different star systems to seed our world. Coming about due to great calamities, many of those worlds had actually survived the catastrophic times. At the time of migration, these worlds had suffered destruction for a great deal of time, some due to nature, and others to the actions of mortals. Again, the Pleiadians were mentioned as being among the systems which had been partially destroyed, and they had come when a turnaround of their situation didn't seem possible. The story was much the same for all the extra-terrestrials represented here, without exception.

Returning inside the temple to retrieve me, my spouse took my hand, again flying us towards the exit. Turning to witness the dove in the sky which had reappeared, it again exploded in another cloud of gold dust which began showering the temple from the sky. Finally dissipating, the dove was no longer visible.

A rushing torrent of energy retrieved my soul, grasping me quickly away from the man whose hand I held, and sending my spirit through the tunnels of time to return to my Earthly abode.

****

Unaware of how our souls had made this grand journey, Andy and I continued soaring towards the star room where the pilots of many spacecraft from various civilizations throughout the Universe were gathered to visit with one another. Humans, as well as, extra-terrestrials were gathered, but despite this very interesting spectacle before me, I couldn't take my eyes off a huge runway which lay in the other direction.

Noticing our Earthly space vessel, it had just undergone extensive repairs. Perhaps we had ridden this vehicle sub-consciously? Set to go at the entry to the runway, I grabbed Andy's hand, and we began running towards it. Entering this very small saucer-shaped vessel, it ran itself, starting its ignition and soaring down the runway at voluminous speed.

Words cannot express the wonder and awe experienced in our ascent to the stars. Before us lay the unadulterated Universe, and the stars sped by us like snowflakes on the windshield of a car. Heavenly bodies could be seen from great distances, their colors brilliant and defined. Galaxies in the distance held every possible hue of white, purple and blue, while the sun and stars emanated orange, red and white. Surprised, I looked in a direction I hadn't yet peered through to notice that the Earth was in our view. At a good altitude above it, something was beginning to go wrong with our vessel. Noticing a star-station in the near-distance, it was our best hope of assistance. As the craft was obviously failing, my eyes fell to what appeared to be a rotating pastel mist of color. If we could get the ship into and underneath this mist, the star station would pull us into its orbit, and eventually down into the bough. Maneuvering the craft towards this star station, we were able to accomplish this feat easily.

Pulling in, the craft was controlled by a force within this grand space airport, leading us to a safe landing. Exiting the ship, I noticed a group of people very obviously from the 19th century being led on a tour. Remaining sub-conscious for this journey, the extra-terrestrials were seeding them with knowledge to hopefully assist them in their current time-frame below on the Earth.

Offering Andy and I the opportunity to take a short journey on one of their crafts which were distinctively more advanced than our own, we accepted their kind gesture and soared through the take-off pod at a speed which cannot be expressed. After experiencing the take-off, however, the ship returned of its own accord to the star-station wherein we were led into a re-materialization chamber to prepare for our return to our Earthly bodies. As would be expected, we became sub-conscious, only to return to Earth, relishing the opportunity we'd been given to leave behind our Earthly craft for a moment, and experience the heavenly vehicle of the stars. For a moment, we had become Galactic!
****

Roaring blew in from overhead as a pulsing energy heralded the vessels in the night sky. Although the spaceships are silent in the physical environment, they are distinctively loud in the realm of the spirit, and their rhythm moves deeply within your molecular structure. Now in my spiritual body, I hovered over to the window to look at the first vessels to arrive. A flat base with an enlarged dome at the top, a pulsating red light came from several points along the seam between the two parts of the ship. Several more were to follow, a rectangular ship which was huge and seemed to fill the sky, as well as, a whole host of Pleiadian vessels. Having seen the Pleiadian ships many times, they were very familiar. A rounded upper part glowed in purple upon a flattened metallic center plate which beheld another rounded lower metallic piece.

Before I could ascertain my situation, a large white globe of light came from the Pleiadian vessels, approached my spirit and entered my head; not once, but several times with each onslaught of ships. As it entered, a tremendous pulsation could be felt within my head. As this continued for quite some time, I found myself becoming exhausted by the continual onslaughts of energy, although there was exhilaration, as well.

Preparing to leave, a bright light came from below one of the Pleiadian ships as two very small creatures descended from the vessel. No more than two feet high, they were wearing the brown robe's of an Earthly monk. Standing on two legs, their skin was sheer and off-white. Several wrinkles formed around their mouths, and their eyes were very large and brownish-black.

Finding them to be very cute, I almost regarded them like little pets, but in order to quell any such arrogance, they conveyed that my time had come to learn from them. Meanwhile, I must be alone to receive them because other people would be unable to tolerate their energy. Before I could respond, they were sucked back into the ship, and the entire battalion of ships sped off into the night.
****

Walking along a deserted valley road, I looked up towards a large orb in the sky. Huge, it was about eight times the size of the Earth's moon and lit up the entire atmosphere. Broad daylight, this orb was clearly visible at midday upon the backdrop of a light blue sky. Wonder and brilliance filled my soul, as I wandered closer, first walking, and then beginning to run towards it. "I should go there!" I thought.
****

CHAPTER SIX
Epochs of the Earth

****

Appearing to me as a human, the commander of this unearthly vessel was a man with a powerful presence. Taking me through a series of epochs in the life of our planet, I was horrified to witness century after century of brutality, hardship and war. Exploring the ages of tyranny in our world, he took me through time to witness world wars, national wars, guerilla operations, and multitudes of prisoner of war and refugee camps all over the world throughout every possible time zone.

As we had crossed through the relevant time periods, he showed me a total of three anti-popes, men who wore the garb of the Bishop of Rome and to the naked eye appeared to be holy men. But the extra-terrestrial commander allowed me to witness their energies which were dark and foul.

All throughout our journey, as I witnessed the sad and desperate state of affairs of a humanity which had clearly been lost throughout many epochs of time, there was a tiny strand of humanity which remained and had been recaptured by various saints and holy people throughout the aeons. As I was given to see this miraculous happening, a sad and desolate melody played repetitively in the heavens around me lamenting the status of mankind. "Earthly remnants of love, Earthly remnants of love, Earthly remnants of love . . ." It went on into the night, filling my soul with a great dismay over the little love which remained active in our world, and a determination to do all that the Lord would deign to allow me, to restore that which had been lost.

Among similar lines, my spirit was then led to witness an enigma of all that had been shown to me. Before me stood a unique looking demon, who apparently was involved in much warring in our world. Clearly he was not limited to global catastrophe, because I was shown that he worked on individual souls to wreak havoc among families and/or communities, as well.

Manifesting as a very large man with large muscles like a body builder, he wore jet black pants while his chest remained bare. Upon his chest were a myriad of depressions which bore no particular form, but reminded me of the states within our country and their various shapes. Eight of them penetrated his chest, each representing a particular aspect of the vice of rage. Each represented one of the eight aspects of rage which could be ignited in this demon who was also surrounded by a very huge force of jet black energy. Every word which proceeded out of the mouth of this creature came at you like a torrent of rage, surrounded by a black vortexing cloud of endless demise.

In battling this horrendous creature, I found that de-energizing him was no easy task. Approaching him with the opposite virtue of the particular rage manifestation he would present, you had to simultaneously push upon the matching depression in his chest. Difficult to do, containing his rampant energies was very hard. Presenting quite a challenge to those of us upon this Earth, it was no wonder that the Earthly remnants of love were squandering for fertility and life. Each and every soul capable of being fertile for the growth of love must do so in order to energize a force large enough to counter this creature who has dominated the history of the Earth.

****

As my spirit was led through an inexplicable experience, I found myself in the service of two extra-eterrestrial souls who had been born as males upon the Earth. Their destiny was to guide a group of about two hundred people to perform a very important work for God. Now that the two men had achieved adulthood, it was necessary for them to be united upon the Earth in order to energize this further task. Throughout the night, I wandered back and forth between these souls energizing lighted links which were being provided as a homing beacon to them.

Awaiting me to finish, a spectacular angelic guardian patiently hovered in the stars. Arrayed in magnificent light which shone outwards from her soul for several yards, this very old woman was a spiritual guardian to the two hundred remaining souls who would eventually be linked with the original two men. In order to bring this union about, the Lord bestowed upon my soul some very unusual spiritual gifts which I would be wont to describe and simply cannot. Somehow, through these gifts, I was able to take each of these two souls on a vast journey through a deep wilderness along the light trails of the energies which had been previously set up. After uniting the men in spirit, we followed a myriad of other trails set up by the angelic guardian which eventually led them to the two hundred remaining souls they were meant to guide in a work for the Lord. Making it possible to link all 202 souls, my inexplicable gift united them in purpose each requiring a myriad of light trails in order to energize fruition. Quietly smiling, the magnificent heavenly host met us, and the inexplicable spiritual gifts which had been given me were immediately energized.

Handing the two men over to her, an indescribably beautiful geometric form of brilliant light ignited lines from her to them, and then throughout the multitude. As soon as this specific purpose was completed, the inexplicable spiritual gifts were taken from me as the purpose for their manifestation had been fulfilled. At this moment, I was swiftly removed from the scene.

Now alit in the wonder of heaven, my soul looked upon a tremendous pathway which seemed to go on into infinity. Nearing ever closer, I noticed that this pathway began down below upon the Earth in the location of my current home. Flitting ever upwards towards the skies, it wavered and meandered, continuing up into the starry realms and the galactic mists beyond my current conception. In the distance, though well beyond view, my soul heard from the mouth of a heavenly host. "This path continues all the way to heaven." As I neared closely enough to vision the purpose of this mystic trail, I suddenly noticed that it was comprised of books.

Leading me to a particular position upon the trail high above the cloudy sky and permeating the galactic havens, I knew it to be resonant of my current status upon the path. Before me were beautiful books covered in exquisite artwork depicting the life of our Lord Jesus Christ, but the pathway was composed of the ancient sacred texts and writings of the prophets, mystics, saints and sages of all world religions; the various meanderings left to us in print by those among us who have moved onward to another higher reality. In the writings of the ancient sacred texts, we were given the opportunity to share the journey of those who had passed beyond the Earthly gates, and thus, be so honored as to receive of the wisdom of their flight. If only other souls knew the tremendous gift of these vital etchings left behind by the prophets, mystics, saints and sages, perhaps they would seek them out.

Looking heavenward at the continuing path of knowledge laid out for me to traverse and the books before me arrayed in beatific artistry of the image of Jesus Christ, I knew that He was the center of my journey, and as my eyes pierced forward, upwards toward the celestial city, my heart instinctually knew and felt the biblical words: "I am the Way, the Truth, and the Life. No one comes to the Father but by Me."

****

Arriving without my foreknowledge, a spaceship had hovered over my house and landed in my backyard. Sub-conscious astral reporters had come to see what was happening and were inquiring with me regarding the unusual compression they had noticed in and around my house which would indicate an area of extensive psychic travel. Explaining to them that this compression had come about so that I may travel to other realms, I asked them if they might be interested in learning the deeper knowledge contained within the mysteries of the redemption. Ascertaining quickly that their interest lay only in a nebulous, intellectualized perception of psychic phenomena, rather than a true spiritual thrust which would include deep moral and ethical considerations and lengthy self-examination, I escorted them away and turned to greet my extra-terrestrial visitors who had remained unseen by these sub-conscious travelers during their short visit.

****

As my eyes opened to the spirit world, they took in a sight unimaginable in the human terms of my own day. Perhaps a future time would not find this vision quite so unusual, but during my time, it was astonishing. Circling my home and filling the clouds around my house were spaceships from many different star systems, apparently having come to give welcome. For a moment, my spirit was lifted out of my body and began flying around the room under the power of the extra-terrestrial beings, as I laughed in the pure joy. Returning my soul to form, they conveyed, 'When it is that your time comes to die, we shall be there to bid you welcome to the galactic heavens.' Honored, I thanked them and bid them adieu.

****

Watching in the distance over the desert oasis, my spirit observed as six fighter jets approached their target and bombed a city. After the place was obliterated, they flew away while I continued to watch the clouds of destruction dissipate.

Finally, a huge craft of obvious extra-terrestrial origin appeared and flew over the scene several times, sometimes slowly and sometimes very fast. Emitting great power, the craft was shaped somewhat like an Earthly airplane, long and conical; but it was completely silver, had no wings, and was covered in a variety of metal plates which resembled the exoskeleton of a grasshopper. Overseeing events in the world, I knew that they were watching carefully the decisions of mankind, but that only my eyes were able to see them at this moment. (A moment of great import, the world was in the midst of making the decision of whether or not to invade Iraq which was being ruled by an evil dictator.)

Returning to form, an obviously demonic presence manifested before my face, that of a woman with black hair and canine teeth. In annoyance, I calmly said, "Get a life, Satan."

As she instantly disappeared, the image of my white-winged horse, St. Harmony Crystal Fire, appeared before my vision, wings flapping in the wind. Feeling the immense power, St. Harmony Crystal Fire passed by me in a wind of ethereal power as I reached to touch a feathery wing which swept across my face as he passed.

****

Running towards what appeared to be a small bathtub of some kind, I knew that somebody was in grave danger. Before I could reach him, though, the tiny little fetus had fallen into the water. A man approached from the other side carrying some type of surgical tool in his hands, and despite my best efforts, I reached for it much too late. Below the surface of the water, the tiny fetus had been beheaded. As the soul of the baby hovered and sat next to the bathtub feeling the peace and tranquility of God, I raced to the aid of his war torn body. Taking his head and reattaching it to his body, I stood watch over him. The man approached again, trying to mash the baby's skull, but I grabbed his hand shouting, 'No!' With great effort and stillness, I waited at the baby's side because I'd been instructed by the eternal that this child could be healed if he were allowed the proper time to recover. Backing off, the man who had instigated the initial injury saw determination in my face and held back, although he seemed a bit confused.

Suddenly, in the sky appeared a series of ships which I knew to be of extra-terrestrial origin. Shaped much like the planet Saturn, they were globular with rings around the center. But rather than being orangish in color, they were a bluish violet. As they hovered above us, we felt their energies come into us and both myself and this man were immediately filled with the Holy Spirit of love. They, too, were standing in guard of this precious young life, but their presence had awakened the man who stood before me to this truth. "Do you remember them?" He asked me in a state of awe. "Yes, I do," I said, "but from where I cannot recall."

Instantly, the man began to assist me in trying to help this very young fetus to survive. Using his skills to help rather than hurt, he started to repair the damage which had been done to such an innocent body. As he did so, I held the tiny hands of the fetus and watched as his spirit observed this from aside and made way to re-enter his body. On a sub-conscious level, this doctor had experienced the horror of abortion and had now been implanted with the knowledge to cease such harm and attend to helping instead. And then, suddenly, I was somewhere else.

A female duck was sitting on a nest filled with eggs and I'd arrived just in time to witness her moving aside to allow them to hatch. To my surprise, however, ducks did not emerge from her eggs, but rather, kittens. Iridescent kittens with white fur, they were lightly shadowed in individual effervescent colors of yellow, blue and violet. They were so adorable and cute; I wanted to cuddle them myself. But the mother duck was as much a mother to these kittens as she would have been had they been ducks, and she protected and nurtured them as any mother would. In her eyes, it was irrelevant that they were not ducks; they were still as much her children as any natural child would've been. And what was very clear was that they were meant to be together just as much as any other mother/child relationship, despite the fact that they were obviously not biologically related. At this time, she allowed me to pick up one of her kittens, and I did so. A cute little white kitty with iridescent yellow streaks in her fur licked my hand as I held her. In this moment, I understood the beauty of adoption and how it fits perfectly into the will and greater plan of God. And then I was gone . . .

"There is a world of bodies, another of imaginings, another of fantasies, and another of suppositions, but God is beyond all worlds, neither within nor without them. Now, consider how God controls these imaginings by giving them form without qualification, without pen or instrument. If you split open your breast in search of a thought or idea and take it apart bit by bit, you won't find any thoughts there. You won't find any in your blood or in your veins. You won't find them above or below. You won't find them in any limb or organ, for they are without physical quality and are non-spatial. You won't find them on your outside either. Since His control of your thoughts is so subtle as to be without trace, then consider how subtle and traceless He must be who is the Creator of all this. Inasmuch as our bodies are gross objects in relation to ideas, so also subtle and unqualifiable ideas are gross bodies and forms in relation to the subtlety of the Creator."

Signs of the Unseen, Jalalludin Rumi, Discourse 23, (Islamic: Sufi, Words of Rumi)
****

As my vision was directed by an unseen force towards the back window, my spirit began to gaze at the cloudy sky behind my home. Suddenly, the presence of several races of alien life was felt profoundly and the sky lit up from many locations. Music began to emanate from the skies, as I smiled in a state of transfixed bliss upon the spectacle. A soulful chant was played out in harmonic feminine voices, singing of the shortness of time each of us have upon the earth to fulfill the calling of our destiny. As the lightning storm of light continued, I looked and listened in utter silence as a vague download began to enter into my soul. Some type of information regarding alien races and 'The Urantia Book' were being given to me, although in a very unconscious way.

*"True and holy are Thy continents and universes; true and holy are Thy worlds
and the forms created by Thee"*
Sri Guru Granth Sahib, Volume II, Raga Asa, Page 981 (Sikhism)
****

CHAPTER SEVEN
The Galactic Council

****

My bridal gown and veils were flowing in the wind as my spirit was traveling at light speed towards a destination unknown. Plain and empty grass fields passed by my vision on both sides as I contemplated the aloneness I had found in this journey. But up ahead there was something of great importance.

Before I was to arrive, I was to make a final stop at what appeared to be an ancient sacred text shop. Walking around aimlessly, I didn't have anything in particular that I was looking for so I casually glanced at those things on the shelves, much of which were texts I already owned or had read before. Getting tired from this long journey, I sat down on a bench and awaited further instruction. It didn't occur to me how odd it was that I continued to be wearing a brightly white wedding gown with a veil over my face.

A very small and thin older gentleman approached me and said nothing. But in his hands he bore some things beyond words. Handing them to me, I said nothing also but stared at the documents in disbelief.

The first text he'd handed me was a careful preservation of all the ancient Hebrew texts of the bible and the biblical region. These were not translations, mind you, but the actual papyrus placed in a protective receptacle in the book. Leafing through it, I did not speak.

But as I gazed upon them, I realized that my journey had already encompassed their contents. (With the hopes that what I might share does not sound arrogant), I instinctively understood that these represented a road already traveled. And with that interior understanding made very clear to me, I would leave them here for somebody else who might still have need of them.

Three other books lay in my lap beyond anything I could've imagined. They appeared to be a set . . . of galactic origin. Encompassing the knowledge of the other races within the Universe, they went beyond this in that they were ancient sacred texts of these other worlds and planets. Holding them and looking within their pages, I saw pictures of many different extra-terrestrial races. (For a moment, I remembered how long ago in 'Galactica' I'd been shown the galactic ancient sacred texts and how they were aeons above from those we had upon the earth.) One race in particular was pointed out to me by this quiet man, a race with unusually square-ish looking heads, slits for mouths and eyes. For a moment, I morphed into that species as if being reminded of another time and place . . . or perhaps a future time? But I knew that this race was somehow related to my soul's origins and I understood that I was to prepare to bring something of these other world's ancient sacred texts into our own.

My spirit was swept into them as a giant gale wind took me to my final destination for the night.

At the end of the road was an unimaginable natural wonder. In the very rock of the earth was a cyclone of brownish energy spinning in a circular fashion. Knowing it to be a gateway to another level of some kind, I was not given to know of what. But I did know that it had nothing to do with the lower realms within the earth. Wondering, I couldn't help but imagine that it might have something to do with death . . . surrendering the earthly body to the ground in order that the soul might be transformed into its next life and destiny for God. After all, I was dressed for the marriage of the bride to the bridegroom.

Without warning, I was instructed to remove the gown. "The marriage of the bride to the bridegroom has been accomplished," the voice said, "discard the gown and take the next step." As I became naked, I stared at the swirling brown cyclone on the ground as it suddenly moved from the earth to the horizon and turned to white light. I instinctively knew that I was being beckoned to dive into it. But I did not . . .

Unable to respond, I disappeared from the scene because something remained which was holding me back. Something karmic . . .
****

My presence did not appear expected this night at the 'Galactic Council,' the highest council of civilizations around the Universe. My journey would begin with a local universal group originating in Washington D.C., United States. It was one of the most highly top secret gatherings in our world.

About 200 dignitaries had come from around the world, but the Lord bid to take me on a journey of such profound intensity, I can scarcely tell of it or restate it to those among the living in our world of mankind.

Someone was there who represented the Holy Priesthood of the Catholic Church, but I knew him. He had aborted his mission with the Lord and our Galactic allies months ago. He was shocked to see me at a meeting of such important caliber. Because all of the current attendees were men, it seemed odd that I waited there to receive my leave from the Lord to speak.

Before I could speak, however, my spirit was whisked to a room below ground. Down there was an alien life force being held down by ropes and ties on a hospital like bed.

Odd in appearance, I knew him to be a member of our federation. He had a long 2-3 foot spout for a nose, his skin was amphibious and looked pink at the moment. He was writing and trying to break free from the ropes, but something was wrong. There was a reason that God had allowed me here at this top secret Galactic Federation tonight with full consciousness and memory about to take place.

In the distance, I could hear her. She was a dark one, and she was hissing. But her hiss went above the din of the normal ordinary waking world. And in the din, no one could trace that her hiss was sending a dark wave of transformative power throughout the building.

She had taken our ally captive, and he was turning a bright red. I knew this to be very serious at that moment, but not yet why.

Within moments, I was again taken upstairs to see that our Galactic brothers and sisters had arrived from all over the galaxy and the universe. I was no longer the only woman. But I knew that I was here because I was AWARE, I was conscious. Many others were in the deep sleep of unconsciousness and completely vulnerable and asleep to what was about to happen. It was my job to bring the inbreath . . .

Going back downstairs, I began to blow the Holy Spirit upon the alien. He stood upright, had a normal face except for his two foot long spout-like nose, and he was wearing no clothes. His sex was not obvious. His species had a pot belly and a long tail.

As I blew the inbreath upon him, he began to change into the shade of light blue, which I knew to be the correct and holy understanding coming from the energies of the holy mother of God, the blessed virgin herself.

This other creature, the human-formed female of demonic origin, was suddenly multiplying into beasts of various kinds, and huge insects, spiders and bugs.

We raced to the upper room where the gathering was taking place as a battle began to ensue beyond my wildest dreams. It went on for hours before the outcome could even be predicted, much less known as fact.

The beasts had already begun to turn into serpentine slitherers through the crowd while I still had to await my command from God allowing me to act. I was quiet and sitting in a corner waiting for this word, when a man of very high stature in the Galactic Council came to me and told me that someone wished to speak with me.

Walking over to a table of the top scientists in the human world, they were at odds. Unable to differentiate between good and evil, the beasts were coming their way and they had to make decisions fast. Conveying to them some words of importance, I noticed that the man who had aborted his mission with the council upon the earth was staring at me as I spoke to them. He could not yet understand why I was being given such high authority and such importance in this discussion of the utmost of significance for worldly affairs. Neither could I . . . but I did as I was told. Nothing more, nothing less.

The men of science were listening intently to me, and they understood my words. As they did so, they began to turn a light blue of the power of the Virgin Mother of God. But the beasts had already begun their work through the room. And others were turning dark red and a violent color of the beast.

"Use the outbreath!" I shouted to them as we all began to move about the room carrying within us the holy breath from the Virgin Mother of God, and sending it outward until its effects were clearly seen in the transformation of the colors of these various men and creatures from all over the Universal Spheres of God's kingdoms into the holy color of light blue, the color of the Blessed Mother, the Holy Virgin of God.

Walking over to a group of guards and officers, I was able to distinguish a demonic packet of blood within the pocket of the source of this demonic infestation - a single man with contamination towards destructive sexual energy beyond the gull - he had denied his mission for sexual temptations! I was disgusted! He had taken every guard down with him and this was the way in which the demonic woman and her beasts had entered into this highly secret and vastly important galactic organization.

Rather than guarding the Holy Grail of Universal Peace and Unity, they had been taking the life blood of women that they lusted after by playing games of lust and sexual desire with those who came through the halls, but had no business learning of what lie beyond them. I took in the breath and began blowing upon the source of this madness and upon all whom he had taken down with him and slowly but surely their colors turned from the brightest of reds to the light blue of the Madonna.

This procedure continued throughout the room as I was shown various vices that had taken down members of the Galactic Council who were like blistering bellies of sin covered in a red inflammation that was infectious to all around them. It was frightening to see, because the demons multiplied around us as quickly as they could be breathed upon by another. Fortunately, so the in and outbreath of the Madonna that I and the scientists carried was equally powerful and those who turned light blue from our intervention also began to also multiply and breathe upon one another the outbreath of the great and holy Madonna spreading the truth among our brothers and sisters mired and lost in sin. He who had aborted his mission I would not again see this night, my work was intense and extremely exhausting. I knew I must leave no creature this eve left in the mire of the inflammatory sinful state.

Each of them had fallen for different reasons, one of the deadly sins or another stemming from one of these, but none could stand against the outbreath of the most Holy Virgin, the Madonna.

Let me make it clear, however, that this was not an easy task. This outbreath was exhausting my soul, and every one of these took a different amount of time and wind. Some of them stayed inflamed in sin so long, I thought I would run out of breath before their conversion could commence. But I never did . . . even though I came close many a time.

She was not just an earthly Madonna, for this I was sure. She was a being of great magnitude in the universal spheres and the worlds of the galactic heavens, every world.

For a moment, I remembered seeing her arrive aboard the Plieaidian spaceship as 'The Lady in Light.' In this moment, I KNEW her power was quite beyond our world.

But I had not time to contemplate it. For some reason, I carried within me her outbreath. I couldn't explain it, understand it or even ask of it; but somehow I knew that I was connected with her in a profound way, and my duty was great! With this duty came great responsibility, and no one under my care could abort a mission of such magnitude. It was unacceptable.

I understood.

So I carried on and my brethren all followed suit in carrying on. It was a battle to the very end as I came upon a priest I had recently been made to know. It was shocking to see that he was covered in the blackness of something I could not identify, because I had seen his holiness upon the ground already. But I blew the outbreath of the Madonna upon him, and he took upon him the colors of light blue.

In that moment, I knew something of great importance beyond my ability to comprehend. It was made known to me interiorly in that moment that my work in the world was quite unseen. But it was absolutely beyond description in its power. The outbreath from myself had converted this priest . . . but how I knew not. But I did know that I was the instrument. This shocked me. And I must not give up . . .

In the world, my outbreath would remain unseen. But here in the world of spirit, this outbreath was determining the destinies of those upon the ground. And those who took the inbreath upon themselves were thereby converting more and more souls to the outbreath of the holy Madonna.

It literally took us many hours, and I saw so many different creatures from so many worlds. But we fought the good fight, and in the end, the beast was taken captive. I breathed him in, as his manifestation had lost all power of deception and his beastly creatures and the she-demon had all transformed into one body of himself.

As I breathed him out, he had turned a pale blue and lay before me lifeless on the ground. His eyes opened a tiny slit. Everybody, the hundreds and thousands in the Galactic Council, had been transformed and reawakened somehow to mission. And they knew they had fallen from grace, that they had allowed themselves to be lost in the mire of sin. "Our great work must continue!" I shouted, "We all know of its importance!" It was of vast, vast importance, and it cannot be explained in human words. But we all knew it.

Shouting at the beast, I said, "Go on, then, you disgusting creature." He did nothing but lay there as if mortally wounded. "Shall I beat you more with the soles of my feet!?!?!" I shouted, as I took my foot and roughly placed it upon his head. "Shall I beat you *more*, beast!?!?!?!?!?

He was surrounded by the entire Galactic Federation, all the souls who manifest in worlds around the universe and are working together towards the peace and unity of all God's creatures. We were the best among the best, the most powerful among the silent powerful of God's unseen workers in different worlds. We were the top secret agents of God who were holding worlds and peoples in place despite their own wicked choices and decisions to follow sin, destruction, vice and wickedness, WICKEDNESS! It was our moment to confront the beast who dared to enter into the holy confines our Council declared holy by the Lord, chosen by the Lord, consecrated and consumed entirely in the Lord's service!

"SPEAK, BEAST!" I shouted in disgust, "Before I spit you out before your own wolves in sheeps clothing and allow them to devour you as I would devour you before God if He gave me permission!" I looked towards the guards who had fallen to the temptation of lust in anger. They had allowed our protection to be compromised. Suddenly, permission from God came through me in a giant galewind of the outbreath from the Madonna through me.

I felt as if my own spirit would be depleted by this outbreath, but it came out in a monsoon wind which took the beast by total surprise. In his compromised position, he was battered, abused and tormented as he was whisked into infinity and disappeared into the hands of God to receive what He might so deign. He disappeared in the spot he had lain, as I and my scientists looked upon our brothers with great seriousness and foreboding.

No words were exchanged. They had all turned the proper shade of light blue indicating their royal servitude to our Lord. But I and my comrades showed anger in our faces. We were the quiet ones in the group, and these were not accustomed to hearing us speak or having us dominate a meeting.

But they stood there in shame as they knew of their sins and their evil turning away from God by taking in the outbreath of the enemy!

"Know this!" Came the voice of God from the heavens as I listened. "Know this!!!!" Falling to my knees, I shouted, "I will know it, Father!"

Suddenly, my spirit stood upon Mount Sinai as wisdom was being transferred into my etheric substance energetically. And as this was happening, an angel appeared who carried a beautiful pitcher filled with 'heavenly nectar.' It was pink, and she poured and poured and poured it down my throat as my spirit seemed unable to absorb enough. But after several minutes she was gone and I had now been transported to a small gathering of people.

I didn't notice the older gentleman sitting to my right until he got up to leave. He was wearing the garb of a regular person of his age, but when he stood, I suddenly recognized him. It was Pope John Paul II, and he turned to wink as he stood to leave. He didn't speak, I had not recognized him quickly enough. But it was clear that he was trying to show me his ordinariness outside of his Pope's garb. And that it was clear that he would not be noticed in a crowd if he were dressed as a common man. Something was important about this. But I didn't have time to think about it, because I was whisked quickly through the galactic heavens and back to my earthly abode.

Moments later, I awakened in shock. I had spent seven hours with the Galactic Council, something of which I'd only been shown tidbits over the years. But now I'd seen it in its entirety, now I knew my responsibility with them. There would be no more excuses, I must go to my brethren and get to work.

****

Destiny and Prophecy

Mystic Knowledge Series

Compiled and Written by Marilynn Hughes

The Out-of-Body Travel Foundation!

www.outofbodytravel.org

PART I
CHAPTER ONE
The Difference Between Knowledge and Knowing in the Determination of your Destiny.

****

There is a difference between knowledge and knowing. Knowledge is acquired intellectual learning, whereas knowing is experience with God, union with God. The two are entirely different experiences in that the first can contain much false knowledge, while the second is absolute truth containing no falsehood beyond all words. This kind of knowing cannot be put into words, and if any attempt is made to do so, it is no longer knowing. This is so because it becomes contaminated by the intellect and worldly concepts which cannot contain the all-powerful essence of God.

As you try to discern what it is you'd like to do with your life, I recommend that you step back. Does your ego get involved when you think 'callings' in that certain things are more 'noble' in your mind so that whatever you think might be the most 'noble,' is what you want to do? Contemplate an ancient saying from the Bhagavad Gita which states: If you give up what you are meant to do in order to do something that is not yours, you will lose what which was not yours and that which was yours both.

What does this mean? I guess I'd like you to contemplate a garbage man. Let me ask you this question. If God wishes this man to be a garbage man, is it a higher calling for him to go to medical school and become a doctor? I would hope that you would say no, because God calls us each to things. And despite the way society views certain vocations, the world cannot live without any one of them. Without garbage men, we're all screwed. Forgive my bluntness. We should treat those who do this thankless job with a great deal of respect because not only are they doing a job for which they are not well paid, but they are also often given a certain societal stigma, they are often viewed at the bottom of the totem pole in society and our world can't function without them. In essence, they are sacrificing MUCH more than most of us to do God's will in their life.

Many years ago, we had lived across the street from a family of five kids who had all witnessed their mother's death in a car accident due to a drunk driver. One of the young sons was nine years old and is now about twenty one. He had suffered minor brain damage, but it affected his ability to learn. Many of us wondered if he'd ever be able to do anything. Recently, I spoke with his mother and found that he's holding a job as a garbage collector, and I was so proud of him. He's living in a group home for the handicapped which provides assistance and he's very happy. His mom said he may never be able to do anything but pick up garbage because of his ability to learn, but he's happy and he's doing God's will. And we are all benefiting from his vocation and sacrifice. No one will ever tout his name like they do Mother Teresa or others of the saints, but God knows his heart and soul. He knows what he suffered, and how he's gained victory since that horrible moment. And God will reward him greatly for his humility, grace and perseverance.

This takes me to the next level. What if you could never do anything at all? What if tomorrow you were paralyzed from the neck down and people had to take care of you? Would your life still have meaning? Or would it not be good enough because you're not doing something mighty and noble like saving Africa? What if that's what God wanted you to do - simply survive and be here? Would it be good enough, or would your ego struggle with that?

So we come back to your vocation in life. I'm not saying that such noble things are not a good thing to think about or to strive for if God so wills. But as long as you strive for them because you believe them to be superior to other paths in this life than you have missed the point. And as long as you discern your vocation in life this way, you cannot find it. Because you must allow God to show you His will, even if He may choose to give you a more humble calling, or ask you to do something that a lot of other people do. What if He needs that from you?

So what's my point? Maybe nothing. But I believe I am trying to tell you that I think it would be very beneficial to you to start approaching your discernment without any preconceived notions about what is more 'noble' or better or holier. Let God tell you where He needs you. In other words, get out of His way. And be ready and willing to accept His call no matter where He leads you, even if to the most humble of places where no recognition will come your way.

Let me ask you to ponder this. When Mary and Joseph were given this great task to care for Our Lord, they knew they would do this all their lives without anybody knowing who they were, no recognition, utter ridicule, a great deal of torturous suffering and their reward would truly be only in heaven. Nobody knew who they were until they were long dead, and many other Christians along with them.

Pope John Paul II had to work in the rock pits and simply survive WWII in Poland before God could even begin with him.

Mother Teresa, one of the greatest saints of our time, did not change the world. After she died, more wars broke out than before. And think deeply on this . . . Jesus Christ did not change the world, either. He made redemption possible, but people are just as corrupt today as they were in His time. This teaches you something. You CAN'T change the world, and it is arrogant for you to think you can when you're own Lord couldn't do it. But you CAN change your own little corner of the world. And through obedience to God's will for you, no matter how humble or exalted a place he gives you in this world, you will find the vocation that will serve God the most and bring the most love to the earth that you possibly can. But you still won't change the world. Even when you're gone, everything will continue; vice, violence, destruction, etc. But you will probably change a lot of individual people's lives by the impact you make on them.

Let me tell you of a mystical experience I had years ago. Several very large angels came to me and showed me the two outcomes of my life. The first was that I would try to change the world. In this image they showed vines and roots coming from below the earth and holding me tight to the ground. I was trapped, suffocated and nothing was truly accomplished. The second was to change my own little corner of the world in which I was shown a very happy, joyous family who had prospered much spiritually and risen above that of this world. I was shown friends and others scattered around the world who would be forever changed by my work, but they were few and far between.

I say the same to you, be happy with whatever God gives you to do. Be joyous about whomever He gives you to serve. Don't count the numbers, don't count the cost, just be blissful every time the Lord places you in a position to fill a need.

God rewards us when we are obedient. He rewards us when we are willing to be patient and wait upon Him. He rewards us when we choose to be joyful about doing His work whether it involves one soul or thousands, whether it involves working with other people or cleaning up trash.

The late Father Eddie used to constantly comment on the holiness of changing a diaper. Find the holiness in your everyday activity, in everything you do, and you will find peace. Find this holiness in following God no matter how great or how humble He asks you to be and you will find peace. Find the holiness in serving in any way that God so chooses. Whether He asks you to cut rocks in a rock pit like John Paul II, or if He asks you to be like Mother Teresa and simply walk into the street and see what is needed.

Remember, that in every age and time different things are needed. I had to totally let go of the great things others did in their day, in order to even become aware of the needs in my own. And it was only God who could reveal to me that doing my writing could fill some very important needs for people all around the world, but scattered, few and far between. And He did this when I was physically incapacitated. It was in my complete disability, that my soul became open to hearing the words of the Lord in visions and ecstasies. So was my physical incapacity of no worth? I would say not. The Lord asks us to see the value in every path, every person, every soul . . . and even every failing. Because without the failings of others, we have no vocation. Without those who need my guidance in the spiritual realm, I have no vocation. Without my children who need someone to teach them and care, I have no vocation. Learn to truly love those you serve as being even greater than yourself, because without them, you have no vocation. God has given them to you as a gift, just as much as He has given you to them as a gift.

Never forget to see Jesus in every face, every calling, and every task you (or anyone else) may do in a day. The practice of contemplation is much like this. You learn to be in the presence of God throughout every moment of your day, whether in trouble or in bliss. You learn to be in the presence of God even as someone is losing their temper with you, and to feel compassion for their pain. Practice the presence of God in all you do, let go of your ego, and let God tell you what to do. Stop telling Him what you want to do.

****

CHAPTER TWO
A Vision of Destiny as a Child, Understanding Others as Personal Calling, Book Prophecies, Blocks to Destiny, Eternal Contracts, Live in these Mountains and Remember Things, Silence, the East and the West, Prophecy of World Events, Taking Salvation to a Higher Level, Call of Jesus.

****

"Out of my distress I called to the Lord, and He answered me. From the midst of the nether world, I cried for help, and You heard my voice."
New American Bible, Old Testament, Jonah 2:2, (Christianity, Catholic)
"I give praise to you, Father, Lord of heaven and earth, for although you have hidden these things from the wise and the learned you have revealed them to the childlike."
New American Bible, New Testament, Matthew 11:25, (Christianity, Catholic, Words of Christ)

Not long after my spirit had been sleeping, I began to hear the roaring sounds of a thunderous uprising in the heavens. Although I was unaware of the mechanism of this vision, somehow my spiritual eyes opened to a sight unimaginable prior to this awakening.

The clouds had parted to reveal gold and marble steps leading high up into the sky, and at the top of this amazing spectacle was a throne. The Lord God sat in this seat, appearing to me in a human form wearing a white robe. Aside Him was the lamb, Jesus Christ who would remain silent for this very first vision. Angels were flying all around the holy sight, singing and performing celestial music of praise to the Lord. The power of God was so strong in this vision, that it cannot be expressed in words. "Holy, holy, holy," I thought. Humbling myself, I bowed in spirit form, to the Lord, my God.

Motioning me to come forth, the Lord presented another vision that somehow overlapped this one. In it, the cross was on fire, and I was trying to put it out. Certain people in the world could only see the fire, not the cross. As a result, every time I put the fire out, they would re-light the flame to the cross. Battling our fundamental differences seemed to continue without end, but finally, due to the grace of God, I was able to put the fire out completely, allowing the cross to stand tall.

The Lord spoke to me, "The fire represents ignorance, and the cross, awareness." He conveyed that there would be much fire in my life, but that I would bear the cross. Many people would never see it, and this would cause frustration. Pausing, I bowed again to His majesty. "At a future time, you will take that cross to the world and present it as a living vision of the reality of God. Though others may think you are foolish, you are special."

Thunder struck and the heavens began to close. As I watched the heavenly messengers and the Lord disappear behind the clouds, I bowed to them. The Lord had filled my spirit with a love I could not describe. During a time when my life was filled with Godlessness, it had given me a certain peace to withstand the times. I was nine years old.

"In a dream, in a vision of the night, when deep sleep falleth upon men, in slumberings upon the bed; Then he openeth the ears of men, and sealeth their instruction."
King James Bible, Old Testament, Job 33:15-16, (Christianity)

****

Lying amidst a stone complex, I awaited the guidance of someone to come. Resting peacefully, the spirit who had run with me on the racetrack of life appeared.

"In order to understand the true reality within your conflicts, you must see the window of perception that others see through." Projecting images of the way somebody I knew perceived reality, I immediately understood why we misunderstood one another. "Allow yourself to tune into other people's perceptions, so that you may understand the parameters of their vision. Love all beings, despite their present manifestation, as love is the only reality." He disappeared.

"There is nobody who lives happily with anger. Hence the enemy, anger, creates sufferings such as these, but whoever assiduously overcomes it finds happiness now and hereafter."
A Guide to the Bodhisattva's Way of Life, Chapter VI, No. 5-6, (Buddhism, Tibetan, Author: Shantideva)

****

After assisting a soul in flight techniques, I was taken into an ancient looking bookstore. Noticing a large stack of books, it became known to me that they were my own. An astral publisher came in, sub-conscious astral, and handed one to me. The old and tattered book he gave to me had brown, taped pages. It appeared ancient. Looking up in surprise, I said, "Even this was completely pre-planned, was it not?" "Yes," he said, "All your experiences have been orchestrated to write a book written aeons ago." Then it was made known to me that Andy was the 'Dreammaker,' which meant he assisted in bringing my work into ground level manifestation.

****

"The experience of prophecy must come about through intermediaries. Man cannot attach himself directly to God's Glory, or perceive it as one sees a man standing in front of him. The perception of God involved in true prophecy must therefore come about through God's servants, whose task it is to provide such a vision."
The Way of God, Part 3, Chapter 3, No. 5, Paragraph 1, Page 208, (Judaism, Author: Rabbi Moshe Chayim Luzzatto)

Standing before a large murky lake, another woman was with me for whom I was to take to a very special place. An octopus emerged from the waters and pointed to the far left of this body of water. "It is that way, my friend." He said. Thanking him, I wasn't quite sure what he meant, but I created a thought-form boat to take us in that direction. Getting into the boat, the woman with me spoke of how she didn't like this lake because it was so murky. "Well," I said, "we have to work through the things that aren't so clear in order to find true vision."

Floating along, we saw another boat up in the distance. A man was guiding it along and a monkey was hanging over the side. Waving wildly to me, the monkey called out, "Come on, it's that way, follow the glistening stars." Pointing to the sky, sure enough, on one side of the lake, though it was not night, the stars glimmered like emeralds.

Changing my direction to follow them, the woman began arguing with me. "I don't want to follow those, let's go in the other direction!" Coming upon a river that scurried out from the lake, a small wooden sign pointed in its direction, 'To Crystal Forest,' it said. The woman immediately jumped out of the boat just as it got caught in the flow of the river. "Come on," I shouted, "come with me. I will take you to the golden river." "No!" She cried out, "I want to stay on the lake." Creating herself a thought-form boat to take her back to shore, she climbed aboard and went backwards. (Conceptually, as well as, physically.)

Not much time passed in my journey before the river waters became a beautiful iridescent golden color. In excitement, I glimmered at the beauty of the Crystal Forest where the trees were pastel pink, their leaves pastel violet, and the ground a pastel blue. Quasar was beckoning from a not so distant shore, and as I no longer needed my boat, it disappeared and I was completely immersed in the golden waters of the river. One of the musicians I had been working with was with Quasar, and he began singing a song called, 'Destiny.' As he did, his light began growing wildly in proportion to what it had been. Quasar called out, "Come on, remember your destiny!" As my soul began to feel the universal tug dragging me away, I allowed the energetic current of my destiny to become one with my night wind, and then I was gone.

"Their reward is with their Lord: Gardens of perpetuity wherein flow rivers, abiding therein for ever. Allah is well pleased with them and they are well pleased with Him."
The Holy Qur'an, Part XXX, Chapter 98, No. 8, (Islam, Words of Mohammad)

****

A transmitter fell into my hand as my spirit rested among the stars. Pushing a button on the side, I said, "Hello?"

A voice returned the call. "It is Jozukel, I call from Jupiter." He said. "Ask whatever you wish and the answer will be yours." "You mean anything I ask will be answered?" I asked. "Yes." The dry voice came from the other end. "What is my biggest blockage to growth at this time?" "Stubbornness and inflexibility." "Okay, what can I do to help that?" "You need to see the value of relationships in their proper time perspective." Apparently, I had trouble letting go when it was time. Becoming very serious, the voice said, "There is so much that you are destined to do, and still you sit and do nothing." Surprised by this, I asked, "Tell me, what am I destined to do?" "Many higher selves are calling to retrieve the information we have given you, three hundred incarnate spirits have already contacted you on many levels asking to become creative containers of expression for different aspects of your knowledge, and still you sit and do nothing."

Angered by this criticism, I responded like a moron. "Fine! If I am doing such a terrible job, remove me from this planet and take me back!" Calmly and without emotion, he said, "Yes, we can do that." Realizing my stupidity, I humbled myself. "I'm so sorry. What is it that I need to do?" A faint buzzing came from the device along with the now fading voice. "You will know when you listen to your inner wisdom. There is much to create, do not waste time on worry and unworthiness. Do not sit and do nothing." Then the voice was gone.

"The Adjusters accept a difficult assignment when they volunteer to indwell such composite beings as live on Urantia. But they have assumed the task of existing in your minds, there to receive the admonitions of the spiritual intelligences of the realms and then to undertake to redictate or translate these spiritual messages to the material mind."
The Urantia Book, Paper 108, No. 5, Paragraph 1, (Christianity, Urantia)
****

And it came to pass that I was shown the actual eternal contracts I had in regards to the salvation of souls. On each of them were written these words:

"Tiniest spark
Light cometh
I abide"

Within my sleeping, words and chants would constantly be filling my ears. I began writing some of them down. Rescinding form, a light figure was skipping by the sky. "Where are you going?" I asked. "I am off to the land of the rebels," he said, "the land where reason lies." Words began to flow from his soul to mine:

"Light befalls the virgin eye, dispensate all crowning lies
Fortune comes on velvet masts, the truth of souls encased
In the evening bronze, the night wind sings
Chanting visions and songs, calling forth the Nefertiti wings"
"Calling bird release the past, ancient memory come to see
Circling nature come to pass, spirit reason lingers free
A voice must be listened, the calling be seen
Perpetually unfolding, within the light beam"

"Who can I be? And where is the door?
What are the answers? And what is this for?
I am the light! The door is inside!
The answer is love, to bring dawn to the night!"

"But the wise, whose wisdom makes them full of eyes, pierce through the garment to the very essence of the word that is hidden thereby. And when the word is momentarily revealed in that first instant of which we have spoken, those whose eyes are wise can see it, though it is so soon hidden again . . . In the course of such passages a secret emerges from its sheath, and as soon as it has been revealed returns thereto and once more conceals itself therein."
The Zohar (Kaballah), Volume III, Mishpatim (Exodus), Page 300, Middle, (Judaism)
****

Taken to a mountain hold where I saw a monk sitting in the clearing reading an ancient sacred text, wings began to emerge from my back, as a voice called from the distance echoing the Old Ones. "You are already so open to your memory. That's all you need to do, live in these mountains and remember things."

Past programs began to come out of me, old beliefs, thought patterns and horrid memories. "It is a purging," the voice said, "these things must come out, but you needn't analyze every piece. You must simply let them come out because they are no longer compatible. What was before will become as a past-life, a veil will actually proceed to fall. You will leave that life, as it will no longer be your concern."

A buffalo appeared who was in labor, struggling to give birth. Trying to assist, aspects of my past pushed me aside, and the calf was stillborn. "Let this be a warning to you, your past life must die in order for your new life to be birthed."

When you walk with the eternal, you can enter the world of noise to fulfill your mission, completely protected. But if you act on your own, you go alone. Because you are not energized properly, you become open to invasion, losing focus and losing your head. World's noise and silence seldom intersect.

If you truly want the wisdom of the silence, you must live there for you cannot leave silence, live the noise, and then teach of silence. It is like discussing a far-away world that becomes a myth. And the messenger of the far away world becomes the fool. The silent one does not fit into the world of noise, he becomes an anomaly, an oddity, seen by those without true reason as being unreasonable in their claims of a higher world.

By leaving the peaceful reason of silence, the silent one becomes clouded with noise, thus, becoming confused and losing his reason . . . and ultimately his head. Silent ones cannot live in the world of noise, it is not compatible to who they are; although they may assist when properly energized for eternal functions. Noisy ones, though they may be intrigued with the oddities they may see in the silent ones, cannot go where the silent ones live. For the walk towards this silence is not just a passing fancy, it is a journey and a commitment. Traveling through much noise in order to find silence, when you arrive you will join many majestic beings in their silence: mountains, rivers, streams, oceans, stars, moons, trees, bushes, flowers, herbs, deer, elk, squirrels, buffalo, wind, rain and snow. And the elements of the earth, fire, air, earth, and water, all remain profoundly silent.

"Listening is understanding the mystery of vibration because listening has to do with the inner vibration of the descending intelligence of the moment.
Meditators become silence so that they can go to true vibration, which becomes the audible workings of vibration, of which ideas are made. Inner listeners, or people who are continually listening to life as it is unfolding, are true humans because they are picking up vibrational messages before the messages become crystallized energy or perceptual forms that can then be articulated by the brain."
Being and Vibration, Chapter 2, Page 67, Paragraph 2-3, (Tribal, Tiwa, Author: Joseph Rael)

****

For several nights, I awoke with voices in my ears. "The eastern star has come to keep the native going." "Reading Buddhist texts will make you fly more." And the following night, "Unite the East and the West, the religions of the world. Darkness and light exist within all of them, illumine the four quarters." Conveying to me that it was my task to discover and distribute such knowledge, and bring unity to the people, I understood.

"Then, pointing to His wounded Heart: 'This wound is the fiery furnace to which chosen souls, especially the brides of My Heart, must come to enkindle theirs. This wound is theirs; It belongs to them with all the graces it contains, that they may distribute them to the world, to the many souls who do not know

where to seek them, and to so many others who despise them.'"
The Way of Divine Love, Page 405, Paragraph 7-8, (Christianity, Catholic, Words of
Christ, Author: Sister Josefa Menendez)

****

Standing outside of form, the Lord made it known to me that He wished for me to sing as music began echoing through my vocal chords. Up until now, the Lord had not given me any indication as to whether He just wanted me to write these hymns, or if He also wanted me to use the voice that He had given me to perform them in some way. "It is My wish," He conveyed, "that you use the voice I have given you to exalt My name, and as prayers of deliverance for souls on Earth and in lower realms." Conveying His wish, He began to magnify the energy within my vocal chords until my vocal range expanded and my voice became electrified with power.

"For I don't believe it is news to you that a certain omnipotence in singing is
usually granted the Muses. If I am not mistaken, this is what is called Music."
The Fathers of the Church, Volume 4, On Music, Book 1, Chapter 1, Last paragraph,
(Christianity, Catholic, Author: St. Augustine)

****

Unable to overshadow that which was to come, the grand vista of the canyon shuddered as the first blast came unexpectedly, the sound of it deafening to the human ear. Falling to the ground, I held to the Earth as several others ran off, the ground shaking in their wake. Covering my eyes, the light from the blasts was so blinding I was afraid I would lose my sight. Fighting off tears, the impending destruction shocked me. A prophesy of that to come? I didn't yet know. (Two years later, the World Trade Center fell on 9/11/01.)

Moments later, I was flying high above New York City as the darkness had taken such a hold on this place that the only way I could even fly through the crowd of demons in the air was to constantly and repeatedly recite Christ's name, over and over. Reciting the Savior's name held off the constant barrages of dark energy momentarily, but the infestation was so rampant, it could not be dissipated. Parasites and gargoyles were everywhere. Demons had taken charge; humanity had given away its soul.

Feeling very quickly fatigued from this constant battling, I tried desperately to continue my flight, as I knew my job was to bring more light in to attempt a turnaround on the ground. Questionable whether this could be done, ghouls, demons, goblins, ghosts were all around me, demanding my destruction. "In Jesus Christ's name, I demand for you to leave. In Jesus Christ's name, I demand for you to leave. In Christ's name, leave! In Christ's name, leave!"

Just then I thought of these demons, wondering who would pray mercy for *them*? Beginning to pray mercy for the demons and their charges, my spirit began flying high above the murky cloud of evil. In sorrow, I turned away as no more could be done energetically tonight. All I could do was pray . . . and prayer was enough.

"And corruption hath laid hold upon all things on Earth, and the Providence of
the True encompasseth, and will encompass them."
The Divine Pymander of Hermes, The Fifteenth Book, No. 39, (Mystery Religions,
Egyptian/Hermetic, Words of Hermes)

****

Again, I was experiencing the coming times, the aftermath of a war. Looking for shelter, I could find none amidst the horrid chaos, but a native man approached me with peace, leading me to shelter in a cave. "You must understand the Jewish connection," he said, as I bowed in peaceful acceptance of his words. (9/11)

"Fortunate is he who greeted him with 'Peace,' and to whom he responded
'Peace.'"
The Siddur, Zemiros for the Departure of the Sabbath, Page 629, Stanza 7, (Judaism)

****

Swept into the coming changes prophesied by the millennium, a war was raging, and I'd been captured and held prisoner. As the bombs would approach in the distance, everyone was instructed to close their eyes so as not to become blind. Laser beams were constantly hitting the Earth from an unknown source, casting burns and horrid injuries to all. Over time, after having been taken as prisoner of war, I became somewhat immune to pain and to torment. As I looked upon the face of one of the captors, I saw above him a horrid looking circular spindly creature, a demon.

Looking upon him, I spoke loudly so he would hear what I was saying to my fellow prisoners. "Our saving grace is that our captors are just as miserable as we are." The profundity of this was made clear to me in an epiphany of awareness, as I recalled the Exodus, the deliverance from a state of mind or perception. Our captor approached me with a whip, as I looked directly into his eyes. I recognized the demon who lived within him. "Race is thy justifier, accursed angel." I said. (Two years before the World Trade Center fell; this was the soul of Osama bin Ladin.)

Bowing his head down in shame, he walked away. Perhaps a prophecy . . . and a depiction of the karmic battle which occurs within each soul to overcome its unfortunate state?

"There is another type of dal, the poor in intelligence, and his lot is the worst of all. Chazal have declared (Nedarim 41a): 'No one is poor except the one who lacks in wisdom.' Here there are many classes. A person has foolish ideas, has strayed from the true path and become wicked. In this case, one has to think of ways to make him repent, how to restore him to the correct path. The merit for such an act is extremely great. The Zohar Chadash expresses it in these words (Lech Lecha): 'R. Eliezer said: How great is the reward of a person who causes another to repent.'"

Ahavath Chesed, Chapter 7, Page 221, Paragraph 2, (Judaism, Author: Chafetz Chaim)
****

As the coming changes filtered through my soul, I watched as two distant tornadoes ravaged everything in sight. Awesome power was displayed before me, as I sat helpless, acknowledging the power of the Lord. Now dwindling, I looked outside to notice that a rainbow with eight rings of color (the immortal) was shining brilliantly in the sky. Immediately, a voice spoke these words from the Old Testament in my ears:

"And I will establish my covenant with you; neither shall all flesh be cut off any more by the waters of a flood; neither shall there any more be a flood to destroy the earth. And God said, This is the token of the covenant which I make between me and you and every living creature that is with you, for perpetual generations: I do set my bow in the cloud, and it shall be for a token of a covenant between me and the earth. And it shall come to pass, when I bring a cloud over the earth, that the bow shall be seen in the cloud. And I will remember my covenant, which is between me and you and every living creature of all flesh; and the waters shall no more become a flood to destroy all flesh. And the bow shall be in the cloud; and I will look upon it, that I may remember the everlasting covenant between God and every living creature of all flesh that is upon the earth."

King James Bible, Old Testament, Genesis 9:12-16, (Christianity)

My heart understood the sign. The millennium would bring either great destruction or great movement within the soul of humankind, but God would not destroy all flesh, for many would remain to renew His covenant upon the earth.

"To live in the world or to leave it, depends upon the Will of God. Therefore work, leaving everything to Him. What else can you do?"

Teachings of Sri Ramakrishna, The Worldly Minded, Page 96, No. 276, (Hinduism, Words of Sri Ramakrishna)
****

Shooting began between the world powers, as the planes were now overhead as the war had begun. "It is coming," I said to those around me. Mocking me, I quietly repeated with renewed vigor, "It is coming," as the Earth began to shake.

"In the name of Allah, the Beneficent, the Merciful. When the earth is shaken with her shaking, and the earth brings forth her burdens, and man says: What has befallen her? On that day she will tell her news, as if thy Lord had revealed to her. On that day men will come forth in sundry bodies that they may be shown their works. So he who does an atom's weight of good will see it. And he who does an atom's weight of evil will see it."

The Holy Qur'an, Part XXX, Chapter 99, No.'s 1-8, (Islam, Author: Mohammad)
****

Thrown into the center of the millennial disasters, a blizzard had come upon a mountain whose destruction was so severe that nothing remained. Entering a small cave where some survivors had gathered, I was grateful for the blankets they offered because I had been wandering in the snows for at least two days without shoes on my feet, only socks. When the snows came, everything had been destroyed; buildings, vehicles, they'd all been simply crushed by the winds and the weight of the snow. Ancient sacred texts were now buried beneath the ground by a heavy blanket of this snow. And this snow was not just snow, it was something else, but I couldn't yet define its substance. It was almost like ash. (This vision occurred about two years before the fall of the World Trade Center towers.)

During my stay within the cave, I began talking to the people about God and His ways, and that perhaps those among us who had not believed in Him, had now reconsidered because His power had been shown with such might. A particularly irreverent atheist immediately proclaimed his disbelief in God, and his view that those who did believe in such a myth were morons. Making several arrogant statements, I interrupted, "Be careful of what you say during this time of God's chastisement," I said, "or you will be stricken down like many of the others." Other people in the cave were uncomfortable with me being so blunt about the truth, and began saying that we all had a right to believe as we shall choose. Correcting them, I replied, "For how do you think our world came upon this great chastisement, if not for the cowardice of God's people to insist upon respect for the Creator? It is, indeed, valid to offer freedom for people to believe as they wish, but it is not wise to sit aside as you do now, in the midst of the chastisement, and still proclaim man's rights above those of God. And if you refuse to proclaim Him, if you have not the courage to stand for Him, you, too, will follow in the fate of the atheist and those who do not respect God."

Angry, they kicked me out of their cave, expecting me to die in the snows. Walking alone, I had an interior knowing that God would allow no more blasphemy from their lips, for as soon as the chastisement had begun, I had an interior knowing to this effect. Passing the cave at a later juncture, I didn't hear any noise. About a mile further down, I saw blood in the snows, and when I swept the bloody snows away, the face of the atheist. Other bodies were scattered about in the snow, all killed in the collapse of the cave. I cried. (In hindsight, one can see that these were the Al-Qaida in Afghanistan, whose lives were snuffed out when their caves were blown to bits by the American military.) Humankind had forgotten the Lord and become arrogant.

As I wandered down the mountain, I saw a heavenly body (an asteroid or a star) falling towards the Earth from the heavens, and I knew that with it much tribulation would come upon the world.

"In the spiritual world stars appear to fall from heaven to the earth there whenever knowledges of good and truth are rejected."

Apocalypse Revealed, Chapter 6, Verse 13, No. 333, (Christianity, Swedenborgianism, Author: Emanuel Swedenborg)

"And every free man, hid themselves in the dens and in the rocks of the

mountains. And said to the mountains and rocks, Fall on us, and hide us from
the face of him that sitteth on the throne, and from the wrath of the Lamb."
King James Bible, New Testament, Revelations 6:12-16, (Christianity)

****

      Swept into the potential coming changes, I stood aside a singular bomb. Set to take off in an hour, this was apparently America's response to an attack on its soil. (This occurred two years before the fall of the World Trade Center and the subsequent war on Afghanistan.) Waiting with several people in a bomb shelter for this momentous event which would alter the course of all of our lives, we were talking. Some were saying that the United States should make an all-out attempt to destroy everything, send off all nuclear missiles and completely destroy the country which would not give in to our demands. Others were chastising them, saying we should forgive them completely for their actions and leave them alone, despite their attempts at world tyranny. Calmly looking at them, I said, "But neither of your solutions is feasible, for there is a middle way." Intrigued, I continued, "A balance exists between justice and mercy, wherein a soul can offer absolution, but refuse to allow further harm."

      Coming to life, the singular missile began its birth pangs as the seed of destruction had been born, and began its flight. Moments later, we were standing amidst the aftermath, as a cloudy vaporous substance, much like fog, filled the air with its horrible stench.

"Even in time of dispute and quarrel, we should treat intimates and enemies
alike and never think of retaliation. In the thinking faculty, let the past be dead.
If we allow our thoughts, past, present and future, to become linked up into a
series, we put ourselves under restraint. On the other hand, if we never let our
mind become attached at any time to any thing, we gain emancipation."
A Buddhist Bible, Sutra Spoken by the Sixth Patriarch, Chapter IV, Page 524, Paragraph
1, (Buddhism)

****

      Amidst the spectral of the future, I was shown my life resume. Upon it were many entries, most of which were voluntary posts, unpaid services the Lord wished for me to render to my fellow man. Others among them were tasks the Lord wished for me to fulfill for specific individuals who would come and go from my life through the years. So I would not lose sight of the natural exchange in such matters, the Lord made me to see that I would also benefit and learn from those He sent to me. What stood out the most, however, was the entry stating that I would spend a great deal of my life in helping other couples to stay together, making use of the knowledge I'd obtained through my own fall from grace.

"When a man is beloved of God, He sends him poor men as gifts; if the man aids
them, God places upon him a thread of mercy, marking him as beyond the touch
of the Angel of Punishment."
The Talmudic Anthology, No. 108, Stanza 5, Zohar, i, 104a, (Judaism)
"The Master is always with you. You have many more things to accomplish for
the welfare of the world."
Teachings of Sri Sarada Devi The Holy Mother, Chapter X, No. 4, (Hinduism, Words of
Sri Sarada Devi)

****

      Red and in full bloom before me, the roses were dripping blood. In moments, the roses metamorphosized into a pencil drawing. Blood no longer fell from its petals, as it had become an engraved image within my soul and the souls of those who were required to make such a sacrifice for the betterment of knowledge and the attainment of the Lord's will.

      In Catholic mystical literature, to receive a vision of a red rose means 'martyrdom.' At the time of this vision, my physical ailments remained undiagnosed, and I was unaware of the path that lay ahead. Time would reveal the meaning of this vision.

"The bodies of other martyrs will be torn with iron, but thou wilt be transfixed, and martyred in thy soul."
Victories of the Martyrs, Appendix, Part II, Paragraph 4, (Christianity, Catholic, Author: St. Alphonsus Liguori)

****

Alighted in flame were the souls of the future, ignited in the flame of knowledge which had given them repast. But amongst them were a few seeds of darkness, who had come to bring disharmony to this future harmonious time. Occurring beyond a war, wherein many souls were lost, some of the good seed had been preserved to begin a new covenant upon the earth. As I gazed upon these souls, I became astonished, for what lay in their laps were scriptures for their time. In a shocking moment, I realized that they were my own writings.

Experiencing a euphoric energy of knowledge, it imprinted upon every cell of my being the importance of these words, that each must be chosen so carefully so as to represent the truth, and that no words be given or interpreted in error. But there was a greater felicity to be attended to. Among the souls who'd been seeded to cause discord, I became aware of two souls who were to make a final attempt to thwart the new peace of the world by questioning the origin of these 'scriptures.'

"It must have been written as a fiction for the entertainment of the weak," one stated. If not for this warning given to my soul about this future, their efforts may have succeeded. But given such warning, the Lord bid me to state very clearly these two things. 1) Every word of which you read in this text is true to the best of my knowledge, as every experience did, indeed, occur to my soul in visions and out-of-body travel, and 2) Every word of which you read was written under divine inspiration, for the purpose of His greater glory. Although I remain a sinner, and I mistrust my own discretion, I do trust in the Lord. Let it be known . . . so that there may be no doubt.

"There are moments when I mistrust myself, when I feel my own weakness and wretchedness in the most profound depths of my own being, and I have noticed that I can endure such moments only by trusting in the infinite mercy of God."
Divine Mercy, Notebook II, No. 944, (Christianity, Catholic, Words of St. Faustina)

"In their blind deception they follow darkness as their light, taste the bitter as sweet, take deadly poison for remedy of their souls . . . In thy actions take counsel first of all from the interior knowledge and light communicated to thee by God, in order that thou mayest not go blindly forward; and He shall always grant thee sufficient guidance."
The Mystical City of God (Abrid.), The Coronation, Chapter III, Page 640, Middle, (Christianity, Catholic, Words of Mary)

****

Standing amidst a heavenly abode, my soul began to float upon the ethers in a state of perfect bliss. All around were celestial sights, which confirmed the status of where I had traveled. Music was penetrating me at severe depths, as I allowed it to fill my soul with warmth and light.

Suddenly an inspiration came upon me. Knowing that the next song to play in the celestial spheres would be an answer to a question I'd asked in prayer, I remembered what I had asked of the Lord. 'For what have I been placed upon the Earth, and what is God's purpose for my life.' A musical symphony began to fill me as I began to listen to the words of a woman who sang with force and dignity. At first I began to think I was listening to a Christian song because it spoke of the salvation of men, but then I realized there was a great deal more. As the song progressed, it became clear that the words being used were similar to the type I use in my own writing. She spoke of 'being the light,' and 'taking salvation to a higher level.' My soul actually experienced the two levels of salvation of which she spoke in the music. There is a salvation which comes to a Christian based on redemptive suffering of the Lord, and there is a higher salvation which comes to a soul after this who overcomes himself.

As her voice continued and my soul was filled with a huge awareness and bliss of God's will and purpose for my life, a tremendous light came from the sun of heavens towards my spirit. "The purpose of your Earthly existence is to take salvation to a higher level, which is encompassed within 'The Mysteries of the Redemption." Unable to be clearer, I was thrilled to know this. Surrounded in the cosmic energies of bliss in the heavenlies, I felt utter peace, realizing that though my words do not coincide perfectly with Catholic teaching, they define purification and purgation within the Earthly sphere. Reincarnation and redemption are inextricably bound on Earth because our world *is* one of the purgatorial realms, wherein a soul must continue to return until he gets it right.

In the larger sphere involving the actual mechanics of existence, there was no contradiction. Knowledge and mechanism are one, and they operate in a continuum beyond Earthly dogma.

Waking from this experience, I was filled with peace, and I *knew* beyond any shadow of doubt that the path I was following had been ordained by God for His greater glory.

****

Her face was glowing in the astral sky as I met Grandma Hornik for the first time. My husband Andy's grandmother had died long before we'd even met, but she had come to share with me her joy in our union. She especially appreciated the spirituality that I had brought back into Andy's life, as well as, that of her great-grandchildren. Her smile was endless as her joy was deep, and it felt so wonderful to be loved so deeply by this matriarch of one side of our family.

Traveling deeper into the cosmos, I had various experiences which were showing my incompatibility to the physical world. As I had again been questioning whether I should try to get back into the workforce and make some money, the Lord showed me each of these options and how it would interfere with my true destiny. If I didn't do what I do, being a mom, recluse, hermit and writer, I would forget to care about other people and the important issues in life.

Finally, my spirit was taken through a wild mountain woodland, where the destination was a grand lake. But when we reached the lake, it was empty, showing the barren and empty spirit which would result from me following such a path. Sitting on the dry ground of the lake bed, I understood. The spirit within me would not remain active if I were to drain it of its sustaining inflow from the spirit world. In order to continue to bring heaven to earth, I must remain as a recluse and not of the earth. In this, I could continue to sustain the inflow from the heavenly spheres and work towards reanimating the spirit of the world and bring back the water which was sadly missing.

"But as one that looks up to the heavens and sees the splendour of the stars thinks of the Maker and searches, so whoever has contemplated the Intellectual Universe and known it and wondered for it must search after its Maker too. What Being has raised so noble a fabric? And how?"
Plotinus, The Enneads, III.8, (Mystery Religions)
"Myriads of mystic tongues find utterance in one speech, and myriads of hidden mysteries are revealed in a single melody; yet, alas, there is no ear to hear, nor heart to understand . . . Purge thy heart from malice and, innocent of envy, enter the divine court of holiness."
The Hidden Words, No. 16, 42, (Bahai', Words of Baha'u'llah)

****

Entering into the cyclone that was surrounding our reality right now, I understood it to be related to some circumstances which plagued Andy at his job. Seeing the grand destructive nature of this cyclonic energy, I rushed over to shield Andy from another onslaught which was heading his way.

It became known to me that the goal of his current job situation was to eventually retire and leave the cyclone of energy to pursue another path. But he had to make preparations to do this at some point.

As I pulled him away from the cyclone, he was relieved and very excited about how it felt to be relieved of the bondage of it. Within a moment, we were both running joyfully up a hill on a green meadow. Wildflowers decorated the landscape, as above us the gates of heaven were open. Staring ecstatically at this gate of heaven, we ran with our faces lifted up towards the sky, unaware of our destination. Many Missionaries of Charity shared the hill with us and surrounded us in their joy. Mother Teresa approached me with a very important message about our future work for God, but I cannot recall her words at this time. In her voice, I felt the urgency and the need for a change to take place in our future which would allow God to use us in a different way.

Continuing to gaze upon the sky, I didn't want to take my eyes off the heavenly gate because I knew I could only view it for a short time and it was so exquisitely beautiful. The clouds had parted to reveal a gateway full of light where lightning and electrical energy was continually expressing itself.

Gradually, we began to disappear from that realm, re-entering the physical world.
****

Sitting in classroom on mathematics, I was busily notating words and instructions which came as an influx from above, and as a result, was not paying attention to the class. Receiving instructions as to several new editions of my books to put out and in what manner, I heard nothing in the room. As I finished my notations, I realized that the teacher was finished and I panicked, worrying that I would be unable to do the math homework which I thought was a task of great importance. But an interior knowing came over me that this was unimportant in my task, and that especially with my unique health issues, I needed to place my focus only on that influx from above. This came at a time when I had been questioning whether I should go back to college or not, and it was a clear indication that I should not for it was not my path.

At that moment, thunder struck and a huge torrent of rain began falling all around the building outside. As the class began to scatter, I suddenly found myself alone trying to find my way back down the stairs to the exit of the building. When I arrived, however, I was shocked to find that all was again sunny and dry.

Suddenly, I began to hear the voice of Christ. It wasn't explained to me, it was just something I knew. Speaking in Aramaic, He was telling me famous verses from the bible in His native tongue, and then repeating them in English. This mesmerized me to a point of ecstasy and I continued to walk forward as I listened to His beautiful voice. Before He appeared to be finished, He had gone through about fifteen of the major bible verses and with each one I had been given an energetic influx of the deeper interior meanings of the words.

Ahead of me was a huge city, and I heard Christ say, "Start walking . . . " Interiorly, I understood that He was sending me to this city and I began to walk. But I saw a car drive by and quietly asked, "Could I possibly get a ride?" At that instant, I was hovering above the car and Jesus Christ appeared in the passenger seat. Wearing robes of blue and red, his face looked older than I'd seen him in many paintings. His hair was very dark and there were lines of age within His brow. Although I was outside the vehicle, it was as if I were inside with Him and we began to drive in the direction of the huge city.

"For this reason do I send you forth." He said. "To tell the good news to all nations and peoples . . ." Interiorly, I understood that He wished for me to go forth into the world with my message in a more profound way, much of which would be fulfilled in these new editions of my books which were to be released worldwide.

Gazing upon His countenance for one last millisecond, I saw the city ahead, prepared to go, and disappeared.
****

The Secret Prophecies

INTRODUCTION:
The Secret Prophecies

As per the command of the Lord, I have written these prophecies down and kept them in a sealed document. Unable to fully understand or comprehend what they truly mean, and because it is entirely possible that I may not fully comprehend these events even at the time of my death, I offer myself as the Lord's servant, recording them and commenting no further.

Let them remain sealed as per order of the Lord, until He commands their release.

NOTE:

November 7, 2007 - Let it be done according to thy will. They shall now be opened . . .

And so it came to pass that the Lord asked me to open the sealed book of the Secret Prophecies here in this place, and it is now presented to you in its entirety.

The only comment I will offer is that to this day I do not know their import or understand their meaning. It is my assumption that I will not fully understand until the days of my children are done. I present it as it was given and experienced with only the knowledge that I cannot know their meaning and a firm belief that every child that is born bears within them this same profound holy potential if we would only cultivate their natural affinities. I can only share the experiences . . .

I am reminded of the experience wherein Christ took me to meet one of the many 'unknown messiah's. It was made known to me at the time that there are many who are called to be a messiah to others. In fact, they may be innumerable. Some are well-known saints, others are completely anonymous people who walked the earth and did the Lord's bidding quietly.

Perhaps the meaning of these experiences lies in the fact that the potential exists within every one of us and our children to become a 'messiah' in our own way, in our own corner of the world. Just as each of us can choose to be creator or destroyer at any given moment.

If we look at that potential purely, perhaps we will see that as parents we wield a great amount of power in the future of our world. What will we do with our children? Will we raise them to be messiah's, or will we encourage them to continue karmically circling and return again and again? Are we as parents willing to put in the time and effort it requires to bring out the highest potential in each and every one of our children to become the sons and daughters of Christ that they already contain within them at birth?

We go now back in time. It starts when I was undergoing the Rites of the Ascension. I was given to walk into a statue of the Blessed Virgin Mary, and initiated into 'Holy Motherhood.' This didn't make me special, it just gave me a unique responsibility with my children.

Our story begins three years before the birth of my middle daughter, Mary (now 12), and six years before the birth of my youngest son, Jacob (now 8). We are going back now fourteen years. My oldest daughter was five at that time . . .

CHAPTER ONE
Mary's Birth
"And Jesus said unto them, Verily I say unto you, That ye which have followed me, in the regeneration when the Son of man shall sit in the throne of his glory, ye also shall sit upon twelve thrones, judging the twelve tribes of Israel."

Appearing to me for many years before the events were to take place, a baby boy and girl, so similar in spiritual station that they were like twins, were to be born unto my womb. Different than me, my husband and my eldest daughter, Melissa; they were to be of higher spiritual station. Seven years passed between the birth of my first daughter and the continuing revelation which then began to manifest on the ground.

****

In the distance, a silhouette of twelve Indian chiefs flowed behind a young Indian man. As his deeply intense eyes caught mine, the young man said, "My name is Son of the Twelve Chiefs." Knowing him to be my future son, he disappeared.

****

"It has been prophesied," burst the voice of the old ones over the majestic mountain. Feelings of holiness filled me as I saw Son of the Twelve Chiefs again. A white door opened in the side of the mountain. "He who is known as Son of the Twelve Chiefs," the voice continued, "is to be born a master. He will be unlike the others for he comes through a different door. He will be born without karma." For only a moment, Son of the Twelve Chiefs spoke to me. "I leave you with this," he said, "for some; music is the expression of noise. But for you, mother, music is the expression of silence." Nodding, I understood that he spoke of the hymns the Lord revealed to me.

"He holds the twelve diadems of Light, and before Him stand twelve great ones, His own sons, like twelve bright forms (cihrag) of the Father of Light. Many gods, deities and jewels have been created, called forth and set up as attendants of the Lord of Paradise. And beside them (there are) the twelve great firstborn kings and rulers . . . Exalted is the praised Realm of Light where you dwell, pure and bright, beautiful and calm, full of joy, peace, and hope, life, ambrosia and fragrance . . . "
Gnosis on the Silk Road, Chapter 1, Page 31, No. 3, No.'s 1-3, (Christianity, Gnostic/Essene/Parthian, Harper San Francisco)

****

Awaking, Andy's face held shock and holy wisdom as he related a vision he'd just had: Four green spaceships were escorting a center white spaceship. Coming ever closer to the Earth, Andy and I were in the green spaceships, of the Earth. But the center ship carried a very important and holy being - Son of the Twelve Chiefs. As he watched the guardian ships escort the lighted being, he *knew* that he had sworn allegiance to the death for the safety of this master. Much like the ancient samurai warrior, where no sacrifice could be too great, power radiated to all who witnessed as a complete knowing, as if there was *no doubt* as to the magnitude of he who was to be protected. It was as if he was stating simply, directly, powerfully and with no mistake, "I am here." Continuing their slow approach as Son of the Twelve Chiefs was getting ever closer to the Earth, this was to be a voluntary mission for he was coming into this world without karma.

****

Two spotted Cheetah's faces hovered in the sky as I looked upon the vision outside of form. Spots merged as the faces slowly became one. All at once, they were now singular. Soaring to the ground, he became a lithe and swift being. "He is to be born under the sign of the Cheetah," the voice from the sky sounded as if it came from a very ancient old man.

****

Son of the Twelve Chiefs appeared wearing full headdress. "I am charity," he said, "charity I cannot stop in myself." He paused. "In a sense, I am your son and you are my daughter, because in our unity we give birth to one another," he disappeared.

****

Time stood still as I was transported to a place of many clouds. Peace and serenity filled me as the angels surrounded me in a blanket of their golden wings. A moment passed, and the angels began to part for the entrance of another.

Walking with quiet and reverence towards me, the Mother Mary said nothing at first, as her white and pale blue robes blew in the spirit wind. Displaying effervescent serenity, her eyes were astonishing. "If you are to birth the son," she said, "then it will be most vital to begin your retreat."

****

Andy awoke with eyes peeled to heaven as he relayed his vision. Looking down upon our wedding rings, simple bands that bore the sign of the cross, he said: "Zooming inside the ring, I was taken back to a village setting like that of ancient Jerusalem. The people were dressed as shepherds and townspeople of that time. Suddenly, a cross appeared in the ether above the people, a pale silver cross like that in our wedding bands. Appearing in a sitting lotus position, a man appeared in the sky with his palms outstretched and open. Unquestionably, he was a very holy being and one whom upon reflection *I knew* to be Son of the Twelve Chiefs. Feeling that he was similar to Christ in his love, power and wisdom, I was very humbled by his presence."

****

Despite the abruptness of being snatched from form, I felt no harm and surrendered to the will of God. Taking me through many layers of existence, we finally stopped when we reached a completely white building that shone with iridescence.

Leading me to a room, the invisible spirit placed a cross about my neck made of green stone with an angel etched in gold. Leaving, the doors closed and I waited as the light cascaded through the single window.

Much time had passed before anyone came to greet me, but I'm sure it wasn't as long as it had appeared. Without notice, the door began to open slowly.

Bowing and falling to one knee, Christ entered the room wearing a white robe. Conveying as He approached, He placed His hands upon my stomach. As He did this, white light began to shine from all about Him and His hands and into my stomach. "I am filling you with the Holy Spirit," He said as His demeanor changed to a very stern and serious composure, "you are not to concern yourself with anything but birthing My son." Calmly placing me down upon my knees, knowing that the Holy Spirit was within me, I understood that he wanted me to nest . . . like a chicken . . . for the pregnancy I now bore may be troublesome. Going over my stomach again as light continued to pour into me, I humbly spoke, "I am your servant." Quietly, he left the room.

Immediately there were dark vulturous creatures looming outside the window. Now that I had been implanted with the Holy Spirit, those demonic beings would try ever harder to stop God's mercy from being born again. A black-winged human-like figure and another short impotent demon banged relentlessly on the window. Instinctively and without understanding of why I chose to do this, I took the cross about my neck and showed it to them. "We are of the deer, elk and bear clans," I said. Speaking the words without knowing their meaning, I was surprised to see that the demons disappeared as soon as they were spoken.

"And Jesus had not told his disciples the total expansion of the emanations of the treasury, nor their orders, how they are extended; nor had he told them their saviours, according to the order of every one, how they are; nor had he told them what guard is at every (gate) of the Treasury of the Light; nor had he told them the region of the Twin saviour, who is the Child of the Child . . ."

Pistis Sophia, First Book, Page 2, Paragraph 1 (Christianity, Gnostic/Essene)

****

"Mommy, mommy!" Melissa, our seven-year-old daughter called to me upon waking. "I had a dream." "Oh, what did you dream?" "I went in the sky to the mountain. All the animals were there, and God and Mary and Jesus were there." "Oh, really?" I replied. "God told me you were going to have a baby, and that he is Jesus' son." My eyes perked as she relayed her story. "God said his name will be Jacob."

(Let it be said that we are all sons and daughters of Christ, too.)

"When a child says one or two wonderful things by accident, then we may be confident that he will one day teach the Torah in Israel."
The Zohar, Volume V, Balak (Numbers), Page 269, Paragraph 1, (Judaism)

****

On August 7, 1994, my eldest daughter, Melissa's, birthday, it was revealed to us that I was pregnant. Mary was expected to arrive on May 13th, 1995.

****

An angel arrived very silently as she guided my spirit into my own body and within my womb and allowed me to observe my baby in her peaceful amniotic sac. But darkness lurked, and the dark side was continuing to try to harm this child in whatever way they could. Panicking, I thought, 'How can I protect such a small creature from forces so determined to destroy it?'

As I prayed, I began hearing the sounds of angels singing ancient Gregorian chants. Conveying the importance of remaining in retreat, I vowed to remain unmoved. Whisked away, I suddenly stood in the center of a large and beautiful cathedral. A Jewish Rabbi came forward and looked at me sternly, indicating the need for quiet in this matter until the Lord so deigned otherwise.

Walking forward, the angel was holding another baby in a respectful manner, as she handed a boy unto me. Reaching lovingly, the rabbi spoke, "Blessed is she who births a messiah, you shall name him Jacob." Handing the baby back to the angel, knowing it would be returned to me at its appointed time, I turned.

"He said, also, that a star would arise unto Jacob, which was Christ, who arose to reign forever in the house of Jacob (Luke 1, 32)."
The Mystical City of God, The Incarnation, Chapter VI, Paragraph 1, (Christianity, Catholic, Author: Venerable Mary of Agreda, TAN Books)

****

Appearing amidst a place entrenched in sin; I didn't know how I might add light to this quagmire. Hundreds of souls were there, and I had to do something. Standing up, I prepared to sing some hymns I had been given, but as I stood, my robes became blue and white as I was transformed into an emissary of Mother Mary. Angels began forming all around the sky, thousands or more who were singing. Every single soul in this place of sin looked forward. Moving aside, they created a clear path from the deepest pits of the place to the exit.

As I looked, I saw him at the end of that hall. Appearing much like Jesus but with shorter hair, my son awaited me in robes of white and began walking towards me. Arms outstretched, I began to cry at this vision of him. When he reached my hands, he embraced me and led me through what had now become a column of souls watching him. Walking slowly and then ascending into the sky, my spirit rose to meet the angels as they began singing over and over . . .

'My eyes have seen the glory of the coming of the Lord
Glory, Glory, Hallelujah
Glory, Glory, Hallelujah
His Truth is Marching on'

Hovering above them with thousands of angels and my son, I knew that deliverance was possible from any state of sin, and the mercy of the Lord is unfathomable for those who reach to it in pure contrition. Praise be to you, my Lord.

****

Traveling the fourth realms, my spirit was suddenly hit by a 'gunshot.' Attacks from the dark side can be felt as sudden extreme pain in a certain area, and I'd just been hit in the buttocks. Falling to the ground, I was lying on the floor, bleeding profusely from the area in which I'd been hit. The injury was causing pains in the lower pelvic floor, and was threatening to push me into premature labor. My soon to be daughter was not yet due for two months.

A 'doctor' approached me almost immediately, "We have to deliver the baby right here and now," he said, "the wound is bleeding too much and if the bullet were to move it could enter the womb." Inherently, I knew which master he served. "You WILL NOT deliver the child now!" I spoke to him ferociously, "I will not move until the child has been in my womb long enough to be born healthy." "But you could die," he spoke with frustration at how quickly I recognized his purpose. "Then I will die, but this baby will not be born until its time has come."

Approaching in the form of a woman, a servant of the light approached as I grabbed a piece of paper and wrote, 'The Golden One.' Pointing to my womb which would eventually hold the golden one (but currently held his predecessor), she immediately understood and ran quickly to get help. In moments, she returned with a gleaming golden blanket with which she wrapped around my wounds and womb. Healing me, I was immediately transported from that place to what appeared to be a large celebration.

Thousands of servants of God were gathered to celebrate the child's imminent arrival into the world. Process nearing completion, several monks approached me with amazing joy in their eyes. In a consensus consciousness voice, they proclaimed joyously the future birth of a world messiah, the Golden One. Making mention of three prophesied returns (Maitreya for the Buddhists, Son of the Twelve Chiefs for Native Americans, and Christ for the Christians) I only stared at them in disbelief. Speaking of the pregnancy which was yet to come, the full magnitude of what they were saying hit me like a ton of bricks and dumbfounded me. In moments, I began to disintegrate and return home, prepared to focus on this first birth.

****

Shooting through space, I had been guided to go to what looked like a regular classroom with the exception that its ceiling was open to the dark of the night sky. Servants of the Lord were gathered; about thirty had come for this event. Sitting with three women, I remembered who they were beyond the veil, but did not know them in this physical life. All in the room were manifesting special divine gifts from God in their present Earth-walk.

About four seats down from us sat two men, one of whom manifested a very holy gift. As my thoughts were wandering, three people entered the room to preside over the group. Pointing towards this man, they indicated that he was going to demonstrate his very special and holy gift.

Standing up, his spirit became white light and within moments fiery bursts of immortal energy began enveloping his presence. I'd only seen this once before, when Christ became the messiah and accepted the living immortal energy. Before anyone could blink an eye, he began running around the room as a fiery ball of light, totally aflame. Overwhelmed and frightened, I was intimidated by his power.

Coming towards me, my fear took over as I ran and ran from him, but his pursuit knew no end. Encouraging this rather than asking him to stop, those who presided over the gathering were egging him on. "Come on," he said, "you need to experience this up close." "Listen," I replied, "I'm not comfortable being really close to you, okay. So why don't we compromise and I'll just hang out over here at this end of the room, while you show me what you want to show me from way over there." Pointing to the farthest corner of the room, his laughing continued his pursuit, relentlessly chasing me for another fifteen minutes or so.

"Okay, I have an idea," he said, "is anyone else willing to volunteer to demonstrate this?" One of the women responded immediately, taking his hand and beginning to fly. As my fears subsided a bit, he finished his short demonstration, looking towards me with expectancy. "Okay," I said, walking towards him.

Placing his arm around my waist gently, we began to lift up into the air and fly across the room. Excitement overtook me as I began doing double-flips in the air, and as we flew, my own energy began emerging from my hands and feet into much smaller flames than his. But the excitement of igniting this immortal energy within my own soul thrilled me. On the other hand, I also felt inadequate in realizing how much more advanced his energy was than mine.

Without warning, he stopped dead in his tracks still floating midair. All was calm within the room and my fears had been diffused. Feeling only exhilaration at the ignition of immortal energies within, I was surprised when he pulled from his pocket a diamond ring with a beautiful golden band which he placed on my right hand. Speaking to the group, he said, "This is the woman that I am going to meet and marry someday." His announcement confused and dumbfounded me. "We will have more than a marriage, as our eternal union will be a perfect uniting of souls. I will ignite within her the living immortal energy, and she will teach me of the knowledge. It will be a different kind of a marriage, a different kind of union." With this odd announcement, I stared at him confused. Quietly, we hovered to the floor.

With no further adieu, he walked away, rejoining his friends as if he had never come. Looking at the golden band upon my finger and the living immortal energy he had given to my soul, I knew. "The Golden One." I thought. A different kind of a union, a union of mother and child in the work of the Lord. Bowing at this revelation and prophecy, I quietly accepted his words and turned to go.
****

Torrential energies overtook my soul as I awoke to the spirit. Returning in a spectacular manner, my future son and three other native souls, a young woman, middle-aged man, and an Old One with short gray hair, came to take my soul to the top of the mesas outside.

Converting himself into living immortal energy, he showed me the technique used in making that conversion. Tired and exhausted from the pregnancy (I was in my eighth month); his request to do as he did seemed overwhelming. So I watched as he lay on the ground face-first with his arms outstretched, spread-eagle. Beginning to generate energy first from his outstretched arms, his molecular structure began to liquefy. Becoming liquid molecules, he shot upwards into the sky flying and immediately spinning like a never-ending vortex of energy beyond any power I'd ever imagined.

Finishing, he came to me and requested that I do as he had done. Placing a white powdery substance upon my stomach, he told me to alter my molecular structure as he had just done. But my exhaustion was clear as I sighed heavy breaths of fatigue. Holding my face in his hands, he placed his eyes near mine and said, "You are going to be healed through this." Immediately, I perceived that he spoke of a spiritual healing and pulled within all remaining strength to do as he said, beginning to focus my attention on altering my molecular structure.

Becoming liquid molecules, I began to fly. As he joined me in flight, we flew from mesa to mesa as I watched him spin like a vortex in complete awe. Although I was able to achieve this molecular state, I couldn't achieve the energy necessary to create this whirlwind of power that surrounded him, and it honored me to know that this was to be my son. Acknowledging my absolute fatigue, he flew over to assist in my landing. Generating this state had taken any remaining source of energy completely from me, and I couldn't keep my eyes open.

"It's okay," he said quietly as he laid my soul to rest upon the red earth of the mesa. Watching with utter respect and awe of his divine power, the three natives were silent. "Everything's going to be okay." For a moment, I opened my eyes and looked upon his face.

His adult face became that of a baby. Even as an infant, you could see the wisdom and power in his eyes. 'He really will be different,' I thought. Changing to the persona of a toddler, his hair was longer but his face held a similar impression. One thing stood out, and this was that his physical strength apparently matched his spiritual strength. Returning to the adult image, I closed my eyes to the realm we now occupied.

Waking, Andy opened his eyes, too, and relayed that he had also seen our child. "I got the impression that he would have unusual physical strength," he said, "and that we would have to be very careful so that he would not hurt himself or others." I nodded.

****

Rumbling and shaking from within like an earthquake, the mountains emitted a powerful voice, "The Earth prepares to receive the son." Winds picked up and became like a typhoon as the night sky became brilliantly violet. Turning away from the sky for a moment, explosive and violent sounds louder than any thunderstorm I'd ever heard came from all sides. But as I looked to find their cause, I could not. All I could see was the Earth shaking violently and the winds uplifting the world.

Turning up to the heavens, the stars themselves seemed to be blown by the winds. In fact, it appeared that the heavens were being *blown* all the way to the Earth! Stars were exploding, several at the same time; super nova's brilliantly showered their sparkles towards the ground. Before the stars exploded they briefly resembled the star of Bethlehem; a bright, triangular-shaped star lighting the sky with its embers. But within moments, the shapes would become more circular and deep blue, purple, green and red. As the colors encompassed the exploding super novas, they blasted into tiny particles of light which quickly hurled towards the earth creating monstrous winds and thunderous noise.

Echoing behind me the voice said, "The son comes." "Our son?" I asked. Due to give birth any day now to my daughter, this Universal spectacle amazed me in that it was presented in regards to the upcoming birth, which would fulfill the first phase of the coming. "God sends his son." Shocking, but eminently eternal and beautiful, I bowed as the winds began to cease.

Again, I saw the calamities which would hit the Earth, which years later I recognized as those belonging to the time of the fall of the World Trade Center Towers and the subsequent wars. "Preserve the ancient sacred texts, and all that is sacred." Knowing that the second part referred to my children and their destiny in the world, I realized the importance also of preserving the texts. "What good are the things that preserve the body, if that which resurrects the soul is lost?" Bowing, I nodded.

Going into labor that night, Mary Elizabeth was born the following day, May 8, 1995.

"Some have said that a holy woman will appear and be recognized as the [second] incarnation of the Christos. Others have said that a holy woman will attain supernal consciousness, give birth to a daughter, and it will be her daughter who is the Christ-bearer. In modern times, prophets of the Bride's reception have seen a different vision. It is the vision off a matrix of the Christ-presence embodied by a number of holy women. Thus, seers in our age speak of the Second Coming as brought about by many holy women, not a single woman

alone . . . Just as the First Coming transpired through manhood and Christ was received as a holy man, until a holy woman is received as the Christ-bearer in the same way Yeshua was received, the fullness of the Christ Revelation is incomplete."
St. Mary Magdalene: The Gnostic Tradition of the Holy Bride, Cycle Five, The Second Coming: Reception of the Holy Bride, Page 124, Paragraph 1 (Christianity, Gnostic/Essene)

God Sends His Son, By Marilynn Hughes

CHAPTER TWO
Jacob's Birth
"Krsna and Yogamaya appeared as brother and sister - the Supreme Powerful and the supreme power. Although there is no clear distinction between the Powerful and the power, power is always subordinate to the Powerful."
KRSNA, Chapter 2, Page 26, Paragraph 3, (Hinduism, Author: A.C. Bhaktivedanta Swami Prabhupada, Bhaktivedanta Book Publishing)

Traveling through the Buddha lands, Andy related that he had been shown the wonders of the Buddha's teachings, their vastness and depth. Suddenly, a voice began repeating over and over again . . . "The five tathagatas, the five tathagatas, the five tathagatas." Inherently, he knew that the five

tathagatas were our family, that one member had not yet been born. Tathagatas, according to Buddhist tradition, are the unborn . . . the Buddha's.
****

Appearing for only a moment, the Dalai Lama said, "One has yet to be born; the five tathagatas are much stronger together than as separate parts. The youngest two will be of higher knowledge than the others."
****

Listening to music, I saw Jacob, full-grown, playing the electric guitar. Implanting deliverance to mankind through music, a spiritual guardian walked forward calmly and laid out all that would have to come to pass before Jacob would be born. "Jacob will be different than Mary," he said, "although they come to fulfill a similar purpose, her essence does not hold all that Jacob's will hold."

"Some day a real musician may appear on Urantia (Earth), and whole peoples will be enthralled by the magnificent strains of his melodies. One such human being could forever change the course of a whole nation, even an entire civilized world. It is literally true, 'melody has power a whole world to transform.' Forever, music will remain the universal language of men, angels, and spirits."
The Urantia Book, Section 2, Paper 44, Part 1, Last Paragraph, (Mystery Religions, Urantia, Uversa Press)
****

Several monks had met me high in the mountains instructing me to go to a place of retreat. High in the mountains and away from the coming changes. Suddenly my soul was elsewhere in a prophetic dream.

People were killing each other in the streets, and the battle was raging from all sides. Fighter jets were flying back and forth, dropping bombs and killing people at random. Machine gun fire was everywhere, as there was no peace to be found. There was a woman with short blonde hair who had led this fierce attack with a younger man. Looking into this woman's eyes, I was filled with shock that a *woman* could be so dark and such a personification of vile destruction. But her attacks were relentless, and no matter what, she wouldn't stop. A young pilot was preparing to drop a bomb upon them, knowing that this bomb could well kill all of them and maybe some of our own, as well, but there seemed to be no other option.

Another woman came rushing to me through the streets, her intention to find me a safe place because my womb did bear the holy infant (Although in the physical realm, I was not yet again pregnant.) But at the same time, I was watching from the future, and Jacob was simultaneously a full-grown man caught amidst this chaos. Few places of safety could be found, so she directed me to take cover underneath a small wooden bookcase (which was presented as an allegory to the ancient sacred texts).

Moments before the bomb was to be dropped, time entered slow-motion. As it began to fall, I was transported below the plane to watch the raging fireball plunge to the Earth in tears as the finality of it was unbearable.

An explosion was heard around the world, the devastation was enormous. Now standing before the front lines, I watched the evil woman's life-force slowly leave her physical form. Burning bodies filled the empty charred hole which had opened the Earth. Horrendous in its smell, the atomic bomb bore fumes that could not be described. Survivors were getting ill and dying very slowly on all sides of this war from the radiation poisoning and the fumes.

Returning, the woman who was trying to protect me and child within me shouted, "You'll die! And the life within your womb will be destroyed." Shock filled my face, as I ran. "I'm still pregnant aren't I?" I shouted. Looking grim as another man ran towards us, he said, "I found Jacob's body near the border," he said, "he's gone."

Screaming, I shouted, "I'm still pregnant aren't I?" Solemnly, the woman replied, "No life remains in your womb." Reaching my hands to the sky, I screamed, "NO!!!!!!!!!"

Understanding, I must stay in retreat so that Jacob could be born, raised and grow into manhood safely to fulfill his destiny.
****

Before my eyes, the two military rocket airplanes were about to take off. Highly advanced in their nature, they could take off like a rocket straight up into the sky. But something happened within seconds of takeoff and they plummeted to the ground from high up in the sky causing an explosion that rocked the world.

Coming nearer to the sight of the explosion, a man requested my presence for he had news to tell me. "Marilynn, it is time for you to know," he said," that your medical condition was caused by the chemical spill you were exposed to ten years ago. There was much more damage done there than your government will allow you or anyone else to know. Eventually, Marilynn, you will die from your condition."

As soon as we began driving, a bomb went off somewhere in a small town nearby. Confused by the fact that it didn't do much damage to property, the horrible smell was like a death gas. Another went off within minutes and the air was filling more and more with the coming of the dangerous fumes.

Deciding I would find a safe place in the mountains, Jacob and Mary would be protected there through the coming times. For the end can come like a thief in the night, just as Christ had prophesied two thousand years before, and we must choose to be prepared.
****

Flying away from an alteration one night, my son was in my perimeter. I was alone and he was around me, but I was yet unaware of His presence. Coming from behind, he put his arms around me. "Do not be apprehensive," he said, "for the seed will not come in the next six months . . ." I knew that he was speaking of the seed of Jacob, the pregnancy with son, "or the next six months after that." Indicating that the actual physical pregnancy would begin around September of 1998, he spoke of energies which were coming into me now to prepare for this. "For the meantime, you must concern yourself with the life of seclusion and solitude. Focus on inner things, and do not concern yourself with the coming of the seed for there is no rush. Love will come to your soul at that time." I would only understand much later that the coming of the seed would precipitate a huge surge of love within me as I would experience a love unlike any I'd previously known through this child.
****

Taken into the energies of Christmas, Andy had an experience. Surrounded by the amazing excitement and wonderment of the birth of Christ, he was then taken into the energy of the second Christmas, the birth of our son. "It was just as amazing, exciting, wonderful and spectacular, if not more in some ways," he said. Conveying that he saw light rays coming from the sun down upon him, a spiral of sparkly light was born in front of him and encompassed him entirely. In ecstasy over these wonderful miraculous Christmas days, he was in awe of the birth.
****

Splendor and grace filled me as I was shown an elite starship from a Universal federation which had appeared in the sky. Speaking to me in a loud magnetic voice, they warned me that I'd only be able to remember a portion of what they shared.

Speaking of their origins, I was surprised to note that they came from a star system I'd never heard of and one that was far away. As a very advanced spiritual society, they spoke of my oldest daughter, Melissa, and her wondrous destiny upon the Earth. Energetically, it was conveyed that she could far surpass me spiritually if she used the tools given her. Evolution is meant to go this way, as I was born into a family of great darkness, and proceeded towards the light, she had come from this light and could proceed to even greater heights than I might be able to accomplish.

Conveyed to me through words and energies, these heights were astonishing. Honored to witness her path, she had come from their star system which was a secondary alliance to Venus and these beings were higher than any extra-terrestrial life I'd experienced to date.

Having been born into great karmic difficulty from previously Earthly incarnations, because of our diligence together in ridding herself of karmic malaise during her childhood, she'd energized the capacity to come into a greater, fuller and more significant aspect of her soul.

Oh, how I wish I could remember their words, for they were powerful, vast and beautiful. For now, I accept this knowledge as a great gift, and will continue to honor the holy union between the three children to be born of my womb.

****

Having been captured by several dark men, I was looking for an avenue of escape. Although pregnant in this vision, I was not yet pregnant in the physical. Waiting for me to find him, a very holy Native American man was hiding behind a tree. Giving me several petals from a red rose, he told me to place them in my mouth, "They will protect you from bullets," he said. "The child in your womb will also protect you as his identity, when revealed, will frighten your captors."

Placing the rose petals in my mouth, a spray of bullets came towards me, but I was protected. Continuing to walk, my potential captors were attempting to negotiate with me regarding my release from their grasp. Looking at my swollen stomach in horror, one said, "Who do you bear in your womb?" "Maitreya," I said, "the Buddha to come." Shaking in fear, they moved aside as I walked quietly away and then disappeared.

Standing in the middle of the woods, a Native American woman showed me a simple wooden cross covered in blood. Searing pain was felt across my belly as I became aware that my son may have to undergo tremendous sufferings to fulfill his task. "Let it be done according to thy will," I thought quietly.

****

Andy had an experience: "A Caucasian man with reddish brown hair and beard was walking in a cave wearing a loincloth. His very existence and who he was infuriated the masses, whose rage would manifest as gnashing teeth and eyes around his body. I don't know if they were actually biting him, but it seemed - at least energetically - that they were attacking him from all sides. Surrendering completely to this torment, he didn't fight it at all. As a result of this repulsion from the crowd, he went into a posture of crucifixion, to which he also surrendered and offered no resistance. Readily and willingly, he gave himself totally - bodily, spiritually - to the rage of the people as a sacrifice to God."

"What struck me the most was the level of rage the people had towards him just by him being who he was because he hadn't done anything wrong. His mere existence was enough to infuriate them to a state of wanting to crucify him, wanting him dead. It seemed like this was our son, but I don't know for sure, and that's all I remember."

****

After witnessing a marvel and spectacle of the heavens as the Mysteries of the Redemption were played out in the heavenlies, a holy message appeared, written in light upon the nighttime sky:

JESUS SENDS DOWN
THY KINGDOM COME HEAVENS SON

Words cannot express what I have seen and been made to know, all of it was inexplicable, and I am without words.

****

Mary was giving birth to a small jelled statue of the sphinx, and I immediately knew that this being was an extra-terrestrial. Upon the sphinx's back was Christ crucified, and above its head, an angel.

****

Meeting me as a full grown man, my son appeared as the living immortal energy. A bit taller than me, he had wavy brownish-blonde hair and a somewhat pale complexion. Hair at neck length, he expressed a deep love for me which filled me with joy. Both of us were joyous to be together again for a short time before the incarnation was to begin.

Continuing throughout the night, I learned secrets of his incarnation and of the quiet nature of his life until his mission were to be manifest. Shown to me that many might perceive him as a fool, the disguise intended for his true mission was so good that only the wise and discerning eye would be able to see through the guise he'd intended. Others would see him as a simpleton. Fascinating depth existed between the guise he'd created and the true depth of his purpose. It was shown to me as a comparison between a purse maker - the guise, and a secret agent - the reality.

Coming times were shown very blatantly, where the possibility for war and other forms of world destruction could be possible. Falling within that time-frame, much of his purpose was to assist in the effort to avoid such strife if it came to pass. Not able to understand most of what I was shown, I accepted continued ignorance.

****

As the night wore on, I found myself suddenly surrounded by the holy energies of the conception, gestation and birth of Jesus Christ. A very sacred energy surrounded and filled me with visions of such a time. And as I experienced it, I knew that my womb was being spiritually prepared for the birth of Jacob. This very night, my womb conceived certain energetic aspects of Jacob which were vital to occur before the physical conception could take place. Much too holy to describe, my soul was surrounded in three qualities; conception, gestation and birth, as energetic spirals surrounded my body and soul filling me with vibrational ecstasies.

****

Andy had an experience: "Your hands were wrapped around your stomach and you said, 'Not to worry, God has already implanted the seed within me.' It wasn't necessarily that you were pregnant already, but it was more like some spiritual aspect of it was already within you, almost like they didn't *need* me."

****

Melissa (Now ten years old) had an experience: "Mary appeared to me the way she appeared at Fatima. 'Everyone will conceive the Immaculate Conception,' she said as she disappeared, only to reappear dressed in a blue robe with a red coat, a crown of glory over her head, an angel under her feet, and angels all around her. And then as soon as soon as she appeared, she left, because I was scared."

****

Two men were fighting in the wild outdoors, but all I could think of were the poor tiny creatures like the mice and chipmunks who were in danger of being squashed during this brawl. Scooping up the tiny creatures in my hands, I suddenly noticed in the dirt a very unusual thing.

Appearing to be an archeological find, it was a clay ceramic doll. "That was intentionally dropped into your lap, and it is a fertility doll," a male spiritual guardian said, as I noticed an ancient text with pictures of the many Incan artifacts next to the doll.

Suddenly, my soul waited in line to board a space transport vehicle. Walking towards our freedom, I carried the fertility doll with some books. When I boarded, we began spinning like a vortex for a very long time and when it was finished, I looked around me at my totally new surroundings. A space man approached, "When a woman is *in* eternity, it grows up to influential infinity." Then he was gone.

****

Amongst the multitude, he called me into his service. No one else could see him or hear that which he had spoken. "I wish to take your soul into a state of prophecy," he said, as he placed a gift in my hands; a rough-hewn stone which became clear and smooth upon closer inspection. I remained quiet. Filling me with knowledge, the stone emanated the concept of speaking when directed by the will of the Lord, and remaining quiet at all other times. And it emanated refinement, in one's character and one's words. Saying much more, all that remained was inexplicable.

Again amongst the multitude, someone asked the man of whom they'd suddenly become aware a question. "Will the Messiah come again?" "The second coming of this I know for a certainty will come, but the messiah?" The second coming comes to each one of us as we accept the spirit of Christ within us. Interrupting him, I spoke suddenly as my spirit was now watching the future as if along the lighted lines of a dream. "Oh, yes," I said, "I've been told a messiah will come." With this, all were silent.

Piercing a line of prophecy, it appeared only to my eyes moving my soul along a line which followed its precepts. Along the way, I was told of two things important in his return, renunciation and resuscitation (regurgitation). Entering an ecstatic state, I followed this line of inquiry in a private manner.

Moving through walls and other solid items, my soul moved without its own cognition following this line of prophecy which only I could see. Heavenly music seared my soul in a state of rapturous peace as the prophecies regarding the return of a messiah, the deliverer, were played to me as if by symphony. Others followed my movements with their eyes, unaware of the significance.

Following with a special attention because only he and I knew of his destiny or his importance, the others no longer saw him or knew of his import. Pleased of my recognition of him and the prophecies regarding his birth, he was joyous that I had followed completely in the energy of the prophecy allowing myself to be moved according to the will of God. "Let it be done according to thy will." I quietly spoke, as my soul became transparent.

****

Andy had a vision: "Showing me two large pure white crucifixes, one was behind the other. The one on the wall was of Christ and the one hanging on the doorknob in front of the other one appeared initially to be the same thing. Upon looking closely at the second one I noticed that it was Mary holding the baby Jesus. Upon reflection, I knew the message was that Marilynn's cross was to bear and guide our children."

****

Swishing through the atmosphere, the Pleiadian ship began its descent towards me. From my vantage point, I saw about five beings standing with their backs turned to me wearing brown robes similar to that of a monk. In my excitement, I edged closer to the hangar, where a singular Pleiadian being approached me. As she lowered her hood, I saw who it was and was astonished. My oldest daughter, Melissa, looked me in the eye and then returned to her ship having casually revealed another extra-terrestrial liaison.

****

Returning, the Pleiadian ships filled the galactic night sky with tens of ships. Many were circular, but there was a huge rectangular ship amongst them which took up much of the sky. Images of two babies were beamed at me in the sky. The first was a constant image which never wavered. The second, however, faded in and out of view. Inherently, I knew this to mean that we were definitely going to have a third child, but the question of whether we would have a fourth, had not yet been decided.

****

There was great suffering amongst this multitude of laity who resided at a convent of nuns amongst the stars. Many of these souls were the troubled souls, who had gotten caught up in their own confusion, causing distress to others in their midst. Having been here before, I remembered it although its memory had just emerged within my soul.

Wearing the habit of a nun in the color of gray, I spent the day with about thirty children who were immersed in karmic confusion, and all of whom seemed to calm their energies in my presence. Mother Superior was watching me, but said nothing about my arrival or my work. Quietly and without interruption, she allowed me to take my solitary post amongst the troubled children and begin my work in calming their souls and teaching them about Jesus.

One young boy demonstrated a great interest in the second coming of Christ. "Whoever encompasses Him will be great, indeed." "Yes," I replied, "they will. But it will not happen as you seem to believe." Thinking that someone would *contain* the messiah, rather than inherently *be* it. Or that messiah's must come in only one form, shape and size; rather than encompassing many important missions in the world. He had a misunderstanding.

Helping them to reach more harmonious and humble states, there seemed to be a great issue among them regarding the over-development of their ego's which led them to perform rash and extreme acts in the world, causing themselves and others great suffering. Wanting to prove they were special and unique, they believed they could only do this through extraordinary means.

After a while, the children rejoined the other sisters and Mother Superior for their lunch. Unbeknownst to me, the little boy who had asked about the second coming of Christ had gone rather berserk and had placed the Mother Superior in a great deal of danger. Causing a raucous with the other children and adults, it had become somewhat violent. Mother Superior handled it with ease, however, and they all returned safely. But when they had returned, I noticed something different about the little boy. Becoming rambunctious again, he began speaking and I noticed that his voice kept altering, which indicated demonic possession. Walking over to him, I placed my hands around him and began repeating, "In the name of Jesus Christ, I demand that you leave."

Surreptitiously, he tried to repeat the words as I spoke them, but found it difficult at first because he was overtaken by the demon. But as I kept repeating the words, and he repeated after me, his voice became stronger until suddenly the demon was completely extricated from his soul.

Everyone who had watched was relieved, but I was now nervous that the Mother Superior might be angry at my interference. Taking me aside, the Mother Superior began walking with me quietly. "I've been watching you," she said, "and you are very good with the children. You teach them well, and your influence is good upon them." "Thank you," I replied, grateful that she wasn't angry. "You've made a significant influence on this troubled boy, amongst the others, and I am very grateful for that," she said. "Do you remember when you were with us last?" Interestingly, I did. Speaking of a young man I'd come to help long ago, she said, "Salieri did well in your presence." "Thank you," I replied, "did he continue doing well when I left?" "No," she said politely. "He thrived in your presence, but couldn't hold onto it when you were gone. That's why he incarnated with you this time as your eldest daughter, so that your influence would be of a longer nature, with the hope that such influence might catapult this soul into an eternal destiny."

"Please stay and help us with the children as much as you can," Mother Superior said, "you are welcome here. And when you go, remember that the Lord will give you a place among the angels." Thanking her profusely, I was gladdened that this heavenly monastery accepted nuns of all types who served the Lord, disregarding their doctrinal status.
****

Andy had an experience: "Standing in a bedroom in our home, my attention became immediately focused on a very sweet, peaceful, elderly woman with radiant reddish brown hair that glowed almost as if she were surrounded in a fluorescent light. Sitting next to our bed, she wore dark-rimmed glasses and had shoulder length, thick curly hair. Focus and attention were completely on the bed where I noticed Marilynn, but she appeared more in the shape of an energy than as a physical being. Manifesting as this energy, Marilynn was lying down on the bed with her hands over her stomach and appeared to be resting peacefully. Watching over Marilynn, the elderly woman was an angel, and she informed me that you were pregnant and that the pregnancy was 'in the patches.'"

"Noticing that the bed had a cover over it with many shapes embroidered in the material, I didn't understand what she meant by this, but the feeling was that she might be referring to a very early stage of actual pregnancy or a pregnancy to come and that it was important for Marilynn to stay in bed and rest a lot. Captivated by the presence of love, peacefulness and wisdom, it was an experience that I'll never forget."
****

The Mother Mary appeared to Andy as the Lady of Guadalupe, except *all* in blue, as energies came from both hands in a circular form of energies surrounding our family. Instinctively, he knew it to be protection.
****

On October 29, 1998 we found out we were five-weeks pregnant.
"This occurs in the entrance of the Messiah in this period - 1998."
Edgar Cayce's Story of the Origin and Destiny of Man, Inside Cover, (Christianity, Metaphysics, Words of Edgar Cayce, Berkley Books)
I was given to be with the baby while my body was sleeping.
****

Hitting with full force, I became very sick due to an undiagnosed rare complication of pregnancy. Because it was undiagnosed, it remained untreated and I was on constant bed rest.

After walking in a thrift store in the astral state, I was led to the back where I was given three blankets by a generous older lady, a grandmotherly type. The first blanket rendered the Way of the Cross which was placed over my shoulders in representation of the path I now walked. The second bore the mantle of Job, placed atop the first blanket as a sign of the honor of this journey into suffering. The third held the image of the Blessed Mother of God, and was placed upon the other two as a sign of her glorious protection during this trying, difficult and somewhat treacherous time.
****

Taken to watch an in-depth play regarding the Way of the Cross, it was performed at an old time 19th century theatre. Extremely intense, energetic knowledge entered through my pores.

Observing every station of the cross as if it were truly happening in front of me today, every few moments I had to remind myself that it was being depicted on a stage. Showing me the path I was following, I understood it to be a

good and holy thing, despite its outward appearances to others.
****

During my seventh month of pregnancy, a huge grand white deer with striking antlers, which alone were about two feet high, appeared to me. Giving indication of great purity and grace, I understood these to be qualities held within the soul of our child.
****

Having spent the night being attacked by a whole squadron of demons who surrounded me and were levitating and chanting all sorts of horrid things, these demons appeared in human form but bore the energy of the satanic cult and witchcraft crowd. Trying to overcome me with their sheer numbers, they had me surrounded. Because I said nothing, they began to think that they had won me over to their way and were very pleased. Surprising them, I began to sing the 'Hallelujah' chorus from 'The Messiah' by Handel. Pulling away, one male demon remained.

Coming closer, he looked like he was unsure, as if he really didn't know for sure the significance of Jacob but was perhaps suspicious of his import. "Why are you so excited about Jake being born?" he asked. Pausing, I acted dumb, "I don't know." Exasperated, the demons left in confusion.
****

Shown to me as a kangaroo with a baby in her pouch, the Lord allowed me to see a symbolical rendering of how close my son and I would be when he was born.

After this, Jake and Mary were shown to me as transparent and invisible buck deers with tall antlers of whom only Andy and I could see. Mary and Jacob were portrayed as being the eldest children with Melissa as the youngest, to give indication of the varying levels of soul evolution.
****

Melissa had a few experiences: "After undergoing a transformative encounter on the ground, Christ appeared in the sky wearing the crown of thorns, and at each side of Him stood an angel. Turning, I then saw Him standing on the Mount of Beatitudes."

"Awaking in the middle of the night, I saw the shadow of a shepherd holding a staff watching over Mary as she lay sleeping. Although at first I was afraid, I felt a sudden surge of peace, which made me feel safe."

"Reading bible stories in a dream, I looked out the window and saw Jesus walking with two angels who were watering our flowers as the Lord blessed them."
****

Jacob was born June 29, 1999 at 12:38 A.M.

CHAPTER THREE
Jacob's Infancy, Mary's Toddlerhood, Melissa Discerns

At eleven days, Jacob and I were sleeping together in bed as he took me for an extended journey. Amongst our destinations, he showed me the state of many souls who were close to me. After partaking of this knowledge and being given information regarding the redemption of such states, we entered a holy place.

Flying in his tiny newborn body, wearing a blue-green nightgown, Jacob took me to a most wondrous location; a gathering of about 100 holy and wise men. Amongst them were many Native American Medicine Men, Padre Pio, and off in the distance, Jesus. Padre Pio was the focus of this journey, however, and I spent much time listening to him speak. Unfortunately, I was unable to recall what he had spoken to me about upon return, but I distinctly remembered that his customary sternness was not present. Very calm and accepting, he expressed love and acceptance to my soul. Guiding me in regards to Jacob, it carried great import, but was taken from my mind upon return.
****

Jacob and I slept together much in these early weeks so that I might protect him from demonic attacks. One particular night at about three and a half weeks, Jacob was sleeping and began jumping and moaning. Comforting him, I chose to stay awake for a time. When I did fall asleep, however, several demonic intrusions were occurring.

Opening the door, a large black bat-winged creature with the body of a man and wings of a bat lunged at me with a huge knife. Through heavenly intercession, I was spared.

Later that same night in the sleep state, I found myself with Jacob in a haunted mansion inhabited by a demonic spirit. Looking over towards Jacob, the demonic entity had tried to suffocate him in his own feces by placing a dirty diaper over his nose and mouth. Immediately, I removed the item and slammed the demon with the might of God.
****

At nine weeks, I had an amazing experience wherein I was shown my hands as having holes in them much like the stigmata. But rather than blood pouring out of these wounds, breast milk came from them. (Interestingly, I would end up breastfeeding Jake for 21 months.) Feeling the Lord's contentment in our bonding, I awoke.
****

Satan appeared at the foot of my bed at about ten feet tall with greenish-gray skin and small horns sticking out of his head. As his face is part beast and part man, he always appears in an exaggerated body type, almost as if he were a wrestler on steroids.

Yelling and screaming at me, I couldn't definitely ascertain his problem, but soon realized that he was mad because I was making an all-out war effort against him and his minions for the soul of my oldest daughter, Melissa, who was struggling with her dark side. Jesus and I were winning, and little Lucifer was upset about that.
****

Having taken Jacob to a mall in the astral state, I was returning to my car. Immediately realizing that someone had broken into the car, it appeared that they'd tried to steal the stereo. An unassuming police officer approached with the express intention to help. But within moments, I noticed that there were two thugs hanging out not far away.

Instinctively, I realized that all three were demons and confronted them. "So what are you doing here?" I asked. "We are here for the boy," they said, "you shouldn't have taken him here; we're going to take him now." As the police officer backed away, one thug pulled out a huge butcher knife, threatening me with it. As I grabbed for the knife, he said, "You won't kill me, you don't have it in you." Addressing my abhorrence for violence, he'd forgotten that I was a mother protecting her young. "Try me! Go ahead and try me! I WILL TAKE YOU OUT TO PROTECT MY SON!" Unflinchingly, he said, "We are taking the baby." Reaching for the knife, I shouted, "YOU ARE NOT!" Looking around, there were many people wandering around ignoring our situation, but I shouted to the Lord for help and was immediately delivered.

****

Whisked off to the first home where my husband and I had lived, several elderly ladies had lived in that neighborhood most of whom had passed away shortly after we had moved. Waiting for me as I arrived, they wished to see me. "Have you met the three kids?" I asked. Very happy at our reunion, they replied, "Yes, we have seen them, and they are doing wonderful . . . especially the Supreme Tathagata!" Knowing that they were referring to Jake, they were talking in an almost joking, but yet serious, manner.

****

Appearing to be about twelve years old, Jacob displayed the features of a person from India, although in his physical waking life he was light-skinned and blue-eyed. I was utterly obsessed with him.

Noticing a man overhead him sitting in lotus position in the sky, Jake referred to him as another father. It seemed that I might have peered into one of Jake's nightly journeys with one of his spiritual teachers or guardians.

****

The knock at the door did not indicate the holy presences who awaited us. Someone came to tell me that Pope John Paul II was at the door to see me. Worried because I hadn't showered yet, I rushed to get ready and greet him. Having come by boat, his boat was just outside the door on a river which doesn't really exist in front of our house, but did exist in the astral.

Mother Teresa was with him and I was initially confused because I thought they were there to see me, and they walked right past me in search of my eldest daughter, Melissa. Talking quietly amongst themselves, it soon became apparent that they were discussing her potential future vocation. But it was not definite. Pointing out some of her issues, they observed that destructive tendencies would be her greatest obstacle to overcome in attaining to such a destiny. But they also made it quite clear, by the look upon their faces, that they felt my responses to her destructive tendencies were overdone. As my daughter appeared quite angelic, I was moved to tears that they were watching over her precious soul.

****

At ten months of age, my little sweetheart appeared to me as a young child of about two or three. Standing very coyly, he looked at me with his sweet smile holding his hands together in front of him. On his back were a set of wings which were identical in energy to the wings of St. Michael. Showing the power hidden within the simplicity, they glowed with bright light as I cooed at my sweetheart.

****

Melissa told me of a most profound experience wherein she woke in a dream state and looked outside her back window. Behind our home were about 2,000 deer, lying in wait in several herds upon the ground. Amongst the deer were about 200 angels dressed in robes like shepherds, wearing a veil around their heads and carrying staffs. Although the robes were white, they wore a veil of blue on their heads that was tied around the top. Although they emitted a brightly glittering auric field, they did not display wings. Ministering to the deer, they were feeding them grain and giving them water. Melissa expressed her awe at this sight, but then turned to look in the direction of the altar in her room as she noticed that one of the shepherd angels was standing by her side as she watched.

A life-size painting of Jesus appeared in the ether and came to life, materializing in front of her as Jesus spoke to her soul. "These deer are the flocks of the world. They are the souls that need to be taken care of by mature shepherds given by the Divine Father," Although He had spoken much more of deep profundity, she could not recall any more of His words. At her side, a shepherd angel continued to stand, keeping her company throughout the visitation.

Preparing to leave, Jesus filled her heart with an explosion of love which made her love Him in a way she had not yet experienced, and with this came a desire so strong to do His holy will and to discover His will for her in her life. Returning to her bed, she awoke in a state of wonder and awe.

Days later, she awoke in the night with fear in her heart, a fear of the darkness. Calling out to me for help, she said I appeared in a white robe surrounded in light, thus diminishing the darkness in her room. "Don't be afraid, I am always with you." I said. Talking for a few minutes, I conveyed to her that she needn't be afraid because God is always with her and she always has her guardian angels protecting her. As she calmly fell back to sleep, she saw a brush of angel's wings.

Years later, she's graduating from nursing school and is ready to live out her vocation to serve the sick in the world.
****

Three monks were sitting in my living room, watching Jacob play in the center of them. Wondering if Jacob might be one of them someday, they disappeared.
****

My spirit was given a very large book entitled, 'Priest-ology.' Ironically, I'd just found this old text at a thrift store, and it contained within it lectures from divinity school, presumably for me to teach Jacob.
****

Breastfeeding in bed, my little sweetheart and I were doing bed bun (also known as breastfeeding in bed) and we fell asleep together. Entering into energy, I saw the two of us lying together on the bed witnessing the Living Immortal Energy as it circled around Jacob and into me and back again in a circular pattern of yellow light. Very intense and wonderful, I'd always known there was a special energetic exchange which occurred during this process, but now it had been confirmed.

Because I'd been diagnosed with Peripartum Dilated Cardiomyopathy and accompanying heart failure, it seemed that my deteriorating physical health had sealed our family's fate, that of five members. Whatever question there had been at the time of the visitation of the Pleiadians when they had shown me a possible fourth child, appeared to be firmly sealed.

CHAPTER FOUR
Turning Three and Beyond

Praying with Jake at bedtime, Andy was finishing up when Jake said, "Now we need to thank Jesus for the light in mommies room." Having just returned from a profound heavenly visitation, I had been asleep. No one else knew about my visit to the light . . . but Jake did.
****

Little Mary had a dream the same night in which I had met with all the prophets and saints to discuss my occupation in life. Seeing me soar through through the heavens as an angel, she thought I might have died, but within minutes I came back to the Earth and transformed back into her mommy again.

Realizing that I was very much alive, she also became aware that I traveled back and forth to different worlds throughout the day and night, but that didn't mean I was in danger. "I still have heart failure," I told her in her dream, "but I have a lot of energy now."
****

Mary had an experience: Walking amongst a vast desert wasteland, Mary (now seven) was walking with Jacob (now three years) looking towards a man who was planting seeds. For some unknown reason, the seed man began to chase them away from his garden, and as the two ran, Mary began to wonder if they were in the 'right' place, the place where God would have them be.

Just as she began to think such thoughts, she saw a great light appear upon a nearby mountain of which she knew to be the light of Jesus. 'Perhaps they were in the place God wanted them to be, after all,' she thought, 'despite the symbolism of the spiritually barren lands they inhabited. Maybe it was God's wish for them to fill this barren land with spiritual life at some future juncture, to the protestations of the masses.'

Mary and Jacob arrived at home where the power had suddenly gone out leaving everything dark. Hearing the voices of many ghosts and dead people communicating in the house, she was frightened. So she called out to Jesus for help as He immediately appeared.

Surrounded by a huge light which filled the house, He walked towards her as the disciple Thomas appeared at His side. No longer afraid, Mary began to enter into the mysteries of Christ's life and death. (This may mean that she will share the mystical gift that I have harbored during my life, being able to communicate with the dead, and that she needn't be afraid because Jesus will light her way and show her how He would like her to help them.)

Thomas approached Jesus and said, "Are you going to live forever?" Jesus nodded quietly that He indeed must die, saying, "No, I will be giving my life for your sins very soon."

At this moment, Mary joined Jesus at the Last Supper where she sat next to Christ and watched him break a very large piece of bread. Within moments, she was kneeling at the foot of the cross as Mother Mary stood with her. Before the great moment began, the Blessed Virgin turned to Mary and said, "Did you know that we share the same name?" Seconds later, they grieved Christ's sacrifice of which she knew had been for her and the souls of all humanity. (Jesus was showing Mary that this 'gift' would also be her cross to bear in this life, in order to serve Christ Crucified who died for her and to distribute the graces which had come from His sacrifice, she must give to those lost souls who had not yet received them.) Within a moment, Mary had returned to her bed to see the face of Jesus watching over her as she lay sleeping.
****

Waking up, Jake had a dream. "I had a dream about a tiger. The tiger was playing with me, and he said I was a funny boy. Then I giggled." "Did your tiger have stripes?" I asked him. "No's," he said, "he had spots." Giggling myself, I wondered if his 'tiger' was actually the Cheetah prophesied many years before as his medicine animal.
****

Amidst a profound journey, I saw a stout, grayish older woman stealing something from the spirit world which was not hers to take. Although she had already taken that which was not hers to take, she also began to reach and claw towards Mary, who was portrayed as a small vulnerable embryo in my hands. Protecting Mary with my life, this woman had attempted to take her from me unlawfully. In the process, Mary's tiny body had been injured which now appeared to be enflamed.

Having gone into the spirit world on a lawful journey, the old woman had seen a special holy gift personified in Mary. But rather than honoring these gifts and the will of God in regards to such matters, she wanted those spiritual gifts for herself and others, and had attempted to take them by grasping it from Mary's vulnerable soul; although she knew it violated eternal law.

Entering an old building, the architecture of the building and dress of the people dated the time as late 1800's or early 1900's. A group of people had gathered for 'spiritualistic' teachings. Women filled the room, all richly adorned with long dresses, ornate hats, and make-up and jewelry to excess. A few men were scattered about the room amongst the two or three hundred person crowd. In the streets outside, horse-drawn carriages rode by on the mixture of brick and paved streets.

Having been called in to assist, myself and another soul had been given engraved invitations from the eternal so that we might be given entry to pursue the mission to retrieve that which had already been stolen. For the moment, the old woman didn't notice my presence, and thus, didn't recognize me. Although I didn't have a true sense of what we were looking for, we knew that we would recognize it when we found it; an eternal directive would immediately make us aware.

As we listened to the speakers talking about relatively unimportant issues, we were sitting by a woman who wore two large dangling diamond earrings. Becoming synchronistically aware of the radiation coming from the earrings she wore, we were both given interior awareness that the two large diamond earrings were the items we had been sent to retrieve; they were receivers to the world of the dead, tools to communicate with the spirit world.

Realizing that this was the gift that these souls were attempting to use unlawfully, and which rightfully belonged to my daughter, Mary, we both reached quickly towards her and grabbed the diamond objects which were radiating into the spirit world. Beginning to run, we needed to escape from this torrent of souls who would attempt to regain ownership of this unlawful spiritual gift which is only bestowed when and how God pleases.

But we weren't quick enough and the old woman who had initially committed this act against eternal law summoned everyone to stop us. They had been *using* a holy and spiritual gift, playing around with as if it were meant to be a parlor game.

Continuing to run, we were both stunned when the all-holy God intervened. A light descended from the heavens causing all of the hundreds of people to be unable to move. Frozen in place, they could still talk and many of them were shouting at us, asking us what was going on.

Flying towards a horse-drawn carriage which awaited our exit, we jumped in and were carried away from the scene within moments. Given a further spiritual gift of being unrecognizable to any of the people who had been at this gathering, this would protect us from further harm.

Mary's gift (her ability to see into both worlds) was returned to her soul *and* to the spirit world to be given by God in the manner in which He might choose. Further, Mary would be instructed in the manner of holiness and proper use of spiritual power, so that when her gift did mature, she would use it according to the will of the Lord, as opposed to the trivial and shallow will of the masses.

On the following night, Jacob was shown to me as a tiny fragile preemie weighing about one pound. Trying to protect him, my physical and spiritual presence overshadowed his small and vulnerable form. Over time, he became a strong baby. Jake was now three years old and was very physically strong, but I took these messages to mean that our children remain very fragile in their spirit and body, and their destiny requires astute protection.
****

Jake, now 3 1/2 years old, began relating his own mystical experiences to me. Most of them seemed to involve battling dark forces, prevailing with the aid of St. Michael and Jesus.

On one occasion, he told me a lengthy battle between himself and a large creature, when St. Michael descended and vanquished the foe. Another occasion, Jake was battling soldiers at the foot of our driveway, and he prevailed. Jesus appeared to him and asked how he had banished this entire army. Jacob proceeded to explain to Jesus how he had done so with the aid of his innate spiritual gifts.

To even describe the hundreds of battles he engaged in at this time would be impossible as it would fill so many volumes. But Jake was very actively engaged in demonic warfare in the astral, and saw St. Michael frequently during this period of time.
****

After being shown the potential ravages of a world destruction, I was given to witness the infertility and inability to reproduce which became rampant among man and beast, facilitating a crisis which could lead to the end of the world as we know it. If they were to happen, I was shown the approximate time the changes that might lead up to destruction of such magnitude would begin .
****

After being assaulted by a witch, a demon came after me and threw a two foot long dragonfly-like creature onto my chest. The black creature had two large wings, rather than four smaller ones. Melissa immediately appeared on the scene, ran towards me and grabbed the creature, throwing it off into the abyss and probably saved my life.
****

On another occasion, I was attempting to save two young men who had become involved with a satanic group. Trying to leave the group, their lives were in danger and I was called in to assist them in their escape. Unfortunately, the demons behind the assault to come were very powerful and I was unable to save the lives of these two courageous souls, although their salvation had been attained.

Realizing that I had been defeated, the demons then came towards me. Knowing my life was in great jeopardy, I hadn't yet had a chance to call for help when my four-year old son appeared with another boy his age and went after the demons. One cannot explain how cute and funny it was to see these two tiny boys whipping the large and powerful demons with their mere presence.

Walking towards the demons, Jake's mere presence completely annihilated them and sent them immediately hissing back into the abyss. Reveling in the cuteness of this, I almost lost the powerful nature of the moment because he was so adorable. But upon reflection, I was able to realize just how amazing this moment had really been.

Jake would speak about this little boy, who he called Charlie, for a couple of years as being a constant companion, teacher and fellow warrior in the battles beyond the veil. Charlie sometimes also appeared to him as a grown man, usually in a police uniform, watching over him as he slept and vanquishing demons who attempted to disturb his sleep.
****

Mary, now eight years old, had an experience about two weeks after the passing of our priest: "I was sleeping in the night. Suddenly, I was wakened by a light coming through my window. I saw angels around my bed, and standing inbetween them was Jesus. He said, 'Do not be afraid, Mary, you will have a new priest and the new priest I will give you will be a very good one.' Then it all faded into the ether."
****

Jake, now four years old, had an experience the following night: "Me and Mommy were at home in the backyard. I felt the presence of the baby Jesus in the manger. And then Jesus was talking to me and you from the sky. (Apparently, as an adult.) He said, "The below world is ruled by Satan and the above world is ruled by God. You are going to get a new priest who is ruled by God."

****

Melissa, now sixteen, had an experience that same day: "In my dream, my mom called Mary and I to go talk with her about an experience she had about our well-being. In this dream, I saw her astral notes and the first one was a letter to my sister (Mary) from Jesus, telling her about how special she is and how Jesus loves her so much. On the second part, it related to the fact that I had become so mean-spirited towards my sister that I did not realize how hateful my actions had become. I suddenly realized what the true impact of my words and actions had truly been on my sister's self-esteem and that I needed to fix that."

****

Jake, still four years old, had some experiences one night: "I heard the sounds of a war that sounded like thunder. Then I looked in the direction of the noise and then I saw two red eyes, his head was big and he was looking (sneering) at me like this. And then I wen't over to him and I saw him roar at me again, and I told him not to mess with me. And he told me that there's nothing that's better than *not* having a Jesus picture, that Jesus pictures are dumb. (We have Jesus pictures all over our house.) But then I told him that Jesus pictures are good and then he told me not to mess with Jesus pictures because they're dumb, but I told him that if you don't stop saying that kind of stuff I'll kick you back into your own world. I dug a big hole and kicked him back into his world." On the same night, Jake had this experience: "I heard a big noise, so I saw it was the same demon and he had brought some other demons through the hole into our realm. Mommy was sleeping, and I yelled, "Mommy," and she woke up and came over. Mommy jumped on them and kicked their butt and they fell back through the hole. "

****

Experiencing a very close call in regards to my health, I was ready to give up on my battle for life and surrender to death. In my bodily poverty, my life had been drained out of me during a horrible bout of incessant vomiting matters, which left me dehydrated and my heart struggling to continue forth.

In my hazy fog of pain, it was difficult to see beyond my own boundaries; because my head felt like it was exploding, my stomach was truly exploding, my other end was truly exploding and my chest was searing with agonizing pain. I could barely even get up. But out of the corner of my eye, I noticed little Jacob crying quietly on a chair, because he was afraid of losing his mommy.

Without a second thought, I pulled myself out of this fog and sat upright. "For you," I said to my little sweetiepie, "I'm gonna come back and get all better. For you . . . " The little sweetie rushed over to me and smiled, hugging me tightly. As I quickly grabbed the glass of water next to me, I determined that I would rehydrate myself somehow and make it back. No matter how close to the edge I was . . .

The next two nights were filled with battles to keep me going and to bring me back, but we did succeed. And the following night, I saw my little sweetie pie sitting in lotus position in the back of a van. Sitting before him, I was swooning in my love for him as I kissed his hand repeatedly.

I find it interesting that giving birth to my son was the action that brought about my serious health status of heart failure, but my son's existence also gives me a strength I never had before to live on a daily basis in spite of it. The instrument of my 'downfall,' has also been the ultimate instrument of my own redemption. His birth marked the beginning of many births that have come since to bring me closer to the love of God; beginning with the unusually deep love my son and I have for one another but sustaining itself in the continual blossoming of an ever greater love between each of the members of our family for one another.

I can honestly say that I was reborn on the day that Jacob was born, and if it hadn't been for his birth, we would have all missed so much. The illness itself has been an instrument in the hands of God to bring about things within us for which we would have never before conceived; among them a much deeper love, compassion, caring and unity within our family.

Because of this illness, I have found within myself strength I'd not known existed, and have also discovered a greater and more profound trust in the higher power that guides us all, along with the higher purpose for all that happens to us in this mortal life to prepare us for that life immortal beyond this one.
****

Jake (now four) had this dream when we were going through a difficult time in regards to employment:

"Well the general idea was we couldn't find any homes so we were walking through the woods and then we decided to rest in a cave. Then you were asleep. Then this big old demon came in and he sounded like thunder growls and when he stomped, dirt would tremble people down into the dirt and he had a big humped head and big eyes which were really wide. He had one eye as wide as his head, and his nose was pointy and narrow and would breathe out arrows. And then an evil snake came with an apple that would make me know evil and good. And I knew it was a bad apple so I didn't eat it. So then this demon was talking and he said, 'You'll see how powerful your mother is, I bet she's not very good at it.' But you were, cause, so . . . okay, then I woke you up and told you. And then you got up and got him. You jumped on him and then he ran away.

But the second dream, it was the same demon, but you didn't kick his butt. You didn't, but *I* did. Cause you know where demons are scared of the word, 'Jesus,' so I just yelled, 'Jesus, Jesus, Jesus.' And then I said, 'Enough of annoying.' Then he ran away, and then that's the whole dream.
****

Jake (now five) had two dreams after we had overcome our adversity in regards to employment and had found a new place to live:

"It was weird. Dad let me and Mary out to look out through the fence. Then I saw a cloud around us, and then far away but close, we saw a smoke fire in our town that went towards me. And then when I ran out, Mary was like, 'Looks like you're right, there is a fire.' Because I saw flames going straight up like a volcano. But Mary said it was a fire, not a volcano and she was right.

Then it got put out. After the fire, we looked through my window, we saw shooting lightning from the moon and it shot out lightning everywhere. And it might've hit Dad's truck, but it didn't catch on fire. And then what happened, Mary had a bad idea. 'Let's go hunting for one of those lightning bolts.'

Then these demons came down and created fires which made people bad. Me and Mary ran out, and I was like, "Where are you going, we're going to have to give everybody warnings about this so they don't get in trouble with their parents and their parents don't get in trouble with the fires and the children." I stopped Jake here and he explained this.

"Because the children would be tempted by the fires, and then they would tempt their mom and dad with power."

Then the demons floated back to hell." I stopped Jake and asked him to explain how this happened. "Me and Mary put out the fires that would hold them up here and we put them out while the demons were in the fires. So the fires brought the demons back to hell."

Jake had another dream the following night:

"These demons were after me and Mary and then what happened . . . they were after me. So I was running back home. I saw an airplane and they were shooting metal knife shooters and arrows that would catch the knife shooters and go through the clouds, trying to hit me.

Mom was there trying to find a way to make them stop shooting those things, but then what happened was I talked to them about being bad and then they understood about not being bad. So they then went after Satan and were trying to get Satan to stop doing bad things. Mom was happy that I was able to stop them from shooting their bad things.

****

Mary (now nine years old) was given a temptation in a dream (through a friend) to go into a movie depicting sexuality in an inappropriate way and declined to go, thus turning this sinful option away. As a result, she had a subsequent experience:

"I was looking out my window and I saw five caves. One said, 'You must be kind.' Another said, 'You must tell the truth.' Another one said, 'You must love your neighbor.' Another one said, 'You must not steal.' The last one said, 'You must be caring.'

Then I went outside remembering the caves. I went into each one and when I went into them, they showed me an example of what I must be like in regards to each cave's saying. I thought, 'I need to change, big time.' (Because she felt the energy of those qualities in the caves as she was there.)

Finally, I was telling a friend of mine who had been involved in the previous temptation dream about the caves and I shared with her the dream and took her into each cave. She finally understood that she was going down a false path and she energetically changed. I took this as a sign that I should share these things with her."

****

Mary and Jacob both had powerful experiences the night before last. Mary was in school and received a note that she must go find Jesus. She wandered into the woods and found underneath a tree the Nails and Crown of Thorns. She knocked on the tree and Jesus came out of a door in the tree to greet her. He handed her the robe he wore during his passion, and said to her (in regards to my apparent impending doom) 'Do not fear, child, for no matter what happens, I will always be with you.' He gave her the Crown of Thorns, the nails and His robe to take with her and to keep safe in her closet for a time. She was given a vision of me in heaven wearing a robe of white surrounded by what she described as the bliss and ecstasy of heaven. She said she knew that when I died I would still be right there with her just as powerfully as I was while on earth."

The same night, Jake had a dream. He said that he saw me lying in bed dying, and he looked out the window and there was a huge cloud of darkness and fire trying to drag us all into hell. But there was a light between me and the light which would not allow it to take us. Jake said there was a particularly gruesome demon who was enraged that he could not take me, and Jake said he stuck his tongue out at the demon and closed the window blind coming back to my bedside.

****

The knock at the door did not indicate the holy presences who awaited us. Someone came to tell me that Pope John Paul II was at the door to see me. Worried because I hadn't showered yet, I rushed to get ready and greet him. Having come by boat, his boat was just outside the door on a river which doesn't really exist in front of our house, but did exist in the astral.

Mother Teresa was with him and I was initially confused because I thought they were there to see me, and they walked right past me in search of my eldest daughter, Melissa. Talking quietly amongst themselves, it soon became apparent that they were discussing her potential future vocation as a Missionary of Charity, but it was not definite. Pointing out some of her issues, they observed that destructive tendencies would be her greatest obstacle to overcome in attaining to such a destiny. But they also made it quite clear, by the look upon their faces, that they felt my responses to her destructive tendencies were overdone. As my daughter appeared quite angelic, I was moved to tears that they were watching over her precious soul.

****

Sitting quietly on a park bench in a city, I noticed a group of Missionaries of Charity walking towards me across the street. Melissa, my eldest daughter, was leading about fifteen other sisters through the city. As they walked by, I grabbed her hand for a moment to say hello, but knew that she must continue forward in her quest and quietly let go as she passed with a quiet smile my way.

****

Riding the wanton train through the astral wonderland, my eldest daughter, Melissa - now seventeen, was sitting patiently as an angelic guardian opened her head and programmed within it a psychic shift.

Many hardships began to follow, apocalyptic in nature. Locusts surrounded the compartment of our train, and although were protected in this small space, it was clear that something that was to come relied entirely on Melissa, myself and this male angelic guardian.

On some level, I understood our apocalyptic mission, but Melissa did not. It would take more time for her to understand.

****

Jake had two dreams: (5 1/2 years of age) "God told me that when I grow up, I would have to stop a war. Then me and Mary flew over to the place where the war was going on where I saw that one of the people who was being bad read mommies books and he stopped being bad. Then God gave me power and I used the power he gave me to restore all the buildings and houses for the people."

****

Mary and Jacob continued to have profound experiences regularly with the heavenly hosts and with the souls of those beyond.

A couple of short examples are these:

Jacob said (Age 5): "I'll tell you how it came true. When I once had a dream that came true and I saw the heavens on a cloud and I saw Jesus and I also saw all the angels and St. Michael."

Mary said (Age 9): "I was with Mom in our house and we went into the canyon. She found a demonic green buffalo that she made go away. Then she showed me another buffalo which was brown and black. When she touched it, she was filled with the Holy Spirit and came into her power." (Buffalo medicine is that of prayer)

Mary said (Age 9): "There was a container on the table filled with water. Suddenly, a picture of our house comes into the container. Inside our house has been changed into a monastery."

Mary said (Age 9): "My mom has died and in a vision she says she will be with us forever, even though she is a spirit in heaven."

Mary said (Age 9): "I was able to be in St. Maria Gorretti's life. And after she was stabbed and died she came to me and said I should not be worried about what kind of death I might have because God will bless me no matter how it may come."

Mary said (Age 9): "There was a mirror underground. Demons had been coming out and making people lost souls. When the demons came to our house, though, Jesus and an army of angels defeated them and did not let them enter."

Mary said (Age 9): "I was on my way to the top of a mountain. But when I reached my goal, demons tried to take me. When my parents saw what I was doing, and were concerned, I told them that I'd realized that I had been trying to reach my goal too soon to prove to people that I was special."

Mary said (Age 9): "My dad had gone to work. When he got to his office, I saw many angels sitting there helping him in his work for the Lord."

Mary said (Age 9): "I was praying and Jesus came and blessed me."

Mary said (Age 10): "Dad was in court. And he won the trial. Angels came and said they would help him throughout his life and work and then he was in his office and he was helped very well and he learned many lessons."

Mary said (Age 10): "I was sleeping and Jesus came to me in a glider and He took me to my future to what I could choose to be. And the answer was that I was to be someone, a religious person, who taught the Words of Christ and taught children how to become closer to Christ. Jesus showed me the results of what would happen if I accepted and followed my mission."
****

Both Jake and Mary would continue to have profound experiences.

Mary began battling dark forces before she turned twelve, and she was shown that I would not survive the entire time of tribulation and the battle between good and evil to come because my body was beginning to give out, but that she and the rest of the family would carry on forward the mission that had been set forth.

Melissa was now soon o graduate nursing school, planning to serve the flocks of Christ in whatever way He would lay it out for her in the years to come.
****

Just as with all of us, each born into the holiness that God allows us in our innocence, that holy spark is either maintained or destroyed throughout our childhood and then finally determined by our own individual free will.

What will they choose? What will they do with these gifts the Lord has given them? Will they fulfill whatever these prophecies proclaim? Or will they, like so many others, fall off of the path of spirit and follow the temptation of the world to become shallow and dense.

It is my opinion that these Secret Prophecies portend only the true destiny of all children who given the right circumstances of childhood and choice, have the potential to become everything spoken of in these pages. We are all potential messiah's to everyone we meet, and each one of us chooses either the shallow or the deep waters.

Prophecies about who we are to become can only be fulfilled by the subsequent choice of free will. I remember once being told that Potentials Unfulfilled have no meaning, while Potentials Fulfilled are eternal! And isn't it true that the Lord has shown throughout the centuries that anybody who chooses Him over the world, becomes a bit like Him - they become His sons and daughters.

And each time one of these appears, it is a Second Coming - Moses, Elijah, Jeremiah, St. Francis, St. Catherine of Siena, St. John of the Cross, St. Therese, Milarepa, Rumi, Paramahamsa Yogananda, Thoth/Hermes, Sri Ramakrishna, John Wesley, Baha'u'llah, Martin Luther, Master Dogen, Maitreya, Buddha, Nostradamus, Saint Mother Teresa, Saint Padre Pio . . . the list of them is endless and goes beyond the bounds of any one religion. They exist in every region of the world carrying the banner of every religion; the royal family of God. And they embody and take within themselves all that is holy around them, making themselves a vessel of splendor and grace in a myriad of ways through a kaleidoscope of spiritual and other gifts.

Perhaps the Secret Prophecies only portend the *divine potential* of every child born to this world . . . including yourself and your children. And each one of us is given the opportunity to receive the messiah through others and to be a messiah to others every day of our lives if we choose to see clearly.

Create the auspicious circumstances for yourself and your children, and make it possible for yourself and each of them to choose the depths rather than the shallow waters. Then shall these prophecies be fulfilled . . . as each of us grabs a hold of our greatest potential and seeks to fulfill it in others, as well. Let no one be left behind as we strive to bring the Second Coming of Our Lord Jesus Christ into every man, woman and child born of this earth.

If it comes in this manner, than the gospel shall truly have been fulfilled in its entirety.

****

Initiations into the Mysteries

Mystic Knowledge Series

Compiled and Written by Marilynn Hughes

The Out-of-Body Travel Foundation!

www.outofbodytravel.org

CHAPTER ONE
Warning as you Enter the Mysteries, Guardians of the Sky, Temples in the Sky, The Death Song, Cygnus and the Circles of Fire, the Way of Wa and Da, St. Francis and the Cycles of Time

****

"'The Counsel,' he said, 'alludes to the sublime mystical knowledge which remains hidden and undisclosed save for those that fear the Lord continuously and thus prove themselves worthy of these secrets and able to keep them.'"

The Zohar (Kaballah), Volume IV, P'Qude, (Exodus), Page 299, Bottom, (Judaism)

(A word of caution: Do not believe that because you read these experiences you will obtain the full knowledge of them. As with all visionary experiences, there is an energetic influx of pure knowledge containing transformative vibrations which cannot be put into words. In essence, you may obtain a general map of how to get there, but if you wish to obtain the full knowledge of them, you must then take the journey yourself. As per order of the Lord, some information has been omitted and destroyed to protect it from being misused.)

<u>IMPORTANT NOTE:</u>

In the ancient mysteries, you will find many references to spiritual beings who come in the form of mythical gods of the ancient Greeks, Egyptians, etc. It is important to know that these beings are NOT gods, but rather; 1) people who used to walk the Earth, but now serve God by guarding a particular mystery or rite of passage, or 2) spirits who have always guardianed particular mysteries or rites of passage, whom ancient peoples became aware of through visions, and mistranslated them as gods due to their own perceptions that any spiritual beings were indeed such.

<u>*It is not my intention to portray any of these spiritual beings as anymore than angelic hosts, spiritual guides, or guardians of particular rites, mysteries or realms, who serve God in their own unique fashions. God is ONE, and there is only ONE God.*</u>

****

Entering into the energies of the clouds, I became aware that they were the Guardians of the Sky, the painters of the sky who reveal images to mankind which are often unnoticed and unseen. But within these images, lie hidden meaning, mysteries and secrets to worlds beyond.

And so it came to pass that I was taken through several passages regarding thunder, lightning, rain and clouds.

Hovering amongst the clouds, a thunderstorm was in progress and I soared to the midst of it. Pulsating rapidly with the vibrations of the storm, the raindrops would fall intermittently through my transparent self. With each bolt of lightning, an energy surge gyrated through my arms and into my head. With the thunder, my spirit exploded into the majesty of the clouds. Each movement of the clouds carried with it a distinct feeling within my soul. For a moment, I listened, as the prayers of humanity were traveling from Earth to Heaven on the heels of thunder and lightning.

A tiny raindrop beckoned. Quickly, I jumped into it and felt myself fall lightly to the ground and dissipate. Surrounded by my fellow water spirits in a puddle, I looked around. "My, how big everything looks." Suddenly, I was sucked under. Below ground, a grass blade had pulled me up through its roots and before I knew it, I evaporated back up into the sky where the clouds were making way for the sun to shine through. Peaceful gratitude filled me.

"As long as you live outside the house of maya, as long as there exists the cloud of maya, you do not see the effect of the Sun of Knowledge."

The Gospel of Sri Ramakrishna, Chapter 30, Page 583, Paragraph 16, (Hinduism, Words of Sri Ramakrishna)

****

*"Said the old man: 'O ancient, O ancient, upon what a task hast thou entered!
Thou hast plunged into the great sea, and now perforce must swim on till thou
shalt have gained the farther shore! On, then! And if he take him another . . .
How many ancient mysteries never revealed before, regarding transmigration are
indicated here! All the matters of which I am about to speak are perfect truth
not deviating by one hair's-breadth from the path of truth."*
*The Zohar (Kaballah), Volume III, Mishpatim (Exodus), Page 299, Paragraph 1,
(Judaism)*

Overlooking a large ravine, a tall male spirit approached me, holding a golden stick of incense, the tip searing with the light of a small flame. "This is a very powerful ceremony, are you sure you wish to embark upon this journey?" "Yes," I said excitely, "but please tell me what to expect." Direct and serious, he spoke few words. "This incense will take you to the threshold of death. There you will witness ancient mysteries. Your spirit will be in a state of timelessness for several days in time. We will watch over you until you return from your journey. Then you will be returned to the appropriate day in the structure of time to re-associate with your body." "Okay," I said thoughtfully, "I'm going to be seeing a lot, how will I remember it all?" "You will not," he responded in quietude, "in timelessness you will encounter much but take with you only a little. This is the way it must be for now."

Lifting the golden incense to the sky, he touched it lightly to my arm. "I will stay with you for the first vision, but after witnessing the temples, you will be taken into timelessness and I will be gone." Entering a beautiful state, I felt as though my spirit was a thought-form on the patterns of a mystery. Floating motionless, I began to witness the temples in the sky!

*"Each of the elders held a harp and gold bowls filled with incense, which are the
prayers of the holy ones."*
New American Bible, New Testament, Revelations 5:8, (Christianity)

From the depths of the ground a large column of pink coral rock began to ascend, several hundred feet wide and about thirty feet tall. One side of the rock had the letters HDA engraved within the stone, and directly beside them were three tunnels opening to other worlds. Above each tunnel was a separate single word, and they appeared in this order: Here, There and Always. Temples in the sky were serenaded by the deep pink sky, and they included pyramids and a sphinx. Amethyst began emerging from the ground.

A princess of immense beauty appeared in the sky, her dark Amazon hair blowing in the wind. Silently on her forehead, lay a golden crown surrounding her sparkly face. Filling half the mystical sky, her presence was ominous. Chiming questions to my spirit, her magnetic voice chimed, "Which do you choose?" she said, "Here, There or Always?"

'Here' was the choice of remaining in spirit on the Earth, perhaps to stay with a loved one or stay in fear as a lost soul. 'There' was a choice to enter the astral side of the earth-plane, (fourth realm) and this was a typical choice of many who left their lives in a state of total slumber, giving them time to reacquaint the spirit with the knowledge of truth, while retaining the safe identity of a fragment, or a personality. 'Always' was to slip into timelessness, and to reunite with God. "Always!" I shouted.

"Chant the ancient tonelage!" She chimed, as instantly my inner spirit began to search for the remembrance of this. Eyes shooting to the stone letters emblazoned in the rocks, "HDA! HDA!" I cried out, chanting to the being in the sky. Repeatedly, I continued chanting as my soul entered a state of bliss and shot towards the third tunnel, falling into timelessness.

Entering a state of wandering, I soared to many vast worlds. But the spirit who sent me told me the truth, I would only remember a little bit.

Stopping at one point in timelessness, I appeared to be in ancient Egypt. The pyramid builders were working to construct what would become, in the proper state of time, an ancient mystery. Some of the pyramids were finished, but many were left undone, and a young man was sitting quietly taking a break on a large stone. Behind him, a half-built pyramid stood. Wearing a metal covering on his head with feathers at the top, he wore a skirt made of large metal fringes.

Appearing to him in timeless spiritual form, I sat next to him. "Excuse me, sir, I'm very sorry. I will get off your stone and let you return to work." Intensity filled his eyes, and I *knew* that he understood that I was a spiritual manifestation, rather than a physical one. This was not surprising to him, and that surprised me. Taking my hand, he smiled at its transparency. "I want not off, for I need no rock cut by stone, but love created through life!" Intrigued with his words, I smiled, but had no chance to respond before being pulled away.

Inside a pyramid experiencing a spiritual ecstasy, I listened to those outside who were speaking. "She needs more moments in timelessness," one said to the other, "to regroup for return to the physical." For a moment they were discussing the unusual nature of my journey, and a woman commented that I was the first soul allowed to travel during life . . . this far beyond the doorway of death. "How much will she remember?" The woman asked, "Not much," he responded, "but she will remember the HDA, and the Here, There and the Always." Speaking silently, the woman did not want me to hear. "Will she remember the death song?" "Aaaah," he responded, "a part of it she will take back."

Intrigued, I peeked through a window. The two who spoke were honey-colored with long black hair, the man wearing only a red covering around his groin, but the woman was dressed like a princess.

Moments continued to pass, but I felt no time. Coming out of the intense state, my keepers came to release me. "You have one more stop on the way back." They said, as they raised their arms. Shooting out of the pyramid city, I entered a very unusual realm.

Swaying in the flow with resembled the ocean's current, the cloudy substance which enveloped me was a mist which was wet . . . but also dry. Beginning to hear a man's voice in the distance, he was singing a very soulful and mystical chant. An unusual vibration accompanied his singing, which I could only describe as a transition into timelessness. These were the words he spoke:

"The timeless moon doth ocean sway tide
Holding tight to beachhead reign
But ne'er be near the stillness of time
Crossing to regions of lingering plane"

"Sing in spirit to mountains that speak
The crestful longing of manner abode
A place where time ends is what we seek
The endless journey, along the lighted road"

"The Death Song?" I thought wistfully, as I dizzily re-entered my physical body.

"When a true seeker determineth to take the step of search in the path leading to the knowledge of the Ancient of Days, he must, before all else, cleanse and purify his heart, which is the seat of the revelation of the inner mysteries of God."
The Kitab-I-Iqan, Page 192, Paragraph 1, (Baha'i, Author: Baha'u'llah)
****

Following my inner spirit, I was led to a place within a deep forest. Several fire pits were arranged in a circle, all appeared ready to be lit. All of them were piled with wood, except for the last one which was filled with charcoal. A temple guard stood at this spot, un-moveable and guarding this ancient rite. Looking to me, his dark eyes and golden metallic armor entranced me as he spoke. "Ignite the ancient flame." He said, as I created thought-form matches. Nodding, 'No,' he said, "Give them the BREATH of life."

Inner understanding took over as I walked over to the first pit and blew into it. Rising up in flames, I continued with each of the wood pits and did the same, as they rose in flame. When I arrived at the charcoal pit, I was confused. Blowing and blowing, it would not light. Looking into the starry sky, the guard was emotional as he pointed to a constellation in the North, "Call to Cygnus to complete your circle of fire."

Gazing at the stars, it took me a moment to properly *feel* what I must do, but when I began *feeling* it, the stars seemed to ignite just for me and the shape of a swan appeared in the night sky. "How beautiful!" I cried. Taking my next breath, I raised my arms in the direction of the constellation. "Cygnus!" I called, "please help me complete the circle of fire!" Blowing directly into the coals, smoke began stirring from within. Fire began brewing as I stood in the center of this circle. Sending thanks to Cygnus, the flames grew to several feet high.

"My spirit, you have ignited the ancient flame! Look!" Pointing behind me, I looked and saw a beautiful flowing river and above it . . . an entrance; a tunnel of the brightest blue was apparent, and I began to move towards it. Holding me back, the guard pointed to the gorgeous swan which flew through the tunnel and disappeared from sight. "Behold the mighty Cygnus!" He said.

Wanting to follow, he held me back. "You cannot go, yet," he said, "you have brought together the circle of time. By igniting the ancient flame, you have entered timelessness. Cygnus will be back, but only when he is certain that your heart is pure." Turning to leave, I paused to ask one final question. "What lies beyond that tunnel?" Smiling, he said, "Ancient Temples."

"If, then, the soul withdrew, sinking itself again into its primal unity, Time would disappear: the origin of Time, clearly, is to be traced to the first stir of the Soul's tendency towards the production of the sensible Universe with the consecutive act ensuing."
Plotinus: The Enneads, Seventh Tractate, Page 267, Paragraph 4, (Mystery Religions, Greek, Author: Plotinus)

****

Appearing in the starry night sky was a golden, luminous and transparent pyramid with an ocean flowing from within. Knowing this to be the doorway from the previous night, I quickly leapt inside as a voice with no apparent body filled the place, "All who live sleeping, sleep for the purpose of mankind. If only they would awake in their dreams, they would find themselves in another world." Looking around to find the source of the words, the voice continued, "All life, like all quasars, had really worth still traveling. You can tear away at everything, but the pull of the body within calls for silence."

Integrating the knowledge being expressed, an internal awareness instructed me. A quasar star, much like life, is in constant motion and evolution. Life requires that movement, that traveling, to progress. The intellect tears at things in its effort to understand, but timeless wisdom is attained by silencing the intellect, and allowing wisdom to emerge.

Silence remained until a light descended and the voice called again. "The Omnipotent One calls the presence of within. Come forth!" Knowing that this was a call for the higher soul within me to emerge, I stepped forward. "You stand before the Titan (One of the elder gods in Greek mythology; refer to note at beginning of mysteries) will you choose the way of WA or DA?!"

WA represented the path of life, the way of service to God; DA represented the way of spiritual death, the spiritual death of those who choose forgetfulness. "I choose WA!" I shouted.

Immediately, a huge triangular stone stood before me which looked like an opening to a vault. Ancient inscriptions on the door were written in languages I didn't understand. Appearing as a huge lighted man, the Titan placed his hand on the stone and looked my way. "This is beyond the Here, There and the Always, it is beyond the death song. This is the doorway to eternity. Those who pass through this gate ascend their spirits to light."

Pausing to feel the stone, I touched the ancient inscriptions. Power pulsed through me. "Remember the ancient words of service, you have spoken them often." An immense flow filled my soul, as my spirit remembered these words:

"Perchance, tonelage striving, the mighty worker of light
Perceive the distant calling, send thine eyes to sight
Church bonds tutelage, sacred bonds of fire . . ."
(Per order of the Lord, I have omitted and destroyed the last stanza)

Holding silence, feelings of immense gratitude and love for God rushed through me, as the Titan placed his massive hands on my shoulders. Light poured through my soul, and I shed tears of joy to be seeing this beautiful place again. Eyes searing with intensity into mine, the Titan said, "Commit to cross the isle, dear spirit." With massive force, my spirit called forth the words of commitment to cross the isle:

"I have mastered that which is on the wall
The Mayan cards of walking stone
All who dwell here call to Saul
Meet the mercy all alone"

His hands were now held to the wall, "Come, Felicia, open the door! I stand at the isle of death!" Opening slowly, beautiful Felicia stood there waiting as I shot into the tunnel. My friend who had passed away in a car accident stood there waiting. Holding a life chart, he showed me thirty boxes, twenty-eight of which had been fulfilled. There were unusual symbols in the two remaining boxes. "This one means that you will express your knowledge before leaving the earth-plane." Pointing to the second, he said, "And this means that you will express the music of your soul. But now, you must return as the gate summons you back to form."

Flying of God's accord through the stone gate and back into the pyramid, I called out my thanks as I returned to my body in peace.

"I would it were possible for thee, O my Son, to have wings, and to fly into the Air, and being taken up in the midst, between Heaven and Earth, to see the stability of the Earth, the fluidness of the Sea, the courses of the Rivers, the largeness of the Air, the sharpness and swiftness of the Fire, the motion of the Stars, and the speediness of the Heaven, by which it goeth round about all these."
The Divine Pymander of Hermes, Book Five, No. 21, (Mystery Religions, Egyptian/Hermetic, Author: Hermes)

****

A prophet of old wearing a tattered robe tied at the waist stood before the pyramid carrying a staff of wood. Laced with gold, the luminous steps led to the top and back down the other side. Looking at me with his intensely green eyes, he touched his hand lightly to mine. "Wilst thou come with thee?" He said. Nodding, we walked hand in hand up the etheric creation that lay before us. "Each step represents a cycle of time," he said, "the circular motion of an energy form that recreates until the cycle is complete." "What exactly do you mean?" I asked. The abiding spirit did not speak, but knowledge entered into me. In evolution, there are given certain periods of time wherein a soul may repeat a pattern of behavior over and over again, usually something delusional, without fault being attributed because of their ignorance. But when this cycle of evolutionary time is complete, if the soul still circles in the same delusion, it energetically changes. No longer protected from their own ignorance, they are required to be held accountable for any damage done. Applying also to eternal creations, we are given a cycle of time in which certain aspects must be completed, if they are not, the eternal program can either be aborted, or depending on the will of God, receive an extension.

Leading me down the steps on the other side of the pyramid, he asked me, "Do you know what this represents?" Nodding no, he began to chant:

"Perchance, by moments velvet form
Relinquish not for velvet's sake
Only moments all alone
Breaking distance soul awake"

"Who, but I, can travel far
Beneath the distance of the Way
Trembling chasms set to soar
Hawk spent demons cast away"
"Illusions cast, my soul seeks rest
All libacious form retreat
Sails of light, exuding masts
Light calls forth from God's great feet"

As he chanted, we continued to the bottom of the pyramid into a deep, light-filled cavern. Two huge candles, about five-feet high, were lit around the lighted form of a very holy being. Wearing white glowing robes, his hair had become curly and silver. A band was strewn around his head, and in his hand was a staff. Both of us stopped as we took in the holiness of St. Francis of Assisi. "Do you know what this spirit speaks?" St. Francis asked, in relation to what the spirit aside me had just chanted. "Yes," I replied, "it is the remainder of the death song." Smiling, he mysteriously asked, "Then you know the last stanza? Speak the words to forage all that light retreats!" Bursting to my knees, I began to chant the final words:

"Cyclic change to earth renowned
Casts foreseen a timely rain
Come to cleanse immortal soul
Time will end, but stay the same"

Smiling, St. Francis pointed his staff at me. As soon as he did, I became sub-conscious for the remainder of my travels that night.

The following night, I was sent to recall the word of release to end a cycle of time, words which would end the circular motion and spinning of karmic energies, forcing a birth-point. Those words were 'Chorub Lee.'

"List ye, O man, to the depth of my wisdom, speak I of knowledge hidden from man. Far have I been, on my journeys through SPACE-TIME, even to the end of the space of this cycle. Found I there the great barrier, holding man from leaving this cycle. Ay, glimpsed I the HOUNDS of the Barrier, lying in wait for he who would pass them. In that space, where time exists not, faintly I sensed the guardians of cycles."

*The Emerald Tablets of Thoth the Atlantean, Tablet VIII, Page 45, Paragraph 6,
(Mystery Religions/Egyptian Hermetic, Words of Thoth)*

****

CHAPTER TWO
Frequency of Otara, Secrets of Nor, Key to the Temple, Five Concentric Circles, Secrets of Disintegration, Watchers of the Earth, Immortals, Guardian of the Rite of the Light of the Sun, Elementals, Crystalline Eve.

****

And so it came to pass that I learned more about the frequency of Otara (the high G), which calls the angels into service. In the midst of a holy work to assist a young girl, I called the angels by this tone as the sign again appeared as huge light in the sky; a brilliant, diamond-shaped star, as legions of angels came to our aid.

****

Entering into a tiny passageway, my spirit felt as if it were being turned inside out, like a reversed vortex. As the energies spun to completion, I found myself standing before a small, stone gate. An angel stood with a staff at the gate. "Within lie the secrets of Nor." She said. "Call to the hosts of heaven abide, the light of expansion yearns with a sigh." A geometrically sectioned, snow-tipped mountain appeared behind me, with lines divinating various locations upon it. Flying towards it, I danced in the monolith. "Take a little walk in the movement today," the angel said.

Suddenly words began entering my soul, and as I spoke them, they would occur all around me. "Lilac melt the velvet mist, spirit light relinquish form. From whence, the sacrament to deities divine, postulate season, sing in sighs." Lilacs appeared as the snow melted. My spirit became only a light with no features. Speaking of the sacrament, I knelt to the ground and watched the spring season dawn as angels began appearing and singing, their voices like holy sighs. Again, the angel spoke, "I love to feel the washing stone, kneading out the hardened stain. Mankind's mirth is ground in fine, boding forth new clean slate." Expressing her love of the purification process, she spoke of cleansing the delusion which is ground deeply beneath mankind's joy.

"Find in your imagination words to prolong the truthly hour." Realizing that I must remember the chant required to continue in this land of Nor, I began speaking again. "All to pass in timelessness, Gregorian chants afire. Cretan mammoths linger, but all be gone in time. Passwords movement follows, to find the ancient rest. Hombre' calls to Quetzlcoatl, are you real or dead?" Shouting, the angel said, "Behold! The Chant of Nor!" Beginning to sing an almost involuntary ancient Gregorian chant, I repeated it three times. Standing at the gate of the mysteries, I began speaking the words to open the door:

"Temple of mysteries, open thine door. Pure heart awaiting, centrifugal fate.
All manners cast in tunnels abide, open all ancients, reveal what you hide
Rite of passage, gleaming stone, heartfelt distance, angel zone
(Per order of the Lord, I am leaving out and have destroyed the final stanza)"

As I spoke these words, I received entry into the initiations to come.
"By the act of thought we are, as it were, collecting together things which the memory did contain, though in a disorganized and scattered way, and by giving them our close attention we are arranging for them to be as it were stored up ready to hand in that same memory where previously they lay hidden, neglected."
The Confessions of St. Augustine, Book X, Chapter 11, (Christianity, Catholic, Author: St. Augustine)

****

"Followed, I then, the path to the star planes; followed I, then, the pathway to LIGHT. Deep into earth's heart I followed the pathway, learning the secrets, below as above."
The Emerald Tablets of Thoth the Atlantean, Tablet V, Page 29, Paragraph 3, (Mystery

Religions,
Egyptian/Hermetic, Words of Thoth)
"Only those who are initiated into the divine mysteries can comprehend the
melodies uttered by the Bird of Heaven . . ."
The Kitab-I-Iqan, Page 191, Paragraph, 1, (Baha'i, Author: Baha'u'llah)

Standing amongst the stars, I rode the wings of a swan. Cygnus took my soul on a flight through the universe and then became only light as we arrived at a gateway. Knowing this to be initiation's door, I remembered the words that would gain me entry into the worlds of the mysteries: "Whereupon, the icy bank, a memory lit the cold to shine. In the stillness, thoughts swept forth, fragments of moments, no longer in time. Temple staircase, lead me deep, to the midst of all divine, beyond the veil of mystery, words and thoughts emitting light."

Cold swept over my body, and then an incredible warmth. Beginning to hear voices, I saw the doorway open as my spirit was led inside where many temples awaited my arrival. Merely looking upon them, my soul was immediately immersed in water and began soaring to the depths of a great sea. At the bottom was a stone temple emitting light, and I kneeled before it. Hundreds of stone pillars with words inscribed upon them lay before me:

"Journey, my soul, to places of deep, our thoughts be revealed to you now
Grasp what you may, unravel and keep, remember to use thoughts of the Tao
You will be returning, for this place you have found, holds wisdom of night
winds, foretold
Find fragments and moments, but each hold a clue, to mysteries beyond what
you know.
Seer of thought, call out my name, divine words will enter the mind
This place you now come, where shadows call truth, means nothing to those of
the blind
Fear not the answers of symbolized truth, mysterious shadows restore
Initiate of Mysteries, holder of light, remember the corners of four"

As I read the words upon the monument, I watched an image of Cygnus form in the front of the temple. Wings outstretched, the swan was standing perched upon the flowing waters of the sea with a symbol engraved upon its chest; a triangle with a circle inside.

"After this I saw four angels standing at the four corners of the earth, holding
back the four winds of the earth so that no wind could blow on land or sea or
against any tree. Then I saw another angel come up from the East, holding the
seal of the living God."
New American Bible, New Testament, Revelations 7:1-2, (Christianity, Catholic)
****

Standing before a body of water, an invisible entity conveyed that I must go through this water rite in order to find the key to the next passage.

Jumping into the water, I found myself consumed in a body of ether. Dancers were there to assist me in this rite, and they bent over in backbends forming a tunnel of light-bodies. Swimming deeply into the tunnel they'd formed, I emerged on the other end to notice that I was now holding a small metallic and rectangular object.

Instantly appearing, an old woman spoke. "The initiate has retrieved the key to the temple." Handing me a pile of books made solely of light, I was given to look upon their titles which indicated divine mysteries for which I was being given initiation: 'The Secret of the Sphinx,' 'The Secret of Ain Soph (Eternal State of all Things),' 'The Secret of my Spirit,' 'The Secret of my Inner Song,' 'The Secret of Bath.' Others were present which I was told not to mention.

Pointing to a hinge on the metallic object I'd retrieved, the old woman and I were taken away by a powerful spirit wind as soon as I touched it.

Flying to the sphinx, a doorway blew open. Temple guards stood by this door and all throughout the hallowed halls within. As we went inside, another sphinx appeared which revealed additional qualities of wings and two bull horns. Conveying to me that these aspects were present in the etheric plane on the sphinx, the old woman said that few living souls had ever seen it. Immediately, I noticed that the original sphinx held the image of the lion and man, while the formerly invisible horns symbolized a bull and the wings were that of an eagle. "The Four Corners of Creation," the old woman conveyed into my mind.

"In the center and around the throne, there were four living creatures covered with eyes in front and in back. The first creature resembled a lion, the second was like a calf, the third had a face like that of a human being, and the fourth looked like an eagle in flight."
New American Bible, New Testament, Revelations 4:6-8, (Christianity, Catholic)

Suddenly, an Indian man appeared before me, as the old woman quietly said, "He'll show you the five concentric circles . . . the secret of disintegration." Five circular ropes, hanging separately in the heavens, appeared. Another woman appeared and began to soar quickly through these loops, and as she did so, she disappeared. "Go!" The Indian shouted. "Within lies a secret, one that you must know. Go quickly or it will not work."

Walking over to the ropes, I began my ascent into them, but quickly fell to the ground because I was going too slowly. "The loops of dimensions will take you very far!" Calling out to me, the old woman encouraged me not to give up. Trying again, my spirit filled with strength as I soared through the loops, disappearing to the former dimension.

Before me was a pyramidal tomb chamber whose doors had flung open as I arrived. Quietly walking through the door, the triangular walls were speaking to me of the 'Watchers of the Earth:'

"Through their eyes, the Gods peer through, lighting forth Eternal Flame
Looking, staring, observing earth's youth, Watchers of the day
Ancient tonelage comes with a sound, a blink, a nod and a hoo (an owl)
The feathered beings peacefully observe, at night when they seclude

The wise one leads the many troops, the beasts, the trees and man
Through the eyes of innocence, the lighted beings glance
The leaf bearing beings, beneath the ground, feel all that lies under the dirt
At one with vibration, cognizant of Source, all are Watchers of the Earth
Two eyes adorning, from every place, the birds, the sheep and the mule
Even the cows, regarding their secret, all are Watchers of the Earth
The watchers stand stall, their beauty enhanced, by lights that fill up their eyes
Earth watcher vessels, in semblance form, their vision holds light of the wise"

Rumbling and quaking hit the room, as I noticed that the actual bodily chamber was placed in the center of the tomb, tightly sealed. A white lion appeared and roared very loudly, but I felt absolutely no fear of him. "Seer of thoughts," he said, "divine they may be . . . reach into your heart at this time, for what you are about to see holds mysteries . . . but the tomb will be empty." Unsealing and falling to the floor, the stone coffin was empty. "The immortal is what you've become!" the Lion shouted majestically, as the pyramid wall opened and guided me to exit the tomb.

"The King's and Queen's Chambers each contained an empty plain sarcophagus . . . Lack of inscription and decoration reveals that no royal mummies were ever placed in either of these two coffers . . . The presence of these . . . 'open tombs' indicates that the final state of everlasting life symbolized in these chambers will be attained through resurrection."

Pyramidology, (On the Great Pyramid), Book I, Chapter 4, Page 64 - 65, (Christianity, Pyramidology, Author: Adam Rutherford)

****

Standing before a huge stone wall, there were three choices engraved thereon. Allowed to remember two, they were 'Hoonlicha,' the way of life, and 'Horus,' the way of death. (Horus was the Egyptian god of light, who overcame darkness. He did this by dying a violent death, but was resurrected through the prayers of Isis, his mother.) The way of life presented a way to learn the same knowledge, with less suffering. Choosing 'Hoonlicha,' the stone wall opened.

"Descending passages, representing the way of death, are to be found in all Egyptian pyramids. But ascending passages leading to chambers up in the above-ground masonry, symbolising the way of life, exist in the Great Pyramid only."
Pyramidology, (On the Great Pyramid), Book I, Chapter 4, Page 63, Paragraph 2, (Christianity, Pyramidology, Author: Adam Rutherford)

****

A vortex appeared in the sky and as I soared to it, I was taken to my backyard where the gateway appeared. An Indian woman came through the gateway, holding her hands closed in front of her. Opening them, she held eternal waters which were formed in bodies, which she promptly gave to me. Closing her hands and soaring back through the gateway, a deer bobbed its head to see above the brush.

"Then the angel showed me the river of life-giving water, sparkling like crystal, flowing from the throne of God . . ."
New American Bible, New Testament, Revelations 22:1, (Christianity, Catholic)

"He said to me, 'They are accomplished, I am the Alpha and the Omega, the beginning and the end. To the thirsty I will give a gift from the spring of life-giving water. The victor will inherit these gifts, and I shall be his God, and he will be my son."
New American Bible, New Testament, Revelations 21:6, (Christianity, Catholic, Words of Christ)

****

Led by an unseen force towards the sun, a huge angel was sitting on a throne next to the solar orb, the 'Guardian of the Rite of the Light of the Sun.' Beginning to fly around the sun over and over again, fireballs of light began popping from its surface and into my soul. Taking in the immortal ethers, the Guardian remained silent until my time was finished. When this was so, she raised a single hand, as I was sent soaring back towards the Earth.

Hovering above my bed, seven angels appeared holding a clear cistern of the immortal waters which swayed to and fro like the ocean. Pouring this holy water down my throat, the level of the water inside the cistern never changed, as its supply was endless. Continuing for quite some time, my spirit felt as though it were being healed and replenished. Finished, they all began to glow brightly before they flew away.

"In front of the throne was something that resembled a sea of glass like crystal."
New American Bible, New Testament, Revelations 4:6, (Christianity, Catholic)

"Everyone who drinks this water will be thirsty again; but whoever drinks the water I shall give will never thirst; the water I shall give will become in him a spring of water welling up to eternal life."
New American Bible, New Testament, John 4:13-15, (Christianity, Catholic, Words of Christ)

****

Soaring to an ancient native pyramid site, tribal leaders who called themselves 'elementals,' stood around a fire pit. The first one said, "I am the mortal, I am the earth." The second one rose, "I am oneness, I am the water." The third one spoke, "I am the ascension, I am fire." And the fourth said, "I am immortal, I am the air." Singing an ancient native song, I listened intently and was pushed by an energy force to the floor, as they quickly picked me up and placed me by the fire.

Another native approached, "I image the heavens. I am Many Cloud." Beginning to change forms, Many Cloud slowly became a formation of clouds, as the other elementals immediately pushed my hand into this cloud. Feeling the mist, I also noticed a small metallic object which I pulled from the inside of the cloud which was a key of some kind.

Stepping forth, the immortal elemental said, "I am the choice you have made, let me show you all that will now change." With one feather in his hair, he stood before me, but began to shape-shift. First, he became a white-winged horse; second, he became an eagle; and third, he became a star. Chanting native songs, they began generating energies that were affecting my interior. Slowly, I began to shift into a white-winged horse, then an eagle and finally a star. Filling me with a profound understanding of the energetic properties in regards to the evolution of consciousness, it was clear to me that I was experiencing (in an energetic and elemental sense), the evolution of the spirit. (The white horse in revelations was described as faithful and true, which are elements required to begin the spiritual path. The eagle flies high above the delusions of the world, seeing things from the perspective of truth. And the star is the living life-force of all mortal life, capable of influencing the destiny of entire planetary systems.)

Growing very loud in their chanting, my spirit felt very strong at this moment. The elemental of air handed me a peace-pipe. As I smoked it, I became a huge oak tree. "You have taken the smoke of the mysteries," he said, "The oak tree is the father of the unknown." An owl appeared on my branch and began to sing songs: "Shamanic healing life-force pulse, feel the energy of the few, who reach by night to mighty stars, and bring to Earth the chosen few." As my spirit was being pulled away from the sight, the air elemental said with deep mystical import, "I wish I could lift the memory of the souls."

"The Universe, say the Desana, is made up of four basic elements: land, water, air and energy. These four ingredients are ordered and arrayed in an infinite number of combinations and constitute the essential ingredients of the entire cosmos and of the life-forms - including human beings - that animate it."
Wisdom of the Elders, The Building Blocks of the Universe, Page 57, Paragraph 1, (Tribal)

"Concentration is their citadel, empty silence is their palace, with the armor of benevolence, the sword of wisdom, the bow of mindfulness, the arrows of insight, they spread the canopy of spiritual power on high and raise the banner of knowledge."
The Flower Ornament Scripture, Chapter 38, Detachment from the World, Page 1132, Stanza 2, (Buddhism, Mahayana)

****

Thrust into a deep underworld ghetto, a man in a car was chasing me and shooting at me with a gun. Hitting my spiritual body, my spirit rose as if in death, but I failed to understand what was happening. Inherently, however, I realized that I had failed the first test. Knowledge entered, and I realized that in order to pass this rite, I had to ascend the body, rather than just allowing my form to die. Running through the streets as the man in the car again shot me, I used my will to alter my molecular structure and transfer form.

Immediately, I was on an island with two other men who asked me about what I do. "I live on the earth-plane, just as you might, but at night I go astral and learn of the light." Jumping in the water, we swam below the ethereal space cleansing our souls of the previous rite of passage. But upon return to the shore, I noticed a clam seashell. Opened, it had many tiny seashells inside of it. Showing it to my friends, they were intrigued, but afraid. Suddenly I felt knowing, and that I was being led into another ritual passage.

Holding it, I vibrated with purpose and was immediately transported back to the ghetto. Knowing that a 'Crystalline Statue of Eve' had been hidden by the Lord, I sought to find it so that my illusions would be broken and the mysteries revealed. Accompanying me, the two men who had been with me on the island were no longer able to recognize who I was, and would not be able to do so until I retrieved the 'Eve.'

Running through the streets alone, I was no longer afraid. Seeing the men up ahead, I ran towards them, but they didn't know who I was. Turning to go, I suddenly noticed something in one of their pockets, a shattered 'Crystalline Eve.' In thousands of pieces, only fragments remained of the solid form. Mourning the loss of this mystery, I suddenly realized that the 'Eve' was fully completed inside my own heart. Their shattered image was their own, for each of us has our own 'crystalline Eve.' Imagining the 'Eve' and I as one, the 'Crystalline Statue of Eve' appeared in my hands. Made of white quartz, her hair was blowing in the wind.

Everything suddenly froze in a time warp continuum, as a voice told me that the statue would remain with me as a symbol of my attainment, 'Master of Creation.' Remembering sacred words, I spoke them to receive further passage:

> "Whereupon, the days I mesh, into the stillness of the night.
> Forms of lifedom gaining quest, son of self, relinquish fright."

Sitting in lotus position again in the glen facing the invisible masters, a voice echoed. "Remember the moon, the sacred oath of the seer; never interfere with the laws of nature. In the natural selection, the free will of life, the 'Eve' manifests, only when asked. And most important, the seer must know, to *feel* a pure heart, and one not in growth." Vowing to heal souls, I bowed to the invisible masters, because I felt their presence. "You felt us," they said, "your oneness is wise." Reiterating their calling, the moon conveyed, "Your energy must protect the laws of nature." Asking for a solemn vow to serve the Earth from the energetic realms, I said, "I'll remain pure, I'll follow the law." "Remember the law is not always the same," they said, "purification requires many things." Energy determines validity of action, not moral judgment. Agreeing, I disappeared.

As Eve was the first to eat of the tree of the knowledge of good and evil, the world of karma, she guardians the journey for descendants. While a soul remains in karmic multiplicity, the 'Crystalline Eve' is shattered into hundreds of pieces, much like the soul; but as a spirit becomes pure it regains wholeness. And as we have been led upwards by those above, so shall we lead those below, in order to give back to evolution what it has given to us.

"When God created the universe, He ordained that this world should be served from the world above. Hence when mankind are virtuous and walk in the right path, God puts in motion the spirit of life from above . . ."
The Zohar, Volume 1, Bereshith, Page 186, Paragraph 1, (Judaism)

****

Seven angels came and placed a golden crown upon my head which was like an auric addition. "We give you the crown." They said, as they left me in peace.

"Let souls who are striving for perfection particularly adore My mercy, because the abundance of graces which I grant them flows from My mercy. I desire that these souls distinguish themselves

by boundless trust in My mercy. I myself will attend to the sanctification of such souls."
Divine Mercy, Notebook V, Page 560, Paragraph 2, (Christianity, Catholic, Words of Christ)
****

CHAPTER THREE
The Star Chamber, the Sacred Quartz Ball and the Mystery of Kaballah, the Seven Seals.

****

Looking ominous, I was afraid to go into the Star Chamber, which held within it stars traveling beyond light speed and interstellar forces of grand proportions. In order to pass beyond this point, I had to jump unafraid into the powerful energies within the chamber. One simple step would lift me up into a frenzied flow of stars at speeds beyond light. With caution, I stepped.

Swirling through what seemed like the outer reaches of space, the result was immediate, although I was actually in an enclosure of some kind. Stars cascaded throughout my form, as the energy of the stars permeated my spirit. Holding the vision, it passed just as quickly as it had come.

New chambers of passage appeared, as geometric crystals surrounded me and I began to melt into non-physical liquid ether. Flowing into and inside the interstellar crystals, my liquefied self meshed and took on the properties of their existence.

Pouring rapidly out, my now liquid soul formed a pool in the following chamber. Slowly solidifying, I watched a scene play before me in a 'Prehistoric Chamber.' Fighting for his life, a brontosaurus was fighting for his life against a large insect-like creature. Biting a part out of the brontosaurus's back, the battle continued. Mortal realms are by nature predatory, and it serves an evolutionary function.

Ceramic people with no heads appeared, as I quickly lifted the medicine to shoot a beam of light to destroy these false faces of humanity. Exploding everywhere, the false faces were destroyed as delusion ceased and reality set in. Stopping, I stood quietly upon the bank of the 'Black Hole Chamber.'

Looking down within it, I was overwhelmed, "I don't know if I can do this," I said. Taking one step forward would lead your soul to spiral down this black hole at speeds unimaginable in form. The final chamber was also the most frightening, but if I could only take just one step . . . it would be finished . . . I stepped.

Swirling down the vortex, I tumbled downward through the black hole where there was nothing but empty black space. Beginning to feel dizzy and euphoric, I was going really fast. Because the Star Chamber hadn't lasted very long, I expected this would be over soon. Swirling and swirling, however, I soon realized that there appeared to be no end to this black hole.

Panicking, I wondered, 'Could this be an infinite black hole? What have I done?' Dizziness beginning to change into an almost nirvanic Zen state, I began to laugh uncontrollably as I plunged. Everything was suddenly hilarious, and it felt as if a heavy burden had been lifted up off of my soul.

Thrust into a large room, a spiritual guardian awaited my descent, as I entered in a hysterical state of laughter. Many who had passed through before me were in a daze, having passed beyond the wild laughter stage and recouping their awareness. Within moments, I, too, was thrust into balance.

"Then Sudhana Climbed the path up the cliff of the mountain, a mass of razor edges, and threw himself into the fire. As he was falling he attained an enlightening concentration called 'well-established.' On contact with the fire he attained an enlightening concentration called 'mystic knowledge of the bliss of

tranquility.'"
The Flower Ornament Scripture, Entry into the Realm of Reality, Page 122, Paragraph 3, (Buddhism, Mahayana)
****

Seeking the sacred quartz ball, I knew I must find it to be delivered into the next level, and away from the energies of the past life I had chosen to leave behind. A golden pendulum hung around my neck, it was circular and upon it were inscribed holy words in Hebrew. It was the first of the two objects I had to retrieve for this unknown purpose.

Holding the golden pendulum around my neck, I began running almost aimlessly to find the sacred quartz ball, with the destructive energies from the world in quick pursuit behind me. If I didn't find it soon, I might lose this opportunity. Climbing the stairs of a long and darkened building, I could hear the pursuit behind me of that which sought to stop me in my quest. Increasing my speed, I sought out the highest point within the building, a closet within the attic.

Opening the creaky old door, I looked towards the top of the otherwise barren closet. In the farthest corner, a shimmering could be seen. Stepping up, I reached for the white ball I had found, inscribed with ancient Hebrew lettering. Holding it in one hand, I touched the golden pendulum in the other. As I did, a gate appeared before me with two indentations. One held the shape of the quartz ball and the other of the golden pendulum. Quickly placing the two objects within the gate, I disintegrated, and disappeared just in time, before the worldly sweep could stop me from my quest.

Entering a magnificent space without form or substance, within it was only knowledge. A voice told me, "You have entered into the mystery of the Kabbalah." Entering this mystery had sealed my Exodus, my exile was now complete.

"'Ye truly virtuous, enter and see, for permission is given you to enter as far as the place where the curtain is hung, happy is your lot!'"
The Zohar (Kaballah), Volume V, Shelah Lecha (Numbers), Page 133-234, Bottom & Top, (Judaism)

"When the Holy One created man He set in him all the images of the supernal mysteries of the world above, and all the images of the lower mysteries of the world below, and all are designed in man, who stands in the image of God."
The Zohar, Volume III, Jethro (Exodus), Page 229, Paragraph 2 & 4, (Judaism)
****

Placing a seed into my consciousness, I awoke with an interesting morsel of knowledge forming within my mind. However, I must beg you to take note that this is an attempt to interpret something given to me energetically, and the interpretation is not absolute as I share with you my simple understanding of a *small* part of the seed given to me regarding a *small portion* of the mystery of the seven seals in the book of Revelation, and it remains only a *miniscule* part of the mystery.

The seven seals, the seven chakras, the seven virtues, the seven major prophets, and the seven churches are the cornerstone of the sacred seals, according to what was shown my soul. Each of the seven seals represents a chakra, a virtue, a prophet and a church. The tribulations are the unique battles associated with the opening of that chakra in the body of an individual. The messages to the churches are not only messages pertaining to each of the great seven religions, but hidden messages regarding the keys each of the great religions hold to the awakening of the particular chakras they represent, and beyond this, the particular tribulations involved in the opening of each particular chakra. Each of the seven churches, the world's great religions, represents a tribulation (a soul struggle, if you will), which brings about one of the seven virtues, thus the opening of a chakra. This is why the seventh seal brings about the final peace, because it heralds completion; immortality, ascension, freedom from karmic circling. Thus, it leads to the eight; the Book of the Eights, which is the Book of Life or the Book of Immortals.

Although each religion honors the seven virtues or qualities individually, each of them hold a particular seal to one of the qualities, an energy of attainment, which is the cornerstone or 'key' of their teaching. (This can be interchangeable in regard to individual experience.) In order for a soul to comprehend the seven seals, he must first break the seals of the seven holy prophets, which unleashes the seven virtues, the seven chakras and the seven attainments. In doing so, a soul may then become able to grasp the energetic essence of their particular key of knowledge.

Unloosing the seven seals, brings about completion, a washing in the blood of Christ which cleanses our Earthly garments to white.

In order to understand this, you must follow the seven seals in sequence, the theological virtues in sequence, the manifestation of the prophets of God and their religions in sequence, the chakras, from the foundation to the crown, and their attainments in sequence. Beyond this, you must also follow it as a sequence of the evolution of humanity, gauging things as historical *and* spiritual evolution. For the Bible does not contain mere historical facts, but an allegorical tale of the evolution of individual souls.

Beginning with the seals, prophets, religions and virtues, afterwards I will outlay the chakras. In order to properly understand, you must conceive of the entire Revelation as an allegory of the initiation of a soul from karmic bondage to immortality. The words of the seals pertain to the natural base inclinations of individual chakras before they are opened properly.

(All of the following biblical quotes are from the King James Version of the Bible.)

"Write the things which thou hast seen, and the things which are, and the things which shall be hereafter; The mystery of the seven stars which thou sawest in my right hand, and the seven golden candle-sticks. The seven stars are the angels of the seven churches: and the seven candlesticks which thou sawest are the seven churches. (Chakras)"
Revelations 1:19-20

"And I saw in the right hand of him that sat on the throne a book written within and on the back side, sealed with seven seals. And I saw a strong angel proclaiming with a loud voice, Who is worthy to open the book, and to loose the seals thereof?"
Revelations 5:1-2

"And I saw when the Lamb opened one of the seals, and I heard, as it were the noise of thunder . . ."
Revelations 6:1

FIRST SEAL - Krishna (About 3000 B.C.) - Hinduism - Prudence

Krishna appeared upon the earth about 3000 B.C. In his teachings, which are documented in the Bhagavad Gita and other texts, he stressed our duty in life; in essence, prudence. As he spoke of reincarnation, the message of prudence became even greater, as he stressed how our deeds follow us from lifetime to lifetime. In order to transcend this Earthly rebirth, Krishna stated that one must become prudent enough to cease karmic activity through meditation and love of God. The goal, according to Krishna, *"O sinless one, the mode of goodness, being purer than the others, is illuminating, and it frees one from all sinful reactions. Those situated in that mode become conditioned by a sense of happiness and knowledge." Bhagavad Gita 14:6 (Translation by A.C. Bhaktivedanta Swami Prabhupada) But* before a soul may achieve such a state, he must first conquer his evil inclination. *"Sometimes the mode of goodness becomes prominent, defeating the modes of passion and ignorance, O son of Bharata. Sometimes the mode of passion defeats goodness and ignorance and at other times ignorance defeats goodness and passion. In this way there is always competition for supremacy."* Bhagavad Gita 14:10 *(Translation by A.C. Bhaktivedanta Swami Prabhupada)*, in this we see that prudence is vital to overcoming karma, and that a soul must be willing to go forth and conquer himself through prudence in order to transcend Earthly rebirth.

"And I saw, and beheld a white horse: and he that sat on him had a bow; and a crown was given unto him: and he went forth conquering, and to conquer."
Revelations 6:2

SECOND SEAL - Moses (About 1500 B.C.) - Judaism - Justice

Moses appeared on the Earth about 1500 B.C. In his teachings, which are documented in the Torah of the Old Testament, Moses was the vessel of Gods justice, as God said . . . *"When Pharaoh does not heed you, I will lay My hand upon Egypt and deliver my ranks, My people the Israelites, from the land of Egypt with extraordinary chastisements. And the Egyptians shall know that I am the Lord, when I stretch out My hand over Egypt and bring out the Israelites from their midst."* Exodus 7:4-5 *(Translation by the Jewish Publication Society according to the Masoretic Text)* And Moses fulfilled this command along with bringing in the direct commandments of the Lord which are contained in the Torah and explained by the ancient Jewish Rabbi's in the Talmud. Moses said, *"And if you do obey these rules and observe them carefully, the Lord your God will maintain faithfully for you the covenant that He made on oath with your fathers: He will favor you and bless you and multiply you."* Deuteronomy 7:12-13 *(Translation by the Jewish Publication Society according to the Masoretic Text)* God's justice and His commands regarding every aspect of our lives and our behavior are documented in the Torah, and explained beautifully by the Talmudic sages, along with the punishment which the Lord deemed worthy of each offense, and how this justice of God should be carried out. The laws of the Talmud are rigorous, and their punishments strict, many of them carrying a punishment of death. Because this was a warring time, the people were ensconced in battles amongst each other, but this battle is also an allegorical one which occurs within oneself, because every soul must slay their passions, their vice, their sin and their will, in order to be able to face divine justice.

"And there went out another horse that was red: and power was given to him that sat thereon to take peace from the earth, and that they should kill one another: and there was given unto him a great sword."
Revelations 6:4

THIRD SEAL - Zarathustra (630-550 B.C.) - Zoroastrianism - Temperance

Zarathustra appeared upon the earth about 630 - 550 B.C. He began to receive revelations from Ahura Mazda which translates to Lord Wisdom. In these revelations, Zarathustra was taught that there is a delicate balance between the forces of goodness and evil in our world, and that we must carefully guard our thoughts, words and deeds so as not to be tempted by forces of darkness. In the Avesta, Zarathustra taught, *"Each of the two spirits created in turn, the One created life and the other created absence of life, and this determined how the last shall be, the worst life for the wicked, the Best Mental State for the holy."* The Avesta 30:4 *(Translation by Ernestine G. Busch) Thus,* Zarathustra taught the delicate balance between light and darkness, temperance.

"And when he had opened the third seal, I heard the third beast say, Come and see. And I beheld, and lo a black horse; and he that sat on him had a pair of balances in his hand."
Revelations 6:5

FOURTH SEAL - Buddha (563 - 483 B.C.) - Buddhism - Fortitude

The Buddha appeared upon the earth about 563 -483 B.C. From the time he was a young man, he displayed a tendency towards deep meditation and reflection. Throughout his life, the Buddha displayed a most intensive fortitude in his search for the truth. One of his great epiphanies came about as he reflected deeply on a dead body. In this meditation he discovered that all life is impermanent and filled with suffering. Because the Buddha also taught reincarnation, he said that in order to end this round of rebirths, we must conquer the passions, subdue the cravings, and recognize through meditation on our own corpse, the impermanence of this life, nothing in this world is permanent, and all destiny in this mortal realm ends with death. The Buddha taught a very deeply reflective process of meditation which would extinguish the causes of rebirth, and subsequently, death. *"Through the total fading away and extinction of Ignorance, however, the Karma-formations become extinguished; through extinction of the Karma-formation: Consciousness (in a new birth); through extinction of Consciousness: Mind and Corporeality; through extinction of Mind and Corporeality: the Six Bases; through extinction of the Six Bases: Impression; through extinction of Impression: Feeling; through extinction of Feeling: Craving; through extinction of Craving: Clinging; through extinction of Clinging: the Process of Becoming; through extinction of the Process of Becoming (Karma-Process): Rebirth; through extinction of Rebirth: Decay and Death, sorrow, lamentation, pain, grief and despair. Thus takes place the extinction of this whole mass of suffering."* Path to Deliverance C Wisdom, S XII 17, Page 154, Paragraph 1 (Sutta Pitaka from the Pali Canon, Translation by Nyanatiloka) The Buddha showed immense fortitude in his determination to win the greatest battle of his life, conquering himself, and by doing so, conquering death. Some of the practices which are practiced by Buddhists and other religious orders to conquer these cravings are mortification's of the body, fasting, and deep reflection with the intent to subdue the beasts of vice which control our world. In so doing, they overcome death by overcoming craving to the mortal life and all that sustains it.

"And I looked, and beheld a pale horse: and his name that sat on him was Death, and Hell followed him. And power was given unto them over the fourth part of the earth, to kill with sword, and with hunger, and with death, and with the beasts of the earth."
Revelations 6:8

FIFTH SEAL - Jesus Christ (32 B.C.) - Christianity - Faith

Jesus Christ, the Messiah, appeared around 32 B.C. One of His greatest marvels was how He healed the sick through their faith in Him and the Father. He taught, among other things, that faith is what would bring the children of God back into His fold. *"Arise, go thy way: thy faith hath made thee whole."* St. Luke 17:19, Words of Christ (Translation: King James Version) The entire faith journey can be one of tribulation and suffering, until a soul cleaves to their faith in the Lord, and finds peace even amidst the suffering. *"It is a fearful thing to fall into the hands of the living God. But call to remembrance the former days, in which, after ye were illuminated, ye endured a great fight of afflictions; Partly, whilst ye were made a gazingstock by reproaches and afflictions; and partly, whilst ye became companions of them that were so used. For ye had compassion of me in my bonds, and took joyfully the spoiling of your goods, knowing in yourselves that ye have in heaven a better and an enduring substance. Cast not away therefore your confidence, which hath great recompense and reward. For ye have need of patience, that, after ye have done*

the will of God, ye might receive the promise . . . the just shall live by faith . . . "
Hebrews 10:31:38 (Translation: King James Version) Because of their faith, Christian martyrs went to their deaths confidently and with reverence. They had the greatest faith of all; they were willing to die for their God.

"And when he had opened the fifth seal, I saw under the altar the souls of them
that were slain for the word of God, and for the testimony which they held."
Revelations 6:9

SIXTH SEAL - Mohammad (570 - 632 A.D.) - Islam - Hope

The prophet Mohammad appeared upon the earth around 570-632 A.D. With him, he brought a message of hope regarding social and economic justice for all men. The world of Mohammad's era was deeply afflicted with vice and evil. Mohammad chastised the inequity between social classes and the injustice within the whole of their society. But for those who heeded his warning and listened to his words, Mohammad gave hope . . . *"O you who believe, if you keep your duty to Allah, He will grant you a distinction and do away with your evils and protect you. And Allah is the Lord of mighty grace." The Holy Qur'an, Part IX, Chapter 8, Section 4:29 (Translated by Maulana Mohammad Ali) "And Allah would not chastise them while thou wast among them; nor would Allah chastise them while they seek forgiveness." The Holy Qur'an, Part IX, Chapter 8, Section 4:33 (Translated by Maulana Mohammad Ali) For* those who were willing to stand amidst a world of peril, alone in righteousness, justice and equity, Mohammad brought hope. But for those unwilling to follow the commandments of the Lord, Mohammad did not bring hope, but fear and trembling. *"And those who break the covenant of Allah after its confirmation, and cut asunder that which Allah has ordered to be joined, and make mischief in the land, for them is the curse, and theirs is the evil end of the Abode." The Holy Qur'an, Part XIII, Chapter 13, Section 3:25 (Translated by Maulana Mohammad Ali)* Hope comes with a blessing and a tribulation, for to abolish evil in a soul requires great movement, trembling and change, for every part of the soul must be altered from that which it was before.

"And I beheld when he had opened the sixth seal, and, lo, there was a great
earthquake . . . And the heaven departed as a scroll when it is rolled together;
and every mountain and island were moved out of their places."
Revelations 6:12 & 14

SEVENTH SEAL - Baha'u'llah (1863 A.D.) - Baha'i - Charity, Love

Baha'u'llah appeared upon the earth around 1863 A.D. Baha'u'llah's message can be summed up in three words; charity, unity and love. Urging every man to guard his own conscience, he implored charity to one's fellow man. *"The word of God which the Supreme Pen hath recorded on the third leaf of the Most Exalted Paradise is this: O son of man! If thine eyes be turned towards mercy, forsake the things that profit thee and cleave unto that which will profit mankind. And if thine eyes be turned towards justice, choose thou for thy neighbour that which thou choosest for thyself. Humility exalteth man to the heaven of glory and power, whilst pride abaseth him to the depths of wretchedness and degradation." The Tablets of Baha'u'llah, Kalimat-I-Firdawsiyyih, The Third Leaf, Page 64 (Translated by Habib Taherzadeh) "We enjoin upon them that are the emblems of His names and attributes to firmly adhere henceforth unto that which hath been set forth in this Most Great Revelation, not to allow themselves to become the cause of strife." The Tablets of Baha'u'llah, Kalimat-I-Firdawsiyyih, Eleventh Leaf, Page 72 Translated by Habib Taherzadeh)* He implored people to honor and hold sacred all religions and to seek unity among them. *"He is, in truth, the Speaker on Sinai Who is now seated upon the throne of Revelation. He is the Hidden Mystery and the Treasured Symbol. All the former and latter Books of God are adorned with His praise and extol His Glory. Through Him the standard of knowledge hath been planted in the world and the ensign of the oneness of God hath been unfurled amidst all peoples."* The Tablets of Baha'u'llah, Tajalliyat, The First Tajalli, Page 50 (Translated by Habib Taherzadeh) Baha'u'llah, in his writings, speaks urgently of the need for souls to seek God themselves, and for them to embrace the merciful, charitable nature of the Lord, who requests only that we ask. *"O brother, we should open our eyes, meditate upon His Word, and seek the sheltering shadow of the Manifestations of God, that perchance we may be warned by the unmistakable counsels of the Book, and give heed to the admonitions recorded in the holy Tablets; that we may not cavil at the Revealer of the verses, that we may resign ourselves wholly to His Cause, and embrace wholeheartedly His law, that haply we may enter the court of His mercy, and well upon the shore of His grace. He, verily, is merciful, and forgiving towards His servants."* The Kitab-I-Iqan (The Book of Certitude), Page 217, Paragraph 1 (Translated by Shoghi Effendi) This unity, brings peace to all that is above and all that is below.

"And when he had opened the seventh seal, there was silence in heaven about the space of half an hour. And I saw the seven angels which stood before God; and to them were given seven trumpets. And another angel came and stood at the alter, having a golden censer; and there was given unto him much incense, that he should offer it with the prayer of all saints upon the golden alter which was before the throne. And the smoke of the incense, which came with the prayer of the saints, ascended up before God out of the angel's hand."
Revelations 8:1-4

The first seal and chakra, *prudence*, the base chakra - foundation.
The second seal and chakra, *justice*, the sexual centers, - morality.
The third seal and chakra, *temperance*, the emotional centers - balance.
The fourth seal and chakra, *fortitude*, the heart center - endurance.
The fifth seal and chakra, *faith*, the throat center - the Word.
The sixth seal and chakra, *hope*, the third eye chakra - knowledge.
The seventh seal and chakra, *charity/love*, the crown chakra - unity.

With the opening of the crown chakra and the unitive virtue, all is silent in heaven. After all the seals have been loosed in Revelations, the elect stand before God, marked with the holy symbol of immortality.

"After this I beheld, and, lo, a great multitude, which no man could number, of all nations, and kindreds, and people, and tongues, stood before the throne, and before the Lamb, clothed with white robes, and palms in their hands . . . And one of the elders answered, saying unto me, What are these which are arrayed in white robes? and whence came they? And I said unto him, Sir, thou knowest. And he said to me, These are they which came out of great tribulation. and have washed their robes, and made them white in the blood of the Lamb."
Revelations 7:9 & 13-14

The angels are then commanded to begin the final plagues which must hit the earth. But they are commanded to torment only those without the sign of God. The torments are not heavenly chastisements, but rather, the simple result of karma. Those engaged in vice and deadly sin, will reap the rewards of vice and destruction, until they turn to God.

"And it was commanded them that they should not hurt the grass of the earth, neither any green thing, neither any tree; but only those men which have not the seal of God in their foreheads. And to them it was given that they should not kill them, but that they should be tormented . . ."

Revelations 9:4-5

And the sign on the forehead is revealed in the spiritual or third eye which Paramahansa Yogananda called the seat of Christ Consciousness.

"The telescopic gaze of intuition. During deep meditation the single or spiritual eye becomes visible within the central part of the forehead. Great yogi's who live unbrokenly in the state of God-consciousness are able to behold it whether meditating or carrying on ordinary activities."

Man's Eternal Quest, Man's Greatest Adventure, Page 61, Footnote, (Hinduism, Author: Paramahansa Yogananda)

And the seven plagues which the angels were then commanded to let loose upon the earth are the fruits of the seven deadly sins: Gluttony, Lust, Greed, Pride, Sloth, Vanity and Avarice, and are as much an allegorical rendering of the actual appearance of a soul impaled by vice to heavenly forces, as it is a prophecy of the coming chastisements from God, plagues within a man's soul, which remain until they have been justly purified.

Within the seven seals of the Revelations there is great tribulation, but beyond the tribulation lies the reward of fighting the good fight, thereby, conquering the soul. And when a soul is conquered, it finds unity.

"Now there are diversities of gifts, but the same spirit. And there are differences of administrations, but the same Lord. And there are diversities of operations, but it is the same God which worketh in all . . . For to one is given by the Spirit the word of wisdom; to another the word of knowledge by the same Spirit; To another faith by the same Spirit; to another the gifts of healing by the same Spirit; To another the working of miracles; to another prophecy; to another discerning of spirits; to another divers kinds of tongues; to another the interpretation of tongues; But all these worketh that one and the selfsame Spirit, divine to every man severally as he will. For as the body is one, and hath many members, and all the members of that one body, being many, are one body; so also is Christ . . . For the body is not one member, but many. If the foot shall say, because I am not the hand, I am not of the body; is it therefore not of the body? And if the ear shall say, because I am not the eye, I am not of the body; is it therefore not of the body? If the whole body were an eye, where were the hearing? If the whole body were hearing, where were the smelling? But now hath God set the members every one of them in the body, as it hath pleased him . . . But now are they many members, yet but one body. And the eye cannot say unto the hand, I have no need of thee: nor again the head to the feet, I have no need of you . . . And whether one member suffer, all the members suffer with it; or one member be honoured, all the members rejoice with it. Now ye are the body of Christ, and members in particular."

1 Corinthians 12:4-27

"On earth God is trying to evolve the universal art of right living by encouraging in men's hearts feelings of brotherhood and appreciation . . . He has therefore permitted no nation to be complete in itself. To the members of each race He has given some special aptitude, some unique genius, with which they may make a distinct contribution to the world civilization . . . It is important to note that the great saints of history have personified the ideals of all lands, and have embodied the highest aspirations of all religions."

Sayings of Paramahansa Yogananda, Page 46, Stanza 2, (Hinduism, Kriya Yoga, Words of Paramahansa Yogananda)

Unity . . . the end point.

****

CHAPTER FOUR
Passing on the Knowledge, the Palace of Ancient Knowledge and the Task at Hand, 100 Steps to the Tree of Knowledge and Five Keys to Open it's Door, Stairway to Heaven.

****

Entering into the sky, my soul was quickly hoisted to a small location out of sight of the roving eyes of sub-conscious astral souls. Contained within this small room were several initiates into the mysteries who were now to receive certain energetic gifts and superhuman powers to assist the Lord of all creation.

The first initiate approached as I opened my hands, allowing the light to shine upon him. A breastplate and a staff appeared upon him; the shield of the Word, and the staff of knowledge. Bowing humbly, he turned to allow the next come forth.

A young woman approached who knelt before me as I placed my hand upon her back. Given the gift of wings and superhuman flight, she would work wonders and miracles with her ability to fly in the worlds beyond.

In a surprise move, the eternal suddenly beckoned me to a young boy whose mission in life had already begun. Wishing for the family of this ten-year-old boy to witness his initiation sub-consciously, father, mother and sister waited with eyes wide and open. Unaware of what was about to take place, I entered quietly and touched their boy. As I did, light befell him and he was filled with the power of speech. Skeptical of what had happened because there were no outward signs upon his body; the family didn't know what to think. Being given the gift of words through my hands, he shared a destiny similar to my own, except that he would use words in a different manner, that of speech. Because of the family's unbelief, I was directed to give them another sign that I had come on behalf of the Lord.

Soaring into the sky, above the trees and eventually above the clouds, they watched. And as they watched me fly, something clicked within their sub-conscious minds and they no longer entertained doubts. Sub-consciously they understood and they believed.

As my tasks with his family were finished, I quietly met with the boy alone to give him counsel. His eloquence was already manifesting, so my counsels only made him more aesthetically pleasing to God. Smiling with joy at this young charge of the heavens, I placed my hand on his shoulder in a loving gesture before I left him on my final flight home.

"Constantly with tactful methods he shall fearlessly preach the Law and lead incalculable beings to attain perfect knowledge."
The Threefold Lotus Sutra, The Sutra of the Lotus Flower of the Wonderful Law, Chapter VIII, Page 174, Middle, (Buddhism, Mahayana)

****

For several nights, my soul was given to observe aspects of my next task. Frantically writing, the energy seemed somehow different. Entering into the Palace of Ancient Knowledge, gold and white filled the space which was ornately decorated. Staircases of a grand whiteness were inlaid with gold as the oldest scrolls were kept on the first floor.

Taken immediately to a place within the palace I had not yet seen, my spirit was surrounded by filing cabinets stacked from the floor to the ceiling which was about thirty feet high. Every available space in this basement was filled, and I looked upon the cabinets with expectancy. A man and woman were waiting my arrival, immediately showing me a set of two smaller filing cabinets. "I've been summarizing all of these filing cabinets into two," the woman said, "and I'm almost finished. I'll be giving them to you very soon."

Allowing me to look into one of them, there were tens of manila folders, each labeled with deep aspects of many manifold spiritual mysteries. An element of science emanated from them, as well, which excited me. Looking at lists of spiritual/scientific concepts which were to come, I nodded that I would be patient.

Suddenly, my attention was drawn towards the other direction which was no longer part of this enclosed building, but a scene from somewhere . . . sometime. A man wearing the uniform of a revolutionary war soldier was running frantically across a grassy field towards me, calling out to me as if I were his daughter and he was trying to get to me before it was too late. Before he made it across the field, however, a shot rang out and he fell, almost as if in slow-motion, to the ground. In that millisecond, he was gone, and the mystery of his beckon would remain so . . . for now. Before long, such ancestral surges through the mists of time would again emerge to reveal their purpose.

The following night, a tiny animal which looked like a furry version of a prairie dog scurried in front of me, and as he passed, a series of ancient texts appeared. Encompassing the greater secrets hidden within the mysteries, he conveyed, "Although such things are available in your world, they are not well written. You are going to write about the mysteries and make them understandable to mortal men." Nodding in acceptance of this new task, he finished, "Remember what I said, it's important." Scurrying off into the night, energetic loops entered into my spirit from the ancient texts which lay before me, filling me with the energy of mystery . . .
****

Gathering amidst the ancient library, I found my soul drawn towards a large set of old texts which were about 8 inches in height and off-white in color. At the side of the room, a set of about twenty exquisite and large ornate Catholic statues of Jesus, Mary and various saints, were lined and painted with the utmost care and beauty. Observing their holiness, I continued towards the texts.

Appearing to be a series of papers on the mysteries, I walked towards them, suddenly noticing that upon the wallpaper of this deep cellar, an image of a secret door was opening. White and blue stripes lying vertical from the ceiling to the floor began appearing, overlaid by a mystic image in the shape of a square filled with angels, cherubs, gateways, golden ribbons, and other mystical mirages moving on the wall, as if it were a doorway.

Reaching towards it, I turned to notice that many of the Catholic statues had disappeared and only a few remained. Of those few, the paint was dripping off of them as if they'd been kept out in the rain before the paint had a chance to dry. 'I understand,' I thought, 'in my journey into the mysteries, I must be very careful not to lose the truth, not to allow it to be *watered down* by nebulous intellectualisms in my inquiry.' Loosening, the gateway which merged into the wall became fluid and penetrable.

Beginning to open the secret door, I suddenly noticed a man in a business suit approaching. *Instantly*, I *knew* he represented pure evil, but before I had a chance to respond, I was hit. Shuddering from the force of the attack, I awoke and began vomiting violently. Somebody, or perhaps some dark force, did not wish for me to enter into the mysteries and reveal them to the world.
****

And the filing cabinets of knowledge began to open:

Gazing across a large rocky plateau, there were a series of steps ascending in circular fashion towards a center point. At the center, there was a huge area of flat rock with a singular tree in the very center. A voice said, "There are 100 steps to the Tree of Knowledge." Pausing, it continued, "There are five keys to opening its door; Knowledge Wisdom, Understanding, Joy and Peace." As I gazed upon the mystical mirage before my eyes, the mists enveloped my spirit and whisked me away.

"Hear ye, these words of wisdom, hear ye, and make them thine own, find in them the formless, find ye the key to beyond. Mystery is but hidden knowledge,

know and ye shall unveil, find the deep buried wisdom, and be master of darkness and light. Deep are the mysteries around thee, hidden the secrets of Old, search through the KEYS of my WISDOM, surely shall ye find the way."
The Emerald Tablets of Thoth the Atlantean, Tablet VIII, The Key of Mysteries, (Egyptian: Hermetic, Words of Thoth)

"Within the mental sheath, made up of waves of thought, there is contained the sheath of wisdom. It has the same form, with faith as the head, righteousness as right arm and truth as left. Practice of meditation is its heart, and Discrimination its
foundation. Wisdom means a life of selfless service."
The Upanishads, Taittiriya Upanishad, 4.1-5.1, (Hinduism, Translator Eknath Easwaran)

"The Supreme Personality of Godhead said: It is said that there is an imperishable banyan tree that has its roots upward and its branches down and whose leaves are the Vedic Hymns. One who knows this tree is the knower of the Vedas."
The Bhagavad-Gita As It Is, Chapter 15, Text 1, (Hinduism, Translator: A.C. Bhaktivedanta Swami Prabhupada)

"Say: Is that (doom) better or the Garden of Immortality which is promised unto those who ward off (evil)? It will be their reward and the journey's end."
The Meaning of the Glorious Kuran, Surah XV, No. 15, (Islam, Translator: Marmaduke Pickthall)

"Say to Wisdom 'You are my sister!' Call Understanding, 'Friend.'"
The New American Bible, Old Testament, Proverbs 7:4 (Christianity, Judaism, Words of Solomon)
****

As my health had been deteriorating again, my doctor had made it clear I must get more rest. 'This could be the end,' I thought, but then paused. 'But it's more likely the beginning . . . ' I thought to myself, remembering how the Lord often brings me into much deeper levels of illness in order to make it possible for my soul to travel to ever deeper mysteries and realms of knowledge. Perhaps, the Lord again needed me to be on the edge of life and death, so He might be able to communicate with me all the better.

When you stand in the borderlands, on the wing of an angel leading to heaven but holding tight to the material realm for the sake of your children, something profound happens. You become a part of both worlds at the same time and knowledge can travel from heaven to earth through you.

Slipping off into a deep sleepy night, I awoke to notice that the huge Sacred Heart of Jesus banner on my bedroom wall was alit in golden yellow energy emanating from within and to the without. A staircase was inside the center where the picture of Christ is so carefully embroidered. It was so beautiful, I just looked at it awestruck. It was like being in an ecstasy.

I'd seen this once or twice before when I'd been shown a special mission being ignited between my son and certain priest. I enjoyed the vision of beauty as long as God would allow, and then I slipped back into sleep.

To my surprise, I was awoken again and saw the same thing. Again, I slipped back into sleep. And again, I was awoken about eight times that night to see this beautiful gateway in my bedroom.

First, I thought that certainly these were the stairs I would take at the moment my earthly sojourn was over to go meet my beloved Lord.

But secondly, I thought something else. Perhaps I was right. My illness had brought me back into greater seclusion and I required much more sleep. I was standing at the borderland, and the Lord was showing me a gateway to 'The Mysteries of Our Lord.'

Excitement filled me at the thought of being allowed to traverse those steps at some point and learn of those mysteries.

The golden glowing yellowish light continued as I slipped off into my final veil of sleep for the night grateful to witness the stairway to heaven which was now present and visibly placed within my own room.

And it was a heavenly witness to the fact that the initiations into the mysteries of our Lord and the universe in which we live are endless and they never end.

****

Visions of Jesus and the Saints

Mystic Knowledge Series

Compiled and Written by Marilynn Hughes

The Out-of-Body Travel Foundation!

www.outofbodytravel.org

CHAPTER ONE
Meetings with Jesus Christ, Star of Jesus, Place of Crucifixion, Holy Family, Blessed Virgin.

****

Entering into a realm of existence whose beauty was beyond words, the angel who had come for me and I sat atop two large gray rocks atop a hill in an iridescent plain of green grass and trees. Blue emeralds seemed to dot the sky as stars shot constantly to and fro across the dark sea-colored horizon. Feelings of love rushed through us; a playful, joyful love. And for a moment, I thought to myself that this place reminded me somewhat of the hill in Galilee where Christ taught.

Up in the distance, a man wearing a white robe and clutching a tall cane began to approach. "Oh, my God!" I thought, "Could it be?" Jesus of Nazareth approached as light emanated from every oracle of his bountiful spirit. Smiling peacefully, he sat on a rock in front of us and began to telepathically convey.

"My dear child, you asked to be filled with My spirit and I have come to fill you. I am the pulse of life and love. All that I Am is all that you can be." (Christ was not saying that I could be God, like Him, but rather, that the qualities that He personified in His existence as Jesus of Nazareth could be imitated by those of us on the Earth.) Responding, I cried, "I want to be like you, Jesus. I want to personify love." Lifting his arms up to the sky, I noticed the intensity of all that he created with a single movement of his arm. Shooting stars paraded from the sky like a palisade of ice in a winter mountain cathedral. "What I am is a thought on the canvas of life; I cannot be described in words, but felt through the soul." Intrigued, I said, "It is hard for me to understand. I am beginning to truly *feel* all that you have spoken. But it confuses me that so many speak your words with little or no feeling. I feel no understanding coming from them. Why?" Patiently, he replied, "The words of my incarnation as Jesus of Nazareth are vast and well-spoken among men, but their meaning is felt by only a few who have opened their hearts. Love is all that I am and everything I will always be, concepts cannot enclose me for I am vast when set free in the heart of man." Quieting, his light never waned in brilliance. "How can I become more like you, my Lord?" I asked. "Very good, my dear child!" he said, "a true yearning to know the truth. An open heart will hear the truth in whatever form it comes." A pause. "Set out to know me, not as a concept, but as a light within darkness, a touch when you're all alone, a true existence in the realms of consciousness. I am not dead, for I live in every crevice of every rock, in the rushing water of the streams, and all the pulsating rhythms of life. I am the consciousness of one known as Christ, and I love you greatly. Hear me call your spirit into service." "I hear you," I cried in ecstasy, "I want to serve God." "I know, my dear child, I know. What I am cannot be expressed through anything but love. Open your spirit and my spirit will flow ever so gracefully with your own for we are truly one. My guidance will help you in times of confusion." Reaching out to touch my shoulders, I knew His love was vast enough to encompass every living soul who only so much as asked for his true guidance, not out of fear, but out of love for Him. His peaceful eyes met mine, and I began to disappear.

"Jesus said, 'Come to me, for my yoke is easy and my mastery is gentle, and you will find rest for yourselves.' They said to him, 'Tell us who you are so that we may believe in you.' He said to them, 'You examine the face of heaven and earth, but you have not come to know the one who is in your presence, and you do not know how to examine this moment.'"

The Gospel of Thomas, No. 90-91, (Christianity, Gnostic/Essene, Words of Christ)

****

"The door of the lodge is soon opened for the second time, representing the coming of the purifying Power of the north, and also we see the light which destroys darkness, just as wisdom drives away ignorance."

The Sacred Pipe, Black Elk's Account of the Seven Rites of the Oglala Sioux, Chapter III, Inipi, Page 40, Paragraph 3, (Tribal, Oglala Sioux, Words of Black Elk)

And so it came to pass that my soul was honored with a vision beyond all lights. An ancient wooden door surrounded by sturdy beams was closed, and the Titan was portrayed in a statue of silver riding a winged-horse. Captured looking to the rear of the horse with an intense glaze in his eyes, I remembered the words of release. "Chorub Lee! Open forth the door of light!" Kneeling to the ground, I knew that what lay beyond this door was sanctified. "Bringeth forth the light of the planes!" I said, as the wings began flapping slowly . . . and then more . . . . increasing until they were flapping wildly and the horse and rider came to life and moved aside. Beginning to open, the ancient entry began to gleam with light as it burst through the cracks as the door slowly unsealed.

Standing in awe at what lay before me, tears were streaming down my eyes, as the most magnificent diamond shaped star appeared. Immediately, I knew it was the star of Bethlehem, the star of Jesus. A whooshing sound was heard as the star burst forth with light and filled me. Attempting to walk into the door, my spirit was pushed back by an unseen force. Solemn grace filled my soul.

"Where is the newborn king of the Jews? We saw his star at its rising and have come to do him homage."
New American Bible, New Testament, Matthew 2:2, (Christianity, Catholic)

"And behold, the star that they had seen at its rising preceded them, until it came and stopped over the place where the child was. They were overjoyed at seeing the star, and on entering the house they saw the child with Mary his mother."
New American Bible, New Testament, Matthew 2:9-11, (Christianity, Catholic)

****

Upon entering the place of initiation into the mysteries of the crucifixion, I was intrigued to note that one of the thieves who died next to Christ was the guardian of this ritual passage. Handing me paintings of Christ's death, I was horrified by the magnitude of his injuries and suffering. Beginning to cry uncontrollably, the guide told me that the cross represents the earthly life, while the nailing to the cross represents surrender to the divine will. Crucifixion is also symbolic of the soul's journey, in that the fragment must die to contain the Christ, the higher self. Showing an aura of blue around His head and face as He was crucified, it was brilliant and emitted passionate love for mankind.

Wishing to show them to others as they arrived, the paintings changed and became floral prints. Chastised for attempting to share them with the uninitiated, I became aware that energetic knowledge can be misused. (As per order of the Lord, no more shall be said).

"I have told you this so that you may not fall away. They will expel you from the synagogues; in fact, the hour is coming when everyone who kills you will think he is offering worship to God. They will do this because they have not known either the Father or me."
New American Bible, New Testament, John 16:1-3, (Christianity, Catholic, Words of Christ)

"So they took Jesus, and carrying the cross himself he went out to what is called the Place of the Skull in Hebrew, Golgotha. There they crucified him, and with him two others, one on either side, with Jesus in the Middle."
New American Bible, New Testament, John 19:17-18, (Christianity, Catholic)

****

"O ye My Branches! A mighty force, a consummate power lieth concealed in the world of being. Fix your gaze upon it and upon its unifying influence, and not upon the differences which appear from it."
The Tablets of Baha'u'llah, Chapter 15, Kitab-I-Ahd, Page 221, Paragraph 3, (Baha'i, Author: Baha'u'llah)

"For the yoke that weighed on it, the bar across its shoulders, the rod of its

oppressor, these you have broken . .
."

New Jerusalem Bible, Old Testament, Isaiah 9:3, (Judaism)

"Beloved, we are God's children now; what we shall be has not yet been revealed. We do know that when it is revealed we shall be like him, for we shall see him as he is. Everyone who has this hope based on him makes himself pure, as he is pure."

New American Bible, New Testament, 1 John 3:2, (Christianity, Catholic)

Soaring to a celestial realm beyond time and space, shooting stars cascaded across a deep emerald oceanic sky. Waves of rhythm could be felt in the canvas of sky that serenaded my soul as I stood on the ethereal ground below my feet.

Walking with peace towards the holy family, the sacredness of the moment filled me with a reverence for the Lord. The Holy Mother Mary, Joseph, and their son, Jesus Christ, were sitting upon a large stone bench amidst a plain of grass and trees. Jesus sat on the ground at their feet, looking upon them with reverence and love. As their robes lay motionless and surrounded in light, they looked up towards me. Mary gave me a peaceful smile, Joseph, a knowing look, and the savior emitted a familiar beckon.

Joseph calmly arose and walked towards me, his calm gaze never wavering. Opening his hands, he held a sacred amulet that had a large faceted diamond in the center, and a string of exactly eight small diamonds that surrounded it (which represented the immortal). Hanging this around my neck, I was surprised that it felt weightless. "You are now immortal," he conveyed to me, "there is only life, now." Intuitively, I reached into my own pocket, retrieving a heart-shaped rose-quartz pendant. Hanging it around Joseph's neck, I replied, "We are now forever love."

"Jesus said, 'Fortunate are those who are alone and chosen, for you will find the kingdom. For you have come from it, and you will return there again.'"

The Gospel of Thomas, No. 49, (Christianity, Gnostic/Essene, Words of Christ)

****

Night fell in the spaces beyond time, as a formless hand led my soul to a mysterious corridor. Unable to break free from the impending importance I felt, I began soaring down a blue-green tunnel until I reached a set of barren bleachers and sat alone. Out of the ether, the spirit of Jesus Christ appeared, his face exhibiting tremendous pain and torment, his hands and feet bound in metal shackles. But despite his tortured demeanor, light glowed all around him. A white robed man surrounded in light with a very long beard sat next to Jesus, whose features were barely perceptible. "It is your purpose," he said, "to release the bondage Christianity has put upon Christ's spirit." His powerful comment shocked me, and I didn't know how or what he had in mind. As I gazed upon Jesus' tortured countenance and his beckoning eyes, they both disappeared into the ether.

"But the seed of man hath not understood all of which Thou hast made it heir, neither have men known Thee whensoever Thou hast spoken."

The Dead Sea Scriptures, The New Covenant, Page 438, Paragraph 1, (Christianity, Gnostic/Essene)

Appearing from behind, another spoke. "Look at me!" he commanded, as I turned to look into his deeply intensive eyes. "What you have come to do carries a far greater significance than you know. Do you realize how rare it is to have someone with full consciousness on both sides of existence who resides primarily in the physical?" I'd taken that for granted, since it hadn't occurred to me that others did not live in this manner. "Express the music of your soul, your time has come." Beginning to waver into the ether, he whispered these words over and over again, "Far Greater Significance, Far Greater Significance, Far Greater Significance . . . ," and then he was gone.

"The psychic race is like light from a fire . . . through a voice it was instructed

*and this was sufficient, since it is not far from the hope according to the
promise, since it received, so to speak as a pledge, the
assurance of the things which were to be."*
The Nag Hammadi Library, The Tripartate Tractate, No. 14, Page 94-95, (Christianity,
Gnostic/Essene)
****

*"Do not think lightly of merit, saying, 'It will not come to me.' By the constant
fall of waterdrops, a pitcher is filled; likewise the wise person, accumulating
merit little by little, becomes full of merit."*
Dhammapada, Canto IX, No. 122, Page 51, (Buddhism)
"Behold the Lamb of God, which taketh away the sin of the world."
King James Bible, New Testament, John 1:29, (Christianity)

As I stood outside of my body upon the earthen bank, my spirit was directed to look towards the sky. My face became ecstatic, staring in a fixed state upon the heavens with joy and elusive wisdom. Utter peace filled me as the skies began to whirl and heave. A purple, blue and white vortex began swirling as the clouds began to part. From beneath their depths, the Mother Mary appeared.

Angelic mercy strewn towards me, my ecstatic state grew deeper. 'A New Journey.' She wrote with her finger into the clouds, 'The Final Chapter.' Nodding, the vortex pulled Mary back towards heaven. Feeling her winds slowly release my soul, I fell to the ground in awe. The next day, I found out that I was pregnant with my second child, a daughter, Mary.

*"If the most pure Mary has reached the highest pinnacle in the ranks of the just,
She may also on this very account be considered as the instrument or the motive
power through which the saints themselves have reached their station."*
The Mystical City of God (Abrid.), The Transfixion, Page 400, Paragraph 1,
(Christianity, Catholic, Author: Ven. Mary of Agreda)
****

On the ground below me I suddenly noticed two feet wearing old, old sandals. Looking up to see their bearer, Jesus Christ stood with light glowing all around His white flowing robes. Conveying to me great and wonderful things, He spoke of what I must do to fulfill them. Bowing to the ground, the Lord Jesus honored my soul with secret tasks. In obedience, I lowered my head to acknowledge my duty.

As the Earth began to tremble, a powerful being appeared before Him whose essence was airy and white. "I am Yammeth/Symmeth, he who controls the movements of the Earth." "Will you come with me to Exodus?" he asked. Not understanding what this meant, I simply replied, "Yes, I will." "You and I will go to Exodus alone!" he commanded, as the rumbling increased and he disappeared.

Jesus directed me to stand, and as I did He transformed what I was wearing into a gleaming white robe, much like His own. Feeling unworthy, I bowed my head down. "Retrieve the ancient texts," He said, as my mind filled with the vision of the sacred texts of all the world's religions throughout time, "all of them." Energy pulsed through me, as the Lord directed me to consider the part-time job I had recently taken. "I fear it was not well chosen," he said, "you now begin your Essene training; you must allow no defilements in your retreat." A huge pink and glistening cross appeared in the sky, adorned with jewels. "You shall never make a living from the cross," he said, as I began to understand that I was never to consider my work for the Lord as a means of financial support. "There are many ways in which abundance can come to you." Seeing financial support coming from many different avenues, but none from my own work, He began to disappear. "Retrieve the ancient texts," He repeated, and then He was gone.

*"Every man who in this world does not wrap himself in the ceremonial garb and
clothe himself therewith, when he enters the other world is covered with a filthy*

garment and is brought up for trial. Many are the garments prepared for man in this world, and he who does not acquire the garment of religious observance is in the next world clad in a garment which is known to the masters of Gehinnom, and woe to the man who is clad therein, for he is seized by many officers of judgement and dragged down to Gehinnom, and therefore King Solomon cried aloud, 'At all times let thy garments be white.'"
The Zohar (Kaballah), Volume V, Shelah Lecha (Numbers), Page 236-237, Bottom & Top, (Judaism)

"When God saw that his people would perish because they did not see the Light of Life, He chose the best of Israel, so that they might make the Light of Life to shine before the sons of men, and those chosen were called Essenes, because they taught the ignorant and healed the sick, and they gathered on the eve of every seventh day to rejoice with the Angels."
The Essene Gospel of Peace, Book Three, Page 19, Prologue, (Christianity, Gnostic/Essene)

****

His body was writhing as my soul watched this ancient sacred event taking place upon the Earth from above. Energetic bursts pierced His soul like lightning, as His body hurled and purged, accepting the living immortal energy that was now being forced into His body from His Father. Violently, He was accepting the finality of His destiny, relinquishing the parts of Him that were not ready for such an immense task.

Sweat poured from His brow into His thick mustache and beard, as more pulses of energy hit Him. He *knew* what the acceptance of these final vibrational thrusts would mean, that the Messiah would indeed be birthed and He would die to achieve the destiny of His coming. As the energy pulse slowed in completion, Jesus Christ allowed Himself to have one last peaceful slumber. In honor, I bowed to the invisible guardian who allowed me to bear witness to this incredible moment, and then I was gone.

"Watch and pray that you not come to be in the flesh, but rather that you come forth from the bondage of the bitterness of this life. And as you pray, you will find rest, for you have left behind the suffering and the disgrace. For when you come forth from the sufferings and passions of the body, you will receive rest from the good one, and you will reign with the king, you joined with him and he with you, from now on, for ever and ever. Amen."
The Nag Hammadi Library, The Book of Thomas the Contender, Page 207, Paragraph 3, (Christianity, Gnostic/Essene, Words of Christ)

****

Spiraling rock walls circled themselves until they reached a center point within. The ancient monument had secret columns and passageways below ground where I stood, but only the initiated knew how to get to them. Energies came and hit like torrents of wind from the ground beneath my feet, and the earth began to shudder and shake. Crevasses opened within the Earth and ancient artifacts were exposed to the top-most layer of the ground. Looking at them, I knew they held secrets and wisdoms from the ancient past. Little did I know, I was about to meet some members of God's royal family.

The earthquake ceased, but its quaking had laid me upon the ground, so I looked up, preparing to stand. Two bare feet stood before me with a singular hole in the center of each. I knew who had come, as I whisked myself to my feet so that I could bow to Christ, my divine visitor. Beginning to walk together, we quietly followed the spiraling columns from the farthest point out to the farthest point within, the core center. When we had reached this point, we stopped walking and Christ began to mutter sacred words. As He did, we immediately fell through the rock into the secret columns below ground.

Absolute calm was inside as hundreds of monks from all religions of the world were there awaiting our arrival. As the abbot approached, I noticed that some of the monks glowed very brightly with light, while others did not glow at all. It didn't seem to matter which faith the monks were from, for there were glowing and non-glowing monks of all faiths. Christ conveyed to me that the monks who glowed were true monks, while the others who did not were still in training to become 'true' monks.

Looking at me deeply in the eyes, he motioned to the monks who did not glow, "One must understand the isness. They do not understand the isness." Reaching to take my hand, I placed mine in his as Christ disappeared.

"Every perfect being naturally communicates itself to others so far as is possible, and this belongs to each thing in imitation of the first perfect being, namely God . . . but the good of a person is communicated to others both as regards being and as regards knowledge."

On Evil, Question IX, Page 339, Reply to 3, (Christianity, Catholic, Author: St. Thomas Aquinas)

****

CHAPTER TWO
Meetings with the Buddha, Christ, the Essene Christ, Beatitudes, Holy Rabbi's, Casket of the Dalai Lama's, Pistis Sophia, Mother Teresa, St. Francis of Assisi, Blessed Virgin, Bhikku Nanomali.

****

Brilliant air filled my soul, as the song of a particular Buddhist Sutra began exploding in melodious streams all around me, 'A Guide to the Bodhisattva's Way of Life,' also called, 'Bodhisattvacharyavatara;' the epitome of self-sacrifice on behalf of other living beings. My soul began dancing in flight to the musical stream. But almost as quickly as it had come, it stopped.

In the distance, I saw the outline of the Buddha sitting in a lotus position. The white descended. As it did, the Buddha approached me, floating through the air in the same position. Pulsing white energy throughout my spirit, I immediately felt complete and total calm. Conveying to me that he was now going to place me within the actual energy of three qualities of attainment, I surrendered in awe as the white and absolute serenity covered me in a blanket of solitude.

First, I was surrounded in wonderment.

Then, devotion.

And last, humility.

In these spaces, I knew isness.

With this experience also came a deep sorrow, humility and repentance for all I had done in my many lifetimes that caused harm to others.

Inherently, I understood that all religions serve a pathway, a cause in evolution. Following these very high roads requires a sense of true devotion in order to be understood, followed and embraced. Because they are ensconced in karmic purification, most souls cannot yet understand true devotion. Because their minds are deluded and misled, they may *intend* to be devoted, but their minds are incapable in their present state, of the discipline required to attain true devotion. A karmic soul serves the will of the self, while an eternal soul serves the will of the Lord. As Christ said:

"Thou shalt love the Lord thy God with all thy heart, and with all thy soul, and with all thy mind. This is the first and great commandment. And the second is like unto it, Thou shalt love thy neighbour as thyself. On these two commandments hang all the law and the prophets."

King James Bible, New Testament, Matthew 22:37-38, (Christianity, Words of Christ)

In the white energies of wonderment, devotion and humility, I saw my own vices and how displeasing they were to God, and in the same breath I was given to observe true virtue as it manifests among the heavenly realms. Looking upon great holiness and purity of heart, I yearned for it . . .

"The truly awake know all things, are nondual, beyond duality, all equal, inherently pure as space, not distinguishing self and nonself. As the ocean reflects beings' bodies and is therefore called ocean, enlightenment reflects all mental patterns and hence is called true awareness."
The Flower Ornament Scripture, Manifestation of the Buddha, Page 1011, Stanza 1-2, (Buddhism, Mahayana)

****

Thunderous roaring was heard in the backdrop as a column of monks quietly walked forward chanting the mystical songs of their secret knowledge. Lightning flashed, and rain began to fall as a monk approached and took my hand. "Come," he said, as he led me away.

A flash of light knocked me flat on my back. Looking up, Christ was standing above me waving his arms over my body and soul, exuding vibrational power beyond any I'd ever known. As he continued, my soul became more and more detached from worldly vices; lust, greed, vanity. "What are you doing?" I asked Him. "Purification." He replied, conveying that final purification is a process one undertakes when true devotion is finally achieved. Coming about not of your own hands, but by the hand of God, it comes when a soul is truly repentant and seeking only God's will. When one attains true devotion, this alters the path of the seeker from walking in selfishness, to walking with God.

As Christ continued laying his hands upon me, I felt absolutely tranquil. Going on for hours, when it was over, He quietly said, "You will not be able to explain, it cannot be understood unless you have passed through it." Nodding, I made a move to get up. "Retrieve the ancient prayer books," he said, as suddenly I was whisked into the energy of the Rosary Novenas. So holy that they swept my soul into the air in a state of levitation, I'd never seen them before, but knew they were of the Catholic faith. Overwhelmed, I grasped onto the wisp at the end of their holy reign. "I will." I said. Smiling, Jesus disappeared.

"(Let) the greatest sinners place their trust in My mercy. They have the right before others to trust in the abyss of My mercy. My daughter, write about My mercy towards tormented souls. Souls that make an appeal to My mercy delight Me. To such souls I grant even more graces than they ask. I cannot punish even the greatest sinner if he makes an appeal to My compassion . . . before I come as a just judge, I first open wide the door of My mercy. He who refuses to pass through the door of My mercy must pass through the door of My justice . . ."
Divine Mercy, Notebook III, No. 1146, Page 420, (Christianity, Catholic, Words of Christ, Author: Sister M. Faustina Kowalska)

****

Hovering over my sleeping body, the Buddha transported me into the white spaces. Various alternating patterns of energy barraged me for hours as I saw three frames of energy depicted in pictures, whiz by me over and over again. The first was two Buddhist priests, and one martial arts master. The second was two martial arts masters, and one Buddhist priest. The third, I can no longer remember. Alternating for several hours, the patterns changed back and forth between each vision.

When it was over, the Buddha disintegrated and a Buddhist priest arrived with no fanfare. Wearing a simple brown monk's robe, his serenity was complete. Bowing to him, he said, "I will take you into the energy of the 'Absolute Dissolution of Body and Mind,'" he said, as I bowed again.

Five white energy vortexes surrounded me all at once, spinning a power I could never have fathomed. Becoming the most profound experience of my life to date, the energies of the Absolute Dissolution of Body and Mind relinquished all personality, mind, ego, and self, placing me directly within the mind of God where my soul had begun.

In this space, my wholeness and unity with God was so complete, there was no me; and therefore, there were no desires emanating from me. From this absolutely clear vantage point, I viewed my life and found that despite the fact that I'd always considered myself a reasonably good person, *everything I'd ever done in my life was wrong.* Even those things I'd done to help others bore selfish desire whether it was the need for approval or wanting to be perceived in a certain way, nothing I had ever done in my life had been done for the sole purpose of glorifying the holy will of God; not one thing. Even acts of goodness were done to fortify myself, and despite the fact that some good intentions did exist, every act of my life was tainted by selfish desire.

Bowing in shame, I was overwhelmed by the selfishness of my life. But in this space there wasn't judgment, only compassion and understanding. God knows the path a soul must take to reach the absolute. My walk into karma had been necessary in order to emerge into the light, but a soul cannot serve itself *and* God.

Coming out of the absolute dissolution of body and mind, the Buddhist priest was quiet and calm. "Please!" I begged him. "Show me how I may repent, how may I purify myself of these things?!" Pausing, he placed his hands upon my shoulders. Holding a serious and ominous look, as if he was afraid for me, replied, "You seek a very high level of purification, few seek this level, most retain much darkness within their souls." His face told me that he was trying to convey more than he had already shown and this frightened me. "I want to purify *all darkness* within my soul." I said. Nodding, he replied very calmly, "A dark goddess lives within you, and you must force her out."

Panicking, I tried to remain calm, but this revelation shocked me. Beginning to feel the essence of this dark creature rising from deep within my stomach, the priest walked forward and began performing an exorcism. Feeling her come upwards through the energy centers of my soul, she reached my vocal chords in a plaintive wail. Not wishing to be forced out, sweat poured through me as my thoughts raged towards God's will. After what I had seen and felt about my selfish soul, I could never turn this process back, for the presence of such darkness appalled and shamed me. When her screams had stopped, I turned to the priest. "Is she gone? Is she completely gone?" "These things take time," he said.

"Thy will be done!" I shouted to the Lord, as I awoke.

"Jesus, on seeing a crowd rapidly gathering, rebuked the unclean spirit and said to it, 'Mute and deaf spirit, I command you: come out of him and never enter him again!' Shouting and throwing the boy into convulsions, it came out . . . When he entered the house, his disciples asked him in private, 'Why could we not drive it out?' He said to them, 'This kind can only come out through prayer."
New American Bible, New Testament, Mark 9:25-29, (Christianity, Catholic, Words of Christ)

****

As I stood amongst a crowd of hundreds, despite my wretchedness, the Lord still saw fit to allow me to wear the white robe of Essene training that Christ had given to me. Even so, I felt extreme sadness, as the sins I had committed against my Father seemed too great to bear. Offending Him, offended me. Remorse total, I'd sunk into a state of total depression.

Off in the distance, I saw Jesus administering to the multitudes. Turning, He came to me. "You know why I am so pleased with you, Marilynn." "I do?" "Yes." Looking down, I bowed in shame. "You could not possibly be, my Lord. I have sinned against my Father with selfishness and pride." Christ smiled. "The wretchedness you feel is an essential part of purification, but it is not how you are perceived by your Father." "Oh?" I replied softly, as His beautiful lips formed a smile. Taking my hand, we flew through the white ether. "I'm taking you to meet one of the messiah's," He said.

Sitting upon a rock, Christ conveyed the importance of a man who had lived during the 20th century in Europe without renown. Recently, he had passed over.

Calling him a messiah, the man began to speak of my recent initiations, when he suddenly paused and spoke very slowly. "You know, I wanted to be a professional tennis player." Remembering my own desire to be a professional musician, I listened carefully. "But then I took ill." Realizing our similar plight, I noticed that he paused for a very long time. "The Lord has a way of healing us," he said. Stopping, he turned as if to leave, but for a moment looked my way again. "Then I became a messiah to the people." He disappeared.

God's will is unseen and moves mysteriously to the ways of the world. Christ placed me back into my body, and He was gone.

"And Jesus had not told his disciples the total expansion of the emanations of the Treasury, nor their orders, how they are extended; nor had he told them their saviours, according to the order of every one, how they are."
Pistis Sophia, First Book, Page 2, Paragraph 1, (Christianity, Gnostic/Essene)
****

Death came suddenly in the night as a plummet through worlds. Knowing not where my soul would go, I was not afraid, but within the recesses of my mind, I did not know if this was a true physical death, or yet another spiritual one. Unknowing made my emergence into the ancient cave all the more grand.

Above me on a ledge, ancient robed beings stood in a circle surrounding me. Holiness apparent, I was humbled and I bowed to pray. As one, they spoke. "We are the Beatitudes." They said. Honor amassed within me, as I realized that the words of Christ known as the Beatitudes were not just words, but an actual energy of attainment. Hearing the words resonate within my soul, I bowed as they disappeared.

"Blessed are the poor in spirit, for theirs is the Kingdom of Heaven. Blessed are they that mourn, for they shall be comforted. Blessed are the meek, for they shall inherit the Earth. Blessed are they which do hunger and thirst after righteousness, for they shall be filled. Blessed are the merciful, for they shall obtain mercy. Blessed are the pure in heart, for they shall see God. Blessed are the peacemakers, for they shall be called the children of God. Blessed are they which are persecuted for righteousness sake, for theirs is the Kingdom of Heaven. Blessed are ye, when men shall revile you, and persecute, and shall say all manner of evil against you falsely, for my sake. Rejoice, and be exceedingly glad: for great is your reward in heaven: for so persecuted they the prophets which were before you."
New American Bible, New Testament, Matthew 5:3-12, (Christianity, Catholic, Words of Christ)
"May my life be loyal and true, that in death I may find only beatitude."
The Way of Divine Love, Chapter VI, Page 161, Paragraph 3, (Christianity, Catholic, Author: Josefa Menendez)

Jesus Christ and the Buddha were floating towards me in a cavern. Christ was bearing a hymnal, and I could hear angelic choirs begin singing a very simple but powerful hymn. In four part harmony, the angels resonated throughout heaven in a resounding chorus of 'Holy Love.' Handing the hymnal to me, I understood his wishes. Opening the hymnal, the angels began singing even louder. "Holy love . . . holy love . . . holy love . . . holy love - Gloria!" Looking up at Jesus and the Buddha, I understood that there was a oneness between their paths. Although Christ was indeed the Messiah, it was made known to me that the Buddha was a significant teacher within the Royal Family of God. (The Royal Family of God consists of the prophets, saints, mystics and sages of all the world religions, as well as, the holy hidden ones, people who serve the Lord without notice.) Beyond this, there was a oneness within all of God's holy paths. "I understand." I said, closing the hymnal. "I will bring in your hymns, Jesus, and I will unite the East and the West." Smiling in approval, Jesus said, "Your writings will be as scripture to the next millennia, and your hymns a pathway to the eternal." They disappeared.

As I returned to my body, an angel began repeating the first stanza of the Lord's Prayer into my ears: "Our Father, who art in Heaven, Hallowed be thy name. Thy Kingdom come, Thy will be done, on earth as it is in Heaven . . ."

"We, verily, have made music as a ladder for your souls, a means whereby they may be lifted up unto the realm on high; make it not, therefore, as wings to self and passion."
The Kitab-I-Aqdas, Page 38, No. 51, (Baha'i, Author: Baha'u'llah)

****

Walking quietly into the past, the marketplace was not overly crowded. Gazing at a very old apartment building, I was looking from the back at two balconies, one on each of the two levels. A golden door and window adorned the upper level, and those made of old and beat up wood on the floor below.

Turning away from the building, I walked towards the traders and buyers in the streets, selling their wares and sacred items from the temples and synagogues. Up in the distance, I saw a sight that immediately caught my full attention, a rabbi in full ceremonial dress. Approaching me, his holiness was so apparent that I was staring. My rude gaze did not disturb him, but rather, he quietly pointed to a book sitting on a table in front of me. Its title read, 'Exodus.'

Picking it up, I felt disgust, horror and filthy rage all at the same time. Articles of clothing from Jews who had died during the holocaust of World War II were pasted on each page. But my initial grisly response waned, and in its place I felt a certain elevation. Knowing that this book held a great secret, I waited.

In the book, the 'Exodus' was death, and death was deliverance. Perhaps the greatest act made by the souls of the Holocaust was their surrender to God's will amidst the great evil that would be their end. In the face of torture and death, they loved the Lord thy God with all thy heart, with all thy soul, and with all thy mind. Fearing nothing but His abandonment, walking forth to their torturous deaths, they were unmoved in their faith, love and devotion to Him whom they served.

Perhaps this was the difference between the first and second level of the apartment building, some experienced this horrible outrage on the ground, while others were elevated to a holy sacrifice because of their faith. Some achieved the Exodus even before they died.

"So far concerning this mystery. Old man, old man! As thou has started to sail on the wide sea, go on boldly in all directions and breast its waves! I have now to reveal something more. I said that the 'redeemer,' when he enters into the 'vessel,' lets his spirit cleave to that 'vessel,' so that nothing is lost, not even the breath of the mouth. This is quite correct. Old man, old man! If thou art to reveal mysteries, speak out without fear!"
The Zohar (Kaballah), Volume III, Mishpatim (Exodus), Page 309, Paragraph 1, (Judaism)

****

Kneeling before a holy altar, awe filled me as I looked upon a magnificent golden engraved casket. A very ancient man stood at guard before this oval casket, I knew this by the garb he wore and the expression upon his face. Indicating that he'd guarded this it for a very long time; he motioned me to rise from my humbled position. "This is the casket which holds the energies of all the Dalai Lama's throughout time." Motioning me forward, he continued, "In recognition of your service to the Lord, you are being given this gift. You may proceed forth and *touch* the casket." Magnificence filled me as this was a remarkable honor, and I understood that the casket contained the energy of the *knowledge* of all the Dalai Lama's. Walking forward, I bowed down, rose again, and gently placed my hand on the lid of the casket. Tears struck my eyes as the vibration filled me, but I could only stay for a moment. Granted only a moment of the thunderous vibrations, the ancient man nodded as I turned to leave the holy place. Nodding back, I conveyed gratitude.

"The founder of our spiritual legacy, the mighty Buddha Shakyamuni, first gave birth to the altruistic aspiration to achieve highest enlightenment in order to be of maximum benefit to all living beings . . . All of his teachings can be subsumed under two categories: those of the Hinayana, or Smaller Vehicle; and those of the Mahayana, or Great Vehicle . . . In the first of these vehicles he revealed the means of achieving nirvana, or liberation from cyclic existence, which is accomplished through transcending the belief in a truly existent self . . . In the second category of teachings . . . the Buddha mainly emphasized the methods for eliminating the self-cherishing attitude and replacing it with universal love and compassion."
Training the Mind in the Great Way, Point One, Page 45-46, Bottom & Top, (Buddhism, Tibetan, Author: Gyalwa Gendun Druppa, The First Dalai Lama)

"When seeing a Buddha's tomb, they should wish that all beings be honored as a shrine and receive the offerings of celestials and humans. Reverently gazing at the shrine, they should wish that all beings be looked up to by all celestials and humans. Bowing their heads to the shrine, they should wish that all beings be exalted beyond the view of gods and men. Circumambulating the shrine, they should wish that all beings act without offense and develop omniscience. Circling the shrine thrice, they should wish that all beings diligently see the Buddha's path without indolence of mind."
The Flower Ornament Scripture, Purifying Practice, Page 328, Stanza 1-5, (Buddhism, Mahayana)

****

Taken to a theatre where a band was performing, they sang of only one topic, the 'Pistis Sophia.' In their songs, they told the story of a young woman who would sing of the Way to bring others to it. Living by a lake, one day she walked into the lake with her beloved singing for the deliverance of mankind. But on this day, the bank had changed dramatically and she fell off of the edge into the depths of the waters. Sinking very rapidly, she was gone too quickly for her beloved or anyone else to save her. Pistis Sophia did not struggle, but surrendered her spirit to the depths. As she fell to the bottom of the lake, she never stopped singing of the Way and she dedicated the vessel of her former life to the development of the Way in others. It is said, according to their song, that you can hear her soulful chanting in the wind when it sweeps across the lake; and that if you hear her, that Pistis Sophia is calling your soul to the development of the Way.

Swaying to the beautiful, yet eerie sounds, I hardly noticed it when my hands began to bleed as if two nails had been plunged right in their center. Knowing this to be a grand honor, I looked upon my hands with shock, and the band members began to come towards me, despite the fact that I was sitting amongst hundreds of souls. In joy and elation, a woman from the band said, "It is said that if your hands bleed when we sing of her, that you are the Pistis Sophia." Two other women in this crowd bore the sign, as well.

All of a sudden I saw an image of the Buddha and the Pistis Sophia blending together into one being. Not understanding any of what was going on; all I knew was that the Pistis Sophia is an ancient sacred text.

In the Pistis Sophia, Pistis Sophia is not a person, but rather, a guardian of the twelfth realm of lights who seeks to attain to level thirteen. Because her power in the twelfth realm can only be given by Christ, and there was a time when Pistis Sophia failed to live the Way and her divine protection was removed, she became vulnerable to the chaos realms below. Awakening, Pistis Sophia awakened and sought deep repentance. Praying that Christ would save her from the destruction and chaos, He listened and returned her as guardian to the twelfth realm with all the divine protection the post afforded. However, in order to earn this protection and redemption, she had to unravel several mysteries that lay within the Psalms of the Bible. In those Psalms, according to the Pistis Sophia, lie the map of the eternal order and the mysteries of heaven.

One more question was posed to my soul. "Do you have a little girl of holy birth?" As my second daughter Mary, had been announced by the Holy Mother, I nodded, 'Yes.' Saying that this was the second sign of the Pistis Sophia, she handed me a small statue of the Virgin Mary and requested service of me.

"And at the commandment of my Father, the First Mystery which looketh within, I myself went down into the chaos, shining most exceedingly, and approached the lion-faced power, which shone exceedingly, and took its whole light in it and held fast all the emanations of Self-willed, so that from now on they went not into their region, that is the thirteenth aeon. And I took away the power of all the emanations of Self-willed, and they all fell down in the chaos powerless. And I led forth Pistis Sophia, she being on the right of Gabriel and Michael. And the great light-stream entered again into her. And Pistis Sophia beheld with her eyes her foes, that I had taken their light-power from them. And I led Pistis Sophia forth from the chaos, she treading under foot the serpent faced emanation of Self-willed, and moreover treading under foot the seven-faced basilisk emanation, and treading under foot the lion and dragon-faced power. I made Pistis Sophia continue to stand upon the seven-headed basilisk emanation of Self-willed; and it was more might than them all in its evil doings. And I, the First Mystery, stood by it and took all the powers in it, and made to perish its whole matter, so that no seed should arise from it from now on."
Pistis Sophia, Second Book, Page 117-118, Bottom & Top, (Christianity, Gnostic/Essene, Words of Christ)

****

And so it came to pass that I was whisked away by a Buddhist priest into a deep space. Beginning to manipulate the physical form of my spirit, he formed my body in several postures to achieve states of concentration. "You will now experience the seven levels of concentration," he said. When we reached the seventh level, my head was bent backwards towards my legs which had pulled upward in the form of an oval. Each level of concentration brought more peace and serenity to my mind, and this practice seemed to actually transform seeds of rage and violence that lay within me. As my spirit began its descent back into the body, a brilliant bright purple and green light began pulsating before my vision. Sucked directly into this light, my spirit underwent a very different vibrational raising as I became one with these lights.

Upon return to my body, the purple and green light transformed itself into a huge yellow golden orb. Seeing within its mass several Buddha worlds or aeons, I observed the heavenly realms with wonder and delight.

"It is only the Tathagatas and Bodhisattvas who are firmly established on the seventh stage who can fully understand its workings. Those earnest disciples and masters who wish to fully understand all the aspects of the different stages . . . by the aid of their right-knowledge must do so by becoming thoroughly convinced that objects of discrimination are only seen to be so by the mind . . ."
A Buddhist Bible, The Lankavatara Scripture, Chapter VIII, Page 324, Paragraph 2, (Buddhism)

****

In my bedroom, I had not yet separated from form when I saw some people coming after me who had wanted me to remain trapped in the world of vice. Quickly, I darted out of my body, trying to gauge what I should do.

From behind me, someone grasped my arm and gently pulled me away. Looking upon his face, I sighed in wonder. The Dalai Lama, the fourteenth, was leading me to safety. "I will take you into exile . . ." he said, fulfilling the prophecy that I would go to Exodus alone. In a moment, I was stashed safely away in a Lamasery, a cave where monks often go to meditate.

"It is better to lead a solitary life; there is no companionship with a childish person! Let one live alone committing no sin, having few wishes . . ."
Dhammapada, Canto XXIII, No. 330, Page 129, (Buddhism)

******

Wandering through a high mountain in a rainstorm, a man appeared beside me to take me to an unknown destination. Following him, he led us to a white building sitting atop the crest of the mountain. Inside, there was a small room whose walls were covered with my future paintings. "They appear to be dry," I said to the man, "would it be alright if I take them home, now?" He nodded that I could.

In the corner of the room there was what appeared to be a doll house, but when you got closer, you could see that it was a replica of a nun's convent. On the front of the house, there was a plaque that read, "Sisters of Charity." I recognized that name, as they were the nuns who'd worked on behalf of Mother Teresa to help the poor all over the world.

As soon as I opened the tiny front door, Mother Teresa appeared at the other side of the room. Looking up to see her glowing eminence, I immediately began sobbing great tears of joy and holy honor. Walking quietly, no one could mistake the obvious relevance she had to God, as this was a truly holy woman.

Stepping softly so as not to disturb her, I came closer and held out two stones as gifts; an amethyst and a crystal. Falling to my knees, I bowed at her sanctity. Turning to look at me, I instinctively handed her the two stones. "No," she said without reproach, "take an ordinary stone, my child." Placing a simple rock into my hand, its edges were rough. "Hold it within your hand," she said, "rub it and caress it so that someday from the wear of your hands it will be smooth. By the time that rock is smooth, my child, you will know what God wants you to do . . . you will know." Smiling, before she quietly walked away, she left behind her sacred message of simplicity.

"Let Him empty and transform you and afterwards fill the chalice of your hearts to the brim, that you in your turn, may give of your abundance. Seek Him. Knowledge will make you strong as death. Love Him trustfully without looking back, without fear. Believe that Jesus and Jesus alone is life. Serve Jesus, casting aside and forgetting all that troubles or worries you, make loved the love that is not loved."

The Love of Christ, Part III, Page 75, Paragraph 3, (Christianity, Catholic, Words of Mother Teresa)

******

In our side yard was a huge pig-pen; inside it, a pig about twenty feet tall. Serenely, the Lord Jesus walked towards the gate conveying that this pig was the true energy of people attached to the world, who despite His constant efforts, continued to deny God. Opening the gate, the pig ran away, disappearing into the ether. "Let the pig go." The Lord Jesus instructed.

"Do not give what is holy to dogs, or throw your pearls before swine, lest they trample them underfoot, and tear you to pieces."

New American Bible, New Testament, Matthew 7:6, (Christianity, Catholic, Words of Christ)

Our new baby appeared on my lap, as I was hugging and loving her. Multitudes appeared before me, complaining that I must do more, that taking care of my children was not enough. The Lord Jesus approached the multitudes, "Look how she loves this child, how she cares for this seed from My own mind. It is good." Disappearing in annoyance, the people were gone.

"What else do you do, my child?" Jesus asked. Shrugging my shoulders, I conveyed that I surely didn't do enough. "Let me tell you what you do," the Lord said, "you maintain a breathing operation, your job is to spin the wheel of karmic retribution, and you are the overseer of the souls coming and going." Honored, I stared at Him in silence.

Knowing that it did not matter what Earthly men could see, I realized that all that mattered was that I continue to do God's will, unseen and unheard, as only a quiet whisper upon the wind when Earthly souls would begin their crossings, and as a loud thunderous thud of karmic retribution when God guided them to awake. Before He left, He asked that our home be transformed into a monastery for the Lord.

"Those in this stage, worthy of human and celestial respect, become lords of the heaven of timely portion, carrying out celestial justice; they withdraw beings from the tangle of views and accumulate good for the sake of enlightened knowledge."
The Flower Ornament Scripture, Chapter 26, The Ten Stages, Page 735, Stanza 4, (Buddhism, Mahayana)

****

Christ stood at the foot of my bed when I awoke. Seeing Him made me feel joy, and I begged to ask Him a question. "My Lord," I asked quietly, "am I fulfilling Your will, am I doing what You wish for me to do?" Entering into a portrait that I had painted of Him, He lifted the lips to create a smile, as suddenly, a wave of information came upon me. Gladness exuberated from Him in regards to the fact that I had a true desire to fulfill His will. Fulfilling things according to His wishes, He also wished to convey that despite the simplicity of my paintings, they contained within them the life of the spirit. They were as He wished. Bowing to Him, He disappeared.

"Many times a deep and fervent gaze upon Christ is the best prayer. I look upon Him, He looks upon me, is the most perfect prayer."
The Love of Christ, Part I, Page 6-7, Bottom and Top, (Christianity, Catholic, Words of Mother Teresa)

****

Preparing to enter a bus, I was wearing a white robe and waiting my turn. All the others in the line walked quickly by the driver who presented them with a stole, and walked further onto the bus. When I entered the bus, I saw the driver and bowed to him in tears. St. Francis of Assisi placed an all-white stole around my neck to match my Essene robes. "I am honored," I said.

Sitting down in a prayerful position, St. Francis glanced over at me and began to come closer. Feeling the honor of receiving this stole from the beloved saint, I noticed that I was beginning to disintegrate. Looking up at him one last time, he whispered, "Pray for souls." It was a gift given to my soul honor of prayers made on behalf of others. At that moment, I fully understood how powerful intercessory prayer truly is, and that it brings about awakenings that arguments never could.

"A soul of prayer can make progress without recourse to words, by learning to listen, to be present to Christ, and to look toward Him."
The Love of Christ, Part I, Page 6, Paragraph 3, (Christianity, Catholic, Words of Mother Teresa)

****

Listening to prayers and recitations in the out of body state, the Dalai Lama arrived with two women who had very long black hair. Demonstrating a proper respectful posture towards God, they called it a 'Muslim' look. Conveying that there are times when this is called for, the Dalai Lama changed the music to some very serious chants. As they began, he started singing "Falalalalalalalala," in a simple scale pattern, laughing in its wake. Conveying to me the balance of sacred respect, repentance, and reverence; he then reminded me that God also wants us to be joyful in His name.

"That joyous happiness of yours would be a source of joy, not something prohibited, a precept given by the Excellent Ones and a supreme (means) for assembling others."
A Guide to the Bodhisatva's Way of Life, Chapter VI, No. 77, (Buddhism, Tibetan, Author: Shantideva)

****

Getting lost in a dark realm, some nasty spirits had come to trick me. Confused and scared, I didn't have any idea how to escape from this plight, so after running this way and that, I simply stopped. Allowing the weight of my spirit to completely surrender, I expected to fall to the ground in a huge thud, but instead, as I surrendered to Christ, I shot like a rocket away from this horrible place, now standing in the center of two large mountains.

A doorway of light opened in the sky as Mary quietly appeared. Taking me on a journey to all the sites of her visitations in the 20th century, she allowed me the grace of seeing her as she had appeared in each place. Humbled, I asked, "What may I give to you, Holy Mother, for this wonderful grace you have given me?" "Pray for souls," she conveyed as she disappeared.

Standing before my spirit, the Lord Jesus was asking me to do something for another soul. Expressing hesitation because of my illness, which remained undiagnosed, I knew doing this would cause me great pain and suffering. "Nothing is ever too much to give," He said. Nodding in shame, I apologized for my momentary selfishness. Appearing with a picture of the Pieta, a statue formed by Michelangelo depicting the scene where Christ lay dead in His Mother Mary's arms, two angels handed it to me. "This is a gift given to those who understand the true meaning of sacrifice."

Holding the picture, Jesus began walking towards me, and in His arms, He carried the Blessed Virgin as a baby. "I am as much a father to her, as she is a mother to me." He said. "In a sense, she is my daughter and I am her son, because in our uniting, we give birth to one another."

"By the law of nature, there is no pleasure in suffering; but Divine Love, when It reigns in a heart, makes it take delight in its sufferings."
The Voice of the Saints, The Meaning of Suffering, Page 122, No. 5, (Christianity, Catholic, Words of St. Alphonsus Liguori)

****

Surrounded in the vile defilements of sin, I didn't know what to do, so I called out and surrendered to Jesus, as I immediately soared to a place within a mountain's hold. Although it wasn't our present home, it appeared to be one we might live in someday. (We were being given the initial clues which would eventually lead us to this place, which we have since done, and we remain there.) Inside, there was a small plaque that represented my work with music. But looking outside the window, the ancient sacred texts appeared to be the size of mountains and they completely surrounded the house like a cloak of armor. It appeared that the Lord was conveying that my musical path was small in comparison to the work involving the ancient sacred texts.

Soaring outside, a cloaked man stood in the mountain path. Initially, I reach toward him to unveil who he was, but then stopped. "I don't want this," I said, "I only want Jesus." Appearing in the sky and enveloping its entirety, His image was displayed much like an old Catholic icon. At his feet was a message. "JESUS. Sitting Sin Stings." Chastised for my recent vanity, Jesus knew that I'd gained a great deal of weight since pregnancy which I'd been unable to get off. Annoyed that I had given so much time to such a vain pursuit, rather than accepting my imperfections and focusing entirely on God, I didn't yet understand the meaning of 'Sitting Sin Stings.' 'Sitting in Sin Stings?' I thought, not understanding the message it held for my soul, but I soon would. "I'm sorry, my Lord," I sighed to the heavens. Afraid to find the mysterious meaning of this message, I awoke ashamed and fearful of its impending truth.

"The death from which you flee, that will surely overtake you; then you will be sent back to the Knower of the unseen and the seen, so He will inform you of that which you did."
The Holy Qura'n, Part XXVIII, 62:8, (Islam, Words of Mohammad)

****

Wandering outside of form, my experience in regards to sitting in sin had plagued my mind, and my fears being diminished, I now truly wanted to understand the deeper meaning of the message Christ had come to give. Recognizing the monk who walked ahead of me, he had passed from the Earth two decades earlier, and was responsible for translating several of the most important Buddhist texts from the Pali canon into English. Wearing modern clothing, his head remained shaven in the acceptable manner of a Buddhist monk. Turning to me, he conveyed that I should study his translation of the work, 'The Path of Purification,' also known as the 'Visuddhi Magga.' Bowing to him, I nodded that I would. "Your writing, as it is done at this time, will be completely redone, and the Lord wishes for you to add quotations from the ancient sacred texts of all world religions to the current work." Further clarifying that the work was to be done with the basic theme of Purification as expressed in the Visuddhi Magga, the work should illustrate the ancient texts experientially.

Studying the text made me aware of ignorance remaining within my soul which was causing the rise of karma. Dependent Origination, a Buddhist concept, became known to me. All phenomena arise from causes which we generate. Rather than panic because of Christ's message, I now sought to know it deeply. Because in seeking to unite with God, we cease generation of karmic result, energizing the proliferation of ignorance, whose causes must surface in order for them to be overridden in the quest for a higher destiny.

"With the arising of cankers, there is an arising of ignorance."
The Path of Purification, Chapter XVII, No. 36, (Buddhism, Theravadan)
"Ignorance is an outstanding cause of kamma that leads to unhappy destinies . .
. But craving for becoming is an outstanding cause of kamma that leads to
happy destinies."
The Path of Purification, Chapter XVII, No. 39-40, (Buddhism, Theravadan)
****

In peaceful surroundings, the monasteries upon the top of the mountains had beckoned my soul as the snow had blanketed us in. No man aside from the monks roamed these solitary areas. Visiting both Buddhist and Christian monasteries, I went to several that night where I learned of the many practices, prayers and rites that the monks were to follow.

Following their lead, I fell to the ground in hours of meditation, prayer and various penances for the Lord, but in each place, a number of the monks were impure, and indicated that such a level of discipline was unnecessary. Staring at me while I was bowed in prayer, I wouldn't leave my position of communion with God. Approaching to tell me that although this was the way the practices were meant to be done, there was no need for me to do them with such zeal. Discipline weak and hearts not purified, these monks were untrue.

Among the Buddhist and Christian monasteries, I realized that they were very much alike, and among the *true* monks, there was very little difference between them. (In my waking life, I didn't observe such a strict discipline as I am a mother.)

Preparing to leave, an old Catholic monk came to me whose hair had long since vanished, a few white strands remaining. Removing his cloak, he placed his hand upon my shoulder and with great sincerity, he said. "You are a true monk, you are the Lord's child, I see," concern filled his eyes, as he continued, "but the fact that some monks are not purified, makes an Earthly monastery incompatible to you. It is this that makes it important that you create your own monastery wherein you may serve God as God pleases." Directing me to be aware of the solitude of these places, the mountainous snowy setting was secluded from mankind. "You must live as they do, but in your own setting. You must be prepared to make great changes on behalf of the Lord." With this, my spirit was sent away. (Again, he is referring to the home we did eventually find and make into our own monastery.)

"The Lord himself knows that in the last period there are (to be) wicked monks
who do not understand mysterious speech. One will have to bear frowning
looks, repeated disavowal (or concealment), expulsion from the monasteries,
many and manifold abuses. Yet mindful of the command of the Lord of the world
we will in the last period undauntedly proclaim this Sutra in the midst of the

congregation."
Saddharma-Pundarika or the Lotus of the True Law, Chapter XII, Page 261, No.'s 16-18,
(Buddhism, Nepalese)
****

CHAPTER THREE
Meetings with the Druid, Padre Pio, Mother Teresa, Jesus, Paramahamsa Yogananda, St. Joseph, St. Michael, Mother Mary, Writer of the Urantia Book, Sri Ramakrishna, Devaki - Mother of Krishna, Abdu'l Baha, Baha'u'llah, St. Therese of Lisieux .

****

As my spirit was hurled down a waterfall, an old white-haired druid with a long beard appeared above. Handing me a large staff, I knew that it represented the energies of the ancient sacred texts throughout time, which the Lord had ordered me to retrieve. Reaching, I grasped tightly to the end of the staff as I accepted their energies and the responsibility that entailed.

But just before I was outside of hearing range, the druid spoke. Conveying to me a sacred responsibility regarding the texts, I accepted and understood.

Suddenly, I was dead, and my tasks were complete. Although it appeared that I had died before my work was finished, this was not the case.

"The Torah remains only with him who is prepared to slay himself for its sake."
The Talmudic Anthology, No. 370, Stanza 1, Zohar, ii, 158b: c, 279a, (Judaism)
"Therefore, in order to benefit all beings I shall give up this body without any attachment . . ."
A Guide to the Bodhisattva's Way of Life, Chapter VIII, No. 184, (Buddhism, Tibetan, Author: Shantideva)
****

A vision of light which honored my very tears at his presence, Padre Pio, the stigmatized priest who was truly a saint of our century, appeared to me conveying many things. Many tears were falling down his face and as he wiped them away, he told me that his tears had come about because of people's indifference to Jesus' pain.

Still suffering from his wounds (stigmata) which were given to him during his life, Padre Pio looked very frail and ill. Asking him if praying for him would help, he told me that we should always pray for people because sometimes the Lord grants what we ask. "Your devotion is good in God's eyes," he said, "a soul who thinks about God is dear to Him." Wanting me to know that he had been watching over my soul long before I even knew of his existence, he said that he had given me his blessing November 7, 1995, over 1 1/2 years ago. Honored by his care for us, even before we knew of his holy existence, I bowed to him in thanks.

"'How careful men should be,' he said, 'to abstain from sin and to watch their actions, for at many periods the world is judged and every day deeds are placed in the balance and examined on high and recorded before the Almighty; and when the deeds of men are not approved before the King, wrath arises and judgment is awakened. But if when the executioners of judgment are ready to strike and wrath impends, there is found in the generation a righteous man who is inscribed above, then God looks upon him and His wrath is mollified."
The Zohar (Kaballah), Volume V, Korah (Numbers), Page 239, Paragraph 3, (Judaism)
****
"A man who has obeyed one commandment is helped by Heaven to obey many commandments."
The Talmudic Anthology, No. 108, Paragraph 7, Mekilta Beshallah, (Judaism)
"People say: be the first to tell the low thing about thee."

The Talmudic Anthology, No. 146, Humility, Page 195, No. 2, Baba Kamma, 92,
(Judaism)

My impatience could not be paled as I awaited the arrival of the supremely holy guest. Padre Pio was coming and this large gathering of sub-consciously astral souls were awaiting his guidance about their spiritual journey. When he arrived, however, many were quite disappointed.

Padre Pio arrived with no fanfare, and sat upon a stone underneath a podium. Many souls were kneeling before him, as he gave them the blunt truth regarding their souls. As one brother approached, the Padre made no excuse for his directness. "You are a user, and you cause all sorts of harm to others to get what you want. You will crap all over anybody to get what you want." Furious, the man left. Another approached, and Padre Pio had little to say. "For you, there is nothing at all. Nothing is there at all." The voidness of her soul was clear from his words.

As my turn to listen to the saint came, I was unconcerned. After all I'd been through, I thought I was truly pure and purely clean, so his words came as a stunning surprise. "Your practices are better than nothing," Padre Pio said, "but most of your practices are much too shallow. You should get into the practices much deeper." My thoughts were scattered and worried, "Better than nothing?" I asked, as the Padre offered no comfort to my soul in realizing that my efforts towards God were still quite minimal. "Practices?" I thought, "What does he mean by practices?"

Determining to spend more time in prayer and meditation, I also begged to do my daily duties with more fervor and focus. Everything that we do can be uplifted to a higher deeper level, by making God a part of it.

"They, however, heavy with sleep, hardly hear the voice of Jesus, they barely perceive Him as a faint shadow, so much so that they are not aware of His countenance all disfigured from the internal agony which tortures Him."
The Agony of Jesus, II, Page 22, Paragraph 2, (Christianity, Catholic, Author: Padre Pio)

"This life is a master novel, written by God, and man would go crazy if he tried to understand it by reason alone. That is why I tell you to meditate more. Enlarge the magic cup of your intuition and then you will be able to hold the ocean of infinite wisdom."
Sayings of Paramahansa Yogananda, Page 66, Article 2, Paragraph 2, (Hinduism, Kriya Yoga, Words of Paramahansa Yogananda)

****

Mother Teresa approached me quietly, "I want you to experience the Presence within the Eucharist." She said, as she quietly turned to walk away.

"Divine Blood, spontaneously Thou flowest from the loving Heart of my Jesus; the flood of pain, the extreme bitterness, the steadfast perseverance which He sustains press Thee from that Heart, and sweating from His pores Thou dost flow to wash the earth!"
The Agony of Jesus, IV, Page 32, Paragraph 1, (Christianity, Catholic, Author: Padre Pio)

****

Soaring through space, my soul was led on a journey to the places upon the Earth wherein Jesus had walked during his life. Remembering many flashes of scenes before His tomb, Gethsemane, and places he had walked, I was only allowed to remember that this had occurred, but the details were taken from me. Jesus had spoken to me, but I wasn't allowed to hear what He had said.

"For God so loved the world that he gave his only Son, so that everyone who believes in him might not perish but might have eternal life. For God did not send his Son into the world to condemn the world, but that the world might be saved through him."
New American Bible, New Testament, John 3:16, (Christianity, Catholic)

****

Pulling me from within the confines of sleep, people from India were awaiting me with many other souls who were here to be shown truth of a profound nature. Standing beside six crypts, they began to talk of the saints of the Hindu faith. Telling us about their countries of origin, their deeds and their lives, I found myself immediately enamored and fascinated by them.

Without warning, they opened the first of the six crypts. Inside the crypt was the body of one of these Hindu saints, completely incorrupt, completely intact. "Praise be to Him," a woman spoke, "for when a soul finds something they didn't previously know, it is grand." Looking at his body, the Hindu saint looked as though he had just passed, although his death had taken place long before. I was stunned, because the question of the Catholic incorruptibles had been on my mind for quite some time. Opening the other five crypts, the remaining Hindu saints were found to be preserved in a similar fashion.

Several of the souls who had been led to witness this miracle were asking questions, and I awaited my opportunity to ask mine. Coming towards me, the leader said, "You have a worthy question, ask it." "Well," I responded, "this incorruption has occurred in Catholicism to its saints for thousands of years. From what I am being shown it appears that this incorruption occurs to saints of other world religions, as well." Pausing, I tried to form my thoughts. "I wonder what this means?" The male guide took my hand and smiled as my soul filled with questions. Honoring the importance of my inquiry, he led me closer to look upon the body of the first saint. At the time I didn't know who he was, but later upon seeing a picture, I knew it to be Paramahansa Yogananda. About to answer my question, my soul began feeling the pull and tug of the eternal. "No, please!" I shouted. "Let me stay long enough to find the answer to my question!" But my spirit was tugged back to my body.

"The Great Being saith: O well beloved ones! The tabernacle of unity hath been raised; regard ye not one another as strangers. Ye are the fruits of one tree, and the leaves of one branch."
The Tablets of Baha'u'llah, Chapter 11, Lawh-I-Maqsud, Page 164, Top, (Baha'i, Author: Baha'u'llah)

****

A narrow pathway had led me to small house in the woods. Upon the door, it said, 'The House of Jesus.' Walking in, it was a beautiful monastery in honor of Jesus, and especially of His sacred heart. Reminding me of my own home which had been turned into a personal monastery, a large statue of Jesus was placed on an altar in front of me. Arms outstretched, Jesus' sacred heart was shining from His chest like a beacon of light.

Becoming animated, Jesus stepped off of the altar and came towards me. Smiling, He conveyed happiness in regards to my devotion to making our home a monastery in His honor. Holding a T-shirt in His hand, it had written upon it biblical words, 'Upon this rock, I will build my church.' Instantaneously wearing it, the words were emblazoned upon my back. Smiling again, He turned to re-enter the altar. "You may rest here in My house." Jesus said.

For many weeks following, I awoke each night in this holy House of Jesus, greeted by the outstretched arms of my Lord, wherein He conveyed to me how much we must change in order to become compatible to the holy kingdom, for each of us is wretched in our own right and none of us pure enough to enter without intensive alterations which can only come about through divine intervention inspired by prayer.

Allowing me to see some of the Christian martyrs, their holiness filled me as he gave me the name for my house, 'Many Mansions Monastery.' Created to honor all of God's holy religions, the many sacred receptacles throughout time were brought together in this house.

"Jesus Christ, addressing Peter, said, 'Thou art Peter, and upon this rock I will build my church.' This utterance was indicative of the faith of Peter, signifying:

*This faith of thine, O Peter, is the very cause and message of unity to the nations
. . ."*
*The Promulgation of Universal Peace, 30, April, 1912, Page 65, Middle, (Baha'i, Words
of Abdul Baha')*

****

Standing before a stage, a small upright piano was placed on the floor below in this darkened theatre. An old man had come as my teacher, and he insisted that when it came to words, I was failing. Initially, I didn't believe him, but as he continued to insist, I realized that it must indeed be true. How I was failing at words was a mystery to me. Insisting that if I were willing to go through a long and arduous process, I could pass 'words' with flying colors, I agreed, feeling within me the hard and long path that lay ahead. Leading me to the first of a series of ritual passage, the old man stood before me as a large monolith of sentences appeared.

Cylindrical and round, much like a Buddhist prayer wheel, words were boxed into little compartments on a circular base which turned and spun. Apparently, these were my words, and the old man began highlighting my mistakes all of which were descriptives and adjectives. Angry at his seeming severity with my words, he had highlighted *so* much, but as I thought more carefully, I came to a state of acceptance. Eventually, it was abundantly clear that I was doing something inappropriate with words, although I didn't yet understand what it was. Reflecting upon the 'prayer wheel' from which the words came, it occurred to me that all of our words could be considered as prayerful, since they do ascend into the ether. If this were so, then *all of* my words could be deemed prayerful. And if this were so, then my words were most definitely failing, because I'd spent much too much time in idle conversation and, unfortunately, gossip.

Awakening in an icy river which also had flames coming from it, I was almost naked, wearing only my underwear. Sitting amongst this extreme hot and cold, I thought of the saints who had undergone severe austerities on behalf of others. Getting up, I returned to the old man who was awaiting me on the bank. "Enduring severity will be required in your path in life," he said. A set of steps appeared from the piano to the stage and they were shaped very much like pyramidal steps to a higher point. Handing me a container of liquid filled to the top, the old man had me begin walking, spilling a tiny bit. Immediately reproaching me, the old man said, "You cannot spill any of it." I would have to walk these steps from the floor of the theatre to the stage without any agitation or lack of focus, because the water was of the Holy Spirit and our journey to God could not be taken properly without total focus and the will to maintain every single drop of this great grace.

As I passed to the stage, a huge textbook landed upon my lap and the keys to the piano became large enough to walk upon. Carrying the huge and very heavy textbook which contained knowledge in the proper use of words, I began walking from the midpoint of the keyboard towards the high notes. Careful not to overlap any of the keys, with each step the contents of the textbook came into my soul. Despite this energetic journey, I was not allowed to actually *read* any of the book. Later, I would discover that this holy book was the Talmud (Jewish Writings of the Ancient Rabbi's), which contains detailed instructions in the use of words and proper speech, among other things. Attaining to the highest note, I stood upon the stage again in a place the old man called the world of dreams.

In front of me lay three sets of clothing strewn on individual chairs, each representing a choice. The first was very ornate Victorian clothing which I immediately knew to mean opulence and greed. The second was a pair of pajamas which I immediately knew to represent love and comfort. The third was a set of work clothes, whose meaning I didn't immediately understand. My instinctual drive was to go towards the work clothes because they seemed the most appropriate in our world, but the old man gave warning. "*Those*, I know, will take you into a spiral of chaos." Realizing they represented worldliness, I turned towards the pajamas. "Well," I said, "it seems obvious to me now, the only way into the world of dreams is through the pajamas." Putting them on, I was given a small blank card which held three separate distinct lines, and on them I was to write my three greatest dreams in the order of their importance.

Thinking of music, I inherently understood that my choices must be of a higher quality to pass through this ritual. On the first line I wrote, 'wisdom.' On the second line I wrote, 'love.' Pausing, I was unsure of the third line, but then it came to me. 'Service,' I wrote. Issuing from above with a very cryptic message, a voice said, "Go give service, then you will know how the Lord wishes you to serve."

Returning to sleep that same night, it was conveyed that I had undergone one hour of a two hour rite and was halfway through it.

Swept away to help a woman who was dabbling in the occult, I reached her just as she was about to try to communicate with the dead relatives of two women who had approached her in her séance. Appearing to her in native dress, I had come as a Medicine Woman. "Never try to speak to the souls of the dead if you don't know whether or not any of them are damned." I said.

Shocked by this revelation, she backed off, but she wanted to know the meaning of my attire. "Live as the Indians did, but within the modern world, this will bring balance."

Swept before the entry of our home, an amazing sight stood before my soul. About forty feet high, St. Michael stood as a winged man wearing the garments of a warrior. But his essence was a dark, smoky substance which I knew to be the energy of the wrath and justice of God. Behind him, St. Joseph appeared twice, as if there were two of them, one on each side of St. Michael. Holding the infant Jesus, St. Joseph remained silent, but exhibited the power of no words . . . perhaps in this there lay a clue, perhaps my words were not well chosen because there were too many of them. In my encounters with others, I had a tendency to get involved in debates over the Lord.

"If silence be good for wise men, how much better must it be for fools!"
The Talmudic Anthology, No. 323, Stanza 5, Peshahim, 98b, (Judaism)

St. Michael *moved* with the mind of God, and although he seemed to embody God's justice and wrath . . . there was no wrath. St. Michael crushed demons with no emotional attachment, it was simply his purpose. His power was so great; he could crush a demon with a single sweep of his hand, sometimes with only a thought. But St. Michael exhibited peace in his work and was not angry, he just did his job of crushing darkness and their consorts with no emotional concern. Handing me a report card, I got all 'A's with one exception. For 'words' I had merited a 'B.'

St. Michael then allowed me to witness one of his prime functions. Taking me to an energetic prison, St. Michael showed me that the souls of incarnate mankind who are chaotic and dangerous are held energetically. St. Michael energetically prevents them from causing the total mass destruction they would cause if left to their own will. Allowing me to participate in restraining them, I quickly realized how difficult this was. So violently out-of-control, it took a great deal of concentration to hold them in place and to restrain their destructive impulse.

As I was easily overcome, St. Michael took pity on me and restrained the prisoners with only a thought, demonstrating to me the huge grace that the Lord had given this special angel.

Saying nothing, St. Michael and St. Joseph disappeared, but left behind them three huge statues that showed protection before our front door. Bowing to the Lord, I thanked God and His many angels for His protection.

"Man's power of speech is a spiritual force and it has great effect in the higher spheres. Consequently, the damage wrought by improper speech in the higher worlds is severe and awesome. And the greater the damage, the greater is the punishment."
Taharas Halashon, Chapter 2, Page 28, Shmiras Halashon, Sha'ar Hazchirah, Chapter 1, (Judaism)

"I tell you, on the day of judgement people will render an account for every careless word they speak. By your words you will be acquitted, and by your words you will be condemned."
New American Bible, New Testament, Matthew 12:36-37, (Christianity, Catholic, Words of Christ)

****

Paramahansa Yogananda, the Hindu saint, appeared to warn me of distraction in meditation and spiritual practices.

"Paramahansaji frequently warned disciples of the dangers of spiritual idleness.'The minutes are more important than the years,' he would say, 'If you do not fill the minutes of your life with thoughts of God, the years will slip by; and when you need Him most you may be unable to feel His presence. But if you fill the minutes of your life with divine aspirations, automatically the years will be saturated with them.'"
Sayings of Paramahansa Yogananda, Page 102, Stanza 1, (Hinduism, Kriya Yoga, Words of Paramahansa Yogananda)

****

Flying gracefully through the vociferous mountain skies, the breeze blew by my spirit in a rush of wind, and the smells of the woodland in my spirit body were magnified and more intense. Noticing an amazing spectacle before my eyes, a banner rose from beneath the ground, bordered in roses and beaming in brilliance. Mary appeared upon this banner, looking directly at me. Taken aback, she was ever so holy and beautiful that I could not speak. Another banner rose from the ground beside her. Upon it were also many roses and Jesus appeared in the center. Manifesting as the Lady of Grace, Jesus was wearing white robes. Both of their arms were outstretched and their eyes were upon me.

Unable to speak, I just stared, my soul paralyzed in wonder and undeserved honor. Several more banners began emerging from the ground, showing different manifestations of Mary and Jesus. Gazing upon them all, I never spoke. But as I looked, I began hearing a hymn entitled, 'One and Only Mary.'

Nodding to Mary and Jesus, I knew what would be required of me to render to God for allowing me such a spectacular vision. Preparing to return to form and write the new hymn, my soul was lit alight into the wondrous treetops to smell again the holy aroma of God's green Earth. Thanking them telepathically, it was acknowledged by a nod from the holy duo.

"She composed hymns of praise to the Divinity and the most holy humanity of Christ, while the angels set them to music and were sent with them to congratulate Him for the blessings won for the human race."
The Mystical City of God (Abrid.), The Transfixion, Book 5, Chapter VI, Page 446, Top, (Christianity, Catholic, Words Regarding Mary)

****

"All phenomena, existing and apparent, are ever transient, changing, and unstable; but more especially the worldly life hath no reality, no permanent gain (in it). And so, instead of doing work that's profitless, the Truth Divine I'll seek."
A Buddhist Bible, Life and Hymns of Milarepa, Page 569, Stanza 2, (Buddhism, Words of Milarepa)

Up ahead, his eminence was quite profound. Padre Pio stood before a line of fifteen golden confessionals. Coming to approach him, I closed my eyes as required, moving into position before the golden confessional which I instinctively knew to belong to myself. Beginning to move, I knew I had to go ten paces, but I had moved forward rather than sideways. Opening my eyes, I had moved *beyond* the golden confessionals, and was disappointed. Allowing me to try again, I moved back ten paces, closed my eyes and tried again. Coming to the proper place before the tenth confessional, a nun was standing beside me at the ninth, telling me it was good I had made it to the proper confessional, because different nuns and priests owned the other confessionals, and if I'd landed on theirs, I would have lost my own.

Padre Pio was wearing the robes he would normally have worn at mass, and he looked spectacular. As he stood before the confessionals, his energy was very much focused on the truth, his face stern and foreboding. Frightened a bit, because I knew the wretchedness of my soul, I was afraid God's wrath might come upon me through this priest. However, I couldn't have been more wrong, as he exuded nothing but forgiveness, understanding and love. Happy that I had made it to my proper confessional, he was quiet. I looked at the very ornamental confessional in awe.

"It is the Blood of His well beloved Son, Who came down to purify the earth; It is the Blood of His Son, the God-Man, which ascends to His throne to pacify His justice, offended by our sins. He is superabundantly satisfied."
The Agony of Jesus, Part IV, Page 32, Paragraph 2, (Christianity, Catholic, Author: Padre Pio)

****

Plentiful in attendance, I'd mingled with the crowd as I overheard some souls discussing the holy truths found within 'The Urantia Book.' Gleaming of gold as they spoke of its vastness, I wandered amongst the others. The gathering was plentiful in attendance and I mingled. Seeing a table in the distance, several stacks of Baha'i texts appeared on the table, and as I looked at them, I noticed another small book entitled, 'The Magnificat.' A vision of Mary amongst the clouds being assumed into heaven appeared before me as I stared in awe. Wearing a singular white robe, her eyes looked towards heaven. Angels held her from below and gazed upon her countenance from above, as a singular cloud opened, making way for the great light to penetrate. The vision disappeared.

Noticing another table which was filled with the books of Paramahansa Yogananda, a large image of the glorified Ramakrishna (a Hindu saint) floated above. Gleaming with golden light, I was honored to witness their holiness.

"My soul doth magnify the Lord, and my spirit hath rejoiced in God my Savior. For he hath regarded the low estate of his handmaiden: for, behold, from henceforth all generations shall call me blessed. For he that is mighty hath done to me great things; and holy is his name. And his mercy is on them that fear him from generation to generation. He hath shewed strength with his arm; he hath scattered the proud in the imagination of their hearts. He hath put down the mighty from their seats, and exalted them of low degree. He hath filled the hungry with good things; and the rich he hath sent empty away. He hath holpen his servant Israel, in remembrance of his mercy; As he spake to our fathers, to Abraham, and to his seed for ever."
King James Bible, New Testament, Luke 1:46-55, (Christianity, Words of Mary, The Magnificat)

****

Three trees were displayed before me, each in a succession from below. The lowest of the trees was small with only a few leaves, not yet strong enough to bear much. The second tree was a step above the former, with more greenery and quite a bit larger. The third tree stood above all the rest, its branches and abundance of leaves displayed outward in a fashion of praise, the trunk a solid and thick foundation. Reaching out to touch all life, I was told that this tree's name was 'Devaki.' And Further, I was told that its holy symbolism contained within its confines an element denoting the Baha'i faith.

Devaki was the holy mother of Krishna, the manifestation of God honored by the Hindu faith.

> *"Devaki, the mother of Krsna, offered her prayers . . . Devaki said, 'My dear Lord, Your eternal forms . . . and millions of similar incarnations emanating from Visnu, are described in the Vedic literature as original . . . Such eternal forms are ever cognizant and full of bliss; they are situated in transcendental goodness and are always engaged in different pastimes. You are not limited to a particular form only; all such transcendental, eternal forms are self-sufficient. I can understand that you are the Supreme . . ."*
>
> *KRSNA, Book 1, Chapter 3, Page 51, Paragraph 1, (Hinduism, Words of Devaki)*

****

Enraptured in shock and elation, my holy love appeared to me without warning. Jesus appeared to me in the manner in which he often is seen in portraits with one exception. His skin was darker, as you would expect of somebody born in the region from whence He had come. Standing at the foot of my bed and smiling at me, he appeared for only a moment, and then He was gone.

> *"He said that He would return, and He did return, because the Holy Spirit came not alone, but with the power of the Father, and the wisdom of the Son, and the clemency of His own Essence."*
>
> *The Dialogue of St. Catherine of Siena, A Treatise of Discretion, Page 88, Middle, (Christianity, Catholic, Author: St. Catherine of Siena)*

> *"Heaven and earth shall pass away: but my words shall not pass away. But of that day and that hour knoweth no man, no, not the angels which are in heaven, neither the Son, but the Father. Take ye heed, watch and pray: for ye know not when the time is. For the Son of man is as a man taking a far journey, who left his house, and gave authority to his servants, and to every man his work, and commanded the porter to watch. Watch ye therefore: for ye know not when the master of the house cometh, at even, or at midnight, or at the cockcrowing, or in the morning: Lest coming suddenly he find you sleeping. And what I say unto you I say unto all, Watch."*
>
> *King James Bible, New Testament, Mark 13:31-37, (Christianity, Words of Christ)*

****

'Abdul' Baha', the son and successor of Baha'u'llah was walking quietly; his back turned to me. Suddenly, he turned to look upon my countenance, his face radiant, peaceful, serene. Appearing at the age of about thirty, his white turban had fallen on one side just slightly. Information was imparted to me about Baha'u'llah and his successor, 'Abdul' Baha', but I was not given leave to remember any of it. Remembering his face, it held a silent witness to the power, glory, serenity and love of God. Turning to go on, I watched him walk slowly away.

> *"The denizens of this plane speak no words - but they gallop their chargers. They see but the inner reality of the Beloved. To them all words of sense are meaningless, and senseless words are full of meaning."*
>
> *The Seven Valleys and the Four Valleys, The Four Valleys, The Third Valley, Page 55, Paragraph 4, (Baha'i, Author: Baha'u'llah)*

****

Slightly opening in this vast expanse of sky, the portal which would show me the truth in regards to the question of Christ and Baha'u'llah had emerged. For those of you who don't know, Baha'u'llah had claimed to be the second coming of Christ, and I'd prayed earnestly in regards to this claim.

The holiness, sanctity, and absolute wonder of Christ and His purpose on our earth came through in a flash of light as my soul was made to experience energetically the function of our divine Savior.

And then, my soul was filled with an intense knowledge of the true station of Baha'u'llah and the Bab. Although they were not a manifestation of the second coming of Christ, they *were indeed* the promised Qa'ims of Islam.

Having understood the true station of Christ as Messiah and Redeemer, they made this claim based on the understanding of Christ laid out by the Muslim faith. This view is that Christ was a prophet, but not the Son of God.

In this space, the true loftiness of the Christ was laid before me, and His station which surpassed all men, all prophets and all divines. Standing on a pedestal aeons above the others, He stood high above all the holy men throughout time. Oh, allow me to expand on the great effervescent energies, so powerful and secure, I felt regarding the mystery of Christ. There are no words to describe the holiness of His mission, and the greatness of the wonder of His coming. Christ was above all the prophets, so much higher than all of them, and this was shown to me this eve in an indescribably profound and obvious manner. Christ bore aeons above them because He was the Messiah, and he *is* exactly what He said He was, the Son of God.

Descending further down, I was shown the station upon which Baha'u'llah and the Bab stood, which was a very hallowed place, but aeons below that of Christ. Allowing me to witness the holiness of their writings, the Lord wished to make exception of one particular text; a book of law and rule which was called the 'Most Holy Book' or the 'Kitab-I-Aqdas' by his followers. An impure text, it was conveyed that rules and laws which require payment to a religious organization for sin or transgression of its laws, are not inspired by the Lord. There were other such impurities in this text which were typical of the day and age of their writing.

Eternity is beyond the superstitious structures of humanity, and souls who bear the mark of holiness eventually experience the expansion of understanding which takes them far beyond all Earthly concern, understanding or pretense, into the realm of the unknowable, the absolute. Religious structures among mortal realms are necessary for the guidance of souls unable to lead themselves, the masses; but when a soul seeks to attain immortality amongst the worlds of eternity, he must go beyond their fetters and boundaries to unleash his ancient soul, and thrust it upon the paradise realms which, amidst Earthly delusions, structures and limitations, remain unseen.

Manifestations of God and holy souls bear this one trait of similitude, their knowledge of this truth. It is mortal man's false interpretations of their words, and their unwillingness to acknowledge the humanity and fallibility of such manifestations, which causes the hard-won absolutism of religion. Even Moses, the man who spoke to God face to face, was punished by God for his sin. His imperfection disallowed his entry into the Promised Land.

"You shall die on the mountain that you are about to ascend, and shall be gathered to your kin, as your brother Aaron died on Mount Hor and was gathered to his kin; for you both broke faith with me among the Israelite people, at the waters of Meribath-kadesh in the wilderness of Zin, by failing to uphold My sanctity among the Israelite people. You may view the land from a distance, but you shall not enter it - the land that I am giving to the Israelite people."

The Torah, Deuteronomy 32:50-52, (Judaism, Words of God to Moses, Translator: Jewish Publication Society)

Knowledge in mortal realms is not absolute, but continues to grow and expand as understanding increases. Let thy will be done, and may any soul who may be offended by my words forgive me for my purpose, and that which I must do to fulfill the will of the Lord within the context of my own revelation which remains fallible due to the human counterpart used in bringing it about.

I fear not being wrong. I fear not being right. I only fear in being stuck, therefore, in not attaining to the glorious paradise I seek. My only concern is that my words, whether they be wrong or right (or just misinterpreted), never be used to halt the progress of a people, of a world, or of a single soul. Let it be known that I harbor not this intention; my only intention is to provide a guide for those who wish to cross. But I wish for them to follow such guidance with their own eyes and ears open, so that God may lead them in His own inexplicable manner towards the specific destiny and path He has laid for them. A guide, a guide . . . not a sword.

"O Friend! In the Bayan We directed everyone in this Most Great Revelation to see with his own eyes and hear with his own ears. However, when the horizon of the world was illumined with the resplendent light of this Revelation, many people forgot this divine commandment . . ."
Tablets of Baha'u'llah, Excerpts from other Tablets, Page 236, Paragraph 3, (Baha'i, Author: Baha'u'llah)

"Though my body be pained by the trials that befall me from Thee, though it be afflicted by the revelations of Thy Decree, yet my soul rejoiceth at having partaken of the waters of Thy Beauty, and at having attained the shores of the ocean of Thine eternity."
Prayers and Meditations, LX, Paragraph 3, Page 96, (Baha'i, Author: Baha'u'llah)

"Let there be nothing we know of which it would be a service to the Lord for us to do, and which, with His help, we would not venture to take in hand."
The Way of Perfection, Chapter 16, Page 122, Paragraph 1-2, (Christianity, Catholic, Author: St. Teresa of Avila)

And let it bear repeating for every soul who seeks to overcome this crust upon himself that no coward may cross this gate, only the courageous with the will to look upon himself, his family, his culture, his religion and his world . . . with honesty:

Original sin is transmitted through the seeds of the seven deadly sins, is implanted through habit, is cultivated by tolerance, and grows through the mass ignorance of humanity. Original sin can only be transformed through the seeds of the seven virtues, implanted through habitual choice, cultivated by discernment, and grown through the singular awareness of an individual soul. Beyond our individual karma and vice, lies the original sin of mankind. We partake of it because of our own humanity, so we must transform it because of our own divinity.

"They also lamented the sins of their parents, as if knowing that all kinds of evils had descended to them through their progenitors, as if through them they were still in possession of the sad heritage of sin."
The Life of Jesus Christ and Biblical Revelations, Volume II, From the Second Feast of Tabernacles to the First Conversion of Magdalen, No. 1, Page 380, Paragraph 1 (Christianity, Catholic)

****

Watching the childhood home of St. Therese of Lisieux, it appeared in Claymation as the children went about their day and mother watched over them with loving care. Bade to witness Therese's decision to become a nun, as I watched, I felt her simple holiness which was filled with childlike joy and innocence. Energetically, Theresa gave this gift of her simplicity to me, as I was filled with peace.

"That great soul must stand pictured before another soul, one not mean, a soul that has become worthy to look, emancipate from the lure, from all that binds its fellows in bewitchment, holding itself in quietude. Let not merely the enveloping body be at peace, body's turmoil stilled, but all that lies around, earth at peace, and sea at peace, and air and the very heavens. Into that heaven, all at rest, let the great soul be conceived to roll inward at every point, penetrating, permeating, from all sides pouring in its light. As the rays of the sun throwing their brilliance upon a louring cloud make it gleam all gold."
Plotinus: The Enneads, Fifth Ennead, First Tractate, No. 2, Paragraph 3, (Mystery Religions, Greek, Words of Plotinus)

****

The clouds parted making way for a light to permeate the high heavens and down into this realm below. As the hole emerged, the light sprung forth before my eyes in a splendid array, while a marble staircase became visible from this source of light. An inexplicable experience ensued wherein several aspects from my earlier life emerged energetically, descending the staircase and entering within to fill me with the energetic sense of those happenings which occurred in my late teens and early twenties.

Andy and I had come together, very much out of necessity, when I had been turned away by others after I'd lost a job. Recalling the aloneness I'd felt and the turmoil and ruckus of the time and being alone in the world, that all ended when Andy and I came together. Choices which I'd questioned over and over again were apparently not all based on choice, but necessity . . . and destiny.

Unfolding before me, I understood that the mysteries of God's redemption were working in me even when I was unaware of it, and that despite my many regrets about my past, *that very past* with all its mistakes and regrettable choices, was very necessary in the attainment of my redemption. When Andy had entered into my life so quickly, it had been a signal grace from God. Thanking God, I bowed to the ground.

"And he said unto them, Blessed are they who suffer many experiences, for they shall be made perfect through suffering; they shall be as the angels of God in Heaven and shall die no more, neither shall they be born any more, for death and birth have no more dominion over them."

The Gospel of the Holy Twelve, Lection XXXVII, No. 2, (Christianity, Gnostic/Essene, Words of Christ)

Descending from the steps was a man, and behind him, several nuns. In front of him was a spiritual guardian, who conveyed that this man was the soul who had originally 'translated' the 'Urantia Book' from the heavens into the Earthly realm. Because he had done so with conservatism and traditionality, it had been done in a slightly tainted and wordy manner. Showing me how the wordiness of the book could be changed into shorter, more precise sentences, the guide made me to understand that it was my task to write another translation of this book, a task I had begun years ago (What would become 'The Mysteries of the Redemption'). Both books contained within them the mysteries of the redemption, although in the 'Urantia translation', these mysteries were given in an intellectual manner, wherein in my 'translation', these mysteries were experiential, showing through visionary experience the process of the redemption from beginning to end.

Having tampered with the text slightly due to his own views, the translator concurred, wholeheartedly agreeing and expressing a singular wish that I should help him by weeding out the falsehoods he had added due to his own impetus. These included the denial of reincarnation, the dark side or lower realms, perceptions on racial superiority, the denial of the unique sacredness of the holy family, and the belief in the falsehood of mystical vision. Mostly found in the third and fourth parts of the book, the first two parts on angelic kingdoms had been 'translated' with few flaws.

Due to the most holy nature of this text, I consider myself unworthy to read it, much less to correct it. But let it be known that we should never allow the fallible aspects of ancient sacred texts, to deter us from relishing the most holy true aspects. Truth is a difficult business and you may never fully know the absolute, until you have left this realm through death.

When they were finished rectifying his error; the nuns, the man and the guide, without any display of emotion or thought, all turned to the marble staircase in the sky, walked into the cloudy veil of light and left me spellbound by the sight.

"We incline to the belief that the eternal future will witness phenomena of universe evolution which will far transcend all that the eternal past has experienced. And we anticipate such tremendous adventures, even as you should, with keen relish and ever-heightening expectation."

The Urantia Book, Part I, Paper 23, No. 4, Paragraph 6, (Christianity, Urantia)

****

CHAPTER FOUR

Meetings with the Holy Mother of God, Holy Family, Jesus, Holy Shephards, Don Bosco, Mystical Jesus, Philothea, Swami, Last Supper and Crucifixion of Jesus Christ, Burial Cloth of Jesus, Therese Neumann - Catholic Stigmatist.

****

Appearing very much as the Lady of Grace, the Holy Mother of God had her arms outstretched and was wearing a pink robe, the robe of the redemption. Embroidered with gold and white, upon her head was a gilded golden crown. Brown and streaked with gold, her hair was blowing in the spirit wind as her hands remain outstretched to the world. Waves of light came from her hands, and she conveyed that I would change the title of my books to reflect the mysteries of the redemption. Pausing to consider such grandeur, I gazed upon her most beauteous countenance as a yellow lily, another sign of redemption, appeared in her hand.

> *"I was transported to a high place between Heaven and earth. I saw the earth below me gray and somber, and above me Heaven where, among the choirs of angels and the orders of the blessed, was the Blessed Virgin before the throne of God. I saw prepared for her two thrones of honor . . . and they were formed out of the prayers of earth. They were built entirely of flowers, leaves, garlands, the various species typical of the different value and characteristics of the prayers of individuals and of whole congregations. Angels and saints took them from the hands of those that offered them and bore them up to Heaven."*

The Life of Jesus Christ and Biblical Revelations, Volume I, Section 3 - The Most Holy Virgin, No. 5, Paragraph 8, (Christianity, Catholic, Author: St. Anne Catherine Emmerich)

****

Sent upon a vast pilgrimage, my soul was sanctioned to follow Jesus, Joseph and Mary as they traveled across the desert to Bethlehem. Beginning in ancient times, I was preparing foodstuffs for the long journey. Because I was able to move from each destination point in a flash of moment, I was leaving supplies and food at each post along the way.

Interiorly, I gained a deep understanding of the process that was initially begun two thousand years ago. Joseph would always protect the child Jesus, while Mary would always obey Him. This was the intricate balance required between the two holy parents in order for the redemption to reach fruition on the ground.

Leaving the heavenly abodes, I was given paupers robes to wear as I began my journey across the desert to the first pilgrimage site. Surprised at what I found, my spirit was now ensconced in a maze below a towering rock within the deep desert. Having ridden a donkey, I had no idea what lay ahead. Up until this juncture, I had experienced all the treacheries that the true Mary and Joseph might have known in their time, but most powerfully, the spitefulness of the king and the suffering of the desert. Made especially aware of the safety issues in regards to Mary and Joseph, it was vital that they reach the desired destination where the birth would occur.

As I approached the towering rock in the desert, I entered the maze below it, as suddenly everything was transformed in a great flash of light.

Watching a different time, Mary and Joseph were now children. Observing them, I noticed that they were very charitable and quick to help others. Despite this, no matter how deeply obvious the circumstances of those around them (in terms of sin), they were not quick to judge anybody. Humbling me, I had struggled with making rash decisions about others, and sometimes it had proven incorrect. 'Forgive me, Lord,' I thought. Very much like other children, they bore very distinctly developed aspects of holy of charity and love - manifested through kindness and lack of judgment.

Mary was helping a fellow friend who was engaging in sin, by taking away a sinful object. Choosing not to reveal her friend's shame to anybody else, her charitableness was revealed even further. Quiet assistance from the young Madonna, was quite enough to turn her friend towards virtue. Able to affect great change in their contemporaries by a singular act of love with no words being required or necessary, both Mary and Joseph had this unique gift. Fascinating and most humbling, I watched Joseph helping puppies by taking them to a safe place, out of reach of some particularly violent people who would've harmed them. Immediately, this scene was followed up by a remembrance of Joseph protecting the baby Jesus from the hands of the King, and leading his family to safety. Further scenes were shown of the protection he afforded the child Jesus throughout His life, to keep Him safe from the dark forces who continually sought his downfall through people or circumstances as they presented themselves. I also saw that people were often enraged by Jesus' display of holy wisdom, which others instinctually knew came from God, but convicted them deeply of sin.

Upon leaving this first destination, I was pleased to find that the food I'd earlier prepared for each leg of the journey remained. Continuing my journey on the back of a camel, and sometimes a jeep, I was surprised that despite everything having been prepared ahead of time, this journey was deeply grave. Feeling the difficulty of this path for Mary and Joseph, I experienced extreme empathy for the most Holy Mother in being pregnant and traveling the desert in such a way.

As I traveled, I felt a vague impression of the coming Disciples of Christ, and how they were all inexorably linked to every move of Mary and Joseph. Their destinies were deeply entrenched in how this journey would unfold, which would determine the fate of them all.

"The pillar arose through the center of the church and there, like a tree, divided into several branches. Upon these branches stood the members of the Holy Family and their relatives. They stood as if on the stamens of flowers . . . But above them all, on the very summit of the tree sat the Child Jesus in unfading splendor, the imperial globe in His hand. In adoration around these groups, were the first choirs of the Apostles and disciples . . ."
The Life of Jesus Christ and Biblical Revelations, Volume I, Part III - The Most Holy Virgin, No. 4 , Page 145, Top & Bottom, (Christianity, Catholic, Author: St. Anne Catherine Emmerich)

Flashing back to the scene of Mary and Joseph as children, I was astounded that they chose to link their energies to mine by blending their holy soul's lights to my own. Experiencing their unity for only a moment as man and woman, I felt the oneness between Mary and Joseph, who were twin souls, eternal flames. They were united in body, mind and spirit, and this surprised me because of certain doctrines which support their virginity. Although I could certainly not say whether or not they remained virgins during their marriage, I experienced the aspect of unity and oneness - mind, body, and soul - which resonated between them, and I felt how holy, pure and uncalculated it was. Spirit born, their union contained no self-interest. In a certain sense, their journey and union were a blending of the divine into the soul of mankind as their entire lives were a sacrifice for God. Giving back to him in flesh, in Word, in energy, in power, and in intrinsic substance, these things were inexplicable for their souls were *not* the same as the rest of humanity. Despite their appearance to the eyes of the undiscerning, these were immortals.

Returning to the camel and the jeep, I continued my pilgrimage into the desert, noticing how the food became scarcer into the journey and their sufferings increased. An absence of food was indicated, but there was also an absence of an energetic link-up to other people on the ground, which was so vitally needed in such a grand redemptive effort. Skimming from their supplies, they supplied for all that was wanting in each location of their journey, and they made what they had be enough, rather than ask for more, which they could have easily done to bring about this great event.

Mary and Joseph were shown to me as being very normal and simple, but immensely kind. Through their kindness you witnessed their splendor; otherwise you might not have noticed their holiness amongst the masses. Part of their purpose was to blend in, so as to protect the identity of the child they raised until He was of age to perform His great redemptive act.

Among the three of them, Mary, Joseph and Jesus, there was a great and lofty ideal which caused each member to give all in order to make it happen. This ideal was the mystery of the redemption which had been revealed to all of them in different ways. Because it was only a concept to them at the time, it seemed all the more incredible that they could understand such lofty subjects, because the people of their times were simple nomadic desert dwellers. But Mary and Joseph, and others who were a part of the redemption, became conscious of this knowledge aeons before their time.

Swept to another location deeper within the desert, I watched as another mystery of the redemption unfolded before my eyes.

Watching Jesus digging in the ground with His raw hands, the dirt below Him stirred and swirled almost like a whirlpool as it became mud and then volcanic ash. Below ground at this holy Mount of Sinai, was the great item He sought to find, and Jesus was bound and determined to remove it from this holy place. Seeking something I immediately understood to be 'The Coffin of the Redemption,' He was looking for a simple wooden casket which contained a holy energy of great import. Only knowing that this holy item was vital to the next link of the redemption, connecting the works of the Patriarchs, Moses, and the Ten Commandments, to the coming of the Messiah to redeem all mankind, it bore some connection to the Ark of the Covenant. As He pulled the simple wooden coffin from below ground, the sky turned pink and Jesus turned to look directly into my eyes as I gazed through this portal to the past.

"On the same night that Moses took possession of the Holy Thing, a golden casket shaped like a coffin was prepared, in which at their departure the Israelites took it with them . . . In the center of this coffin-like chest, was placed a little golden casket wherein was contained the Holy Thing . . . Only afterward on Mount Sinai, was made the chest inlaid with gold inside and outside, and in it the golden mummiform coffin with the Holy Thing was placed."

The Life of Jesus Christ and Biblical Revelations, Volume I, Part II - Sin and its Consequences, No. 17, Page 108-109, (Christianity, Catholic, Author: St. Anne Catherine Emmerich)

Waving His arms, we suddenly stood before a great sky portal. Standing in the heavens trying to decide what sacrifice He could make on behalf of mankind, the Lord Jesus Christ was seeking the lofty ideal of the redemption of mankind. Trying many things, he went through every possible sacrifice that could be made, known to heaven and man. But in the end, a great sheath of red blood fell over the sky, and it was clear that the only sacrifice that would be sufficient was His most holy blood, and He was pleased to give it.

As I stood there in the sky looking upon the most holy countenance of the Lord Jesus, covered in a sheet of red, I wept at what He must choose to endure for my sake. As my tears fell, a great sheath of blood came in the form of a gigantic wave towards me and covered my soul. Instantly, I awoke.

"Many times did He beseech his eternal Father not to allow the sins and the ingratitude of men to hinder their Redemption. As Christ in his foreknowledge was always conscious of the sins of the human race and of the damnation of so many thankless souls, the thought of dying for them caused Him to sweat blood many times on these occasions."

Mystical City of God (Abrid.), The Transfixion, Chapter III, Paragraph 2, (Christianity, Catholic, Author: Ven. Mary of Agreda)

****

Amidst the company of several wise men of old, my eyes still hold the vision of their flowing robes around their tall bodies as they stood before me. One's back faced me, as the other two magi looked upon my countenance. Much like shepherds, they stood around me for a great part of the night, as I felt serenity. Teaching me of things, I have not been given leave to remember even one word of their teaching, just the holy wonder and peace . . . peace . . . that I felt in the presence of these shepherds this night.

"And this is that holy and loving inebriation which causes the blessed to lose memory of themselves, to give themselves wholly to praise . . ."
The Soul Sanctified, Chapter 30, Page 84, Paragraph 1, (Christianity, Catholic)
****

A black and white picture of Don Bosco stood before me, the founder and saint of the Salesian missions. As it appeared, I heard a voice repeating over and over, "Blood Eucharist, Blood Eucharist, Blood Eucharist," as my soul felt the longing to partake of this holy sacrament which it seemed would never be mine to taste.

"This Divine Bread is eaten, but it is not changed, because it assumes no other form in him who eats it. It transforms the worthy receiver into Him whom it contains."
The Blessed Eucharist, Chapter 13, Page 188, Paragraph 1, (Christianity, Catholic, Author: Fr. Michael Muller, C.S.S.R.)

Suddenly walking briskly with Albert Einstein, I said, "Boy, you sure look like my father," I said, as he spoke not. "It's interesting," I added, "how you blended science with Christianity." Looking at me, his face didn't change; he had a very mystical sort of presence. Within a moment, he was gone.
****

Given to witness an enigma, a mystery of which I could discern little, I looked upon the cosmic Christ as if through a microscope. Naked and walking towards a door on the right, his eyes were dreamy and mystical. The room had green walls and was covered with images which I believed to be Gnostic symbols, and I was seeing the Christ as they had; naked, pure, untouched and yet imprisoned within form, to fulfill the grand works of the redemption. Observing Him, a hymn began playing, 'He was a being devoted to all the worlds of the dream.'

He, too, received communication through the dream world, and that in His life; He was a very mystical man, far beyond what Christianity perceives of Him. Dreams vivid and prophetic, they led His path through Earthly life.

Holding a surreal quality in this image, His eyes energetically implanted within my soul another side of Jesus. Perhaps it was a mixture between His human and divine, but I don't know exactly what that quality truly meant. But I did know that it was related to His nakedness, as He was exposing *all* of Himself to me by allowing me to see the mystical side of His essence.

Looking upon Him, I felt that there was more to know about His life. Filling me with questions, I began to think. 'Was there some truth to the statements made regarding certain scrolls found of late that He might have had siblings, that He might have been married, or that His birth may have come about through normal means as opposed to the virgin birth? Or perhaps even still, the truth may lie between the lofty divinity and the simple man.'

For a moment, I knew that the truth was depicted in the loftiest degrees of his spoken divinity in Catholicism, to the Gnostic view of the simple man. *Both* were somehow true, both somehow held energetic currents of the actual. Inexplicable, I *knew* the truth of them both, and in this knowing, these truths did not contradict one another.

Most primarily, I felt that there was more to know about His life, that His true life story had been somehow skewed, either through the historical destruction of many Apostolic and Gnostic documents by various parties including the church, or misinterpretations of His teachings due to our own limited understanding. This mystery was *the key* to the chains which Christianity had put upon His soul, and it was vital to their release.

Balance between the human and divine, His humanity was very normal, although His divinity was greatly exalted. Perhaps the truth lay within the knowledge of His natural manhood and the normalcy of His life to all outward appearances, and His supernatural divinity which was the exalted station of Himself invisible to the masses, yet seen by faith among the chosen.

If we allow any part of His history to be untrue, it disturbs the truth of the whole energetic seed of knowledge which comes to us as the mysteries of the redemption through the images of His exterior world. So be it! I say! The Lord of the eternal, the Lord of the redemption has unified the elements of discord. Allow them to be so, and allow the truth of their essence to be understood by men. May they perceive the inexplicable renderings of truth which the Lord deigns to release.

"In the second confession more emphasis was placed upon the combined nature, the supernal fact that he was the Son of Man and the Son of God, and it was upon this great truth of the union of the human nature with the divine nature that Jesus declared he would build the kingdom of heaven."
The Urantia Book, Section IV, Paper 157, No. 5, Paragraph 2, (Christianity, Urantia)
****

Thrust upon the holy time of Jesus' conception, gestation and birth, I was again stunned by the sacredness of this time, but yet, placed within the context of perceiving that there was more to this historic time than I knew. Again, the knowledge was placed within my mind that there was more to Christ's birth than our world currently knows. Again, the answer lay between the Catholic divine of the virgin birth, and the Gnostic human of the natural. The definitive answer was not to be given, however, just the understanding that there was more normalcy in the human element than we had been led to believe. Normalcy allowed the holy family to remain under wraps, beyond suspicion of any such grand event, but this normalcy in no way diminished the holiness of the Christ and His mother.

The truth of these particulars lay within an energetic liaison between the divine and human, Catholic doctrine's highest exaltation and the Gnostics simplest humanity. Together they energetically formed a complete understanding of this mystery of the incarnation of the Lord Jesus. Were natural elements to be added to His exterior life, they would in no way alter the divine mystery that lives within Him of the redemptive act itself. The divine holiness of such a thing is a hidden mystery witnessed and understood only within the energetic realms. The humble natural, also is a hidden energetic enigma understood only within the realms of God. Inexplicable . . .

"More than this cannot be told, for the Holy Streams will take you to that place where words are no more, and even the Holy Scrolls cannot record the mysteries therein."
The Essene Gospel of Peace, Volume 4, The Holy Streams, Page 44, Paragraph 1,
(Christianity, Gnostic/Essene, Words of Christ)
****

As I awoke in bed, I looked up to notice that the Mother Mary was standing before one of the altars in my bedroom formed in her honor, looking upon it. Wearing light blue and white robes, she never turned to glance at me, but kept looking at the altar. Staring at her for several minutes, I turned to go back to sleep.

"She seeks for those who approach her devoutly and with reverence, for such she loves, nourishes, and adopts as her children."
The Voice of the Saints, Chapter 17, Page 135, No. 5, (Christianity, Catholic, Words of St. Bonaventure)

****

Oh, my goodness, to look upon it! How could I bear such beauty and radiance before my eyes? The souls who traveled with me this eve seemed unaffected by that which was affecting me and everywhere my eyes could look, I saw images of the most Holy Mother of God! But what was very odd was that some of these images would begin of her, and then become something ordinary.

Several hundred yards in front of me, I saw a towering image of her most holy essence, at least one hundred feet high. Wearing dark robes, she wore black with a blue interior, much like a nun.

As I began running towards it, however, something odd began to happen. While running, I could hear a distant woman's voice whispering, "Philothea, Philothea . . ." Following the beckon ever closer to what I had seen, when I arrived it had become a rather tall building. My momentary euphoria was not lost, as I began to hear the words echoing in the sky yet again.

On top of a nearby hospital, I saw her image radiating towards me, arms outstretched. Wearing transcendent white laced with gold, her arms reached to me and I saw her lips move. "Philothea, Philothea . . ." Following the beckon, I ran in fury to find the Blessed Virgin, but as I came nearer, I suddenly saw many statues and images of Her most holy essence which had now appeared . . . everywhere! In front and on top of buildings, in the windows, everywhere! Astounded, I said nothing but fell to my knees in fatigue and wonder. "Philothea, Philothea . . ." She continued to call as I got back up and ventured towards the hospital.

Within only a moment, a most beautiful song began playing to my soul from the heavens on a harpsichord, 'Holy Mother of God.' Relishing the beautiful sound, my soul was swept away. All was gone now, except for the whispering words, "Philothea, Philothea . . ."

For those who do not know, Philothea is the original title of a St. Francis De Sales text, 'An Introduction to the Devout Life,' and it means, 'Lover of God.'
"You aim at true devotion, my dear Philothea, because, as a Christian, you know how acceptable it is to the Divine Majesty. But inasmuch as trifling errors at the outset of any undertaking are wont to increase rapidly as we advance, frequently becoming almost irreparable, it is needful that, first of all, you should ascertain wherein lies the virtue of devotion; for there are many counterfeits, but only one true devotion; and, therefore, if you do not find that which is real, you will but deceive yourself, and vainly pursue an idle, superstitious form."
An Introduction to the Devout Life, Page 1-2, (Christianity, Catholic, Words of St. Francis De Sales)

****

Sitting upon the top of a small pyramid, whose point had been carved out to fit his buttocks in meditation, the swami never said a word, but glared right through my soul with his eyes. As he looked at me, my soul went into a deep transcendental state and received guidance regarding the next steps I must take to begin the next leg of my journey. Amongst the guidance, was a stern directive towards more astute meditation, which I agreed to immediately.

Swept more deeply, my agitation and confusion disappeared. But all that lay ahead remained unknown and mysterious to me. A magnetic electrical surge posited between his eyes and mine, as he quietly reached his hand toward me. My soul then went sub-conscious.

"He took hold of me, saying, 'My beloved! Behold, I shall reveal to you those (things) that (neither) (the) heavens nor their archons have known . . . I (shall) reveal to you him who (is hidden.) But now, stretch out your (hand). Now take hold of me.'"

The Nag Hammadi Library, The Second Apocalypse of James, Page 274, Paragraph 1,
(Christianity, Gnostic/Essene, Words of Christ)

****

All those who had received revelation regarding the life of Christ were now waiting here in this spot, each revealing the particular aspect of the truth which had been shown to them. Interestingly, the truth appeared in the form of several small books, each heralding one revelation of the life of Christ. Among them were also bottles, each containing small pills which represented aspects of the truth of Jesus' life and resurrection from the dead. Five different versions of the story were presented here, each with their successive authors, but after careful evaluation of all of them, I was strongly led towards one particular individual who bore a shorter version than some of the rest.

In an inexplicable eternal sense, all of these versions were true, but this particular version was different than the others, and I had not heard it before. Having approximately thirteen bottles containing pink pills regarding such truths, and four volumes; as opposed to the others which ranged from six to twenty six bottles, the colors of white to various shades of blue, and anywhere from one to ten volumes, this was the truth which the Lord wished for me to see this fortnight.

Meeting the man who was about to present me with aspects of this truth, he was a thin but tall gentleman with dark brown hair. Dressed in modern day attire, he introduced himself to me kindly, expressing his interest in showing me his truth. Sincerity grand, I found him to be too humble about his revelation. "May I witness to your truth of the life of our Lord?" I asked. Assuring me kindly that I had reached the proper spot, the humility of this gentleman bore witness to his truth. Gathering around him were people who were calm and accepting, harboring a deep profound peace amongst themselves regarding this revelation. It was not important for those interested in this man's revelation to be 'right,' only to find God's truth. So many on the Earth fight about being right, that what is true gets lost in the quarrel. The egos of these souls were contributing to their inability to find the absolute truth, because their own foundation was so shallow that any disagreement with their former views would be Earth-shattering for them.

Presenting me with the first two bottles of his truth, they consisted of the incarnation of God in Jesus the man. Bidding me to sit, I called Andy over to sit by me. A re-enactment ensued of the days just prior to and after the birth of Jesus Christ, and they were portrayed to me almost as if by live dramatic endeavor. Sitting in my seat, I was whisked by the breezes upswept by the coming of Herod's army for the slaughter of the innocents. Becoming nauseous at the reverie of this horrid event, the horses and the soldiers swept by, as suddenly a quiet overcame the room. Standing before a small altar of the birthplace of Christ, the man showed me a tiny pill from the bottle lying in the manger, which represented the body and life of the baby Jesus. Quietly retrieving two more pills from within the bottle, he placed them to the side of Jesus as beautiful majestic music filled the scene. Instantly, I knew beyond all doubt that these represented two siblings which Jesus had in the flesh, a sister and a brother born to the blessed Mary and Joseph. Rejoicing at this revelation to my soul, the scene began to slowly dwindle and disappear.

Finding these texts in physical form, they were entitled, 'The Life and Teachings of the Masters of the Far East." Because I found them in a used book store, there were four volumes, although the complete version contains five or six. Presenting a wholly unique perspective on Christ, the books hold Him to be a living master, still visiting, teaching and helping many souls in our own time in his resurrected body.

"He saw that man must learn that ignorance is disregard and lack of
understanding both of Divine Mind as the Creative Principle, and of his relation

to that Principle. He saw that man may have all intellectual knowledge and be versed in worldly affairs, yet if he does not recognize the Christ as the living, vitalizing essence of God within him, he is grossly ignorant of the most important factor governing his life."
The Life and Teachings of the Masters of the Far East, Volume II, Chapter XI, Page 108, Paragraph 2, (Anthology)

****

Given to witness the chaos and confusion regarding the times of Christ's sufferings, torments and crucifixion, it was a horrid time. A great deal of hypocrisy was in the air, and it was easy to see how Peter fell so quickly into denying the Christ, because it was such a bloodthirsty calculated event that placed everyone who loved Him in a sort of state of suspended animation.

All along, it seemed that His followers truly believed He would come out of this unscathed, because they believed in His ability to save Himself. Chaos was so high; followers were looking for opportunities to leave the city that night so as not to be added to the roster of victims.

Experiencing what was very much like being in the body of one of his followers, the imminent peril seemed to close in on them, each and every one. In a split second, it became unlawful to follow Jesus, and in the moment, those who had followed Him, responded in a very instinctual fashion. There were those who found ways to disguise themselves, by denying Him and the like, but the majority were thinking on ways to leave the city that night and escape recognition. Chaos and confusion were abundant, and the confidence many of them had in Christ's unction to save Himself was deathly shattered upon hearing of His death. They didn't understand why He wouldn't use His omnipotence to save Himself.

For those who left the city, it was portrayed as if they were skiing down a fast hill, making a fast smooth break. Many waited on the borders of town for fellow Christians, and among the group I saw one individual who was not a Christian and was trying to go with them to spy. Looking at him, I let him know that I knew who he was and said, "Well, this time you'll be outnumbered by the Christians. It'll be more difficult for you to accomplish your purpose." Apparently he'd caused problems for the Christians before.

No longer witnessing this historic time, I had rejoined a league of guardian angels. Preparing for a week in special training, I noticed quickly that we were a highly trained organism of angels who worked in league towards the betterment of mankind. Three to four hundred angels worked in our league, as I enjoyed this remembrance of one of my liaisons in the spirit.

"Jesus recognized this, and He could have saved Himself the Calvary experience. Had He wished to use His power, his enemies could not have touched Him. He saw there was a great spiritual change taking place in His body; and saw that if this was brought about, among those He knew and loved, without some outward change, a great many would not recognize the spiritual import, but would still cling to the personal. He knew that He had the power to overcome death, and He wished to show those that He loved that they had the same power; so He chose the Calvary way, the way they could see; and seeing, they would believe. He also wished to show that He had so perfected His body, that should His enemies take His life . . . still He, the true Self, could, raise His real or spiritual body above all mortal limitations."
The Life and Teachings of the Masters of the Far East, Volume I, Chapter XXI, Page130-131, (Anthology)

****

Amidst the spectral future, my soul was swished back through time to gaze upon a moment of infinite beatitude. The gathering of disciples had another guest visiting from the future, yet only the Messiah seemed to know this. Walking with Jesus among the last few days of his life, this momentous experience resulted in the last supper. But before the supper, my soul was given to witness the event which led to the death of Jesus.

Feeling uncomfortable with His first declarations against the Jewish authorities and their coldness to the people, He was saying this in regard to their attitude about the healing of people who suffered greatly on holy days and the Sabbath. But there was more to His accusation than this, as it seemed that He was accusing them of not caring for the sick even through their own regular means on certain holy days like the Sabbath. My discomfort was caused only by my own wimpiness in such matters of direct confrontation, although my soul recognized the truth of the Messiah's words.

After a short period of time, my courage began to grow within me. The Lord had given me the duty of care giving to a woman who was very ill and appeared to be dying of an open wound in her head. Caused by a disease rather than an injury, Jesus' anger had resulted from the cold and compassionless response of those who insisted that even such a one as her should not be healed on a holy or Sabbath day. Apparently, they had also neglected to give her the proper ordinary care she required, as well.

Confrontation had been with someone in the Sanhedrin who had previously supported Jesus, and actually loved Him very much, but taking such a verbal reprimand was difficult for his ego, and would eventually be enough to make him turn on Jesus, despite his love. This betrayal was as great as that of Judas, because this man loved the Master and knew who He was in his heart. It was an open rebellion against the Son of God, rather than an ignorant reprisal done in anger. Open rebellion was broad and wide amongst the people on this last night following the confrontation; it felt like violence was actually energetically placed in the air.

Making it to the place where the last supper was about to begin, Jesus spoke of the man he had rebuked openly in the streets, and said with great confidence that this man loved Jesus with all of His heart, but despite this, his pride had been challenged and he would have a change of heart which would lead to the bloodshed of many. Speaking of His death with great calm, the disciples didn't seem to allow the truth of it to soak in. But they *felt* the energy in the streets, the violence of the people amongst themselves. Jesus spoke of how others were going to die this night, as well, for there was open battling among many in the streets. Great excitement filled the air, fear and righteous concern.

Turning my head, I was shown a vision inside the vision. Outside the gathering place of the disciples, the sick and suffering were gathering and this was a grand sight. Amongst the chaos were these pockets of the sick, who seemed to carry with them an energy of great courage and peace. Even amongst the disciples at the last supper was a majestic peace, despite the chaos that now surrounded them in all avenues of the city.

As I sat with the other disciples, they spoke to me of the teachings of Jesus, and I tried to listen intently, but couldn't because I found it so shocking that they all were in complete and total denial that Jesus was actually going to die. Although there was probably nothing they could do to prevent it, they simply couldn't imagine this God-man being subject to death, as they didn't yet understand the grand purpose of the death and subsequent resurrection of Christ.

Suddenly, Jesus took me aside, and now with a swift change in energy, He began talking to me as if the present time and the past were overlapping. "All of my disciples will be misled," He said, "Through no fault of their own; they will go in a different way than I have taught them. Only you among my disciples, can I trust, to stand true to the teaching I have given."

Shocked by this revelation, I nodded that I would. I felt the energies of the mysteries and mechanics of existence (i.e. reincarnation), that such things might have been too complex for the people of Christ's time to fully understand, but the time for the fullness of the Master's teaching had come. Face filled with urgency, His arm touching my own with a sureness and forthrightness I cannot explain as He wasn't simply making a statement, He was pleading with me to fulfill this important task.

Knowing in my heart the courage that would take on my part, I would have to challenge the beliefs of a multitude, in order to hopefully reach a few who were willing to embrace the fullness of the Master's truth.

Speaking openly to me of His death, He again shared that it would occur because of this person who had once loved Him, who had a change of heart in order to save face. Feeling in my heart what a horrible betrayal this was, he took me back to the others who were still laughing and making merry.

They began speaking of the commandments and the beatitudes which filled my soul with peace. Looking across the table to my most blessed Jesus; I gazed upon His infinite beauty with a joyous sense of love. It was an honor to be held as one amongst this table. I would worry another night and spend this night in a joyous reunion with my Savior.

"I tell you truly, in the daylight hours are our feet on the ground and we have no wings with which to fly. But our spirits are not tied to the earth, and with the coming of night we overcome our attachment to the earth and join with that which is eternal. For the Son of Man is not all that he seems, and only with the eyes of the spirit can we see those golden threads which link us with all life everywhere."
The Essene Gospel of Peace, Vol. 4, Page 15, Paragraph 1, (Christianity, Gnostic/Essene, Words of Christ)

"And it came to pass that Jesus gathered the Sons of Light by the shore of the river, to reveal to them that which had passed, and each one was ripe for truth, as the flower opens from the bud when the angels of sun and water bring it to its time of blossoming . . . And for seven years the unknown angels of the Heavenly Father had taught them through their sleeping hours. And now was the day come when they would enter the Brotherhood of the Elect and learn the hidden teachings of the Elders, even those of Enoch and before."
The Essene Gospel of Peace, Vol. 4, Page 10, Paragraph 1-2, (Christianity, Gnostic/Essene)

****

Amidst the mountainous waves I came upon the treasure in the out-of-body state. On a small island, no more than 10' X 10' wide, lay the burial cloth of Jesus Christ. By looking at it, you would probably never know what it was; you had to have been brought here with the knowledge implanted within you to have understanding. It was a plain white cloth with no unusual markings except for blood stains. Because this island was in the center of the ocean surrounded by voluptuous waves, there was great effort and sacrifice involved in coming here to see it, and indeed, in remaining here to witness its splendor. Interestingly, every time the waves swelled and I became fearful of the water around me, the cloth would begin to bleed. A connection existed between the sufferings of Christ and the sufferings required of a soul to come to this hidden remote place of passage to witness the splendor of such a gift.

A hymn began singing as I awaited the final waves which came in such a fury; the entire island was obliterated . . . at least for now. As my body swelled beneath the waters, I fought to survive the thrust and return to the surface. Wondering what had become of the burial cloth, inside I knew that this washing away was only symbolic of the washing of the sins that occurs when one witnesses such a marvel.

Swimming to shore, I could no longer see any remnant or vestige of the island of passage, or its contents. Pondering on the cloth that would bleed at any sign of suffering, I began to write the hymn down.

"Yes, O Jesus, it is for Thee to drink the chalice to the dregs, Thou art now vowed to the most terrible death. Jesus, may nothing be able to separate me from Thee, neither life nor death. Following Thee in life, affectionately bound to Thy

suffering may it be granted to me to expire with Thee on Calvary in order to ascend, with Thee to glory . . ."
The Agony of Jesus, Chapter IV, Page 36, Paragraph 2, (Christianity, Catholic, Words of Padre Pio)

****

Coming and going with might, the Pleiadian vessels had come and gone all night, filling my eyes with visions of wonder. Every time they came, the sound of their vibrations resonated across the heavens, as the vessel held your eyes to it as if in some kind of trance.

Outside a denominational church we waited, while several devotees of this church also looked on. Turning a stormy purple-blue, the skies were filled with color. Winds picking up, our skin became elastic as an especially beautiful music of the spheres began playing, and radio energy showers began falling. Waiting aside a sturdy wall, the skies parted for a huge Mother Ship.

Emanating from the underside of the vessel was a light beam, and a beautiful lady was immediately transported to the doorway of the church. Exquisite, she was wearing a white robe with a gilded golden white and sky blue crown, and everyone called her "The Lady in Light." These words were spoken with inherent and instinctual understanding and respect.

Nearby, I moved closer to her and was able to touch her robe, but I couldn't see her face, for she was looking in the other direction. Unable to let go, the vibration was so eminently pleasing. As we walked into the room, all the members of the church were immediately mesmerized. Bowing to her, as she suddenly turned and bowed back five or six times, I was stunned, shocked, and exasperatingly excited!

"My God!" I shouted to her most beauteous face, "you're the Blessed Virgin Mary!" Smiling in knowing, the most Holy Virgin had come to us from the stars, in a spaceship that still hovered in the sky between two light portals. Saying nothing, she only smiled in happiness at my observation, as I began to disappear and return to my physical Earthly craft.

"The local universe Mother Spirit thus acquires a personal nature tinged by that of the Master Spirit of the superuniverse of astronomic jurisdiction."
The Urantia Book, Paper 34, No. 1, Paragraph 3, (Christianity, Urantia)

****

Stunned by the brightness of this immensely holy being, I found myself humbled when I realized who it was. Therese Neumann, the Catholic stigmatist (one who mysteriously bore the wounds of Christ) from Germany who lived in the mid-twentieth century, was looking upon my countenance with a glowing eminence which overwhelmed me. An aura of light shone around her form which seemed to go on forever. Only her smile could surpass the radiance of her mere presence. Glowing at me with love, she conveyed to me that my soul was not in a good place because I'd begun reading some books by a particular author. "Do not follow the New Age or other false paths," she said, "the time is coming for you to become Catholic." Surprised by this pronouncement, I shouted to her as she began to fade from view. "Does that mean that reincarnation is untrue?" She smiled as if to convey that this was not relevant, and that I simply must obey the holy command. Nodding back to her, I watched her disappear from my view, taking the ominous light with her.

****

Awaking in sleep, I found my soul had entered into an all-white room where a table had been placed. At the other end of the room by the table was a large, magnificent painting of Jesus wearing the robes of white and red, His Sacred Heart emanating from it brilliantly. Having approached the table, I noticed that there were several old wrinkled photographs lying next to this painting on the table. Immediately picking them up, they were pictures of Therese Neumann and her family. Because her life as a stigmatist had been filled with criticism and controversy, the Lord wished to convey to me that she was a legitimate messenger of Christ. There would be no doubt as to the authenticity of the message I'd received at her hand, as this was no deception of the enemy. "Thank you, Jesus." I prayerfully said, bowing to the picture which now became animate.

Without words, Jesus conveyed to me that I must embrace my reclusive lifestyle as He had chosen me to be a contemplative in order to fulfill His will through my writing. Further, I was to raise my children, in His eyes an exalted role. Reaching my hand to touch His, my spirit became invisible to the room.
****

CHAPTER FIVE
Meetings with the Blessed Virgin, the Buddha, Avalokiteswara, Zarathustra, Babaji, Indira and Mahatma Gandhi, Cross of Jesus, St. Paul, St. Michael and Heavenly Hosts, St. Patrick, Dalai Lama, St. Elizabeth Ann Seton's Schoolhouse, Padre Pio Celebrating a Mystical Mass in the Heavens.

****
Within the depths of the night, they came towards me like a swarm of bees, angered at the spiritual changes which were being wrought within my soul. Five ugly reptilian demons had come after me followed by a huge vortex of black energy which carried with it the most horrendous humming sound. Individual molecules of evil could be seen within the cloudy vortex. Feeling immediately overwhelmed, I called out to Mary, Mother of God, to assist me in this battle in which I was obviously outnumbered.

Appearing in the heavens before me, she wore a five pointed crown on her head and was covered in a swirling robe of blue. Awestruck by her beauty, I didn't immediately notice that the demons with their energized black vortex of evil had immediately disappeared as soon as she had come. When the moment had passed, I was filled with amazement at how quickly she had vanquished them.

Whenever I've been in trouble, it is the members of the royal lineage of souls upon whom I call for assistance; Jesus, Mary, Buddha, Zarathustra, Avalokiteswara, etc. Perhaps this is a lesson in *true* significance, rather than that which is vainly perceived through worldly eyes.
****
Long black mane blowing in the wind, the master Babaji was soaring through the stars. 'Babaji' is a well known master from India, and quite familiar to those who've read the books of Paramahansa Yogananda. Very, very old (several hundreds of years), he is said to be able to travel between realms, appearing at one moment as a physical being, appearing in another as a spiritual essence at will, manifesting in and out of realities.

Although I saw him soaring, I was unable to keep up with him and stopped to catch my breath. Not my physical breath, mind you, but a breath it is, despite its immateriality. Hovering in the heavens, I noticed that a tiny three-foot high witch had appeared in the sky in front of me. Attempting to dissuade me from finding the great master, she said, "I have much to teach you of sorcery." Laughing at her suggestion, I replied, "Sorcery is a practice which violates eternal law, and don't you think that the green pointy hat and straw-like hair is a bit obvious?" Frowning at this, she disappeared, as a disgusting gull demon appeared. Gulls are the demons of destructive sexual energy who appear as humans with bat-like wings and such. Often, but not always, their hair is greased back. As would be expected of such a demon, he began to make sexual gestures towards me, as I pushed him aside, declining his offer of vice.

As Babaji was now long gone, I began flying in search of him or someone who could lead me to him. As the stars passed by my vision like snow on a windshield, I finally noticed up ahead a golden temple. Approaching the huge gold/marble door, it bore a sign which read, 'Temple to the Masters.' I was elated!

Knocking upon the door, I was not given entrance. Disappointed, I recognized my unworthiness, but was happy that I was allowed to look upon a set of pictures. About thirty masters resided in this temple, and they were shown in their entire splendor. Babaji was not among them, and I noticed that these masters were different than the others I'd already encountered. Bearing an adventurous quality to them, they seemed to be energized in a truly unique manner. Unlike the masters, saints and prophets of the Earth, whose holiness was calm, serene and effulgent, these were powerful stewards of creative energies, almost reminiscent of the Assisi Marauders (who rode white-winged horses with whom I'd encountered long ago.). Active and highly energized, these masters seemed to be involved in energetic action, while the other equally holy ones seemed to be more involved in 'being' with God.

Humbled and in awe, I quietly left this golden marble temple without entering, and continued my quest for Babaji.
****

Traveling with my vision removed, the spiritual world was taking me through the aeons to a very holy place. As my vision was restored, I struggled to regain consciousness in the realm I now occupied. An image of holiness and splendor arrayed in such simplicity lay before me, that of Indira Gandhi, the wife of Mahatma Gandhi. Dressed in an exquisite, but very simple, immaculately white wedding gown, her holiness could never be expressed. Stunned, humbled and moved, a voice spoke, "Gandhi was a saint, not just to the Hindu and Indian people, but to God. The people of the world must know this, especially those in the Christian world who do not believe that a Hindu man could not only go to heaven, but be a *true saint* in the eyes of the Lord." Having known some Christians to say such things, wouldn't it be interesting if they were given a moment to compare their own status in the eyes of God, with such a man as this? Perhaps they would be greatly humbled and deeply troubled by their lack of insight.

Indira was just as holy as her husband, and in some respects, she was even more so due to her silent but powerful influence during life in supporting her husband. She was his strength, courage and stronghold. Literally glowing with light, Gandhi suddenly appeared next to her. Very friendly and hospitable, he was anxious to talk to me. Other sub-conscious astral souls were in the room who did not recognize the obvious level of his saintliness. Disappointed by this, I pointed it out to them because they were completely unaware of the great honor which had been bestowed upon them. Indira and Mahatma Gandhi had lowered themselves from their usual place within the high heavens to deign to speak to a lowly worm such as myself.

Gandhi walked quietly over to me in the same humble manner he bore in life, wearing traditional Indian garb and adorned with a smile which could only speak of the eternal happiness which had been bestowed upon him and his wife for their courageous and holy efforts to save a people through non-violence. Showing me the similarities between the Catholic and the Hindu religion, his purpose was to discard the differences and begin a peaceful discussion with the hopeful conclusion of achieving understanding and unity between peoples. Pointing out that both the Hindu and Catholic religions honor an incarnation of God and a divine mother, he also noted a similarity between the mantras of the Hindus, and novenas of the Catholics. Both honored many symbols, pictures, images and statues of the holy divinities and/or saints, and each religion had an extensive theology of demons. Pointing out the different spelling, the Hindu spelling would be 'daemons.' Finally, Catholics pray to saints for intercession, while Hindu's pray to demi-gods for intercession, which is just another word for saints.

In order to express this unity in a more meaningful way, the entire gathering of people, who had now become completely enamored of this saintly simple man, performed several Hindu mantras together following this holy ejaculation with several Catholic prayers. As we prayed the Hindu mantras, Gandhi made appear Hindu icons and pictures, and when we began the Catholic prayers, he changed the pictures and icons to those of the Catholics. Engaged by the holiness of the moment, I was taken by surprise when I began to fade from this realm.

Waving good-bye to these two amazing souls, I couldn't help but shed a tear as my final breath took me away. Awaking, I had no words, but chose to remain silent for a very long time in honor of this amazingly holy visitation.
****

Walking along an old dusty road, a large convention center loomed ahead. Announcing that a New Age convention was in progress, a large banner was displayed near the doorway. Going towards this building, I began running as I planned to go inside and see what might be happening. When I came near, however, an invisible force resisted my attempts. No matter how hard I might try, I couldn't go in due to an immense force-field which had been placed upon my path.

Suddenly in the sky above me, something began to form. In bright yellow-white light, the aura of a starry emerald phantasm came from the heights of heaven. Waiting to see what it might become, I was humbled and a bit ashamed when the image became clear. The cross of our Lord Jesus Christ hung in the sky at least a mile long and a half mile wide. Instantly, I knew that I was not to 'enter' into anything New Age again. Profoundly intense, this was not a friendly reminder, but a stern reprimand. Bowing to the Lord's wishes and looking down in embarrassment, I began to disintegrate.
****

My soul was honored to observe the last days of St. Paul; his life, death and a small part of what seemed to be his journey into heaven . . . and a resurrection. Beginning my journey this eve, I was allowed to inhabit the body of St. Paul in a way which permitted me to experience the history of this man as if I were living it myself. Inhabiting the body of another disciple of Jesus in a similar fashion, my husband, Andy, was with me. St. Paul was speaking quite verbosely regarding the resurrection of Christ, condemning the actions of His executioners with extreme flame and fury. A plot was being hatched behind St. Paul's back to poison him to death, but St. Paul seemed to have a foreknowledge of their affairs. Telling those gathered that he, too, would die and be resurrected; he was speaking of the resurrection of the spirit.

Following St. Paul after his death, somebody had poisoned both him and his disciple (whom Andy was traveling through) on the day of his death. Following their spirits beyond death, we came upon an interesting gateway which seemed to be a borderland into heaven. As the two had died they reawakened on a beach. Next to the beach, was a huge wall of water bearing onto the sands at least one thousand feet high. Filled with oceanic life, this wavy mirage was a self-contained body, as though it wasn't really water, but perhaps an energy field waving to and fro like an ocean. Knowing he would be transported to heaven as soon as he stepped in, St. Paul did not step. Rather, his soul was resurrected automatically into the spheres, as was the soul of the other disciple.

Andy and I reappeared in the physical world, sitting naked upon each other's lap. A sign of purity, it was now the 20th century.

Because there was a great deal more to this experience which is totally inexplicable, I have left it unsaid.

Flown around the world to witness a marvel of the present age, Pope John Paul II stood atop every mountain and high point of the world waving to the people. Holy eminence a sight to behold, I flew above him in the realm of the blue-green ethers as my soul was somehow receiving of the sacred embers which came from his hands to the people of the world.

****

In the darkness of the night, her image appeared before my soul. Ten feet high and framed in gold, the Blessed Virgin Mary wore a sky blue robe over the inlaid white one below. Stars appeared all about her garments, and cherubim were singing and playing musical instruments, mostly harps and trumpets. Below her was an emblem which read, 'Our Lady of the Rosary.'

Unable to remove my ecstatic and fixed gaze from her beauty, she withdrew with this simple message of the importance of this magnificent Catholic prayer. Thunderstruck, I breathed for the first time since her appearance, and drifted back to sleep.

****

In a desert like oasis, something amazing and spectacular emerged. Standing upon the edge of a beautiful sand dune, a large gathering of heavenly hosts appeared before my eyes. Appearing in human form, their bodies were composed of white light. Heading the most sacred ensemble was Jesus Christ; at his side St. Michael the Archangel. Standing humbly behind them, the Blessed Virgin Mary stood before a gathering of a literal torrent of saints. Angels surrounded the holy ensemble, as they all stared at me with intensity. No words or thoughts were emitted as they stood amongst the desert sage and tumbleweeds.

Because this experience seemed so conscious, I became confused and began to look for a camera in my purse. 'With the level of brightness these hosts are emitting,' I thought, 'they will most assuredly show up on film.' Walking towards my Lord Jesus and St. Michael, I snapped a picture of them as they instantly vanished along with the entire host.

****

Entering unaware of what lay before me, the production was in full force. A group of actors had been preparing for a grand production about the life of an Irish psychic from long ago. Many of the women were arrayed in various veiled outfits, while others were dressed as belly-dancers. Immediately, I was approached by the producer of this grand gala, who grabbed me excitedly, exclaiming that he had saved the title role for me! Not quite sure what was happening, he shoved a picture in my face of the psychic he wished me to portray. Although the man was clearly not evil or dark, I noticed a wild hairdo and that a great dramaticism had been played out within his life. Unfortunately, this dramaticism had leaked into the portrayal of his psychic gifts, as well.

Looking up at this anxious man who assumed I'd be honored to partake of this role, I quietly said, "I'm so sorry to disappoint you, but I don't feel that I can play this part." Looking confused, he waited for me to explain. "I have a very deep and innate feeling that St. Patrick would have whipped this guy's bootie," I said.

St. Patrick, the Catholic Patron Saint of Ireland, had been taken by the Irish as a slave while a young boy, but as he worked in isolation tending to the sheep, he began to undergo grand spiritual changes which were noticed by many. As a result, he became known as the holy youth, because of the virtuous life he lived.

Many had become aware of his mystical experiences which were leading him ever closer to his Lord, Jesus Christ. Beginning to have visions, he was led by them to escape back to his native England. Despite this escape, shortly after he returned from Ireland, he had a vision which told him that he would someday go back to convert the Irish to Christianity, and that someday he'd be the Bishop of Ireland.

Years passed by in a monastery before this opportunity came, but when it did, he jumped on the chance to fulfill the vision of his youth. All these years, he had practiced great austerity, penance, obedience and virtue and had led a very holy life. When he returned to Ireland, the Druids were the primary religious body in the country, and among other things, they practiced human sacrifice, divination, prophecy and the use of magical or mystical powers.

Miracles of amazing stature are reported in regards to St. Patrick, who overturned the rule of the Druids in a very short time. Among the legends, it is said that St. Patrick became immaterial when his former slave owner tried to kill him with a sword, and the sword passed right through his body. The Druid High Priests attempted to poison him, and he was unaffected. When the Druids challenged him to a trial by fire, which was their ultimate test of whose God was supreme; they demanded that he send one of his followers because they believed that St. Patrick was practicing some form of high magic. St. Patrick's follower came out unscathed, wearing the mantle of Patrick upon his shoulders. The Druid and his belongings never came out.

Although suffering a great deal from many persecutions, some from his own church, he never wavered in his great faith and commitment to God. Despite the fact that he was Bishop, he never ceased participating in the difficult daily chores which he could have easily given to others, like building shelters, feeding livestock, or gathering water or food.

Standing before me confused and lost, the man who was to run this production was completely clueless. He didn't know the difference between a saint and a psychic! So I began to convey to him some of the elements of importance. "A psychic," I shared, "is someone who has received a spiritual gift. That is all. Being psychic does not denote that someone is leading a virtuous or holy life, because the gift itself is not related to any merit on their part. We cannot even be sure with such cases wherein the spiritual gift is coming, as it could be coming from either side, God or Satan. 'You may judge them by their fruits,' as Jesus said. Manifesting in a life ever deepening in virtue and holiness, and in the lives of those they aid with their gift, a similar response, another fruit would be modesty and humility in their appearance, as opposed to, excessive displays of vanity to make them stand apart. They would not be guiding people to riches, sex or fame, but rather to simplicity, purity and selflessness."

"A saint may display many spiritual gifts, but they are not a saint because of these spiritual gifts. Living a life of heroic virtue is what defines a saint, although it may also be said that it is likely that such saints receive so many spiritual gifts because they use them for the sanctification of souls. The Lord Jesus said in the parable of the talents that He would give more talents to those who used the first talent He had given to them faithfully. A great energetic chasm exists between saints and psychics, which cannot be understood through mere words. I can't for the life of me understand why there are those who seem to perceive that having a spiritual gift, in and of itself, denotes holiness. It doesn't denote evil, either; but it is a talent, a gift, which can be used for good or ill."

Having made my point as best as I could for the moment, I shook the man's hand and thanked him for his kindness in offering me the part. "I'm gonna stick with the saints." I said, as I disappeared.
****

Beyond the barrier which lay in front of me was a place which filled me with fear. The Lord called it 'the bowery,' and His internal voice directed me to invoke the protection of the Blessed Virgin Mary before entering by saying one 'Hail Mary.' As I did, I became invisible, in the sense that I was protected from danger, although the people in this place were able to see me.

Coming into the bowery, I was to see what was perhaps the poorest and most violent, criminal infested and dangerous part of the city. Former tall buildings lay in ruins before me, partly torn down with windows and doors missing in most places. Rotting on the inside, the buildings were infiltrated by an unusually gross mold.

Passed out or high on drugs, most of the people who lived in this place were just mere shells of the beautiful creation the Lord had intended them to be. Their surroundings could easily be called 'Hell on Earth' without any fear of exaggeration. Bodies broken down from drug and alcohol abuse, hunger, poverty and insanity, the people reached out to me asking me to tell their story so that those who had forgotten about them might try to help. But amidst this horrible display of degradation, I felt totally helpless, and I didn't know what to do.

Speaking in my ear, the voice of Jesus Christ whispered, "Pancreas of Flowers, pancreas of flowers, pancreas of flowers . . ." Repeating this many times, over and over, my spirit began ascending.

Filling me with understanding, I had an internal visual already in place. Bizarre as it may sound, the pancreas produces insulin in the body. Without insulin, the body is ravaged and slowly destroyed by diabetes. Many diabetics eventually have limbs removed, piece by piece, because of the ravages of the disease, and it is impossible to number all of the body systems which are slowly destroyed; the eyes, heart, kidneys, limbs, etc.

Similarly, the people in the bowery were ravaged by hunger, illness and drug abuse, but their poverty was as beautiful as a garden of flowers to Our Lord. As He spoke the words in my ears, I could feel His tremendous and unending love for these poor, forgotten people.

My soul returned to my home.

****

Joining a group of souls praying the rosary, we were being led into a chapel by a group of older ladies. Beautiful and ornate, the church was filled with paintings and images of angels which were surrounding Jesus Christ and His Mother Mary and was appropriately called, 'Our Lady of the Angels.' Stone pillars framed the entrance to this wondrous abode.

Inside the chapel, I looked intently at pictures and mementos of a great bishop, as I suddenly noticed his spirit standing in front of me. Peacefully, the bishop had a simple message to impart to me. "If you are praising the Lord with other Catholics," he said, "feel free to go ahead and pray the rosary together, but if there are Protestants in the group, it is not necessary to convert them. Focus on your mutual love for Jesus and praise Him in a way which is comfortable for both." As our group had been praying the Rosary, we immediately changed our prayers as a group of Protestant souls arrived, joining together in a mutual expression of love and unity for God. He disappeared.

After a short period of time, there were several hundred souls praising the Lord in a unity of spirit, irregardless of their dogmatic or doctrinal differences.

In an interesting dichotomy, my soul was led a fortnight later to another Christian church. Inside the building, a woman's spirit was wandering around the vestibule seeking ways to 'bewitch' the holy tabernacle. Within my soul, I was given immediately to know that this woman, who had once followed a path towards God, had strayed by following witchcraft, and thus, partaking in a pact with the devil.

Another older woman was sitting quietly at a desk when a sudden and odiferous presence made itself known to her. Before she had a moment to ascertain what was happening, she fell to the floor having a full-blown heart attack. Quickly, several more angelic hosts arrived to tend to this poor woman's needs as I was summoned to follow the witch throughout the church and abort any satanic missions she would attempt. Entering into the church library, the witch was trying to place a bewitched book upon the shelves. Grabbing it from her, she then fled to the nursery wherein she attempted to place bewitched baby blankets. Continually going in and out of demonic control, this woman's spirit was almost completely possessed. She would seem normal one moment, and then her face would contort horribly as the demons inside of her would regain control.

Beginning to perform an exorcism, I noticed that her possession was not yet complete, and that she was not totally convinced of her decision to serve the ogre. Becoming disoriented, going back and forth from herself to demonic entities, I told her that I sensed great confusion on her part. "You are divided!" I shouted, "Satan does not want a servant who is divided!" Pausing a moment, the Holy Spirit came upon me and impressed me with a message for this poor lost soul. "Jesus wants *you*. Yes, Jesus does." Matter of fact and very calm, her face contorted for a moment to that of Satan, before he left her body for good and my task was complete.

Waking to the presence of a small being laying next to me on the bed, I first believed it to be that of my second eldest daughter, Mary. Coming over to hug her, I quickly noticed that it was an imp. Chastising the foul creature, I ordered it to leave my home under the authority of Jesus Christ as it scurried off into the night.
****

Hovering amongst the clear blue sky above ancient Egypt, the Dalai Lama appeared to give me instruction. "You need to look for the invisible upon that which is visible," he quietly stated. As my eyes were directly looking upon the side of an ancient pyramid, an image began to slowly appear from invisibility. Upon one side of the rock face was a large eye, just as I'd seen during my journey through the mysteries. "Come," the Dalai Lama replied, "I will take you somewhere where I can show you how to do this." In an instant, he had taken me to a huge wilderness wherein I became sub-conscious for the remainder of the journey.

On a subsequent night, a very saintly nun appeared to me saying, "You need to sit still and meditate on the life of Our Lord; His passion and death."
****

If only the human language could encompass what I've seen this night! My soul was taken over the threshold of death to witness many beautiful and rapturous things, almost none of which I have been allowed to retain in memory.

While enjoying the freedom of spirit, however, I asked Jesus, "Would it be possible for me to see something very holy? It doesn't matter to me what it might be, just as long as it's very holy."

Soaring towards space, approaching what appeared to be a 19th century schoolroom, it was steadily afloat amongst the stars as if it had been given immortal status. Landing inside, the schoolhouse was filled with happy children playing. Sitting down quietly, I was unsure of what to expect.

Before I was to be made aware of the purpose of this flight, a very attractive *appearing* man approached, attempting to entice me sexually. Apparently, he didn't want me to see this grand holy thing, and had come to detract my attention on something foul instead. Annoyed, I grabbed his hand and threw it towards him, away from myself. Holding a firm grasp, I shouted, "In the name of Our Lord Jesus Christ, I command you to leave!" At this command, he turned into a disgustingly grotesque gull demon, angry and writhing. Repeating my command, he lifted his grip, and at the third command, he thankfully disappeared.

Having passed through the throes of temptation, I looked again at the room which lay before me. An old man appeared in the room as an almost ghostly figure. Like an apparition, his human form was all in white. Wearing the coveralls of a man from the 19th century, he was almost completely bald. Many children were sitting down at their desks now which were neatly gathered at the sides of the room. Approaching the older man, I asked him politely if he knew where I might be. "Why, you are in the schoolhouse of St. Elizabeth Ann Seton," he said as he bid me to lie down on the floor.

Following his directive, he told me that the Lord was aware of my desire to know what it was like to die, and that he was going to allow me to experience it in part. Surprised by this revelation, he continued, "I'm going to allow you to experience a death somewhat like Mr. Seton," he said, referring to the saint's husband who had passed away after a short illness (This was prophetic in nature, although I didn't know it.). "Mr. Seton actually passed while his body was being ritually prepared for burial," the old man said, indicating that he was actually in a coma when he'd been pronounced dead.

As his words became an echo from another world, I began to see and feel my soul entering into a lightly blue-green misty place wherein I was slowly beginning to feel the closure of breath. Frightening me a little bit, I shouted to the old man, "I don't want to *really* die, you know!" As I said this, the state was immediately lifted and the old man had disappeared.

Annoyed at myself for making this comment which had indicated my fear of undergoing this experience, I knew I had to find the old man in order to try again. As I began running into a back room, I saw him behind a counter. "There you are," I said, "I'm sorry I messed things up, could we try again?" Without saying a word, I was immediately transfixed back into the state I'd been before.

Interestingly, there was a transition between life and death which was different than what I'd experienced in the astral state. Deathly aware of each system of my body shutting down, most primarily breath and heartbeat, I was still a bit afraid. As the body systems slowed to a stop, I felt a sense of concern over the difficulty one might encounter in adjusting to this different state of existence, sans body functions. Everything vibrated around me, as if I'd become aware of the molecular structure of ether and all spirit life.

Within a few moments, the old man slowly bid my soul return. In his hands, was a large chart. Showing me a graph of what he had done, there were several categories of experience involved in the bringing on of death categorized in the numbers one through six. Six, he explained, would indicate irreversible death, and he had taken me to a level four. "If someone had seen your body while this was going on," he said, "it's not likely they would have noticed these changes in your body. But if they looked closely, they would've noticed the respiration and heartbeat were significantly close to stopping." Interested in this chart, I shared with him how I'd experienced a small panic when my breathing and heart rate slowed. Nodding, he indicated that this was not uncommon, although this transition in true death took only a few moments. As a result, many souls didn't even notice it as they were dying because they'd passed through it so quickly.

As is *quite* usual, he began smiling as his spirit began to waver in and out of my view.

****

Hearing a summon from the Master, I immediately followed this beckon to see where it might lead. Traveling towards the stars, I found myself ascending a large mountain. Halfway to the top, I came upon a messenger who had come on behalf of the Lord, carrying a large binder full of instructions. "The Master is in need of you," he said, as he directed my attention to continue towards the summit of this snow-capped mountain.

Going with him, he took me to a large spiritual community which resided at the crest of this beatific peak. Marble temples had been erected in this magnificently sunny and bright realm, and I understood that the sky was lit with the light of God.

A gathering had assembled of about fifty people as I was led to take a seat next to a woman of whom I did not immediately recognize. Being the only newcomer, the others were natives to this place. Instructing the group from the front of the assembly, a beautiful lady appeared with long, slightly wavy, light brown hair which flowed halfway down her back. Speaking of living in harmony with one another, they began singing a song about how they all worked together to take care of the needs of each individual, and how all that they had was to be used for the community. The next song was about the fire which came down from heaven through the angels, to seed eternity upon the Earth.

When they'd finished singing, the woman openly introduced me to the group as a newcomer. Saying nothing, I noticed that when she mentioned that I'd come directly from the Earth, the lady beside me was upset and began to protest that I'd been allowed to come here at all. In a confrontational manner, she asked, "How many training sessions have you been to?" As I'd been to none, I didn't immediately respond, but the woman at the head replied, "Well, this is a humble soul who has learned through self-seeking and humility." Quiet remained in the room, as I became red with embarrassment. Beckoning me to come forward, I began to walk towards her. "Besides," she said, "the Master has need of her." Feeling a rush of tremendous awe and honor, I felt unworthy of this grand statement. 'How could I, a lowly, wretched human, be of any help to my Lord?' I thought.

Approaching the front of the assembly to join us was a young girl of about thirteen years of age. Reaching her hand to mine, she said her name was 'Lisao.' In awe, I recognized her as being one of the guardian angels of my second eldest daughter, Mary.

Asking Lisao with whom she would like to partner, without hesitation, she asked for me as I knew that I was to be a mother to her in some way, I was adopting her.

"There is to be a marriage today," the lady again spoke, "those who are to be married, please approach." Sitting directly in front of her, I instinctively stood up and a lone, tall, red-haired, skinny man had approached, now standing alone and staring at me. Whispering into the lady's ears, she openly replied to him, "Don't worry, she's stood up. But she's confused and doesn't fully know what is to take place." Taking my hand, the lady placed his in mine as I stood there, confused. Looking towards this man, I replied, "I have three kids, and apparently now, four, as I have adopted Lisao." Very quick to agree to adopt all of my children as his own, he seemed perturbed at my lack of understanding.

Despite this, the ceremony continued as I quietly pondered in my mind what could possibly be happening. It was also clear that this person was living on the other side, and not physically present upon the Earth. (Although I didn't know it at the time, I was meeting somebody who might become more important to me in my after-life. But because there were medical problems which remained undiagnosed, I didn't realize the potential momentousness of this revelation. In a short time, my status would be revealed and their import would become clearer.)

Lisao, this young man and I had wandered off together as the gathering concluded. Looking upon the sky which did not bear a sun but was aflame from the light of God, I hesitated to leave, but knew that I must. Releasing this young man's hand, I looked into his eyes which mirrored back to me an intensive longing on his part for me to remember who he was, something I sadly could not give him at this time. Meekly, I bid them both good-bye, releasing his hand to soar down the mountain.

As I began to soar, my spirit found itself waiting in a mountain temple with marble beams jutting high into the sky. Awaiting me was a young woman who appeared to be of royal descent. Looking as though she might have come from India, her long black hair was pulled back into a casual braid. A very simple golden band was formed around her head, and she wore an exquisite and colorful Indian garment, which was shimmering with pinks, purples and blues.

In her hands was a golden gilded book which she immediately handed to me. Inside was the text of 'The Mysteries of the Redemption,' along with the imprint of a publisher. "I have a message for you from the Master," she said, as she pointed to the name of the publisher. Flipping through the golden gilded book to a page in the back, she handed it to me to read. 'Let Jesus take care of everything,' it said.

Looking up at this royal young lady before me, she closed the golden book, placing it in my hands for me to keep. Quietly, she turned and walked away, as the spirit wind took her essence into a molecular cyclone which then spun upwards towards heaven.
****

Alit by the sun, the clouds were glorious as I arrived without foreknowledge of how I'd made my journey to this abode. Two priests were calmly awaiting my arrival, wearing the robes which are normally worn for the performance of the Mass. Today, they wore the color green. Hovering in the heavens, the priests directed my gaze in another direction wherein I immediately noticed a glorious stairway from the sky into deep space. Turning towards the steps, the priests handed me a stack of 8 X 11 cardboard markers which were to serve in some manner in the journey of which I was about to undertake.

A ritual process followed, as I instinctually threw the cardboard markers up the steps, tossing them into the heavens. It was absolutely vital that a correct synchronization between these markers and the steps occur before I could continue on my way. Coming together in the heavens, the markers synchronized into the first ten steps, as an angel appeared. "You've missed a few steps," she said. Gathering up and looking at the ten markers more carefully, I noticed that several appeared to be stuck together, so I prepared them properly and again flung them towards the heavens directly at this heavenly stairway which led into deep space. Counting, I gathered that I had now acquired twenty-one steps. Very patiently, the angel conveyed, "You have still missed some steps as there are a total of fifty four." Again, I gathered up and looked at the markers, focusing more intently on the hidden meaning that they might, as I flung them again towards the heavens along this galactic stairway. Watching in awe, they magically formed into a grandiose series of fifty-four steps into the heavens, beckoning me to follow. Imprinting themselves upon each of the etheric steps, they had become deeply imbedded a beautiful heavenly image of which I was not yet allowed to see. All I knew was that they followed a sequence of events.

Standing on each side of me, the priests had approached as if to protect me from the thrust which was about to overtake us as we prepared to enter upon this pathway into deep space. As they took my hands, one on each side, the images upon the steps became clear to me and I shuddered at the import of their meaning. Upon each of the fifty four almost invisible, etheric steps, were very distinct images showing the sequence of the holy mass. Jesus Christ appeared in robes of red and white, taking the place of the priest in the performance of the Latin rite, as His sacred heart blazed forth a reddish light which glowed in heavenly proportions. Each of the stages presented, brought about an energetic thrust within the souls of those who were open to them as they attended the mass.

Without a word, my spirit was immediately swept up into galactic space, as my soul followed the fifty-four steps of the Holy Mass undergoing a voluminous transformation as I traveled at the speed of light towards the stars. A rushing torrent of influential energies filled me with a solemn knowledge of this holy rite, and transformed my spirit as I followed its pathway.

Before I had the time to ascertain the meaning of this torrential flood of energy, my spirit came to a sudden standstill. Inside a very solemn and holy cave which held reminiscences of the sacred tomb of Christ, we were hovering in deep space. Because I had been swept up in a whirlwind of white energies, my spirit could not ascertain the path I had taken to enter this tomb. But as I stood here, I felt the coming together of each step of the journey. Each unique and individual image of Christ performing the fifty-four stages of the Latin rite of the mass at the sacred altar had been thrust into my soul.

Standing before me in an epiphany of light, the priests were preparing to finish this sacred ritual by consecrating the Eucharistic host into the body and blood of Jesus the Christ. Before I could ascertain any more, I noticed a holy visitor who had come to join us for this final procession of our faith. Standing beside the priests, placing his holy hands upon their shoulders, Padre Pio looked up to peer deeply into my eyes. Stunned by his entrance, I didn't know what to do or say. But before I could think, the spirits of the priests became ablaze with sparkly blue lights, permeating throughout their spiritual forms and encompassing the robes they wore. All around them, the sparkly blue lights were aglow as they began to speak the sacred words of consecration, which held within them great power now translated into my soul in a lightning-storm of power.

Huge power came from within the priests manifesting as a magnificent and large beam of blue light coming from their hands, entering directly into the sacred host which immediately came alive, bursting with blue energy and light. For a moment, I remembered long ago when I had been taken through the rites of the crucifixion and had been shown images of Christ during his passion. Interestingly, his body had been surrounded by beautiful blue energies, very similar to those which had now overtaken the Eucharistic host. Overcome with holy energy, the entire tomb was filled with an electric silence, the most notable being that of Padre Pio. My mind took note of the appropriateness of his presence, in that as a bearer of the stigmata (the sacred wounds of Christ); he had journeyed through his life as a living crucifixion. In this holy tomb, we had just experienced Christ's resurrection . . . and the most amazing thing about it was that every single soul upon the Earth could experience this magnificent moment any day of the year by attending the holy mass.

A flash of light occurred as our spirits were immediately transported into deep space, hovering amidst the stars. Padre Pio's back was turned to me, as he sat silently in a very still and meditative position. Feeling compelled to talk with the priests who had completed the mass, I was wondering if they had seen the magnificent energy and power which had come from them during the consecration. Because I'd not seen astonishment coming from their faces as all of this had occurred, I'd considered that maybe they'd experienced it in the mundane, the manner in which it is physically experienced on Earth. But gazing upon the back of Padre Pio, I had an inherent feeling that he might consider such a discussion disrespectful in regards to the holy moment of which we had just been allowed to partake.

Keeping my amazement to myself, I sat quietly in respectful obeisance to the Lord, and gazed upon the back of the holy man who was to grace my presence for only a moment more. In a flash, my spirit disappeared, returning to my familiar Earthly abode.
****

"Padre Pio has accepted you as a spiritual child," the voice said, as an invisible hand gave me a relic of the saint. Awaking at San Giovanni Rotondo, I meditated quietly in a room alone all night.
****

Waking up in the back seat of a car, two other people were being driven around a ghetto with me. Stopping in an especially scary location, the driver asked all of us to get out of the vehicle. One exited the car immediately, while the other stayed put.

Looking more closely at the driver, I suddenly recognized him as Padre Pio. Because of this, I made a quick decision. 'Padre Pio wouldn't leave me here in this dangerous part of town,' I thought, 'I think I'll take my chances and remain in the car.' Not moving from my position, the Padre began driving quietly without saying a word. "Those who truly love you," Padre Pio conveyed, "will not put you in harms way." Referring to those who wished for me to continue to provide things to them that I had done before becoming ill, it was very clear that if they truly loved me, they would encourage me to fight for my life, and be unconcerned about the things I could no longer do for others.

****

CHAPTER SIX
Meetings with Jesus, Prophets, Saints, Mystics and Sages from all over the World from All Time, Ancient Biblical Patriarchs, Paramahamsa Yogananda, Pope John Paul II, Mother Teresa, Sai Baba, Crucifixion, St. Veronica.

****

Having appeared to me in the splendor of white, I was stunned by His presence, and overwhelmed by his purpose. Throughout the night, the Lord Jesus repeatedly took me out of my body to observe what my husband and children's lives would be like when I was gone. Literally driving me somewhat crazy, I would try to bring myself back and wake up my spirit so that I wouldn't have to bear witness. "Don't you understand? I don't want them to grow up without me!" I shouted at the Lord, as He responded in understanding and patience. But each time I returned to sleep, Jesus calmly took me back out and allowed me to observe my family in my absence. Ironically, they seemed okay despite my loss.

Very calm throughout, the Lord had wished me to see that my family would be okay without me, and He also filled my spirit with an indescribable peace about the will of God. Conveying that this experience was vital to the spiritual formation of my children, it was an experience which would help form their destiny in adult life. (As always, the Lord never revealed if or when I would truly die, just that whether I or not I died or experienced disability for years, it was the will of God.) Wishing for me to know that my family would be fine if I did pass on, this was very hard for me. Because I most certainly wanted them to be okay, it was hard for me to accept that I may not be present at least while they were growing up. Frankly, I was afraid of being forgotten by my children, and of being replaced by somebody else who might enter their lives as a step-mom. Feeling tremendous guilt for this, I knew that if I were unable to be there, I'd want them to have a motherly figure to love. But I'd always assumed that it would be me . . . apparently arrogantly so.

Waking from this traumatic event, I accepted the peace Our Lord was giving to me as a gift, and I understood that when the time had come in which it was appointed for me to die, that I would be grateful to know that they would be okay, despite the fact that they would be okay *without me.*

That very morning, my middle daughter shared that she had a dream where she was playing in the front yard. A man with long brown hair, a beard and moustache, dressed in white and red robes came walking up the street towards her. "Are you Jesus?" Mary asked. Replying that He was, He played with her in the yard for some time before taking her back into her bedroom where He watched her while she slept, disappearing only in the morning when it was time to get up.

****

Standing amidst the galactic heavens, my soul awaited that for which I had come, although I was unaware of what that might be. Because I'd recently considered getting a job due to financial matters, I had been thinking about things I might still be able to do in my current condition. Suddenly surrounded by a crowd of very colorful spirit beings, I looked among them. Recognizing them as the prophets, saints, mystics and sages of all ages and from all over the world, I was honored and quite amazed.

Feeling a powerful rush of energy, they all began to enter into me energetically, like a bolt of lightning. But this power burst lasted for only a moment as I began to hear above me a resonant and holy voice which came across as 'a mouthpiece of God.', "You are the voice of the prophets and saints. You speak for us in the physical world . . . and this is your occupation." Demonstrating how they were able to use me in the physical world to accomplish the will of God, I was a vessel, a sieve. Without saying so, I knew that I was being directed not to pursue any type of job at this time, and it was further shown to me in another manner that most of the jobs I might be able to acquire would be too physically demanding in my condition and put me at risk of death.

Gazing upon this amazing gathering of souls, a vortex of energy began to circle around and through them into me, as my soul became a rocket burst of light! An incandescent smile lit upon my face to imitate the grand smiles coming from each of them. Marveling at the gathering, I was able to observe that there were prophets, saints, mystics and sages from every world religion represented. So many were there, I felt sure there were those representing smaller sects present, but I wasn't as familiar with what these special souls had looked like during their lives. Among them were Babaji, Paramahamsa Yogananda, various Old Testament guys, some very amazing Jewish sages, a particularly interesting Sufi who I believed might be Rumi, some Buddhist monks of whom I knew to be among the saints of that religion (one of them I believed to be Milarepa and others among the patriarchs), and various monks, saints, nuns, mendicants, hermits and priests of the various religions, as well. In this whirlwind of energy, my spirit was rushed away to return to the Earth and remember my incredible journey this eve.
****

Standing before the ancient patriarch, his ochre robe was draped over his body all the way down to his feet. In his hands, he bore the 'Catechism of the Catholic Church,' from which he was teaching me. Focusing primarily upon the entries regarding Abraham and the patriarchs, he was having me read the inter-dimensional version of the Catechism which explained the metaphysical and multiple mystical meanings which were hidden within the words. Looking upon the inter-dimensional text, some of it would wave in and out of view, and therefore, I was reading slower than usual. Meanings were hidden within the words, deep, mystical and difficult to comprehend. As he finished, the patriarch was pleasantly surprised to realize that I was indeed listening and taking in the words of his teaching, because he was unsure if any of it was penetrating. Although I would be want to explain any of these deeper meanings, my soul went into a meditative state contemplating these new understandings.
****

Lying in bed, I looked up to notice that the ceiling overhead had begun to swirl. As it did so, the walls of the room became transparent and my vision soared to that of the now swirling clouds above my home. Parting, the clouds opened to reveal an image of the heavens as a parade of bluish-white, life-size statues appeared in succession. Showing the history of salvation, it began with the Old Testament patriarchs and prophets and continued through the life of Jesus, finalizing at the ascension of Christ which was portrayed by a bluish-white statue of Him ascending to heaven with a large white-winged angel standing aside.

After this final statue was depicted, there was a large cliff which fell fifty to one hundred feet below. Above the statues was the entrance to heaven which was clearly in view and depicted as a bluish-white, swirling cloud with light. Below the statues and standing below the cliff were thousands of people all reaching to the heavenly gate. These were souls in purgatory, who regretted the missed opportunities in life which would have allowed them to enter heaven immediately upon their death. Although they did not appear to be suffering in any obvious physical way, they exhibited very clearly that they were undergoing a mental suffering in being able to see the gate of heaven, but being unable to penetrate it as of yet.

Following the exquisite salvation history of mankind through the parade of statues backwards and then forwards again, I marveled at this grand plan of the Lord.

****

Traveling the galactic heavens one fortnight, my spirit noticed a familiar soul wandering the heavenly pathways ahead of me. Running to catch up to him, Paramahansa Yogananda immediately seated himself in a lotus position in midair and looked at me expectantly as if waiting for me to pose a question. Bowing before him, I got on my knees. "My question to you, Master, is this. Over the last year, I've experienced and understood that many people die young, either through illness or accident, and don't seem to get the opportunity to finish what they start. Because of this, Master, I am struggling with the feeling that life appears quite meaningless to me."

Calmly, and with no change of expression on his face, he replied, "You must lower your desires and relinquish all things. Allow God to lead your soul to where the meaning lies." Our beatings within the Eucharistic Tabernacle served the purpose of impermanence, renunciation and detachment. Nodding that I would do this, I got up onto my feet and turned to go.

****

Having sat down to talk with this young woman who had recently gone through a bout of non-invasive cancer, I found that my words were not very effective in my attempts to guide her. Next to her, an image of a person began to slowly materialize into the realm in which we occupied, and I became quiet to see who it might be. Within moments, Pope John Paul II had appeared in his white robes with a simple white cap, sitting next to the woman very quietly. "You can not talk to her," he said, "because she has not yet discovered her destiny." Understanding, it was clear that it was pointless to try to talk to this person at this time because of her spiritual status.

****

Walking slowly wearing the garment of a nun, I was amidst a long line of Missionaries of Charity and monks who were engaged in spiritual practice. Mother Teresa was overlooking our practice and guiding us as we went.

Because of my clumsiness, I experienced repeated accidents; falling down, tripping out of line, knocking something over, etc. Each time, I felt so badly about myself because the monks and nuns around me were so very intensely mindful and full of peace. It seemed my soul was trying to overcome some remnants of agitation which remained within it. But each time, Mother Teresa gently came over to me, and took my hand in hers. "I love you," she said, as she gazed into my eyes with utter peace.

As she did so, I felt totally loved and strong enough to get back up and join this line of prayer and contemplation, working towards removing my fetters and agitated qualities which prevented my practice from being as penetrating as these souls who walked with perfect calm and precision.

"I shall share with you fully what I know. Meditation, control of the senses. And passions, and selfless service of all are the body, the scriptures are the limbs and truth is the heart of this wisdom."

The Upanishads, Kena Upanishad, #8, (Hinduism, Translator: Eknath Easwaran)

"Lord! By my inmost mind am I contemplating Thee! This helpless one in Thy Shelter keep. Grant union: my life with love for Thee is brimful. My self ever Thy beauty is contemplating; by realization of the Lord attracted. Lord! You are

protector of the devotees' esteem, shatterer of suffering, fulfiller of all desires.
May the auspicious day arrive when the Lord to my bosom be clasped."
Sri Guru Granth Sahib, Volume II, Raja Asa, Page 980, (Sikhism)
****

In the distance, I saw him sitting in a very peaceful lotus position. Paramahamsa Yogananda was meditating quietly and I was facing his side. As I watched, I was given to see how he was able to tune into any realm, much like a radio, at will. Ringlets of light and laser beams of energy were moving from his third eye and crown chakra into many differing realms, sometimes all at one time. Nodding my observation, I was taken elsewhere.
****

"And those persons who only believe in perception by the senses, those monks, nuns, male and female lay devotees who by the sage were admonished of enlightenment."
Saddharma Pundarika or the Lotus of the True Law, Sadaparibhuta, No. 8 (Buddhism: Mahayana)

"O Brother! Not every sea hath pearls; not every branch will flower, nor will the nightingale sing thereon. Then, ere the nightingale of the mystic paradise repair to the garden of God, and the rays of the heavenly morning return to the Sun of Truth - make thou an effort, that haply in this dust heap of the mortal world thou mayest catch a fragrance from the everlasting garden, and live forever in the shadow of the peoples of this city. And when thou hast attained this highest station and come to this mightiest plane, then shalt thou gaze on the Beloved, and forget all else."
The Seven Valleys and The Four Valleys, The Valley of True Poverty and Absolute Nothingness, (Bahai', Words of Baha'u'llah
****

For weeks, I had been honored to see Christ almost nightly as He gave me further instructions on the final publications of my works. Every detail was covered in exquisite detail, and if I missed something, He would tell me of it the next night. Finally, it appeared that I might be wrapping up the work on the previously written books when He came again.

"We have much to do and not much time left within which to do it." He said, conveying great urgency. Sharing instructions on how I might reorder my life to accommodate a coming onslaught of energies and intensive work, He made me to know that we were going to work together to finish the Palace of Ancient Knowledge. A flurry of instructions began to follow nightly as to which texts I was to study that day and the work began with a pulsating roar . . .

"It is the virtue of teachers to aim not at praise, nor at esteem from those under their authority, but at their salvation, and to do every thing with this object; since the man who should make the other end his aim, would not be a teacher but a tyrant. Sure it is not for this that God set thee over them, that thou shouldest enjoy greater court and service, but that thine own interests should be disregarded, and every one of their built up. This is teacher's duty."
The Complete Writings of the Early Church Fathers, Nicene and Post-Nicene Fathers, Volume 13, Homily VIII, (Christianity, Catholic, Author: St. John Chrysostom)
****

It was the last thing I expected to see or run across in my mystical world, an encounter with Hindu Avatar Sai Baba. Why? Well, let me explain.

Having studied the Hindu Avatar Sai Baba for about a year, I'd ran across many books in support of him and many which discounted him as a sorcerer or a 'false prophet.' Years ago, I'd discounted him myself, never really thinking of him again. He was prominent in India in the mid 1900's, passing from this life into the next in the late 1960's or early 1970's.

One of the difficulties I had with him was the simple understanding of the Hindu people that he was an incarnation of God. I didn't believe that then, nor do I now. But in Hinduism, Krishna was an incarnation of God. And in their belief system, those whom we might consider as saints in subsequent generations can be considered as another subsequent incarnation of God. So that is the Hindu belief, although I do not share it. And because of this, I held Sai Baba as highly suspect.

But another Hindu concept is that of the Avatars and the great Yogi's. These include those such as Babaji (the immortal Avatar), Paramahamsa Yogananda (the Hindu Incorruptible Yogi Saint), and others like them.

After my experience last night, I believe that Sai Baba was an Avatar, and a valid one. Though I still hold within myself the studies and research that I did which showed me he was an imperfect being, but one gifted with unusual gifts.

He was known for healing people and creating miraculous objects of devotion out of the ether. Many followed him, some rejected him, and nobody could explain the miraculous ash that would come forth from his mouth during healing ceremonies except that it is a common miraculous occurrence among Hindu saints.

The first thing I recall when I first saw Sai Baba coming toward me in the ether was his calming voice and the powerful, mind-blowing vibration of his soul. His words were without blame because of my prior judgment upon his soul. "Isn't it true," he said, "that Anna Maria Taigi and many other Catholic mystics were called sorceresses in their lifetime?"

I remembered. During the life of Blessed Anna Maria Taigi, who had been blessed with many visions of great importance to the pontificate of her day, was indeed thought to be a sorceress by many who lived near her, despite her obvious holy nature and many good works.

Without any further question, Sai Baba, the Avatar, came upon my soul. And it was truly a 'coming upon' if I may use this analogy. Without hesitation, I knew immediately that he was not as I'd judged him, that he was a holy man. Instantly, I knew that I'd been wrong. And before I knew it, his holy vibration encompassed my very soul and we began to soar into the mysteries of knowledge . . .

The power cannot be expressed or contained, and if I had known where this journey would lead, I would have been surprised that he had been chosen as its emissary. But at this moment, I didn't yet know where we were going.

It was an exterior and interior experience at the same time, although my body was completely asleep. My soul was filled with his soul, but he was showing me things exteriorly, as well.

We came across several intersections in the galactic heavens of knowledge, and within them were mysteries contained in energetic receptacles of which he allowed me to partake. As we continued, I felt more and more the holiness of this man (who I knew to be a man, not an incarnation of God) and I began to FEEL knowledge rather than KNOW it.

Each subsequent body of wisdom filled me with a greater tranquility and peace, but at the same time, an indescribably powerful energy that I had never before experienced.

It went on for hours as the energies would climb and subside, climb and subside. And interiorly, I just understood.

But the final turn in our journey was unexpected, although perhaps upon reflection it should not have been so. This night journey was taken two nights after an attack was made to the mosque on the Holy Mount in Jerusalem, the site of the original Temple of the Ark of the Covenant. The subsequent day, many mosques all over the Arab world had been attacked by suicide bombers and many people killed. And, of course, this was all happening at a time when my own nation was at war with Iraq.

The horrendous reality of the lives that had been lost during these wars and terrorist attacks is unfathomable to man, how must God see such things?

And then to have the Muslim people, Shiites and Sunni's, desecrating the mosques of their fellow Muslim's? Such craziness was only mirrored by the not long distant fighting, desecration and bloodshed between the Protestant and Catholic Christians of Ireland.

Despite this, Sai Baba was focused on something much smaller, although it became clear to me that these recent desecrations had been a catalyst for my journey with him this eve. Sai Baba took me into a small localized Christian Catholic church. Inside, he showed me something of great importance because it explained the type of mass desecration and violence which was now going on all around me. And in that moment, I realized why God had sent Sai Baba to show this to me; rather than somebody I had accepted, not judged or rendered false according to my own limited capacity to know (like a Catholic Saint, for instance).

Inside the small Catholic Church was being committed a sin akin to murder according to the Jewish Talmud. In the writings of the Talmud, there is a section devoted exclusively to a sin called by the name of 'Lashon Hara' and/or 'Rechilus.' Remember this name well.

Lashon Hara and/or Rechilus are gossip and slander of a fellow human being. And as Sai Baba stood above this small Catholic Church, I saw within him a holy rage begin to emerge identical (I interiorly knew this.) to the rage of Christ at the temple when he shouted, "My Father's House is a HOUSE OF PRAYER!" I felt this holy rage of God at the outrage being committed in an institution called by His name and it filled me like a powerful vibration.

Slander, in the Jewish Talmud, is the cause of ruining another man's reputation. In the Jewish tradition, to destroy a man's reputation is to destroy his ability to make a livelihood. And to destroy someone's ability to make their own livelihood is akin to murdering him.

And in that moment, I saw the correlation between what was happening in a small Catholic church through the mouths of some who were present and participating in Lashon Hara, and the destruction of God's holy temples in other parts of the world. They were one in the same, and one led to the other.

"As for me and my house," I shouted to Sai Baba, "we shall serve the Lord." A huge torrent of energy like a tsunami whizzed through my spirit as I said this. Sai Baba looked at me so intensely, I cannot describe his eyes. And I realized that Sai Baba had come to deliver this message to me, because he was a servant of God that I had judged wrongly; falsely perceived as false. It was my own judgment against him that was false. I was wrong, but had truly and honestly felt that my judgment was correct.

In the mouths of those committing a similar lack of discretion or mistake, was a similar confidence in their correctness. They had no idea the damage they were doing to those of whom they spoke. And the holy rage I was experiencing as if it were Christ's rage when He was at the temple mount which had just literally been desecrated again had been generated by the fact that they didn't care . . .

It was not important enough to them to even consider the damage that their words might do to another fellow brother or sister in Christ. It was not important enough to them to even consider the possibility that they might be wrong about somebody or something and actually INTERFERING with the Will of God!

And it was this arrogant ignorance that was also responsible for the warring of the nations, the desecrations of the Holy Mount and all the Mosques across the Middle East the previous day.

As I stared into Sai Baba's eyes, he didn't ask for apology on my part. He didn't ask for anything. He conveyed . . . and what he conveyed was the Holy Rage of God at each and every person of faith who enters into a house of prayer, whether it be Christian, Jewish, Muslim, Buddhist, Hindu, or any other; and desecrates it with his words or his internal hatred of his brothers and sisters.

And it went without saying that this holy rage extended to those who took it to the higher level by actually desecrating holy places with violence.

I FELT the Holy Rage. And it became a part of me. He wouldn't allow me to speak of my own false judgment of him. He was not willing to waste time on any apology I might have to offer him, because he held no anger at me for this misjudgment. All that mattered to him was that I FEEL the Holy Rage of God and SEE the desecration of this sin and how it had infiltrated so thoroughly into the hearts of so many people of faith, in every religion. So I internally apologized to the Lord, and vowed to never desecrate the holy temple of any of my brothers or sisters, anywhere in the world of any faith with the inappropriate use of words again.

Sai Baba was not yet satisfied. He knew of my sincerity and he was unconcerned. Pointing down below, he showed me my other brothers and sisters so negligently continuing in their acts of 'Lashon Hara' and/or 'Rechilus.' Nodding, I finally understood. He wanted me to tell them, too. This message was not just for me, but for all of us.

Thou shalt NOT bear false witness against they neighbor and Thou shalt not judge that which you don't understand.

In his eyes, I knew that I was not held accountable for making a false assumption about his soul. He was totally unconcerned with this because he knew that I'd done a great deal of discernment and I'd never slandered him. I'd kept my thoughts about him to myself. But he'd come to show me the faulty nature of human understanding.

That which is impossible to man is not impossible to God. That which is understood by God, is not always understood by man.

And it was this that was causing so much warfare in our world. It all began with the inappropriate use of words. From the slanders and blasphemies committed in God's name by those who consider themselves His servants to the bitter and violent struggles of actual warfare in the Middle East. They all had one root; prideful, arrogant, misuse of words.

Sai Baba showed me something else. It concerned a situation wherein such 'Lashon Hara' was resulting in the will of God being usurped in a small community. Imagine the ramifications of this, if you consider all of the small communities put together.

It was a reprehensible act of negligence to the Holy House of God, which no matter what the religion, is meant to be a House of Prayer.

Filling me with one final rush of purpose, he withdrew from my soul only after he knew that I would convey this message to everyone concerned. And it appears that that would be every single one of us.

In honor of this message delivered to me by the holy avatar Sai Baba, the 'Other Voices' section in this issue contains three writers who speak eloquently and powerfully on the subject of violence in our world and the responsibility of every single one of us to stop that violence from within ourselves so that we may become a part of the solution.

Sai Baba was often asked while alive about the miracles that were attributed to him. His response was this. "It is wrong to call them miracles for they are only evidence . . . not an exhibition." Speaking of his devotees, Sai Baba said, "I give them what they want so they will want what I have come to give, a deeper understanding of ourselves."

In the future, perhaps we should ask ourselves to deeply think upon these questions. If something is incompatible with our faith, as it stands now; like Galileo's discovery in his time that the Earth circled the sun and not vice versa. How do we know whether or not we have the wisdom to determine if it is incompatible with God?

And in the words of the great Buddhist Monk, Thich Nhat Hahn, "Peace is Every Step." And I might add . . . every word.
****

Beyond infinitum, my spirit began soaring into the sky and then the heavens, soon to be greeted by the welcoming hand of Jesus Christ my Lord. Taking my hand, He flew me to a sunny oasis, wherein we stopped and I waited to see what was to come.

As we stood there for several moments, the ethers were stirring. But in my heart, there stirred the greatest love as I admired and looked upon my Lord and Saviour. Gazing at Him, He also gazed at me with a huge and voluminously joyous smile. Which was odd considering the sad sight which was about to appear before us. But because I did not yet know, I just stared at Him, with the knowledge of the moving ether around me, but happy and content in the presence of my one and only true love. The skies around us were filled with light and a light blue color sweeter than any earthly sky.

Within moments, four huge crosses appeared in the sky before me. Christ was upon each of the crosses in one of the stations of his agony and death upon the cross. In the first station, his head was upright as he'd just been placed upon it. In the second, it had dropped a few inches down to the right. In the third, his head was at neck level in its drooping and in the fourth, his head rested against his shoulder in death. Observing these four stations, I interiorly understood this to be a penitential observance to be called the 'Watch and Wait.'

Interiorly, I understood that He had felt very alone and abandoned at this time. Although St. John and the Holy Women had stayed, all the other Apostles and followers of Christ had left Him at this difficult time of His suffering and death.

But there was a hidden mystery in this waiting to be revealed. I was unable to take the next step in my white bridal gown because something remained in me that was holding me back. It was not yet something I knew or could even predict, but it would come in its own time so that I might purify myself of it and be ready to jump into the next sphere when given the next opportunity to do so. Perhaps then . . . I could bring back the sacred galactic texts?

Winds began to blow my spirit back into its earthly receptacle as my hand was released from that of my Lord. "I wish others to do this, too." He said, as I began to blow away because of the sudden and intense spirit wind . . . "Tell others this . . ." As He spoke, I nodded in understanding as He disappeared into the ether and I was replaced into my physical receptacle upon the earth.

Watch and Wait

Four Stations

Stand at the Foot of the Cross with St. John and the Holy
Women Between Twelve Noon and Three P.M. Good Friday.

****

Sitting at the piano in the church I was playing and singing the Mass. I noticed quickly that about thirty or forty deceased priests, bishops and monks were sitting in the center pew of the church gathered together. But what struck me was a beautiful voice I heard from my side.

Turning, I saw a woman hovering as if sitting in midair before the statue of the Blessed Virgin. "Who are you?" I asked. "Don't you know me?" She responded. "No." I replied. "I am Veronica, I help you to sing." "Are you *St. Veronica*?" I asked, as she nodded in acknowledgement that she was the woman who had wiped the face of Christ on his Way of the Cross. Awed, I turned and noticed that as she sang, the religious who sat in the pews could hear her, but not see her. They were frightened by it. A sound of a heavenly organ came from the back of the church, and again they felt fear. "Don't worry," St. Veronica said, "I will help you to sing. And many may disapprove of what you do. But it is because they cannot see me and they do not understand that which I am doing. I will stay with you, and I will help you."

She disappeared in a simultaneous wisp with that of my own soul as I left the world of the night to the physical world below.
****

Ascension

Mystic Knowledge Series

Compiled and Written by Marilynn Hughes

The Out-of-Body Travel Foundation!

www.outofbodytravel.org

CHAPTER ONE
The Path of Purification, Discrimination and Discipline.

****

As a child, angels would whisper in my ears, "Born of darkness . . . into light," proclaiming this coming path of purification and entry into the mysteries of the redemption within my soul. But as I became an adult, my life was spent enraptured in vice, lost in delusion, selfishness and mortal desire; I no longer knew virtue, but deluded myself into thinking that what I perceived, felt, and wanted, was virtuous. My choices were reasoned, well-thought out, and filled with intellectual integrity. Their only flaw was that they were not true. Because I was so lost in my own stupidity, pride and arrogance, I couldn't have possibly even fathomed that my soul was in such desperate need of something as grand as the redemption. I was unaware of my iniquities, and I was lost.

Truth has many layers, and although the epiphany of all knowledge cannot be obtained in our limited human form, when you ascend the layers and reach various epiphanies along the way, some of those previous layers may no longer appear to be true, but their truth lies in the evolutionary context of a soul's journey. If you take a hardened sinner and make him into a saint, there will be many different levels in-between the current state and the goal, and those levels will be no less significant because they don't contain all knowledge.

And so the Lord, in order to guide us gently and with mercy, peels each layer of our humanity one at a time allowing us to view it in its truth, thus taking in the knowledge of ourselves and our flaws. And as each layer subsides, so, too, do our worldly passions and clingings. For *all* who are born to the Earth are born of darkness (the stain of karmic delusions and original sin) . . . but not *all* are reborn into the light. Purification heralds the soul's reckoning . . . thus, energizing it to participate in the greatest mystery of this Earthly realm, the Mysteries of the Redemption!

May I offer you the hand of a wretched soul lifted by grace? May I share with you the journey of one who was "Born of darkness . . . into light?"

"Blessed are they who wash their robes so as to have the right to the tree of life and enter the city through its gates."
New American Bible, New Testament, Revelations 22:14, (Christianity, Catholic, Words of Christ)

"Christian Soul! If you seek to reach the loftiest peak of perfection, and to unite yourself so intimately with God that you become one in spirit with Him, you must first know the true nature of perfection of spirituality in order to succeed in the most sublime undertaking that can be expressed or imagined."
The Spiritual Combat, Chapter 1, Paragraph 1, (Christianity, Catholic, Author: Dom Lorenzo Scupoli)

"I, Thoth, have ever sought wisdom, searching in darkness, and searching in Light. Long in my youth I traveled the pathway, seeking ever new knowledge to gain, until after much striving, one of the THREE, to me brought the LIGHT. Brought HE to me the commands of the Dweller, called me from darkness into the LIGHT. . . Each soul on earth that loosens its fetters, shall soon be made free from the bondage of night."
The Emerald Tablets of Thoth the Atlantean, Tablet V, Page 28, Paragraph 5-6, (Mystery Religions, Egyptian/Hermetic, Author: Thoth)

"Then, the crown prince Manjusri said to the Licchavi Vimalakirti, 'Noble sir, how does the bodhisattva follow the way to attain the qualities of the Buddha?' Vimalakirti replied, 'Manjusri, when the bodhisattva follows the wrong way, he follows the way to attain the qualities of the Buddha.' . . . . Manjusri: 'Noble sir, one who stays in the fixed determination of the vision of the uncreated is not capable of conceiving the spirit of unexcelled perfect enlightenment. However, one who lives among created things, in the mines of passions . . . is indeed capable of conceiving the spirit of unexcelled perfect enlightenment . . . For

example, noble sir, without going out into the great ocean, it is impossible to
find precious, priceless pearls. Likewise, without going into the ocean of
passions, it is impossible to obtain the mind of omniscience."
The Holy Teaching of Vimalakirti, Chapter 8, Page 64-66, (Buddhism, Mahayana)
"God therefore arranged and decreed the creation of concepts of both perfection
and deficiency, as well as a creature with equal access to both. This creature
would then be given the means to earn perfection and avoid
deficiency."
The Way of God, Part I, Chapter 2, No. 2, Paragraph 4, (Judaism, Author: Rabbi Moshe
Chayim Luzzatto)
"One must deliver himself with the help of his mind, and not degrade himself.
The mind is the friend of the conditioned soul, and his enemy as well. For him
who has conquered the mind, the mind is the best of friends; but for one who has
failed to do so, his mind will remain the greatest enemy."
The Bhagavad Gita As It Is, Chapter 6, Dhyana Yoga, Text 5-6, (Hinduism, Words of
Krishna
"Allah causes the night and the day to succeed one another. Surely
there is a lesson in this for those who have sight."
The Holy Qur'an, Part XVIII, Chapter 24, Section, 6, Verse 44, (Islam, Author:
Mohammad)
"'Announce the praises' of him who called you out of darkness into his
wonderful light."
New American Bible, New Testament, 1 Peter 2:9-10 American Bible (Christianity,
Catholic, Words of the Apostle Peter)
"As the door of the lodge is opened, all the men cry: 'Hi ho! Hi ho! Thanks!' and
the men are all happy, for they have come forth from the darkness and are now
living in the Light."
The Sacred Pipe, Chapter III, Page 42, Paragraph 2, (Tribal, Oglala Sioux)

"Born of darkness . . . into light."

Allow me to explain a simplified version of how we may understand the varying realms in which we are going to travel. Perhaps this can give you a point of reference in which to understand the make-up of various realms. Please feel free to use the illustration located in the back of the book, 'Universal Sphere of Realms,' to picture this image in your mind.

Various realms of existence can be compared to a series of concentric circles which begin in the center and continue to expand outward into larger and larger spheres. The center point of those concentric rings would be the point of total and imminent darkness, as each of the successive rings outward would represent a greater attainment of light.

Numbering the realms, you would begin in the center, starting with the number one and moving outward with each ring. Using this process 1) realms one and two represent the lower and hell realms, 2) realms three and four are mortal realms (third & fourth-dimensional reality, our world), and 3) realms five and above represent the heavenly realms, continuing to expand outwards into greater and greater attainments of light.

With this understanding, we continue towards the three major paths outlined in this book, which coincide with several monastic traditions.

The journey begins on the Ascension pathway (Purification) in realms five and above, the heavenly realms. It continues on the Alteration pathway (Discrimination) in realms three and four, the mortal realms (third & fourth-dimensional worlds, the Earth). Finally, it concludes on the Absolution pathway (Discipline) in realms one and two, the lower and hell realms.

Within most monastic/mystical traditions, you will find that there are three grand phases of soul development. In the Buddhist tradition they are referred to as Purification, Discrimination, and Discipline. In the writings of the Early Christian Church Fathers they are referred to as Purification, Enlightenment and Union. You will find these three phases, using Buddhist terminology, within these pages, as well.

<u>Purification</u> deals with reincarnation, personal karma, and misunderstandings about the true nature of eternal love. Karmic misunderstandings resonate towards darkness, even if they originate from ignorance, thus, purification seeks to alter personal thrusts which resonate toward delusion, self-gratification and vice. In purifying these aspects of habitual sin, the Lord redirects the soul towards paths of virtue.

The path of Purification leads to the Ascension of the soul. (In the Ascension Pathway, you will encounter eight phases of the Purification process: Awakening, Co-creation, Surrender, Rites of Passage and Initiation into the Mysteries, Emergence of Karma, Mirroring of Karma, Ignition of the Eternal Flame, and Ascension.) The soul travels this path by beginning to explore the heavenly realms, realms five and above, the worlds of life and light, for the purpose of discovering the true nature of eternal love.

<u>Discrimination</u> deals with dark and light forces in the Universe, and becoming energetically capable of recognizing and altering them at God's command. Being able to identify the serpent from the lamb is the first goal, but then the seeker begins to take on the knowledge of energetic evolution in regards to mortal beings, and how to affect it in ways which lead souls, including their own, towards progress.

The path of Discrimination leads to the Alteration of reality, in energy and on the ground. (In Part II of this text, you will encounter three phases of the Discrimination process: Rites into the Medicine, Rites of Evolution, and Alteration of Reality.) The soul travels this path by beginning to explore the mortal realms, realms three and four (third & fourth-dimensional worlds, the Earth), for the purpose of attaining spiritual discretion and the ability to alter negative thrusts.

<u>Discipline</u> deals with sacred practices and teachings from the prophets, saints, mystics and sages of every world religion throughout time. Intensive self-scrutiny and disciplined techniques lead the soul ever deeper into the knowledge of darkness and evil, heaven, purgatory and hell, and the continual combat that rages in every soul between these forces.

The path of Discipline leads to the Absolution of the soul, an interior cleanliness which serves God (In Part III of this text, you will encounter five phases of the Discipline process: Ancient Sacred Paths, Entry into the Knowledge of the Lower Realms, Self-Scrutiny, Original Sin, and the Mysteries of the Redemption.) The soul travels this path by beginning to explore the lower purgatorial and hellish realms, realms one and two, the realms of dominant darkness and pure evil, for the purpose of intensive physical, spiritual and mental discipline, which is achieved through the deep examination of evil in the self and the world.

Among the out-of-body/mystical experiences you are about to read, you will find paintings of various things I've seen in the spiritual world, music of various melodies I've heard while traveling, and pictures of some of the prophets, saints, mystics and sages who grace the pages of my book with their words. These can all be found in the back with descriptions of who they are, and from what religion they have come.

For those who will never see during their lifetime what I have seen, may I provide you with a window? For those who will, may I give you a map? For those who seek comfort in the world beyond, may I hand you a warm blanket? For those who just want to know, may I ask you to come with me . . .?

THE ASCENSION PATHWAY - PURIFICATION
Karmic Purification

This path of purification begins with the ascent into the upper worlds of light, the heavenly realms; five and above, whose ascent aids the traveler in understanding the true nature of eternal love.

1) Awakening
2) Co-Creation
3) Surrender
4) Rites of Passage and Initiation into the Mysteries
5) Emergence of Karma
6) Mirroring of Karma
7) Ignition of the Eternal Flame
8) Ascension

THE ALTERATION PATHWAY - DISCRIMINATION
The Knowledge of Darkness and Light

This path of discrimination begins with the journeying into the border worlds where the battles between light and darkness occur, the mortal realms, three and four (third & fourth-dimensional worlds, the Earth), for the purpose of attaining spiritual discretion and the ability to alter negative thrusts.

1) Rites into the Medicine
2) Rites of Evolution
3) Alteration of Reality

THE ABSOLUTION PATHWAY - DISCIPLINE
Dissolution into the Will of God

This path of discipline begins with the descent into the lower worlds of darkness, the lower and hell realms, one and two, the realms of dominant darkness and pure evil, for the purpose of intensive physical, spiritual and mental discipline.

1) Ancient Sacred Paths
2) Entry into the Knowledge of the Lower Realms
3) Self-Scrutiny
4) Original Sin
5) Mysteries of the Redemption

****

CHAPTER TWO
Personal and Planetary Ascension, the Book of the Eights, Buffalo Medicine, Angel of Ascension, Gateway of the Ascension, Implanting the Seed of Ascension.

****

My husband, Andy had a dream wherein I wanted to buy myself a gift consisting of a set of engraved porcelain steps. Each step was engraved with a spiritual quality that my soul was seeking, and although Andy didn't initially want me to buy the gift because of its great cost, Emmanuel stepped in and told him that these steps represented the journey of my spirit which was a very important gift for me to give myself. Realizing its importance, Andy bought it for me, awaking with a newfound attitude towards our journey.

"Your life consists in drawing nearer to God. To do this, you must endeavour to detach yourself from visible things and remember that in a short time they will be taken from you."

The Voice of the Saints, Chapter 2, Page 13, Stanza 3, (Christianity, Catholic, Words of

Blessed John of Avila)
**"Consider the shortness of time, the length of eternity, and reflect how
everything here below comes to an end and passes by."**
*The Voice of the Saints, Chapter 2, Page 12, Stanza 4, (Christianity, Catholic, Words of
St. Gerard Majella)*

****

And so it came to pass that an Indian man came to me bearing two blue balls, one was light blue and the other dark blue. "The two earths," he said.

Transformed into a fabulously white wedding gown, I was preparing for the marriage of the spirit.

Handing me three paintings, the first was of an Indian chief with a large headdress made of white feathers who stood facing me with his arms outstretched. The second was a native woman with long graying braids, looking down, her hands folded together. The third was a young native man with a single feather attached to his hair blowing in the wind whose arms pointed off into the distance. "These spirits are one in their story." He said. "They all saw the same thing and tried to affect change. They are of the Thunder Tribes." Handing them to me, he said, "Show these to the residents of the Earth." He walked away.

A young Indian boy came with one final painting. Saying nothing, he gave it to me and left. On it was an Indian man and a woman, and below the picture it said, 'The Great Day of Purification.' Suddenly, the native woman came to life in her painting and said, "All we have seen in the past comes to pass in the present." Resuming her non-assuming stance in the portrait, all was quiet.

Startled by a sudden sound from behind, the Chief had jumped out of his painting to speak, "The Mulrabe stand by sacredly, open the lid of repression." Looking at him, I asked, "What is the significance of the three?" He said nothing, but soared back into his picture as the young native jumped out. "We represent breath, life and death!" He said, "The Chief holds his arms out for breath, I point forth the direction of life, and the shamaness holds somber the moment of death." At that moment, the shamaness created two rattles which she began to shake in a rhythmic beat. "She holds rattles to mourn the death of the spirit." Clinging to her incessantly mournful chant, he continued. "The Mulrabe will come on eight winds. (There are 8 phases in the ascension pathway.) Each wind will contain six qualities of spirit. The breath will bring it within." Breathing loudly, the Chief reached for the sky in his painting. "Each of these eight winds will contain a higher frequency of these six qualities: Friendship, Peace, Justice, Piety, Temperance, and Virtue." All became still.

**"Entering the variety of six courses of migration of life, craving being the
moisture, ignorance the shade, action the field, consciousness the seeds, name
and form the simultaneous sprouts - Thus do they see beings in the world,
beginningless and endless. Those beings' minds are full of the action of
afflictions, according to patterns of habit."**
*The Flower Ornament Scripture, Chapter 26, The Ten Stages, Page 786, Stanza 1-2,
(Buddhism, Mahayana)*

****

**"Wisdom's voice rings out from behind the doors of the righteous; wherever the
godly foregather (is heard) her song. Whenso they eat and are filled, the word is
of her; when they drink in fellowship together, their talk is of the lore of the
Most High; the aim of their discourse is to further the knowledge of His power . .
. Bless ye, the Lord, who redeems the humble from the grasp of the proud."**
*The Dead Sea Scriptures, Poems from a Qumran Hymnal, II, No. 12-18, Page 220,
(Christianity, Gnostic/Essene)*

Hundreds of spirits were gathered, but no one was paying attention to one another and there appeared to be no way to exit this building. Noticing a woman who walked by, she had a symbol emblazoned on her forehead which I immediately knew to be the sign of attachment. A sideways triangle with an arrow running through it, I shouted, "You are Romulet!" Turning to meet my gaze, she replied, "You recognized me, my friend. I will tell you of the crossing."

Moments later, we stood before a pyramid. "Prepare for the next rite," Romulet said, as a thought-form began before me. Standing at the side of a busy road, a tiny child was running towards the traffic. Stopping her with a wave of energy coming from my hands, I said, "When making the crossing, it's very easy to be like a tiny child, naive and unknowing of what happens next. For this reason, you must remain far to the side, because when you are truly ready to cross, the movement will take you. But if you linger at the border when you're not yet ready to pass, the energies (like the cars), will hurl you far away from the crossing." Romulet smiled, "The time must be right, and the danger only comes when you try to force the movement."

Movement beginning, we were taken to the outer perimeter of the pyramid. Above the pyramid was a very real human eye, and in the center of the pyramid was an unusual sign which I recognized as the sign of the eights. Looking like an 'h' with a low hanging left hook, the top of the pyramid glowed with golden light. Understanding the pyramid to be a symbol of God's creation, we entered the empty tomb chamber within.

"The hub and center of the entire pyramid symbolism is Christ . . . If you were to read through the Bible from cover to cover, and ascertain the plan of God therein, and then attempt to draw a diagram of that plan in such a simple way that a child could understand, you could not do so any more simply and accurately than it is portrayed in the Great Pyramid . . . "
Pyramidology, (On the Great Pyramid), Book I, Chapter VII, Page 106, (Christianity, Pyramidology, Author: Adam Rutherford)

A man materialized and joined us in this room where a stone casket lay unopened. Also carrying a sign on his head, a number eight was surrounded by a black circle. Saying nothing, they stood together as if they expected something from me. "The signs of attachment," I pondered. "You're not wearing them right. The signs represent the masculine and feminine, and they are switched, are they not?" Amused, the signs switched foreheads, the man now wearing the triangle with the arrow, and the woman the eight surrounded by a circle.

"The Holy Scriptures are like a large house with many, many rooms and that outside each door lies a key - but it is not the right one. To find the right keys that will open the doors - that is the great and arduous task."
On the Kabbalah and its Symbolism, Chapter 1, Page 12, Bottom, A Quote from Origen, Selecta in Psalmos, (Judaism, Author: Gershom Scholem)

Knowing they wished for me to explain the meaning of the signs, I began. "The eight is immortal," I said, "and the circle represents the circle of life. The feminine energy has the higher potential to touch immortality, but is held back by its attachment to karmic circling." I paused. "As for the masculine, the arrow shoots upward from the pyramid base straight through the top-point which is oneness, thus the masculine energy can be focused on the goal, but remains attached at the base of the triangle, which is the expansion of oneness into multiplicity, the endless cycles of lives, karma." Smiling, they reached for the stone that covered the casket.

Pulling out a book, its title read, 'The Book of the Eights.' Falling in unison to the floor, we were all deep in a prayerful state. Upon the cover, was the same sign that had been in the center of the pyramid; the sign of the immortals. "This book contains the names of all those who have achieved the ascension," he said, as he began chanting: "The book of the crossing, the Book of the Eights, reminds us of those who have passed through Your gates. Into the realm of spiritual ether, the realm of immortals, the world of hereafter. Who among us knows the name, of one passing through the gateway of the Eights?"

Handing me the book with great sanctity, he said, "Inside you will find the names of those who've descended the Holy Christ Spirit. This sacred book is given to those who embark upon the path of the ascension. You passed through many trials, and now you are an initiate to the worlds of the wise." "But what is this symbol," I said, pointing to the symbol of the immortals on the cover. He wouldn't say.

Gleaning no more from this journey, they left me with a warning to be careful as I passed through the mass retain (astral energy zone containing the thoughts of humanity) on my journey back to my body. Surrounding me with white light, they sent me back.

"I saw the dead, the great and the lowly, standing before the throne, and scrolls were opened. Then another scroll was opened, the book of life. The dead were judged according to their deeds, by what was written in the scrolls . . . Anyone whose name was not found written in the book of life was thrown into the pool of fire."
New American Bible, New Testament, Revelation 20:12, 15, (Christianity, Catholic)
****

Beckoned towards a gateway I could not attain of my own merits, the Assisi Master Sage, who had taught the Assisi Marauders, took my hand and led me to the gate on *his* merit.

Awaiting me beyond the doorway was an ancient Indian village, while a young warrior bowed to me with respect. "Buffalo woman, we welcome you!" Acknowledging his polite welcome with a nod, the master and I followed him, as he took us to a prayer lodge.

Buffalo skins were hung with great care around a large fire in the center, and all who were present addressed me as 'Buffalo Woman.' Bowing to offer respect in return, the master sage waited until nightfall to take me outside so that I might find my medicine, my power.

Painting the sky in the dead of night, the full moon and bright stars shimmered so brightly that I almost didn't notice a shimmering on the ground. But when I did, I bent over to pick up seven very large feathers. "Buffalo feathers!" I cried out. Lifting them to the moonlight, they held the seven colors of the rainbow (representing karmic purification, a mortal quality). "I have found my medicine." I mused.

Returning to the lodge, it was still warm as the fire glowed brightly awaiting our return. Sitting next to the flame, sacred emotion filled me. Gazing at the master beside me, I felt the holiness of our bond. "The Buffalo is your medicine!" A medicine man said from behind, as a woman instantly appeared and began to act aggressive, obviously wishing to fight with me. Displaying her own medicine, she lifted the shields of the Lion, of which she was using for backwards (or dark) purposes. True medicine is given by the Lord and helps them to achieve His will. When properly used in a sacred manner, medicines promote the spiritual life and harmony among the tribes of the earth.

Quickly grasping my own power which was that of the seven feathers; I approached her. "Your power is not real," I stated, as I was surprised by her immediate disappearance into the dust. Turning, the medicine man shouted. "You are of the medicine! You are of the medicine! The Buffalo Woman is sacred, her medicine is of prayer. The Lion medicine can also be sacred, but it is a teaching in the proper use of power. When one uses the medicine to overcome others, it is no longer sacred." Aging eyes gazing deeply into my own, he continued. "The power of prayer is true and cannot be harmed by any other medicine . . . prayer of the living, it is immortal." Prayer contains a quality of immutability, it simply *is*.

As he spoke, lightning struck, as the master sage and I romped through a golden wheat field. A heavenly golden hue exuded from this celestial wheat, and the buffalo feathers were now attached to my hair, while the master had his own set of buffalo feathers about his waist in the form of a belt.

"Plans made after advice succeed; so with wise guidance wage your war . . . Say not, 'I will repay evil!', Trust in the Lord and he will help you . . . To do what is right and just is more acceptable to the Lord than sacrifice."
New American Bible, Old Testament, Proverbs 20: 18 & 22 & 21:3

"Suchness is said to be similar to the substance of gold because this essence is immutable, perfectly pure and most noble."
The Changeless Nature, Buddha Nature, Page 66, No. 148, (Buddhism, Words of Arya Maitreya, Author: Acarya Asanga)

****

Hovering while she descended, this extra-terrestrial woman seemed very familiar. Coming upon me with peace, tranquility and love, her body was of shimmering light and she wore an iridescent pale green gown. Blue eyes framed by an overly large head, she placed her hand upon my forehead sending light through my spirit. "It will be done." She said. "What will be done?" I asked quietly, not wishing to appear stupid. A barely perceptible smile could be seen from her thin mouth. "You have made the choices that have brought you to this point. You will accomplish everything in this lifetime, you have reached the ascension." "Who are you, and where are you from?" I asked. Manifesting a golden lamp in her hand, she replied, "Express the music of your soul." Turning to re-enter her ship, she had nothing more to say.

"Through being completely under your care I shall benefit all with no fears of conditioned existence; I shall perfectly transcend my previous evils and in the future shall commit no more."
A Guide to the Bodhisattva's Way of Life, Chapter 2, Stanza 9, (Buddhism, Tibetan, Author: Shantideva)

****

The gallery was inlaid with gold and the stairs were of marble. Huge paintings on the wall depicted God's most beautiful creations. Three entities approached, wearing black hooded robes, their faces the image of skeletons and their hands white bones. Surrounding me on each side and to my back, I recognized them as the 'Angels of Death.' "Who are you here for?" I asked, thinking that meeting one angel of death would be quite significant, but three? "We are here for you," they thought simultaneously, "but another comes." "Another?" I thought.

Approaching with eminence in his mysterious form, his robes were as white as snow. But they could not overshadow the faceless being who exuded light but no features. "I am the 'Angel of Ascension.'" He conveyed. Bowing lightly, I looked deeply into his faceless image. "Clearly you must know," he thought, "that ascension is becoming reality for you. You must translate the Book of the Eights . . . finish the Book of the Eights." Confused by this command, I didn't know what he meant. "When this is complete," he thought, "you may choose to stay or go from this realm at anytime." Raising his invisible arm to the sky, he pointed directly at my heart sending light through it. My astral form began to disintegrate until I was only a skeleton, then my bones turned into dust, and in moments, I became only white light.

Quietly, he turned and walked away with the three angels of death. Watching the angel of ascension soar upwards, he became particle energy and dissipated into a thought within the mind of God.

"Now, what is this 'Book of the Hidden Mystery?' Said R. Simeon: 'It contains five sections which are to be found in the midst of a great Hall, and whose wisdom fills the whole earth.' Said R. Judah: 'If this book of wisdom is enclosed in that Hall, it is of more worth than any other to me.' 'Verily,' returned R. Simeon, ' it is so, for one who is used to passing in and out of the courts of wisdom, but not to one who rarely or never enters into that Hall."
The Zohar (Kaballah), Volume IV, Terumah (Exodus), Page 112, Middle, (Judaism)

****

Embarking upon the sacred violet tunnel which led to the 'Universal Sun,' I could see its emanation from a distance. Crystal angels appeared in the tunnel, one holding her hand to me with a luminous smile. Going towards her, she grasped my hand and took me deep within and beyond the borders of these realms. Tears of joy streamed my face as I beheld that which I so desired, the essence of God, living and beautiful. Bathed in the light of silence, I stayed for hours in my private mass with the Lord.

"Then from the midst of the Fire came a voice, 'Behold the Glory of the First Cause.' I beheld that light, high above all darkness, reflected in my own being. I attained, as it were, to the God of all Gods, the Spirit-Sun, the Sovereign of the Sun spheres."
An Interpretation of the Emerald Tablets Together with the Two Extra Tablets, Tablet XI, Page 58, Paragraph 1, (Mystery Religions, Egyptian/Hermetic, Words of Thoth)
"This ultimate truth of the spontaneously-born is to be understood through faith alone - The orb of the sun may shine but it cannot be seen by the blind!"
The Changeless Nature, Buddha Nature, Page 68, No. 153, (Buddhism, Words of Arya Maitreya, Author: Acarya Asanga)

Taking me yet deeper within, we stood before a gate. Seeing the higher and finer frequencies of light gleaming from beyond, the angel spoke. "This is the 'Gateway of the Ascension,' you may go now if you wish, but make sure that if you do, it's what you really want." Looking deeply inside, I was honored to be allowed to enter and yearned to go. But something deeper held me back. "No. I don't really want to go, yet." Squeezing my hand with love and understanding, almost as if to say that she was pleased with my decision, she said, "Then return to the earth knowing that the love of the light is always with you no matter where your consciousness may lie."

"Two angel messengers stand at the gate of Paradise and call aloud to the chieftains who have charge of that spot in Gehinnom, summoning them to receive that soul, and during the whole process of purification they continue to utter aloud repeatedly the word 'Hinnom.' When the process is completed, the chieftains take the soul out of Gehinnom and lead it to the gate of Paradise, and say to the angel messengers standing there: 'Hinnom (lit. here they are), behold, here is the soul that has come out pure and white.' The soul is then brought into Paradise."
The Zohar (Kaballah), Volume IV, Vayaqhel (Exodus), Page 219, Middle, (Judaism)
****

Riding the wild stallion through the arid desert, I suddenly stopped as a spaceship was waiting. Two emerged from the vessel to greet me, a man and a woman. Stepping forward, the woman took hold of my hand. "I implant you; I give you the seed of ascension. As I pass this energy through your hands, you will also pass this to those you touch." Stepping forward, the man took my other hand. "I give you the ethereal water to fill the seed with growth, allow it to flow within you, beginning the birth of this seed." Letting go of my hands, they calmly turned and walked towards the spaceship, turning into particle energy and disappearing before my eyes.

"Jesus said, 'If you bring forth what is within you, what you have will save you. If you do not have that within you, what you do not have within you (will) kill you.'"
The Gospel of Thomas, No. 70, (Christianity, Gnostic/Essene, Words of Christ)
****

Leading me to a sacred place where statues of immortal beings throughout time were displayed, Odyssey took me to a holy image of Christ. "Enter it." She said. Walking into the stone encasement, I was given the gift of the Christ energy. Leading me to a holy statue of Mary, she said, "Enter it." Walking into the stone encasement, I was given the gift of holy maternity. Pointing to an elaborately decorated piece which stood upon a pedestal, it was formed like a small temple and a door upon it held words in hieroglyphs. I opened it. Lying inside was an ancient book written in an unfamiliar language. My eyes dropped as I read the only part written in my own language. 'The Book of the Eights.' It said. "Translate it." Odyssey said. In order to translate the book, I would have to experience the rites of passage within it. "I will translate it."

"Thereupon the old man took me by the hand and led me towards the spacious

temple; and after he had duly performed the rituals of opening the doors and of making the morning-sacrifice, he produced from the secret recesses of the shrine certain books written in unknown characters. The meaning of these characters was concealed, at times by the concentrated expression of hieroglyphically painted animals, at times by wreathed and twisted letters with tails that twirled like wheels or spiraled together like vine-tendrils - so that it was altogether impossible for any peeping profane to comprehend. From these books the high priest interpreted to me the matters necessary for my mystic preparation."
The Ancient Mysteries, The Egyptian Mysteries of Isis and Osiris, Page 188, No. 22, Paragraph 4, (Mystery Religions, Mediterranean)
"Come, mother of the seven houses, that thy rest may be in the eighth house."
The Apocryphal New Testament, Acts of Thomas, Second Act, No. 27, (Christianity, Gnostic, Words of St. Thomas)
****

"Then he said to me, 'Do not seal up the prophetic words of this book, for the appointed time is near. Let the wicked still act wickedly, and the filthy still be filthy. The righteous must still do right, and the holy still be holy."
New American Bible, New Testament, Revelations 22:10, (Christianity, Catholic)
And so it came to pass that I entered into the contents of the Book of the Eights, which came as a sequence of experiential energies which began and fulfilled the final throes of ascension's path.
"When that time comes, your own people will be spared - all those whose names are found written in the Book."
New Jerusalem Bible, Old Testament, Daniel 12:1 & 4, (Judaism)
****

CHAPTER THREE
Brotherhood of the White Wolf, The Golden Angels - Sisters of the Sacred Rite of the 23rd Dimension, Mandor - Goddess of Ancient Knowledge, Key to the Passages, River of the Doors of Limitation, Mud of Murky Thoughts, Web of Negative Thinking, Seeders of Ascension, Whirling into Invisibility.

****

Soaring across the arctic snow country, my glistening white paws were enmeshed in the white snow, as my fellow white wolves gathered around. Pouncing across the icy waters that had once been a fluid lake, we trekked across the great arctic to our destination inside the caves where the great white wolf lived.

Everything was white and covered in snow, including the above which appeared to have no rock enclosure, only the white which seemed to go on forever.

A large white wolf approached from an inner cavern. "We are the wolf people, the teachers of the tribes of man. We are the white brotherhood of all life; we seek to teach the living of life, and the dead of the re-birth." "But why am I here?" I thought to him." He paused. "You are here to receive the teaching of the white wolf so that you may encompass and become it. Then you will give it to others who will do the same. It is simple. The wolf teaches of freedom and brotherhood, a union and a separation, a balance." Karmic relationships have a tendency to be all-consuming, but eternal unions serve God, and thus they serve both unitive and individual goals. Gazing about the space, my brothers pierced my eyes with their own iridescence. "Thank you, great white wolf and all my wolf brothers for having me in your pack tonight. It is a memory I will treasure." Turning to begin our trek back across the snowy arctic, we crossed the frozen lake, the pines aside it swaying in the wind.

"Embedded within the Chewong notion . . . is the conviction that what each

creature sees through its eyes constitutes a 'truth' equivalent to that of human experience."
Wisdom of the Elders, Each Species Sees the World Through its own Eyes, Page 110, Paragraph 1, (Tribal, Chewong)
"Faithful words are often not pleasant; pleasant words are often not faithful. Well informed men do not dispute; men who dispute are not well informed. The wise man is not always learned; the learned man is not always wise."
A Buddhist Bible, Tao Teh King, Chapter 81, Paragraph 1, (Buddhism, Taoism)
****

Swollen at the stomach which was the sign of the pregnancy I bore, I carried within me the spirit of love about to be born within the world. As a sister of the sacred order, I had seen the four flames; the violet, blue, green and red. Knowing of the crossing, I had been there. In the essence world, I encompassed the order, living the sacred rites of the 23rd dimension. Here, I was to seed the birth and begin the descent of spirit into the third dimension. My spirit had become the golden angel, the eternal manifestation of Odyssey.

Dashing through the wilderness fall, I witnessed ancient wisdom. The hill I bore was seeking downwards into a golden ravine. Faces emerged from every point, hundreds of wolves peered out upon me as if in a mad dash. Blowing endlessly in the wind, my dress had become a burden in this holy place, but I bore it not. The people at the top of the forest hill beckoned my return.

From behind a clump of rocks, however, surprise echoed through the wilderness as a black wolf came with a dash towards me and held me in a deadly jaw lock about my head. Blood was dripping slowly from my face and the pain echoed an inner stillness. Playing dead, I did not move, hoping the wolf would release me to my death. But he did not, and those atop the hill offered no help. A lone teardrop fell on my face in my moment of confusion, but a knowing came to me in a dreamy and dazed state. Between worlds, I was given the knowledge of the black wolf.

Reaching up, I grasped each of the wolf's jaws separately with each hand, disabling his only weapon against me. As I did, the wolf became limp and powerless. Inner compassion told me of the rightful place of the animal as I sought to go further into the wilderness. Though the blood still fell from my wounds, my only concern was that the animal live, grow and evolve into its highest potential. "Sister of the sacred order," the animal limply spoke, "I know of your power." "It is my power to understand that you know of, wolf." I said. "Yes," he replied, "but it is your power to understand that gives you courage to realize that I come as a black wolf because my potential has not been realized." Pausing, he added, "You are of the great white wolf clan." "Yes," I replied, "the great white wolf is realized potential; he understands that which is eternal . . . and that which is not." Wolf looked pensive now, almost ashamed. "You are of the wolf clan, too, but you are of a different tribe of teachers. You have shown me never to fear unrealized potential, but to guide it to a place of nurturance and growth where it may fulfill itself."

Entering a mountain setting deep in the wilderness, the swaying winds blew to and fro as I transformed into my truest self. Glistening robes surrounded my lithe airy form. "It is only ignorance that harms us," I said. Running my hands over the gaping wound in my head, I reached to the black wolf as he licked the blood off, cleansing them. "This is my life-force; I give it to you to help you attain life." As I did this, I turned to see the four flames; violet, blue, green and red as they appeared in a gateway in the sky, it was the entrance to the 23rd dimension.

"While that woman lived, some evenings or nights - especially cold nights - you could hear the wolves howl for her. They missed her. But that's the way things go. Man and animal are closely related, and once in a while the animals show their affection this way."
Walking in the Sacred Manner, Chapter 6, Page 117, Paragraph 1, (Tribal, Plains)

****

Mandor, the goddess of ancient knowledge, had arrived upon her white stallion named Adrid. A blonde beauty dressed in a buckskin dress carrying a bow and arrow, she stood in the light-filled plain which sparkled with trees. Magical and mystic, I climbed onto her horse as Mandor shot an arrow into the trunk of a tree.

Surrounded by every crystal formation of the Earth, the light emanated from all locations creating an essence of peace; purple, pink, blue, green, all the eternal colors were represented. Leading me to an unusual stone, a huge crystallized formation sparkled with black and white, karma and purity.

Taking my hand, she placed it on the stone and as I touched it, Mandor said, "Hold the quality and it will transform you." Feeling myself balance, understanding was becoming one with me. A light flashed and we were now surrounded in complete white. Opening a pathway, Mandor was now holding an aquamarine crystal ball. Placing it in my hand, I looked into it and saw the people of the Earth turning into dolls . . . they were not real. "This is the vision of the light," Mandor said, "it will show you only the truth." Gazing inside the crystal again, the people became dead fish. "You see the dearth of your world, so many have forgotten the water of life, and no longer swim within it. The water is the spirit and the spirit dies for false love." My mind momentarily lapsed as it swirled through time in the aquamarine cloud of truth.

Upon reaching awareness, I found myself standing on Easter Island before the legendary stones that had been erected there. In a raging torrent of light, the stones became animated ancient faces, and I was surrounded by a council of twelve.

Beginning to speak, I realized that they were living, breathing beings and this caused many of them to giggle at my surprise. Speaking amongst themselves, I listened but didn't understand them. A female stone spoke out, "You are confusing our guest. It is simple; we must help her to see." The Council Master smiled at the stone lady, "Cescina, your wisdom is great indeed. It is true, and I believe you know her wisdom." "Yes, indeed, I do." Cescina spoke to me, although I was still awestruck at watching their faces move on the stones just like any other living creation. "You have come to us seeking a quality, and yet, you already possess the quality you seek." Confused, I thought about the meaning of her words: I had come seeking knowledge, and it had already been given me. I had come seeking strength, but I had come to possess it. I had come seeking my destiny, but it had already been shown me. "I understand," I said. Cescina smiled, as I was again surrounded by the aquamarine clouds.

In a moment, I stood atop Adrid, Mandor awaiting my return. But nothing more was said.

"Inasmuch as His so great goodness is omnipotent, He can accomplish good even from evils, whether it be by forgiving them, or by healing them . . ."
The Father's of the Church, Volume 14, St. Augustine - Treatises on Various Subjects, Continence, Chapter 6, No. 15, Page 206, Bottom, (Christianity, Catholic, Author: St. Augustine)

"He is ever the stay of my right hand. The path beneath my feet is set on a mighty rock unshaken before all things. For that rock beneath my feet is the truth of God, and His power is the stay of my right hand; from the fount of His charity my vindication goes forth."
The Dead Sea Scriptures, The Hymn of the Initiants, Page 141, Stanza 1, (Christianity, Gnostic/Essene)

****

Coming for only a moment, he called himself 'Key.' With a click of his fingers, he altered all things, moving mountains, traveling light years . . . The Key master had come to show me through the maze to the place of passage. "One who seeks passage must hold the key to the Universe," Key said, "the maze of dimensions and realms." All worlds and universes spun around us in this cosmic space; stars, planets, cloudy mists, suns, moons, trees, lakes, oceans, realms and every known and unknown manifestation. "You must follow this key in order to learn to master knowledge." Nodding, I began to follow him, and within a snap of his fingers, everything disappeared.

All was quiet, all was black, and we were now in a place of no-existence. "This is where we will start," Key said, "where nothing exists, all creation is potential." In laughter, he pointed his finger at me, causing my spirit to soar into the 'Maze of Earthly Realms.' Now I was alone, and I shouted out for key. "What is the key, Key master?" Symbols were scattered all around the walls and corridors, but I didn't understand them. Key master reappeared, "What will be, will be. Immortality is forever. The passage teaches of one who sought, and in the seeking found nothing, but yet found everything. Tell me, ascended one, what is the Key?" Opening my hand, I was surprised to see a golden key lying within my palm. "Key master, what I know can be summed up in but a few words which carry the energy of a meaning far beyond them. Change is the only constant of the eternal; therefore, life has no conclusion for it is a continuum. In one moment, lies all eternity." Smiling, the Key master closed my fingers around the key and he disappeared.

"Then from the throne there poured a great radiance, surrounding and lifting my soul by its power. Swiftly I moved through the spaces of Heaven, shown was I the mystery of mysteries, shown the Secret heart of the cosmos."
An Interpretation of the Emerald Tablets Together with the Two Extra Tablets, Tablet XI, Page 58, Paragraph 3, (Mystery Religions, Egyptian/Hermetic)
****

And so it came to pass that my soul was allowed to cross over the gates of death, although my body had not truly died, and as I crossed, I witnessed the truth of existence being formed in every cell of my being. In order to fully separate from the physical body, however, I had to pass through three rites of passage to transform my cells into light.

THE RIVER OF THE DOORS OF LIMITATION gave the will strength to tear down all limitations, beginning in utter darkness, there were many doors which opened to deeper levels of light until I reached THE MUD OF MURKY THOUGHTS, wherein all blotches within my auric field were removed, and as my soul began to go higher, I came upon THE WEB OF NEGATIVE THINKING which was a place ensconced in total darkness, wherein I faced it and ripped it away. In a spiral of light, my soul was now transformed by death, into life.

Sucked out of this pressurized chamber, my life-force had been removed from the physical, transferred to spirit, and replaced in form again as only a hologram of light; fully spirit, love, light, ascendant.

Returning from the other side, a nurse was waiting to release me. "What do I tell them?" I asked, "I've crossed over, yet nothing was wrong with me. I did not die, I am not ill." Taking my blood pressure, the nurse smiled. "You've crossed over so many times, and there has never been anything wrong with you. What do you say to those who do not see where you've been? You tell them firstly, not to fear death, for it is a beautiful transformation; secondly, that death is easier experienced when one awakens in life; and thirdly, that breaking down the river of limitation, the mud of murky thoughts, and the web of negative thinking is the only way to awaken life." Pausing, she looked upon me with great intensity. "Tell them the truth, sister, that life is only a short pause from reality, and in order to ascend, one must die first."

"I approached the confines of death . . . and borne through the elements I returned."
The Ancient Mysteries, The Egyptian Mysteries of Isis and Osiris, Page 189, No. 23, Paragraph 4, (Mystery Religions, Mediterranean)
****

Boarding the space vessel flown by the 'Seeders of the Ascension,' the male approached me. "I know you, I know of your destiny." He said. "What one seeks is usually right before their eyes, and in the seeking of higher fulfillment, the essence of all that we understand expands into what we've always known. Sometimes you must fly away from home to truly value home; sometimes you find that your true heart was always there."

Everybody disappeared, and I was now standing in a river. Struggling to get to the bank, a gentle man pulled me onto the shore. "Where am I?" I cried out, joyfully. Waving his arms across the sky, swirls of vortexes began to move all around us. "Watch closely, for these are the mechanics of creation, and as you watch, you will take on the knowing of the mechanics of life." All I had experienced became a whole as the energetic knowledge entered into me. "Immortality," he said, "is the transformation from the limited being that exists in fragmentary identity to the whole of consciousness that encompasses all life in one thought, all being in one breath, and all that is holy as everything." With that, he was gone.

"Then did I pass round the circle of eight, saw all the souls who had conquered darkness, saw the splendor of light where they dwelled. Longed I to take my place in their circle."

An Interpretation of the Emerald Tablets Together with the Two Extra Tablets, Tablet XI, Page 58, Paragraph 4, (Mystery Religions, Egyptian/Hermetic, Words of Thoth)

****

Having a totally inexplicable experience, it occurs to me that this has become the normal type of energy I now traverse. Circling like a group of whirling dervishes, I was with a group of tens of souls. Rapidly spinning as a great electrical current of ecstatic energies was generated; it caused some of us to be transformed into a greater higher vibrational pattern of which I cannot define. And the others . . . well, they seemed to have died.

In partial understanding, I knew that some souls attain to the heights when they give it their all, and others simply cannot handle the higher energies and do not reach such a high station. Grateful to have survived the process and to have been transformed into something higher, I couldn't help but wonder if this was a true death or, perhaps this was not as it seemed. In failing to achieve this higher vibratory nature, perhaps those souls who appeared to have died, had really only disappeared to our view. Because their frequencies do not intersect, it is often true that those with higher and lower vibrations cannot even 'see' one another; but it is equally possible that those who seemed to have 'passed,' only failed at their first attempt to unify the energetic influx which was generated from the group as a whole.

"When you have a desire to go somewhere, your heart goes first, sees the place and finds out what it is like; then it returns and takes the body there. People are all 'bodies' in relation to the saints and prophets, who are the world's 'heart.' First they come out of their humanity, flesh and skin, and travel to the other world. They observe both the other world and this world high and low and traverse many leagues until they find out how to get there. Then they return and invite the people."

Signs of the Unseen, No. 44, Page 176, Paragraph 5, (Islam, Sufi, Words of Rumi)

****

UNIVERSAL SPHERE OF REALMS

Realms:

Center, 1 and 2 = First and Second Dimension/Lower Worlds (Total Darkness) = Below Veil of Illusion

3 and 4 = Third and Fourth Dimension/Border Worlds (Light and Darkness) = Below Veil of Illusion

5 and above = Fifth Dimension and Above/Upperworlds (Light) = Above Veil of Illusion

Suffering and Sickness

Mystic Knowledge Series

Compiled and Written by Marilynn Hughes

The Out-of-Body Travel Foundation!

www.outofbodytravel.org

St. Benedict Standing Over Sick Man

PART I
When Tragedy Strikes

What can I possibly say to you in light of Suffering and Sickness in our world? All I could think of was silence . . . nothing . . . emptiness . . . but one strand of thought kept rippling through my mind which was this. "What is there to say except to make a profound restatement of our faith?"

Incidents like these happen throughout time and history and great minds have said great things. Among them are these:

"It is only when our rights are invaded or seriously menaced that we resent injuries or make preparation for our defense." **President James Monroe**

"The world will little note nor long remember what we say here, but it can never forget what they did here. It is for us the living rather to be dedicated here to the unfinished work which they who fought here have thus far so nobly advanced. It is rather for us to be here dedicated to the great task remaining before us - that from these honored dead we take increased devotion to that cause for which they gave the last full measure of devotion - that we here highly resolve that these dead shall not have died in vain, that this nation under God shall have a new birth . . . With malice toward none; with charity for all; with firmness in the right, as God gives us to see the right, let us strive on to finish the work we are in; to bind up the nation's wounds; to care for him who shall have borne the battle, and for his widow, and his orphan - to do all which may achieve and cherish a just and lasting peace among ourselves, and with all nations." **President Abraham Lincoln**

"I am tired; my heart is sick and sad. From where the sun now stands, I shall fight no more forever." **Chief Joseph, Nez Perce**

From the Funeral Oration for President Garfield, 2/27/1882: "Garfield was slain in a day of peace, when brother had been reconciled to brother, and when anger and hate had been banished from the land. Great in life, he was surprisingly great in death. For no cause, in the very frenzy of wantonness and wickedness, by the red hand of murder, he was thrust from the full tide of this world's interest, from its hopes, its aspirations, its victories, into the visible presence of death - and he did not quail. Not alone for one short moment in which, stunned and dazed, he could give up life, hardly aware of its relinquishment, but through days of deadly languor, through weeks of agony, that was not less agony because silently borne, with clear sight and calm courage he looked into the open grave. What blight and ruin met his anguished eyes, whose lips may tell; what brilliant, broken plans, what baffled, high ambitions, what sunder of strong, warm manhood's friendship, what bitter rending of sweet household ties! Behind him a proud, expectant nation, a great host of sustaining friends, a cherished and happy mother, wearing the full, rich honors of her early toil and tears; the wife of his youth, whose whole life lay in his; the little boys not yet emerged from childhood's day of frolic; the fair young daughter; the sturdy sons just springing into closest companionship, claiming every day and every day rewarding a father's love and care; and in his heart the eager, rejoicing power to meet all demands. And his soul was not shaken. His countrymen were thrilled with instant, profound and universal sympathy." **James G. Blaine**

"In Bunyan's 'The Pilgrim's Progress' you may recall the description of the 'man with a muck rake,' the man who could look no way but downward, with the muck rake in his hand; who was offered a celestial crown for his muck rake, but who would neither look up nor regard the crown he was offered, but continued to rake himself the filth of the floor. In 'The Pilgrim's Progress' the man with the muck rake is set forth as the example of him whose vision is fixed on carnal instead of spiritual things. Yet he also typifies the man

who in this life consistently refuses to see aught that is lofty, and fixes his eyes with solemn intentness only on that which is vile and debasing. Now, it is very necessary that we should not flinch from seeing what is vile and debasing. There is filth on the floor, and it must be scraped up with the muck rake: and there are times where this service is the most needed of all the services that can be performed. But the man who never does anything else, who never thinks or speaks or writes, save of his feats with the muck rake, speedily becomes, not a help but one of the most potent forces for evil . . . The foundation-stone of national life is, and ever must be, the high individual character of the average citizen." **President Theodore Roosevelt**

"The world must be made safe for democracy . . . It is a fearful thing to lead this great peaceful people into war." **President Woodrow Wilson**

"I believe you can do nothing with hatred . . . I believe in the law of love." **Clarence Darrow, Attorney During the Civil Rights Movement**

"Where there is no vision the people perish . . . We must act and act quickly. We face the arduous days that lie before us in the warm courage of national unity, with the clear consciousness of seeking old and precious moral values, with the clean satisfaction that comes from the stern performance of duty by old and young alike." **President Franklin D. Roosevelt**

"You are not all going to die. Only two percent of you right here today would die in a major battle. Death must not be feared. Death, in time, comes to all men. Yes, every man is scared in his first battle. If he says he's not, he's a liar. Some men are cowards but they fight the same as the brave men or they get the hell slammed out of them watching men fight who are just as scared as they are. The real hero is a man who fights even though he is scared . . . " **General George S. Patton Jr.**

"We must assist free peoples to work out their own destinies in their own way." **President Harry S. Truman**

"I know war as few other men now living know it, and nothing to me is more revolting." **General Douglas MacArthur**

"Let us never negotiate out of fear. But let us never fear to negotiate." **President John F. Kennedy**

"I have a dream that one day every valley shall be exalted, and every hill and mountain shall be made low, the rough places will be made plain, and the crooked places will be made straight, and the glory of the Lord shall be revealed and all flesh shall see it together . . . Free at last, free at last. Thank God Almighty, we are free at last." **Dr. Martin Luther King Jr.**

"These are the enemies: poverty, ignorance, disease. They are our enemies, not our fellow man, not our neighbor. And these enemies, too - poverty, disease and ignorance - we shall overcome." **President Lyndon B. Johnson**

"Why should they ask me to put on a uniform and go 10,000 miles from home and drop bombs and bullets on brown people in Vietnam while so-called Negro people in Louisville are treated like dogs and denied simple human rights? No, I'm not going 10,000 miles from home to help murder and burn another poor nation simply to continue the domination of white slave masters of the darker people the world over. This is the day when such evils must come to an end. I have been warned that to take such a stand would cost me millions of dollars. But I have said it once and I will say it again. The real enemy *of my people is here. I will not disgrace my religion, my people, or myself by becoming a tool to enslave those who are fighting for their own justice, freedom and equality. If i thought the war was going to bring freedom and equality to 22 million of my people, they wouldn't have to draft me, I'd join tomorrow. I have nothing to lose by standing up for my beliefs. So I'll go to jail, so what? We've been in jail for 400 years."* **Muhammad Ali, Boxer**

"My favorite poem, my favorite poet was Aeschylus. And he once wrote:

'Even in our sleep, pain which cannot forget

Falls drop by drop upon the heart,

Until in our own despair,

Against our will, comes wisdom

Through the awful grace of God.'

What we need in the United States is not division; what we need in the United States is not hatred; what we need in the United States is not violence and lawlessness: but is love and wisdom, and compassion toward one another, and a feeling of justice toward those who still suffer within our own country." **Senator Robert F. Kennedy**

"You have lost too much, but you have not lost everything . . . A tree takes a long time to grow, and wounds take a long time to heal. But we must begin." **President Bill Clinton after Oklahoma City Bombing 4/23/1995**

"Indifference is always the friend of the enemy . . . Indifference can be tempting - more than that, seductive. It is so much easier to look away from victims. It is so much easier to avoid such rude interruptions to our work, our dreams, our hopes. It is, after all, awkward, troublesome, to be involved in another person's pain and despair. Yet, for the person who is indifferent, his or her neighbors are of no consequence. And, therefore, their lives are meaningless. Their hidden or even visible anguish is of no interest. Indifference reduces another to abstraction . . . In a way, to be indifferent to that suffering is what makes the human being inhuman. Indifference, after all, is more dangerous than anger or hatred. Anger can at times be creative. One writes a great poem, a great symphony. One does something special for the sake of humanity because one is angry at the injustice that one witnesses. But the indifference is never creative . . . Indifference elicits no response. Indifference is not a response. Indifference is not a beginning; it is an end. And, therefore, indifference is always the friend of the enemy, for it benefits the aggressor - never his victim, whose pain is magnified when he or she feels forgotten. The political prisoner in his cell, the hungry children, the homeless refugees - not to respond to their plight, not to relieve their solitude by offering them a spark of hope is to exile them from human memory. And in denying their humanity, we betray our own. Indifference, then, is not only a sin, it is a punishment. What about the children? Oh, we see them on television, we read about them in the papers, and we do so with a broken heart. Their fate is always the most tragic, inevitably. When adults wage war, children perish. We see their faces, their eyes. Do we hear their pleas? Do we feel their pain, their agony? Every minute one of them dies of disease, violence, famine. Together we walk towards the new millennium, carried by profound fear and extraordinary hope." **Elie Wiesel, Survivor of Auschwitz**

These words are profoundly true today as yesterday and they will be again on another tomorrow. But what I want to share with my readers at this time is that this is, in part, the reason for the profound faith which sets us apart.

Because if we understand it, in a true and meaningful way, then nothing - even the greatest acts of evil - can harm our souls. Yes, they can harm our bodies, they can kill our loved ones, they can do great calamities upon this earth and will continue to do so because we live in this mortal realm wherein the battles between good and evil will continually rage.

But in our hearts, if we know the truth, none of it can change that which we are in the spirit. In the words of Our Lord (New American Bible, New Testament, Matthew 10:28) "Do not fear those who deprive the body of life but cannot destroy the soul. Rather, fear him who can destroy both body and soul."

By saying this, I do not mean in any way to deny our grief. Our grief is powerful and necessary. Grief can be a great harbinger of changes in the soul, and a powerful stimuli for greater understanding. It can also be a sword that is placed in the heart and never given rest. It is the Way of the Cross, the Way of Our Lord. So we embrace it. But what I am saying is that there really is nothing more profound that can be said other than to restate our belief and that which we already know to be true as spiritual seekers of the kingdom.

PART II
CHAPTER ONE

****

Standing before an aging storefront, a soul who had been struggling with terminal illness for several years awaited my arrival. Diabetic and in kidney failure, she couldn't survive without undergoing the rigors of dialysis three times a week.

Owning the store in my vision, I would go there every day and wait for the winds to pass. Kicking up about three in the afternoon, they'd remain deadly for several hours until they died down. Staying inside the store, we hoped that the windows would not be blown out. "Why don't we just go live in another town?" I asked her one day, "This is ridiculous, going through natural disasters every single day. There must be some other place we can go where this doesn't happen." Calmly she said, "I cannot go anywhere else."

Knowing that the winds were going to be especially treacherous and dangerous one day, she had a very small little house that lay within a ravine aside the store. Having only one room, it was built with wooden shutters which could block the windows and the door in case of a day like this. Urging me to join her in the house to withstand the winds, I agreed as the clouds did look ominous.

Entering the small room, I almost felt like I was suffocating because it was so small, but I entered anyway because I knew that it was the only way. Bolting the two different doors that overlapped, we closed most of the shutters around the windows, too, but left a couple of them open so that we could watch the impending storm. The winds picked up quickly and dramatically as a woman who'd been walking along the parking lot knocked on the door, but my friend called out to her that we couldn't open the door because of the pressure. "But go run into the store," she said, "it's open. And run to the far end of the building away from the glass." Doing so, we watched her running and struggling to get there. Momentarily relaxing when she made it, all of a sudden we saw a huge funnel cloud approaching us directly. The house began blowing around in circles and bumping on the ground. Quickly jumping up, I ran to her window and closed the wooden protective barrier. "I don't want you to get glass in your eyes," I said, as the funnel cloud whipped up the building, tossing us on our heads and all about.

Remembering that Andy and my daughters were in a house nearby, I panicked. "What can I do?" I thought. "I can't do anything to protect them from this!" No element remained within my control, and I could do nothing. We bopped around for quite some time before the funnel dropped us onto a very busy city street. Feeling that the winds were dying down, I'd opened the window behind me just a crack. Glass was broken and vehicles were coming towards us very quickly. Would they stop? Or were we about to be smashed to bits? It was out of our control and we couldn't do anything.

Before we could panic too badly, several city buses surrounded the little house to protect us from oncoming traffic. As we slowly exited through the door, many stood aside and clapped as they were grateful we had survived this awful day. Andy stood among them and walked forward, as my relief could not be measured. Taking his hand, we were suddenly walking in the parking lot of the store.

The windows had been completely blown out and debris was blocking many of the fallen windows. In a panic, we ran towards the building hoping to find the woman we had sent there for safety. Andy blocked my path. "I'm sorry, Andy. I didn't mean to put myself in harms way." "No," he said, "it's okay. You have to feel the pain."

Realizing suddenly the pain of those with terminal and chronic illness, I saw the analogy of their fight, of battling the destructive natural disaster that hits them every day with valor and courage. 'How stressful it would be to have to join this woman in her battle everyday!' I thought. Overwhelming and constant, she had no choice in seeking a more amenable environment. She couldn't escape her own body, except were she to die. In the meantime, she must accept her fate and the fact that it was something she could not leave. "You have to feel the pain and fight the good fight," Andy said, "and in so doing, you will be sanctified and brought ever closer to holiness."

People with chronic and terminal illnesses serve a purpose for the remainder of us who do not yet suffer so. They teach us to be more compassionate, but because of their long-suffering, they also teach us about true courage, perseverance and sacrifice. Shared pain deepens love.

"At Christmas I was talking to our lepers and telling them that the Leprosy is a gift from God, that God can trust them so much that He gives them this terrible suffering . . . and one man who was completely disfigured started pulling at my sari. 'Repeat that,' he said. 'Repeat that this is God's love. Those who are suffering understand you when you talk like this, Mother Teresa.' Christ is really living his passion in these homes. In our people you can see Calvary."
Prayertimes with Mother Teresa, Week Seven, Page 29, (Christianity, Catholic, Words of Mother Teresa)

****

Peering from above in the out-of-body state, I watched myself interacting with some friends I'd known in my past. As we were all going to go to sleep on this floor, I gently laid a blanket upon myself and immediately fell asleep. Stirrings began immediately and soon went out of control as a nightmarish memory from a past rape emerged. Yelling and screaming in my sleep, I begged the perpetrator to leave me alone, to get away from me. He did not. While looking from above, I couldn't help but be a bit embarrassed because in my sleep I was revealing to my on-looking friends this nightmarish part of my past. But I had no control over the horrid tremblings that overtook my soul upon the ground.

A nearby friend was concerned at these unconscious cries for help from this unknown assailant and went to find a counselor. When they returned, I was still murmuring in my sleep about the rape, and the counselor understood their meaning. Awaking, on some level I had known that I'd revealed my inner secret, but acted as if I didn't know, because I was ashamed.

Only a moment passed before I was swept off into a classroom with a childhood teacher and friends. Receiving an eternal message for one of my classmates, I asked the teacher for permission to give the written message to him in private. Declining, she insisted that I read the message aloud to the class. Becoming enraged, I screamed, "How dare you try to control me and the eternal in this way?" Quickly, I was out of control and enraged in my insistence. Subconscious intention obvious, I tried to control *them* instead. Remaining calm, but concerned about my rage, the teacher called in another one to help her. Although I wouldn't have hurt anyone, my rage was intense enough to make her wonder if I could.

Calming myself as the other teacher arrived; he looked at me with kindness and patience. "Mother Teresa once told me that when you make chocolate chip cookies, you will inevitably burn them sometimes. But we are not to be choosy, we should eat them anyway." Cowering in shame, I felt only compassion from the eternal. Because of these acts that occurred to me in childhood, I had tried desperately not to be controlled by others, even in circumstances where obedience required. By raging at others when they didn't understand something from the eternal, I defiled the very message that I was meant to give. In order to do a good deed, I committed a vile act which far surpassed the goodness of the original intent. In fulfilling the Lord's requests, we must fulfill them with temperance, obedience and prudence in mind, as well as, respect for both the message and for whom it is intended. If it cannot be given in the original manner intended, then pray . . . for the Lord shall surely find another way.

"My Father, I humbly pray and bow before you and ask for your forgiveness for my inexcusable conduct on many occasions. It is unforgivable to defile a holy grace in this manner, but through your divine mercy, I ask for this stain to be purified and redeemed into a higher domain, so that I may humbly fulfill your will in the manner in which you ask. At no time, Lord, have I earned the incredible graces you have bestowed upon my soul. Please forgive me, my Lord."

Standing in my backyard as an Aurora Borealis began to merge with the night sky, the moon began to change image, and the colors of purple and blue began shooting across the sky in the form of lights. Ancient writings and letters appeared aside the moon in the sky as I watched in holy wonder.

"But, if they were not thus clothed with My Will, in true humility, they would often offend against their own perfection, esteeming themselves the judges of those who do not walk in the same path."
The Dialogue of St. Catherine of Siena, A Treatise of Prayer, Page 211, Middle,
(Christianity, Catholic, Author: St. Catherine of Siena)

****

As debris was everywhere, I began obsessively cleaning everything in sight, thinking that this might please my friend when she returned. Because it was her reality I was cleaning up, I thought she would be very excited. When she returned, however, she wasn't as pleased as I'd expected. "You forgot to clean the most important part," she said, as suddenly I saw two large ugly tarantulas inside of my body. Knowing that this was another remnant of my days wandering in darkness, I ordered them out. They began walking, one through each arm, until they left my body through each hand.

Disgusted and grossed out, my friend looked at me with care and consideration as there was no judgment, it just simply had to be done. In our efforts to help others with their defilement, we mustn't forget our own. In the end, we are all individually responsible for what lies within us, and we cannot purify another, just as another cannot purify us.

"If one runs after that which is not his, it flies from him, and what is more, he loses his own as well."
The Zohar (Kaballah), Volume V, Korah (Numbers), Page 238, Paragraph 2, (Judaism)
"And no bearer of a burden can bear the burden of another."
The Holy Qur'an, Part XV, Chapter 17, Section 2, No. 15, (Islam, Words of Mohammad)

****

Wearing a pink cloak, a man approached and looked deeply into my eyes. Pulling down his coverlet, I could see his brown eyes and hair. "The A and the B, the I and the AM is calling you into service. Listen to Him." I turned.

Suddenly within a church where many people were gathering, I noticed that everybody was bringing injured people into the building on stretchers. Saying nothing, I felt my soul being sucked away as the power of the Lord entered my spirit and took over my spiritual body, as I observed from above. Speaking amazing profundities through my mouth, the Lord spoke as most in the room scoffed. Two or three of them, however, realized that the Lord had come among them. As the words flowed from my mouth, many of the injured were healed and His Presence awoke a few. The Lord called my spirit back to my body five or six times, and entered five or six times, and each time was unexpected and amazingly powerful.

When it was over, I uttered not a sound. Praying to the Lord quietly, I said, "I am unworthy of Your presence within me, Lord. But I thank you for purifying me, and for applying mercy to my sinful soul. I know, Lord, that it is not through myself, but through You alone that it has become possible for my body to become a temple for You." Bowing in prayer, I was suddenly whisked back to form.

"You have 159 days left before you die. Use them wisely," a voice whispered in my ear. For now, I didn't know if this were to be a true physical death, or yet another birth into higher mind. Waiting . . .

"And Moses said unto God, Behold when I come unto the children of Israel, and shall say unto them, the God of your fathers hath sent me unto you; and they shall say to me, What is his name? What shall I say unto them? And God said unto Moses, I AM THAT I AM: and he said, Thus shalt thou say unto the children of Israel, I AM hath sent me unto you."
King James Bible, Old Testament, Exodus 3:13-14, (Christianity, Judaism)
"There are twenty-two letters by which the I am, Yah, the Lord of hosts, Almighty and Eternal, designed, formed and created by three Sepharim, His whole world . . ."
Sepher Yezirah, Chapter VI, Section 9, (Judaism)

****

"'As it hath been said: 'Now Thou drawest me to the summit of glory, again Thou castest me into the lowest abyss.'"
The Seven Valleys and the Four Valleys, The Second Valley, Page 53, Paragraph 1, (Baha'i, Author: Baha'u'llah)

As I had been sitting in sin, and such a state would indeed sting, I broke out in a rash all over my body. Open bloody sores pierced my legs, feet and groin, while the hives lingered on every other part of my body.

As my physical body got sicker and sicker (still undiagnosed), and my blood pressure soared, it began to appear as if I could die. In this moment, when all else seemed out of my hands, my death became real and haunting as the Lord began to open my eyes. It was the week of the 159th day . . . the day of my death.

In that week, the Lord made it possible for me to see the true grossness of vice, in particular, that of vanity, a vice I was taught by the world and indulged in all of my life. Perhaps words cannot express what I now felt, but I saw vanity from God's eyes, and was horrified by its disgusting nature. Vanity is so very ugly. But beyond this, that week had been a true battle between me and darkness, as they were trying very hard to overcome my physical strength and do me in. These are my thoughts as they occurred on day 159:

I'm very sick as I write this, but I feel I must leave these final words, whether I truly die today or not, for they speak of this horrible truth that every soul must face when they look upon their own death, and when they enter into the abyss of their own sin. The Lord has shown me many things, things that could be of value to every soul to know.

As horrible dark creatures have been purged of my soul these past few months, I have gone through repeated temptations and glimmerings into the workings of temptation. I have seen that I am and always have been very attracted to vanity and destructive sexual energy and it is these energies that have allowed the presence of spindly demons, tarantulas, spiders and bees. I have seen that my attraction to this came from a sexual crime which was perpetrated on me long ago, and I have been given the grace to see the vileness of that act and how the Lord looks upon this sin by the perpetrator.

But I have been given this grace from a vantage point of detachment, wherein I see that my vices are still my own, and despite their origination, it is my duty to God to discover the truth and amend my own life, irregardless of what others may have done.

"In the other life, a person never suffers punishment because of inherited evil, because it does not belong to him. That is, he is not at fault for being what he is in this respect. Rather, he suffers punishment because of the realized evil that does belong to him - that is, the amount of inherited evil that he has made his own by his life activities."
Heaven & Hell, Chapter 37, No. 342, Paragraph 3, Page 258, (Christianity, Swedenborgianism, Author: Emanuel Swedenborg)

Having seen that to judge and hold anger is a grave sin which pulls a creature far away from God, doing so allays the application of mercy to your own soul. Now I truly know what it means, 'Judge not, lest ye be judged.' And the horrid creatures, now that they are all outside of me, my body feels almost like acid has burned it from the inside out, as if the exit of such vile substance was as traumatic as their existence. And repeatedly, the creatures have come after me in my sleep and in my wakefulness, for I see them as if they were physical. Bees hit my chest with the ferocity of a lightning-bolt, as my blood pressure soars and I feel pains from inside out. I've never felt such pain . . . or disgust.

"And why beholdest thou the mote that is in thy brother's eye, but perceivest not the beam that is in thine own eye?"
King James Bible, New Testament, Luke 6:41, (Christianity, Words of Christ)

Through the Lord's eyes, I have come to know the vileness that we are surrounded in our world, the disgusting nature of the lives we lead. It is so hard to express, and I'm certain, hard to understand from the other side of this view. For before I had seen it . . . I did not see it. Before I had felt it, I didn't feel the absolute nausiousness and pounding head pain that accompanies the mere resolution that has come to my vision of the disgusting nature of my own crimes against God, and the way our world pollutes the beauty of all the Lord has created. All is vanity, all is vanity. There is nothing more profound than viewing your own sins from the purity of God's eyes and seeing who you really are, rather than what you believe yourself to be. I've come to know that all humans have a very untrue perception of themselves, shadowed by many layers of self-delusion, which if revealed, would shock every one of them into a state of repentance.

My entire delusion about the purpose of life has also been shattered. I've entered a limbo about the reason for existence, as all that I now see within our world with very little exception, is so meaningless in God's eyes. How much time we waste on useless things, my feelings of disgust for the things of this world are deep at this moment. The vain renderings of flattery, pursuing unworthy goals which attend to self-glorification or self-gratification, lustful attempts to attract the opposite sex; where is the pursuit for the attainment of God, eternal love and mercy? The purification of our souls must surely be the only reason for our existence in these mortal realms; the purification of vice and the perfection of virtue. My children are so important to me now, because I don't know if I will live to raise them. Oh, how important the Lord considers our sacred obligation to the little ones.

"How much more reprehensible are those whose thoughts and deeds are concentrated upon their bodily desires and the time's vanities, whose souls do not ponder the fear of God nor draw it intimately into the fabric of their heart and of their innermost being, nor into their regularly appointed contemplations . . ."

The Gates of Repentance, Second Gate, IX, First Paragraph, (Judaism, Author: Rabbeinu Yonah of Gerona)

Grace and the strength of Christ have kept me alive through this, for this experience has been paralyzing and hard to accept. But I do not feel that I will remain sick forever, I feel that this sickness is being taken from me, and thus, I will someday feel anew. Then I will again be able to feel the love, joy, harmony and mercy of all that which is true. In the meantime, I must accept what is true within me, although it is the most difficult thing to do. For how can anyone see such filth within themselves, know it to be true, see how vile it is, feel the disgust with which God sees it, and then go on? It is a *true* death, one of which I do not yet know how to transcend. For there is a true dying occurring within both my body and soul.

Perhaps the monk who told me in regards to exorcizing dark things from within, 'these things take time,' misspoke the enormity of the task, for indeed an eternity would not be enough.

I am consoled only by the reminder from the Lord that He knows that we cannot ever attain eternal love if we don't first attempt imperfect love. Some people feel it would be best to deny love than ever take the risk of offending God with imperfect love. I believe this offends God more. In this hour of misery, I cannot get out of my head the saving word that delivered me from hell, 'Mercy.'

If every one of us were to see ourselves as God sees us, we would be implicitly merciful to all, no matter what their sin. For to judge another, is to be blind to the truth of yourself. Blessed are the merciful, for they shall obtain mercy. In my hour of wretchedness and death, surrounded by the realization and knowledge of all that is vile within me, all I can ask for is mercy, and hope that God grants more mercy to me than I have shown my fellow man. For vice and corruption are truly not seen in those who are filled with it. I did not see it, until now. And now that I see it, I am so overwhelmed; I cannot even give the words to express what I feel. Pain fills my body and mind, and the assaults of the demons who wish to hold these crimes against God within me forever, if only they knew what I know. Mercy.

"And when ye stand praying, forgive, if ye have ought against any: that your Father also which is in heaven may forgive you your trespasses. But if ye do not forgive, neither will your Father which is in heaven forgive your trespasses."
King James Bible, New Testament, Mark 11:25-26, (Christianity, Words of Christ)

For now, I must die. All that is within me, is worthy of death. It must be plucked out like a cancer destroying my very soul. And in the ashes, I will rise again.

Mercy, mercy, mercy.

Last night, as the horrid bee stung my heart I called to Christ for His grace and strength. My strength was gone, and I was surrounded by an all-out affront from the demonic, surrounded in only vile things. All alone, I asked Christ to sustain me through the battle, and He did. The Lord's Presence came strongly, with the knowledge that this battle was one I must fight, that I was indeed very vulnerable and close to death, and that it was not known who would win this battle. If I were to die, it would mean I had failed, so therefore, I fight, for the beast will not tear down this temple of the Lord, just as it has finally achieved its greatest victory, the knowledge of itself! For now, this temple can rise again and be true!

"And he said unto me, 'My grace is sufficient for thee: for my strength is made perfect in weakness.' Most gladly therefore will I rather glory in my infirmities, that the power of Christ may rest upon me."
King James Bible, New Testament, Galatians 1 12:9, (Christianity, Words of Christ)

Still, I fight. If I were to pass from this world today, I ask only one thing of those I leave behind. Please forgive me, if you can. I truly forgive all now, because I know what forgiveness really means. Sin isn't personal, it's ignorant. To think how vain, how arrogant it was that I could even have thought that you might need forgiveness from a soul as wretched as my own. I have been humbled by the Almighty One.

"And whosoever shall exalt himself shall be abased; and he that shall humble himself shall be exalted."
King James Bible, New Testament, Matthew 23:12, (Christianity, Words of Christ)

Satan wants people to despair and believe they are out of reach of the love of God. Having looked upon the bees and tarantulas, I realized that the bees were more assaultive and quick, while the tarantulas were more subtle and sneaky. Bees hit you right in the heart and other vital organs with lightning bolts of destructive energy, while the tarantulas prefer to enter while you are asleep, unaware, working a slower, more precise destruction from within.

As I'd looked upon them, I suddenly felt compassion. "Isn't it a horrible existence to be like you?" I asked, as they had cowered slowly. "To live solely for the purpose of the destruction of souls; the dismantling of all hope and love within humanity. That is so sad." Becoming more shadowed, I continued, "You know, I'm absolutely certain that even *you* could be redeemed, even a demon, if you turned to God. Jesus would have mercy on even your souls, if you would let Him deliver you from this abyss." With this, I felt their sadness, but also knew that they were unwilling to make this turn, despite their tremendous despair.

From that moment on, I felt no more fear of them. Going to the abyss taught me compassion for those who must live within it always, because they are too frightened or remote from the ways of God's love.

"A holy man was coming that way one day, and the cowboys warned him of the serpent. 'My children,' said, the holy man, 'I am not afraid. I know Mantras to protect me from harm of all kinds.' And he continued his way and the snake attacked him with upraised hood. On the incantation of some charm by him the snake fell helpless at his feet. 'Why do you,' said the holy man, 'go about doing evil to others? Let me give you a holy name (of God) to repeat always, and you shall learn to love God, and your desire to do evil to others will leave you.' So saying he gave him the holy name and went away."
Teachings of Sri Ramakrishna, The Worldly Minded, No. 285, (Hinduism, Words of Sri Ramakrishna)

It is in that moment of realization, when our despair and pain mount to a level indescribable at our offenses to the Lord, that God loves us the most. When a soul no longer believes it is worthy of God's love, it actually becomes the most worthy, for it has attained humility, a virtue beautiful in the eyes of God. The gravest sin, I have been shown through the Lord, is not to forgive. Forgive them, even if they are unable to acknowledge the harm they do, forgive them.

"And Jesus answering said unto them, 'They that are whole need not a physician: but they that are sick. I came not to call the righteous, but sinners to repentance.'"
King James Bible, New Testament, Luke 5:31-32, (Christianity, Words of Christ)

Allow me to clarify what forgiveness is. It is a choice to bear no ill will or desire for revenge towards a person who may have caused you harm, whether intentionally or inadvertently. When forgiveness is given to a remorseful and repentant offender, it is a way of saying that you accept their imperfection as a human being. When forgiveness is given to an unremorseful and unrepentant offender, it is a way of saying that you accept their inherent ignorance, and their inability to recognize their impact.

But in such a case, you must also draw a strong and bold line. For souls who do not recognize their impact upon others can become the most dangerous of people, and forgiveness does not mean allowing dangerous people to remain in your life, or affording them the freedom to continue causing harm in society. If mercy were absolute, there would be no hell. There is a hell, just as there are prisons, because there are souls who refuse to take responsibility for their acts. Forgive them, but don't allow darkness to reign by removing consequences.

Lord, I love thee with all my heart and soul and mind. Please Lord be more merciful upon me than I deserve and purify my soul of the stains of sin in which I sit. Born of mercy, by mercy, for mercy, for the greater glory of God. Forgive me, if you can. Mercy, mercy, mercy. Forevermore, mercy. Forgive me. Forgive me. Forgive me.

"You suffer, for Satan and his diseases torment your bodies. But fear not, for their power over you will quickly end . . . by your fasting and your prayer, you have called back the lord of your body and his angels. And now Satan torments you so grievously, for he feels that the end is come. But let not your hearts tremble, for soon will the angels of God appear, to occupy again their abodes and rededicate them as temples of God."
The Essene Gospel of Peace, Book Four, Page 30-31, Bottom & Top, (Christianity, Gnostic/Essene, Words of Christ)

****

Standing at the foot of a huge mountain, I noticed that it was covered in snow. Knowing the journey would be difficult; I realized it had to be undertaken. About twenty friends were with me at this point, but as I began to climb, they remained in the foothills. Within moments, I stood at the top of this highest peak alone. Andy was there, but in the background, for this journey had been a solitary one.

Appearing from inside a cave, a man took me hostage. Intending to kill me, this demon wanted me dead simply because I had reached the pinnacle of God's holy understanding. If the demon allowed me to descend this mountain, he knew I would tell of this holy knowledge of virtue and vice to those below. Knowing that I would speak of how we mustn't allow ourselves to walk in the acceptance of vice, but rather, travel the painful, heart-wrenching path of awakening and remembrance; demonic forces would prefer that we tell everyone that whatever they do is okay, but this is not God's will.

The demon at the top of the mountain tried to kill me, but failed, and I descended the mountain to tell the others of what I had found. When I got there, everyone had left me behind, for they were afraid of this descent into the deeper reaches of my soul. Fearful of this dark night of the soul, they walked away, afraid that being near me would bring the truth of these matters into their awareness. Unwilling to acknowledge that darkness remained within them, as well; they had convinced themselves that this abysmal path was my own and had nothing to do with them.

He shows us our sin and our corruption, but still, we must cleanse it. It will not just be taken from you, you must be willing to give all you have to satisfy the purification of your own corruption; herein lies deliverance, by the power of God, but through your own hand. Herein lies the purpose of the dark night of the soul.

"This divine purge stirs up all the foul and vicious humors of which the soul was never before aware; never did it realize there was so much evil in itself, since these humors were so deeply rooted. And now that they may be expelled and annihilated they are brought to light and seen clearly through the illumination of this dark light of divine contemplation. Although the soul is no worse than

before, neither in itself nor in its relationship with God, it feels undoubtedly so bad as to be not only unworthy
that God should see it but deserving of His abhorrence."
The Collected Works of St. John of the Cross, The Dark Night, Chapter 10, No. 2,
(Christianity, Catholic, Author: St. John of the Cross)
"When thy passions rebel, do thou rebel against them. When they fight, do thou fight them. When they attack thee, do thou attack them. Only beware lest they conquer thee."
The Voice of the Saints, In Temptation, Page 65, No. 4, (Christianity, Catholic, Words of St. Augustine)

****

CHAPTER TWO
The Will of God, Crashing Under the Weight of Suffering, Demonic Attacks and Suffering, Earning the Cross, Tyranny, Sickness as Purgation, Temptations Under Suffering, Understanding Suffering as Christ Understands it.

****

Coming to me in the night with a message to impart, he said, "You have Lupus, and everything is going to be okay because it is God's will." Having contracted it during a huge chemical spill years ago, he bade me to accept it and do my best to live within its confines. Thanking him, he disappeared.

****

Behind me, the old casket they bore was heavy and old. The funeral procession was long and arduous, following many miles of hills and valleys. Ahead of me, a young minister was walking, and I knew immediately the state of his soul. Although he had a sincere heart, he'd also had weaknesses towards lust which had kept him from perfection. Those who carried the casket were energetic and strong, but I was falling weak. Journeying this procession had left me sick and tired, and I turned to give them a warning look. My eyes told them I didn't know how much longer I could go on.

The abyss had weakened me, and I could no longer carry the casket which contained the deadness which had been purged. Suddenly, I collapsed to the ground, unable to go any further. After all the battles I'd undergone with the demonic, I was now failing from sheer exhaustion, which I'm sure made the demons joyous.

But before anyone could respond, a huge light began shining in front of me. Looking up, it came towards me at a speed indescribable and entered into my soul. As it did, my spirit was lifted up off the ground and began floating forward in the direction of the procession. Smiling with glee, I knew that my body did not move of its own accord, and that in my weakest moment, when there was only a little further to go, the Lord God was carrying me the rest of the way, so that I could bury my past properly.

The minister fell to his knees in worship of the obvious presence of the Lord. Others fell, too, somehow conveying to me that this act of God had shown them how deeply God must love me, which had changed their view of me as a soul. As they were mortal, they had judged me according to appearances, and my honesty about my status as a sinner. The lengths in which I would go to confess made them look down upon me.

As I was carried, the Lord made to know that the minister had tried to hide his lust and imperfection, and that despite my own sins of a similar nature; it was my humility and clear confession of those deeds which made me more loveable to Him. Because of this, He wouldn't allow my own weakness to hinder completion of this phase.

As God carried my soul, I shed tears of gratitude and joy, for he wouldn't allow me to fall, he wouldn't allow me to fall . . .

"They went into another garden and saw there people digging graves and dying immediately, and coming to life again with holy, luminous bodies.'What does this mean?' they asked. He replied: 'They do this every day. As soon as they lie in the dust the evil taint which they received at first is consumed and they rise at once with new and luminous bodies, those in which they stood at Mount Sinai. As you see them, so they stood at Mount Sinai, with bodies free from all taint; but when they drew upon themselves the evil imagination, they were changed into other bodies."

The Zohar (Kaballah), Volume V, Shelah Lecha (Numbers), Page 234, Top, (Judaism)
****

And so it came to pass that Satan and his forces made continual assaults on my body. At night, they would grab my legs and refuse to let go, until I ordered them to leave in Jesus' name. One night in particular, Satan came with hundreds of his demons trying to have me killed, but I remembered how powerful God is, and simply ordered them to leave again, in Jesus' name. Amidst these assaults, I found that whenever any demon or dark force is near, attacking you, or even just trying to tempt you, you may order them to leave in the name of Jesus Christ, and they *must* obey. Several times, the really sick ones would come and tell me to do evil things, which angered me even more, but it helped me to understand how Satan works within those whose hearts are ignorant or already darkened enough to respond to these sub-conscious promptings. They feed on your anger towards others, your feelings of hopelessness, and your vice.

Energizing your weaknesses, they tempt you to commit acts of evil, from slander to murder, by making you feel that vengeance is your own, rather than God's. But again, I simply ordered them to leave in Jesus' name. Many times, they would come in disguises, but as soon as they were ordered to leave in Jesus' name, they would metamorphosize back into their demonic form, look annoyed and disappear by the power of God.

On one occasion, someone had come to me from my past, offering an insincere apology, but I didn't recognize its insincerity and I accepted it. As soon as I did, a stick bug demon attempted to enter my neck. Pulling it off, I glanced at this person whose motives were clear. The serpent comes in many faces.

On other occasions, demons would take the form of my husband, Andy, and it would only be through my energetic awareness that I could identify what was happening. One time, a demon disguised as Andy came on to me sexually, but I immediately knew it was not him. Seeing a cross manifest in the sky, I knew I was under temptation and ordered him to leave. Revealing himself as a slimy green with pointy ears and horns, he left.

Interestingly, when we seem to have overcome temptations on a conscious level, there still lies beneath the surface of our souls subtler levels of vice which must be purified. We must purify our souls on all levels, mind, body and soul, the physical, our thoughts, and our dreams, in that order . . . and to do this is a great task, for our tendencies, karmic and otherwise, run deep.

"Many think that merely refraining from adulteries in the body is chastity, when yet that is not chastity unless there is abstention in the spirit also."

Marital Love, Chapter VI, Page 213, No. 153, (Christianity, Swedenborgianism, Author: Emanuel Swedenborg)

"The tempter, ever on the watch, wages war most violently against those whom he sees most careful to avoid sin."

The Voice of the Saints, In Temptation, Page 64, No. 2, (Christianity, Catholic, Words of St. Leo the Great)

"The devil is only permitted to tempt thee as much as is profitable for thy exercise and trial, and in order that thou, who didst not know thyself, mayest find out what thou art."

The Voice of the Saints, In Temptation, Page 64, No. 3, (Christianity, Catholic, Words of St. Augustine)

"The spiritual combat in which we kill our passions to put on the new man is the most difficult struggle of all. We must never weary of this combat, but fight the holy fight fervently and perseveringly."

The Voice of the Saints, In Temptation, Page 64, No. 4, (Christianity, Catholic, Words of St. Nilus)

****

Swept within a church wherein an angel of the Lord gave me a huge painting of the passion, she said, "You have earned the cross." Continuing, she conveyed, 'If you look towards darkness, then darkness shall look towards you. If you look towards the light, then the light shall look upon you. If you carry within you understanding, than no matter where you must look, whether it be the highest heaven or the lowest hell, you will see God. In this, you will always know what service to render to evolution.' Vowing to guard the direction of my eyes, she disappeared.

"During the past, this mind of mine roamed freely as it liked, as it desired, at its own pleasure. But today, I shall fully keep it in check, even as the elephant driver with the point of a goad controls an unruly elephant in rut."

Dhammapada, Canto XXIII, No. 326, Page 129, (Buddhism)

****

"And the Lord passed by before him, and proclaimed, The Lord, The Lord God, merciful and gracious, longsuffering, and abundant in goodness and truth, keeping mercy for thousands, forgiving iniquity and transgression and sin, and that will by no means clear the guilty; visiting the iniquity of the fathers upon the children, and upon the children's children unto the third and to the fourth generation."

King James Bible, Old Testament, Exodus 34:6-7, (Christianity)

"Lead me from darkness to light. Lead me from hatred to love. Lead me from limitations to Thine inexhaustible power; lead me from ignorance to wisdom. Lead me from suffering and death to everlasting life and enjoyment in Thee. Above all, lead me from the delusion of human attachment into realization of Thy love eternal, which plays hide and seek with me in all forms of human love."

Man's Eternal Quest, Looking at Creation with Seeing Eyes, Page 260, Paragraph 2, (Hinduism, Kriya Yoga, Words of Paramahansa Yogananda)

My soul had again entered deep illness, and in my sleep I was taken into an energetic powerhouse. Vibrating at speeds I'd never before fathomed, I was stunned by this overwhelming frequency with which I'd made contact. "You're illness is an initiation into the Kabbalah," a voice said, as many energetic currents overtook my soul and my sick and wretched form surrendered to the flow of divine influx. The clouds above me became immersed in lights, and my soul became content in wonder. Unaware of it at this moment, my journey into the Kabbalah was about to take me into the mystery of original sin.

"The more illuminating the exposition given of the Torah, the more those clouds are lit up, and they become more and more transparent until the veil becomes visible, and from the midst of that veil they see a light brighter than that of all other lights, and this is the face of Moses. No one actually sees his face, but only the light which proceeds from the veil behind all the clouds . . . When they emerge from the Academy of Moses they fly to the Academy of the firmament, and those who are qualified fly to the highest Academy. Of that generation it is written: 'Happy is the people that is in such a case, yea, happy is the people whose God is the Lord."

The Zohar (Kaballah), Volume V, Shelah Lecha (Numbers), Page 235-236, Bottom & Top, (Judaism)

****

Faced with absolute tyranny, I looked upon a concentration camp from World War II. The desolation confounded me, and I felt immense sorrow when I looked upon four black hats often worn by Hasidic Jews, lined up aside a grave site which was burrowed next to an oven. Such scenes only remind us of the true mystery behind the redemption of mankind, and the mysterious ways through which the will of God are fulfilled despite the tyranny and evil of humanity. No words, no words . . .

"And thy Lord will surely pay back to all their deeds in full. He indeed is Aware of what they do."

Holy Qur'an, Part XII, Chapter 11, Section 10, No. 111, (Islam, Words of Mohammed)

"'How abundant is Your goodness that You have concealed for Your reverent ones,' and it is written: 'He guards all his bones, even one of them was not broken.' May it rest secure, alone, and serene, from fear of evil . . . May his/her soul be bound in the Bond of Life. And may it be brought back to life with the Resuscitation of the Dead with all the dead of Your people Israel, with mercy. Amen."

The Siddur, Death and Bereavement, From the Prayer for the Deceased, (Judaism)

****

For several years now, my soul had heralded momentary glimpses into the world of pain and suffering due to the still undiagnosed illnesses (Lupus) which had clung to my soul. Wondering why such an affliction might be necessary, I began to pray and ask for wisdom as to the purpose of my own particular suffering, and also to know in some general sense, the purpose of the many sufferings which are placed upon the people of God during their Earthly sojourns.

Immediately, I began to hear the voice of an unidentified saint as if speaking over a radio. Speaking of the importance of overcoming vanity, I instantly realized that my current illness was connected with her words. Making it difficult to be vain as my body was continually covered in rashes, sores or other disgusting maladies, it was forcing my spirit to let go of this sin.

A method of purging myself of all vanity - a sin which was great within me - this was to be accomplished in two ways. First, by the nature of the physical disgustingness of the maladies themselves which precluded vanity, and second, by being in a situation for which I could not control, the discharge of the vanity of self-control and self-destination.

"Illness and tribulations, being teachers of piety, are not to be avoided."

A Buddhist Bible, The Supreme Path, No. V. No. 5, (Buddhism, Tibetan)

"When God gives you something to suffer, says St. Augustine, He acts as a physician, and the suffering He sends it not a punishment but a remedy."

The 12 Steps to Holiness and Salvation, Chapter 12, Page 188, Top, (Christianity, Catholic)

Padre Pio was standing behind the counter, as I had emerged in a new place. Immediately watching him from afar, I reveled in this holy man who had received the stigmata, bearing the wounds of Christ.

Approaching him, I said, "I have something to tell you, Padre." Looking up, he waited for my words. "I love you," I said. Smiling for a moment, he then spoke. "Good," he said, "that's good . . . for now."

"Wherefore, every blessed soul will lose all her own desires and will have no other desire but to love God and to be loved by Him, and knowing that she is sure of ever loving Him and of being ever loved by Him, this very thing will be her blessedness . . ."

The Soul Sanctified, Chapter 30, Page 84, Paragraph 2, (Christianity, Catholic)

****

About six months pregnant with my third child, who would be Jacob, I'd been ordered to bed rest. A serious undiagnosed condition remained beneath the surface, however, one which would not be discovered for another two years. But when it would be discovered, it would affect my life in a huge way.

Falling off into a deep, ecstatic, transcendental state, my soul was hovering amongst the stars. Honoring my soul in this brilliant and peaceful place with the presence of my two daughters, Melissa and Mary, we hovered together for hours absorbing the celestial impetus given us by the Lord. Being able to watch my two jewels made this heavenly experience all the more joyful, and I thanked the Lord for his kindness.

****

Taking my soul on a hellish journey, the disgusting ogre had arrived with permission from the Lord to make an effort to tempt me to despair. Because I'd been so sick throughout my pregnancy, I'd already been struggling with depression, and Satan felt that he knew just what might take me over the edge.

Reaching his hand to me, I refused to take it, looking at him as though he were delirious. "I will go with you, because it has been ordered by the Lord. But I shall at no point touch you," I said. Acting insulted, the devil began falling as if he were traveling through an endless pit. Without any conscious participation on my part, I fell in line with him as we entered into the deepest caverns of the Earth.

Arriving at two pits of fire, the horrific stench was only outdone by the moans heard in the darkness. Deeply touched, I remained unmoved in my countenance refusing to look upon the face of the ogre; but inwardly, I mourned and lamented the existence of this hell realm, and beyond this, the terrifying reality that some souls actually condemned themselves to such a place.

Everything was as dark as the deepest of caverns, the soil and pith sloppy and gooey, like mud beneath your feet. Filled with the energy of evil, these were the pits of fire.

Looking to Satan, he was waiting expectantly for a reply, or even better, a horrified reaction to his kingdom. Looking at him emotionless, I said, "The Lord does not wish us to despair, but rather, to focus on heavenly things . . . hope." Looking deeply disappointed, he didn't move, but his face showed no more sarcasm. Continuing, I quietly replied, "And that is exactly what I intend to do." Immediately, I disappeared.

Aboard a huge circular craft, several hundred sub-conscious astral souls were soaring through the heavens to bear witness to some of the wonders of God. Immediately, I noticed that we were all wearing inflatable socks upon our feet and lower legs to battle the cold of outer space. Holding a book in their hands, a group of human looking spiritual beings showed it to us, communicating that this was to be given to the extra-terrestrials at the space station, which was apparently our destination. Sacred and holy, I couldn't help but open my naive mouth, querying their disapproving faces. "Why haven't you also brought them ancient sacred texts?" Immediately I understood that they had brought some of the ancient sacred texts to them. Looking at me as if it should be obvious, they said, "As pertains to the galactic heavens, some of the ancient sacred texts upon the Earth are out of date. Although some things, such as the Bible and other holy scriptures, remain timeless and relevant wherever they may be, there are others which are obsolete in our realms, although highly relevant to those of you remaining on the Earth." Embarrassed, I could *feel* the highly evolved nature of these galactic beings who far surpassed any intelligence I'd ever seen.

Unfortunately, they didn't expand on this because the time had come to look upon our destination. Following their instructions, I looked out of the window in our craft. To our right, was a magnificent space station, much larger than the one I'd seen recently. But what absolutely confounded me in a state of wonder and bliss was my witness to a most profound debacle of heavenly beauty filled with knowledge of great galactic significance. Surrounding the space station were huge magnificent paintings with gold frames, encircling the city with their holy protection and filling us travelers with the wisdom that they had been placed upon the sky to impart. As these paintings hovered in the heavens, they seemed to be attached only to the heavenly landscape. Stars cascaded around them as if they were somehow alive, and indeed, in an inexplicable way they were.

Enraptured by the brilliant artistic renderings of Jesus Christ, Mother Mary, the Twelve Disciples, St. John the Baptist and a panoramic display of the Life of Christ, they had been placed in chronological order and completely surrounded the space station. Profound but simple was their message, Jesus Christ was just as significant to the galactic heavens as He had been to the planet Earth and His life on Earth was a great galactic and Universal moment! Seeding us to one day become a part of this much larger, universal, grand and galactic union, this amazing redemptive journey had been etched upon the stars with a patient knowing. Someday, the tribes of the Earth would awaken, and grasp the knowledge of the spheres . . . that of Galactica!

****

As I was reading the following passage from a vision beheld by the most saintly Padre Pio, a most amazing consolation was given me by the Lord:
"My soul was suddenly carried away by a force stronger than itself into a very large room illuminated by a very bright light. On a high throne studded with jewels was seated a lady of rare beauty. This was the most holy Virgin who held in her arms the Child of majestic mien, his face more resplendent and luminous than the sun. All around them was a great multitude of very beautiful Angels. At the end of this large room there were two small beds, in each of which was a person who, to judge by appearances, must have been in great suffering. One of them was suffering so much as to seem on the point of bidding farewell to this life. Before the throne on which the Virgin was seated there was another person, completely absorbed in contemplation, who was the personification of happiness. The Child came down from the Virgin's arms, and followed by his Mother and the Angels approached the person wrapt in prayer. He threw his arms around that person, clasped her to his breast, kissed her an infinite number of times and bestowed on her innumerable other caresses. The Virgin and the Angels did likewise. Then he went towards the beds of the two sick persons. To one of these, who was sitting up in bed, the Child addressed just a few words of comfort, rather coldly and unceremoniously. At the other sick person who lay at full length in the bed and had greater need of comfort, he did not deign even to glance, and as if he hated even to punish her, he ordered the Angels to beat her. These did not hesitate to carry out his orders. They approached the sick person, one of them took her by the hand and the others began to punch and kick and slap her. This scene seemed very cruel. But what a strange and wonderful thing! The poor creature did not complain, but in a very weak voice exclaimed: 'O most gracious Jesus, have mercy on me while the time for mercy still lasts. Do not condemn me, most sweet Jesus, when you come to judge me, for I should not be able to love you anymore. O most compassionate Jesus, if your severe justice intends to condemn me, I appeal to your most loving mercy.' The Child turned to me and said, 'Learn how one should love.' I understood nothing. This sight made me tremble like a reed exposed to a violent wind, for I expected this soul to be rejected by Jesus. But alas, how different from the reality is the sensual man's estimation of spiritual things! Wretched me! For many years I have attended the school of suffering without learning anything. May the infinite mercy of our God be eternally blessed for his great goodness and patience in bearing with me! But to banish all fear from my heart the Lord willed to show me also the souls of these three persons. How beautiful are the souls in whom the heavenly Spouse reigns! If all were to be shown this beauty, we should certainly not see so many of our foolish brethren hastening to where God is not to be found. All three of these angelic creatures were in God's grace; all were adorned with merits, though not in equal measure, for the third was more fully adorned by merit than the second and the second more than the first. Since I could not understand why the Lord treated in such different ways these dear spouses of his, he was pleased to

come to the aid of this wretched creature and by a clear and explicit interior locution he began to say to me: 'The first was a soul still weak and in need of caresses, otherwise she would have turned her back on him; the second soul was less weak and to keep her in his service she still needed some little sign or affection; the third was a beloved spouse of his, because, in spite of the way he afflicted her, she remained constant in her service and faithful in love.'
Padre Pio of Pietrelcina - Letters, Volume 1, Letter 139, Page 436, (Christianity, Catholic, Words of Padre Pio)

As I read this vision of Padre Pio, I allowed myself to consider that maybe this sort of thing was happening to me. After all, I started out my spiritual life receiving many consolations in the form of visions and holy dreams, but now was very often left to battle the wretch on my own, not to mention that I'd been suffering great illness. But I didn't want to be presumptuous, so I began to let that thought go, when suddenly . . . a light from heaven came down and surrounded my whole body.

Immediately wrapped in a state of ecstatic bliss, all around me began to glow with light, even down to the last particles. Molecular light was filling the air around me as a spectacular shower of white glowing dust fell from the heavens to the floor of my bedroom. Literally *feeling* the Holy Spirit come into me like a torrential flood of energy, I immediately became aware of the presence of the Lord Jesus at my side. 'I wish for you to read this as a consolation to your own soul,' He said. Reassurance that my sufferings were not an indication of God's wrath, but rather, an indication of God's confidence in my loyalty to Him, despite the active purgation being experienced in my body, was undeniable.

Knowing without *any doubt* that the Lord was happy with me, He still loved me, despite the just consequences of my former sins. In that moment, I realized that it was through *these very consequences* that my soul was becoming sanctified. Perhaps this is one of the ways God heals us, as suffering with grace brings its own reward. Knowing the sincerity of my contrition, the Lord conveyed that my sins had been blotted out, but purgation was under way.

Surrounded by this heavenly light for about ten minutes, I cannot even describe the eternal ecstasy which I experienced within that time. In this totally conscious, physical waking state, the presence of Jesus was so comforting and clear, and the light had manifested to my physical vision. The Lord had not left me to muddle in the quagmire of past sins, but rather, was preparing me to receive of heaven! Having grown up in the Lord, it was time for me to *stand tall* for the Lord, irregardless of heavenly consolations I did or did not receive.

Receiving a similar ecstatic consolation two weeks later while watching the holy mass on television, the priest had spoken about those who were unable to attend mass (due to personal illness, taking care of babies, or attending to the sick). Saying that Jesus was with us in our suffering, I immediately felt peace and saw as heavenly hosts appeared visibly in multitudes around the room. The Lord conveyed that He not only *approved* of my absence from the holy altar, but *preferred* it, because it was a sacrifice. Given for the benefit of my children or on behalf of souls when I was sick, the heavenly lights descended from heaven, and I was *completely filled* with the presence of the Lord. "I prefer sacrifice and surrender," Jesus said, "to the strict adherence of rule."

As the lights began to lift in the room, St. Patrick appeared (Patron saint of Ireland), hovering in the air above the floor. Nodding quietly in approval of my sacrifice, he disappeared as the entire heavenly host vanished.
****

CHAPTER THREE
The Reward, the Powerful Spirit Underlying those who Suffer Much, Heavenly Healing Help, Warnings from Heaven about Physical Sickness, Insensitivity Posed by Others when we Become Sick, Meeting Gabriel.

****

After several months of chronic pain and various infections, I found myself in a ballpark wearing the robe of a monk. Head pounding with a migraine, my neck was sore, and I was coming down with another high fever. Andy was sitting on the bleachers a few feet in front of me, while I was standing in the wings trying not to make my discomfort obvious. One of the ballplayers left the field, coming directly towards me. "You poor thing," he said, "always trying to smile, even though the pain never goes away." Emanating great compassion, my soul was immediately transported to a very glorious place.

Amongst the celestial heavens, stars cascaded around the metaphysical convent as a very old woman came towards me wearing a nun's habit. Blue-green skies shimmering, her long gray hair and deep blue eyes held compassion in this magnificent cathedral which claimed the stars as its walls and the cosmos as its altar.

Coming towards me, she reached out her hand to mine as I eagerly grasped it. Tears filled my eyes. "Why are you crying?" she asked very sweetly. Not knowing quite what to say, my embarrassment eluded the fact that I was just ecstatically happy to remember her. "I'm home," I said quietly, accepting the momentary reunion as a gift in reward for perseverance.

****

Given entry into this man's life only days before he was to die, I was astounded to witness the level of suffering from which he was about to be freed. Debilitating and fatal, his condition was shown to me in a graphic display as I looked upon his soul. In the symbolic image given me, I noticed that his spinal column traveled upwards from his tailbone to his neck . . . and then it continued down his left arm all the way to his hand. Unable to ascertain his exact disease, I knew it to be related to a spinal deformity.

For only a moment, the Lord allowed me to experience the pain this poor man was undergoing as his final death watch had begun. Unable to describe such pain in words, I can only say that it was deafening.

Having been taken care of by his mother all of his life, he was a grown man in his early twenties. Able to see her, although she was completely unaware of my presence, my purpose this eve was to die *with* this young man and bring him over the divide, assuring that his journey was completed properly.

As soon as his mother left for work that morning, his soul and body became transfixed in an unusual way, as if he were seeing into two worlds. It was at this time that he first became aware of my presence. Immediately as our eyes met, there was a confounding joyous love that we shared, as if we had perhaps known each other from before.

Allowing me a singular gift, the Lord permitted me to see beyond his very visible physical deformity, and peer within to witness his absolutely spectacular soul. Breathtakingly beautiful, I was able to see his overlapping spirit as it began its preparations to leave. Although his deformity was really quite difficult to look at physically, his soul was magnificently beautiful.

Knowing this beauty had come about through the experience of such a difficult life, he'd been trapped in a body which was both unappealing and non-functional. Quite a trial for this soul, his spirit radiated empowered masculinity and strength. Although some people think that such afflictions are brought about by the way people think, lack of faith or karmic retribution, it was evidently clear that this was not at all true in this person's case. Clearly enunciated by the Lord, the purpose of this incarnation was for this very masculine, virile and powerful soul . . . to experience abject powerlessness and being despised by his fellow man. Karmic aspects were not relevant. Wow, what an amazing thing this was to see.

When a soul requires a certain experience to affect spiritual elements within their character, they have the experience irregardless of karma or other such matters. Learning absolute humility from this experience, this humility was all the more striking because I was witnessing it, side by side, with the true power and magnitude of his soul. Magnified by the attainment of the necessary virtue of humility, this power was actually strengthened from the experience of total helplessness, abjection and having to be cared for by others in every way.

No words can express the intense love I felt for this soul, as we spent these few days in timelessness (one night astral time) laughing and discussing his current life and my own. Our time together was made more special because there were many people, gratefully not including his mother, who were anxious for him to leave. Many considered him a burden and wished for him to hurry up and die. This was so sad, I cannot even express it. So many people think that when a person is obviously deformed, handicapped, chronically or terminally ill, or mentally challenged, that they are not aware of how others feel about having to care for them. But in this case, he was definitively aware and deeply troubled by the burden his existence placed on others.

When souls are near death, while their spirit is going back and forth from the physical body to their soul, they are often quite lucid and aware during the times in which they enter into the awareness of their spirit. Our time of death is a very important time, and most of us would like to have the opportunity for proper good-byes, Lord willing. Most of us would like to leave this world in peace, knowing our loved ones are at peace with us. It's painful to leave knowing resentment remains because of the manner in which you left this world.

After spending several days in timelessness together with this wondrous being, the Lord, through a great and merciful act, allowed me to experience his death alongside him as if I were also leaving the world. Feeling every pain right alongside him, I felt every system shut down. Amazed at the incredible amount of pain this man had lived with, I was grateful to have this window into the severity of the suffering of others. Experiencing this generated a great deal of compassion within me towards the sick. Although I'd had my own share of suffering in this life due to my disease, this was a totally different kind of suffering. Deformity is a cross in itself, but his condition caused constant extreme pain in the head, spine, back, and arms. Although my own suffering could be severe, it was usually transient, appearing in cycles, giving me breaks between severe bouts of pain. Giving a chance for regeneration between them, this is distinctly different from being worn down continually by severe pain that never leaves.

Feeling the body systems shutting down as the process of death continued, I again noticed that the most difficult adjustment for me was the cessation of breath, although I felt all of the systems shut down. It was as if there were a psychic bond between the soul and the various parts of the body, because you could definitely ascertain such things as the liver, the intestines, the pancreas, kidneys, etc., all shutting down. During this experience, they seemed to occur one by one, beginning with the cessation of breath, and then the heartbeat, followed by the remaining bodily organs and systems.

Entering eternity, I was surprised that this man had crossed over with his disability intact. Before I had a moment to contemplate this any further, we immediately began flying.

Mountainous and serene, we stood amidst a large desert valley in the center of a cathedral of peaks. A large, rectangular, crystal, transparent enclosure was graciously encased before us in the sand. Approximately twenty feet long and ten feet wide, the energy from this enclosure immediately pulled his soul inside, as he now appeared to be lying down within the confines of the crystal. Restoration the purpose, I watched as a beautiful light lit the heavens, surrounding him and myself as he fell into a deep sleep within the enclosure.

Although I had a great desire to wait here so that I might be present upon his waking, the arrival of a disc-shaped flying ship seemed to direct my attentions elsewhere. Four men exited the spaceship, wearing the clothing of common men. Knowing them to be angelic hosts, I found their humanness astonishing. Swift to let me know that I must now return to my body, my protestations were of no avail, as they firmly directed a wave of their hands towards my spirit. Within less than a second, I was gone.

****

Melissa, my daughter, had an experience (March 1, 2001):

"You, Dad and I were riding down a snow-covered hill upon a large inflatable sled. Before we knew it, we had suddenly gone into deep water and all had been submerged. Somebody was pulling me above the water, and when I emerged from the depths, I shouted out for you and Dad. Dad was walking towards me . . . on the water . . . but you were nowhere to be found. Going underneath the water, I found your body and lifted it up above the water, but realized that you had died."

"Up in the distance, Dad and I were stunned, as we watched your spirit walking towards the sunset, which was of an unusual brilliance. An outline of a gate, perhaps the gates of heaven, was outlined in the sky and lit by the light of the sun. Beautiful music of angels singing could be heard coming from beyond heaven's gates in welcome. Wearing a robe of gleaming and pure white, you turned to us and waved good-bye. Asking me to watch out for my little brother and sister, you shouted, "I love you!" as I shouted it back. "You'll have to look out for yourself now, and learn to handle problems without my guidance." Dad was just looking towards the scene with shock, as if he couldn't believe that this had happened so quickly and unexpectedly."

This moment marked the time that I decided I must push my doctors to figure out what was wrong with me, and when they finally identified the anomalous illness, a shockwave would burst throughout our home.

****

Although I was not yet aware of what really plagued my potential corpse, my mortality was beginning to seem very real to me. Coughing uncontrollably for several weeks before, I was also experiencing severe chest pain.

As the death knoll began, I began to leave my body, immediately noticing an older man and woman quickly approaching my spirit. Emotionally wrapped up in the bliss of separation, I could still feel the pain of my body, however, as they came nearer. "We have to do something," the woman said, "she's leaving her body." Immediately I knew that she was not concerned about me taking a little journey, but that I might be leaving my body in a more permanent way through death. Without any further adieu, the man came towards me with a needle containing adrenaline and another drug which began with an 'F' and had a very long name. Interrupting his approach, I said, "Wait a minute, I think I'm having a stroke. Don't give me anything that would make that worse." Looking at me hastily, he conveyed that he knew what he was doing, and without waiting a second longer, he plunged the needle into my arm. At that very second, my eyes popped open in the physical realm.

****

Alit with warnings regarding the dangerous state of my health, angels shouted in my ears, *"Emergency, Emergency,"* as they showed me a picture of my heart. Something was deathly wrong. "You must accept that you are very sick, and do *absolutely* nothing!" Appearing as if I was pushing myself too hard, I agreed as the angels disappeared.

Finding out the next day that I was in severe heart failure due to a condition known as Peripartum Dilated Cardiomyopathy, my heart was enlarged, functioning poorly, thinned out, and suffering from a generally terminal heart muscle disease, which they believed had been caused by a rare complication of pregnancy. Preparing to be evaluated for heart transplant, I allowed the news to sink in.
****

Approaching me in liturgical robes of the purest white, I recognized him as a priest who had spent his lifetime fighting for the rights of the unborn. Coming to embrace me, he conveyed, "I am joyous that you are willing to sacrifice your life, so that Mary and Jacob may live." Because my illness had come about due to pregnancy, he seemed to understand that when my time of death did come, that it would be a sacrifice. In the meantime, my daily life as someone who had become greatly disabled due to heart failure would also be an offering to the Lord.

Looking at my three children through a clear pane of glass, an old nun was carefully watching over them. "If you are to die," she conveyed, "they will be all right."
****

Although my soul bore no memory of the journey to reach this highest of places, I awoke to find myself conscious in the top floor of what was presented to me as the highest building on Earth. Looking down, I noticed that my soul was adorned in a robe of the whitest white with a deep red sash around my shoulder and waist side. Knowing immediately that these robes were energetically linked to the Sacred Heart of Jesus, my soul became radiant with the light of the beatific vision, as all the scars of my worldly life had been removed. Because of the Lupus, I sometimes had visible signs of disease on my body, but these were now gone.

Reveling in this newfound freedom of soul, I received a phone call from below from someone in my current life who was very much caught up in karmic circling. Speaking with urgency, I listened to her with calm and peace, but noticed that as I did, my face began to break out in a rash. Exhaustion began to overtake me, as I politely hung up the phone. Quickly realizing that I must stay off the phone which was linked to those remaining below, communicating on that level appeared to drag me back into the world of death. Because they were trapped in karmic malaise, they had needs which they wished for me to fulfill which caused this affect. Souls who called wishing me well or desiring to know my status did not cause this phenomenon.

As soon as I understood this mechanism, I was led to the door. Looking below, I noticed that this 'building' was a way-station floating above the clouds in the sky. Without further adieu, I became unconscious.
****

Surprisingly, I felt more pressure to perform once I got seriously ill, than I had before getting sick, and it appeared to be due to people's general judgment of everything I did or didn't do. Now under close scrutiny, everything was subject to a general appraisal of whether or not I was fighting hard enough, being sufficiently positive, or feeling sorry for myself.

Because it is one of the worst things that can happen to you, I found that most people generate little compassion and can be quite insensitive to such serious illness. Although they seem quite capable of feeling compassion for much smaller issues, things they can relate to, death can be a very humbling experience, because the world lets you know that it'd be fine with them if you should slip quietly off into the night, not bothering them with the difficulties encountered in disability, or the grief you may feel about your own demise.
****

Many people can be insensitive, although I'm sure unintentionally, when someone is passing from this world.

There are two things a person who is leaving this world needs to know: 1) that their existence had meaning, to themselves and to others, and 2) that their death will not go unnoticed.

People who are dying, especially those who are unusually young or leaving children behind, need to know that others consider their death tragic, rather than insisting that they must see something good and wonderful in their demise. Rather than being helpful, telling a dying person all the 'positive' ways they can see their own demise is insulting and negates the seriousness of their loss. Invalidating the meaning behind the person's life, it forces them to feel that their existence really doesn't matter all that much to others, and it shoves the soul prematurely into the humbling realization that they, too, shall die, and the world will go on as if they'd never lived.

Allow me to give you a listing of things that are always said to terminal patients, which should be abandoned: 1) Everybody's going to die, I could die before you do. 2) Everybody has their problems, just get over it and move on. 3) If only you thought more 'positive,' had more 'faith,' engaged in proper 'conduct,' practiced the correct 'religion,' thought 'properly' or took this 'supplement,' you would be healed. 4) Just get up and force yourself to go on, stop being lazy. 5) You are feeling better, aren't you?

Telling a person that anybody could go at anytime is insensitive and invalid. A terminal patient is facing death at *this* moment, and unfortunately, because terminal patients rarely know exactly when their demise shall come, death becomes an inseparable part of their lives; because it could happen at any time, or it could be delayed for years.

Aside from this, terminal patients usually face physical disability during this time-frame, and the pain and limitation they experience almost constantly, remains a continual reminder that their body is slowly failing and death will eventually occur. Somebody who goes suddenly, usually does not know that it is coming for more than a few minutes, and they are usually not already disabled and in mourning over the life that they've lost to the illness.

Subsequently, many terminal patients have no choice but to ask for help from people who may resent their need. Ironically, this resentment sometimes builds as the patient fights to live . . . and does. Because many people unconsciously project onto the seriously ill patient that it would be more convenient to others if they would either hurry up and have a miraculous and complete recovery or . . . die; survival, at the expense of remaining sick or disabled, can be used against you. And it is common to feel this from family, caregivers *and* medical professionals, as a patient may feel guilty about requiring assistance from the very busy medical profession.

Comparable only to a doctor telling someone that they *may* statistically die in a car accident or of a terminal illness sometime before they turn ninety-five, such analogies should never be used with someone who faces imminent illness and death.

Judged as having brought this calamity upon themselves either by wrong thinking, insufficient faith, or incorrect religious beliefs, they may also be regarded as lazy by those who have never experienced an illness which slaps you right down on your butt, making it impossible to do the things you once did with ease.

In order to insure that you don't express the sometimes sad reality which occupies most days due to your illness, people will say, "You *are* feeling better, aren't you?" As if 'not feeling better' somehow indicates a failure on your part, this is also taken as a warning not to 'go there,' so the patient behaves and says, "Oh, of course." Despite the obvious reality that a terminal illness is so because it has no cure, it will continue as is or will progress until you die (unless you are one of the people who is honored to receive a miraculous intervention from the Lord). Allow me to make this clear; it doesn't improve, the patient remains sick and disabled according to their disease, and it is likely to get worse, rather than better.

Because most people haven't experienced illness which does not go away, they keep wondering why you won't just get better, and in order to quell the terror they have of their own mortality, they revert back to the incorrect thinking which got you into this mess in the first place. After all, if you do everything wrong and they do everything right, than they are safe from this ever happening to them. Right?

Talking about death is absolutely forbidden with most people, even those close to you, and doing so puts you at risk of being accused of not 'fighting the good fight,' not being 'positive,' and being 'morbid.' Although this begs the obvious question, wouldn't you have to be a total moron not to *even consider* your own death, if you have an 85% chance of meeting it within five years? Perchance, it should be considered that our death is the most significant spiritual event of our lives, and in the case of a terminal patient, it is imminent and impending. Wanting to know the prognosis, seeking statistics, or wishing to discuss what will happen to your body as the disease progresses, is also a no-no; although most terminal patients genuinely need this information in order to battle their disease and prepare for what is to come.

A person faced with terminal illness faces the difficult task of balancing fight and hope with preparation for death. Because it is deemed a probability, those who shirk speaking about death to their loved ones, simply ignore a true, meaningful need. Although the living may not be comfortable talking about death, the dying *need* to talk about it, just as a bride wishes to speak of her upcoming wedding, and a couple needs to speak of marriage. People need to talk about what they are going through, and the very best thing you can say to someone faced with a catastrophic moment in their lives (whether it be a terminal illness, or another catastrophic loss or event) is that it sucks! As opposed to being negative, this validates the pain and suffering involved, and the loss of something as great as a life. When validated, tragedy can be processed productively. Invalidated, it remains as a searing pain upon the soul.

The most difficult aspect of a terminal diagnosis is that a patient must prepare for life and death at the same time, having no idea when the moment shall come. Losing their future, their dreams, and the plan they had for their life, the terminal patient must also prepare to lose *every single person* in their life. As opposed to the one loss that will be suffered by those they leave behind, the dying patient loses all their loved ones in one fell swoop, in this lifetime and this world. Anticipating a future in both worlds, accepting the limitation of disability, you must prepare to continue a fruitful and rewarding existence while living in a precarious limbo.

It is in these moments that true epiphanies arise in most every soul, things which those of us not yet at this juncture could gain from, true knowledge behind the mystery of our existence . . . if we would but listen. (Many souls are very compassionate to those in their suffering, but I share with you not only my own experience, but the identical thoughts shared with me by several other terminally ill patients. Because many people don't know what to say to someone who faces a catastrophic situation, I thought it would be helpful for people to understand what is going through *their* mind, and the things that can be hurtful if said at this time. Hopefully, this gives a better perspective on that which is helpful to a person facing a life crisis, and makes it easier to avoid the unintentional invalidations which occur regularly amidst our society.)
****

Although I had never played the trumpet before, beautiful and celestial music came from the instrument which now adorned my lips. My instruments had been the flute, bassoon, guitar and piano, but never the trumpet. Looking around me, I realized that I was playing with a celestial band of some sort.

A very tall man with short brown feathered hair was conducting, and he wore royal navy-blue clothing which was designed in galactic fashion. Rims around the shoulders to indicate high rank, the clothing itself had the consistency of vinyl.

As the band stopped playing for a moment, I heard a complaint from the back of the room. Noticing the person who expressed concern, I recognized him. 'Has he died?' I thought. "What's she doing playing the trumpet?" he protested loudly, "she's only played the flute in the past, she will ruin our sound!" Surprised by this unwelcome response, I was quiet. Replying immediately, the conductor said, "I have given her a special gift," he said very calmly, as I took notice of how well I had been playing despite my total lack of experience. "She is here because I wish her to be here. She has accomplished many things on subtle levels of energy which qualifies her to be here."

Boldly, I turned to the conductor who appeared so majestic. "Who are you?" I asked. Pausing a moment, he looked directly into my eyes. "Gabriel," he said, "as in the Archangel . . . Gabriel." Dumbfounded, I stared at him but said nothing more as my soul was whisked into a school building.

On the walls were hundreds of signs, all reading, 'Don't lose Hope. Remain Positive.' Walking over to the registration desk, I was fearful of acknowledging my status because I thought I was too sick to be accepted. "All who come here are in catastrophic situations," the lady said, "I believe you are here because you are waiting on a heart transplant?"

Looking at her with horror, my medications had helped my heart to function better. Although I'd been evaluated for transplant, and those with my condition almost always eventually need one (or die first), I was considered 'stable,' for the moment. Another possible obstacle was Lupus, in that it is a systemic disease which could disqualify me from having one altogether.

Saying nothing, I turned to notice that several people had arrived, including the person who had been unkind. Coming to apologize they expressed their loyalty to Archangel Gabriel. Apparently, it was their duty to apologize for their insolence. Quietly nodding my acceptance of their apology, I was gone.

Awaking in astral form in my bedroom, my spirit walked over to a mirror and noticed that my body had swelled up as if in acute heart failure. Returning to bed, I awoke.

Although my body was not swelling in any unusual way, I'd had a lot of chest pain recently and knew this to be a warning about the vulnerability of my body, and the need for caution and care. This began the now continual process which would be my life from here on out, going back and forth from relative stability to severe illness to the doorway of death . . . and back. For the remainder of my life (unless I got a transplant someday), I would ride the gateway between worlds on a daily basis.
****

CHAPTER FOUR
The Massacre yet Holiness of Illness, Beauty of the Way of the Cross, Learning to Deal with Ever Increasing Levels of Pain, Compassion for those who have not yet Underwent the Fires of Suffering, the Unspoken Love and Concern of Others, Keeping up the Fight.

****

Showing me the scene of a massacre, it clearly represented what had happened to our family since the diagnosis. As it was completely restored, I felt the presence of someone very holy.

Catapulted into the presence of Padre Pio, I couldn't see him, but *felt* him filling every corner of the room. Enveloping me in love and acceptance, he conveyed to me a certain peace about my condition, and that it was, indeed, God's will. "I implore you to be at peace regarding your illness. I, for one, am elated and joyful that you have been allowed to share in the sufferings of Christ, totally without merit on your part."

An angel came down from the sky with a gift for me which I *knew* to be from Jesus. Handing me a beautiful medal of Padre Pio, it slowly transformed into a Padre Pio rosary which was identical to the St. Francis rosary I currently owned. Feeling his presence around me, he conveyed, "You are following the way of the cross." As it was an honor to share in the sufferings of Christ, he was guiding me through his letters which contained much advice regarding suffering and the holy state with which we can be endowed when we come to such a juncture in our own lives.

Unexpectedly, a life-size statue of the Virgin Mary appeared in front of me in the image of 'Our Lady of Guadeloupe.' Having been painted rather sloppily, I thought how disrespectful this was of its benefactress. Around the eyes, the paint overlapped and bled into the cheeks and there were no clear lines in the paint job.

Having immediately bowed before the statue, I knew that Mary was present in the room. Within the distorted image, I felt the full presence, power and fullness of the Mother of God, despite these flaws. Mary wished for me to see that an imperfect body does not disguise a soul reaching for perfection. The suffering demonstrated on the image of the Blessed Mother, represented the spiritual transformation which we undergo . . . through the sufferings of this world.

Without warning another full-size statue appeared, this time in the image of 'Our Lady of Fatima.' Exquisite and painted to perfection, I again bowed, realizing that the true beauty of a soul is always realized by God, despite the horrific image which suffering may make upon our bodies at the time of its fruition.

Whole and complete, Mary's immensity filled me yet again, as I stayed on my knees in the power of her presence. "Your suffering comes about through the absolute will of God, and you are to be at peace. I am pleased with the manner in which you have endured your trial, and the Lord is pleased in that which you are learning." Love, peace, joy and calm came from the Creator, through the Blessed Mother and Padre Pio.

Giving thanks, I lowered my head in humility at her presence as they disappeared.
****

Entering into a religious bookstore which seemed to be placed in a happenstance manner along the parkway, an old woman approached me. Showing me a white casket, she spoke in a very serious tone. "Your grandmother has a burial site for you." (My grandmother is deceased.) Placing a medal around my neck, I observed that it was an image of the Divine Mercy, a special Catholic devotion especially suited for the suffering and the dying.

Awaking in a dream, I instinctually looked downwards towards my feet which were pitch black, much like that of a decomposing body. Surrounded in light and wearing a gown of the most subtle and pale blue, a woman stood at the foot of my bed quietly. Though her skin was fair and very beautiful, she lifted her hands which had been hidden at her sides. Upon her palms was a thick layer of black paint which resembled my feet. Showing them to me, I understood.

It has become interesting to me in my journey of death to realize that between illnesses, accidents, malfeasant acts, etc., that there are a great many people on this Earth who do not live very long. Some die in childhood, and others sometimes pass during their twenties or thirties. Despite this constant reminder of our own mortality, I have noticed that very few people seem to actually contemplate their own death, but rather, they are constantly thinking of their future plans in this world. This is interesting because any one of us could be standing at the judgment seat of God within one or two minutes of any given moment.

If you were to die right this minute, would you be ready to stand at the judgment seat of God . . . right now?! Though we must take care of matters which deal with our continued existence upon the earth, we must never forget that this is a temporary abode from which we can be snatched at any given moment. At that moment, all that we have upon this earth will be spontaneously taken away. Only those things we have done which hold eternal value will come with us, and all of our future plans will be irrevocably altered.

As the bible states so very clearly, death is appointed for all . . . and then the judgment.
****

Pounding fiercely to demonstrate my palpitations, the metallic body also had an approximately one and a half foot in diameter metal patch in the center of the chest which protruded outward from the body to demonstrate the enlargement of the heart and the power of the palpations. Next to it was a metallic body which represented a normal, healthy person. Pointing to the metallic form whose heart was pounding, the scientist standing next to it said, "How long do you think *that* can go on?" Despite reassurances from my doctor that I had a while to live, it seemed I was being warned that my future was not so set in stone. Vowing to be more careful so this status would occur as infrequently as possible, I heeded the warning.
****

Taken to a warehouse, many things had been stored here, but I immediately noticed that amongst the various garbage of this realm . . . were huge statues of exquisite beauty representing the Way of the Cross! Approaching, the first one I noticed was a bigger than life size depiction of a scene of the Blessed Virgin Mary bowing before the tomb of her son as two twenty-foot high angels stood before it. But as I looked upon this, I noticed that others had been well-hidden behind other things. Looking upon them, statues began to materialize all over the place. Life size, the Way of the Cross appeared first in complete order. Touching the thorns upon Christ's head on the statue which depicted the crowning with thorns, I found myself especially drawn to Jesus Carrying His cross.

Internally, it was conveyed that the hugeness of these statues represented the prime force which suffering was now taking in my own life, my own Way of the Cross. As this path was forged all around me, life-size statues of various saints began to appear and I mused in wonder at them.

A band of roving thieves had come upon the warehouse with evil intentions to cause me harm, and I began shooting them with a tranquilizer gun. As they lay sleeping on the floor before me, a voice said, "You may fight your disease and put it to sleep at times, but you cannot destroy it. It will come again."

Gazing upon Jesus Carrying His cross, I fantasized about having such a marvelous remnant in my own yard to constantly remind me of the glorious nature of this path of suffering. Perhaps, I could gather these stone figures within my soul to remind me of such things. "God is good," I thought, as I continued to repeat this over and over even as I awoke. "God is good, God is good, God is good . . . "
****

Given to witness how another person might respond to the level of pain I experienced on a regular basis, I was surprised to see that this male individual for whom I was given to watch was screaming out in agony. "You are a very strong person to be able to endure such increasing levels of pain," an angel said, "and others might very well be shocked to feel what goes on beneath the surface while exteriorly you are able to conceal the pain as if you are in perfect health." Grateful for this, I nodded.

Several days later, my spirit was led through the experience of a 'sudden death.' Within less than a moment, my transcendental nature had been separated from my body and I was hovering in a very soothing dimension imbued with the color of peaches upon the horizon. Despite this environment, I was anything but soothed, as I began to fight to return to my bodily form in the other world. Knowing I must return to my children, I fought with my entire strength, but the divide was sealed and there was nothing further I could do.

For this moment, I experienced the amazing shock of sudden death. Lamenting the loss of my life with my husband and children, a voice echoed across this peach-colored horizon. "Your chest pain is not 'Nothing,' it said, in response to what I'd been told by my doctors, "Your doctors have missed something, and you are at high risk of sudden death. Be very careful . . ."

Feeling the presence of my friend trying to protect me from this imminent destiny which had taken her, the divide opened and I turned to cross.
****

Concluding many things, I observed several truths which are relevant to us all. Firstly, until somebody has truly undergone the purifying fires of suffering and death, either through their own mortality or that of somebody very, very close, they simply do not understand the catastrophic nature of terminal illness. Secondly, people choose not to go there because of their unwillingness to face mortality and death in their own life, and being judgmental of those who are walking this road is a very convenient method of denying that death, too, comes to us all. Thirdly, to face such things is a true gift from God, because it completely severs our belief in our own self-sufficiency, and makes us render to God what is His. Fourthly, to experience the loss of life and the loss of property simultaneously creates a very healthy awareness of the impermanence of this life and everything in it, reminding us that our heavenly homeland is our true destination, and that we must not rely or allow ourselves the delusion of feeling safe in a world which guarantees only one thing, that no one will get out of it alive.

Continuing to observe my soul being battered within the confines of the Eucharistic Tabernacle, I gave great thanks for this unusual experience, because it carried with it the greater knowledge of life . . . and death. And as I sat observing this phenomenon, it became clear to me that we truly had been blessed above all others in our suffering, because it had been in this journey into losing everything, that we had become whole and our love for one another had increased tenfold. Detachment was now a daily aspect of our lives, and in this we had brought eternity into the confines of our family from what had previously been a limited, confined and selfish love. Agape had come down from heaven and entered into all of our hearts. God is always good, and infinite in His wisdom, and it is wonderful to realize this amidst tragedy when we are usually confounded rather than enlightened.
****

Accompanied by a male angel, a woman who had died of heart failure came to encourage me to fight. Showing me a heart transplant in progress, it was indicated that two major complications could arise in my case, but I should accept a transplant if it were to be offered. "Do this for your children," she said.
****

Entering into a house, I saw four people I'd known in the past arrive at my door and leave something underneath it. When I went to retrieve it, I was surprised and moved to find that it was a set of cards with lists of hundreds of names of people I had known throughout my life, many of whom had recently found out about my condition, all expressing concern and sorrow. As I held the cards, I felt their concern deeply and realized some very important things.

Although people may say or do weird things in such a situation as this, it doesn't necessarily mean that they care any less. Even those who say things that come across as hurtful probably don't really mean the things they say. Because it is an awkward situation for both parties, the sick person feels like they must constantly validify how they're handling it, what they're doing about it, and whether or not they have the proper mental attitude; while those who come to visit have no idea what they should say. As a result, the *oversensitivity* of the terminal patient can make the visitor feel more *self-conscious* about their words, and that *sensitivity* can make the terminal patient more *self-conscious* about every word that is said. People do really care, which is what is truly important, although the way they show it can sometimes appear otherwise.

****

Running through the canyons, I was deep in the crevasse of rock. Another angelic guardian ran beside me, repeating over and over, "Keep pushing! Keep pushing!" Continuing to run, my spirit wasn't finished until the end of the night. As I finally had run all the way back to the top of the deep canyon, my spirit and body were exhausted. "Keep pushing," she repeated with a smile as I breathed loudly.

In her eyes was a message; my spirit and body were being brought back, and the Lord wished for me to push myself in order to recondition my body which had been deteriorating for so long due to heart failure.

Suddenly, I was back. After a three-hour surge of heat had entered my body and filled it a week or so before, the Lord was bringing me back from the threshold of death, and preparing me to get to work on my next task. "Keep pushing," she repeated with a knowing smile as we both disappeared.

****

Images and mirages penetrated my vision as the Lord filled me with a deeper understanding of my next task. Worried that I may not be able to contain what had been shown to me, I pondered before leaving the mystical realm as to how I would bring it back into the physical world and remember it. Despite my best efforts, I returned with no further memory of the experience beyond the profound knowledge that I'd seen something of magnificence and great import.

Returning to the spirit world, my soul was taken to join the members of a large family. Two parents and six children, I was saddened to learn that one of the older boys who appeared to be in his early twenties was dying of Cardiomyopathy, a disease I shared. Talking with him, he said, "My doctors have told me that there is nothing more we can do, I am close to death."

Having walked that road myself, I was deeply moved by the sorrow of this family. At the dinner table, I sat next to him and his mother, and quietly listened as they spoke of the hardship of this cruel situation. Placing my arm around her shoulder, I spoke to his mother. "Several weeks ago, I was in the same position." I said. "And today, the Lord has brought me back. Do not lose hope." (My condition had improved in part due to a change in medication, but it was my sincere belief that there was also divine intervention [an episode of heat] involved because it had improved so dramatically that the medication change seemed an unlikely source of the entire transformation. My belief was that I'd improved dramatically due to both factors, and that God was bringing me back to some degree, perhaps to make it possible for me to continue working; but to what level or for how long, we didn't yet know. My condition remained terminal but stable for the moment, and hopefully for years to come.)

My words were not that helpful, and I fully understood, because I'd been in their shoes just weeks before. When actually engaged in the battle, you have no idea of how it will end. You cannot expect people engaged in warfare for the life of themselves or a loved one, to focus on hope alone.

A grieving process is underway which is normal and required, in order for the soul to prepare for whatever outcome may cross their doorstep. Because

statistically speaking, death is very often a greater probability than a healing of any kind, and death is a journey which is usually taken without the traveler's conscious consent.
****

Appearing in a flash of white, the doctor came towards me with a gleeful smile adorning his face. A grand energy of power came with him as he began to relate to me how well I had done in my fight to live. "You've really fought the good fight," he said, "and you've done a lot of good things along the way." Looking at him, my gaze conveyed, 'Oh, really?' Speaking of some of the doctors that I'd had over the past couple of years, he said, "You've taught them so much, and this will help them in the future with other patients. Do you really have any idea how well you've done?" Nodding 'No,' he continued, "I've had five other patients with the same condition you had and they are all dead. You have a *huge* will to live. God is pleased with you!" Smiling, I began to loosen up a bit.

Deep in my heart I was very happy to realize that, in God's eyes, I had really put up the good fight; although at the same time I realized that my survival was also an incredibly merciful act of God granted through the prayer of others. My choices and actions helped me in my fight to live, but they did not determine the outcome. God alone determined that outcome. So many people put up the good fight when faced with incredible odds and they still die through *no* fault of their own. Death in and of itself is not a failure, because we all will eventually lose that fight. But for the moment, God was allowing me to enjoy the momentary and meaningful victory which had prolonged my life in the meantime.
****

CHAPTER FIVE
How People Want you to Keep Doing Things that you can No Longer Do, Experiencing What it's Like to Live in a Body Devoid of Mental and Physical Function, Sensing Love, Hate and Indifference, Perception of Laziness, Isolation, Getting Worse and Getting Better, Heavenly Helpers, True Discipleship - Doing that which is Needed Rather than that which You'd Prefer, Deterioration, Surrendering the Physical Vessel to Weakness.

****

Lying in the middle of the room in an easy chair suspended in space, all those who could not understand my condition were gathering around me in agitation. "We need to build a hospital over there," one said, as another pointed in the same direction and said, "and a school there!" Completely unconscious, I was unable to respond. "Why won't she get up and *do* something?!?!?!?!" One said to the other, as she responded with equal disdain and confusion.

Suddenly, out of the ether began to appear angels. Three or four Female angels with white robes and wings were gathered in a small circle around my chair watching over me. As the people continued to ask over and over, "Why won't she get up and *do* something?!?!?!?!" the angels replied, "Because her heart doesn't work." Although they said it many times, it appeared that I was the only one who could see or hear them. Smiling at me, they filled me with assurance that I was not lazy, just sick.
****

In the spirit world, I was taken into the heavens to receive a message. We'd been reaching out to somebody on the Earth in regards to our mission with the music which had been given to me, and this person came to me in the astral and said, "Let's go ahead and do a demo and see what happens." Smiling with glee, I turned to my left and saw my former priest hovering in the heavens. Wearing his green robes, he smiled hugely and gave me a thumbs up. Ecstatic, I understood that because he had died and crossed over, he now understood my purpose and was supporting me. Giving him a thumbs up back, a small cell phone which had been attached to his garment began ringing. As it rang, I saw an image of the old woman calling. Father smiled and said, "Gotta take this, still a priest, you know." Understanding, I left him to assist.

Suddenly, my spirit was in the body of an older person who was unable to respond to external stimulus. For several moments, I experienced what it felt like to be in that body. Interestingly, I was very much aware of all that was going on around me, although I could not speak or move my body in any way in and of myself. In a nursing home environment, there were many people who were saying things all around me. Noticing that many said very unkind things, this was very hurtful. When one woman came over and spoke to me with kindness and tenderness, her act of generosity meant so much to me. Although I remained unable to respond, I understood the energies of love and hate that were coming towards me and others in the home. What an eye-opening experience this was to see that even those who may be so sick that they are completely unable to utilize their physical or mental faculties understand the energies of love, hatred or indifference which come towards them. They feel it profoundly.

Returning to consciousness for only a few moments, I drifted back into the astral states to experience a warning. As I was getting up to tend to my son, I was walking towards his bedroom when suddenly time became suspended and appeared as if in slow-motion. In an instant, I was experiencing everything from outside of my body, as I watched my body fall in slow motion to the floor. I didn't feel the impact. My husband was kneeling over my body saying, "Oh, no. I think it's time to call 911." "Oh, no," I shouted to him, "I'm right here, I'm fine." But as I said this, I realized that I was sitting outside my body and my body was truly dead. Feeling the profundity of the warning, I knew that I must never take for granted my physical health because it was still very tenuous.

Before I could think or respond to this situation, a huge demonic attack ensued. An invisible demonic force had taken control of my body and was throwing me around the room, as I no longer had control of my spiritual being. Repeating over and over, I said, "I command you to leave in the name of Jesus Christ, I command you to leave in the name of Jesus Christ, I command you to leave in the name of Jesus Christ . . ." But I was making little or no progress, until my eldest daughter appeared on the scene. Noticing my condition, she knelt on the floor and began to pray with me. In a few moments, I was liberated from the demonic attack. A Satanist had recently begun harassing me through the internet because of his hatred for God and those like me doing His work. I was made very much aware that this assault had come from him. Taking note, I arose feeling unwell but rested up and prepared for what may be to come.
****

Standing behind our home in the astral state, I was wearing a flimsy white gown staring off into the distance. All was well behind our home, but I noticed that somebody else's yard was now next to ours and that a huge tidal wave was coming towards it.

This person was a very kind and generous person, but had fallen prey to suggestions of demonic persecution. As a result, she had become very unkind to us, spreading gossip and rumors about me not really being very sick, but just lazy. Because this gossip had continued to spread, I had lost many friends and acquaintances. People I had to deal with in daily life like teachers and other medical or religious personnel developed preconceived notions about me that I could not suppress. Those who had previously come to visit, no longer did so. Their suspicions had been aroused and no matter what I would say or do, I couldn't undo the damage of the frothful words that had been spoken of me. So, she really had done some harm.

But I had chosen to generally forget about it, because I knew that many people who face long-term catastrophic illness are easily misunderstood. It is one of those things in life that cannot be known unless one has traveled its road. At some point, you either accept that many people will judge and misunderstand you and be okay with that; or you drive yourself crazy trying to change what usually cannot be changed.

What happens in such cases of 'demonic persecution' is that those people who do not guard their minds, who do not recognize dark forces which can interfere with their thinking; become very easily manipulated by them as they make suggestions to them about other people, situations, etc., which may very well be untrue. Demons will present it to a person as if it were their own thought. Because it is also then presented to them as a strong gut feeling, or a powerful feeling of enmity; they may choose to believe it to be true and proceed forth from there. In this way, many 'demonic persecutions' are undertaken by the dark side.

Literally, they gather around a person or place in hordes and continually suggest falsehoods about a colleague, a friend, a neighbor, or anybody for which they've received permission from God to 'try by fire.' Those who are not paying attention and carefully scrutinizing their thoughts will most likely immediately fall right into line with the 'demonic persecution.' Those who take the time to think carefully about whether or not what is coming into their head makes any sense or has any basis in fact may be able to realize that it is a demonic suggestion and refuse to participate. It is all about free will, choice and discernment.

Suddenly, my family was in a room with this woman and her family and friends. She began to again go on and on about all the things I should be doing, how lazy I was, and what a rotten mother I was for not doing this or that (despite the fact that I couldn't physically do them), etc. etc. Walking closer to her, I said, "You really should be ashamed of yourself." Continuing in a very calm and quiet way, I continued, "Your entire life's work centers around the importance of families and taking care of their needs, but you have allowed yourself to be so influenced by dark forces as to be unable to generate a single ounce of compassion for a mother of three young children with a terminal illness."

A huge bolt of lightning came down from heaven and struck her with force. As she stared forward in a daze of shock, I waited for a reply. But it took many moments for her to respond. "Oh, my God!" She cried. "I'm so sorry, I'm so sorry." Placing her hands over her face, she began to cry uncontrollably as the lightning bolt had awakened her from her sleep, making her realize that she had truly totally misjudged our family and had been deceived. This was difficult for her to accept, because she didn't previously think she could have been capable of making a bad judgment such as this.

Everybody got very quiet as she continued to bawl. Finally, I went over to her and picked her up and placed my arms around her. Hugging her tightly, I said, "It's okay, we understand. We forgive you." After she began to calm down, I said, "You know the funny thing about this is that you and I probably would've been great friends if it hadn't been for this stupid thing which has always been in the way." (We had a lot in common, actually.) "Maybe now that it's out of the way, that can happen." She nodded, still in tears, as if she were open to that happening. Again, I hugged her, "It's okay." I repeated. "We truly do understand. It's okay . . ."

"Now if any one should wonder, whence those who had at first been of this last class, now are so different, let him learn that affliction was the cause, affliction, that school mistress of heavenly wisdom, that mother of piety. When riches were done away with, wickedness also disappeared."

The Complete Writings of the Early Church Fathers, Nicene and Post Nicene, Volume 11, Homily 7, (Christianity: Catholic, Words of St. John Chrysostom)

"For the dreams that disturbed them had proclaimed this beforehand, lest they perish unaware of why they suffered ill."
The New American Bible, Old Testament, Wisdom 18:19, (Christianity, Judaism)
****

Standing in the canyon with the mesa's surrounding me, I suddenly heard a beckoning female voice. "The spirit is calling you from the Earth." She said. Within moments, buffalo in motion began appearing out of the ether until there was a gigantic herd of several thousand all around me. Looking upon the buffalo with a sense of holiness, I knew great meaning lay beneath their appearance. Gratitude for gifts received and a beckoning call to return those gifts to others filled my spirit. Sometimes we are called to pray, and sometimes we are called to become an answer to someone else's prayers. At this moment, I felt a call to both.

Before I could ascertain all that was coming to pass, a wall of water came crashing towards us. The wave took myself and the buffaloes into its current as we began traveling 'into the spiritual waters' towards an unseen destination.

Recently, a woman with an advanced disease had come into my life. It felt to me that the medicine women from throughout the ages were calling me to be her friend for she had been praying for one. In a subsequent experience, I was instructed to treat her as family. And it would be so . . .
****

Entering my former home which was no longer compatible to me, I was shown some things about my own reality which were important for me to observe. The doors locked behind me as I entered and I became almost completely isolated. Realizing that the lack of social life and relationships among friends had caused in this previous location the absence of a vital energetic requirement for my life-force to remain healthy and vigorous; it was shown to me that this vital energetic requirement was better in our current location, but still required improvement.

Because I am a mother of three responsible for my children 24 hours a day and seven days a week, I entered my isolation with a certain sense of resignation. And there was purpose to this isolation; it was simply out of proportion to the needs of my soul. My isolation provided a monastic environment for which I was able to study and write. But as I stood alone in the house, a guide came into the home.

Appearing as a man in about his forties, he had dark black hair but was slightly balding. Wearing a baseball uniform, he was laughing and cracking jokes among his friends who had come with him. Inexplicably, I began laughing and falling into a state of relaxation with them. Despite my usual solitary manner, I experienced for a moment how refreshing and fun it could be to be able to have friendly outlets from my continually serious existence in raising three children, reading ancient sacred texts and never leaving the house. Allowing me to observe, it became clear that this need to have human contact and friendships outside of my marriage and family was not wrong on my part. Despite the recent temptation which had come through another person in the form of the carnivorous demon, denying myself of all friendships was causing me actual physical and spiritual harm.

There is a time in the spiritual life when absolute solitude is not only preferred but necessary; when the soul is young and inexperienced in the riding of temptation. In this solitude a soul is able to cultivate the virtues and extricate the vices, becoming a better shepherd of its senses. But as the soul progresses, sometimes the Lord calls the soul out of that solitude, asking it to trust again in itself and its ability to discern and disarm temptation as it may arise . . . for the purpose of fellowship.

"Be well prepared and well minded; join your hands: he who is affectionate and

merciful to the world is going to speak, is going to pour endless rain of the law and refresh those that are waiting for enlightenment."
Saddharma Pundarika or the Lotus of the True Law, Introduction, No. 99, (Buddhism: Mahayana)

"Come aside to me, you untutored, and take up lodging in the house of instruction; How long will you be deprived of Wisdom's food, how long will you endure such bitter thirst? I open my mouth and speak of her: gain, at no cost, wisdom for yourselves. Submit your neck to her yoke, that your mind may accept her teaching. For she is close to those who seek her, and the one who is in earnest finds her."
The New American Bible, Old Testament, Sirach 51:23-26, (Christianity, Judaism)

****

As my medical condition appeared to continue to improve, I was taken to observe a map. Upon its fetters was a line drawn showing the journey we had taken from our previous home to our new location. Looking upon the map, my attention was drawn to a schoolroom around me which represented our former home. Teachers were gathering their books to close out the school year and janitors were preparing to close up the building. One of the very humble janitors approached. 'Class is dismissed,' he said. As he said this, I began flying simultaneously at the speed of light towards the location on the map which represented our new home. In the distance, I felt bliss much like that of approaching the Promised Land. The desert oasis in the distance was a liberation from the extended stay we had experienced 'being beaten up inside the Eucharistic Tabernacle,' something which had been shown to me in 'Galactica.' We appeared to be leaving the land of persecution to the land of light. In the distance, the desert oasis beamed with light.

Suddenly, I was standing in our new home. Outside, my huge living room crucifix had been nailed to a large pole. Winds began to stir around it, and I became nervous and afraid that it might blow off the pole and shatter. As the winds picked up, a short but powerful gust blew it off the pole. But rather than shattering, it gently landed on its feet, standing solidly on the ground by a mystical force. A sense of wonder filled me as I heard a voice in the wind. "You have been taken off the cross," it conveyed. "And rather than being shattered to pieces, you stand tall." Indeed, the crucifix stood tall in the distance as I watched in awe.

Although I still technically had heart failure and would continue to take many meds, I was realizing that in some energetic way I had been taken down from the cross for a time to finish certain heavenly tasks. My condition had improved in a miraculous way and I was doing things now that I never thought I would have been able to do again. Somehow, my life had been restored by God's holy will. Dumbfounded by this phenomenal gift of grace from God, I could only stare. No words came to my lips as I remained silent.

****

Within days of this profound experience, I began to cough up small amounts of blood.

Entering into a deepened state, my spirit began to vibrate as the vision of the angels came near to my conscious view. All around me, the spirit wind vibrated with light and my soul entered into an ecstatic view of peace and silence beyond my pain and agitation.

Gently lifting my feet, the angelic forces began to move and manipulate my body in ways which were healing and helpful to my current crisis. In the distance, I could still hear them thinking to one another. "She's experienced bleeding in her lungs, what should we do about this?" One thought, as the other began to instantly respond with energetic assistance to various parts of my body including the chest. It was conveyed to me that I had done the right thing in asking for the divine physician in prayer.

My soul was almost as if in rapture, as utter peace and serenity surrounded me. Continuing to move my limbs and sending vibrations throughout my body, I surrendered to their assistance as I suddenly noticed my spirit was heading towards some type of gate or door. As I headed towards it, my vision began to go black and I instantly understood I was approaching death.

Uncertain as to whether this death was going to happen or not, I began to observe the goings on. As I came closer to the gate, it seemed as though my physical vision was going further and further black, as if in reference to the process of turning from one state of consciousness to another. Instinctively, I knew that if it were to go full black that I would be dead and ready to begin seeing in my new spiritual vision.

But as I headed towards about 90% black and noticed there was only a small light still shining through my earthly vision, an angel very calmly and quietly approached me and said, "Not yet." Without having a moment to think, I began going back towards the other direction although I was still very unable to associate myself with my earthly self and still regarded myself as bordering on the 'dead.'

Pointing towards my physical body and the Earth which lay almost as if in overlay above it, I looked to see what she wished me to look upon.

My husband was sitting beside the bed waiting. Although I knew he couldn't hear me, I was so happy that he had come and began to speak to him. "I'm so happy that you cared enough to be here for this," I said, "I love you." But he just smiled at me with love, because he couldn't hear me.

Two friends approached, trying to wake my physical body, but unable to do so. As they turned to walk away, one said, "I think she's truly going this time." Although they were very much at peace, I felt their sadness and a certain loss to their souls in my absence which could in some way be necessary or required for their further movement forward.

Lunging forward, I realized that I could not yet surrender to death. By lunging so, I pulled myself out of the 'death' vibration and back into my physical body. For many moments, I struggled to bring myself back to consciousness. But as I did, the angels hovered above me smiling.

Conveying to me, I felt a sense that despite my exhaustion and fatigue in my earthly burden and battle, there was much more to be done. It appeared to be their wish that I push forward and not give up the fight, and they were prepared to hold me up with supernatural force despite the terminal conditions which raged within my body. Nodding that I understood their wishes, and their calling to come and aid me in times of greater danger, I listened. "God wishes it so," they said, as they whisked off into the heavens and I awoke to greater strength. Immediately, I understood that I wasn't finished yet.

"For he had found many a secret justice in this seeming tyranny of the watchman, and seen how many a mercy lay hid behind the veil. Out of wrath, the guard had led him who was athirst in love's desert to the sea of his loved one, and lit up the dark night of absence with the light of reunion. He had driven one who was afar, into the garden of nearness, had guided an ailing soul to the heart's physician."
The Seven Valleys and The Four Valleys, The Valley of Knowledge, (Bahai', Words of Baha'u'llah)
"Ward off the grief from your heart and put away trouble from your presence, though the dawn of youth is fleeting."
The New American Bible, Old Testament, Ecclesiastes 11:10, (Christianity, Judaism)
****

As I'd recently been trying to get some volunteers together to organize a ministry providing for some of the unmet needs of the sick, primarily that of friendship, I'd been inundated with people who felt they weren't 'called' to such a thing, or that they were too 'busy' to sit with a homebound individual who just needed a friend.

Exhausted, I'd gone to sleep flustered in the reality of realizing that I was probably the only one who understood these needs and it would be very difficult to get such a ministry going without the help of others. The problem was, however, that those who had never experienced catastrophic illness just didn't understand or 'get' the needs of those who had them. And those who had catastrophic illnesses, such as I, were generally too sick to do anything requiring endurance or reliability. When you're sick yourself, you never know which days you'll be functional and which ones you will not, so you can't plan ahead or plan to care for another person with any degree of reliability.

Floating around a particular minister's church, I was lying flat on my back indicating the nature of my fatigue. The members were discussing discipleship and seemed utterly obsessed with gaining converts to the faith. Trying to get their attention, I wished to help them understand 'true discipleship,' but they couldn't hear me. As I whisped in frustration, several angels appeared. "You will not live to see this ministry completed." They said. "It must go into the hands of those physically able to accomplish it. Tell the ministers that Discipleship is not about doing what you like to do best, but about doing what needs to be done. This is the sacrifice which makes it pleasing to God. Ask if someone is willing to receive this torch because it needs to be taken, not because the task at hand is pleasing." Nodding yes, I turned.

Suddenly, my body was lying flat but being held partially upright by a group of many angels who began to sing songs. Asking them questions about my family and other earthly concerns I'd had, they began to sing a song which surprised me. "You'll soon be passing away . . . don't worry about it. It is no longer your concern . . . "As they sang, peace filled me and a detachment from earthly things. Faces of many people I'd known during my life who had passed away appeared before me. Some of them were teachers from my childhood, but they all turned to acknowledge my presence and smiled in welcome. Falling into the music of the angels, I allowed my spirit to rest in their hands.
****

Sitting quietly in my home preparing to go back into my body, a doctor who had seen me once appeared in my room with great urgency. His sub-conscious astral soul appeared to have a message for me, but I was confused by this since we had barely known each other. "Why would you receive a message for *me*?" I asked. "We barely even met." Breathless in his urgency, he said, "What you must understand is that when two people bond through caring, an energetic union is formed which creates such a possibility. Although you were unaware of how much I had chosen to care about your situation, I energetically latched on with great fervor to your well-being." "Wow." I said with surprise. "I had no idea how much you had cared. After all, I'm just one of many patients. But tell me, what message do you have for me?" "It is this," he replied. "If you continue to work as hard as you have been doing, you will most assuredly die prematurely. You must balance the creative energies that work through you to create more balance." Pausing, I thought of those creative souls throughout time who had literally worked themselves to death by not properly balancing the great eternal impulse which worked through them. Mozart, for instance. "Thank you," I said, "thank you so much. You're very right, I have been working too compulsively, and I must find more balance. Thank you!" Again, I disappeared and awoke within my body.

"By the Star when it setteth, Your comrade erreth not, nor is deceived; Nor doth he speak of (his own) desire. It is naught save an inspiration that is inspired, Which one of mighty powers hath taught him, One vigorous; and he grew clear to view when he was on the uppermost horizon. Then he drew nigh and came down till he was distant . . . And He revealed unto His slave that which He revealed. The heart lied not (in seeing) what it saw. Will ye then dispute with him concerning what he seeth? And verily he saw him yet another time . . . The

eye turned not aside nor yet was overbold."
The Meaning of the Glorious Kuran, Surah LIII, No. 1-17, (Islam, Translator: Marmaduke Pickthall)

"See for yourselves! I have labored only a little, but have found much . . . Work at your tasks in due season, and in his own time God will give you your reward."
The New American Bible, Old Testament, Sirach 51:27, 30, (Christianity, Judaism)

"As to more than these, my son, beware. Of the making of many books there is no end, and in much study there is weariness for the flesh. The last word, when all is heard: Fear God and keep his commandments, for this is man's all."
The New American Bible, Old Testament, Ecclesiastes 12:12-13, (Christianity, Judaism)

"And now the hand can write no more, and pleadeth that this is enough. Wherefore do I say, 'Far be the glory of thy Lord, the Lord of all greatness, from what they affirm of Him."
The Seven Valleys and The Four Valleys, The Fourth Valley, (Bahai', Words of Baha'u'llah

****

Suddenly, I was spun forth from this lofty sphere into the valleys of the earth below wherein I began to experience a set of frames.

My body was limp as if in Pieta, lying in the arms of this priest in our parish church. Swirling white energies surrounded this scene which was filled with a raw but yet patently quiet emotion. As this scene entered into center frame, several new frames appeared around it of myself with this priest in different locations within the church, the rectory and its offices. They were a continuum, but of what I could not yet ascertain. But I could feel this continual raw yet patently quiet emotion, as if it were to pierce me in crucifixion. From somewhere in a palliatively etheric realm, I heard a resounding echoing voice, "You've got to take care of her, you've got to take care of her . . . "

****

And so it came to pass that I began to wander back into the realms of spirit, experiencing things of wonder and awe - like traveling through the starry realms all night; the moon, the sun, the star tunnel - and things of concern.

As my health was going up and down, I entered into a deterioration cycle. My spirit was taken to a jailhouse wherein a man was being held. Satan spoke through him, and St. Michael spoke through me. But my strength waned unexpectedly, and for the first time, I lost a battle with the demonic realm. I couldn't extricate the demonic force from the man, and I felt saddened by this defeat.

In prayer, however, I simply asked for God's will to be done; that I be used for however long I might be of service to the Lord, but that at such a time as my bodily vessel became too weak to follow that warrior path, that I be replaced by younger, healthier trainees to do the work that I may no longer be able to do.

In a subsequent experience, my prayer was answered me in that I was shown that this weakness was not due to a moral flaw, but only to aging and weakness of the body. I was not to concern myself with it, as God would ordain and send me as He so wished. Perhaps he wished for me to visually experience this waning in spiritual thrust, so I could know and understand that it was a natural part of the path. As none of us can do everything at each stage of our journey, we allow God to determine our portion as we go.

****

PART III

Suffering:

The Fruits of Utter Desolation

INTRODUCTION:

Suffering:

The Fruits of Utter Desolation

The Lord came upon me in the night during an unusually difficult time in my life. What type of suffering I was undergoing really doesn't matter, but be assured that my health, my physical well-being, my marriage, my children's welfare, my ability to hold a job, my husband's lack of a job and its subsequent loss of medical insurance during a crucial medical crisis were all contributing to the shambles of my life in that moment of my reckoning. And I felt very abandoned by a great deal of my friends and family. Whether or not this was actually true, I felt it to be true at that moment, just as we all do at random difficult moments in our lives.

My great Lord awoke me in the night with a simple command, "Write," he said, "write about the things I am trying to show you through Utter Desolation."

I began to write . . .

CHAPTER ONE
What is God trying to show me through Utter Desolation?

It seems that God is trying to show me several things through utter desolation:

1.) Most people really don't care that much.

2.) True friends are few.

3.) Most things don't really matter.

4.) Everything outside of God is totally nothing.

5.) Religion, when practiced as 'religion' in a legalistic way, is purely heretical and completely contrary to the teachings of the Prophets and the Messiah, Jesus Christ.

6.) Religion, when practiced from a mystical point of view, becomes divine and all-seeing, knowing, feeling and all-powerful.

7.) Priests are not God men; very few have become true Alter Christus - either perfectly or imperfectly.

8.) Hypocrisy rules much religion and many Churches.

9.) It's not okay that this is so.

10.) The moneychangers are in the temple . . .

CHAPTER TWO
If these Suppositions are True, then are these Conclusions also True?

1.) The lies that people believe about you don't matter if God knows they are not true.

2.) There is nothing in this earth that can come close to the beauty of Our Lord.

3.) There is no earthly love (except perhaps between mother and child to some degree) that can come close to the love you experience when you are standing in the Presence of God.

4.) Therefore, ALL ELSE, EXCEPT THE SEEKING OF GOD, has no meaning.

5.) In God's Presence, nothing earthly or physical may change, but everything BECOMES peace.

6.) People who practice Religion very rarely KNOW God.

7.) Those who KNOW God cannot practice Religion well because they MUST move with the spirit.

8.) If they do not move with and become one with the Spirit, they will die.

9.) They will die because once you've KNOWN God, nothing else is sufficient.

10.) So in order to live, they must 'die' to this life and all of its peculiarities, rituals, false piety, falsehoods, random show - and meet God ALONE.

11.) And when we meet God ALONE, chaos subsides, love becomes all that remains and we cease fruitless movement and activity.

12.) If God is there, it doesn't matter if anyone else is. He is sufficient.

CHAPTER THREE
If these Suppositions are True, then how do we teach worldly souls to cease seeking Him only in ritual and to thirst for private communion with Him?

1.) It would seem that it can only be sought by a few, because too many are attached to worldly views and distractions.

2.) I MUST SEEK MY ONE TRUE LOVE, my Lord, and stay with Him at all times.

3.) His spirit must take me away from the chaos and into the peace.

4.) I MUST STOP SEEKING GOD'S CHARITY IN HUMAN BEINGS, but only in Him ALONE.

5.) I must give Him my whole self - so that whether others choose to do so or not - that I may embody God's charity and be that light that can rarely be seen on earth to my fellow suffering brethren.

6.) I need to give myself completely to my Lord accepting NO intermediaries. This does not mean I cease to honor the position of men who stand in His Presence, but it means that I listen to God first.

7.) I must STORM THE GATES OF HEAVEN with love for my fellow suffering brethren and for His children and DEMAND that they ALL be saved.

8.) But I must do this mystically, so that my steps may be set aright and God's purpose be fulfilled.

9.) I must release all need to be understood, cared for, loved, or for any need and I must do so in total resignation to the Passion of Our Lord Jesus Christ - in that it will be in suffering that the Lord will become able to move in me. Therefore, if suffering is required to make this possible, I must resign myself totally to His will.

10.) I MUST BE HIS SLAVE, willing to accept whatever hardships He deems necessary.

11.) I must resolve to BECOME the compassion to others which has been denied to me, to BECOME the love which has been denied to me, to BECOME the hope, the faith, the understanding that has been denied to me and to my suffering brethren.

12.) I must STAND for those who cannot, PRAY for those who cannot and EMBODY the Gospel of Jesus Christ by knowing profound desolation and abandonment in times of suffering. I MUST BECOME FOR OTHERS all those things which in this moment I feel have been denied to me.

13.) By so doing, GOD TRIUMPHS in my weakness and HIS LOVE will reach from Heaven to earth through me because He has honored me by allowing me to KNOW utter desolation. Can anyone understand desolation lest they've truly walked the path?
14.) By KNOWING utter desolation, God prepares me to help others in utter desolation.

15.) In the end, we will heal ourselves by healing one another.

CHAPTER FOUR
If these Suppositions are True, than how do we answer the question of suffering in the world?

1.) We answer that God is good and true - no matter what suffering we or any other may endure.

2.) God remains faithful even in desolation.

3.) He is the one light that never dims, the one heart that never stops loving, the one mind that never ceases to understand.

4.) God is the answer.

5.) No other answer can be sufficient.

CHAPTER FIVE
Epiphany!

1.) Desolation is the door!

2.) Desolation makes it possible for us to see God.

3.) God is present in all things, but it is in desolation that we become most able to find Him ourselves.

4.) Desolation is a gift!

5.) Desolation brings us back to our core of mortality.

6.) Desolation forces us to come down from all of our earthly delusions as we are reduced to dust.

7.) What can be humbler than dust?

8.) By becoming dust, our eyes may be suddenly opened and we are then able to SEE the face of our Beloved.

9.) And it is only then that we finally and truly KNOW love.

10.) I shall receive desolation with honor because it is known to bear great fruit.

CHAPTER SIX
Deliverance!

1.) My desolation has become my deliverance!

2.) How can I reject it?

3.) It has opened a door and I don't want to close it.

4.) It has given me understanding.

5.) I no longer need to be understood.

6.) It has given me . . . all I need by taking away everything I did not need.

7.) I stand face to face with my Lord and I know all has been ordained for my greater good.

8.) I KNOW HE is my true spouse.

9.) He provides for all that has been wanting.

10.) And I FEEL now, that He loves me profoundly and it has pained Him to see me suffer.

11.) But we stand in triumph together because our marriage has borne great fruit.

12.) Now, I must wait. For now, we are together silently because words are unnecessary.

CHAPTER SEVEN
Peace!

1.) And all is peace!

2.) My gracious and loving Lord, who has stood with me from the day of my birth and has never left me no matter how many others did, stands alone with me.

3.) I finally realize my past, present and future is with my beloved heavenly spouse.

4.) And although he chastises me when I need it, He NEVER leaves.

5.) In this moment, I realize that what I've been seeking has always been there.

6.) And He says, "Now, go. Help others to see this, too." For I know that My Lord loves all His children in this way.

7.) And then I understand the equation:

Desolation = Doorway = Emptiness = Heavenly Visitation = Translation of suffering into . . . MISSION!
8.) God allows us to experience desolation so that we completely feel, understand and know the needs of our brethren.

9.) By KNOWING this, we are then enabled to become a vessel of God's grace to our fellow suffering brethren.

10.) Some of us will be freed of our sufferings and given the opportunity to physically help our brethren with our newfound understand of their needs.

11.) Some of us will not survive those sufferings and it is these who are even more BELOVED of God. Their offering of prayer and loving submission to His will, in concert with the offering of their daily pains, becomes a bouquet of flowers soaring to heaven on the incense cloud of prayer.

12.) And when we are able to realize that we love our heavenly spouse even more because He has taken everything meaningless away and allowed us to suffer for our good and the good of others, we can confidently approach the table of the heavenly banquet with our empty plate and know that it is full in the eyes of Our Lord.

13.) The Lord gives, the Lord takes away . . . . Blessed be the Name of the Lord.

14.) In my ecstasy, I find suffering to be preferred, because I now understand how my suffering pleases and assists my beloved.

15.) By offering my own suffering, and allowing my soul to be permanently etched with the knowledge that suffering affords, I allow my beloved to make my life a sacrifice to Him.

16.) I now plead with my Lord to simply allow me to become a sacrifice for Him. I do this because I love Him so deeply, that I wish to give Him anything and everything He could ask of me.

17.) I desire to bring all those who are lost back to Him. I desire this profoundly.

18.) I desire it because I love Him with all of my heart, and I know He loves them with all of His.

19.) I want Him to have all of his beloved, and I'm willing to give him anything He asks so that it may be done.

20.) Then I realize: Love = Sacrifice

21.) I will give all to my beloved and continually plead that He makes my sufferings fruitful for all mankind . . . OR for one soul. It may be great or small, it doesn't matter.

22.) Religion = Rules, Ritual

23.) God = Love

24.) I CHOOSE YOU, GOD!

CHAPTER EIGHT
Embracing the Suffering!

I gladly walk through the door of desolation. I *want* to share your agony! I want to wipe the sweat off of your brow and give you consolation.

I know you are waiting. I've left you for a time, thinking that religion alone was the way to you. But in my misunderstanding, I lost Your presence because I sought worldly things, people and places.

Thank you for always letting me come back to you, my beloved God!

Religion is a PATH, it is NOT the TRUTH! The TRUTH IS YOU! I'd already had You, how foolish of me. Make me an instrument, my beloved Lord.

"Brothers and sisters: Therefore, since we have been justified by faith, we have peace with God through our Lord Jesus Christ, through whom we have gained access by faith to this grace in which we stand, and we boast in the hope of the glory of God. Not only that, but we even boast of our afflictions, knowing that affliction produces endurance, and endurance, proven character, and proven character, hope, and hope does not disappoint, because the love of God has been poured out into our hearts through the Holy Spirit that has been given to us."

The New American Bible, New Testament, Romans: 5:1-5

Mystical Poetry

Mystic Knowledge Series

Compiled and Written by Marilynn Hughes

The Out-of-Body Travel Foundation!

www.outofbodytravel.org

PART I
FROM BOOKS

THE HOLY GRAIL
Deep in the soul of man
Lies the holy grail of wisdoms chance
The tempest storm of reasons past
Seeks the sign of an angry man
In the dark of the moon, hold my hand

Night holds a seekers glance
Begging, calling for one last chance
Death is a hungry bird
No more time, join with mirth
In the dark of the moon, there's rebirth

Seasons change the Holy Grail
Hark the night the words prevail
No more chance, life is frail
Find the wisdom of the Holy Grail

Far in the ancient cave
The words of knowledge etched with grace
Reason holds a hungry man
Knowledge fills his empty hands
In the dark of the moon, it is man
In the light of the sun, life's begun

Seasons change the Holy Grail
Hark the night the words prevail
No more chances, life is frail
Find the wisdom of the Holy Grail

THE TWIN TREES
Two trees stand tall in the woods, one a birch and one a pine
The pine tree is taller to show the effect of time
The birch tree looks up to the pine and turns to call her friend
She says, 'I love you very much but I must sing my own song.'

'I want to grow up towards the sky, and see the flocks of birds!
I want to grow above the woods, and see the prairie herds!'
The pine responds lovingly, 'Go, pursue your dreams,
But don't get struck by lightning, like all the tallest trees!'

'Growing tall may be it for you, but me, I'll stay right here.
I'm safe beneath the tallest pines, but do what you must, my dear.'
The birch grew taller over the years, she grew towards the sky
She saw the prairie herds afar, and she watched many birds fly by

One day she looked down towards her friend, buried beneath the trees
'Oh, lovely pine, I love you so, but I have learned to be.
It's time for me to move along, I've grown, so, as a tree
Tomorrow, I will end my stay, as there is much more for me to see!'

A storm was brewing the very next day, and the birch was not surprised
A lightning bolt hit her branch, and the birch tree quietly died

The loving pine cried softly, as she could not understand
When suddenly she felt a touch, on her branch she felt a hand

She looked below her branches, to find the source of the touch
A human being sat next to her, eating a bagged lunch
The human looked up at the pine and smiled the biggest smile
'It's good to see you, friend, it has been quite a while!'

'It could not be,' the pine tree thought, 'my dear old friend is dead.'
But doubt crept away, light shone in her eyes and knowing came instead
The tears flowed long from the pine trees eyes, but the pine tree was not sad
She spread her branches and began to grow, through the forest roof above her head

The pine grew tall over the years, she grew towards the sky
She saw the prairie herds, afar, and she saw the birds fly high
Then one day, the clouds came in, and a storm began to brew
The pine was struck by lightning, its eternal life ensued

She looked down from the heavens to find her human friend
Her friend appeared beside her, and reached out to her a hand
They smiled at each other with wisdom, as they now understood the divine plan
'Come on, friend,' said the human, and they went to earth as man

THE SEASHELL

What, before the sea, lies a creation as timeless as man?
Beckoning, Yearning, as the tide forever takes it on its path
The circling chambers, they run to completion like life itself
If ever you've wondered, the answer you'll find in the ocean's seashell

The seashell, beauty to few, home to many
Within lie the secrets of time long due
Listen and learn, the ocean speaks volumes through its spiraling bough

Lying quietly, the peaceful being awaits to be heard
If only a moment, before tide comes to heed natural course

SPIRIT VOICES

The voices in the anteroom, are priceless like an old heirloom
The message in the words they say, remind me not to lose my way
Though many do not hear a sound, let me tell you what I've found
The voices speak of things to come; they tell me that my path is love

And down the path, I've had to free the spirit voices inside of me
Yearning and longing to truly know love, I follow the path of the golden dove
Inside, I know that all that I see, is only the spirit inside of me
Wherever I go, the path is now clear, I follow love and dispose of my fear

I WISH YOU COULD SEE THROUGH MY EYES JUST ONE TIME

I wish you could see through my eyes just one time
See where I go, what I've seen, where I fly
If you could peek through the windows of my minds' eye
You'd never again ask yourself why

The beauty you'd see, the love you would feel
The knowing, the adventure, the freedom to heal

All that you've wanted to believe could be true
Lies waiting inside, just waiting for you
Close your eyes softly, and allow yourself sight
Crystal forests, winged horses and long, holy nights
There's nothing to fear, there's no need for fright
Love is all that remains when you enter the light

Let go of the fear, let go of your pain
Release yourself from the illusory game
When it comes right down to it we're all the same
Let the spirit descend as your consciousness wanes

I wish you could see through my eyes just one time
See where I go, what I've seen, where I fly
If you could peek through the windows of my minds' eye
You'd never again ask yourself why
You'd never again ask yourself why

THE CALL OF WAR

Why do you shout the call of war, tell me friend, what is it for
In fear, we cry damnations name, in love, we join our brother, tamed
All is well beyond the veil, the call of swords linger in still
Temptations tempest calls the young, but in our hearts we are but one

What is the fight, the cause you seek, to quell the thoughts of different speech
Or are you fighting for what you are, and if so, what is your cause
For who you are is what I am, all life joins as one in the land
Who you are is what I seek, share your beauty, don't fight with me

Tell me of your earnest dream, and I'll tell you of what I see
Beyond the veil, we know each other well; love brings mirrors to us all
Mirror your dreams; I'll catch their glare, the vision of a bright, white, eagle feather
I'll mirror back all that I view, the beauty that I've found in you
The mirroring started, memories begin, love's veiled tempest starts again
All we are as bearers of light, together, our vision will dawn the night

THE DOVE SONG

Destiny's wind came calling, you listened to the voice
You heard the cry of freedom, for a moment, released the noise
Our paths of light have crossed, and love's been shared and embraced
Tomorrow, you'll remember, your purpose in this race

But in your heart, remember
With every passing sound
Flying on the wind stream
The dove follows you around

Part of me is with you, my spirit knows your place
Inside my soul remembers, every single face
No matter where life takes you, your path is not alone
For many walk beside you and fly just like the dove

I'm hidden in your spaces, but I'm always by your side
Open to my presence and find where love abides

Remember in the darkness, that life is very near
I come to you as a dove, for your soul I shed

SUNSTREAMS

Lying in the sunstream, beauty lies to vision seek
All that bears the skin to warmth, holds my heart in raptures keep
Sunstreams, light-filled fantasies, flowing to the gentle force
Senses swaying, songs of the breeze, finding those deep in my heart

Yellow beams of sensual flair, calling cells, reaching out
Ray beings send my soul to haste, sunstreams blending every part
Memories glistening, calling forth, passions flowing, drawing near
From the deep-filled ember hearth, all who dwell inside are dear

No one calms him, words cry out
The sunstreams purpose follows prose
The lighted glisten heralds praise
Spirit enters sunstreams throes

WALKING IN THE SHADOWS

Here I am, walking in the shadows, doing my best to see the light
Here I am, walking in the shadows, when I look, the glare's too bright
I know there's something to making dreams come true
I feel your presence and inside, I remember you

Feeling the power of the universal flow
The energy comes through me and is awesome in its show
And somehow when you're near me, I hear the night wind cheer
"A spirit's discovered illusion and reality is now clear!"

But here I am, walking in the shadows, doing my best to see the light
Here I am, walking in the shadows; I wonder why the glare's too bright
Only fear blocks my sight, from now on I'll follow the path of the light
Submitting to trust as fear is illusion, it's time to end this path of confusion

And somehow when you're near me, I hear the treetops roar
"A spirit is now conscious, and fear presides no more."
Here I am, walking in the shadows, the shadows of my spiritual guides
Here I am, love belongs beside me, because I

LITTLE GIRL WARRIOR

Who are you, sad Indian face? You stare at me through eyes of grace.
A noble child, your breed stood tall. Amongst the thieves, you held to the soil.
Your painted cheeks cry out to me, create a dream, curiosity
Surrounds your face, hair long and black. In my mind, I look back.

There was a day when you were here. Your beauty shows a tiny tear.
The way of love destroyed by man, they took it all, they took the land.
Speak to me, little girl warrior. I know your face tells a story.
Your spirit calls to all mankind, "Open your eyes, listen for the signs!"

"The day has come for my return. The ways of old will spark and burn.
All that I am, an Indian child, returns again with passion wild."
The voice rescinds, my heart stirs. Her heart speaks out, but no one hears.
A knowing look, I glance her way. "I hear

MY MESSIAH

Destiny calls the night wind's cause
The birth of wisdom flies in the stars
The name emblazoned, a holy being
My Messiah, you've come again
Flutes fill the spaces deep in my heart
But travelers reckon the pathways to chart
The vision of love, the glory of light
My Messiah, My Lord, I saw you tonight

Embers of knowing and truths of the past
The spirit of love fills lands with its cast
The eyes hold a vision, the seer of thoughts
I call for your wisdom, my Messiah, you're home

A moment is captured, a moment of love
Reuniting, assembling, returning to God
My thanks fill the hour with all that's divine
My Messiah, you've come, you knew it was time

DAWN OF NIGHT

Resurface moon, dawn of night, feel the stars, address their light
Time is nigh, the pathway cleared, leave the form, and enter sheer
All is past, all is now, the future exists in the center of the Tao
Go to reclaim a birthright vast, to reason, strange, a conscious clash

Flight of the wind becomes your own, the spirit light lays seeds to sow
Drop seeds of light on mankind's heart, a beautiful gift, a wondrous art
Back to the stars in essence form, there's someone there at the doorway home
Who are you familiar face, a dear old friend exists in grace

The moon recedes and day draws near, the spirit's called, the spirit hears
Return to form, awake to day, remember none but illusory clay
But next night draws, plan spirits return, a place forgotten, the pathway home
Resurface moon, dawn of night, feel the

GUARDIANS OF THE SKY (THE CLOUD BEINGS)

A voice, a presence, a surge from above, a willowy wisp, the spirit of love
An inner knowing, I looked way up high, lo and behold! The Guardians of the Sky!
The light shone through, a pathway cleared, but my spirit, afraid, was frozen in fear
The beauteous forms, of clouds floating by, yearning to know, my call came as a sigh

Peering, I thought, 'Why do I hold back?' A voice rang in my head, up, my head snapped
A majestic sound filled my brain, thunder and lighting, and then there was rain
Magnetic voices said, 'It is I, remember, you know me, I'm Guardian of the Sky.'
The cloud slowly spoke, but only I heard, people walked by, they didn't hear a word

'Trying to reach you, I create many scenes like pathways and tunnels and velvety rain.
Right there above you, remembrance brews, I show you the beauty, that beauty is true.'

'Constantly changing, manipulating form, there is no limit to what I adorn.
I mirror the universe, all that there is, and then I send rain in the form of a kiss.'
So awesome a message, such beautiful words, looking about me, still, only I heard
I spoke to the cloud, I asked him, 'Why me? If no one else hears, could this really be?'
The cloud began changing, a tunnel emerged, the sun's ether pathway in brilliance, immersed
'I show you the pathway, my dear little one, many don't see it, but it will take you home.'

I reached out my arm to feel what he said, but suddenly an energy shot through my head
My eyes sprung open in brilliance of light, the power of God, I felt it that night
Turning to leave, I waved to the earth, 'Thank you for teaching me, and for my rebirth.'
As I looked behind at the clouds in the sky, "Will you come with me?' I asked with a sigh

A gentle nod, 'No,' the cloud was sincere. 'I have many to reach, to the earth I'll stay near.'
'My beautiful spirit, you've found your way home, There's much more to learn, through the universe you must roam.
Please understand,' said the cloud with a tear in his eye, 'It gives me great joy to be Guardian of the Sky.'
He turned to the earth and began to create, a beautiful display for the human race
Few took the time to notice the art, but someday another, would see the sky through his heart

VISION BIRD
A bird with wings is a joy indeed; he fills the earth with emerald seeds
A flight through clouds, leads to clear skies, the vision bird, thunder and lightning nigh
A crack of thunder, awareness begins, a flash of lightning, who have you been
I asked a star, 'Who am I?' He replied with a fury and filled me with light

A sound I felt but never heard, a breeze blew by, the vision bird
Star-filled visions filled my soul, no longer one, but part of the whole
A spirit light flies through my brain, to clear perceptions, a summer rain
A light, a soul, a part of God, stopping rain, recedes the cloud

The star looked down, 'Now you know, my beautiful spirit you've entered the flow.'
A bird flew by and said with a sigh, 'You and I, we are alike!'
'But Vision Bird,' I called to him, 'You have wings, you fly with the wind.'
'Aaaaah, yes I do,' the Vision Bird claimed, 'my vision is yours, go, dance in the rain.'

I took to the dance and to my surprise, my spirit shot up in a frenzy of flight
Looking below me, I heard a voice cry, 'Vision Bird . . . will you teach ME to fly?'

THROUGH THE EYES OF A RAINDROP
The eyes of a raindrop, what would it see, a cloud burst created, the spirit is me
Falling through skies, looking below, the earth it comes closer, to thunder it roars
Green tops cascading, what could they be, reaching them quickly, oh, it's a tree

Passing them by, I whir to the ground, 'my, that was quick,' the grass makes a sound

A slight tiny whimper, a quenching of thirst, I enter the ground and am sucked up by roots

Now what I am is a blade of grass, looking around me, I grow very fast
My brothers beside me connected in form, our oneness apparent, dominion the norm
My journey moves upward, I sweat through the blade, and enter a puddle, to liquid I'm made

No lines to separate the spirits in form, one loving mass, in water adorned
The water keeps falling, but now I have seen through the eyes of a raindrop, my spirit is serene
The universe shudders in awesome delight, the oneness experienced, a beautiful sight
There's more to it though, than beauty alone, an awakening has surfaced, a spirit's gone home

SPEAKING THUNDERCLOUDS
I'm roaring, I'm reaching, I'm trying to feel, trying to discover what holds you back still
My thunderous voice, the lights I display, should awaken your longing to return home someday
Mass retain holds your energy tight, no room to feel, and no room for flight
But remember, my dears, it's you that I am, there's no separation between you and the land
Reach out and have it, it's yours if you ask, open to feeling all that you mask
For where you belong, in spiritual form, your trueness embraced, your beauty adorned

Return to the state of flowing with love, feel who you are, look up above
I thunder again to show you the way, the power you hold, the games that you play
Calling from the sky, from where you belong, I love you so much, where have you gone
FEEL who I am, don't ask yourself why, you know in your heart, I'm Guardian of the Sky

Remember the day you entered the earth, I told you then there'd be a time for rebirth
I call in the storm, and my voice never stills, in your sleep, you'll remember the higher will
Love never fades, and we always express all that we are, our happiness
There are no limits, no egos to check, we simply love you and we want you back

THE WIND
To ponder the wind, unmask what emotes, I quiet the conscious and feel gentle strokes
The swaying of grass, the shudder of trees, the clouds billow faster, I fall on my knees
The voice gently soothing, touches my heart, the sounds rise and fall as the leaves play and dart
Swishing about me, the flow and the cool, the movement of energy, of sweethearts and fools

Singing above me, our voices enmesh, as the wind blows harder and becomes one in bliss

As tree branches sway, the spirit is seen, not noticed in stillness but felt in the wind

Movement is calming, clouds billow away, the trees stop their shudder, grass ceases to sway

The energy stills and becomes only light, but it will return to bring movement in the night

THE VIBRATIONAL BEINGS (The Trees)

The vibrational beings of the underworld, responding to movement beneath the earth

Limbs pulling forth, displayed in the fashion, meanders of praise, reaching out in passion

Limbs pulling inward, the vibrational sound, a love of the inner, knowledge of profound

The outward display of trees reaching high, encompassing allness, blessing all life

The fragmented gypsies, who tremble at form, display the confusion of the earth-plane

All display signs of universal praise, remember their creator, reminding those in a daze

The limbs reaching out like arms on a man, reaching for allness, being all that they can

Next time you look at a group of trees, see their display of vibrational praise

SKYLIGHTS (A Thunderstorm Speaks)

Lights in the sky, a billowing mesh, a voice tells of one and calls to the nest

Furrowing feathers and leaves blowing by, the voice calls out loudly, 'Come, spirit, fly!'

A knowing unanswered, a call of one's own, to render the knowledge, a question bestowed

'Where will you take me?' the spirit retorts, a smile never seen but felt in the heart

The trust gently soothing, relinquish all doubt, there's no room to question, it's time to get out

A body now solid, relinquishes mass, to light particles enter, from earth-plane detach

The movement directed, release to the sky, a spirit gains freedom, a soul gains insight

Through gateways they enter to planes unexplored, beyond illusions, beyond heavenly doors

The love gently swaying, returns to the gate, all movement remembered, a moment with fate

Call to the moment, removing the past, the spirit in freedom blends into the mass

JULIOSA

For to tell a soul such things, for to spread the righteous wings

How shall I, a mortal strand, seek to know a heavenly man?

My joy's complete for but a time, for earth's return must end my flight

I'll gaze upon this familiar face, and allow the movement to fill my haste

And tomorrow morn, when I awake, I'll remember him, I'll know his face
But who am I to know his reason, who am I, Lord, I'm pleading
Beyond my morn, beyond the flesh, I find the souls, the fragments rest
But here beyond, oh Lord, I cry, seek to

LORD OF CREATION
My soul, my soul, I've found my soul, my love, my love, I've found my love
My heart, my heart, I've found my heart, My

PAINTED LILACS
Painted lilacs in the sky, emitting tones of misty sighs
Controlling none but moments rest, the sky painting leads me on a quest
Pinks and purples emanate tones; my spirit sings the sounds of loons
The love cry of a world so vast, hiding midst the thick veiled cast
Searching deep within my soul, the lilac triggers love of old
Beauty taming worlds of fear, forget me not, a tiny tear
Setting sun unites with one, emanations of a holy God
 The lilacs part to greet the night, stars fill heavens with lighted might

THE MESSIAH POEM
I come to you on a breath

Through lilac rivers, velvet streams, the walking plain abode
Fly above the starry realm, this is where I call home
Know me not in terms of flesh, fine in spirit abiding soul
Beyond the grave, beyond the death, the Messiah calls you home

If name be known beyond the body, then let it be of One
Who I am is Starlit Son; the Son of Man has come
Remember me, my dearful soul; the Messiah calls your birth
It was I, the babe who received, gifts of gold and myrrh

Feel the passion, feel the strength, beauty find unfolding
The energy of light divine, cannot be contained or molded

Whence upon the earth, many years ago, I walked with my feet upon the rocks.
Traveling, beholding and doing all that I knew to fulfill the purpose of my
coming. Through the work which was a joy, much came forth. But much was
lost as well.

In judgment, men have lost their souls, Fear abiding, in time, fragments,
They look to their brother and see nothing, when in truth, it is a mirror
It is through judgment that men have lost their souls
The beauty adorned, forgotten, unseen, the many who look, look no more
For what they find, is not what they want to believe?
Woe to all those who choose the path of blindness
And unloving ways
For it is they who choose to fast, the fast of no love in their days

The sadness that they see in life, images inner pain
Bottled, capped and tossed, the soul no longer remains
Love and sadness, emotion call, find creation, call St. Paul
Sink to depths, but ne'er be near, for the rise will occur another year

In judgment we go beneath the soil, in love we rise above it all
Who among us has never done wrong, then they may cast the judgment stone

Though sadness lingers because of the fear, the judgment unanswered brings plights to the dear
The joy ever spiraling rises so high, truly find life, in a joyful sigh
When a spirit releases, all needs coalesce, they rise to occasion and become one with Godness
Then all is answered, the prayers come divine, I plunge from the heavens, and release the joyful sigh
Hear, then I call you, we say, I love you, thank you for hearing all that is true
Spread to my brothers whatever you may; help them recover where it is that they stray

Subtlety beckons, questions cannot be ignored, but the truth will answer and open the door
Inside of the heart, the blood-beating pulse, the God force is calling, please, please join us
There lie the answers, divinely inspired, no need for confusion or eternal mire
Hosts of angels await the call, of brothers in form, who stop and remember Saul

Impulse of the heart, is the life of the light, it belongs to each man, it's heard in the night
I am but a vision, a vision of life, a man who once walked the earth day and night
I was much like you, but relinquished all sighs, my fragment begot, the consciousness of the Christ
You who listen can contain me now, if your vessel is open beyond the shroud

Relinquish all doubt and move into the force, energy awaits upon the white horse
Fly in the night, wings taking stride, they'll guide you to heaven, they'll take you tonight
Whereupon the ancient days, breathtaking beauty, soul arise
Who among us knew the sage, who among us knew the rite?
Rite of passage, words forgot, wheretofore, the memory naught
In the days beyond the veil, timelessness lingers and beauty prevails

Who among us carries the sign, the sign of Otara, the golden shine?
Calling all angels, and singing the tone, why have you forgotten, where is your home
If time were to stop and linger behind, would all be for naught, or would there be kind
Where is the purpose of each spirits path, a hidden direction lost in the mass?
Find, Remember, Forget Not, Open

If in time linger, where do you pray, in timelessness, God, or judgment day
What are you saying, what do you believe, if there is no answer, then try a new sieve
Pray to the truth, pray to divine, call for our answers with no limits on line
Memories will come, moments will cease, a version recalled, time moment decease
Timelessness' purpose, reaches its end, centrifugal beginning must seek to bend
Whereupon nightmares, cast out of the way, angelic dreaming becomes the way

Who upon the earthen shore is gathered near the marble stone?
Call Otara, frequency Nor, Ask the angels to come again
All that has come, has already been, all that has been, will happen again

THE ANGELS
Where is the sound that pulled me inside?
It is the frequency of Otara that calls the sleeping to service

Who is calling out the name, if not the spirit, mankind's mind?
Asking for our star seed aid, remit old patterns, turn to gold
Where amidst the cloudy realm, to find the saucer of the star
A spirit force lies at the helm, with tides of love, it traversed far
Love of lifedom travels far, amidst the starry realm of sky
All will purge the thought-swept fear; your earnest spirit brings us all

Where in mass can beauty find, a place where moments linger deep?
Shining starlet, climbing vine, see to all of God divine
Sole survivalist tendencies, beneath the vision of the moon
High crest waves linger to naught, pulling towards the singing loon
Every mass rekindles soul, the treatment of divine interplay
Be a temple, be a shrine, be a light of God divine

THE MIGHTY QUEST
The mysterious winds call forth the night, dawning those in stillness lay
Blanket spirits cover the earth in white, the isolated create in play
(Initiation into the mysteries is imminent, dawning humanity to movement. A
purification is at hand, to come about from the play of mankind.)
Oedipus began the mighty quest, upon the earth millennia ago
The retiring wind pointed to his absence, as other forces retained the flow
(The mysteries have been traversed for ages (Oedipus was an ancient Egyptian
prince who solved the mystery of the sphinx), as those who have moved beyond
the earthly realm have energized others to retain the movement of evolution
upon the earth.)
Call Otara (High G) and we will arrive, parting veils of mystery
Relinquish illusion; find the life, call to allness, cast souls free
(Ask, and ye shall receive of the mysteries and be freed of karmic delay. Pray,
and ye shall be cast into freedom.)
Call to movement, call to quest, rescind the voice of fragmentness
(Ask, and ye shall receive. Respond to the movement, rather than karmic
personality.)
Movement renders the mighty flow, quest becomes a purple glow
Quest in movement, long abide, freedom's spirit will not hide
(Entering the movement energizes higher wisdom . . . a long journey which leads
to freedom of the soul.)

THE DEATH SONG
The timeless moon doth ocean sway tide, holding tight to beachhead reign
But ne'er be near the stillness of time, crossing to regions of lingering plane
Sing in spirit to mountains that speak, the crestful longing of manner abode
A place where time ends is what we seek, the endless journey along the lighted
road
Perchance, by moments velvet form, relinquish not for velvets sake
Only moments all alone, breaking distance, soul awake
Who, but I, can travel far, beneath the distance of the way
Trembling chasms set to soar, hawk spent demons cast away

Illusions cast my soul seeks rest, all libacious form retreat
Sails of light, exuding masts, light calls forth from God's great feet
Cyclic change to earth renown, casts foreseen a timely rain
Come to cleanse immortal soul, time will end, but stay the same

Forage all that light retreats

POETRY FROM THE INITIATIONS INTO THE MYSTERIES
"Perchance, tonelage striving, the mighty worker of light
Perceive the distant calling, send thine eyes to sight
Church bonds tutelage, sacred bonds of fire . . ."
(Per order of the Lord, I have omitted and destroyed the last stanza)

"I have mastered that which is on the wall
The Mayan cards of walking stone
All who dwell here call to Saul
Meet the mercy all alone"

"Tiniest spark
Light cometh
I abide"
"Light befalls the virgin eye, dispensate all crowning lies
Fortune comes on velvet masts, the truth of souls encased
In the evening bronze, the night wind sings
Chanting visions and songs, calling forth the Nefertiti wings"

"Calling bird release the past, ancient memory come to see
Circling nature come to pass, spirit reason lingers free
A voice must be listened, the calling be seen
Perpetually unfolding, within the light beam"

"Who can I be? And where is the door?
What are the answers? And what is this for?
I am the light! The door is inside!
The answer is love, to bring dawn to the night!"

"Journey, my soul, to places of deep, our thoughts be revealed to you now
Grasp what you may, unravel and keep, remember to use thoughts of the Tao
You will be returning, for this place you have found, holds wisdom of night
winds, foretold
Find fragments and moments, but each hold a clue, to mysteries beyond what
you know.
Seer of thought, call out my name, divine words will enter the mind
This place you now come, where shadows call truth, means nothing to those of
the blind
Fear not the answers of symbolized truth, mysterious shadows restore
Initiate of Mysteries, holder of light, remember the corners of four"

"Whereupon, the days I mesh, into the stillness of the night.
Forms of lifedom gaining quest, son of self, relinquish fright."

DEATH
So many things come today which blend so nice with never to be

Find within the beating heart, all four chambers holding tight
Calling out to journeys start, find new worlds of inner beat
Excuse me, for I mean no fright, only call to one I love
Surprise at the dead is a humorous sight, for knowing tells you we are still one

Create some drama, fear abide, rescind the voice of terror's gain
But still . . . I am . . . despite the hour, calling forth the victory gain

The might is real for but a time; timeless change deflates its form
Spirit light holds much more shine, fear replaced by truth adorn
(Karmic purification requires the dramatic. As the voice of terror rescinds (the inner voice of karmic delusion), the seeker sees that he still exists, he still IS, despite the death of delusion and personality. A higher birth has taken place. I am, I exist, and this is immutable. Karmic delusion appears real for a time, but timeless energies deflate its appearance of reality. The spiritual truth is immutable, and the seeker eventually recognizes and replaces the fearful karmic delusion with the truth of God.)

Final endings chosen swell, look for reasons to be afraid
But inner sounds emit the tone, final journey, in the heart, be found
All you hear are releasing sighs, the remembrance of the dying souls
In oneness return to world abide, return all reason, remember the goal

(The final purification is amplified dramatically as the seeker looks for reasons to be fearful. All the while, the inner world amplifies the tones which energize the truth, and the seeker releases those fears, finding the journey within his own heart. As the dying souls remember the truth of God, they sigh at the beauty of it. Higher reason returns to them and they remember the purpose of the Earth walk.)

In understanding, find the stain; increase the memory of the deceased
Ask their light to retrieve the chain, return to states of joy and peace
Gentle bidding bonds with time, but timeless winds call only truth
Reach for sunsets filled with shrines; find all moments, ready birthed

(As understanding comes to them, they remember the stain of karmic delusion. The memory is gently increased to contain the multiplicity of existence and lives. Remembering the chain of events in their own evolution, they are then ready to return to peaceful, after-death states. While encapsulated in time, gentle bidding is employed to call our spirits back to God. The timeless winds, the movement, call out the truth to all of humanity, and those who hear must reach to the timeless, the ancient temples and shrines of truth that are visible as the sun sets within our consciousness. As the sun is immortal energy, in timelessness, one finds that all that has ever been or ever will be, has already occurred.)

Some who watch, watch from the sky, some who breathe fear not to die
Some who call resound in fear, but all who sing to God are dear
Love remains beyond the veil, increased by knowing of divine
Talk to me, I linger more, nothings changed but matter and time

(Some guide others from above, while others reincarnate and try again, this time with decreased fear of death. Some remain in fear, whether they are in spirit or reincarnated. But all who seek God, no matter their state of evolution, are greatly loved, gently guardianed and guided towards higher understanding. Love remains . . . but it is increased by the acceptance and entry into eternal love, a much higher love than human love can fathom.)

MY BROTHER, WE ARE ONE
I see you in the distance, your hair so long and black,
The wind streams catch its glisten; it flows along your back
Feeling my stare you turn, your olive face confused
But behind my eyes I'm dreaming and the dream is captured in you

My mind holds many faces, of spirits in my heart
And times among the prairie's and wooded lands of earth
The music fills my spaces, you look at me confused
But dreams can never shatter, in my mind ring sounds of flutes

The wanton memory aroused of all you now possess
A part of me now missing, the Indian blood caressed
Your face wonders at my vision, but I cannot reveal the cause
My brothers I am crying, in my heart I know we're one

The joy that fills my vision, the part of me you are
I call to spirits gleaming, my brother, we are one

INNOCENCE
The sadness lingered in my heart, the thoughts of dying souls
Releasing all of innocence, fragment embers coals
But glazing through the windowpane the light poured through the glass
The mighty oak tree's innocence, the sunlight calling mass

Beneath the essence of the light, the joy filled all my cells
'Sun being teach me innocence and show me where you dwell.'
Shining brightly in my eyes the being glowed with tones
'The innocence you seek is gone; you've remembered all the souls.'
'But dearest soul, your sadness swells, empathic child you are.
The oneness and the love are filled with passions of a star.
Your purpose is not to maintain unknowing in your form.
But grasp for the knowledge you have sought, you've called your eternal home.'

The message stopped, but light retained
The gleaming essence of ONE
My sadness swelled into a tear
At the message of the Sun

THE LAND OF THE UNION
The long black hair, a tiny trace, the darkened eyes, the love-filled face
Meeting the moment, my eyes touch your own, but my heart raptures, I feel so alone
When will you know me, and feel my heart pulse, do your eyes see my spirit, does your heart know the source
Free spirits roam, and loves calls a sigh, when will you come home, do you remember tonight
Do your eyes hold visions of all that I see, do you remember love, do you remember me
Or is your heart blank, do your eyes wonder still, for the land of the union lies waiting for you

MANNER OF THE EAGLE
In the manner of the eagle, the sacred rite begins
Wings span many distances, the destiny, re-live
All who walk the way, of eagle flight adorned
Return them to their graves, from their home they have been torn

I call from the ground, the site of the dead, the bones have been moved, the people misled
The fire of your heart calls out your fate, return us to earth, give our spirits peace

Have you whispered the song of life or do you lay there weeping
The cross and crow call you to wake, no need for slumber's sleeping

THE CALLING WIND

The calling wind has spoken, did you hear it in your ear
Karmic love is closing in, do you now see clear
The songs of time play radiantly, the wind blows forth the sounds
Deep inside spirit memory, the calling wind cries out

A soul's been lost in timelessness, so time must find the cause
Where in time do you hide; come out, I'll help you home
The calling wind cries out your name, the soul cry passes light
The time we've shared in memory, is surfacing in our hearts

WHO AM I TO YOU DEAR SOUL?

Who am I to you, dear soul, what mirror do you see
Is it love, or is it fear, what image do you perceive
I call to you in oneness; I call to you in light
I sing the song of brothers, I dance the shaman rite
Beyond the veil I fly to stars and soar to crystal cities
Winged horses carry me to light and tunnels lead me to infinity
I call to you the spirit sound, varying vibrations of light
Egyptian blood or Incan tempest, which part do you see tonight
My image veils eternity to aid your silent call
But veils are made for seeking what lies beyond the wall
See beyond the shadows, the illusions of the flesh
I'm hiding in my mirror; release me from your past

FATE WINDS FIRE

Light fills the destiny of fate winds fire, prosaic incursions of the earthly hour
Beaming white heavens, the dust from the sword, monuments standing of our days on the earth
Gleaming tears streaming, fires of the heart, memories enraptured, remember the good part
Love-filled illusions shared on the plains, regardless of reason, love always remains

Peering in the eyes of the fate winds fire, the scenes come in flashes, scenes from afar
The winds of fate, drawing them near, the deepest of unions, all becomes clear
I see your trueness, you've envisioned mine,
We've recognized each other, within the confines of time

ANGELS TWILIGHT GLEAMING

Hidden in the twilight, the masters show the Source
Hidden in our fears, we find our highest course
The gleaming light of one, my aura's seen the star
The angel's purpose followed, now the two must part

Angels in the twilight, spirits seeking home
But pathways merge and pathways cross, some take different roads
Can I give them freedom, and, therefore, free myself
Or will I hold to past good-byes and fear the coming path

Love the angel's twilight, release them on new flight
Send them off with gratitude, and take your path to light

YOU'LL FOLLOW

There are times in your life when you follow your heart,
Though you don't know the answer, you follow.
Many paths may be calling and your mind knows not why,
But your heart tells the answer and, you follow.

Sometimes there are those who wait patiently aside,
Watching the path and beside you, they follow.
These are the special ones, who know not why,
But because they love you, they follow.

I cannot tell you why or where the path will lead,
But in my heart I know you'll follow.
And because our love is patient, love is never lost,
Our spirits, merged as one, will follow light.'

SWORDSMAN

The life of one remained unseen, an anger swelling deep
A Scottish swordsman, death wish keep, a woman's love foreboding
Lingering love, why do you weep, he's left you for your honor
The ties of life bring memories back, the mysteries of consciousness deep

In time, you held a key to life, allowed me bid you love
But then you took that love away, at the hands of a long, steel knife
I feel it now; the pain is new, a surging in my heart
Intense emotions, the falling rain, for hundreds of years, it brewed

A memory now, no more mystery, this fear of smothering love
With freedom comes the safety sign, from the consciousness of my sea

MIRROR OF GRATITUDE

A mirror of my gratitude to all who've shared my path
All the angels coming forth from the recesses of my past
Do you know your gifts to me, every face I've known?
If only for a precious moment, you've led my path to home

I think of childhood fantasies, playmates running still
Within the recesses of my mind, those moments are surreal
Friends and lovers, paths foretold, all who bared their soul
And all who've shared my war torn lives, in love we're one forevermore

This moment filled with gratitude to spirits floating by
Lost souls, friends and spirit guides, the angels in my life
Mirrors of all I've held inside, the angels brought them forth
In return, this moment stills, gratitude flows through my pores

Angels, angels, angel light
Eluded for so long
But now I see your truthful self
Thank you, angel sons

There is no greater teacher than a mirror of oneself
A mirror teaches wisdom and shows the higher path
A moment spent in solace, alone with thoughts of life
Will imitate the mirror and show the path of light

To those who've been a mirror, and shown me where I'm frail
I thank you for the wisdom
I thank you for the Way

HEAVEN DAWN
Out in the night, the wind streaking still, I call out your name from my hearts deepest fill
It rides on a moonbeam straight into your thoughts; I've known you forever, not a moment less
Stars glitter waning, the sun starts to rise, the flaming horizon holds images of your psychedelic eyes
Intense time-filled spaces, I sense them right now, they exist in my future, but I feel you somehow

Where do you call from, I'll find you in space, the moonbeams allude to the aura of your face
I'll follow the sunrise, the fiery mirth, to the dawn of heaven, to recapture the soul's birth
And there in our essence, I'll look in your eyes, and find the answers amidst heavenly skies
So ride on your moonbeams, and fly in the stars, stare from the sunrise, I feel you, Heaven Dawn

DAWNING THROES
Heaven's throes awoke me, a dawning in the night
In my mind a vision flew, your face soared through my eyes
And as it passed, my heart swelled up, a tear fell down my cheek
Sighing as the feeling passed, I felt your soul's mystique

Wondering at the passion flare, I asked my soul explain
I heard majesty, and a sound, it filled me with your pain
I felt the sorrow of your soul, filled so deep with love
Reaching, yearning, calling out, to find no one at home

Where in time, could it be met, emotions masked by men
Passion's wisdom burns within, I'm here I feel your pain
Dawn within, the time is now, you'll find the hearthstone warm
The home of souls within the night, I'm tuned into your heart

Turning eyes are closing now; your face lingers at my touch
I love you now, I loved you then, forever, I've loved you so
Remember in the distance, heaven's dawn is near
A heart to touch is always close, though our bodies may be far
My sleeping soul remembers, as I soar the skies
The one who's held my heart forever with his psychedelic eyes
There are no more mysteries, the secrets have been found
Love within the light of wisdom, and trust

LIFE IN YOUR EYES
I caught a glimpse of life today, the memory of your eyes,
The piercing vision now as one, you've come into my life
Moments spent in time, wondering at your cause
Feeling all the beauty and the love inside me pulse

Wondrous light-filled memories and visions of the now
Fill my heart with glory, I shed tears of love

One's been found who was lost to me, a bearer of my soul
My heart, my love, your freedom's safe, I love you, Heaven Dawn

WHO ARE YOU

Who are you
One who holds my sight?
What does it mean
When I think of you all night?

Sentinel caller
Tells me your many names
I feel your passion
And I acknowledge your face

But, who are you
Behind the mask you wear
I see love
So deep in there

Angelic mercy
Strewn all about my world
I see your face
But I gaze right in your soul
Why are you
A question pondered still
Why are you
The one who gives me chills

Intrinsic mercy
I ask to please restrain
The fire inside
So I will not burst into flame

Do you feel me?
Do you wear the mask I hold?
Pretending, quelling
The passions of the soul

Touch me
So I may feel your light
I see you
So totally in the night

I know you
You're the deepest part of me
As tears fall
I touch your endless sea

Don't go
Your heart is safe inside
I love you
My soul beats at your side

A heartbeat
The moment lingers still

My memory
Holds your face as my heart spills

A moment
A gift of divine love
I thank you
I touched a part of Heaven Dawn

THUNDER LIGHTS

Thunder lights the passion glaze, all goes dark but bursting light
Screeching caller, booming throes, tainted eyes begin to sigh
A moment now, alone at last, no one's music by my own
What does glisten from my spheres, your vision face, and then your soul?
Hidden message comes to naught, amidst a bolt of lightning spray
I feel your power absorbed by dark, and in the essence, we're one again
Spirit lingers with my own, no physical form to hold a stare
But my heart knows the vibration's yours, and as it thunders, you sit here

Amidst the power and dark, I see an essence sharing all I am
Thank you God for all to be, and all the light here in my hand
Your hand reached to touch my own, a spirit light with sparkly fire
Loving embrace, I feel you now, and in the dark there is no fear

Gazing essence, I see your eyes, their beauty paled by no known jewel
Psychedelic in their spirit light, a relic to the ides of fools
Don't go away velvet, thundering rain; your power held wisdoms from worlds of love
When the light blasted, I felt the pain; my soul rode moonbeams straight from above

But moments may linger, and then go away
The messenger's wisdom imparted with care
Please return this love to earth
As the powerful lightning journeys away

NIGHT WIND SOUL

There's a presence in the night wind, I feel the searing pulse
A movement follows thundering eyes, a soul has entered course
Beating heart, thrash to still, its innocence foretold
The lingering essence of the man, known to me as Lavelle

Searching pulse, a throbbing heat, pouring through my heart
Please don't go, I feel you now, a blessing, a miracle, a fire
Stay with me, night wind soul, I'll feel you ever more
Don't leave the place I seek to find, the oneness with your soul

KARMA
Part I

To surrender to spirit, the traveler must find
The inner self dancing, to songs of the mind
Relinquish repression, and follow the heart
Expressive emotion is a good place to start
Through this you will find, the answers you seek
The hidden, un-trodden, karmic mystery

Part II
The emergence of our karma, comes with mighty force
The doorway has been opened; the soul must find its course
But doorways left still open, still hold clues behind
Though we may try to close them, it's too late, we will find
Though passion springs eternal, on earth, there is much more
Secrets still lay hidden, behind that opened door
Travelers seek the wisdom, passion seeks its own
Knowledge seeks redemption, karma seeks to know

Part III
In the foyer of the pathway, the searcher finds true cause
Hidden deep within the past, salvation's secret laws
All who bid the silence will find eternal cause
The truth of all existence, the love of all for God
The angels in the twilight, hiding beneath their veil
Guide you to the answers that free your soul to sail
The blessings always hidden, under karma's foolish disguise
But once it has been altered, you'll see through different eyes

Part IV
The silence of knowing is the space of reality where unconditional love resides
Silence takes form in love and love takes form in silence
Knowing becomes wisdom and wisdom is always silent
Part V
Immortality is transformation from the limited being that exists in fragmentary
identity to the whole of consciousness that encompasses all life in one thought,
all being in one breath, and all that is holy, as everything.

THE FLOWER IN THE VALLEY
There's a flower in the valley, whose hair is dark as night
Her smile is bright as sunshine, and her spirit's filled with light
In essence, she's an angel, traveling earth in keen disguise
But her heart reveals her nature, as all is good and fine

Inside her suffering corridors are images revealed
Of God's profoundly mystic and unmistakable things
She walks her day with Jesus, His suffering and cross her plight
But beneath this solemn torment, lies true scarlet that's been made white

She wears her crown of thorns, with dignity, upright
And though many do not see it, God uses her to purify the night
We all walk with more stature because of the sacrifice she makes
Her offering to Heaven is every breath she takes

Welcome home, flower of the Valley, you've been missed it is so sure
But know we see your beauty with which God filled you to the core

PART II
FROM HYMNS

I FEEL THE CHANGE

There's a change, it's a coming, within sight of our lives
I can feel it in the darkness of the night

The sky is on fire, from the hatred of the land
I can feel it in the darkness of the night

It's a crazy thing, but I feel it, and it tatters my soul
It's the helpless feeling of a people who've been bought and sold

There's a change, it's a coming, from inside of our souls
We must cherish our differences I'm told
Rage is a fire, that's put out with love
Let there be peace and justice in the world

Exalt in the exposition, dream of only God's
ambition, sing of the mission of the soul
Exalt in the Word revealed, dream of only high ideals, make His life unite us one
and all
Tear the wall, of domination, there'll be no more to overcome
Just a people who love one and all

ETERNAL PATHWAYS

If you haven't found the place that you want to be
It's time to follow your heart, find it naturally
Eternal pathways, will lead you to the sky

If dreams seem distant and far away
Seek to find them in a quiet place inside
Find the pathway, and you will learn to fly

Maybe you, need a clue
Seek the silence of your heart
Come to me, naturally
And I, will come, to you

Eternal pathways leading me higher, the whole world can be brighter
Eternal memories, I'm feeling lighter, the universe is wider

I'll see you, I'll see you, I'll see you, on the pathway to life

THE NOTABLE ONE

Traveling through a timewarp, passing through the age
I seek a notable one, a wise man, a sage Seeking the knowledge, the reality I
gauge Upon finding the answer, I turn the page, I turn the page

He lives deep in the monolith, the ancient stones disguise
And if you seek to find him, you'll reach the other side
Seeking the notable one, the ancient truth abide
The pages are now flying, he's inside, he's inside

Passing through the ages, I seek another time
A place where love is written, on the pages of all life
Finding it inside me, I shift to natural course Let it be noted on the pages, I left
this world, I left this world

The notable one
The notable one

SKY

In the mist there's gold . . . and hues to hold . . .
when you fly . . . the sky
2. Scenes span a lifetime's gaze, flight is the eagle's
way
Here in my heart is flight . . . sky
4. Night's fill the eyes with love, realms of the lighted
ones
Go where your dreams will fly . . . sky

I AM THE GRANDFATHER

I am the grandfather, old and wise
I know the answers you just can't deny
But you haven't found me yet
But you haven't found me yet

YOU'RE NOT ALONE

I see you in a dream, you look so tired and meek
Your tears glow in the light, you feel alone tonight
You're not alone, you're not alone

I reach to touch your skin, your sadness pulls me in
I know you can't see me, I hope you feel me breathe
You're not alone, you're not alone

I know, you feel alone
In your eyes, it sure seems true
But I'm here, at your side
Loving you, Ooh

I catch the tears that fall, I hold them in my palm
Though we may never meet, if only you could see me
You're not alone, you're not alone

ANCIENT THOUGHT

In an ancient thought I feel the mists of time
A memory from a world I've left behind

There's a face I see sometimes whose eyes hold a clue
A master of disguise, he reveals not when or who

He bears a secret, a key to time, and I know not why
He hides his wisdom, it's easy to see, the truth sets you free

In an ancient cave I see the words of old
A carving on a wall that tells of the soul

I turn to see his face, it glows in the dark
He reaches to touch me, I seek from my heart

STALLION OF THE LAKE

Fly to the lake, my little stallion, fly to the lake for me
Fly to the sky, my winged companion, fly to the sky with me

I'm a flyer in the sky, can you see me

Sing to the wind, my little stallion, your voice echoes in the sea

GRIDIMARIA

She lives all alone
In castles of stone
Who is this queen
Gridimaria

GYPSY

Whisper wind the ancient sign Find her there, enraptured with time
Hair billows in the wind
A voice, I now hear again
Gypsy

Timely quest towards visionhold
Ancient logs begin to be told
But you cannot hear
You try, but there's something you fear
Gypsy

Gypsy . . . Gypsy . . . Gypsy . . . Gypsy . . .
Gypsy . . . Gypsy

Dark eyes turn, the vision fades
Night is gone, it's onto the day
Her face held no regret
And you could never forget
Gypsy

IN YOUR NAME
(Jesus pronounced, Haysoos)

Come to me, Oh Jesus of man's desiring Come to me, Oh caller of the rain
Come to me, we'll walk on skies of thunder Fly to worlds of wonder in your
name

Sing to me, my quiet stillness calling
Sing to me of the silence you sustain
Sing to me, let our voices join together Harmonize forever in your name

Follow me, oh sun without a flower
Follow me, you can stop the parting rain Follow me, like the soul within the hour
Seeks unearthly power in your name . . . in your name

Fly with me, to pearly gates of heaven
Fly with me, on angel wings we'll go

Fly with me, the righteous call your mission Where angels seek admission in your name

SPIRIT CRUCIFIED ON EARTH

I would gladly fly away, I really thought that I could stay
I can stay for but a day, but I'll be back this way

I've known passion, as well as pain, seen the sunshine, held the rain Felt the spirits torment strain, but I'll be back this way

Pain and passion, joy and mirth, spirit crucified on earth

I would gladly fly the skies, beyond the sunset,
Heaven rides
Blend my soul into the light, then I'd be back
tonight

Take a part of sky with me, blend it with eternity Give to earth all that I see, then I'd be back . . . free

ONCE IN A LIFETIME

Once in a lifetime, the gift is given to you
Once in a lifetime, the gift of all eternal truth

Nights in a beggars dream, the heart unfolds its mighty quest
Days with the dancing queen, beauty shows its gift to us

Hand you the light, on this very night
Hold the flame, in your heart

Sing to the lighted ones, courage holds their
mighty quest
Laugh with the ghostly ones, for soon you will be their guest

BUILD A BRIDGE

Build a bridge to the stars from your eyes
Brick by brick build a bridge to the sky
Paint it with colors of celestial sighs

Build a bridge, build a bridge, build a
bridge, be free

Find all the stones that will pave your way home
Settle for nothing but angelic zones
Step on the ether, the home of the soul
Step on the bridge and complete the phase
The bridge will then take you to a world of malaise
All in your past was illusion's haze

BEFORE THE DAY YOU DIE

I've come a long hard road, travelled through waves
Searching for a lost soul, whose come awake

Followed an eternal dream, sought my desire
Igniting a part of me, an inner fire

Reach for the setting sun, reach for the sky
Reach to the far beyond before the day you die

Hope for a brighter dream, seek and ye shall find
Heighten what remains of thee, before the day you die

THE WHOLE OF LIFE

Aren't you afraid if you open your eyes You'll remember, you'll remember
The whole of life

There's a time, when you recall
All the joy, of brothers and friends
Every day, that passes by
Will make you cry, cause you need a hand

Cause all God's people, will come to an end And when we die, the angels will
send
For us
All God's love, and His merciful hand
All our loved ones, so we can make amends
There's a place, in your heart
Which recalls, our brothers and friends
And if you, will recall
All that matters, is love and amends

There's a time, in our lives
When we cry, for brothers and friends
Oh time, passes by
And we find, it's too late for amends

Then we'll wonder, if it's too late to find
Resurrection, in their eyes
Then we'll reach out, from beyond our grave
But they won't hear us, cause it's now too late

LISTEN TO THE WIND

Forevers something you may never find
You try too hard to tear at something right
No one could ever blame you, I won't even try
It's something you hear when you listen to the sky
It's something you hear when you listen to the sky

Love is something you can't pick and choose It comes to those who recognize it's
truth
No one can show you, I won't even try
It's something you hear when you listen to the sky
It's something you hear when you listen to the sky

You've given up and you've held on
You've tried so hard to carry on

If you care enough to try again
Listen to the wind
Forever's something you must seek to know It's not so much longevity, but in
your soul No one can find it for you, I won't even try It's something you hear
when you listen to the sky
It's something you hear when you listen to the sky

GRAND AWAKENING

Grand Awakening, Grand Awakening,
Grand Awakening . . . to love

An image floats before me, a vague but gentle face
It's essence guides me, to remember

A place in spirit rises, the movement slow
But I do want to know it, to remember

There's a seed of knowledge that grows as I seek
It's now inside of me

The core of wisdom, lies with the answer
To live, love and to be

The movement penetrates me, towards the core of memory
I am waking, I remember

All light is still within me, I seek to know the wisdom
Will you tell me, do you know it

WHITE WOLF

He lives in the caves of love, the deep grass ember
He bays at the moon at night, to call the stars He speaks to humankind in our
dreaming It's time to awake to who we are in light
We live in a world of hate and fearful people We scarcely recall the spirit we hide
within We don't think about the pathway called eternal
It's time to recall the source of all that is

White wolf, the healing teacher
Teach the ways of the wild and the ways of the native son
White wolf, seeks tribal leaders
Who will hear what he says and spread the light to the world
White wolf
He lives in our hearts and souls, the dreampath finder
He is love and wisdom, of knowledge way
A deliverer waits to see you, to give direction You are so much more than earthly
dirt and clay

TO RETRIEVE A GOLDEN ANGEL

To retrieve a golden angel, to light the pathway home
To call the flame of zion, to sing an angels song

I'd give everything, in the world, just to see . . . a golden angel

A seekers glance ignites the flame, calling to the Source
The knowledge gained is happenstance, no longer use the sword

For all I have seen, I seek eternity, in a golden angel

Take me home, angel zone, to the place where love abounds

In the sky, I see you fly, your wings aglow with the sun
To retrieve a golden angel, a sister of the sacred rite
Pass through the flaming gates, seek the 23rd dimension tonight

And love everything, just enough to see . . . a golden angel

GOTTA WAKE UP

Gotta wake up, to the day gone melody
Gotta wake up, to mortality
My day's a distant memory, my future far away
My life has come to nothing but my soul has much to say
It's the same old situation, my dreams will never die
And tomorrow I'll be sitting here still waiting to fly
I've simply got to find a way to make my heart sing clear
I know that I have much to give the Earth I hold so dear
It won't be the same tomorrow, cause my dreams have come alive
And tomorrow I'll be dancing to the music in the sky

FOR THE ASCENSION

One more time for the ascension
One more time for the accused
One more time for the transfiguration

Just in time, we don't mind . . . Lord . . . pull us out of the blues

One more time for the redemption
One more time for the abused
One more time for the transfiguration
No more doubt, I'm getting out . . . Lord . . . it's you that I choose
I'm not afraid, I've got it made . . . Lord . . . on my side I've got you
Don't you fear, can't you hear . . . Lord . . . He's calling to you

CHANGE THE WORLD

They tell me, I'm the angry one
They say things to compromise, what I'm thinking of
They tell me, it's not your problem
They say don't worry, it's okay, though it may be unjust

They say you can't change the world, that's just the way that it is
Just take care of yourself, and forget it

He tells me, don't listen to them
He says things about truth and love, let justice rise again

He tells me, it is our problem
He says we are our only hope, because we all are
one

He says I can change the world, with just one caring thought
Best take care of your world, or you can forget it

He asks me, will you find one more, who cares the way you do
I don't know, could it be you
He shows me a world at peace, a place of love and truth
Well do you, do you believe it, too

Do you believe, that you can, change the world
Well, do you, do you care too
Do you believe, that you can, change the world
Well, do you, do you care too

THUNDER TRAVELING TO LOFTIER HEIGHTS

Thunder traveling to loftier heights Thunder traveling to loftier heights

A vision, a man held the vision of wisdom He shared it with all of the world
In his time they deceived him, and took his heart away
His vision, remained even after his passing Remains in my heart on this day
His name perceived his vision,
Heinmettooyalakekt

Chief Joseph, a heart in the likeness of spirit A man who instilled in him wings
No one could compromise him, his conscience was his guide
Chief Joseph, remains even after his passing Remains in my heart on this day
His name perceived his vision,
Heinmettooyalakekt

APOLOGY

On behalf of the white men, who choose not to understand
On behalf of the white men, who desecrate your land
On behalf of this race, ignorant and cruel I'm so sorry what my race has done to
you
Thunder travels higher, when beckoned in the wind
And torment be forever, with unacknowledged sins
Though few will ever say it, I say this to you I'm so sorry what my race has done
to you

I'm sorry for the hatred, and stealing Indian land I'm sorry for the torture, and
the murder at our hands
I'm sorry for the vengeance and discrimination, too
I'm so sorry what my race has done to you I'm sorry for the anguish, and the
lives you lost too soon
I'm so sorry what my race has done to you

On behalf of the people, who respect and value life
We will vow to come together, and to change the wrongs to right
On behalf of the people, who care just as I do We will give to you our lives to
make it up to you
We will give to you our lives to make it up to you

WAGE PEACE INSIDE

The world is at one with the tides of time
Where is your heart and your soul and your mind
Seek the light and you'll find the sky
The time has come for all to wage peace inside

Who will you be in the coming days
Someone at peace or a mad, angry rage
Will you seek life or destructions ways
The time has come for us to pray for a better day

How much blood will reprieve our hate
Will we even cry on Our Father's grave
Will we bow down in shame on judgment day
The time has come for all to wage peace inside

We can be the hand of eternal grace
Or we can be lost in evil's malaise
What will you choose on your dying day
The time has come for all to wage peace inside

THE GHOSTS OF LONELY CHILDREN

One day I met a child
He seemed so lonely, he seemed so tired
He wept, and then he asked me
Who are you, are you my mommy

I looked upon his face, and then I reached to him with grace
But my hand went right through him, he was the ghost of lonely children
Spirit child, tell me what you see
Don't fly away, until I know your legacy
Are you here just to show me the child in everyone
Or the heart of all the people turning to stone

He stared into my eyes, the gaze of a lonely child
And he spoke so quietly, when he said these words to me
I'm not what I may seem, I am the voice that fills your dreams
And when you hear me crying, please comfort me, the heart of humanity

In my hand, he'd placed a key
To the heart of all who'd see
Don't you know, we all are brothers
Here to love every earth brother

I held my hands to me, and vowed to love him inside of me
That lonely child no longer lingered, he'd grown to be all of earth's people

STORMS OF THE RED HAWK

Wings of the nightbird, come to my night Follow the vision, sing to the light

Storms of the Red Hawk, inspire the rain Redeem the wisdom, come back again

Storms of the Red Hawk, come to my night

Born to destruction, birthed by the rain Seek resurrection, be born again

THE SONG OF LIFE

Sing to the valley, sing to the trees, sing to the oceans and streams

Ride on a mountainside, glide on the breeze, fly on a moments glance with me
Sing to the night, the song of the sea
Sing to the day, let freedom ring
Sing to the sky, the song of life
Sing to me

Call to the nightwind, sway with the leaves, hark to the angels sing

LOOK AWAY, WINDOW HEART

There's a window of light, where the truth is shown
May we all have the courage to find our own

There's a sword in the earth, that's been placed there by man
Who once were the stewards, now are the death

Look away from your conscience
Look away from the land
Look away from the water
In God's hand
Look away from the mountains
Look away from the stars
Look away from your neighbor
Look away from your heart
Look away Window Heart
Your heart is the window where truth can be known
It's your fear to feel it that let's it go on

God's creatures are dying, at the hands of the feared
Why aren't you crying, where are your tears

ANGEL WOMAN

I know a woman, who talks to the sky
Some say she's holy, some say she lies
Angel woman much more than she seems

I know a woman, who sings to the sea
Some think she's crazy, some say she's naive
Oh, angel woman much more than she seems

I know a woman, whose been to the stars
Some say she's dreaming, some say she's inspired
Angel woman much more than she seems

I know a woman, who talks to the sky
Some say she's holy, some say she lies

Angel woman much more than she seems
Angel woman much more than she seems

HALLELUJAH TO THE LORD

We're not watching for a win tonight
We've all come to dominion
And there's no one who prefers to fight
We prefer to undo harm
There's a light in the soul's interior
And his name is Jesus Christ
And because He simply loves us
He saves all souls who ask

Hallelujah, no one will get burned tonight
Hallelujah, all souls will survive
Hallelujah, hallelujah, hallelujah to the Lord
Hallelujah, hallelujah, hallelujah to the Lord

HEAL THYSELF

Heal thyself and
Heal thy wealth and
Heal the soul inside

Change the world and
Change your world and
Change your inner light

Come to God in a dream
In heaven all souls gleam
In pure light

Heal thy chain and
Heal thy rain and
Heal the soul of the eye

Let it see and
Let it be and

Let it bear heaven's sign

ACROSS THE RIVER

In a haunted woodland, I saw my Father
Gazing through the bush, next to the water
I watched the river run, cascading water glide
His hands were pointing to the other side
Across the river

As I began to walk, the thrashing current flow
My spirit soared, in going home
Stepping on the shore, His hand reached to me
Knowing all there was, He set me free
Across the river

When I cross the river, I'll be on the other side
And all my illusions will be washed away, behind
Across the river

In a haunted woodland, I saw a river
And it took me to the other side
In a haunted woodland, I saw a river
And it took me to the other side
Across the river

AND THE LIGHT CAME TUMBLING ON IN

Hallelujah, and the light came tumbling on in
Hallelujah, and the light came tumbling on in

Love, light and harmony, it's a triumph for the angels
Wasted nights and wasted dreams, only you can help the angels

Love, light and harmony, as words they have no meaning
But in the hearts of those who seek, the angels fill with reason

Hallelujah, and the light came tumbling on in

PRAY FOR THE SOULS WE'VE LOST TO DARKNESS FROM THE LIGHT

Sing to salvation, redemption of the blind Pray for the souls we've lost to
darkness from the light

People pray, people pray for those who sleep
To the sky, to the Lord salvation's keep People pray to God to save the souls
Who've wandered from the light
And our prayers must reach the highest peak
To bring souls home tonight

MOTHER EARTH

Walls of illusion have come crashing down All I see is the fire all around me
Moment of truth carries all the weight of the world
Why don't they see it with the eye of the wise
Why don't they hear it, the sounds of the sighs
Where are you going, do you know the master you serve
It's a hard luck story . . . of the earth
I know the glory is rebirth Seekers tremble with the dirt
While the blind ones till the hurt
Mother earth
Why must I share all the promises that you break
Why can't you live with the promises that you make
Is it just a dream, or can it be held back It's a hard luck story . . . of the earth
I know the glory is rebirth

Raging volcano speaks the truth of the land Earthquakes rumble to the beat of
quicksand All around you, she speaks in language unheard
Nobody knows it but the ones who have sight
Nobody hears it lest they listen at night
A seekers vision can become his greatest curse

HOLY LOVE

Holy love
Holy love
Holy love
Holy love (Gloria)

EXODUS

I'm soaring up a mountain, illusions far behind
The woodland seems to touch the sky Exodus the mission, ascension is the flight
Liberation calls me nigh

Deliverance from what I perceive, deliverance to
God's will in me

Liberation comes
To me
When I release my earthly love
Replace it with love from above
Liberation shines
Through thee
When you release your earthly will
Replace it with one higher still
Up at the top where God resides
You'll find the will of love inside

TIME

Time, gives us our lullabies
It sings, right as we grow
Time, precedes all last good-byes
Which linger in our soul

Sing, to glorify His name
Praise, Him all day long
Remember, Him in all life's things
For He, has called your soul

Just give me time, I'll give you a reason
It'll all be fine, Just give me a sign
Just give Your love, and I can fight demons
I'll surrender my will . . . on . . . high

Time, can lead a heart astray
And time, recaptures souls
And time reminds of the Way
Which lingers in our souls

You, can find your soul again
No, it's not too late
Time, will lead you back to when
The child . . . within you . . . reigned

Lord, please bring my soul to you
Lord, forgive my sins

Lord, bequeath my love to you
Sing, our praise to heaven

IT WAS ALL OVER YOU

I've tread down narrow pathways of innocence and youth
I tried my hand at hard times and Lord I made it through
Along the way I found, the solitary voice, of You

I followed a redeemer into the darkest night
When I emerged from this, my Lord, I found the greatest light
Along the way I found, a power most profound, on high

So long to the shadow
Farewell to the prattle
The silence settles in
I'll give my final breath to realize
My Lord God of Heaven inside
It was all over You
It was all over You

I walked into the distance, alone and confused
Directly to the fire, the sins of my youth
Along the way I found, the solitary voice, of You
Following the vision, I vanquished my soul's plight
On the fires of Your mercy, I laid my soul aright
Along the way I found, a power most profound, on high

WHEN GOD WILL STEP IN

Come on stand up, from your weakness
Give your cares to God above
Shout His name out, shout it loudly
So He'll know how much you love
Don't keep crying
Don't keep hiding
From His love

Come on reach out, from your smallness
Reach high above to find the Way
Then look for Him, look real closely
He'll be there to guide to the way
Don't you turn now
There's no return, Pal
From His love

There's a great revelation
In His malaise
There's a great inspiration
In His face
There's a great occupation
In His grace
Don't give up now
It's hard to tell

When God will step in

I AM

| Time, on a wall, to recall, Her honor Pray through the night, to requite, the
Father

Mary wants me to sing, songs everlasting, songs that would take you to heaven
The wind holds her song, and the night goes
along, singing her soulful . . .
remember

You - want me - to be - your Mother

Who is this man I see, riding the walls with me, talking of things of hereafter
No one must know his name, most just think he's insane, I see his eyes hold
forever

You - want me - to be - your Mother

| Ride, on a wave, to reclaim, Her honor
Seek, ye shall find, and remind, of the Father

Now I call Christ to me, and His mother Mary, knowing their presence, I'm
honored
For who could be worthy, of His divine mercy, bow to their presence, surrender

You - want me - to be - your Mother

What is this sight I see, appearing before me, I see that God's presence is
furthered
The I and the AM call me, a rainbow appears 'fore me, to service I go, with fervor
You - want me - to be - your Mother

| God, enters me, just to see, my heart
Pure, it must be, or He, will part

I
AM
I AM
Is calling
I
AM
I AM
Is moving

MORE OF YOU

More of you, I still need more of you, more of you, within my soul
More of you, I need the Lord of you, more of you, in my heart
More of you, I must have fortitude, in my
heart

I followed you, in a dream at night
You said to me, pray for souls, make things right
Seek, ye shall find, knock it shall be opened
You reached to me, I took your hand, in the light

You said to me, pray without ceasing
I bowed to you, and received, Christ's Passion
Seeing His torment, I recall in the vision
Christ looked at me, and told me His wisdom

MARY, JESUS

Mary, Jesus
Your faith has born the other one
Oh Mary Jesus
For you have both been born
In the star tonight
Born, by the Lord this time
Born in the Lord's design

So Mary, Jesus
Who will bear the other one
For Mary, Jesus
Your faith has made you one
In each other's eyes
One, in the Lord's design
One, in the earthly sign

So come, blessed virgin who carries forth the
holy lamb
And come, our redeemer, who bears the yolk of all to come
Oh Lord, give us mercy and show us how to mend our lives
Oh lord, give us wisdom, to emulate their lives
Mary, Jesus
Your birth has born you both tonight
And Mary, Jesus
You both shall be the child
In each others arms
Strength, for the other one
Love, when the light is gone

Mary, Jesus
Oh Lord, give us wisdom to emulate their holy lives

GO, AND SIN NO MORE

There's an angel on your window
And you've noticed her before
Please don't crash and burn between us
For she dearly loves your soul

So your life is complicated
We've been down that road before
If you would put your trust in Jesus
There'd be mercy for your soul

Give it light, and give it to Jesus
Give His blood, and send it on high
Give Him love, and give Him your freedom
And Go, and sin no more
So you followed an illusion

And you broke so many rules
You don't think He can redeem you
For you wear a sinner's shoes

In your heart you have a yearning
You now seek to know the truth
And you seek to find redemption
From the depth of love's rebuke

VOICE OF THE STILL ONE

Voice of the still One
Voice of the Ancient One
Voice of the Still One
Voice of the Ancient One

I don't want to give my soul alibis
I don't want to tell myself ugly lies
All I want is to be true to You
My Lord, to be true to Your truth
My Lord, to be true to You

Give me something to remember You by
Give me wisdom to change my life
All I want is to be true to You
My Lord, to be true to Your truth
My Lord, to be true to You
I don't want to force others to fly
I don't want to make anyone cry
All I want is to be true to You
My Lord, to be true to Your truth

My Lord, to be true to You

WHO AM I TO SAY

Sometimes it seems, like a million dreams have gone by
Sometimes I stray, when I think I know but then who am I to say

Sometimes I ask for forgiveness
Gratitude other days
Then I just get quiet . . . cause . . .
Who am I to say, who am I to say

Sometimes I bleed, like a prayerful plea to
someone
Sometimes I pray, when I want to know because who am I to say

MAYBE MY SAVIOUR'S GONNA BE WITH ME TONIGHT

I kneel beside my bed post
And look towards the sky
My palms will come together
My soul pours forth tonight
I look towards the window

And then I look inside
Cause maybe my Saviour's gonna be with me tonight

I turn to face the Justice
But mercy's all I see
Beyond a sinner's fury
Lies God's eternity
I look towards the window
And then I look inside
Cause maybe my Saviour's gonna be with me tonight

Maybe my Saviour's gonna be with me tonight
Roll out the carpet, turn down the lights
It's gonna be a high time for praying
It's gonna be a high time for staying
In the light

I crouch under the covers
The night is fully lit
I reach towards salvation
From the earthly pit
I look towards the window
And then I look inside
Cause maybe my Saviour's gonna be with me tonight

LIFE'S SHORT LITTLE DANCE

Where does love go, it's a truth I have to know
When you don't have the chance to say goodbye
Do you laugh or do you cry, do you smile or do you hide
When they ask, are you allright

How much can a heart sustain
When all that's left of love is pain
Cut the cord so I may live again
How long can I be
Married to a memory
My life has been a short little dance

It all seems like a dream, it's so hard to believe
No I'll never live to be with someone like you
It all happened so fast, my life's short little dance
No I'll never have a chance to love someone like you

Life comes and it goes, I guess you never know
How much time you really have left, or if you'll grow old
In God's master plan, we're all dealt different hands
Until He takes us home from life's short little dance

So tell me, where does love go
Does it die or does it grow

Are we really all alone, in this life

THE PATRIARCHAL SWOON

Climb the heights of Israel
Sing the patriarchal tale
Look upon the wisdom trail
Everyone's looking at Abraham, Allelu

Alleluja Allelu
Alleluja Allelu

To tell the story of the soul
Start with testaments of old
All begins in Israel
Everyone's looking at Abraham, Allelu

The allegory holds the key
Secrets of eternity
It all began as history

Everyone's looking at Abraham, Allelu

ONE AND ONLY MARY

Praise the Lord so hard . . . we cry
Even until we die
Nothing good has ever come from sin
Praise Him for His gift . . . today
In every single way
His Holy Mother falls upon our lips

Let there be . . . one and only Mary

See Her in the sky . . . tonight
Healing every plight
No one loves us as Our Mother's Son
See them both arise . . . today
In each and every way
The Son of God, and His Holy Mother come

Let there be . . . one and only Mary Let there be . . . one and only Mary

See Her in my eyes . . . tonight
I saw her just last night
Her holy essence graced my humble skin
I saw Him as She rose . . . today
In many holy ways
Appearing to me, they touched my soul with bliss

STARLIGHT

I'm talking about starlight
Shining every way
Starlight
Shine my path today

Sing of the freedom
The flight the soul must take
Follow the ether
And fly your soul awake

Beyond all the mountains
The beauty pales my soul
Beyond all the summits
My soul is being called

Flying to heaven
See it face to face
Relinquish the pathway
And bring your soul to grace

WESTWIND

I closed my eyes and now I'm feeling great I felt the power of the Lord quake
Feels like the westwind is falling down on me

Waiting for a summit of the light I feel vibrations as they come tonight
Feels like the westwind is falling down on me

Falling down on me
Falling down on me

I close my eyes and see the Prophet's eyes Within his gaze I know he's come inside
Feels like the westwind is falling down on me

There are no words cause all's conveyed inside
The prophets wisdom rides a wave of light Feels like the westwind is falling down on me

So beckon tonight
For this light
And tomorrow you'll find
The Kingdom inside

Reach for the sky
And Reach for God
And reach for the Prophet
In the land of Abha
Reach for the sign
Conveyed in the sky
And reach for the Glory
In the land of Baha

I see the sunset and I feel his eyes
I know tomorrow he'll remain inside
Feels like the westwind is falling down on me

I WISH I WERE AN ANGEL

I wish I were an angel
Putting God's word upon the street

I wish I were a prodigal
New to salvation's mystery
Maybe then you'd be amazed
At all the Lord has done for me
I wish I were an angel
I wish I were an angel

I wish I were an angel
With God's mercy to reveal
And if I were an angel
I'd spread God's hidden mysteries
Maybe then you'd be afraid
But your eyes might finally see
I wish I were an angel
I wish I were an angel

I wish I were an angel
Putting God's words out on the street
New to Salvation's mystery
But not for long

I wish I were an angel
I wish I were an angel

I wish I were an angel
Who could hear God every day
I wish I were a prodigal
Whose temptations had been slain
I wish I were a holy man
Whose soul had crossed the gate
I wish I were an angel
I wish I were an angel

If I were an angel
I'd bring God's joy to every thing
If I were a prodigal
Of salvation I would sing
Maybe then you'd be amazed
And you'd rejoice with me
I wish I were an angel
I wish I were an angel

I wish I were an angel
Who could hear God every day
Whose temptations had been slain
For eternity

I wish I were an angel
Bringing God's joy to every thing
Of salvation I would sing
For eternity

I LOVE THE LORD

Would it be selfish, for me to ask
What I'm dreaming of

Would it be possible, for me to return
Where my soul just was

Would it be prudent, would it be wise Could it be possible, for my eyes Just one
more time Lord, Just one more time
May I return, Lord, to the sky

I love the Lord, I love the Lord I love the Lord, I love the Lord I love the Lord, I
love the Lord I love the Lord, the Lord, the Lord
The Lord

Wouldn't it be ungrateful, to see such things
And turn one's head to earth
First through the matrix, then the stars
The yellow, red and blue

Mind not my impatience, when I pray
And ask to see such signs
My Lord, you are merciful, to bid me see
The gate of Paradise

HOLY MARY

Holy Mary Mother of God
Forgive our sins and please pray for us

SING TO JESUS

Sing to Jesus when your heart may be blue Sing to heaven, God will listen to you
Sing His name out so the world may know There's a redeemer whose mercy
holds all

Praise God, Praise Jesus, Praise His Mother

I pray to Jesus when I'm down on my knees
I pray to Jesus when I walk down the street My mind sings praises when I'm
singing in church
When I'm working, when I'm sick or I hurt
No one can see
All the joy
He brings to me
There's a place
In my soul, that can't bear
Another moment

Another moment, another day spent, any time away from You

THE MYSTICAL JESUS

His words were calm, almost surreal
He was a being devoted to all the worlds of the dream
He said, stand up, stand up, come on, allright
Wake up to the dream world and find the light

His way was kind, almost sweet
He was a being devoted to lifting people's pain

He'd say stand up, stand up, come on, allright
Wake up to the healer, whose with you tonight

Oh mystical Jesus, your reign is forever

His soul was free, and yet He was bound
He was a being devoted to all soul's, lost and found
He'd say, stand up, stand up, come on, allright
Your sins are forgiven you, your free from your plight

PEACE ON EARTH UNFOLDING

I hear the peace on earth unfolding
Peace for you and me
I hear the bells of heaven tolling
Call to you and me
I hear the sound of new beginnings to resound on
high, on high

I hear the watcher make his movement
Watching you and me
I feel the ether's undercurrent
Moving you and me
I hear the sound of new beginnings to resound on
high, on high

Beyond the fragments of the earth
Lay the soul of all rebirth
And the seed of God's mirth

I hear the infant cry beholding
Cry for you and me
I feel the movement quite unfolding
Move for you and me
I hear the sound of new beginnings to resound on high, on high

HOLY MOTHER OF GOD

I came across the Virgin Mary standing over me
Her essence was extraordinary, she came to life for me
There were no words required of her, her beauty said it all
As she returned to statuary, I returned to home

Holy Mother of God

My thoughts were guided rightly, softly, to follow virtue's ways
My inner inclinations were found to follow much malaise
I vowed to her to try to right it, all these thoughts of mine
And make my mind and spirit purely golden, sweet, sublime

Another spectral moment fills my memory this eve
Her essence held the glory of the newborn son, the babe
In all my worldly wanderings I'd never seen such bliss
All the world could never convey, the love in just her kiss

THE WISDOM OF THE GURU

I don't know the meaning of the Word
I don't know the knowledge of all truth
I don't know the path to be observed
I don't know the wisdom of the guru
The wisdom of the guru

I don't know the secrets in the sky
I don't know the highest energy
I don't know the greatest place to fly
I don't know all the realms of mystery
The realms of mystery

What's going on in my belated mind
Will I ever find what I seek to find
Where is the doorway to the Absolute
Where is the pathway to unbridled truth
Where is the Heaven that I yearn to move

GET DOWN ON MY KNEES

I'm gonna get down on my knees and pray
To the Lord up in the sky
I'm gonna fly all night with wings astride
Till I reach salvation's sight
I'm gonna get down on my knees
I'm gonna fly all night with wings
I'm gonna get down on my knees
And pray

I'm gonna go on down to the altar ground
And kneel before the signs
I'm gonna fly all night till the morning light
Till I've left this world behind
I'm gonna get down on my knees
I'm gonna fly all night with wings
I'm gonna get down on my knees
And pray

I'm gonna go on high to the worlds of life
Until I see an angels face
Then I'll fall down as the sights abound
And behold all heaven's grace
I'm gonna get down on my knees
I'm gonna fly all night with wings
I'm gonna get down on my knees
And pray

Hold, Tight, World, Abide
Sing, High, Angels, Sigh
Cry, For, Salvations, Door
No, Fear, in Getting, Here

I WANT TO BE LIKE JESUS

All my life I've misunderstood
All that time I was seeking God outside
Of my life
Time has come where the truth reveals
And my soul must break the seal of itself
Inside

Break that seal of pride
Humility to find

I want to be like Jesus
I want to be like Jesus
I want to be like Jesus
On the cross

HE WAS THERE

Her face was worn and tattered
Her eyes a hazy green
Life was warm and willing
As she prepared to leave

Her life had been a long one
Filled with surprise
There were many who had loved her
And he the one who died
He died when she was twenty
She bore his only son
The simple ring he'd given her
Was still the only one

Her son had never known him
But as he held her hand in tears
He knew he'd come to get her
When a smile replaced her fears

Not many had known him
But she remembered still
And as her life was passing
He was there, he was there

He held her hand in passing
As she gently let it go
Another hand had taken hers
He felt it in his soul

And when he went to sleep that night
He saw them in a dream
She'd never looked so beautiful
As she waved farewell to him

He was there, he was there, he was there, he was there

OPERATOR OF THE SKY

Where in this dream, can new skies take hold
An illusion, of light, in your dream

Where in my heart, can I find the seed
A beginning, of love, taking hold

Operator of the sky, here's my question in the night
No more sorrow, alibis, just dreams
Perpetrator of the sun, I see that life has just begun
The answer lies at one, humanity

Where in my mind, can I find the truth
Just a moment, of light, in my soul
Operator of the sky, teach my soul to see the light
No illusions of light, just reality
Operator of my mind, teach me to recognize the signs
And reach to destinies untamed, in my dreams

MODERN DAY SLAVES

Peeking between the bar frames
Seeking to find the light
Hoping that time will free them
They live in a world of plight

The faces they see don't feel them
They don't recognize their face
The soldiers of shade act as masters
To the modern day slaves

When will we free them, who are we to choose
All life is sacred, not meant to be abused

They live in many cities
In dictatorial states
No one knows how to save them
They're modern day slaves

Jailed for their uniqueness
Their lives a whirlwind fate
No human life is sacred
They're modern day slaves

He's speaking through the bar frames
Would you look into his eyes
His pain is just like yours and mine

WHAT YOUR EYES WILL NEVER SHOW

You can wear those dark sunglasses
And the clothes you just bought
You can smile at all the people
And walk big and tall
You can act all calm and happy

Live your life on the go
But nothing can hide
What your eyes will never show

You can walk right by a homeless man
Just a beggar on the street
You can drive right through the poor side of town
Cause you've got food to eat
You can tell yourself it's hopeless
There's nothing you can do
But no words will ever hide
What your eyes will never show

It's a hateful world we live
And it's up to us to change
We cannot simply give in
Let's care enough to change

Let's take off our dark sunglasses
And look at our world
We war with our neighbors
And the Earth we call home
You can pretend it's okay
But your heart will always know
And no words will ever hide
What your eyes will never show

It could be a whole new world
Where love would always reign
Where tears would never hide
To disguise, all the pain

Let's put down the wall of silence
That blocks love's flow
I can see it peeking slowly
From your eyes, yeah, it shows

You can walk right by your neighbor
But, honey, it still shows

YOU COULD BE A FANTASY

You could be a fantasy to me
You and me could reach for eternity
To find a star in you
Fly harmony in the sky and you will see Soar evermore on the wings of white
horses
To see a star in you

I'm a rider, I am a rider, Assisi rider]
I'm a rider, I am a rider, Assisi rider

You could be a reality to me
You have become as one in imagery
We've become reality, in God

I'm a rider, I am a rider, Assisi rider I'm a rider, I am a rider, Assisi rider

Take me home, take me home, Assisi brother Take me home, take me home, Assisi brother

I BELIEVE IN LOVE

I believe in love, in love
I believe in love, in love

There's a cold wind in the moonlight
That chills the heart of me
I feel so much excitement, my spirit's feeling free
Cause deep in my heart, I feel so much joy
That's where the love is, I believe in joy

DREAM WITH ME

Where is your dream, that you can become
A World . . . as one
Reach to the stars, lighted realms lay
Fly from the ground, remember the way
Dreamer live on, in oceans and streams
Dreamer, dream high, dream with me

RIVER TAKE ME HOME, COUNTRY ROAD

It was an old country road, that I walked down all my life
It was the way I'd always go, when things didn't go quite right
A river ran on that grassy hill, I'll always follow . . . that old country road

There was more to that place, it was to me a sacred ground
I felt the calming grace, and dancers came without a sound
A river ran on that grassy hill, I'll always follow . . . that old country road
River run, river follow me, river take me home
River run, river follow me, river take me home . . . to that old country road

That old dirt road is far away, but in my heart I see it still
It will always be my place, to set my restless spirit still
A river ran on that grassy hill, I'll always follow . . . that old country road

ANGEL IN WAITING

Trailing . . . Sailing . . . Wailing . . . in the night

I'm falling down a mountain, a victim's disguise
Urging life within me to fly

Trapped between the heavens and the earth below
I'm an angel in waiting, so slow

Flying . . . Sighing . . . Crying . . . Please make it right

Between the night and sunrise, you'll hear my bells
I'll call to you in music, please help

I'm circling you in neon, a lighted malaise
I look into your eyes, they're glazed

You'll hear me in the ether, I feel your regret
No need to sign your sorrow, it's not over yet
When will you hear me, the call of earth's design
Return to the master . . . and fly

BREEZE IN THE WILLOW

There's a breeze in the willow, the gentle flight
There's a seed with the fellow, who rides the sky

The land here is fertile, but dry from no rain The seed must be planted, to flourish in the vein

It's a seed of life, a seed of eternity
It's a seed of love, one more time for humanity

There's a man in my window, who calls my name His eyes fill with tears, when he sees the pain

He told me once it could change
He begged me please won't you see, you are my only link

Who . . . will . . . you . . . be
Will you care about humanity

There's a song in the soul of man, a song of love
It's hidden from the conscious mind, by deception's blood

There's a breeze in the willow, there's a breeze in the willow

GREEN PEACE

To ride a mustang in the night
A sigh, an eagle in flight
To swim, aside a dolphin's fin
Climb a mountain's tip
Ocean's in the wind
A dream, or so it seems
A tree, dropping heaven's leaves
A sky, filled with cloudy lies
No one answers why
Mother Earth must die

You see
Men can hardly read
The message of the sea
The wisdom of a tree
Oh oh oh, Green peace
Let's create, Green peace

To care, each one of you I dare
To share, our planet with our heirs
To find, a part of you inside

That no longer hides
Seeks to make things right

To be, the message of the sea
To plea, we need the air to breathe
To unite, humans with all life
The air with the sky
Mother Earth will smile

ADALEDA OF GOD

There's a face in my memory, I see in my mind
sometimes
A gentle melody, I recall the voice in the night

Her image grows ghostly, as her pale white linen
blows
No one else sees her, but I always hear her voice

She calls out Adaleda, Adaleda, Adaleda,
Adaleda of God

Night is for the fleeting glance, the world beyond our senses comes alive
Angels sing their soft romance, hidden in their song is life

They are with us, we need to hear them, angels of God, hear them call

LIFE ABOVE ME

Sometimes I fight the changes, sometimes I hide
Sometimes I run from danger, sometimes I cry
Late at night I reach to old ones, in a mountain hold
Then I wake and greet a new day, wisdom's lot foretold

And I think about life . . .in the valley
Life . . . in the trees
Life . . . in the oceans
And life . . . above me

Sometimes I grab the new day, on its breath I glide
Sometimes I reach to heaven, that's when I fly

Early dawn I grasp the essence, my soul takes a ride
The strands of life melt right into me, that's when I take flight

H IGH ROAD

She's driving down the road, just following the wind
She's headed for a mountain, where all her dreams have been
She's searching for the high road, a place where new lives begin
She's waiting there for no one, but she . . . may come back again

Searching for the high road
The place where she'll come alive
Searching for the high road
Where all her dreams reside, where all her dreams reside

She's heading for a valley, but she knows it's on the way
If she's going to reach that temple, she's going to pass through some mistakes
She's gonna take the high road and understand the plan
She's got a ways in front of her, but she . . . may come back again

VISIONTOWN

Welcome to Visiontown, please enter without a sound

Night is brewing, spirits moving, vision comes in the night

Waitings ample, movement samples, silence in Visiontown
Wisdom enters, here in the dark, here in
Visiontown

Many come here, many forget . . . Visiontown

LIFT UP YOUR HEARTS

Lift up your hearts, it's Jesus's nation
Lift up your voice, it's a celebration

There's a power in God's forgiveness
There's a light come from on high
There's the Word of God incarnate
Who can teach us to fly

There's a kindness in His passing
And the Word of God revealed
There's much joy in resurrection
Through which we've all been healed

Come the Kingdom of Heaven
Into my mind's eye
Let me feel it, and worship You
Teach me to fly
In the ways of the Prophets, Lord
Teach me to see
Beyond all earthly vices
Lord, make my heart clean

BORN BENEATH THE SOUL

Born beneath the soul
Born beneath the soul
Born beneath the soul
Oh, oh, oh, the soul is waiting

CAN YOU FEEL IT IN YOUR SOUL

The tallest trees guide some of our nighttime stars
A gentle breeze moves the clouds so very far
It's not hard to see how life flows in all things
Can you feel it in your soul

The solar rays provide food for all that's green
And every life finds its needs met through the rain
It's not hard to see how life flows in all things
Can you feel it in your soul

Beyond natural senses where vibrations hold
the key
That's where you'll feel it
That's where you'll know it in your soul
Among the mountains, lie shelter for the wild
And in the nighttime we are guided by the stars
It's not hard to see how life flows in all things
Can you feel it in your soul

DREAMQUEST

There's a voice that calls to me in the night
 Asking me to see
 Beckon sounds from the fiery sky
 The spirit quest to be

The howling wind requests the rite
 Swaying pines retreating
 The gateway serves to call the light
 A forest face is bleeding

A misty face fills the green
 The forest image so serene
 Magical lace enshrines the thought
 The end of the old I saught

Tomorrow's vision seeks the day
 A dawn of new awakening
 Cloudy sunsets, immortal rays
 Old illusions shaking

A dreamquest filled with colored eyes
 Seeking truth beyond me
 No more visions of shadowed lies
 I know I believe I see

 I know
 I believe
 I see

I REMEMBER HIS NAME

He came to this world as a child
Before he reached manhood, he died
The vision and memory still clear
But yet I don't remember the year

But I remember his face, and the laughter
I remember the grace of his smile
I remember his way of turning sorrow to gladness
I remember his name

My brother and he were a pair
_Children playing without a care
They grew, graduated, got a job
For a time, though, their lives did part
In a river once, I nearly died
He pulled me out and saved my life
The phone call came, left me in shock
He had died, it broke my heart

Now I see him in my dreams
He lets me know that he's still okay

HAUNTED BY A MEMORY

Haunted by a memory
Haunted by what used to be
Haunted by a hologram
Of a child, of a child

Rainy days and stormy nights
Haunted Scenes fill the twilight
Your face won't go, it's a mystery
True love never dies

True love never dies
I'll be haunted all my life
Fading scenes of the lonely one
My own image in the sky
Haunted by a memory
Haunted by one who loved me
Haunted by my own ignorance
God sent her away
Sleepless nights, remembering
Lonely days, forgetting
Wishing I could go back in time
And help her choose another way

ORPHAN IN YOUR DREAM

Deep in the night, I hear the sounds of your
cries
An ocean apart, another world
You call to me, as if I hold a key
Reach for my hand and it's yours

But I'm an orphan
Yes, I'm an orphan
In your dream

You look in my eyes, there's no way I can disguise
Feelings inside . . . of me
You are in pain, life has turned into a game
Somewhere in time you reach to me

I'm still an orphan
Yes, I'm an orphan
In your dream

There's a world that is your own
And a world I know as true
Orphan, orphan

You're far away, I know I can't really stay
The ocean blocks me from your view
Stay, hold my hand, remember all that we had
Tomorrow, you'll wake and you'll know

That I'm an orphan
Yes, I'm an orphan
In your dream

ANCESTRAL IMAGE

All around me's just another world
Men and women, boys and little girls
Running before me are all my dreams
Ancestral image within my reach
Those behind me must be seen
In the light
I go where the movement flows
I see
They're free
And they're me
I go where the sunset rolls
I fly
So high
In the sky

Beyond all I had seen
I'd never known their face
And their image retains
Their vibrations through space
But through silence comes their wisdom
Let their soul release the dream
Our hearts be born together
Through the pain

There's a fire in my heart
That can bring me to sight
In the world of the night
God leads souls to flight
But the rain must come to guide us
And the seeds must fill the rain
Our hearts be born together
Through the pain

FACES AND SOULS

A scene fills my mind, my soul goes back in time
Wandering through years, through faces and fears

Who am I now, I will go home somehow
Have I learned from the pain, am I still the same

Who will I be tomorrow
Who will I be in a year
All that I know, are the faces and the souls
Of those who've walked with me

Reaching through time, I seek another sign
Your image so clear, though you're no longer here
You exist in a space, where the mist hides your face
You are my guide, take my hand on this night

JOURNEY THROUGH A TEAR

I once knew a man who would ride the sun He followed a road I could never see for long
He was a mysterious man, a mystical man, to me
Finally, I see
I once held an image of love inside my heart Then life came and hardened the very core, I'd gone too far It was a mysterious thing, a mystical thing, to me
Finally, I see

Life is an ocean, a journey through a tear It's love that comes to free us, and tear away the fear
I once felt the world was at fault for lives gone wrong
But now I see life as an angry child, begging for love
It's not such a mysterious thing, a mystical thing, at all
Not at all

FOR THE OLD MAN

One more time for the ocean, one more sigh for the sky
One more sigh for the old man who died

One more breath for the water, one more breath for the seer
One more breath for the old man . . . who cared

One more sigh, one more tear, one more drop of water to bear

TIME IMMEASURABLE

Time, immeasurable as time will always be
Time's been good to me
You, a memory flicker past that lives in time
A time you were alive
Ride the wave of time

Love, it feels so real when I look your eyes
A picture of surprise
Truth, I thought I saw it all in you
God, we sure loved you

Now, I see the writing on the pages of all time
What you were and what you are are now are different states of mind

But time holds the memory
In time it will always be . . . love

Time's been good to me
Ride the wave of time

WHEN I DREAM

What does it mean when I dream
It's not always what it seems
What does it mean when I dream
About you
In a whisper of a moment
Your face goes by my eyes
You're gone in only seconds
But your soul has touched my life

Another night, another year
Another space that might be clear
Where are you now
Where are you now

My vision fades so slowly
When you phase into my realm
You're gone and yet you're with me
In my dreams, and in heaven

THAT TIME WON'T LEAVE MY MIND

A face I remember down in my dreams
Was it years or forever, so far away it seems
That time won't leave my mind

His eyes were the color of cloudy windswept skies
And deep in his aura, a soul as bright as light
the memory of his face fills me with grace
And deep in my heart we'll never part
I wonder where he is right now
I wonder if he feels me somehow
Can he hear my thoughts and know what I mean
When I say, you are my dream

A child in his essence, hardly knowing how to feel
Reaching for the answers, but fearing them as well
As hard as he tried, he still died

I reached for his spirit, we love him from long ago
Every time he looked at me, I gazed deep in his soul
And whatever you do, we still love you
And deep in our hearts, we'll never part

AND THE DREAM'S STILL ALIVE

My mother was an immigrant
Saw wars and blood and strife

My father was an army man
Who fell for Mom one night

She followed him to America
The land of the free
Dreaming of a brighter place
And children they had three

And the dream's still alive . . . in America
The world across the sea
Celebrations of life and a growing dream
A world . . . at peace

I was the lonely one
To others it seemed so
When I met him I fell adrift
A sea of vision's glow

My girl was born one silent night
Crying confused tears
Sometimes I see so much in her
I wonder what she will be . . .

I'll NEVER WONDER

I've often wondered where you are today
Memories wander to places far away
Nights on oasis where love makes souls fly
Days filled with sadness 'cause we never said goodbye

Whatever you're reaching
Whatever you're seeking
You will find it somehow

I'll never wonder where you are again
I know you're following the light that takes you home
I trust God's wisdom in taking you when He did

I loved you then
I'll see you again
I will meet you there

Whatever you're reaching
Whatever you're seeking
You will find it
And I'll meet you there

FAERIETALE ANGELS

Whatever happened to faerietale angels
Ponies, dancers and wings
Whatever happened to heaven and romance
Whatever happened to me

I dreamed of an angel, with white, golden wings
Behind her were stars and mermaids who sing

Celestial visions of all magnitudes
Behind me, I thought I felt you
Behind me, I was sure it was you

I seem to recall, a day gone by
The stories and visions, the midnight flights
Sweet little girl, it came so easy to you
Remember the world that we knew
Remember the world that we knew

EUCHARISTIC JESUS

I wanna place my arms around you
I wanna wash my sins away
I wanna wrap my arms around you
And fly away . . .

I wanna eat the bread of Heaven
Receive new life and heavenly grace
I wanna ease my pain in Jesus
And fly away . . .

Come to me, dear Jesus Christ
Feed me in your sacrament divine
Fill me
Instill in me
Your life

Is there one worthy to receive You
Are any of us without sin?
But still you offer us the Kingdom
But still you offer to forgive

BORN BENEATH THE SOUL
COME TO WISDOM'S DOOR

Born beneath the soul
Born beneath the soul
Born beneath the soul
Oh, oh, oh, the soul is waiting

Come to wisdom's door
Come to wisdom's door
Come to wisdom's door
Oh, oh, oh, the Lord will show you
Oh, oh, oh, the Lord is waiting

FINAL THOUGHT:
Whispers

I accept the whispers with no need to hold on
I trust the whispers, my heart and they are one
They call to me from the heart space love adorns
I hear them whisper, the truth seeks me again

I feel the longing; I hear whispers of its power
It will be back, whispers the hereafter
I accept the whispers; they are the truth of life
I'll accept the whispers, they love my soul tonight

The Mystic Knowledge Series

In One Volume
Compiled and Written by Marilynn Hughes

The Out-of-Body Travel Foundation!

www.outofbodytravel.org

Author, Marilynn Hughes, *Photo by Harvey Kushner*

The Mystic Knowledge Series in One Volume is a group of compilations of the Mystic and Out-of-Body Travel Works of Marilynn Hughes on various subjects of scholarship so you may have at your fingertips all the Out-of-Body Travel Instructions on a particular area of study.

Out-of-Body Travel
Ghosts and Lost Souls
Spirit Guides and Guardian Angels
Reincarnation and Karma
Spiritual Warfare, Angels and Demons
Death, Dying and the Afterlife
Heaven, Hell and Purgatory
ExtraTerrestrials
Destiny and Prophecy
Initiations into the Mysteries
Visions of Jesus and the Saints
Ascension
Suffering and Sickness
Mystical Poetry

Go to our Website at:
www.outofbodytravel.org
For more information!

BIBLIOGRAPHY

Having made a shortened list of some of the more important texts of the world religions, I've made careful note to include texts which have been drawn to me in sacred vision and have been an integral part of energizing my spiritual path. Most of the texts in the bibliography have been brought to me through eternal guidance.

World Scripture is an excellent starting point, as it contains scripture from all world religions on various subjects, as well as, a detailed listing in back of the prescribed texts from all major and minor world religions.

Scriptural texts are the foundation or the root of knowledge. Visionary texts are the branches of the tree. Lives of prophets, saints, mystics and sages are the leaves.

Words in italics are actual book titles, while the unitalicized words are not title names, but rather authors and saints to glean from.

Hinduism: *The Bhagavad Gita As It Is, Srimad Bhagavatam, Upanishads, KRSNA, Autobiography of a Yogi, The Divine Romance, Man's Eternal Quest, The Gospel of Sri Ramakrishna*

Judaism: *New Jerusalem Bible, The Talmudic Anthology, The Zohar (Kaballah), The Apocrypha, The Lost Books of the Bible and the Forgotten Books of Eden, The Book of Enoch, Sefer haHinnuch, Josephus, Philo, The Way of God, The Path of the Just, The Gates of Repentance*

Zoroastrianism: *The Avesta, The Desatir, A Guide to Zoroastrian Religion*

Buddhism: *A Buddhist Bible, Dialogues of the Buddha, Dhammapada, Threefold Lotus Sutra, Path to Deliverance, The Flower Ornament Scripture, The Holy Teaching of Vimalakurti, Sutra of the Past Vows of Earth Store Bodhisattva, A Guide to the Bodhisattva's Way of Life, Training the Mind in the Great Way, The Life of the Buddha, Moon in a Dewdrop, The Shobogenzo, Tao Te Ching, Chuang Tsu, Analects of Confucius, Wen Tzu*

Christianity: *Holy Bible, Apocrypha, Lost Books of the Bible and the Forgotten Books of Eden, Dead Sea Scriptures, Gospel of Thomas, Essene Gospel of Peace 1-4, Book of Enoch, Nag Hammadi Library, Pistis Sophia, Gnosis on the Silk Road, The Dialogue of St. Catherine of Siena, The Mystical City of God, Heaven & Hell, The Life of Jesus Christ and Biblical Revelations, The Imitation of Christ,* and the writings of the saints with an emphasis on the following: St. Augustine, Mother Teresa, Padre Pio, St. Alphonsus Liguori, Cure' of Ars, St. Teresa of Avila, St. Thomas Aquinas, St. Francis de Sales, St. John Bosco, St. Ignatius, St. John of the Cross, Emanuel Swedenborg, Martin Luther, John Calvin

Islam: *Holy Qur'an, Sahih Muslim* (The Hadith), *Nahjul Balagha, Imam Gazzali's Ihya Ulum Ud Din, The Life of Mohammad (Translation of Sirat Rasul Allah), Signs of the Unseen, The Doctrine of the Sufi's*

Baha'i: *Tablets of Baha'u'llah, Seven Valleys and the Four Valleys, The Kitab-I-Iqan, The Hidden Words, Prayers and Meditations, Selections from the Writings of the Bab, Tablets of the Divine Plan, Promulgation of Universal Peace*

Mystery Religions: *The Divine Pymander of Hermes, The Emerald Tablets of Thoth, An Interpretation of the Emerald Tablets, The Ancient Mysteries, The Secret Doctrine of the Rosicrucians, Secret Teachings of All Ages, Plotinus: The Enneads,*

Tribal: *Book of the Hopi, Secrets of Mayan Science/Religion, Navajo Religion, Encyclopedia of Native American Religions, African Religions & Philosophy*

SOURCE LISTING

African Religions and Philosophy, by John S. Mbiti, Heinerman, 1969

Agony, of Jesus, The, by Padre Pio, Tan Books, 1967

Ahaveth Chesed, by the Chafetz Chaim, Feldheim Publishers, 1967

An Interpretation of the Emerald Tablets, by Doral, Brotherhood of the White Temple, 1992

An Introduction to the Devout Life, by St. Francis De Sales, Tan Books, 1923

Analects of Confucius, The, by Confucius, Translator Arthur Waley, Vintage Books, 1938

Ancient Mysteries, The, Editor Marvin W. Meyer, Harper Collins, 1987

Anguttara Nikaya 1-3, Translator Nyanaponika Thera, Buddhist Publication Society, 1981

Anugita, The, Translator Kashinath Trimbak Telang, Wizards Bookshelf, 1981

Apocrypha, The Editor Manuel Kromroff, Dorset Press, 1992

Apologia Pro Vita Sua, by John Henry Cardinal Newman, Doubleday Image Books, 1956

Aryasura's Aspiration/Meditation on Compassion, by Tenzin Gyatso, H.H. the 14th Dalai Lama, Library of Tibetan Works, 1975

Autobiography of a Yogi, by Paramahansa Yogananda, Self-Realization Fellowship, 1946

Autobiography of St. Margaret Mary, The, by Saint Margaret Mary, Tan Books, 1930

Avesta, The, Translator Rev. Ernestine Busch, Ernestine G. Busch, 1985

Baha'u'llah and the New Era, by J.E. Esslemont, Baha'i Publishing Trust, 1923
Being and Vibration, by Joseph Raphael and Mary Elizabeth Marlow, Council Oak Books, 1993
Bhagavad Gita, The, Translator Eknath Easwaran, Nilgri Press, 1985
Bhagavad-Gita As It Is, Translator A.C. Bhaktivedanta Swami, Bhaktivedanta Book Trust, 1986
Bible in Art, The, Editor Clifton Harby, Garden City Publishing Co., 1936
Birth of Purgatory, The, by Jacques Le Goff, Translator Arthur Goldhammer, The University of Chicago Press, 1981
Black Elk Speaks, by John G. Neihardt, University of Nebraska Press, 1932
Blessed Eucharist, The, by Fr. Michael Muller C.S.S.R., Tan Books, 1868
Book of Discipline, The, Translator I.B. Horner, Pali Text Society, 1938
Book of Analysis, The, Translator Pathamakyaw Ashin Thittila, Pali Text Society, 1969
Book of Enoch the Prophet, The, Translator Richard Laurence, Wizards Bookshelf, 1883
Book of the Hopi, by Frank Waters, Penguin Books, 1963
Buddhist Bible, A, Editor Dwight Goddard, Beacon Press, 1938
Call to Remembrance, by Baha'u'llah, Baha'i Publishing Trust, 1992
Candragomin's Twenty Verses on the Bodhisattva Vow, by Sakya Dragpa Gyaltsen, Library of Tibetan Works and Archives, 1982
Catechism of the Catholic Church, by The Holy See, Doubleday Image Books, 1994
Changeless Nature, The, by Arya Maitreya and Acarya Asanga, Translators Ken and Katia Holmes, Karma Drubgyud Darjay Ling, 1985
Chofetz Chaim Looks at: Eternity, The, by The Chofetz Chaim, Bais Yechiel Publications, 1989
Chuang Tsu, by Lao Tsu, Translators Gia-Fu Feng and Jane English, Random House, Vintage Books, 1974
City of God, by Saint Augustine, Translators Walsh, Zema, Monahan, Honan, Doubleday Image Books, 1950
Classic Midrah, The, Translator Reuven Hammer, Paulist Press, 1995
Collected Works of Saint John of the Cross, The, by Saint John of the Cross, Translators KieranVanaugh and Otilio Rodriquez, ICS Publications, 1979
Complete Artscroll Siddur, The, Translator Rabbi Nosson Scherman, Mesorah Publications, Ltd., 1985
Complete Works of Josephus, The, by Flavius Josephus, Translator William Whiston A.M., Krege, 1960
Concise Book of Mitzvoth, The, Editor The Chafetz Chayim, The Feldheim Publishers, 1990
Confessions of Saint Augustine, The, by Saint Augustine, Translator Rex Warner, Penguin Books, Mentor, 1963
Contemplative Prayer, by Thomas Merton, Doubleday, 1969
Course in Miracles, The, by The Foundation for Inner Peace, Foundation for Inner Peace, 1975
Dead Sea Scriptures, The, Translator Theodore H. Gaster, Doubleday, Anchor Books, 1956
Denkoroku, The, by Keizan Zenji, Translator Rev. Hubert Nearman, Shasta Abbey Press, 1993
Desatir, The, Translator Mulla Firuz Bin Kaus, Wizards Bookshelf, 1888
Devotion for the Dying, by Mother Mary Potter, Tan Books, 1880
Dhammapada, Translator Harischandra Kaviratna, Theosophical University Press, 1980
Dialogue of Saint Catherine of Siena, Translator Algar Thorold, Tan Books, 1907
Dialogues of the Buddha, Translators T.W. and C.A.F. Rhys Davids and Scholars, Pali Text Society, 1921
Diamond Sutra and The Sutra of Hui-Neng, The, Translator A.F. Price and Wong Mou-lam, Shambhala Publications, Inc. 1990
Discourse on the Fruits of Recluseship, The, Translator Bhikku Bodhi, Buddhist Publication Society, 1989
Divine Crucible of Purgatory, The, by Mother Mary of Saint Austin, Helper of Holy Souls, Unknown Publisher and Date
Divine Love and Wisdom, by Emanuel Swedenborg, Translator George F. Dole, Swedenborg Foundation, 1985
Divine Mercy In My Soul, by Sister M. Faustina, Translators Drabik, Pearce, Maguire, Marina Helpers, 1987
Divine Providence, by Emanuel Swedenborg, Swedenborg Foundation, 1764
Divine Pymander of Hermes, The, by Hermes Mercurius Trismegistus, Translator Dr.

Everard, Wizards Bookshelf, 1978

Divine Romance, The, by Paramahansa Yogananda, Self-Realization Fellowship, 1986

Doctrine of the Sufi's, The, by Al-Kalabadhi, AMS Press, 1935

Druids, The, by Peter Berresford Ellis, William B. Eerfdmans Publishing Co., 1994

Echoes in the Heavenly Court, Editor Dean of Machon, Feldheim Publishers, 1994

Edgar Cayce, Modern Prophet, by Carter, Hartzell, Reed, Langley, Gramercy Books, 1967

Egyptian Heaven and Hell, The, by E.A. Budge, Open Court, 1905

Emerald Tablets of the Thoth the Atlantean, The, by Thoth the Atlantean, Translator Doreal,   Brotherhood of the White Temple, 1939

Encyclopedia of Native American Religions, The, by Hirschfelder, Arlene and Molin, Paulette, MJF Books,   1992

Epistle to the Son of Wolf, by Baha'u'llah, Baha'i Publishing Trust, 1941

Essence of Self-Realization, The, by Kriyananda (J. Donald Walters), Crystal Clarity Publishers, 1990

Essene Book of Creation, The, by Edmond Bordeaux Szekely, International Biogenic Society, 1989

Essene Communications with the Infinite, by Edmond Bordeaux Szekely, International Biogenic Society, 1979

Essene Gospel of Peace, The, Vol. 1-4, Translator Edmond Bordeaux Szekely, International Biogenic Society, 1981

Essential Rumi, The, by Rumi, Translator Coleman Barks, HarperSanFrancisco, 1995

Ethics of Spinoza, The, by Baruch Spinoza, Carol Publishing Group, 1957

Fathers of the Church, The, Vol. 2, 4, 11, 16, 60, by Saint Augustine, Catholic University of America Press, 1947-1968

Five Books of Moses, The, Translator Everett Fox, Schocken, 1983

Flower Ornament Scripture, The, Translator Thomas Cleary, Shambhala Publications, 1984

Forgotten Secret of Fatima, The, by Msgr. Joseph A. Cirrincione and Thomas A. Nelson, Tan Books, 1988

Forty Dreams of Saint John Bosco, by Saint John Bosco, Tan, 1969

Four Doctrines, The, by Emanuel Swedenborg, Swedenborg Foundation, 1763

Fox's Book of Martyrs, by John Fox, Whitaker House, 1981

Gates of Repentance, The, by Rabbeinu Yonah Ben Avaham of Gerona, Feldheim Publishers, 1967

General Principles of Kabbalah, Rabbi Moses C. Luzzatto, Translator Dr. Philip S. Berg, Research Centre of Kabbalah, 1970

Glories of Mary, The, by Saint Alphonsus Liguori, Redemptorist Fathers, 1931

Gnosis on the Silk Road, Translator Hans-Joachim Klimkeit, HarperSanFransisco, 1993

Gospel of Sri Ramakrishna, The, by M., a disciple of the holy Master, Translator Swami Nikhilananda, Ramakrishna-Vivekananda Center, 1942

Gospel of the Holy Twelve, The, Translator Rev. Gideon Jasper Richard Ousley, Teofil de la Torre, N.D., O.D., 1954

Gospel of Thomas, The, Translator Marvin Meyer, HarperSanFransisco, 1992

Grace Abounding, by John Bunyan, Whitaker House, 1993

Great Means of Salvation and of Perfection, The, by Saint Alphonsus Liguori, Redemptorist Fathers, 1927

Great Ocean-An Authorized Biography of the Dali Lama, by Roger Hicks and Ngakpa Chogyam, Penguin Books, 1984

Group of Discourses, The, Translator K.R. Norman, Pali Text Society, 1992

Guide to the Bodhisattva's Way of Life, A, by Shantideva, Translator Steven Batchelor, Library of Tibetan   works and Archives, 1979

Guide to the Zoroastrian Religion, A, Translators Firoze M. Kotwal and James W. Boyd, Scholars Press, 1982

Heaven and Hell, by Emanuel Swedenborg, Translator George G. Dole, Swedenborg Foundation, 1976

Hell and How to Avoid Hell, by Fr. F.X. Schouppe S.J. and Thomas A. Nelson, Tan Books, 1989

Hidden Words and Selected Holy Writings, The, by Baha'u'llah, Baha'i Publishing Trust, 1985

Hildegard of Bingen's Book of Divine Works, Editor Matthew Fox, Bear & Co., 1987

History of Witchcraft, The, by Fr. Montague Summers, Barnes & Noble, 1993

Holy Bible, The (King James Version), World Bible Publishers, 1989

Holy Qur'an, by Muhammed, Translator Maulana Muhammed Ali, Ahmadiyyah Anjuman

Isha'at Islam, 1917

Holy Teaching of Vimalakirti, The, Translator Robert A.F. Thurman, Pennsylvania State University, 1976

Hymns of Hermes, The, by G.R.S. Mead, Phanes Press, 1991

Hymns of the RGVEDA, Translator Ralph T.H. Griffith, Motilal Banarsidass, Date Unknown

Ihya 'Ulim-Ud-Din, by Imam Gazzali, Translator Al-Haj Maulana Fazal-Ul-Karim, Kazi Publications, Date Unknown

Imitation of Christ, The, by Thomas A. Kempis, Barbour & Co., 1984

Interior Castle, by Saint Teresa of Avila, Translator E. Allison Peers, Doubleday Dell, Image Books, 1961

Introduction to Saint Thomas Aquinas, Editor Anton C. Pegis, Random House, 1945

Itivuttaka, The, Translator John D. Ireland, Buddhist Publication Society, 1991

Jesus Christ 1 and 2, by Ferdinand Prat S.J., Translator John J. Heenan, S.J., Bruce Publishing Co., 1950

Kabbalah, by Gershom Scholem, Penguin Books, Meridian, 1974

Khutubat-I-Jumu'ah, Editor Maulana H. Ashraf Ali, Sh. Muhammad Ashraf, Date Unknown

KITAB-I-AQUDAS, The, by Baha'u'llah, Baha'i Publications, 1993

KITAB-I-IQAN, The, by Baha'u'llah, Baha'i Publishing Trust, 1931

KRSNA, Translator A.C. Bhaktivedanta Swami Prabhupada, Bhaktivedanta Book Trust, 1996

Kybalion, The, by Three Initiates, Yogi Publication Society, 1912

Large Sutra on Perfect Wisdom, The, Translator Edward Conze, University of California Press, 1975

Legends and Lore of the American Indians, Editor Terri Hardin, Barnes & Noble, 1993

Life and Glories of Saint Joseph, by Edward Healy Thompson M.A., Tan Books, 1888

Life and Holiness, by Thomas Merton, Doubleday, 1962

Life and Teaching of the Masters of the Far East, by Baird T. Spalding, DeVorss &Co., 1948

Life of Jesus Christ and Biblical Revelations, The, by Ven. Anne Catherine Emmerich, Tan Books, 1914

Life of Muhammad, The, Editor A. Guillaume, Oxford University Press, 1995

Life of the Blessed Virgin Mary, The, by Ven. Anne Catherine Emmerich, Translator Sir Michael Palairet, Tan Books, 1954

Life of the Buddha, The, Translator Bhikku Nanamoli, Buddhist Publication Society, 1972

Little Flowers of Saint Francis, The, by Brother Ugolino di Monte Santa Maria, Translator Raphael Brown, Doubleday Image, 1958

Living Buddha, Living Christ, by Thich Naht Hahn, Parallax Press, 1995

Lost Books of the Bible/Forgotten Books of Eden, Translator World Bible Publishers/Alpha House, World Bible Publishers, 1926

Love of Christ, The, by Mother Teresa, Translator John A. Otto, Harper & Row, 1982

Maggid of Dubno and his Parables, The, by Benno Heinemann, Feldheim Publishers, 1967

Mahabharata, The, Editor C. Narasimhan, Columbia University Press, 1965

Man and God, by Voctor Gollancz, Houghton Mifflin, 1950

Man's Eternal Quest, by Paramahansa Yogananda, Self-Realization Fellowship, 1975

Mansions of the Soul, by H. Spencer Lewis, Supreme Grand Lodge of AMORC, 1930

Marital Love, by Emanuel Swedenborg, Swedenborg Foundation, 1768

Masters of the Path, by Dr. Javad Nurbakhsh, Khaniqanhi-Nimatullahi Publications, 1980

Meaning of Life, The, by Tenzin Gyasto H.H. the 14th Dalai Lama, Wisdom Publications, 1992

Mediaeval Legends of Christ, by A.S. Rapport Ph.D., Nicholson, Ivor, & Watson, 1934

Meditation Prayer on Mary Immaculate, by Padre Pio, Translator Laura Chanler White, Tan Books, 1974

Moments Divine Before the Blessed Sacrament, by Fr. Frederick A. Reuter K.C.B.S., Tan Books, 1922

Moon in a Dewdrop, Editor Kazuaki Tanahashi, North Point Press, 1985

My Utmost for His Highest, by Oswald Chambers, Barbour and Co., 1935

Mystical City of God, by Ven. Mary of Agreda, Translator Fiscar Marison, Blue Army of Our Lady of Fatima, 1949

Mystical City of God, The, Abridged, by Ven. Mary of Agreda, Tan Books, 1978

Mystical Life of Jesus, The, by H. Spencer Lewis, Supreme Grand Lodge of AMORC, 1929

Mystical Visions, by Hildegard Von Bingen, Bear & Co., 1986

Nag Hammadi Library, The, Translator Coptic Gnostic Library Project, Harper Collins, 1978

Nahjul Balagha, by Imam Ali Ibn Abu Talib, Translator Sayed Ali Reza, Tahrike Tarsile Qur'an, Unknown

Native Religions of North America, by Ake Hultkrantz, HarperSanFransisco, 1987

Navajo Religion, by Gladys A. Reichard, Princeton University Press, 1950

Nectar of Devotion, The, by A.C. Bhaktivedanta Swami Prabhupada, Bhaktivedanta Book Trust, 1970

Nectar of Instruction, The, Translator A.C. Bhaktivedanta Swami Prabhupada, Bhaktivedanta Book Trust, 1975

New American Bible, The, World Bible Publishers, 1970

New Jerusalem Bible, The, Doubleday, 1985

New Oxford Annotated Bible, The, Oxford University Press, 1946

On Christian Doctrine, by Saint Augustine, Translator D.W. Robertson Jr., Macmillan, 1958

On Evil, by Saint Thomas Aquinas, Translator Jean Oesterle, University of Notre Dame Press, 1995

On Free Choice of Will, by Saint Augustine, Translators Anna Benjamin and L.H. Hackstaff, Library of Liberal Arts, 1964

On the Kabbalah and its Symbolism, by Gershom Scholem, Translator Ralph Manheim, Schocken Books, 1965

Orations of Muhammad, The, by M. Muhammad Abaidul Akbar, Sh. Muhammad Ashraf, 1954

Our Lady of Fatima's Peace Plan From Heaven, Tan Books, 1950

Padre Pio: The True Story, by C. Bernard Ruffin, Our Sunday Visitor, 1982

Path of Discrimination, The, Translator Bhikku Nanamoli, Pali Text Society, 1991

Path of Purification, The, by Bhadantacariya Buddhagosa, Translator Bhikku Nanamoli, Buddhist Publication Society, 1975

Path of the Just, The, by Rabbi Moshe Chaim Luzzatto, Feldheim Publishers, 1966

Path of the Righteous Gentile, The, by Chaim Clorfene and Yakov Rogalsky, Feldheim Publishers, 1987

Path of Yoga, The, by A.C. Bhaktivedanta Swami Parbhupada, Bhaktivedanta Book Trust, 1971, 1979

Path to Deliverance, by Nyanatiloka Mahathera, Buddhist Publication Society, 1952

Path to Enlightenment, The, by Tenzin Gyatso, H.H. the 14th Dalai Lama, Snow Lion Publications, 1995

Philosophies and Religions of India, The, by Yogi Ramacharaka, Yogi Publication Society, 1930

Pilgrim's Progress, The, by John Bunyan, Barbor & Co., 1993

Pistis Sophia, Translator G.R.S. Mead, Kessinger Publishing Co., Date Unknown

Plotinus: The Enneads, by Plotinus, Translator Stephen MacKenna, Larson Publications, 1992

Prayers and Heavenly Promises, by Joan Carroll Cruz, Tan Books, 1990

Prayers and Meditations, by Baha'u'llah, Translator Shoghi Effendi, Baha'i Publishing Trust, 1938

Prayers of Saint Francis, The, Editor W. Bader, New City Press, 1988

Prayertimes with Mother Teresa, by Eileen and Kathleen Egan, Doubleday, 1989

Preparation for Death, by Saint Alphonsus Liguori, Translator Robert A. Coffin, Tan Books, 1857

Promulgation of Universal Peace, The, by Abdul-Baha, Baha'i Publishing Trust, 1982

Prophet, The, by Kahlil Gibran, Walker & Co., 1923

Purgatory, by Fr. F.X. Schouppe S.J., Tan Books, 1926

Pyramidology (Three Volumes), by Adam Rutherford, Institute of Pyramidology, 1957

Pythagorean Sourcebook and Library, The, Translators Guthrie, Taylor, Fairbanks, Phanes Press, 1987

Rama Story, The, by Bhagavan Sri Sathya Sai Baba, Translator N. Kasturi, Sri Sathya Sai Books and Publications, 1981

Red Record, The, Translator David McCutchen, Pavery Publishing Group, Inc., 1993

Reincarnation, An East-West Anthology, Editors Head and Cranston, Theosophical Publishing House, 1961

Revelations of Divine Love, by Juliana of Norwich, Translator M.L. del Mastro, Image Doubleday, 1977

Revelations of Saint Bridget, by Saint Bridget, Tan Books, 1965

5

771

Rosary Novenas to Our Lady, by Charles V. Lacey, Benziger, 1926

Sacred Pipe, The, by Joseph Epes Brown, Norman & London, University of Oklahoma Press, 1953

Saddharma-Pundarika or the Lotus of the True Law, Translator H. Kern, Dover Publications, 1963

Sahih Muslim (The Hadith, Volumes 1-4), by Imam Muslim, Translator Abdul Hamid Siddiqi, Nusrat Ali Nasri for Kitab Bhavan, Date Unknown

Samyutta Nikaya 1-3, Translator John D. Ireland, Buddhist Publication Society, 1981

Sayings of Paramahansa Yogananda, by Paramahansa Yogananda, Self-Realization Fellowship, 1952

Science of Being and Art of Living, The, by Mahrishi Manhesh Yogi, International SRM Publications, 1966

Secret Doctrine of the Rosicrucians, The, by Magus Incognito, Yoga Publication Society, 1949

Secret Doctrines of Jesus, The, by H. Spencer Lewis, AMORC, 1937

Secret of Divine Civilization, The, by Abdul-Baha, Baha'i Publishing Trust, 1957

Secret of the Rosary, The, by Saint Louis Mary De Montfort, Translator Mary Barbour, Montfort Publications, 1965

Secret Teachings of All Ages, The, by Manly P. Hall, Philosophical Research Society, 1977

Secrets of Mayan Science/Religion, by Hunbatz Men, Translators Diana Ayala and James II Dunlap, Bear & Co., 1990

Sefer haHinnuch, Ascribed to: Rabbi Aaron of Barcelona haLevi, Feldheim Publishers, 1523

Selections from the Writings of the BA'B, by The BA'B, Translator Habib Taherzadeh, Baha'i World Centre, 1976

Sepher Yezirah, Translator Dr. Isidor Kalish, L.H. Frank & Co., 1877

Sermon on the Mount According to Vedanta, The, by Swami Prabhavananda, New American Library, 1963

Seven Valleys and the Four Valleys, The, by Baha'u'llah, Baha'i Publishing Trust, 1945

Shobogenzo-Zuimonki, Translator Shohaku Okumura, Kyoto Soto-Zen Center, Date Unknown

Sign of Contradiction, by Karol Wojytla (Pope John Paul II), Seabury Press, 1979

Signs of the Unseen, by Rumi, Translator W.M. Thackston Jr., Threshold Books, 1994

Sinner's Guide, The. by Ven. Louis of Granada, O.P., Tan Books, 1883

Some Answered Questions, by Abdul-Baha', Baha'i Publishing Trust, 1930

Son of the Sun, by Savitri Devi, Supreme Grand Lodge of A.M.O.R.C., 1946

Songs of the Soul, by Paramahansa Yogananda, Self-Realization Fellowship, 1983

Soul Sanctified, The, Tan Books, 1873

Speaking in Tongues, by Felicitias D. Goodman, University of Chicago Press, 1972

Spiritual Combat, The, by Dom Lorenzo Scupoli, Translators William Lester and Robert Mohan, Tan Books, 1945

Spiritual Doctrine of Saint Catherine of Genoa, The, by Saint Catherine of Genoa, Tan Books, 1874

Spiritual Exercises of Saint Ignatius, The, by Saint Ignatius, Translator Anthony Mottola Ph.d, Image Books, 1964

Sri Guru Granth Sahib, (4 Volumes), Translator Gurbachan Singh Talib, Publication Bureau, Punjabi University, 1995

Srimad Bhagavatam (Volumes 1-3), Translator A.C. Bhaktivedanta Swami Prabhupada, Bhaktivedanta Book Trust, 1972

Srimad Bhagavatam (Part One), Translator A.C. Bhadtivedanta Swami Prabhupada, Bhaktivedanta Book Trust 1975

Srimad Bhagavatam (An Abridgement), Translator Swami Prabhavananda, Sri Ramakrishna Math, Date Unknown

Saint Antony of the Dessert, by Saint Athanasius, Translator Dom J.B. McLaughlin, Tan Books, 1924

Saint Athanasius On the Incarnation, by Saint Athanasuis, Translators Religious of C.S.M.V.A., Saint Vladimirs, 1944

Saint Francis of Assisi, by Saint Francis of Assisi, Thomas Nelson Publishers, 1989

Saint Michael and the Angels, Compiled from approved sources, Tan Books, 1977

Story of A Soul, by Saint Therese of Lisieux, Translator John Clark .C.D., ICS, 1975

Strive for Truth, Volumes 1-3, by Rabbi Eliyahu E. Dessler, Feldheim Publishers, 1978

Sutra of the Past Vows of Earth Store Bodhisattva, Translator Heng Ching, Buddhist Text Translation Society, 1974

Tablets of Baha'u'llah, by Baha'u'llah, Translator Habib Taherzadeh, Baha'i Publishing Trust, 1978

Tablets of the Divine Plan, by Abdul-Baha', Baha'i Publishing Trust, 1977

Taharas Halashon, Translator David Landesman, Feldheim Publishers, 1994

Talmud, The, Classics of Western Spirituality Series, Paulist Press, 1989

Talmudic Anthology, The, Editor Spitz Newman, Behrman House, Inc., 1945

Tao Te Ching, by Lao Tsu, Translators Gia-Fu Feng and Jane English, Random House, Vintage Books, 1972

Tao Te Ching, by Lao Tsu, Translator Victor H. Mair (from the Ma-Wang-Tui Manuscripts), Bantam, 1990

Teachings of Lord Caitanya, Translator A.C. Bhativedanta Swami Parabhupada, Bhakivedanta Book Trust, 1985

Teachings of Lord Kapila, Translator A.C. Bhativedanta Swami Parabhupada, Bhakivedanta Book Trust, 1977

Teachings of Queen Kunti, by A.C. Bhativedanta Swami Parabhupada, Bhativedanta Book Trust, 1978

Teachings of Sri Ramakrishna, by Advaita Ashrama, Swami Mumukshananda, 1994

Teachings of Sri Sarada Devi ,the Holy Mother, Editor Sri Ramakrishna Math, Sri Ramakrishna Math, Date Unknown

Teachings of Swami Vivekananda, Editor Advaita Ashrama, Advaita Ashrama, 1994

Theology of Saint Paul, The, by Fernand Prat S.J., The Newman Bookshop, 1926

Therese Neumann, by Adalbert Albert Vogl, Tan Books, 1987

Third Secret of Fatima, The, by Brother Michael of the Holy Trinity, Translator Anne Barbeau Gardiner, Tan Books, 1991

Thoughts and Sayings of Saint Margaret Mary, by Saint Margaret Mary, Tan Books, 1935

Three Pure Land Sutras, The, by Hisao Inagaki, by Nagata Bunshodo, 1994

Three Ways of the Spiritual Life, The, by Rev. R. Garrigou-Lagrange O.P., Tan Books, 1938

Threefold Lotus Sutra, The, Translators Kato, Tamura, Miyasaka, Kosei Publishing Co., 1971

Tibetan Book of the Dead, The, Editor W.Y. Evans-Wentz, Oxford University Press, 1960

Tibetan Book of the Great Liberation, The, Editor W.Y. Evans-Wentz, Oxford University Press, 1954

Torah, The, Translator Jewish Publication Society of America, Jewish Publication Society of America, 1962

Training the Mind in the Great Way, by Gyalwa Gendun Druppa (The First Dalai Lama), Translator Glenn H.   Mullin, Snow Lion Publications, 1993

Travelers Narrative, A, by Abdul-Baha', Translator Edward G.Browne, Baha'i Publishing Trust, 1980

Treasury of Judaism, A, Editor Philip Birnbaum, Hebrew Publishing, 1957

Trinity, The, by Saint Augustine, Translator Edmund Hill O.P., New City Press, 1991

True Christian Religion, The, by Emanuel Swedenborg, Swedenborg Foundation, 1771

True Devotion to Mary, by Saint Louis De Montfort, Translator Fr. Federick Faber, Tan Books, 1941

Twleve Steps to Holiness and Salvation, The, by Saint Alphonsus Liguori, Translators Rev. Paul Leik and Rev. Cornelius Warren, Tan Books, 1986

Udana, The, Translator John D. Ireland, Buddhist Publication Society, 1990

Unknown Life of Jesus Christ, The, by Nicolas Notovitch, Translator Alexina Loranger, Tree of Life Publications, 1894

Upanishands, The, Translator Eknath Easwaran, Nilgiri Press, 1987

Urantia Book, The, by Urantia, Urantia Foundation, 1955

Vedanta-Sutras, by Vyasadeva, Translator George Thibaut, Motial Banarsidass Publishers, 1904

Voice of the Saints, The, Editor Francis Johnston, Tan Books, 1965

Walking in the Sacred Manner, by Mark St. Pierre and Tilda Long Soldier, Simon & Schuster, 1995

Way of Divine Love, The, by Sister Josefa Menendez, Tan Books, 1972

Way of Perfection, The, by Saint Teresa of Avila, Translator E. Allison Peers, Doubleday Dell, Image Books, 1964

Way of the Sufi, The, by Idries Shah, Arkana Penguin Books, 1968

Ways of Reason, The, by Rabbi Moshe Chaim Luzzatto, Feldheim Publishers, 1989

Wen-Tzu, by Lao-tzu, Translator Thomas Cleary, Shambhala Publications, 1991

Whispers From Eternity, Paramahansa Yogananda, Self-Realization Fellowship, 1949

Wisdom of the Elders, by David Suzuki and Peter Knudtson, Bantam Books, 1992

Wisdom of the Idiots, by Idries Shah, Octagon Press, 1969

Wonders of the Holy Name, The, by Fr. Paul O'Sullivan O.P. (E.D.M.), Tan Books, 1946

Word of the Buddha, The, Translator Nyanatiloka, Buddhist Publication Society, Date Unknown

Works of Philo, The, by Philo, Translator C.D. Yonge, Hendrickson, 1995

World Scripture, by the International Religious Foundation, International Religious Foundation, 1991

Zohar, The, Translators Harry Sperling and Maurice Simon, Sonicio Press, 1984

Look for these texts by going to:
www.bookfinder.com
or
www.sacred-texts.com!

Books by Marilynn Hughes:
Come to Wisdom's Door
How to Have an Out-of-Body Experience!

The Mysteries of the Redemption
A Treatise on **Out-of-Body Travel** *and* **Mysticism**

The Mysteries of the Redemption Series in Five Volumes
(Same Book - Choose Your Format!)
Prelude to a Dream
Passage to the Ancient
Medicine Woman Within a Dream
Absolute Dissolution of Body and Mind
The Mystical Jesus

GALACTICA
A Treatise on **Death, Dying** *and the* **Afterlife**

THE PALACE OF ANCIENT KNOWLEDGE
A Treatise on **Ancient Mysteries**

Touched by the Nails
(Watch and Wait)
A Karmic Journey Revealed!

PRINCIPLES OF THE WORLD BEYOND DEATH

Books of Terror
Evil Exists, it's Closer than you Think
Based on the Visions of Mary Hughes
By Marilynn Hughes

Michael Jackson:
The Afterlife Experiences
A Theology of Michael Jackson's Life and Lyrics

Michael Jackson:
The Afterlife Experiences II
Michael Jackson's American Dream to Heal the World

Michael Jackson:
The Afterlife Experiences III
The Confessions of Michael Jackson

Comparative Religious Mystical Theology
Out-of-Body Travel in World Religion

Forgotten Mystics in World Religions
Lesser Known Out-of-Body Experiences

Selfishness and Self-Will
The Path to Selflessness in World Religions

A Life of Cultivation

Near Death and Out-of-Body Experiences
(Auspicious Births and Deaths)
Of the Prophets, Saints, Mystics and Sages in World Religions

The Voice of the Prophets
Wisdom of the Ages - Volumes 1 - 12

At the Feet of the Masters

Miraculous Images:
Photographs Containing God's Fingerprints

Suffering:
The Fruits of Utter Desolation

We are all Shadows

The Overview Series
The Oral Transmissions of the 52 Soto Zen Buddhist Ancestors
The Doctors of the Catholic Church
The General Councils of the Catholic Church
Marian Apparitions in the Catholic Church
Heresies in the Catholic Church
Miraculous Phenomena in the Catholic Church
Fascinating Figures in World Religion
Practices, Prayer, Ritual, Liturgy, Sacraments and Theology in the Catholic Church

Mystic Knowledge Series:
Out-of-Body Travel
Ghosts and Lost Souls
Spirit Guides and Guardian Angels
Reincarnation and Karma
Spiritual Warfare, Angels and Demons
Death, Dying and the Afterlife
Heaven, Hell and Purgatory
ExtraTerrestrials
Destiny and Prophecy
Initiations into the Mysteries
Visions of Jesus and the Saints
Ascension
Suffering and Sickness
Mystical Poetry

Teaching Stories of the Prophets in World Religions!
(Ages 10 to Adult)

World Religions and their Prophets!
(Ages 2 - 8)

CHILDREN'S BOOKS

The Former Angel! - *A Children's Tale*
(Ages 2 - 8)

The Mystery of the Key to Heaven!
(Ages 2 - 10)

Streams in the Willow

The Story of One Family's Transformation from Original Sin

COMPILATIONS

Out-of-Body Travel and Near Death Experiences: Compiled Works
through 2006

World Religions and Ancient Sacred Texts: Compiled Compiled
Works through 2006

**The Voice of the Prophets:
Abridged Lesser Known Texts**

The Out-of-Body Travel Foundation Journals

*Journal One: The Importance of the Seven Virtues and Vices in Understanding the Practice
of Out-of-Body Travel!*
Journal Two: My Out-of-Body Journey with Sai Baba, Hindu Avatar!
Journal Three: The History of 'The Out-of-Body Travel Foundation!'
Journal Four: A Menage of Wonderful Writers and Artists!
Journal Five: The Stories of Cherokee Elder, Willy Whitefeather!
*Journal Six: Discerning your Vocation in Life by Learning the Difference Between
Knowledge and Knowing!*
*Journal Seven: When Tragedy StrikesJournal Eight: Comparing the Buddhist
Avalokiteswara's Descent into Hell with that of Jesus Christ!*
*Journal Nine: Huzur Maharaj Sawan Singh - Sant Mat (Sikh) Master Guru and Grandson
Maharaj Charan Singh - Sant Mat (Sikh) Master Guru*
Journal Ten: The Great Beyond
Journal Eleven: Ghosts and Lost Souls: Our Responsibility
*Journal Twelve: The 800th Anniversary of Jalalludin Rumi, and the True Spiritual Heritage
of Afghanistan and the Middle East*
Journal Thirteen: Pensatia – Forgotten Rosicrucian Mystic
Journal Fourteen: Reverend John Macgowan – Forgotten Protestant Mystic
Journal Fifteen: A. Farnese – Forgotten Mystic Amanuensis (to Franchezzo)
Journal Sixteen: Comte St. Germain – Forgotten Immortal Mystic of the Mystery Schools
Journal Seventeen: Franz Hartmann – Forgotten Mystical Adept
Journal Eighteen: SA'D UD DIN MAHMŪD SHABISTARĪ –Forgotten Islamic Sufi Mystic
Journal Nineteen: Dionysius - Forgotten Christian Mystic of the Early Church
Issue Twenty: Acvaghosha - Forgotten Buddhist Mystic of the Mahayana Path
Issue Twenty One: Bishop Shelemon of Armenia – Forgotten Nestorian Christian Mystic
Issue Twenty Two: Abú Sa'íd Ibn Abi 'l-Khayr– Forgotten Islamic Mystic
Issue Twenty Three: Rev. G. Vale Owen - Forgotten Christian Mystic
Issue Twenty Four: Swami Abhedânanda- Forgotten Hindu Mystic
Issue Twenty Five: Moses Maimonides - Forgotten Jewish Mystic
Issue Twenty Six: The Bab - Forgotten Baha'i Mystic

Mystics Magazine

Go to our Web-Site:

The Out-of-Body Travel Foundation!

http://outofbodytravel.org